THE FLOWER PAINTERS

The Flower Painters

An Illustrated Dictionary

Elisabeth Hardouin-Fugier
Etienne Grafe

Edited by Peter Mitchell

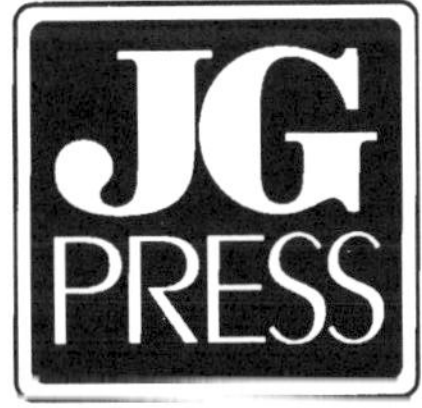

This book is dedicated to the memory of André and Hans Grafe

Published in the USA 1996 by JG Press
Distributed by World Publications, Inc.

The JG Press imprint is a trademark of JG Press, Inc.
455 Somerset Avenue, North Dighton, MA 02764

Published by special arrangement with W.S. Konecky Associates, Inc. and Philip Wilson Publishers Ltd.

ISBN: 1-57215-215-X

Printed and bound in Italy

Contents

List of Colour Illustrations

Plate 14: Jean Benner

Oil on canvas, 78 3/4 X 57 3/4 in.
(198.5 x 145.5 cm.),
signed and dated 1866,
Paris Salon: 1866
Mulhouse,
Musée de l'Impression sur Etoffes

Plate 15: Antoine Berjon

Oil on canvas, 42 1/2 X 34 1/2 in.
(108 x 87.5 cm.),
signed, Paris Salon: 1819
Philadelphia Museum of Art
(Edith H. Bell Fund)

FOLLOWING PAGE 144

Plate 16: Antoine Berjon

Oil on canvas, 39 1/4 x 30 in.
(99.4 x 76 cm.), signed
Private Collection,
Courtesy John Mitchell & Son

Plate 17: Pancrace Bessa

Watercolour on vellum,
4 1/2 x 6 1/2 in. (11.5 x 16.5 cm.),
signed. A drawing for the
Herbier Général
de l'Amateur, 1810-1837
Private Collection, U.S.A.,
Courtesy John Mitchell & Son

Plate 18: Pierre Bonnard

Oil on board laid down on cradled
panel, 16 1/4 x 20 3/4 in.
(41 x 53 cm.),
signed and dated 1900
Courtesy Sotheby's, New York

Plate 19: Francois Bonvin

Oil on canvas, 21 1/4 x 13 1/4 in.
(54 x 34 cm.)
signed and dated 1878
Private Collection,
Courtesy Wheelock Whitney & Co.

Plate 20: Pierre Bourgogne

Oil on Canvas, 76 x 49 in.
(193 x 124.5 cm.),
signed and dated 1879
Courtesy Christie's, London

Plate 21: Gustave Caillebotte

Oil on canvas, 24 1/2 X 18 1/4 in.
(61.5 x 46.5 cm.)
Estate stamp lower left:
'G. Caillebotte', 1881
Private Collection

Plate 22: Madeleine Carpentier

Watercolour on board, 17 1/2 x 14 in.
(44.5 x 35.6 cm.), signed
Avignon, Musée Calvet

Plate 23: Eugéne-Henri Cauchois

Oil on canvas, 27 3/4 x 19 3/4 in.
70.5 x 50 .5 cm.) signed
Private Collection,
Courtesy Daniel B. Grossman Gallery,
New York

Plate 24: Paul Cezanne

Oil on canvas, 18 1/4 x 21 3/4 in
(46.5 x 55.5cm.), c. 1885
Courtesy Sotheby's New York

Plate 25: Jean-Antoine Chazal

Oil on canvas, signed and dated 1830;
inscribed ' à Gérard van Spaendonck,
decédé Paris le 11 mai 1822'
Tourcoing, Musée des Beaux-Arts
(photo: Giraudon)

Plate 26: Eugène Claude

Oil on canvas, 38 x 51 in.
(97 x 130 cm.), signed
Collection Mrs Georgette Misbacher,
Courtesy Christie's, London

Plate 27: Louis-Aristede-Léon Constans

Oil on canvas, one of a pair, 32 x 26 in.
(81.5 x 65.5 cm.), signed and dated 1842,
Courtesy Richard Green Gallery

Plate 28: Jean-Francois van Dael

Oil on canvas, 79 x 60 in.
(198 x 150 cm.),
signed and dated 1804
Musée National du Château de Malmaison

Plate 29: Ferdinand-Victoire-Eugène Delacroix

Oil on canvas, 29 x 36 1/2 in.
(74 x 92 cm.) c. 1842
Vienna, Österreichische Galerie

Plate 30: Emma-Andrée-Felicité Desportes de la Fosse née Beuselin

Watercolour on vellum,
31 1/2 x 24 1/2 in.
(80 x 62 cm.), signed and dated 1836
Private collection,
Courtesy John Mitchell & Son

Plate 31: Narcisse Virgile Diaz de la Peña

Oil on canvas, oval, 24 1/2 x 19 1/2 in.
(61.8 x 49.5 cm.), signed
Glasgow Art Gallery and Museum

FOLLOWING PAGE 216

Plate 32: Paul Gauguin

Oil on canvas, 37 1/2 x 24 1/2 in.
(95 x 62 cm.), signed, c. 1895
Private collection

Plate 33: Jean-Georges Hirn

Oil on canvas, 47 1/4 x 37 in.
(120 x 93 cm.),
signed and dated 1829
Colmar, Musée d' Unterlinden

Plate 34: Alexis Kreyder

Oil on canvas, 41 x 33 1/2 in.
(104 x 85 cm.) signed
London, Noortman London Ltd.

Plate 35: Victor Leclaire

Oil on canvas, 47 x 60 in
(119.4 x 152.3 cm.), signed
Courtesy Sotheby's, New York

Plate 36: Madeleine-Jeanne Lemaire

Oil on canvas, 39 1/2 x 29 1/2 in.
(100 x 75 cm.), signed
Mulhouse, Musée de l'Impression sur Etoffes

Plate 37: Francois Lepage

Oil on canvas, 12 x 19 1/2 in.
(30.5 x 23.5 cm.), signed and dated 1826
Private collection,
Courtesy Sotheby's, Monaco

Plate 38: Claude Monet

Oil on canvas, 39 1/4 x 31 1/4 in.
(100 x 80.7 cm.), signed
Malibu, J. Paul Getty Museum

Plate 39: Adolphe-Joseph-Thomas Monticelli

Oil on panel, 24 x 18 1/2 in
(61 x 47 cm.), signed
Reproduced by courtesy of the Trustees,
National Gallery, London

Plate 40: André-Benoit Perrachon

Oil on canvas, 45 3/4 x 35 in.
(116 x 89 cm.), signed
Lyon, Musée des Beaux Arts

Plate 41: Eugène Petit

Oil on canvas, 22 1/2 x 28 1/4 in.
(57 x 72.5 cm.), signed
Private collection, U.S.A.,
Courtesy John Mitchell & Son

Plate 42: Camille Pissarro

Oil on canvas, 28 x 23 in. (71 x 58.5 cm.),
signed and dated 1876
Private collection
(photo courtesy Marlborough Fine
Art (London) Ltd.)

Plate 43: Jean Louis Prévost

Watercolour and bodycolour with gold
highlights on paper, 7 1/2 x 10 1/2 in.
(19.2 x 26.8 cm.), signed
'Prévost le Jeune 1810'
Cambridge, Fitzwilliam Museum
(Broughton Collection)

Plate 44: Elise Puyroche-Wagner

Oil on canvas, 13 x 9 3/4 in
(33 x 24.8 cm.),
signed
Private collection

Plate 45: Ernst Quost

Oil on canvas, 18 x 21 1/2 in.
(45 x 54 cm.), signed
Paris, Musée Marmottan
(photo: Studio Lourmel, © SPADEM)

Plate 46: Jean-Francois Raffaëlli

Oil on canvas, 53 x 37 1/4 in.
(134.5 x 94.5 cm.),
signed and indistinctly dated '77
Courtesy Sotheby's, London

FOLLOWING PAGE 288

Plate 47: Jean-Marie Reignier

Oil on canvas, 7 1/2 x 9 1/2 in.
(19 x 24 cm.),
signed and dated 1864
Private collection

Plate 48: Germain-Théodore Ribot

Oil on canvas, 18 x 15 in.
(46 x 38 cm.), signed
Private collection

Plate 49: Philipe Rousseau

Oil on canvas, 36 1/2 x 48 3/4 in.
(92.5 x 124 cm.),
signed and inscribed 'Monsieur
Rousseau à Acquigny'
Courtesy Sotheby's, London

Plate 50: Simon Saint-Jean

Oil on canvas, 35 1/4 x 28 1/2 in.
(84.5 x 72.4 cm.), signed
Reproduced by permission of the Trustees,
Wallace Collection, London

Plate 51: Georges Seurat

Oil on canvas, 18 1/4 x 15 1/4 in.
(46.4 x 38.5 cm.), c. 1879-1881
Fogg Art Museum, Harvard University
(Bequest: Collection of
Maurice Wertheim, Class of 1906)

Plate 52: Vincent van Gogh

Oil on canvas, 28 x 36 1/2 in.
(71 x 93 cm.), signed
Private collection

Plate 53: Corneille van Spaendonck

Oil on panel, 25 x 20 1/2 in.
(63.5 x 52 cm.), signed
Private collection,
Courtesy John Mitchell & Son

Plate 54: Pierre-Jean Francois Turpin

Pencil and watercolour, 22 x 17 1/2 in.
(56 x 43.5 cm.), signed and inscribed
Private collection

Foreword

To all those interested in the history of flower painting or in the achievements of the Lyon School in every genre, Elisabeth Hardouin-Fugier and Etienne Grafe are well known and admired. Their exhibition of 1982, devoted to the Lyon School of flower painting, is an outstanding memory of my long involvement in this field. The catalogue of that exhibition is a model of scholarly care and thoroughness. From this strong footing in Lyon, their energies and devotion have now reached out to embrace the whole of France in the 19th century. The result is an unprecedented achievement—not only a standard work of reference but also a very beautiful book.

As might be expected in such a large project, the transformation from seed to full flowering has been lengthy and not without dormant periods. Suffice it to say that my involvement began by transplanting the project from impoverished and unsuitable ground to fertile and highly receptive terrain. We shall always be grateful to Philip Wilson and Anne Jackson for the decisive and enthusiastic way in which they took up my proposal that they publish this Dictionary on a scale appropriate to the text. It was agreed that I should be responsible for selecting and obtaining all the illustrations, both colour and black and white, and for adding artists who came to light in the course of doing so. The opportunity to edit and add to individual entries, whether selected for illustration or not, information gained in the course of picture research has, of course, been fully taken. This editing has been carried out, in large measure, by Judith Carmel, of whom more anon.

The delay referred to above has certainly not been without substantial benefits. It has now been possible to include the great names (e.g. Renoir) and the major artists, not born in France: Gérard and Corneille van Spaendonck, Redouté, Van Dael, and Van Gogh. In several cases they are illustrated by magnificent examples which have only recently become accessible. Thus the entries include specialist flower painters of every status from Cauchois to Fantin-Latour, great artists where, although flowers may form only a small part of their œuvre, their achievements are remarkable and their influence far reaching, and artists, again of every status, who occasionally painted flowers to good effect. While not wanting to venture formally into the applied or decorative arts, reminders of the work of flower artists as applied to ceramics and fabrics are included. We have drawn strongly upon the Broughton Collection of flower drawings in various media because, largely unpublished, they reflect the strength of this tradition throughout the century—the long shadow of Redouté. The important contributions of women artists are particularly apparent in this context. Where the choice has lain between illustrating an interesting picture or broaching the 20th century, the decision has been to illustrate. Otherwise the period of the Dictionary has been respected. Where the work of unrecorded or little-known artists has been encountered, it has been illustrated in the hope of finding more works and documentation through doing so. All entries not written by the authors are, of course, initialled and identified in the list of contributors.

For ease of reading, the authors have streamlined the entries. Abbreviations of sources, salons, museums, departments, media, etc., have been made as much as possible and fully keyed in the list of abbreviations. Except in the case of recorded salon titles or museum catalogues, or instances where a descriptive title has been effective in identifying the work, titles have been omitted throughout the illustrations in accordance with modern practice. LIT., should be understood as select bibliography, including, in many cases, works providing a more extensive bibliography. The reader's attention is particularly drawn to the use of semi colons separating exhibits.

Superfluous material in the entries has been omitted. The inclusion, in its entirety, of Madame Fantin-Latour's catalogue of her husband's work, a rare book today, is very valuable. In the same way, the complete salon records with original descriptions have been given in the case of important artists, e.g. Spaendonck, Redouté, Van Dael, etc., rather than the maddening practice of referring the reader to *Bellier*. Given the contemporary importance of the salons in the careers of artists and the attitudes of the public, any alternative would be inadequate. The alphabetical format of a dictionary produces stimulating juxtapositions. These reflect, to some extent, the style and hanging of collections in the period. They also serve to remind us that the 'popular' artists were known and admired throughout France, at a time when Monet, Renoir, and their friends enjoyed but a fraction of their present day celebrity.

Private collecting in France has always been just that, and no less admirable for its discretion. Thus it has proved impossible to locate examples of a number of artists who merit illustration but whose work is today neither in museums nor appearing at auction. Many, many flower paintings, once exhibited to the public in Parisian and provincial salons, must now be enjoyed by one family alone. In any case, the aim has been to draw upon museum examples as much as possible for obvious reasons. Clearly it was impossible to check the museum notations of every entry, but, from the experience of hundreds of photograph requests, there is a considerable discrepancy between existing records and the actual holdings in the museums today, as anticipated. War, fire, flood, and deterioration, have taken their familiar toll. However, the loss of museum paintings lent to municipal and regional authorities seems regrettable and unnecessary. Equally to be anticipated, the need for drawing up comprehensive inventories, cataloguing, photographing and conservation, is hampered by lack of funds and motivation—a situation certainly not unique to France.

This is one of many reasons why no pioneering dictionary of this kind may lay claim to be complete or definitive. No doubt its publication will stimulate interest throughout the world and bring forth 'new' artists, 'unknown' works, new source material, and so renew even the most seasoned observer's astonishment at the depth of France's riches in this period.

In the task of illustrating this superb text, I have been helped by many people, as the reader may well imagine. First among them is Judith Carmel. She is a post-graduate student preparing a doctoral thesis and a skilled researcher. In the last seven months, she has worked unceasingly, monitoring a large correspondence and innumerable telephone calls to France. Judith has given much of her own time to the project and taken responsibility for selecting the Broughton illustrations and writing those entries, as well as liaising constantly with auctioneers, dealers, and collectors, extracting photographs, often painlessly. She has put up with problems as a part-timer and borne up under conditions which were stressful and frustrating at times and occasionally farcical. I remember particularly shouting down the phone against the cacophony of pneumatic drills in Bond Street to a rather startled man in the Pyrénées-Atlantiques, no doubt confirming the eccentricity of the English in his judgement. I am very grateful to Judith Carmel.

The following deserve my special thanks: Throughout the latter, vital months of preparation two delightful young ladies, Alice Aitken, my ever-cheerful colleague, and Jane 'Gordon' Bennett of Philip Wilson's; my shipper in Paris, Bernadette d'Ussel of Jet-Art Services, appointed one of her colleagues, Yvette Gardon, to deal with all expenditure in France on our behalf; Chantal Mauduit and her assistant Stéphane Pinta for constant research and support; Veronique Tellier of Sotheby's, London; Jovan Nicholson, Christie's, London; Ian Brunt of Wildenstein, London; David Scrase of the Fitzwilliam. I would like to express my appreciation to Robert Gordon, Gabriel Weisberg, Sarah Lidsey (Phillips, London), Giselle Haag (Giraudon, Paris), William Hanham and Claudia Brigg (Christie's, London), John Sunderland, Jane Rick (Victoria & Albert Museum); Peter John Gates. My friends and colleagues have given generous help: Philippe Brame, Richard Green (Selena Evans), Robert Noortman and John Whately, Martin Zimet, Jack Baer, Evert Douwes, Ivo Bouwman, Walter Feilchenfeldt, Thomas Gibson (Maria Gottesman), Nial Hobhouse, Alain Letailleur, Kate Maclean, Nicholas Ohotin (Daniel Grossman, Inc.), Stoppenbach & Delestre, and Mary Miller (Marlborough Fine Art).

The following officers and staff of museums and institutions, nearly all in France, have put up with persistent letters and phone calls with great courtesy and, mostly, good humour: In an ideal world, I would leave tomorrow to drive slowly around France visiting every one of their collections to thank them personally: Madame le Docteur Madeleine Caillot, Albi; Marc Bordreuil, Alès; Françoise Lernout, Amiens; Viviane Huchard, Béatrice de Chancel, Angers; Annick Davy, Arras; Matthieu Pinette, Autun; Marie-Pierre Foissy-Aufrere, Avignon; Hugues de la Touche, Avranches; Vincent Ducourau, Bayonne; Nathalie Javalet, Belfort; Francoise Soulier-Francois, Chislaine Courtet, Besançon; Nicole Riche, Béziers; Martine Tissier de Mallerais, Blois; Sabine Ganidel, Bordeaux; Marie-Francoise Poiret, Bourg-en-Bresse; Claire Moser, Brive; Alain Tapié, Caen; David Scrase, Melissa Dalziel, Jane Munro, Cambridge; Edgar Peeters Bowron, Cambridge, Mass; François Nedellec, Cannes; Jean-Louis Auge, Castres; Armand Amann, Mireille Vedrine, Chambéry; Amelie Lefébure, Chantilly; Marie-Agnès Sonrier, Chaumont; Marie-Claude Fontaine, Clamecy; Étienne Martin, Christian Heck, Colmar; Christian Lapointe, Compiègne; Corinne Legout, Dax; Pierre Bazin, Dieppe; Noël Durand, Digne; Catherine Gras, Dijon; Maryvonne Marmet, Dole; Regis Fabre, Madame Colette, Draguignan; Gérard Guillot-Chene, Evreux; Professor Marti, Glarus (Switzerland); François Davoine, Gray; Serge Lemoine, Frédérique Deutch, Grenoble; Françoise Cohen, Le Havre; Madame Jorrand, Laon; Madame Anneu, La Rochelle; Michèle Bordier-Nikitine, Le Mans; Annie Scottez-De Wambrechies, Lille; Chantal Meslin-Perrier, Veronique Notin, Limoges; Rosario Asevedo, Lisbon; Mlle Pourreau, Louviers; Philipe Durey, Dominique Brachlianoff, Lyon; Evelyne Gaudry-Poitevin, Lyon (Musée des Tissus); Jean-François Garmier, Mâcon; Leticia Wheeler Kollgaard, Malibu; Gérard Hubert, Malmaison; Marie-Paule Vial, Bénédicte Pradie, Marseille; Magdeline Joly, Metz; Madame Husson, Montargis; Florence Viguier, Montauban; Martine Feneyrou, Montpellier; Françoise Daniel, Morlaix; Jacqueline Jacqué, Mulhouse; Claude Petry, Nancy; Henry-Claude Cousseau, Nantes; Sylvie Saint-Martin, Narbonne; Élise Colombel, Nevers; Jean Forneris, Nice; Monsieur Lassale, Nîmes, Madame Tixier, Niort; David Ojaloo, Orléans; Professor Yves Laissus, Catherine Hustache, Bibliothèque Centrale du Muséum National d'Histoire Naturelle, Paris; Michèle Nespoulet, Jacqueline Mallet, Museum National d'Histoire Naturelle, Paris; Geneviève Bonté, Conservateur en chef de la Bibliothèque au Musée des Arts Decoratifs, Paris; Marie-Noelle de Grandry, Sonia Edard, Musée des Arts Decoratifs, Paris; Caroline Genet, Musée Marmottan; Madame Ann Roquebert, Musée d'Orsay, Paris; Monsieur Soubeyran, Périgueux; James White, Pittsburgh; Edda Maillet, Pointoise; Nicole Amprimoz, Le Puy; Francois Pomarède, Reims; François Bergot, Madame Chevalier, Rouen; Pascal Aumasson, Saint-Brieuc; Maurice Frechuret, Saint-Étienne; Marianne Thaure, Saintes; Madame

Levavasseur, Saint-Malo; Eric Hild, Saint-Tropez; Monique Jacob, Saumur; Mlle Moreau, Sens; Monsieur Freises, Sète; Tamara Préaud, Sèvres; Madame Speroni, Strasbourg; Claudine Sudre, Monsieur Milhau, Toulouse; Chantal Rouquet, Troyes; Isabelle Dulac-Rooryck, Mlle Roux, Tulle; Mr Koens, Utrecht; Mlle Creusot, Varzy; Alain Girard, Villeneuve-les-Avignon; Beverly Carter, Washington, DC.

The authors would most especially like to acknowledge their gratitude to Madeleine Rocher-Jauneau, Conservateur Honoraire du Musée des Beaux-Arts de Lyon, for her help and encouragement during the early stages of the project. They also place on record their thanks to M.F. Aufrère, H. Boissier, H. Bringuier, C. Charignon, M.C. Chermat, S. Giagnorio, D. Gros, P. Héritier, I. Lajut, M. and J. Stirt-Grafe, I. Sulier, P. Vallet. Etienne Grafe wishes to acknowledge the assistance of the Trustees and staff of the Maison de l'Institut de France à Londres (Fondation Edmond de Rothschild).

My secretary, Malcolm Uttley, a veteran of many campaigns, has typed and re-typed letters in English and French, the bibliographies, this foreword, new entries, and much besides, with characteristic care, amid countless interruptions.

Finally, I wish to record my heartfelt gratitude to the authors, my friends Elisabeth and Étienne. I have been greatly touched by the trust they have placed in me in so many respects over the last four years. Such help as I have been able to give them has been far, far outweighed by the privilege and excitement of being close to their magnificent achievement.

PETER MITCHELL
London, October 1988

Note on the text

It has always been difficult to give titles to flower paintings. The banality of *Roses, tulips and other flowers in a glass vase* dear to auctioneers' catalogues has been rejected here. By the same token, the reader is left to recognise that Van Gogh's subject (page 225) was irises. Because it was impossible to give identifications to the hundreds of paintings reproduced here, it was felt that the full analysis of one bouquet would serve as a guide to the variety, subtlety and complexity of the flower painters' task.

In order to illustrate museum examples, to balance the many privately owned works, it has been necessary to include some paintings where old, discoloured varnishes have prevented ideal reproduction.

References to colour illustrations within the dictionary are marked with a dagger in the margin.

The flowers depicted in Antoine Berjon's flower-piece (see colour illustration on page 96), are as follows:

1 Rembrandt Tulip *Tulipa* hybrid.
2 Iris *Iris germanica* L.
3 Madonna Lily *Lilium candidum* L.
4 Peony *Paeonia lactiflora* hybrid.
5 Hollyhock *Althaea rosea* Cav.
6 Lilac *Syringa vulgaris* L.
7 Gallica Rose *Rosa* hybrid.
8 Hedge Bindweed *Calystegia sepium* (L.) R.Br.
9 Poppy leaf *Papaver ? orientalis* L.
10 Single Rose *Rosa foetida* Bast.
11 Pot Marigold *Calendula officinalis* L.
12 Night-scented Stock *Matthiola longipetala* (Vent.) DC. subsp. *bicornis* (Sibth. & Sm.) P. Ball
13 Single Rose ? *Rosa rugosa* Thunb.
14 Oriental Poppy *Papaver orientalis* L.
15 Rudbeckia *Rudbeckia laciniata* ? L.
16 Blue Bind-weed *Ipomoea tricolor* Cav.

We are grateful to Brian Mathew at The Royal Botanic Gardens, Kew for providing this analysis. P.M.

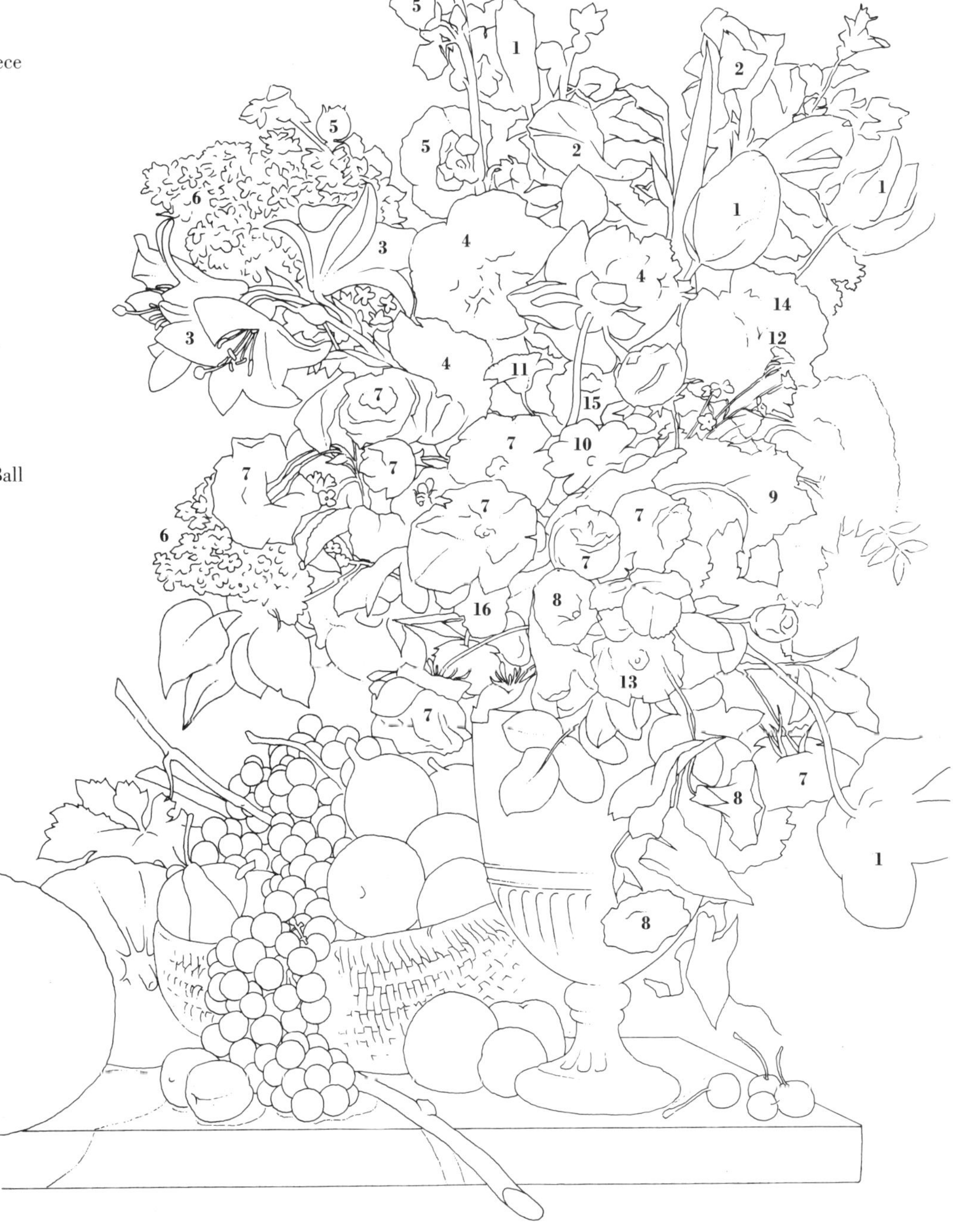

Contributors

AC: Andrée Cormier
BG: Bruno Gaudichon
BJ: Bernard Jacque
CL: Christine Lamarre
FU: Françoise Uny
G and LT: Gabrielle and Louis Trénard
IG: Isabelle Girardet
JLC: Judith L. Carmel
JLM: Jean-Luc Mordefroid
JPB: Jean-Paul Bouillon
MTC: Marie-Thérèse de Contenson
MW: Maurice Wantelet
PM: Peter Mitchell

Unsigned entries are by Elisabeth Hardouin-Fugier and Etienne Grafe

Introduction

Flower painting in 19th-century France has a complex history. The most diverse styles flourish side by side, overlap and disappear, only to surface again in the most unlikely ways and places. There were plenty of schools of flower painting in 19th-century France, and some artists were undoubtedly influential, but by no means every painter belonged to one. Many did for reasons that will be explained; others, among the most famous, did not. We shall set about coaxing order out of chaos, using chronology as a loose thread.

Needless to say, many 19th-century flower painters were born in the previous century and worked in the idiom that had always been theirs. Some, like Jean-Baptiste Pillement (d. 1808), Jean-Louis Prévost le jeune (d. 1810), Pierre Leriche (d. 1811) or Anne Vallayer-Coster (d. 1818), only belong to the century in their late works. Pillement painted and drew his *Fleurs idéales* to his dying day, and Leriche had no reason to give up turning out his charming bread-and-butter overdoors. Some influential teachers, like Thérèse Baudry de Balzac (d. 1831) or Pierre-Toussaint Déchazelle (d. 1833), carried on 18th-century traditions well into the following century. Like many others, both of these looked back to the cradles of European flower painting—Flanders and Holland.

THE NEO-DUTCH TRADITION

The Dutch painters Jan van Huysum and Rachel Ruysch and their followers, with their analytical approach, opulent compositions, unerring eye for refined detail, unparalleled craftsmanship and high finish, all influenced French painters well into the century of Delacroix and Courbet, as evidenced by salon handbooks.

Though in the previous century the Dutch-born Gérard van

Spaendonck had been elected a Royal Academician, flower painting still ranked low in France by 19th-century Academy standards. None the less, while large, uplifting history paintings still held pride of place in the annual Paris or provincial Salons, flower-pieces along with portraits and genre paintings—still called *petit genre* in the 1820s—continued to sell well and grace many an elegant room. Their modest size made them suitable for smaller rooms with a *cabinet* atmosphere. Patronage was seldom lacking, though the flower painter as such had no official training. Unlike history, portrait or landscape painting, flower painting was not taught at the Paris École des Beaux-Arts, and of course it lacked the incentive of the Prix de Rome. But though officially underrated, it was far from ignored, being useful in many fields such as botany at the Jardin des Plantes, porcelain painting at Sèvres, and the textile industries in Lyon, Saint-Etienne or Mulhouse, whose flower designers exhibited their easel paintings at Salons.

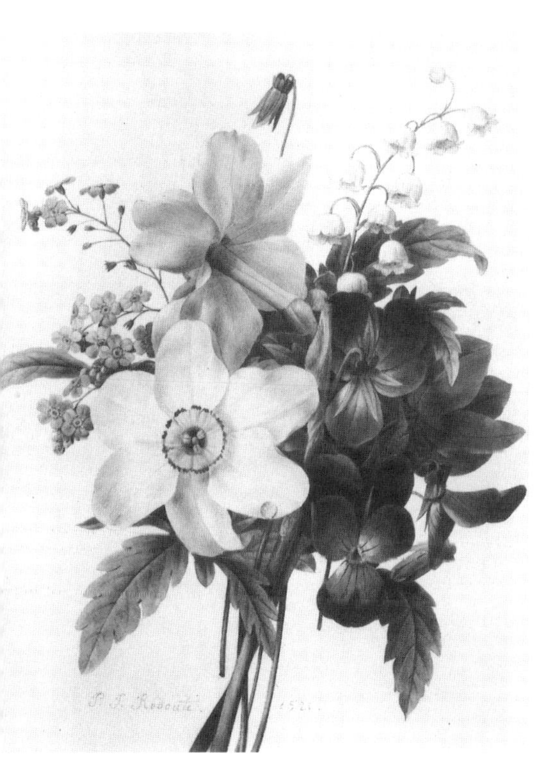

Pierre-Joseph Redouté

Watercolour on vellum, $7\frac{1}{2} \times 6\frac{1}{2}$ in. (19 × 16.3 cm.) signed and dated 1821
Private collection

Understandably, French critics, such as the revered Landon, saw flower painting in these limited terms. The Paris Salon of 1812 is typical in that it featured only three flower-pieces by French painters—one by Deharme, Jean-Georges Hirn's *Fleurs sur les ruines d'un autel antique*, and another piece by Marie Victoire Jaquotot. The other flower painters were all Dutch or Flemish-born. Jean-François Eliaerts contributed *Fleurs, fruits et animaux*, Spey a flower-piece, Van Dael *Fleurs et fruits*, Van Os a flower-piece, and Corneille van Spaendonck three.

Such Dutch and Flemish supremacy is understandable, given the standards of excellence set by their flower painters, and they found French patronage increasingly available as their native countries came under Napoleonic rule. Incidentally, Hortense, Queen of Holland, Napoleon's stepdaughter and sister-in-law, was an amateur flower painter and influential art patron.

Corneille van Spaendonck was active at Sèvres, and his brother Gérard at the Paris Muséum d'Histoire Naturelle (Jardin des Plantes) where he was succeeded as professor of botanical drawing ('iconographie végétale') by another Flemish-born artist, Pierre-Joseph Redouté, the 'Raphael des roses'. Jean-François Eliaerts, also born in Flanders and a naturalized Frenchman, a regular Paris Salon contributor, spent many years teaching art at that most exclusive of all French girls schools, the Saint-Denis Institution de la Légion d'Honneur. In the same institution, the neo-Dutch tradition was carried on in the 1830s by Thérèse Baudry de Balzac, a pupil of Van Spaendonck who published a self-teaching method, *Cours d'iconographie ou l'art de dessiner d'après nature les fleurs, fruits, etc.* (1830). Clémentine de Bar was active at the same school in the 1840s and Marie Guignebert in the 1880s.

In Lyon, a stronghold of Dutch-inspired flower painting, the thirty or so flower-pieces by David de Heem, Van Dael, Van Brussel, Mignon and their likes purchased by the city's art gallery (or bequeathed to it by civic-minded townspeople) were used as reference works and models by the aspiring flower painters and textile designers of Lyon. Even Antoine Berjon, perhaps the most eminent flower painter of his time, is known to have copied Van Dael's *Tubéreuse cassée*. When the Dutch and Flemish works went on permanent show at the Lyon museum in the Salon des Fleurs, opened in 1808—the only museum room in France entirely devoted to flower paintings—their influence extended far beyond local textile designers, reflecting the taste of the time. Elisa Bertrand, for example, painted Dutch-inspired flower-pieces throughout her life, often featuring a central figure or scene within a wreath; and at the 1846 Paris Salon her contemporary, Henriette de Longchamp, exhibited an *Offrande à la Vierge*, no doubt inspired by Simon Saint-Jean's highly popular 1842 exhibit. Arthur Chaplin (b. 1869) carried the neo-Dutch tradition, albeit in a weakened form, far beyond the turn of the century.

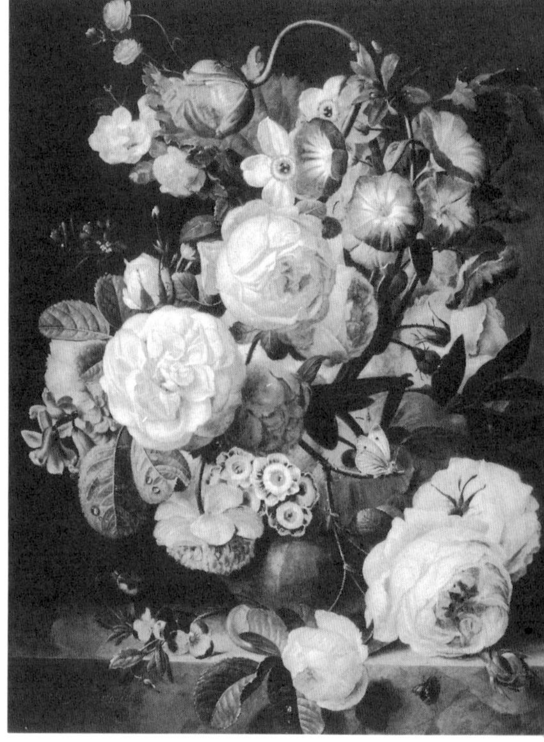

Jean François Eliaerts

Oil on canvas, 19 × 14¼ in. (48 × 36.5 cm), signed
Courtesy Sotheby's, London

At the beginning of the 19th century, several Dutch or Flemish masters had well-attended studios in Paris. Among Van Dael's many pupils were Bonneval and Brienne together with a number of female painters such as Adèle Riché, Madame Deharme (née Laugier) and Elisa Bruyère (née Le Barbier). The latter exhibited widely both in Paris and in the provinces (especially at Lyon and Rouen) and her works in the Dutch idiom were admired and copied extensively. Another pupil of Van Dael's, the Vicomtesse Decaux (née Milet de Mureau), opened a fashionable ladies' academy of flower painting in Paris.

Still more successful as a teacher was Gérard van Spaendonck, who had scores of pupils both at the Paris Jardin des Plantes and at his private studio. Along with skills such as singing, dancing and embroidery, flower painting had long been one of the standard accomplishments expected of young ladies, and at the most fashionable teaching studios such as those of Van Spaendonck, female pupils far outnumbered male. German-born Jacob Ber, alias Jacobber, made his name as the most popular porcelain painter of the century; Antoine Chazal too was successful. The Marquise de Grollier, Henriette Vincent Rideau du Sal, Ernestine Panckoucke, Mélanie de Comoléra and Thérèse Baudry de Balzac are among the best-known female painters taught by Van Spaendonck; after his death, most of them studied under Redouté and became teachers themselves.

REDOUTÉ AND HIS PUPILS

Redouté's influence on 19th-century French flower painting was due not only to his own artistic achievements, but also to his long teaching career. In 1786 he had been appointed draughtsman to Queen Marie-Antoinette's Cabinet, though he was never the Queen's drawing master. A few years later Empress Josephine, a flower-lover and keen botanist, employed him, making him virtually the head of an active team of botanical artists working at Malmaison. It is not known whether Redouté gave tuition at the various studios he occupied first at the Louvre (1798–1805) and then at the Hôtel d'Angiviller, rue de l'Oratoire (1805–7). What is certain is that his country studio at Fleury-sous-Meudon and the town studio he opened in 1807 at the Hôtel Mirabeau, 6 rue de Seine, Saint-Germain, attracted many pupils.

The studio at Fleury-sous-Meudon was attended by wealthy country neighbours such as Adélaïde de Pastoret, and that at the Hôtel Mirabeau by aspiring artists ranging from gifted amateurs such as the Comtesse de Mulinen and Aurore Poniatowska to highly professional artists like Antoine Pascal or Pancrace Bessa. Redouté succeeded Gérard van Spaendonck as professor of botanical drawing at the Paris Muséum d'Histoire Naturelle in July 1822, and he taught there thirty hours a week for the last sixteen years of his life. He gave beginners and students of average ability tuition in drawing and watercolour painting on paper, providing drawn and engraved models for them to copy from in winter, and flowers from the Jardin des Plantes as models during the spring and summer. He insisted on accuracy, draughtsmanship, and composition. Echoes of his teaching method will be found in Jules Dumas' *Redouté des Dames*. At the Jardin the master would teach the technicalities of watercolour over pencil, hence the very small number of oil painters working in his circle. Forty or so painters, most of them female against seven men only, have been listed to date amongst his pupils; some of the men (e.g. Brienne and Chazal) who had studied under Van Spaendonck were proficient in oils. The others worked in Redouté's favourite medium, watercolour, sometimes on vellum, thus carrying on the tradition of the Vélins du Roy, the collection of botanical designs commissioned by Gaston d'Orléans and continued by Louis XIV, Louis XV and Louis XVI. Though most botanical artists of the time listed by Nissen (see Bibliography), such as Claude Victor de Boissieu, Pierre Boitard, Jean-Baptiste Bory de Saint Vincent, the Cloquet family or Desmaisons (the engraver), owed little to Redouté, some pupils of his, like Antoine Poiteau or Alfred Riocreux, became successful botanical artists, designers or decorators at Sèvres or at the Gobelins tapestry factory. Others still had successful teaching careers. Camille de Chantereine, amongst many others, deputized for Redouté while Jules Cloquet taught at the École des Mines and Augustine Dufour privately, as did Huberte Gérono, Elisabeth Lemire and Adèle Riché in the 1840s. Pancrace Bessa became Redouté's colleague at the Muséum d'Histoire Naturelle and Ange-Louis Guillaume Lesourd de Beauregard his successor.

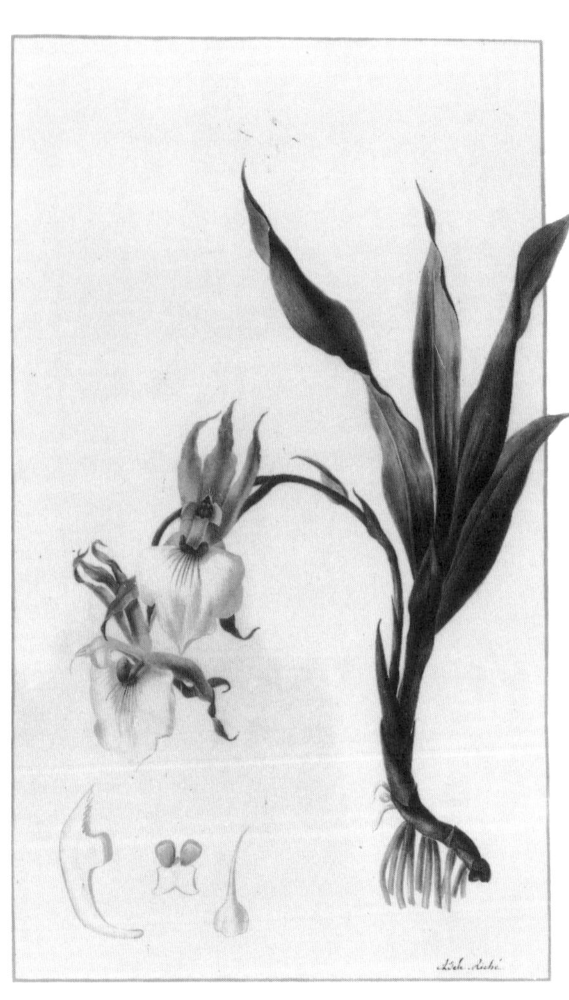

Adèle Riché

Watercolour, signed
Paris, Bibliothèque Centrale du Muséum d'Histoire Naturelle

Porcelain painting also provided traditional flower painters with work. The Sèvres factory was, of course, the Mecca and stronghold of Dutch-inspired flower painters, and Jacob Ber alias Jacobber was the most accomplished of them all. An outstanding technician, he painted flowers and fruit on large porcelain plaques, masterpieces of dazzling draughtsmanship and brilliant colouring, worthy in every respect of Gérard van Spaendonck, his teacher. Jacobber spent over thirty years of his life working at Sèvres and exhibited his opulent *tours de force* from the early 1820s to the 1855 Paris Exposition Universelle. Among his many pupils were Fanny Burat, Charlotte Hublier, Jean-François Philippine and Julie van Marcke. Philippine and Julie van Marcke both worked for Sèvres along with Abel Schilt and scores of lesser artists.

Another minor but still interesting feature of the time is the link between flower painting and portrait or miniature painting, bouquets, wreaths or single flowers being as popular accessories as ever before. Some portrait or miniature painters exhibited flower-pieces as a side-line—Jean-Pierre Barrois, Louis-Léopold Boilly, Auguste Garneray (painter to both Queen Hortense and the Duchesse de Berry) and Amanda Girault de Saint-Fargeau produced lovingly accurate flower paintings in the neo-Dutch idiom. Conversely, Antoine Berjon was also active as a portrait and miniature painter, which takes us back to the Lyon School.

FLEURS DE LYON

Though flowers had been painted and drawn in Lyon for perhaps fifty years, the Lyon School as such materialized during the reigns of Louis XVIII and Charles X. The aim of the École des Beaux-Arts at Lyon was to train textile designers in the two disciplines essential to the silk industry: flower design and *mise-en-carte*, i.e. the design and preparation of squared pattern cards. Antoine Berjon was professor of the class of flower design from 1810 to 1823. He was a demanding, temperamental and unpredictable teacher whose own works speak for themselves. He insisted on sound draughtsmanship and luminous colours, and to these he added, in his own works, the kind of quietly mysterious quality to be found in some of the best 17th-century Dutch flower-pieces. His class was attended by about twenty pupils each year, some of whom spent several years studying flower design. In all he had nearly two hundred pupils, most of them born between 1795 and 1805, and after retiring he went on teaching privately but had very few regular pupils.

Berjon was succeeded at the Lyon École des Beaux-Arts by Augustin Thierriat, one of his former students, who held the

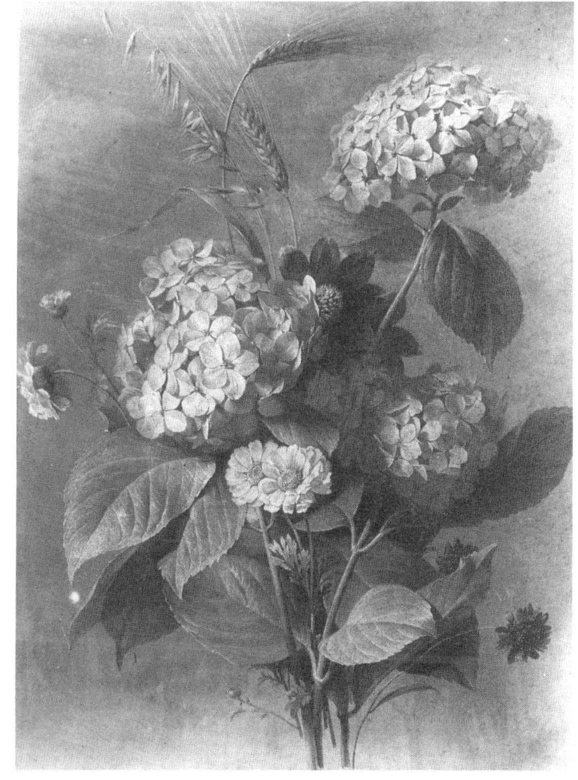

Antoine Berjon

Black chalk heightened with white on buff paper, 24¾ × 20 in. (63 × 51 cm.), signed
Lyon, Musée des Beaux-Arts

professorship of flower design from 1823 to 1853. He proved a gifted, more tolerant teacher than Berjon and most of the works of his five hundred or so pupils do him proud indeed. Like their predecessors, their flower studies, flower-shop bouquets and votive flower-pieces are noteworthy for their sound draughtsmanship, clever composition and, above all, high finish. Dewdrops, flies, and all sorts of insects are often worthy of their Dutch models, but their fine craftsmanship and sometimes uneasy combination of flamboyant arrangement and wistful sentimentalism are distinct Lyon features. Painters of the Lyon School went on turning out such works well into the 1860s, long after they had gone out of fashion in Paris.

The Lyon creed was spread far and wide by two popular self-teaching methods, the *Méthode Grobon frères* published in the late 1840s in Paris and London and, twenty years later, Chabal Dussurgey's more substantial *Études et compositions de fleurs.*

WINDS OF CHANGE

Though no overnight stylistic change was noticeable at the time, the deaths of certain flower painters of the old school somehow seemed to toll the knell of an era. Jean-Georges Hirn died in 1830, and, sadder losses, Corneille van Spaendonck, Jean-François van Dael and Redouté all died in 1840 and Berjon three years later. Significantly Julie Abner, Amélie Birat, Thérèse Herzog, Elisa Lemire, Esther de Maulnoir, Madame Rebours, Jules Baget, Charles Charbonnel and Auguste Gobert, all of them connected with Redouté's circle or pupils of the master, had works refused by the 1843 Paris Salon selection committee. Likewise, though Simon Saint-Jean had so far exhibited to great critical acclaim, his 1845 exhibition was murdered by Baudelaire: 'Saint-Jean . . . is of the School of Lyon, the penitentiary of painting, the corner of the known world in which the infinitely minute is wrought the best . . .' *(Le Salon de 1845)*. Redouté had fallen from grace, too. In his review of the 1847 Paris Salon for *L'Artiste*, Clément de Ris called the late Redouté's flowers waxen compared with Philippe Rousseau's. The same reviewer praised Delacroix's flowers: 'They are so lifelike, so solid, so true in colour that I would fain try and lift up one of his roses.' These two reviews are typical of the time in that they herald a change in vision, a new preference for painterliness, broader treatment and bolder brushwork.

But paintings of the old school did not, as has already been said, vanish overnight. At the 1846 Paris Salon, Antoine Chazal, Madame Colombet, Amédée Damis, Jean-Marie Reignier, Simon Saint-Jean and a few more represented the neo-Dutch trend along with watercolourists such as Brienne or Madame Girardin. Nevertheless, Jean Benner, Faustin Besson, Frédéric Grobon, Charles Node and others, some of them specializing in flower painting, all of them newcomers, exhibited flowers in the new, more painterly idiom, aiming at a stronger decorative effect. None of them, of course, was as boldly modern in outlook as Delacroix, but, at a time when flower painting stood at a crossroads, all of them had, so to speak, taken the road to freedom from botanical accuracy. Many more were to follow this direction in the years to come. For the rearguard the future looked bleak indeed. In his review of the 1859 Salon for the *Gazette des Beaux-Arts*, Paul Mantz had a bone to pick with the Lyon School: 'A flower is a living thing . . . M. Saint-Jean cuts out in a material that is neither paper nor cloth the unhealthy-looking plants of an impossible flora.' In these early years of pre-Impressionism, the artificiality of art was a controversial issue and argument waxed fierce. In 1860, again in the *Gazette*, Lagrange contrasted the meticulousness of the old school of flower painting with the new *paysagiste* approach, emphasizing the variations of light and a more sensual interpretation of flowers. Some painters saw the writing on the wall, others did not. Amongst those who did not Lesourd de Beauregard, Pauline Allain, Etienne Corpet and their likes continued to propagate their traditional approach either as teachers or government officials. The large number who did included Delacroix, Courbet, all the Impressionists and their heirs, but though many Impressionists occasionally painted flowers, none of them can be called a flower painter in the strict sense. Meanwhile, the so-called *fleuristes*, who had always been treated as poor relations by Salon officials, were to suffer further humiliations.

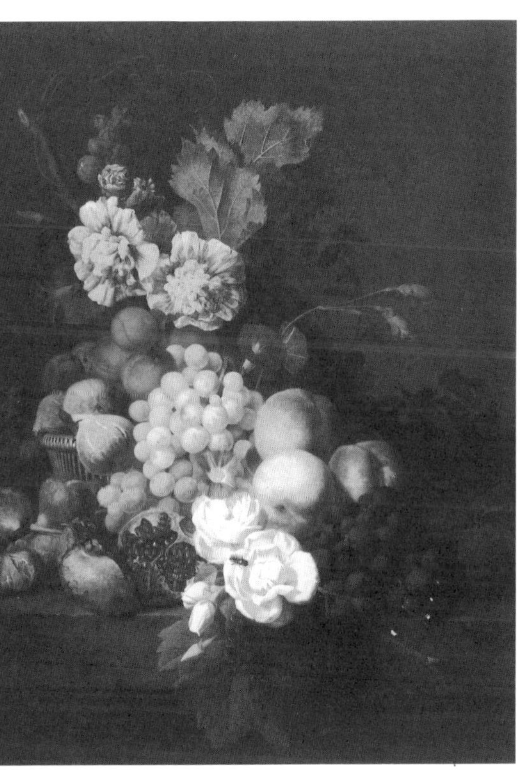

Charles-Joseph Node

Oil on canvas, $30\frac{3}{4} \times 23\frac{1}{2}$ in (78 × 60 cm.), signed and dated 1843
Montpellier, Musée Fabre

CUT FLOWERS

Among those who exhibited flower paintings at the 1855 Paris Exposition Universelle were Adèle Delaporte, Louise Durat-Lassalle, Honorine Emeric-Bouvret, Paul Faivre, Mme Alfred-Elaine Girbaud, Node Saint-Ange, and an unusually strong group of Lyon painters including Mathieu Berger (two exhibits), Chabal-Dussurgey (two), Fleury Chantre (two), Deyrieux (three) Laÿs (three), Remillieux (two), Saint-Jean (nine) and Elise Wagner (five). Though badly lit, a usual complaint with Salon exhibitors, Saint-Jean's exhibits brought him a gold medal and his Lyon friends and colleagues asked him to plead the cause of his fellow flower painters: 'The flower painters have been stripped of the first medal ... they are the only ones to be deprived of the honour; they are thereby placed lower than the lithographers and miniature painters.' And as a final blow in the face for the old school, the well-established artist Lesourd de Beauregard, Redouté's successor at the Jardin des Plantes, whose exhibits had so far been exempt from the selection committee's seal of approval, had two works of his rejected by the 1867 Exposition Universelle, which slight alone reveals French *fleuristes* as the Cinderellas of 19th-century painting.

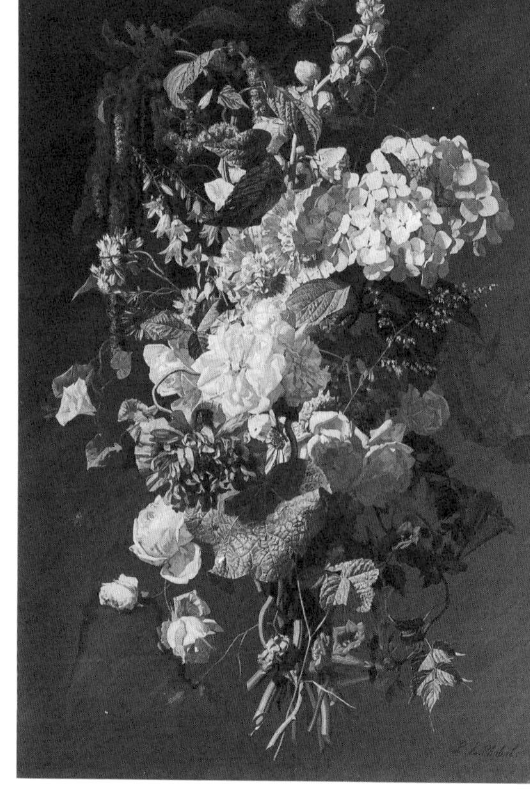

Pierre-Adrien Chabal-Dussurgey

$32\frac{1}{4} \times 23\frac{1}{4}$ in. (82×59 cm.), signed
Angers, Musée des Beaux-Arts

However, flower painting continued to provide countless artists, both Parisian and provincial, with a living. The Lyon artists for whom (Simon Saint-Jean and André Perrachon being exceptions) flower painting was a side-line and flower design for the silk industry their main source of income, were in a class of their own. The 1830s, 1840s and 1850s saw the birth of a number of highly professional flower painters who were to make their name in the second half of the century. Amongst these are Pauline Allain, the Biva brothers, Pierre Bourgogne, Achille Cesbron, Charles-Etienne Corpet, Georges Jeannin, Joanny Maisiat, Eugène Petit, Ernest Quost and, of course, Fantin-Latour and his wife, Victoria Dubourg. Jean-Alexandre Couder, their senior by many years, is interesting as an early example of a genre and history painter who devoted part of his time to flower painting. This Jack-of-all-trades opened the way to scores of artists such as Fabius Brest, Narcisse-Virgile Diaz de la Pena and Paul Huet, mostly landscape painters;

Blaise-Alexandre Desgoffe, Philippe Rousseau and Antoine Vollon, mostly still-life painters; and, as said before, the Impressionists.

Even eminent figure and genre painters, such as Jules Breton, Edouard Debat-Ponsan or Auguste Toulmouche, turned to flower painting more than occasionally, as did scores of portrait painters (including Léon Bonnat), animal painters (Euphémie Muraton and Edouard Traviès), poster designers (Jules Chéret), or even sculptors (Jean-Baptiste Carpeaux). Thousands of amateurs did likewise, in France as elsewhere. From Louise and Marie-Amélie d'Orléans to Anna de Noailles, aristocratic women found flower painting a welcome, eminently lady-like pastime. They were painters of widely varying distinction, and included representatives of every walk of life: the politician Marc Caussidière, the ceramist Camille Moreau-Nélaton, the draughtsman Hansi, and, of course, members of the Vilmorin family of seed and nursery fame—all painted flowers, often in watercolours, gouache or pastels, more seldom in oils.

FLEURS DES SALONS

As long as the Paris Salon remained the shrine of conservative painting, flower painters, most of them working in the traditional neo-Dutch style or in a more free and painterly idiom, continued to be treated as poor relations. As a matter of course, selection committees favoured academic trends in every field of painting. When seceding members founded the Salon des Indépendants in 1884 and the Société Nationale des Beaux-Arts in 1890, more wall space was given to flower painters not only because selection committees were more tolerant, but because flower painting, having evolved towards a looser treatment, had become accessible to more artists. Grégoire Chapoton and Mathieu Battaglia, two founding members of the Salon des Indépendants, were full-time flower painters. Typically, this was the Salon where flower-pieces were made especially welcome; scores of exhibitors, most of them obscure, with no mention of teacher or address, would send one or two paintings and then vanish into thin air, which seems to indicate more or less gifted amateurs. The old Salon, renamed Société des Artistes Français, could in the 1880s and 1890s, unlike its competitors, boast well-illustrated handbooks and even issued postcards of the most popular exhibits—Edmond Allouard was a favourite exhibitor and his *plein air* flowers were reproduced nine times in fifteen years (1883–98). His works, like Achille Cesbron's *Fleurs du sommeil* (1886), are fine specimens of wistful, moody, playful or swooning turn-of-the-century taste.

Another feature of the Paris art scene towards the end of the century was the emergence of two Salons whose exhibitors were mostly women: The Union des Femmes Peintres et Sculpteurs and the Salon du Noir et Blanc. The former tended to be for the professionals, whereas the latter was a favourite with art teachers and their amateur pupils. A number of artists exhibited at both Salons.

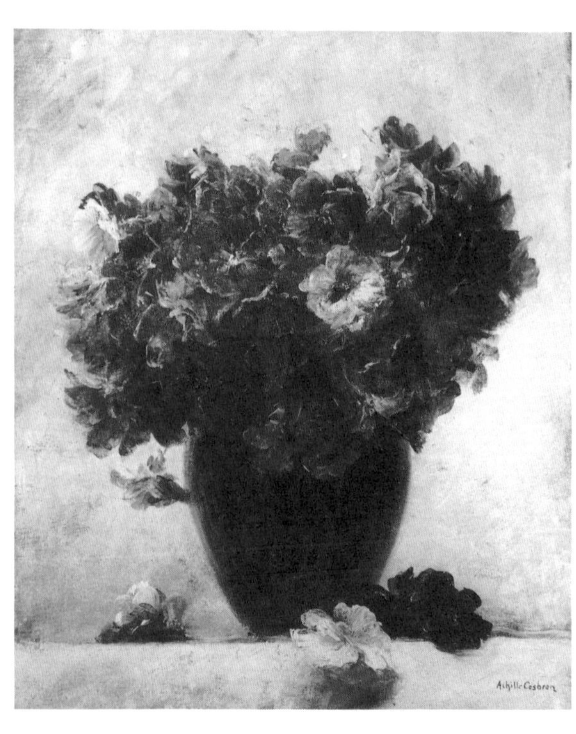

Achille-Théodore Cesbron

Oil on board, 18 × 15 in. (46 × 38 cm.), signed
Paris, Musée d'Orsay

STATE COMMISSIONS AND PURCHASES AFTER 1845

The comparatively few recorded state commissions and purchases of flower paintings reflect the scant proportion of these paintings exhibited at the Paris and provincial Salons. Officials would, of course, consider more favourably works exhibited at the conservative Salon (later Salon des Artistes Français) than those shown at the more adventurous Société Nationale des Beaux-Arts where state purchases were to become more frequent in the early 20th century. Thus Ruth Mercier, a regular Salon exhibitor, had several works purchased by the State. Never favourites as government purchases, flower paintings, however, fared from bad to worse. Even Pierre Bourgogne, a well-known, respected specialist, who repeatedly applied for state purchases, was turned down nine times in the 1880s and 1890s. Ernest-Ange Duez had several exhibits of his purchased but none of these was a flower-piece. Sometimes a theme flower painting would attract some reviewer's attention—thus in 1890 *Le Centenaire* pressed for the purchase of Georges Jeannin's *Buste de la République dans une couronne* (1882) for the Musée du Havre. Watercolours, being both inexpensive and unobtrusive, made suitable consolation prizes and, as such, were popular as government purchases. But even old favourites such as Eléonore Escallier had to suffer the humiliation of fierce bargaining. She wanted 4,000 to 5,000 francs for her Paris Salon exhibit of 1865 and was offered a mere 1,500 francs for it five years later. Achille Cesbron was less demanding: his *Metempsychose* (1884) was acquired for 1,500 francs, his *Fleurs du sommeil* (1886) for 1,800 francs, his *Bouquet de roses* (1897) for 1,500 francs and his *Roses à la guirlande* (1898) for 1,000 francs.

As a rule, most flower paintings bought by the State in the 1880s averaged 1,000–1,5000 francs, seldom exceeding 2,000 francs. Among the most expensive of them were Jundt's *Fleurs de mai* of 1876 (2,000 francs) and Pierre Bourgogne's *Panneau décoratif* of 1885 (2,500 francs). Watercolours were less expensive—Delphine de Cool was paid 1,200 francs for hers in 1890, and Pierre Bourgogne 1,000 francs in 1890 and 800 francs for his *Fleurs de printemps* (1896) and *Fleurs d'eté* (1897).

Flower painters applying for government purchases often had to muster support from ministers, deputés of the Assemblée Nationale, or Ministry of Agriculture officials. Thus the influential critic Charles Blanc recommended Charles Nicolas Lemercier's *Fleurs et fruits* in 1849, a flower-piece by Eléonore Escallier in 1878, and bought flowers from Jean-Alexandre Couder's widow in 1879. Georges Jeannin's supporters included such leading figures as the painter Robert-Fleury and the politicians Félix Faure, Jules Siegfried and Comte Fabre de l'Aude. No wonder he was awarded the Légion d'Honneur in 1903. At the turn of the century another powerful critic, Léonce Bénédite, supported scores of flower painters.

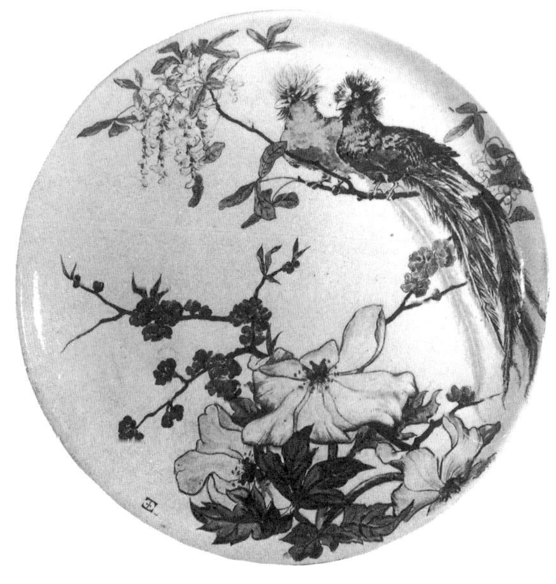

Marie-Caroline-Eléonore Escallier

Earthenware plate, decoration in relief, painted and underglazed, diameter 23½ in. (60 cm.), Paris, Musée des Arts Décoratifs

Most flower paintings bought by the State were sent to provincial museums or public buildings. They would grace innumerable small-town art galleries such as Issoudun, Tulle, La Ferté-Macé, so that to this day even the tiniest, most remote town can boast at least one *fin-de-siècle* flower painting in the town-hall *salle des mariages*, or in some petty official's dusty office. Of course some more fortunate works found more flattering destinations. Claire Lemaître's *Fleurs d'automne*, purchased in 1892 for 1,200 francs, was sent to Toulouse's town-hall on Senator Hébrard's oddly-worded recommendation: 'Quite an effective work, this would be no disgrace to the Capitole.' Among the flower paintings sent to more exotic destinations were Alfred Rouby's Salon exhibit of 1890 (800 francs), sent to the French Embassy in St Petersburg, and Pierre Bourgogne's *Fleurs de printemps*, presented to the Emperor of China in 1897.

NEW TEACHERS

In mid-19th-century France as elsewhere the prosperous middle classes, reaping the benefits of the industrial revolution, provided flower painters with ever-welcome incentives and outlets.

First and foremost, flower painting ranked more highly than ever among the fashionable lady-like pursuits, and a growing need for teachers made itself felt. What used to be taught privately, or at a few exclusive girls' boarding schools, came to be more and more widely taught as more schools opened to cater for the needs of the growing middle classes. When school attendance was made compulsory in France in 1882, it became available to innumerable students, hence the rash of more or less proficient turn-of-the-century works gracing proud parents' sitting-rooms.

Eléonore Escallier, a popular porcelain painter with long Sèvres associations, aware of the importance of flower painting both as a female prerequisite and as a means of livelihood, as early as 1865 offered to teach the subject free of charge at the École Impériale de Jeunes Filles. Escallier realised that the unprecedented development of arts and crafts in the second part of the century would give flower design and painting a corresponding importance, and that more and more women would be needed as teachers and factory workers. In the 1880s, many women exhibited at the Union des Femmes Peintres et Sculpteurs and at the Noir et Blanc Salon, the latter featuring many works by elementary, secondary and École Normale teachers. Others taught privately—Madeleine Carpentier, Uranie-Alphonsine Colin-Libour, Eugénie-Juliette Faux-Froidure and Louise-Marie Trébuchet were four influential turn-of-the-century art teachers operating well-attended Paris studios. Similarly most provincial towns had their own locally established, often female art teachers whose studios were patronised by young ladies of varying talent. Typical of such teachers was the Lyon artist Thérèse Guérin, who for more than forty years taught scores of middle-class girls the gentle art of flower painting. The Paris Académie de la Plante and the Société des Peintres de Fleurs both evidence the never-flagging interest in flower painting and design. Best-known among Paris specialist schools was the Atelier des Gobelins, headed by another Lyonnais, Pierre-Adrien Chabal-Dussurgey. In the last decades of the century Chabal's influence made itself felt mostly in the south of France where he had been appointed director of the Nice École des Arts Décoratifs. His students remembered him as an uncompromisingly demanding teacher. Equally demanding were his Lyon colleagues, Berjon's successors at the chair of flower painting in the Lyon École des Beaux-Arts, Thierriat, Reignier and Castex-Dégrange; hence the generally high standards of flower painting in the silk capital where several Écoles Municipales de Dessin taught flower design as well. Neighbouring Saint-Etienne, with a prosperous ribbon industry, also had its own art school, with a flower design class in the Lyon tradition. Its first professor was Achille Chaine, best-known as a genre painter, who had trained as a textile designer; Joseph Dupasquier, another Lyonnais, succeeded him. From 1867 to 1880 the head of the school was Jean Champier, a portrait and landscape painter, the flower painter Laÿs's brother-in-law. His successor was Alexandre Beauderon, who had studied under Thierriat and was later appointed director of the school

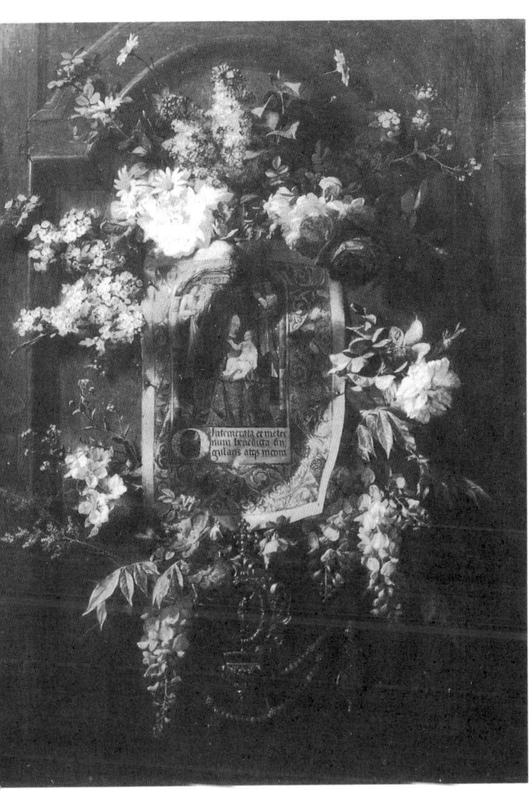

Jean-Marie Reigner

Oil on canvas, $47\frac{1}{4} \times 36\frac{1}{4}$ in. (120 × 92 cm.)
signed
Le Mans, Musée de Tessé

Though the Lyon and Saint-Etienne textile industries did provide local flower painters with more or less secure employment, it would be misleading to see flower painting in mid-19th-century France as a mere branch of the decorative arts, requiring industrial training schools. Indeed many flower painters received tuition from artists who hardly ever painted flowers. Just as Ernestine Panckoucke had studied under Prud'hon earlier in the century, Jean-Alexandre Couder was a pupil of Gros, and Fantin-Latour a pupil of Lecoq de Boisbaudran; Achille Cesbron, Gustave Caillebotte of Bonnat, Armand Leleux of Ingres. Bouguereau, Cabanel, Gleyre and Gustave Moreau all ran popular studios attended by many flower painters whose vision was no doubt broadened by such many-sided tuition. This and the influence of major artists such as Delacroix, Courbet and, later, the Impressionists may account for the more painterly idiom adopted by flower painters in the second half of the century. Last but far from least, a few flower painters, among them Albert-Tibulle Furcy de Lavault at La Rochelle, Augustin Dumas at Arles and Alexis-Marie Lahaye at Nîmes, were active both as teachers and as museum curators, and this too may have contributed a further broadening of approach.

TOUR DE FRANCE DES FLEURS

Very few French flower painters active in the second part of the century were born abroad. Achille Parvillée born in Istanbul, Amélie La Cazette born in Cuba, Eugène Morand born in St Petersburg, Blanche Roullier born in San Francisco, Joseph-Eugène Racine born in Guadeloupe, Blanche Pierson born in La Réunion and a few more, all of them exceptions to the rule, later settled in Paris for most of their working lives. The capital naturally attracted many provincial flower painters, though, as already seen, a few provincial towns could boast well-established, consistent schools of flower painters. Also linked with textiles but far less important in size than Lyon, the Mulhouse School, headed by the Benner family, Schilt and their fellow painters, is conspicuous for its consistency and the works painted there have a charm of their own. The Mulhouse speciality being printed cottons and wallpapers manufactured at nearby Rixheim—incidentally, Eugène Ehrmann worked for the Rixheim Zuber factory—local painters favoured a broader, more flexible idiom than their Lyon counterparts. The textile designers of Lyon were trained to meet the exacting requirements of designing for the limits imposed by Jacquard loom weaving. Mulhouse-born painters regularly exhibited at the Paris

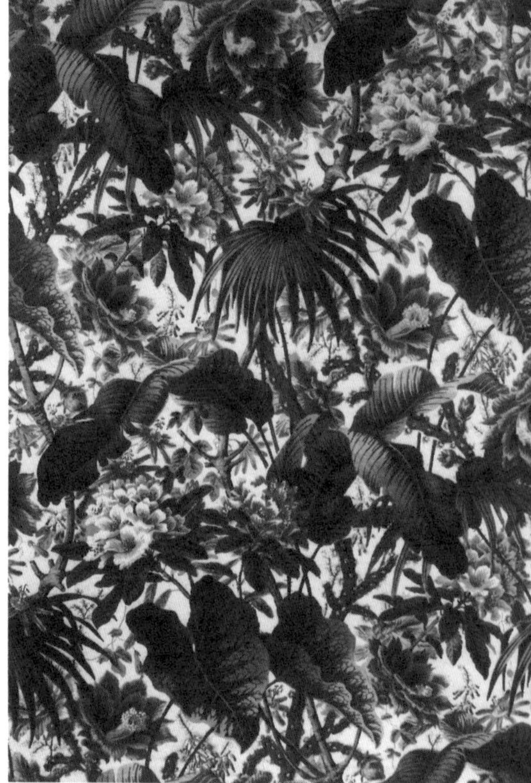

Jean-Ulrich Tournier

Glazed percale (composition by J.U. Tournier, manufactured by Schwartz-Huguenin, Mulhouse, *c.*1850) Mulhouse, Musée de l'Impression sur Etoffes

Salon, and frequently at the Lyon Salon in the 1860s and 1870s. Another link between the two textile cities was provided by Adolphe Braun, the Mulhouse-born painter and photographer who issued early photographic flower studies, many of which were used by the textile designers of Lyon. Chabal-Dussurgey, who for some time worked for Braun in Paris, is another interesting link between flower painting and the printing and photographic industries.

The neighbouring city of Metz could boast the Maréchal stained-glass factory where decorative flower design must have proved useful indeed. Mélanie Paigné and Octavie Sturel (née Paigné), both of them pupils of C. L. Maréchal, are two major names among the many flower painters of the area.

The Strasbourg Salon handbooks of the mid-century list a number of local flower painters, and the busy city must have provided them with a ready market. Besides, earthenware, a century-old Strasbourg speciality, may have proved more important to flower painting than has hitherto been realized. When Germany claimed the city after the French defeat of 1870, some flower painters left their home town to settle in Paris (e.g. Marie Cornélius) or, more often, Nancy, where Emile Gallé, whose activity as a flower painter is often overlooked, opened his vastly successful factories. For many years flower design, first of the accurately botanical type, later in the stylized Art Nouveau idiom, played a significant part in the decoration of his earthenware, glassware and marquetry. Incidentally Gallé's *Écrits sur l'art* reveal a keen, knowledgeable botanist and flower lover.

The Dijon Salon handbooks list so many flower-pieces as to place this Salon second only to its Lyon counterpart. Scores of flower painters, ranging from Laurent Adenot and Jeanne Berthet to Berthe Vincendon, exhibited there, mostly after 1870, along with painters active elsewhere such as Castex-Dégrange or Alexis Kreyder, and, as elsewhere, standards varied greatly but compare well with those of other provincial Salons of the time. Many of the exhibitors active in the 1870s and 1880s worked in a style featuring fluid brushstrokes and moderately thick impasto. Thanks to Brune's dictionary and J.L. Mordefroid's studies, the painters of the area are somewhat better known than others. Few of them seem to have specialized exclusively in flower painting. Thus Camille Dolard, born at Lons-le-Saunier, the photographer-painter, whose figure and genre paintings sold well, painted some flower studies for his *Arums dans une pièce d'eau* (1881). Eléonore Escallier, born at Poligny, the only local flower painter with a national reputation, is the exception to the rule.

The entries in our dictionary show a more or less similar situation in Grenoble and Chambéry, where about a hundred artists, many of them landscape painters, occasionally produced flower paintings in the second part of the century. Among these Charles-Philippe Blache had many friends in Paris artistic circles but his works were less popular than those of Ernest Filliard, who exhibited in Paris at the turn of the century, thus unsuspectingly opening the way to Jules Flandrin and Jacqueline Marval, the two figure-heads of the local modernistic movement. But for a slightly above-average number of exhibits featuring gentians, edelweiss and sundry alpine flowers, the local output seems to have lacked specific characteristics. Being within easy reach of Lyon, even in those days of comparatively slow trains, the Grenoble Salon was, of course, a favourite with Lyon flower painters such as Claudia Bret-Charbonnier, Pierre-Nicolas Euler, Thérèse Guérin, Charles Jung or François Rivoire, which brings us back to Lyon once again.

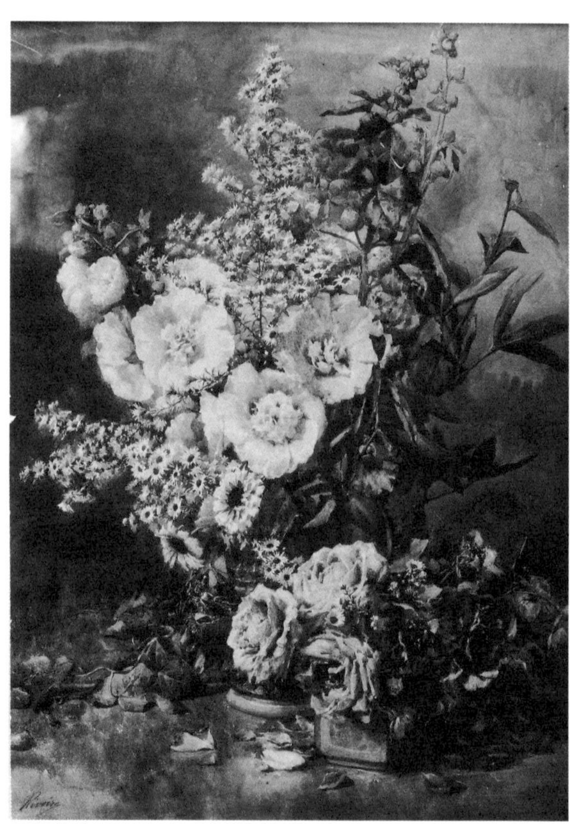

François Rivoire

Watercolour, $21\frac{1}{2} \times 15$ in. (55×38 cm.), signed
Formerly Paris, Musée du Luxembourg

In the second half of the century attendance figures of the flower design class at the Lyon B.A. school reflected the critical situation of the silk industry due to the loss of the American market during the Civil War, silk-worm disease, the fashion for plain materials, and the general trend towards less luxurious, cheaper materials than silk. Significantly Thierriat's successor, Jean-Marie Reignier, had only 130 pupils over a teaching career spanning thirty years, whereas his predecessor, whose teaching career was equally long, could boast four hundred or so, while his own successor Castex-Dégrange trained about two hundred students over the same number of years.

Far from heralding a decline of interest in flower painting the varying fortunes of the local textile industry coincided with a striking revival of the art. The demanding, intolerant, staunchly conservative, severely criticized methods of Reignier gave way to

Castex-Dégrange's more flexible approach pioneering Art Nouveau stylization and more luminous colouring. He and his many students exhibited to great critical acclaim at the local and Paris Salons and at the 1889 and 1900 Paris Expositions Universelles. Female students who were still denied access to the École des Beaux-Arts would flock to the several Écoles Municipales de Dessin, which also had classes of flower design and painting. Some influential private teachers, like the rose specialists André Perrachon and Thérèse Guérin, Jules Médard of camellia fame, Claudia Bret-Charbonnier, Charles Jung the thistle king, and François Rivoire, famous for his flowers in watercolours, operated most successful private studios. As a result, their students exhibited hundreds of works in the 1880s and 1890s. Critics, preaching in the desert, complained of a surfeit of flower-pieces. In nearby Saint-Etienne, where the situation was much the same, Eugène Brosse's virtuoso flower-pieces, painted in dazzling impasto, stood high above the flood of well-meaning but often uninspired local works.

Moving further south, one finds that flower painting undergoes some changes. In the strong, vibrant light so gloriously rendered by Van Gogh and Cézanne, colours become more vivid, and something of a Latin dash can be found in the brushwork of artists such as Monticelli or Ziem. Next to the usual flowershop bouquets in vases, flowers would be painted out of doors growing in gardens or on terraces, sometimes with a sea background.

With Marcel Arnaud, a self-styled Cézanne disciple, as a possible exception, the influence of the master of Aix made itself felt long after his death and his uncompromisingly personal flowers which owe so little to traditional flower painting remain in a class of their own. Back in the mainstream of contemporary flower painting, Nice is conspicuous as the birthplace of the *envoi de Nice*, the ubiquitous composition featuring a bulrush basket overflowing with bunches of locally grown violets, carnations, mimosas or roses. This arrangement was popular from the early 1870s to the 1930s, and thousands of amateurs depicted it. Influential local teachers include Carpentras-born Jules Laurens and Paul Vayson, born at Gordes. As already pointed out, the Nice École des Arts Décoratifs under the direction of Chabal-Dussurgey trained many a flower painter, but the two major names of the time are Avignon-born Antoine

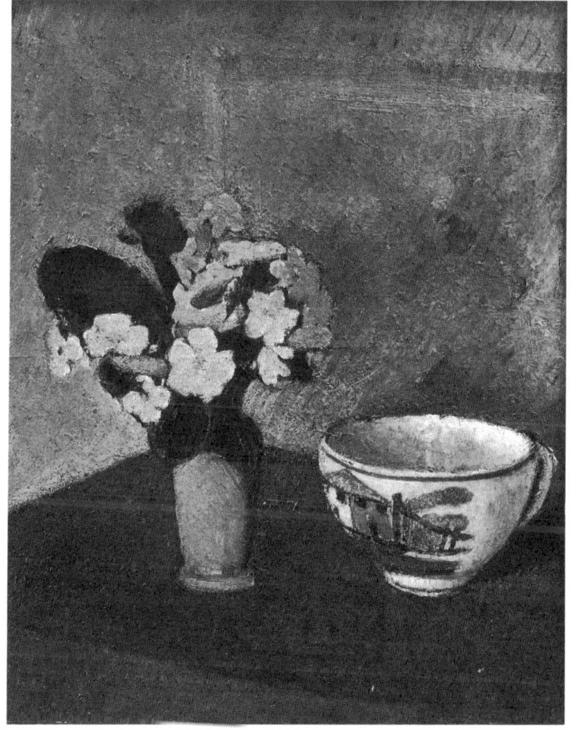

Emile Bernard

Oil on canvas, 1887,
Vincent van Gogh Foundation/National Museum
Vincent van Gogh, Amsterdam

Grivolas and Eugène Claude, born at Toulouse, both flower specialists who exhibited extensively to great critical acclaim.

Further north in the Limoges area, as can be seen in the local art gallery, flower painting, a vital branch of porcelain painting, was popular. Many artists studied at the local École des Arts Décoratifs. Limoges-born Renoir painted his first flowers on porcelain plates and dishes. Another native of Limoges, Louis Désiré Billotey, made his name in Paris as a virtuoso flower painter on silk, gauze and velvet, working for Worth and later Poiret.

Heading further north towards another flower-growing region, the Val-de-Loire, one comes to Blois, birthplace of the unique Vélins du Roy collection of botanical designs. Something of the glorious local past will be found reflected in the exciting collection of flower paintings exhibited nearby at Azay-le-Féron. The original watercolours for one of the most important mid-century flower books, the *Album Vilmorin*, have been kept to this day at La Ménitré, near Angers, the native city of one of Redouté's most gifted pupils, Héloïse Girault née Lesourd-Delisle.

No brief survey can do justice to the many painters born in Brittany, Normandy and the north of France or working there. The latter have been listed and studied by L. and G. Trénard. From Émile-Théophile Blanchard, a pupil of Van Spaendonck, botanical artist and illustrator, to Émile Bernard with his long Pont-Aven associations, they have little in common except that they were full or part-time flower painters. Countless flower painters exhibited at Rouen, Le Havre, Lille, and other towns in the area, and sold their works locally. Far from all local Salon handbooks have been examined closely, but those that have reveal at least one certainty: 19th-century flower paintings travelled far and wide, and comparatively few painters exhibited only locally. Jean Dablin, an art teacher at Valenciennes and Saint-Etienne, is a typical case in so far as he exhibited in Paris and Saint-Quentin amongst other places. Achille Cesbron's *Fleurs du sommeil* was exhibited in 1886 in Paris and at Nantes; the work was purchased by the State and considered for the Lyon museum with Bordeaux as a possibility, only to end up at Rennes. A survey of French provincial museums, one of the many original contributions of the 1982 Saint-Tropez exhibition, would prove a most instructive index of a painter's popularity. For instance, one of the most successful flower painters of his day, Jean-Alexandre Couder, had works purchased for the Dinan, Laval, Orléans, Périgueux, Rennes, Saint-Denis, Tours and Vitré museums. Later in the century another most popular flower specialist, Pierre Bourgogne, had works purchased for Béziers, Blois, Issoudun, Morlaix, Rennes, Toulouse and Tulle.

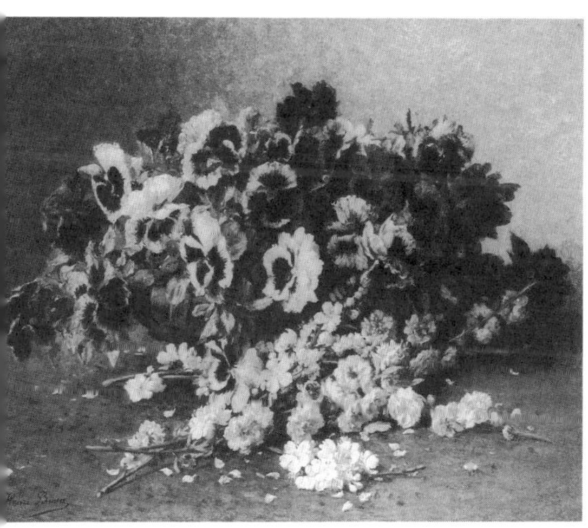

Henri Biva

Oil on canvas, 20½ × 24½ in. (52 × 62.5 cm.), signed
Paris, Galerie du Lethé

This brings us to the comparatively few flower painters who enjoyed a nation-wide popularity in the last thirty years of the century. Chabal-Dussurgey, the Second Empire flower painter *par excellence*, remained active to his last day. His rivals were the Biva brothers, Pierre Bourgogne, Eugène Claude, Georges Jeannin, Madeleine Lemaire, Eugène Petit and Ernest Quost, all of them born in the 1840s. They have much in common—extremely sound workmanship and prolific output ranging from competent to dazzling. Their approach was always highly decorative and their fluency obvious. At their best their most unpretentious flower studies have an easy-going charm all of their own, whereas their opulent, large-scale compositions cry out for the lush, over-decorated rooms they once adorned. Most of their early works were still solidly painted against often dark backgrounds.

Later, most of these painters turned to ever-lighter colours as rooms became more and more crowded with furniture and knick-knacks of every description and their atmosphere more and more claustrophobic. Those who favoured light, airy, sparsely furnished rooms were a tiny minority, their influence outside the very limited anglophile circle of the Paris bourgeoisie and aristocracy being hardly noticeable before the very last years of the century. Though the study of flower design applied to the decorative arts lies beyond the scope of this survey, it should be pointed out that the influence of the sparse Kate Greenaway or Boutet de Monvel style of room was slow to make itself felt in France outside the nursery. Unlike Germany or Austria, France had no organized Arts and Crafts movement in the 1880s; hence the slowness of change in interior decorating fashions. Hence too the lasting popularity of middle-of-the-road flower painters whose works were accessible to a wide range of buyers, who relished the paintings of Pierre Bourgogne or Eugène Claude, combining instantly recognizable craftsmanship with a sensible, readily acceptable painterliness and flattering colours. Compositions ranged from the deceptively simple country *jeté* to the highly opulent flowershop arrangement. The Second Empire revival of interest in 18th-century fashions being far from extinct, flowers in stone or bronze vases painted against outdoor backgrounds complete with stone balustrades and cloudy skies were still popular as large-sized decorations suitable for panelled rooms in the Louis XV or Louis XVI styles. Equally proficient in oils and watercolours, the Biva brothers and Madeleine Lemaire enjoyed lasting popularity; their output was huge and still more uneven than that of their contemporaries, but their works are typical of the heady, swooning *fin-de-siècle* mood.

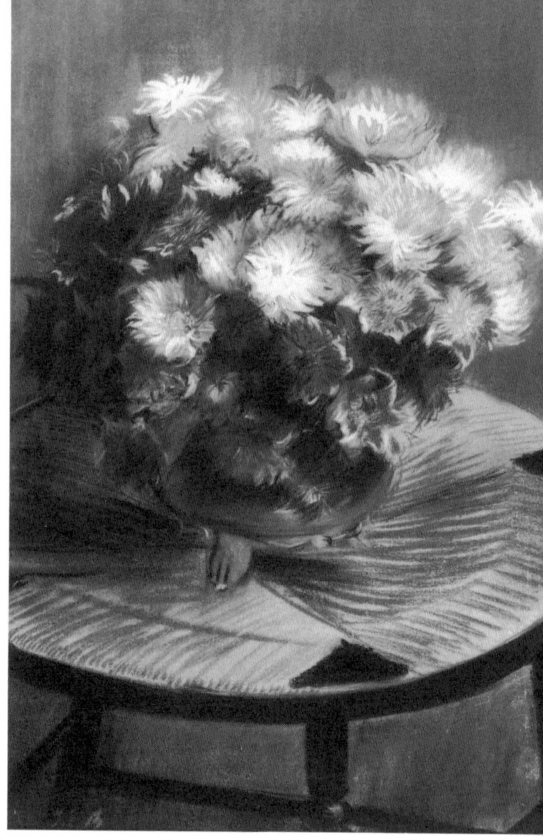

Jacques-Emile Blanche

Pastel, $24\frac{1}{2} \times 15\frac{3}{4}$ in. (62×40 cm.), signed with initials
Courtesy Sotheby's, London

FANTIN-LATOUR

Nothing could be more alien to the mainstream of late 19th-century flower painting than the flowers of Henri Fantin-Latour. Though in the 1860s he shared with his contemporaries a fondness for rich, dark, mellow tones, his later works stand in a class of their own. However opulent his arrangements are never showy, and even the more elaborate of them owe little to his forerunners or contemporaries. Their splendour is something deeply vital, not contrived. No wonder his luminous, truthful works appealed to English taste. Fantin's works have the quiet, moving charm of old cottage gardens and their deceptive simplicity echoes treasured memories of sunny afternoons. Even his peerless silvery greys are more at home in the land of misty twilights than in their native country.

Fantin-Latour had mixed feelings about flower painting. At first, he loathed the commercial side of it: 'I have never had more ideas than now and am obliged to paint flowers! While doing so, I keep thinking of Michaelangelo.' Seignemartin felt likewise: 'I don't want to spend the rest of my life between a carnation and a rose.' Over the years Fantin's reluctance gave way to a more relaxed approach: 'I am going to have a restful time at Sunbury and am looking forward to painting flowers very slowly—I will try to do something worthwhile ...' Later on, according to Vauxcelles, Fantin came to 'love painting flowers as much as he loved music'.

Between 1860 and 1870 Fantin painted about four flower-pieces a year. His meeting with Edwin Edwards and his marriage (1876) to Victoria Dubourg, herself a flower painter, were to prove such strong incentives that he painted over two hundred and fifty flower-pieces between 1870 and 1880. Thereafter his output dwindled as he turned to allegorical painting. Indeed Madame Fantin points out that her husband painted no flowers at all in 1896, 1897 and 1901. According to her Fantin may have painted five hundred flower-pieces whilst other biographers suggest a more likely six hundred.

First and foremost, as Jacques-Émile Blanche, one of his pupils, observed, Fantin was a peerless painter of roses: 'He knew roses better than anybody else ...' He hardly ever painted any before 1871 but in his work of 1885 and 1889 the rose reigned supreme. His wife's Buré garden was full of them, popular 19th-century varieties such as Maréchal Niel, Gloire de Dijon, Céline Forestier, and so on. Before leaving for his holiday in the country, Fantin would paint spring flowers bought in Paris—hyacinths, primroses, periwinkles, narcissi, daffodils and other wild and garden flowers. Unlike so many of his more fanciful forerunners, he painted only actual arrangements. Larger flowers such as chrysanthemums, peonies or zinnias were often painted on their own, seldom with other flowers. Chrysanthemums appear in 1861, before roses, and among Fantin's other early flowers are dahlias and sunflowers (1860); zinnias had to wait until 1881. Other favourites include hollyhocks, phloxes, poppies, larkspurs, carnations, gladioli and, more frequently, pansies, whose pensive associations (the flower is called *pensée* in French) must have appealed to Fantin's taste for remembrance and memorials. Greenhouse or hothouse flowers such as azaleas and camellias are exceptional, so are southern flowers such as mimosas. Vases, some of them presents from Edwards, change according to period, blooms and moods. The round glass bowl appears in 1864, the dark blue glass in 1869; these are succeeded by white porcelain or earthenware vases and a crystal and worn silver jardinière. However, Fantin's favourite containers are drinking glasses, which come in many shapes and sizes, plain and straight in 1866, tall in 1871. Wine and champagne glasses all make Fantin's flowers quietly familiar in their arrangement and approach. Flowers lying on tables next to vases are more unusual, potted flowers more frequent.

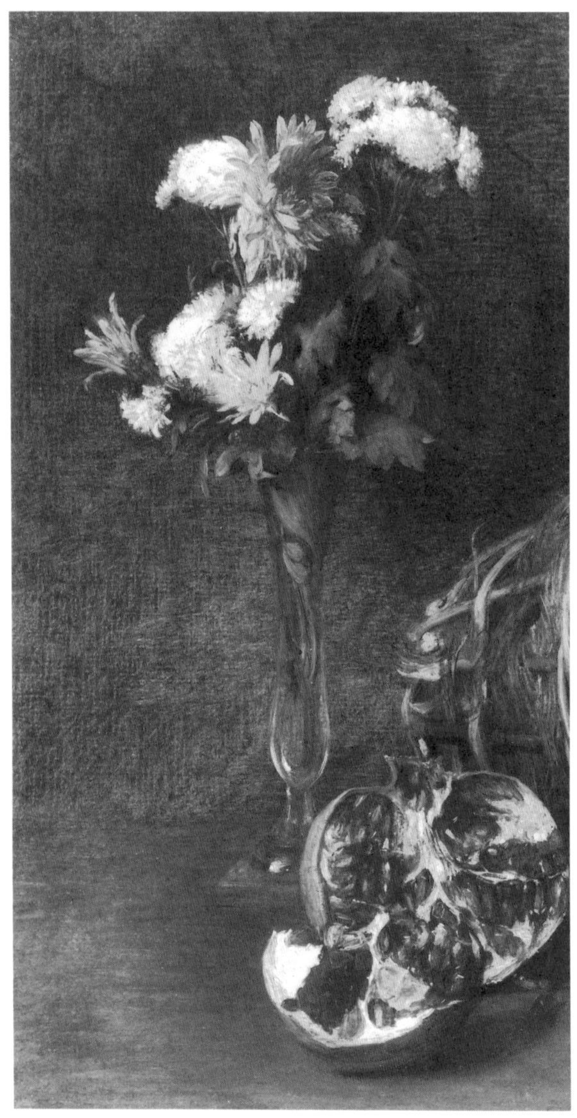

Victoria Dubourg, Mme Fantin-Latour (detail)

Oil on canvas, 18 × 21 in. (46 × 53.5 cm.), signed and dated 1875
Courtesy Robert Noorman and Gebr. Douwes Fine Art, London-Amsterdam

Fantin's style and technique are masterfully unobtrusive and inimitable. According to Jacques-Émile Blanche in *La Revue de Paris* of 15 May 1906:

> Fantin suffused his blooms with light and air, scraping through layers of paint to bring out the absorbent canvas, thus letting the painting breathe free. Unlike Courbet who, with his palette-knife, kneads the paint, forces it into the canvas and whips up the magnificently shining onyx and marble surface.

Fantin seldom used preparatory drawings. When he wanted to start a painting, he would prepare his palette on the previous evening, cut his flowers in the morning and arrange them most carefully. He would paint the canvas with an absorbent preparation over which he would apply a slightly tinted layer of paint; adding siccative to his colours allowed him to work quickly. His vision is so truthful, his technique so subtle, that the canvas seems to mirror his flowers like still pond water. His flower paintings have a vibrant charm of their own due to his unique handling of blooms and backgrounds. Depth is suggested by a sheet of often greyish paper pinned to the studio wall, with the utmost attention to the source of light, and it seems that Fantin sat close to his flowers while painting.

In France Fantin's flowers did not attract much critical attention before 1900, but they had been great favourites with English art-lovers for the previous forty years. Whistler, whom Fantin met when he was copying works in the Louvre, Seymour Haden and Ridley, then a young painter, were his early links with England. In 1859 Ridley seems to have introduced Fantin to Edwin Edwards, then a recently retired lawyer, who was to become his life-long friend, patron and agent. From that year onwards Fantin spent many a holiday with the Edwardses at Sunbury and was a regular contributor at the Royal Academy. There he exhibited the following (after Algernon Graves's list):

1862	Still life
1862	Flowers
1865	Fruit and flowers
1869	Fruit and flowers
1870	Autumn flowers
1877	Gilly flowers and Cherry blossoms
1878	Roses
1879	Spring flowers
1880	Roses. Peonies
1881	Pluie d'or, lilas et fleurs d'arbres fruitiers
1882	Peonies
1883	Fleurs d'automne – passe-roses. Fleurs
1884	A medley. Roses
1885	Chrysanthemums. Roses
1886	Double larkspurs. Roses. Lilies
1887	Fleurs variées
1888	Fleurs de Normandie
1889	Roses. A posy. Verbena
1890	Chrysanthemums etc. Roses
1891	Roses et capucines. Here are the flowers of middle summer. Carnations
1892	Peonies. Larkspurs. Here, without a thorn, the rose
1893	Asters. Flowers of all hues. Phlox
1894	Zinnias. Roses. Sweetpeas
1895	Gift of the mellowed year, a nosegay
1896	High midsummer pomp, gerbe de roses
1897	Roses. Zinnias
1898	The rosy wealth of June. Chrysanthemums
1899	June, la coquette des blanches. Zinnias
1900	Pieds d'alouette. Roses

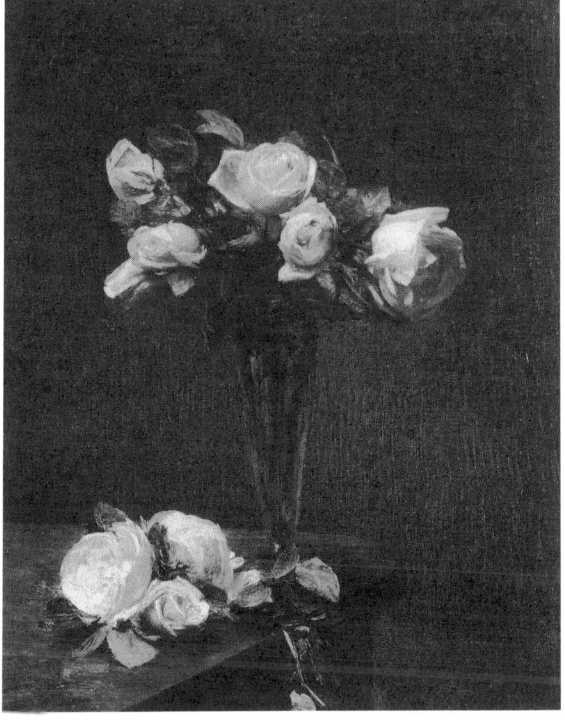

Henri Fantin-Latour

Oil on canvas, 17½ × 15 in. (43.9 × 38 cm.)
signed and dated 1877
Private collection

Fantin's flowers delighted many English collectors such as Sir William Boxall the portrait painter, Elmore the genre painter, Sir Henry Thompson, Ionides and, of course, Edwin Edwards. Prices for them ranged from about 1,200 francs in 1890 to 3,100 francs in 1900, a steep rise considering the 300 francs they commanded in the 1870s. At a 1906 sale, many flower-pieces from the Buckler collection fetched from £36 for small, sketchy works to £399, whereas at the same time large compositions would fetch up to 10,000 francs in Paris. Among the London dealers who had works by Fantin were Agnew, Allard & Noel, Gooden & Fox, Goupil, Knoedler, and last but not least, Obach. Among French owners of Fantin's flower-pieces were Bonjean, Darrasse, Ferdinand Dreyfus, Blanche Marchesi, the famous singing teacher, and A. Tavernier. Fantin's Paris dealer was Tempelaere.

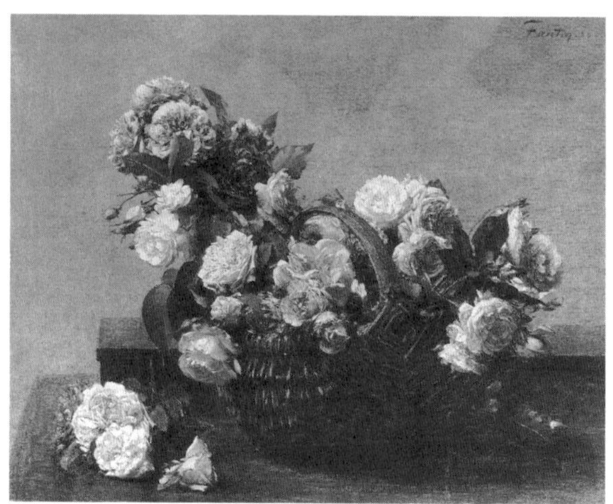

Henri Fantin-Latour

Oil on canvas, 24 × 28¾ in. (61 × 73 cm.), signed and dated 'Fantin. 80'
Courtesy Christies, London

In his home country Fantin's flowers, though not unnoticed, received, as already pointed out, little critical attention before the end of the century. However Philippe Burty, the most perceptive critic of his time, singled out Fantin's 1874 Paris Salon exhibit and praised the 'sweet and proud treat that English art lovers have been privileged to enjoy for some time'. At the turn of the century and even more so during the 1906 posthumous exhibition, French critics went into raptures over Fantin's flowers, smothering them with eulogies of the 'painting flowers is not enough, one must love them' type (Hérémence in *Le Lys*). Meaningless comparisons were not lacking either: 'His wild flowers, his white carnations ... are as forceful as any *Déjeuner sur l'herbe*' (Alphone Derveux in *Arts et Lettres*, November 1906). Fantin's English reviewers proved far more perceptive in their understated way. Many of them praised Fantin's exquisite draughtsmanship, his unique feeling for harmony and tone, his truthful, unaffected approach and thoughtfully chosen backgrounds. Most of them pointed out the innate dignity and restraint of Fantin's flowers, a quality so seldom found in flower painting. In a late (1909) article, the *Times* reviewer contrasted Fantin's flowers with his forerunners':

> ... older painters whose flowers for the most part ignore one another. In a Van Huysum bouquet they bloom, so to speak, in airtight compartments; and this is, to a certain extent, the case even in so fine a modern piece of flower painting as the picture by Courbet recently on show. They do not

breathe a common air and share, like real flowers, the mystery of life with us. It is in his more initimate feeling for nature and growth and personality of flowers that the charm of Fantin-Latour's pictures consists. In his chosen apprehension (which is more akin to that of the poet than that of the peeping botanist) the life of the flowers, with what they have of refreshment and consolation to the human spirit, is rendered intelligible and expressive.

TECHNICALITIES

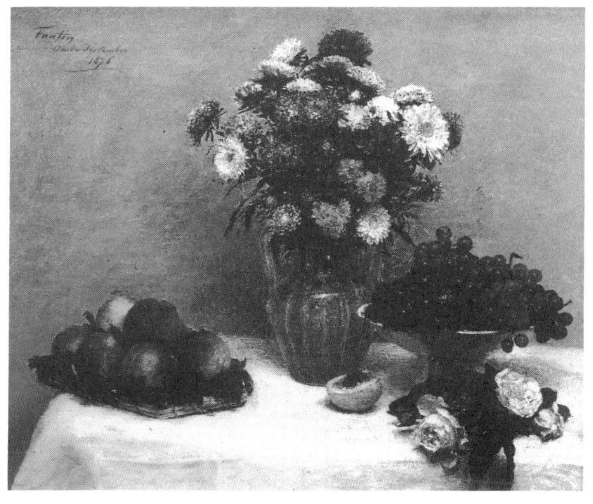

Henri Fantin-Latour

Oil on canvas, 24 × 28¾ in. (61 × 73 cm.), signed and dated 'Fantin aout-Septembre 1876'
Courtesy Christies, London

Though flowers in oils never went out of fashion and gouache was a favourite medium with textile and wallpaper designers and decorators in general, the 19th-century saw the triumph of flowers in watercolours. The medium was, of course, popular with Redouté and his circle. The demanding technicalities of watercolours on vellum ventured far beyond their Mecca, the Paris Jardin des Plantes, but gradually lost their appeal in the second half of the century. Among later exponents were Anaïs Bernard, Marie-Firmin Bocourt, Madame Clamoran, Armand-Lucien Clément, Charles-Émile Cuisin and Lesourd de Beauregard, whose works can be seen at the Jardin des Plantes.

Watercolours on paper were less demanding, especially when applied over a pencil drawing, though pure watercolours required far greater skill. Innumerable artists produced flowers in watercolours throughout the century and their number increased considerably from the 1860s onwards. The annual Salon des Aquarellistes held in Paris was their shrine and its handbooks, along with Paris and provincial Salon catalogues, are telling evidence of a lastingly popular medium. The turn-of-the-century bible of all amateur flower painters was Georges Fraipont's *L'Art de peindre les fleurs* (Paris, Laurens, n.d.), a masterpiece of dainty prose, accurate advice and efficient self-teaching method:

> A woman's hand is wonderfully suited to holding the flower as well as the brush which is to render its elegant forms and gorgeous colours ... how tempting flower painting is; how convenient, too, as it can be indulged in comfortably, at home, with everything at hand; no tiresome carrying of box and easel, no rain or sunshine to fear. It is, indeed, but how difficult if you want to do it well.

Instructions take the aspiring painter through various stages, like the buying of materials and choice of twenty colours: ivory black, warm sepia, bistre, burnt sienna, Van Dyck brown, yellow ochre, chrome lemon, yellow chrome, Indian yellow, Naples yellow, red lead, vermilion, crimson lake, rose madder, emerald green, Verona green, olive green, French ultramarine, cobalt and Persian blue. The step-by-step method emphasizes correct position and lighting and advises watercolourists to sketch with shadows laid in first. Later shading, modelling and glazing will be applied according to the flowers to be painted. Advice on flower design and painting in the decorative arts is also provided. Throughout his manual, Fraipont insists on careful observation and correct draughtsmanship and provides illustrations showing the same flower first outlined, then painted in watercolours.

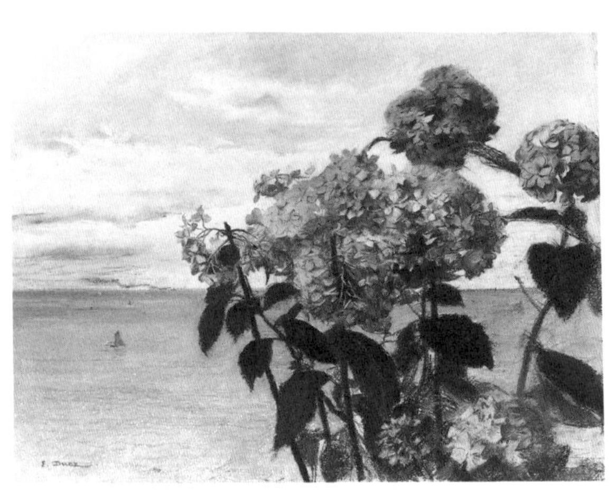

Ernest-Ange Duez

Pastel, $21\frac{1}{4} \times 29$ in. (54 × 73.5 cm.), signed
Private collection, England
(photo: Hazlitt, Gooden & Fox)

Fraipont's book went through many editions and must have helped thousands of aspiring flower painters. Considering how uneven the output of, say, Madeleine Lemaire is—and she was the most proficient and prolific of all turn-of-the-century watercolourists—no wonder the standards of flowers in watercolours varied greatly, ranging from highly accomplished to downright amateurish. In this respect the systematic copying of chromolithographed models, often German or Swiss imports, would have proved a mixed blessing. It must have improved the standards of draughtsmanship to some extent but can't have done much good for colouring.

FASHIONABLE FLOWERS

Most garden flowers remained popular throughout the century. Of course, roses never lost their appeal. The small moss rose and the fleshy cabbage rose along with scores of other centifolias were great favourites in the first half of the century and even later. More and more sophisticated hybrids were painted towards the end of the century and while white, pink or red roses never went out of fashion, the 1870s and 1880s favoured the rich yellow and orange blooms painted by Georges Jeannin, André Perrachon and their likes. Remontant rose trees and more and more sophisticated greenhouses and hot-houses would provide painters with blooms well into the cold months of the year. Likewise the white lily in its various guises, with its royal and virginal associations, remained an all-time favourite, but, while orange or tiger-lilies had been painted mostly by botanical artists in the early part of the century, they were to enjoy a much wider popularity in the 1870s and 1880s. Violets of the wild or cultured variety (Toulouse or Parma) were more popular than ever during the First and Second Empires, as were the crown imperial and the hortensia. The 1830s saw the heyday of the dahlia. The camellia, still a rarity at the beginning of the century—it was virtually unknown in Lyon—became popular in the 1830s to such an extent that in the 1870s some painters, led by Jules Médard, made it their own. Tea-roses and carnations came into fashion from the 1860s onwards thanks to the new railway network which brought them from their native Midi to eager painters throughout the country in a matter of days. Wild flowers had their own painters, Jean-Alexandre Couder being prominent among them. The chrysanthemum fashion started timidly in the 1830s, almost vanished during the following three decades, and raged through the last forty years of the century, carried by the tidal wave of *Japonisme*. In the 1880s Bleton, the influential Lyon critic, found the surfeit of chrysanthemums nauseating. Greenhouse or hot-house flowers, like orchids, long the botanical designer's preserve, came out as comparative novelties in the 1850s but somehow failed to become really popular outside narrow aesthetic circles.

In 19th-century France as elsewhere, the flowershop bouquet or posy in a vase was by far the most popular. Vases vary greatly. Marble, alabaster, terracotta or crystal vases, though great favourites in the early part of the century, never went out of fashion and glass vases provided many a painter with a bravura piece throughout the century. Bronze suited opulent, and earthenware plain, more rustic arrangements especially when these came back into fashion in the 1840s and 1850s, simultaneously with the Barbizon School of landscape painting. So did flowers in pots, mugs or watering-cans.

The traditional bouquet or posy suspended in mid-air against a plain, often greyish background was a more or less compulsory set-piece taught by most private teachers and art schools. It was widely

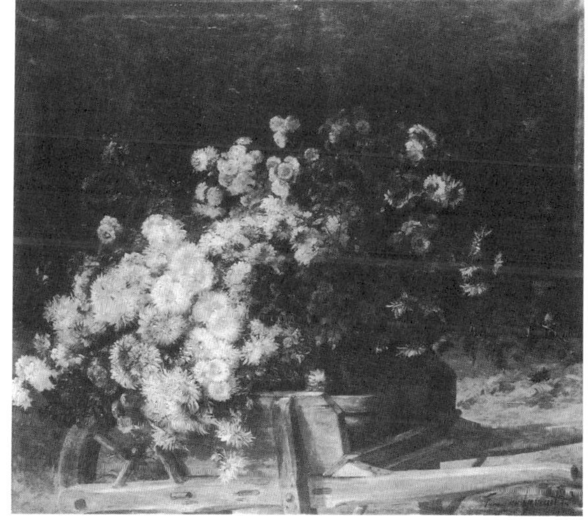

Albert-Tibulle Furcy de Lavault

Oil on canvas, 43 × $49\frac{1}{4}$ in. (109 × 125 cm.)
Courtesy Sotheby's, London

used both for studies and highly finished Salon exhibits. Though all the rage in the early decades of the century, its popularity extended far beyond the 1850s and must have been sustained by scores of engraved, lithographed or photographic models used for teaching purposes. Antoine Berjon's deceptively simple *Fleurs sur un fond blanc* (Lyon, Musée des Beaux-Arts) shines as a supreme specimen of flower painting at its purest.

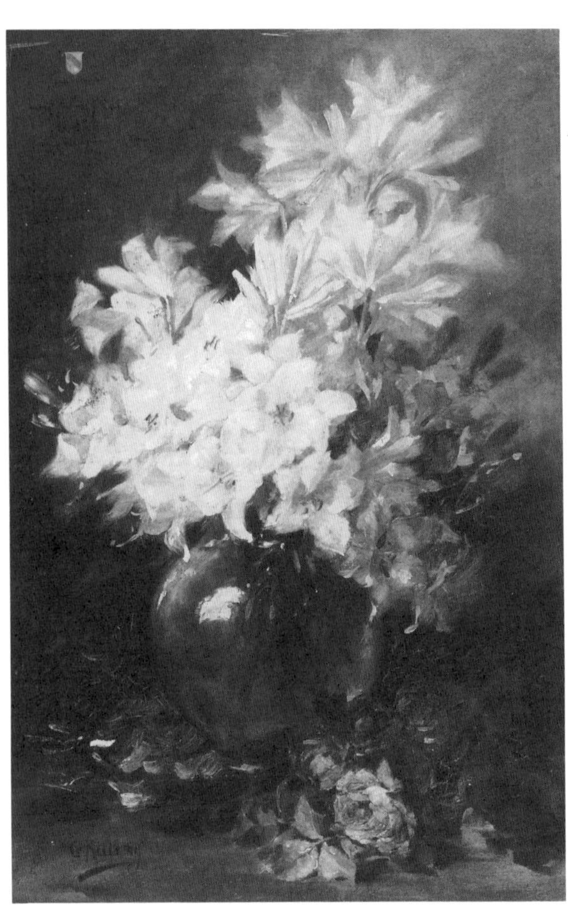

Georges Ritleng

Oil on canvas, 31 × 21¼ in. (80 × 54 cm.), signed
Strasbourg, Musée d'Art Moderne

The century's most original contribution to composition seems to have been the *jeté* or *jonchée* showing armfuls of flowers lying on the ground, on a table or ledge. Some forerunners of such arrangements are to be found in the previous centuries, but the fashion really caught on in the 1830s. So did flowers painted *in situ* in gardens, borders, along walls, by roadsides, on balconies. Some Lyon painters like Simon Saint-Jean loved flowers growing by river banks. No doubt they found the wistful association of short-lived blooms and running waters appealingly sentimental. The seemingly artless *fouillis* showing entangled wild or garden flowers, which required a very skilled hand, became briefly popular in the 1860s to such an extent that it was, for a few years, a set-piece for the Lyon Beaux-Arts students.

Wickerwork baskets, though less popular than vases, never quite went out of fashion. As already pointed out, the oblong bulrush basket, *bourriche*, was a standard feature of the turn-of-the-century *envoi de Nice*. Those proficient in the decorative arts, such as Chabal-Dussurgey or Castex-Dégrange, painted opulent garlands fastened by ribbons in the seventeenth- and eighteenth-century styles. Wreaths on their own or surrounding portraits or statues were the main features of many a votive or allegorical flower-piece. Many of them, like Simon Saint-Jean's *Hommage à la Vierge Marie* (Musée des Beaux-Arts, Lyon, 1842) look back to 17th-century Dutch models. Others are more fanciful: Georges Jeannin and Chabal-Dussurgey both painted figures of the Republic within wreaths of roses and other flowers. Some are funereal, others of the commemorative or festive type. Many paintings feature the 'language' of flowers and leaves, such as laurels for glory, pansies for thought, forget-me-not for remembrance, or ivy for lasting loyalty. These were particularly popular with the painters of Lyon but are to be found elsewhere too.

Fantin-Latour painted *Bouquet de fiançailles* in 1869 and Achille Cesbron *Fleurs du sommeil* in 1886. Between 1870 and 1914, following the loss of Alsace, anti-German feelings gave birth to a number of patriotic paintings featuring flowers such as Fillat's *Les trois couleurs* (1880). Grandville's eccentric *Fleurs animées* (1847) seem to have had few followers as such, but many *fin-de-siècle* allegorical works featuring water-nymphs with irises or narcissi, and luscious dark-haired nudes clad in poppy petals or holding poppies, may derive from them. Literary flowers such as Joseph Perrachon's *Suicide par les fleurs*, inspired by Zola's *La Faute de l'abbé Mouret*, were mercifully few. Gardeners, flower boys and girls, still exceptional in the 1840s, became commonplace in the 1870s. More than in any other period, the language of flowers was widely understood and Charlotte de la Tour's *Le Langage des fleurs*, illustrated by chromolithographs, replaced the many unillustrated, prim little books that had found their way into countless libraries.

Flowers now no longer spoke the esoteric language of previous centuries. The symbolic gave way to an openly allegorical, easily understandable, often purely sentimental language, something within everybody's reach. However, as the century drew to its close, aesthetes *à la* Des Esseintes would favour flowers speaking a more esoteric, less obvious language than the mere forget-me-not. Drowsy poppies with their opiate associations, fleshy irises growing by ponds or streams swarming with nymphs and dragonflies, armfuls of heavily scented roses held against panting breasts, virginal lilies and sexy orchids became popular within *fin-de-siècle* circles whose artistic gospel was the Art Nouveau movement. So did sickly brambles, nettles and puny, half-wilted wildflowers. These were to be painted as accessories only, Sâr Péladan, mystic, master of the occult and author of the Décadence Latine novels, having banned still-lifes as being too vulgar for his uplifting Rosicrucian doctrines. Wistaria and laburnum were favourites, used as shades to filter the suitably rosy, mauve or golden sunlight or, even better, twilight. Georges de Feure, Edmond Aman-Jean and Lucien Lévy-Dhurmer spread such unlikely trends well into the 20th century, but their decorative works hardly belong to flower painting at all.

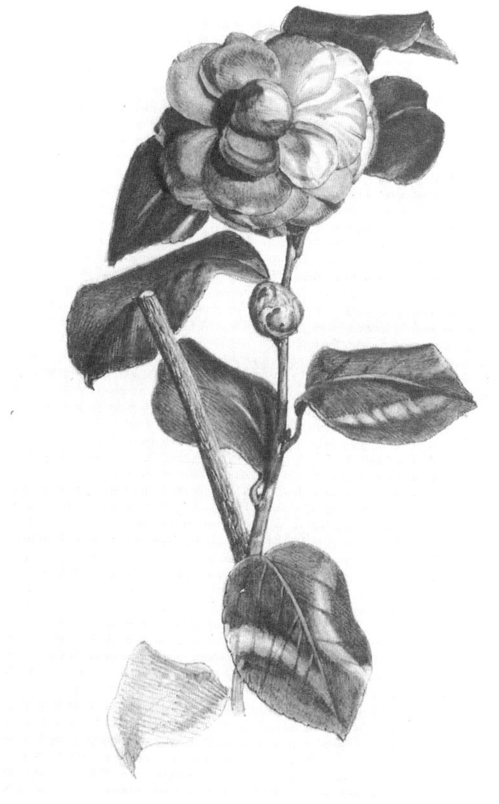

Jean-Ignace-Isidore Grandville

Watercolour over traces of graphite, $9\frac{3}{4} \times 7\frac{1}{2}$ in. (24.5 × 18.7 cm.), *c.* 1846, stamped, 'Vente de 1853' Nancy, Musée des Beaux-Arts

FLEURS DU SIÈCLE

The neo-Dutch idiom so popular in the first decades of the century, the favourite of Redouté and his circle, of botanical illustrators and the early Lyon School, a style combining meticulously realistic draughtsmanship enhanced by life-like colours, never quite lost its appeal. Outside the narrow circle of botanical artists bound by tradition to such a demanding, timeless style, a few artists continued the endeavour to meet the standards of 17th and 18th-century Dutch painting well into the 1880s. Prominent among these was Jean-Claude Pizzety whose 'unbearably perfect' Lyon Salon exhibits were ridiculed in the 1890s.

What Delacroix and Courbet owe to the Flemish tradition is obvious. The painterliness they added to it speaks for itself; so does their strongly personal vision. Both opened the way to countless, less strikingly original painters, to such an extent that by the late 1870s their idiom had become standard for many flower painters. Works by Bonvin, Ribot or Vollon derive from the Delacroix-Courbet mainstream to which Cauchois also belongs. Hundreds of such works, often painted against dark backgrounds, feature moderately thick impasto and fluid brushwork, and none is highly finished. The overall vision is solidly decorative and the painters' aim is to give a rough impression of the blooms they have arranged rather than a detailed, accurate rendering of their shapes, colours and textures.

At the other end of the spectrum, the Impressionists, under the spell of all things fleeting, could not resist flowers. For some like Manet, Renoir or Monet, painting flowers was a favourite activity, for others only a side-line. As already pointed out, though many did paint flowers, none was a flower painter in the narrowly specialized sense of the word.

Going far beyond the meticulous vision of earlier painters and the Impressionists' concern with the interplay of light and form, Fantin-Latour stands head and shoulders above his contemporaries as a supremely independent and personal figure, perhaps the one and only real flower painter in late 19th-century France. For him a

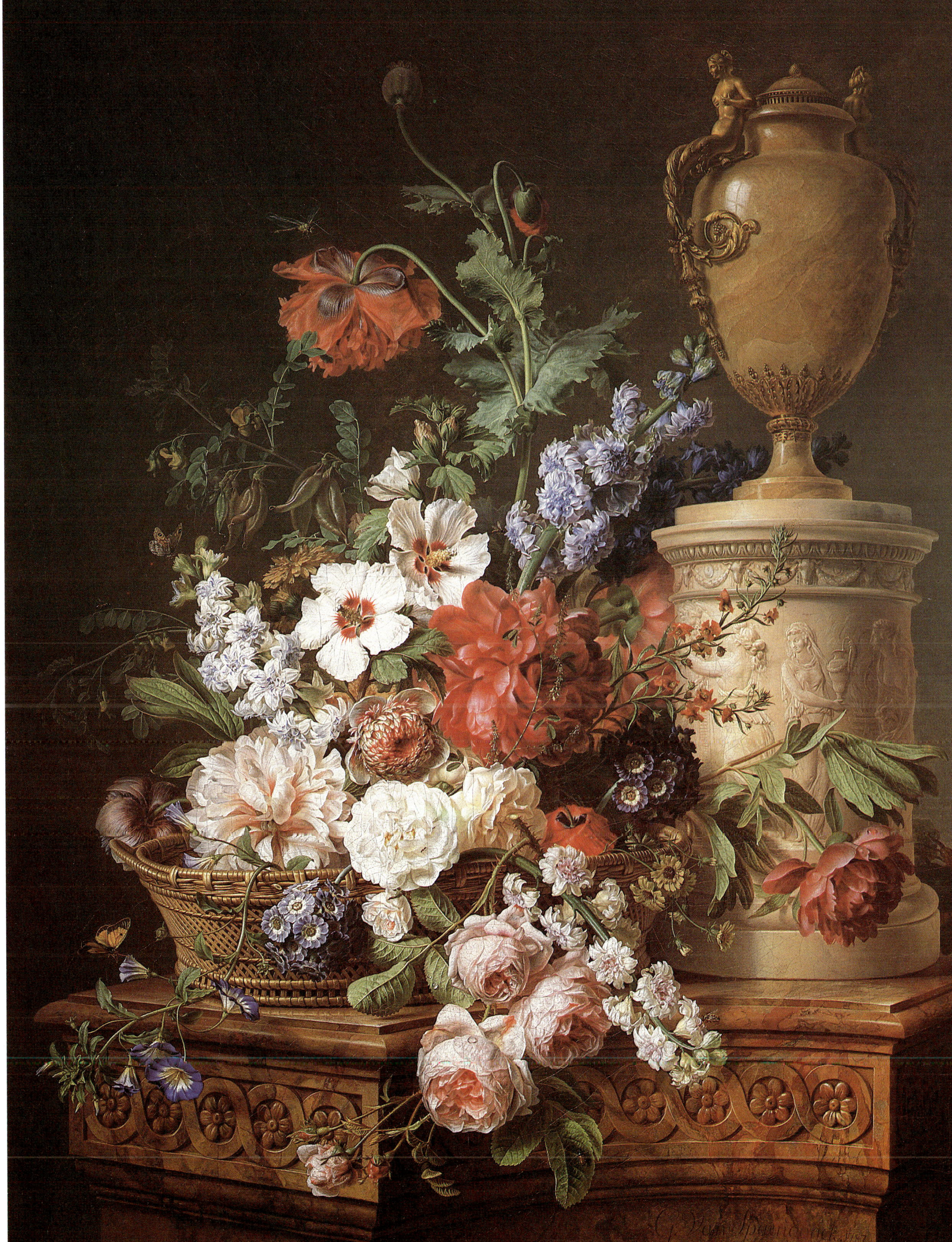

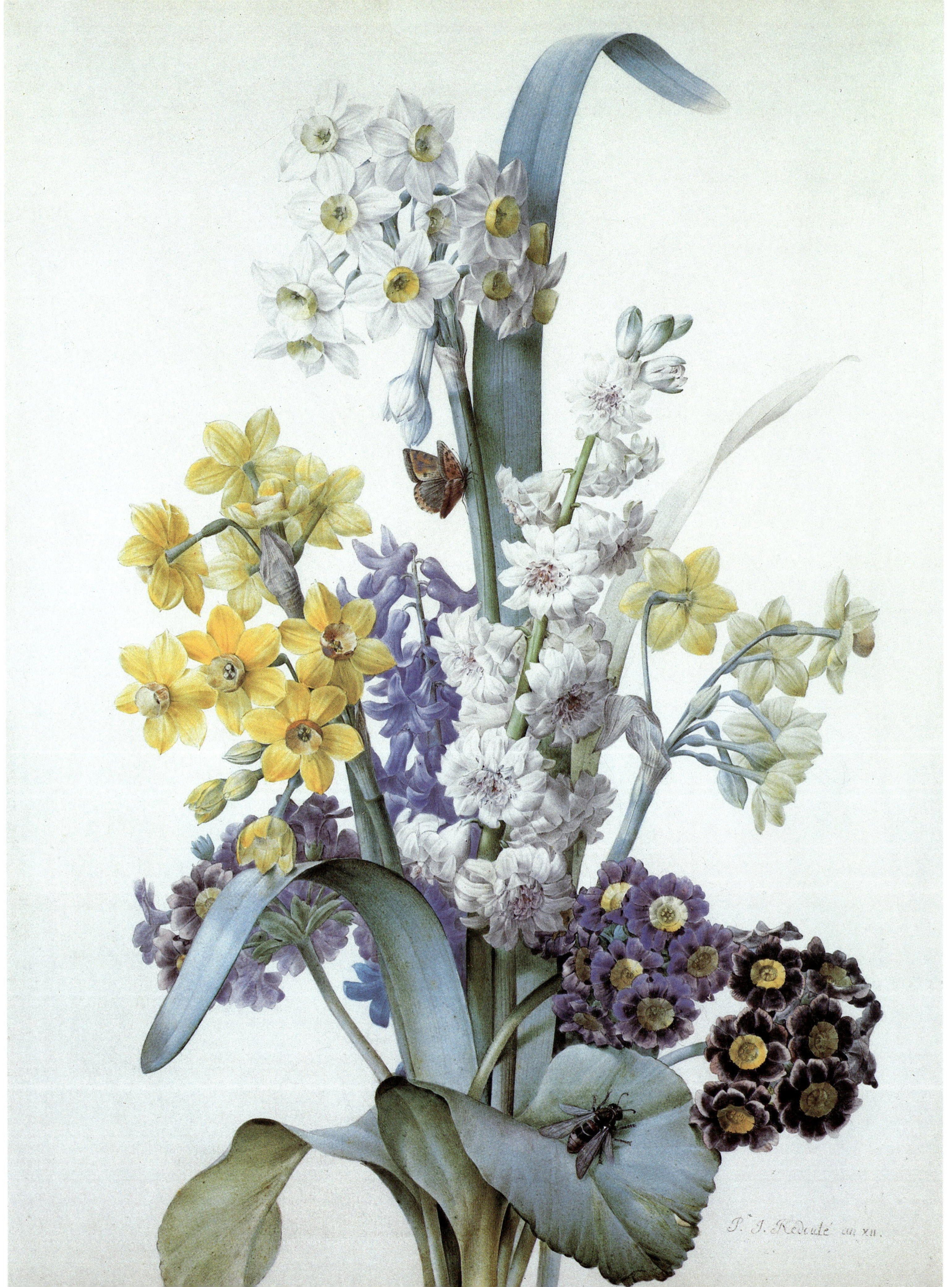
P. J. Redouté an XII.

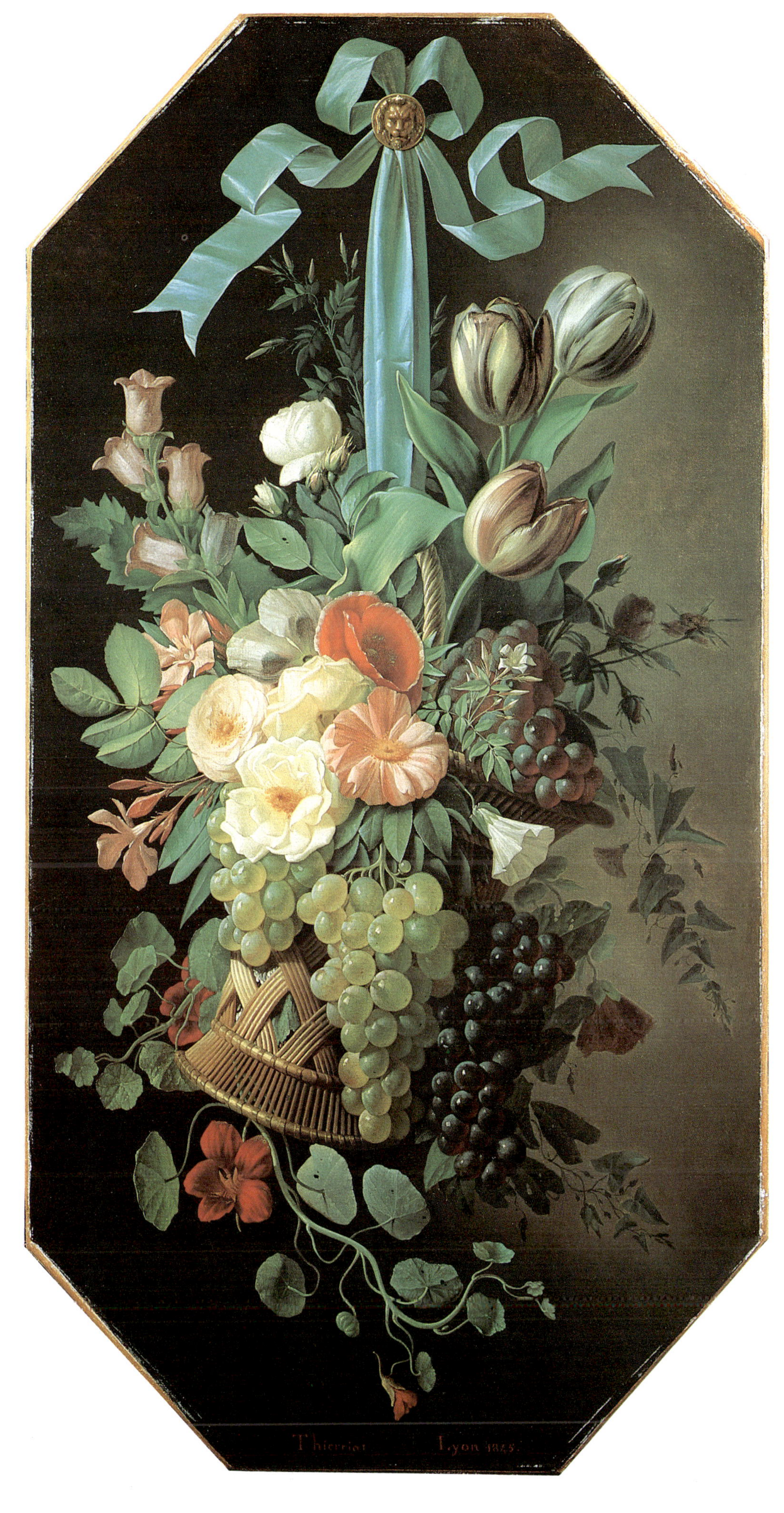
Thierriat
Lyon 1845.

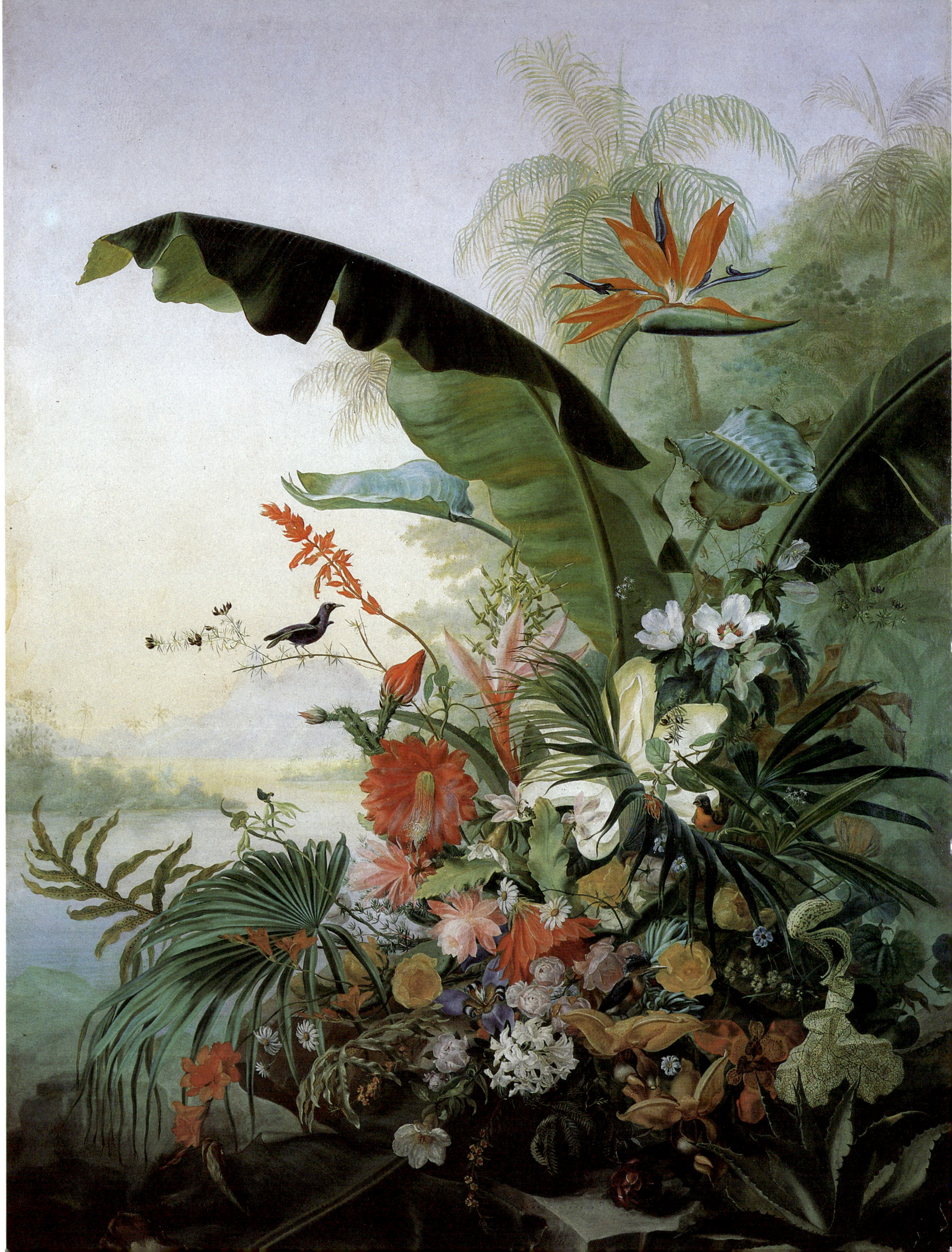

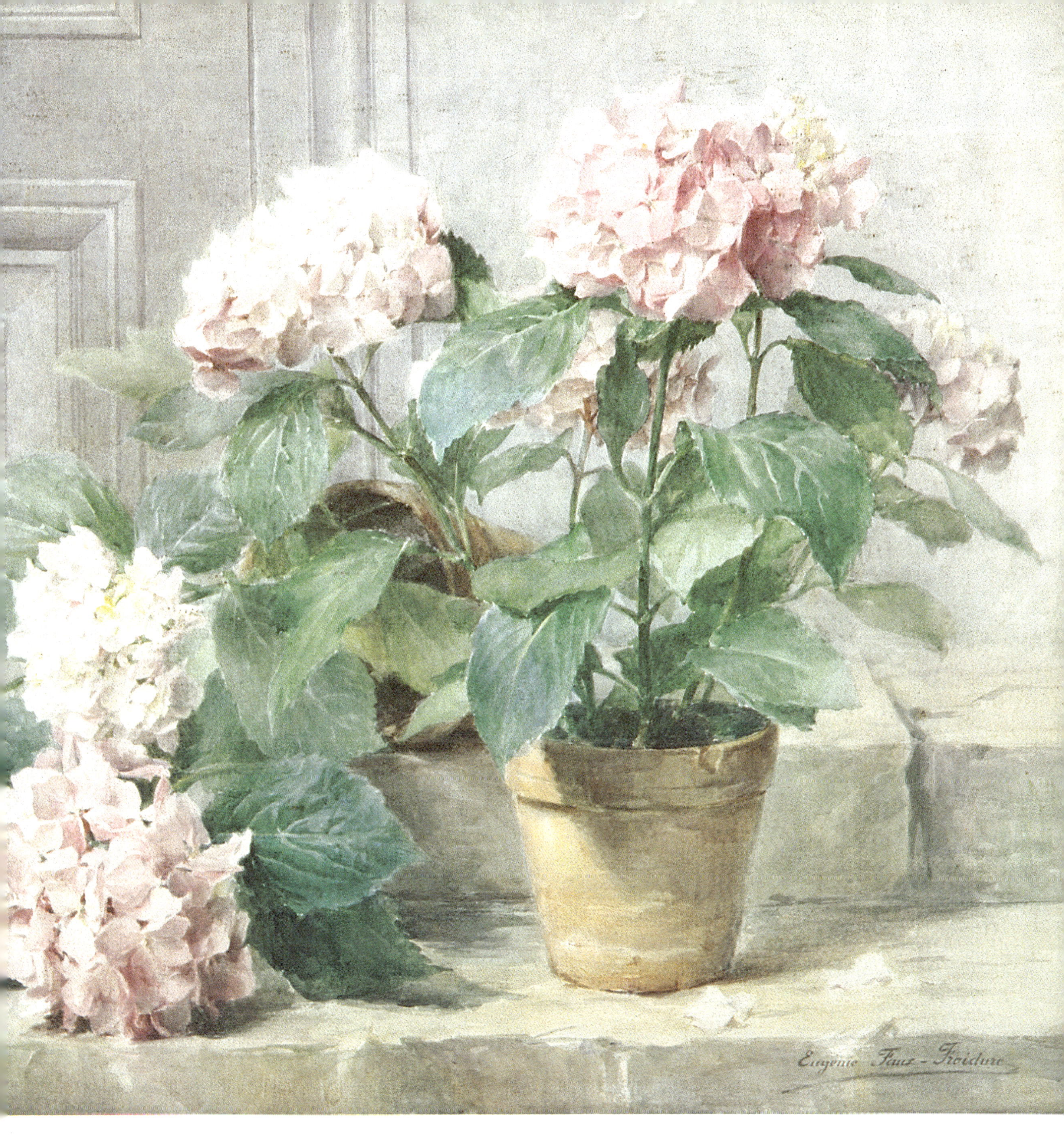
Eugenie Faux - Froidure

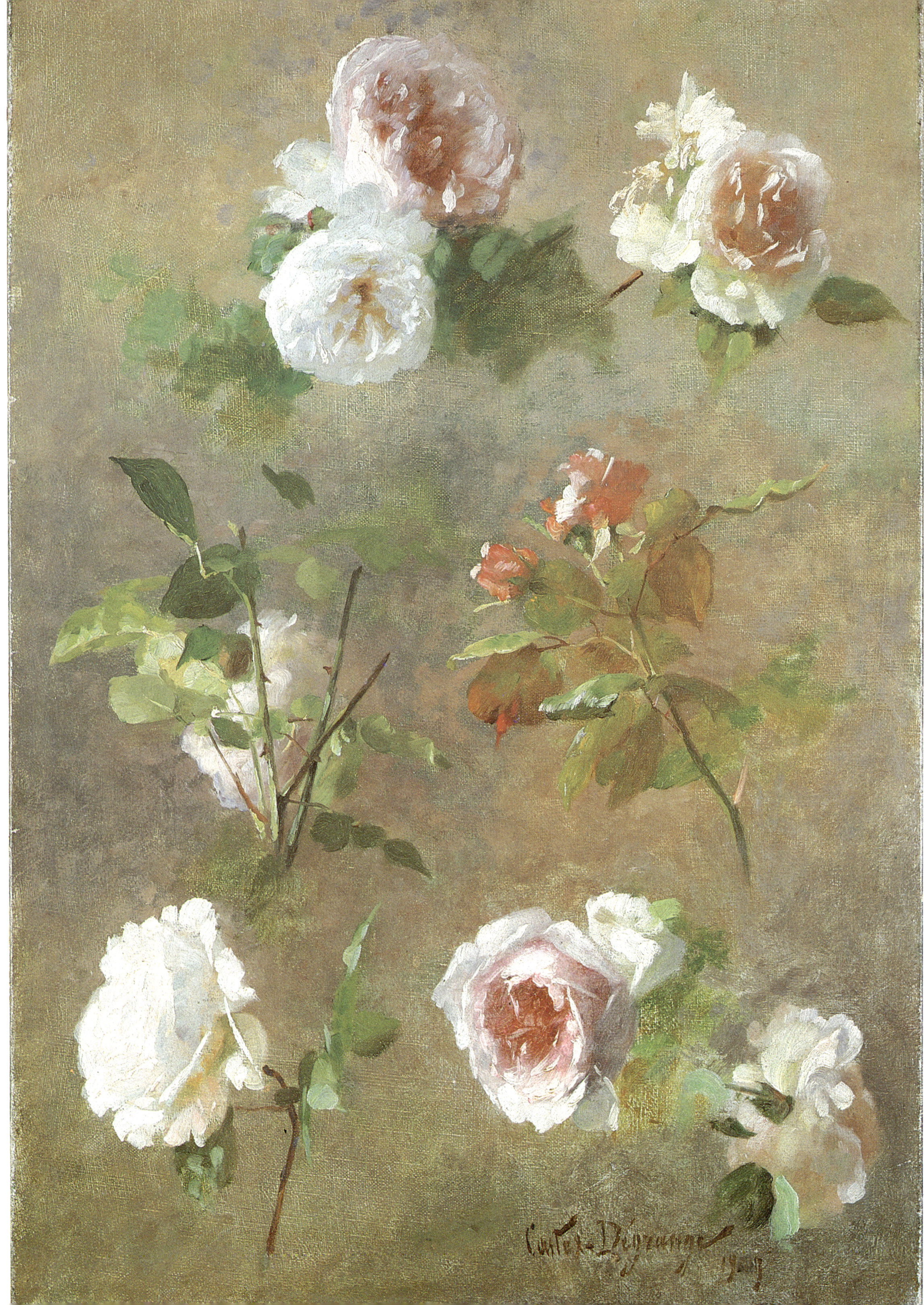

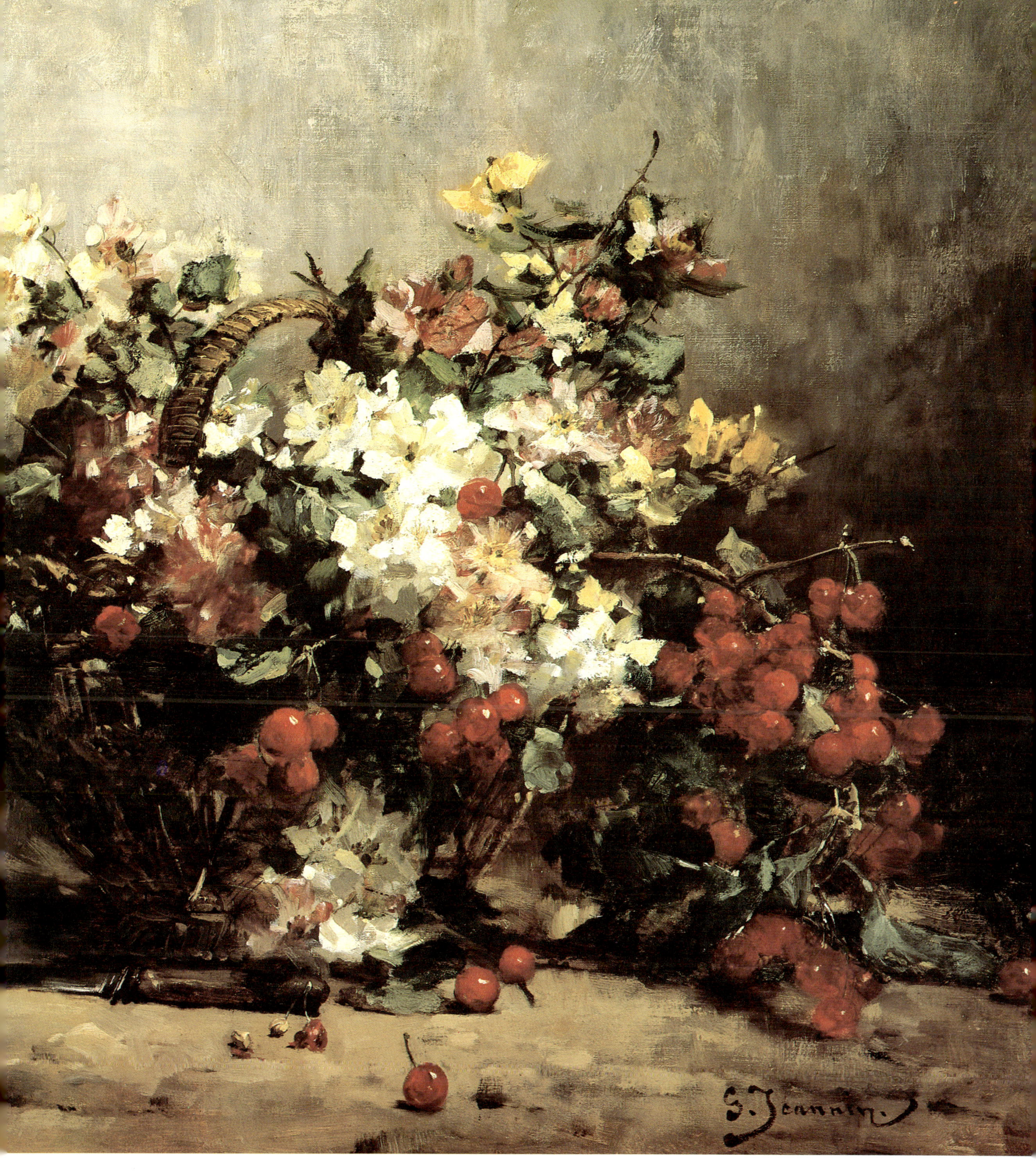

Fantin - 90

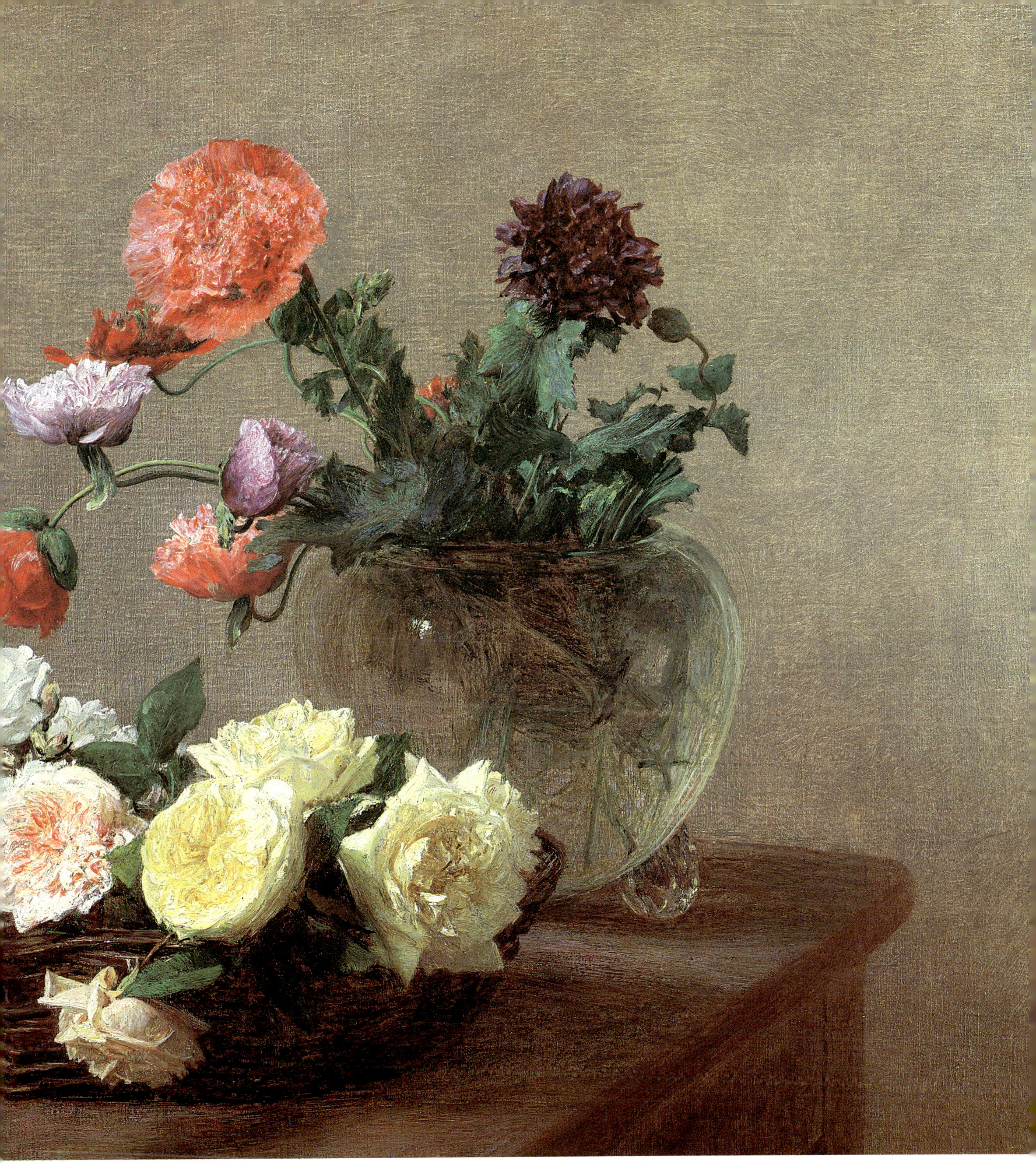

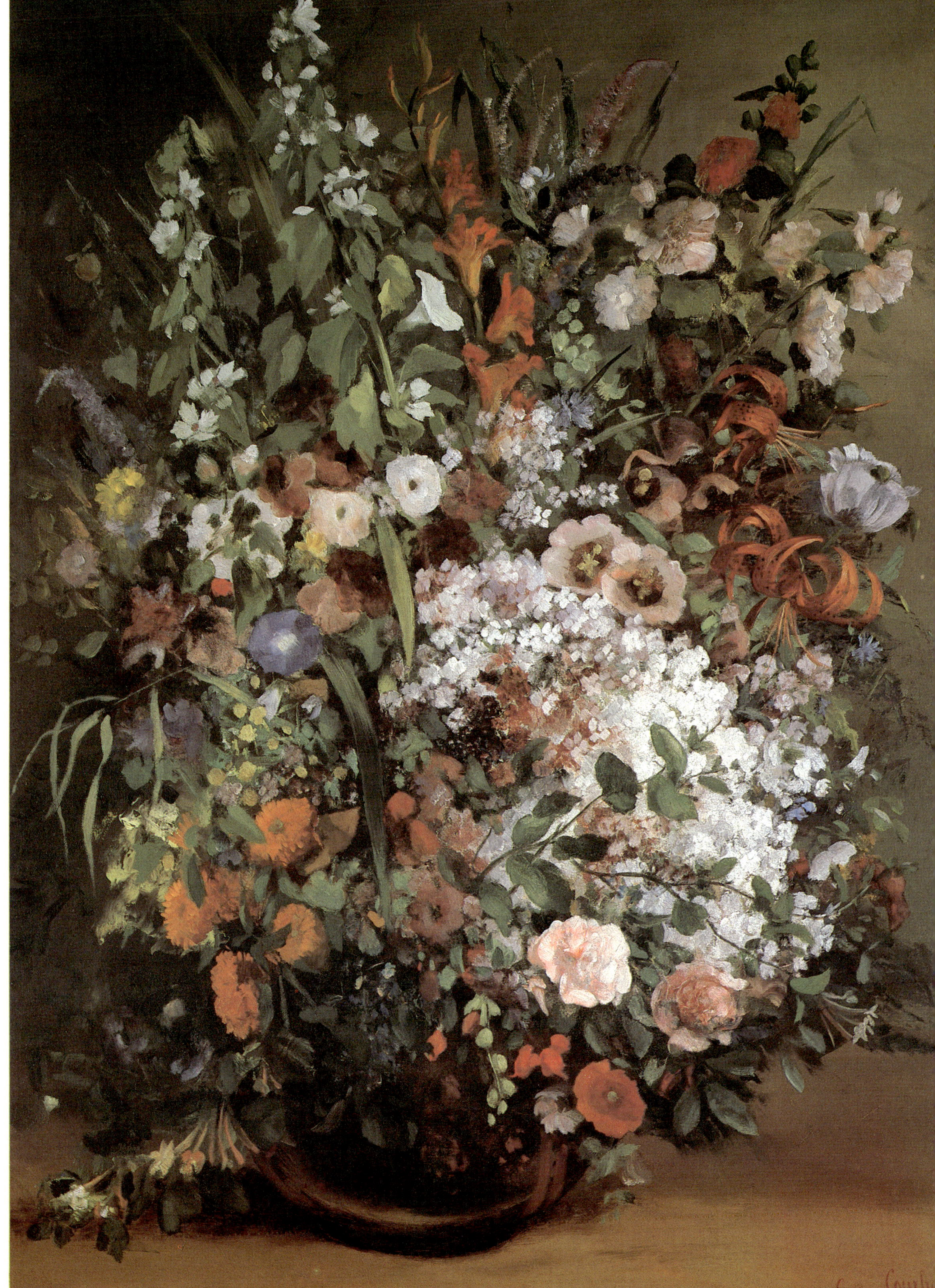

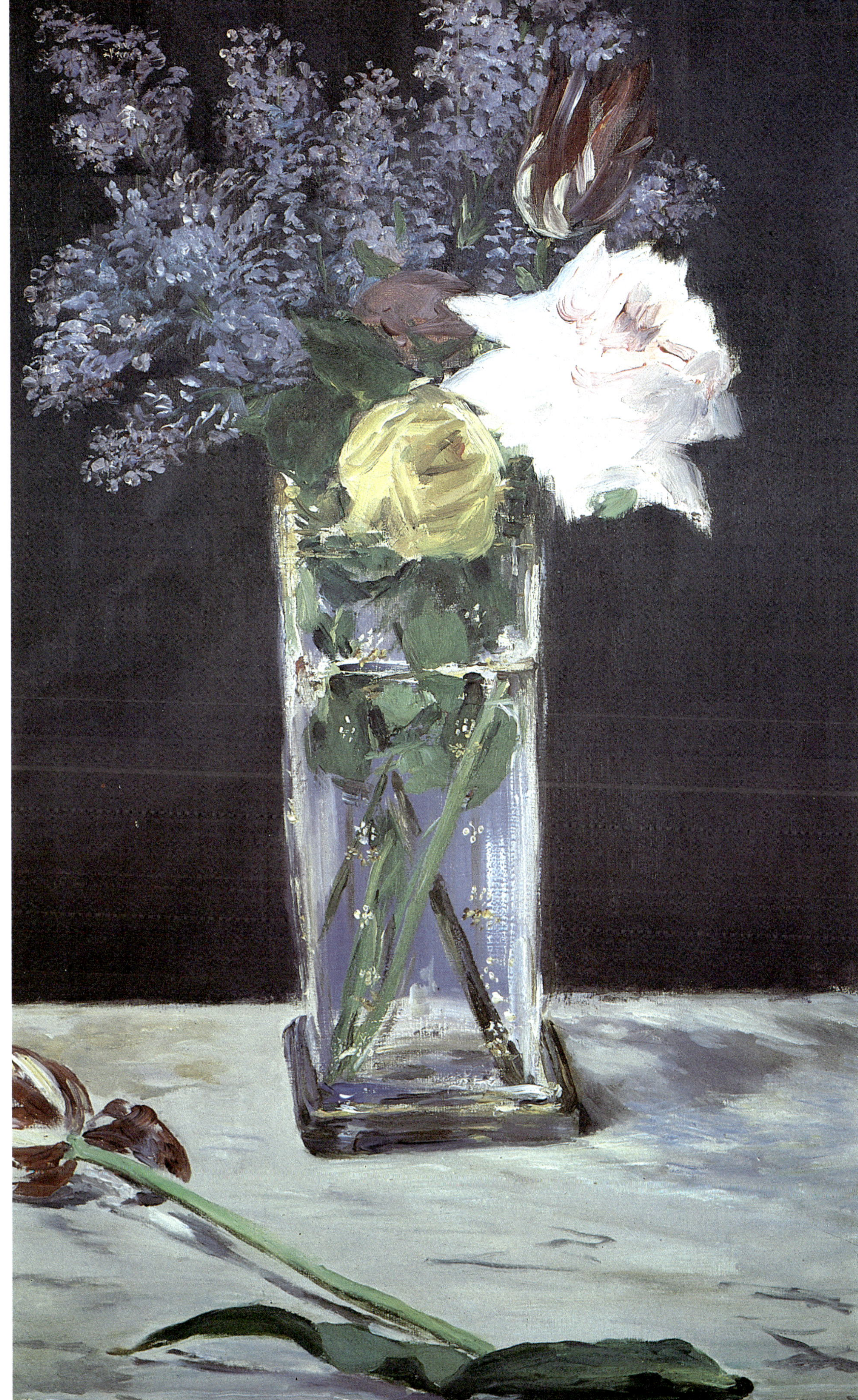

Renoir.

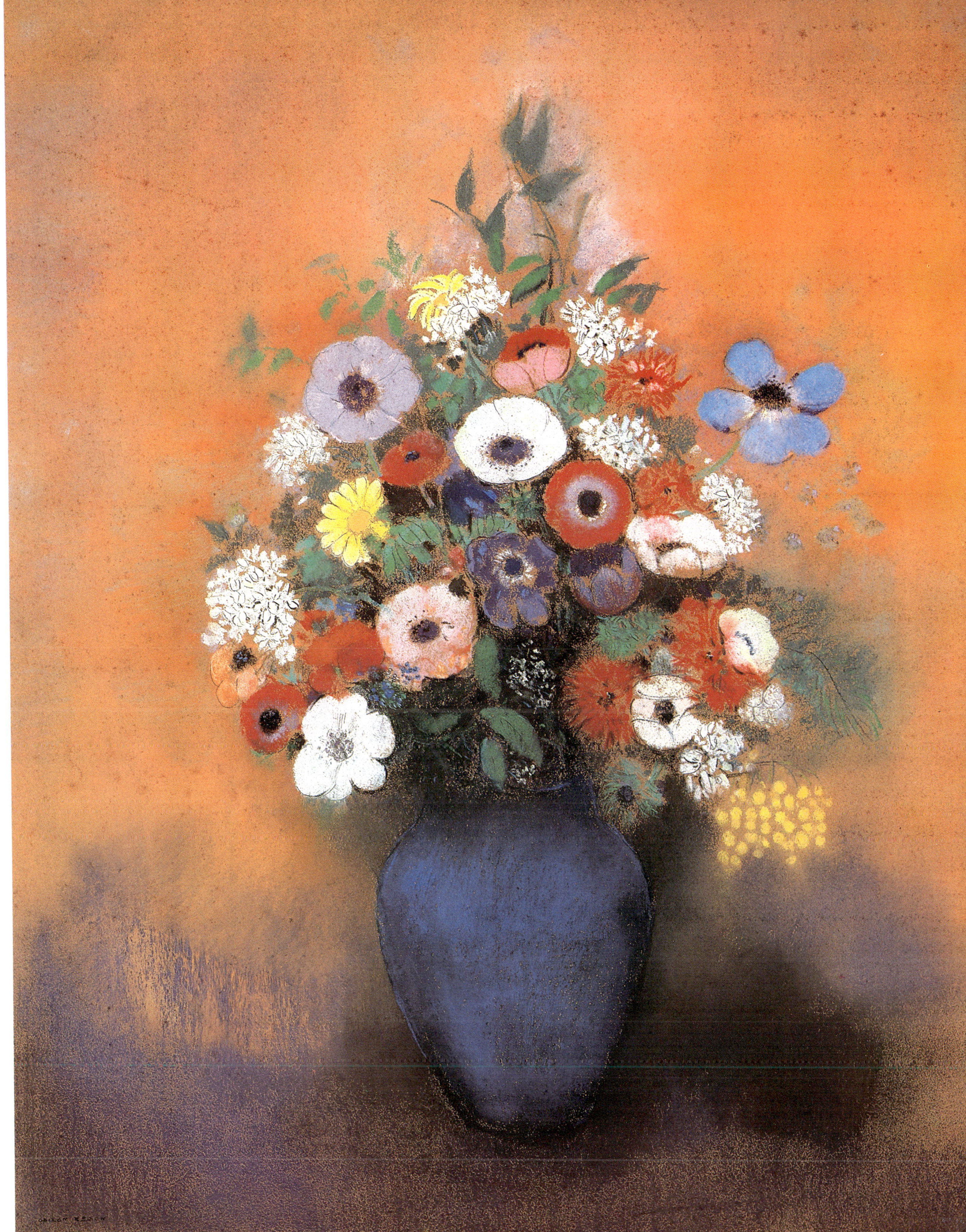

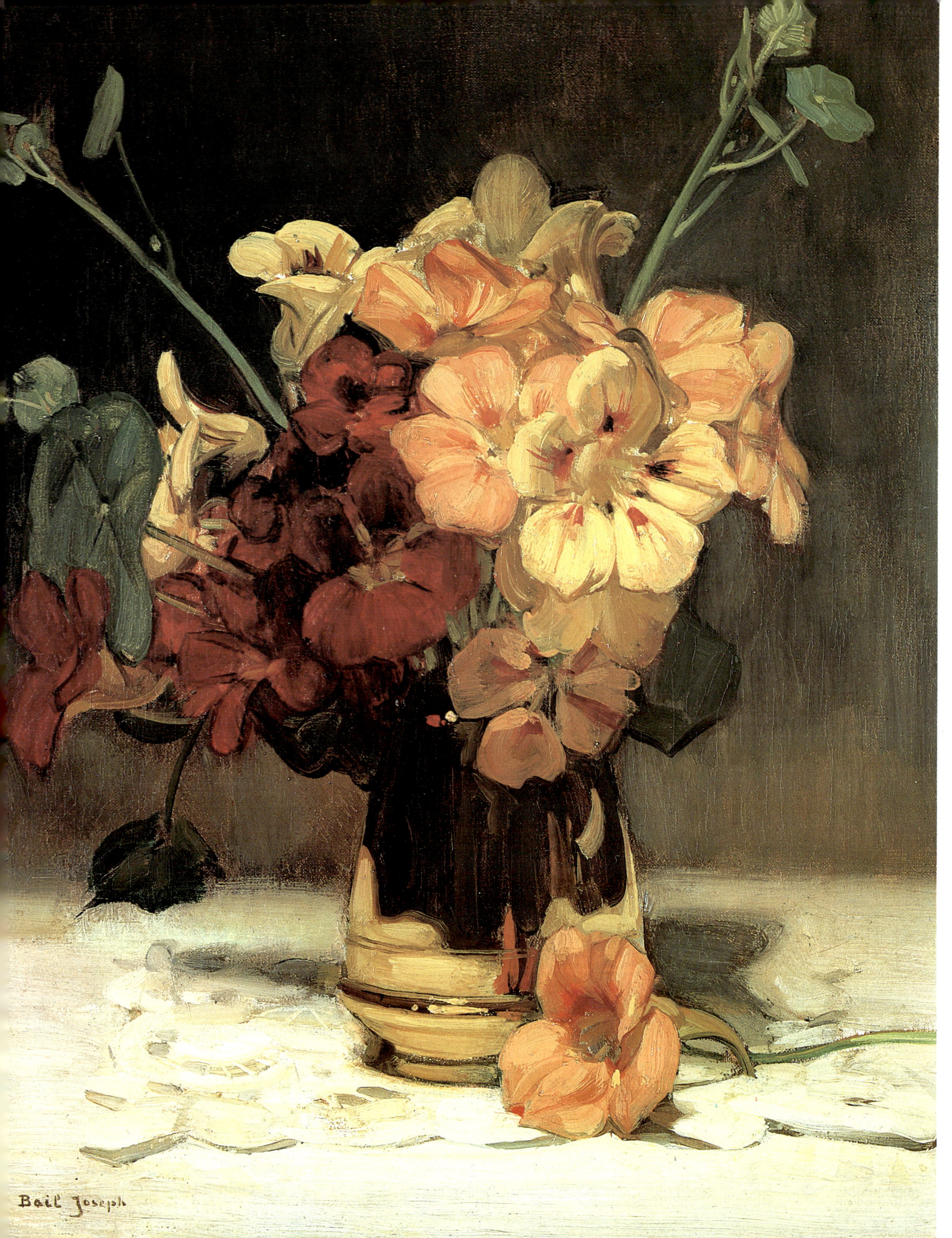
Bail Joseph

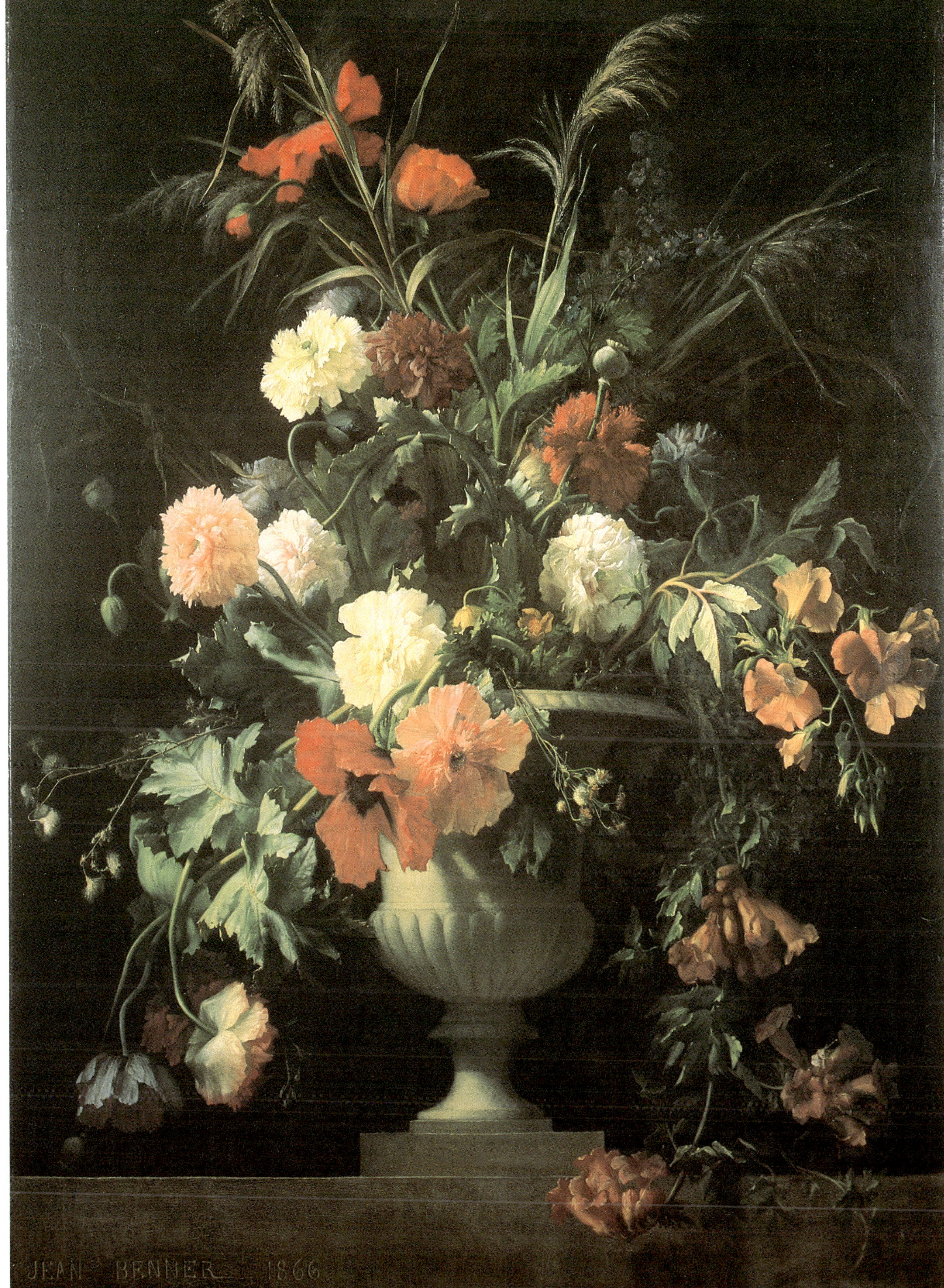
JEAN BENNER 1866

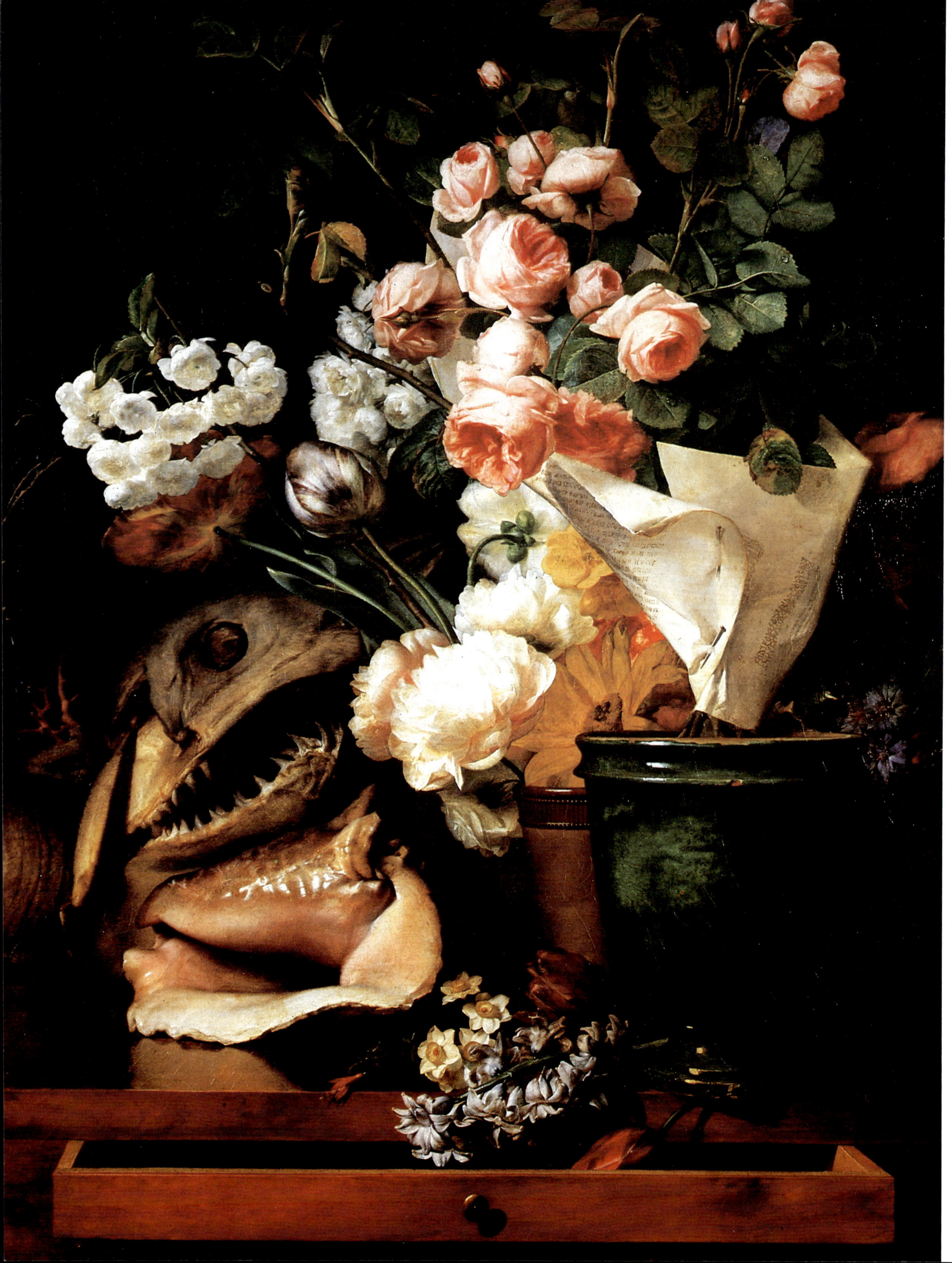

flower is as individual, as unique as any sitter; he, more than any other painter of his time, has achieved the miraculous balance between the short lived and the eternal. So far as flower painting is concerned his contemporaries, however gifted, however bold, display artistry, whereas he seems to reach quite effortlessly the mysterious yet familiar shores of art. Using a very different idiom, the same brilliance is attained by Odilon Redon, whose flowers breathe a life of their own, both peaceful and incandescent, familiar yet remote. For most major painters, flowers were an excuse, a mere object lesson in style. Not for Fantin and Redon, whose concern with the very essence of the flower outweighs every other stylistic consideration. Not for them the highly finished, ultra-realistic botanical approach of their traditional forerunners, the strong brushwork and impasto of Delacroix or Courbet, and their tonal contrasts of dark and light values. Not for them the Impressionists' immediacy, light tone, and high-key colour. They had little in common with the Pointillistes' obsession with the decomposition of light conveyed through mosaic-like brush-strokes. The ruthlessly synthetic approach and strong outlines of the Cloisonnistes or the snug vision of the Nabis were equally alien to them. Their flowers are what they should be: forever fresh and soulful. This is what Redon's message means: 'Flowers born where the two rivers, image and memory, meet. They are the very land of art, the good earth of reality harrowed and furrowed by the spirit.' This seems to echo Swinburne's moving tribute to Fantin-Latour's flowers:

Deep flowers, with lustre and darkness fraught,
From glass that gleams as the chill still seas
Lean and lend for a heart distraught
Heart's ease.

ELISABETH HARDOUIN-FUGIER

ETIENNE GRAFE

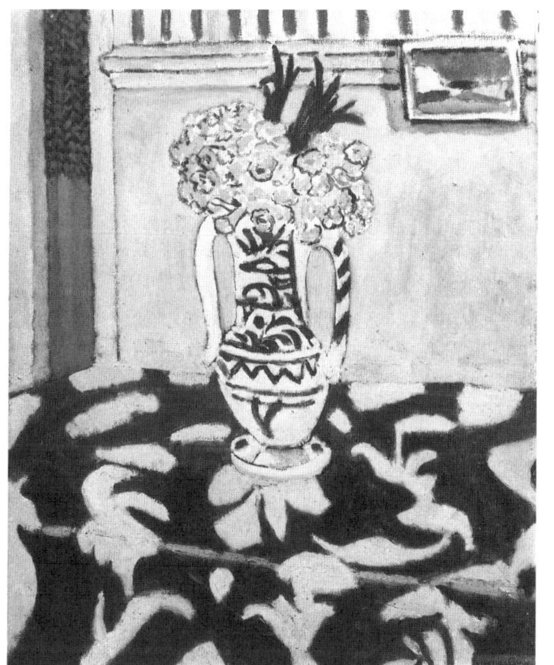

Henri Matisse

Oil on canvas, 32 × 29½ in. (81 × 65 cm.), signed and dated 1911
Courtesy Christie's, London

The Dictionary

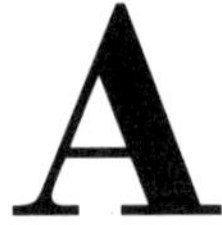

A

ABBÉMA, Louise ***1858–1927***
b. Etampes (Essonne). Pupil of Chaplin. Henner and Carolus-Duran. Sarah Bernhardt's friend and favourite painter. Occasionally painted flowers e.g. *Roses*, Dijon Salon 1880; *Gardenias*, Lyon Salon 1881. Musée de Limoges, *Capucines* (gift of the State 1906).
LIT *L'Art*, V, 253; *Bellier*; *Bénézit*; *Dijon Salon* 1880; G. L. Lecocq *Abbéma*... Paris (Librairie des Bibliophiles) 1879; *Lyon Salon* 1881; *Orsay*; Paris Arch. Nat. F21:4163; *Schurr* I, 107; *Thieme*; *Witt*

ABEILLE DE FONTAINE
Flowers on vellum, Paris Muséum d'Histoire Naturelle
LIT *Faré* 1962, p. 247

ABNER, Sophie
Pupil of Redouté. Exhib. flowers, wc, Paris Salon 1842
LIT *Paris Salon* 1842

ABOURY, Marie
b. Paris. Pupil of Mlle Burat. Exhib. Paris Salon *Roses*, fan-leaf, and *Fleurs sauvages*, 1879, *Fleurs variées*, wc, 1880
LIT *Bellier*; *Paris Salon* 1879–1880

Caroline Adrien

Watercolour and bodycolour on vellum, $16\frac{1}{16} \times 12\frac{11}{16}$ in. (40.7 × 32.3 cm.), signed and dated 1830
Cambridge, Fitzwilliam Museum
(Broughton Collection)

ACARIE
Painted and lithographed flowers. Paris BMAD (Maciet coll.)
LIT *Paris BMAD*

ACCARD, Eugène ***1824–1888***
b. Bordeaux (Gironde). Pupil of Abel de Pujol, Puvis de Chavannes and Carrière. Exhib. flowers e.g. *Bouquet de la Mariée*, Strasbourg Salon 1862; *Fleurs et coquillages*, Lyon Salon 1877
LIT *Bellier*; *Bénézit*; *Lyon Salon* 1877; *Marseille Salon* 1858; *Schurr* V, 107; *Strasbourg Salon* 1862; *Thieme*; *Witt*

ACELLY, Alfred
b. Paris. Pupil of A. Rousy. Exhib. Paris Salon 1890
LIT *Bénézit*; *Paris Salon* 1890

ACHINTRE, Armand-Louis ***b.1812***
b. Versailles (Yvelines). Pupil of Thierriat, Lyon BA (CFD 1832)
LIT *Hardouin-Fugier Grafe*

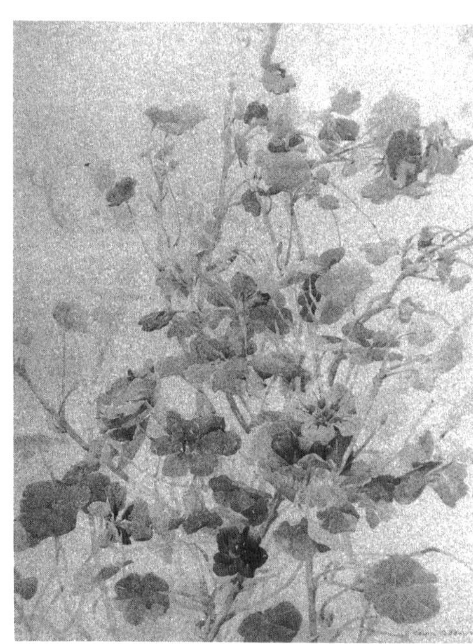

Louise Abbéma

Watercolour, $29\frac{1}{2} \times 23\frac{1}{2}$ in. (75 × 60 cm.), signed
Limoges, Musée Municipal

ACOQUAT, Louise-Marie
b. Pontivy (Morbihan). Pupil of Mme Dumoulin and Luigi Loir. Exhib. Paris Salon gouaches e.g. *Buisson d'églantines*, 1879, *Fleurs des champs*, *Roses et lilas*, 1880, and pastels e.g. *Laurier rose et blanc*, Paris Noir et Blanc Salon 1886
LIT *Bellier*; *Bénézit*; *Paris Salon* 1879, 1880; *Paris Noir et Blanc* 1886

ADAM, Nanny
Painted landscapes and, occasionally, flowers e.g. *Fleurs*, Paris UFPS 1896
LIT *Bénézit*; *Paris UFPS* 1896; *Witt*

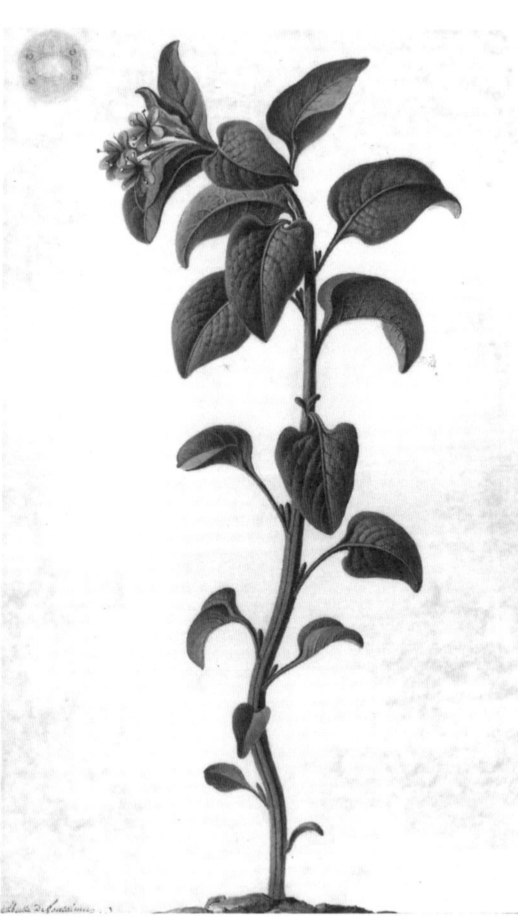

Abeille de Fontaine

Watercolour on vellum, Vélins vol. 22, no. 78, signed
Paris, Bibliothèque Centrale du Muséum National d'Histoire Naturelle

ADAM-MONCEAU, Clémence
b. Paris. Pupil of MacNab and de Champeaux. Exhib. Paris UFPS *Géraniums*, *Roses*, *Panier de zinnias*, wc, 1896; *Pivoines*, *Géraniums*, *Vase de roses*, wc, 1898
LIT *Paris UFPS* 1896, 1898

ADAN, Félix-Louis
b. Paris. Pupil of H. Adan. Exhib. flowers, Paris Salon 1880
LIT *Bellier*; *Paris Salon* 1880

ADÈLE, *fl.c.1820*
LIT *Hardouin-Fugier* 1981; *Witt*

ADELEN, Mlle de
Exhib. *Gloxinias*, *Géraniums*, *Pavots*, Lyon Salon 1857
LIT *Lyon Salon* 1857

ADELINA, Mlle
Exhib. Strasbourg Salon e.g. *Bouquet de fleurs*, 1853 (200 francs), *Roses*, 1855 (125 francs), *Pavots d'Orient et pivoines*, 1856, *Fleurs*, pastel, 1857 (200 francs)
LIT *Strasbourg Salon* 1850–1857

ADELON, *see* DONEAUD

ADENOT, Laurent *b.1848*
b. Nuits-Saint-Georges (Côte-d'Or). Pupil of Gaitet and Rondot. Exhib. *Chrysanthèmes*, Dijon Salon 1887
LIT *Bénézit*; *Dijon Salon* 1887. CL

ADER, André *b.1806*
Pupil of Berjon, Lyon BA (CFD 1822)
LIT *Hardouin-Fugier Grafe*

ADORNE, *see* EGLÉE

ADOUR, Pauline-Françoise
Pupil of M. Carpentier, R. Colin and J.-P. Laurens. Painted landscapes. Exhib. *Roses trémières*, wc, *Boules de neige*, pastel, Paris UFPS 1886
LIT *Bénézit*; *Paris UFPS* 1896

ADRIEN, Caroline
b. Paris. Possibly a pupil of Redouté. Exhib. flowers, wc, Lyon Salon 1837, 1839. A protégée of Comtesse de Montalivet. *Centifolia roses with buds*, and *Spray of Flowers*, 1830, Fitzwilliam Museum, Cambridge (Broughton coll.)
LIT *Hardouin-Fugier* 1981 (two works reproduced); Louvre Arch.; *Lyon Salon* 1837, 1839; *Pavière*; *Thieme*
See illustration on page 64

ADRIEN, Marie
b. Nantes (Loire–Atlantique). Pupil of Mme Bernard and F. Rivoire. Exhib. e.g. *Roses*, wc, Paris Salon 1885; Paris Noir et Blanc Salon *Bouquet de violettes*, 1886, *Panier de roses*, 1888; *Panier de rhododendrons*, wc, Dijon Salon 1892; *Reines-marguerites et dahlias*, wc, Paris UFPS 1896; Paris SNBA, *Roses et ronces*, wc, 1898; *Fleurs de printemps*, 1899
LIT *Bellier*; *Dijon Salon* 1892; *Paris Noir et Blanc Salon* 1886, 1888; *Paris Salon* 1885; *Paris UFPS* 1896; *Paris SNBA* 1898, 1899

AGARD, Charles-Jean *1866–1950*
Pupil of Bonnat. Painted landscapes, still-lifes and, occasionally, flowers
LIT *Bénézit*; *Schurr* II, 122; *Thieme*; *Witt*

AGASSIS, *see* COLLOMB

AGESSY, Thérèse d'
Exhib. Dijon Salon *Bouquet de violettes et primevères*, 1890, *Lilas jeté sur un banc de pierre*, 1892
LIT *Dijon Salon* 1890, 1892. CL

AGNÈS, Ferdinand *b.1866*
b. Lyon. Pupil of Castex-Dégrange. Lyon BA (CFD 1891)
LIT *Hardouin-Fugier Grafe*

AGUETTANT, Denis
Pupil of Thierriat, Lyon BA (CFD 1824)
LIT *Hardouin-Fugier Grafe*

AGUTTE-SEMBAT, Georgette *1867–1922*
b. Paris. Pupil of Gustave Moreau. Founder of Paris Salon d'Automne. Exhib. portraits and, occasionally, flowers. Two late flower-pieces in the Musée de Grenoble
LIT *Bénézit*; *Grenoble Musée doc.*; Paris Arch. Nat. F21:4163; *Schurr* I, 141; *Thieme*

AIMÉE, Louise
Pupil of Mme Trébuchet. Exhib. Paris Salon *Fleurs*, gouache, 1878, *Lilas*, gouache, 1880
LIT *Bellier*; *Paris Salon* 1880

ALAUX, Mme L.-D.
Exhib. Paris SNBA, *Glycines*, 1897, *Chrysanthèmes*, wc, 1898, *Oeillets*, 1899
LIT *Paris SNBA* 1897, 1898, 1899

ALBANS, *see* JOUFFROY

ALBERT, Adolphe *1853–1938*
b. Paris. Exhib. Paris Indép. and Paris SNBA, occasionally flowers in oils or wc, e.g. Paris Indép. 1889
LIT *Bénézit*; *Paris Indép.* 1889; *Schurr* V, 153

ALBERT, Ernest
b. Paris. Pupil of Sieffert, Pipard and Mathieu. Exhib. Paris Salon *c.*1870–1880
LIT *Bellier*

ALBERT, Fx (Felix ?)
A lithograph after a flower piece by Fx Albert in Paris BMAD (Maciet coll.)
LIT *Paris BMAD*

ALBY, Jules
b. Marseille. Pupil of Cabanel. Exhib. Paris Salon e.g. *Fleurs rustiques*, wc, 1890
LIT *Bellier*; *Bénézit*; *Paris Salon* 1890; *Thieme*

ALDA, Marie-Céline
Pupil of F. Rivoire. Exhib. *Chrysanthèmes et grenades*, wc, Paris Salon 1890
LIT *Paris Salon* 1890

ALEXANDRE, Eugénie or Eva
b. Limoges (Haute-Vienne). Pupil of the Limoges École d'Art. Exhib. Professor at École Nationale des Arts Décoratifs de Limoges, 1886; Paris Noir et Blanc Salon 1888; Musée de Limoges, *Roses trémières*, wc, *Chrysanthèmes en bouquet dans un vase*
LIT *Bénézit*; *Limoges Musée doc.*; Paris Noir et Blanc Salon 1888

ALLAIN, Pauline, *née* Jamet
Pupil of Lesourd de Beauregard, Chabal–Dussurgey and Rosa Bonheur. Exhib. Paris Salon *c.*1848–1868 e.g. *Panier de fleurs et de fruits*, 1852; *Fleurs, fruits au bord de l'eau*, Paris Amis-des-Arts 1856; Paris Salon *Fleurs des champs*, 1857, *Offrande à Flore*, 1859, *Couronne de roses*, 1864; *Roses et narcisses*, Lille Salon 1866; *Fleurs*, after Saint-Jean, Roubaix Salon 1866; *Jacinthes, violettes et coquelicots*, drawing, Paris Salon 1868; *Le bouquet à la Sainte Vierge*, Amiens Salon 1868
LIT *Amiens Salon* 1868; *Bellier*; *Bénézit*; Delécluze in *Le Journal des Débats*, 16 Apr. 1848; *Louvre, Paris* (*Amis-des-Arts*) 1855, 1856; Paris Arch. Nat. F21:114, 450; *Thieme*

ALLAIS, *see* REYS

ALLARD, Charles
Pupil of Lyon BA. op. Decorator. Exhib. flowers e.g. *Pivoines*, *Ellébores*, Lyon Salon 1873
LIT *Hardouin-Fugier Grafe*; *Lyon Salon* 1873–1877; *Thieme*

ALLARDET, Jacques-Claude *b.1832*
Pupil of Thierriat, Lyon BA (CFD 1850)
LIT *Hardouin-Fugier Grafe*

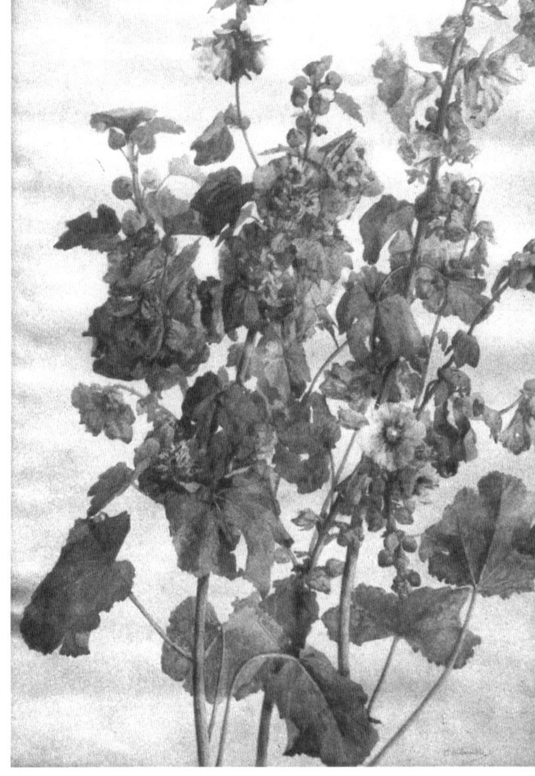

Eugénie or Eva Alexandre (*above*)

Watercolour, 35½ × 24¾ in. (90 × 63 cm.), signed
Limoges, Musée Municipal

Georgette Agutte-Sembat

Oil on canvas, 32 × 39½ in. (81 × 100 cm.), signed
Grenoble, Musée de Peinture et de Sculpture

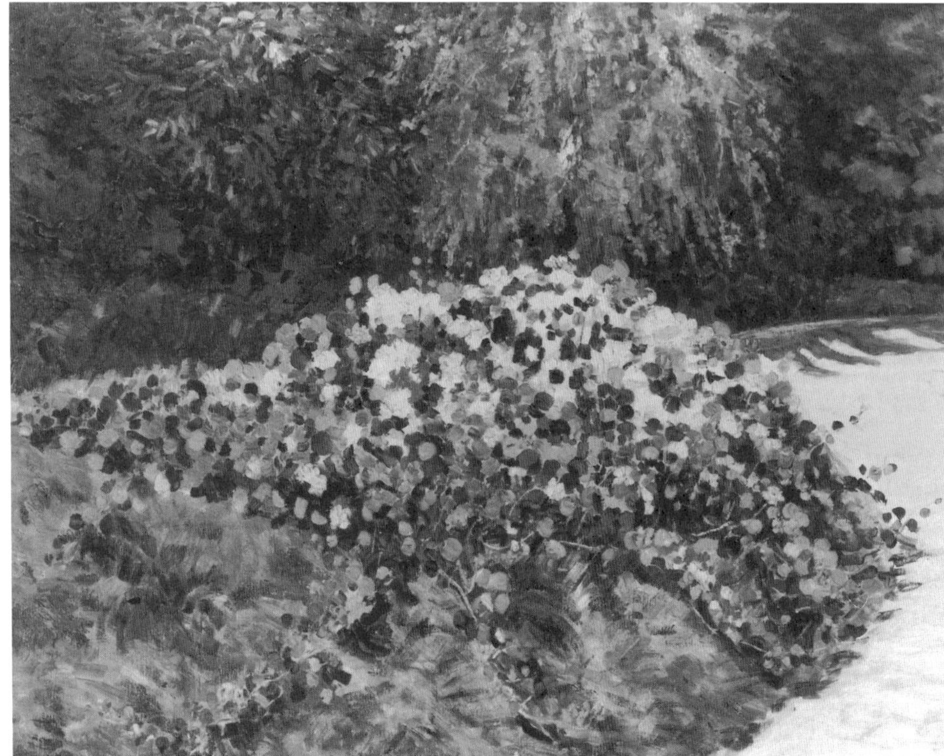

ALLOUARD, Edmond ***fl.1880–1915***
b. Paris. Pupil of Lechevallier-Chevignard. His 1880 *Fleurs et fruits* after Van Dael, was bought by the government (500 francs). Exhib. Paris Salon from 1881 e.g. *Fleurs d'été*, 1883, *Rhododendrons*, *Fleurs de printemps* and *Fleurs l'hiver*, 1885, *Ondée au printemps*, 1888, *Pivoines* 1894, *Fleurs au crépuscule*, 1896, *Près de la source*, 1898; *Iris au crépuscule*, Dijon Salon 1897. His *Iris au réservoir* once listed in the inventory of the Musée Bonnat, Bayonne, is untraceable. Works often reproduced in Paris Salon handbooks e.g. 1883, 1885, 1894–1899
LIT *Bellier*; *Bénézit*; *Dijon Salon* 1897; Paris Arch. Nat. F21:190, 4164, 4500; *Paris Salon* 1883, 1885, 1888, 1894, 1896, 1898; *Thieme*

ALLOUIS, Jeanne
Exhib. *Roses*, on porcelain, Dijon Salon 1897
LIT *Dijon Salon* 1897

ALOZIO, Clarisse
b. Lyon. One of Castex-Dégrange's private pupils. Exhib. Paris Salon 1876, 1878; Lyon Salon 1876
LIT *Hardouin-Fugier Grafe*; *Lyon Salon* 1876; Picard "les artistes lyonnais à Paris" in *La Revue du Lyonnais*, 1878 II, p. 223

ALVAR D' ***see*** **FOYOT**

ALZINE, Henri
Pupil of Thierriat, Lyon BA (CFD 1826)
LIT *Hardouin-Fugier Grafe*

AMAND, Gaspard ***b.1793***
Pupil of Berjon, Lyon BA (CFD 1810–1813)
LIT *Hardouin-Fugier Grafe*

AMAUDRY, Marie
Exhib. *Fleurs*, Dijon Salon 1887, *Primevères*, Poitiers Salon 1887
LIT *Dijon Salon* 1887; *Poitiers Salon* 1887. BG

AMELLER, André-Jean-Isidore ***b.1834***
Pupil of Thierriat, Lyon BA (CFD 1849)
LIT *Hardouin-Fugier Grafe*

AMEN, Jeanne ***1863–1923***
b. Belleville-sur-Saône (Rhône). Pupil of A. Grivolas. Exhib. Dijon Salon *Quand les pêchers sont en fleurs*, 1890, *Pavots*, *Lilas*, 1894; *Orchidées et chrysanthèmes*, Paris UFPS 1896. Her *Pivoines et aubépines* was bought for the Musée de Langres (800 francs) and her *Les lys et la mer*, for the Musée de Mâcon (1,000 francs)
LIT *Bénézit*; *Dijon Salon* 1890, 1894; *Hardouin-Fugier Grafe*; *Langres Musée doc.*; Paris Arch. Nat. F21:2129, 4164; *Paris Salon* 1890; *Paris UFPS* 1896, 1898; *Thieme*

AMIARD, Henriette-Eugénie
Pupil of Mlle Delmas. Exhib. *Primevères*, Paris Salon 1898
LIT *Bénézit*; *Paris Salon* 1898

AMPENOT, Edouard-Gabriel-François
b. Paris. Pupil of Lucas and Maillard. Worked for the Gobelins tapestry factory. Exhib. Paris Salon 1879–1881. Painted flowers and landscapes. Curator of the Musée de Coulommiers
LIT *Bellier*; *Bénézit*; *Thieme*

AMSINCK D', ***see*** **DOUTRELEAU**

ANDERS, Marie-Josèphe ***née*** **Hésèque**
Pupil of Delorme and, possibly, Redouté. Exhib. 1875–1880 e.g. *Roses dans une potiche*, Paris Salon 1879
LIT *Bellier*; *Bénézit*; *Paris Salon* 1875–1880; *Thieme*

ANDIGNY, Jenny d'
b. Paris. Pupil of E. Claude. Exhib. *Pensées*, Paris Salon 1873
LIT *Bénézit*; *Paris Salon* 1873

ANDRÉ, Benjamin-Marie-Albert ***1869–1954***
b. Lyon. Studied Académie Julian and under Benjamin Constant and Bouguereau. This post-Impressionist painted flowers e.g. *Pétunias*, 1893, Museum of Fine Arts, Boston; *Pivoines et lys de Dieppe*, 1894; Exhib. *Fleurs de Lyon*, 1982. A friend of Renoir, Albert André copied the master's *Gladioli* exhib. Tooth, London 1964. *Vase de fleurs*, Park Bernet, New York, 16 Dec. 1977, lot 23
LIT *Bénézit*; J.G. Besson in *Fleurs de Lyon* (*Hardouin-Fugier Grafe* 1982); M. Mermillon, *A. André*, Paris (Crès) 1927; *Paris Indép.* 1896; Saint-Denis Musée, *A. André* 1970; *Schurr* I, 129; *Thieme*; *Witt*

ANDRÉ, Jean-Isidore ***b.1834***
b. Lyon. Pupil of Thierriat, Lyon BA (CFD 1849). *Branche de camélia* by André was won at the 1852 Lyon Société des Amis-des-Arts raffle
LIT *Compte-rendu annuel de la Société des Amis-des-Arts de Lyon*, Lyon Perrin 1852; *Hardouin Fugier Grafe*

ANDRÉ, Jenny
b. Neuilly (Hauts-de-Seine). Exhib. *Roses trémières*, pastel, Paris Noir et Blanc Salon 1888
LIT *Paris Noir et Blanc Salon* 1888

ANDRÉ, Suzanne
b. Paris. Pupil of Valentino and F. Rivoire. Exhib. *Roses*, wc, Paris Salon 1890
LIT *Paris Salon* 1890

ANDRÉ DUHAMEL, Mme
Exhib. *Fleurs*, wc, Lyon Salon 1874
LIT *Lyon Salon* 1874

ANDUC, Charles-Jean ***b.1827***
b. Lyon. Pupil of Thierriat, Lyon BA (CFD 1844)
LIT *Hardouin-Fugier Grafe*

ANGLADE, Gaston-Vincent ***b.1854***
b. Bordeaux. Pupil of Baudet and Pelouse. Watercolourist. Very successful at Bordeaux with landscapes; rival of Didier-Pouget
LIT *Bénézit*; *Schurr* II, 37. PM

ANGRAND, Charles ***1854–1926***
b. Criquetot-sur-Ouville (Seine-Maritime). The now well-known post-Impressionist was one of the founding members of the Société des Artistes Indépendants with Seurat and Signac and befriended Van Gogh. Painted landscapes, figures and may occasionally have painted flower pieces. Exhib. Paris Indép. from 1884 e.g. *Dans le jardin*, 1884
LIT B. Welsh-Orcharov, *The Early Work of Charles Angrand*, The Hague, 1971; J. House *Angrand* in Post-Impressionism, London RA, 1979–1980; F. Lespinasse *Angrand* Rouen (Le Cerf) 1982

ANNE, Marie ***fl.c.1845–51***
Lived Mainz 1845. Most probably a pupil of Redouté. Exhibited two watercolours of flowers at the Paris Salon 1845. Her work was included in a Royal Academy exhibition, London, 1851. Two watercolours are in the Victoria and Albert Museum: *Dahlias*, *Tecoma Jasminoides*. Cambridge, Fitzwilliam Museum (Broughton Coll.): *Spray of*

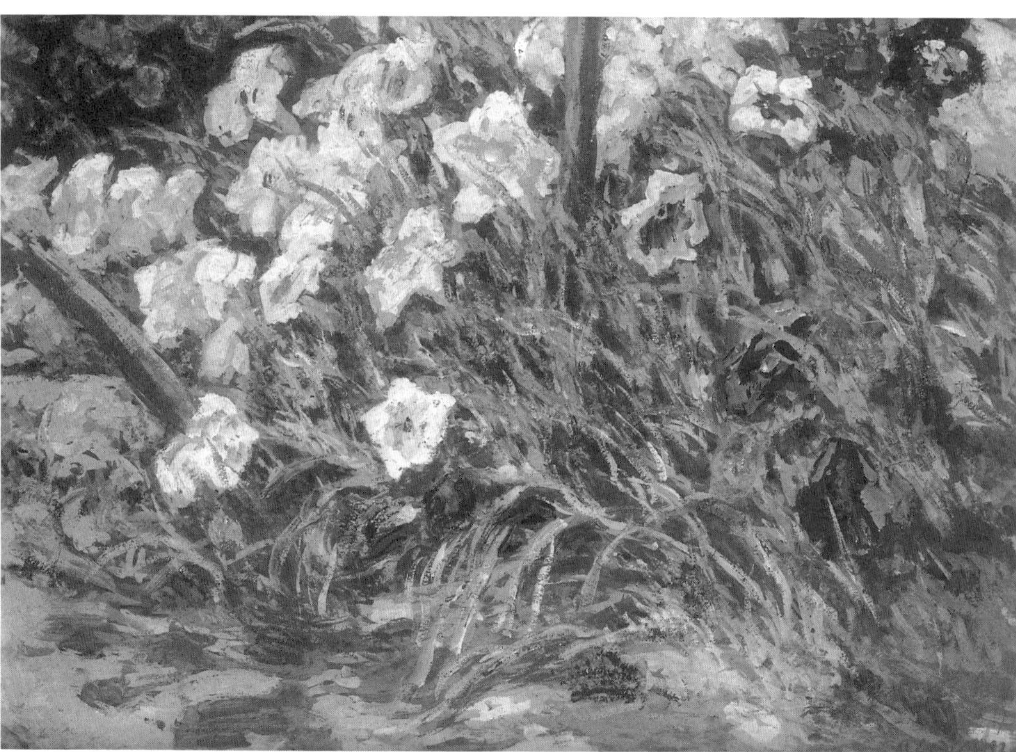

Benjamin-Marie-Albert André

Gouache on paper board mounted on panel, $19\frac{1}{4} \times 25\frac{3}{4}$ in. (48.8 × 65.5 cm.), signed and dated 1892
Boston, Museum of Fine Arts

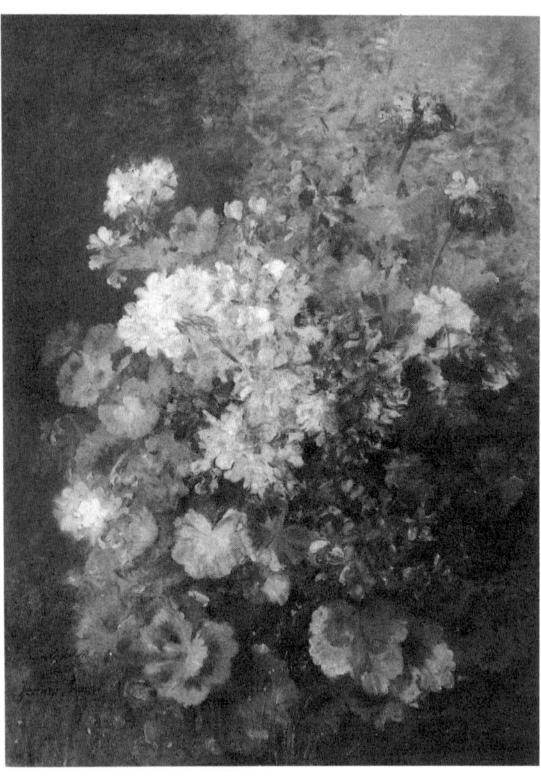

Jeanne Amen

Oil on canvas, $28\frac{3}{4} \times 21\frac{1}{2}$ in. (73 × 54 cm), signed and inscribed 'à Monsieur Chincholle du Figaro'
Private collection

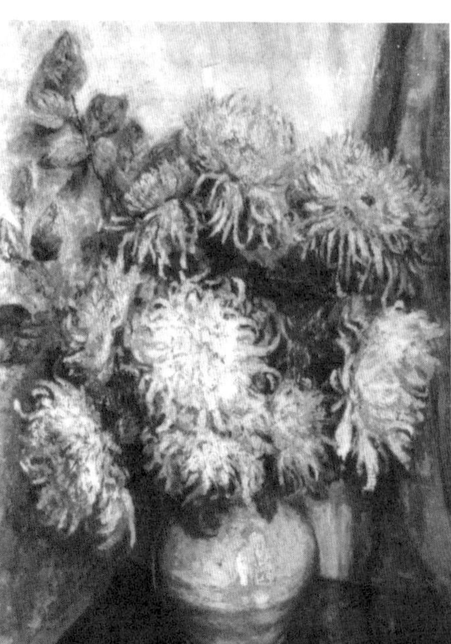

Gaston-Vincent Anglade

Oil on canvas, $32 \times 23\frac{3}{4}$ in, (81 × 60 cm.), signed and dated '27
Private collection

Flowers including viola, chrysanthemum and rose, 1823, wc, *Nerium Oleander*, wc, *Gay Flowers*, wc
LIT *Paris Salon* 1845; *Bénézit*; *Hardouin-Fugier*, 1981 (ill.); *Broughton*, 1983 (ill.). JLC

ANNET, *see* BERGUIGNAT

ANQUETIN, Louis *1861–1932*
b. Etrepagny (Eure). Pupil of Bonnat and Cormon. Painted townscapes, figures, portraits and, occasionally, flowers. Invented Cloisonnism. Exhib. Paris Indép.
LIT J. Ajalbert *Anquetin*, Paris (Rey) 1930; E. Bernard "Anquetin" in *La Gazette des Beaux-Arts* 1934; H.H. Hofstätter *Geschichte des Europäischen Jugendstilmalerei*, Köln (Dumont) 1972, p. 59; M.A. Stevens "Anquetin" in *Post-Impressionism*, London (RA) 1979–80; *Schurr* I, 121; *Thieme*; C. Versini *Anquetin* (Bordeaux, Centre Régional de Documentation Pédagogique) 1965

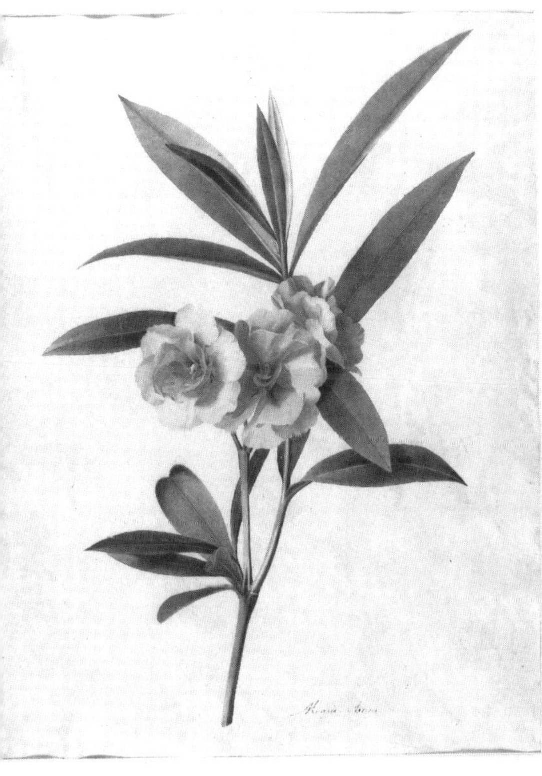

Marie Anne

Watercolour on vellum, 15¾ × 12¼ in. (39.9 × 31.1 cm.), signed
Cambridge, Fitzwilliam Museum (Broughton Collection)

APOIL, Suzanne-Estelle *née* Béranger *1825–after 1874*
b. Sèvres (Hautes-de-Seine). Pupil of A. Béranger, her father. Married painter Charles-Alexis Apoil. Op. Sèvres. Exhibited flowers Paris Salon 1845–1855, 1861–1863, and Bordeaux 1862
LIT *Bénézit*; *Bordeaux Salon* 1862; *Faré* 1962, p. 242; *Thieme*

APPIAN, Jacques-Barthélémy *alias* Adolphe *1818–1898*
b. Lyon. Pupil of Thierriat's CFD at Lyon BA. Well-known as a landscape painter, he produced some (mostly early) flower-pieces e.g. *Fleurs dans une haie*, Lyon, private coll.
LIT *Audin Vial*; *Bénézit*; Hardouin-Fugier Grafe, *Répertoire des peintres lyonnais du XIX siècle en Bugey* (Lacoux) 1980; *Schurr* I, 59; *Thieme*; *Witt*

ARBANT, Louis
b. Mâcon (Saône-et-Loire). Pupil of Lyon BA. Exhib. Paris Salon 1849–79. This still-life painter produced some flower-pieces
LIT *Bellier*; *Bénézit*, *Paris Salon* 1868, 1869, 1877, 1878; *Thieme*

ARBINET, Jane
Pupil of Jannot. Exhib. *Pensées*, wc, Dijon Salon 1894
LIT *Dijon Salon* 1894. CL

ARCHAMBAULT
Exhib. flower design for a table top, wc, Paris Salon 1835
LIT *Paris Salon* 1835

ARGUILLÈRE
b. 1830. Pupil of Thierriat, Lyon BA (CFD 1847)
LIT *Hardouin-Fugier Grafe*

ARMAND, Charles
Lyon textile designer, fl.*c.*1838
LIT *Audin Vial*; *Hardouin-Fugier Grafe*

ARMAND-DELLILE, Ernest-Emile *1843–1883*
b. Marseille. Pupil of Mme Armand-Dellile and Gérôme. Exhib. flowers Paris Salon 1875, *Pavots et Pivoines* 1876
LIT *Bellier*; *Bénézit*, *Paris Salon* 1875, 1876

ARNAUD, *see* WEBER

ARNAUD, Marcel *1877–1956*
May have produced some early (c.1900) flower-pieces. A self-styled Cézanne follower. M. Saint-Tropez, *Roses dans un vase*, 1918
LIT Eric Hild "La peinture de fleurs en Provence 1870–1920" in Saint-Tropez, *Fleurs de Fantin-Latour à Marquet, 1982*, Musée de l'Annonciade 1982, (ill.); *Schurr* I, 74; Witt

AROSA, Marguerite *veuve* Barria
b. Paris. Pupil of Maver, Barrias and Armand Gautier. Exhib. *Roses*, wc, Saint-Etienne Salon 1882; Dijon Salon *Coquelicots*, pastel, 1894, *Lilas en fleurs au Parc Monceau*, 1897
LIT *Bénézit*; *Dijon Salon* 1894, 1897; *Noir et Blanc Salon*, Brussels exhib. 1892; *Saint-Etienne Salon* 1882

AROUD, Antoine ***b.1820***
b. Saint-Etienne (Loire). Pupil of Thierriat, Lyon BA (CFD 1838)
LIT *Hardouin-Fugier Grafe*

ARSON, Olympe-Marie-Alexandrine ***1814–after 1870***
b. Paris. Pupil of Redouté and his "déléguée au cours d'iconographie végétale du Jardin des Plantes". Exhib. *Flowers*, wc, Paris Salon 1834, 1835, Dijon Salon 1837; *Roses*, wc, Lyon Salon 1837; *Roses et violettes*, wc, Dijon Salon 1840; *Vase de fleurs*, wc, Lyon Salon 1841. Contributed designs to most of Chavant's lithographed flower sets *c.*1837. Cambridge, Fitzwilliam Museum (Broughton coll.): *Potted Hydrangeas*, *Four Tulips*, both oil on paper, *Centifolia Roses*, 1832, WC
LIT *Bellier*; *Bénézit*; Broughton 1977; *Dijon Salon* 1837, 1840; *Hardouin-Fugier* 1981; *Lyon Salon* 1831; *Paris Salon* 1834, 1835, 1837; *Pavière*

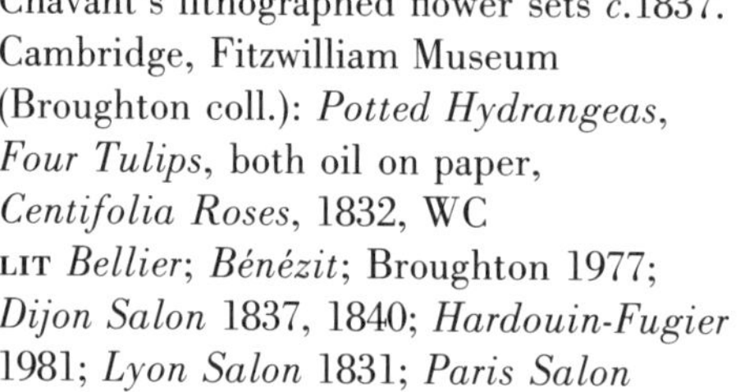

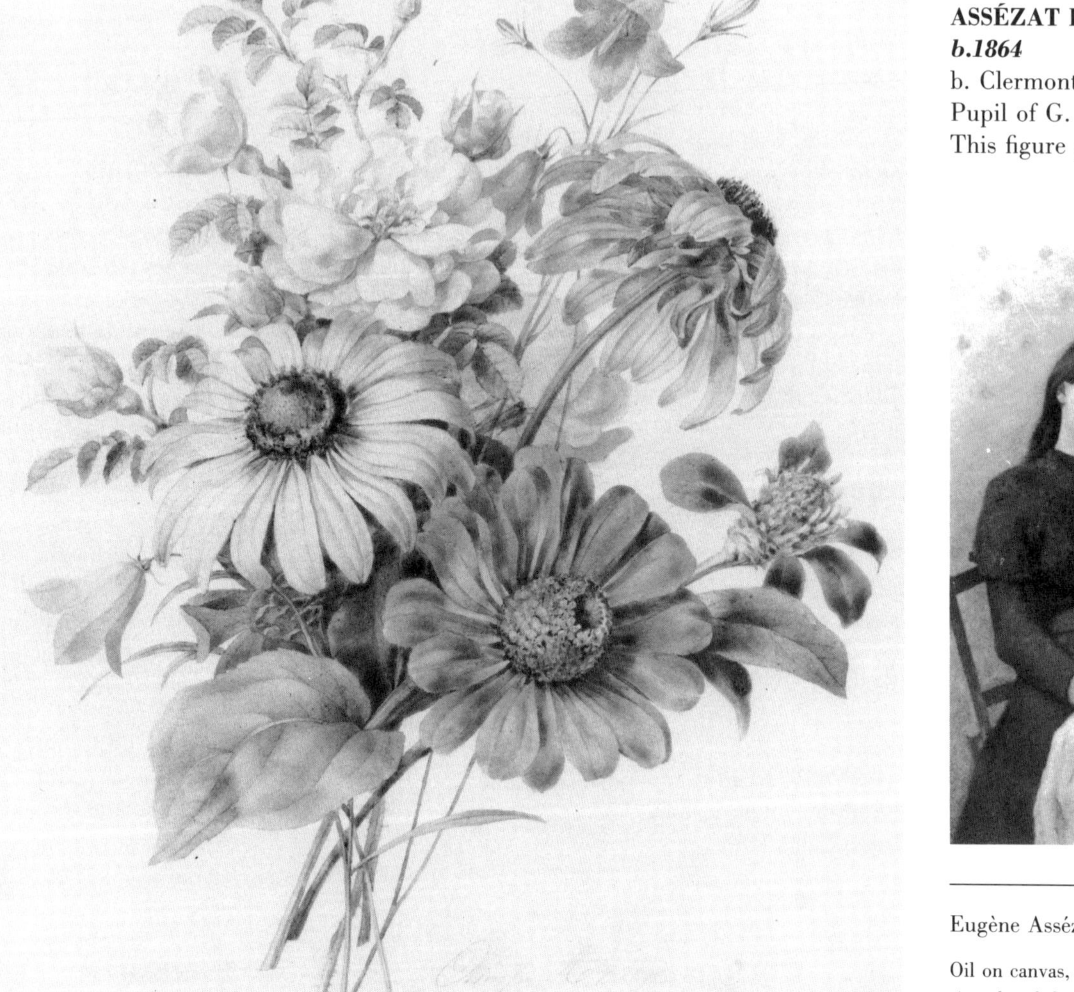

Olympe-Marie-Alexandrine Arson

Watercolour on vellum, 10½ × 8½ in. (26.5 × 21 cm.), signed and dated 1836
Private collection, Switzerland

ARTIGUE, Albert-Emile
b. Buenos Aires, fl.*c.*1875–1901. Pupil of École Municipale de Bordeaux and Cabanel. This figure painter occasionally produced some flower-pieces e.g. *Lilas*, Paris Salon 1877
LIT *Bellier*; *Bénézit*; *Thieme*; *Witt*

ARTRU, Alexis ***b.1872***
Pupil of Castex-Dégrange, Lyon BA (CFD 1892)
LIT *Hardouin-Fugier Grafe*

ASH, Thomas ***b.1842***
b. Philadelphia (USA). Pupil of Reignier, Lyon BA (CFD 1867)
LIT *Hardouin-Fugier Grafe*

ASSCHE, ***see*** **VAN ASSCHE**

ASSÉZAT DE BOUTEYRE, Eugène ***b.1864***
b. Clermont-Ferrand (Puy-de-Dôme). Pupil of G. Ferrier, T. Robert-Fleury. This figure painter whose works

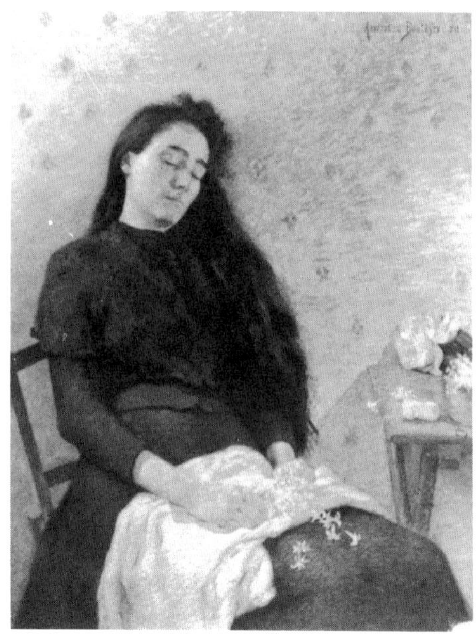

Eugène Assézat de Bouteyre

Oil on canvas, 45½ × 35½ in. (116 × 90 cm.), signed and dated 1892
Le Puy, Musée Crozatier

sometimes feature flowers may have produced some flower-pieces. His *Fleuriste endormie* exhibited at Le Puy Salon 1894 was bought for the Musée du Puy
LIT *Bénézit*; *Le Puy Musée, doc.*; *Schurr* IV, 132

ASTIER, Jeanne
b. Paris. Exhib. *Anémones*, *Azalées*, wc, Dijon Salon 1892
LIT *Dijon Salon* 1892. CL

ASTRUC, Pauline-Hélène
b. Angers (Maine-et-Loire). Pupil of Zacharie Astruc and Hermann Léon. Exhib. *Gloxinia*, *Bouquet de giroflées*, Paris Noir et Blanc Salon 1888; *Roses*, wc, Paris Salon 1890
LIT *Paris Noir et Blanc Salon* 1888; *Paris Salon* 1890

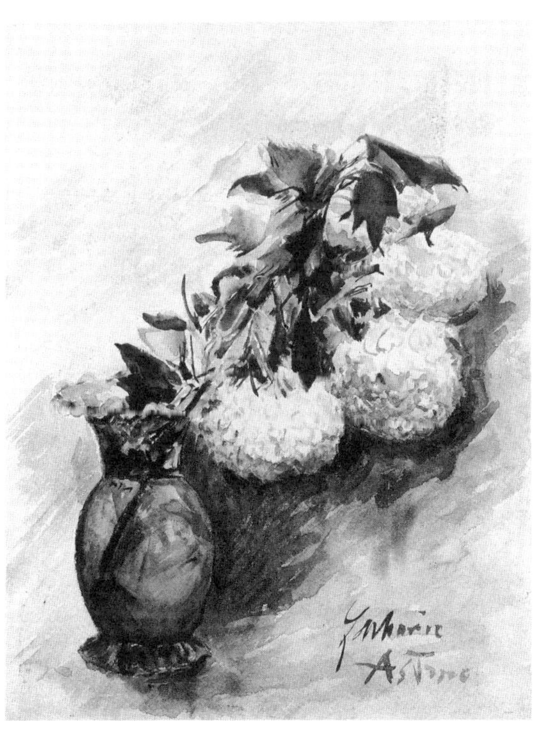

Zacharie Astruc

Watercolour over pencil, 14½ × 11¼ in. (37.2 × 28.5 cm.), signed
New York, Metropolitan Museum of Art

ASTRUC, Zacharie ***1835–1907***
b. Angers (Maine-et-Loire). Sculptor and illustrator. Exhib. flowers e.g. *Pivoines dans un vase du Japon*, wc, Paris Salon 1890. His six decorative flower designs *Géraniums*, *Dahlias*, *Tournesols*, *Roses trémières*, *Roses*, *Hortensias* were bought in 1892 for the Musée de Saint-Etienne (9,000 francs); Metropolitan Museum, New York *Roses*, wc, and *Flowers in a vase*
LIT *Bellier*; *Bénézit*; S. Z. Flescher *Astruc* ... New York, London (Garland) 1978; *Orsay*; Paris Arch. Nat. F21:2119, 4165; *Paris Salon* 1890; *Schurr* IV, 137; *Thieme*; *Witt*

ATTENDU, Antoine-Ferdinand ***b.c.1845***
b. Paris. Pupil of Mettling. Exhib. Paris *c.*1870–1905. Painted still-lifes and flowers
LIT *Bellier*; *Bénézit*; *Schurr* III, 69; *Thieme*

AUBÉ
The French government granted this most shadowy flower painter a pension
LIT Paris Arch. Nat. F21:287

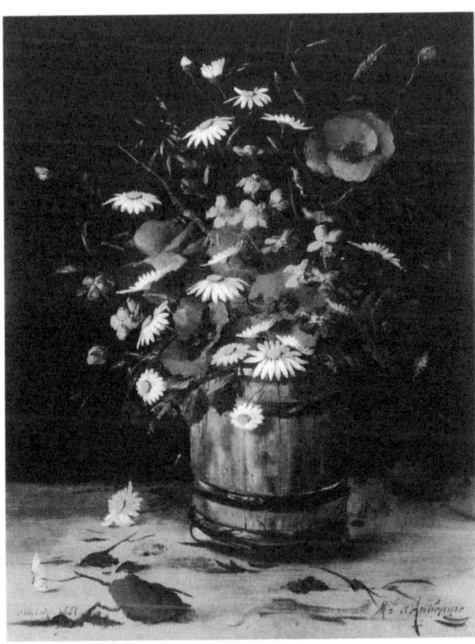

Marcel-Jules-Gingembre d'Aubépine

Oil on canvas, 21 × 17 in. (53 × 43 cm.), signed and inscribed 'Biarritz 1884'
Courtesy Christie's, London

AUBÉ, Gabrielle
b. Paris. Pupil of Accard. Exhib. *Fleurs*, Paris UFPS 1888
LIT *Paris UFPS* 1888

AUBÉ, Valentine
b. Paris. Pupil of Julia Beck, Exhib. *Chrysanthèmes*, *Roses thé*, *Pensées*, *Géraniums* etc. Paris UFPS 1896
LIT *Paris Noir et Blanc Salon* 1888; *Paris UFPS* 1896

AUBÉPINE, Marcel-Jules-Gingembre d' ***b.1843***
b. Habsheim. (Haut-Rhin) Painter and engraver, lithographer of landscapes and occasionally flowers. Made a series of

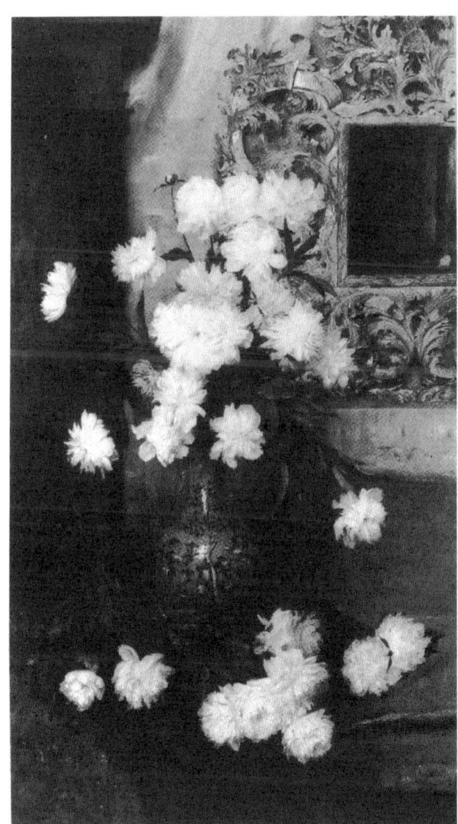

Albert Aublet

Oil on canvas, 78 × 45½ in. (198 × 115 cm.), signed and dated 1887
Courtesy of Sotheby's, London

engravings of Biarritz for Queen Victoria. Exhib. Paris Salon *c.*1892
LIT *Bénézit*. PM

AUBERGEON, Marie-Madeleine
b. Luc-sur-Mer (Calvados). Pupil of Carbillet. Exhib. Paris Salon 1877–1882, figures, genre and, occasionally, flowers
LIT *Bellier*; *Bénézit*; *Thieme*

AUBERT, Maximin ***b.1847***
b. Lyon. Pupil of Reignier, Lyon BA (CFD 1861–1862)
LIT *Hardouin-Fugier Grafe*

AUBLET, Albert ***1851–1938***
b. Paris. Pupil of Jacquand and Gérôme. Exhib. Lyon Salon. *Chrysanthémes*, 1875, *Giroflées*, 1876; Paris SNBA *Roses jaunes*, 1894; *Dans les roses trémières*, wc, 1894 *Vase de pivoines*, 1887, Sotheby's, New York, 21 May 1987, Lot 93
LIT *Bénézit*; *Lyon Salon* 1875, 1897; *Paris SNBA* 1891–1895; *Schurr* II, 102; *Thieme*; Witt

AUBRY, Eugène
Exhib, *Ange groupé avec des fleurs*, wc, Dijon Salon 1849
LIT *Dijon Salon* 1849

AUCTA ***b.1837***
b. Orléans (Loiret). Pupil of Reignier, Lyon BA (CFD 1854)
LIT *Hardouin-Fugier Grafe*

AUDENIS
b. Lyon. Exhibt. *Groupe de fleurs dans un vase*, Lyon Salon 1842
LIT *Audin Vial*; *Hardouin-Fugier Grafe*

AUFFRAY, Georges ***1869–1942***
Painted *Pichet de roses*, Versailles sale, 24 Feb. 1974
LIT *Orsay*; *Schurr* III, 43

AUMONT, Augustine
Pupil of Jacobber
LIT *Faré* 1962, p. 246

AURE, Mme d' ***née*** **Catherine Passy** ***b.1833***
b. Evreux (Eure). Pupil of O. Roland. Exhib. *Fleurs et fruits*, Paris Salon 1866
LIT *Bellier*

AUREL, Paul d'
b. Paris. Exhib. Paris Salon *Violettes*, fan-leaf, 1878, *Eglantines*, 1880
LIT *Bellier*

AUTEROCHE, Eugénie Venot d'
Pupil of Léon Cogniet. Exhib. flowers and portraits Paris Salon 1876–80
LIT *Bellier*; *Bénézit*; *Thieme*

AUTHIER, Henriette
b. Moulins (Allier). Exhib. Paris Indép. *Chrysanthèmes*, 1887, *Calendrier de Flore*, 1888, *Lilas, jacinthes*, 1889, *Bouquet de fleurs*, 1891
LIT *Bénézit*; *Paris Indép.* 1887–1889, 1891

AVELINE or AVELYNE, Clotilde-Eugénie-Victoire ***1873–1940***
b. Plancy (Aube). Pupil of Royer, Nanny Adam and Faux-Froidure. Exhib. *Chrysanthèmes*, *Iris et violettes*, wc, Paris UFPS 1896, Musée de Troyes, *Oeillets dans un panier*, wc
LIT *Bénézit*; *Paris UFPS* 1896; *Troyes Musée doc.*

AVIGNON, J.B. d'
b. Avignon (Vaucluse). Exhib. *Géraniums en plein soleil*, Paris Indép. 1894
LIT *Paris Indép.* 1894

AVRARD, Berthe
b. Versailles (Yvelines). Pupil of E. Bazin and E. Richard. Exhib. Paris Salon *Reines-marguerites*, on porcelain, 1880, *Fleurs de printemps*, on porcelain, 1882
LIT *Bellier*; *Paris Salon* 1880

AYNARD, ***see*** **JONNART**

Clotilde-Eugénie-Victoire Aveline or Avelyne

Watercolour, 15 × 21¾ in. (38 × 55 cm.), signed
Troyes, Musée des Beaux-Arts

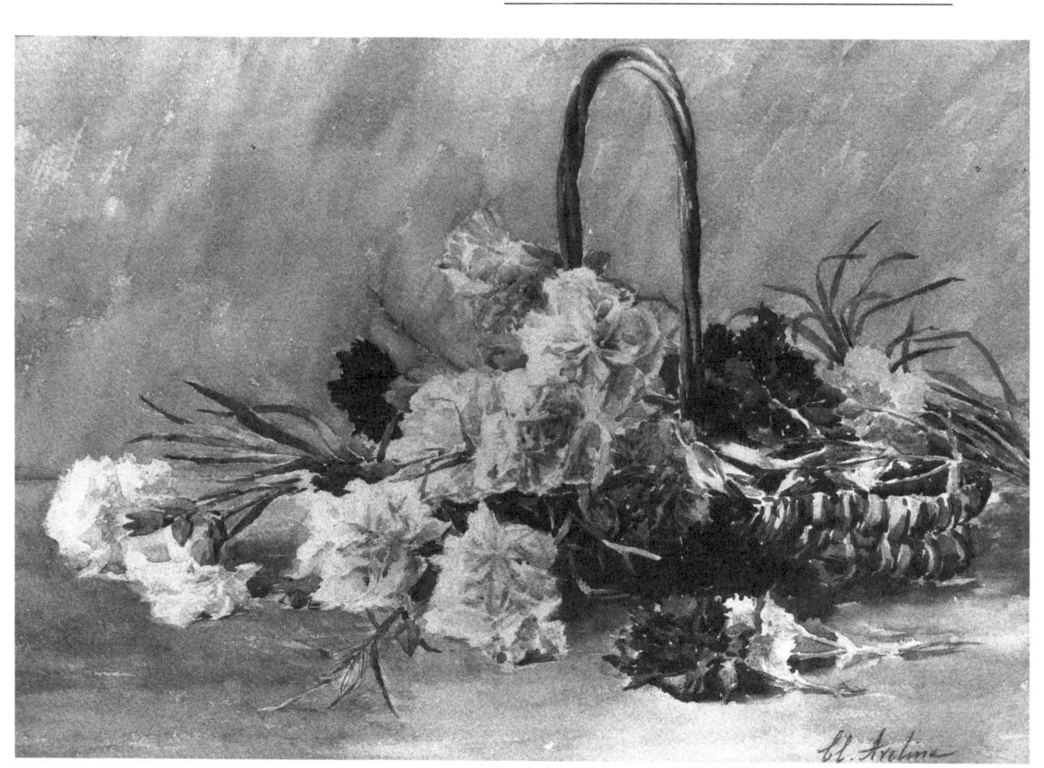

B

B
Exhib. *Roses de Dijon*, gouache, Lyon Salon 1858
LIT *Lyon Salon* 1858

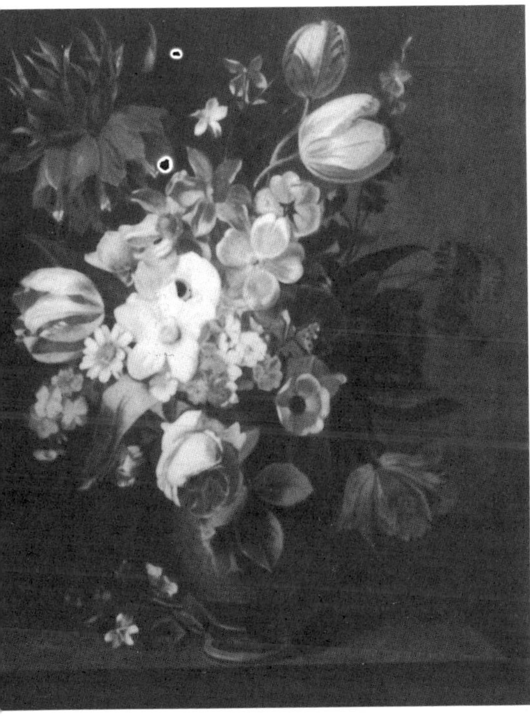

Claude Bachelut

Gouache, 30 × 25½ in. (76 × 64 cm.), signed and dated 1842
Private collection (photo: Musée des Beaux-Arts, Lyon)

BACCARD, Joseph ***b.1843***
Pupil of Reignier, Lyon BA (CFD 1861). Exhib. Lyon Salon 1880
LIT *Bénézit*; *Hardouin-Fugier Grafe*; *Lyon Salon* 1880

BACHELARD, Marcelin ***b.1816***
b. Lyon. Pupil of Thierriat, Lyon BA (CFD 1834–1857). Exhib. Lyon Salon 1837–1850)
LIT *Audin Vial*; *Bénézit*; *Hardouin-Fugier Grafe*

BACHELUT, Claude ***1824–1893***
A gardener's son. Pupil of Thierriat, Lyon BA (CFD 1843). Entered 1845–1846 FDC; op. textile designer
LIT *Hardouin-Fugier Grafe*; *Hardouin-Fugier Grafe* 1982 (ill.)

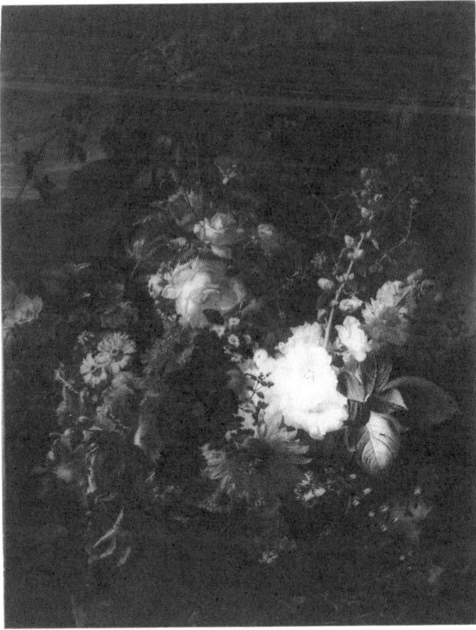

Jacques-Joseph Baile

Oil on canvas, 32¼ × 24 in. (82 × 61 cm), signed and dated 1851
Lyon, Musée des Beaux-Arts

BADINAND, Jean-Claude
Exhib. *Pivoines*, Saint-Etienne Salon 1891
LIT *Hardouin-Fugier Bringuier*; *Saint-Etienne Salon* 1891

BADOIS, Jeanne
b. Paris. Exhib. Paris Indép. *Vase de tulipes*, *Corbeille de mimosas*, 1893, *Oeillets*, pastel, 1894; *Corbeille de mimosas*, Dijon Salon 1894
LIT *Bénézit*; *Dijon Salon* 1894; *Paris Indép.* 1893, 1894

BADY
Pupil of Thierriat, Lyon BA (CFD 1835)
LIT *Hardouin-Fugier Grafe*

BAGARY, Jean-Antoine ***b.1827***
Pupil of Thierriat, Lyon BA (CFD 1847)
LIT *Hardouin-Fugier Grafe*

BAGET, Jules ***1810–1893***
Pupil of Redouté. Exhib. Paris Salon 1836, 1837. Contributed designs to some lithographed flower sets published by Chavant (*Naissance des Fleurs* etc.)
LIT *Hardouin-Fugier* 1981

BAGNIARD, Alfred-Adrien ***b.1826***
b. Paris. Pupil of Charlet. Textile designer, of Mulhouse
LIT *Histoire Documentaire*. BJ

BAIL, Antoine-Jean ***1830–1918***
b. Chasselay (Rhône). Exhib. decorative flowers. Lyon Salon 1870. Genre and still-life painter
LIT *Bellier*; *Bénézit*; *Hardouin-Fugier Grafe*; *Lyon Salon* 1870; *Schurr* I, 63; *Thieme*; *Witt*

BAIL, Franck-Antoine ***1858–1924***
b. Paris. Pupil of Antoine-Jean Bail, his father. Portrait, still-life and flower painter
LIT *Bénézit*; *Schurr* IV, 120; *Thieme*

BAIL, Joseph ***1862–1921***
b. Limonest (Rhône). Pupil of Antoine-Jean Bail, his father, Carolus-Duran and Gérôme. Painted genre, still-lifes and, occasionally, flowers. Exhib. *Chez le peintre de fleurs*, Dijon Salon 1887
LIT *Bellier*; *Bénézit*; *Dijon Salon* 1887; *Hardouin-Fugier Grafe*; Pavière; *Schurr* I, 65; Weisberg, G., *Chardin and the Still-Life Tradition*, Cleveland, 1979; Weisberg, G., *Arts Magazine*, 1981; *Thieme*; Valmy-Baysse, *Joseph Bail*, Paris (Juven) 1910

BAILE, Jacques-Joseph ***1819–1856***
Pupil of Thierriat, Lyon BA (CFD 1836) and Lepage. Textile designer. Exhib. Lyon Salon from 1840, Paris Salon 1844, 1846, 1850. His 1851 *Fleurs sur un rocher* is in the Musée des Beaux-Arts, Lyon, and his 1853 *Fleurs et fruits* was exhibited at the 1855 Paris Exposition Universelle
LIT *Hardouin-Fugier Grafe*; *Hardouin-Fugier Grafe* 1982 (ill.)

BAILLY, Antoine
Pupil of Berjon, Lyon BA (CFD 1810)
LIT *Hardouin-Fugier Grafe*

BAILLY, Bernardine
Exhib. Dijon Salon *Bouquet-de lilas*, 1885, *Un panier de primevères*, 1887
LIT *Dijon Salon* 1885, 1887

BAILLY, Félix ***1822–1892***
b. Troyes (Aube). Painted landscapes and flowers e.g. Musée de Troyes, *Fleurs des champs* and *Roses dans un vase*
LIT Saint-Tropez, *Fleurs de Fantin-Latour à Marquet*, Musée de l'Annonciade, 1982, no. 2 (ill.)

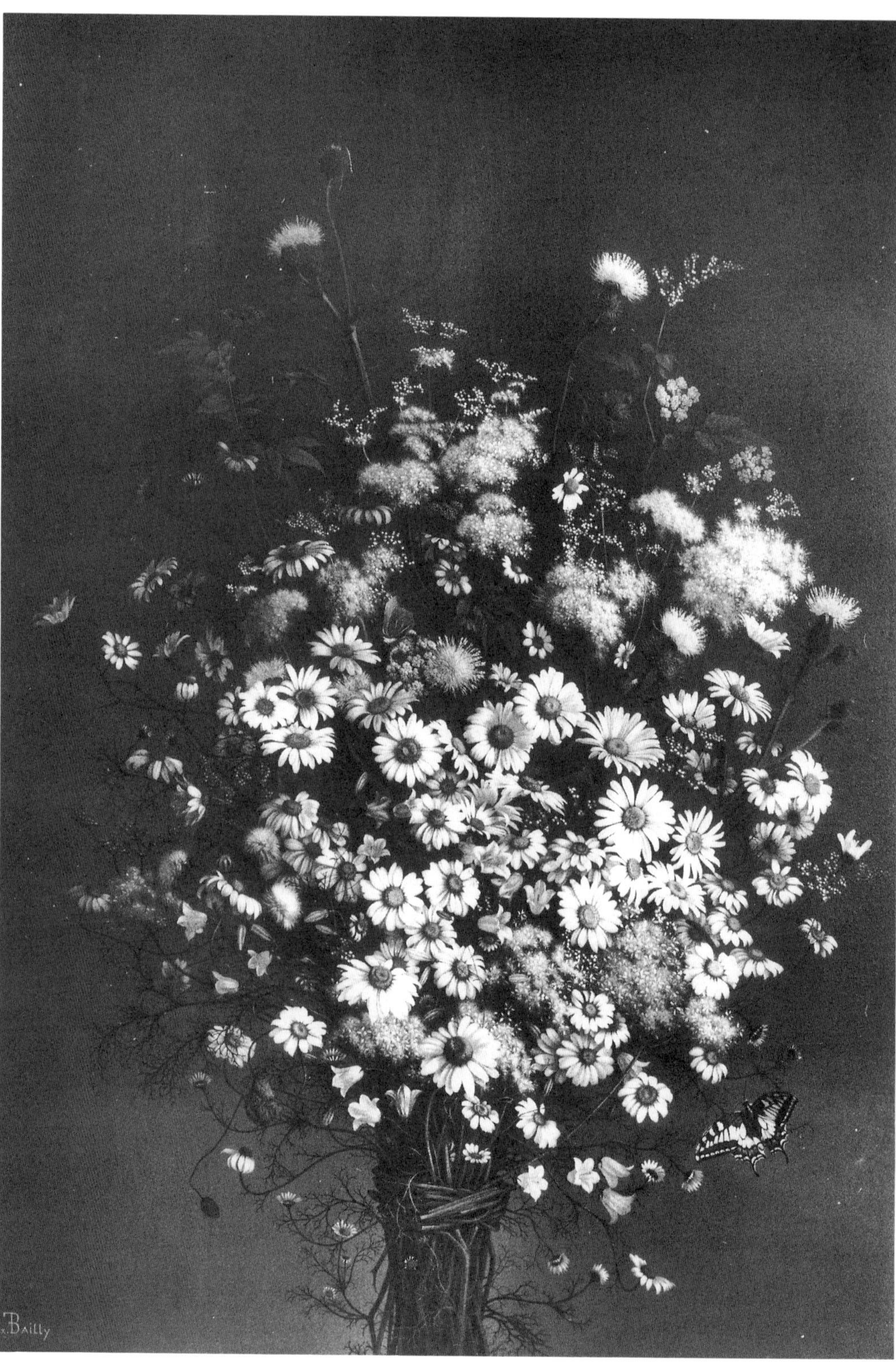

Félix Bailly

Oil on panel, $40\frac{1}{4} \times 28$ in. (102×71 cm.), signed
Troyes, Musée des Beaux-Arts

BAILLY-MONTAGNARD
Lyon textile designer, fl.1838–1853
LIT *Hardouin-Fugier Grafe*

BAINATHUN, Eugénie-Marie-Marguerite
b. Boulogne (Hauts-de-Seine). Pupil of Trébuchet. Exhib. *Eglantines*, Paris Salon 1880
LIT *Bénézit*; *Paris Salon* 1880

BAL, Jean-Claude *1864–1884*
Lyon textile designer
LIT *Audin Vial*

BALANÇA, Jean *b.1826*
Pupil of Thierriat, Lyon BA (CFD 1844)
LIT *Hardouin-Fugier Grafe*

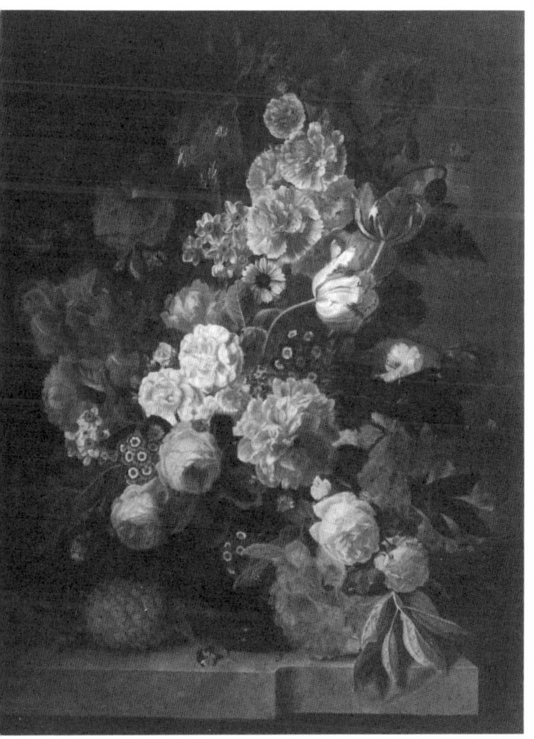

Juliette de Bansy

Oil on canvas, 45¼ × 33½ in. (115 × 85 cm.), signed and dated 1863
Castres, Musée Goya

BALANÇA, Pierre
Pupil of Berjon, Lyon BA (CFD 1822). Textile designer
LIT *Hardouin-Fugier Grafe*

BALESTAS, Esther-Marie
b. Grenoble (Isère). Exhib. *Iris*, wc, Grenoble Salon 1899
LIT *Grenoble Salon* 1899. MW

BALET, Isabelle
b. Paris. Pupil of Sousselier and Chaumet. Exhib. *Gerbe de chrysanthèmes*, Paris UFPS 1896
LIT *Paris UFPS* 1896

BALEYGNIER, Jean-Marie *b.1837*
b. Saint-Etienne (Loire). Pupil of Reignier, Lyon BA (CFD 1857)
LIT *Hardouin-Fugier Grafe*

BALLANDRIN, Jules-César *d.1886*
b. Lousance (Jura). Drawing-master at Poligny (Jura) 1860–1884. Occasionally painted flowers, e.g. *Bouquet des champs*
LIT *Brune*

BALLAVOINE, Jules-Frédéric *b.1855*
b. Paris. Pupil of Pils. Exhib. 1869–1882 e.g. Paris Salon *Bouquet de fête*, 1874, *Bouquet de fiancé*, 1876. Mostly a portrait and genre painter
LIT *Bellier*; *Schurr* II, 89; *Witt*

BALLEROY, Charles
b. Limoges (Haute-Vienne). Pupil of Balleroy, (1828–1873), his father and Gérôme. Exhib *Cinéraire*, wc, Paris Salon 1880
LIT *Bénézit*; *Paris Salon* 1880

BALLET, Léon-Victor
b. Paris. Pupil of Riottor. Exhib. flowers on porcelain. Paris Salon 1872, 1880, 1882
LIT *Bellier*

BALLUE, Pierre-Ernest *1855–1928*
This landscape painter occasionally painted flowers
LIT *Bellier*; *Bénézit*; *Orsay*; *Schurr* IV, 68; *Thieme*; *Witt*

BALOUZET, Armand-Auguste *1858–1905*
Lyonnais landscape painter who occasionally produced some flower-pieces
LIT *Bénézit*; *Hardouin-Fugier Grafe*, *Répertoire des paysagistes lyonnais du XIX° siècle en Bugey*, (Lacoux) 1980; *Schurr* IV, 96; *Thieme*

BALPETRÉ, Jean-Pierre *b.1819*
Pupil of Thierriat, Lyon BA (CFD 1838)
LIT *Hardouin-Fugier Grafe*

BALPEYRE
Entered the 1840 Lyon FDC
LIT *Hardouin-Fugier Grafe*

BALZAC de, *see* BAUDRY

BANSY, Juliette de
A copyist. Recommended to Nieuwerkerke by Prince of Schleswig-Holstein. A copy of a flower-piece by Van Dael in the Louvre was commissioned from her and completed in 1863. It was sent to the Musée de Castres in 1869. Juliette de Bansy then copied figures until 1869.
LIT Paris Arch. Nat. F21:443, 116

BAR, Clémentine de ***1807–1856***
b. Paris. Pupil of Paulin Guérin. Drawing mistress at the Légion d'Honneur school. Painted portraits, genre and, occasionally, flowers, e.g. *Pensées d'après nature*, Paris Salon 1840
LIT *Bellier*; *Bénézit*; *Paris Salon* 1840; *Schurr* V, 16; *Thieme*

BARABAN-CAHAGNET, Blanche-Marie
Pupil of Mme Dury-Vasselon, Henner and Fougerat. Exhib. *Chrysanthèmes* (200 francs) Poitiers Salon 1887
LIT *Bénézit*; *Poitiers Salon* 1887. BG

BARBAUD-KOCH, Marie-Elisabeth-Marthe ***1862–after 1928***
Pupil of Sophie Olivier, Elie Laurent and Jules Médard. Exhib. Lyon from 1887; Dijon Salon *Pivoines*, *Panneau de fleurs*, 1892, *Chrysanthèmes*, *Pavots*, 1897. Her 1901 *Chrysanthèmes* was bought by the City of Lyon
LIT *Dijon Salon* 1892, 1897; *Hardouin-Fugier Grafe*; *Hardouin-Fugier Grafe* 1982 (ill.)

BARBÉ, Jules-Edouard-Désiré
b. Paris. Pupil of Diéterle and Séchan. Exhib. Paris Salon 1865–1876. Painted still-lifes and, occasionally, flowers
LIT *Bellier*; *Bénézit*; *Thieme*

BARBEQUOT, Louis-Joseph ***b.1825***
Pupil of Thierriat, Lyon BA (CFD 1843)
LIT *Hardouin-Fugier Grafe*

BARBEREL, *see* CUROT

BARBERIS
Painted flowers on porcelain (Sèvres)
LIT *Orsay*

BARBERY, Clotilde
b. Septeuil (Seine-et-Oise). Pupil of Birat. Exhib. 1880–1892 e.g. *Fleurs de printemps*, on porcelain, *Fleurs d'été*, wc, Paris Salon 1880
LIT *Paris Salon* 1880

BARBIER, *see* THIERCELIN

BARBIER, Antoine ***1858–1948***
This distinguished landscape painter and watercolourist occasionally produced flowers
LIT *Bénézit*; *Hardouin-Fugier Grafe*

BARBIER, Ernest ***b.1859***
b. Chartres (Eure-et-Loire). Pupil of Valton and Hareux. Painted landscapes and, occasionally, flowers. Exhib. *Fleurs*, *Fleurs et fruits*, Paris Indép. 1892
LIT *Bénézit*; *Paris Indép.* 1892

BARBIER-DEROVE, Marie
b. Paris. Exhib. *Roses à la fontaine*, *Pavots*, Paris Salon 1885
LIT *Paris Salon* 1885

BARBOU, Mlle ***fl.c.1820***
LIT *Hardouin-Fugier* 1981

BARCET
Pupil of his father. Exhib. *Corbeille de fleurs*, ink drawing, Paris Salon 1801–2
LIT *Paris Salon* 1801–1802

BARDE, see LEROY, N

BARDOUX, Laure ***née*** **Vivier**
Pupil of Gérôme and Regnard. Exhib. *Iris*, *Tulipe*, on porcelain, Paris Salon 1882
LIT *Bellier*

Marie-Elisabeth-Marthe Barbaud-Koch

Oil on canvas, 59 × 74¾ in. (150 × 190 cm.), signed and dated 1901
Ville de Lyon (photo: Musée des Beaux-Arts, Lyon)

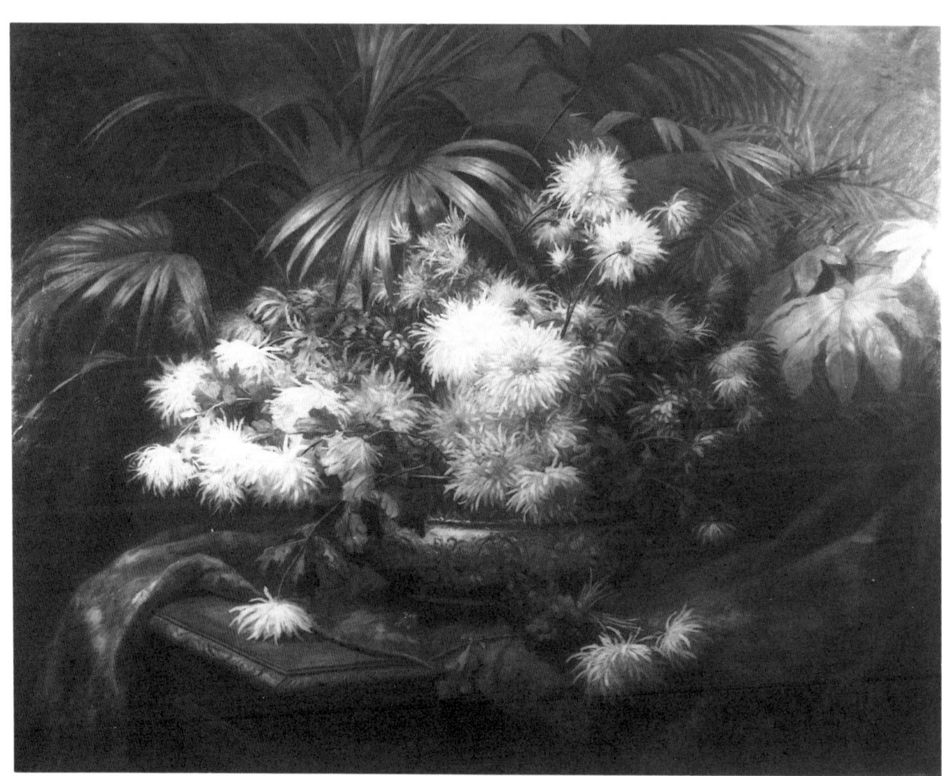

BARILLOT, Léon ***1844–1929***
b. Montigny-lès-Metz (Moselle). Pupil of his father, a Metz wallpaper manufacturer. Mostly a landscape painter. L. Barillot produced some wallpaper designs. Exhib. flowers Metz Salon 1865
LIT *Bellier*; *Bénézit*; *Metz Salon* 1865; *Thieme*; *Witt*

BARILLOT-BONVALET, Léonie ***d.1901***
b. Montigny-lès-Metz (Moselle). Pupil of Léon Barillot, her brother, Jules Lefebvre and Benjamin Constant. Exhib. Paris Salon from 1878 e.g. *Roses et giroflées*, 1878, *Roses trémières*, 1880, *Fleurs de printemps*, 1881, *Camélias*, *Chrysanthèmes*, 1882, *Pensées*, 1890, *Oeillets*, *Roses et renoncules*, 1898; *Carnations in a vase*, Sotheby's, London, 28 Nov. 1984, Lot 450
LIT *Bellier*; *Bénézit*; *Paris Salon* 1880, 1882 (ill.), 1886, 1887, 1890, 1895; *Thieme*; *Witt*

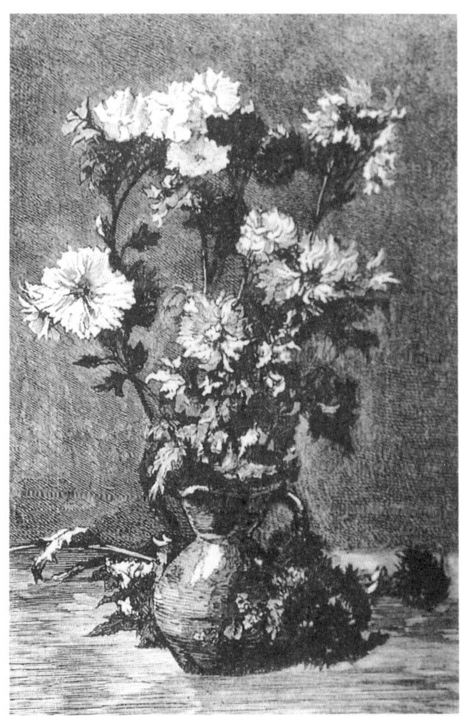

Léon Barillot

Engraving after, 6 × 4 in. (15 × 10 cm.)
Paris, BMAD (Maciet Collection)

BARLA, J.B. ***1817–1896***
b. Nice (Alpes-Maritimes). Designed plates for *Flore illustrée de Nice*, Nice, 1868
LIT *Nissen* I, 78

BARNICHON, Aurélie
Exhib. *Chrysanthèmes*, Dijon Salon 1890
LIT *Dijon Salon* 1890

BARNOIN, Adolphe ***b.c.1878***
b. Avignon (Vaucluse). Pupil of Cabanel. Exhib. *Fleurs*, Dijon Salon 1897
LIT *Dijon Salon* 1897; *Schurr* IV, 130. CL

BARNOVIN, Julie
Copied *Fleurs et fruits*, after Van Os for the Saint-Denis Légion d'Honneur School
LIT Paris Arch. Nat. F21:205

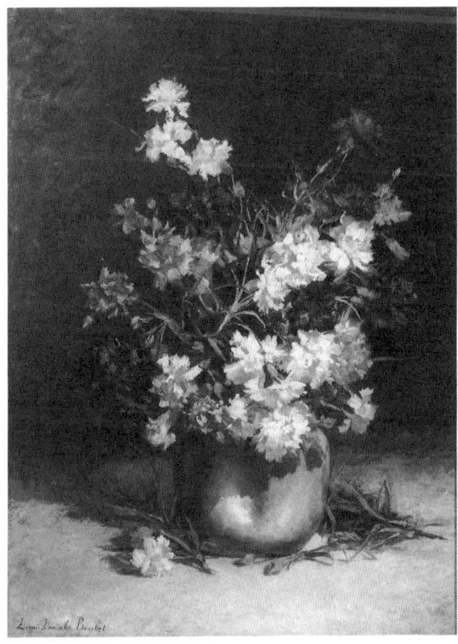

Léonie Barillot-Bonvalet

Oil on canvas, $28\frac{1}{4} \times 20\frac{3}{4}$ in. (71.5 × 52.5 cm.), signed
Courtesy Sotheby's, London

BARON, Henri-Charles-Antoine ***1816–1885***
b. Besançon (Doubs). Well-known genre painter and engraver exhib. two designs for overdoors *Le bouquet*, *Le toucher*, Paris Salon 1855
LIT *Bellier*; *Bénézit*; *Béraldi*; *Brune*; A. Estignard *H. Baron* ... Besançon (Louys) 1896; *Witt*

BARON, Pierre ***b.1802***
Pupil of Berjon, Lyon BA (CFD 1822). Exhib. *Vase de fleurs posé sur une colonne*, Lyon Salon 1828
LIT *Hardouin-Fugier Grafe*

BARONNET, Marie
One signed gouache has appeared at auction recently. Sotheby's, Monte Carlo, 26 June 1985, Lot 373. PM

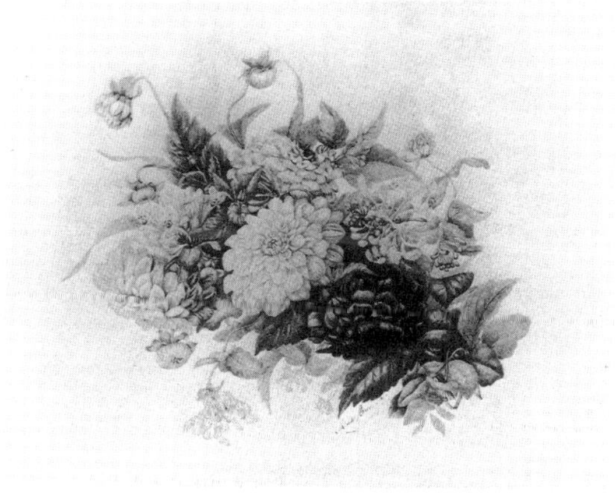

Marie Baronnet

Gouache on vellum, $17\frac{1}{2} \times 22$ in. (44.5 × 56 cm.), signed
Courtesy Sotheby's, London

BARQUI, Jean-Baptiste-Alexandre ***1828–1898***
Pupil of Thierriat, Lyon BA (CFD 1844), succeeded Béraud as designer to the Schultz textile factory. His *Soleil d'orchidées* is in the Musée Historique des Tissus, Lyon
LIT M. Jay in *Fleurs de Lyon* (*Hardouin-Fugier Grafe* 1982 ill.); *Hardouin-Fugier Grafe*

BARRABAND, Jacques ***1768–1809***
b. Aubusson (Creuse). Pupil of Aubusson Art School and Malaine. op. Gobelins, Sèvres and Paris Muséum d' Histoire Naturelle. Painted birds and flowers. Appointed professor of flower design at Lyon BA in 1807. Works formerly in Lyon École Nationale des Beaux-Arts
LIT *Audin Vial*; *Bénézit*; *Hardouin-Fugier Grafe*; *Hardouin-Fugier Grafe* 1982; *Witt*

BARRAL, François-Baptiste ***b.1839***
Pupil of Reignier, Lyon BA (CFD 1855)
LIT *Hardouin-Fugier Grafe*

BARRAL, Joseph-Auguste ***b.1817***
Pupil of Thierriat, Lyon BA (CFD 1843)
LIT *Hardouin-Fugier Grafe*

BARRÉ, Louis-Désiré ***1844–1881***
op. Sèvres 1872–81
LIT *Bénézit*; *Brunet Préaud*; *Thieme*

BARRET de, *see* CHARMY

BARRIA, *see* AROSA

BARRIAT, Charles
op. Sèvres. Painted orchids on a vase (1854) for the Belgian Royal family. A namesake or the same artist exhib. landscapes Paris Salon 1851, 1855, 1865
LIT *Bellier*; *Bénézit*; *Brunet Préaud*; Sèvres Arch.; *Thieme*

BARRIÉ, Claude-François
Pupil of Thierriat, Lyon BA (CFD 1830)
LIT *Hardouin-Fugier Grafe*

BARROIS, Jean-Pierre-Frédéric ***1786–1841***
b. Paris. Pupil of Fontallard and Hersent. This miniature and genre painter exhibited *Fleurs et fruits*, Paris Salon 1836 and 1841
LIT *Bellier*; *Bénézit*; *Paris Salon* 1841; *Schidlof*; *Thieme*

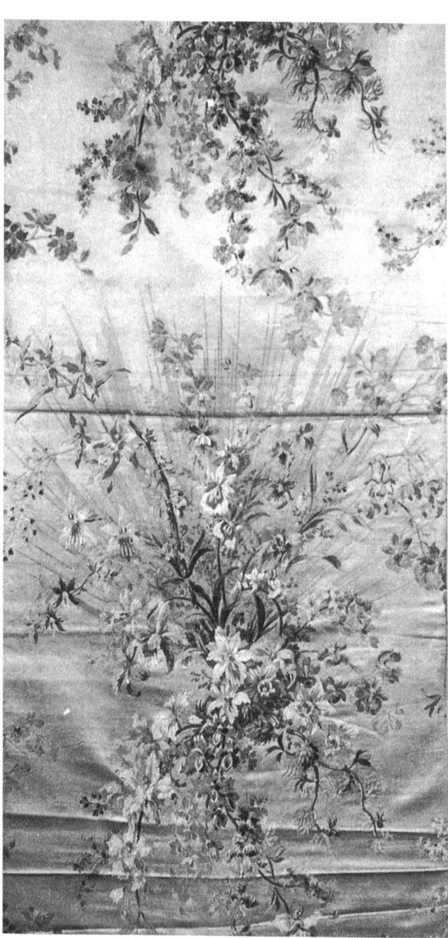

Jean-Baptiste-Alexandre Barqui

Brocade silk with satin braid, woven by Schulz, Gourdon & Cie, Lyon, $78\frac{3}{4} \times 25\frac{1}{4}$ in. (200 × 64 cm.), Lyon, Musée Historique des Tissus

BARTHÉLÉMY, Angèle
Pupil of T. Robert-Fleury, Barrias, Henner and Carolus-Duran. Exhib. Paris UFPS *Bourriche de pensées*, *Roses et statuette Tanagra*, 1986, *Anémones*, wc, 1898
LIT *Paris* UFPS 1896, 1898

BARTIER-DEROCHE, Marie
b. Paris. Exhib. *Roses gloire de Dijon*, Dijon Salon 1883; *Roses près d'une fontaine*, *Pavots*, Paris Salon 1885
LIT *Dijon Salon* 1883; *Paris Salon* 1885. CL

BASCHET, Ludovic
b. Paris. Pupil of Couture. Exhib. *Fruits et fleurs*, Paris Salon 1868; *Pêches et fleurs*, Lyon Salon 1869
LIT *Bellier*; *Lyon Salon* 1869

BASSET, *see* BOIRIVENT

BASSO, François-Jacques ***b.1856***
Pupil of Reignier, Lyon BA (CFD 1871)
LIT *Hardouin-Fugier Grafe*

BASTIAN, Georges
Textile designer, Lyon 1835–1844
LIT *Hardouin-Fugier Grafe*

BATTAGLIA, Mathieu ***b.1870***
b. Brusimpiono (Italy). Naturalized French. Founder-member of Paris Indépendants where he exhibited flowers almost every year from 1884. e.g. *Fleurs*, 1884, *Roses*, *Iris*, *Coquelicots*, *Coin de Jardin*, *Roses*, 1892, *Roses*, 1895, *Coin de jardin* 1900
LIT *Paris Indép.* 1884, 1895, 1900, 1926; *Thieme*

BATTANCHON, Marie
Exhib. *Anémones et mimosas*, Dijon Salon 1890
LIT *Dijon Salon* 1890. CL

BATTANDIER, Jules-Aimé
Designed plates for *Atlas de la Flore d'Algérie*, 1886–1920
LIT *Nissen* I, 94

BATZ, Marthe de
One pair of signed watercolours on vellum is known to date, typical of the Redouté-inspired works so numerous in the first half of the century. PM

BAUCHANT, André *1873–1958*
b. Château-Renault (Indre-et-Loire). Nurseryman and market-gardener. Though no early flower-piece by this now well-known painter has been traced so far, he may have produced some
LIT *Bénézit*; *Mitchell* (ill.)

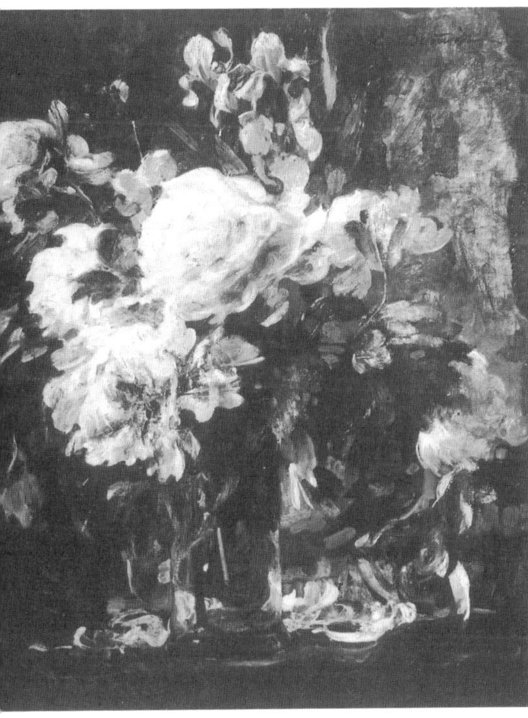

Eugène-Benoit Baudin

Oil on canvas, 36¼ × 28¾ in. (92 × 73 cm.), signed
Lyon, Musée des Beaux-Arts

BAUDIN, Eugène-Benoit *1843–1907*
b. Lyon. Pupil of Reignier, Lyon BA (CFD 1859) and Guichard. Graduated 1865. Worked for the Marc Bruyas design studio. Went into wallpaper designing and manufacturing, then back to textile design. A most successful designer. Exhib. flowers Lyon Salon 1863, 1882, 1884, 1888, 1901, 1904, 1905. Paris Salon 1902, 1904; Paris Indép; Saint-Etienne Salon 1882 *Vase de fleurs*, Palazzo Strozzi, Florence, 1967, 88. M: Louvre, *Camélias dans un vase bleu et blanc*, 1901; Lyon, *Pivoines*, 1892; Reims, Bagnols-sur-Cèze
LIT *Bénézit*; C. and E. Bidon *E. Baudin*, Lyon PUL 1983; C. and E. Bidon *Baudin* Lyon, Musée des Beaux-Arts 1983; *Hardouin-Fugier Grafe* 1979 (ill.); *Hardouin-Fugier Grafe* 1982 (ill.); *Saint-Etienne Salon* 1882; Saint-Tropez, *Fleurs de Fantin-Latour à Marquet*, Musée de l'Annonciade, 1982 (ill.)

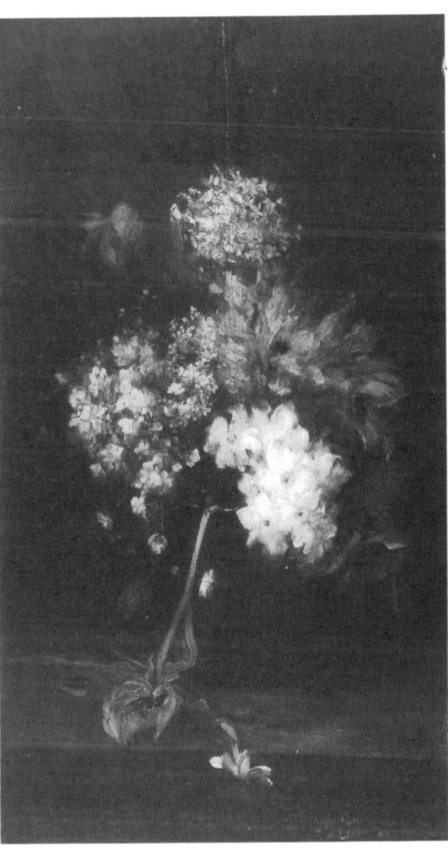

Jean-Baptiste Baudin

Oil on canvas, 29½ × 19¼ in. (74 × 49 cm.), signed and dated 1886
Marseille, Musée des Beaux-Arts

BAUDIN, Jean-Baptiste *1851–1922*
b. Marseille. Pupil of Jeanron at the École des Beaux-Arts, Marseille. Honorable mention at the Exposition Universelle 1900. *Lilas et Anémones*, 1886 was purchased that year (200 francs) by the Musée des Beaux-Arts, Marseille.
LIT *Musée de Marseille doc.*; P. Auguier, *Catalogue du Musée de Marseille*, 1908

BAUDRIER, Gustave-Louis
b. Paris. Pupil of Bergerot. Exhib. *Fleurs des champs*, Paris Salon 1880; *Lilas*, Dijon Salon 1883; *Fleurs et fruits*, Dijon Salon 1890
LIT *Bellier*; *Bénézit*; *Dijon Salon* 1883, 1890; *Thieme*

BAUDRY, Marie-Adélaïde
Exhib. *Bouquet de dahlias et de glaïeuls*, *Bouquet de camélias*, *Bruyère rose et violettes de Parme*; *Bouquet de géraniums roses et blancs*, *giroflée rouge*, *primevères foncées*, Paris Salon 1850
LIT *Paris Salon* 1850

BAUDRY DE BALZAC, Caroline-Catherine later Mme Cerrès *1798–1844*
b. Metz (Moselle). Pupil of Gérard Van Spaendonck. Drawing mistress at the Légion d'Honneur school. Exhib. *Chapeau de paille rempli de fleurs*, Lille Salon 1826; Paris Salon *Groupe de fleurs sur une table de marbre*, 1833, *Fleurs*, wc, 1836. Niece of Thérèse Baudry de Balzac. May have been a distant relation of Balzac, the novelist. Musée de Metz, *Fleurs et fruits* (currently untraceable)
LIT *Bellier*; *Bénézit*; *Faré* 1962, p. 245; Genaille J. "Baudry de Balzac ..." in *Archives de l'Art français*, Paris, (de Nobele), 1978, pp. 301–305; *Thieme*; *Witt*

BAUDRY DE BALZAC, Thérèse-Antoinette ***1774–1831***
b. Paris. Pupil of Van Spaendonck and the sculptor Pecquinot. Painted flowers on vellum for the Paris Muséum d'Histoire Naturelle. Exhib. Paris Salon 1800, 1806–1810. Drawing mistress at the Légion d'Honneur school (Saint-Denis and Écouen) 1807–1823. She worked as drawing mistress, settled at Sèvres, but does not seem to have worked for the porcelain factory. Designed plates for the *Annales du Muséum d'Histoire Naturelle*, ninety-nine botanical drawings on vellum
LIT *Bellier*; *Bénézit*; *Faré* 1962, p. 245; *Gabet*; J. Genaille "Baudry de Balzac ..." in *Archives de l'art français*, Paris (de Nobele) 1978, pp. 301–305; *Laissus*; *Thieme*

BAUDRY-VAILLANT, Adélaïde
Pupil of T. Robert-Fleury. Exhib. *Fleurs d'automne*, wc, Saint-Etienne Salon 1882
LIT *Saint-Etienne Salon* 1882

BAUME, Berthe de la ***1860–1911***
fl.*c.*1890. *Still-Life of Flowers*, formerly New York, and *Four Seasons*, Sotheby's, London, 24 June 1987, lot 254, are two known works by the artist
LIT *Connoisseur*, Jan. 1970; *Witt*

BAVOUX, Charles-Jules-Nestor ***1824–1887***
Pupil of Besançon BA and Picot. Professor at Besançon BA 1852–1872. Painted still-lifes (often featuring grapes), landscapes and, occasionally, flowers e.g. *Marguerites*, Nancy Salon 1874; *Fleurs*, Lons-le-Saunier Salon 1876; *Fleurs*, Lyon Salon 1877
LIT *Bellier*; *Bénézit*; *Brune*; *Lons-le-Saunier Salon* 1876; *Lyon Salon* 1877; *Nancy Salon* 1874

BAYE, Alphonse-Pierre
b. Paris. Exhib. Paris Salon 1878–1882 e.g. *Anémones*, gouache, 1878, *Pivoines*, 1879, *Boules de neige et pivoines*, 1879, *Fleurs*, wc and gouache, 1881, *Roses*, gouache, 1882, *Dahlias*, Dijon Salon 1897
LIT *Bellier*; *Dijon Salon* 1897

BAYLE, Georges-Bertrand ***1788–1851***
b. Santo Domingo. Pupil of Gérard Van Spaendonck. A naval officer. Exhib. Paris Salon *Fleurs dans un vase étrusque*, 1843, *Fleurs, images de la vie humaine*, 1844, *Fruits et fleurs*, 1846. His 1843 flower-piece featuring butterflies and insects is in the Musée de Narbonne
LIT *Bellier*; *Bénézit*; *Faré* 1962, p. 245; *Pavière*; *Thieme*

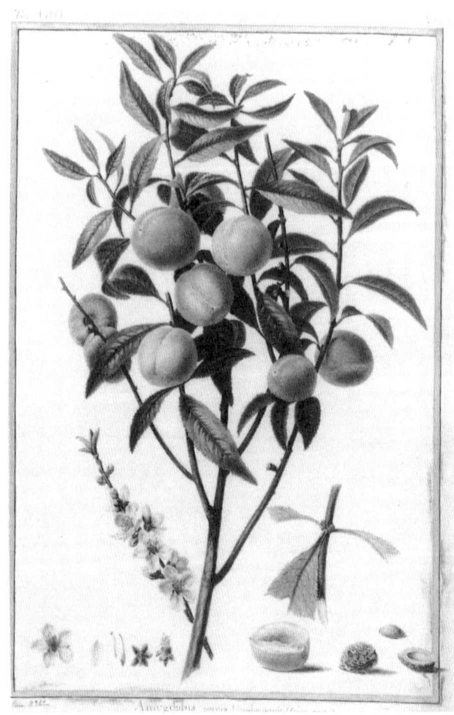

Thérèse-Antoinette Baudry de Balzac

Watercolour on vellum, Vélins vol. 53, no. 57, signed
Paris, Bibliothèque Centrale du Muséum National d'Histoire Naturelle

BAYON, Antonie
Pupil of Jules Médard. Exhib. Lyon Salon e.g. *Chrysanthèmes*, 1894
LIT *Hardouin-Fugier Grafe*

Berthe de la Baume

Oil on canvas, 35 × 46 in. (89 × 117 cm.), signed
Formerly the Incurable Collector Inc., New York

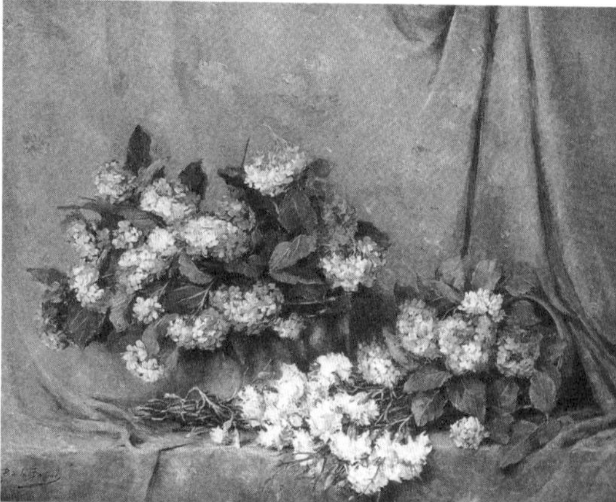

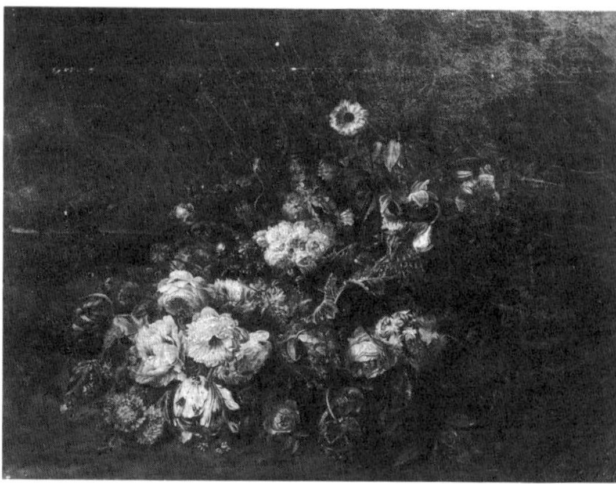

Georges-Bertrand Bayle

Oil on canvas, 39 × 51½ in. (99 × 131 cm.), signed and dated 1843
Narbonne, Musée d'Art et d'Histoire

BAZELLAIRE, Isabelle
Exhib. Paris Salon *Azalées et rhododendrons*, wc, 1880, *Fleurs de printemps*, wc, 1881
LIT *Bellier*

BAZILLE, Jean-Frédéric *1841–1870*
b. Montpellier (Hérault). Pupil of Gleyre. Shared rooms with Monet, befriended Cézanne, Alfred Stevens and Renoir. Was painted by Fantin-Latour (*Un atelier aux Batignolles*). Painted figures, portraits, landscapes, nudes and occasionally flowers e.g. *Pots de fleurs*, 1866 (Daulte 18); *Fleurs* (Paris Salon 1868, Daulte 147); *Négresse aux pivoines* (Montpellier, Daulte 51, 52); *Fleurs*, c.1870 (Daulte 53/54); *Lauriers Roses* (Daulte 26); *Fleurs* (Grenoble, Daulte 30); M: Grenoble *Fleurs*, 1868, Montpellier
LIT F. Daulte *Bazille et son temps*, Genèva (Cailler) 1952; Paris, Grand Palais, 1979, *L'Art en France sous le Second Empire*, p.251f.; Saint-Tropez, *Fleurs de Fantin-Latour à Marquet*, Musée de l'Annonciade, 1982, No.4; *Witt*

BEAU, Charles
Exhib. flowers Lyon Salon 1873
LIT *Hardouin-Fugier Grafe*

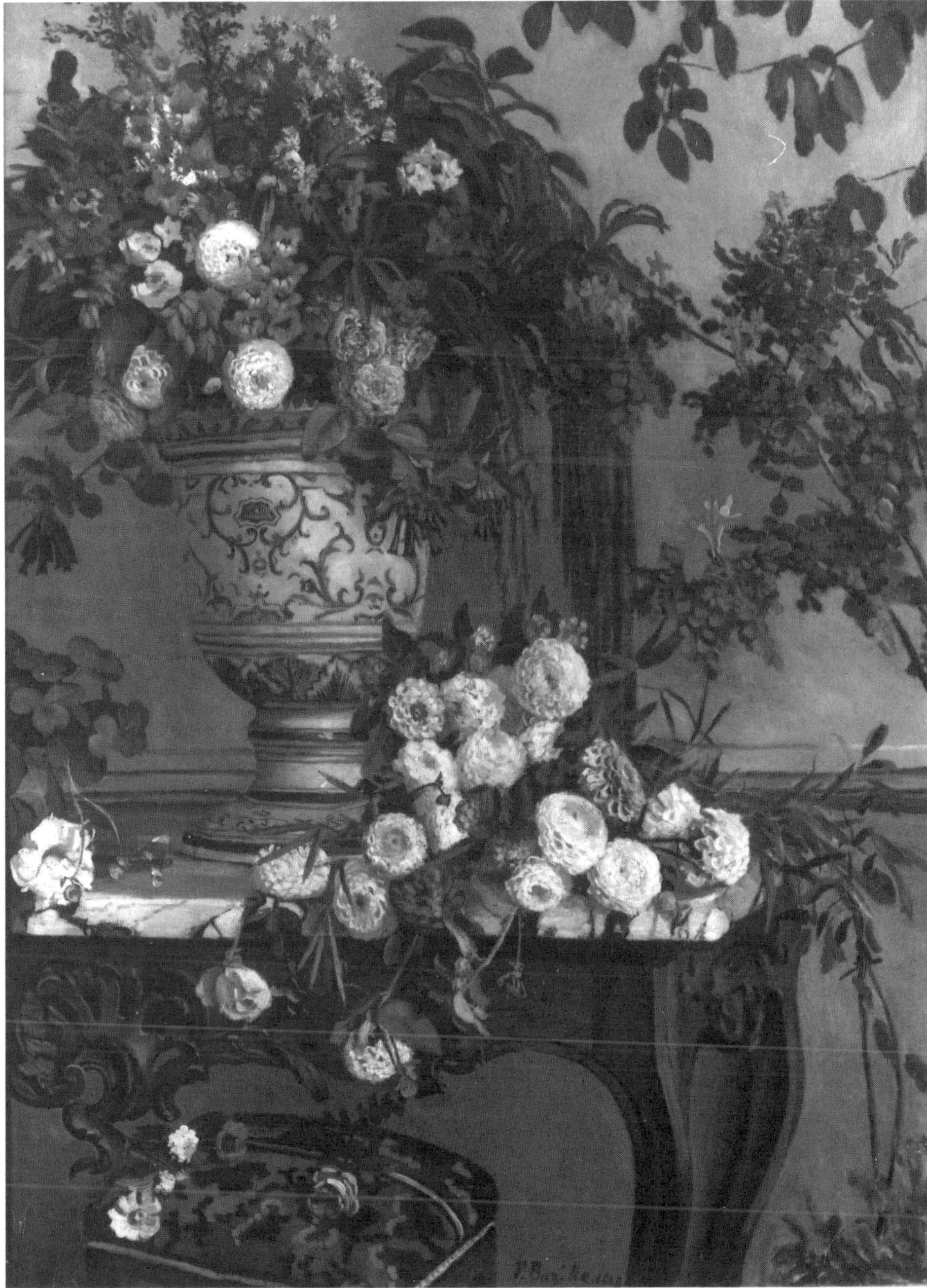

BEAUCÉ, Vivant *1818–1876*
b. Nolay (Côte-d'Or). Painter and wood-engraver. Painted on porcelain. op. St Petersburg 1853–1868. Exhib. flowers, Paris Salon 1867
LIT *Bénézit*; *Paris Salon* 1867; *Thieme*

BEAUCHARD-MASSON, Angelina
b. Lyon. Pupil of Midy, de Beauregard, D. de Cool. Exhib. *Pavots*, gouache, *Roses*, on porcelain, Paris Salon 1880; *Fleurs*, Paris UFPS 1898
LIT *Hardouin-Fugier Grafe*; *Paris Salon* 1880; *Paris UFPS* 1898

BEAUCOURT, Joseph-Emile *b.1823*
Pupil of Thierriat, Lyon BA (CFD 1843)
LIT *Hardouin-Fugier Grafe*

BEAUDENEAU, Marie-Julie
Pupil of Mayeux and École Élise Lemonnier. Exhib. *Chardon, étude décorative*, Paris Salon 1898
LIT *Paris Salon* 1898

BEAUDERON, Alexandre Adolphe *1822–1898*
b. Aubusson (Creuse). Studied Lyon BA 1840. In Thierriat's CFD 1842. Lived in Paris 1849–1859. Taught figure and flower painting at Saint-Etienne BA. Director of the school 1881–1884. Curator of the local museum. Painted landscapes à la Diaz, murals, theatre sets and, occasionally, flowers
LIT *Audin Vial*; *Bénézit*; *Hardouin-Fugier Grafe*; *Thieme*

BEAUFORT, Vicomtesse Jeanne de
b. Paris. Pupil of Marest. Exhib. Paris Salon 1881 *Jacinthe et tulipe*, on porcelain
LIT *Bellier*

Jean-Frédéric Bazille

Oil on canvas, $51\frac{1}{4} \times 38\frac{1}{4}$ in. (130 × 97 cm.), signed and dated 1868
Genoble, Musée de Peinture et de Sculpture

BEAUGEAN or BAUJEAN
b. Marseille. Designed flowers for lithographer Delaunois
LIT Paris. Bibl. Nat. Est. Jd 59

BEAUHARNAIS, Hortense de, Queen of Holland *1783–1837*
Pupil of Isabey. Must have met Redouté at Malmaison where two flowers in wc by her can be seen
LIT *Hardouin-Fugier* 1981 (ill.)

BEAUHARNAIS, Joséphine-Hortense de *née* Tascher de la Pagerie *1763–1814*
Pupil of Isabey. Possibly a pupil of Redouté. The Empress was a flower lover and keen botanist but no flower study by her has come to light yet
LIT *Hardouin-Fugier* 1981; Paris Muséum Arch.

BEAUMONT, Hughes de *b.1874*
b. Chouzy (Loir-et-Cher). Pupil of Gustave Moreau, Chartran and A. Maignan. Portrait, genre and flower painter. Exhib. Paris Salon from 1892. His still-life in the Glasgow Art Gallery features a few flowers
LIT *Bénézit*; *Thieme*; *Witt*

BEAUREPAIRE CHACERÉ de, Appoline-Marie-François *later* Gaillard *alias* Lucy de Beaurepaire
Pupil of Redouté. Exhib. flowers in wc, Paris Salon 1835, 1839, 1842 and *Roses des bois, fleurs des champs*, wc, *Marguerites et dahlias*, wc, Dijon Salon 1840. Contributed about fifteen flower designs to Chavant's *Naissance des fleurs* set. *Bunch of mixed roses*, including a yellow rosa hemispherica and *Vase of Flowers including rose and lilac*, wc, 1841, are in the Fitzwilliam Museum, Broughton coll., Cambridge
LIT *Dijon Salon* 1840; *Hardouin-Fugier* 1981; Broughton 1977; Broughton 1978

BEAUSSIER, Émile *1874–1944*
b. Avignon (Vaucluse). Pupil of Lyon BA and J.P. Laurens. Painted landscapes, seascapes and flowers. Exhib. Lyon and Paris from 1892
LIT *Bénézit*; *Hardouin-Fugier Grafe*; *Thieme*

BEAUVAIS, Anaïs *d.1898*
Pupil of Carolus-Duran and Henner. Exhib. *Perles et roses*, Lyon Salon 1881; Dijon Salon *Bouquet de pivoines*, 1883, *Bouquet de chrysanthèmes*, 1887
LIT *Bénézit*; *Lyon Salon* 1881; *Dijon Salon* 1883, 1887

BEAUVOISIN, Mme
Exhib. *Pivoines*, wc, *Bouquet*, wc, Paris Salon 1833
LIT *Paris Salon* 1833

BECQ DE FOUQUIÈRES, Louise-Marie *née* Dedreux *1825–1892*
Painted portraits, landscapes and flowers. Exhib. Paris Salon *Fleurs d'automne*, 1877, *Pavots roses*, 1880
LIT *Bellier*; *Bénézit*

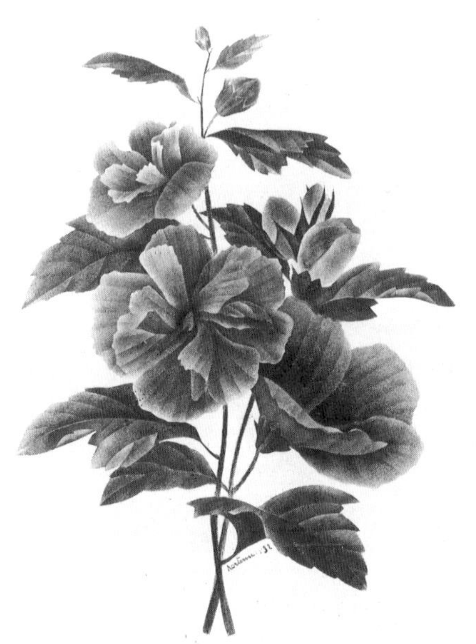

Hortense de Beauharnais, Queen of Holland

Watercolour, $10\frac{3}{4} \times 8\frac{1}{4}$ in. (27.5 × 20.7 cm.), signed and dated 1832
Rueil-Malmaison, Musée National du Château de Malmaison

BEINDER, Jules *b.1796*
Pupil of Berjon, Lyon BA (CFD 1813)
LIT *Hardouin-Fugier Grafe*

Hugues de Beaumont

Oil on panel, $6\frac{3}{4} \times 7\frac{3}{4}$ in. (17.5 × 19.8 cm.), signed
Glasgow Art Gallery and Museum: McInnes Bequest

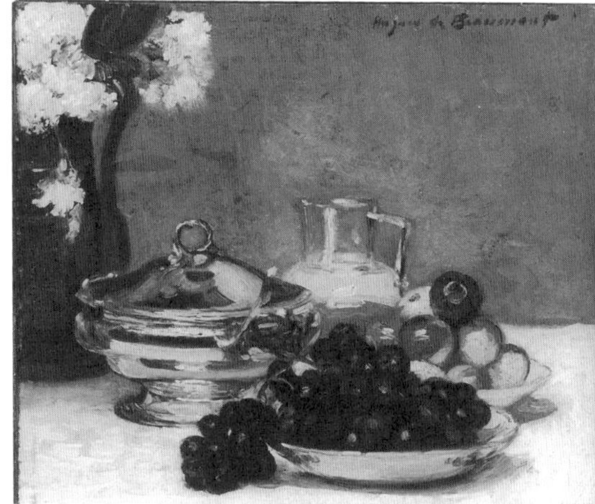

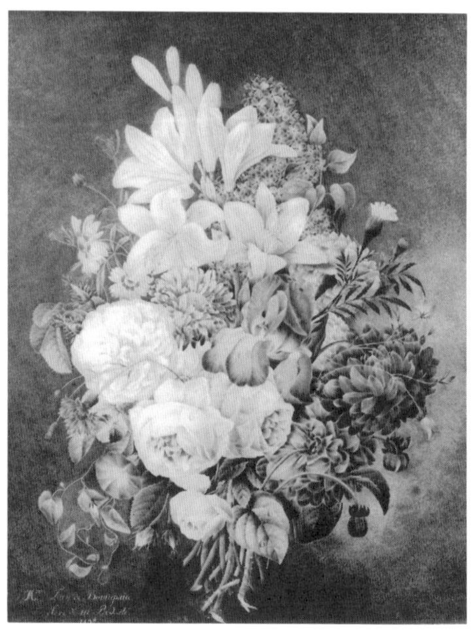

Lucy de Beaurepaire

Watercolour on vellum, $23 \times 19\frac{1}{4}$ in. (58.5 × 49 cm.), signed and dated 1837
Private collection (photo: Jeremy Ltd, London)

BEKE, Marguerite
Exhib. *Coquelicots et marguerites*, wc, Saint-Etienne Salon 1882
LIT *Hardouin-Fugier Bringuier*; *Saint-Etienne Salon* 1882

BELIN, Jeanne
Exhib. *Etude de pensées*, Dijon Salon 1897
LIT *Dijon Salon* 1897

BELLANGER, Caroline
Exhib. *Branche de camélias*, wc, Paris Salon 1837
LIT *Paris Salon* 1837

BELLECOUR, *see* BERNE

BELLECOURT, *see* VÉRON

BELLET, Marie
Exhib. Dijon Salon e.g. *Lilas*, *Chrysanthèmes*, 1890, *Bouquet de roses*, 1892, *Fleurs des champs*, 1894
LIT *Dijon Salon* 1890, 1892, 1894

BELLEUSE, *see* CARRIER

BELLIVAUX *or* BELLIVEAUX, Léonard *1821-1894*
b. Lyon. Pupil of Bonnefond at Lyon BA (1837) and Drolling. Exhib. Lyon Salon 1842, Paris Salon from 1847. Painted figures, portraits, landscapes and, occasionally, flowers
LIT *Bellier*; *Bénézit*; *Thieme*

BELOUS, *see* HODIEUX

BENARD, *see* LEMARCHAND

BENIER, Jenny
Worked in Lyon as a drawing mistress 1861–1865. Exhib. Lyon Salon 1873
LIT *Hardouin-Fugier Grafe*

BENNASSI, Alphonse
Exhib. *Fleurs et fruits*, Paris Salon 1850
LIT *Paris Salon* 1850

BENNER, Aline
b. Modersheim-près-Mulhouse (Haut-Rhin). Exhib. *Verveines* (200 francs) *Chrysanthèmes* (100 francs), Strasbourg, Salon 1891
LIT *Strasbourg Salon* 1891

BENNER, Emmanuel *1836–1896*
b. Mulhouse (Haut-Rhin). Pupil of his father, Jean Benner-Fries, Eck, Henner and Bonnat. Textile designer. Painted landscapes, genre and, occasionally, flowers. Exhib. Paris Salon from 1867, sometimes flowers and game e.g. *Fleurs et gibier*, 1867. M: Mulhouse *Fleurs en pot*, 1868, and *Chrysanthèmes*, acquired 1889
LIT *Bellier*; *Bénézit*; *Mulhouse Musée doc.*; Paris Arch. Nat. F21:2055; *Paris Salon* 1867; *Sitzmann*; *Thieme*. BJ

BENNER, Jean *1836–1909*
b. Mulhouse (Haut-Rhin). Twin brother of Emmanuel Benner, son of Jean Benner-Fries. Pupil of his father, Eck and Pils. Worked in Mulhouse as designer for the textile printing industry. Flower and landscape painter. Exhib. Paris from 1857 e.g. *Roses*, 1861, *Vase de fleurs*, 1866, (Musée de Mulhouse), *Fleurs et fruits sur des livres*, 1868, *Hommage à Jeanne d'Arc*, 1888, *Chrysanthèmes*, 1890. (Fourteen works in M: Mulhouse) *Anémones* was acquired by the Musée des Beaux-Arts, Caen, in 1883 (destroyed). Nice, *Pavots*
LIT *Bellier*, *Bénézit*; *Mitchell*; Paris Arch. Nat. F21:2055; *Paris Salon* 1861, 1885, 1890; *Pavière*; *Sitzmann*; *Thieme*; *Witt*. BJ

BENNER-FRIES, Jean *1796–1849*
b. Stauffberg (Switzerland) or Guebwiller (Haut-Rhin). Pupil of Van Dael and Van Spaendonck. A successful Mulhouse textile designer, specializing in chintz. Worked in Paris, England and Mulhouse. Father of Jean and Emmanuel Benner. Exhib. Paris 1837–49 e.g. *Fleurs*, 1838, *Fleurs et fruits*, 1841, *Vase garni de fleurs*, 1842. M: Mulhouse, *Fleurs exotiques*, 1836, Carpentras, *Tulipes*
LIT *Bellier*; *Bénézit*; *Faré* 1962, p. 247; *Mitchell*; *Paris Salon* 1838, 1841, 1842, 1843; *Pavière* III, pt. 1 (ill.); *Thieme*

BENOIST, Léon
Exhib. flowers Dijon Salon 1881
LIT *Dijon Salon* 1881. CL

BENOIST, Marie-Augustine
Exhib. *Pavots*, Paris UFPS 1898
LIT *Paris UFPS* 1898

BENOIST, Théophile-Maximilien
b. Paris. Exhib. flowers Paris Indép. 1889, 1890
LIT *Paris Indép.* 1889, 1890

BENOIT, Félix *b.1794 or 1795*
Pupil of Berjon. Lyon BA (CFD 1813)
LIT *Hardouin-Fugier Grafe*

BENOIT, Jean-Baptiste *b.1845*
Pupil of Reignier, Lyon BA (CFD 1869)
LIT *Hardouin-Fugier Grafe*

BENOIT, Mme *fl.c.1814*
Two works in Cambridge, Fitzwilliam Museum, Broughton coll.: *Sprig of pansies*, wc, and *Flower Study—Double Hyacinth*, wc
LIT *Bénézit*; *Thieme*

BENSA, François *b.1811*
b. Nice (Alpes-Maritimes). Porcelain painter
LIT *Bénézit*

BER, ***see*** **JACOBBER**

BÉRANGER, ***see*** **APOIL**

BÉRARD, Denis-Joseph ***b.1829***
Pupil of Thierriat, Lyon BA (CFD 1845) and Guy. Textile designer. Painted landscapes
LIT *Bénézit*; *Hardouin-Fugier Grafe*

BÉRARD, Désiré-Honoré ***1846–1932***
Grenoble address, Pupil of Guichard, Cabanel and Yvon. Though only late (e.g. *Roses*, Grenoble Salon 1913) flowers have been traced so far, may have produced early flower-pieces
LIT *Grenoble Salon* 1913; *Schurr* I, 32

BÉRAUD, Gabriel-Louis ***b.1860***
Pupil of Reignier, Lyon BA (CFD 1878). A flower-piece by this artist was won at the 1884 Lyon Société des Amis-des-Arts raffle
LIT *Hardouin-Fugier Grafe*

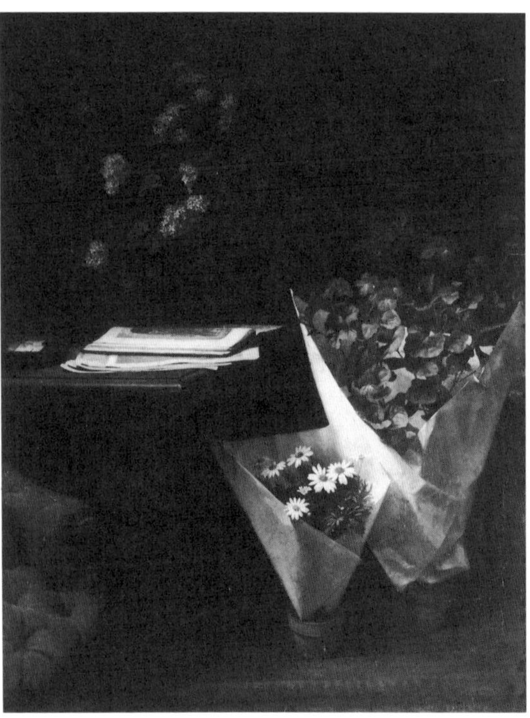

Emmanuel Benner

Oil on canvas, 64½ × 51¼ in. (164 × 130 cm.) signed and dated 1868
Mulhouse, Musée de l'Impression sur Etoffes

BÉRAUD, Michel ***1810–1882***
Pupil of Thierriat, Lyon BA (CFD 1827–1829). This outstanding Lyon textile designer's best-known work is the coronation cloak for Empress Eugénie
LIT *Hardouin-Fugier Grafe*

Mme Benoit

Watercolour on paper, 7 7/16 × 5¾ in. (19 × 14.5 cm.), signed
Cambridge, Fitzwilliam Museum, (Broughton Collection)

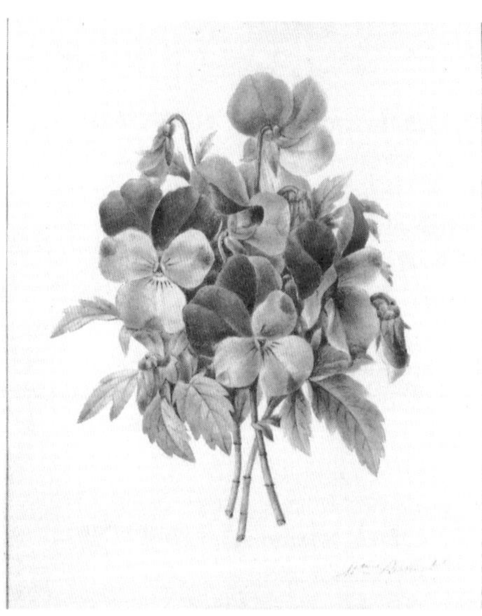

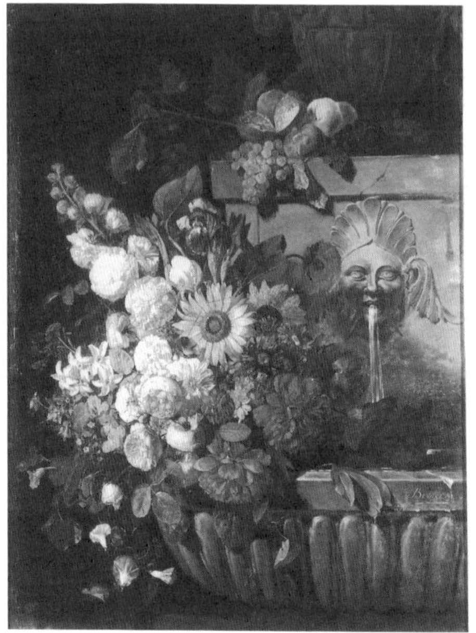

BERCHÈRE, Narcisse ***1819–1891***
b. Étampes (Seine-et-Oise). Pupil of Rénoux and Rémon. Painted landscapes, figures, still-lifes and, occasionally, flowers
LIT *Bellier*; *Bénézit*; Paris, Galerie Fischer-Kiener, May 1983; *Schurr* I, 34; *Thieme*; *Witt*

BERCIOUX, Jean-Charles
b. Paris. Exhib. *Roses trémières*, Paris Salon 1880; Paris Indép. *Chrysanthèmes*, 1884, *Roses trémières*, 1890, *Pensées*, 1892, *Fleurs*, 1894
LIT *Bénézit*; *Paris Indép.* 1884, 1890, 1892, 1894; *Paris Salon* 1880

BERGER, Elisa
Pupil of N. Cabane. Exhib. Lyon Salon *Vase de fleurs*, gouache, 1883. *Fleurs*, gouache, 1884
LIT *Lyon Salon* 1883, 1884

BERGER, Jean-Baptiste ***1832–1886***
Pupil of Thierriat, Lyon BA (CFD 1849). Exhib. flowers in gouache Lyon Salon 1858, 1866; Paris Salon 1866
LIT *Bénézit*; *Hardouin-Fugier Grafe*

BERGER, Mathieu ***b.1807***
Pupil of Thierriat, Lyon BA (CFD 1824–1826). Textile designer. Exhib. Lyon Salon 1828, 1833, 1836, 1839. His 1836 *Fleurs dans le bassin d'une fontaine*, exhibited at the 1855 Paris Exposition Universelle is now in the Musée des Beaux-Arts, Lyon
LIT *Bénézit*; *Hardouin-Fugier Grafe*; *Hardouin-Fugier Grafe* 1979 (ill.); *Hardouin-Fugier Grafe* 1982 (ill.)

Mathieu Berger

Oil on canvas, 43 × 32¼ in. (109 × 82 cm.), signed and dated 1836
Lyon, Musée des Beaux-Arts

BERGER, Jenny ***née*** **Desoras**
Painted portraits, genre and flowers e.g. *Jacinthes, étude*, Paris Salon 1817
LIT *Bellier*; Paris Salon 1817; *Thieme*

BERGER, Nicolas-Elisée ***1811–1836***
Pupil of Thierriat, Lyon BA (CFD 1832). Exhib. *Fleurs et fruits*, Lyon Salon 1836
LIT *Hardouin-Fugier Grafe*

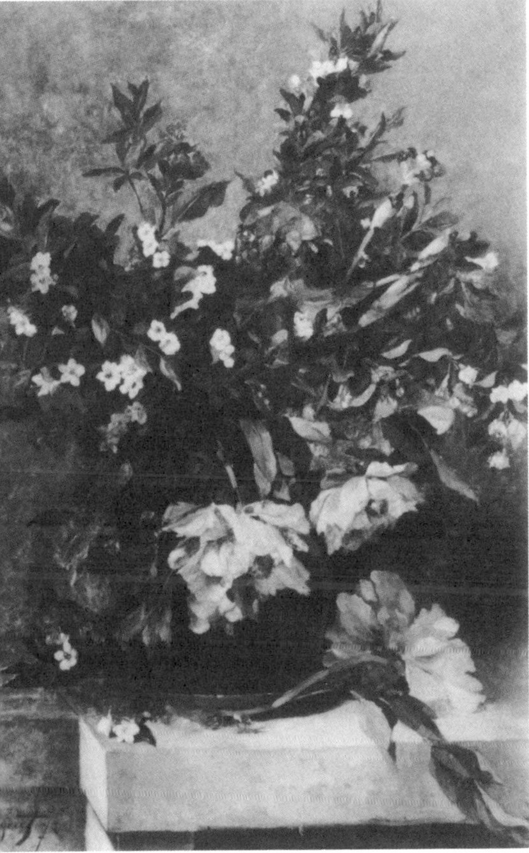

Denis-Pierre Bergeret

Oil on canvas, 39 × 27½ in. (99 × 70 cm.), signed and dated 1872
Courtesy Sotheby's, London

BERGERET, Claude ***1831–1891***
Pupil of Lyon BA. This Lyon textile designer who was librarian at the Palais-des-Arts owned a collection of drawings and may have produced some flower-pieces
LIT *Audin Vial*; *Hardouin-Fugier Grafe*; *Pavière*

BERGERET, Denis-Pierre ***1846–1910***
b. Villeparisis (Seine-et-Marne). Pupil of Eugène Isabey, was influenced by Vollon. Exhib. Paris Salon 1870–1908, mostly still-lifes including flowers and fruit, vegetables, fish, game or shrimps. Exhib. a few flower-pieces, e.g. *Gerbe des prés*, Paris Salon 1882. *Still-life of Flowers*, Sotheby's, New York, 27 May 1982, lot 103
LIT *Bellier*; *Bénézit*; Cleveland Museum. *The realist tradition* ... 1980; G. Weisberg, *Chardin and the Still-life Tradition*, Cleveland, 1979 (ill.); *Thieme*

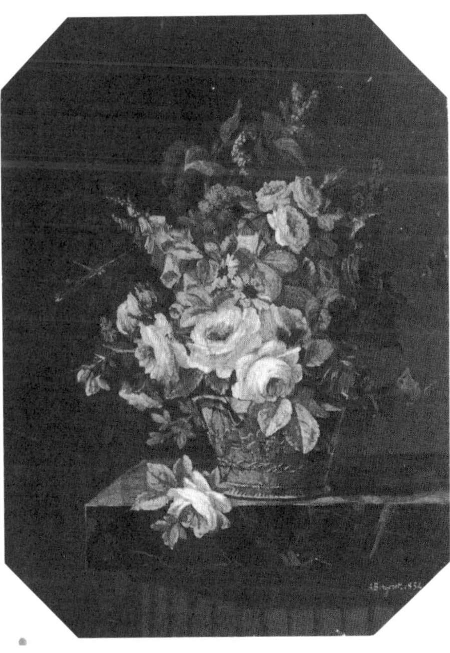

Jean-Jacques-Arthur Bergeret

Gouache, 8¼ × 6 in. (21 × 15 cm.), signed and dated 1854
Private collection

BERGERET, Jean-Jacques-Arthur ***b.1831***
b. Paris. May have been one of Thierriat's private pupils and went straight into his CFD at Lyon BA (1848). Exhib. landscapes and flowers Lyon Salon 1860–1873
LIT *Bénézit*; *Hardouin-Fugier Grafe*

BERGERON, B.
Painted with E.M. floral designs on vellum for the Paris Muséum d'Histoire Naturelle. Both artists signed with M and B intertwined
LIT *Paris Muséum MS 2376*

BERGERON, Mme Victor
b. Lyon. Exhib. *Roses et éventail*, Lyon Salon 1885
LIT *Lyon Salon* 1885

BERGEROT, Louise
Pupil of D. Rozier. Exhib. Dijon Salon *Fleurs de mai*, 1890, *Panier de roses*, 1897; Paris UFPS *Fleurs de Nice*, *Roses cent feuilles*, 1896, *Vierge aux roses*, *Dernières fleurs*, 1898
LIT *Dijon Salon* 1890, 1897; *Paris UFPS* 1896, 1898

BERGIER, Joseph-Jacques ***b.1834***
Pupil of Thierriat, Lyon BA (CFD 1852)
LIT *Hardouin-Fugier Grafe*

BERGUIGNAT-ANNET
b. Rive-de-Gier (Loire). Exhib. *Fleurs et fruits*, Saint-Etienne Salon 1882
LIT *Hardouin-Fugier Bringuier*; *Saint-Etienne Salon* 1882

BERJON, Antoine ***1754–1843***
b. Lyon. Pupil of Antoine-Michel Perrache. Textile designer. Settled in Paris 1794. Miniature painter. In Lyon 1810. Provided designs for Bony's raised-velvet factory and succeeded him as a professor of flower design at Lyon BA, 1810, resigning in 1823. Though temperamental, a much-loved teacher. Had about 200 pupils over his thirteen years of teaching. Exhib. Paris Salon 1791, 1796, 1798, 1799, 1804, 1810, 1817, 1819, 1842. Exhib. Lyon Salon 1822, 1836, 1837, 1843 (memorial exhibition). As a designer, a many-sided and outstanding artist. As a flower-painter, the most eminent of all Lyonnais flower painters. M: Bagnères-de-Bigorre, Cambridge, Fitzwilliam Museum, Broughton coll. (three works); Lyon, Paris (Louvre), Montpellier, Philadelphia Museum of Art
LIT G. Guillot, "*Les Solitaires de Lyon*, Apollo, 1964; *Hardouin-Fugier Grafe* 1982, pp. 72–86 (an original contribution featuring the list of the paintings and drawings found in Berjon's studio after his death as well as a bibliography)

BERLIOZ, Mme C.
Exhib. *Marguerites*, *Chrysanthèmes*, *Lilas*, *Roses*, Paris Indép. 1896
LIT *Paris Indép.* 1896

BERNAMONT, Clarisse
b. Chatillon-sous-Bagneux (Hauts-de-Seine). Pupil of Thoret and A. Leloir. Exhib. Paris Noir et Blanc Salon e.g. *Fleurs ornémentales*, *Seau de pivoines* 1886 and UFPS. A design by C. Bernamont is in the Paris BMAD (Maciet coll.). Her *Panier de pivoines blanches* was bought for the Musée de Bagnères-de-Bigorre, wc
LIT *Bénézit*; *Orsay*; Paris Arch. Nat. F21:4500; *Paris BMAD*; *Paris Noir et Blanc Salon* 1886

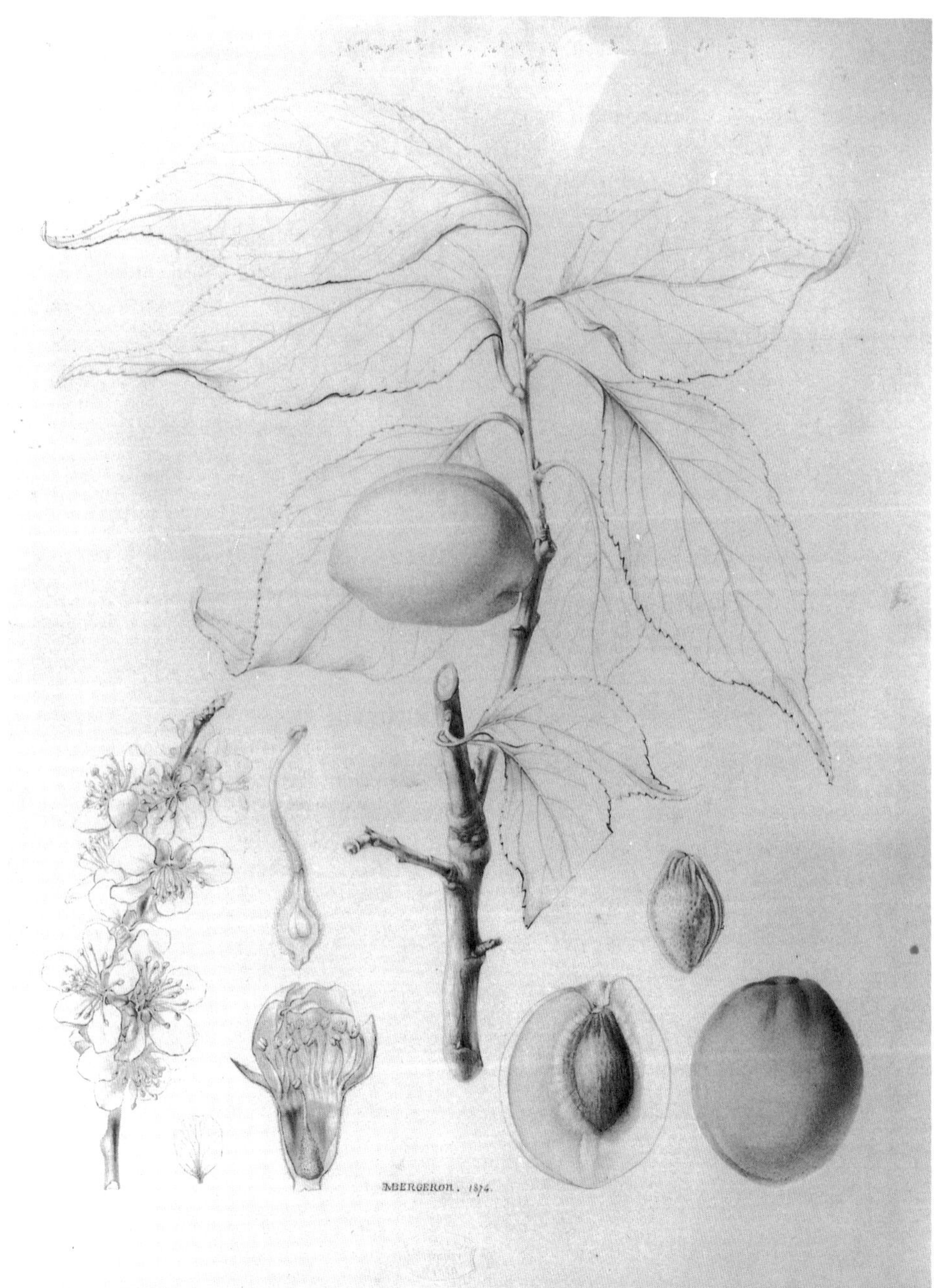

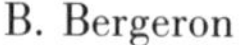

B. Bergeron

Watercolour on vellum, Vélins, Ms. 2346, no. 8, signed and dated 1874
Paris, Bibliotèque Centrale du Muséum National d'Histoire Naturelle

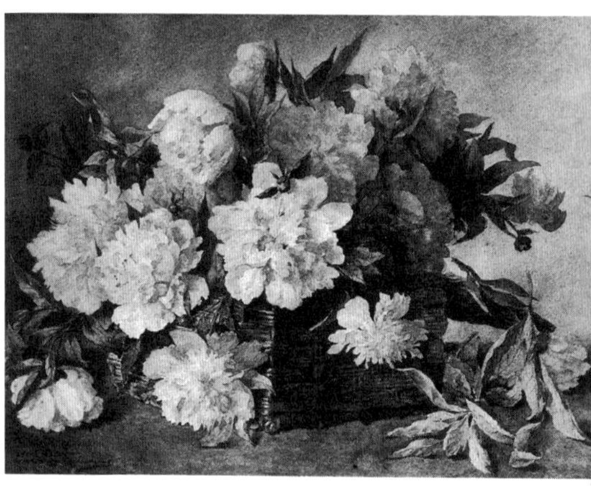

Clarisse Bernamont

Watercolour, signed
Bagnères-de-Bigorre, Musée Salies

BERNARD, Anaïs *née* Desgranges *b.1825*
b. Bernay (Eure). Pupil of Pauline Girardin. Exhib. *Bouquet: reines marguerites, fuchsias*; *Bouquet: camélias, bruyère, pensées*, Lyon Salon 1854; *Bouquet d'iris, Bouquet de pensées*, Paris Exposition Universelle, 1855. Exhib. Paris Salon *c.*1851–72 mostly wc e.g. *Bouquet de dahlias et de chèvrefeuilles*, 1857, *Bouquet de lilas*, 1867, *Bouquet de fleurs des champs*, 1872. Painted flowers on vellum for the Paris Muséum d'Histoire Naturelle (now untraceable). Collette lithographed some of A. Bernard's designs
LIT *Bellier*; *Bénézit*; *Faré* 1962, p. 247; *Lyon Salon* 1854; *Paris Exposition Universelle* 1855; Paris Bibl. Nat. Est.; *Paris Salon* 1867

BERNARD, Benoit *b.1828*
Pupil of Thierriat, Lyon BA (CFD 1852)
LIT *Hardouin-Fugier Grafe*

BERNARD, Delphine *1825–1864*
b. Nancy (Meurthe-et-Moselle). Pupil of Maréchal (Metz). Portrait, genre and flower painter. Exhib. Paris Salon from 1848. Her letters were published by Jules Breton
LIT *Bellier*; *Bénézit*; *Schurr* II, 20; *Thieme*

BERNARD, Emile *1868–1941*
b. Lille (Nord). Pupil of Paris École des Arts Décoratifs and Cormon. Cézanne's friend's influence made itself felt on the Pont-Aven school. Painted landscapes, figures, still-lifes and, occasionally, flowers e.g. *Vase de tulipes*, 1887 (Bremen), *Fleurs*, 1889, Paris Galliera 1 Dec. 1969. M: Amsterdam
LIT Auxerre, *E. Bernard*. Musée des Beaux-Arts 1968; *Bénézit*; Bremen Kunsthalle, *E. Bernard ... 1967*; Lille, *E. Bernard* ... Musée des Beaux-Arts, 1967; *Orsay*; Saint-Fargeau, *E. Bernard*, Musée des Beaux-Arts, 1980; M.A. Stevens in *Post-Impressionism*, London, RA, 1979–1980
See illustration on page 41

BERNARD, Jean-Marie *b.1820*
Pupil of Thierriat, Lyon BA (CFD 1837)
LIT *Hardouin-Fugier Grafe*

BERNARD, Jules-François *1849–1917*
b. Grenoble (Isère). Pupil of Paris BA, Pils and Hébert. Exhib. *Fleurs des champs*, Grenoble Salon 1899
LIT *Grenoble Salon* 1899. MW

BERNARD, Louise
Exhib. *Roses*, Lyon Salon 1877
LIT *Hardouin-Fugier Grafe*

BERNARDIN, Emilie-Camille
b. Rambouillet (Seine-et-Oise). Pupil of Saintpierre and Henry E. Delacroix. Exhib. Paris UFPS *Botte de roses*, 1896, *Pavots*, 1898
LIT *Bénézit*; *Paris UFPS* 1896, 1898

BERNE-BELLECOUR, Etienne *1838–1910*
b. Boulogne-sur-Mer (Seine-Maritime). Pupil of Picot and Barrias, Paris BA. This genre and military painter occasionally painted flowers e.g. *Bouquet*, wc, Paris Exposition Universelle 1878
LIT *Bellier*; *Bénézit*; *Schurr* I, 87

BERNHARD, Hilaire
Exhib. *Bourriche de pensées*, Dijon Salon 1892
LIT *Dijon Salon* 1892. CL

BÉROUJON, Régis
b. Lyon. Pupil of F. Vernay. Exhib. flowers and still-lifes, Lyon Salon from 1884
LIT *Bénézit*; *Lyon Salon* 1884

BERR DE TURIQUE, Jeanne
b. Paris. Pupil of Colin-Libour. Exhib. *Oeillets et violettes*, wc, Paris Salon 1895
LIT *Bénézit*; *Paris Salon* 1895

BERRIA-BLAN, Béatrice
Exhib. flowers Paris Indép. 1887
LIT *Paris Indép.* 1887

BERRIAT, Charles-Joseph
b. Bourg-Saint-Andéol (Ardèche). Exhib. *Magnolias*, Paris Noir et Blanc Salon, 1880
LIT *Bénézit*; *Paris Noir et Blanc Salon* 1880

BERRUET, Jacques-Florent *1842–1911*
Pupil of Lyon BA. Exhib. Lyon Salon from *c.*1870
LIT *Bénézit*; *Hardouin-Fugier Grafe*

BERRY, Jean *d.1889*
Textile designer, Saint-Etienne
LIT *Hardouin-Fugier Grafe*

BERRY, Duchesse de, Marie-Caroline-Ferdinande-Louise *1798–1872*
Pupil of Bessa (1820). A competent rose grower, the Duchess had a few lessons with Redouté
LIT *Hardouin-Fugier* 1981

BERTAUD, Louis
op. textile designer, Lyon *c.*1827
LIT *Hardouin-Fugier Grafe*

BERTHELIER, Jean-Marie *b.1834*
b. Lyon. Pupil of Reignier, Lyon BA (CFD 1854). Exhib. Lyon Salon 1860, 1869, 1877; Paris Salon 1866–1874 e.g. *Fleurs*, 1868, *Fleurs et fruits*, 1873
LIT *Bellier*; *Bénézit*; *Hardouin-Fugier Grafe*

BERTHET, Jeanne
Exhib. *Roses et liserons*, *Roses et lilas*, on porcelain, Dijon Salon 1897
LIT *Dijon Salon* 1897, CL

BERTHOD, Cécile
op. Lyon. Exhib. flowers in oils, wc and pastel Lyon Salon 1859–1876 e.g. *Bénitier entouré de fleurs*, 1859, *Vase de fleurs*, 1860, *Vase de roses*, 1865, *Panier de fleurs*, 1866, *Fleurs*, 1873. Her exhibits sold well and her 1865 flowers were singled out by Lyonnais art critics
LIT *Bénézit*; *Hardouin-Fugier Grafe*

BERTOLONI, Anna
Exhib. *Oeillets et mimosas*, Paris Noir et Blanc Salon 1886
LIT *Paris Noir et Blanc Salon* 1886

BERTRACHON ***b.1835***
Pupil of Thierriat, Lyon BA (CFD 1851)
LIT *Hardouin-Fugier Grafe*

BERTRAND, Elise ***fl.c.1840–1851***
op. Copyist and flower painter. Applied for a state commission (1843) and suggested a figure surrounded by a wreath (Hospice Civil, Albi). Her 1844 *Christ in a wreath* was painted for the Anguery church. Seems to have produced a few more religious subjects within wreaths, termed old-fashioned in 1846. Exhib. *Fleurs diverses dans un vase de terre*, Dijon Salon 1840; Paris Salon *Groupe de fleurs dans un vase*, 1841; *Fleurs et animaux*, 1845. M: la Rochelle, Lons-le-Saunier, Narbonne
LIT *Bellier*; *Bénézit*; *Dijon Salon* 1840; *Faré* 1962, p. 242; Paris Arch. Nat. F21:15; *Paris Salon* 1841, 1845; *Thieme*

BERTRAND, Félix
Pupil of Lyon BA. Exhib. *Fleurs*, Lyon Salon 1884
LIT *Lyon Salon* 1884

BERTRAND, Georges-Jules ***1849–1929***
Pupil of Yvon, Barrias and Bonnat. Painted genre and, occasionally, flowers e.g. *Roses*, Paris Salon 1879
LIT *Bellier*; *Bénézit*; *Witt*

BERTRAND, Joseph ***b.1845***
Pupil of Reignier, Lyon BA (CFD 1861)
LIT *Hardouin-Fugier Grafe*

BERTRAND, Mlle M.
Exhib. *Fleurs*, Dijon Salon 1890
LIT *Dijon Salon* 1890. CL

BERTRAND, Pierre ***b.1797***
Pupil of Berjon, Lyon BA (CFD 1812)
LIT *Hardouin-Fugier Grafe*

BERTRIX, Auguste ***b.1834***
b. Nevers (Nièvre). Pupil of Lyon BA. Exhib. *Fleurs*, gouache, Lyon Salon 1855
LIT *Hardouin-Fugier Grafe*

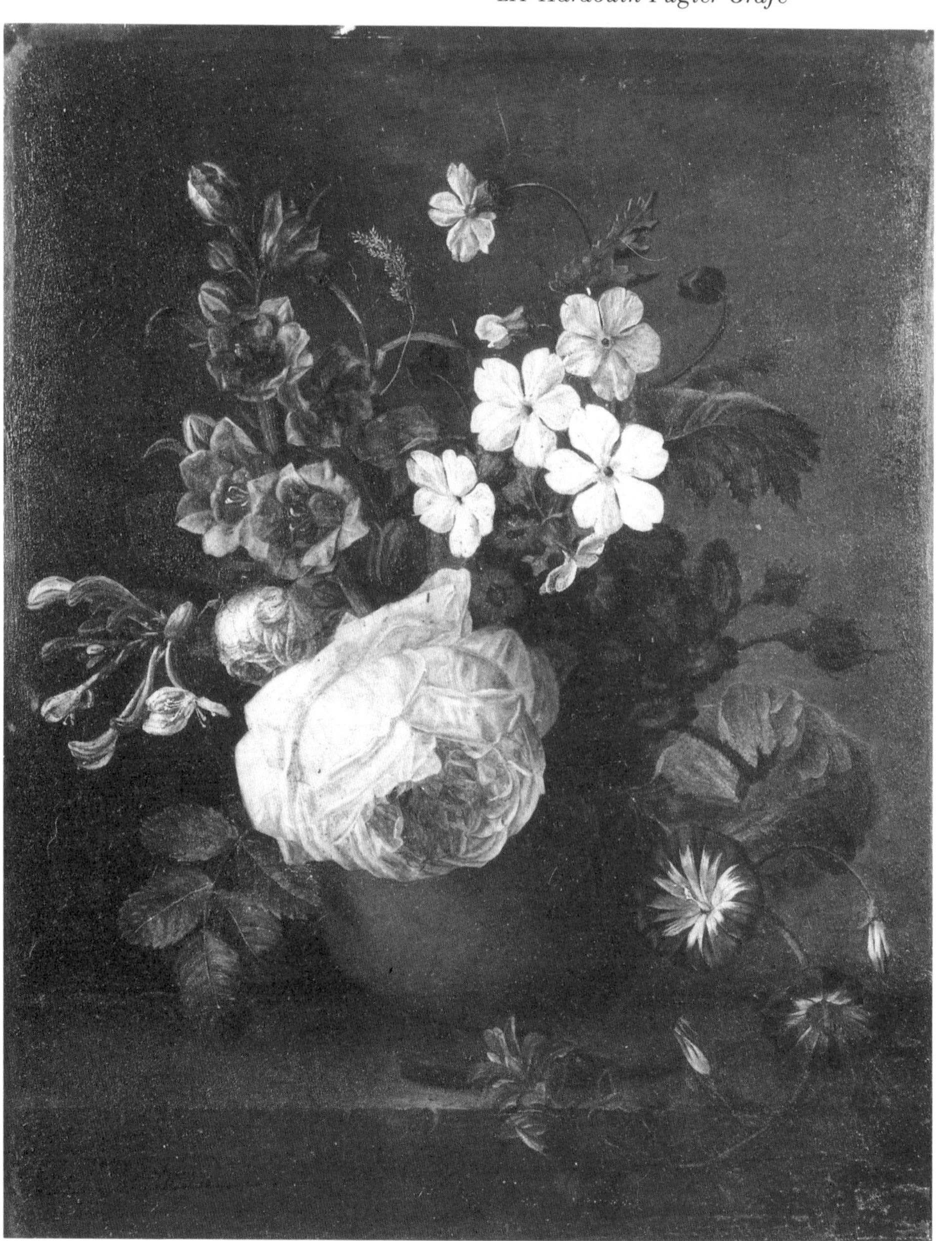

Elise Bertrand

Oil on panel, 16½ × 13 in. (42 × 33 cm.), signed
Narbonne, Musée d'Art et d'Histoire

BESSA, Pancrace ***1772–1846***
Pupil of Van Spaendonck and Redouté. Exhib. flowers in wc. Paris Salon 1806–14. An eminent botanical artist. Bessa contributed designs to many works e.g. *Nouveau Duhamel*, *Mordant de Launay*, *Herbier de l'Amateur*, *Volière des dames*, *Album de roses* etc. Engraved Redouté's *Roses*. Flower painter to the Duchesse de Berry (1816) and her drawing master (1820). Works in Fitzwilliam Museum, Broughton coll. Cambridge; Paris BMAD, Paris Muséum d'Histoire Naturelle
LIT *Hardouin-Fugier* 1981 (ill.); *Mitchell*

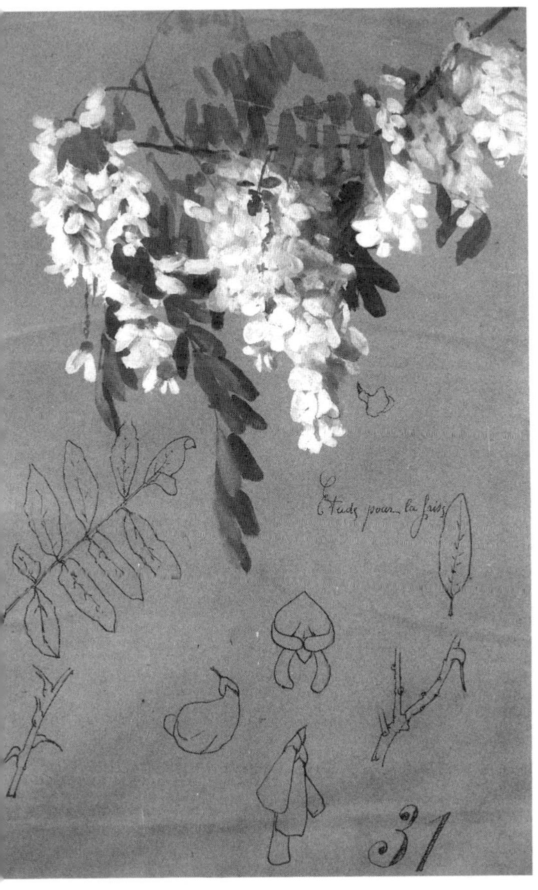

Jean-Benoit Frédéric Besson

Gouache, 21¼ × 14 in. (54 × 36 cm.), signed, inscribed '*Etudes pour la frise*' and numbered 31
Private collection

BESSET, Gilles
b. Saint-Cernin-Du-Plain (Saône-et-Loire). Exhib. *Bouquet*, Paris Indép. 1893
LIT *Paris Indép.* 1893

BESSIN, *see* DELAPORTE

BESSON ***b.1838***
Pupil of Reignier, Lyon BA (CFD 1854)
LIT *Hardouin-Fugier Grafe*

BESSON, Charles-Martial-Auguste, *alias* Jacques ***1839–c. 1905***
b. Lyon. Pupil of Reignier, Lyon BA (CFD 1858). Exhib. Lyon Salon 1880–1903 e.g. *Fleurs*, 1880, *Fleurs de printemps*, *Fleurs d'automne*, 1885, *Fleurs*, Dijon Salon 1892
LIT *Bénézit*; *Dijon Salon* 1892; *Hardouin-Fugier Grafe*; *Lyon Salon* 1880, 1884, 1885

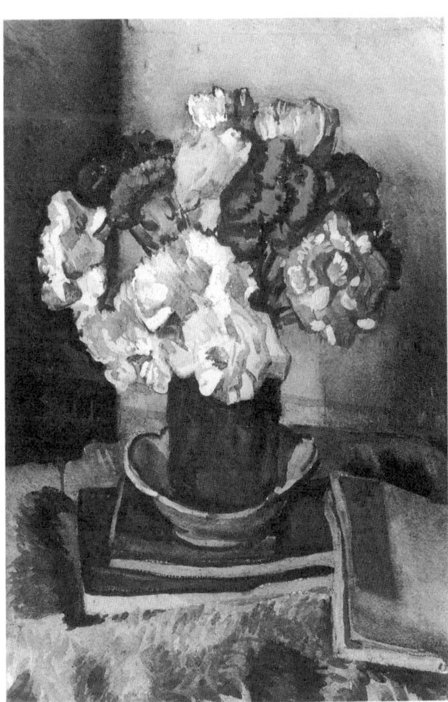

Charles-Théodore Bichet

Watercolour, 19 × 12¼ in. (48 × 31 cm.), signed, La Rochelle, Musée d'Orbigny-Bernon

BESSON, Faustin ***1821–1882***
b. Dôle (Jura). Pupil of J.S. Désiré, Decamps. A. Brune, Gigoux. Exhib. Paris Salon, *Fleurs*, 1846, *Bouquet de pervenches*, 1851. Was curator of the Musée de Dôle, where his works are kept
LIT *Bellier*; *Brune*; *Paris Salon* 1846, 1851; *Schurr* I, 51

BESSON, Fleury
Pupil of Albano of Florence. Exhib. *Roses et marguerites*, Lyon Salon 1884
LIT *Lyon Salon* 1884

BESSON, Jean-Benoit-Frédéric ***b.1886***
A pupil of Castex-Dégrange in 1904 (in Lyon CFD under Castex)
LIT *Hardouin-Fugier Grafe*. PM

BESSON, Joseph ***b.1830***
Pupil of Thierriat, Lyon BA (CFD 1846)
LIT *Hardouin-Fugier Grafe*

BETHMONT, E.
op. Sèvres *c.*1800—has 180 floral designs in the Sèvres archives
LIT *Orsay*

BÉTHUNE; Gaston ***1857–1897***
b. Paris. Pupil of Noél, Giraud and Bonnat. Exhib. Paris Salon from 1876, mostly landscapes. *Fleurs d'été*, Paris SNBA 1893
LIT *Bénézit*; *Paris SNBA* 1893; *Schurr* III, 66; *Thieme*; *Witt*

BEUSELIN, *see* DESPORTES

BEYSSON or BESSON, Louis-Antoine ***1856–1912***
b. Lyon. Pupil of Lyon BA and G. Poncet. Exhib. Lyon Salon 1880–1903, Paris from 1903. Painted flowers, still-lifes, landscapes, portraits and, later, trains and railway stations
LIT *Bénézit*; *Hardouin-Fugier Grafe*; *Thieme*

BEZARD, Léontine-Marie
Exhib. Dijon Salon *Fleurs de lilas et magnolias*, 1880, *Bouquet de roses*, 1885, *Lilas*, 1890
LIT *Dijon Salon* 1880, 1885, 1890. CL

BIARD-JEANDEL
Chrysanthèmes dans un vase, Musée d'Auxerre
LIT *Auxerre Musée doc.*

BICHET, Charles-Théodore *1863–1929*
b. Paris. Pupil of Lechevallier-Chevignard. Drawing master Paris, then Limoges École d'Arts décoratifs. Painted flowers in wc. M: La Rochelle, *Fleurs*
LIT *Bénézit*; Moisy. *Catalogue du Musée de la Rochelle*, 1974; *Schurr* III, 140

BIDAL
Fifty-seven floral designs *c.*1900–1910 in the Sèvres Archives
LIT *Orsay*

BIDAU, Eugène
b. La Roche-sur-Yon (Vendée). Pupil of Lechat and Alexandre. Exhib. Paris Salon *c.*1867–*c.*1900 e.g. *Le panier renversé*, 1867, *Fleurs et bijoux*, 1880, *Camélias et violettes*, 1885, *Fleur*, 1899. Bidau's *Touffe de violettes de Parme* was in the Sarah Bernhardt sale. Paris, 11–13 June 1923; *Still-Life with Flowers*, 1867, Sotheby's, New York, 24 Feb. 1983, lot 88
LIT *Bellier*; *Bénézit*; *Lyon Salon* 1869; *Paris Salon* 1867, 1880, 1885, 1899; *Pavière*; *Salon Illustré*, 1899, p. 255 (ill.); *Witt*

BIDAULT or BIDEAULT, François c.*1817*–c.*1860*
b. Châlon-sur-Saône (Saône-et-Loire). Exhib. flowers and still-lifes Lyon and Paris Salons 1855–1857
LIT *Bénézit*; *Thieme*

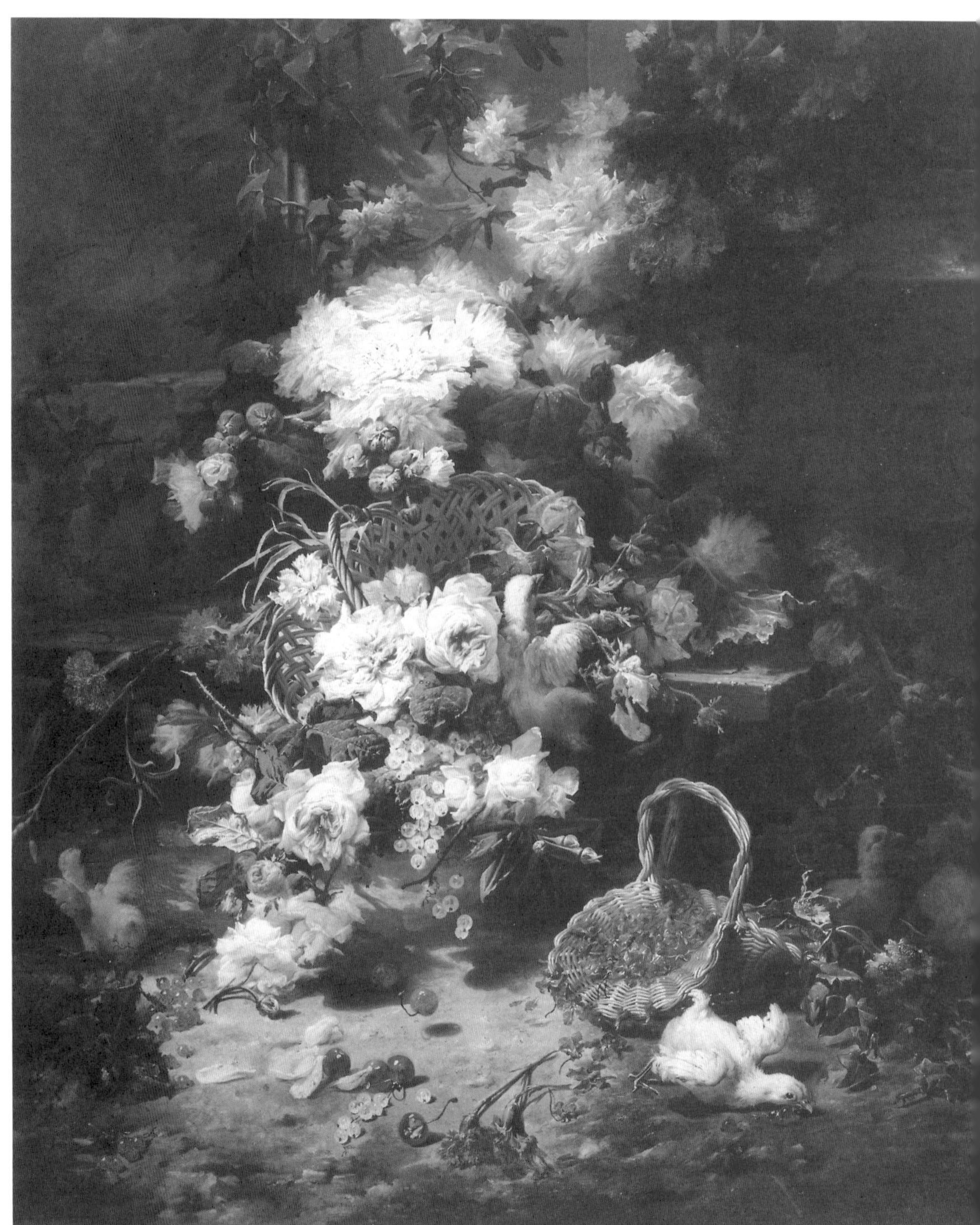

Eugène Bidau

Oil on canvas, $45\frac{3}{4}$ × 40 in. (116 × 101.5 cm.), signed and dated 1867
Courtesy Sotheby's, London

BIDAULT, Jean-Pierre-Xavier *1745–1813*
b. Carpentras (Vaucluse); op. Lyon. Brother of Jean-Joseph-Xavier Bidault, the landscape painter. Painted still-lifes and, occasionally, flowers e.g. Paris Salon *Fleurs*, gouache, 1801–1802, *Fleurs*, 1810
LIT *Audin Vial*; *Bellier*; *Bénézit*; *Hardouin-Fugier Grafe*; *Paris Salon* 1801–1802; *Witt*

BIDLINGMEYER, Jules *1830–1893*
b. Mulhouse (Haut-Rhin). Textile designer. Exhib. *Fleurs*, *Fleurs et fruits*, Strasbourg Salon 1884. A work formerly in the museum at Mulhouse has been untraceable since the war
LIT *Bénézit; Strasbourg Salon* 1884

BIENAIMÉ, *see* GILBERT

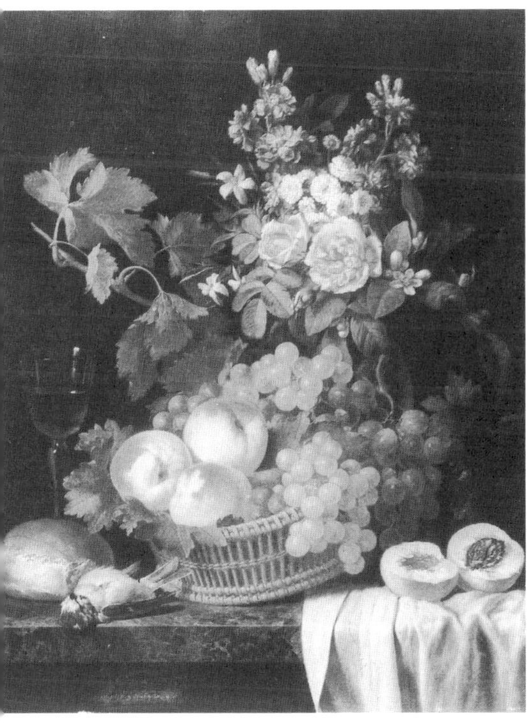

Jean-Pierre-Xavier Bidault

Oil on panel, 20 × 15¾ in. (51 × 40 cm.), signed
Courtesy Sotheby's, London

BIENAIMÉ, Mme
Exhib. *Fleurs d'après nature*, wc, Paris Salon 1834
LIT *Paris Salon* 1834

BIENVÊTU, Gustave
b. Paris. Pupil of S. Petit. Exhib. Paris Salon *c.*1877–*c.*1906 e.g. *Roses et pavots*, 1878; genre, still-life and flower painter. His 1906 *Bourriche de roses* was bought for the Musée de Bourbon-Lancy
LIT *Bellier*; *Bénézit*; Paris Arch. Nat. F21:4500

BIETRIX, Louis
Possibly a pupil of François Lepage. Exhib. Lyon *c.*1855–1898
LIT *Bénézit*; *Hardouin-Fugier Grafe*

BIGOT, Eugénie-Victoire *d.1907*
b. Dinan (Côtes-du-Nord). Pupil of Desportes and Aubé. Exhib. flowers on faience e.g. Paris Salon *Fleurs de printemps*, *Fleurs d'automne*, 1880, *Pensées*, *fritillaires*, *narcisses*, 1882
LIT *Bellier*; *Bénézit*

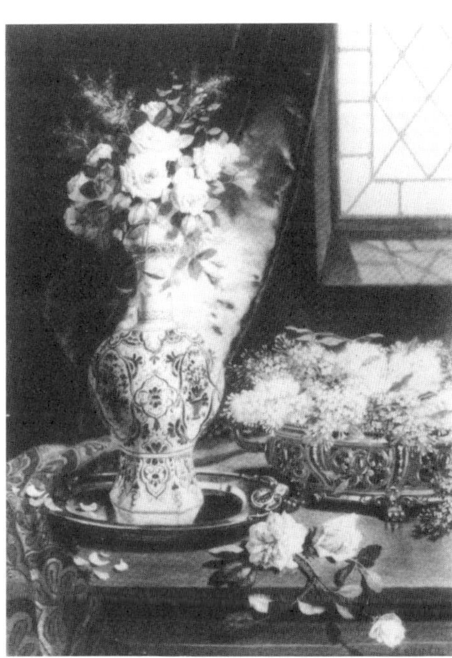

Gustave Bienvêtu

Oil on canvas, 47½ × 35½ in. (120 × 90 cm.), signed
Courtesy Sotheby's, London

BILHAUD, Ernest-Célestin
b. Montmartre (Paris). Exhib. portraits and flowers e.g. *Bouquet de lilas*, Paris Salon 1876; *Lilas*, Dijon Salon 1890
LIT *Bellier*; *Bénézit*; *Dijon Salon* 1890. CL

BILLER, Joseph
b. Neufbrisach (Haut-Rhin). Pupil of Thurner. Exhib. Paris Salon from 1877, e.g. *Coin de jardin*, 1878, *Chrysanthèmes*, 1880
LIT *Bellier*; *Bénézit*; *Paris Salon* 1880

BILLIAN
Exhib. *Fleurs*, Saint-Etienne Salon 1838
LIT *Hardouin-Fugier Bringuier*; *Le Mercure Ségusien*, 5 Sep. 1838; *Saint-Etienne Salon* 1838

BILLOT, Achille *b.1834*
b. Sellières (Jura). Pupil of F. Besson, L. Cogniet, T. Robert-Fleury, J. Perraud, Exhib. *Fleurs de printemps*, Dijon Salon 1880; *Fleurs de printemps*, Lyon Salon 1881
LIT *Bénézit*; *Dijon Salon* 1880; *Lyon Salon* 1881. CL

BILLOTEY, *see* COLOMBO

BILLOTEY, *see* MONTAIGNAC

BILLOTEY, Louis-Désiré
b. Limoges (Haute-Vienne). Pupil of Lequien and Laporte. Exhib. *Pensées*, gouache, Paris Salon 1890
LIT *Paris Salon* 1890

BILLY, Charles-Bernard de
Pupil of Donzel and Levasseur. Painted genre and flowers. Exhib. Paris Salon 1876–1892, e.g. *Fleurs et fruits*, wc, after Maisiat, 1879
LIT *Bellier*; *Bénézit*

BIMAR, Pierre-Charles-Henri
b. Montpellier (Hérault). Exhib. *Fleurs*, Lyon Salon 1872
LIT *Bellier*; *Bénézit*; *Lyon Salon* 1872

BINE, Joseph-Marie ***b.1819***
Pupil of Thierriat, Lyon BA (CFD 1834). Textile designer
LIT *Hardouin-Fugier Grafe*

BINET, Anna-Maria ***née*** **Ménard** ***b.1835***
b. Paris. Pupil of Lesourd de Beauregard and Barye. Painted still-lifes, game and, possibly, flowers
LIT *Bellier*

BINET, Georges-Jules-Ernest ***1865–1949***
Pupil of Cormon, Collin and Thuillier. Exhib. *Azalées*, *Roses trémières*, Paris Salon 1898. Geneva sale, 1–2 June 1988, lot 2, *Roses mousseuses*
LIT *Bénézit*; *Paris Salon* 1898, (ill.); *Schurr* II, 122; *Witt*

BINET, Victor-Jean-Baptiste-Barthélémy ***1849–1924***
b. Rouen (Seine-Maritime). This landscape painter produced some flower-pieces, e.g. *Poppies in a vase*, exhib. Dusseldorf, 1982–1983
LIT *Bénézit*; *Orsay*; Schurr I, 111

BIOTTOT, Adolphe
b. Paris. Pupil of Fontaine. Exhib. *Roses* on porcelain Paris Salon 1880
LIT *Paris Salon* 1880

BIRAT, Augustine-Hélène-Amélie ***née*** **d'Harchies** ***1812–c.1867***
b. Gorizia (Italy). Pupil of Redouté and de Mirbel. Painted portraits and miniatures. Exhib. flowers, Paris Salon 1844, 1846, 1847, 1861–7
LIT *Bellier*; *Hardouin-Fugier* 1981; *Witt*

BIRONNEAU, ***see*** **DUPRÉ**

BIVA, Henri ***1848–1928***
b. Paris. Pupil of Nozal and L. Tanzi. Exhib. landscapes and flowers often in pastel and wc. Paris Salon from 1875. *Anémones et roses*, Lyon Salon 1884; *Les roses du jardin*, Paris Salon 1881 and Dijon 1883; *Roses du matin*, Paris Salon 1885; *Roses de Nice*, Roanne Salon 1890; *Roses et lys*, Dijon Salon 1890; *Dahlias*, wc, Strasbourg Salon (400 francs) 1891; Dijon Salon *Roses et tubéreuses*, wc, 1892, *Violettes et mimosas*, 1894, *Vase de roses*, 1897. A prolific and popular artist. M: Rouen. Rothschild coll., Royal Belgian coll. (untraceable). *Still-Life* Sotheby's, London 28 Nov. 1984, lot 502.
LIT *Bellier*; *Bénézit*; *Dijon Salon* 1883, 1890, 1892, 1894, 1897; *Lyon Salon* 1884; Paris Arch. Nat. F21:2122; *Paris Noir et Blanc Salon*, 1886; *Paris Salon* 1875, 1885; *Roanne Salon* 1890; *Strasbourg Salon* 1891; *Thieme*; *Witt*
See illustration on page 44

BIVA, Paul ***1851–1900***
b. Paris. Pupil of H. Biva and Lequien. Painted landscapes and flowers. Exhib.

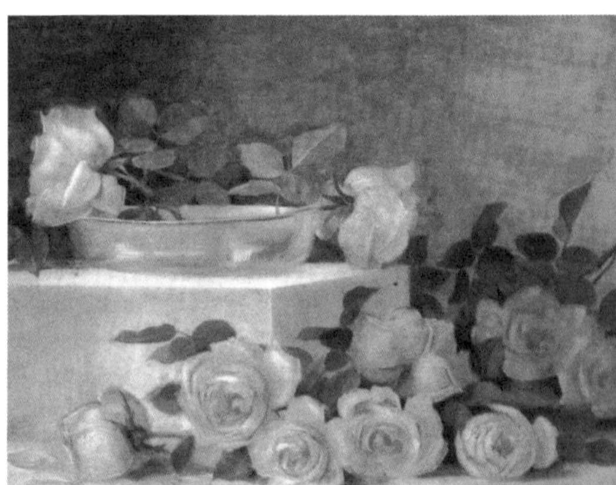

Georges Binet (*right*)

Oil on canvas, $19\frac{3}{4} \times 25\frac{1}{2}$ in. (50 × 65 cm.), signed
Private collection

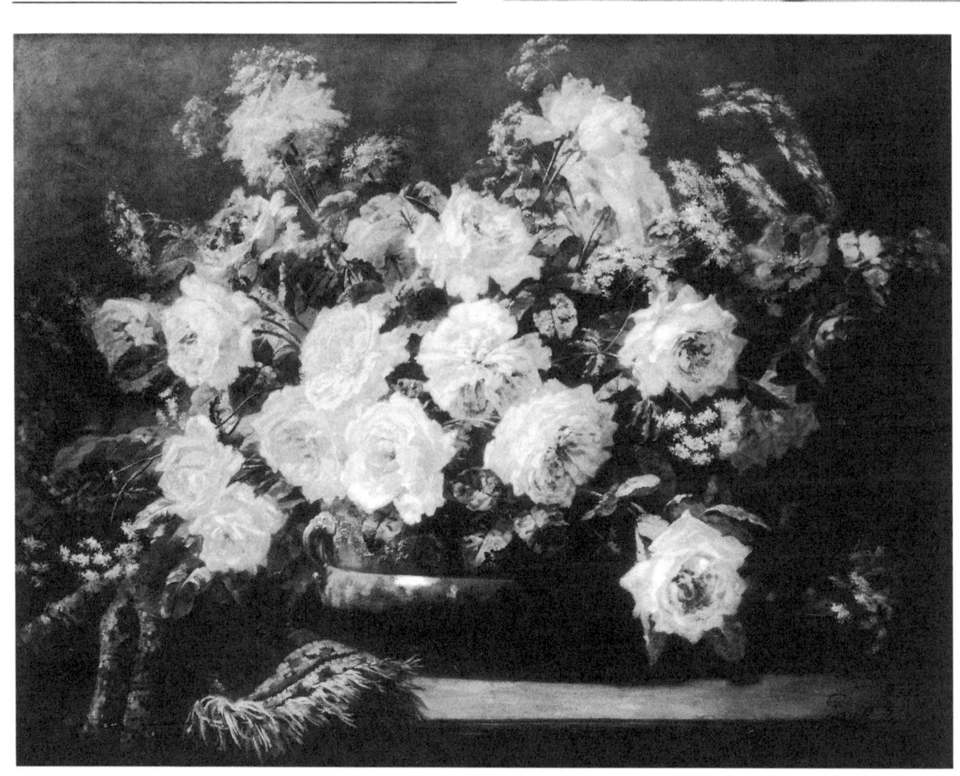

Paul Biva

Oil on canvas, $34\frac{3}{4} \times 44$ in. (88 × 112 cm.), signed
Courtesy Sotheby's, London

Lyon Salon *Roses*, 1879, *Pensées*, 1884; *Pensées*, Paris Indép. 1884; *Fruits et fleurs*, Strasbourg Salon 1884 (350 francs). His *Vase de roses et de tulipes*, wc, was in the 1886 raffle of the Lyon Societé des Amis-des-Arts; Dijon Salon, *Pivoines*, 1890, *Panier de roses*, 1892, *Anémones*, gouache, 1897; *Roses trémières*, Paris Salon 1898. A prolific and popular flower painter. *Roses*, Sotheby's, London, 23 Mar. 1988, lot 485. Musée de Dijon, *Roses*
LIT *Bellier*; *Chronique des Arts*, 1900, p. 241; *Dijon Salon* 1885, 1887, 1890, 1892, 1897; *Lyon Salon* 1879, 1885; Jeanne Magnin *Catalogue du Musée de Dijon* 1933, p. 91; Paris Arch. Nat. F21:2122; *Paris Indép.* 1884; *Paris Salon* 1884, 1889 (ill.), 1890 (ill.), 1898; *Roanne Salon* 1890; *Strasbourg Salon* 1884, 1891

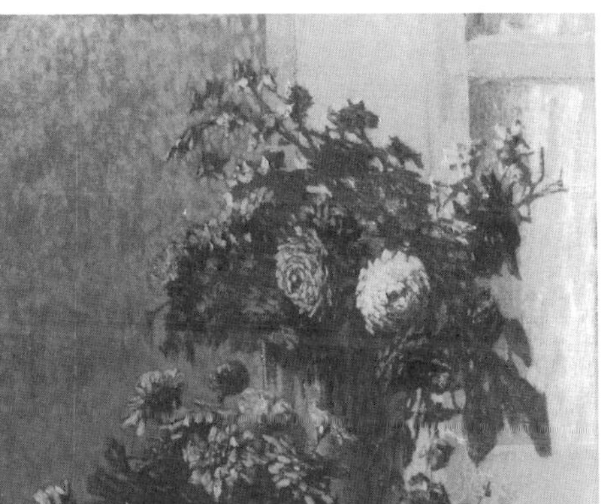

Charles-Philippe Blache

Oil on canvas, 21¼ × 17¾ in. (54 × 45 cm.), signed
Grenoble, Musee de Peinture et de Sculpture

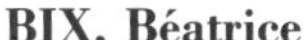

BIX, Béatrice
b. Vendôme (Loir-et-Cher). Exhib. *Fleurs*, wc, Paris Salon 1861
LIT *Paris Salon* 1861

BIZARD, Ferdinand-Alexandre *1820–1879*
Pupil of Rémond. Painted landscapes, still-lifes (Musée de Dijon) and, occasionally, flowers e.g. *Fruits et fleurs*, Lyon Salon 1855
LIT *Bellier*; *Bénézit*; *Lyon Salon* 1855

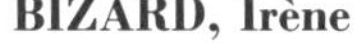

BIZARD, Irène
b. Ourouët (Nièvre). Exhib. *Reines-Marguerites*, pastel, Paris Noir et Blanc Salon 1888
LIT *Paris Noir et Blanc Salon* 1888

BLACHE, Charles-Philippe *1860–1908*
b. Tullins (Isère). Pupil of Paris BA. Exhib. landscapes and flowers, Paris Salon 1879–1881 and SNBA e.g. *Fleurs*, SNBA 1891, *Tulipes le matin*, *Fleurs la nuit*, SNBA 1893, *Fleurs*, SNBA 1895. Blache was friendly with Mallarmé, Bourdelle, Despiau and Degas. Retrospective exhibition Musée de Grenoble 1921. Works by Blache were in the Degas collection. His 1893 *Fleurs au soleil couchant* was bought (1896) for the Musée de Grenoble (600 francs)
LIT *Bénézit*; Grenoble, Bibl. Mun. man. Sainson; Grenoble Musée, *cat.* 1904; Paris Arch. Nat. F21:2123; *Paris SNBA* 1892, 1893, 1895; Paris *Vente Degas* Nov. 1918; *Pavière*

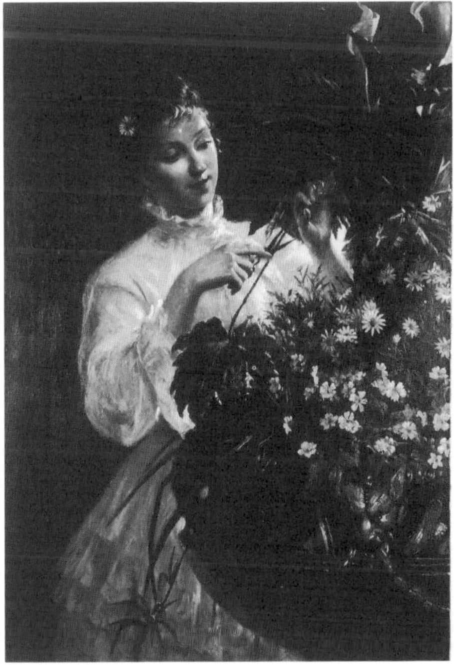

Ernest Blanc-Garin

Oil on canvas, 44½ × 29 in. (113 × 73.5 cm.), signed and dated 1887
Courtesy Christie's, London

BLAGNY, *see* LECHÊNE

BLAN, *see* BERRIA

BLANC, Antoine *b.1810*
Pupil of Thierriat, Lyon BA (CFD 1831)
LIT *Hardouin-Fugier Grafe*

BLANC, Moïse
Exhib. *Fleurs et fruits*, Paris Salon 1841
LIT *Bénézit*; *Paris Salon* 1841

BLANC, Pierre-Louis *b.1839*
Pupil of Reignier, Lyon BA (CFD 1855). Exhib. Lyon Salon 1873
LIT *Hardouin-Fugier Grafe*

BLANC-DUCHÉ, Benoite
b. Roanne (Loire). Exhib. Saint-Etienne Salon *Bouquet de lilas et de seringas*, *Roses trémières dans un vase*, 1882
LIT *Hardouin-Fugier Bringuier*; *Saint-Etienne Salon* 1882

BLANC-GARIN, Ernest *1843–1916*
b. Givet (Ardennes). Pupil of Portaëls (Brussels) and Cabanel in Paris. Painted townscapes, occasionally still-lifes. A Belgian born in France, he opened an academy near Brussels after service in 1870. Exhib. Paris Salon from 1868
LIT *Schurr V*, 22. PM

BLANCHARD, Emile-Théophile *b.1795*
b. Saint-Omer (Pas-de-Calais). Pupil of Van Spaendonck. Botanical designer and flower painter. Exhib. *Fleurs sur une table de marbre*, Paris Salon 1844, *Corbeille de fleurs*, 1850; Designed plates for Jaume Saint-Hilaire, *Plantes usuelles des Brésiliens*, 1824 and *L'Horticulteur Français*, 1851–1872 etc. Flowers on vellum, in the Paris Muséum d'Histoire Naturelle (currently untraceable)
LIT *Bellier*; *Bénézit*; *Laissus*; *Paris Salon* 1844, 1850; *Nissen* I, 1717

BLANCHE, Jacques-Emile *1861–1942*
b. Paris. Pupil of Gervex and Humbert. Painted portraits, landscapes and flowers e.g. *Pivoines, étude pour une composition décorative*, Paris Salon 1885; Paris SNBA, *Bouquets de dahlias*, *Pommes d'api*, 1895, *Pois de senteur*, 1898, 1899. *Vase de fleurs*, Sotheby's, London, 6 Dec. 1973, lot 154. M: Colmar, Paris (Musée d'Orsay)
LIT *Bellier*; *Bénézit*; J.E. Dieppe, *Blanche*, Musée des Beaux-Arts 1954; *Orsay*; *Thieme*; *Witt*
See illustration on page 45

BLANCHEVILLE, Lucie
Exhib. *Chrysanthèmes*, Dijon Salon 1887
LIT *Dijon Salon* 1887. CL

BLANCHEVILLE, Marthe
Exhib. *Chrysanthèmes*, Dijon Salon 1887
LIT *Dijon Salon* 1887. CL

BLAZY, Georges-André *b.1816*
Pupil of Thierriat, Lyon BA (CFD 1834–1836)
LIT *Hardouin-Fugier Grafe*

BLÉCHY, Jean-Claude *b.1829*
Pupil of Thierriat, Lyon BA (CFD 1846). Bléchy et Bourget design studio. op. Lyon 1847
LIT *Hardouin-Fugier Grafe*

BLÉRY, Eugène-Stanislas-Alexandre *1805–1887*
Engraver. Occasionally painted flowers in watercolours
LIT *Bénézit*; *Thieme*; *Witt*

BLET, Laurent *b.1820*
Pupil of Thierriat, Lyon BA (CFD 1837)
LIT *Hardouin-Fugier Grafe*

BLOESCH, Charles *1818–1908*
b. Mulhouse (Haut-Rhin). Pupil of Van Dael. Textile designer Berlin, Paris, Mulhouse and flower painter
LIT *Histoire documentaire*; *MISE cat.* BJ

BLONDEL, *see* DÉSOUCHES

BOCOURT, Marie-Firmin *1819–1904*
b. Paris. Pupil of Abel de Pujol and Drolling. Drawing master. Several flower painters were his pupils. Paris, Muséum d'Histoire Naturelle, wc on vellum, 1852–1869 (not botanical)
LIT *Bénézit*; *Laissus*

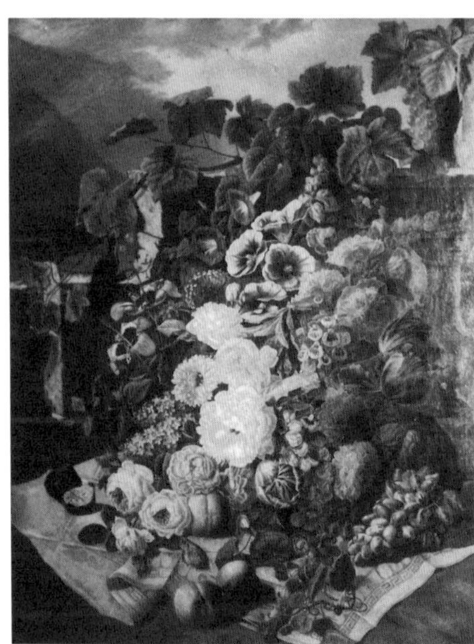

Emile-Théophile Blanchard

Oil on canvas, signed
Paris, Bibliothèque Centrale du Muséum National d'Histoire Naturelle

Eugène-Stanislas-Alexandre Bléry

Etching, 8¾ × 6¼ in. (22 × 16 cm.), signed and dated 1857
Private collection

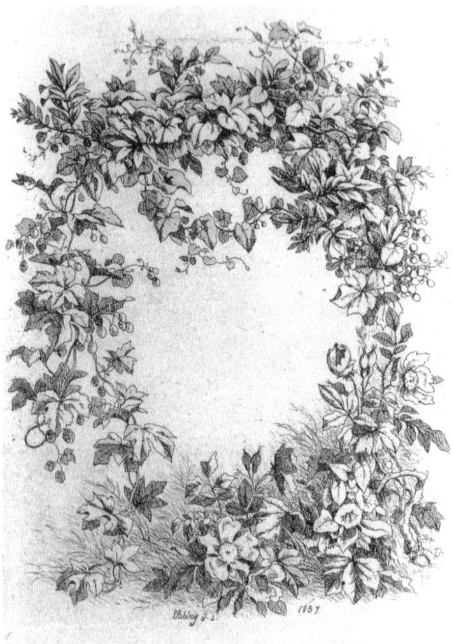

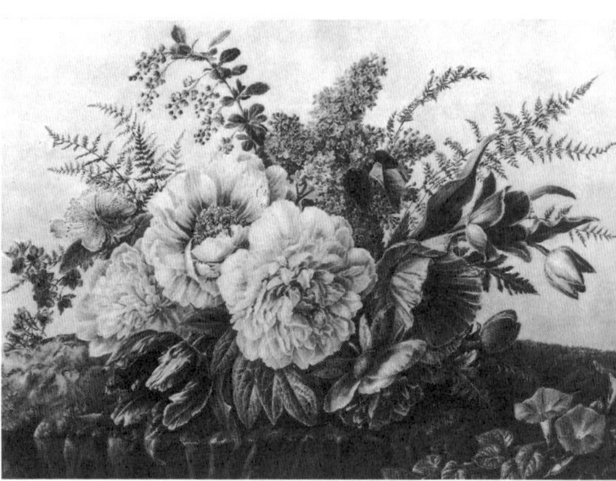

Charles Bloesch

Gouache on beige paper, 20 × 28½ in. (51 × 72 cm.), dated 25 juillet 1885
Mulhouse, Musée de l'Impression sur Etoffes

BOCQUET
op. Sèvres 1808–1813
LIT *Brunet Préaud*

BOCQUET, Louis-Auguste-Henri
b. Paris. Pupil of Adam. Exhib. Paris Salon from 1878 e.g. *Fleurs d'amandier*, gouache, 1878, *Fleurs de pommier*, gouache, 1878, *Fleurs de printemps*, 1880
LIT *Bellier*; *Bénézit*

BOGUREAU
At Sèvres 1896–1908. A plate by this artist is in Paris BMAD (Maciet coll.)
LIT *Orsay*; *Paris BMAD*

BOHLY, Marie
b. Colmar (Haut-Rhin). Pupil of Lousteau. Exhib. Paris Salon *Fleurs*, 1861, *Fleurs et fruits*, 1863, *Roses trémières*, 1864, *Lilas et roses*, decorative panel, 1865, *Fruits et fleurs*, decorative panel, 1866
LIT *Bellier*; *Bénézit*; *Paris Salon* 1861

BOICHARD, Henri
b. Versailles (Yvelines). Pupil of Cogniet. Exhib. flowers. Lyon Salon 1874, 1876
LIT *Lyon Salon* 1874, 1876

BOILEVIN, J.A.
b. Alger (Algeria). Valence address. Exhib. *Fleurs décoratives*, wc, Saint-Etienne Salon 1886
LIT *Saint-Etienne Salon* 1886

BOILLAT, Mlle Lucie
b. Paris. Pupil of Jumon and Donzet. Exhib. *Fleurs*, gouache, Paris Salon 1880
LIT *Bénézit*; *Paris Salon* 1880

BOILLY, Louis-Léopold ***1761–1845***
The famous portrait, figure and genre painter produced some flower-pieces e.g. *Fleurs dans un vase* (Harisse 912), *Roses sur une table de marbre* (Harisse 913), *Fleurs et fruits*, miniature (Harisse 914). Some have been on the art market e.g. *Fleurs et oiseau*, W. Wheeler, London 1951, *Roses*, Galerie Giroux, Brussels, 29 Nov. 1956, and *Garden flowers in a vase*, Sotheby's, New York, 3 June 1988, lot 11; Cambridge, Fitzwilliam Museum (Broughton coll.): *Vase de fleurs*
LIT *Bellier*; *Faré* 1962, p. 242; H. Harisse *L.L. Boilly* ... Paris (Société de propagation des livres d'Art) 1898; *Witt*

BOIREAU, François-Charles ***b.1810***
Pupil of Thierriat, Lyon BA (CFD 1830)
LIT *Hardouin-Fugier Grafe*

BOIRIVENT-BASSET
Worked in Lyon. Exhib. *Fleurs*, Roanne Salon 1890
LIT *Roanne Salon* 1890

BOIRLEAU, Marie
b. Limoges (Haute-Vienne). Pupil of Mme Baraton and Dalpayrat. Exhib. Paris Salon 1878–82. *Lilas*, Dijon Salon 1890
LIT *Bellier*; *Dijon Salon* 1890. CL

BOIRON, Antonin ***b.1834***
Pupil of Thierriat, Lyon BA (CFD 1851)
LIT *Hardouin-Fugier Grafe*

BOIRON, Jean-Baptiste ***b.1818***
Pupil of Thierriat, Lyon BA (CFD 1837). Textile designer. Entered 1838 Lyon Salon FDC
LIT *Hardouin-Fugier Grafe*

BOIS DE SACÉ, Marguerite
Exhib. *Fleurs*, pastel, Paris SNBA 1894, *Pivoines*, wc, 1896
LIT *Paris SNBA* 1894, 1896

BOISLECOMTE, Marie-Félix-Edmond de ***1849–1923***
Pupil of J.P. Laurens and Rivey. Exhib. *Le rosier*, Dijon Salon 1892
LIT *Bénézit*; *Dijon Salon* 1892

BOISSIÈRE, Jean-Antoine ***b.1814***
Pupil of Thierriat, Lyon BA (CFD 1835)
LIT *Hardouin-Fugier Grafe*

BOISSIEU, Claude-Victor de ***1784–1869***
Pupil of J.J. de Boissieu, his uncle. Designed botanical plates for his own *Flore d'Europe*, Lyon 1805–1806
LIT *Bénézit*; *Hardouin-Fugier Grafe*; *Répertoire des Peintres lyonnais du XIX° siècle en Bugey*, Lacoux, 1980; *Nissen* I, 191

BOISSIEU, Jean-Jacques de ***1736–1810***
b. Lyon. The well-known engraver and painter produced some flower designs e.g. *Mauves*, ink, Audin Vial, p. 101
LIT *Audin Vial*; *Bénézit*; *Witt*

BOISSON, *see* VIDAL

BOITARD, Pierre ***1787–1859***
b. Mâcon (Saône-et-Loire). Designed plates for *Botanique des dames*, 1821 and *Botanique des demoiselles* (Paris), 1835–1880
LIT *Nissen* I, 192, 193

BOITELET, Marie-Louise
b. Guéret (Creuse). Pupil of Carolus-Duran and Henner. Exhib. flowers, Paris Indép. 1892
LIT *Bénézit*; *Paris Indép.* 1892

BOMBLED, Louis Charles ***1862–1927***
b. Chantilly. Principally a painter of military subjects and well-known illustrator. Occasionally painted flowers. Exhib. S.F.A.
LIT *Bénézit*, *Schurr* II 17

BOMBOY, Jean-Claude-Simon ***b.1826***
b. Lyon. Pupil of Thierriat, Lyon BA (CFD 1843). Exhib. flowers Lyon Salon 1853–1856. Drawing master
LIT *Bénézit*; *Hardouin-Fugier Grafe*

BOMPARD, Maurice ***1857–1936***
b. Rodez (Aveyron). Pupil of Boulanger and Jules Lefebvre. Painted genre, portraits, marines, occasional flowers. Salon debut 1878. Legion of Honour, 1914
LIT *Bénézit*. PM

BONAMY, ***see*** **VILLERMEUIL**

BONET, Emile-Michel ***b.1806***
Pupil of Thierriat, Lyon BA (CFD 1826)
LIT *Hardouin-Fugier Grafe*

BONHEUR-GERMAIN, Mme ***née*** **Ulysse Bernard**
Pupil of U. Bernard and Germain Bonheur. Painted landscapes and, occasionally, flowers e.g. *Encadrement de plantes décoratives*, Paris Noir et Blanc Salon 1888
LIT *Bellier*; *Bénézit*; *Paris Noir et Blanc Salon* 1888; *Thieme*

BONIROTE, Emilie
Exhib. flowers Lyon Salon 1882–1885
LIT *Lyon Salon* 1882–1885

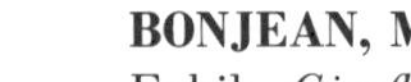

BONJEAN, Marie-Antoinette
Exhib. *Giroflées*, Paris Salon 1879
LIT *Bellier*

BONNARD, Antoine-Claude ***b.1835***
Pupil of Thierriat Lyon BA (CFD 1854)
LIT *Hardouin-Fugier Grafe*

BONNARD or BONARD, Benoit-Noël ***b.1821***
Pupil of Thierriat, Lyon BA (CFD 1840). Entered 1841 FDC. Exhib. Lyon *c.*1860
LIT *Hardouin-Fugier Grafe*

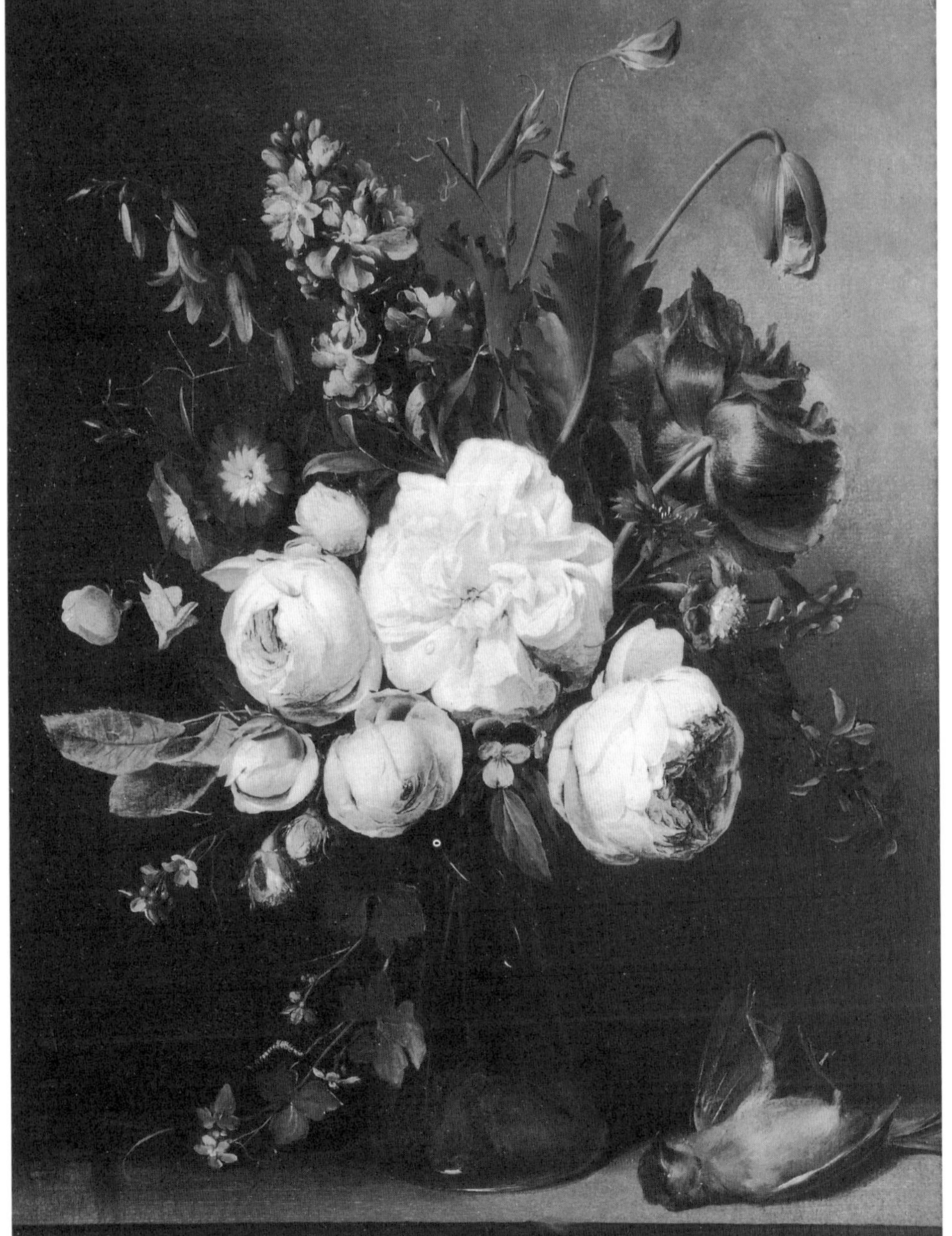

Louis-Léopold Boilly (*left*)

Oil on paper mounted on canvas, 18 × $13\frac{1}{4}$ in. (46 × 33.5 cm.), signed
Cambridge, Fitzwilliam Museum
(Broughton Collection)

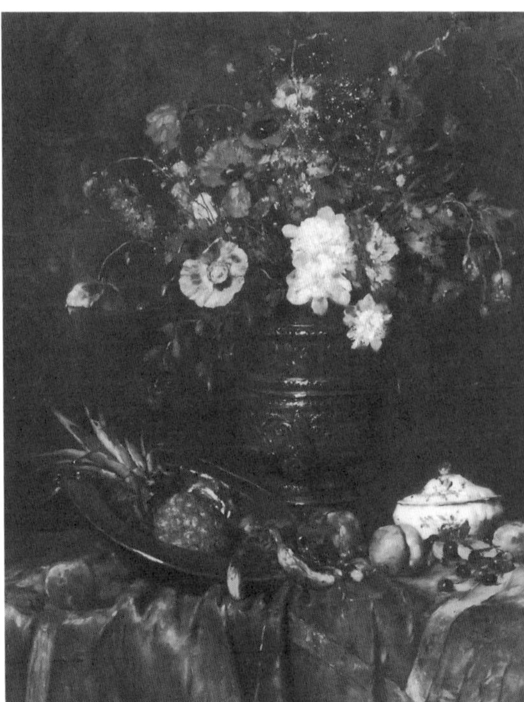

Maurice Bompard

Oil on canvas, $43\frac{1}{4}$ × $33\frac{1}{2}$ in. (110 × 85 cm.), signed and dated 1897
Courtesy Sotheby's, London

BONNARD, Mme Georges
b. Paris. Pupil of Médard and Loubet. Exhib. *Fleurs*, Lyon Salon 1885
LIT *Lyon Salon* 1885

† **BONNARD, Pierre** ***1867–1947***
b. Fontenay-aux-Roses (Hauts-de-Seine). Pupil of Paris BA and Académie Julian. Though Bonnard's early landscapes e.g. *Paysage aux coquelicots*, 1890, or portraits e.g. *Portrait de Berthe Schaudlin*, feature blossoming trees or flowers, most of his flower paintings are later works. His favourite blooms are snowballs, wild flowers of every kind and, later, mimosa. Among his early flowers are: *Jonquilles dans un pot vert*, *c.*1887 (D. 1696); *Vases de fleurs sur une table*, *c.*1887 (D. 1698); *Bouquet des champs*, *c.*1888 (D. 4); *Bouquet*, 1888 (D. 5); *Bouquet de roses*, 1889 (D. 6); *Boules de neige*, *c.*1891, 1892, 1892 (D. 30, 31, 32); *Branches fleuries*, *c.*1899 (D. 01805); *Bouquet sur une table*, 1900 (D. 01824)
LIT J. et H. (here D.) Dauberville, *P. Bonnard, Catalogue raisonné*, Paris (Bernheim Jeune) 1965; *Pavière III*, pt. 2; *Witt*

BONNARDEL, Alexandre-François ***1867–1942***
b. Pajay (Isère). Pupil of Lyon BA and Zacharie. Taught Lyon BA. Painted portraits, genre and flowers. His wife, Marcelle Bonnardel, also painted flowers
LIT *Bénézit*; *Hardouin-Fugier Grafe*; *Thieme*

BONNARDEL, Pierre-Antoine ***1824–1856***
b. Bonnay (Saône-et-Loire). Pupil of Thierriat, Lyon BA (CFD 1851)
LIT *Hardouin-Fugier Grafe*

BONNASSIEUX, Jules ***b.1873***
Pupil of Castex-Dégrange, Lyon BA (CFD 1892)
LIT *Hardouin-Fugier Grafe*

BONNAT, Léon ***1834–1922***
The famous portrait and figure painter produced some flower-pieces e.g. *Capucines rouges et jaunes dans un vase flammé gris-vert*, Musée Bonnat Bayonne; *Bouquet de fleurs*, Pau Salon 1878
LIT *Orsay*; *Pau Salon* 1878; *Pau, L. Bonnat*, Musée des Beaux Arts, 1978

BONNEFOND, Claude ***1796–1860***
b. Lyon. Studied at Lyon BA from 1808. with Grognard and Revoil. Debut Paris Salon 1817; worked in Paris at the Atelier Guérin. Exhib. Paris from 1824: interiors, genre, landscapes. In 1831 became director of the Lyon BA and teacher of painting. M: Cambridge, Fitzwilliam (Broughton coll.), *Bouquet of flowers against an urn*, 1820, wc.
LIT *Bellier*; *Thieme*. JLC

BONNEFOY, Adrien-Adolphe
b. Paris. Pupil of J.P. Laurens. Exhib. *Chrysanthèmes*, *Roses*, Paris Noir et Blanc Salon 1888
LIT *Bénézit*; *Paris Noir et Blanc Salon* 1888

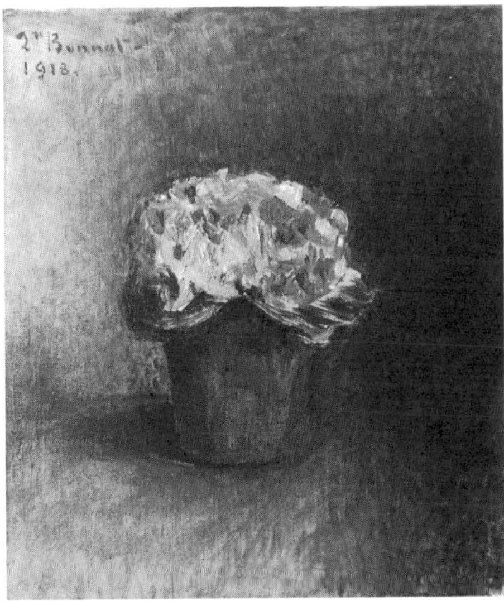

Léon Bonnat

Oil on canvas, 18 × 15¾ in. (46 × 41 cm.), signed and dated 1918
Bayonne, Musée Bonnat

BONNEFOY, Henri-Arthur ***1839–1917***
b. Boulogne-sur-mer. (Pas-de-Calais) Pupil of L. Cogniet. Landscapes and occasionally still-lifes. Paris Salon debut in 1857 with a still-life
LIT *Bénézit*. PM

BONNEMAISON, Georges ***d.1885***
b. Toulouse (Haute-Garonne). Exhib. landscapes and flowers Paris Salon 1874, 1875
LIT *Bénézit*; *Witt*

BONNET, Alfred ***b.1847***
b. Grenoble (Isère). Studied Grenoble BA and Lyon BA. Exhib. *Fleurs* Lyon Salon 1876
LIT *Hardouin-Fugier Grafe*; Lyon Salon 1876; *Witt*

BONNET or BONET, Etienne-Michel
Pupil of Thierriat, Lyon BA (CFD 1826). Exhib. flowers Lyon Salon 1851
LIT *Hardouin-Fugier Grafe*

BONNETON, Joseph-Cécile ***b.1809***
Pupil of Thierriat, Lyon BA (CFD 1827). *Coupe garnie de fleurs près d'une fontaine*, Lyon Salon 1831
LIT *Hardouin-Fugier Grafe*

BONNEVAL, André
b. Saint-Myon (Drôme). Pupil of Van Dael. Exhib. flowers 1795–1799 and 1810 Paris Salon
LIT *Bellier*; *Bénézit*; *Paris Salon 1810*

BONNOT, Albert Louis
b. Paris. Pupil of Gérôme. Exhib. *Chrysanthèmes*, Paris Salon 1876
LIT *Bellier*

BONOME, Adolphine
b. Paris. Pupil of Colin-Libour. Portrait, genre and flower painter. Exhib. Paris Salon *Chrysanthèmes*, 1875, *Pensées*, 1876, *Chrysanthèmes*, 1877
LIT *Bellier*; *Bénézit*; *Paris Salon* 1875

BONTHOUX, Jean-Louis ***b.1828***
b. Lyon. Pupil of Thierriat, Lyon BA (CFD 1844). Exhib. still-lifes and flowers Lyon Salon 1846–1875 e.g. *Fleurs*, 1862. His *Premières fleurs de printemps* was bought by the Lyon Société des Amis-des-Arts (1864). His *Fleurs et fruits* was won by Comte Palikao at the 1866 Lyon Société des Amis-des-Arts raffle. Three more flower-pieces were in the same committee's 1871, 1872 and 1873 raffles.
M: Clermont-Ferrand
LIT *Bénézit*; *Hardouin-Fugier Grafe*

BONVALLET, *see* BARILLOT

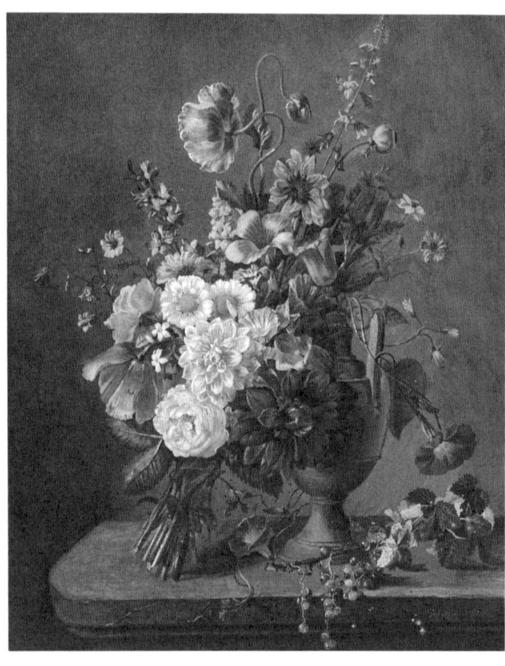

Claude Bonnefond

Bodycolour on vellum, 23¾ × 19 in. (60.9 × 48.3 cm.), signed and dated 1820
Cambridge, Fitzwilliam Museum (Broughton Collection)

BONVIN, François ***1817–1887***
b. Paris. Pupil of Atelier des Gobelins. The well-known portrait, figure and genre painter occasionally produced some flower-pieces e.g. *Fleurs*, Langlois, Jersey 1965, *Roses*, 1878, Galerie Delestre, Paris 1978
LIT *Apollo* Sept. 1965 (ill.); *Bénézit*; *Connoisseur*, Sept. 1978 (ill.); Moreau-Nélaton. *F. Bonvin* ... Paris (Laurens) 1927; *Thieme*; G. Weisberg *F. Bonvin* ... Paris (Geoffroy-Dèchaume) 1979; G. Weisberg *Chardin and the Still-Life Tradition*, Cleveland, 1979 (ill.); Wheelock Whitney, New York, exhib. *F. Bonvin*, 1984

BONVIN, Léon ***1834–1866***
b. Vaugirard (Seine), brother of François Bonvin. Pupil of Cours de dessin, rue de l'École de Médecine, Paris. Painted flowers in oils and wc, eg. *Vase de fleurs*, 1863, wc, and *Flowers at a window*, both Walters Art Gallery, Baltimore
LIT *Bellier*; *Bénézit*; Cleveland, Weisberg, Talbot, *Chardin and the still-life tradition in France*, 1979 (ill.); G. Weisberg, *Léon Bonvin*, Cleveland, 1980 (ill.); *Louvre*; *Thieme*; *Witt*

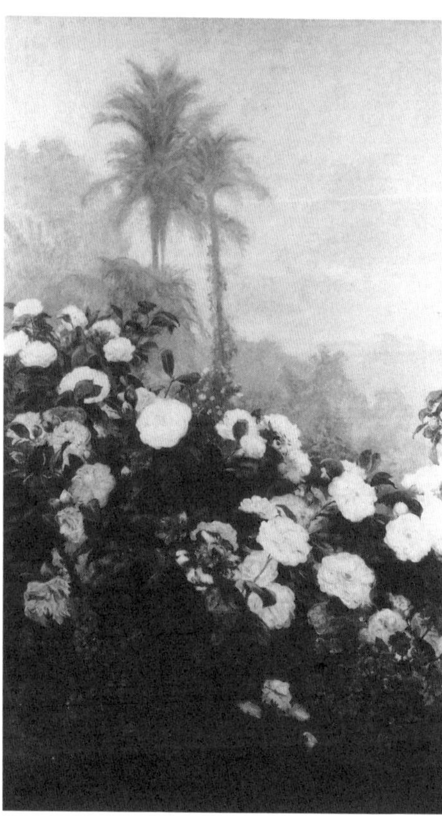

Henri Arthur Bonnefoy

Oil on canvas, 63½ × 34¼ in. (161 × 87 cm.), signed
Courtesy Christie's, London

BONVOISIN, Catherine-Hélie ***née*** **Lassare** ***b.1788***
b. Paris. Pupil of Jean Bonvoisin (1752–1837) her husband. Redouté and Chazal. Exhib. Paris Salon 1831–1837 e.g. *Fleurs*, wc, 1831, *Pivoine de Chine*, 1833, *Bouquet de fleurs de pêcher, roses thé, pivoines*, 1834, *Bouquet de jasmin du Cap, primevères de Chine, oreille d'ours*, 1834
LIT *Bellier*; *Bénézit*; *Faré* 1962, p. 148; *Paris Salon* 1833; *Pavière*

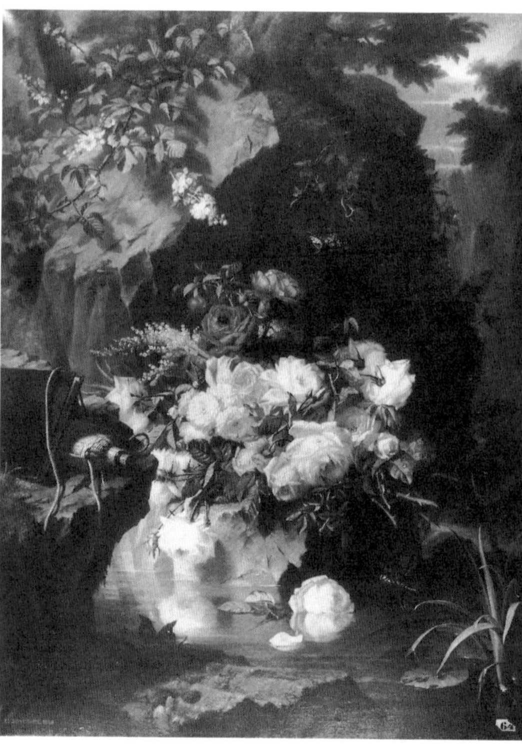

Jean-Louis Bonthoux

Oil on canvas, signed and dated 1868
Clermont-Ferrand, Musée de Bargoin

BONY, Jean-François ***1754–1825***
b. Givors (Rhône). Pupil of Gonichon (Lyon). Textile designer. Professor of flower design at Lyon BA 1809–10. Designed hangings for Saint-Cloud and for Empress Marie-Louise's drawing-room at Versailles. Exhib. flowers in oils or gouache Paris Salon 1819. Bony's *Le printemps* is in the Musée des Beaux-Arts, Lyon. A collection of designs in wc and gouache is in the Musée Historique des Tissus, Lyon. M: Lille, *Coupe de Fleurs et de fruits*, inscribed "Fait par Bony dessinateur de sa fabrique d'etoffes de soie Lyon 1815."
LIT *Hardouin-Fugier Grafe* (ill.); *Hardouin-Fugier Grafe* 1982 (ill.); *Thieme*

BOQUET
At Sèvres 1892–1902
LIT *Orsay*

BOQUET, *see* FAJON

BORD, Léon de
b. Bordeaux (Gironde). Exhib. Paris Salon *Une bourriche de pétunias*, 1866, *Panier de fleurs d'automne*, 1868
LIT *Bénézit*; *Witt*

BOREL, Anna-Jeanne-Charlotte ***b.1869***
b. Lille (Nord). Pupil of Écoles Académiques de Lille and P. de Winter. Exhib. Amiens Salon 1890, Lille Salon 1893
LIT *Bénézit*

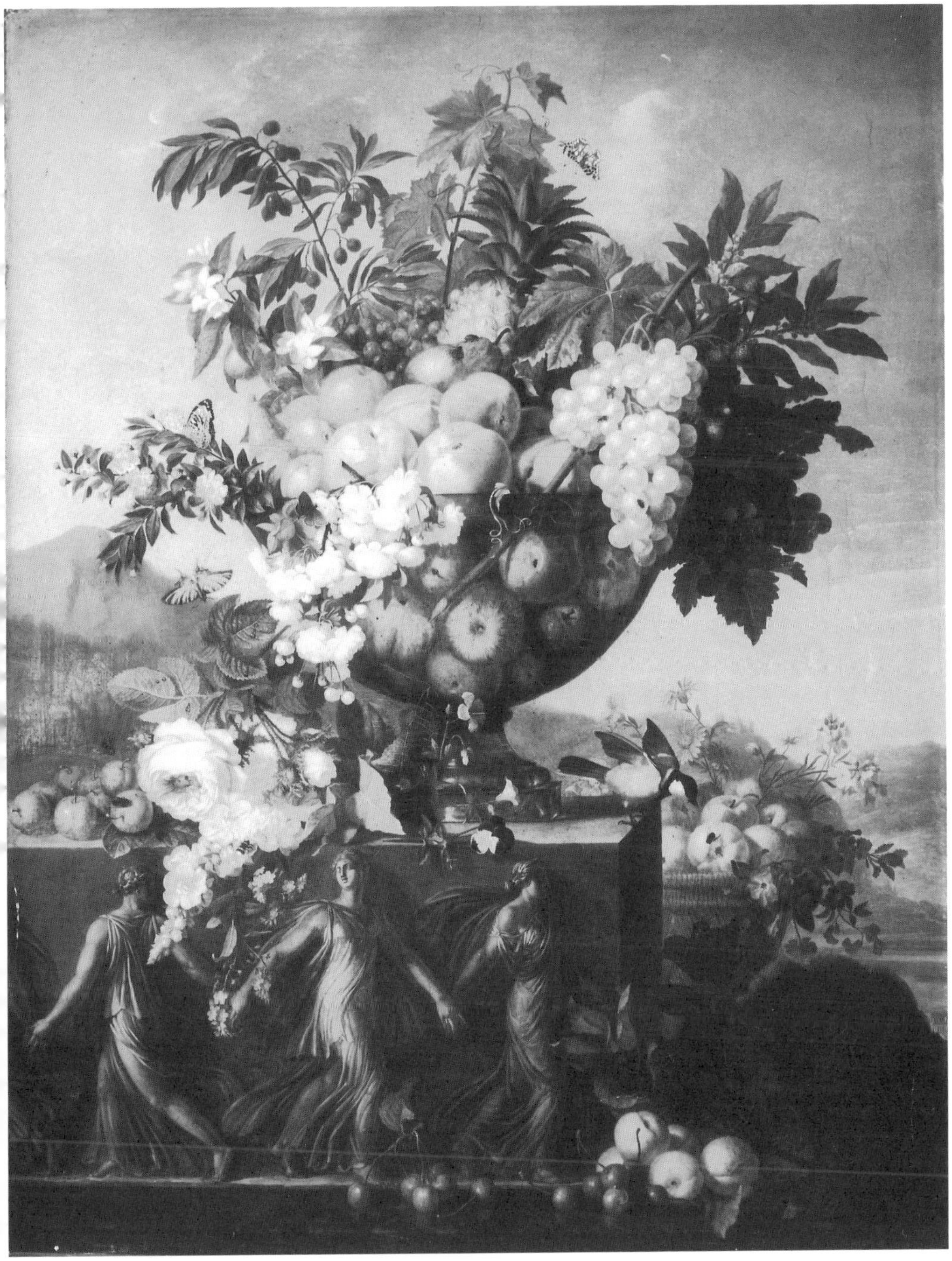

Jean-François Bony (*left*)

Oil on canvas, 45½ × 35¾ in. (116 × 91 cm.), signed, inscribed 'Fait par Bony dessinateur de sa fabrique d'étoffes de soie Lyon'; dated 1815
Lille, Musée des Beaux-Arts

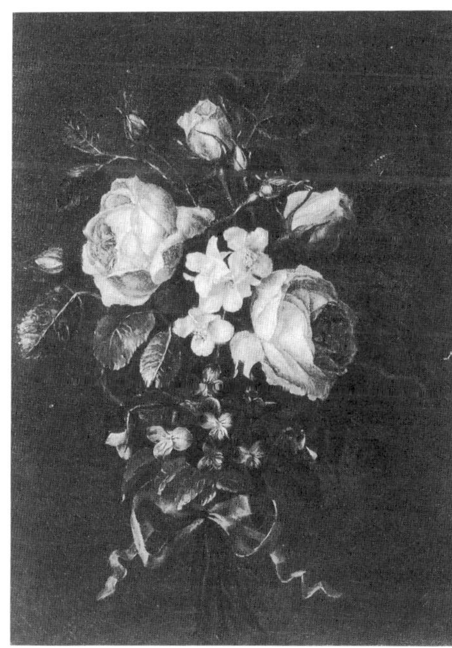

Jean-Baptiste Borély

Oil on canvas, 13 × 9⅞ in. (33.1 × 25.1 cm.), signed and dated 1807
Courtesy S. Nystad, The Hague (photo: RKD)

BOREL, Henriette-Marie-Evelina *b.1871*
b. Lille (Nord). Sister of Anna Borel. Pupil of Écoles Académiques de Lille and P. de Winter. Painted still-lifes, portraits and flowers. Exhib. Paris Salon 1890, Amiens Salon 1890, Lille Salon 1893
LIT *Bénézit*

BORÉLY, Jean-Baptiste *1776–1823*
b. Montpellier (Hérault). *Roses et pensées*, private collection
LIT *Bénézit*; *Mitchell* (ill.)

BORNOT, Jules-Paul-Antoine *1802–1863*
b. Savoisi (Côte-d'Or). Pupil of Gros and Paris BA (1818). Exhib. *Bouquet où la rose fortunée est alliée au lys*, Paris Salon 1822
LIT *Bellier*; *Bénézit*; *Revue Universelle des Arts*, XVL, 355–6

BOROT, Armande
Exhib. Dijon Salon, *Fleurs*, wc, 1837, *Fleurs*, 1840
LIT *Dijon Salon* 1837, 1840. CL

BORROMÉE *d.1850*
b. Paris. Designed plates for J.B. Bory de Saint-Vincent *La nouvelle Flore du Péloponnèse et des Cyclades*, Paris, Strasbourg (Levrault) 1838 and for many other works. More of a zoological artist. Paris Muséum d'Histoire Naturelle, wc on vellum
LIT *Laissus*; *Nissen* I, 213; *Sitwell*

BORY DE SAINT-VINCENT, Jean-Baptiste-Georges-Marcelin *1780–1846*
b. Agen (Lot-et-Garonne). Designed plates for Bélanger's *Voyage aux Indes Orientales*, 1825–1829, and for his *Nouvelle Flore du Péloponnèse et des Cyclades*, Paris, Strasbourg (Levrault) 1838
LIT Paris Muséum d'Histoire Naturelle; *Nissen* I, 126, 213; *Sitwell*

BOS, Camille
b. Grenoble (Isère). Exhib. *Chrysanthèmes*, *Roses*, Grenoble Salon 1899
LIT *Grenoble Salon* 1899. MW

BOSGUERARD, Gabrielle de
b. Fort-de-France (Martinique). Pupil of Mme Gérôme and Regnard. Exhib. Paris Salon *Fleurs*, faience, 1879, *Fleurs et oiseaux*, 1880
LIT *Bellier*

BOSQUIER, Charles-Joseph *b.1824*
b. Paris. Painted still-lifes. Exhib. *Roses et giroflées*, *Fleurs des prés*, Lyon Salon 1869
LIT *Bénézit*; *Lyon Salon* 1869

BOSSER, Eugène
b. Paris. Pupil of Bonnat. Painted landscapes and exhib. *Boules de neige et lilas*, Dijon Salon 1894
LIT *Dijon Salon* 1894. CL

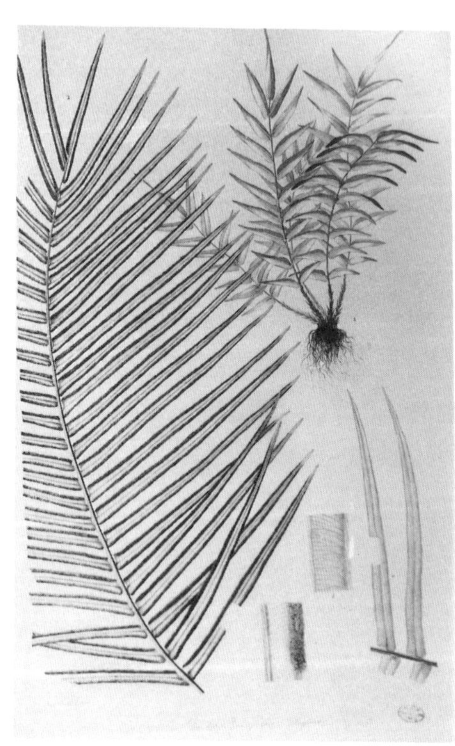

Borromée

Engraving after a drawing, signed
Paris, Muséum National d'Histoire Naturelle

BOST, Antoine or Tony *b.1816*
Pupil of Thierriat, Lyon BA (CFD 1835). Exhib. *Panier de fleurs*, Paris Salon 1864
LIT *Hardouin-Fugier Grafe*

BOST, Jean-Baptiste (?)
Entered gouache in 1842–1843 Lyon FDC. May be the same as J.B. Bost who studied at Lyon BA 1836–1840
LIT *Hardouin-Fugier Grafe*

BOST, *see* SIEFERT

BOSVIEL, Maurice-Marie *b.1835*
Pupil of Reignier, Lyon BA (CFD 1858)
LIT *Hardouin-Fugier Grafe*

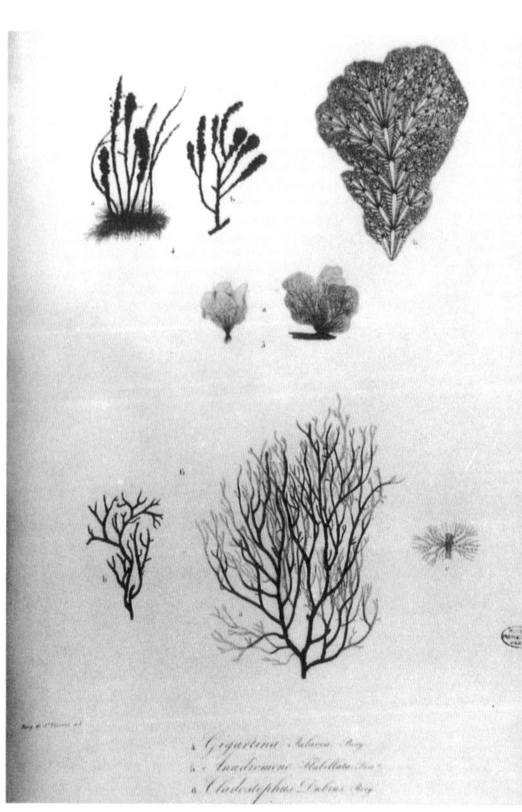

Jean-Baptiste-Georges-Marcelin Bory de Saint-Vincent

Engraving after a drawing, signed,
Paris, Muséum National d'Histoire Naturelle

BOUCHARLAT, Jean-Claude-Marie *b.1826*
Pupil of Thierriat, Lyon BA (CFD 1843)
LIT *Hardouin-Fugier Grafe*

BOUCHARLAT, Pierre
Pupil of Thierriat, Lyon BA (CFD 1825)
LIT *Hardouin-Fugier Grafe*

BOUCHÉ, Philippe
b. Lormes (Nièvre). Exhib. *Panier de bruyères*, Paris Salon 1875
LIT *Paris Salon* 1875

BOUCHER, Guillaume
Pupil of Thierriat, Lyon BA (CFD 1848)
LIT *Hardouin-Fugier Grafe*

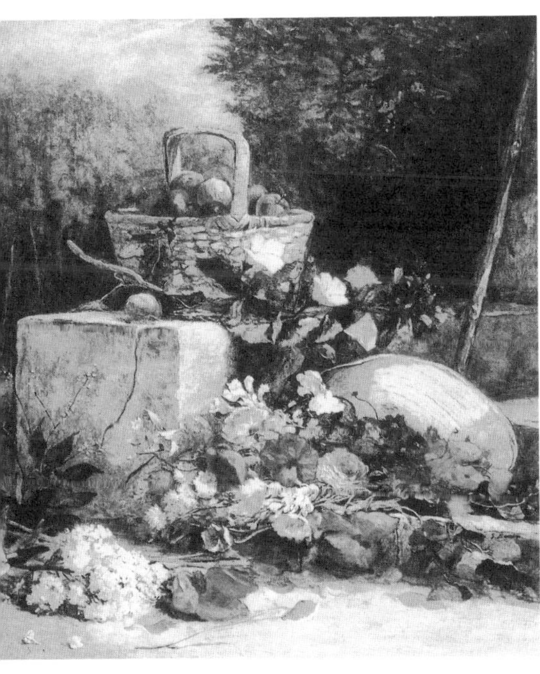

Eugène-Louis Boudin

Oil on canvas, 35½ × 31½ in. (90 × 80 cm.), signed
Courtesy Sotheby's, London

BOUCHER, Urbain *b.1826*
Pupil of Thierriat, Lyon BA (CFD 1844). Exhib. flowers in gouache, Lyon Salon 1850
LIT *Hardouin-Fugier Grafe*

BOUCHEROT, Zulma
Pupil of Mme Voruz. Exhib. Paris UFPS *Iris et boules de neige*, *Lilas*, *Roses*, wc, 1896, *Fleurs de printemps*, *Marguerites*, *Violettes*, wc, 1898
LIT *Paris UFPS* 1896, 1898

BOUCHET-DEDIEU, Jane *d.1926*
b. Paris. Pupil of J. Lefebvre, B. Constant and J. Adler. Exhib. landscapes and flowers, Paris Salon
LIT *Bénézit*

BOUCHIER, Cornélie
Exhib. *Corbeille de roses*, Paris Salon 1850
LIT *Paris Salon* 1850

BOUCHON, Antoine *b.1829*
Pupil of Thierriat, Lyon BA (CFD 1847)
LIT *Hardouin-Fugier Grafe*

BOUCHON, Louise-Marie
Pupil of F. Rivoire. Exhib. *Oeillets*, fan-leaf, Paris Salon 1898
LIT *Paris Salon* 1898

BOUDET, Marie
Pupil of Mme Trébuchet. Exhib. *Roses*, *Paris Salon 1880*
LIT *Paris Salon* 1880

BOUDET, Pierre *1800–1883*
op. Sèvres 1827–1832
LIT *Bénézit*; *Brunet Préaud*; *Witt*

BOUDET, Valentine
Pupil of Lesourd de Beauregard, Gouillet and Levasseur. Exhib. *Dahlias*, Paris Salon 1880
LIT *Paris Salon* 1880

BOUDIN, Eugène-Louis *1824–1898*
The famous landscape painter produced a few flower-pieces e.g. *Vase de giroflées, oeillets d'Inde, lilas*, Musée du Havre, *Fleurs dans un verre*. Fondation Anne et Albert Prouvost, Marcq-en-Bareuil; *Flowers and Fruit in a Garden*, Sotheby's, London, 14 May 1980, lot 209
LIT G. Jean-Aubry *E. Boudin*, Neuchâtel (Ides et Calendes) 1968–1977, Orsay; Schmit, R., *Eugène Boudin: 1824–1898*, three vols (Paris) 1973; G. Weisberg *Chardin and the Still-Life Tradition*, Cleveland, 1979 (ill.); *Thieme*

BOUËT, Marie-Josephe
b. Le Havre (Seine-Maritime). Exhib. *Lys tigria*, wc, Paris Salon 1880
LIT *Paris Salon* 1880

BOUET, Pierre-Henri *1828–1889*
Exhib. Paris Salon 1857–1880. Painted landscapes, seascapes and, occasionally, flowers
LIT *Bénézit*

BOUFFAY, Caroline
b. Haubourdin (Nord). Pupil of Bourgogne and Rigolot. Exhib. Paris Salon from 1879 e.g. *Fleurs d'automne*, 1879, *Pavots*, 1880, *Myosotis et roses*, 1881, *Fleurs de Provence*, 1882; Dijon Salon, *Une touffe d'anémones*, *Roses thé et violettes de Parme*, 1883, *Roses*, 1885, *Fleurs de France*, 1890, *Fleurs de Provence*, 1892, *Buisson de roses*, 1894, *Chrysanthèmes blancs*, 1894; *Paniers de reines-marguerites*, Paris UFPS, 1896
LIT *Bellier*; *Bénézit*; *Dijon Salon* 1883, 1885, 1890, 1892, 1894; *Paris UFPS* 1896

BOUFFÉ, *see* HAQUETTE

BOUGET, Auguste-Amédée ***b.1833***
Pupil of Thierriat, Lyon BA (CFD 1849)
LIT *Hardouin-Fugier Grafe*

BOUHIER, François
Pupil of Thierriat, Lyon BA (CFD 1827–1830)
LIT *Hardouin-Fugier Grafe*

BOUILLAT, Edmé-François ***1741–1810***
Worked at Sèvres. Works in the Musée de Sèvres
LIT *Brunet Préaud*; Sèvres Arch. BVIII

BOUILLET, Alexis ***1848–1899***
Pupil of Reignier, Lyon BA (CFD 1862). Textile designer
LIT *Hardouin-Fugier Grafe*

BOUILLET, Antoine-Joseph
Pupil of Reignier, Lyon BA (CFD 1862)
LIT *Hardouin-Fugier Grafe*

BOUILLET, ***née*** **Angélique Lambert** ***d.1866***
Exhib. Paris Salon *Fleurs et fruits*, 1838, *Médaillon de fleurs*, 1851
LIT *Bellier*; *Bénézit*

BOUIN, Lucie-Alexandre-Antoinette
Pupil of Mlle Mikulska. Exhib. *Fleurs*, gouache, fan-leaf, Paris Salon 1879
LIT *Bellier*

BOUISSET, Etienne-Maurice-Firmin ***1859–1925***
b. Moissac (Tarn-et-Garonne). Pupil of Cabanel, Paris BA. Book illustrator. His *Fleurs animées* is in the Paris BMAD (Maciet coll.)
LIT *Bénézit*; *Paris BMAD*

BOULANGER, Annette ***1804–1853***
Sister of Louis Boulanger (1806–1867). Exhib. Paris Salon 1834–1839 e.g. *Bouquet de fleurs*, wc., 1835, 1837, *Etude de fleurs*, 1837,
LIT *Bellier; Bénézit; Paris Salon* 1835, 1837

BOULARD, Auguste ***1825–1897***
Pupil of L. Cogniet and J. Dupré. Painted landscapes, genre and, occasionally, flowers e.g. *Roses coupées*, *Brassée de roses*, *Pâquerettes dans un vase*, *Jonchée de roses sur le sol*, *Parterre de roses*, *Des roses*, *Fleurs*, *Gerbe de roses*, Boulard sale, Drouot, Paris, 10 Apr. 1900, *Vase de roses*, Galliéra, Paris, 1971, *Roses blanches*, Sotheby's, London, 24 Oct. 1974, lot 5
LIT *Bailly-Herzberg, Daubigny*, 1975, p. 85; *Bellier*; *Bénézit*; *Orsay*; *Thieme*

BOULARD, Auguste ***1852–1927***
b. Paris. Pupil of Auguste Boulard, his father, and Bracquemond. Exhib. Paris Salon from 1874, landscapes, seascapes, genre and, occasionally, flowers
LIT *Bénézit*; *Schurr* II, 50

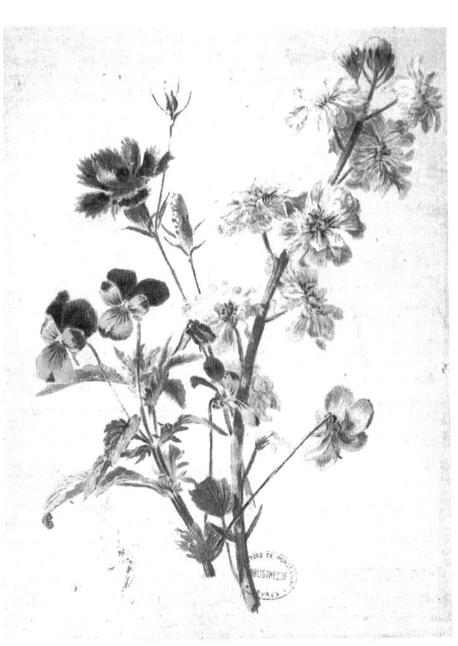

Edmé-François Bouillat

Watercolour on paper
Sèvres, Manufacture Nationale de Sèvres

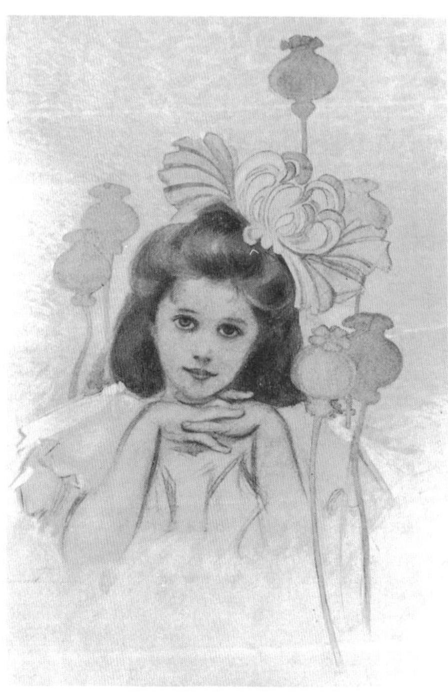

Etienne-Maurice-Firmin Bouisset

Watercolour on paper, 7 × 8¾ in. (17 × 22 cm.), signed
Paris, BMAD (Maciet Collection)

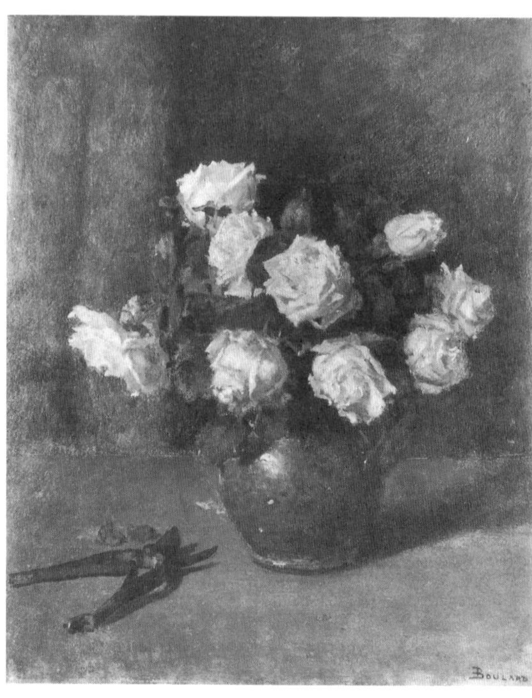

Auguste Boulard

Oil on canvas, 21¼ × 16¼ in. (54 × 41.5 cm.), signed
Courtesy Sotheby's, London

BOULARD, Emile ***1863–1943***
Pupil of Auguste Boulard (1825–1897), his father. Friendly with Joseph (1862–1921) and Franck (1858–1924) Bail. Married Amélie Bail. Painted flowers cf. cat. *Les Amis de l'Isle-Adam*, 1979
LIT *Bénézit*; L'Isle-Adam, *Les Amis de l'Isle-Adam*, Musée Louis Senlecq, 1979; *Orsay*; *Schurr* II, 52

BOULARD, J.B.
Pâquerettes dans un vase, Paris BMAD (Maciet coll.)
LIT *Paris BMAD*

BOULAY de la, ***see*** **CHAMPEAUX**

BOULET, Cyprien-Eugène ***1877–1927***
b. Toulouse (Haute-Garonne). Pupil of J.P. Laurens, R. Collin. Painted genre, portraits and, occasionally, flowers
LIT *Bellier*; *Schurr* III, 21; *Witt*

BOULET, J.
Exhib. *Géraniums*, *Fleurs*, Dijon Salon 1892
LIT *Dijon Salon* 1892. CL

BOULIGAND, D.
Exhib. *Etude de fleurs*, wc, Paris SNBA 1894
LIT *Paris SNBA* 1894

BOULIGAND, L.
Exhib. *Fleurs*, wc, Paris SNBA 1894
LIT *Paris SNBA* 1894

BOULLAY, ***see*** **MAILLET**

BOURBON, Emilie
This needy and disabled flower painter and drawing mistress repeatedly applied for a state allowance from 1860 to 1875
LIT Paris Arch. *Nat. F21:274, 288*

BOURCET, Lucile
Exhib. *Fleurs de printemps*, Dijon Salon 1894
LIT *Dijon Salon* 1894. CL

BOURDET, Joseph-Guillaume ***1799–1869***
Fleurs, 1820, Paris Muséum d'Histoire Naturelle (currently untraceable)
LIT *Laissus*; *Schurr* III, 12

BOURDON, Adine
b. Paris. Pupil of Lesourd de Beauregard, Levasseur and Gouillet. Exhib. Paris Salon 1870–1878 e.g. *Bouquet*, gouache, 1870, *Bouquet de marguerites*, wc, 1872, *Dahlias*, gouache, 1878
LIT *Bellier*; *Bénézit*; *Paris Salon* 1872

BOURET, Jean-Louis-Antoine-Marie
Pupil of Mme Chéron and Dufaux. Exhib. Paris Salon 1876–1879. Painted still-lifes and, occasionally, flowers
LIT *Bénézit*

BOURGEAT, Sébastien ***b.1837***
Pupil of Reignier, Lyon BA (CFD 1860)
LIT *Hardouin-Fugier Grafe*

BOURGEOIS, Anna-Louise
Pupil of Mazerolles and Urbain Bourgeois. Exhib. Paris Salon from 1877 e.g. *Giroflées*, 1877, *Primevères*, 1878, *Giroflées et chrysanthèmes*, 1882
LIT *Bellier*; *Bénézit*

BOURGEOIS, Léon ***b.1834***
Pupil of Reignier, Lyon BA (CFD 1854)
LIT *Hardouin-Fugier Grafe*

BOURGEOIS, Louis ***b.1873***
Pupil of Castex-Dégrange, Lyon BA (CFD 1891–1893)
LIT *Hardouin-Fugier Grafe*

BOURGEOIS, Victor-Ferdinand ***1870–1957***
b. Amiens (Somme). Pupil of École des BA de la Somme and Paris Arts Décoratifs. Friendly with Guillaumin. Painted landscapes and, occasionally, flowers, e.g. *Oranges, figues et fleurs d'oranger*, Drouot, Paris, 5 Dec. 1969
LIT *Bénézit*; *Orsay*

BOURGOGNE, Pierre ***1838–1904***
b. Paris. Pupil of V. Galland, C. Polish and Lequien. Exhib. Paris 1869–1904, Royal Academy (London) 1888, e.g. Paris Salon, *Buisson de roses*, 1875, *Giroflées*, 1875, 1880; *Fleurs*, Lyon Salon, 1881; *Dahlias* (300 francs) Strasbourg Salon 1883; Paris Salon *Fleurs et fruits d'automne*, 1890, *Fleurs et fruits d'éte*, 1892, *Fleurs de printemps*, 1892; *Cueillette au printemps*, 1894; *Premières fleurs*, Dijon Salon 1897. His *Fleurs de printemps* was presented to the Emperor of China by the French government in 1897. Bourgogne provided tapestry designs for the Beauvais factory. A prolific, highly successful flower painter. *Roses and flowers in an urn*, Christie's, London, 21 Oct. 1983, lot 105. Many of his works were bought for French museums e.g. Béziers, *Fleurs de Printemps*, 1888 (exhib. Beziers Salon 1892 and bought that year for the museum by the Béziers Commission des Beaux-Arts); Blois, *1899*, *Étalage de Fleurs* (2,200 francs); Issoudun, 1890, *Fleur et fruits*; Morlaix, 1883, *Giroflées*; Rennes, *Les dons de l'automne*; Toulouse, *Roses Thé*; Tulle, 1889, *Chez la fleuriste* (1,500 francs)
LIT *Bellier*; *Bénézit*; *Dijon Salon* 1890; *Lyon Salon* 1881, 1885; Paris Arch. Nat. F21:2144, 4294, 4500; *Paris Salon* 1875, 1880; *Paris SNBA* 1891, 1892, 1894 (ill.), 1895 (ill.), 1896 (ill.), 1899; *Strasbourg Salon* 1883; *Witt*

BOURGOIN, Désiré
Painted landscapes, figures, portraits and, occasionally, flowers. Exhib. Paris Salon from 1870 e.g. *Bouquet de roses du*

Bengale, wc, 1872, *Fleurs de printemps*, wc, 1872
LIT *Bellier*

BOURGONNIER, Berthe-Claude
1860–1921
b. Paris. Pupil of P. Delorme. Painted flowers and genre. Exhib. *Hortensias*, pastel, Paris UFPS 1898. Musée de Brive, *Tulipes de Chine*, pastel (bought for the museum by the State 1902)
LIT *Bellier*; *Bénézit*; Paris Arch. *Nat. F21:2058, 4500; Paris UFPS* 1898; *Schurr* IV, 120; *Thieme*

BOURLY, Edmond ***b.1835***
Pupil of Reignier, Lyon BA (CFD 1854)
LIT *Hardouin-Fugier Grafe*

BOURNE or BOURNES, Joseph
1740–1808
op. Textile designer. His late works are flower and fruit pieces exhibited after his death. *Fleurs et fruits*, Weinmüller, Munich, 23 Jan. 1974
LIT *Bénézit*; *Thieme*; *Witt*

BOURON, Hélène
b. Agen (Lot-et-Garonne). Pupil of Mme Colin-Libour. Exhib. Paris Salon *c.*1880 e.g. *Pivoines*, porcelain, 1882; *Fleurs de pavots*, wc, fan-leaf, Paris UFPS 1888
LIT *Bellier*; *Bénézit*; *Paris UFPS* 1888

BOUROTTE, Coralie
Exhib. *Un bouquet de fleurs*, wc, Poitiers Salon 1887
LIT *Poitiers Salon* 1887. BG

BOURSEY, Jules
b. Châlon-sur-Saône (Saône-et-Loire). Exhib. *Chrysanthèmes*, Paris Indép. 1887
LIT *Paris Indép.* 1887

BOUSQUET, Hélène du
Exhib. Paris Salon *c.*1890. Painted *Fleurs et nacre*
LIT *Bénézit*

BOUTROUX, Christine-Félicité
Exhib. *Iris et glaïeuls*, Saint-Etienne Salon 1882
LIT *Hardouin-Fugier Bringuier*; *Saint-Etienne Salon* 1882

BOUVAIST, *see* COROT

BOUVERAT, Antoine ***b.1845***
Pupil of Reignier, Lyon BA (CFD 1860)
LIT *Hardouin-Fugier Grafe*

BOUVERAT, Fleury-Hippolyte
Pupil of Castex-Dégrange, Lyon BA (CFD 1894)
LIT *Hardouin-Fugier Grafe*

BOUVERET, *see* DAGNAN

BOUVIER, Alfred
b. Paris. Exhib. flowers and still-lifes Paris Salon 1847, 1848, 1849
LIT *Bellier*; *Bénézit*

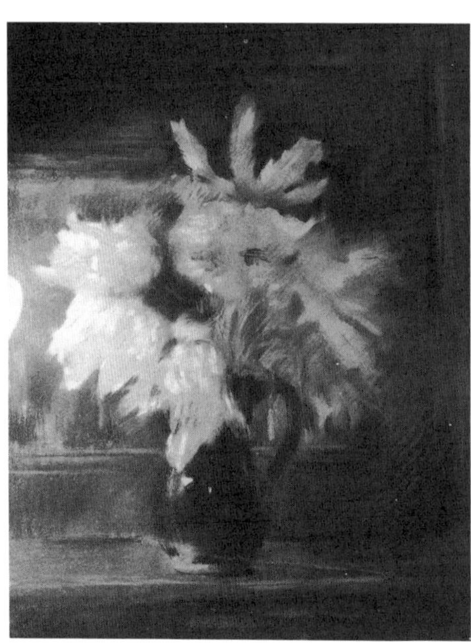

Berthe-Claude Bourgonnier

Pastel on canvas, $25\frac{1}{4} \times 20\frac{3}{4}$ in. (64.5 × 53 cm.), Brive, Musée E. Rupin

BOUVIER, Jeanne
Exhib. *Iris*, Dijon Salon 1894
LIT *Dijon Salon* 1894. CL

BOUVIER, Joseph-Laurent-Daniel
1841–1901
b. Vinay (Isère). Pupil of Capelle. *Vase de fleurs* in Musée de Grenoble (1905 gift

Joseph Bourne or Bournes

Oil on canvas, 20 × 24 in. (51 × 61 cm.), signed
Private collection

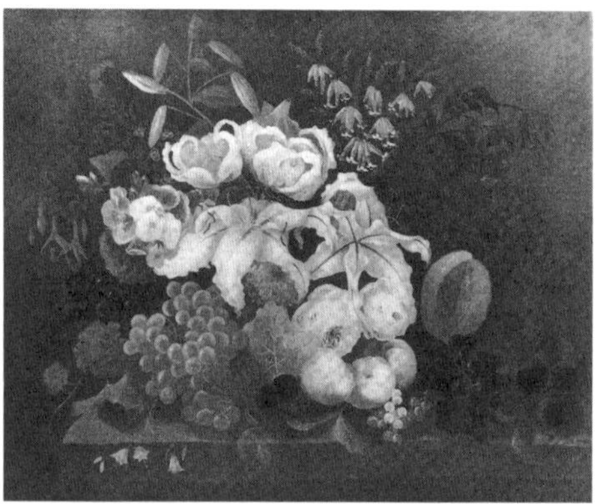

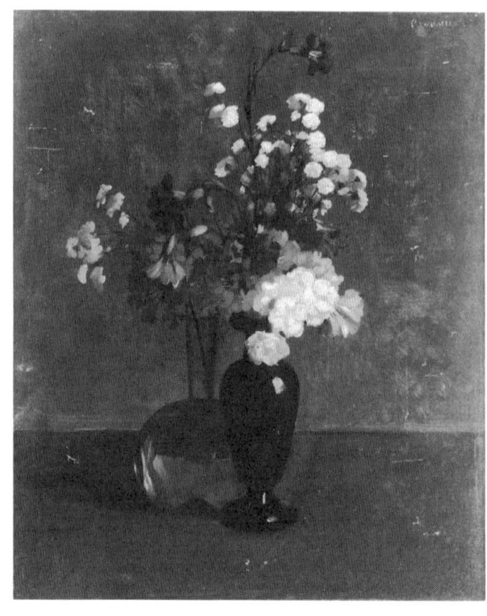

Joseph-Laurent-Daniel Bouvier

Oil on canvas, $21\frac{3}{4} \times 17\frac{3}{4}$ in. (55 × 46 cm.), Grenoble, Musée de Peinture et de Sculpture

from Moreau-Nélaton). May be the same as Laurent Bouvier who exhib. *Vase de fleurs*, Lyon Salon 1868
LIT *Bellier*; *Bénézit*; Grenoble Musée doc.; *Lyon Salon* 1868

BOUVIER, Victorine *1863–1943*
Pupil at Lyon of Loubet and Tollet. Painted portraits, interiors, genre, occasionally flowers. Exhib. Lyon Salon from 1889
LIT *Bénézit*. PM

BOUVRET, *see* EMERIC

BOUZANQUET, Pierre-Benoit *b.1814*
Pupil of Thierriat, Lyon BA (CFD 1831). Exhib. *Fleurs et fruits dans une coupe*, Lyon Salon 1833
LIT *Hardouin-Fugier Grafe*

BOVIER-LAPIERRE, Jeanne *b.1868*
b. Clermont-Ferrand (Puy-de-Dôme). Pupil of C. Barriot, Sarrazin and A. Perrachon, fl. Lyon *c.*1895–1957. Exhib. *La jeune fleuriste*, Lyon Salon 1895
LIT *Bénézit*; *Hardouin-Fugier Grafe*; *Schurr* II, 94

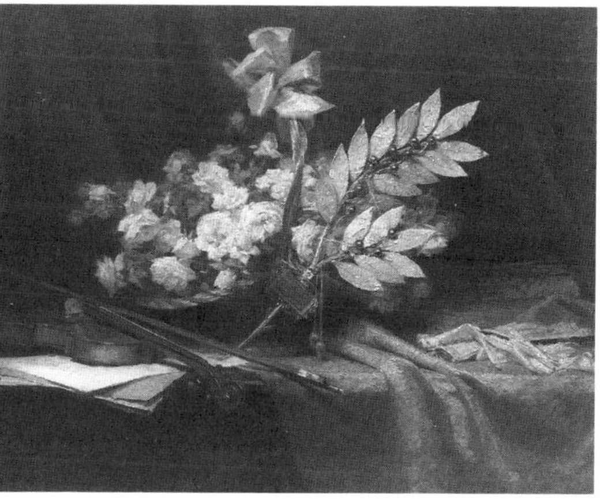

Victorine Bouvier

Oil on panel, 9½ × 13 in. (24 × 33 cm.), signed and dated 1900
Private collection

BOY, Antoine
Pupil of Thierriat, Lyon BA (CFD 1824–6). Painted still-lifes and flowers. Textile designer
LIT *Hardouin-Fugier Grafe*

BOYÉ, Rose-Marie-Emma
Pupil of Balleroy. Exhib. flowers on porcelain, Paris Salon *c.*1875–8 e.g. *Roses de Provins panachées et bluets*, after C. Labbé, 1875
LIT *Bellier*; *Paris Salon* 1875

BOYER, Claude
Exhib. *Chrysanthèmes*, Dijon Salon 1897
LIT *Dijon Salon* 1897

BRACQUEMOND, Félix *1833–1914*
b. Paris. Pupil of Joseph Guichard. Painter, engraver, ceramist and decorator. Produced flower designs (in pencil), wc and engraved for some of his dinner sets 1866–1880 e.g. *Service Rousseau*, 1866, partly inspired by Hokusai's Mangwa. This set was exhibited in 1869 at the Paris Union Centrale des Arts Décoratifs and often re-issued. Designed plates for the 1879 *Service à fleurs et à rubans* made by Barluet (Montereau) for Haviland (Limoges). Designed stylized flowers for typographic ornaments (*Gazette des Beaux-Arts*, May 1884), jewels, furniture and the wood-panelling in the billiard-room of Baron Vitta's Evian villa La Sapinière *c.*1900
LIT J. and L. d'Albis, J.P. Bouillon *Céramique impressionniste*, Paris 1974; *Béraldi*; J.P. Bouillon, *Félix et Marie Bracquemond*, Mortagne 1972; J.P. Bouillon, O. Nouvel, *L'Art françcais sous le Second Empire*, Paris (Grand Palais) 1979; G. Weisberg "Bracquemond et le baron Vitta" in *Bulletin of the Cleveland Museum of Art*, Nov. 1979; L. Vaillat, *Oeuvres de Félix Bracquemond exposées à la Société Nationale des Beaux-Arts*, Paris 1907. JPB

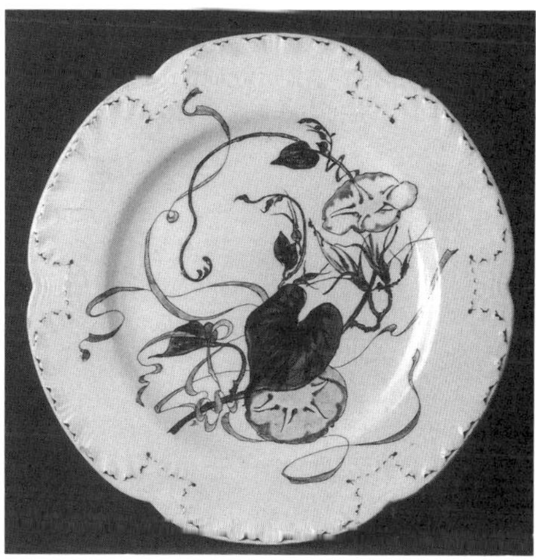

Félix Bracquemond

Plate from a service of eleven; marked: 'Creil B.E.C. (Barluet et Montereau)'
Paris, Musée des Arts Décoratifs

BRACQUEMOND, Marie *1840–1916*
b. Argenton (Finistère). Pupil of Ingres. Wife of F. Bracquemond. Painter, engraver and ceramist. Produced several flower paintings before and during her Impressionist period i.e. after 1880. These were exhibited after her death. *La lettre* (*Madame Bénédict*) Ader Picard Tajan, Paris, Galliera, 2 June 1971, lot 41
LIT J.P. Bouillon, *Félix et Marie Bracquemond*, Mortagne 1972; J.P. Bouillon, E. Kane "M. Bracquemond" in *Woman's Art Journal*, Fall 1984, G. Geffroy *Marie Bracquemond*, Paris 1919; Paris, *M. Bracquemond*, Galerie Bernheim-Jeune, 1962; *Witt*. JPB

BRANTE, Etienne *b.1831*
Pupil of Thierriat, Lyon BA (CFD 1848)
LIT *Hardouin Fugier Grafe*

BRAUER, Germaine de
Exhib. *Fleurs*, Dijon Salon 1890
LIT *Dijon Salon* 1890. CL

BRAZIER, Marie-Caroline
Exhib. wc. Paris Salon 1833–1848 e.g. *Bouquet de dahlias*, *Un dahlia*, *Bouquet composé*, 1834, *Bouquet de camélias*, *Fleurs sur une table*, 1835, *Tulipes, étude d'après nature*, 1836, *Roses trémières*, 1837, *Pivoines d'après nature*, 1839, *Cactus*, d'après nature, 1840

LIT *Bellier*; *Bénézit*; *Faré* 1962, p. 248; *Paris Salon* 1833, 1837, 1839, 1840

BRAZIER, Marie-Julie
b. Paris. Pupil of Aumont and H. Saintin. Exhib. wc. Paris Salon from 1879 e.g. *Chrysanthèmes*, 1880
LIT *Bellier*; *Bénézit*; *Paris Salon* 1880

BRÉMONT or BRÉMOND, Marie-Thérèse
Pupil of Trébuchet. Exhib. Paris Salon from 1878, flowers in wc or gouache
LIT *Bénézit*; *Paris Salon* 1880

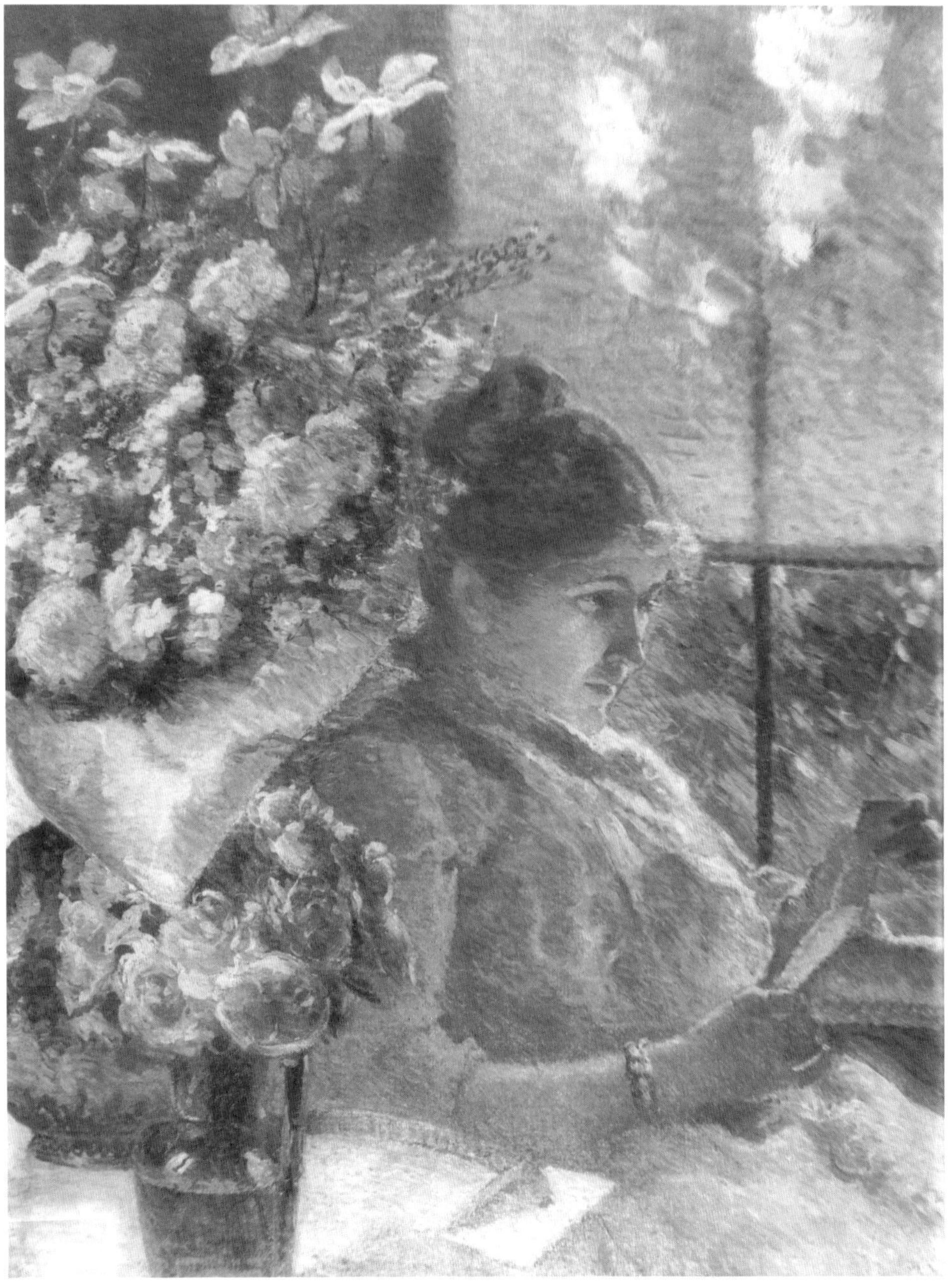

BRESSANT, Paul
b. Basse-Terre (Guadeloupe). Exhib. Paris Indép. *Roses*, 1890, *Fleurs*, 1891
LIT *Paris Indép.* 1890, 1891

BRESSON, Etienne
Pupil of Berjon, Lyon BA (CFD 1818)
LIT *Hardouin-Fugier Grafe*

Marie Bracquemond

Oil on canvas, 32 × 23½ in. (81 × 60 cm.), signed (photo: Ader Picard Tajan, Paris)

BREST, Germain-Fabius ***1823–1900***
b. Marseille. Pupil of Loubon and Troyon. Painted landscapes and, occasionally, flowers e.g. *Pensées*, Nancy Salon 1876
LIT *Bellier*; *Bénézit*; Marseille, *L'Orient en question*, Musée Cantini, 1982; *Nancy Salon* 1876; *Schurr* III, 23; *Witt*

BRET ***b.1823***
Pupil of Thierriat, Lyon BA (CFD 1842)
LIT *Hardouin-Fugier Grafe*

BRET-CHARBONNIER, Claudine, ***alias*** **Claudia** ***1863–1951***
Pupil of Médard, Quost, Thurner, Bourgogne and, possibly, A. Perrachon.

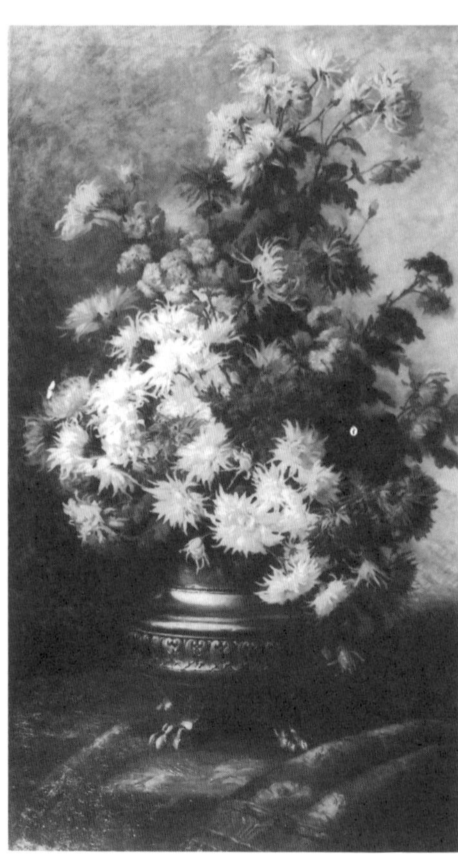

Claudine Bret-Charbonnier

Oil on canvas, 62¼ × 34¾ in. (158 × 88 cm.), signed and dated 1900
Ville de Lyon (photo: Musée des Beaux-Arts, Lyon)

Exhib. Dijon Salon *Roses*, 1890, *Roses trémières*, *Roses thé*, 1892; *Pivoines et lilas*, Lyon Salon 1894. A prolific, successful flower painter and influential teacher. Her *Mare fleurie* was bought by the State for the Musée des Beaux-Arts, Lyon
LIT *Hardouin-Fugier Grafe*; *Hardouin-Fugier Grafe* 1982. (ill.)

BRETILLOT
Exhib. *Fleurs et instruments de musique*, Dijon Salon 1881
LIT *Dijon Salon* 1881. CL

BRETON, Charles-Léon
b. Paris. Pupil of U. Bertin. Exhib. flowers on porcelain, Paris Salon 1874
LIT *Bénézit*

Auguste Piquet de Brienne

Engraving, 8 × 8¾ in. (20 × 22 cm.), signed and dated
Paris, BMAD (Maciet Collection)

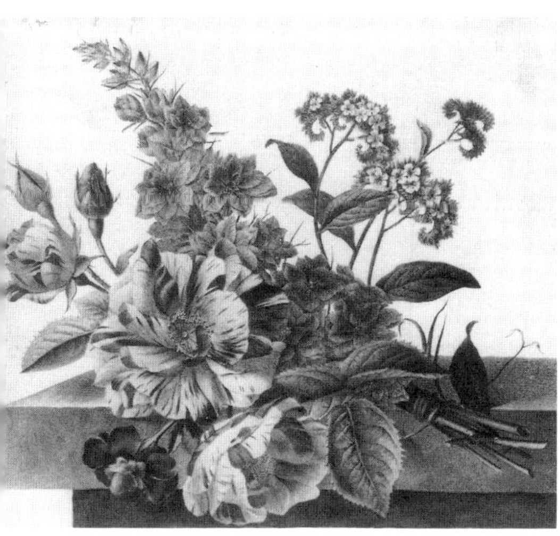

Annica Bricogne (*right*)

Engraving, 78 × 47 in. (203 × 210 cm.), signed
Paris, BMAD (Maciet Collection)

BRETON, Jules-Adolphe ***1827–1905***
The well-known genre and figure painter's *Dernières fleurs* shows snow-covered garden flowers
LIT *Paris Salon* 1889 (ill.); *Witt*

BRETON, *see* DEMONT

BRIAND, Jules
b. Angers (Maine-et-Loire). Pupil of Dupuis. Painted still-lifes and, occasionally, flowers. Exhib. Paris Salon *c.*1870
LIT *Bénézit*

BRIAUDEAU, Paul-Charles-Jean ***b.1869***
b. Nantes (Loire-Atlantique). Pupil of G. Moreau. Painted landscapes and, occasionally, flowers. Exhib. Paris Salon 1896–1898, then Paris Indép.
LIT *Bénézit*; *Thieme*; *Witt*

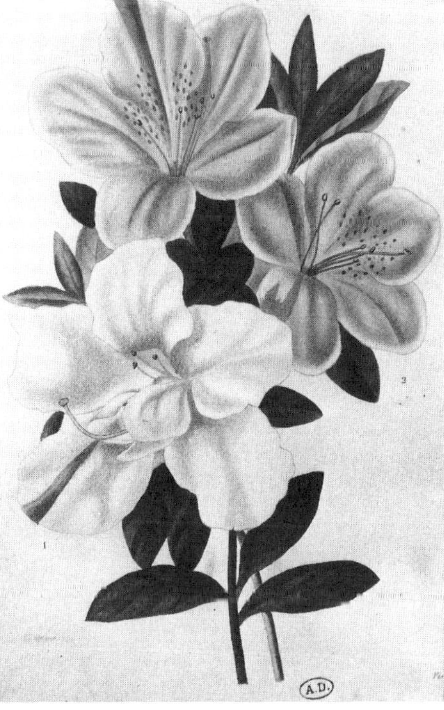

BRICOGNE, Annica
Exhib. Paris Salon *Bouquet composé*, wc, *Rose cent feuilles*, 1845, *Iris*, wc, 1850. Designed plates for *L'Horticulteur français*, Paris, Hérincq, 1851–1872 and *Choix des plus belles roses*, Paris Dusacq 1845–1854. Some plates in Paris BMAD (Maciet coll.)
LIT *Paris BMAD*; *Paris Salon* 1845, 1850; *Nissen*. 2232, 2337n.

BRIDIEU de, *see* BURY

BRIELMAN, Eugénie-Claire, *see* GRUYER

BRIELMAN, Jacques-Alfred-François
Exhib. *Panier de coquelicots*, Roanne Salon 1890
LIT *Roanne Salon* 1890

BRIELMAN, Julie-Eugénie, *see* PIOGÉ

BRIENNE, Auguste PIQUET de ***b.1789***
Pupil of Van Dael and G. Van Spaendonck. Exhib. flowers mostly in wc, Paris Salon *c.*1814–45 e.g. *Fleurs dans un vase*, *Branche de roses*, 1819, *Fleurs et fruits*, 1834, *Etude de pivoine en arbre*, 1839, *Fleurs dans une corbeille*, 1842, *Fleurs et raisins*, 1844, *Fleurs et fruits*, 1845. Provided designs for several flower sets e.g. *Fleurs diverses*, lith. by Engelmann 1821–1829, *Cours de fleurs du Jardin des Plantes*, Paris (Chavant) 1837, *Choix de 15 bouquets de fleurs* etc.
LIT *Bellier*; *Bénézit*; Gabet; H. Jouin, *Nouvelles Archives de l'Art Français*, Paris Charavay, 1890; Paris Bibl. Nat. Est. Dc 138; *Paris MAD*; *Thieme*

BRIGUET, Félix
Pupil of Berjon, Lyon BA (CFD 1815)
LIT *Hardouin-Fugier Grafe*

BRIGUET, Louis ***b.1876***
Pupil of Castex-Dégrange, Lyon BA (CFD 1896–1898)
LIT *Hardouin-Fugier Grafe*

BRINQUANT, ***see*** **VIOLAINE**

BRIZARD, Ferdinand
Exhib. *Vase de fleurs*, Lyon Salon 1862
LIT *Lyon Salon* 1862

BROCHIOUZE, Speranza de
Exhib. *Oiseaux et fleurs*, Paris Indép. 1888
LIT *Paris Indép.* 1888

BROCQ, Ad.
Contributed designs to Bory de Saint-Vincent, *Nouvelle Flore du Péloponnèse et des Cyclades*, Paris, Strasbourg (Levrault) 1838. An engraver
LIT *Nissen* I 213, II 2245; *Sitwell*

BROCQ, Pierre-Jules ***b.1811***
b. Paris. Pupil of Pigal and J. Cogniet. Exhib. Flowers Paris Salon 1852, 1853, 1861
LIT *Bellier*; *Bénézit*; *Thieme*

BRONDELLE, Antoine
Pupil of Thierriat, Lyon BA (CFD 1837)
LIT *Hardouin-Fugier Grafe*

BRONGNIART, Catherine
Exhib. Paris UFPS *Coquelicots*, *Mignardises*, *Roses*, 1896, *Pétunias*, *Roses*, 1898. Her *Grands Pavots*, wc, was bought (250 francs) for the Musée de Bagnères-de-Bigorre in 1898
LIT Paris Arch. Nat. F21:2125, 4500; *Paris UFPS, 1896, 1898*

BRONNER, Henri
Exhib. *Bouquet de fleurs*, Lyon Salon 1870
LIT *Lyon Salon* 1870

BROQUET, Adrien ***b.1872***
Pupil of Castex-Dégrange, Lyon BA (CFD 1890–1891)
LIT *Hardouin-Fugier Grafe*

BROS, Joachim ***b.1806***
Pupil of Berjon, Lyon BA (CFD 1822)
LIT *Hardouin-Fugier Grafe*

BROSSARD, Mme
Pupil of O. Arson. A flower-piece by this artist was rejected by the 1843 Paris Salon selection committee
LIT Louvre. Arch.

BROSSE, Eugène ***b.1855***
b. Rive-de-Gier (Loire). Pupil of Jung. Exhib. Lyon Salon from 1891 e.g. *Phlox*, *Lilas*, 1894; Saint-Etienne Salon, *Fleurs*, *Roses*, 1891. His *Pivoines* was bought for the Musée d'Art et d'Industrie, Saint-Etienne in 1897
LIT *Bénézit*; *Saint-Etienne Salon* 1891; *Thieme*

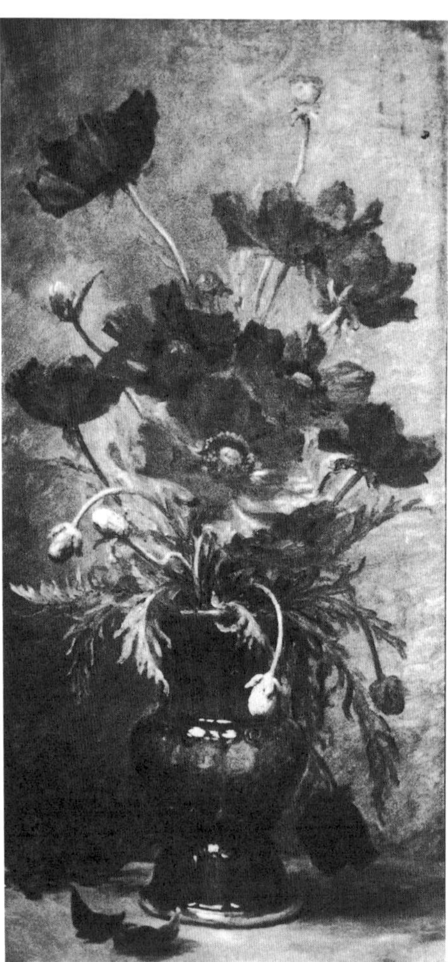

Catherine Brongniart

Watercolour, $39\frac{1}{2} \times 23$ in. (100 × 58 cm.), *c.* 1898, signed
Bagnères-de-Bigorre, Musée Salies

BROSSELARD, Claire
Exhib. Paris Salon *Camélias*, wc, 1843, *Tulipes*, wc, 1844, *Fleurs dans un vase*, 1844; Cambridge, Fitzwilliam Museum (Broughton coll.): *Bunch of Roses, Lilac and Wallflowers*, 1844, watercolour
LIT *Paris Salon* 1843, 1844

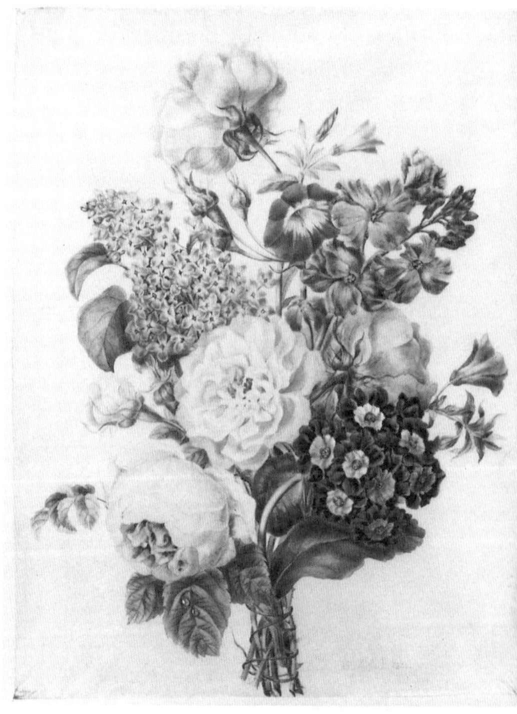

Claire Brosselard

Watercolour on vellum, $13\frac{7}{8} \times 10\frac{7}{8}$ in. (34.2 × 26.5 cm.), signed and dated 1844
Cambridge, Fitzwilliam Museum (Broughton Collection)

BROSSETTE, Jean ***b.1836***
Pupil of Reignier, Lyon BA (CFD 1855)
LIT *Hardouin-Fugier Grafe*

BROU, P.C. de
Exhib. Paris Indép. *Oeillets*, 1892, *Fleurs*, 1893
LIT *Paris Indép.* 1892, 1893

BROUILLET, Pierre-André ***1857–1904***
b. Charroux (Vienne). Pupil of Gérôme. Painted genre, figures, portraits and, occasionally, flowers
LIT B. Gaudichon "La peinture au XIX° siècle ..." in *Bulletin de la Société des Antiquaires de l'Ouest*, 1983

BRU, A.
Reines-marguerites dans un panier, s.d. 1892 with M. Neumann (Marseille) 1982
LIT Neumann, Marseille 1982

BRUDON, Jean
Designed a 19th century Dauphinois broadsheet. This naïvely fanciful wood engraving advertising flower seeds shows the most unlikely flowers. This is the only signed work of its kind. M: Grenoble, Musée Dauphinois (six gouache designs of vegetables and flowers)
LIT Grenoble, *Musée Dauphinois doc.*

BRUN, Antonin
Exhib. Lyon Salon *Pivoines*, wc, *Couronne de roses*, wc, 1862
LIT *Lyon Salon* 1862

BRUN, Edouard ***1860–1935***
Pupil of Achard and Ravier. Painted landscapes and, occasionally, flowers
LIT *Bellier*; *Bénézit*

BRUN, Marguerite
Pupil of A. Perrachon and Thurner. Exhib. Lyon Salon, *c.*1892–*c.*1924 and Paris UFPS. An influential teacher.
LIT *Bénézit*; *Hardouin-Fugier Grafe*

BRUN, Nelly
Exhib. Paris from 1871. Exhib. *Pivoines et boules de neige*, Dijon Salon 1890
LIT *Dijon Salon* 1890. CL

BRUNARD, Joseph ***1821–1892***
b. Saint-Brice (Val-d'Oise). Pupil of Delaroche, E. Rousseau and Pommayrac. Painted portrait miniatures and, occasionally, flowers
LIT *Bellier*; *Bénézit*; *Thieme*

BRUNARD, Lucien
b. Paris. Pupil of Gérôme and de Serres. Painted landscapes and flowers. Exhib. *Fleurs*, pastel, Paris Noir et Blanc Salon 1888
LIT *Bellier*; *Paris Noir et Blanc Salon* 1888; *Thieme*

BRUNE, Adolphe ***1802–1880***
b. Paris. Pupil of Gros and Paris BA (1824). Painted figures, genre and, occasionally, flowers e.g. *Fleurs*, Paris Salon 1863, *Fleurs*, Rouen Salon 1864
LIT *Bénézit*; *Brune*; G. Lacambre in *Société de l'Histoire de l'Art français*, Paris (de Nobèle) 1969, p. 71; *Paris Salon* 1863; *Rouen Salon* 1864

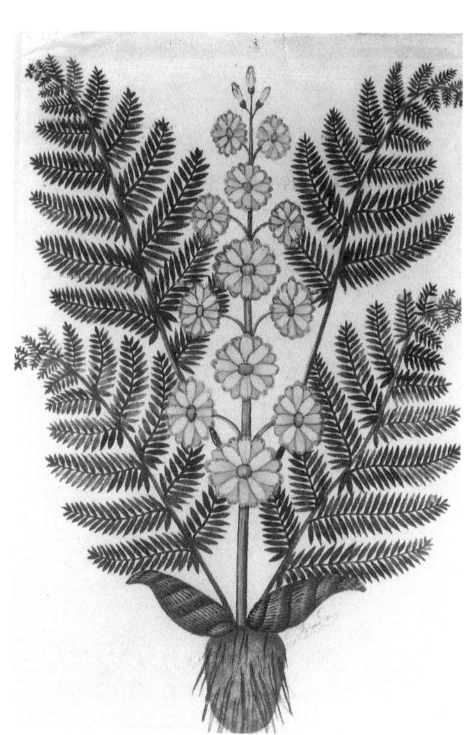

Jean Brudon

Wood engraving, signed
Grenoble, Musée Dauphinois

BRUNEAU, Aurélie or Amélie
Pupil of Mme Girardin. Exhib. landscapes and flowers e.g. Paris Salon *Bluets et marguerites*, wc, 1868, *Dahlias*, 1869
LIT *Bellier*; *Bénézit*

BRUNEAU, Charles
b. Angers (Maine-et-Loire). Pupil of Cabanel. Painted landscapes and flowers e.g. *Bourriche de pensées*, *Roses du Bengale*, wc, Paris Salon 1880
LIT *Bellier*; *Paris Salon* 1880

BRUNEL DE NEUVILLE, Alfred-Arthur ***1852–1941***
Exhib. Paris Salon from 1879. Painted still-lifes, fruit-pieces and, occasionally, flowers e.g. *Fleurs et fruits*, Dorotheum, Vienna, 17–20 Mar. 1970, lot 22
LIT *Bénézit*; *Orsay*; *Schurr* IV, 82; *Thieme*; *Witt*

BRUNET, Elisa-Antonine-Marie
b. Paris. Exhib. *Couronne de bluets et de fleurs des champs*, fan-leaf, Paris Indép. 1890
LIT *Paris Indép.* 1890

BRUNET, Isabelle ***fl.c.1855***
This flower painter also made artificial flowers
LIT Paris Arch. Nat. F21:288, 293

BRUNET, Mme
At Sèvres 1806–1807, 1816
LIT *Brunet Préaud*

BRUNET, Sophie
b. Paris. Exhib. Paris Indép. *Chrysanthèmes*, 1884, *Fleurs de printemps*, *Chrysanthèmes*, 1887, *Roses et lilas*, 1888; Paris UFPS *Pivoines*, 1890; Paris Indép. *Branche de chrysanthèmes*, 1894
LIT *Paris Indép.* 1884, 1885, 1887, 1888, 1894; *Paris UFPS* 1890

BRUNET-DEBAINES, Alfred ***b.1845***
b. Le Havre (Seine-Maritime). Pupil of Pils and Normand. Exhib. Paris Salon from 1866. Painted landscapes and flowers e.g. *Giroflées et pensées*, wc, Paris Salon 1880
LIT *Bellier*; *Bénézit*; *Paris Salon* 1880

BRUNETTON, Joseph-Auguste ***1863–1923***
b. Lyon. Pupil of Lyon BA, Boulanger, Gérôme and Cabanel. Painted portraits, landscapes, still-lifes and, occasionally, flowers
LIT *Bénézit*; *Hardouin-Fugier Grafe*

BRUNIER, Antoine
Exhib. *Fleurs*, Lyon Salon 1863
LIT *Lyon Salon* 1863

BRUNIER, Charles ***b.1818***
Pupil of Thierriat, Lyon BA (CFD 1834)
LIT *Hardouin-Fugier Grafe*

BRUNIER, Joseph ***1860–1929***
b. Chambéry (Savoie). Pupil of Dumas (Lyon BA), Cabanel, Boulanger and Lefebvre. Painted portraits, figures and, occasionally, flowers
LIT A. Germain, *Les Artistes lyonnais*, Lyon (Lardanchet) 1911

BRUNNER-LACOSTE, Emile-Henri ***1838–1881***
b. Paris. Pupil of Georges Brunner, his father, the German flower painter, E. Le Poitevin and A. Faure. Exhib. *Fleurs* (200 francs) Strasbourg Salon 1859; Paris Salon, *Bénitier fleuri*, *Fleurs de printemps*, *Fleurs d'automne*, 1861, *Pavots*, 1867, *Pavots*, 1875, *Marché aux fleurs*, *Roses trémières*, 1880, *Fleurs*, 1876, Libert & Castor, Paris, 26 Nov. 1986; Sotheby's, New York, 29 Oct. 1987, lot 261, *Pink Chrysanthemums*
LIT *Bellier*; *Bénézit*; *Paris Salon* 1861, 1867, 1875, 1880; *Schurr* IV, 81; *Strasbourg Salon* 1859

BRUNO, Emmanuel
Designed plates for André Edouard, *Description des broméliacées ... de la Colombie*, Paris (Masson) 1889
LIT *Nissen* I, 29

BRUYAS, Etienne ***b.1807***
Pupil of Thierriat, Lyon BA (CFD 1827)
LIT *Hardouin-Fugier Grafe*

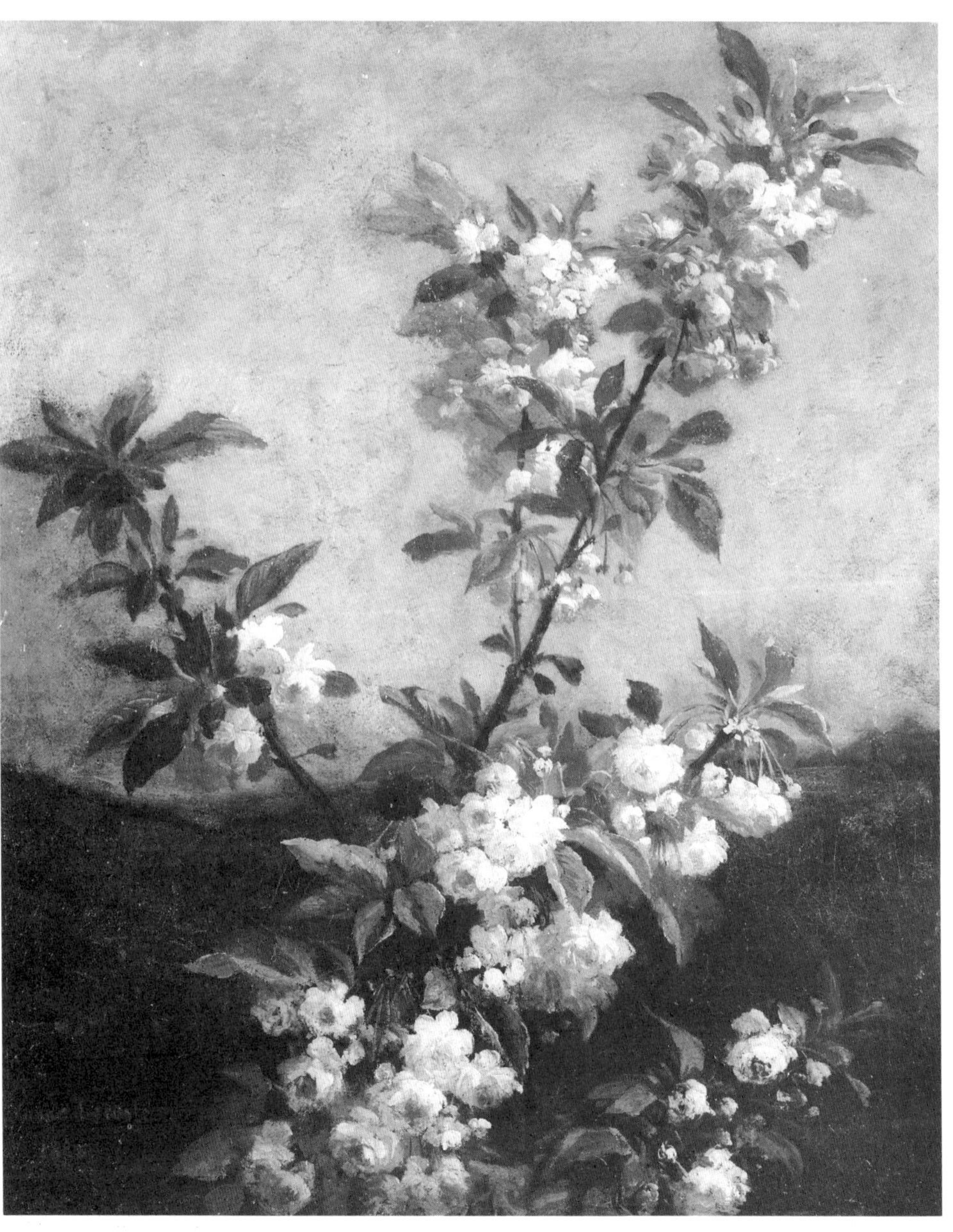

Emile-Henri Brunner-Lacoste

Oil on canvas, 26 × 21 in. (66 × $53\frac{1}{4}$ cm.), signed and dated 1876
Mes. E. Libert et A. Castor, Paris

BRUYAS, Marc-Laurent ***1821–1896***
b. Lyon. Pupil of Thierriat, Lyon BA (CFD 1832) and F. Grobon. Textile designer. Exhib. Lyon Salon 1857–95, Paris Salon 1863–1870 e.g. Lyon Salon *L'oranger fleuri*, 1864, *Corbeille d'orchidées*, 1865; *Roses et fuchsias*, Paris Salon 1867, Lyon Salon 1867; *Fleurs et fruits*, Dijon Salon 1881. Lyon, Musée des Beaux-Arts, *Roses et fuchsias*
LIT *Hardouin-Fugier Grafe*; *Hardouin-Fugier Grafe* 1979 (ill.); *Hardouin-Fugier Grafe* 1982 (ill.)

BRUYÈRE, Elisa or Elise, *née* Le Barbier ***1776–1842***
b. Paris. Pupil of Le Barbier aîné, her father, and J.F. Van Dael. Exhib. Paris Salon *c.*1802–1844, portraits, genre and mostly flowers. Her last flower-piece *Groupe de fleurs dans un vase d'albâtre oriental* was completed by Chazal and exhibited at the Paris Salon 1844 (now in Musée des Beaux-Arts, Valenciennes). A most successful flower painter. M: Lyon, Valenciennes, Rouen
LIT *Bellier*; *Bénézit*; *Faré* 1962, p. 246; *Gabet*; Landon, *Salon de 1819*, p. 107; Marshall Spink *Three centuries of flower and still-life painting*, London 1980; Mitchell (ill.); Paris Arch. Nat. F21:2201; *Paris Salon* 1806, 1819, 1827, 1831, 1834, 1839, 1844; *Witt*

BRUYÈRE, Jacques ***b.1823***
Pupil of Thierriat, Lyon BA (CFD 1840). Textile designer
LIT *Hardouin-Fugier Grafe*

BRUYÈRE, Jeanne-Louise
b. Paris. Pupil of D. de Cool. Exhib. *Azalées, Boules de neige et lilas*, wc, Paris Salon 1890
LIT *Paris Salon* 1890

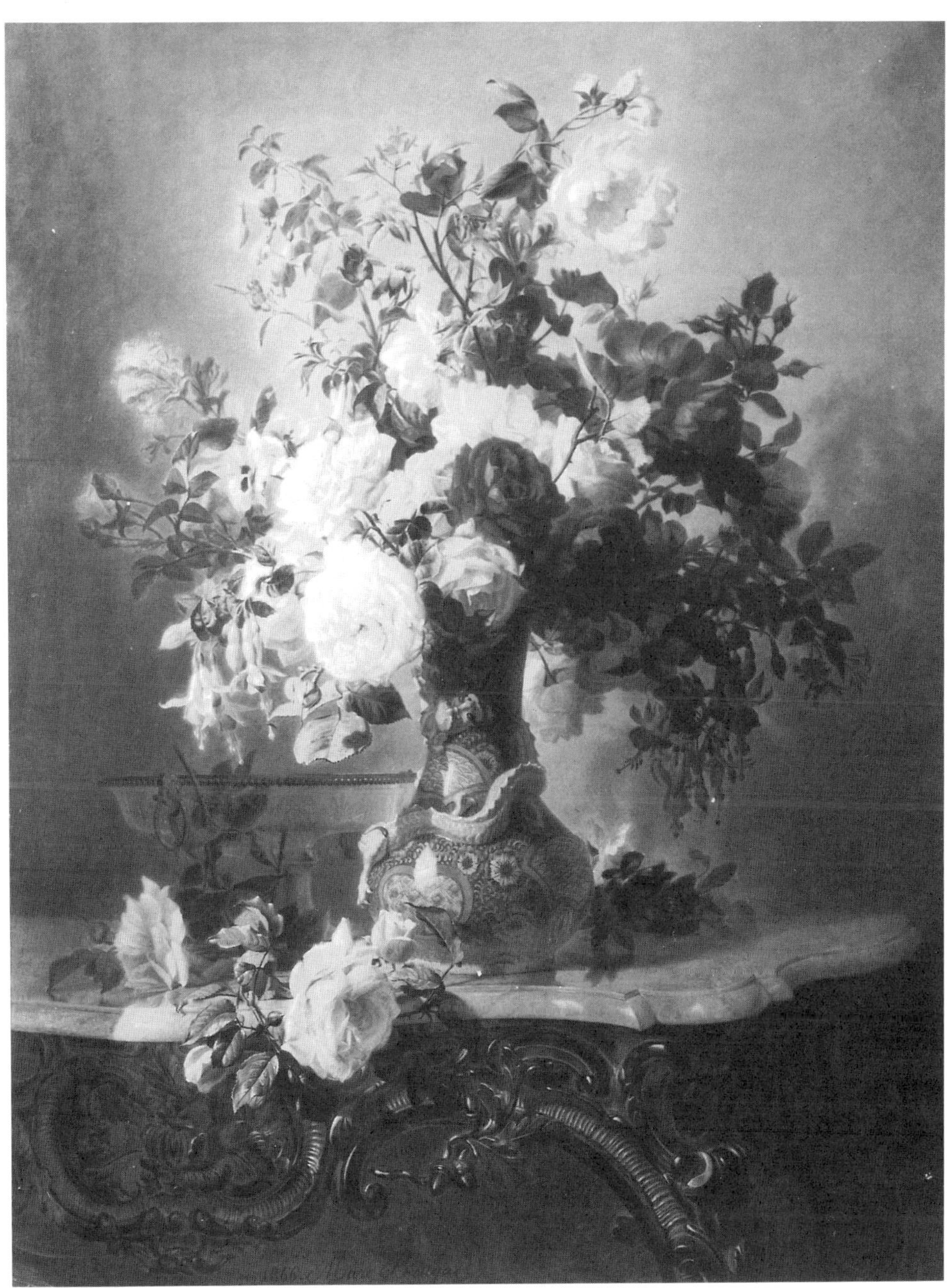

Marc-Laurent Bruyas

Oil on canvas, $42\frac{1}{2} \times 32$ in. (108 × 81 cm.), signed and dated 1866
Lyon, Musée des Beaux-Arts

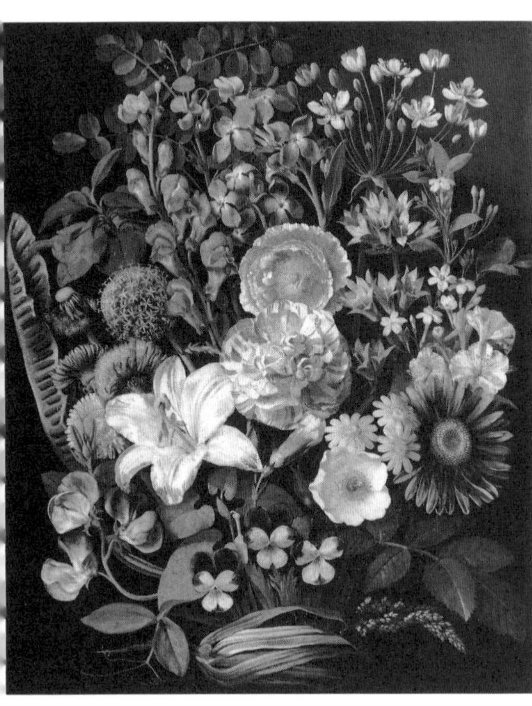

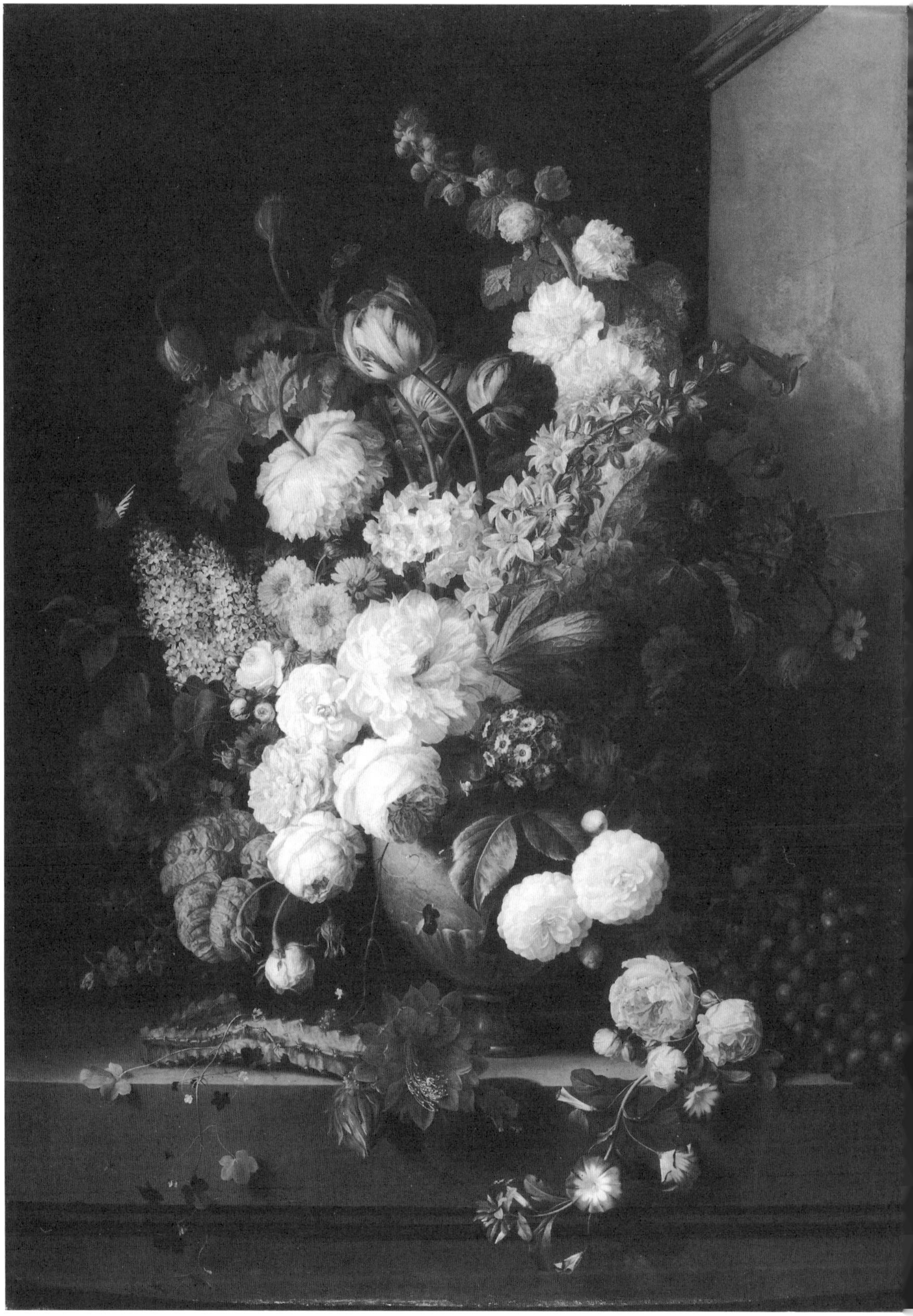

Elisa Bruyère

Oil on canvas, $18\frac{1}{2} \times 15$ in. (47×38 cm.)
Collection Edgar Both

Elisa Bruyère and Antoine Chazal (*right*)

Oil on canvas, *c.* 1844, signed by both artists
Valenciennes, Musée des Beaux-Arts,
(photo: Lauros-Giraudon, Paris)

BUCHÈRE, Marie-Clémentine, *later* Martin *1819–1873*
b. Paris. Pupil of Redouté. Married Amédée-Henry Martin, a drawing master. Exhib. Dijon Salon *Vase de fleurs*, wc, 1840, *Bouquet de roses*, 1841; Paris Salon *Hommage à Redouté*, 1841, and flowers in wc 1841–1849. Cambridge, Fitzwilliam Museum (Broughton coll.); *Damask rose*, watercolour, is the only known work by the artist
LIT *Dijon Salon* 1840, 1841; Broughton 1977; *Hardouin-Fugier* 1981

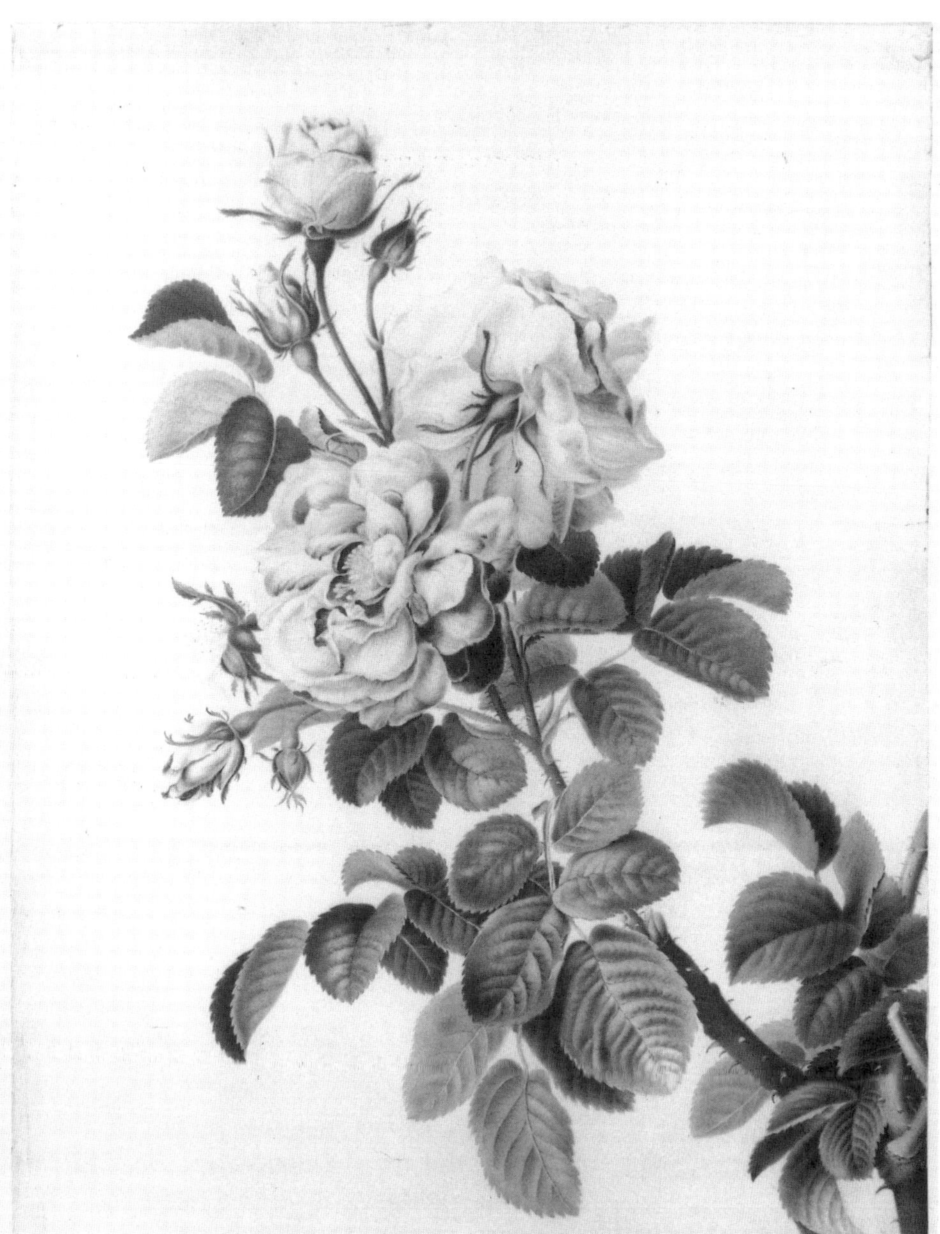

Marie-Clémentine Buchère

Watercolour, 17¼ × 12½ in. (43.4 × 31.9 cm.), signed
Cambridge, Fitzwilliam Museum
(Broughton Collection)

BUCHET, Mme Julie *fl.c.1891–1900*
Exhib. *Chrysanthèmes*, Paris Salon 1891. This was bought (400 francs) by the State for the Musée de Bourges and was transferred to Paris (Louvre) in 1972
LIT Paris Arch. Nat. F21:2125

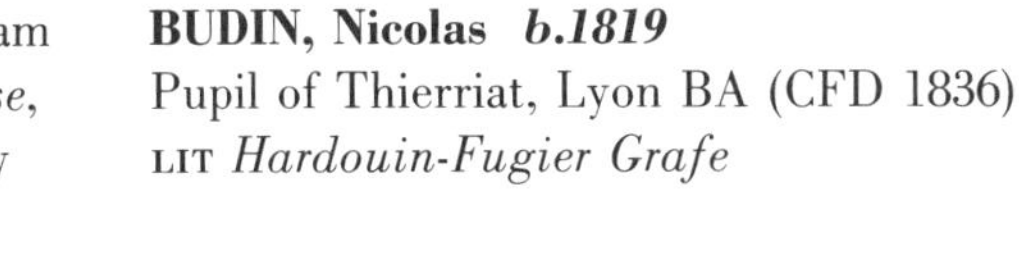

BUDIN, Nicolas *b.1819*
Pupil of Thierriat, Lyon BA (CFD 1836)
LIT *Hardouin-Fugier Grafe*

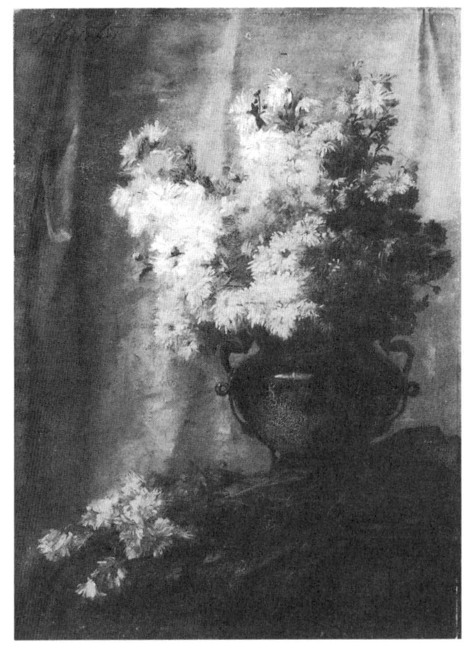

Julie Buchet

Oil on canvas, 48 × 34½ in. (122 × 87 cm.), signed
Paris, Musée du Louvre

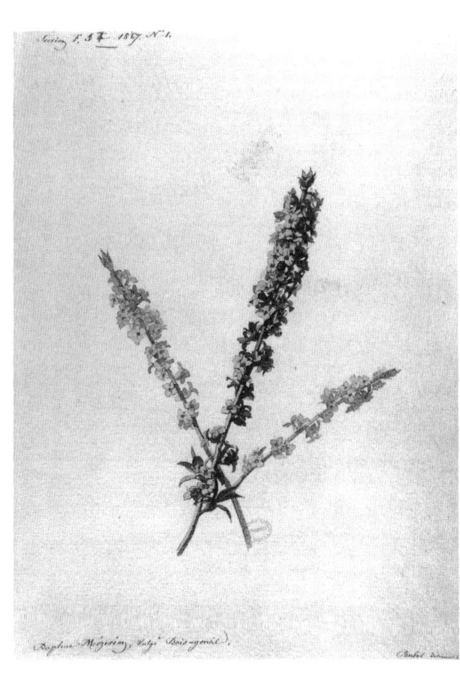

Eugène-Alexandre Bulot

Watercolour, signed and dated 1867
Sèvres, Archives, Manufacture Nationale de Sèvres

BUFFARDIN, Stanislas-Nicolas-Théodore ***1805–1860***
b. Avignon (Vaucluse). Pupil of Monvoisin. Flower and bird painter and lithographer. Exhib. Paris Salon e.g. *Oiseaux, fleurs et papillons*, 1835
LIT *Bellier*; *Bénézit*; *Paris Salon* 1835

BUGHE, François ***b.1821***
Pupil of Thierriat, Lyon BA (CFD 1838)
LIT *Hardouin-Fugier Grafe*

BULLIARD, Pierre
Designed plates for *Herbier de la France*, Paris 1780–1808
LIT *Sitwell*

BULLOT-EICHER, Marie-Louise
b. Paris. Pupil of Busson. Exhib. *Fleurs*, wc, Paris Noir et Blanc Salon, 1888; *Lys* (200 francs) and *Pavots* (150 francs), Strasbourg Salon 1891, *Volubilis*, Paris UFPS 1896
LIT *Paris Noir et Blanc Salon* 1888; *Paris UFPS* 1896; *Strasbourg Salon* 1891

BULOT, Eugène-Alexandre
Pupil of Lejour. Exhib. Paris Salon 1868, 1873. His 1867 flowers, wc, are in the Sèvres Museum. Worked at Sèvres. Decorated two vases presented by Napoléon III to the Czar.
LIT *Bellier*; *Bénézit*; *Orsay*

BUOVOLO, Renée
b. Bône (Algeria). Exhib. *Fleurs d'automne* Paris UFPS 1896
LIT *Paris UFPS* 1896

BURAT, Fanny ***b.1838***
b. Blois (Loir-et-Cher). Pupil of Jacobber. Exhib. Paris Salon, watercolour and porcelain paintings from 1863 e.g. *Fleurs*, wc, 1872, *Roses de Noël*, wc, 1880; *Roses de Noël*, wc, Dijon Salon 1885. Her 1875 flower-piece is in the Musée des Beaux-Arts, Tours
LIT *Bellier*; *Bénézit*; *Dijon Salon* 1885; *Paris Salon* 1872, 1880

BURDIN, Amélie ***b.1834***
b. Lyon. Pupil of Houssaye, Chaplin and Robert-Fleury. Exhib. Paris 1861–1867 and Lyon *c.*1864–1867 e.g. *Fleurs*, decorative panel, Lyon Salon 1867
LIT *Bénézit*; *Hardouin-Fugier Grafe*; *Lyon Salon* 1867; *Witt*

BUREL, Antoine-Alexandre ***1865–1942***
Pupil of Castex-Dégrange, Lyon BA (CFD 1884). Textile designer. Painted flowers in wc
LIT *Bellier; Hardouin-Fugier Grafe* 1978

BURGAT, Eugène ***b.c.1849***
b. Manigod (Haute-Savoie). Pupil of Van Elven and Pils. Painted still-lifes and, occasionally, flowers. Exhib. Paris Salon from 1869
LIT *Bellier*

BURILLON, Jacques-Antoine ***b.1820***
Pupil of Thierriat, Lyon BA (CFD 1839)
LIT *Hardouin-Fugier Grafe*

BURTY, Philippe ***1830–1890***
Pupil of Chabal-Dussurgey at Gobelins manufactory, Paris. The famous art critic was also an amateur flower painter
LIT *Bénézit*; *Orsay*; G. Weisberg, *The early years of P. Burty*, Ph.D. dissertation, Johns Hopkins University, 1967; G. Weisberg, Chardin and the Still-Life Tradition, Cleveland, 1979

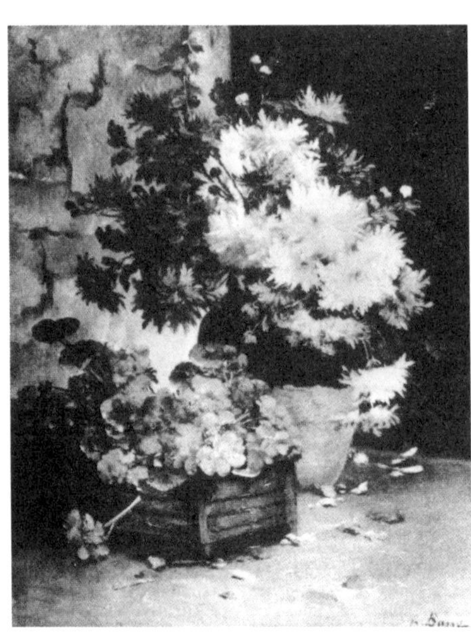

Simon-Albert Bussy

Oil on canvas, $21\frac{3}{4} \times 12\frac{1}{2}$ in. (55 × 32 cm.); signed
Private collection

BURY, Marie-Pélagie-Eulalie, *née* de Bridieu ***d.1849***
b. Vendreuve (Vienne). Contributed flower designs to *Botanic Garden*, London 1825, *Botanist*, 1837–46, *Voyage au Pôle sud*, (vol. III, Botany). Mostly an insect painter. Two watercolours on vellum, s.d. are in the Paris Muséum d'Histoire Naturelle
LIT *Hardouin-Fugier* 1981; *Laissus*

BUSSIÈRE, Gaston ***1862–1928***
b. Cuisery (Saône-et-Loire). Pupil of Cabanel and Puvis de Chavannes. This symbolist painter often associated allegorical female figures and flowers e.g. *Les iris*, Paris Salon 1898 (private coll. Switzerland). Produced some flower studies
LIT *Orsay*; *Schurr* III, 130; *Thieme*

BUSSILLIET, Charles-Onésime ***b.1817***
Pupil of Thierriat, Lyon BA (CFD 1834)
LIT *Hardouin-Fugier Grafe*

BUSSOD, Léon-Pierre ***b.1818***
Pupil of Thierriat, Lyon BA (CFD 1835)
LIT *Hardouin-Fugier Grafe*

BUSSY, Simon-Albert ***1869–1954***
b. Dôle (Jura). Pupil of Gustave Moreau, Paris Arts Décoratifs and E. Delaunay. The well-known landscape, figure and animal painter, occasionally produced some flower studies, mostly late works
LIT *Bénézit*; *Orsay*; *Schurr* I, 96; *Thieme*

BUTEL, Rambert ***b.1824***
Pupil of Thierriat, Lyon BA (CFD 1840)
LIT *Hardouin-Fugier Grafe*

C

C., S, Mme de
Pupil of Médard. Exhib. *Chrysanthèmes du Japon*, Lyon Salon 1885
LIT *Lyon Salon* 1885

CABAILLOT-LASSALLE, Camille-Léopold ***b.1839***
Pupil of L. Cabaillot, his father. Exhib. Paris Salon 1864–1889. Exhib. *Cyclamens et violettes de Parme*, Dijon Salon 1897
LIT *Bénézit*; *Dijon Salon* 1897. *Witt* CL;

CABAN, Eugène-Charles
op. Sèvres 1847–1885. His 1850 flower-piece is in the Musée de Sèvres. Seven flower designs by Caban are in the Sèvres Archives and a bouquet in a private collection.
LIT *Bénézit*; *Orsay*

CABANE, Adda or Adélaïde
b. Saint-Didier-les-Bains (Vaucluse). Pupil of Némorin Cabane, her father. Exhib. *Chrysanthèmes*, Grenoble Salon 1899
LIT *Bénézit*; *Grenoble Salon* 1899; *Thieme*. MW

CABANE, Florian-Némorin ***b.1831***
b. Logrian (Gard). Pupil of Paris BA. Painted landscapes and still-lifes. Exhib. *Fleurs*, Grenoble Salon 1899
LIT *Bénézit*; *Grenoble Salon* 1899; *Schurr* IV, 70; *Thieme*; *Witt* MW;

CABANET, François
Exhib. *Fleurs*, wc, Paris Salon 1846
LIT *Paris Salon* 1846

CABANNE, Pauline, *née* Garnerey
Exhib. Paris Salon *c.*1836–1844 e.g. *Vase de fleurs sur une table de marbre*, *Etude de fleurs*, 1836, *Etude de fleurs*, wc, 1837, *Une rose*, wc, 1844
Cambridge, Fitzwilliam Museum (Broughton Collection): *Oleander*, 1834, wc.
LIT *Paris Salon* 1836, 1837, 1844

CABIÉ, Louis-Alexandre ***1853–1939***
Pupil of Harpignies and Pradelles. This landscape painter occasionally produced flowers e.g. *Bouquet*, wc, Drouot, Paris, 16 Mar. 1972. *Still Life*, Phillips, London, 17 July 1985, lot 123
LIT *Bénézit*; *Orsay*; *Schurr* II, 37; *Witt*

CABUZEL, Auguste-Hector ***b.1836***
b. Bray-sur-Somme (Somme). Pupil of H. Vernet, Cogniet and Toulmouche. Exhib. *Dernières fleurs*, Paris Salon 1880
LIT *Bénézit*; *Paris Salon* 1880

CADET, Marie
Pupil of her father, M. Moreau, C. Gossin and Chaillery. Exhib. *Chrysanthèmes*, Paris UFPS 1890
LIT *Bénézit*; *Paris UFPS* 1890

CADILHON, Pauline
Exhib. Paris Indép. *Chrysanthèmes*, 1894, *Pavots*, 1896, *Pivoines*, 1898
LIT *Paris Indép.* 1894, 1896, 1898

CAGNARD or CAGNIARD, Etienne ***b.1796***
b. Lyon. Exhib. Paris Salon 1841–1851 e.g. *Fleurs*, wc, 1841, *Fleurs*, wc, 1843
LIT *Bellier*; *Bénézit*; *Thieme*

CAHEN, Isaac ***b.1833***
Pupil of Thierriat, Lyon BA (CFD 1849)
LIT *Hardouin-Fugier Grafe*

CAILLAUD, Alfred-Benoit ***d.1940***
b. La Rochelle (Charente-Maritime). Painted landscapes, still-lifes and, occasionally, flowers. Exhib. Paris Indép. *Fleurs*, 1891, *Fleurs des champs*, 1894
LIT *Orsay*; *Paris Indép.* 1891, 1894

CAILLE, Fanny
b. Paris. Pupil of Chaplin. Exhib. *Branche de capucines*, Paris Noir et Blanc Salon, 1886; *Bouquet de pensées*, Roanne Salon 1890
LIT *Bénézit*; *Paris Noir et Blanc Salon* 1886; *Roanne Salon* 1890

CAILLEBOTTE, Gustave ***1848–1894***
b. Paris. Pupil of Bonnat. Though mostly a landscape and figure painter, Caillebotte, like many of his Impressionist friends, was sensitive to flowers. Unlike them, he was a man of means and his Petit Genevilliers garden provided him with many a motive e.g. *Massifs de fleurs*, 1882 (B.215); *Soleils*, 1885 (B.308); *Massif de Jacinthes*, 1890–1 (B.391); *Iris bleus*, 1892 (B.424); *Chrysanthèmes blancs et jaunes*, 1893 (Marmottan, B.457); *Orchidées dans la serre du Petit Genevilliers*, 1893 (B.460). Caillebotte's favourite blooms were garden flowers of the fleshy, opulent kind —dahlias, roses, gladioli and the ever-popular *fin-de-siècle* chrysanthemums. He grew orchids in his hothouse and painted them in 1893 on panels for his dining-room doors (B.465–71). Among Caillebotte's flower paintings are *Panier de fruits et vase de fleurs*, *c.*1878 (B.183); *Giroflées*, 1881 (B.182); *Dahlias dans un vase*, 1881 (B.183); *Roses jaunes dans un vase*, 1882 (B.206); *Reines-marguerites dans un vase*, 1882 (B.207); *Lilas dans un vase*, 1882 (B.242); *Bouquet de roses dans un vase de cristal*, 1883 (B.239); *Nature-morte au vase de lilas*, 1883 (B.240); *Lilas et pivoines dans deux vases*, 1883 (B.241); *Roses rouges dans un vase*, 1883 (B.243); *Bouquet de reines-marguerites, capucines et soleils dans un vase*, 1887 (B.322); *Bouquet de reines-marguerites et soleils dans un vase*, 1887

(B. 323); *Roses jaunes et rouges dans un vase de cristal*, 1887 (B. 324); *Vase de glaïeuls*, 1887 (B. 325); *Iris jaunes*, 1892 (B. 426); *Roses*, 1892 (B. 427); *Dahlias, cactus rouges*, 1892 (B. 428); *Marguerites*, 1892 (B. 429); *Capucines*, 1892 (B. 430, B. 432); *Dahlia rose*, 1892 (B. 433); *Deux dahlias*, 1892 (B. 434); *Dahlias-cactus dans un vase*, 1892 (B. 435); *Dahlias dans un vase*, 1892–1893 (B. 436); *Quatre vases de chrysanthèmes*, 1893 (B. 454); *Chrysanthèmes dans un vase*, 1893 (B. 455, B. 456); *Chrysanthèmes blancs et jaunes*, 1893 (B. 459); *Orchidées jaunes*, 1893 (B. 461); *Orchidées*, 1893 (B. 462); *Orchidées à fleurs jaunes*, 1893 (B. 464); *Orchidées Catleya et Antonia*, 1893 (B. 465); *Orchidées à fleurs blanches*, 1893 (B. 466); *Orchidées et plantes à fleurs rouges*, 1893 (B. 469); *Fleurs blanches et roses, Antoniums*, 1893 (B. 470); *Begonias argentés et cyprièdes*, 1893 (B. 471); *Glaïeuls*, 1893–1894 (B. 472, B. 473); *Penstemons*, 1893–1894 (B. 474); *Orchidées dans un vase*, 1893 (B. 475). M: Paris, Musée Marmottan, Orsay
LIT *M. Berhaut;* (here B.) *Caillebotte, sa vie, son œuvre, catalogue raisonné*. Paris (Bibliothèque des Arts) 1978; London, *Gustave Caillebotte 1848–1894*, (Wildenstein) 1966; New York, *Gustave Caillebotte* (Wildenstein) 1968; K. Varnedoe, *Gustave Caillebotte*, New Haven and London, 1987; Witt. AC, PH

CALBET, Antoine *1860–1944*
Pupil of Cabanel. This figure painter often associated nudes and flowers and produced some flower-pieces e.g. *Vase de roses*, J. Gautier sale, Drouot, Paris, 16 May 1939
LIT *Bénézit*; *Orsay*; *Schurr* III, 120

CALLARD, Jean-Marie Louis *b.1835*
Pupil of Thierriat, Lyon BA (CFD 1853)
LIT *Hardouin-Fugier Grafe*

CALLOT or CALOT, Marie-Evelyne or Elvina
b. Corbeil (Essonne). Pupil of Rivoire. Exhib. Paris Noir et Blanc Salon *Eglantines*, *Chrysanthèmes*, 1886, *Fleur variées*, 1888
LIT *Bellier*; *Paris Noir et Blanc Salon* 1886, 1888

Eugène-Charles Caban (*right*)

Drawing, signed
Sèvres, Archives, Manufacture Nationale de Sèvres

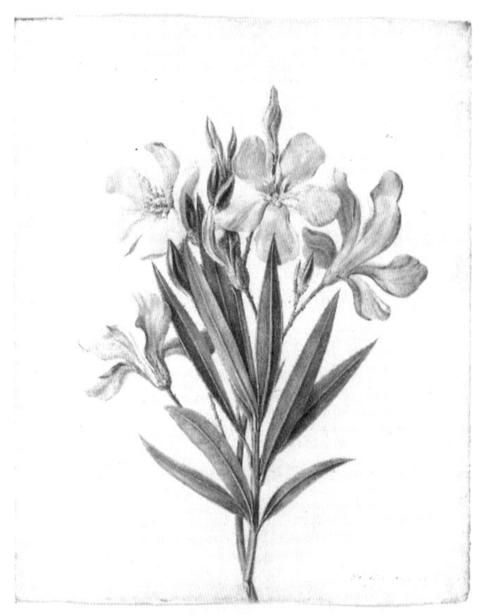

Pauline Cabanne née Garneray

Watercolour on vellum, $10\frac{5}{8} \times \frac{1}{16}$ in. (27.1 × 22 cm.), signed and dated 1834
Cambridge, Fitzwilliam Museum (Broughton Collection)

CALMANT, Eugène-Marguerite
b. Paris. Pupil of Rivoire. Exhib. *Bouquet de roses*, wc, Lyon Salon 1878; Paris Salon *Bourriche de pensées*, wc, *Pot de giroflées*, 1879, *Cinéraires*, *Glaïeuls*, 1881. *Fuchsia, white fuchsia and pelargonium*, wc, Sotheby's, London, 8 Oct. 1980
LIT *Bellier*; *Bénézit*; *Lyon Salon* 1878; *Orsay*

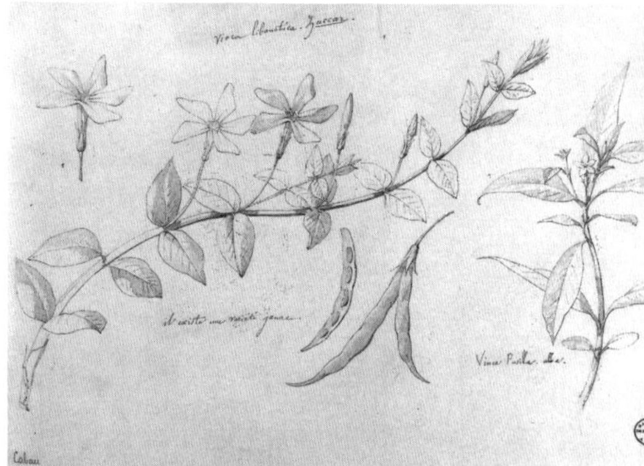

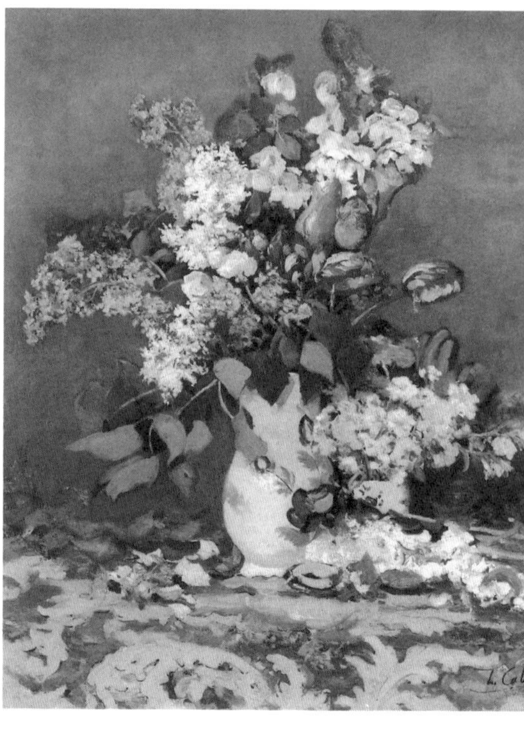

Louis-Alexandre Cabié

Oil on canvas, $28\frac{3}{4} \times 23\frac{1}{2}$ in. (73 × 59.5 cm.), signed
Private collection, Courtesy Phillips', London

CALMBACHER, Jeanne
Pupil of J. Cantal. Exhib. *Chrysanthèmes*, *Fleurs*, wc, Paris UFPS 1896
LIT *Bénézit*; *Paris UFPS* 1896

CALMELET, H.G. ***b.1814***
Two watercolours entitled *Caltha Palustris*, both signed and dated 'mars-avril 1881' in Cambridge, Fitzwilliam Museum (Broughton coll.) may be by the artist b. Lyon 1814, and who exhib. a series of watercolours, primarily landscapes, 1848–1870.
LIT *Bellier*; *Bénézit*; *Thieme*; *Broughton*, 1974; *Broughton*, 1979; *Broughton*, 1983 (ill.). JLC

CALMELS, Henry de
b. Toulouse (Haute-Garonne). Exhib. Paris Noir et Blanc Salon *Pivoines*, 1886, *Coin de mon jardin*, *Verveines*, *Phlox*, *Primevères et laurier thym*, *Roses et croix de Malte*, 1888
LIT *Bénézit*; *Paris Noir et Blanc Salon*, 1886, 1888

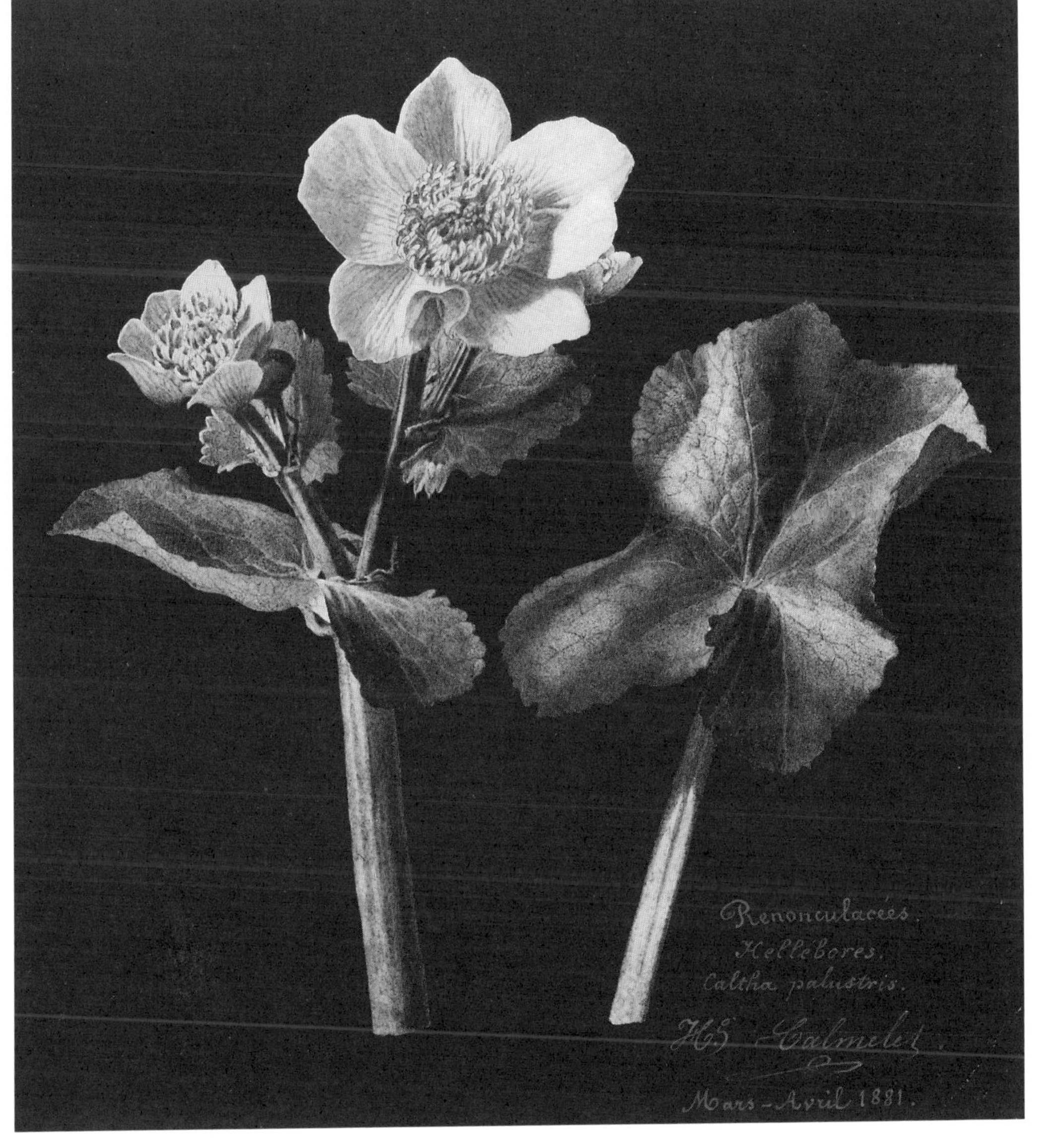

H.G. Calmelet

Gouache on paper, signed and dated 'mars — avril 1881'
Cambridge, Fitzwilliam Museum
(Broughton Collection)

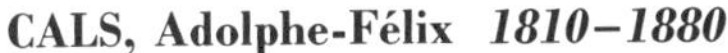

CALS, Adolphe-Félix ***1810–1880***
b. Paris. Pupil of Cogniet. Painted landscapes, portraits, interiors and, occasionally, flowers e.g. *Bouquet de roses*, *c*.1855–1860 (private coll.)
LIT *Bellier*; *Bénézit*; Paris, *A.F. Cals*, François Delestre, 1975; Paris, *A. Cals*, Galerie Jacques Dubourg, 1979; *Schurr* I, 47; G. Weisberg, *Chardin and the Still-Life Tradition*, Cleveland, 1979 (ill.); *Thieme*

CALVÈS, Georges ***b.1848***
b. Paris. Pupil of his father and Lewis Brown. Exhib. *Bourriche de géraniums variés*, wc, Paris Salon 1872; *Azalées*, Dijon Salon 1881; *Glaïeuls*, wc, Lyon Salon 1882
LIT *Bénézit*; *Dijon Salon* 1881; *Lyon Salon* 1882; *Paris Salon* 1872; *Witt*

CALVINIÈRE, Laura-Marie de la
b. Presle (Savoie or Haute-Saône). Pupil of Cogniet. Exhib. *Fleurs et fruits*, pastel, Paris Salon 1880
LIT *Paris Salon* 1880

CAMARET, Mathilde
One signed work of 1888 has recently appeared at auction, Geneva 1–2 June 1988. PM

CAMENISCH, Melchior-Antoine ***b.1818***
Pupil of Thierriat, Lyon BA (CFD 1837–1839)
LIT *Hardouin-Fugier Grafe*

CAMME, Lili
Exhib. *Lilas*, *Roses trémières*, *Violettes*, Paris Indép. 1888
LIT *Paris Indép.* 1888

CANOBY, Marie
b. Paris. Pupil of Colin-Libour and Eugène Trouvé. Exhib. *Pensées et giroflées*, *Violon et pivoines*, Lyon Salon 1879; *Pavots et oeillets*, wc, Paris SNBA 1894
LIT *Lyon Salon* 1879; *Paris SNBA* 1894

CANTEL, Jacques
Designed plates for *Les fleurs dans les appartements*, Paris BMAD (Maciet coll.)
LIT *Paris BMAD*

CAPPE, Mlle de
Exhib. *Vase de marguerites*, Dijon Salon 1849
LIT *Dijon Salon* 1849. CL

CARBET, Jean
Exhib. *Fleurs sur une tombe*, Paris SNBA 1893
LIT *Paris SNBA* 1893 (ill.)

CARDON, Delphine
Pupil of École Professionelle Roquette-Sabourin. Exhib. *Chrysanthèmes*, on porcelain, Paris Salon 1880
LIT *Bellier*

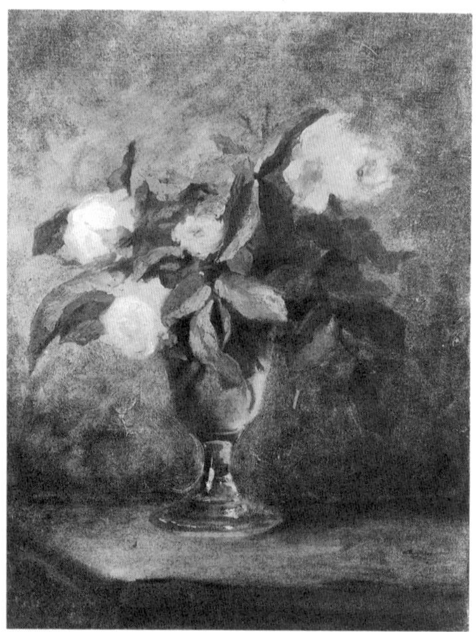

Adolphe-Félix Cals

Oil on canvas, 12 × 9 in. (30.3 × 28.1 cm.), signed, *c.* 1855–1860
Private collection (photo: Stoppenbach & Delestre, London)

CARDOT, Jules
b. Toulouse (Haute-Garonne). Pupil of Toulouse BA. Exhib. *Branche de cerisier*, gouache, Paris Salon 1867
LIT *Paris Salon* 1867

CARLIEZ, Eléonore-Auguste
b. Rouen (Seine-Maritime). Pupil of Pils, G. Morin and Cogniet. Painted landscapes, genre and flowers e.g. Paris Salon *Roses*, wc, 1875, *Fleurs d'automne*, 1880
LIT *Bellier*; *Bénézit*; *Paris Salon* 1875, 1880

CARME, Félix
b. Bordeaux. Active at Bordeaux. Painted still-lifes, interiors. Exhib. 1895–1937. M: Bordeaux
LIT *Bénézit*. PM

CARNOT, G.S.F.
Exhib. *Roses, le soir, Trianon*, Paris SNBA 1899
LIT *Paris SNBA* 1899

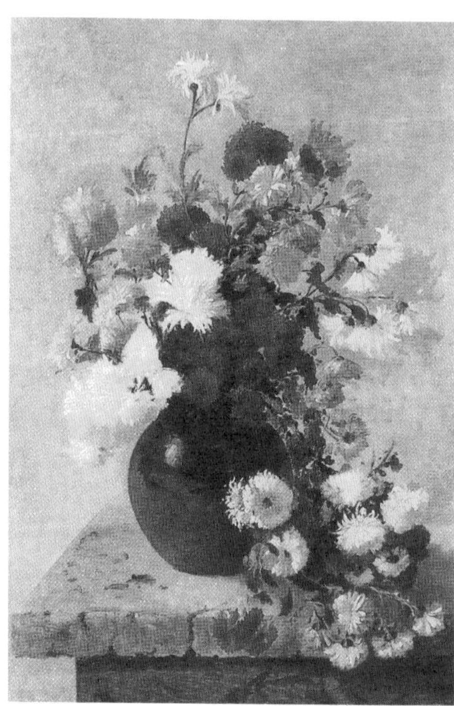

Mathilde Camaret

Oil on canvas, 39½ × 27½ in. (100 × 70 cm.), signed and dated 1888
Private collection

CAROLUS-DURAN, Charles Durand alias *1837–1917*
The famous figure and portrait painter produced some still-lifes featuring flowers e.g. *Carafe, corbeille de fruits renversée et vase de fleurs*, 1864, *Vase, plat, plante verte et fleurs sur une nappe*, 1864
LIT *Bénézit*; *Orsay*; *Thieme*

CARON, Christophe-Ferdinand *1774–1831*
Pupil of J.J. Bachelier and J. Barraban. Painted birds and, occasionally, flowers. At Sèvres 1792–1815
LIT *Brunet Préaud*

CARON, Jules
Poissy (Yvelines). Pupil of Rémond. Exhib. Lyon Salon *Oeillets divers*, 1865, *Chrysanthèmes*, 1867, and 1870, *Giroflées*, 1873, *Lilas*, 1875
LIT *Bellier*; *Bénézit*; *Lyon Salon* 1865, 1867, 1870, 1873, 1875 *Thieme*

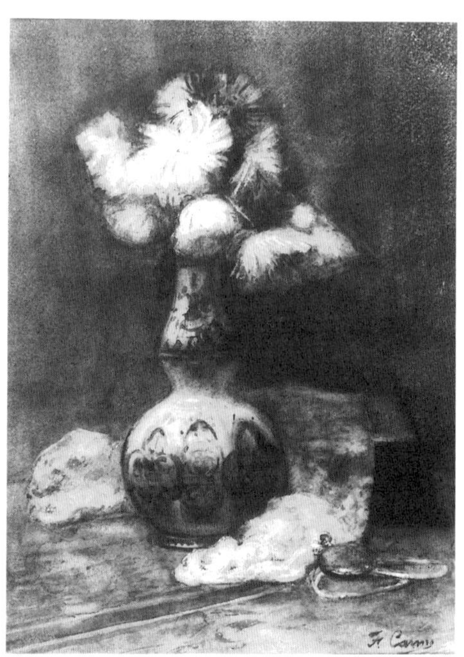

Félix Carme

Watercolour 12¼ × 9½ in. (31 × 24 cm.), signed
Bordeaux, Musée des Beaux-Arts

CAROT, Jules-Etienne
b. Paris. Pupil of Kreyder. Exhib. Paris Salon from 1877 e.g. *Pour faire un bouquet*, 1878, *Fleurs de printemps*, wc, 1880
LIT *Bellier; Bénézit; Paris Salon* 1880; *Thieme*

CARPEAUX, Jean-Baptiste *1827–1875*
b. Valenciennes (Nord). The famous sculptor occasionally painted flowers e.g. *Roses dans un verre, Bouquet de lilas* etc. Paris atelier sale 1913. M: Paris. Petit Palais, *Fleurs des champs, Bouquet de muguets*, 1874; Valenciennes, *Bouquet de lilas*, 1874
LIT *Courbevoie, J.B. Carpeaux*, Musée des Beaux-Arts, 1975–1976; Nice, *J.B. Carpeaux*, Musée des Ponchettes, 1980; *Orsay*; Saint-Tropez, *Fleurs de Fantin-Latour à Marquet*. Musée de l'Annonciade, 1982, no. 8 (ill.)

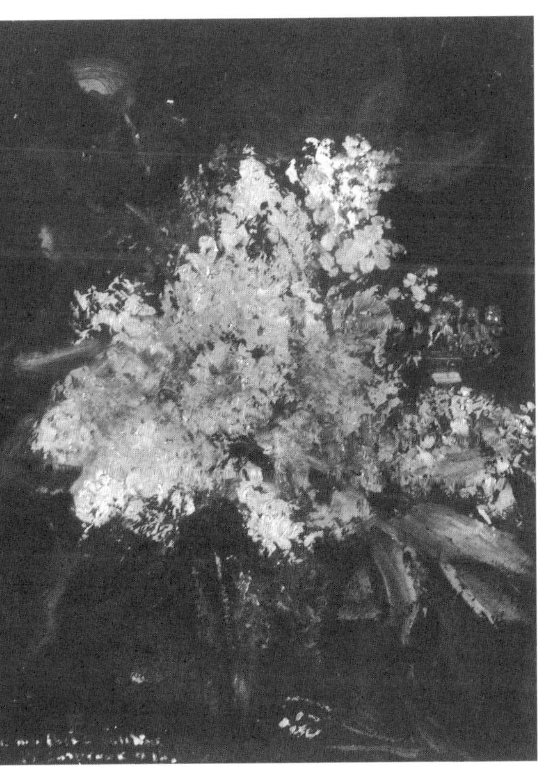

Jean-Baptiste Carpeaux

Oil on canvas, 16¼ × 13 in. (41 × 33 cm.), signed and dated 1874
Valenciennes, Musée des Beaux-Arts

CARPENTIER, Madeleine *b.1865*
b. Paris. Pupil of A. Bonnefoy, J. Lefebvre, B. Constant, E. Luminais. Painted to support bankrupt relatives. Painted genre, still-lifes and flowers e.g. Paris Salon *Primevères*, wc, 1885, *Giroflées*, wc, 1895. Her *Marché de fleurs aux Halles*, wc, was bought in 1899 for the Musée d'Aurillac (1,500 francs); *Violettes et roses jaunes*, wc. Musée Calvet, Avignon
LIT *Bellier*; *Bénézit*; Paris Arch. Nat. F21:2126; *Paris Salon* 1885, 1895; *Schurr* II, 93; *Thieme*

CARQUILLAT, Joseph *b.1826*
Pupil of Thierriat, Lyon BA (CFD 1844)
LIT *Hardouin-Fugier Grafe*

CARRAND, Louis-Hilaire *1821–1899*
The now well-known Lyonnais landscape painter occasionally painted flowers e.g. *Roses*, Lyon Salon 1896
LIT *Hardouin-Fugier Grafe*; *Witt*

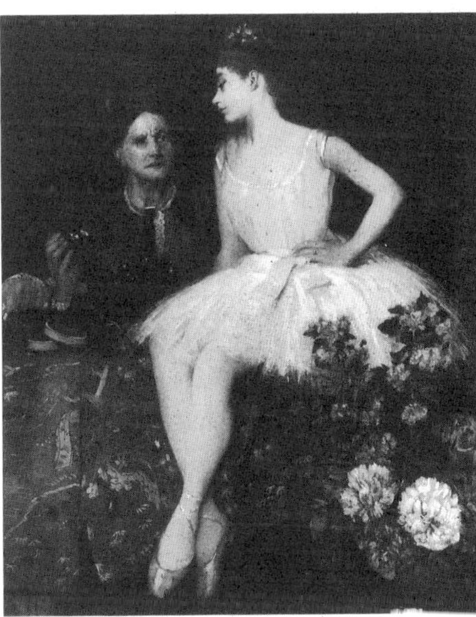

Henriette Carrier-Belleuse

Oil on canvas, 23 × 18½ in. (58.5 × 47 cm.), signed and dated 1888
Courtesy Christie's, London

CARREY, Louis-Jacques *1822–1871*
b. Rouen (Seine-Maritime). Pupil of Thierriat, Lyon BA (CFD 1842) and Saint-Jean. Exhib. Lyon Salon 1843–1868, Paris Salon 1857–1865. Painted still-lifes and, occasionally, flowers. His *Roses* was in the 1860–1861 Lyon Société des Amis-des-Arts raffle
LIT *Audin Vial*; *Bénézit*; *Hardouin-Fugier Grafe* 1981; *Thieme*

CARRIER-BELLEUSE, Henriette
b. Paris. Pupil of A.E. Carrier-Belleuse, her father, and Cottin. Married Joseph Chéret. Exhib. *Primevères*, Paris Salon 1874, 1879
LIT *Bellier*; *Bénézit*; *Thieme*

CARRIÈRE, Eugène *1849–1906*
The famous portrait and figure painter occasionally produced still-lifes featuring flowers e.g. *Vase de fleurs*, Drouot, Paris, 17 May 1900, *Fleurs*, Madrid, Duran Senano, 31 Jan. 1973
LIT *Bénézit*; J.P. Dubray "E. Carrière", *Paris Séheur*, 1931; G. Geffroy, *L'oeuvre de Carrière*, Paris 1901; *Orsay*; *Thieme*; *Witt*

CARRIÈRE, Léo *b.1874*
Pupil of Castex-Dégrange, Lyon BA (CFD 1894)
LIT *Hardouin-Fugier Grafe*

CARRIÈRE L., *see* DEVOLVÉ-CARRIÈRE

CARRILLON, François *b.1826*
Pupil of Thierriat, Lyon BA (CFD 1842)
LIT *Hardouin-Fugier Grafe*

CARTERON, Marie-Zoé, *née* Valleray *b.1813*
b. Paris. Pupil of Granger and Cogniet. Painted portraits, still-lifes and, occasionally, flowers. Exhib. Paris Salon 1839–1880
LIT *Bellier*; *Bénézit*; *Faré* 1962, p. 242; *Thieme*

CASPERS, Pauline
b. Paris. Pupil of Lemaire and Hanter. Exhib. *Primevères de Chine*, Dijon Salon 1890; Paris Salon, *Chrysanthèmes*, 1890, *Chrysanthèmes et grenades*, 1898
LIT *Bénézit*; *Dijon Salon* 1890; *Paris Salon* 1890, 1898; *Thieme*

CASTAGNARY, Marie-Amélie, *née* Viteau
b. Saint-Mandé (Val-de-Marne). Pupil of Maillard, Henner and Carolus-Duran. Painted portraits and flowers. Exhib. Paris Salon from 1883. Musée de Saintes, *Pivoines*
LIT *Bénézit*; *Thieme*

CASTETS, Henri *1797–1870*
Pupil of Thierriat, Lyon BA. Textile designer
LIT *Hardouin-Fugier Grafe*

CASTEX-DÉGRANGE, Adolphe-Louis-Napoléon Dégrange *alias* *1840–1918*
b. Marseille. Pupil of Reignier, Lyon BA (CFD 1854). Succeeded Reignier as professor of the CFD at Lyon BA, 1884 to his death. A prolific, distinguished flower painter and influential teacher. Exhib. Lyon Salon from 1858, Paris Salon from 1874 e.g. *Buisson de roses trémières*, Lyon Salon 1872; *Buisson de roses*, Lyon, Paris Salon 1876; Paris Salon *L'eventaire de la bouquetière*, 1877, *Avant le marché*, 1881, etc. Musée des Beaux-Arts de Lyon, *Ma table à modèles*, 1885
LIT *Hardouin-Fugier Grafe* (ill.); *Hardouin-Fugier Grafe* 1979 (ill.); *Hardouin-Fugier Grafe* 1982 (ill.); Pavière III, pt. 1

CATENOD, François-Marie-Joseph *b.1828*
Pupil of Thierriat, Lyon BA (CFD 1846)
LIT *Hardouin-Fugier Grafe*

CATTAERT, Auguste-Joseph-Antoine
b. Lille (Nord). Exhib. *Fleurs de printemps*, *Cueillette du jardinier*, Lille Salon 1881
LIT *Lille Salon* 1881. G and LT

CAUCHOIS, Eugène-Henri *1850–1911*
b. Rouen (Seine-Maritime). Pupil of Duboc, Cabanel and Quost. Exhib. Paris Salon from 1874. A prolific painter. *Culture de pavots*, Saint-Etienne Salon 1891; Paris Salon *Après la pluie*, 1893, *Pour l'autel*, 1894; *Géraniums*, Dijon Salon 1897; *Roses de septembre*, Paris Salon 1898. M: Chatellerault, Rouen, Louviers, Musée Municipal: *Bouquet de fleurs des champs* (two examples), *Chrysanthèmes*, *Fleurs*, *Chez le jardinier*. *Nature morte aux bouquets de fleurs et fruits* (Daniel Grossmann, Gallery, New York, 1987),
LIT *Bellier; Bénézit; Dijon Salon* 1897, *Hardouin-Fugier Bringuier; Orsay; Paris Salon* 1893 (ill), 1894 (ill), 1898 (ill) *Saint-Etienne Salon* 1891; *Schurr* II, 64; *Thieme*; *Witt*

CAUCHY, Mme Emile de
Pupil of Armand Leleux and Mlle Burat. Exhib. Paris Salon *Fruits et fleurs*, on porcelain, 1876, *Géranium*, wc, Paris Salon 1878
LIT *Bellier*

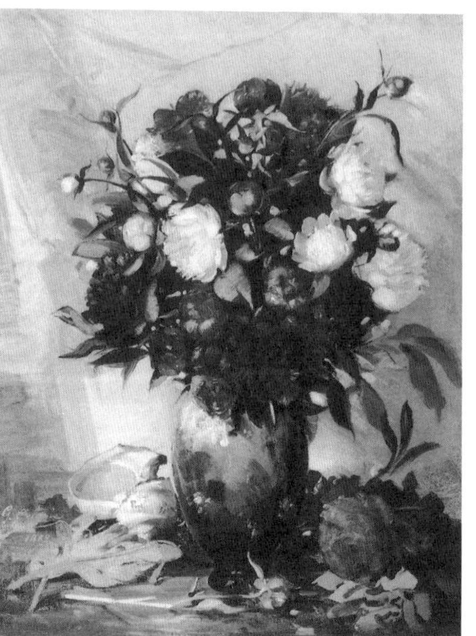

CAUSSIDIÈRE, Marc *1808–1861*
Pupil of Berjon, Lyon BA (CFD 1821). Textile designer and politician
LIT *Hardouin-Fugier Grafe*

CAVAROC, Honoré *1846–1931*
b. Lyon. Pupil of Lyon BA (1866). A life-long friend of Seignemartin and F.Vernay. Photographer. Painted landscapes, portraits and flowers. Exhib. Lyon Salon from 1872 e.g. *Fleurs*, 1875
LIT *Bénézit*; *Hardouin-Fugier Grafe. Lyon Salon* 1875; *Thieme*

CAVÉ, Jules-Cyrille *b.1859*
b. Paris. Pupil of Bouguereau and Tony Robert-Fleury. Painted genre and flowers e.g. Paris Salon *Première gelée*, 1891, *Moisson de fleurs*, 1899
LIT *Bellier*; *Bénézit*; *Thieme*

CÉLARIÉ, F.F-Gaston
b. Homps (Gers). Pupil of Cormon. *Peonies in a vase*, 1882, Sotheby's, London, 20 June 1979
LIT *Bénézit*; *Orsay*

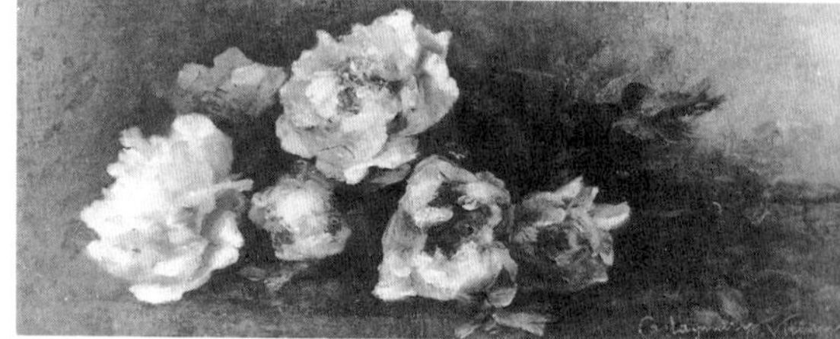

Marie-Amélie Castagnary

Oil on canvas, $11\frac{1}{2} \times 26\frac{3}{4}$ in. (29 × 68 cm.), signed
Saintes, Musée des Beaux-Arts

F. F-Gaston Célarié

Oil on canvas, $35\frac{1}{2} \times 28$ in. (90 × 71 cm.), signed and dated 1882
Courtesy Sotheby's, London

CERCLEUX, Pierre-Antoine *1828–1892*
b. Marseille. Pupil of Thierriat, Lyon BA (CFD 1844)
LIT *Hardouin-Fugier Grafe*

CERNIT, Jeanne de
Pupil of Trébuchet. Exhib. *Fleurs*, gouache, Paris Salon 1880
LIT *Paris Salon* 1880

CERRÈS, *see* BAUDRY DE BALZAC

CESBRON, Achille-Théodore *1849–1913*
b. Oran (Algeria). Pupil of Bonnat and Cormon. A most successful flower painter. Exhib. Paris Salon from *c.*1877 e.g. *Roses et pavots*, *Le reposoir*, 1881, *Metempsychose*, 1884, *Fleurs du sommeil*, 1886; *Chrysanthèmes*, Dijon Salon 1892; Paris Salon *Trois dahlias jaunes*, 1895, *Rosier blanc*, 1898. With G. Jeannin, painted decorative panels for the Paris Hôtel de Ville. His 1884 *Metempsychose* was bought for the Musée d'Angers. His 1886 *Fleurs du sommeil* (1,000 francs) is in the Musée de Riom. Other works, M: Gray, Paris, Musée d'Orsay, *Pensées dans un vase*, exhib. Saint-Tropez 1982
LIT *Bellier*; *Bénézit*; L. Lambeau *L'Hôtel de Ville de Paris*, Paris (Laurens) 1908; *Orsay*; Paris Arch. Nat. F21:2126, 4287; Saint-Tropez, *Fleurs de Fantin-Latour à Marquet*, Musée de l'Annonciade, 1982, no. 10 (ill.); *Schurr* II, 88; *Thieme*
See illustration on page 32

CÉZANNE, Paul *1839–1906*
b. Aix-en-Provence (Bouches-du-Rhône). Pupil of Académie Suisse, Paris. Friend of Pissarro and Guillaumin. After countless failures, retired to Aix. Owned a watercolour of flowers by Delacroix. A slow worker, he found painting flowers difficult. Among his flower paintings are: *Dahlias dans un pot de Delft*, 1873 (Louvre, O. 213); *Fleurs dans un vase*, 1873–1875 (Leningrad, O. 215), *Vase de fleurs, bouquet au petit Delft*, 1873–1875 (Louvre, O. 216); *Géraniums et coreopsis*, 1873–1875 (O. 214); *Vase de fleurs*, 1875–1877 (O. 224); *Fleurs dans un vase de verre*, 1875–1877 (San Diego, O. 225); *Vase de fleurs*, 1873–1877 (O. 217); *Les deux vases de fleurs*, 1873–1877 (O. 219); *Fleurs dans un vase vert*, 1873–1877 (Philadelphia, O. 220); *Vase de fleurs sur une table ronde*, 1873–1877 (O. 218); *Pétunias*, 1875–1876 (O. 221); *Pot de fleurs*, 1875–1876 (O. 222); *Le vase rococo*, 1876 (Washington, O. 223); *Nature-morte, fleurs et fruits*, 1879–1882 (Paris, Musées Nationaux, O. 486); *Vase de fleurs*, 1879–1882 (Los Angeles, O. 487); *Fleurs dans un vase*, 1879–1882 (O. 488); *Le vase bleu*, 1879–1882 (O. 489); *Fleurs dans un vase bleu*, 1879–1882 (Paris, Musée Nationaux, coll. Guillaume, O. 490); *Fleurs dans un vase vert*, 1883–1887 (O. 491); *Vase de fleurs et pommes*, 1883–1887 (O. 492); *Le vase bleu*, 1885–1887 (Louvre, O. 493); *Fleurs et fruits*, 1888–1890 (Berlin, O. 819); *Pot en terre cuite et fleurs*, 1888–1890 (Merion, O. 820); *Fleurs et fruits*, 1890–1894 (O. 821); *Pots de géraniums et fruits*, 1890–1894 (New York, O. 822); *Vase de tulipes*, 1890–1894 (Chicago, O. 824, O. 825); *Grand bouquet de fleurs*, 1890–1894 (O. 826); *Vase au jardin*, 1895–1900 (O. 827); *Bouquet de pivoines dans un pot vert*, c.1898 (Paris 1878, 30); *Fleurs et verdures*, 1900 (Moscow, O. 828); *Vase fleuri*, 1900 (Merion, O. 829). M: Berlin; Chicago Art Institute; Leningrad Hermitage; Norton Simon Foundation, Los Angeles; Barnes Foundation, Merion; Moscow Pushkin Museum; New York Metropolitan Museum of Art; Paris, Orsay; Philadelphia Museum of Art; Timken Art Gallery, San Diego; Washington National Gallery
LIT S. (here O.) Orienti, *Tout l'œuvre peint de Cézanne*, Paris (Flammarion) 1975; Paris, *Cézanne, les dernières années*, Grand Palais, Réunion des Musées Nationaux, 1978; Witt. AC

CHABAL-DUSSURGEY, Pierre-Adrien *1819–1902*
b. Charlieu (Loire). Pupil of Thierriat, Lyon BA (CFD 1836). Exhib. Lyon Salon from 1839, Paris Salon from 1842 where Baudelaire praised his 1845 exhibit: "A conscientious and pleasant gouache flower piece." Professor of flower design at the Paris Gobelins school from 1850 (tapestries and designs Paris, Mobilier National). Provided designs for Beauvais and Gobelins tapestries e.g. for Empress Eugénie's Tuileries drawing-room. An influential teacher whose best-known pupil was Burty, the art critic. Designed a set of plates for his own *Etudes et Compositions de fleurs*, Paris *c.*1868. First exhib. flowers in gouache, later in oils. Founded the Nice École des Arts Décoratifs (1881). Musée d'Angers, *Fleurs*, gouache; Musée de Limoges, *Fleurs*; Cambridge, Fitzwilliam Museum (Broughton coll.) two watercolours signed "Dussurgey" may be by the artist; Musée d'Art et d'Industrie, Saint-Etienne, *Le printemps*, 1863; Musée des Beaux-Arts, Lyon, *Concordia*, 1878; Musée Chéret, Nice, *Un rosier de mon jardin*, 1879
LIT Hardouin-Fugier in *Fleurs de Fantin-Latour à Marquet*, Musée de l'Annonciade, Saint-Tropez, 1982 (ill.); *Hardouin-Fugier Grafe* (ill.); *Hardouin-Fugier Grafe* 1979 (ill.); *Hardouin-Fugier Grafe* 1982 (ill.); O. Nouvel, *L'Art français sous le Second Empire*, Paris, Grand Palais, 1979; *Thieme*

CHABOURET-LATOUR, Raymonde *1865–1930*
Painted flowers *c.*1900
LIT *Orsay*

CHADE, Jules *1870–1942*
b. Clermont-Ferrand (Puy-de-Dôme). Painted decorative flowers *c.*1900
LIT *Orsay*

CHAGOT, Edmond ***b.1832***
Pupil of Durand-Brager and Ziem. Exhib. Paris Salon 1864–1885. *Bouquet de fleurs*, 1877 (private coll.)
LIT *Bellier*; *Bénézit*; *Orsay*; *Schurr* III, 54; *Thieme*

CHAILLERY, Eugène-Louis
b. Angers (Maine-et-Loire). Exhib. Paris Salon 1870–1880 e.g. *Giroflées*, 1879
LIT *Bellier*

CHAINE, Achille ***1814–1884***
Pupil of Thierriat, Lyon BA (CFD 1834). Painted figures, genre and, occasionally, flowers
LIT *Hardouin-Fugier Grafe*; *Hardouin-Fugier Grafe* 1981

CHALAMEL, Claude or Claudius-Pierre
Pupil of Thierriat, Lyon BA (CFD 1841). Entered 1842–1843 Lyon FDC (flowers in gouache). Exhib. Lyon Salon 1842–1859
LIT *Hardouin-Fugier Grafe*

CHALEYÉ, Jean-Baptiste or Joannès ***1878–1960***
b. Saint-Etienne (Loire). Pupil of Castex-Dégrange, Lyon BA (CFD 1897–1899), then Gérôme and Cormon. Art-teacher (Le Puy and Roubaix). Most of his flowers are later works (e.g. *Bouquet de Roses*, 1931) but he may have produced some early ones
LIT *Hardouin-Fugier Bringuier*; *Hardouin-Fugier Grafe*; *Schurr* III, 148; *Witt*

CHALLIÉ, Alphonsine de
b. Château de Gaultret (Deux-Sèvres). Pupil of Chaplin. Painted genre and flowers. Exhib. Paris Salon 1878–1882 e.g. *Premières roses*, 1880
LIT *Bellier*; *Bénézit*; *Thieme*

CHAMBARD, Edouard-Jean-Baptiste-Gaspard ***1806–1890***
b. Saint-Amour (Jura). Textile designer, Lyon. Painted flowers in wc
LIT E. Davies-Legouis. Private correspondence

CHAMBINIÈRE, Maurice
b. Niort (Deux-Sèvres). Exhib. Paris Salon from 1879. Painted portraits and flowers e.g. *Tulipes*, wc, Paris Salon 1880. *Mixed flowers in a vase*, Sotheby's, London, 5 July 1979, lot 249
LIT *Bénézit*; *Paris Salon* 1880; *Witt*

CHAMBON, Marie
Pupil of Rivoire. Exhib. *Pivoines*, wc, Paris UFPS 1898
LIT *Paris UFPS* 1898

Jean-Baptiste Chaleyé (*right*)

Oil on canvas $21\frac{1}{4} \times 32$ in. (54 × 81 cm.), signed and dated 1931
Le Puy, Musée Crozatier

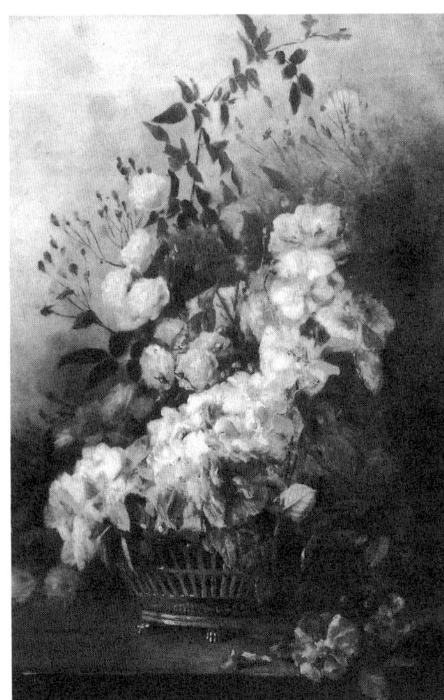

Maurice Chambinière

Oil on canvas, $33\frac{1}{2} \times 23$ in. (85 × 58 cm.), signed
Courtesy Sotheby's, London

CHAMEAU, Etienne ***b.1795***
Pupil of Berjon, Lyon BA (CFD 1813). op. Textile designer. Exhib. Lyon Salon 1843, 1844
LIT *Hardouin-Fugier Grafe*

CHAMECIN, Adèle
b. Lyon. Pupil of Guichard, Miciol, Carolus-Duran, Henner, L.O. Merson. Painted figures, portraits and flowers. Exhib. Lyon Salon from 1884
LIT *Bénézit*; *Thieme*

CHAMECIN, G.
Exhib. *Fleurs*, Grenoble Salon 1880
LIT *Grenoble Salon* 1880. MW

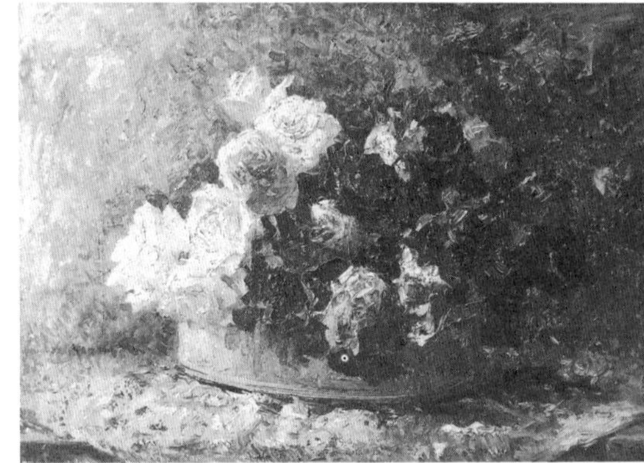

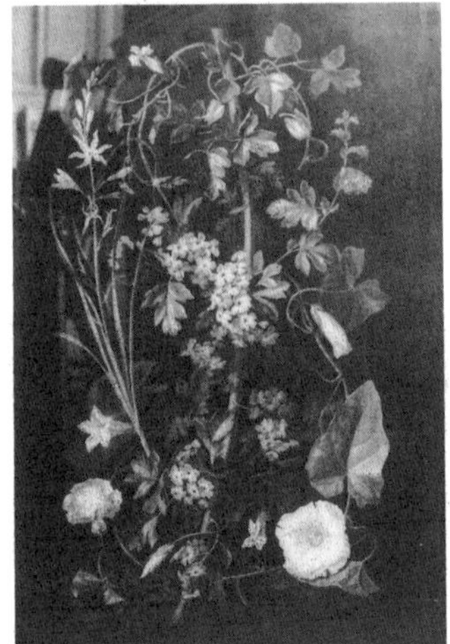

Etienne Chameau

Gouache and gum arabic, $23\frac{3}{4} \times 15\frac{3}{4}$ in. (60 × 40 cm.), signed
Private collection

CHAMONARD, Marie-Guillaume *b.1813*
Pupil of Thierriat, Lyon BA (CFD 1835)
LIT *Hardouin-Fugier Grafe*

CHAMONARD, Paul *b.1867*
Pupil of Castex-Dégrange, Lyon BA (CFD 1889)
LIT *Hardouin-Fugier Grafe*

CHAMPCLAUX, Célina-Marguerite
b. Neuilly-le-Réal (Allier). Pupil of Thoret, Dessard and Blanchard. Exhib. Paris Salon 1877–1880 e.g. *Fleurs*, porcelain, 1880
LIT *Bellier*; *Paris Salon* 1880

CHAMPCLAUX, Hyacinthe-Constance
b. Neuilly-le-Réal (Allier). Pupil of Thoret, Dessard and Blanchard. Exhib. Paris Salon 1877–1882 e.g. *Bouquet de fleurs*, gouache, 1878.
LIT *Bellier*

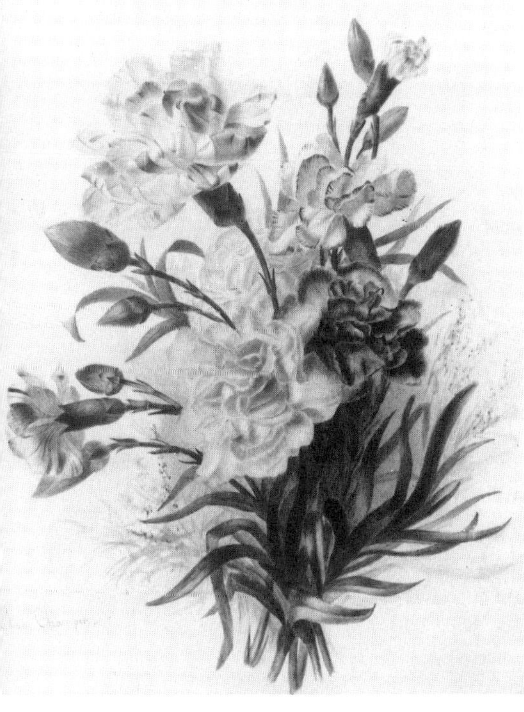

Elisa-Honorine, Champin

Watercolour on vellum, signed
Courtesy Maître Martin, Versailles

CHAMPEAU, Mlle
Designed botanical plates for H. Jaubert, E. Spach *Choix de plantes ... de l'Asie Occidentale*, Paris Roret 1842–1857
LIT *Nissen* I, 985; *Sitwell*

CHAMPEAUX DE LA BOULAYE, Octave de *1827–1903*
b. Orléans (Loiret). Pupil of Diaz. Exhib. *Anémones*, Dijon Salon 1885
LIT *Dijon Salon* 1885; *Thieme*. CL

CHAMPIN, Elisa-Honorine, *née* Pitet *d.1871*
b. Paris. Pupil of A. Riché. Exhib. Paris Salon from 1834 e.g. *Bouquet de fleurs*, wc, 1834, *Bouquet de dahlias*, wc, 1842, *Vase de fleurs et ananas*, wc, 1844, *Groupe de fleurs et de fruits*, wc, 1845. Designed plates for *Album Vilmorin*, 1853. One signed work, a watercolour on vellum, has recently appeared at auction. Versailles, 12 June 1988.
LIT *Album Vilmorin*; *Bellier*; *Bénézit*; *Faré* 1962, p. 248; *Hardouin-Fugier* 1981; *Paris MAD*; *Paris Salon* 1834, 1837, 1842, 1844, 1845; *Thieme*. PM

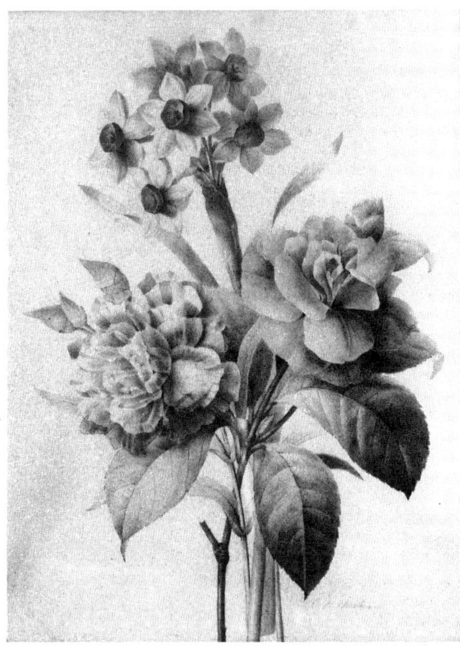

Camille de Chantereine

Watercolour, signed
Tours, Musée des Beaux Arts (on deposit Château d'Azay-le-Ferron)

CHAMPION, Edmé-Théodore
b. Paris. Pupil of Touillon. Exhib. Paris Salon 1874–1882 e.g. *Fleurs de printemps*, wc, *Fleurs d'automne*, wc, 1880
LIT *Bellier*

CHAMPION, Eugène-Desiré
b. Valençay (Indre). Exhib. *Fleurs de printemps*, wc, *Fleurs d'automne*, wc, Paris Salon 1880
LIT *Paris Salon* 1880

CHANET, Gustave-Frédéric
b. Paris. Pupil of Cormon. Exhib. *Oeillets*, wc, Paris Salon 1895; *Bouquet d'oeillets*, wc, Dijon Salon 1897
LIT *Bénézit*; *Dijon Salon* 1897; *Paris Salon* 1895. CL

CHANTEREINE, Camille de *d.1847*
b. Paris. Pupil of Redouté. Exhib. Paris Salon 1827–1844 and *Bouquet de fleurs*, wc, Dijon Salon 1840. Contributed designs to Redouté's *Cours des Fleurs du Jardin des Plantes*, *Choix de 15 bouquets de fleurs*. M: Tours (on deposit at Château d'Azay-le-Ferron), Cambridge, Fitzwilliam Museum (Broughton coll.)
LIT *Dijon Salon* 1840; *Hardouin-Fugier* 1981 (ill.); Broughton 1979

CHANTON, *see* LAMBERT TRISTAN

CHANTRE, Fleury ***b.1806***
b. Lyon. Pupil of Thierriat, Lyon BA (CFD 1825). op. drawing master. Painted flowers and fruit pieces. Exhib. Lyon Salon 1848–1859 e.g. *Roses au bord de l'eau*, 1856, *Roses et bleuets*, 1857, *Raisins et liserons au bord de l'eau*, 1858
LIT *Bénézit*; *Hardouin-Fugier Grafe*; *Thieme*

CHANTRE, François ***d.1859***
b. Lyon. Musée de Bagnères-de-Bigorre, *Bouquet de roses*, wc
LIT *Bénézit*; *Thieme*

CHANTRE, Jean-Marie ***b.1810***
Pupil of Thierriat, Lyon BA (CFD 1830)
LIT *Hardouin-Fugier Grafe*

CHANTRON, Alexandre-Jacques ***1842–1918***
b. Nantes (Loire-Atlantique). Pupil of Picot, T. Robert-Fleury and Bouguereau. Exhib. *Fleurs de printemps*, Paris Salon 1895. *Roses and Chrysanthemums*, Sotheby's, London, 4 Mar 1981, lot 156
LIT *Bellier*; *Bénézit*; *Paris Salon* 1895; *Thieme*; *Witt*

CHANUT, Alfred-Marie-Claude ***1851–1918***
b. Bourg (Ain). Pupil of Lyon BA and L. Bonnat. Exhib. *Chrysanthèmes*, Dijon Salon 1890
LIT *Dijon Salon* 1890; *Schurr* IV, 114; *Thieme*

CHAPAY, Denis ***b.1825***
Pupil of Thierriat, Lyon BA (CFD 1843).
LIT *Hardouin-Fugier Grafe*

CHAPELON, François ***1815–1872***
A textile designer in Lyon
LIT *Hardouin-Fugier Grafe*

CHAPELON, Joseph
Pupil of Reignier, Lyon BA (CFD 1863)
LIT *Hardouin-Fugier Grafe*

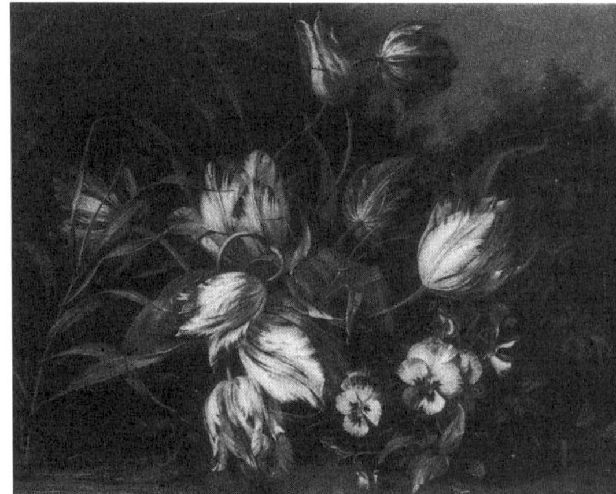

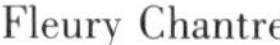

Fleury Chantre

Oil on canvas, 16 × 21¼ in. (40.5 × 54 cm.), signed and dated 1851
Courtesy Sotheby's, London

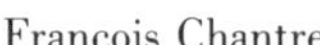

François Chantre

Watercolour, 23½ × 17¼ in. (60 × 44 cm.), signed and dated 1851
Bagnères-de-Bigorre, Musée Salies

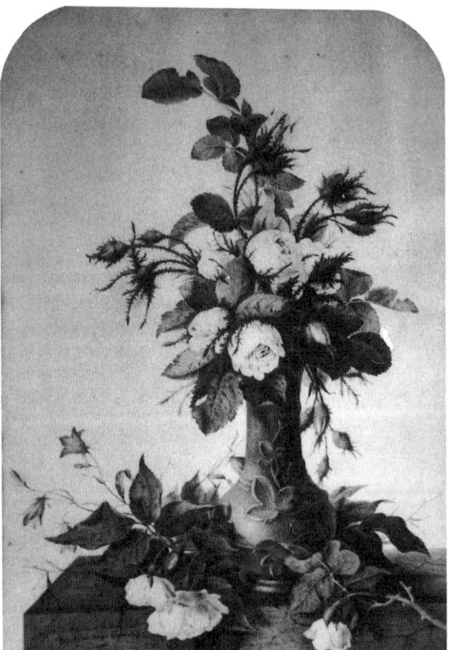

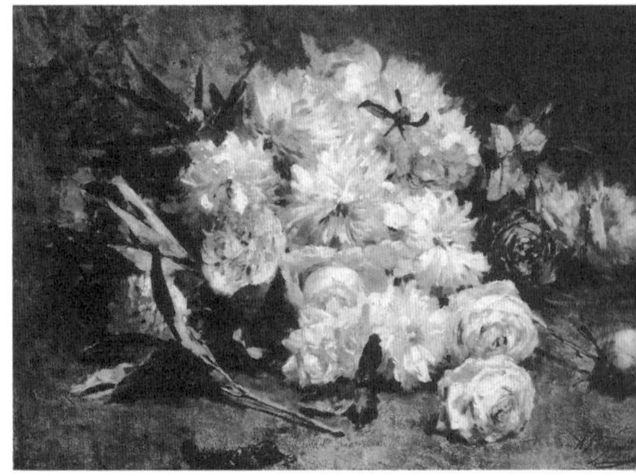

Alexandre Jacques Chantron (*above*)

Oil on canvas, 17¼ × 25¼ in. (44 × 64.5 cm.), signed and dated 1884
Courtesy Sotheby's, London

CHAPLIN, Arthur *b.1869*
b. Jouy-en-Josas (Yvelines), son of Charles Chaplin. Pupil of Bonnat and Bernier. First a decorator, then a flower painter in the Flemish and Dutch styles. Exhib. Paris Salon from 1899. His *Panier de fleurs* is in the Musée du Petit Palais, Paris
LIT *Bellier*; *Bénézit*; *Orsay*; *Thieme*; *Witt*

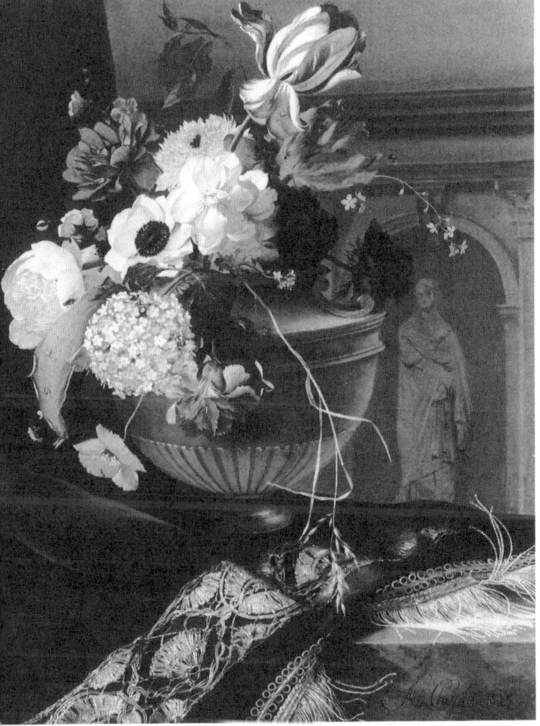

Arthur Chaplin

Oil painting on brass, $21\frac{3}{4} \times 17\frac{3}{4}$ in. (59.7 × 45 cm.), signed and dated 1925
Courtesy John Mitchell & Son, London

CHAPLIN, Charles *1825–1891*
b. Les Andelys (Eure) of British parentage. Pupil of Drolling and Paris BA (1840). The famous portrait, genre and figure painter occasionally painted flowers e.g. for the Tuileries Salon des Fleurs ceiling and overdoors (1861). In his atelier sale (Drouot, Paris, April 1891) were *Roses*, on panel, *Oeillets*, on panel, *Roses et pensées*
LIT *Bellier*; *Bénézit*; F. Masson *C. Chaplin* ... Paris, (Boussod-Valadon) 1888; *Orsay*; *Schurr* I, 85; *Thieme*

CHAPONET, *see* RICHARD

CHAPOTON, Grégoire *1845–1915*
b. Saint-Rambert-sur-Loire (Loire). Pupil of Soulary, at Saint-Etienne, then Reignier, at Lyon BA (CFD 1863). Founder-member of Paris Indép. Exhib. Paris Salon 1870–1880 e.g. *Roses et sureau* and *Une razzia faite au jardin*, 1880; *Bouquet de roses*, Saint-Etienne Salon 1882; *Roses en août*, Paris Indép. 1884; *Végétation cultivée*, Saint-Etienne Salon 1891. M: Laval, Saint-Etienne, *Une razzia faite au jardin*, 1880 (acquired at or just after exhibition at the Paris Salon), and Tours
LIT *Bellier*; *Bénézit*; *Hardouin-Fugier Bringuier*; *Hardouin-Fugier Grafe*; *Paris Indép.* 1884. *Paris Salon* 1880; *Saint-Etienne Salon*, 1882, 1891; *Thieme*

CHAPPET
Pupil of A. Sicard. Exhib. Lyon Salon 1867
LIT *Hardouin-Fugier Grafe*

CHAPPIUS
Pupil of Thierriat, Lyon BA (CFD 1842)
LIT *Hardouin-Fugier Grafe*

CHAPUIS, Pierre *1863–1942*
b. Paris. Pupil of Paris BA. op. Theatre designer and decorator. This many-sided artist painted landscapes and, occasionally, flowers e.g. *Bouquet de fleurs*, no. 59 and 77 of the atelier sale, Drouot, Paris, 8 June 1979
LIT *Orsay*; *Schurr* III, 59

CHAPURLAT, Louis *b.1872*
Pupil of Castex-Dégrange, Lyon BA (CFD 1891)
LIT *Hardouin-Fugier Grafe*

CHARAVEL, Paul *1877–1961*
b. Marseille. Pupil of Bordeaux BA. Friendly with Signac, Valtat, Luce, Cross and Manguin. Painted landscapes and, occasionally, flowers. Atelier sale, Drouot, Paris, 24 May 1967
LIT *Orsay*; *Schurr* I, 109; *Witt*

CHARBONNEL, Charles
Exhib. *Fleurs*, Paris Salon 1838
LIT *Bénézit*

CHARBONNIER, *see* BRET

CHARCOUCHET, Edouard-Joseph *b.1832*
Pupil of Thierriat, Lyon BA (CFD 1850)
LIT *Hardouin-Fugier Grafe*

CHARDERON, Francine *1861–1928*
b. Lyon. Pupil of Rey, Loubet, Hébert and Carolus-Duran. Painted portraits, genre and flowers. Exhib. Lyon Salon from 1885, Paris Salon from 1893; *Roses*, pastel, *Coquelicots*, pastel, Grenoble Salon 1899. M: Lyon, *Petite fille aux roses*, 1897 (exhib. Lyon Salon 1898)
LIT *Bénézit*; *Grenoble Salon* 1899; Hardouin-Fugier Grafe, *Portraitistes Lyonnais*, Lyon, 1986 (ill.); *Thieme*; *Witt*

CHARETTE, F.
Exhib. Lyon Salon *Fleurs et fruits*, *Fruits et fleurs*, 1860; *Fleurs et accessoires*, wc, 1874
LIT *Lyon Salon* 1860, 1874

CHARLES, Marie
Exhib. *Chrysanthèmes*, Paris UFPS 1896
LIT *Paris UFPS* 1896

CHARLES, Mme, *née* Huard
op. Sèvres 1827–1833 and 1837–1841. Exhib. flowers, wc and on porcelain, Paris Salon 1839–1842 e.g. *Bouquet de fleurs d'après nature*, wc, 1841, *Fleurs d'après Van Os*, on porcelain, 1842
LIT *Bellier*; *Brunet Préaud*; *Paris Salon* 1841, 1842; *Thieme*

CHARLIER, Charles-Louis-Henri
Pupil of Ingres. Painted portraits and religious subjects. Exhib. *Fleurs et fruits*, Paris Salon 1845
LIT *Bellier*; *Bénézit*; *Paris Salon* 1845; *Thieme*

CHARMEIL, Mme E.
Flower, fruit and animal painter. Exhib. flowers in wc, Paris Salon 1835, 1838, 1841, 1844 e.g. *Camélia*, 1835, *Fleurs des champs*, 1844. Possibly the same artist as the one who exhibited at the Paris Salon, *Fleurs des champs*, wc, *Anémones*, wc, 1879
LIT *Bellier*; *Bénézit*; *Paris Salon* 1879; *Thieme*

CHARMIER, Claude
Pupil of Berjon, Lyon BA (CFD 1822) and Thierriat, Lyon BA (CFD 1824). Possibly the same artist as Claude Charmier, engraver
LIT *Bénézit*; *Hardouin-Fugier Grafe*

CHARMY, Emilie-Espérance, Barret de *1878–1974*
b. Saint-Etienne (Loire). Pupil of Desvallières. Painted figures, portraits, landscapes, still-lifes and flowers
LIT *Hardouin-Fugier Grafe*; *Orsay*

CHARNIER, Léopold-Marius *b.1860*
Pupil of Reignier, Lyon BA (CFD 1878)
LIT *Hardouin-Fugier Grafe*

CHARON, Pierre
b. Château-Gontier (Mayenne). Pupil of Gérôme, Henner and Barrias. Painted portraits and, occasionally, flowers. *Bouquet de roses*, 1898, Versailles 8 Mar. 1981
LIT *Bénézit*; *Orsay*; *Thieme*

CHARPENTIER, Paul-Alfred
b. Saint-Gervais (Isère). Pupil of L. Salles and Legastelois. Exhib. *Panier de roses*, Grenoble Salon 1899
LIT *Bénézit*; *Grenoble Salon* 1899. MW

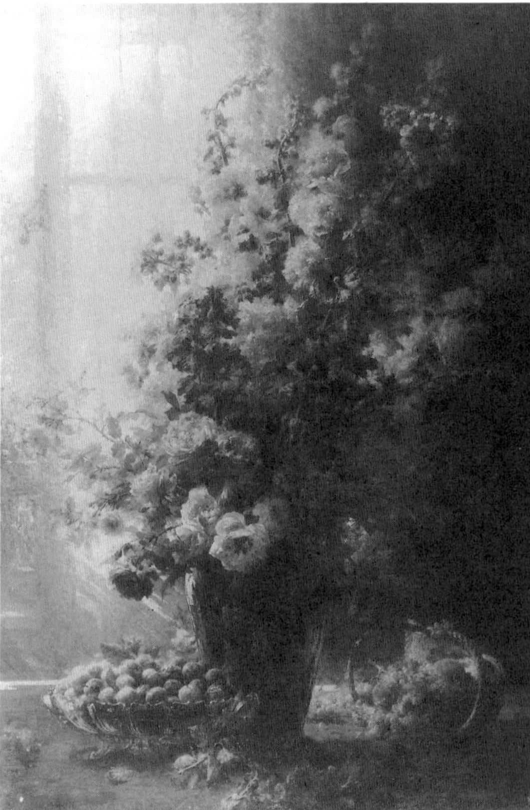

Grégoire Chapoton

Oil on canvas, $73\frac{1}{4}$ × 53 in. (186.5 × 132 cm.), signed
Saint-Etienne, Musée d'Art et d'Industrie

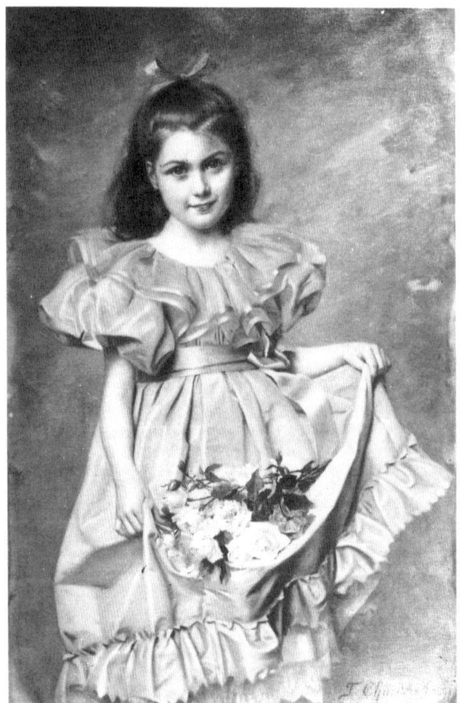

Francine Charderon

Oil on canvas, $45\frac{3}{4}$ × $26\frac{3}{4}$ in. (116 × 67.5 cm.), signed and dated 1897
Lyon, Musée des Beaux-Arts

CHARPINE, Joseph-Marie ***b.1819***
Pupil of Thierriat, Lyon BA (CFD 1840). Entered 1842 FDC. op. textile designer. Exhib. Lyon Salon 1842
LIT *Hardouin-Fugier Grafe*

CHARREL, Louis ***b.1820***
Pupil of Thierriat, Lyon BA (CFD 1838)
LIT *Hardouin-Fugier Grafe*

CHARRETON, Victor ***1864–1936***
Painted landscapes and flowers
LIT *Amis de Victor Charreton*, Paris (Mazarine) 1964–1966; *Orsay*

CHARTON, Edouard ***b.c.1855***
b. Paris. Pupil of Lequien and P. Bourgogne. Exhib. Dijon Salon *Giroflées*, 1887, *Fleurs des champs*, 1890. Musée de Louviers, *Fleurs des champs*
LIT *Bénézit*; *Dijon Salon* 1887, 1890; *Schurr* II, 119; *Thieme*

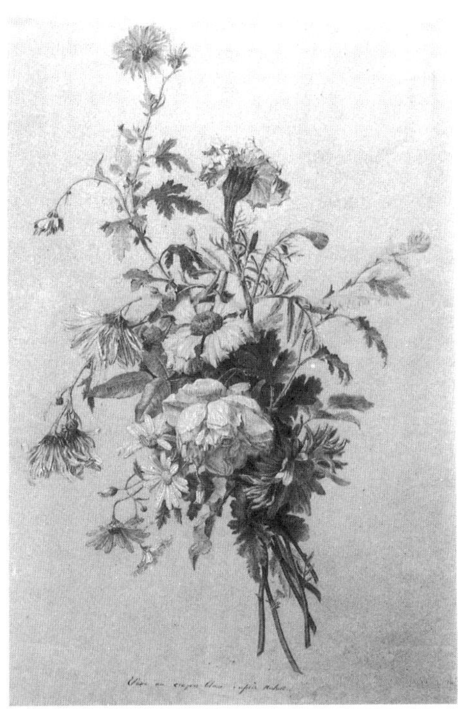

Joseph-Marie Charpine

Pencil heightened with white, $20\frac{1}{2} \times 15\frac{3}{4}$ in. (52 × 40 cm.), signed with initials, dated 1840 and inscribed 'Etude au crayon blanc d'apres nature' Private collection

CHARTON, L. Marius ***b.1856***
Pupil of Reignier, Lyon BA (CFD 1875)
LIT *Hardouin-Fugier Grafe*

CHARVET, Toussaint ***b.1814***
Pupil of Thierriat, Lyon BA (CFD 1833)
LIT *Hardouin-Fugier Grafe*

CHARVOLIN, Félix ***b.1832***
b. Lyon. Pupil of Thierriat, Lyon BA (CFD 1848). Painted flowers and landscapes. Exhib. Lyon Salon from 1858
LIT *Bénézit*; *Hardouin-Fugier Grafe*; *Thieme*

CHASSAGNE-GROSSE, Laetitia de la
Pupil of J. Lefebvre, Bouguereau, G. Ferrier, F. Flameng, M. Baschet. Painted flowers and still-lifes *c.*1890
LIT *Bénézit*

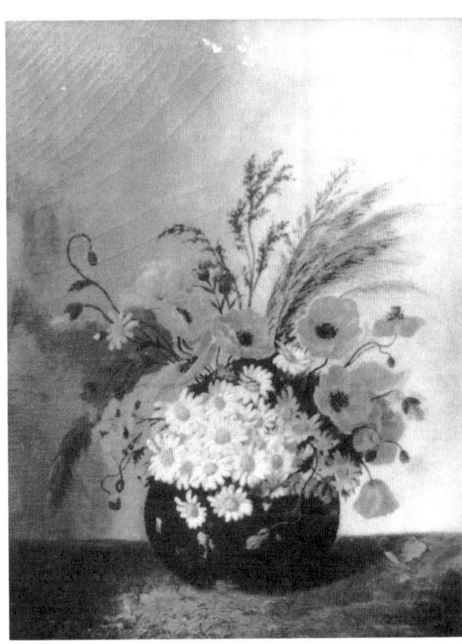

Edouard Charton

Oil on canvas, $28\frac{3}{4} \times 21\frac{1}{4}$ in. (73 × 54 cm.), signed Louviers, Musée des Beaux-Arts

CHASSELAT, Henri-Jean-Saint-Ange ***1813–1880***
b. Paris. Pupil of Guillon-Lethière (Paris BA). Painted genre, landscapes, historical subjects and, occasionally, flowers. Exhib. Paris Salon 1833–1868. Exhib. *Les bluets*, Dijon Salon 1840. *Hunting Scene with Flowers* (exhib. Boston Museum of Fine Arts 1877-1882), Sotheby's, New York, 25 Jan. 1980, lot 261; *Fleurs et melon*, Delorme, Paris 3 Nov. 1986, lot 13
LIT *Bénézit*; *Dijon Salon* 1840; *Schurr* V, 100; *Thieme*. CL

CHATELAIN, Michel ***b.1812***
Pupil of Thierriat, Lyon BA (CFD 1831)
LIT *Hardouin-Fugier Grafe*

CHATILLON, Charles de
Exhib. miniatures, genre and gouaches at the Salon 1795–1808. Portraits of Napoleon (Wallace coll., London) and the Empress Marie-Louise, engraved by Audouin, are attributed to him. *Fleurs*, 1820, wc, in Cambridge, Fitzwilliam Museum (Broughton coll.) may be by this artist
LIT *Bellier*; *Bénézit*; *Busse*; *Thieme*. JLC

CHAUBARD, Louis-Anastase
Designed plates for Bory de Saint-Vincent, *Nouvelle flore du Péloponnèse et des Cyclades*, Paris, Strasbourg (Levrault) 1838
LIT *Nissen* I, 213; *Sitwell*

CHAUDE, Georges ***d.1900***
Exhib. *Les roses*, Paris Indép. 1896
LIT *Bénézit*; *Paris Indép.* 1896

CHAUSSON, Jean-Marie
Pupil of Thierriat, Lyon BA (CFD 1841)
LIT *Hardouin-Fugier Grafe*

CHAVAGNAT, Antoinette
b. Rouen (Seine-Maritime). Pupil of Cliquot and F. Rivoire. Exhib. *Panier de*

roses, wc, *Coquelicots doubles*, wc, Lyon Salon 1884; *Roses et reines marguerites*, wc (150 francs), Strasbourg Salon 1884; Paris Noir et Blanc Salon *Chrysanthèmes*, 1886, *Pivoines*, *roses*, 1888; *Coquelicots*, *Chrysanthèmes*, *Giroflées*, wc, Paris Indép. 1890; *Roses trémières*, Paris Salon 1890; Paris Indép. *Roses*, 1891, *Fleurs de printemps*, *Bégonias*, wc, 1892; *Chrysanthèmes et fontaine en vieux Rouen*, wc, Dijon 1894; *Rose*, *Coquelicots*, wc, Paris Salon 1894, Paris UFPS 1898
LIT *Bénézit*; *Dijon Salon* 1894; *Lyon Salon* 1884; *Paris Indép.* 1890, 1891, 1892; *Paris Noir et Blanc Salon* 1886, 1888; *Paris UFPS* 1898; *Paris Salon* 1890, 1894; *Strasbourg Salon* 1884

CHAVANIEUX, Jean ***b.1865***
Pupil of Castex-Dégrange, Lyon BA (CFD 1888)
LIT *Hardouin-Fugier Grafe*

CHAVANNE, Etienne ***1797–1887***
b. Culoz (Ain). Pupil of Thierriat, Lyon BA (CFD 1831) and Jacomin. Painted genre, portraits, still-lifes and flowers. Exhib. Lyon Salon 1848–1853
LIT *Bénézit*; *Hardouin-Fugier Grafe*; *Thieme*

CHAVANNE, François ***b.1799***
b. Culoz (Ain). Pupil of Thierriat, Lyon BA (CFD 1828)
LIT *Bénézit*; *Hardouin-Fugier Grafe*

CHAVANT, Anna, ***née*** **Picard**
Exhib. Lyon Salon 1838–1850 e.g. *Vase de fleurs d'après nature*, wc, on vellum, 1839, *Un bouquet de bal d'après nature*, wc, 1844
LIT *Hardouin-Fugier* 1981; *Hardouin-Fugier Grafe*; *Lyon Salon* 1839, 1844

CHAVANT, Fleury ***op.c.1837***
This lithographer published sets of plates after Redouté and his pupils e.g. *La naissance des fleurs*, *Le cours de fleurs du Jardin des Plantes*, *Alphabet de Flore*, *Choix de 15 bouquets de fleurs* etc.
LIT *Hardouin-Fugier* 1981

Félix Charvolin

Gouache, 15 × 10¼ in. (38 × 26 cm.), signed and dated 1850
Private collection

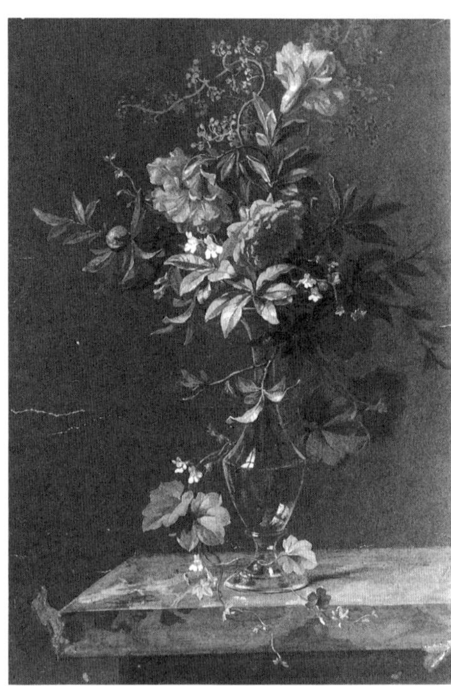

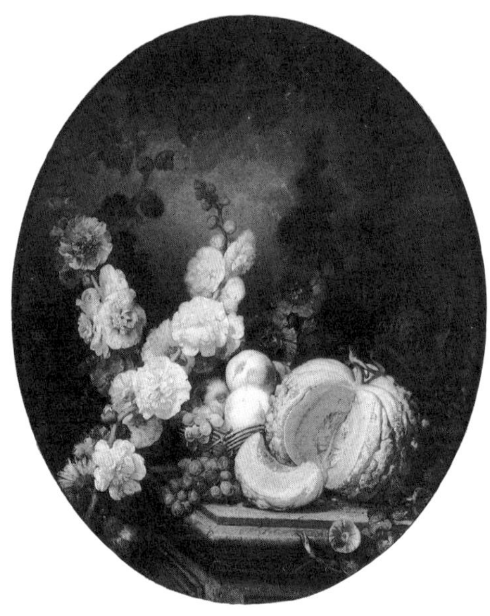

Henri-Jean-Saint-Ange Chasselat

Oil on canvas, 41 × 34 in. (104 × 86 cm.), signed
Courtesy Maître Delorme, Paris

CHAVASSIEUX ***b.1862***
Pupil of Reignier, Lyon BA (CFD 1879)
LIT *Hardouin-Fugier Grafe*

CHAVASSIEUX, Joannès-Marius ***b.1865***
Pupil of Castex-Dégrange, Lyon BA (CFD 1885)
LIT *Hardouin-Fugier Grafe*

CHAVEROT, Théophile
This amateur painter exhibited *Fleurs* at the Saint-Etienne Salon 1891
LIT *Hardouin-Fugier Bringuier*; *Saint-Etienne Salon* 1891

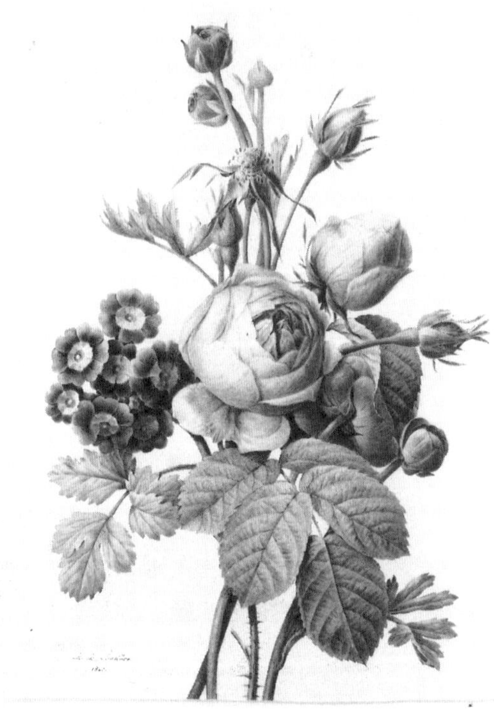

Charles de Chatillon

Watercolour on vellum, 13⅜ × 10⅛ in. (33.9 × 25.7 cm.), signed and dated 1820
Cambridge, Fitzwilliam Museum (Broughton Collection)

CHAZAL, Charles-Camille ***1825–1875***
Son of Antoine Chazal. Exhib. Lyon Salon 1862
LIT J. Adhémar, J. Lethève, *Inventaire du Fonds français après 1800*, Paris Bibliothèque Nationale 1954, p. 111; *Bénézit*; *Lyon Salon* 1862

CHAZAL, Jean-Antoine ***1793–1853***
b. Paris. Pupil of G. Van Spaendonck, Misbach and J. Bidauld. Drawing master, Professeur d'iconographie des animaux at the Paris Jardin des Plantes, 1838. Designed plates for *Voyage de l'Uranie, Paris* 1817–1820, *Voyage autour du monde* ... Paris, 1822–1825, *Flore pittoresque* ... Paris, 1825. A most successful flower painter and much indebted to Van Spaendonck as shown by his *Hommage à Gerard Van Spaendonck*, 1830, Musée des Beaux-Arts, Tourcoing. Exhib. Paris Salon 1822–1853 e.g. *Fleurs et fruits sur une table de marbre*, 1834, *Fleurs et fruits d'automne*, 1842, *Yucca Gloriosa* ... 1845, *Groupe de fleurs près d'une source*, 1852. Lyon Salon e.g. *Groupe de fleurs dans un vase d'agathe*, 1838, *Panier de fruits et groupe de dahlias*, 1846. M: Amiens, Bagnères-de-Bigorre, Cambridge, Fitzwilliam Museum (Broughton coll.), Château-Thierry, Lyon, Musée des Beaux-Arts, Valenciennes; Lexington, Mass., USA
LIT J. Adhémar, J. Lethève, *Inventaire du Fonds français après 1800*, Paris Bibliothèque Nationale, 1954; C. Baudelaire, *Le Salon de 1845*; *Bellier*; *Bénézit*; Dussieux, *Les artistes français à l'etranger* ... Paris, Lyon 1876, p. 11; *Faré* 1962, p. 249; *Gabet*; *Laissus*; *Lyon Salon* 1838, 1846; *Mitchell* (ill.); Paris Arch. Nat. F21:21, 4500,03:1408; Paris Bibl. Nat. Est. Dc 151; Paris Muséum bibl. B6203; *Paris Salon* 1834, 1842, 1852; *Mireur*; *Nissen* II, p. 34, 350n; *Pavière III*, pt. 1; *Sitwell*; *Thieme*

CHAZELLE, Laurent-Léon ***b.1859***
b. Saint-Etienne (Loire). Pupil of Reignier, Lyon BA (CFD 1878). Exhib. *Aubépines et boutons d'or*, Saint-Etienne Salon 1882
LIT *Hardouin-Fugier Bringuier*; *Hardouin-Fugier Grafe*; *Saint-Etienne Salon* 1882

CHAZOT, Antoine ***b.1824***
Pupil of Thierriat, Lyon BA (CFD 1842)
LIT *Hardouin-Fugier Grafe*

CHEDIAC
Co-designed plates for J. Deniker, *Atlas manuel de Botanique*, Paris (Baillière) 1899
LIT *Nissen* I, 469

CHEILLEY, Jeanne
b. London of French parentage. Exhib. *Azalées*, wc, Paris Indép, 1892
LIT *Bénézit*; *Paris Indép.* 1892

CHENAVARD, François-Marie ***b.c.1753***
b. Lyon. op. textile manufacturer. Exhib. *Vase de fleurs*, Paris Salon 1831
LIT *Audin Vial*; *Hardouin-Fugier Grafe*; *Thieme*

CHENEVIER, Frédéric-Antoine
Exhib. flowers (engraved and in ink) Lyon Salon 1842, 1845, 1853
LIT *Audin Vial*; *Hardouin-Fugier Grafe*

CHENOU, Camille, *née* Levesque
Exhib. Paris Salon 1834–1844, mostly flowers in wc, e.g. *Étude de fleurs*, 1834, 1845, *Bouquet de fleurs de printemps*, 1837, *Capucines*, 1841, *Digitales*, *Pois de senteur*, 1834, *Bouquet de roses*, *Glycine*, 1844
LIT *Bellier*; *Bénézit*; *Paris Salon* 1834, 1835, 1837, 1841, 1843, 1844; *Thieme*

CHENU, Marguerite-Marie ***b.1829***
b. Belleville (Seine). Pupil of Gelée and Cogniet. Exhib. *Branche de chèvrefeuille*, Strasbourg Salon 1856 (180 francs)
LIT *Bellier*; *Bénézit*; *Strasbourg Salon* 1856; *Thieme*

CHÉRET, Gustave-Joseph ***1838–1894***
b. Paris. Brother of Jules Chéret. *12 dessins de fleurs*, atelier sale, Drouot, Paris, Dec. 1894
LIT *Bénézit*; *Orsay*; *Thieme*

CHÉRET, Jules ***1836–1932***
The famous poster designer and decorator painted some flowers e.g. *Fleurs*, on panel, Drouot, Paris, 23 Oct. 1970; *Vase de fleurs*, on panel, Versailles, 14 Nov. 1971
LIT *Bénézit*; *Orsay*; *Schurr* I, 102; *Thieme*

CHERPIN-LECOMTE, Alexina ***b.1834***
b. Lyon. Pupil of Baile and Grobon. Exhib. Lyon Salon 1855–1867, Paris Salon 1851–94. *Pivoines et cerises*, *Bouquet de lilas*, Saint-Etienne Salon 1882. Her *Roses* was in the 1861–1862 Lyon Société des Amis-des-Arts raffle. *Couronne de fleurs autour d'une aiguière*, Maison Antique, Prague, 29–31 Oct. 1927
LIT *Bénézit*; *Hardouin-Fugier Grafe*; *Saint-Etienne Salon* 1882; *Thieme*; *Witt*

CHERVET, Mlle
Pupil of A. Perrachon. Exhib. *Fleurs*, Lyon Salon 1877
LIT *Lyon Salon* 1877

CHEVALIER or CHEVALLIER
Illustrated F.F. Chevalier, *Fungorum et byssorum illustrationes* ... Paris, 1837
LIT *Nissen* I, 355

CHEVALIER, Anna
Exhib. *Chrysanthèmes*, Dijon Salon 1894
LIT *Dijon Salon* 1894. CL

CHEVALIER, E.G.
Exhib. *Chardons près de la mer*, Paris Indép. 1892
LIT *Paris Indép.* 1892

CHEVRIER
Co-designed plates for J. Deniker, *Atlas manuel de botanique*, Paris (Baillière) 1889
LIT *Nissen* I, 469

CHICHOUX, Claude ***b.1825***
Pupil of Thierriat, Lyon BA (CFD 1845)
LIT *Hardouin-Fugier Grafe*

CHIPPEL, *see* NEPVEU

CHIRADE-DEVORE, Marie-Denise
Pupil of J. Lefebvre. Exhib. Paris Salon *Chrysanthèmes dans un coin d'atelier*, *Boules de neige*, 1895, *Roses et boules de neige*, 1898, *Camélias et mimosas*, 1899
LIT *Bénézit*; *Paris Salon* 1895 (ill.), 1898 (ill.), 1899 (ill.); *Thieme*

CHIRAT, Benoit ***1795–1870***
b. Lyon. Pupil of Berjon, Lyon BA (CFD 1813). op. textile designer. Flower and fruit painter and lithographer. Exhib. Lyon Salon 1842–1843, Paris Salon 1842–1866
LIT *Audin Vial*; *Bénézit*; *Faré* 1962, p. 256; *Hardouin-Fugier Grafe*; *Schurr* I, 57; *Thieme*

CHIRAT, Benoite-Anaïs, *later* Mme Duchesne ***b.1820***
Daughter of Benoit Chirat. Pupil of Genod. Exhib. Paris Salon 1840–1849 portraits, genre and flowers e.g. *Groupe de fleurs et de fruits*, pastel, 1843
LIT *Audin Vial*; *Bénézit*

CHOISY, Apprien-Julien de
op. Sèvres 1770–1812
LIT *Bénézit*; *Brunet Préaud*

CHOMEL DE PRANDIÈRE
Pupil of A. Perrachon. Exhib. Lyon Salon 1891, 1893
LIT *Hardouin-Fugier Grafe*

CHOPARD or CHOPPARD-MAZEAU, Jeanne
Pupil of Thoret, Carolus-Duran and Henner. Exhib. Dijon Salon *Etude de fleurs*, 1887, *Fleurs d'avril*, 1890
LIT *Bénézit*; *Dijon Salon* 1887, 1890; *Thieme*. CL

CHOSSON, Jean-Marie ***b.1823***
Pupil of Thierriat, Lyon BA (CFD 1841)
LIT *Hardouin-Fugier Grafe*

CHOUARD, Martin-Jules ***1839–1919***
b. Aufferville (Seine-et-Marne). This school-teacher painted fruit and, occasionally, flowers in wc
LIT *Orsay*

CHOUBRAC, Alfred ***1853–1902***
b. Paris. Pupil of Doërr and Pils. Painted genre, figures and, occasionally, flowers. Exhib. *Pivoines* Paris Salon 1875
LIT *Bénézit*; *Paris Salon* 1875; *Schurr* III, 79; *Thieme*; *Witt*

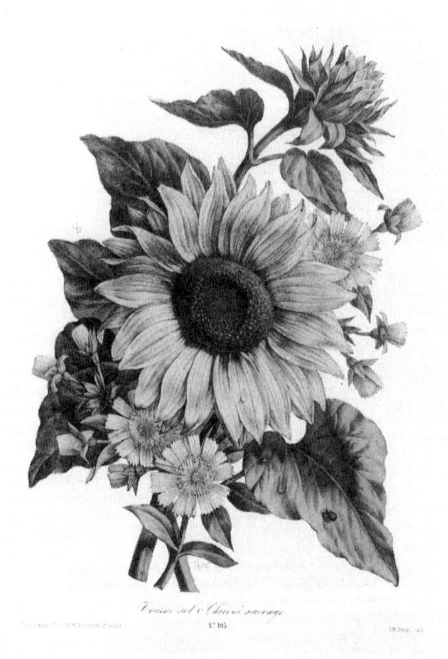

Benoit Chirat

Coloured lithograph, $13\frac{1}{2} \times 10\frac{1}{4}$ in. (34 × 26 cm.), signed in the plate
Private collection

CHOUSSERIE, Mlle de
Exhib. *Lis exotiques*, Dijon Salon 1883
LIT *Dijon Salon* 1883. CL

CHRÉTIEN, René-Louis ***1867–1942***
b. Choisy-le-Roi (Val-de-Marne). Pupil of Bonnat. Painted fruit and, occasionally, flowers. Exhib. Paris Salon from 1889. M: Caen, La Rochelle (Still-life without flowers); Mulhouse, Niort, Reims
LIT *Bénézit*; *Orsay*; *Thieme*

CHRISTMANN
Exhib. *Fruits et fleurs* (450 francs), Strasbourg Salon 1859
LIT *Strasbourg Salon* 1859

CIBOT, Marie
b. Paris. Pupil of Colin-Libour. Exhib. *Pensées*, wc, Paris Salon 1880
LIT *Bellier*; *Bénézit*; *Paris Salon* 1880; *Thieme*

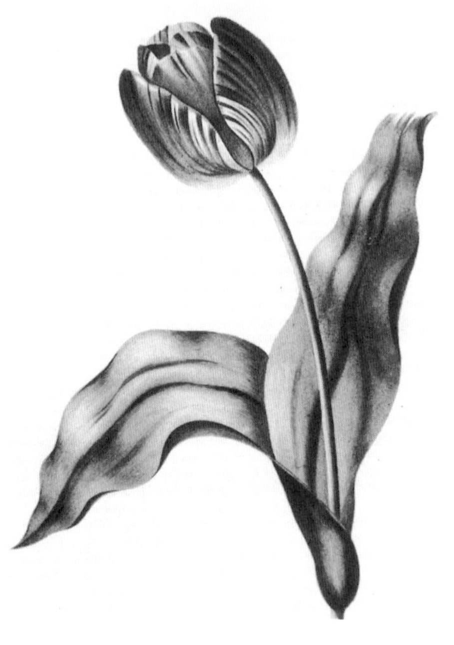

Jean-Marie Chosson

Watercolour on paper, $12 \times 8\frac{3}{4}$ in. (30 × 22 cm.), signed
Paris, BMAD (Maciet Collection)

CINQUIN, Jean ***b.1817***
Pupil of Thierriat, Lyon BA (CFD 1837)
LIT *Hardouin-Fugier Grafe*

CITROEN ***b.1842***
Pupil of Reignier, Lyon BA (CFD 1864)
LIT *Hardouin-Fugier Grafe*

CIZERON, Barthélémy
Exhib. Saint-Etienne Salon *Vase de fleurs*, gouache, 1882, *Fleurs*, 1891
LIT *Hardouin-Fugier Bringuier*; *Saint-Etienne Salon* 1882, 1891

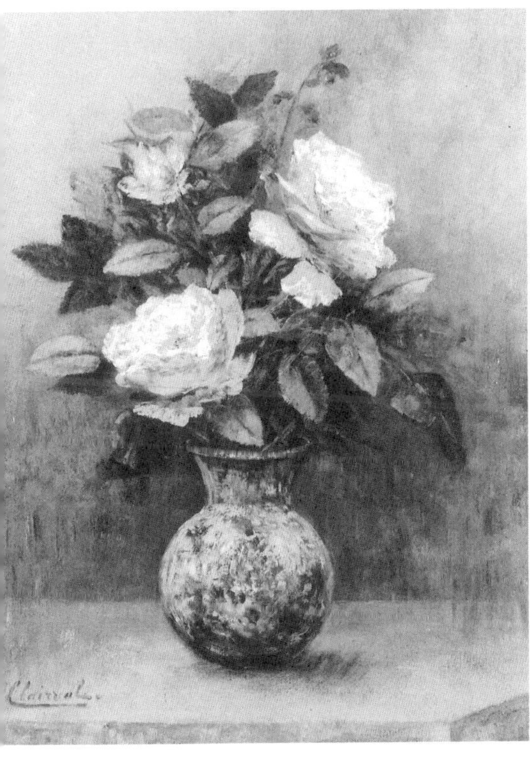

F. Clairval

Oil on panel, 16 × 13 in. (40.5 × 33 cm.), signed
Private collection, Courtesy John Mitchell & Son, London

CLAIRANSON, Charles-Hippolyte ***b.1826***
Pupil of Thierriat, Lyon BA (CFD 1843)
LIT *Hardouin-Fugier Grafe*

CLAIRANSON, Louis ***b.1828***
Pupil of Thierriat, Lyon BA (CFD 1845). Exhib. Lyon Salon 1842–1848
LIT *Hardouin-Fugier Grafe*

CLAIRIN, Georges ***1843–1919***
The well-known portrait and genre painter occasionally produced some flower studies
LIT *Bénézit*; *Orsay*; *Schurr* I, 88; *Thieme*; *Witt*

CLAIRVAL, F.
One signed work by this artist is known, but F. Clairval is probably not the artist recorded in Bénézit, Marie-Thérèse, Vicomtesse H. de Clairval. PM

CLAMORAN, Mme
Painted flowers on vellum (Paris, Muséum d'Histoire Naturelle (not botanical). A flower design (1867) of hers was lithographed by Lemercier
LIT *Faré* 1962, p. 247

CLARY, Juliette
b. Paris. Pupil of Trébuchet. Exhib. *Anémones*, gouache, Paris Salon 1885
LIT *Paris Salon* 1885

CLAUDE, Eugène ***1841–1922***
b. Toulouse (Haute-Garonne). A prolific, successful flower painter. Exhib. *Fleurs*, Lille Salon 1866; Marseille Salon *Marguerites*, *Giroflées*, 1868, *Bouquet de roses blanches*, 1869; *Roses sur une pierre*, Nantes Salon 1872; Paris Salon *Salsifis sauvage*, 1872, *Chrysanthèmes*, *Lilas*, 1873; Lyon Salon *Giroflées*, 1873, *Roses trémières*, 1875; *Fleurs des champs*, Rouen Salon 1876; *Fleurs des champs dans un arrosoir*, wc, Saint-Etienne Salon 1882; *Bourriche d'anémones*, Dijon Salon 1883; *Bouquet de violettes* (300 francs), Strasbourg Salon 1884; *Lilas et pivoines*, Lyon Salon 1885; Paris Salon *Chrysanthèmes*, 1890, *Fleurs d'automne*, 1893; *Giroflées*, Dijon Salon 1897. *Basket of Lilac*, Christie's, London, 26 June 1987, lot 83. M: Abbeville, Alger, Amiens, Arras, Auxerre, Bordeaux, Calais, Reims, Saint-Denis
LIT *Bellier*; *Bénézit; Dijon Salon* 1883, 1897; *Lyon Salon* 1873, 1875, 1885; *Marseille Salon* 1868, 1869; *Nantes Salon* 1872; *Orsay*; *Paris Salon* 1872, 1873, 1885, 1890, 1893; *Rouen Salon* 1876; *Saint-Etienne Salon* 1882; *Strasbourg Salon* 1884; *Schurr* II, 163; *Thieme*

CLAUDOT, Jean-Baptiste-Charles
1733–1805
b. Badonviller (Meurthe-et-Moselle). Painted capricci and overdoors. Musée de Nancy, *Vase de fleurs* (two examples)
LIT *Bellier*; *Bénézit*; *Faré* 1962, p. 242; *Mitchell* (ill.); *Thieme*

CLAUSSE, Mlle
Pupil of Le Besgue-Delbarre. Exhib. *Chrysanthèmes*, wc, Paris UFPS 1898
LIT *Paris UFPS* 1898

CLAVEL, Théodore *b.1817*
b. Avignon (Vaucluse). Pupil of Yvon. Exhib. *Fleurs et fruits*, Lyon Salon 1868
LIT *Bénézit*; *Lyon Salon* 1868; *Thieme*

CLÉMENCET, Louis-Célestin
b. Brussels (Belgium) of French parentage. Exhib. Paris Salon *Fleurs*, wc, 1869, *Fleurs et feuilles*, 1870, *Bouquet de roses*, *Bouquet de Chrysanthèmes*, 1876. A Clémencet illustrated La Brugère, *Ecole du Jardinier Amateur*, Paris (Fayard)
LIT *Bellier*; *Bénézit*; *Paris MAD*

CLÉMENS, L.
Designed plates for *L'Horticulteur français*, Paris Hérincq 1851–1872
LIT *Nissen* 2337n

CLÉMENT, Anne-Clara, *née* Lemaître
1826–c.1880
b. Paris. Pupil of A.F. Lemaitre, her father. Exhib. Paris Salon 1878–1880 e.g. watercolours: *Cinéraire*, *Primevère de Chine*, 1878, *Massif de pensées*, *Bouquet de roses trémières*, 1880
LIT *Bellier*; *Bénézit*; *Paris Salon* 1880; *Thieme*

CLÉMENT, Armand-Lucien
b. Paris. Active at Paris Jardin des Plantes. Painted flowers on vellum and paper 1873–1881 (Paris Muséum d'Histoire Naturelle, not botanical). Exhib. Paris Salon from 1888 and Paris Noir et Blanc Salon from 1892
LIT *Laissus*; *Schurr* IV, 82 (ill.); *Thieme*

CLÉMENT, Mlle M.L.A.
Exhib. *Oeillets*, Paris SNBA 1899
LIT *Paris SNBA* 1899

CLÉMENT, *see* JUSSIOME

CLERC, Jean-Baptiste
At Sèvres 1847–1848. Exhib. *Fleurs et oiseaux*, porcelain, Paris Salon 1844 and 1845
LIT *Bellier*; *Bénézit*; *Brunet Préaud*; *Paris Salon* 1844–1845; *Thieme*

CLERÉ, Louisa
Pupil of Latruffe, Colomb, Cuyer, E. Claude. Exhib. *Fleurs et fruits d'automne*, Paris UFPS 1896
LIT *Paris UFPS* 1896

CLET, Emma
b. Grenoble (Isère). Exhib. *Fleurs*, Grenoble Salon 1899
LIT *Grenoble Salon* 1899. MW

CLISS, Gustave
Exhib. *Fleurs de printemps*, Paris Indép. 1884
LIT *Paris Indép.* 1884

CLOQUET, Anne-Louise *1788–1860*
CLOQUET, Jean-Baptiste-Antoine *d.1828*
CLOQUET, Joseph-Hippolyte *1786–1843*
CLOQUET, Jules-Germain *b.1790*
A family of botanical artists. Jean-Baptiste-Antoine Cloquet or his son Jules-Germain contributed designs to Ventenat, *Description des plantes nouvelles et peu connues dans le jardin de M. Cels*, Paris 1800–1803. Two plates from *Le jardin de M. Cels* are in the Musée de Malmaison: *Statice fasciculata*, *Ruellia varians*
LIT *Hardouin-Fugier* 1981; *Nissen* I, 2048; *Thieme*

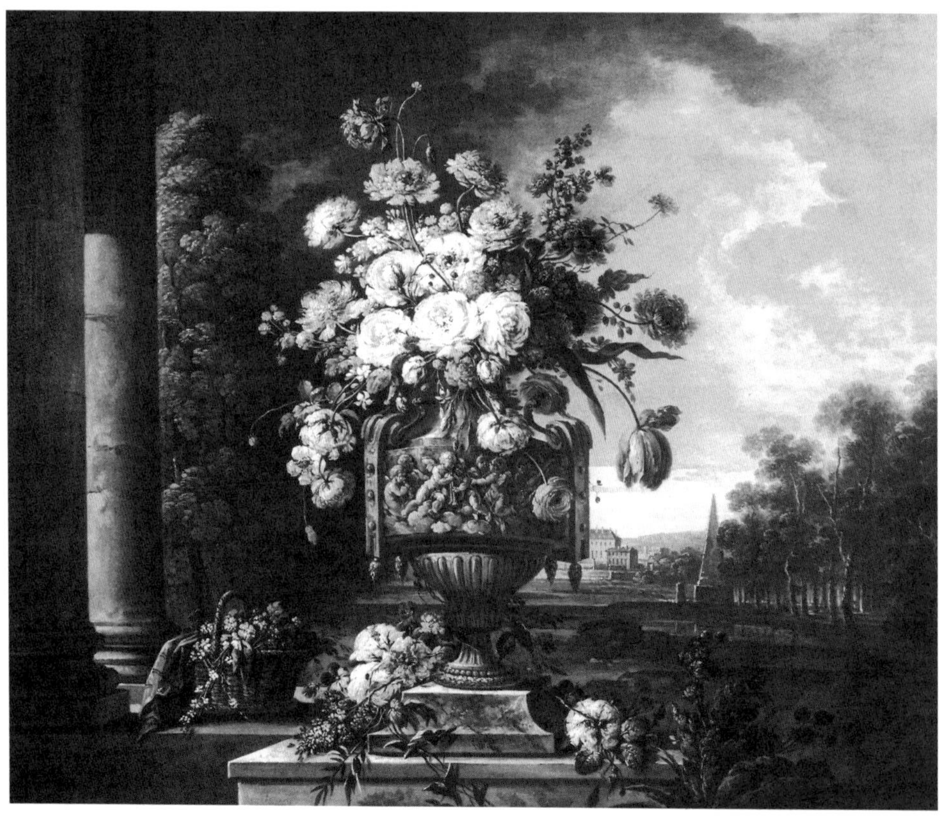

Jean-Baptiste-Charles Claudot

Oil on canvas, 49¼ × 60½ in. (15 × 154 cm.), signed
Nancy, Musée des Beaux-Arts

CLORGET, P.E.
Exhib. Paris SNBA *Roses multiflores, Pensées, Pavots coreopsis, Pieds d'alouette*, wc, 1898; *Hortensias, Pétunias*, wc, 1899
LIT *Paris SNBA* 1898, 1899

CLUGNET, Jean ***b.1819***
Pupil of Thierriat, Lyon BA (CFD 1837). Entered the 1849 Lyon Société des Amis-des-Arts FDC
LIT *Bénézit*; *Hardouin-Fugier Grafe*

COBUS, Adèle
Exhib. *Bouquet, Roses trémières, Capucines, Roses mousseuses et anémones*, wc, Paris Salon 1850
LIT *Paris Salon* 1850

COCHAUX, Clémence
b. Vrigne-aux-Bois (Ardennes). Pupil of Thurner. Exhib. *Envoi de Nice*, Paris Salon 1895; *Roses, Fleurs de printemps*, Paris UFPS 1896
LIT *Paris Salon* 1894; *Paris UFPS* 1896

COCHET, Victor
Pupil of Thierriat, Lyon BA (CFD 1824)
LIT *Hardouin-Fugier Grafe*

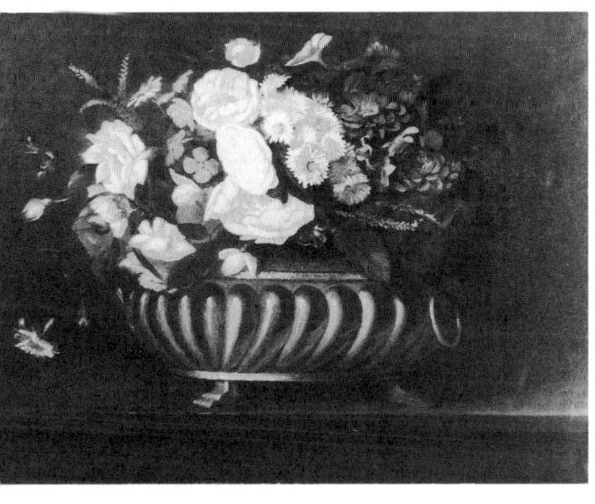

Jules-Jacques-Olivier de Cocquerel

Oil on canvas, 21¼ × 30¾ in. (54 × 78 cm.), signed
Courtesy Maître Blache, Versailles

COCQUEREL, Alfred de ***1876–1940***
Pupil of O. de Cocquerel, his father. Painted landscapes and flowers
LIT *Hardouin-Fugier Grafe*

COCQUEREL, Jules-Jacques-Olivier de ***1838–1903***
b. Saint-Didier-au-Mont-d'Or (Rhône). Pupil of Lyon BA and F. Chenu. Painted still-lifes mostly with fish and, occasionally, flowers. Exhib. Lyon Salon from 1860, Paris Salon from 1876 e.g. *Pivoines*; Lyon Salon 1878. Sale: *Fleurs*, Mme Blache, Versailles, 27 Jan. 1980, lot 63
LIT *Bellier*; *Bénézit*; *Hardouin-Fugier Grafe*; *Lyon Salon* 1878; *Thieme*

COCQUET, Philibert ***b.1808***
Pupil of Thierriat, Lyon BA (CFD 1827)
LIT *Hardouin-Fugier Grafe*

COEUR, Mary
b. Amiens (Somme). Pupil of Pallandre. Exhib. *Chrysanthèmes*, on faience, Paris Salon 1879
LIT *Bellier*

COGNEL, Hélène
b. Strasbourg (Bas-Rhin). Pupil of Moral. Exhib. *Chrysanthèmes*, Paris Salon 1880
LIT *Paris Salon* 1880

COHN, Cécile
Pupil of Sieffert. Exhib. *Fleurs de pommier*, after Beyle, on porcelain, Paris Noir et Blanc Salon 1888
LIT *Paris Noir et Blanc Salon* 1888

COIGNET, Marie
b. Honfleur (Calvados). Pupil of Fouace. Exhib. *Premières fleurs*, Dijon Salon 1897
LIT *Bénézit*; *Dijon Salon* 1897; *Pavière*; *Thieme*

COINDRÉ, Sébastien ***b.1814***
Pupil of Thierriat, Lyon BA (CFD 1834–1836)
LIT *Hardouin-Fugier Grafe*

COIZET, Louis ***1816–1876***
Pupil of Lyon BA. Textile designer. Painted genre, portraits, still-lifes and, occasionally, flowers
LIT *Audin Vial*; *Bénézit*; Lyon Bibl. Mun. *Dossiers biographiques*

COLAS, Jean-Claude ***b.1867***
Pupil of Castex-Dégrange, Lyon BA (CFD 1885)
LIT *Hardouin-Fugier Grafe*

COLAS, Jeanne
b. Lille (Nord). Exhib. *Panier de fleurs*, Lille Salon 1881
LIT *Lille Salon* 1881. G and LT

COLIN, Charles-François ***1795–1858***
Pupil of Garnier. Exhib. *Branche de pêcher, Corbeille de fleurs et de fruits*, Paris Salon 1850
LIT *Bénézit*; *Paris Salon* 1850

COLIN, Paul-Alfred ***1838–1916***
b. Nîmes (Gard). Pupil of his father. Painted landscapes and, occasionally, flowers. Exhib. *Fleurs dans un vase*, Nancy Salon 1872 and 1874
LIT *Bénézit*; *Nancy Salon* 1872, 1874

COLIN-LIBOUR, Uranie-Alphonsine ***b.1833***
b. Paris. Pupil of S. Rude, Muller and Bonvin. Painted genre and flowers. An influential teacher. Exhib. Paris Salon from 1861 e.g. *Chrysanthèmes, Pavots*, wc, 1890; *Coquelicots, Roses et pensées*, wc, Dijon Salon 1892; Paris Salon *Violettes*, wc, 1895, *Fleurs des champs*, 1898. Her *Livre et fleurs* was no. 51 in

the 1887 Drouot sale held in aid of Bonvin in Paris
LIT *Bellier; Bénézit; Dijon Salon* 1892, 1895; *Paris Salon* 1890, 1898; *Thieme*

COLINS, Baron de
A talented nobleman typical of the many artists in Paris, both gifted amateurs and professionals, who followed in the wake of Redouté in the first half of the 19th century, painting in watercolour on vellum—in the case of the one signed work known by the artist, on a large scale. PM

COLLAS, Elise
Pupil of S. Apoil. Exhib. flowers on enamel Paris Salon 1879–1881
LIT *Bellier*; *Bénézit*

COLLET, Eugène-Alexis *b.1862*
b. Paris. Pupil of Castex-Dégrange, Lyon BA (CFD 1886) and Bardey. Exhib. *Fleurs*, Lyon Salon 1885
LIT *Hardouin-Fugier Grafe*; *Lyon Salon* 1885

COLLIGNON
Exhib. *Fleurs et nature morte*, Lyon Salon 1852
LIT *Lyon Salon* 1852

COLLIN, Louis-Joseph-Raphaël *1850–1916*
b. Paris. Pupil of Bouguereau and Cabanel. Painted portraits, genre and flowers. Musée des Beaux-Arts, Liége (Belgium), *Vase de fleurs*; Musée Fabre, Montpellier, *Iris*
LIT *Bellier*; *Bénézit*; Mireur; *Schurr* III, 115; *Thieme*

COLLINEAU, Marie-Emélie
b. Paris. Pupil of M. Carpentier. Exhib. *Verveine*, wc, Paris Salon 1895
LIT *Paris Salon* 1895

COLLOMB-AGASSIS, Louis *b.1857*
b. Lyon. Daughter of draughtsman, J.M. Agassis (1811–1889). Pupil of A. Chaine, Compte-Calix and E. Luminais. Painted portraits, still-lifes and flowers. Exhib. Lyon Salon from 1878, Paris Salon from 1879
LIT *Bellier*; *Bénézit*; *Thieme*

COLMANT, Eugène-Marguerite
Exhib. *Roses et lilas*, wc, *Pensées et lilas*, wc, Paris Indép. 1884
LIT *Paris Indép.* 1884

COLOMBET, Marie
Exhib. Paris Salon 1844–1846 e.g. *Fleurs et fruits, 1844*
LIT *Bellier*; *Paris Salon* 1844

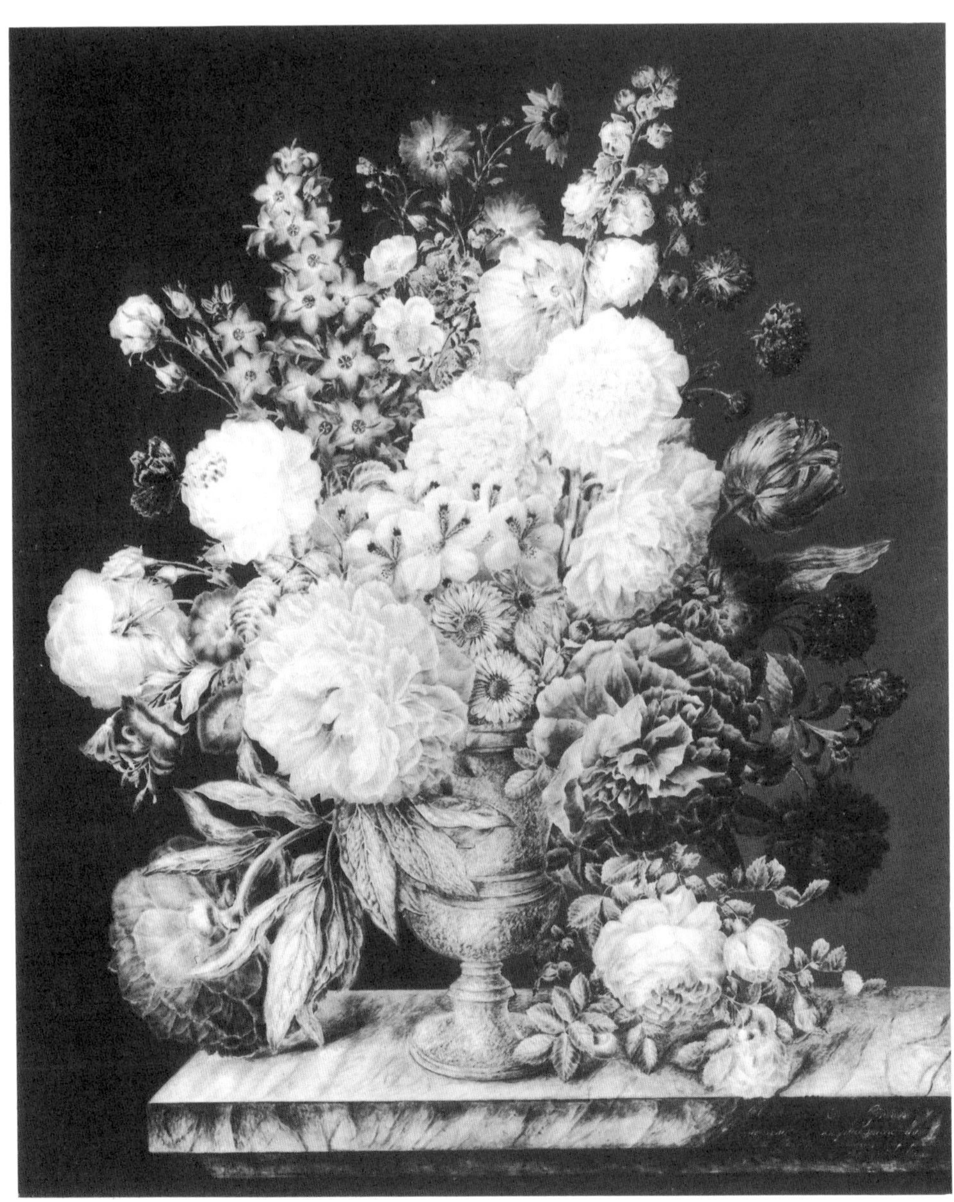

Baron de Colins

Watercolour on vellum, $30\frac{1}{4} \times 24\frac{3}{4}$ in. (77 × 63cm.), signed and dedicated to Monsieur Girardin — 'Souvenir de son plus sincère ami'
Private collection, Courtesy John Mitchell & Son, London

COLOMBO, Aline-Valérie *née* Billotey
b. Limoges (Haute-Vienne). Pupil of her father. Exhib. *Narcisses de Constantinople*, wc, Paris Salon 1885; *Fleurs d'hiver*, gouache, Paris Noir et Blanc Salon 1888; *Fleurs et parfums*, *Violettes*, wc, Paris UFPS 1898
LIT *Paris Salon* 1885; *Paris Noir et Blanc Salon* 1888; *Paris UFPS* 1898

COLONGEAT, Joseph *1827–1896*
Pupil of Thierriat, Lyon BA (CFD 1844). Entered 1846 FDC. op. textile designer. Exhib. Lyon Salon 1848–1851
LIT *Hardouin-Fugier Grafe*

COMBE, Barthélémy
Pupil of Thierriat, Lyon BA (CFD 1830)
LIT *Hardouin-Fugier Grafe*

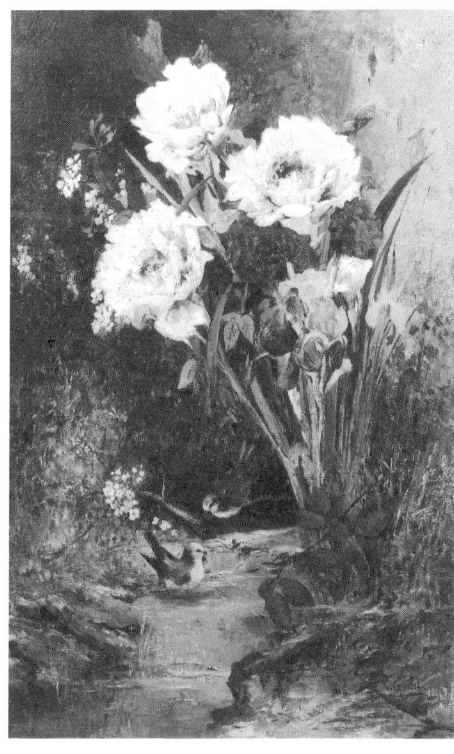

Gabriel Combet

Oil on canvas, 36 × 24½ in. (91.3 × 62.3 cm), signed
Courtesy Christie's, London

COMBE, Joseph-Alexandre-François *b.1824*
Pupil of Thierriat, Lyon BA (CFD 1842)
LIT *Hardouin-Fugier Grafe*

COMBET, Gabriel
b. Salignac (Dordogne). Pupil of Bauduit. Painted landscapes and flowers, e.g. Dijon Salon *Violettes*, *Fleurs d'automne*, 1885, *Roses*, *Myosotis*, 1887. *Flowers and bird*, Christie's, London, 26 Feb. 1988, lot 77
LIT *Bénézit*; *Dijon Salon* 1885, 1887; *Thieme*. CL

COMMERRE, Léon *1850–1916*
b. Trélon (Nord). Pupil of Colas and Cabanel, Paris BA. The well-known portrait and history painter occasionally produced some flower studies. *La mort d'Albine*, 1882 which featured many flowers, formerly in the Musée de Caen, disappeared in World War II
LIT *Bénézit*; G. and D. Commerre, *L. Commerre*, Paris (La presse artistique) 1980; *Orsay*; *Schurr* I, 91; *Thieme*

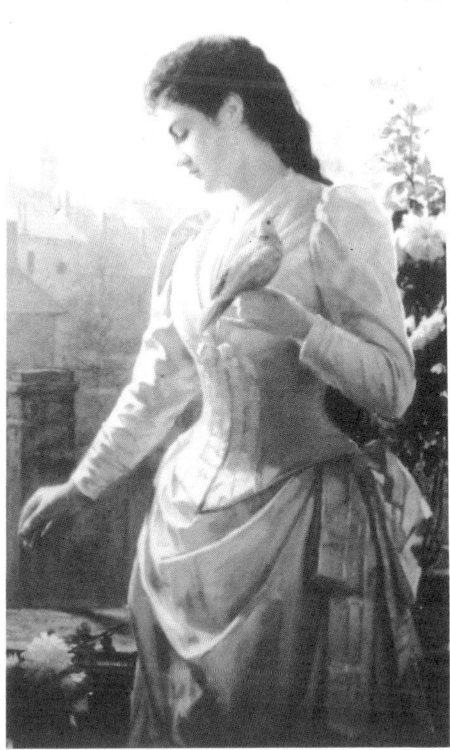

Régina de Coninck

Oil on canvas, 45¾ × 28¾ in. (116 × 73 cm.), Louviers, Musée Municipal

COMOLERA
Pupil of his father and Dumont. Exhib. *Chrysanthèmes*, wc, Paris Salon 1880. Possibly a relation of the other Comoleras or a namesake
LIT *Paris Salon* 1880

COMOLERA, Alexandre-Jean-Louis de *1817–1847*
At Sèvres. Exhib. Paris Salon, *Tulipes*, wc, 1836, *Roses muscades des quatre saisons et héliothrope*, on porcelain, 1845
LIT *Bellier*; *Bénézit*; *Brunet Préaud*; *Paris Salon* 1836, 1845

COMOLERA, Mélanie de
Pupil of Van Spaendonck. op. Sèvres 1816–1818. In London 1827. Flower painter to the Duchess of Clarence, later Queen Adelaide. Exhib. London RA 1826–1854. Exhib. Paris Salon 1817–1839 e.g. *Tableau de fleurs*, on porcelain, 1817, *Roses dans un vase*, 1819; *Groupe de fleurs et de fruits, guirlande de pensées et de myrthes*, for a table top, 1824, *Le rosier symbolique d'Angleterre*, 1837. *Fleurs dans un vase*, Duc de Berry sale 1834; *Flowers in a vase*, Halsbury sale, Robinson-Fisher, London, 23 June 1927, lot 130; M: Cambridge, Fitzwilliam Museum (Broughton coll.); Chatsworth, Duke of Devonshire coll.; private coll., Philadelphia
LIT Angers Bibl. Mun. MS 1055, Grille; *Bellier*; *Bénézit*; *Brunet Préaud*; *Mitchell* (ill.); *Paris Salon* 1817, 1819, 1824, 1837; *Pavière* III, pt.1; *Thieme*; *Witt*

COMPTE-CALIX, Pierre-François *1810–1880*
Pupil of Thierriat, Lyon BA (CFD 1828)
LIT *Bénézit*; *Hardouin-Fugier Grafe*; *Schurr* II, 79

COMTE, Jean-François ***b.1824***
Pupil of Thierriat, Lyon BA (CFD 1842)
LIT *Hardouin-Fugier Grafe*

CONDAMIN, Henry
Pupil of Lyon BA. Exhib. decorative paintings (flowers) for a château, Paris Salon 1875
LIT *Bénézit*; *Thieme*

CONDAMIN, *see* GIRARD

CONIN, Jeanne
b. Paris. Pupil of Corbillet and B. Formstecken. Exhib. *Chrysanthèmes*, Paris Salon 1880 and Lyon Salon 1882; *Fleurs d'hiver*, Paris Salon 1882
LIT *Bellier*; *Paris Salon* 1880; *Lyon Salon* 1882

CONINCK, Régina de
Pupil of her father. Exhib. Paris Salon e.g. *Jardinier préparant son concours*, 1894, *Giroflées Pivoines*, 1898: Dunkerque, *Fleurs* (destroyed); Louviers, *Pour les artistes de la rue*
LIT *Bénézit*; *Paris Salon* 1894 (ill.), 1898

CONSTANS, Louis-Aristide-Léon
Exhib. Paris Salon 1836–1848 e.g. *Fleurs*, after E. Bruyère, on porcelain, 1836, *Fleurs*, after Van Dael, on porcelain, 1837; *Fleurs de printemps et d'été dans un vase d'albâtre*, *Fleurs d'automne dans une corbeille*, 1842, a pair, acquired at the Salon 1842 (o. 409 410) by M. de Wailly, inspector of the Civil List of Louis-Philippe (Richard Green Gallery, London). *Fleurs de printemps et d'été dans un vase de verre*, 1842, *Fleurs d'après nature*, 1844. *Portrait of Nasir Ud-Din Shah within a wreath of flowers*, 1867, Sotheby's, London, 14 Apr. 1976. Two flowers, wc on vellum, Paris Muséum d'Histoire Naturelle
LIT *Bellier*; *Bénézit*; *Laissus*; Paris Arch. Nat. F21:97; *Paris Salon* 1836, 1837, 1842, 1844; *Thieme*; *Witt*

CONSTANT
op. Sèvres 1853–1863
LIT *Brunet Préaud*

CONSTANT, Suzanne
b. Paris. Pupil of Trébuchet. Exhib. *Fleurs*, wc, Paris Salon 1895
LIT *Paris Salon* 1895

CONSTANTIN, Auguste-Aristide-Fernand ***1824–1895***
b. Paris. Pupil of Picot, Couture and Labrouste. Painted landscapes and still-lifes. Exhib. *Pivoines*, wc, Saint-Etienne Salon 1882; *Pivoines et oranges* (400 francs), Strasbourg Salon 1891
LIT *Bénézit*; *Saint-Etienne Salon* 1882; *Schurr* I, 31; *Strasbourg Salon* 1891; *Thieme*; *Witt*

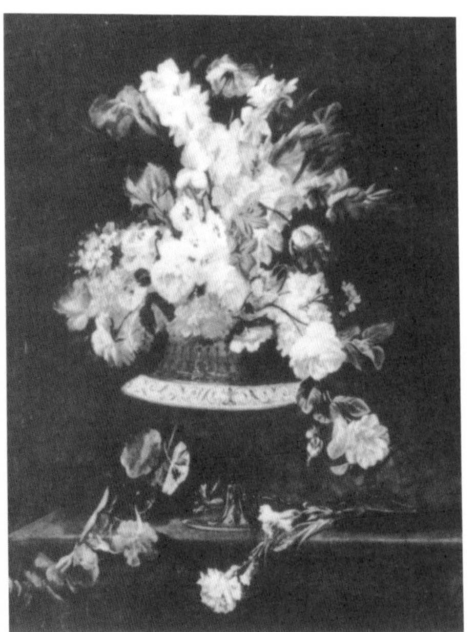

Auguste-Aristide-Fernand Constantin

Oil on canvas, 51 × 39 in. (129.5 × 99 cm.), signed and inscribed 'Paris'
San Francisco, Butterfield & Butterfield

CONSTANTIN, Barthélémy ***b.1831***
Pupil of Thierriat, Lyon BA (CFD 1851)
LIT *Hardouin-Fugier Grafe*

CONTAL, Isabelle
b. Paris. Pupil of H. Le Roux and A. Forestier. Exhib. *Fleurs de mon jardin*, wc, Paris Salon 1895
LIT *Paris Salon* 1895

CONTAL, Jeanne
b. Nancy (Meurthe-et-Moselle). Pupil of Bellay. Exhib. *Fleurs*, pastel, Paris SNBA 1899
LIT *Bénézit*; *Paris SNBA* 1899; *Thieme*

CONTE, Hortense
b. Paris. Pupil of Maisiat. Painted still-lifes and flowers. Exhib. Paris Salon 1870–1881
LIT *Bénézit*

COOL, Delphine de, Mme Arthur Arnould, *née* Fortin, *alias* ***b.1830***
b. Limoges (Haute-Vienne). Pupil of R. Fortin, her father. Headmistress of the Paris École de dessin subventionnée du 20° arrondissement. An influential teacher. Painted copies after various masters, on porcelain. Exhib. Paris Salon 1859–1911 e.g. *Fleurs de mai*, 1881, *Coquelicots*, wc, 1882; *Reines-marguerites mauves et blanches et géraniums*, Paris Noir et Blanc Salon 1886; *Reines-marguerites*, *Violettes*, wc, Paris Salon 1890. M: Limoges, Musée Municipal
LIT *Bellier*; *Bénézit*; Paris Arch. Nat. F21:2128, 206; *Paris Noir et Blanc Salon* 1886; *Paris Salon* 1890; *Schidlof*; *Thieme*

COPPENOLLE, *see* VAN COPPENOLLE

COQUARD, Claude-Jacques-André *b.1827*
Pupil of Thierriat, Lyon BA (CFD 1845). Exhib. Lyon Salon 1848–1877. His *Fleurs et fruits* was in the 1849 Lyon Société des Amis-des-Arts raffle
LIT *Hardouin-Fugier Grafe*

COQUELIN, Théodore-Charles-Ange
Painted flowers and fruit. Exhib. Paris Salon 1885–1901. M: Cannes, Tourcoing
LIT *Bénézit*; J. Forneris in *Renaissance du Musée des Beaux-Arts de Cannes* 1983, p. 142 (ill.); *Thieme*

CORBEAU, *see* ROUSSELIN

CORBIÈRE, Jean-Louis *b.1865*
Pupil of Reignier, Lyon BA (CFD 1884). op. textile designer
LIT *Hardouin-Fugier Grafe*

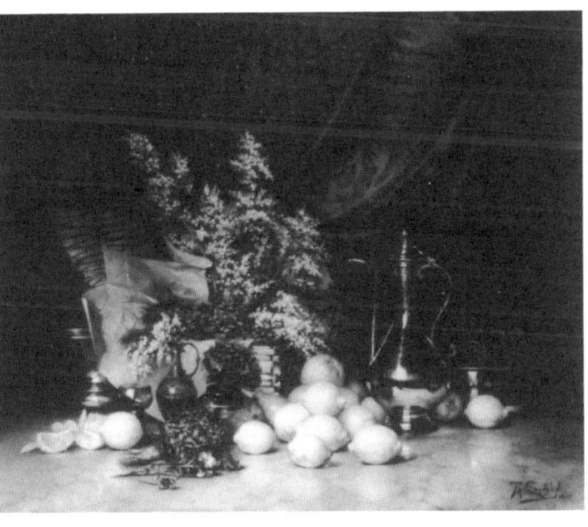

Théodore-Charles-Ange Coquelin,

Pastel on card, 37¾ × 45¼ in. (96 × 115 cm.), signed and dated 1901
Cannes, Musée de la Castre

Jean-Louis Corbière

Watercolour on paper 16½ × 11 in. (42 × 28 cm.), signed
Private collection

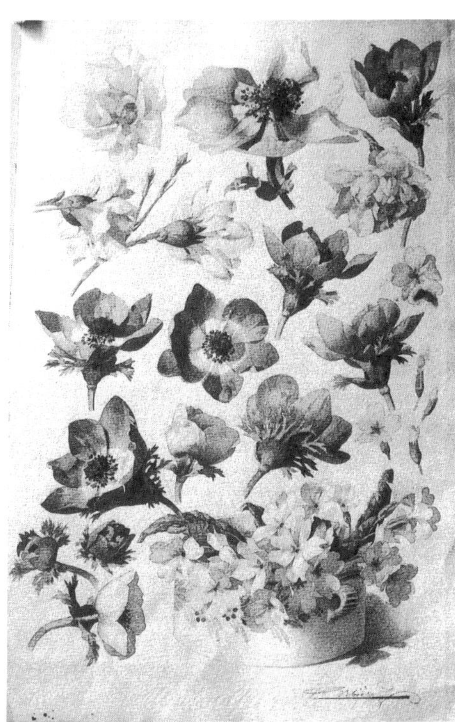

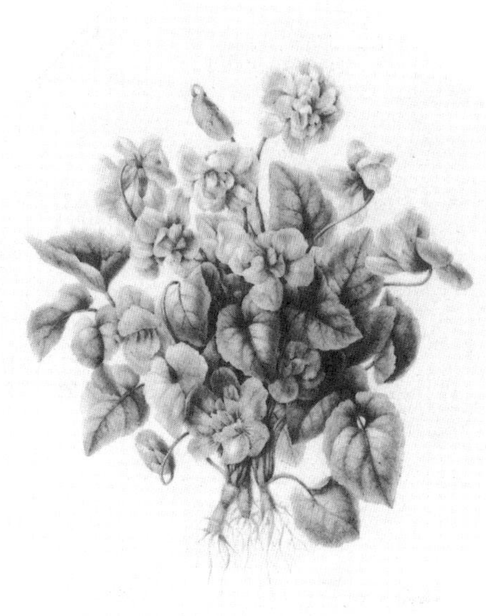

Aline Corbin

Watercolour and bodycolour on vellum, 6¼ × 4¾ in. (16.2 × 12.1 cm.), signed
Cambridge, Fitzwilliam Museum
(Broughton Collection)

CORBIN, Aline
Exhib. flowers in wc, Paris Salon 1835, 1837, 1838, 1848. *Fleurs*, wc, Lyon Salon 1838. *Bouquet de fleurs*, wc, 1835, Versailles Hôtel Rameau, 8 Dec. 1968, no. 93. *Violets*, wc, Cambridge, Fitzwilliam Museum (Broughton coll.)
LIT *Bénézit*; *Hardouin-Fugier* 1981 (ill.); *Lyon Salon* 1838; *Witt*

CORBINEAU, Charles-Auguste *1835–1901*
b. Saumur (Maine-et-Loire). Pupil of Hébert. Painted genre and, occasionally, flowers. Exhib. *Fleurs*, Paris Salon 1872
LIT *Bellier*; *Bénézit*; *Paris Salon* 1872; *Thieme*

CORDENOT, Auguste *b.1867*
Pupil of Castex-Dégrange, Lyon BA (CFD 1887)
LIT *Hardouin-Fugier Grafe*

CORDIER, Albert-Louis *1871–1906*
Pupil of Louis Cordier, his father. Exhib. Paris Indép. *Vase de fleurs*, 1890, *Chrysanthèmes dans une soupière de Saxe*, *Fleurs des champs*, 1898
LIT *Bénézit*; *Paris Indép.* 1890, 1898; *Thieme*

CORMON, Fernand-Anne-Piestre *1845–1924*
b. Paris. Pupil of Portaëls in Brussels, then of Cabanel and Fromentin in Paris. Painted historical subjects, portraits, occasionally still-lifes. Salon debut 1868. Highly successful. Professor at Paris BA; member of the Institut de France; numerous medals
LIT *Bénézit*; *Schurr* III, ill. PM

CORNÉE-VETAULT, Hélène *b.1850*
b. Soulaines (Maine-et-Loire). Pupil of Berton. Musée de Tourcoing, *Fleurs*
LIT *Bénézit*; *Thieme*

CORNELIUS, Marie-Lucie
Fled her native Alsace because of the Franco-Prussian war, moved to Paris. Started painting professionally to bring up her sons, being given government support. Painted portraits and flowers. Exhib. Dijon Salon *Dahlias*, *Roses*, 1887, *Roses*, *Lilas*, 1890; *Lilas*, Strasbourg Salon 1891; Dijon Salon *Dahlias*, *Chrysanthèmes*, 1892, *Lilas*, *Chrysanthèmes*, 1894; Paris SNBA *Bluets et chardons*, *Roses*, 1896, *Chardons*, 1899. A still-life was bought by the State for the Musée de Cannes
LIT *Bénézit*; *Dijon Salon* 1887, 1890, 1892, 1894; Paris Arch. Nat. F21:2128, 4500; *Paris SNBA* 1896, 1899; *Strasbourg Salon* 1891; *Thieme*

CORNILLON, Joannès ***b.1821***
Pupil of Lyon BA and A. Vollon. Entered 1845 Lyon FDC. Exhib. Lyon Salon from 1842. Exhib. Paris Salon from 1868 e.g. *Fleurs des champs*, *Giroflées*, 1873, *Fleurs d'automne*, 1880; *Banc aux roses*, 1882
LIT *Bellier*; *Bénézit*; *Hardouin-Fugier Grafe*; *Paris Salon* 1873, 1880, 1882; *Thieme*

CORNU, Jeanne
b. Paris. Pupil of F. Rivoire. Exhib. *Roses thé*, wc, Paris Salon 1895; Paris UFPS *Roses*, *phlox*, *camomilles*, 1896, *Tulipes*, 1898
LIT *Paris Salon* 1895; *Paris UFPS* 1896, 1898

CORNUARD
b. 1820. Pupil of Thierriat, Lyon BA (CFD 1838)
LIT *Hardouin-Fugier Grafe*

COROT, Jean-Baptiste-Camille ***1796–1875***
b. Paris. Pupil of Michallon. Mostly a landscape and figure painter. *Bouquet de fleurs*, 1871 (Robaut 2152; Galerie Schmidt, Paris, *Corot*, 1971, no.58); *Bouquet de fleurs dans un verre à côté d'un pot à tabac*, 1873–1874 (Robaut 2153; Lefevre Gallery, London, 1954; Chicago Art Institute, *Corot*, 1960, no. 141; Bernkunstmuseum, *Corot*, 1960, no. 96; Marlborough Fine Art, London, 1963, no. 47; Arts Council Loan Exhibition, London, 1965, no. 100; Leymarie, p. 158f., ill.; Preston, p. 45–46, ill. II; private coll., London); *Bouquet de fleurs dans un verre jaune*, 1874 (Robaut 2154; Museo d'Arte, Saó Paulo) are his three signed and fully documented flower paintings
LIT Robaut A. *L'oeuvre de Corot*, Paris, Laget 1965 (reprint). J. Leymarie, *Corot*, Geneva, 1966 (reprint 1979); H. Preston, "Facets of French Art", *Apollo*, January, 1985, pp. 40–7; *Witt*. AC and JLC

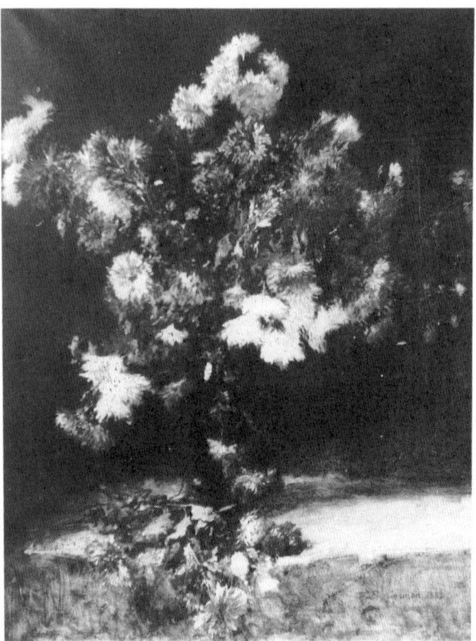

Fernand-Anne-Piestre Cormon

Oil on canvas, $38\frac{1}{4} \times 31$ in. (97 × 79 cm.), signed and dated 1885
Le Mans, Musée de Tessé

COROT, Mme *née* Charlotte-Paule Bouvaist
b. Abbeville (Somme). Pupil of Voitellier and Barré. Exhib. Paris Salon *Couronne de roses*, gouache, *Fleurs des bois*, fan-leaf, 1875, *Roses centfeuilles*, 1880
LIT *Bellier*; *Bénézit*; *Paris Salon* 1875, 1880

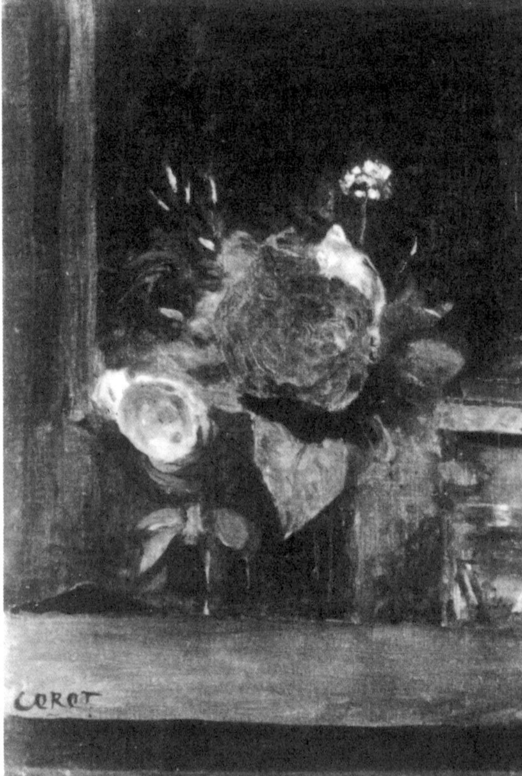

Jean-Baptiste-Camille Corot

Oil on canvas, $12\frac{1}{4} \times 9\frac{1}{2}$ in. (31 × 24 cm.), signed and dated 1874
Private collection

CORPET, Charles-Etienne ***1831–1903***
b. Paris. Pupil of Lesourd de Beauregard and J. Maisiat. Lithographer. Exhib. Paris Salon from 1857, Munich Secession from 1894 and Lyon Salon from 1865. Lyon Salon *Roses trémières*, 1865, *Rosier des quatre saisons*, 1867, *Bouquet d'automne*, 1868, *Glycines et roses*, 1872, *Giroflées*, *Roses de Noël*, 1874, *Premier printemps*, 1875, *Dernières fleurs*, 1877, *Bouquet de roses*, 1878; *Pâquerettes*, Paris Salon 1880; Lyon Salon *Roses*, 1880, *Pavots*, *Roses*, 1881, *Pâquerettes*, 1882, *Roses dans une vasque*, 1883, *Fleurs d'automne*, 1885; *Paris Salon*, *Bouquet de roses*, 1895. M: Gray, *Au Fil de l'Eau*, *Les liserons*; Saint-Etienne
LIT *Bellier*; *Bénézit*; *Faré* 1962, p. 245; *Hardouin-Fugier Grafe*; *Lyon Salon* 1865–1867, 1872, 1874, 1875, 1877, 1878, 1880, 1881–1883, 1885; *Paris Salon* 1880, 1895; Saint-Tropez, *Fleurs de Fantin-Latour à Marquet*, 1982, Musée de l'Annonciade, 1982, no. 2, 12, (ill.); *Thieme*

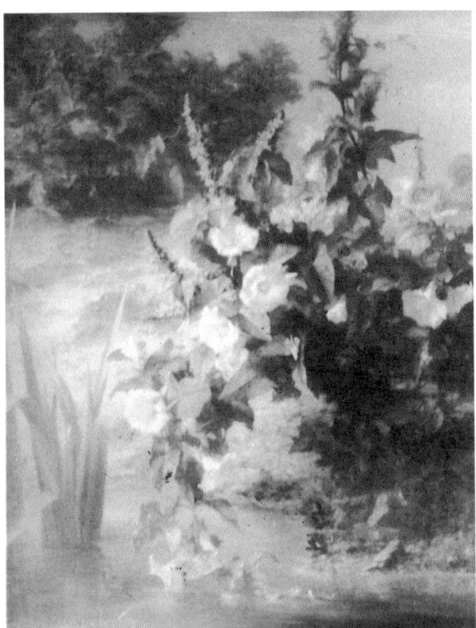

Charles-Etienne Corpet

Oil on canvas, 33½ × 42 in. (85 × 107 cm.), signed Gray, Musée Baron Martin

COSMANN, Hermann-Maurice
Exhib. *Fleurs*, Paris Salon 1850
LIT *Paris Salon* 1850

COSSARD, Amélie
Pupil of J. Cossard, her uncle. Exhib. *Fleurs*, wc, Paris Salon 1833. Musée de Troyes, *Fleurs et fruits* (received by the museum as a gift, 1861)
LIT *Bellier*; *Bénézit*; *Paris Salon* 1833; *Thieme*

COSTE, Numa ***1843–1907***
b. Aix-en-Provence (Bouches-du-Rhône). Pupil of Gibert. The founder of *L'Art libre* was friendly with Zola and occasionally painted flowers
LIT *Orsay*

COSTER, *see* VALLAYER

COTALORDA, Eugénie
Exhib. two flower-pieces, Dijon Salon 1837
LIT *Dijon Salon* 1837. CL

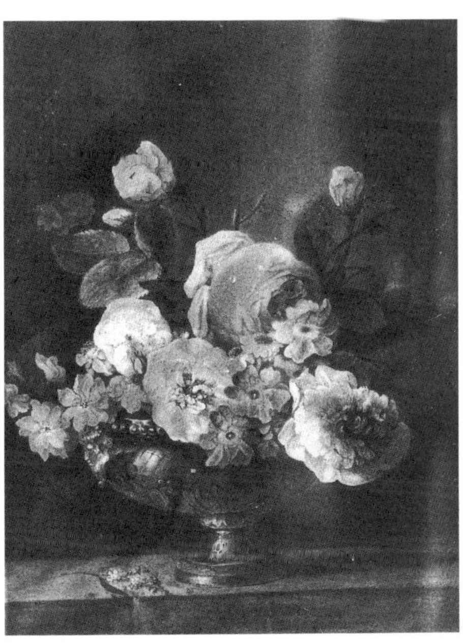

Amélie Cossard

Gouache, 7¾ × 6 in. (19.3 × 15 cm.), Troyes, Musée des Beaux-Arts

COTHENET, Marie
Exhib. Dijon Salon *Lilas*, 1887, *Chrysanthèmes*, 1894
LIT *Dijon Salon* 1887, 1894. CL

COTTAVE, Jeanne
b. Grenoble (Isère). Pupil of Guignebert. Exhib. *Fleurs*, *Cigües et dahlias*, wc, Paris Salon 1895. A J.C. Cottave designed plates for the Vilmorin album
LIT *Paris Salon* 1895

COTTIER, Claude-Marie-François ***b.1824***
Pupil of Thierriat, Lyon BA (CFD 1842)
LIT *Hardouin-Fugier Grafe*

COTTON, Antoine Romand ***alias***
Pupil of Thierriat, Lyon BA (CFD 1838)
LIT *Hardouin-Fugier Grafe*

COUDER, Emile-Gustave ***d.1903***
b. Paris. Pupil of Vasselon. Exhib. Paris Salon from 1869 e.g. *Fleurs de mai*, *Choix de mon jardin*, 1880, *Fleurs de juin*, 1885. His *Primevères de Chine*, formerly in the Musée de Mulhouse, disappeared in the war
LIT *Bellier*; *Bénézit*; *Paris Salon* 1880, 1885; *Thieme*

COUDER, Emile-Hippolyte
b. Paris. Pupil of Lavastre. Exhib. *Fleurs*, Paris Noir et Blanc Salon 1886
LIT *Paris Noir et Blanc Salon* 1886

COUDER, Jean-Alexandre ***1808–1879***
b. Paris. Pupil of Paris BA and Gros. A prolific and popular artist, one of the seven French flower painters who exhibited in Brussels in 1860. Exhib. Paris Salon from 1833 and *Fleurs et fruits*, Lyon Salon 1848; *Fleurs*, Strasbourg Salon 1859; *Fleurs, Fruits*, Paris Amis-des-Arts, 1855; *Fleurs et fruits*, Lyon Salon 1860; *Fleurs et fruits*, Strasbourg Salon 1860; *Fleurs et fruits*, Rouen Salon 1860; *La marguerite, Roses trémières*, Lyon Salon 1861; *Fleurs et fruits*, Moulins Salon 1862; *Fleurs des champs*, Paris Salon 1872; *Vase de fleurs*, Nantes Salon 1872; *Fleurs des champs*, Rouen Salon 1876, *Fleurs des champs*, Reims Salon 1877, *Fleurs des champs*, Pau Salon 1878; *Fleurs des champs*, Nancy Salon 1878; *Fleurs des champs*, Paris Salon 1879. His works were bought by the State for many museums: Armentières, *Fleurs des champs, (1,500 francs), 1872;* Dinan, *Fleurs des champs*, (2,000 francs), 1874; Laval, *Fleurs*; Orléans, *Fleurs*, 1875; Périgueux, *Fleurs et fruits*; Reims, *Roses et fruits* (untraceable); Saint-Denis, *Fleurs et fruits*; Tours, *Fleurs et fruits*; Vitré, *Fleurs des champs*, (600 francs), 1879
LIT *Bellier*; *Bénézit*; *Faré* 1962, p. 242; J.P. Laÿs *Manuscript* (private coll.); *Lille Salon* 1885; Louvre Arch.; *Lyon Salon* 1848, 1859, 1860, 1861; *Moulins Salon* 1862; *Nancy Salon* 1878; *Nantes Salon* 1872; *Orsay*; *Paris Amis-des-Arts* 1855; Paris Arch. Nat. F21:452, 455, 464, 469; *Paris Salon* 1872, 1879; *Pau Salon* 1878; *Reims Salon* 1877; *Rouen Salon* 1876; *Schurr* IV, 80; *Strasbourg Salon* 1859, 1860; *Thieme*; *Witt*

COURAJOD, Louise
b. Saint-Ouen (Seine-Saint-Denis). Exhib. flowers on porcelain, Paris Salon 1877, 1878
LIT *Bellier*

COURBARON, Alexis-Ernest
Exhib. *Fleurs* Paris Indép. 1884
LIT *Paris Indép.* 1884

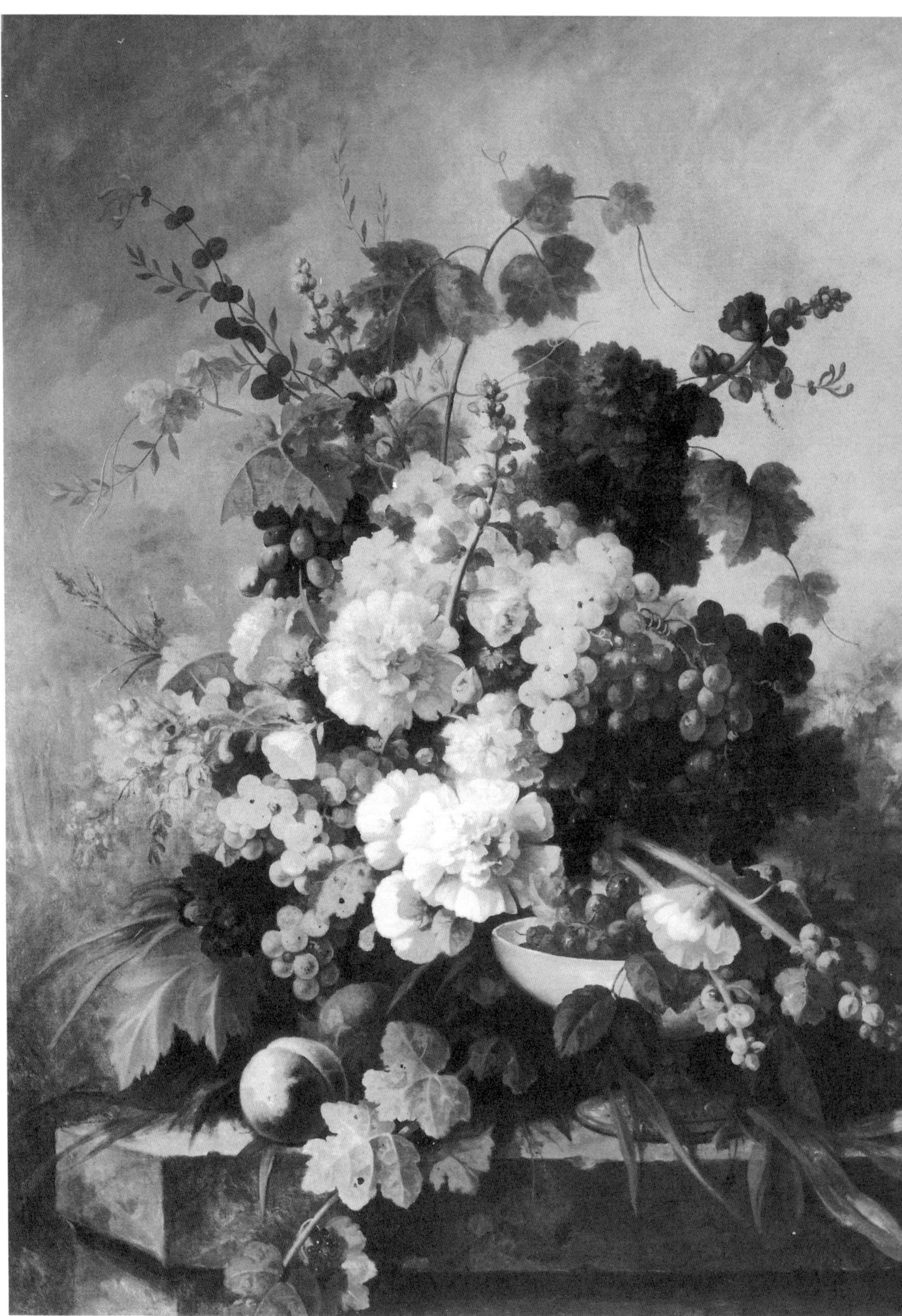

Jean-Alexandre Couder

Oil on canvas, $50\frac{1}{2} \times 37\frac{3}{4}$ in. (128 × 96 cm.), signed and dated 1856
Brussels, Courtesy Palais des Beaux-Arts

COURBET, Gustave ***1819–1877***
b. Ornans (Doubs). Pupil of Steuben and Hesse. Claimed to be self-taught. Mostly a landscape, figure and portrait painter. Many of his flowers were painted in 1862–1863 at Rochemont near Saintes where his friend E. Baudry had his country house. Patrons were not wanting: "Je bats monnaie avec des fleurs" (letter to Isabey May, 1863). His later flowers were painted at the Paris Sainte-Pélagie prison where Courbet served a sentence after the Paris Commune. *Fleurs*, 1855 (Hamburg, F. 182); *Fleurs*, *c.*1855–1860 (Metropolitan Museum, New York); *Bouquet d'asters*, 1859 (Basle, F. 247); *Fleurs sur un banc*, 1862 (F. 229); *Soucis*, 1862 (F. 300, 301); *Bouquet de fleurs dans un vase*, 1862 (F. 302); *Oreilles d'ours et autres fleurs*, *c.*1862 (F. 303); *Pavots*, 1862 (F. 304); *Jeune fille arrangeant des fleurs*, 1862 (F. 306); *Touffe de fleurs*, 1862 (Köln, F. 307); *La femme aux fleurs*, 1863 (Toledo, F. 357); *Nature-morte aux fleurs*, 1863 (F. 360); *Magnolias*, 1863 (Bremen, F. 361); *Iris et giroflées*, *c.*1863 (Glasgow, F. 362); *Pivoines*, 1863 (F. 363); *Vase de fleurs*, 1863 (F. 364); *Fleurs dans un pot brun*, 1863 (F. 365); *Corbeille de fleurs*, 1863 (Glasgow, F. 366); *Branche de cerisier*, 1863 (F. 367); *Branche de cerisier anglais*, 1863 (F. 368); *Bouquet de fleurs*, 1863 (F. 369); *Bouquet de fleurs*, 1871 (F. 781); *Branche de pommier en fleurs*, 1871 (F. 782); *Tête de femme et fleurs*, 1871 (F. 783); *Fleurs dans un vase*, 1872 (Boston, Blondon 27); *Panneau de fleurs*, 1871–1872 (Blondon 6, 9); *Fleurs de pêcher*, 1871–1872 (Blondon 39). M: Musée des Beaux-Arts, Alençon; Kunstmuseum, Basle; Museum of Fine Arts, Boston; Kunsthalle, Bremen; Glasgow Art Gallery; Kunsthalle, Hamburg; Kunsthalle, Cologne; Malibu, J. Paul Getty Museum, Metropolitan Museum of Art, New York; Toledo Art Gallery
LIT Blondon, *Liste des tableaux faits en captivité par Courbet*, MS 2030, Besançon Bibliothèque; R. (here F.) Fernier, *La vie et l'oeuvre de G. Courbet*, Paris, Lausanne (Bibliothèque des Arts) 1977; Paris, *Gustave Courbet*, Grand Palais, Réunion des Musées Nationaux, 1977–1978; *Pavière* III, pt.1; *Witt*. AC.

COURMIER, Marthe
Pupil of P. Dumas. Exhib. *Bouquet de pivoines*, wc, Paris Salon 1898
LIT *Paris Salon* 1898

COURT
Exhib. *Fleurs*, Saint-Etienne Salon 1838
LIT *Hardouin-Fugier Bringuier*

COURTEFOY-COUTURIER, Charles-Louis ***b.1825***
Pupil of Thierriat, Lyon BA (CFD 1842)
LIT *Hardouin-Fugier Grafe*

COURTIN, Alexis
Exhib. *Fleurs dans un vase*, wc, Paris Salon 1844. An F. Courtin is listed as lithographer. A Courtin (no initial given) designed plates for *L'Horticulteur Français*, Paris (Hérincq), 1851–1872
LIT *Béraldi*; *Nissen* 2337n; *Paris Salon* 1844; *Thieme*

COURTOIS, Ernest, Bonnencontre ***alias***
b. Bonnencontre (Côte-d'Or). Painted landscapes. Exhib. *Fleurs*, Dijon Salon 1890
LIT *Bénézit*; *Dijon Salon* 1890. CL

COURTOIS, Gustave-Claude-Etienne ***1851–1924***
b. Pusey (Haute-Saône). Pupil of Gérôme and Jeanneray. Exhib. *Coin de jardin*, Paris Salon 1888; *Lys*, 1872 (Wildenstein) 1973
LIT *Bénézit*; Fondation Wildenstein, *Courtois* ... 1973–1974; *Paris Salon* 1888; *Schurr* I, 27; *Thieme*

COUSIN-FRANQUEBALME, Henriette
She married Ferdinand Franquebalme, a landowner, in 1846. Exhib. genre paintings Paris Salon 1842–1849 and Lyon Salon, *Les fleurs pures et blanches de la Sainte Victime déversent leurs pétales aux pieds de la fiancée* ...
LIT *Hardouin-Fugier Grafe*

COUSTURIER, Césaire
b. Dôle (Jura). Pupil of F. Besson. Painted landscapes and flowers. Exhib. Paris Salon from 1868. Exhib. *Fleurs d'automne*, Bourg Salon 1878
LIT *Bellier*; *Bénézit*; *Bourg Salon* 1878; *Thieme*

COUSTURIER, Lucie ***1870–1925***
b. Paris. Pupil of Signac. Painted landscapes. Among her early flowers are *Les marguerites jaunes*, 1899, *Tulipes dans un vase*, 1900, Geneva, 1968
LIT *Bénézit*; Geneva, *L'Aube du XX° siècle*, Petit Palais, 1968; *Orsay*; Saint-Tropez, *Fleurs de Fantin-Latour à Marquet*, Musée de l'Annonciade, 1982, no. 14 (ill.); *Thieme*

COUTANCE, Joséphine
Exhib. flowers in wc, Paris Salon 1833–1835, 1837, 1840, 1842, 1844. Contributed designs to the Vilmorin album, 1866, lithographed by E. Champin
LIT *Bellier*; *Bénézit*; *Paris Salon* 1833, 1838, 1840, 1844; *Thieme*

COUTIER, Antoine ***b.1837***
Pupil of Reignier, Lyon BA (CFD 1861)
LIT *Hardouin-Fugier Grafe*

COUTURE, Thomas ***1815–1879***
b. Senlis (Oise). The famous figure painter produced some flowers. "Couture fait en plein soleil des études de fleurs délicieuses" (Corvisart to S. Saint-Jean, 24 May 1853 in *Hardouin-Fugier* 1981).

M: Montauban, *Bouquet de pivoines*, *c.*1862 (transferred to the Louvre in 1953); Compiègne, *Bouquet de roses dans un verre*. A still-life with flowers was with Knoedler Gallery, New York, in 1954
LIT Bertauts-Couture, *T. Couture* ... Paris (le Garrec) 1932; *Burlington Magazine*, Sep. 1954; Hardouin-Fugier, *S. Saint-Jean*, Leigh-on-Sea, Lewis, 1981; Pontoise, *T. Couture*, Musée des Beaux-Arts 1972; Senlis, *T. Couture*, Musée des Beaux-Arts, 1980; *Witt*

COUTURIER, *see* COURTEFOY

COUTY, Jean-Frédéric *1829–1904*
b. Issoudun (Indre). Pupil of Billoux and Luminais. Painted landscapes, genre and flowers. Exhib. *Asperges et aubépines*, Dijon Salon 1883; Lyon Salon *Pivoines*, 1884, *Chrysanthèmes*, 1885; Dijon Salon *Giroflées*, 1885, *Fleurs des champs*, 1887
LIT *Bénézit*; *Dijon Salon* 1883, 1885, 1887; *Lyon Salon* 1884, 1885; *Thieme*

COUVREUX, Mme
One signed work dated 1858, a large watercolour on vellum, has recently appeared at auction. L-G-B-T, Paris, 27 Nov. 1986, lot 38. PM

CRESPEL, Berthe-Marie-Henriette, *née* Dauchez
Exhib. *Pivoines*, *Hortensias*, Paris SNBA 1897
LIT *Bénézit*; Paris Arch. Nat. F21:4500; *Paris SNBA* 1897; *Orsay*; *Thieme*

CRESTY, Marguerite, *née* Buret *b.1841*
b. Paris. Pupil of Emeric Bouvret, Français and Kreyder. Exhib. *Fleurs*, Paris Salon 1861 (Buret), *Groupe de fleurs dans une hotte*, Lyon Salon 1874; Paris Salon *Pavots*, wc, 1885, *Roses thé*, wc, 1890; Dijon Salon *Hotte de pavots*, 1892, *Cerises et marguerites*, wc, 1894; Paris Salon *Chrysanthèmes*, wc, 1895, *Hotte de fleurs des champs*, 1898. *Anémone* after Cresty in Paris BMAD (Maciet coll.). Her *Roses trémières*, wc, was bought by the State for the Musée de Nîmes
LIT *Bellier*; *Dijon Salon* 1892, 1894, *Lyon Salon* 1874; Paris Arch. Nat. F21:2128, 1210; *Paris BMAD*; *Paris Salon* 1885, 1890, 1895, 1898; *Thieme*

CRÉTINON, Mlle
Exhib. *Fleurs*, Saint-Etienne Salon 1891
LIT *Hardouin-Fugier Bringuier*; *Saint-Etienne Salon* 1891

CRETU *b.1870*
Pupil of Castex-Dégrange, Lyon BA (CFD 1889)
LIT *Hardouin-Fugier Grafe*

CREUZET, Michel *b.1814*
Pupil of Thierriat, Lyon BA (CFD 1833)
LIT *Hardouin-Fugier Grafe*

CROCHET, Jules *b.1867*
Pupil of Castex-Dégrange, Lyon BA (CFD 1886)
LIT *Hardouin-Fugier Grafe*

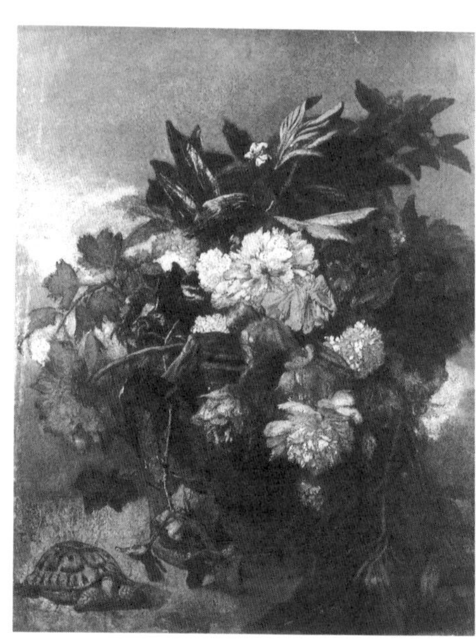

Thomas Couture

Oil on canvas, 32 × 25½ in. (81 × 65 cm), signed, dateable *c.*1862–1863
Montauban, Musée Ingres

CROCHET, Louis *b.1827*
Pupil of Thierriat, Lyon BA (CFD 1844)
LIT *Hardouin-Fugier Grafe*

CRON, Pierre-Etienne
b. Paris. Pupil of his father. Painted genre and flowers. Exhib. *Fleurs*, gouache, Paris Salon 1880
LIT *Bénézit*; *Paris Salon* 1880

CROSNIER, Jules *b.1843*
b. Nancy (Meurthe-et-Moselle). Pupil of B. Menn. Exhib. *Pied de chrysanthèmes*, Paris Noir et Blanc Salon 1886
LIT *Bénézit*; *Paris Noir et Blanc Salon* 1886; *Thieme*; *Witt*

CROSS, Mlle A.
Exhib. *Roses*, *Anémones*, Paris SNBA 1892
LIT *Paris SNBA* 1892

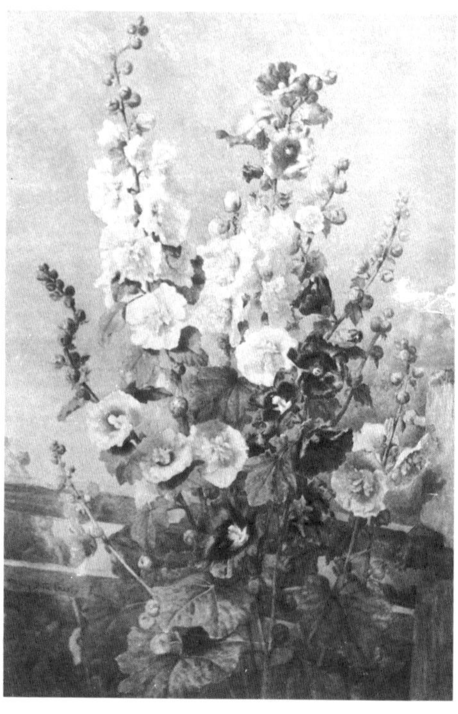

Marguerite Cresty

Watercolour, 39 × 26¼ in. (99 × 66.5 cm.), signed
Nîmes, Musée d'Art et d'Histoire

CROSS, Henri-Edmond, Delacroix *alias* *1856–1910*
b. Douai (Nord). Pupil of Lille BA and F. Bonvin. The well-known pointillist and divisionist may have painted some early flowers e.g. *Bouquet de fleurs dans un pot*, Musée des Beaux-Arts, Dijon (donation Granville) M: Bayeux, Musée Baron Gérard *Fleurs dans un vase*
LIT *Bénézit*; I. Compin *H.E. Cross*, Paris (Quatre Chemins) 1964; Nice, *H.E. Cross*, Musée des Ponchettes, 1972–3; *Orsay*; Saint-Tropez, *Fleurs de Fantin-Latour à Marquet*, Musée de l'Annonciade, 1982, no. 15 (ill.); *Thieme*

CROUAN, Julie
b. Brest (Finistère). Pupil of Colas. Exhib. Paris Salon from 1876 e.g. *Dernier bouquet d'automne* 1878, *Panier de roses*, 1880
LIT *Bellier*; *Bénézit*; *Thieme*

CROZANT, Zoé
Pupil of I. Deubergue. Exhib. *Boules de neige*, *Roses et pivoines*, Paris UFPS 1896
LIT *Paris UFPS* 1896

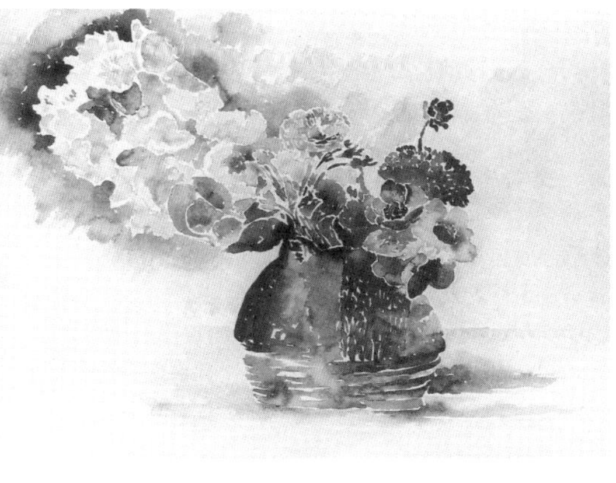

Henri-Edmond Delacroix alias Cross

Watercolour on paper, 11½ × 17 in. (29 × 43 cm.), Dijon, Musée des Beaux-Arts

CROZET
Pupil of Thierriat, Lyon BA (CFD 1827)
LIT *Hardouin-Fugier Grafe*

CRUZET
Pupil of Thierriat, Lyon BA (CFD 1834)
LIT *Hardouin-Fugier Grafe*

CUIRBLANC, Berthe
b. Villiers-Charlemagne (Mayenne). Painted landscapes and flowers. Exhib. Paris Salon 1868–1874 e.g. *Chrysanthèmes et missel*, 1872, *Fleurs et bijoux*, 1874. Her *Fleurs et livres*, 1873 was bought by the State but destroyed during World War II (Musée de Vire)
LIT *Bellier*; *Bénézit*; C. Marumo, *Barbizon* ... Paris (L'Amateur) 1975; *Michelez* 1873, Paris Arch. Nat. F21:207, 475, 477; *Paris Salon* 1872, 1873

CUISIN, Charles-Emile *1832–1900*
Botanical designer and lithographer. Painted flowers in wc on vellum and paper for the Paris Muséum d'Histoire Naturelle, the latest of which is dated 1891 though Thieme claims Cuisin died at an earlier date. Designed plates for E. Bonnet, *Illustrations des espèces nouvelles ... de la Tunisie*, 1892, E. Cosson, *Illustrationes Florae Atlanticae*, Paris (Masson) 1882–1897; J. Deniker, *Atlas manuel de botanique*, Paris (Baillière) 1885–1889
LIT *Laissus*; *Nissen* I, 203, 416, 469; *Schurr* I, 32

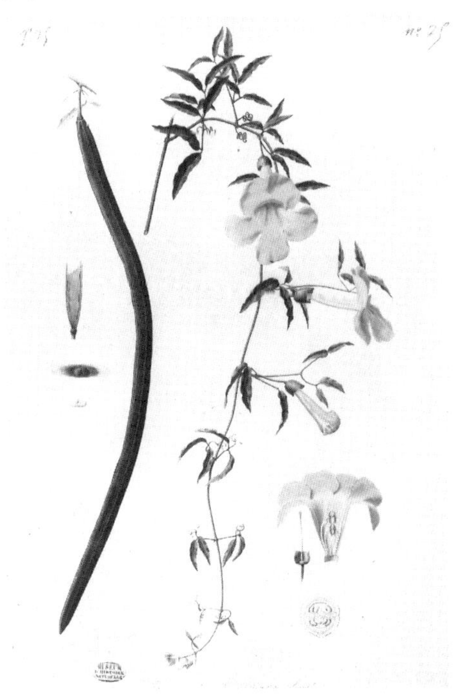

Charles-Emile Cuisin

Watercolour on vellum, Vélins vol. 75, no. 75, signed and dated 1875
Paris, Bibliothèque Centrale du Muséum National d'Histoire Naturelle

CUROT-BARBEREL, Marie-Louise
b. Dourdan (Essonne). Pupil of A. Boulian. Painted portraits and miniatures. Exhib. *Reines-marguerites*, Paris Salon 1880
LIT *Bénézit*; *Paris Salon* 1880; *Thieme*

CURTET, Joseph *b.1814*
Pupil of Thierriat, Lyon BA (CFD 1832–1835). op. textile designer. Exhib. *Fleurs dans un vase*, Lyon Salon 1843
LIT *Hardouin-Fugier Grafe*; *Lyon Salon* 1843

CUSIN, Louis-Antoine *1824–1901*
Designed plates for *Herbier de la Flore française*, Lyon 1867–1876 and *Essai d'une flore élémentaire agricole*, Lyon 1869
LIT *Nissen* I, 444–5

CUSSINET, Jean-Claude *b.1818*
Pupil of Thierriat, Lyon BA (CFD 1837). Engraver
LIT *Hardouin-Fugier Grafe*

CUVILLIER, Marie
b. Paris. Pupil of Barré. Exhib. *Roses et volubilis*, *Fleurs des champs*, on porcelain, Paris Salon 1867
LIT *Paris Salon* 1867

CYBOULLE or CYB, Armand
b. Paris. Exhib. Paris Salon from 1868 e.g. *Roses*, 1879, *Amours et roses*, 1880
LIT *Bellier*; *Bénézit*; *Thieme*

D

D.
Exhib. *Fleurs*, wc, Lyon Salon 1852
LIT *Lyon Salon* 1852

D., J.M.
Exhib. *Fleurs des buissons*, Lyon Salon 1852
LIT *Lyon Salon* 1852

DABLIN, Jean ***1858–1923***
b. Saint-Quentin (Aisne). Pupil of the architect Dablin, his father, Bertin and Henriquel-Dupont. Art teacher at Valenciennes BA and Saint-Etienne BA (1892–1921). (Taught flower design at Saint-Etienne BA.) Painted allegorical subjects, landscapes and flowers
LIT *Hardouin-Fugier Bringuier*

DABNOUR
Botanical draughtsman. Designed plates for *Flore des Antilles*, 1808–1827
LIT *Nissen* I, 2017

DAEL, Jean François (Jan Frans) van ***1764–1840***
b. Antwerp (Belgium). The best pupil in oils of Gérard van Spaendonck began studying architecture from the age of 12 at the insistence of his parents. Despite obtaining first prizes in this discipline at the Antwerp Academy in 1784 and 1785, he left for Paris to become a painter/decorator. 1786: his commissions for work on the interiors of the châteaux at St Cloud, Bellevue, and Chantilly established his ability and began a long career of distinguished patronage. Painted (but did not exhibit) various subjects before devoting himself to flower and fruit, supported and encouraged by Van Spaendonck. 1791: Exposition de la Jeunesse. 1793: Salon debut, lodged in the Louvre. 1799: his most celebrated picture *Offrande à Julie* exhibited at the Salon, painted for Josephine's Malmaison (now lost), passed to her son Eugène de Beauharnais, as did the collection of Redouté's original drawings for the celebrated Liliacées. 1804: a work of similar status *Le Tombeau de Julie*, now at Fontainebleau. The composition and sentiment of these large works were perfectly in harmony with the sentiments of Rousseau. Received gold medals at the Salons of 1810 and 1819; Chevalier of the Legion of Honour (1825); medal of honour from Leopold I; member of the Antwerp and Amsterdam academies, among other learned societies; exhibited Ghent 1812 (Société des Artistes); contributed porcelain designs; presided over a studio at the Sorbonne where Christian van Pol, Elise Bruyère, André Bonneval, and Iphigénie Milet-Mureau were notable pupils. He finished his days in a rural setting where he could cultivate his own models; buried beside Van Spaendonck at Père-Lachaise. Exhib. Paris Salon 1793: *Un vase rempli de fleurs posé sur une table de marbre*; 1795: *Trois tableaux de fleurs, Un tableau de fleurs et de fruits*; 1796: *Une corbeille de différentes fleurs attachée à un chêne, differents fruits peints sur marbre blanc*; 1799: "*Offrande à Flore*"; 1801: *Trois tableaux de fleurs et de fruits, sous le même numéro*; 1804: *Tableau de fleurs, Tableau de fruits*; 1806: *Tableau de fleurs*; 1808: *Un tableau de fleurs*; 1810: *Une croisée sur laquelle on voit un vase de fleurs, Un bocal de cristal rempli de roses avec un groupe de pêches et de raisins, fleurs et fruits, Un tableau de fruits*; 1812: *Tableau de fleurs et fruits*; 1814: *Tableau de fleurs, Tableau de fruits, Tableau de fleurs exposé en* 1810; 1817: *Un tableau de fleurs*; 1819: *Tableau de fleurs, Tableau de fruits, Fruits peints sur marbre blanc*; 1822: *Un tableau de fleurs, Un tableau de fruits, Corbeille de fleurs devant une statue dans une grotte, Corbeille de fleurs dans un fond de paysage*; 1824: *Tableau de fleurs, Tableau de fruits*: 1827: *Tableau de fleurs et de fruits, même numero*; 1833: *Tableau de fleurs.* M: Bruges, Cambridge, Cologne, Compiègne, Florence, Fontainebleau, Liège, Lille, Lyon, Orléans, Rouen
LIT *Bellier*; B. Lossky, "Le peintre fleuriste Jean-François van Dael et ses oeuvres au Château de Fontainebleau", *Bull. de la Société d'Hist. de l'art français*, 1967, p. 122–36; Faré, 1976. PM

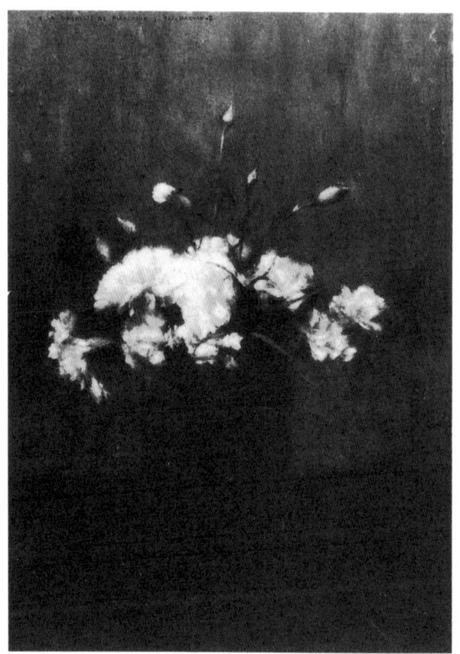

Pascal-Adolphe-Jean Dagnan-Bouveret

Oil on panel, 16 × 12 in. (40.5 × 30.5 cm.), signed and inscribed 'A la Duchesse de Marchena'
Private collection

DAGNAN-BOUVERET, Pascal-Adolphe-Jean ***1852–1929***
Pupil of Gérôme. The well-known figure painter, friendly with Courtois, the flower painter, produced some flowers from 1867 e.g. *Fleurs et oeillets*
LIT *Bénézit*; Dagnan-Bouveret, *Cat. des oeuvres*, Paris (Meunier) 1901, and Paris (Rousseau) 1934; *Orsay*; M.A. Stevens in *Post-Impressionism*, London, RA, 1979–1980; *Thieme*

DAGNAUX, Albert-Marie-Adolphe ***b.1861***
b. Paris. Pupil of Roll. Landscape painter and engraver. Exhib. *Fleurs*, Paris Indép. 1888 and Paris SNBA 1891
LIT *Bénézit*; *Paris Indép.* 1888; *Paris SNBA* 1891; *Thieme*

DAMERON, Emile-Charles ***1848–1908***
Pupil of Albert Adam and Pelouse. Designed fashion plates and posters. Decorator. Painted landscapes and flowers e.g. *Pavots*, *Fleurs des champs*, *Rosiers en fleurs* (atelier sale)
LIT *Bénézit*; *Dameron Atelier Sale*, Paris Drouot 8 Apr. 1908; *Orsay*; *Schurr* III, 39; *Thieme*

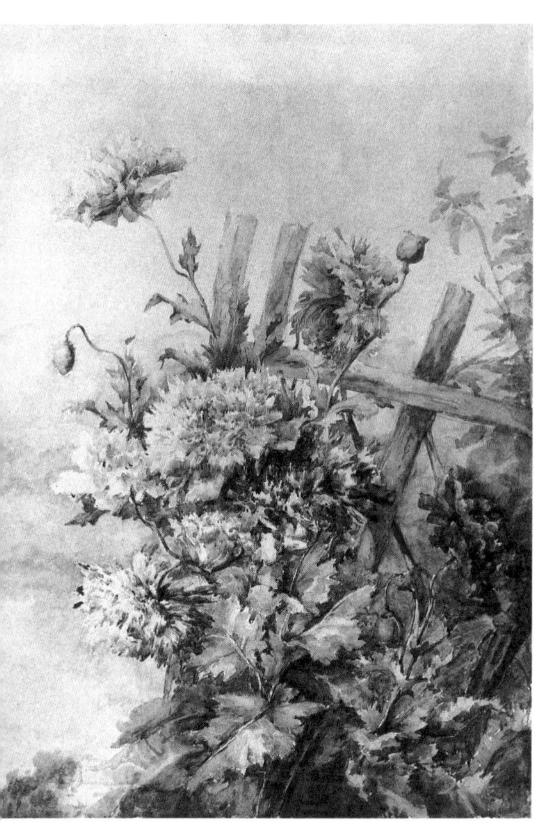

Marie-Céline Dampt

Watercolour, 28 × 21 in. (71 × 53 cm.), signed
Avignon, Musée Calvet

DAMIS, Amédée-Gustave ***1811–1851***
b. Bruges (Belgium). Painter and sculptor. Possibly a pupil of Redouté. Provided a floral design for a Beauvais tapestry cartoon. Exhib. Paris Salon 1846–1848 e.g. *Corbeille de fleurs renversée*, 1846, *Bouquet de fleurs et fruits sur une table*, 1848
LIT *Bénézit*; *Bellier*; *Hardouin-Fugier* 1981

DAMMOUSE, Edouard-Alexandre ***d.1903***
b. Paris. Pupil of Bracquemond. Exhib. *Chrysanthèmes*, pastel, Paris Salon 1890
LIT *Paris Salon* 1890

DAMPT, Aurélie
b. Paris. Pupil of F. Rivoire. Exhib. wc: *Chrysanthèmes*, Paris Noir et Blanc Salon, 1886; *Iris*, Paris Salon 1890; Dijon Salon *Iris*, *Chrysanthèmes*, wc., 1892, *Roses*, *Chrysanthèmes*, wc., 1894; *Iris*, *Soleils*, wc., Paris Salon 1895; *Violettes et roses*, *Roses*, Dijon Salon wc., 1897; *Pivoines*, Paris SNBA 1897; *Roses trémières*, *Verveines*, *Pavots et bluets*, wc., Paris UFPS 1898; Paris SNBA, *Violettes*, wc., 1897, *Oeillets*, *Chardons*, 1899
LIT *Bénézit*; *Dijon Salon* 1892, 1894, 1897; *Paris Noir et Blanc Salon* 1886; *Paris Salon* 1890, 1895; *Paris SNBA* 1897–1899; *Paris UFPS* 1898; *Thieme*

DAMPT, Marie-Céline
b. Paris, sister of Aurélie Dampt. Pupil of J. Lefebvre and F. Rivoire. Exhib. Paris Exposition Universelle 1900. Her *Pavots*, wc, is in the Musée Calvet, Avignon
LIT *Bénézit*; *Thieme*

DANANCHE, Mme Xavier de
Exhib. Lyon Salon *Fleurs et fruits*, 1858, *Fleurs*, 1860, *Vase de fleurs*, 1861, *Fleurs*, 1868, *Fleurs et fruits*, 1877
LIT *Hardouin-Fugier Grafe*; *Lyon Salon* 1858, 1860, 1861, 1868, 1877

DANCAUD, Cécilie
Exhib. *Etude de fleurs*, Amiens Salon 1868
LIT *Amiens Salon* 1868

DANCHEZ, *see* CRESPEL

DANGON, Victor
b. Lyon. Exhib. *Fleurs*, Grenoble Salon 1899; *Asters de Chine*, étude, 1887, Paris BMAD (Maciet coll.)
LIT *Grenoble Salon* 1899; *Paris BMAD*

DANGUIN, Gaspard ***1778–1878***
b. Theize (Rhône). Textile designer.
LIT *Audin Vial*; *Bénézit*

DANIEL, Georges
Exhib. *Fleurs*, Paris Indép. 1890
LIT *Paris Indép.* 1890

DANTAN, Louis-Edouard ***1848–1897***
b. Paris. Pupil of Pils and Lehmann. Exhib. *Chrysanthèmes*, *Roses trémières*, Paris Salon 1895. Exhib. *Le Paradou*, Paris Salon 1883 (after Zola's *Faute de l'abbé Mouret*) featuring many flowers in the foreground
LIT *Paris Salon* 1895; *Schurr* III, 114; *Thieme*

DANTIN, P.
Exhib. Paris Salon *Étude*, featuring potted plants, 1888, *Étalage de fleurs*, 1889
LIT *Orsay*; *Paris Salon* 1888 (ill.), 1889 (ill.)

DANVERS, Juliette
Exhib. *Violettes*, wc, Paris Salon 1898
LIT *Paris Salon* 1898

DARDEL, Claude ***1799–1855***
b. Lyon. Pupil of Van Spaendonck. Mulhouse textile designer
LIT *Histoire documentaire*, p. 637. BJ

DARDEL, Jules
A Lyon textile designer c.1810
LIT *Audin Vial*

DARDEL, Samuel
op. Lyon, textile designer *c*.1810
LIT *Audin Vial*

DARGENT, Edouard-Yan ***1824–1889***
b. Saint-Servais (Finistère). A book illustrator. Painted landscapes and flowers e.g. *Fleurs*, Brest, 17 Dec. 1972
LIT *Bénézit*; *Schurr* III, 34; *Thieme*

DARPY, Lucien-Gilbert ***b.1875***
b. Paris. Pupil of Géry-Richard. Exhib. flowers, Paris Salon from 1897
LIT *Bénézit*

DARU, Louise
b. Neubourg (Bas-Rhin). Pupil of Piette and A. Doré. Exhib. *c*.1864–1880 e.g. *Fleurs des champs*, Paris Salon, 1867; *Fleurs des champs*, Marseille Salon, 1868; *Fleurs des champs*, *Roses*, Rouen Salon 1872; *Le bouquet de la paysanne*, Paris Salon 1875; *Fleurs*, Nancy Salon 1876; *Fleurs*, Limoges Salon 1879. Her *Bouquet villageois* was exhibited at the Évreux Salon 1874 and bought by the State for the Musée d'Évreux (1875, 1,200 francs)
LIT *Bellier*; *Bénézit*; *Limoges Salon* 1879, *Marseille Salon* 1868; *Nancy Salon* 1876; Paris Arch Nat. F21:208; *Paris Salon* 1867, 1875; *Rouen Salon* 1872; *Thieme*

DAUBIGNY, Cécile ***1843–1896***
Daughter of C.F. Daubigny, the landscape painter. Painted *Fleurs des champs*, n.d.
LIT Bailly-Herzberg, *Daubigny*, Paris 1975, p. 79

DAUPHIN, Eugène-Baptiste-Emile ***1857–1930***
b. Toulon (Var). Pupil of Courdouan. Painted landscapes. Exhib. *Fleurs sauvages*, Paris SNBA 1894
LIT *Bellier*; *Bénézit*; *Paris SNBA* 1894; *Schurr* V, 80; *Thieme*

DAVEAUX, Jules ***d.1913***
b. Bordeaux (Gironde). Exhib. *Giroflées*, *Chardons*, Grenoble Salon 1899
LIT *Grenoble Salon* 1899. MW

DAVID Charles-Eugène
Pupil of Leloir, J. Lefebvre, Boulanger. Painted portraits and flowers. Exhib. Paris Salon from 1878
LIT *Bellier*; *Bénézit*; *Thieme*

DAVID, Ernest ***b.1830***
b. Caen (Calvados). Pupil of Guillard. Painted landscapes, genre and flowers. Exhib. Paris Salon 1864–82 e.g. *Fleurs*, 1880
LIT *Bellier*; *Bénézit*; *Paris Salon* 1880; *Thieme*

DAVID, Euphémie-Thérèse, ***née*** **Didier** ***b.1823***
b. Paris. Pupil of Barbier, Grönland and Mme Girardin. Exhib. Paris Salon 1848–*c*.1868 e.g. *Fleurs déposées au pied d'un chêne*, 1852, *Roses*, wc, 1867
LIT *Bellier*; *Bénézit*; *Paris Salon* 1867; *Thieme*

DAVID, François-Alexandre ***1805–1894***
op. Sèvres 1844–82
LIT *Bénézit*; *Thieme*

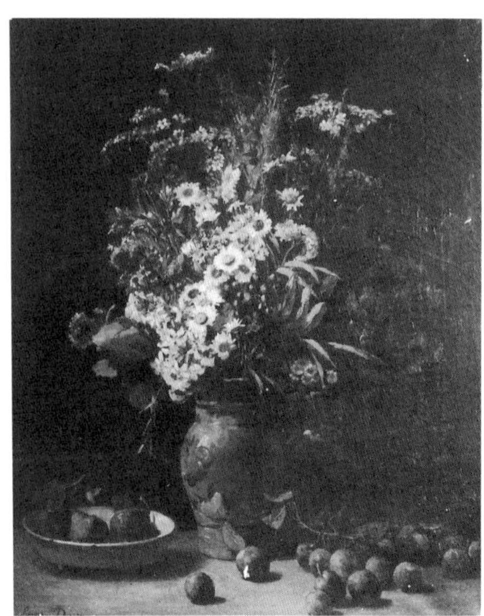

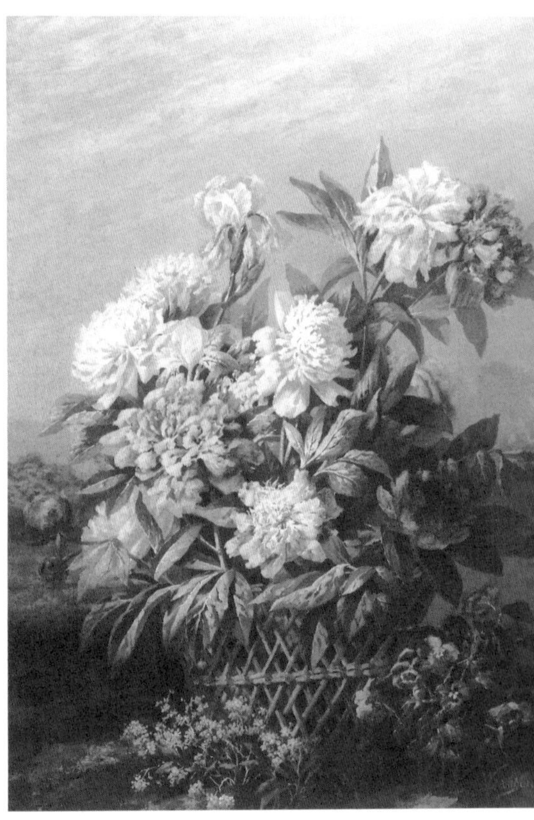

Victor Dangon

Oil on canvas, 50 × 35 in. (127 × 89 cm.), signed and dated 1904
Courtesy Frank S. Schwarz & Son

Louise Daru

Oil on canvas, 39½ × 32 in. (101 × 81 cm.), signed
Evreux, Musée de l'Ancien Évêché

DAVID, Maurice ***b.1868***
Pupil of Castex-Dégrange, Lyon BA (CFD 1888)
LIT *Hardouin-Fugier Grafe*

DAVID DE MAYRÉNA, Clémence-Jeanne, *née* Eymard de Lanchatres
b. Metz (Moselle). Pupil of Bricka. Exhib. Paris Salon from 1875 e.g. *Fleurs*, Paris Salon 1880
LIT *Bellier*; *Bénézit*; *Paris Salon* 1880; *Thieme*

D.C., Mme S.
Pupil of Médard. Exhib. *Chrysanthèmes*, Lyon Salon 1882
LIT *Lyon Salon* 1882

DEBAINES, *see* BRUNE

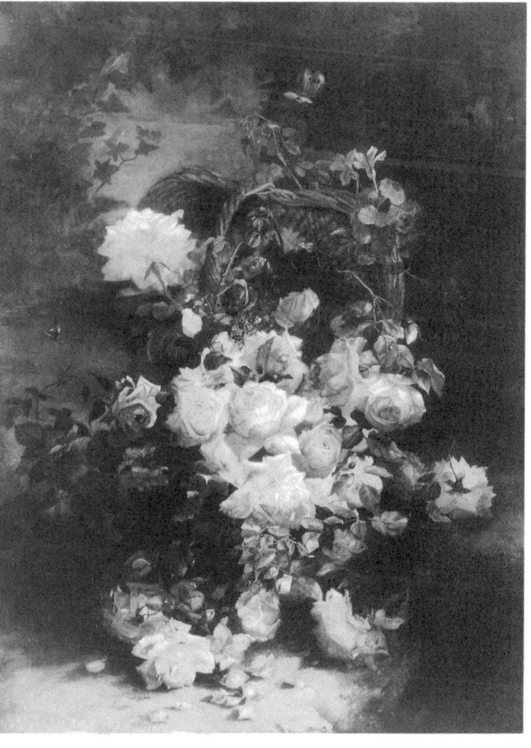

Alexandre Debrus

Oil on canvas, 39¼ × 29¾ in. (100.3 × 75.6 cm.), signed and dated 1896
Courtesy Sotheby's, London

DEBAT-PONSAN, Edouard ***1847–1913***
The well-known figure, genre and portrait painter produced some flower studies e.g. *Bouquet de fleurs*, 1888, for his portrait of Mlle de Vilmorin (1891, Paris Salon). This work is in the Musée des Beaux-Arts, Tours; *Bouquet de fleurs*, for his 1885 portrait of Mme Debat-Ponsan (Paris, Louvre)
LIT *Bénézit*; *Orsay*; *Schurr* III, 113; *Thieme*

DEBAVAY, Auguste ***b.1804***
b. Lyon. Pupil of Berjon, Lyon BA (CFD 1822)
LIT *Hardouin-Fugier Grafe*

DEBELLUT
Exhib. *Lilas*, *Pensées*, Dijon Salon 1885
LIT *Dijon Salon* 1885. CL

DEBRUS, Alexandre
One signed and dated work of 1896 has recently appeared at auction (Sotheby's, New York, 29 Oct. 1987, lot 144)
LIT *Bénézit*. PM

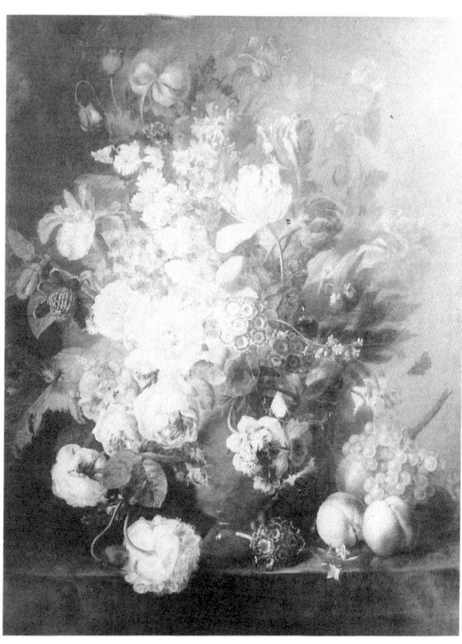

Vicomtesse Iphigénie Decaux

Oil on canvas, 39¼ × 31¾ in. (99.6 × 80.5 cm.), signed
Private collection

DECAISNE, Joseph ***1807–1882***
b. Brussels (Belgium). Designed plates e.g. for B. Delessert, *Icones selectae plantarum* ... Paris, 1820, J.B.A. Guillemin, *Florae Senegambiae* ... Paris, 1830–1833, E. Spach *Histoire naturelle des végétaux* ... Paris, 1834–1848, H.F. Jaubert and E. Spach *Choix de plantes ... de l'Asie occidentale*, Paris (Roret) 1842–1857
LIT *Bellier*; *Nissen* I, 1878, 461, 766, 985; *Sitwell*; *Witt*

DECAUX, Fanny, *née* Michel
Exhib. Paris Salon 1844–1851 e.g. *Une éphémérine ou tradescantia*, wc, *Géranium*, wc, 1844 *Branches d'amandier et de prunier*, 1850
LIT *Bellier*; *Bénézit*; *Paris Salon* 1844, 1850

DECAUX, Vicomtesse Iphigénie, *née* Milet de Mureau ***b.1780***
Pupil of Van Dael, operated a studio. Exhib. Paris Salon e.g. *Fleurs et fruits*, 1808, 1821, 1819. Her *Fleurs dans un vase* was with Knoedler, London, in 1930
LIT *Bellier*; *Bénézit*; *Faré* 1962, p. 246; *Gabet*; *Hardouin-Fugier* 1981; *Paris Salon* 1812, 1819; *Thieme*; *Witt*

DÉCHANIE, Noémi
b. Bapeaume (Seine-Maritime). Pupil of Wurst. Exhib. *Fleurs*, wc, Paris Salon 1880
LIT *Paris Salon* 1880

DÉCHAZELLE, Pierre-Toussaint ***1752–1833***
b. Lyon. Pupil of D. Nonotte and A. Douet. Textile designer. Updated Lyonnais textile design and provided the local silk industry with Dutch-inspired flower designs. A man of many parts and an able flower painter
LIT *Bénézit*; *Hardouin-Fugier Grafe*; *Hardouin-Fugier Grafe* 1982 (ill.); *Thieme*

DECOEUR, Jean-Marie ***b.1822***
b. Lyon. Pupil of Thierriat, Lyon BA (CFD 1839). Exhib. Lyon Salon e.g. *Couronne de fleurs suspendue* ... 1861. *Fleurs des bois*, Musée de Bagnères de Bigorre
LIT *Bénézit*; *Hardouin-Fugier Grafe*; *Lyon Salon* 1861; *Thieme*

DECOMBE, Claude
Pupil of Berjon, Lyon BA (CFD 1813). Exhib. Lyon Salon 1822, 1828, 1833 e.g. *Une tourterelle portant une couronne de roses*, 1833; Paris Salon e.g. *Fleurs posées au pied d'une lyre*, 1824, *Guirlande de fleurs enlaçant une urne placée sur une tombe*, 1824, *Couronne de fleurs*, 1828, *Fleurs devant une coupe de raisins* ... 1828, *Bouquet détaché* ... 1828, *Fleurs dans une coquille*, 1828. His *Guirlande de fleurs*, 1826, was in the Galliera, Paris, 25 Mar. 1969 sale
LIT *Bénézit*; *Faré* 1962, p. 249; *Hardouin-Fugier Grafe*; *Orsay*; *Paris Salon* 1824, 1828

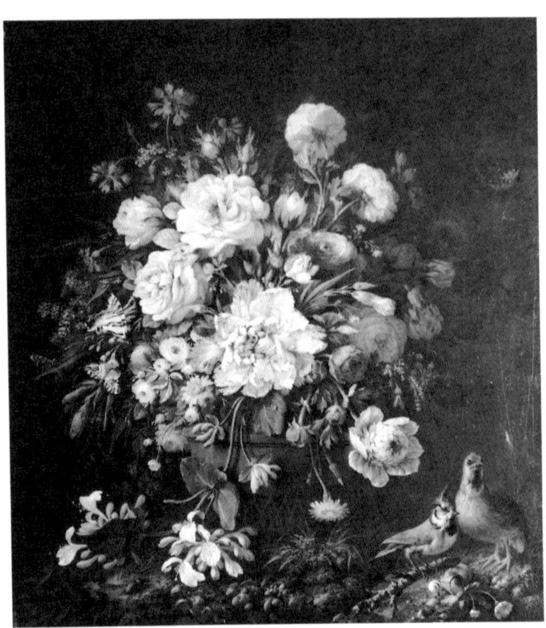

Pierre-Toussaint Déchazelle

Oil on panel, 23¾ × 21 in. (60 × 53 cm.), Private collection, Courtesy Musée des Beaux-Arts, Lyon

DECOREIS, Pierre ***1824–1902***
This Toulon drawing master painted still-lifes and, occasionally, flowers
LIT *Bénézit*

DÉCOT, Mathieu ***b.1868***
Pupil of Castex-Dégrange, Lyon BA (CFD 1886)
LIT *Hardouin-Fugier Grafe*

DECUGIS, M.
Exhib. *Violettes*, wc, Paris SNBA 1899
LIT *Paris SNBA* 1899

DEDIEU, *see* BOUCHET

DEDIEU, Emile
Exhib. *Coin d'atelier, fleurs*, Dijon Salon 1881
LIT *Dijon Salon* 1881. CL

DEDREUX, *see* BECQ DE FOUQUIÈRES

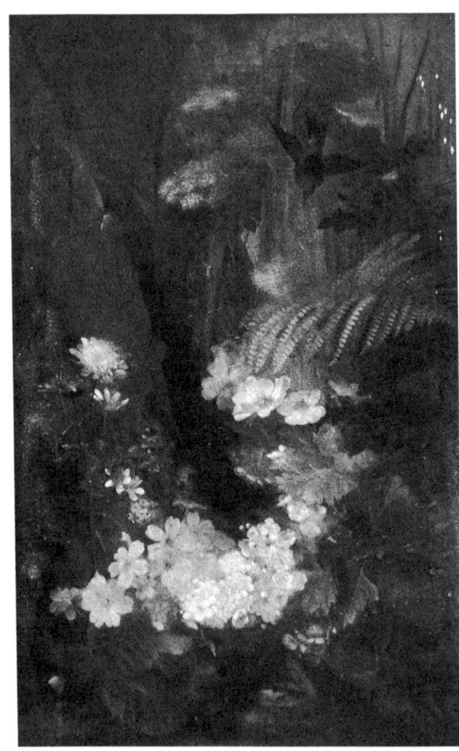

Jean-Marie Decoeur

Oil on canvas, 21¼ × 13½ in. (54 × 34 cm.), signed Bagnères-de-Bigorre, Musée Salies

DEFAUX, Alexandre ***1826–1900***
b. Bercy (Paris XII°). Pupil of Corot. Painted landscapes, genre, animals and, occasionally, flowers e.g. *Fleurs*, Marseille Salon 1877; *Des Fleurs*, Dijon Salon, 1880; *Jeté de fleur*, Sotheby's, Monaco, 22 June 1986, lot 270
LIT *Bénézit; Dijon Salon* 1880; *Marseille Salon* 1877; *Schurr* I, 42; *Thieme; Witt*

Claude Decombe

Oil on canvas, 27½ × 20½ in. (69 × 52 cm.), signed and dated 1826
Courtesy Etienne Ader, Paris

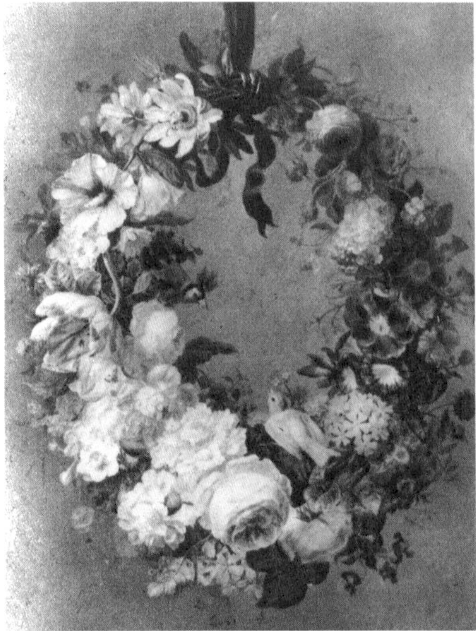

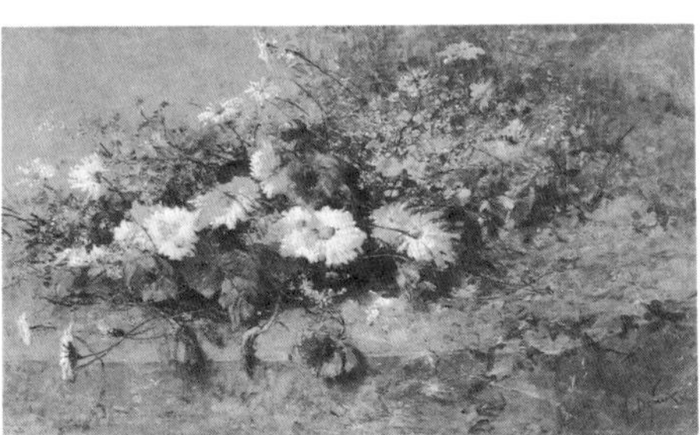

Alexandre Defaux

Oil on canvas, 16¼ × 26¾ in. (41 × 68 cm.), signed Paris, Galerie du Lethé

DEFRETÈRE, Georges ***b.1872***
Pupil of Castex-Dégrange, Lyon BA (CFD 1891)
LIT *Hardouin-Fugier Grafe*

DEGAS, Hilaire-Germain Edgar de Gas or ***1834–1917***
b. Paris. Pupil of Louis Lamothe. Claiming to be allergic to flowers, Degas painted them as accessories only as in *Femme aux Chrysanthèmes*, 1865 (New York, Metropolitan Museum, Minervino 210); *Femme à la potiche*, 1872 (Paris, Louvre, Minervino 341); *Danseuse au bouquet saluant*, *c*.1878 (Paris, Louvre, Minervino 510). M: Metropolitan Museum of Art, New York; Paris, Louvre, Orsay
LIT F. Minervino, *Tout l'œuvre peint de Degas*, Paris (Flammarion) 1974; Paris, *Degas*, Galeries Nationales du Grand Palais, 1988; *Witt*

DÉGRANGE, *see* CASTEX

DEGUERVILLE, Marthe
b. Paris. Pupil of C. Giraud. Exhib. *Bouquet de fleurs*, gouache, Paris Salon 1880
LIT *Paris Salon* 1880

DEHARME, *née* Laugier
Pupil of Van Dael. Exhib. Paris Salon 1810–1824 e.g. *Fleurs*, 1810, 1814, *Fleurs dans une corbeille*, 1812, 1817, *Tableau allégorique de fleurs et de fruits* ... 1819, *Fleurs dans un casque* ... 1824, *Groupe d'iris*, wc, 1824
LIT *Bellier*; *Bénézit*; *Faré* 1962, p. 248; *Paris Salon* 1810, 1812, 1813, 1817, 1819, 1824; *Thieme*

DEHEYDER
Exhib. *Fleurs*, Paris Salon 1842
LIT *Paris Salon* 1842

DEJEAN, Gabrielle
Exhib. *Fleurs*, on porcelain, Dijon Salon 1892
LIT *Dijon Salon* 1892

DELACROIX, Ferdinand-Victor-Eugène ***1798–1863***
b. Charenton-Saint-Maurice (Val-de-Marne). Pupil of Guérin. His strongly painted flower-pieces, whether formal opulent arrangements or more sketchy studies, opened the way to the more adventurous painters of the century. *Bouquet de fleurs*, 1833 (G. 253); *Bouquet de fleurs dans un vase*, 1848 (G. 519); *Corbeille de fleurs renversée dans un parc*, 1848 (New York, Metropolitan, G. 525); *Marguerites et dahlias dans un parterre*, 1848 (G. 526); *Fleurs dans un vase bleu*, 1848 (Montauban, G. 527); *Pavots, roses et dahlias dans un vase*, 1848 (G. 528); *Hortensias sur le bord d'un étang*, 1848 (G. 529); *Corbeille de fleurs posée sur un socle*, 1848 (G. 530); *Fleurs*, 1848 (Lille, G. 532); *Bouquet de fleurs dans un vase*, 1848 (Bremen, G. 533); *Pivoines*, 1848 (Oslo, G. 531); *Fuchsias en pot*, wc, 1855 (G. 47); *Dahlias* (Copenhagen, G. 902); *Bouquet de fleurs dans un vase de grès* (the picture belonged to George Sand by 1844; thereafter in her 1846 sale, lot 8) (Vienna, G. 370); *Paysages et fleurs*, 1863 (G. 682–91). M: Bremen Kunsthalle; Copenhagen Ny Carlsberg Glyptotek; Lille Musée des Beaux-Arts; Montauban Musée Ingres; New York Metropolitan Museum of Art; Oslo Nasjonalgalleriet; Vienna Kunsthistorisches Museum
LIT L.R. Georgel P. Bortolatto, *Tout l'œuvre peint de Delacroix* (here G.) Paris (Flammarion) 1975; L. Johnson, *The Paintings of Eugène Delacroix*, Oxford, 1986; *Witt*

DELACROIX, Gustave
Pupil of Berjon, Lyon BA (CFD 1823)
LIT *Hardouin-Fugier Grafe*

DELACROIX-GARNIER, Pauline ***1863–1912***
b. Paris. Pupil of J. Garnier, her brother, and H.E. Delacroix, her husband. Exhib. *Marie, la jardinière*, Paris Salon 1891
LIT *Bénézit*; *Paris Salon* 1891 (ill.); *Thieme*

DELACROIX, *see* CROSS

DELAHAYE, Adrienne
Pupil of Laugée. Exhib. Paris Salon *c*.1880 e.g. *Fleur d'oranger*, gouache, fan-leaf, 1878, *Giroflée et aubépine*, gouache, 1880, *Violettes et mimosas*, gouache 1880. Eleven flower designs, three on vellum, eight on paper dated 1854–1881 and signed Delahaye may be by this artist or a namesake (Paris Muséum d'Histoire Naturelle—not botanical)
LIT *Bellier*; *Bénézit*; *Laissus*; *Paris Salon* 1880; *Thieme*

DELAHOGUE, Alexis-Auguste ***1867–after 1930***
b. Soissons (Aisne). Landscape painter. Exhib. *Violettes et mimosas*, Paris Salon 1895
LIT *Bénézit*; *Paris Salon* 1895; *Schurr* IV, 33

DELAISSE, François-Laurent ***b.1823***
Pupil of Thierriat, Lyon BA (CFD 1842). Entered 1843 FDC
LIT *Hardouin-Fugier Grafe*

DELANDE, *see* ROBLOT

DELANOY or DELANOYE, Hippolyte-Pierre ***1849–1899***
b. Glasgow (Scotland). Pupil of Lyon BA, Jobbé-Duval, Gleyre, Barrias, Bonnat and Vollon. Exhib. Lyon Salon 1863–1887, Paris Salon 1868–1899 e.g. *Fleurs d'été*, Lyon Salon 1875, *Fleurs d'automne*; *Marguerites et soucis*, Paris Salon 1875. Musée de Clamecy, *Vase de fleurs*

LIT *Bellier*; *Bénézit*; *Hardouin-Fugier Grafe*; *Lyon Salon* 1875; *Paris Salon* 1875; *Schurr* II, 64; *Thieme*

DELANOY, Jacques *1820–1890*
b. Paris. Pupil of Acloque, Vollon, Ferrey and Dussauce. Exhib. landscapes, still-lifes and, occasionally, flowers from *c.*1850, e.g. *Pêches et fleurs*, Paris Salon 1880; *Roses et pêches*, Dijon Salon 1890. Father of H.-P. Delanoy
LIT *Bellier*; *Bénézit*; *Dijon Salon* 1890; *Paris Salon* 1875, 1880

DELAPLANCHE, Mlle A.
Exhib. *Fleurs et fruits d'après nature*, three studies, wc, Paris Salon 1840
LIT *Paris Salon* 1840

DELAPORTE, Adèle
b. Paris. Pupil of Steuben. Exhib. animals and flowers e.g. *Le Mois de Marie*, *Couronne de fleurs*, Paris Exposition Universelle 1855; *Fleurs*, Strasbourg Salon 1862 (100 francs)
LIT *Bellier*; Paris Arch. Nat. 46 AP:3; *Paris Exposition Universelle* 1855; *Strasbourg Salon* 1862

Edgar Degas

Oil on canvas, $25\frac{1}{2} \times 21\frac{1}{4}$ in. (65 × 54 cm.), signed and dated 1872
Paris, Musée d'Orsay

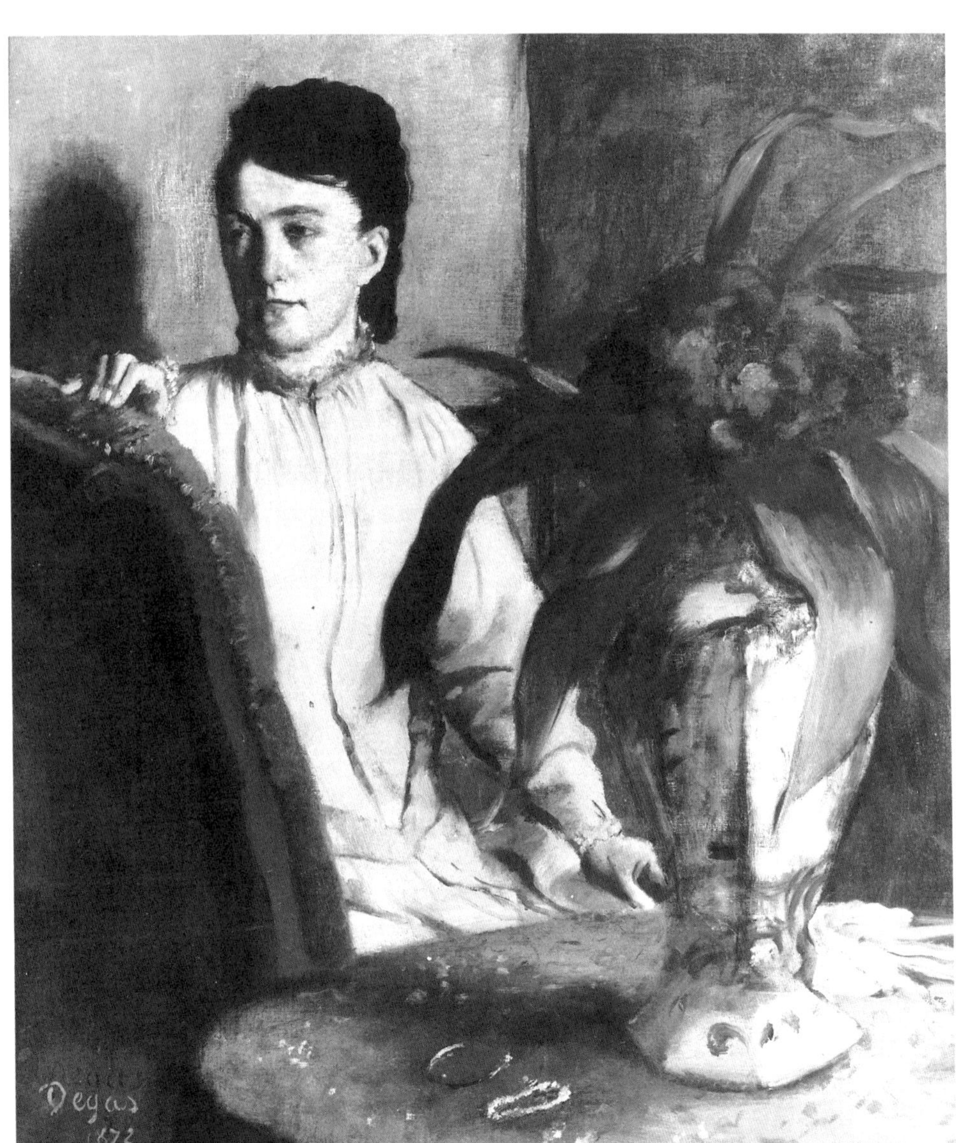

DELAPORTE, Rosine-Antoinette, *née* Bessin *1807–1876*
Pupil of Redouté. Drawing mistress at the Légion d'Honneur school. Contributed designs to Chavant's *Naissance des fleurs* set, *Cours des Fleurs du Jardin des Plantes* etc. Exhib. flowers

Hippolyte-Pierre Delanoy

Oil on canvas, signed
Clamecy, Musée des Beaux-Arts

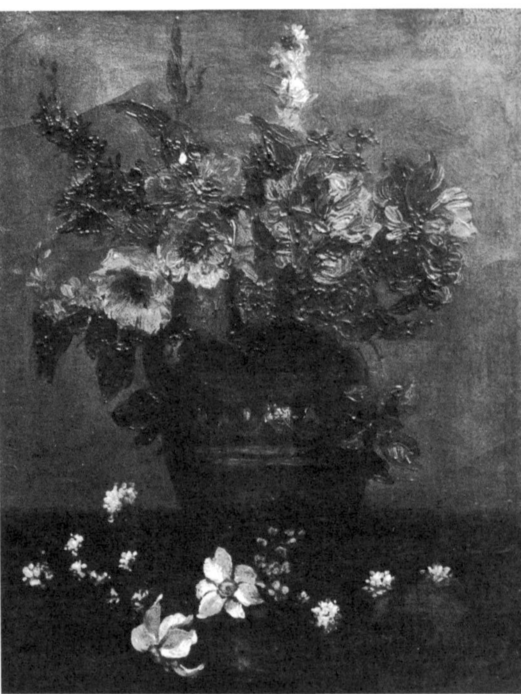

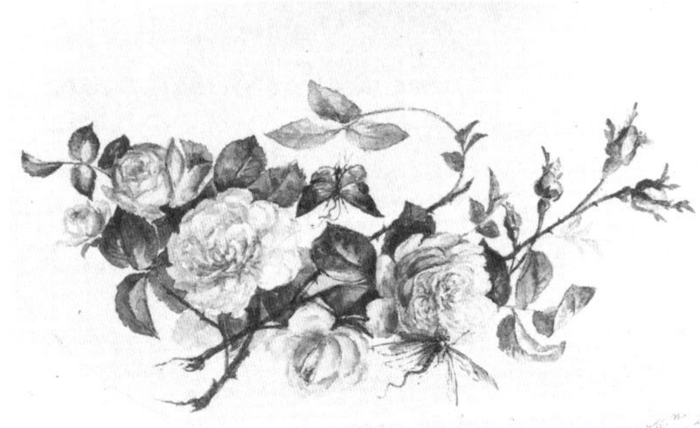

Rosine-Antoinette Delaporte

Watercolour, $12\frac{1}{4} \times 19\frac{1}{2}$ in. (31 × 49.5 cm.), signed
Pontoise, Musée Tavet-Delacour © SPADEM

in wc, Paris Salon 1833–1851 e.g. *Tulipe*, *Fleurs sur un banc*, wc, 1850; *Dahlias*, Cambrai Salon 1843. Was one of Redouté's 'Déléguées au cours d'iconographie végétale du Jardin des Plantes'. One work in Musée de Pontoise
LIT *Bénézit*; *Hardouin-Fugier* 1981 (ill.); *Paris Salon* 1850

DELAROCHE, Honoré-Gaspard *b.1804*
b. Montmorency (Seine-et-Oise). Painted landscapes. Exhib. Paris Salon 1835 and 1866. M: Cambrai *Fleurs*, possibly by this artist
LIT *Orsay*

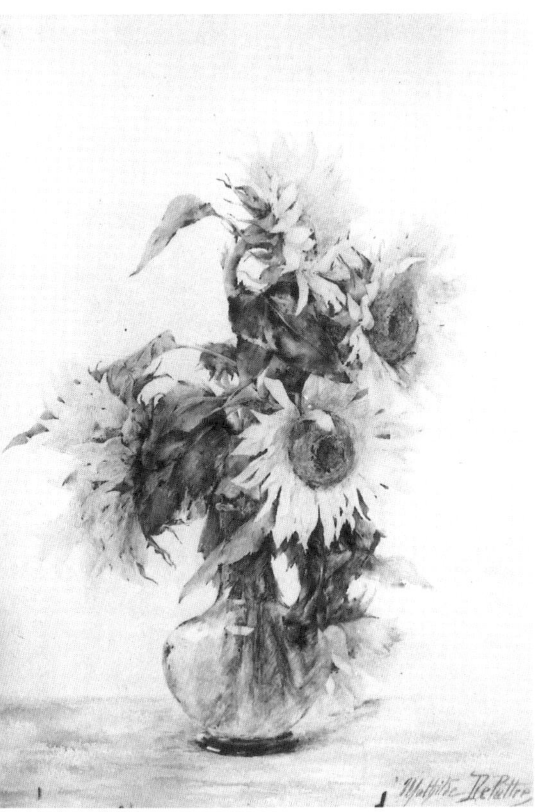

Mathilde-Henriette Delattre

Watercolour, 55 × 35½ in. (140 × 90 cm.), signed
Semur-en-Auxois, Musée Municipal
Inventaire Général, © SPADEM 1988

DELARUE, Claire-Coralie, *née* Lireaux *1821–1906*
b. Rouen (Seine-Maritime). Pupil of Redouté. Grandmother of Lucie Delarue-Mardrus (1880–1945), the poet
LIT *Hardouin-Fugier* 1981

DELATTRE, Mathilde-Henriette *b.1871*
b. Cairo (Egypt). Pupil of Saintpierre and Leroux. Exhib. *Fleurs jaunes et rouges*, wc, Paris Salon 1898; *Pensées*, Paris UFPS 1898. Musée de Semur, *Soleil*, wc, bought by the State in 1898, following exhbition in that year at the Semur Salon
LIT *Bénézit*; *Orsay*; Paris Arch. Nat. F21:2129; *Paris Salon* 1898; *Paris UFPS* 1898; *Thieme*

DELBARRE LE BESGUE, Marie-Louise
Exhib. *Fleurs de Nice*, *Lauriers roses et reines-marguerites*, *Dernières fleurs*, *Chrysanthèmes*, gouache on satin, Paris UFPS 1896; *Fleurs des champs*, *Coquelicots*, Dijon Salon 1897; *Roses trémières*, *Phlox*, gouache, Paris UFPS 1898
LIT *Dijon Salon* 1897; *Paris UFPS*, 1896, 1898

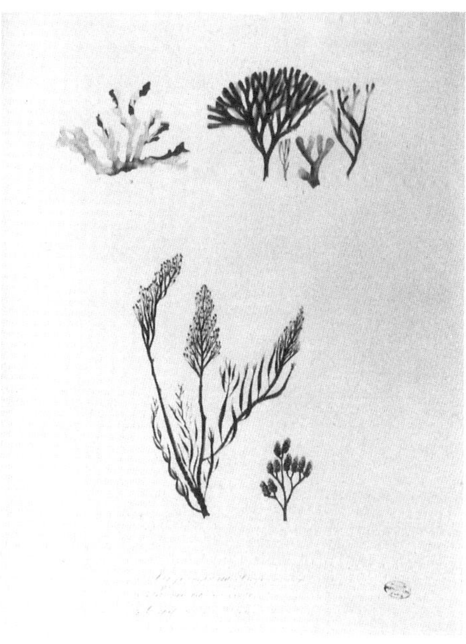

Eulalie Delile or Delille

Engraving after a drawing
Paris, Muséum National d'Histoire Naturelle

DELECROIX, Gustave *b.1857*
b. Tourcoing (Nord). Pupil of Chérier. Painted still-lifes and, occasionally, flowers
LIT *Bénézit*; *Thieme*

DELESSERT, *see* NADEILLAC

DELESSERT, Benjamin *1773–1847*
b. Lyon. The well-known botanist, businessman, philanthropist and politician was an amateur botanical draughtsman
LIT *Nissen* I, 461; Prévost, Roman d'Amat. *Dictionnaire de biographie française*, Paris (Letouzay) 1959; Taylor Baron, *Annuaire de l'Association des Artistes peintres*, Paris, 1845–1852

DELEURY, Laure
b. Luyens (Indre-et-Loire). Pupil of Lesourd de Beauregard. Exhib. Paris Salon from 1876 e.g. *Roses noisettes*, wc, 1876, *Roses et lilas blancs*, 1880
LIT *Bellier*; *Bénézit*

DELFOSSE, Louis-Marie-Lucien *b.1863*
b. Bayonne (Pyrénées-Atlantiques). Pupil of Cormon and Rops. Painted flowers and landscapes
LIT *Bénézit*; *Béraldi*; *Thieme*

DELIERRE, Auguste *b.1829*
b. Paris. Pupil of Ciceri. Painted genre, game, fruit and flowers. Exhib. Paris Salon 1852–1882
LIT *Bénézit*; *Béraldi*; *Thieme*

DELILE or DELILLE, Eulalie
Pupil of P. Bessa. Contributed designs to B. Delessert, *Icones selectae Plantarum* ... Paris, 1820–1846; Saint-Hilaire, *Flore du Brésil*, Paris, 1825–1833; Dumont d'Urville, *Voyage ... de la Corvette* l'Astrolabe ... 1826–1829 Paris 1832–1834; V. Jacquemont, *Voyage dans l'Inde ... 1828–1832* Paris 1841–1844; C. Belanger, *Voyage aux Indes*

orientales (Art Bertrand) 1846; Bory de Saint-Vincent, *Nouvelle Flore du Péloponnèse* Paris, Strasbourg (Levrault) 1838
LIT *Bellier*; *Hardouin-Fugier* 1981; *Nissen* I, 126, 213, 555, 966, 1715

DELINIÈRES, Rémy
Exhib. *Fleurs*, wc, Paris Salon 1850
LIT *Paris Salon* 1850

DELOBBE, François-Alfred *1835–1920*
b. Paris. Pupil of Bouguereau at ENSBA 1853. Painted mythological subjects, genre, and, occasionally, flowers. Salon debut 1861
LIT *Bénézit*. PM

DELON, Jacques-Fréderic *1778–1838*
b. Montpellier (Hérault). Painted landscapes and, occasionally, flowers. Exhib. Paris Salon 1835–1838
LIT *Bellier*; *Bénézit*; *Thieme*

DELONGÉ
Exhib. *Roses*, Saint-Etienne Salon 1891
LIT *Hardouin-Fugier Bringuier*, *Saint-Etienne Salon* 1891

DELORME
Textile designer, Saint-Etienne *c.*1832
LIT *Hardouin-Fugier Grafe*

DELORME, C.
Designed plates for A. Jordan, *Icones ad Floram Europae* ... Paris 1866–1903
LIT *Nissen* I, 1008

DELORME, Lucie
b. Paris. Worked in Geneva. Exhib. Flowers in wc, Paris Salon 1877–1880. Her *Panier de roses* is in the Musée d'Alès
LIT *Bénézit*; *Thieme*

DELORME, Marguerite *b.1876*
b. Lunéville (Meurthe-et-Moselle). Pupil of L.O. Merson, R. Collin, Paul Leroy. Painted landscapes and genre. Exhib. *Quelques fleurs*, Paris UFPS 1896
LIT *Bénézit*; O. Merson in *Le Monde Illustré*, 22 Feb. 1896, p. 143; *Paris UFPS* 1896; *Thieme*

DELORME, René
Pupil of C. Sibuet. Exhib. Lyon Salon 1870–1879 e.g. *Azalées*, 1877, *Giroflées dans un vase*, 1878, *Primevères*, 1879
LIT *Bénézit*; *Hardouin-Fugier Grafe*; *Lyon Salon* 1877, 1879; *Thieme*

DELOY, Georges *1856–after 1930*
b. Paris. Pupil of Collin. Painted landscapes. Exhib. *Lilas*, Dijon Salon, 1890
LIT *Bénézit*; *Dijon Salon* 1890; *Thieme*

DELPUY, L.
b. Paris. Exhib. *Fleurs*, Paris Indép. 1887
LIT *Paris Indép*. 1887; *Thieme*

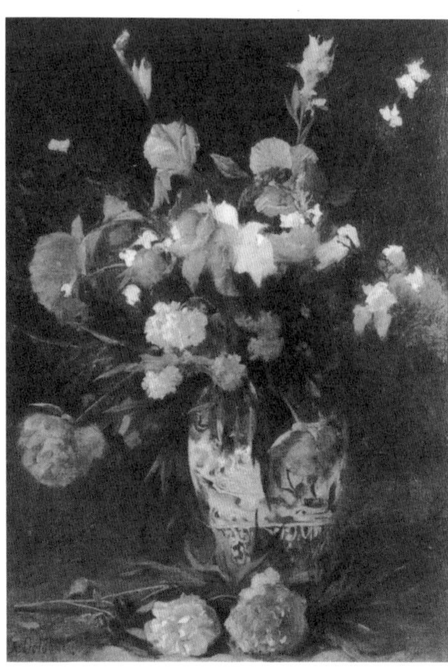

François-Alfred Delobbe

Oil on canvas, $36\frac{1}{4} \times 23\frac{1}{2}$ in. (92 × 60 cm.), signed
Private collection

DELPY, Hippolyte-Camille *1842–1910*
b. Joigny (Yonne). Pupil of Corot and Daubigny. Painted landscapes and, occasionally, flowers
LIT *Bénézit*; *Orsay*; *Schurr* I, 45; *Thieme*; *Witt*

Lucie Delorme

Watercolour, signed
Alès, Musée Municipal

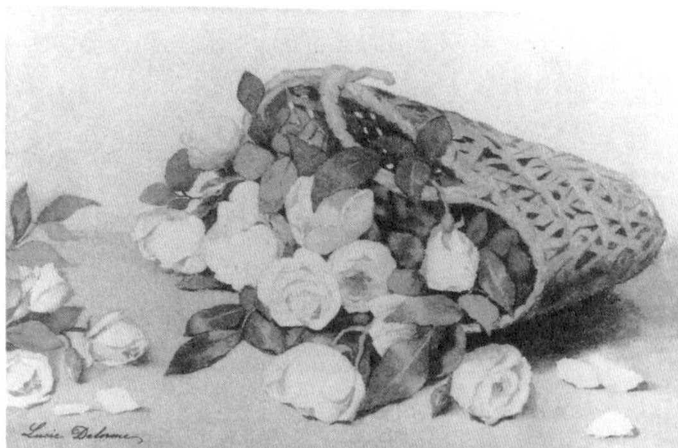

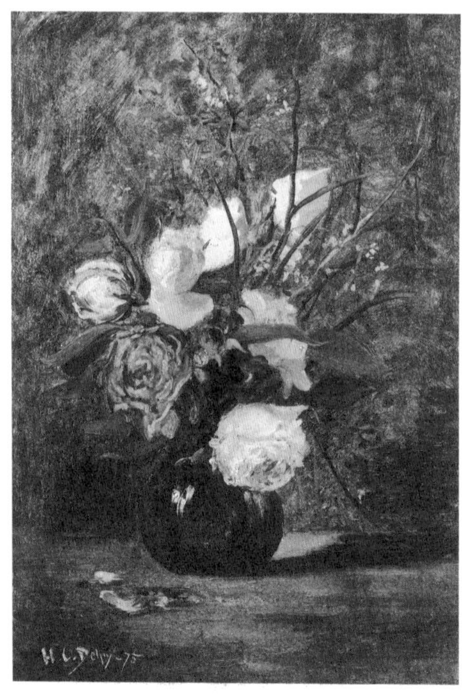

Hippolyte-Camille Delpy

Oil on panel, $20\frac{1}{2} \times 12\frac{3}{8}$ in. (52 × 31 cm.), signed and dated 1875
Private collection, The Netherlands
Courtesy Noortman, London

DELSESCAUX, Charles
b. Mâcon (Saône-et-Loire). Exhib. Paris Salon *Roses*, 1876, *Fleurs d'été*, 1886
LIT *Bellier*; *Bénézit*; *Hardouin-Fugier Grafe*; *Paris Salon* 1886

DEMARÇAY, Camille
b. Paris. Pupil of E. Hautïer. Painted portraits and flowers. Exhib. Paris Salon from 1869 e.g. *Fleurs d'automne*, 1869
LIT *Bénézit*; *Bellier*; *Thieme*

DEMIANNAY, Eugénie, *née* Lachassaigne
Exhib. *Vase de fleurs* after E. Bruyère, on porcelain, Paris Salon 1843
LIT *Paris Salon* 1843

DEMONT-BRETON, Virginie *1859–1935*
b. Courrières (Pas-de-Calais). Pupil of Jules Breton, her father. Painted genre and flowers. Exhib. Paris Salon *Fleur d'avril*, 1880, *Pissenlit*, 1881
LIT *Bellier*; *Bénézit*; *Paris Salon* 1880; *Thieme*

DEMONY, Berthe
Exhib. *Bourriche de giroflées et de pensées*, *Pétunias*, gouache, Dijon Salon 1894
LIT *Dijon Salon* 1894. CL

DEMONY, Julie
Exhib. *Trèfles et marguerites*, gouache, *Géraniums*, gouache, Dijon Salon 1894
LIT *Dijon Salon* 1894. CL

DEMURAT, Antoine-Albert
b. Paris. Pupil of Numa. Exhib. Paris Salon from 1880 e.g. *Fleurs d'automne*, 1880
LIT *Bénézit*; *Paris Salon* 1880

DENIS, Claude *b.1878*
Pupil of Castex-Dégrange, Lyon BA (CFD 1895), L.O. Merson and Gervex. Painted landscapes and, occasionally, flowers
LIT *Hardouin-Fugier Grafe*; *Thieme*; *Witt*

DENIS, Georges
Exhib. *Fleurs*, wc, Dijon Salon 1894
LIT *Dijon Salon* 1894. CL

DENIS, Maurice *1870–1943*
b. Granville (Manche). Pupil of Académie Julian where he befriended Bonnard, Ranson, Sérusier, Vuillard and others. Exhib. Among this prominent symbolist painter's early flowers are *Vase d'iris*, wc, *c.*1884 (Prieuré 4); *Bouquet de lilas*, wc, 1888 (Prieuré 32); *Pivoines*, wc, 1888 (Prieuré 34)
LIT Saint-Germain-en-Laye, *Symbolistes et Nabis, Maurice Denis et son temps*, Musée du Prieuré, n.d.

DENIS, Michel-Pierre-Marie *b.1826*
Pupil of Lyon BA. Exhib. Lyon Salon 1855–61 e.g. *Roses, gloire de Dijon et cerises*, *Vase de fleurs de printemps*, *Le bouquet de fête*, *Primevères en plein champ*, 1861
LIT *Hardouin-Fugier Grafe*; *Lyon Salon* 1861

DENISE, Alexandre
b. La Haye-Descartes (Indre-et-Loire). Pupil of Abel de Pujol. Exhib. Paris Salon from 1879 e.g. *Roses*, 1880
LIT *Bénézit*; *Paris Salon* 1880

DENISE, Marie
b. Paris. Pupil of Dumoulin. Exhib. *Giroflées*, gouache, Paris Salon 1880
LIT *Paris Salon* 1880

DENISSE, Etienne
Draughtsman and lithographer. Designed plates for *Flore d'Amérique*, Paris, Gihaut, 1843–1846
LIT *Nissen* I, 470

DENISSE, Jean-Julien *b.1866*
b. Bordeaux (Gironde). Exhib. portraits, landscapes, still-lifes and flowers, Paris SNBA
LIT *Bénézit*; *Thieme*

DENOIS, Lucile
Worked at Sèvres 1820–1822, 1826–1827. Exhib. Paris Salon 1831–1838 e.g. *Oreilles d'ours*, on alabaster, 1833, *Le printemps*, 1837, *Camélias*, oils on alabaster, 1838
LIT *Bellier*; *Bénézit*; *Brunet Préaud*; *Faré* 1962, p. 218; *Paris Salon* 1833, 1837, 1838

DENOUVION
Exhib. flowers in wc, Lyon Salon 1833
LIT *Hardouin-Fugier Grafe*

DENOYELLE, Paul-Léonard
b. Mony (Oise). Pupil of Bonnat. Painted still-lifes and flowers. Exhib. Paris Salon from 1873 e.g. *Chrysanthèmes*, 1880
LIT *Bellier*; *Bénézit*; *Paris Salon* 1880; *Thieme*

DEPALME, Pierre
b. 1812. Pupil of Thierriat, Lyon BA (CFD 1831–4)
LIT *Hardouin-Fugier Grafe*

DERICHSWEILER, Jean-Charles-Gérard *b.1822*
Worked at Sèvres. Exhib. *Fleurs dans un vase de verre*, on porcelain, Paris Salon 1845
LIT *Bellier*; *Bénézit*; *Brunet Préaud*; *Paris Salon* 1845; *Thieme*

DEROCHE, Marie
Exhib. Strasbourg Salon *Chrysanthèmes à la fontaine*, 1883 (300 francs), *Roses*, 1883 (200 francs), *Roses de Nice*, 1884 (400 francs)
LIT *Strasbourg Salon* 1883, 1884

DEROVE, *see* BERBIER

DESAMIAUX, Joséphine-Esther
b. Paris. Pupil of Bricka. Exhib. flowers on porcelain, Paris Salon 1880
LIT *Paris Salon* 1880

DESAVARY, Charles-Paul-Etienne *1837–1885*
b. Arras (Pas-de-Calais). Pupil of Dutilleux, his father-in-law and T. Couture. Worked with Corot. Drawing master (Arras) and illustrator (*Le Monde Illustré*). Exhib. Amiens Salon, 1868, Lyon Salon, 1872, Arras Salon, 1879, Moulins Salon, 1879, Boulogne-sur-mer Salon, 1881. Musée d'Arras, *Bouquets de fleurs*, 1871, *Fleurs de la mariée*, 1878
LIT *Bénézit*; P. Dutilleux, *Nos artistes peintres*, Lille, 1911; Saint-Tropez, *Fleurs de Fantin-Latour à Marquet*, Musée de l'Annonciade, 1982, no. 17 (ill.); *Witt*

DESBIROUS, Marguerite
b. Paris. Pupil of Riottor and Brollot. Exhib. Paris Salon *Fleurs*, on porcelain 1872, *Roses*, on porcelain, 1880
LIT *Paris Salon* 1872, 1880

DESBORDES-JONAS, Louise-Alexandra *b.c.1855*
b. Angers (Maine-et-Loire). Pupil of A. Stevens. Exhib. Paris Salon from 1876. Exhib. Paris SNBA *Plantes exotiques*, 1890, *Fleurs*, 1894. May be the same as Louise Desbordes who exhib. Paris SNBA *Avril*, 1891, *Fleurs et papillons*, 1892, *Fleurs au bord d'un étang*, 1893 and Dijon Salon 1894; Paris SNBA, *Etang fleuri*, 1895. One work in Musée de Gray (not a flower painting)
LIT *Bénézit*; *Dijon Salon* 1894; *Paris SNBA* 1890, 1891 (ill.), 1892 (ill.), 1893 (ill.), 1894 (ill.), 1895 (ill.); *Schurr* III, 70; *Thieme*

DESBRIAT or DESBRIAS
Pupil of Thierriat. Lyon, textile designer, 1845
LIT *Hardouin-Fugier Grafe*

DESCAMPS-SABOURET, Louise-Cécile *b.1855*
b. Paris. Pupil of Hautier and T. Robert-Fleury. Painted genre and flowers. Exhib. *Fleurs de mai*, Dijon Salon 1883; *Pensées, roses*, Paris Salon 1885; *Chrysanthèmes, Anémones*, Dijon Salon 1887; *Pivoines*, pastel, *Soleils, clématites* on porcelain. Paris Salon 1890. Dijon Salon, *Roses*, 1890, *Bibelots et roses de Nice*, 1892
LIT *Bénézit*; *Dijon Salon* 1883, 1887, 1890, 1892; *Paris Salon* 1885, 1890; *Schurr* IV, 82; *Witt*

DESCELLES, Paul *1851–1915*
b. Raon-l'Etape (Vosges). Pupil of Mirbecks. Painted genre and flowers. Exhib. *Pivoines*, Strasbourg Salon, 1891 (250 francs); *La bouquetière*, Dijon Salon 1892
LIT *Bénézit*; *Dijon Salon* 1892; *Strasbourg Salon* 1891; *Schurr* IV, 115; *Thieme*

DESCHAMPS, Joséphine-Pauline
Exhib. Paris Salon *Groupe de fleurs*, wc, 1835, *Vase de fleurs*, wc, 1836
LIT *Paris Salon* 1835, 1836

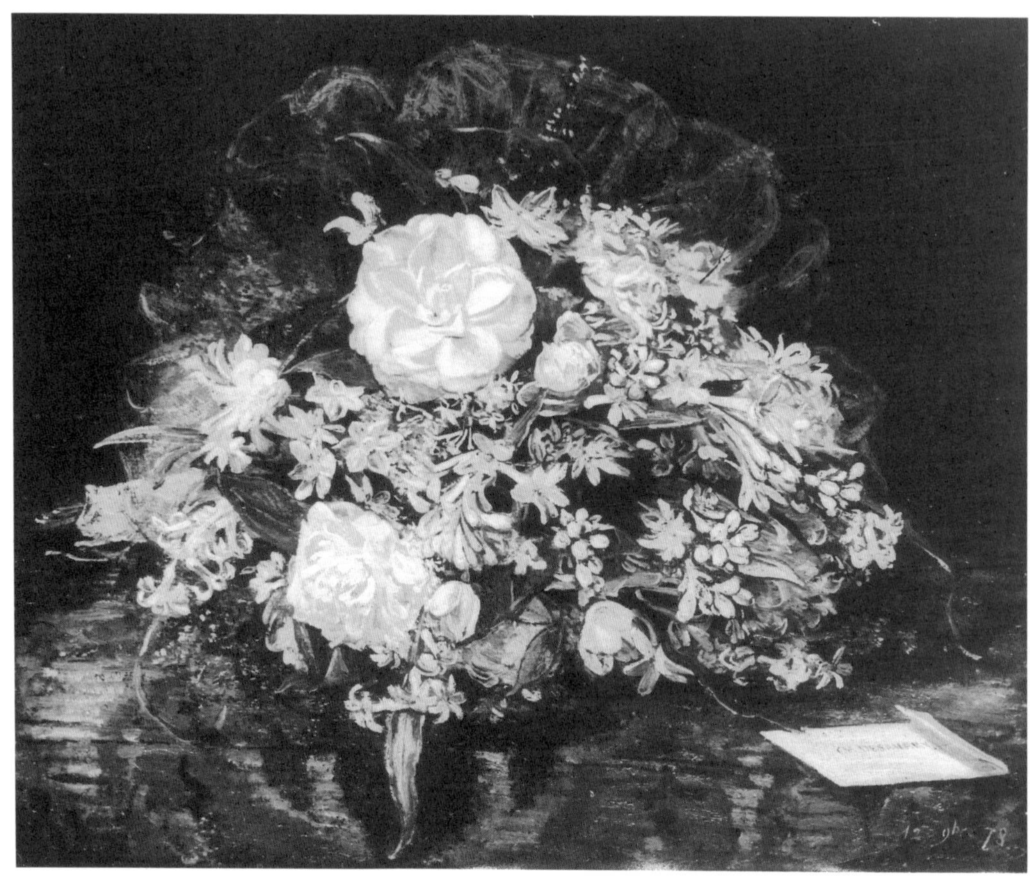

Charles-Paul-Etienne Desavary

Oil on canvas, 15½ × 18 in. (39 × 47 cm.), signed and dated '12 obre 78'
Arras, Musée des Beaux-Arts

DESCHAMPS, Marguerite
b. Paris. Pupil of Hautier. Exhib. *Primevères de Chine, Campanules, Pétunias*, Lyon Salon 1878
LIT *Lyon Salon* 1878

DESCHIENS-ASTRUC, Pauline-Hélène
b.1861
b. Angers (Maine-et-Loire). Pupil of P. Bourgogne and Thurner. Exhib. Paris Salon from 1889 and Paris UFPS *Fleurs*, 1896, *Lilas, Chrysanthèmes*, 1898
LIT *Bénézit*; *Paris UFPS* 1896, 1898; *Thieme*

DESCOURTILZ, Joseph-Théodore
Designed plates for M.E. Decourtilz e.g. *Flore pittoresque et médicale des Antilles*, Paris, 1821–1829; M: *Argémone du Mexique*, Paris BMAD (Maciet coll.)
LIT *Nissen* I, 471; *Paris BMAD*; *Sitwell*

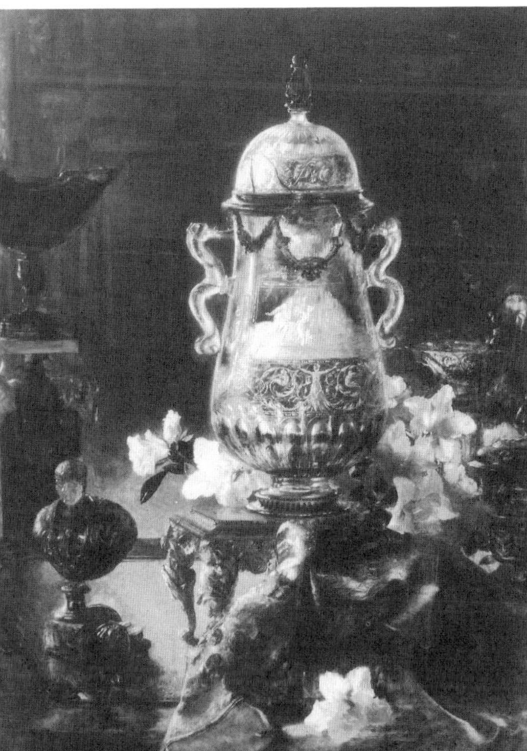

DESCOURTILZ, Michel-Etienne
1775–c.1835
Designed plates for his own *Flore pittoresque et médicale des Antilles*, Paris, 1821–1829
LIT *Nissen* I, 471; *Sitwell*

DESGOFFE, Aline-Jeanne
b. Vierzon (Cher). Pupil of Thoret. Exhib. *Nénuphars et libellules*, fan-leaf, Paris Salon 1880
LIT *Paris Salon* 1880

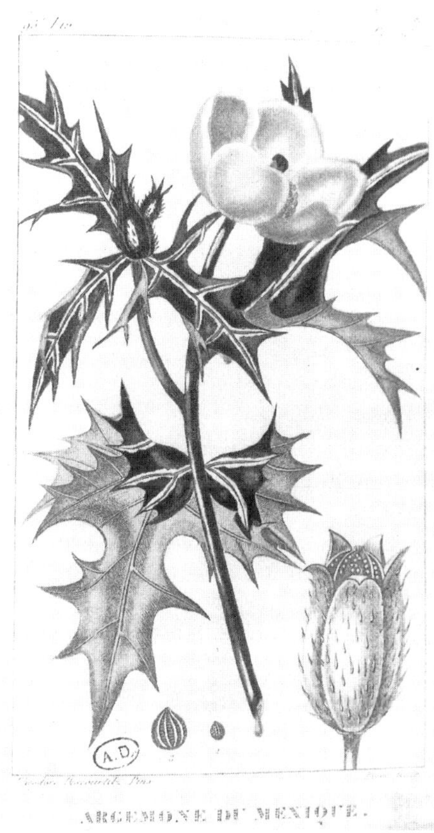

Joseph-Théodore Descourtilz

Engraving, 6½ × 4 in. (16.3 × 9.8 cm.), signed
Paris, BMAD (Maciet Collection)

Blaise Alexandre Desgoffe

Oil on board, 28 × 29¾ in. (71 × 52.5 cm.), signed and dated 1879
Courtesy Sotheby's, London

DESGOFFE, Blaise-Alexandre
1830–1901
b. Paris. Pupil of H. Flandrin. Painted still-lifes and flowers. Exhib. Paris Salon from 1866 often flowers with jewels e.g. *Orchidées, agate, ivoire, cristal de roche* etc., Paris Salon, 1898; *Still-Life with Flowers*, Sotheby's, London, 28 Nov. 1979, lot 58; *Still-Life with Flowers*, Christie's, New York, 27 Oct. 1982, lot 27; *Nature-Morte*, Schwarz, Philadelphia, 1988. A flower painting illustrated by Pavière III, pt. 1, as in Springfield, Mass., is untraceable. M: Chantilly, La Rochelle, Tours (not flowers)
LIT *Bellier*; *Bénézit*; A. Desgoffe, *B.-A. Desgoffe* ... Paris (Mersch) 1888; G. Lacambre "Desgoffe" in *Le Musée du Luxembourg en 1874*, Paris Grand Palais 1974, p. 54; *Paris Salon* 1898; *Schurr* I, 32; *Thieme*; *Witt*

DESGRANGE, Isabelle, *née* Toudouze
Pupil of Mme Toudouze. Exhib. *Roses trémières*, decorative panel, Paris Noir et Blanc Salon 1880. Designs after I. Desgrange dated 1881 are in Paris BMAD (Maciet coll.)
LIT *Paris BMAD*, 421, 470; *Paris Noir et Blanc Salon* 1888

DESGRANGES, *see* BERNARD

DESGRANGES, *see* SELMERSHEIM

DESHAYES, Charles-Félix-Edouard *1831–1895*
b. Paris or Toulon (Var). Pupil of Senequier and Français. Exhib. *Giroflées*, Lyon Salon 1883
LIT *Bénézit*; *Lyon Salon* 1883; *Schurr* III, 53

DESHAYES, Jean-Eléazar *d.1848*
Landscape painter and lithographer. Designed plates for E.A. Duchesne, *Répertoire des plantes utiles et des plantes vénéneuses*, Brussels, 1846
LIT *Bénézit*; *Nissen* I, 537; *Thieme*

DESHAYES, Madeleine
b. Paris. Exhib. Paris Indép. *Bruyère, bluets, pissenlits, Bouquet d'iris*, 1899, *Pavots*, 1900
LIT *Paris Indép.* 1899, 1900

DESLANDES, Elisabeth *d.1896*
Exhib. *Chrysanthèmes*, Paris UFPS 1896
LIT *Bénézit*; *Paris UFPS* 1896

DESLIENS, Cécile *1853–1937* and DESLIENS, Marie *1856–1938*
b. Chavenon (Allier). Pupils of A. Soulié. Painted most of their works (genre, portraits, flowers) together but occasionally, exhib. separately e.g. *Lilas*, Paris Indép. 1889; *Au printemps*, Paris SNBA, 1890 (Cécile). M: Tulle, Saint-Brieuc, Riom. Panels in Tulle town-hall
LIT *Bénézit*; A. Mazeyrie, *Cécile et Marie Desliens*, Tulle 1953; *Paris Indép.* 1889 (ill.); *Paris SNBA* 1890 (ill.); Saint-Tropez, *Fleurs de Fantin-Latour à Marquet*, Musée de l'Annonciade 1982, no. 18 (ill.); *Thieme*

DESMAISONS
Painter and engraver. Exhib. Paris Salon 1780–1834. Some of his bouquets "dessinés d'après nature" were published by Dautry
LIT *Bellier*; Paris Bibl. Nat. Est. Jd 59 b

DESOLME
Pupil of Berjon, Lyon BA (CFD 1810)
LIT *Hardouin-Fugier Grafe*

DÉSOMBRAGES, Joseph *1804–73*
b. Lyon. Pupil of Berjon, Lyon BA (CFD 1820)
LIT F. Desvernay, *Le Vieux-Lyon à l'exposition de 1914* Lyon (Rey) 1914; *Hardouin-Fugier Grafe*

DESORAS, *see* BERGER

DESORMEAUX, *see* PANCKOUCKE

DÉSOUCHES, Léonie, *née* Blondel
b. Paris. Exhib. Paris Salon 1870–1881 e.g. *Vase, écran et fleurs*, 1872, *Roses de Noël*, 1876
LIT *Bellier*; *Bénézit*; *Paris Salon* 1872

DESPORTES DE LA FOSSE, Emma-Andrée-Felicité, *née* Beuselin *1810–1869*
b. Paris. Pupil of Vinchon. Exhib. Paris Salon 1835–1868 e.g. *Pivoines*, wc, *Bouquet de fleurs*, wc, 1835, *Etude de fleurs d'après nature*, 1836, *Fleurs*, wc, 1837, *Vase de fleurs*, wc, 1838, 1840, 1841; *Fleurs*, Paris Exposition Universelle, 1855; *Fleurs et fruits*, 1861. Her *Fleurs et fruits* is in the Musée d'Amiens
LIT *Bellier*; *Bénézit*; Delécluze in *Le Journal des Débats*, 16 Apr. 1848; *Faré* 1962, p. 248; *Paris Exposition Universelle* 1855; *Paris Salon* 1835–1838, 1840, 1841, 1861; *Schurr* I, 30; *Thieme*

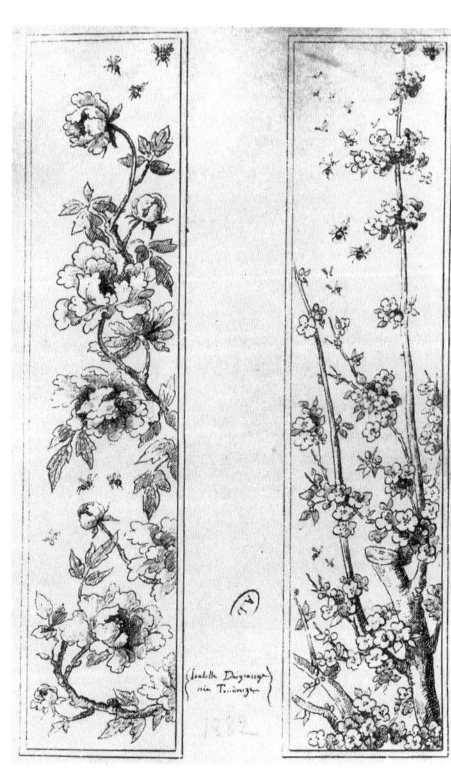

Isabelle Desgrange née Toudouze

Engraving, 6¼ × 38½ in., (16 × 98 cm.), signed
Paris, BMAD Maciet Collection

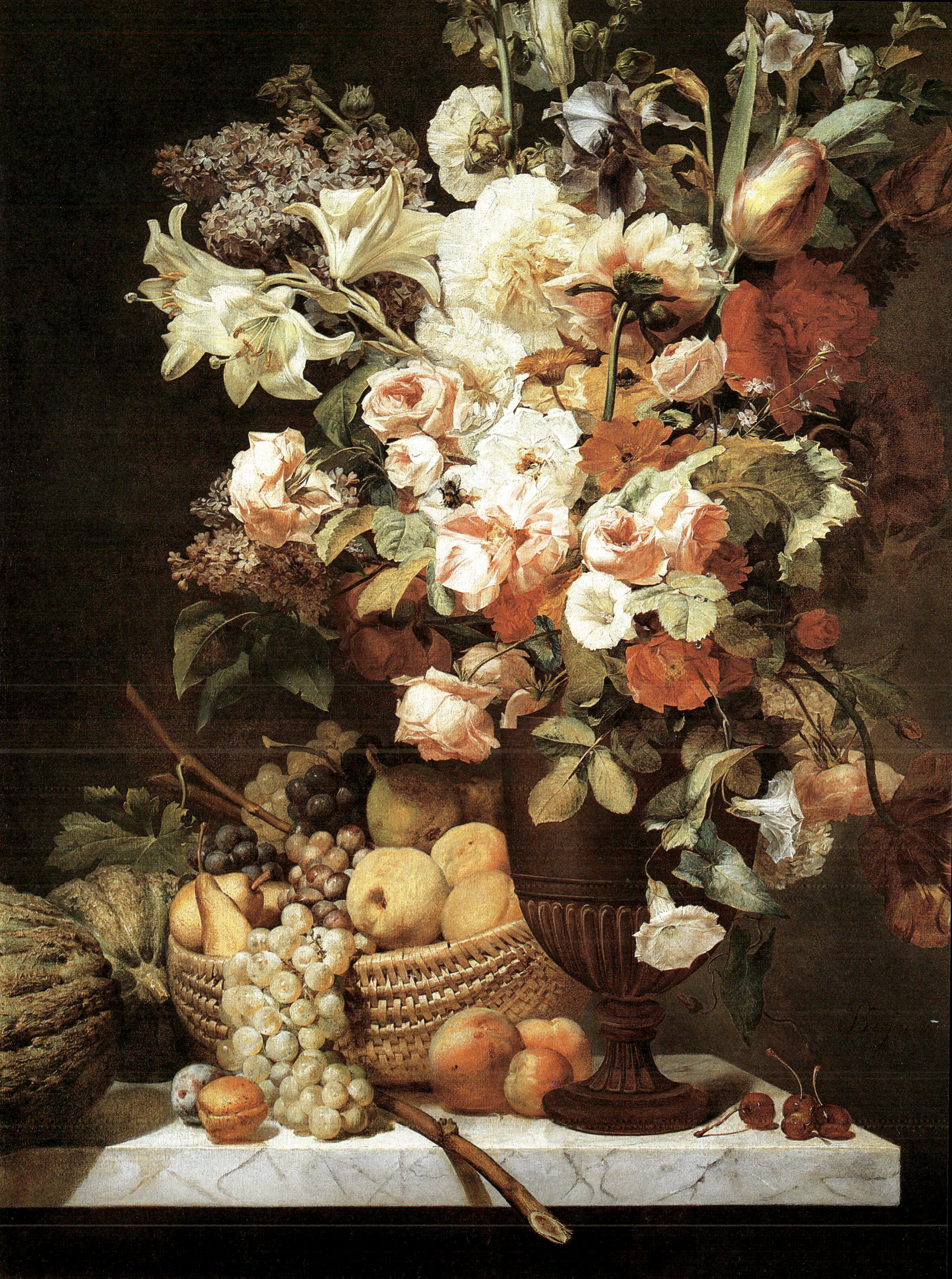

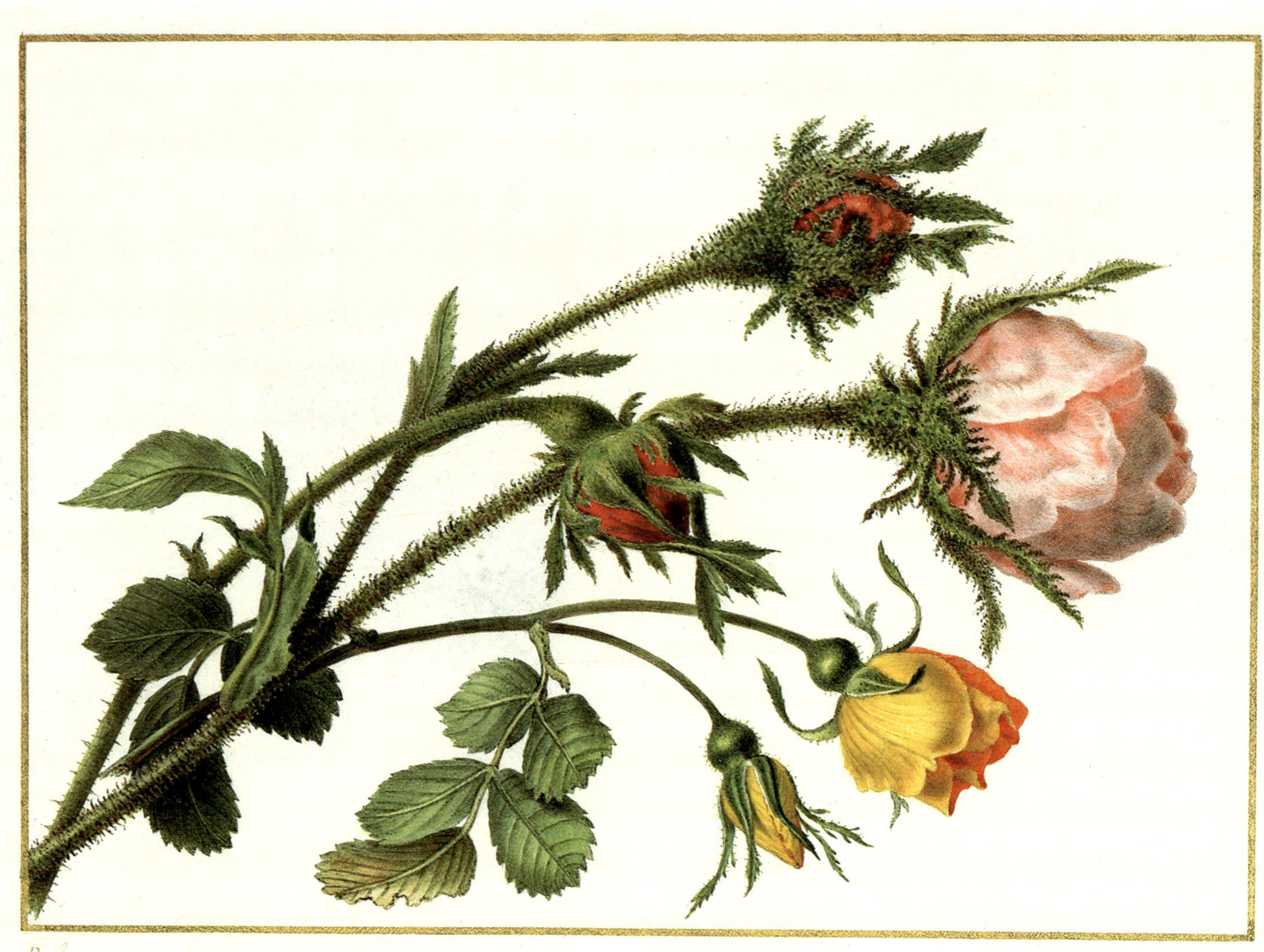
P. Bessa.

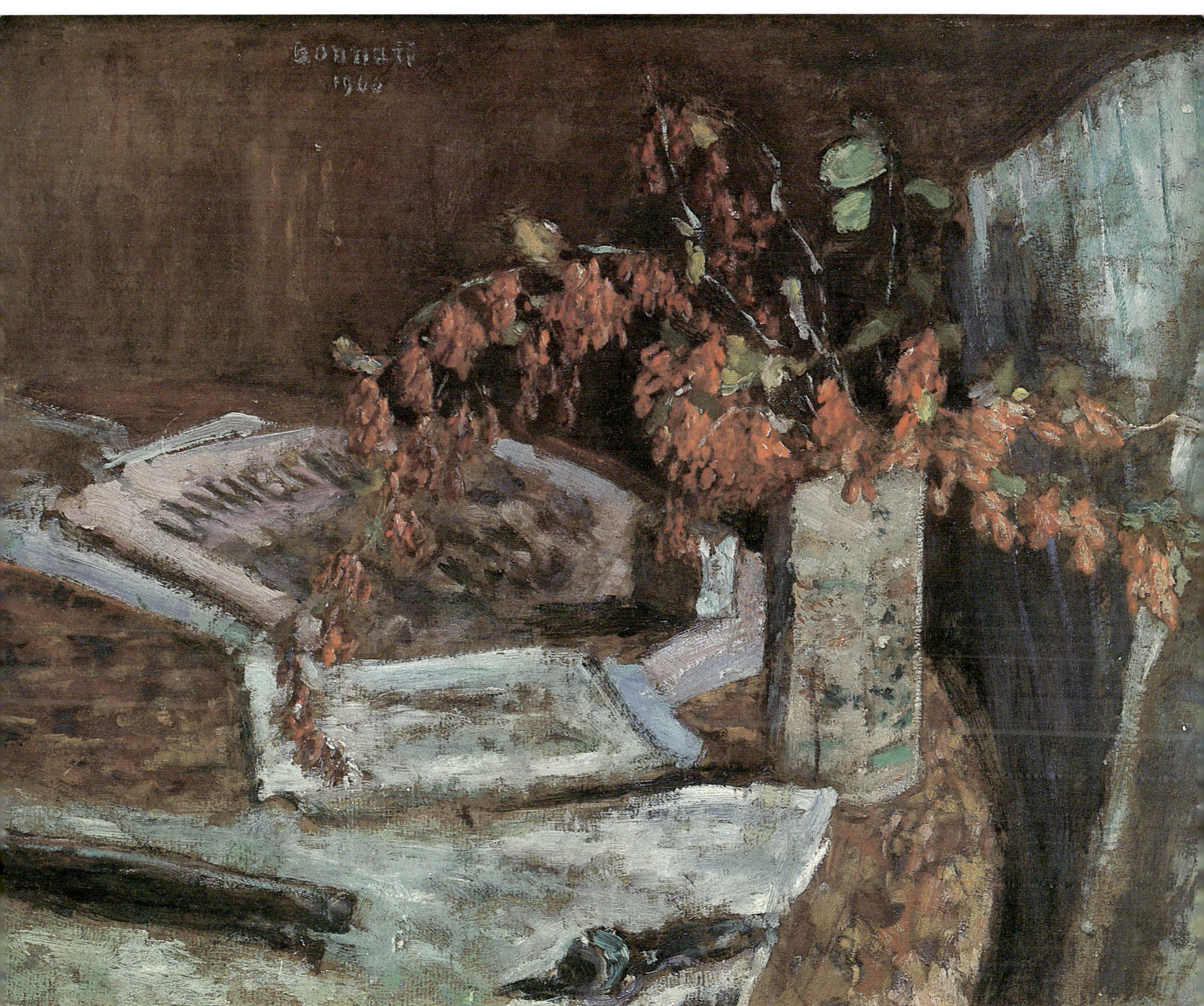

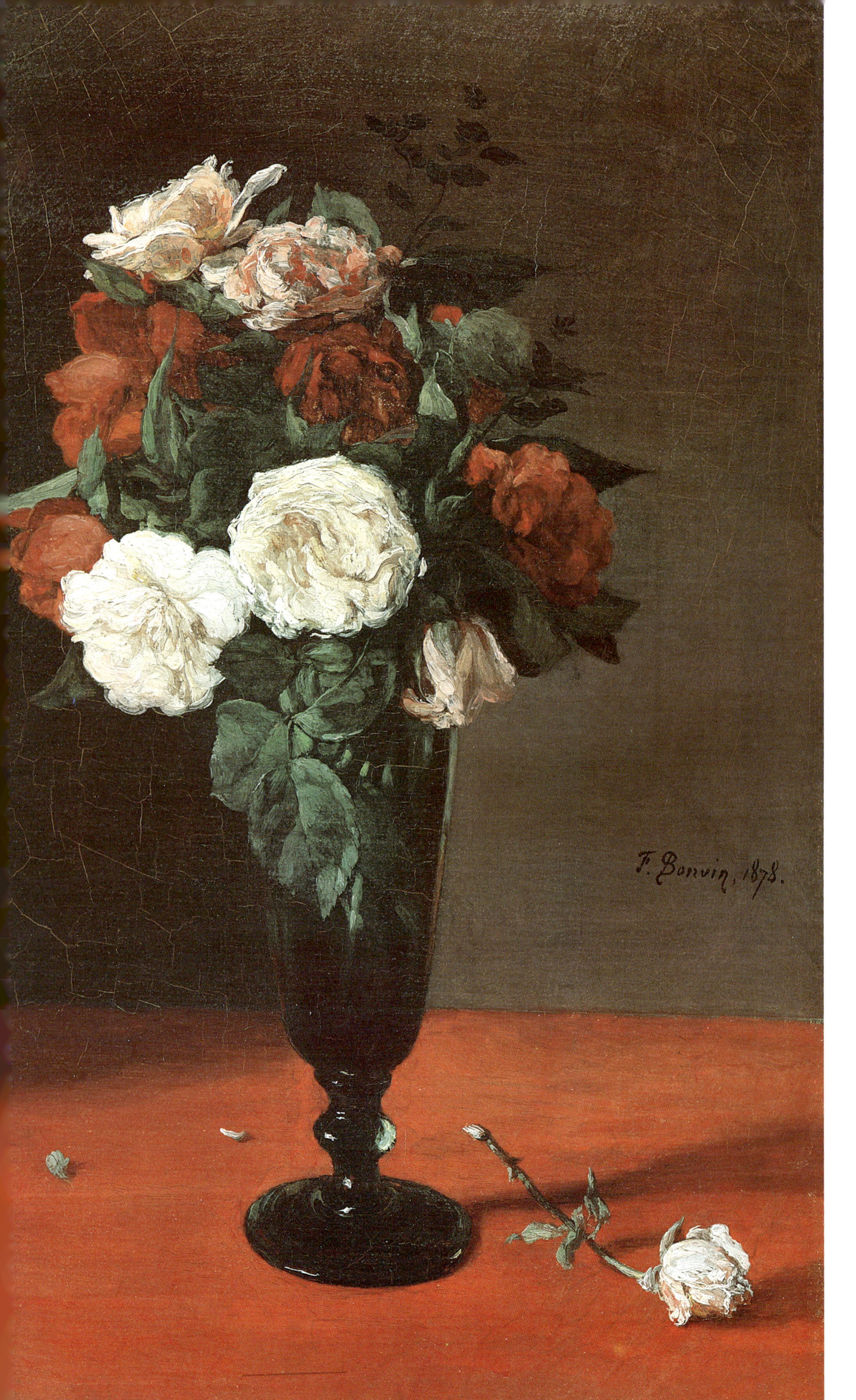
F. Bonvin, 1878.

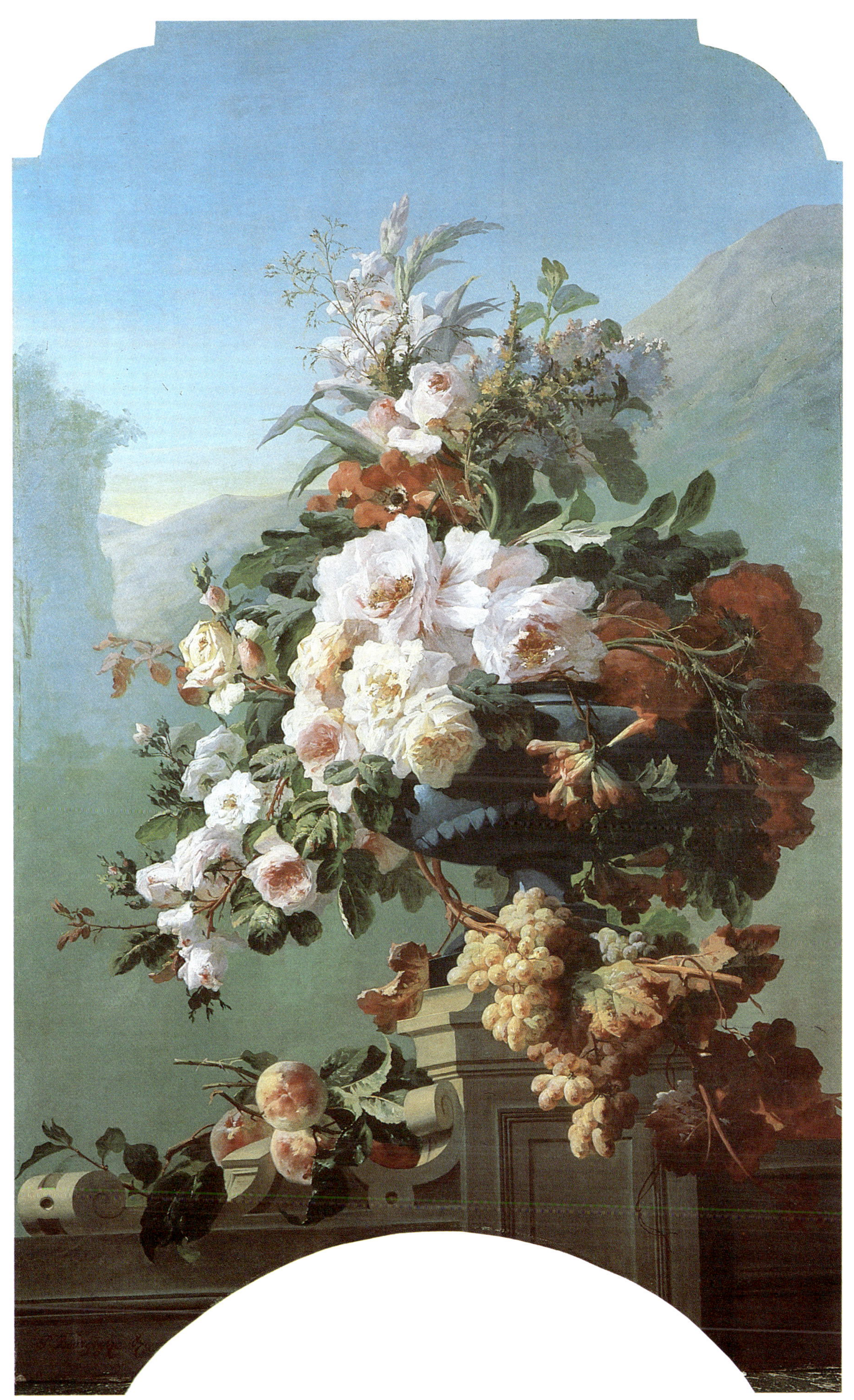

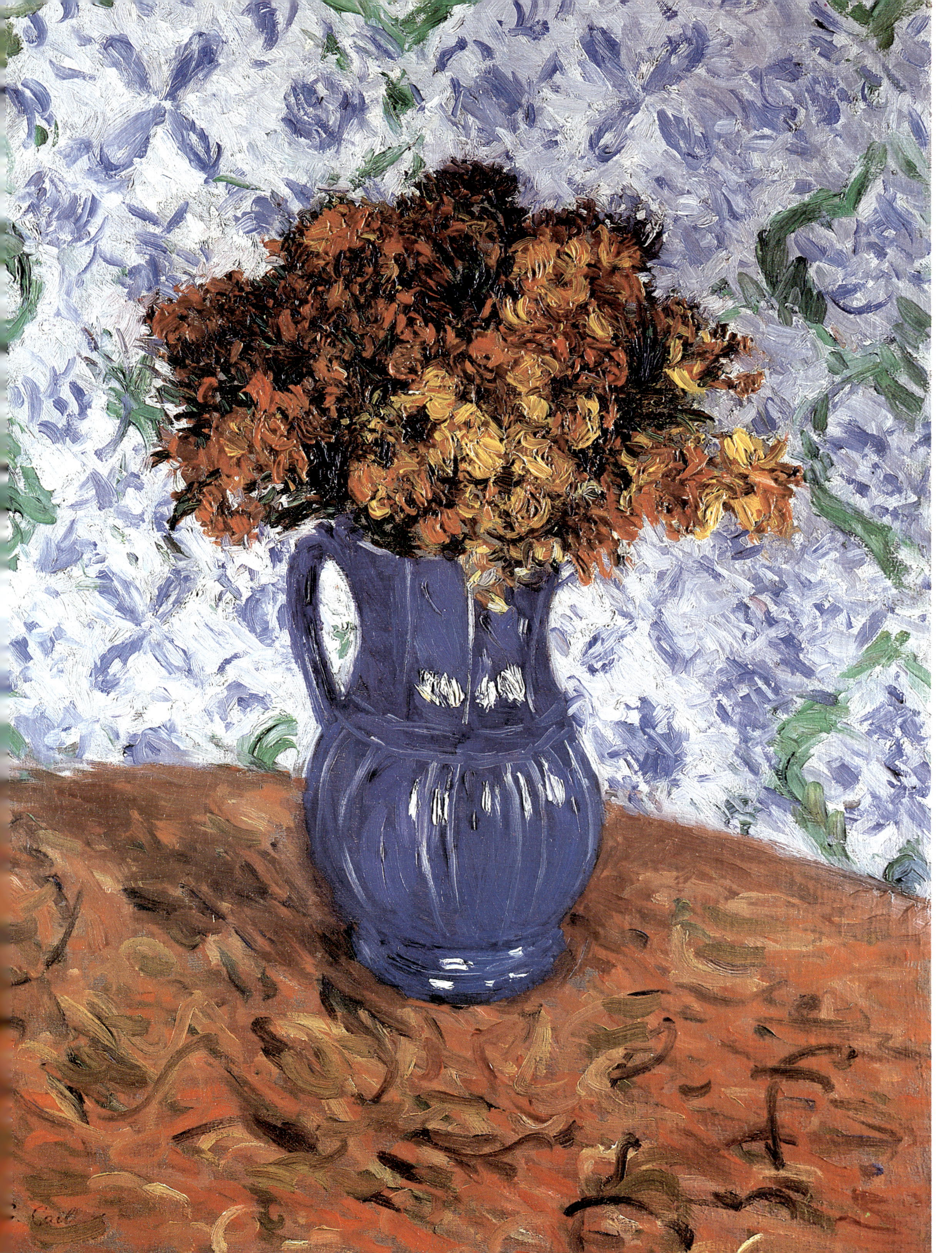

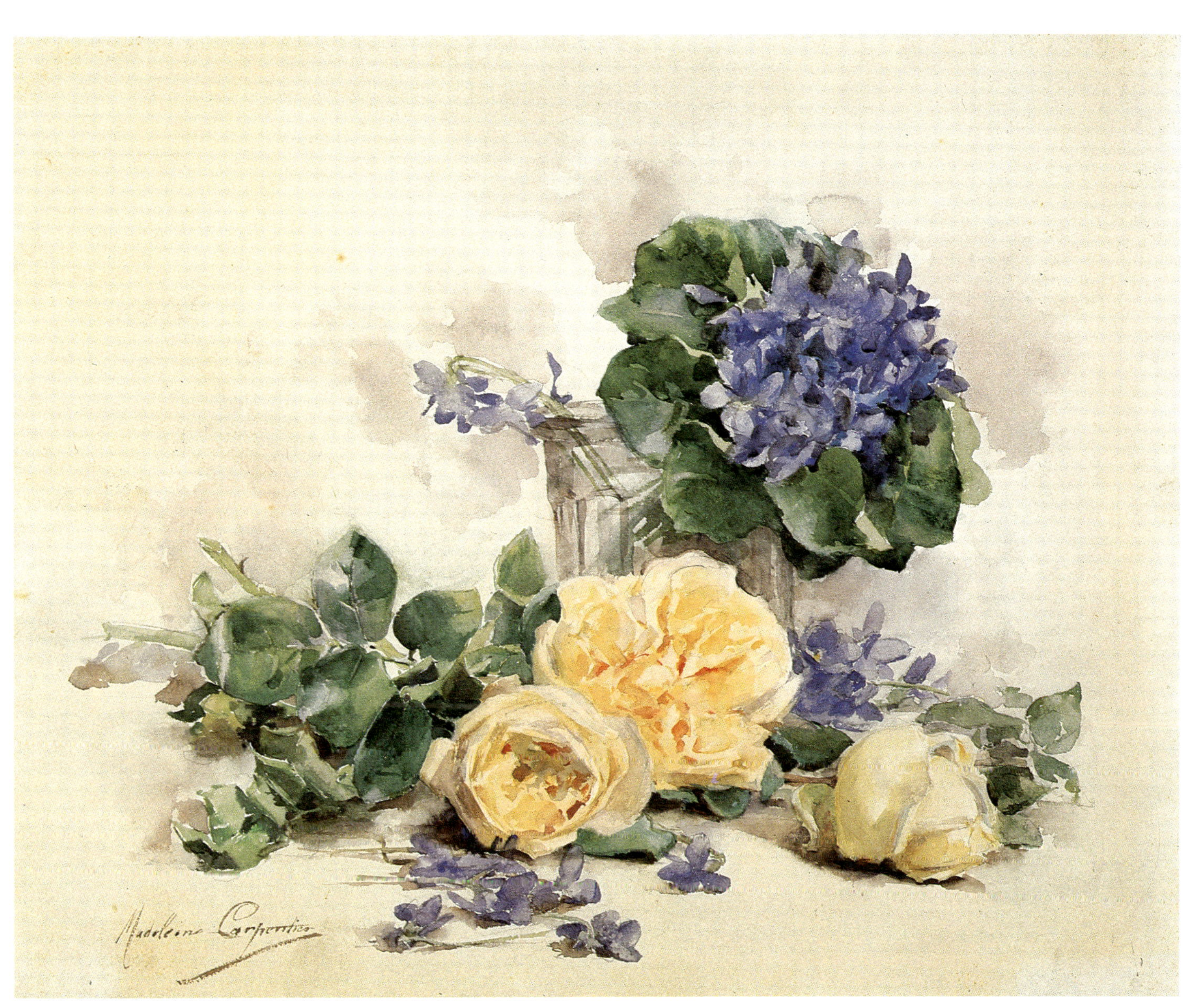
Madeleine Carpentier

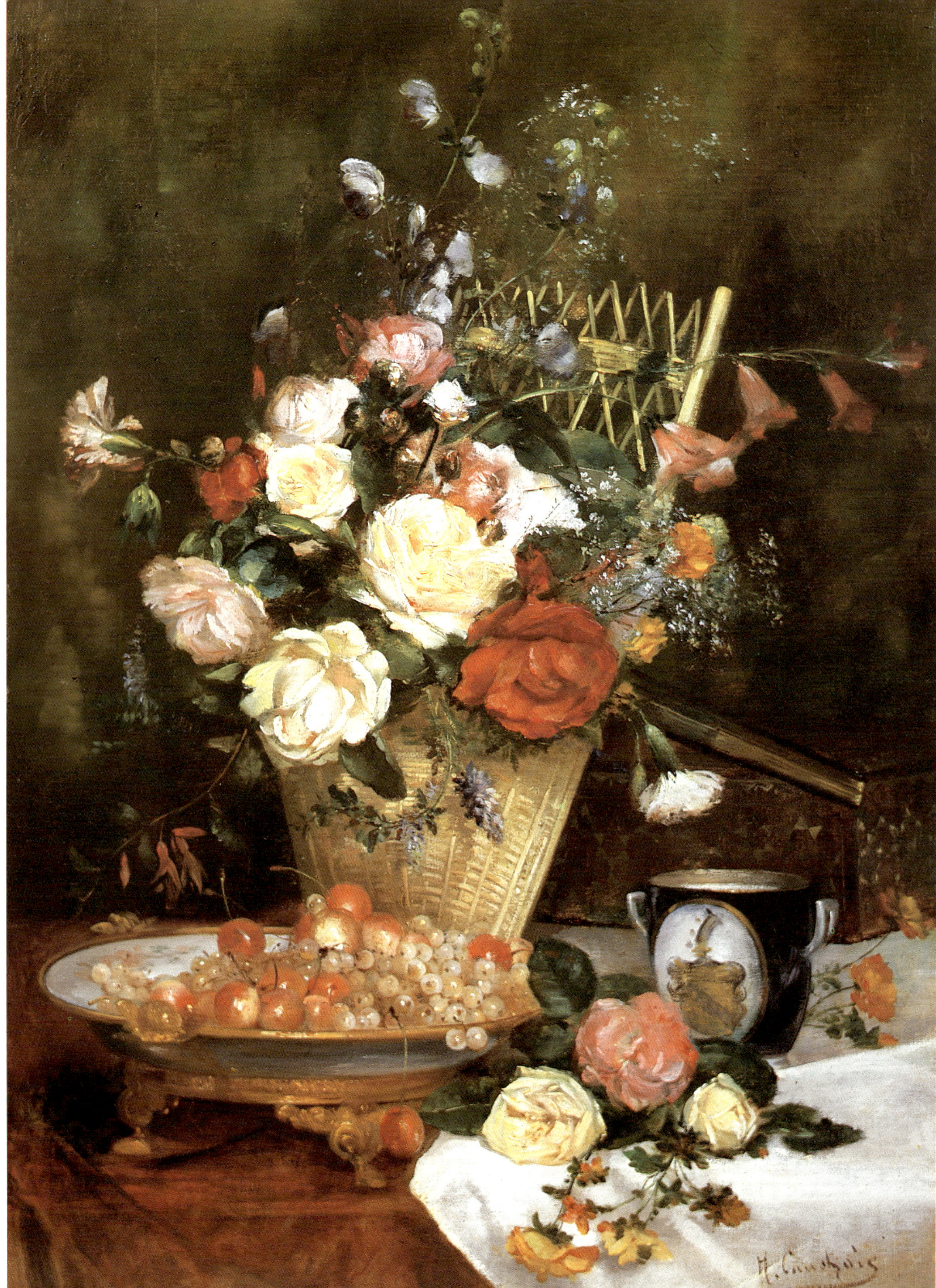

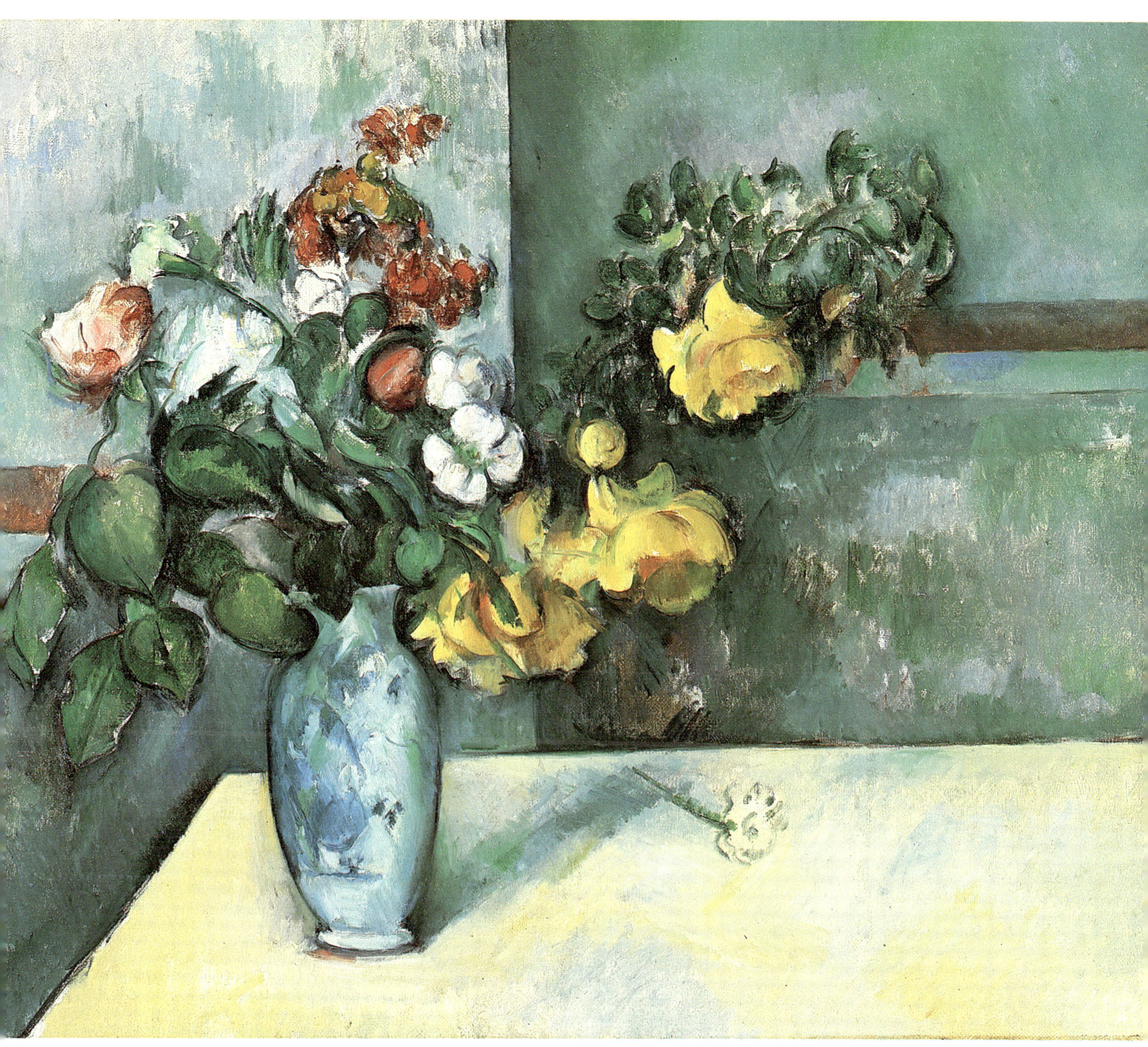

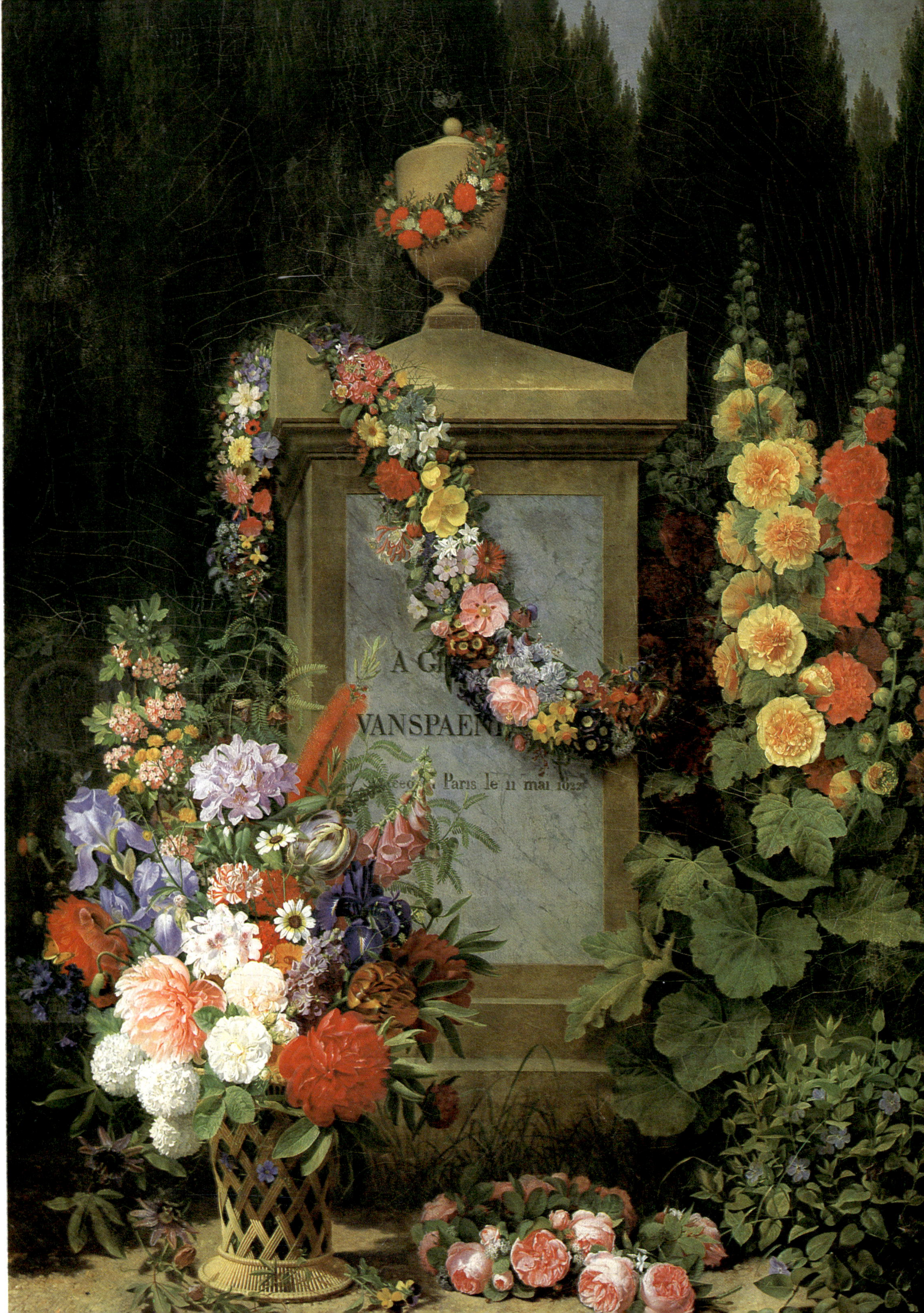
VANSPAEN
Paris le 11 mai

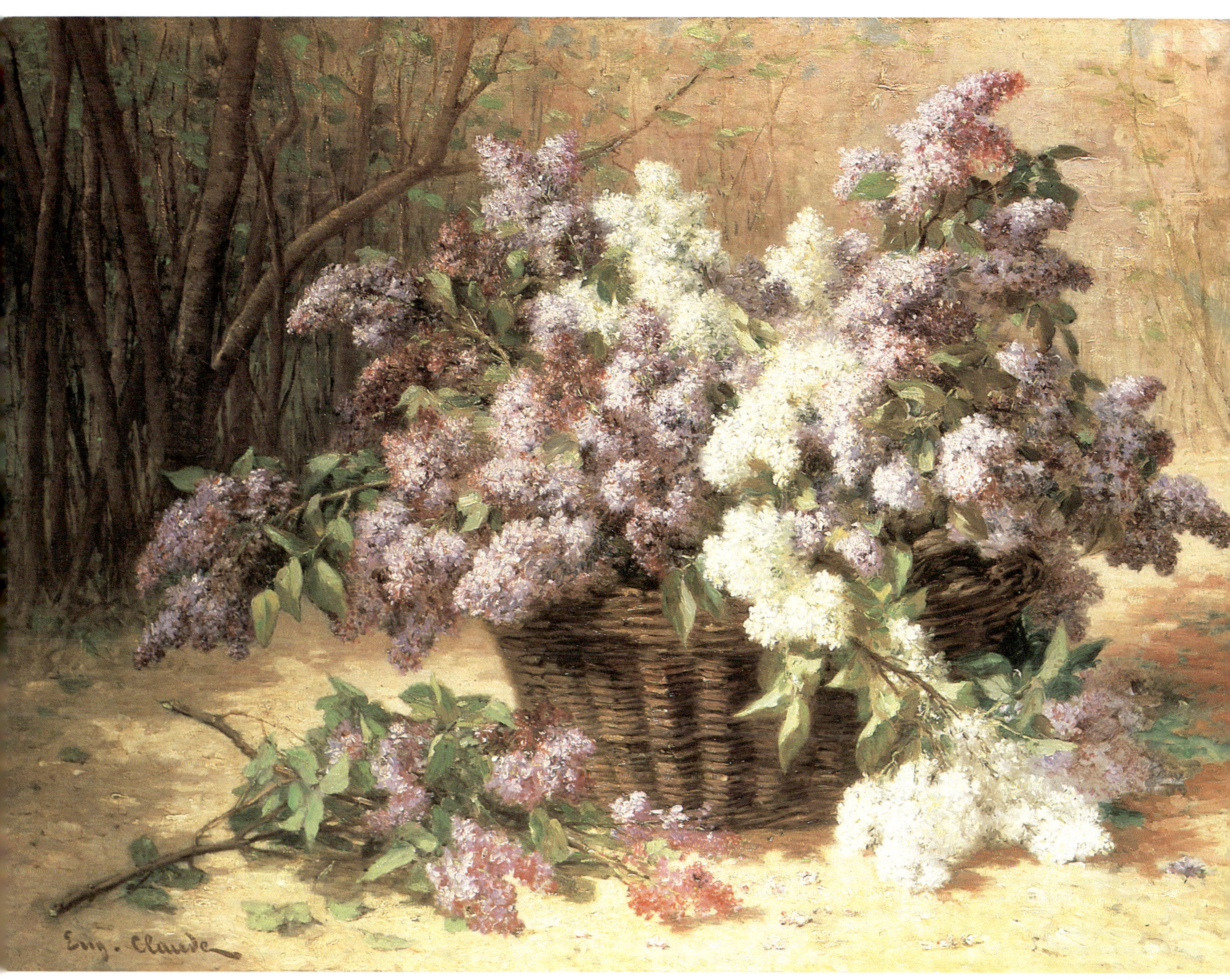
Eug. Claude

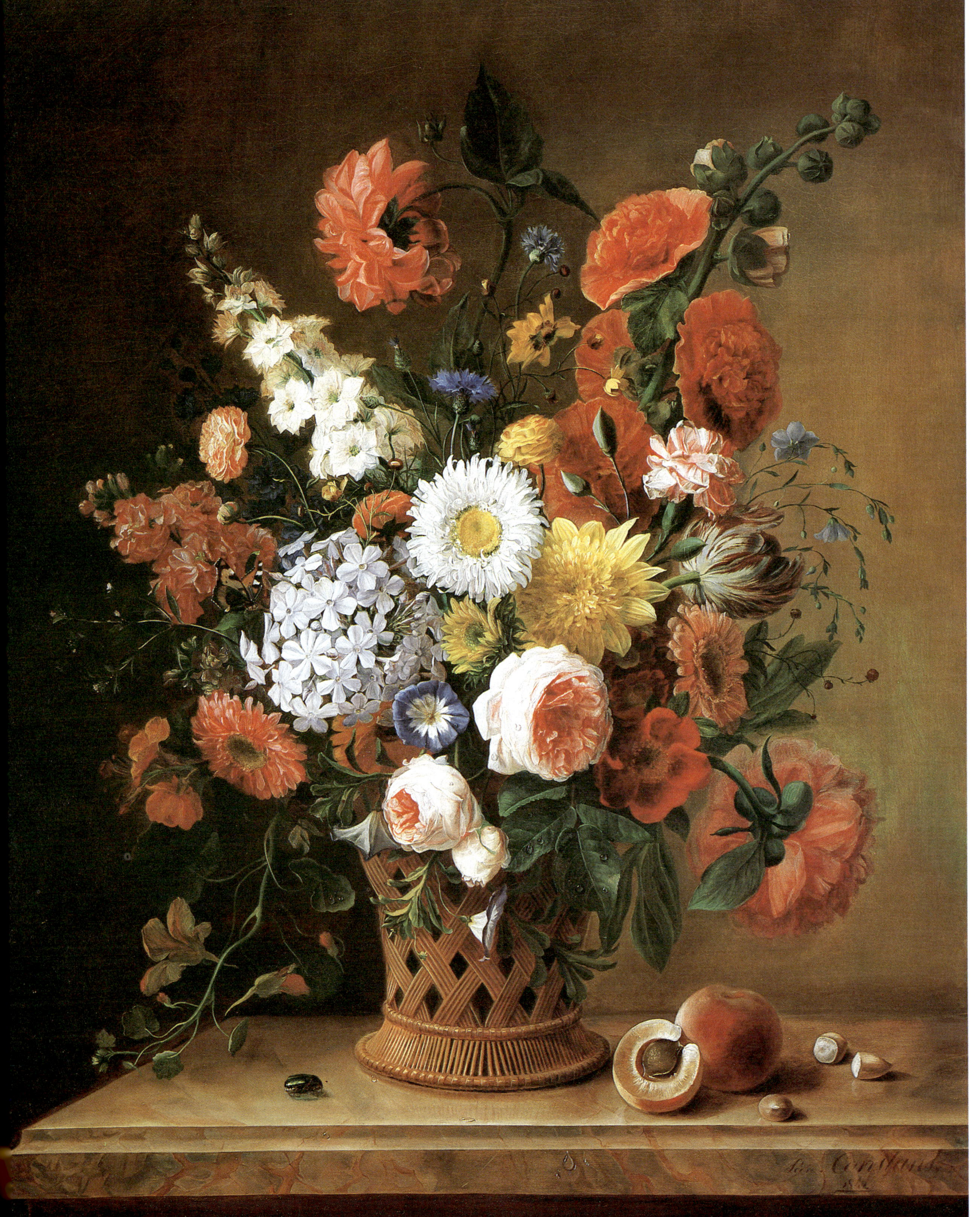

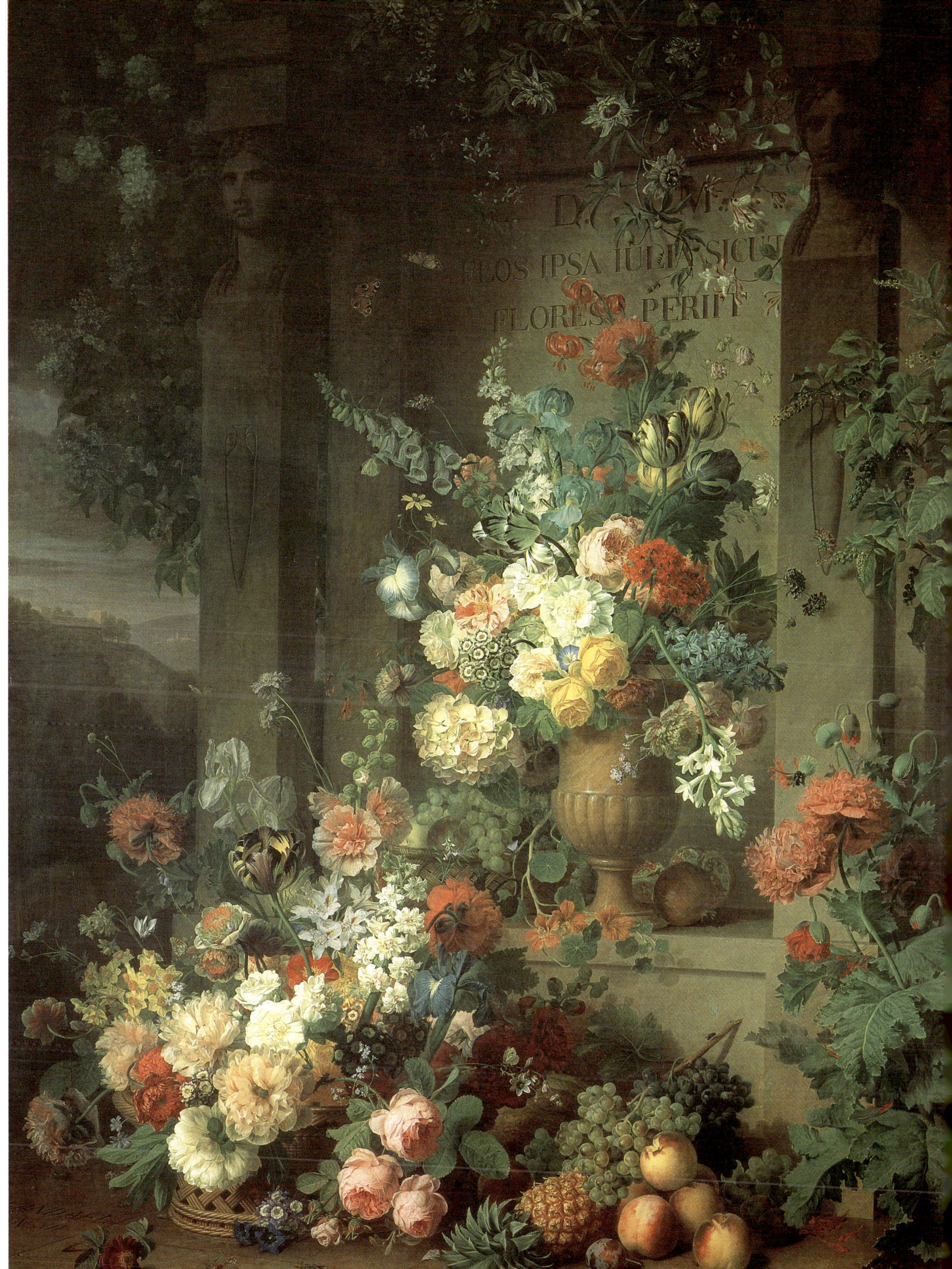
FLOS IPSA IULIA SICUT
FLORES PERIIT

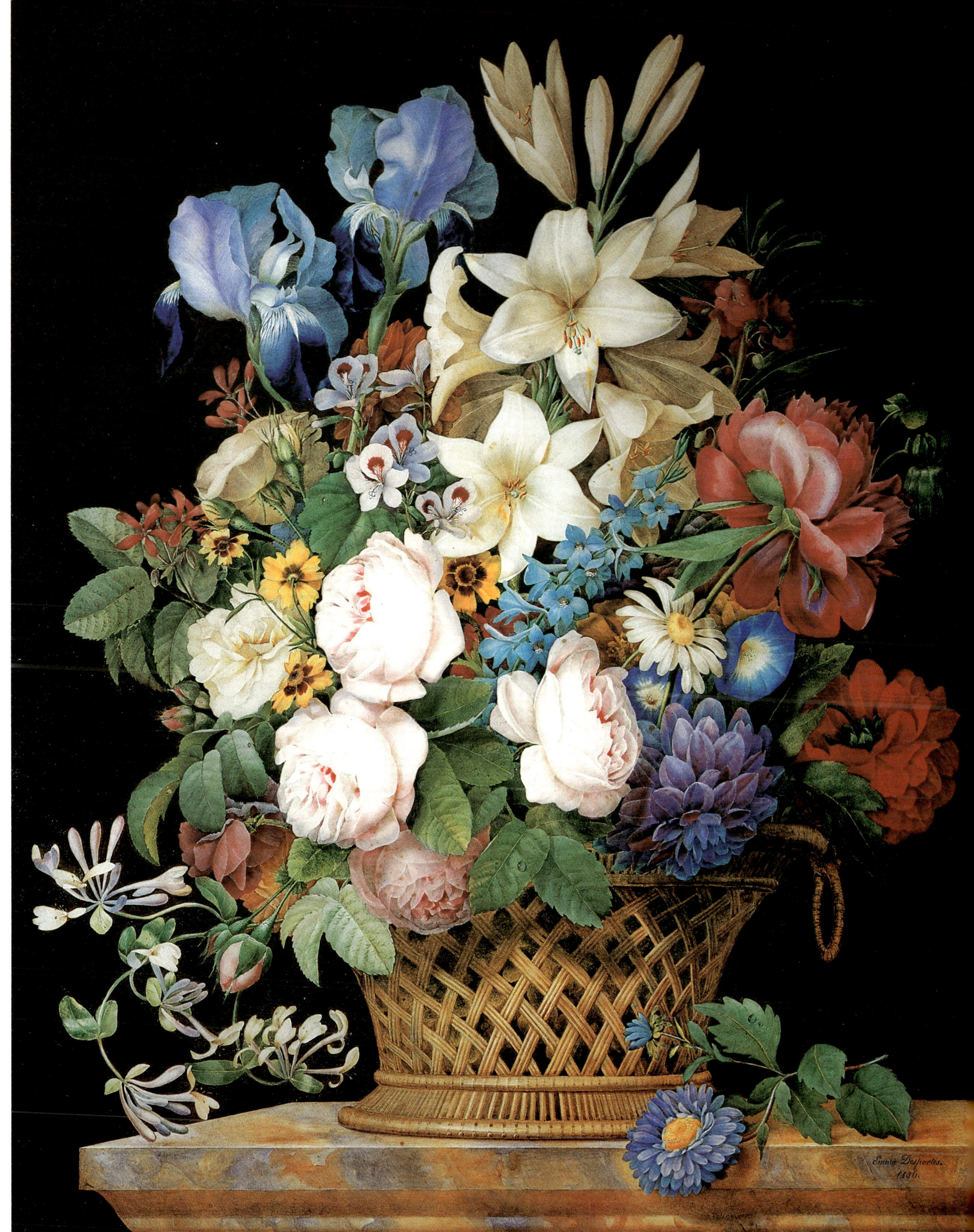
Emma Desportes.
1836.

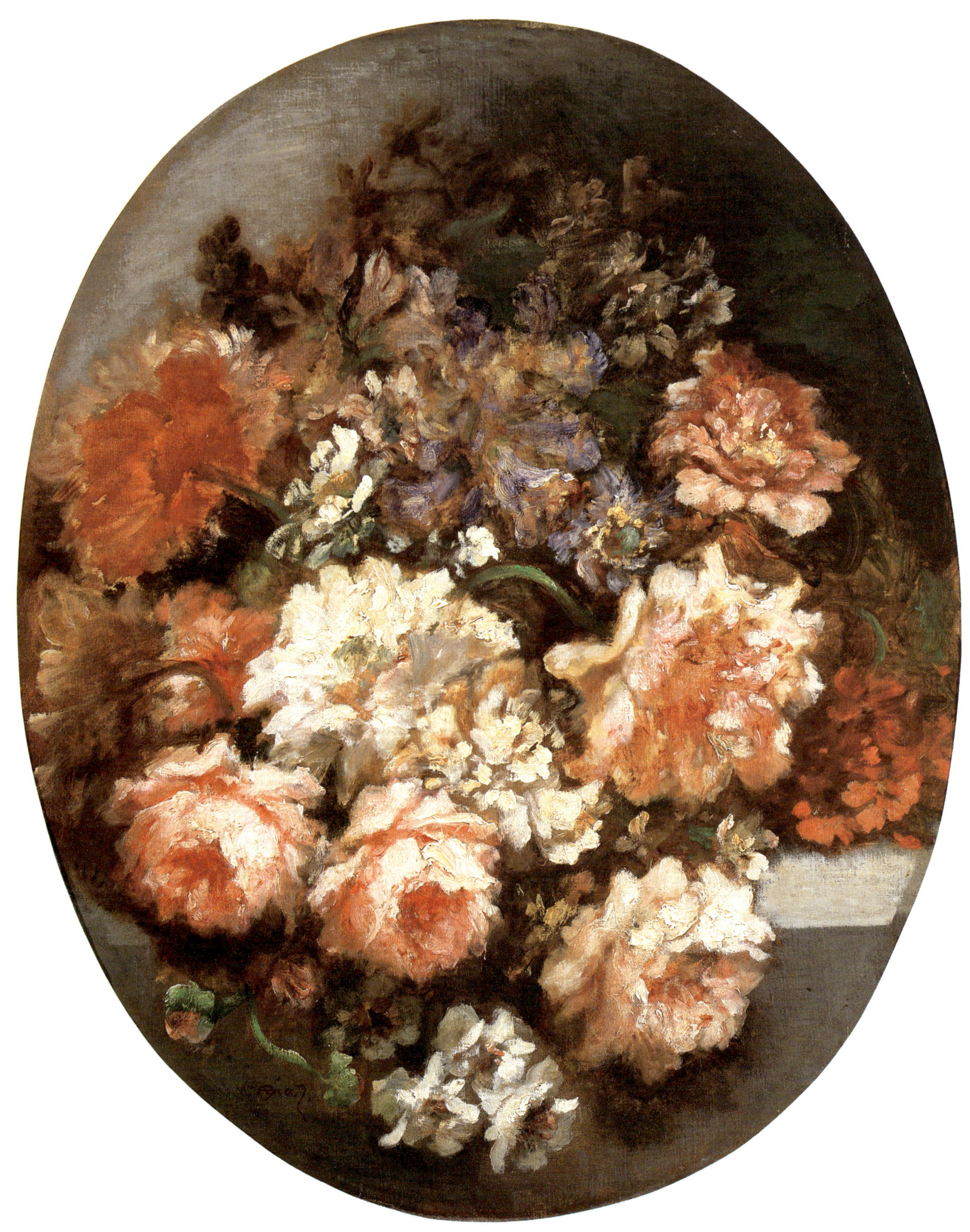

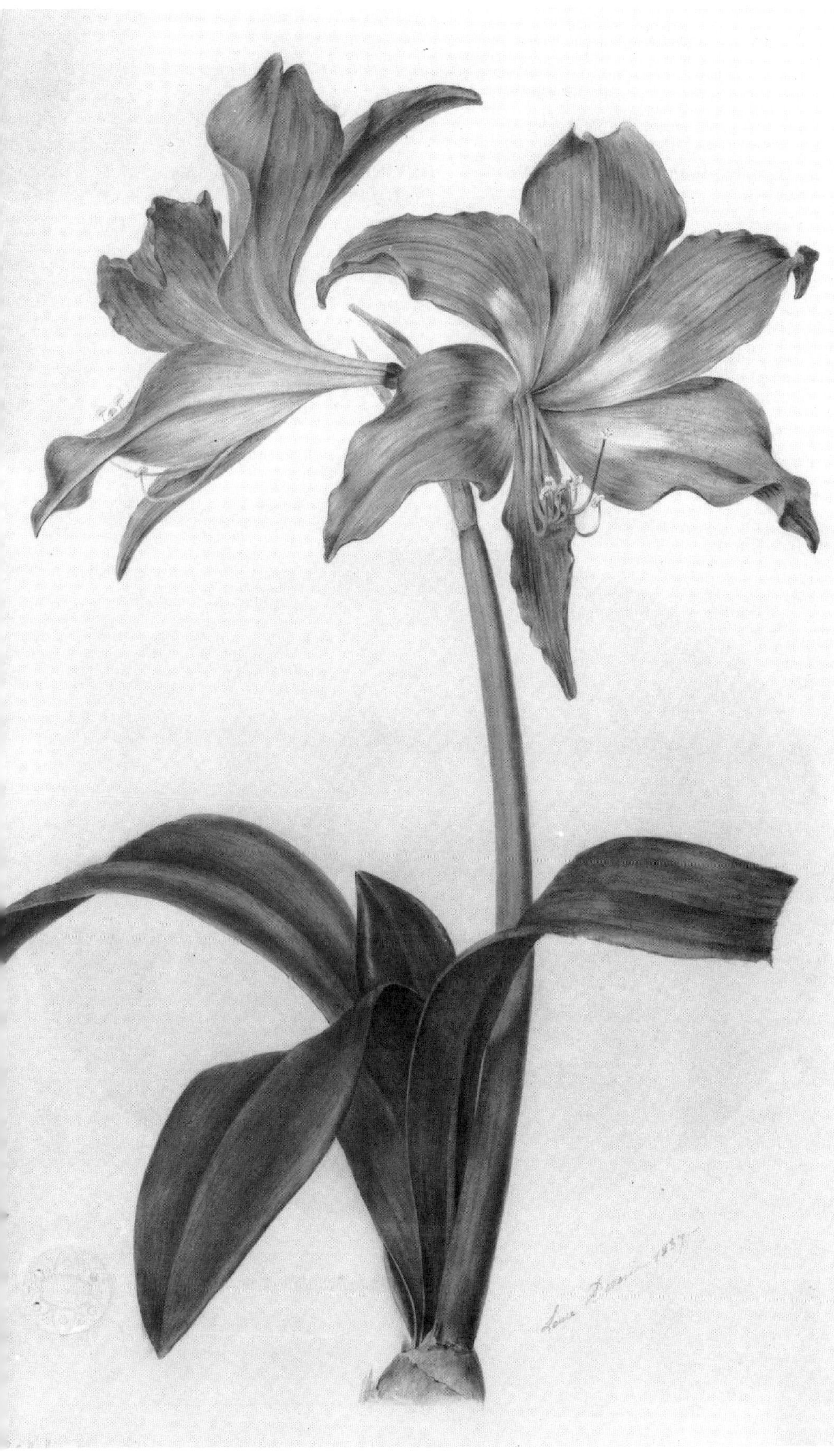

DESPREZ, Marguerite
b. Paris. Pupil of Trébuchet. Exhib. Paris Salon from 1878 e.g. *Roses*, *Lilas*, gouache 1880
LIT *Bellier*; *Bénézit*; *Paris Salon* 1880

DESROCHES, *see* MOISSON

DESTROIS, Alba *b.1863*
b. Paris. Pupil of Faux-Froidure. Painted still-lifes and, occasionally, flowers
LIT *Bénézit*

DESVAUX, E.
Designed plates for C. Gay *Historia ... de Chile*, 1845–53
LIT *Nissen* I, 695

DESVIGNES, Gabrielle-Marie-Thérèse
b. Paris. Pupil of F. Besson. Painted landscapes and flowers. Exhib. Paris Salon 1876–1880 e.g. *Fleurs d'automne*, 1876, *Hortensias*, 1878
LIT *Bellier*; *Bénézit*

DÉTANGER, Germain *1846–1902*
b. Lyon. Painted figures, portraits, genre and, occasionally, flowers e.g. *Fleurs et légumes*, Lyon Salon 1865
LIT *Bénézit*; *Lyon Salon* 1865; *Thieme*

DÉTANGER, Pierre
Pupil of Lyon BA. Exhib. landscapes and flowers, Lyon Salon 1873–1883
LIT *Bénézit*; *Hardouin-Fugier Grafe*; *Thieme*

Laure Devéria

Watercolour on vellum, Vélins vol. 75, no. 82, signed and dated 1837
Paris, Bibliothèque Centrale du Muséum National d'Histoire Naturelle

DEUBERGE, Ida ***b.1857***
Pupil of Carolus-Duran and Henner. Exhib. *Campanules*, *Fleurs de printemps*, Paris UFPS 1896
LIT *Bénézit*; *Paris UFPS* 1896

DEVARENNE, Jean ***1743–1806***
Textile designer. Professor of flower design at Lyon school of flower design and later, head of a class of flower design 1799–1806, prior to the opening of Lyon BA
LIT *Bénézit*; *Hardouin-Fugier Grafe*; *Thieme*

DEVAUD, Georges ***b.1861***
Pupil of Castex-Dégrange, Lyon BA (CFD 1884)
LIT *Hardouin-Fugier Grafe*

DEVELLY, Jean-Charles ***1783–1849***
op. Sèvres
LIT *Bénézit*; Sèvres Arch. BVIII; *Thieme*

DEVÉRIA, Laure ***1813–1838***
b. Paris. Sister of Achille and Eugène Devéria. A famous beauty, Laure Devéria was an able flower painter. Exhib. Paris Salon 1833–8 e.g. *Portrait de femme entourée d'une couronne de fleurs*, 1833, *Fleurs*, wc, 1837, 1838. Provided designs for lithographs. M: Compiègne, Paris, Bibl. Nat. Est., Louvre, Muséum d'Histoire Naturelle
LIT *Bellier*; *Bénézit*; *Faré* 1962, p. 218; *Laissus*; Paris Bibl. Nat. Est. Jd 93; *Paris Salon* 1833, 1836–1838; *Thieme*

DEVOLVÉ-CARRIÈRE, Lisbeth
Pupil of Eugène Carrière, her father. Painted landscapes and flowers. Exhib. Paris SNBA from 1899. e.g. *Anémones*, *Azalées*, 1899
LIT *Bénézit*; *Orsay*; *Paris SNBA* 1899

DEVORE, ***see*** **CHIRADE**

DEYRIEUX, Georges ***1820–1868***
b. Millery (Rhône). Pupil of S. Saint-Jean. His *Couronne de fleurs entourant une croix* (private coll.) won the 1842 Lyon Société des Amis-des-Arts FDC. Exhib. Lyon Salon 1842–1858, Paris Salon 1853, Paris Exposition Universelle 1855
LIT A. Charrin, in *Fleurs de Lyon* (*Hardouin-Fugier Grafe* 1982, ill.); *Hardouin-Fugier Grafe*; *Thieme*

DEYROLLE, Lucien-François ***b.1809***
Pupil of Paris BA from 1832. Worked at Paris Gobelins, producing tapestry designs. Professor at École de Tapisserie des Gobelins and École de Tapisserie de Beauvais. Painted genre and flowers. Exhib. Paris Salon 1840–1867 e.g. *Fleurs et jeune fille*, 1844
LIT *Bellier*; *Bénézit*; *Paris Salon* 1844; *Thieme*

DEYROLLE, Théophile-Louis ***1844–1923***
Pupil of Cabanel and Bouguereau. Exhib. *Chrysanthèmes*, Paris Salon 1895
LIT *Bellier*; *Bénézit*; *Paris Salon* 1895; *Schurr* III, 11; *Thieme*

DHEURS, Etienne
Exhib. *Lilas et giroflées*, Roanne Salon 1890
LIT *Roanne Salon* 1890

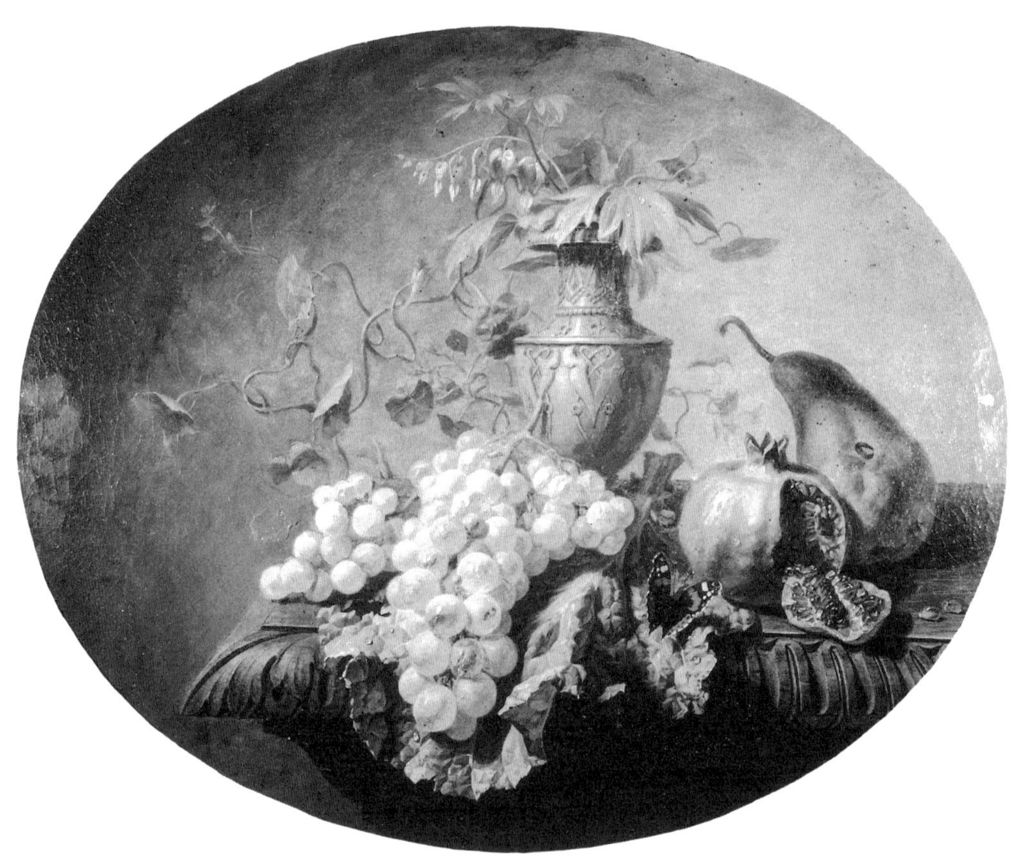

Georges Deyrieux

Oil on canvas, oval, $19\frac{3}{4} \times 24\frac{1}{2}$ in. (50 × 62 cm.), signed
Private collection, Courtesy Musée des Beaux-Arts, Lyon

DIART, Jules-Edouard
b. Berry-au-Bac (Aisne). Exhib. *Fleurs*, Paris Salon 1861; *Fleurs*, Lyon Salon 1862; *Bouquet de Chrysanthèmes*, Dijon Salon 1892. *Grapes, Peaches and Roses*, Christie's, 1980, lot 236
LIT *Bénézit*; *Dijon Salon* 1892; *Lyon Salon* 1862; *Paris Salon* 1861; *Thieme*; *Witt*

DIAZ DE LA PEÑA, Narcisse Virgile *1807–1876*
b. Bordeaux (Gironde). Self-taught. The famous Barbizon painter exhibited few flowers e.g. *Fleurs*, Marseille Salon 1854 but seems to have painted many e.g. *Buisson fleuri*, *Roses*, *Pivoines et campanules*, *Grappe fleurie*, *Pivoines et boules de neige*, *Fleurs dans un vase*, Diaz Exposition Particulière, Paris 1877; *Fleurs*, Cottier sale, Durand-Ruel, Paris, 27–28 May 1892, *Grand Bouquet de fleurs*, Christie's, London, 28 Nov. 1972, 1866; *Flowers*, Parke-Bernet, New York, 15 Jan. 1975, lot 171 etc. Flowers in M: Grenoble, Marseille (Grobet-Labadié). Leeds City Art Gallery, National Gallery of Scotland, Edinburgh, Glasgow Art Gallery; Antwerp etc.
LIT Béziers, *Collections privées de Béziers et de région*, 1961; *Marseille Salon* 1854; *Mitchell* (ill.); *Orsay*; Paris, *Diaz*, Exposition Particulière, *Pavière*, Vol. III, pt. 1; *Thieme*; *Witt*

DELIER, *see* DAVID

DIEMER, Berthe-Georgine
Beuvrages (Nord). Pupil of G. Jeannin and A. Dubos. Exhib. Paris Salon *c.*1890 e.g. *Tulipes et pensées*, wc, 1885, *Panier de roses*, wc, 1890, *Fleurs*, *Chrysanthèmes*, gouache, 1895 and 1898
LIT *Paris Salon*, 1885, 1890, 1895, 1898

DIJON, Martial
b. 1879. Pupil of Castex-Dégrange, Lyon BA (CFD 1898)
LIT *Hardouin-Fugier Grafe*

D'LEINDRE, Zélie-Julie *1795–1858*
b. Blois (Loir-et-Cher). Pupil of Redouté. Exhib. *Panier de fleurs*, Paris Salon 1835. Porcelain painter. Her *Vase de fleurs* was in the Duchesse de Berry's collection
LIT *Hardouin-Fugier* 1981

DOIN, Mme M.
Exhib. *Chrysanthèmes*, *Hortensias*, *Boules de neige*, designs for a screen, Paris SNBA 1897
LIT *Paris SNBA* 1897

DOLARD, Camille *1810–1884*
b. Lons-le-Saunier (Jura). Lyon painter and photographer. Painted figures, portraits, genre and, occasionally, flowers e.g. *Arums dans une pièce d'eau*, Lyon

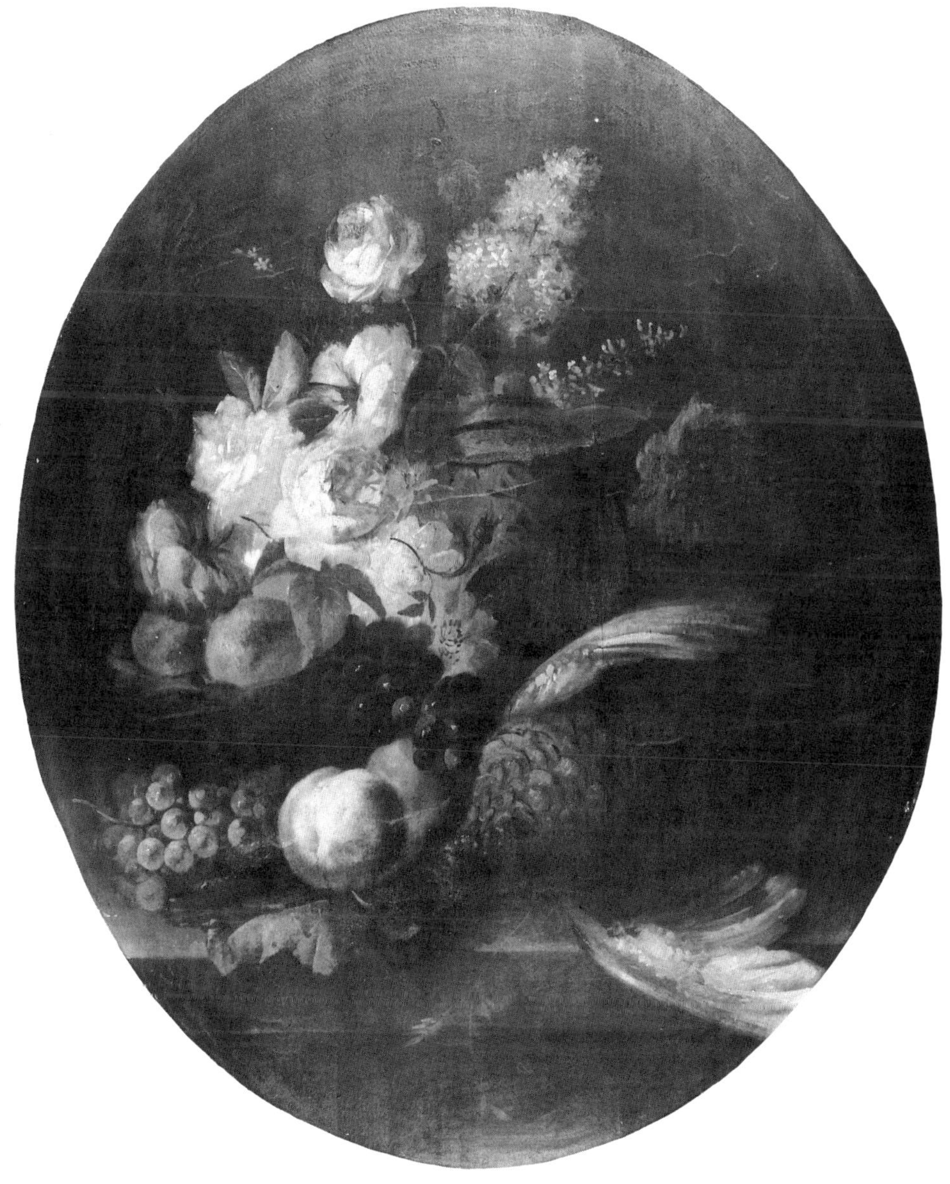

Jules-Edouard Diart

Oil on panel, oval, 31½ × 21 in. (80 × 63.5 cm.), signed
Courtesy Christie's, London

Salon 1881 and wc, Saint-Etienne Salon 1882
LIT *Audin Vial*; *Hardouin-Fugier Grafe* 1981; *Saint-Etienne Salon* 1882

DOLBEAU, Antoine *b.1864*
Pupil of Castex-Dégrange, Lyon BA (CFD 1882–1885). Exhib. Paris and Lyon Salons from 1888
LIT *Bénézit*; *Hardouin-Fugier Grafe*

DÔLE, Berthe
Exhib. *Gerbe de fleurs des champs*, Dijon Salon 1880
LIT *Dijon Salon* 1880. CL

DOLIVOT, Georges-Edmond *b.1843*
b. Paris. Exhib. *Fleurs*, wc, Paris Salon 1870
LIT *Bellier*

DOLL, Mathias *b.1804*
b. Münster (Haut-Rhin). Son of engraver Jean-Jacques Doll. Pupil of Lyon BA. Exhib. *Vase de fleurs et perdrix*, *Lyre entourée de fleurs*, *Vase de fleurs, tulipes et impériales*, Lyon Salon 1828
LIT *Audin Vial*; *Bénézit*; *Hardouin-Fugier Grafe*; *Lyon Salon* 1828

DOLL-PANSERON, Louise
b. Paris. Pupil of G. Jeannin. Exhib. Paris Noir et Blanc Salon *Roses*, fan-leaf, 1886, *Marguerites*, 1888; Paris UFPS *Narcisses, jonquilles*, 1896, *Tulipes*, 1898
LIT *Paris Noir et Blanc Salon* 1886, 1888; *Paris UFPS* 1896, 1898

DOMER, Jean-Barthélémy, *alias* Joanny *1833–1896*
b. Lyon. Pupil of Lyon BA. This splendid decorator produced a few flower pieces e.g. *Fleurs et objets d'art*, *Fleurs et bibelots*, Paris Salon, 1875
LIT *Audin Vial*; *Bénézit*; Hardouin-Fugier *Miniguide de Fourvière*, Lyon (SME) 1983; *Hardouin-Fugier Grafe*; *Paris Salon* 1875; *Schurr I, 63; Thieme*

DOMINO, Jean-Pierre
Pupil of Lyon BA. Exhib. Lyon Salon *Vase de fleurs*, 1846, *Camélias*, 1858
LIT *Hardouin-Fugier Grafe*; *Lyon Salon* 1846, 1858

DONCRE, Guillaume-Dominique-Jacques *1743 or 1748–1820*
b. Zeggers-Cappel (Nord). Active in Arras from 1770. Musée d'Arras, *Fleurs dans un vase*, 1807
LIT *Bellier*; *Bénézit*; *Faré* 1976, p. 330 (ill.)

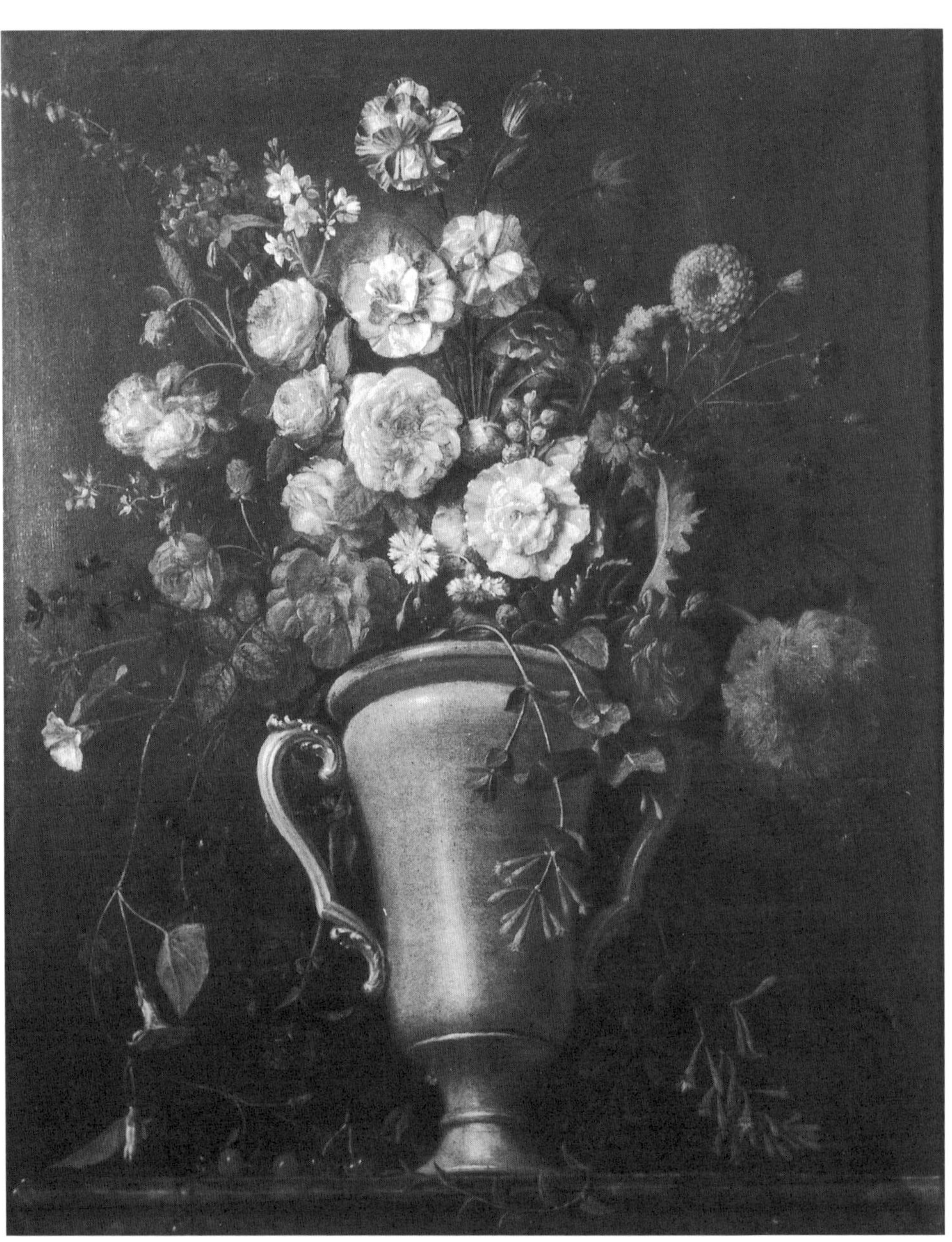

Guillaume-Dominique-Jacques Doncre

$28\frac{3}{4}$ × 23 in. (72.3 × 58.6 cm.), signed and dated 1807
Arras, Musée des Beaux-Arts

DONEAUD, Jacqueline-Cécile, *née* Adelon
b. Dijon (Côte-d'Or). Pupil of Doneaud, her husband, and Rosa Bonheur. Exhib. Paris Salon *c.*1868–75 e.g. *Primevères de Chine*, 1868 and 1875, *Roses Malmaison*, 1870
LIT *Bellier*; *Bénézit*; *Paris Salon* 1875; *Thieme*

DONIN, Laurent
Pupil of Reignier. Exhib. *Pivoines et marguerites*, Saint-Etienne Salon 1882; Lyon Salon *Fleurs*, 1883, *Fleurs au pied d'un vase*, 1885
LIT *Lyon Salon* 1883, 1885; *Saint-Etienne Salon* 1882

DONNEUX-GUICHARD, Jeanne
Pupil of A. Perrachon. fl.*c.*1890 Lyon
LIT *Hardouin-Fugier Grafe*

DONNEY
Pupil of Berjon, Lyon BA (CFD 1813)
LIT *Hardouin-Fugier Grafe*

DOQUIN, Mme
Exhib. *Branche de lilas*, Paris Société des Amis-des-Arts, 1833
LIT *Paris Amis-des-Arts* 1833

DORCEVAL, Mme
Exhib. *Fleurs*, *Fleurs aquatiques*, Lyon Salon 1873
LIT *Lyon Salon* 1873

DOREN, *see* VAN DOREN

DORIAS, François *1855–1936*
Self-taught. fl. Lyon. Painted landscapes and flowers
LIT *Hardouin-Fugier Grafe*

DORNOIS, Marie-Louise
Pupil of Burat. Exhib. *Roses cent-feuilles* after Burat, on porcelain. Paris Salon 1872
LIT *Paris Salon* 1872

DOUARD
fl. Lyon. Entered 1840 FDC
LIT *Hardouin-Fugier Grafe*

DOUCET, Marie
Exhib. *Iris*, *Chrysanthèmes*, Grenoble Salon 1899
LIT *Grenoble Salon* 1899. MW

DOUILLET, Charles *b.1792*
Pupil of Berjon, Lyon BA (CFD 1813)
LIT *Hardouin-Fugier Grafe*

DOUILLET, Etienne
Exhib. *Fleurs et panier de cerises*, Lyon Salon 1831 and 1833. May be the same as Charles Douillet
LIT *Hardouin-Fugier Grafe*

DOUSSEAU
Exhib. *Fleurs*, wc, *Fleurs et gland*, Paris Salon 1833
LIT *Paris Salon* 1833

DOUTRELEAU D'AMSINCK, Mme Agathe
b. Château-de-Vieuville (Ille-et-Vilaine). Exhib. Paris Indép. *Fleurs d'automne*, *Digitale*, 1896; Paris UFPS *Reines des prés*, *Fleurs d'automne*, 1896
LIT *Bénézit*; *Paris Indép.* 1896; *Paris UFPS* 1896

DOYON, Antoine-Louis *b.1826*
op. Lyon. Pupil of Thierriat, Lyon BA (CFD 1844). Entered 1845 FDC
LIT *Hardouin-Fugier Grafe*

DREVET, *see* MANCHICOURT

DREVET, Madeleine
b. Neuilly-sur-Seine (Hauts-de-Seine). Pupil of Mme de Châtillon. Exhib. *Pavots*, Paris Salon 1895
LIT *Paris Salon* 1895

DREVET, Marie-Angélique
b. Chambéry (Savoie). Painted landscapes and flowers. Exhib. *Fleurs de printemps*, Dijon Salon 1887
LIT *Bellier*; *Bénézit*; *Dijon Salon* 1887; *Thieme*. CL

DREVET, Paul b.c.*1820*
Pupil of Saint-Jean. Entered 1840 Lyon FDC with *Couronne de fleurs autour d'un pilier*. Exhib. Lyon Salon 1840–1877 e.g. *Fleurs*, wc, 1861 and 1862. Drawing master *c.*1882
LIT *Audin Vial*; *Bénézit*; *Hardouin-Fugier Grafe*; *Thieme*

DREVET, Pierre *b.1807*
Pupil of Berjon, Lyon BA (CFD 1822)
LIT *Hardouin-Fugier Grafe*

DRIESSCH, Elisabeth de
Exhib. *Fleurs de printemps*, *Fleurs d'été*, *Fleurs d'automne*, Paris Indép. 1884
LIT *Paris Indép.* 1884

DROUET, Gilbert *b.1769*
op. Sèvres 1785–1825
LIT *Bénézit*; *Sèvres* Arch. B.VIII; *Thieme*

DROUET, Louis
b. Niort (Deux-Sèvres). Pupil of A. Delmotte. Exhib. *Fleurs*, Paris Salon 1898
LIT *Bénézit*; *Paris Salon* 1898

DROUIN, Mlle C.
Exhib. *Fleurs et cristaux*, *Fleurs*, Paris SNBA 1895
LIT *Paris SNBA* 1895

DROUVILLE, Mme C.
Exhib. *Bourriche de pensées*, Paris SNBA 1895
LIT *Paris SNBA* 1895

DUBIEZ, Claude, or Claudius
b. Trévoux (Ain). Pupil of Laurent and R. Colin. Exhib. Lyon Salon *Fleurs et fruits*, 1855, *Fleurs*, 1874, 1876, *Vase de fleurs*, 1884; *Glycines*, Dijon Salon 1885
LIT *Bénézit*; *Dijon Salon* 1885; *Hardouin-Fugier Grafe*; *Lyon Salon* 1855, 1874, 1876, 1884; *Thieme*

DUBOIS, Albert ***b.1835***
b. Saint-Lô (Manche). Pupil of G. Jeannin and Levasseur. Exhib. Paris Salon from 1865 e.g. *Lilas et giroflées*, 1879
LIT *Bellier*; *Thieme*

DUBOIS, Gaspard ***b.1823***
Pupil of Thierriat, Lyon BA (CFD 1842)
LIT *Hardouin-Fugier Grafe*

DUBOIS, Maria ***b.c.1845***
b. Meaux (Seine-et-Marne). Exhib. Paris Salon from 1869. *Fleurs de mai*, pastel, 1874, was bought by the State (200 francs) for the Musée de Nice
LIT *Bellier*; *Bénézit*; Paris Arch. Nat. F21:211A; *Schurr* IV, 82; *Thieme*

DUBOIS-PILLET, Albert ***1845–1890***
b. Paris. The pointillist landscape painter, founder-member of Paris Indép. Exhib. flowers e.g. Paris Indép. *Fleurs sur une fenêtre*, 1886, *Fleurs*, 1888, *Marguerites*, 1889, *Marguerites dans un vase de verre*, *Fleurs dans un pot de grès*, *Chrysanthèmes*, 1891; *Bouquet de reines-marguerites à la fenêtre*, 1885, Sotheby's, London, 1 July 1970. His *Giroflées* is in the Musée Crozatier, Le Puy
LIT L. Bazalgette, *A. Dubois-Pillet* ... Villejuif, 1976; *Bénézit*; *Paris Indép.* 1886, 1888, 1889, 1891; *Thieme*; *Witt*

DUBOS, Angèle ***b.1844***
b. Laigle (Orne). Pupil of Chaplin and Hautier. Exhib. Paris Salon from 1866 e.g. *Azalées*, 1880
LIT *Bénézit*; *Paris Salon* 1880; *Thieme*

DUBOSC, Georges
Exhib. *Fleurs et gâteaux*, Paris Indép. 1884
LIT *Paris Indép.* 1884

DUBOST, Michel ***1879–1952***
Pupil of Castex-Dégrange, Lyon BA (CFD 1898). op. textile designer. Succeeded Castex-Dégrange as head of the CFD at Lyon BA. Painted figures, portraits and flowers
LIT *Bénézit*; *Hardouin-Fugier Grafe* (ill.)

DUBOURG, Victoria, Mme Fantin-Latour ***1840–1926***
b. Paris. Pupil of Fantin-Latour, her husband. Exhib. Paris Salon from 1869; *Fleurs et fruits*, Lyon Salon 1872; *Fleurs et fruits*, Pau Salon 1872; *Fleurs et fruits*, Paris Salon 1872, *Fleurs et fruits*, *Chrysanthèmes*, Paris Salon 1873; *Fleurs et fruits*, Lyon Salon 1875; *Oeillets, géraniums* ... Paris Salon 1875, *Phlox, Capucines*, Paris Salon 1890; *Roses, Bouquet de fleurs*, Dijon Salon 1892; *Roses, Panier de fleurs*, Paris Salon 1895; *Dahlias*, Paris Salon 1898. M: Amiens, Château-Thierry, Grenoble, Paris (Jeu de Paume, Louvre, Orsay), Pau, Reims
LIT *Bellier*; *Bénézit*; *Dijon Salon* 1892; *Lyon Salon* 1872, 1875; *Orsay*; Paris Arch. Nat. F21:2131, 4500; Paris, *Fantin-Latour*, Grand Palais 1982; *Paris Salon* 1872, 1873, 1875, 1890, 1895, 1898; *Pau Salon* 1872; *Thieme*; *Witt*
See illustration on page 48

DUBRON, Pauline ***b.1852***
b. Arras (Pas-de-Calais). Pupil of Rozier and J. Bail. Painted still-lifes and, occasionally, flowers. Exhib. Paris Salon from 1889
LIT *Bénézit*; *Thieme*

DUBUISSON, Jeanine
b. Lille (Nord). Pupil of Ghesquier. Exhib. *Panneau d'orchidées*, Paris Salon 1895
LIT *Paris Salon* 1895

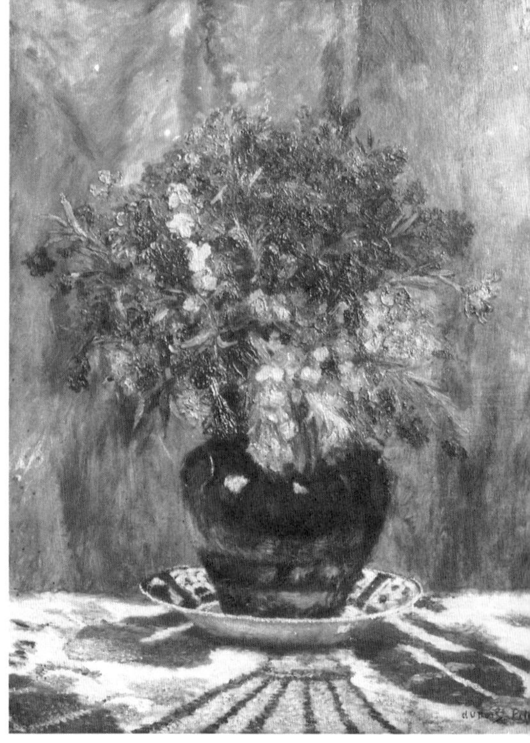

Albert Dubois-Pillet

Oil on canvas, $31\frac{1}{2} \times 24\frac{3}{4}$ in., (80 × 63 cm.), signed
Le Puy, Musée Crozatier

DUBUSSON, E.
Flowers including roses and lilies, 1825, wc, in Cambridge, Fitzwilliam Museum (Broughton coll.). JLC

DUCARUGE, Léon-Pierre *1843–1922*
b. Lavoûte-Chilhac (Haute-Loire). Pupil of Harpignies. op. textile designer 1870–1885 and art teacher (Saint-Etienne). From 1885, painted mostly landscapes
LIT *Annuaire de la Loire*, 1899; *Bénézit*; *Hardouin-Fugier Bringuier*, *Saint-Etienne*, *Paysagistes* ... (Maison de la Culture) 1982

DUCHAMP, Guillaume *b.1797*
Pupil of Berjon, Lyon BA (CFD 1813)
LIT *Hardouin-Fugier Grafe*

DUCHÉ, Jeanne
b. Paris. Pupil of Trébuchet. Exhib. *Fleurs*, wc, Paris Salon 1880
LIT *Paris Salon* 1880

DUCHESNE, *see* CHIRAT

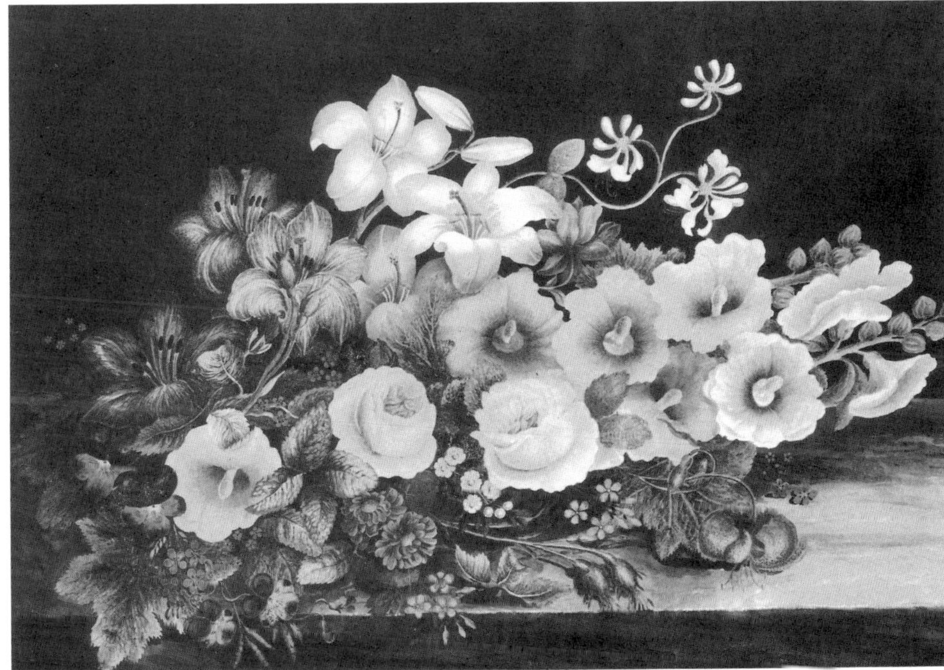

E. Dubusson

Watercolour on paper, 13 × 18½ in. (33 × 45.9 cm.), signed and dated 1825
Cambridge, Fitzwilliam Museum
(Broughton Collection)

Gabriel-Dominique Dudan

Oil on canvas, 19 × 23¾ in. (48 × 60 cm.), signed
Saint-Etienne, Musée d'Art et d'Industrie

DUCHESNE, Louis-Charles *b.1824*
Pupil of Barrias. Painted portraits, still-lifes and, occasionally, flowers. Exhib. Paris Salon 1863–1878
LIT *Bellier*; *Bénézit*; *Thieme*

DUCLOUX-POMEY, Jeanne
Pupil of Pelletier and Dupont. Exhib. *Coquelicots*, Paris UFPS 1896
LIT *Paris UFPS* 1896

DUCROS, Blanche
b. Sarreguemines (Moselle). Pupil of Quost. Exhib. *Fleurs*, Paris Salon 1885
LIT *Paris Salon* 1885

DUCURTYL, Marie
Pupil of Castex-Dégrange. Exhib. Lyon Salon *Fleurs d'automne*, 1876, *Bouquet d'hiver*, 1879
LIT *Hardouin-Fugier Grafe*; *Lyon Salon* 1876, 1879

DUDAN, Gabriel-Dominique
Exhib. *Fleurs*, Paris Salon 1841. Musée d'Art et d'Industrie, Saint-Etienne, *Bouquet de fleurs avec papillon et fruits*, 1844
LIT *Bellier*; *Bénézit*; *Paris Salon* 1841; *Thieme*

DUEZ, Ernest-Ange *1843–1896*
b. Paris. Pupil of Pils. Painted genre, landscapes, figures, still-lifes and flowers e.g. Paris Aquar *Roses trémières au bord de la mer*, *Lys et bourdons*, *Pavots rouges*, *Nénuphars*, *Dahlias*, *Petites roses*, wc, 1883, *Chrysanthèmes jaunes sur la mer*, *Chrysanthèmes bruns sur la mer*, *Hortensias bleus sur le ciel*, wc, 1886; Paris SNBA, *La botanique*, 1892, *Hortensias*, *Pavots*, 1894, *Hortensias*, embroidery design for a screen, 1897. A flower design for a fan-leaf is in Paris BMAD (Maciet coll.)
LIT *Bénézit*, Oxford *Impressionist Drawings*, *Ashmolean*, 1986 (ill.); Paris Arch. Nat. F21:2075, 2131; *Paris MAD*; *Paris Aquar*, 1883, 1886; *Paris SNBA*

1892, 1894, 1897; *Thieme*
See illustration on page 52

DUFAY, Jules-Amédée ***b.1822***
b. Béthune (Pas-de-Calais). Painted still-lifes and, occasionally, flowers. Exhib. Paris Salon 1868–1870
LIT *Bellier*; *Bénézit*; *Thieme*

DUFÊTRE, Pauline
b. Lyon. Pupil of A. Perrachon and T. Tollet. Exhib. Lyon Salon from 1892 and *Groupe de roses*, Dijon Salon 1892
LIT *Bénézit*; *Dijon Salon* 1892; *Hardouin-Fugier Grafe*; *Thieme*

DUFEU, Edouard-Jacques ***1840–1900***
b. Marseille of Egyptian origin. An independent figure largely misunderstood in his lifetime. Painter in oil WC; also engraver of landscapes, portraits, still-lifes
LIT *Bénézit*. PM

DUFEY
op. Sèvres 1813–1816
LIT *Brunet Préaud*

DUFOUR, Augustine ***b.1797***
b. Paris. Pupil of Redouté. Drawing mistress. Wrote *'Art de peindre les fleurs à l'aquarelle* ... Paris 1834
LIT *Gabet*; *Hardouin-Fugier* 1981; *Thieme*

DUFOUR, Joseph
b. Paris. Exhib. *Coquelicots*, wc, Saint-Etienne Salon 1882; *Fleurs*, Lyon Salon 1884
LIT *Saint-Etienne Salon* 1882; *Lyon Salon* 1884

DUFOUR, Marie
One signed work has recently appeared at auction, a gouache on vellum, Sotheby's, Monaco, 23 June 1985, lot 372. PM

DUFRÉNOY, Georges-Léon ***1870–1943***
b. Thiais (Val-de-Marne). Pupil of Académie Julian and Désiré Laugée. Painted genre, landscapes, still-lifes and flowers. Exhib. Paris and Berlin Secession. A selection of later flower-pieces was exhibited at Lyon, Musée des Beaux-Arts
LIT *Bénézit*; R. Déroudille, "Dufrénoy" in *Georges Dufrénoy*, Lyon, Musée des Beaux-Arts, 1983–4; *Schurr* I, 109; *Thieme*

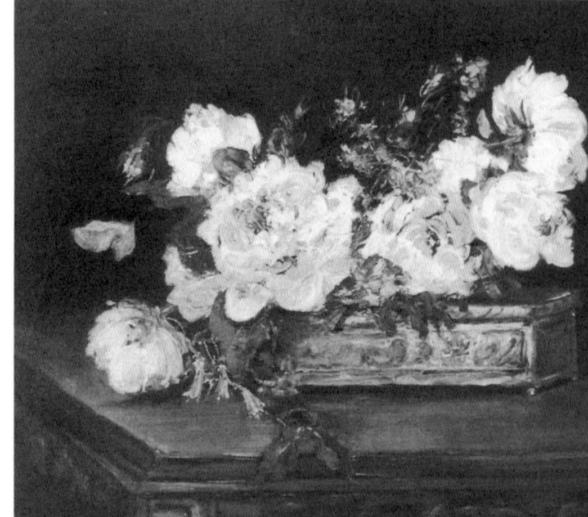

Edouard-Jacques Dufeu

Oil on canvas, $17\frac{3}{4} \times 21\frac{3}{4}$ in. (45 × 55 cm.), signed
Paris, Galerie du Lethé

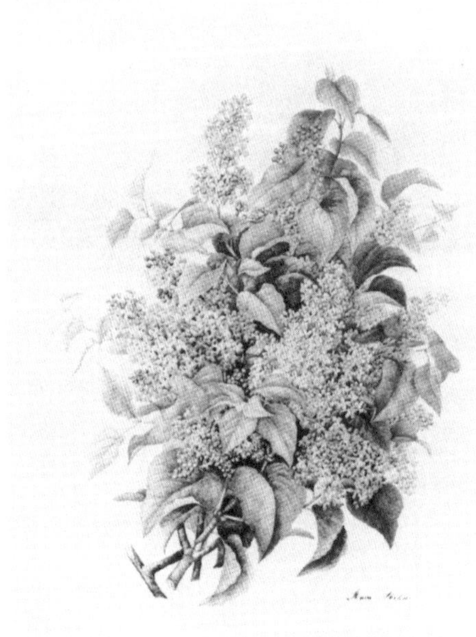

Marie Dufour

Gouache on vellum, $28\frac{3}{4} \times 23\frac{1}{2}$ in. (73 × 59.5 cm.), signed
Courtesy Sotheby's, London

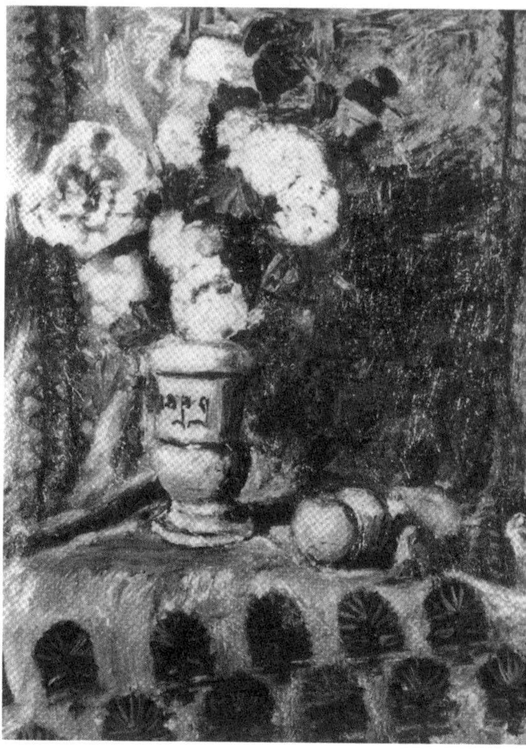

Georges-Léon Dufrénoy

Oil on canvas, $35\frac{3}{4} \times 28\frac{3}{4}$ in. (91 × 73 cm.), signed
Private collection

DUGASSEAU, Charles ***1812–1885***
Pupil of Ingres. Exhib. Paris Salon 1835–1878. e.g. *Vierge aux chrysanthèmes*, Paris Salon 1872, Musée de Boulogne; Musée du Mans, *Corbeille fleurie*, a series of four decorative panels executed in 1865 for Adolphe Singher in Le Mans
LIT *Bellier*; *Paris Salon* 1872; *Schurr* III, 10; *Thieme*; *Witt*

DUHAMEL, *see* ANDRÉ

DUHANOT, *see* MURATON

DUHEM, Marie-Geneviève ***1871–1918***
b. Guimps (Charente). Painted genre and flowers. Exhib. *Pivoines*, Paris SNBA 1899. M: Douai, *Pivoines* 1899, *Boules de neige*, Paris (Louvre, Orsay)
LIT *Bénézit*; *Paris SNBA* 1899; *Schurr* II, 94; *Thieme*; *Witt*

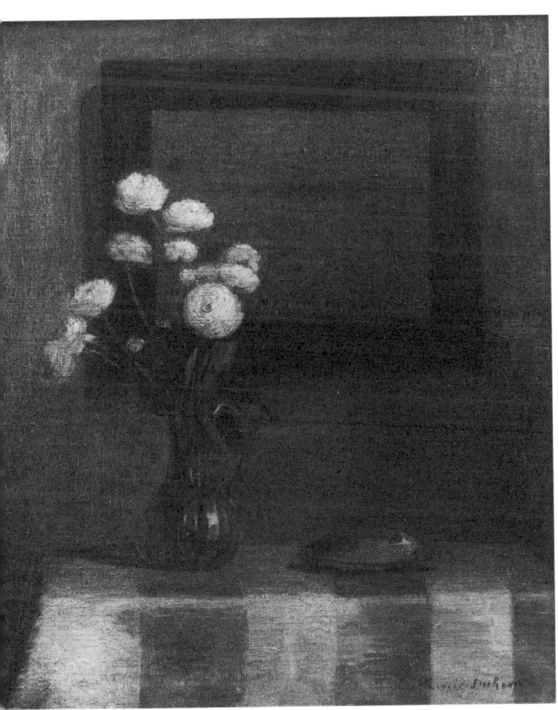

DULONG, Jean-Louis ***1800–1868***
Pupil of Gros and Abel de Pujol. Painted figures, religious paintings, portraits, still-lifes and, occasionally, flowers, e.g. *Fleurs, fruits, animaux*, Paris Salon 1845, *Offrande au dieu des jardins*, Paris Salon 1855
LIT *Bellier*; *Faré* 1962, p. 242; *Paris Salon* 1845; *Thieme*

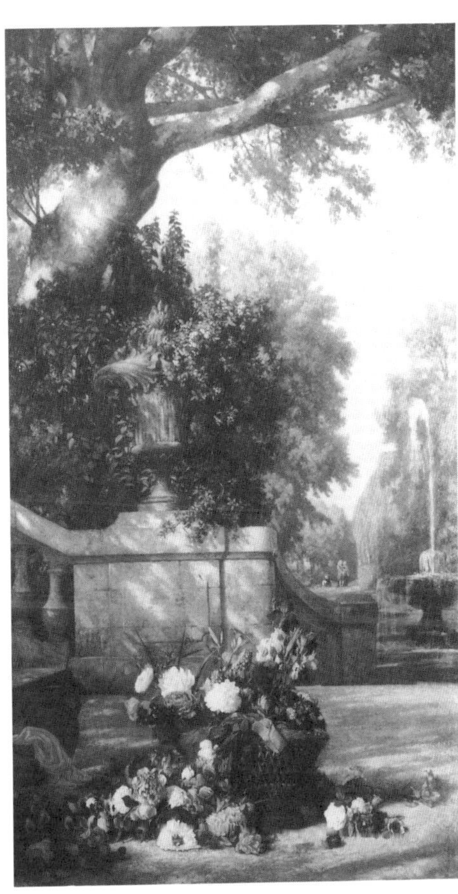

Charles Dugasseau

Oil on canvas, 80 × 44 in. (200 × 112 cm.), Le Mans, Musée de Tessé

Marie-Geneviève Duhem

Oil on canvas, 18 × 15 in. (46 × 38 cm.), signed Paris, Musée d'Orsay

DULUC, Mme Elizabeth
b. Paris. Pupil of Fichu and Redelsperger. Exhib. *Anémones et orange*, wc, Paris Salon 1880
LIT *Paris Salon* 1880

DUMAS, Alice-Claire
Pupil of Académie, 7 quai Voltaire, Paris. Exhib. *Giroflées*, Paris UFPS 1898
LIT *Paris UFPS* 1898

DUMAS, Augustin
Flower and history painter. Head of art school. Curator of Musée d'Arles, 1857
LIT *Bénézit*; E. Parrocel, *Annales de la peinture provençale*, Paris, Marseille (Albessard-Bérard) 1862, p. 431; *Thieme*

DUMAS, Isaline
Active in Paris *c.*1837. Designed plates for *Naissance des Fleurs* and *Musée de la Fabrique*
LIT *Hardouin-Fugier* 1981

DUMAS, Jules
Active in Paris *c.*1837. Designed plates for *Redouté des Dames*, *Naissance des Fleurs* and *Musée de la Fabrique*
LIT *Hardouin-Fugier* 1981

DUMAS, Marie-Marguerite
b. Poitiers (Vienne). Pupil of Couroy-Habert. Exhib. *Fleurs au bord d'un puits*, Lyon Salon 1885; *Fleurs*, Paris Noir et Blanc Salon 1888
LIT *Lyon Salon* 1885; *Paris Noir et Blanc Salon* 1888

DUMAS, Marie-Virginie
b. Lyon. Pupil of Médard. Exhib. *Pavots et chrysanthèmes*, Saint-Etienne Salon 1882
LIT *Saint-Etienne Salon* 1882

DUMONCEAU, F., le Comte
A signed *Flower Study* in oil at Cambridge, Fitzwilliam Museum (Broughton coll.). JLC

DUMOND, Claude
Pupil of Berjon, Lyon BA (CFD 1820)
LIT *Hardouin-Fugier Grafe*

DUMONT, Henri-Julien ***b.1859***
b. Beauvais (Oise). Exhib. Paris Indép. *Fleurs*, 1889, *Printemps*, 1890, *Azalées*, 1891; Paris SNBA *Panier de violettes*, 1893; Paris Indép. *Fleurs*, 1893; Paris SNBA, *Pivoines*, 1897, *Phlox*, *Roses*, *Chrysanthèmes*, *coquelicots*, *Roses*, *Orchidées*, *Tulipes et giroflées*, 1899. His *Monnaie du Pape* was bought by the government for the Musée de Chaumont, and is recorded in the museum's 1912 catalogue, no. 114, but is currently untraceable
LIT *Bellier*; *Bénézit*; Paris Arch. Nat. F21:4500; *Paris Indép*. 1889–1891, 1893; *Paris SNBA* 1893, 1897, 1899; *Thieme*; *Witt*

DUMONT, Jean-Claude ***1805–c.1875***
Self-styled pupil of Berjon. Exhib. Paris Salon 1865 and Lyon Salon 1845–1875 e.g. *Corbeille de roses noisettes*, 1872
LIT *Bellier*; *Bénézit*; *Hardouin-Fugier Grafe*; *Lyon Salon* 1872; *Thieme*

DUMONT, V.
Designed *Roses trémières*, lithographed by Lemercier, Paris BMAD (Maciet coll.)
LIT *Paris BMAD*

DUMOULIN, Alexandrine-Jenny
Exhib. Paris Indép. *Vase de fleurs*, *Fuchsia d'après nature*, on porcelain, 1892, *Fleurs*, on faience, 1894 and 1896, *Tulipes*, *Cyclamens*, 1898
LIT *Paris Indép*. 1892, 1894, 1896, 1898

DUMOULIN, Louisa
Oeillets, 1883
LIT Paris Bibl. Nat. Est. Jd 66

DUNEAU, *see* ROUAIX

DUPART, Alexandre de
Exhib. *Fleurs des champs*, Paris Salon 1850
LIT *Paris Salon* 1850

DUPASQUIER, Joseph-Auguste ***1817–1878***
b. Lyon. Pupil of Thierriat, Lyon BA (CFD 1837). Professor of flower design at the Saint-Etienne Art school *c*.1844. Exhib. Lyon Salon 1848–1874 e.g. *Roses d'automne*, 1856, *Dessus de crédence*, *Glycines*, 1857. Praised by Burty. Musée d'Art' et d'Industrie, Saint-Etienne, *Fleurs*, 1852 (acquired by private legacy 1912), 1867
LIT *Bellier*; *Bénézit*; *Hardouin-Fugier Bringuier*; *Hardouin-Fugier Grafe*; *Thieme*

DUPETIT-THOUARS, Louis-Marie-Aubert ***1758–1831***
Illustrated his own *Histoire des végétaux recueillis sur les isles australes d'Afrique*, Paris 1805
LIT *Nissen* I, 563–564; *Thieme*

Le Comte F. Dumonceau

Oil on canvas, $5\frac{7}{8} \times 7\frac{3}{4}$ in. (14.9 × 19.1 cm.), signed
Cambridge, Fitzwilliam Museum
(Broughton Collection)

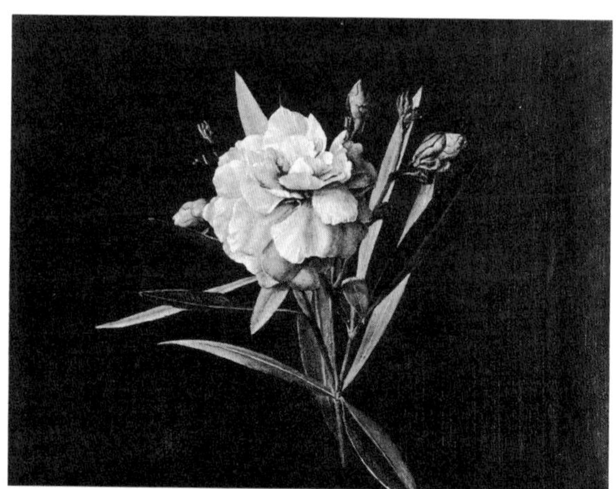

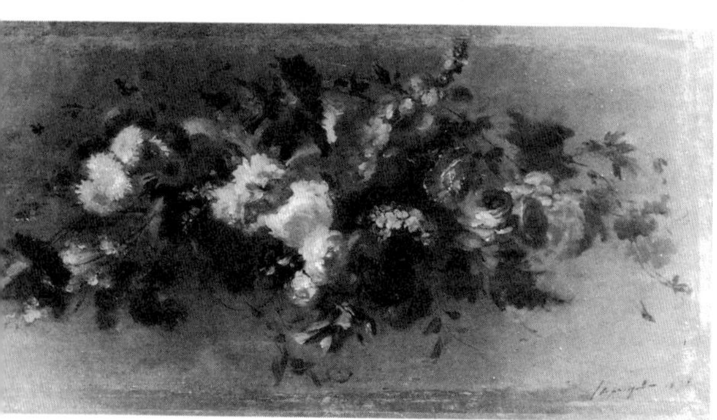

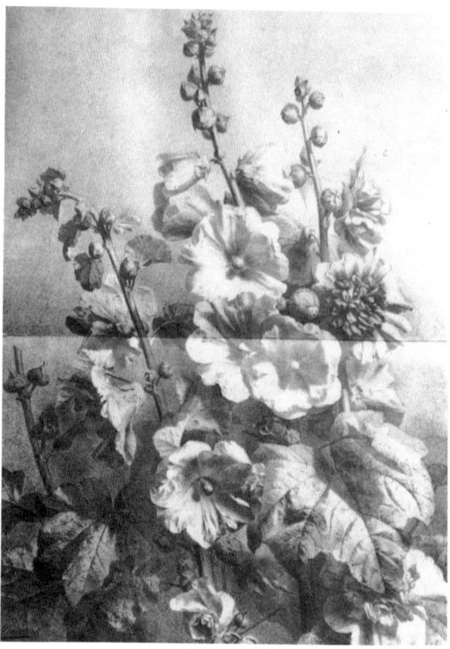

V. Dumont (*above*)

Engraving after a drawing, $24\frac{1}{2} \times 17\frac{3}{4}$ in. (62 × 45 cm.), signed
Paris, MAD (Maciet Collection)

Joseph-Auguste Dupasquier

Oil on canvas, signed and dated 1852
Saint-Etienne, Musée d'Art et d'Industrie

DUMÉNIL, Paul-Chrétien-Romain-Constant ***b.c.1779***
b. Paris. Pupil of Lair and Miquevert. Illustrated e.g. F.F. Chevallier, *Flore Générale des environs de Paris*, Paris 1826–1827. With J. Delarve made ninety-three watercolour drawings, *c.*1848, for P. Duponchel and A. Guénée, *Iconographie et Histoire Naturelles des Chenilles* (Sotheby's, London, 4 Nov. 1983, lot 116)
LIT *Faré* 1962, p. 227; *Nissen* I, 353; *Thieme*

DUMESNIL, Marie ***b.1850***
b. Paris. Painted genre, still-lifes and, occasionally, flowers. Exhib. Paris Salon 1868 and 1870
LIT *Bellier*; *Bénézit*; *Thieme*

DUMESNIL, Pauline
Exhib. *Renoncules*, *Glycines*, Saint-Etienne Salon 1882
LIT *Saint-Etienne Salon* 1882

DUMILLIER, Dominique
Pupil of Reignier. Exhib. Lyon Salon 1857–1892 e.g. *Fleurs diverses*, gouache, *Fleurs des champs*, gouache, 1860. Designer for Lyon silk manufacturers. *Flowering Branch of Snowball Tree*, bodycolour, Cambridge, Fitzwilliam Museum (Broughton coll.)
LIT *Bénézit*; *Broughton* 1976; *Broughton* 1979; *Lyon Salon* 1860; *Thieme*

DUMINI, Eugène-Armand-Marie
Exhib. Paris Indép. *Hortensias*, *Pavot*, 1896, *Lilas de Meudon*, 1898
LIT *Paris Indép.* 1896, 1898

Paul-Chrétien-Romain-Constant Duménil

Watercolour on vellum, (*Iconographie et Histoire Naturelles des chemilles* by P. Duponchel & A. Guenée), $74\frac{3}{4}$ × 53 in. (190 × 135 cm.), signed, Courtesy Sotheby's, London

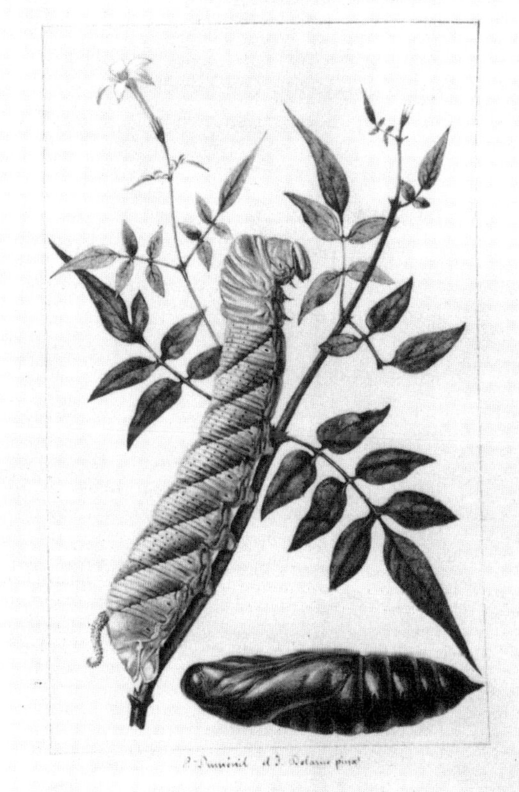

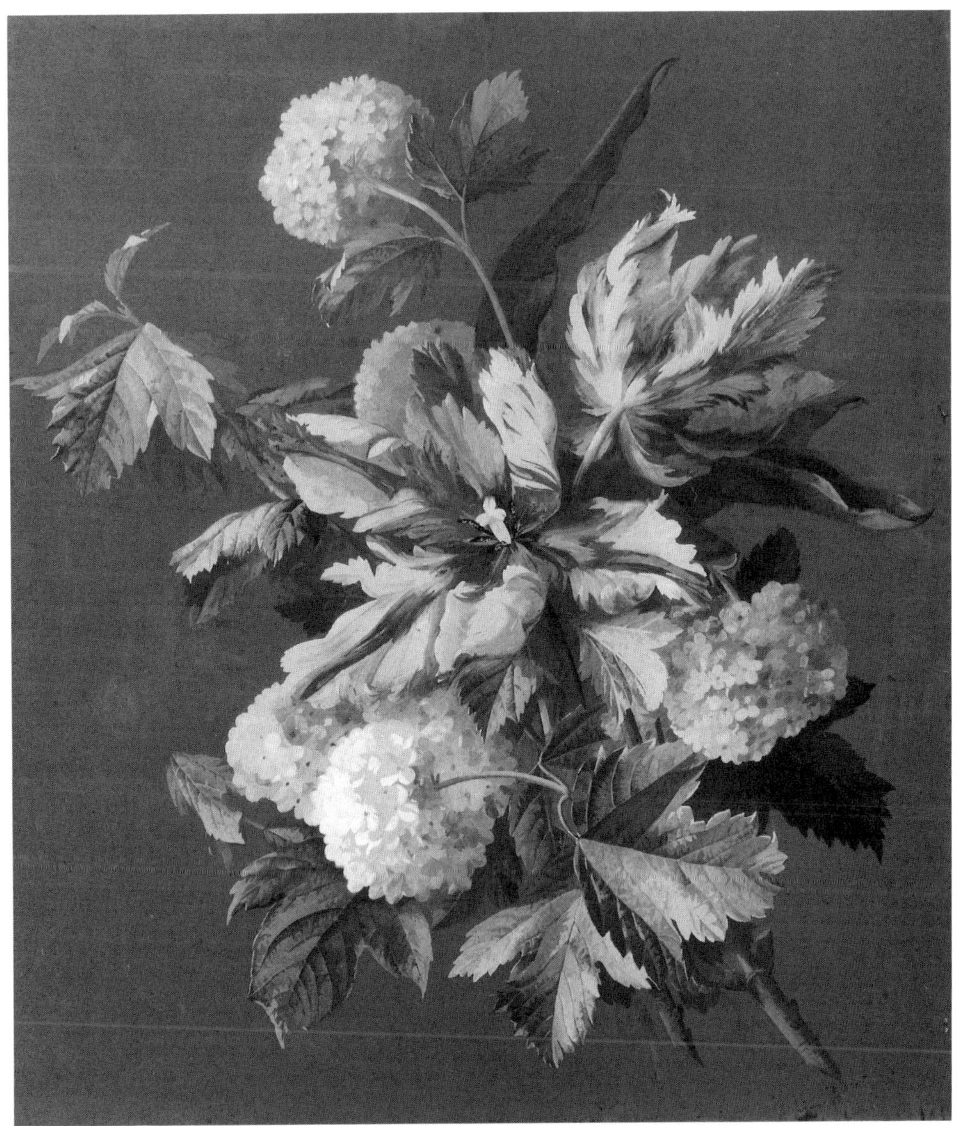

Dominique Dumillier (*left*)

Bodycolour on vellum, $19\frac{1}{2}$ × 17 in. (49.4 × 43.1 cm.), signed
Cambridge, Fitzwilliam Museum
(Broughton Collection)

1886. Musée de Bordeaux, *Fleurs*, 1892 (currently untraceable)
LIT *Bénézit*; *Thieme*

DURANT, Philippe *b.1798*
Pupil of Berjon, Lyon BA (CFD 1813)
LIT *Hardouin-Fugier Grafe*

DURAT-LASSALLE, Louise
Pupil of Grönland. Exhib. *Fleurs et fruits*, Paris Exposition Universelle, 1855; *Fleurs et fruits*, Lyon Salon 1858
LIT *Lyon Salon* 1858; *Paris Exposition Universelle* 1855

DURGIN, Henriette
b. Boston (USA). Pupil of de Cool and F. Rivoire. Exhib. *Chardons*, wc, Paris Salon 1890.
LIT *Paris Salon* 1890

DURIEU, Virginie *b.1820*
b. Nîmes (Gard). Pupil of L. de Mirbel. Painted portrait miniatures and flowers. Exhib. Paris Salon 1845–1852 e.g. wc: *Vase de fleurs*, *Dahlia*, 1845, *Pivoines*, *Roses thé*, 1847
LIT *Bellier*; *Bénézit*; *Paris Salon* 1845; *Thieme*

DURIEUX, Joseph *b.1877*
Pupil of Castex-Dégrange, Lyon BA (CFD 1894)
LIT *Hardouin-Fugier Grafe*

DURNERIN, Mathilde
b. Paris. Pupil of Arnaud. Exhib. *Pivoine*, *Camélias et Azalées*, Paris Salon 1880; *Reines-marguerites*, wc, Lyon Salon 1882
LIT *Lyon Salon* 1882; *Paris Salon* 1880

DURRUTHY-LAYRLE, Zélie *b.1872*
b. Paris. Pupil of Humbert and Thirion. Painted genre and, occasionally, flowers. Exhib. *Roses*, Paris UFPS 1896
LIT *Bénézit*; *Paris UFPS* 1896; *Thieme*

DURY-VASSELON, Hortense
b. Paris. Pupil of A. Vollon. Exhib. Paris Salon *Buisson de roses*, 1889, *Fleurs dans un parc*, 1891, *Pavots et fleurs des prés*, 1893; Dijon Salon, *Fleurs*, 1894; Paris Salon *Corbeille de fleurs et de fruits*, 1894, *Fleurs et fruits*, *Rosiers*, 1895, *Fleurs et fruits*, 1896; Paris UFPS *Azalées*, *Fleurs*, *Vase de fleurs*, 1896, *Roses et oeillets*, *Giroflées et anémones*, *Fleurs et fruits*, 1898; Paris Salon *Roses Malmaison*, *Fleurs et fruits*, 1898, *Roses d'été*, 1899. Musée de Tours, *Roses blanches et pêches*
LIT *Bénézit*; *Dijon Salon* 1894; *Paris Salon* 1889 (ill.), 1891 (ill.), 1893 (ill.), 1894 (ill.), 1895 (ill.), 1896 (ill.), 1897 (ill.), 1898 (ill.), 1899 (ill.); *Paris UFPS* 1896, 1898; *Thieme*

DU SAL, *see* VINCENT

DUSSAUCE. Auguste *1802–1877*
b. Beaune (Côte-d'Or). Pupil of Mathis and Deroche. Decorator. Exhib. *Fleurs et fruits*, Paris Salon 1827 and 1841. Musée de Valenciennes *Fleurs* (disappeared)
LIT *Bellier*; *Bénézit*; *Gabet*; *Thieme*

DUSSAULE, Marguerite
Pupil of Chamecin and d'Apvril. Exhib. *Roses*, Grenoble Salon 1899
LIT *Grenoble Salon* 1899

DUSSIEUX, Louise-Stéphanie, *later* Dussieux-Keller
b. Versailles (Yvelines). Pupil of Fontaine, Pallandre, de Villers and Giacomelli. Exhib. Paris Salon from 1877. *Fleurs des champs*, *Panier de fleurs*, Lyon Salon 1878; *Chrysanthèmes au salon*, *Chrysanthèmes au jardin*, Paris Salon 1880; *Chrysanthèmes au jardin*, Lyon Salon 1881; *Pensées*, Saint-Etienne Salon 1882; *Coucous*, Lyon Salon 1883; Strasbourg Salon *Pensées*, 1883 (150 francs), *Fleurs des champs*, 1884 (350 francs); *Fleurs d'été*, *Fleurs des champs*, Dijon Salon 1885; *Dernières fleurs*, Paris Salon 1885
LIT *Bellier*; *Bénézit*; *Dijon Salon* 1885; *Lyon Salon* 1878, 1881, 1883; *Paris Salon* 1880, 1885; *Saint-Etienne Salon* 1882; *Strasbourg Salon* 1883, 1884

DUSSORT, Claudius or Claude-Antoine *b.1855*
b. Lyon. Pupil of Reignier, Lyon BA (CFD 1872). Exhib. Lyon Salon from 1879 e.g. *Roses*, 1894
LIT *Bénézit*; *Hardouin-Fugier Grafe*

DUSSUC, François *b.1871*
Pupil of Castex-Dégrange, Lyon BA (CFD 1888)
LIT *Hardouin-Fugier Grafe*

DUSSURGEY, *see* CHABAL

DUTROU, Jean-Baptiste *b.1814*
b. Paris. Painted still-lifes and, occasionally, flowers. Exhib. Paris Salon 1869–1880
LIT *Bellier*; *Bénézit*; *Thieme*

DUVAL, L.
Exhib. *Marguerites et fruits*, Dijon Salon 1883
LIT *Dijon Salon* 1883

DUVERDY, Jules *b.1804*
Pupil of Berjon, Lyon BA (CFD 1822)
LIT *Hardouin-Fugier Grafe*

DUVIGNAU, *see* VIGER

DYBOWSKA, Emilie
b. Paris. Pupil of Faguet and Rivoire. Exhib. *Phlox*, *Bouquet des champs*, Paris Noir et Blanc Salon 1888; *Anémones et narcisses*, wc, *Roses et vieux lierre*, wc, Dijon Salon 1892; *Violettes*, wc, Paris Salon 1898
LIT *Dijon Salon* 1892; *Paris Noir et Blanc Salon* 1888; *Paris Salon* 1898

DUPLAY, Mathieu-Philippe ***1844–1908***
b. Saint-Etienne (Loire). Pupil of Lyon BA, Reignier and Bruyas (Lyon) Muller (Paris). Painted flowers
LIT *Bénézit*; *Thieme*

DUPLOMB, Jean-Marie ***b.1827***
Pupil of Thierriat, Lyon BA (CFD 1844)
LIT *Hardouin-Fugier Grafe*

DUPONT, Julie
b. Pontoise (Val-d'Oise). Pupil of Desforges and de Cool. Exhib. Paris Salon from 1877 e.g. *Fleurs*, wc, 1880
LIT *Bellier*; *Paris Salon* 1880

DUPONT-ZIPCY, Emile ***1822–1885***
b. Douai (Nord). Pupil of Souchon and Lille art school. Drawing master. Painted genre, portraits and, occasionally, flowers e.g. *Fleurs, panneaux décoratifs*, Paris Exposition Universelle, 1878; *Pivoines*, wc, Saint-Etienne Salon 1882
LIT *Bellier*; *Bénézit*; *Saint-Etienne Salon* 1882; *Thieme*

DUPRAS, Henri-Théodore-Auguste
b. Domfront (Orne). Pupil of Levasseur. Exhib. Paris Salon from 1880 e.g. *Roses*, *Roses trémières*, wc, 1880
LIT *Bellier*; *Bénézit*; *Paris Salon* 1880; *Witt*

DUPRAT, Sophie
b. Paris. Pupil of Prud'hon. Exhib. Paris Salon 1833–1851 miniatures, religious subjects, portraits and copies after old master paintings, some of them featuring flowers e.g. *Vierge couronnée de fleurs*, after *Rubens*, 1836
LIT *Bellier*; *Bénézit*; *Gabet*; *Thieme*

DUPRÉ-BIRONNEAU, Marie-Blanche
Pupil of T. Robert-Fleury and Donnadieu. Exhib. Dijon Salon *Violettes et oeillets*, wc, 1892, *Violettes*, pastel, 1894; Paris UFPS *Bibelots et fleurs*, pastel 1896, *Fleurs d'hiver*, pastel, 1898
LIT *Bénézit*; *Dijon Salon* 1892, 1894; *Paris UFPS* 1896, 1898. CL

DUPUY, B.
Exhib. *Roses trémières et volubilis*, wc, Lyon Salon 1858
LIT *Lyon Salon* 1858

DUQUENNE, Charles-Alphonse
Exhib. Paris Indép. *Fleurs*, 1892, *Chrysanthèmes*, *Orchidées*, *Reines-marguerites*, *Azalées*, 1893, *Chrysanthèmes*, *Fleurs variées*, *Roses*, 1894
LIT *Paris Indép.* 1892, 1893, 1894

DURAFOUR, Charles-Louis ***b.1838***
b. Saint-Etienne (Loire). Pupil of Reignier, Lyon BA (CFD 1857). Exhib. *Fleurs*, Saint-Etienne Salon 1891
LIT *Hardouin-Fugier Bringuier*; *Saint-Etienne Salon* 1891

DURAND, Gabriel-Dominique ***b.1812***
b. Toulouse (Haute-Garonne). Painted portraits and, occasionally, flowers. Exhib. Paris Salon 1847–1878. His 1844 *Fleurs et fruits* is in the Musée d'Art et d'Industrie, Saint-Etienne
LIT *Bellier*; *Bénézit*; *Thieme*

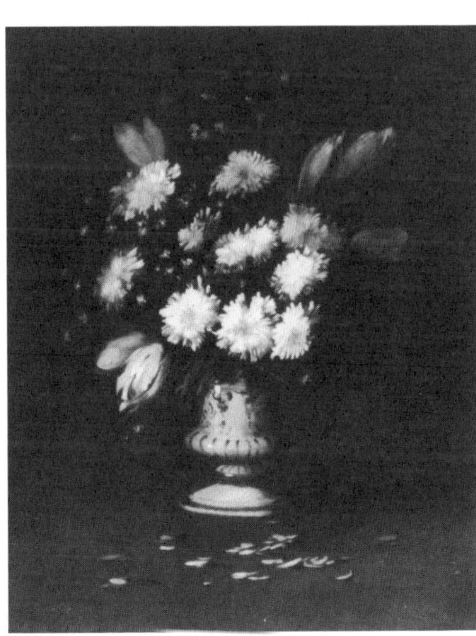

Emile Dupont-Zipcy

Oil on board, 35 × 51 in. (89 × 130 cm.), signed and dated 1878
Private collection, Courtesy Sotheby's, London

DURAND, Joannès ***1873–1914***
b. Lyon. Pupil of Lyon École Municipale de dessin. Friendly with Jean Puy and Paviot. Painted landscapes, interiors and flowers in a bold, colourful Fauve style. Exhib. Paris Indép. from 1901
LIT H. Béraud, *L'École moderne de peinture lyonnaise*, 1912; N. Mas, in *Fleurs de Lyon Hardouin-Fugier Grafe* 1982, (ill.)

DURAND, ***see*** **CAROLUS-DURAN**

DURANDEAU, Auguste-Antoine ***b.1854***
b. Bordeaux (Gironde). Pupil of Cabanel and Galland. Exhib. Paris Salon from

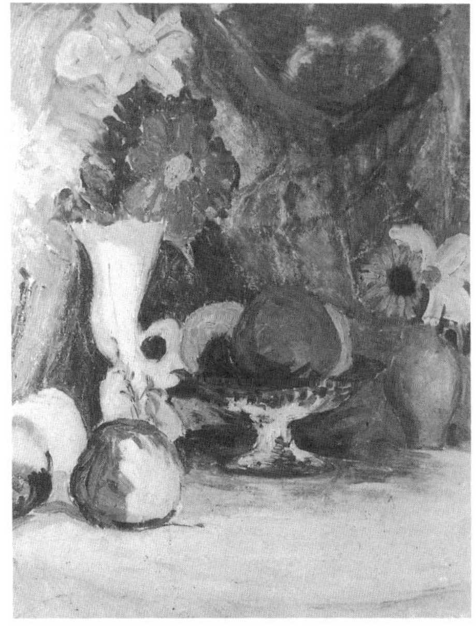

Joannès Durand

Oil on board, 21 × 16½ in. (53 × 42 cm)
Private collection, Courtesy Musée des Beaux-Arts, Lyon

Flowers and fruit, Christie's, London, 16 June 1978. Produced designs for lithographs and chromolithographs
LIT *Bellier*; *Bénézit*; *Faré* 1962, p. 245; *Paris Salon 1843, 1846, 1855 (Exposition Universelle), 1861, 1880; Thieme*; *Witt*

ENFANTO DE SAINTE-MARIE *fl.c.1800–1831*
Pupil of Redouté. Work in Cambridge, Fitzwilliam Museum (Broughton coll.), *Spray of flowers*, 1831, wc
LIT *Hardouin-Fugier* 1981

ENGEL, José *b.1873*
b. Joinville-le-Pont (Val-de-Marne). Pupil of Roll. Painted landscapes and, occasionally, flowers. Exhib. *Chrysanthèmes*, Paris Indép. 1893
LIT *Bénézit*; *Paris Indép.* 1893; *Thieme*

EPINAY, Marie d'
b. Rome (Italy). Pupil of Prosper d'Epinay, her father, and Machard. Painted genre, portraits and flowers. Exhib. Paris Salon from 1893
LIT *Bénézit*; *Thieme*

EPREMESNIL, Jacques-Louis-Raoul
b. Paris. Pupil of Lambotte. Exhib. Paris Salon *Glaïeuls*, wc, 1880, *Fleurs*, gouache, 1885
LIT *Bénézit*; *Paris Salon* 1880, 1885

ERMEL, A.
Exhib. *Fleurs des champs*, Paris SNBA 1890
LIT *Paris SNBA* 1890

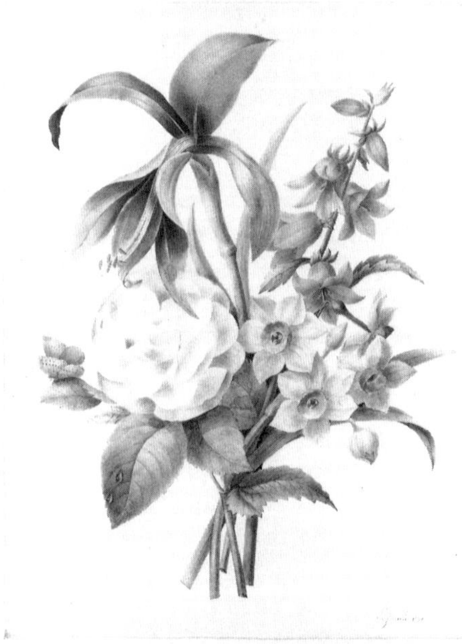

Enfanto de Sainte-Marie

Watercolour on vellum, $12\frac{3}{4} \times 9\frac{9}{16}$ in. (32.4 × 24.4 c.), signed and dated 1831
Cambridge, Fitzwilliam Museum, (Broughton Collection)

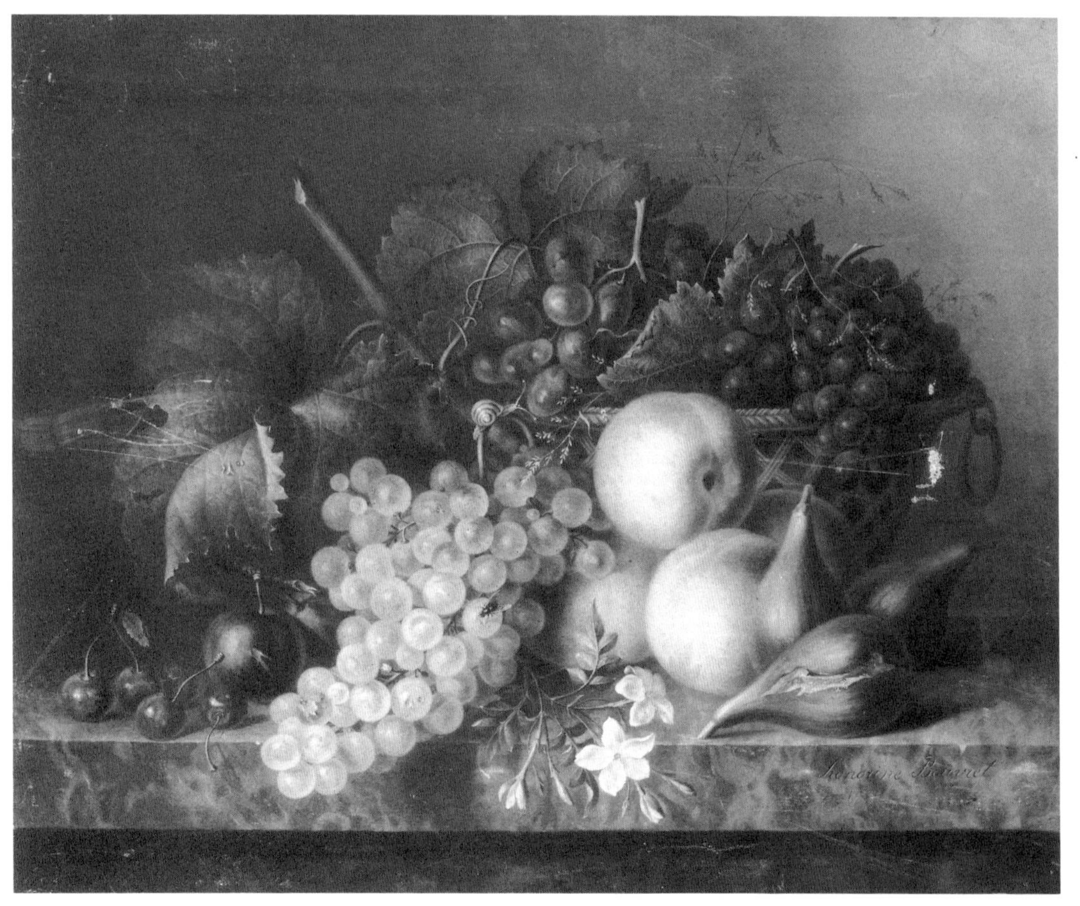

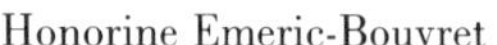

Honorine Emeric-Bouvret

Oil on canvas, $16\frac{1}{2} \times 20\frac{1}{2}$ in. (42 × 52 cm.), signed
Courtesy Christie's, London

E

EDOUARD, E.
Exhib. *Gerbe de Chrysanthèmes*, Dijon Salon 1883
LIT *Dijon Salon* 1883. CL

EGGER, Ida
Exhib. Paris Salon *c.*1834–1838 e.g. *Bouquet de pivoines*, wc, *Fleurs et fruits*, *Fleurs dans un verre*, 1834, *Fleurs et fruits*, *Fleurs*, wc, 1836, *Fleurs de printemps*, *Fleurs diverses*, wc, 1838
LIT *Bénézit*; *Paris Salon* 1834, 1836, 1838

EGLÉ, Louise, *later* Adorne de Tscharner
b. Strasbourg (Bas-Rhin). Exhib. Paris Salon 1848–1851 (Eglé) e.g. *Bouquet de violettes*, 1850
LIT *Bénézit*; *Paris Salon* 1850; *Thieme*

EGLEN, J.E.
Fruit and Nuts in a Basket, 1831, wc, and *Spray of Flowers*, 1832, wc, Cambridge, Fitzwilliam Museum (Broughton coll.). JLC

EHRARD, Anna
Exhib. *Iris et tulipes*, gouache, Strasbourg Salon 1891
LIT *Strasbourg Salon 1891*

EHRMANN, Eugène *1804–1896*
b. Colmar (Haut-Rhin). Wallpaper designer for Zuber (Rixheim). Designed *Isola Bella*, *Eldorado* etc. all featuring flowers
LIT B. Jacqué, "Les papiers peints panoramiques de Zuber au XIX° siècle" in *Bulletin du Musée Historique ... de Mulhouse*, 1981

EICHER, *see* BULLOT

ELIAERTS Jean François or Jan Frans *1764–1848*
b. Deurne (Belgium) 1761, d. Antwerp 1848. A naturalised Frenchman. Painter of still-lifes and flower pieces. Influenced by Jan Van Huysum. Professor at l'Institution de la Legion d'Honneur. Exhibit. regularly at the Paris Salon 1810–1848.
LIT *Bellier; Bénézit*
See illustration on page 21

ELIOT, Maurice *b.1864*
b. Paris. Pupil of Cabanel. Painted landscapes, genre and, occasionally, flowers. Exhib. Paris SNBA *Sauges bleues*, *Glaïeul*, 1892, *Fleurs de pommier*, 1898, *Ombelles*, pastel, 1899
LIT *Bénézit*; *Paris SNBA* 1892, 1898, 1899; *Thieme*

ELRY, Jack
Exhib. *Pensées*, wc, *Azalées*, wc, Paris Indép. 1884
LIT *Paris Indép.* 1884

EMERIC, Jules-Théodore
b. Paris. Pupil of Clérian senior and junior and Grobon. Painted flowers and fruit. Exhib. Paris Salon 1865–1867
LIT *Bellier*; *Bénézit*

EMERIC-BOUVRET, Honorine *b.1814*
b. Melun (Seine-et-Marne). Pupil of Grobon and Lesourd de Beauregard. Exhib. Paris Salon 1843–1880 e.g. *Corbeille de fleurs*, after Van Spaendonck, on porcelain, 1843; *Bouquet sur une table*, 1846, *Bouquet sur la croix*, Paris Exposition Universelle 1855, *Fleurs de printemps*, *Fleurs de serres*, wc, 1861, *Binxias roses*, *Roses thé*, gouache, 1880.

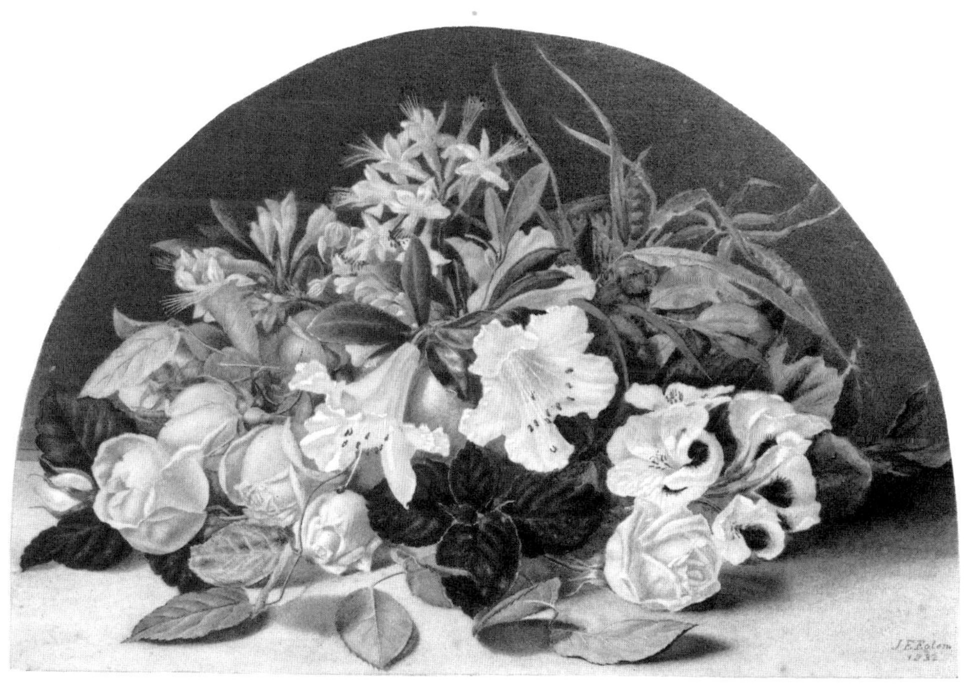

J.E. Eglen

Watercolour on paper, $9\frac{7}{8} \times 14\frac{7}{8}$ in (25 × 37.8 cm.), signed and dated 1832
Cambridge, Fitzwilliam Museum, (Broughton Collection)

ESCALLIER, Marie-Caroline-Eléonore, *née* Légerot *1827–1888*
b. Poligny (Jura). Pupil of Ziegler. op. Sèvres 1874–1888. Produced tapestry design for Beauvais, 1880. Exhib. Paris Salon from 1857 e.g. *Le vase de fleurs*, *Les iris*, 1857; *Les iris*, Lyon Salon 1860; Paris Salon *Panier fleuri*, *Vase de pétunias*, 1861, *Vase de fleurs*, *Coin de jardin*, 1867, *Fleurs de printemps*, 1872, *Coin de jardin*, 1873, *Oeillets de mai*, *Muguets*, *Fleurs d'automne*, 1874, *Panneaux pour le palais de la Légion d'honneur*, *Panier de muguet*, 1875. *Fleurs*, *Fleurs et fruits*, Lons-le-Saunier Salon 1876. A most successful flower and porcelain painter. Her works were bought by the State for M: Bar-le-Duc, Lons-le-

Marie-Caroline-Eléonore Escallier

Oil on canvas, 51 × 36 in. (130 × 91 cm.), signed and dated 1867
Paris, Muséum National des Arts Décoratifs

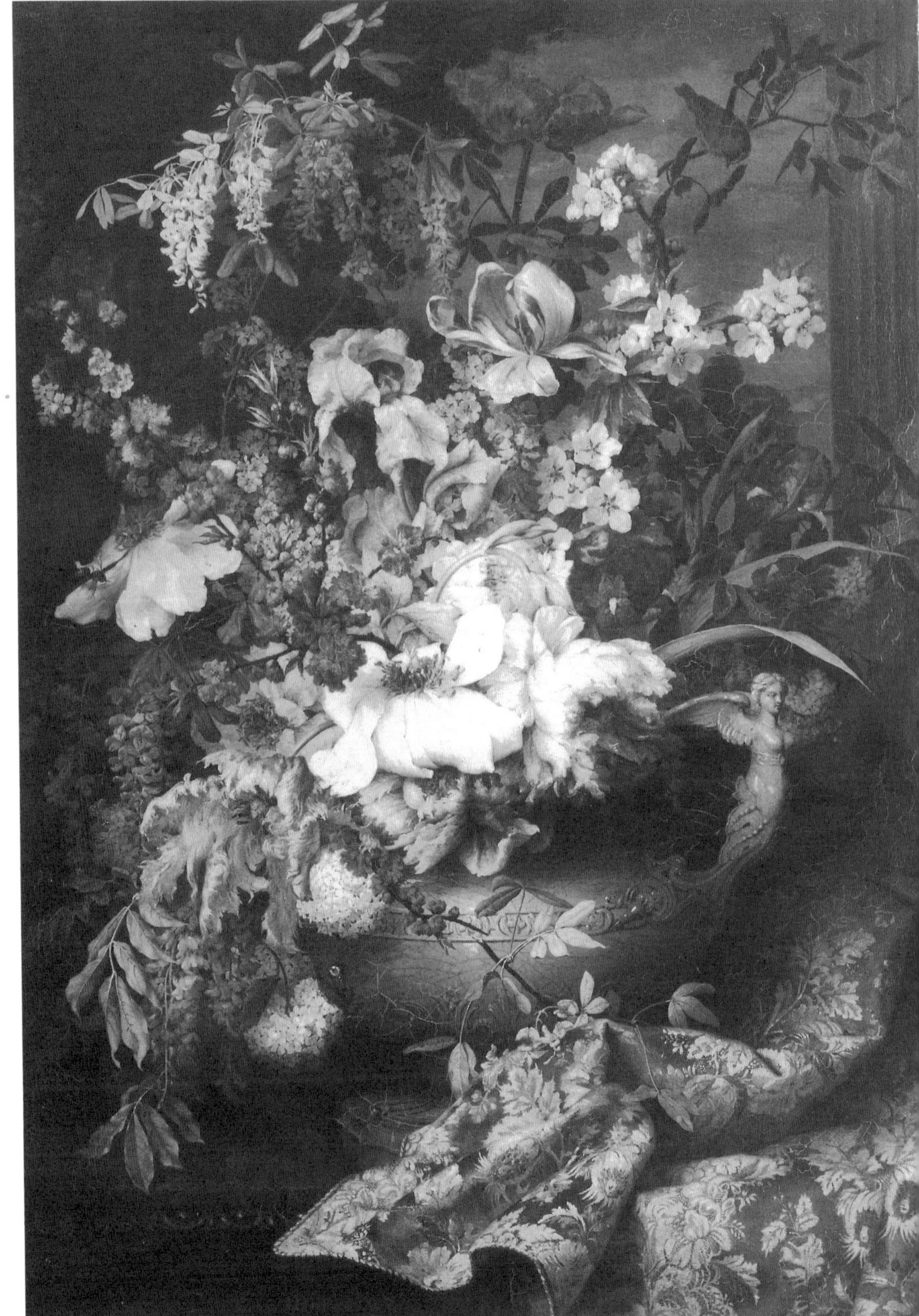

Saunier, Paris (now Orsay), Paris Muséum d'Histoire Naturelle, MAD, Saint-Etienne, Sèvres
LIT *Bellier*; *Bénézit*; *Brune*; *Brunet Préaud*; *Paris. Céramique et verrerie*, 1–15 July 1888; K.B. Hiesinger, "E. Escallier" in *L'Art en France sous le Second Empire*, Paris, Grand Palais 1979, pp. 231–2 (ill.); Paris Arch. Nat. F21:138, 215, 306, 314, 447, 493, 522; Paris Salon 1857, 1861, 1867, 1872, 1873, 1874, 1875; *La Sentinelle du Jura*, 22 June 1888; *Thieme*; *Witt*. FU
See illustration on page 33

ESMÉNARD, Nathalie-Elma, *later* Renaud *1798–1872*
Pupil of Redouté. Exhib. Paris Salon 1822 and 1827 e.g. *Tableau de Fleurs*, 1827. M: seven works in Cambridge, Fitzwilliam Museum (Broughton coll.)
LIT *Broughton* 1974; *Broughton* 1977; *Broughton* 1979; *Hardouin-Fugier Grafe* 1981 (ill.); *Paris Salon* 1827; *Broughton* 1983

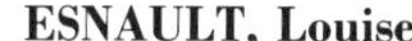

ESNAULT, Louise
Exhib. *Fleurs*, on faience, Paris Salon 1880
LIT *Bellier*

ESPAGNAT, Georges d' *1870–1950*
b. Paris. Painted genre, figures and flowers. Though most flowers by this artist are 20th-century paintings, he may have produced earlier ones
LIT *Bénézit*; *Orsay*; *Thieme*

ESTABLIE
b. Paris. Pupil of J. Gerderez. Exhib. *Bourriche de roses*, Paris Noir et Blanc Salon 1888
LIT *Paris Noir et Blanc Salon* 1888

ESTACHON, Louis-Antoine *1819–1857*
b. La-Tour-d'Aigner (Vaucluse). Pupil of Camille. Painted landscapes and still-lifes and exhibited these subjects at the Paris Salon from 1847–1855
LIT *Bénézit*. PM

ESTACHY, Dominique *1794–1868*
Active in Lyon *c.*1830
LIT *Audin Vial*

ESTIENNE, Giovanni
Exhib. *Fleurs*, Lille Salon 1866
LIT *Lille Salon* 1866. G and LT

ESTRAGNAT, Pierre *b.1874*
Pupil of Castex-Dégrange, Lyon BA (CFD 1892)
LIT *Hardouin-Fugier Grafe*

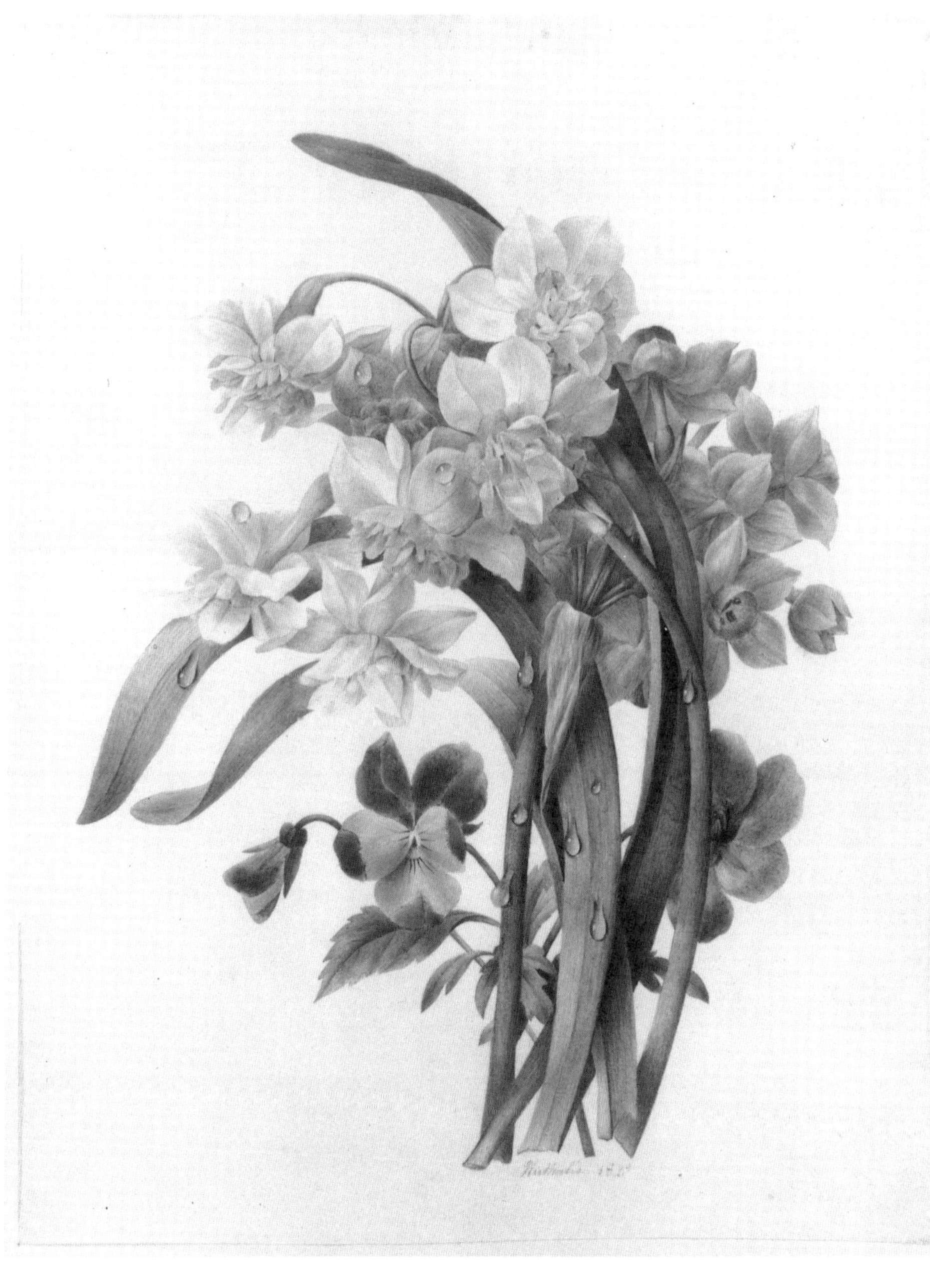

Nathalie-Elma Esménard

Watercolour and bodycolour on vellum, $10\frac{3}{4} \times 8\frac{1}{4}$ in. (27.7 × 21.2 cm.), signed and dated 1823
Cambridge, Fitzwilliam Museum, (Broughton Collection)

ETEVENOT, *see* LESCA

EUDES, Eugène-Jules
b. Choisy-le-Roy (Seine). Painted flowers in wc. Designed plates for *Album Vilmorin*. Exhib. *Pavots*, Dijon Salon 1890
LIT *Album Vilmorin*; *Bénézit*; *Dijon Salon* 1890

EULER, Pierre-Nicolas *1846–c.1913*
Pupil of Reignier, Lyon BA (CFD 1864). Entered 1864 and 1868 Lyon Société des Amis-des-Arts FDC. Textile designer, Lyon and Paris. Exhib. Lyon Salon from 1872 e.g. *Fleurs des champs*, 1875, *Fleurs de printemps*, 1897; *Bouquet de roses*, *Giroflées et violettes*, Dijon Salon 1897; *La Saison des violettes*, Lyon Salon 1898; *Bouquet de roses*, Grenoble Salon 1899; *Cyclamens*, Lyon Salon 1903; *Roses*, Grenoble Salon 1909; *Roses*, *Chardons*, Lyon Salon 1913. His 1898 *Saison des violettes* is in the Musée des Beaux-Arts, Lyon
LIT *Bénézit*; *Dijon Salon* 1897; *Hardouin-Fugier Grafe*; *Hardouin-Fugier Grafe* 1982 (ill.); *Thieme*

EUZIÈRE DE LA VALETTE, Eva
b. Nice (Alpes-Maritimes). Pupil of Leroy. Exhib. *Violettes*, wc, Paris Salon 1880; *Vase de fleurs*, wc, Lyon Salon 1882
LIT *Lyon Salon* 1882; *Paris Salon* 1880

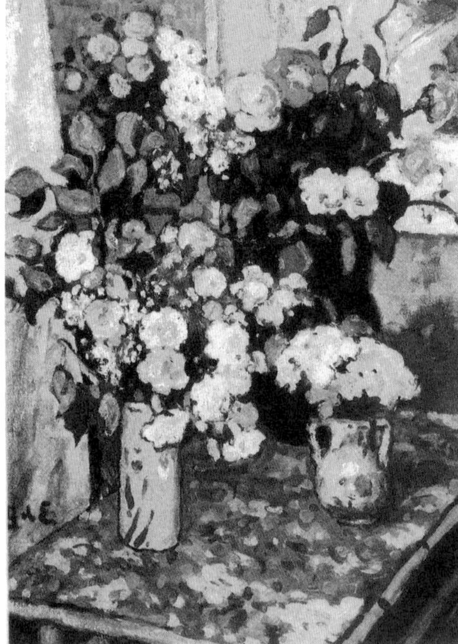

Georges d'Espagnat (*above*)

Oil on canvas, 29⅞ × 22 in. (76 × 56 cm.), signed with initials
Courtesy Christie's, New York

Louis-Antoine Estachon

Oil on canvas, 21 × 17¼ in. (53.5 × 43.8 cm.), signed and dated 1852
Courtesy Christie's, London

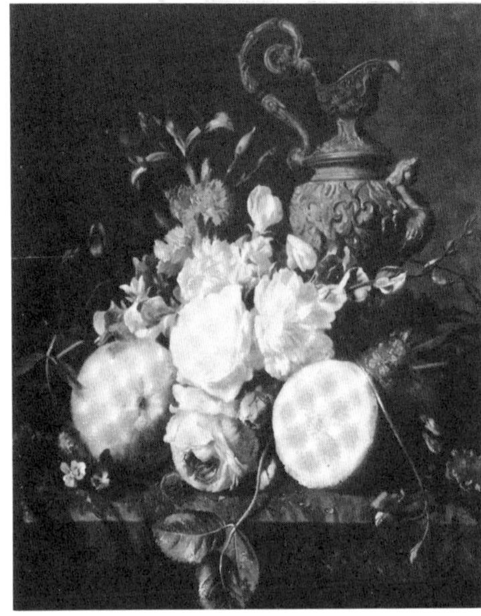

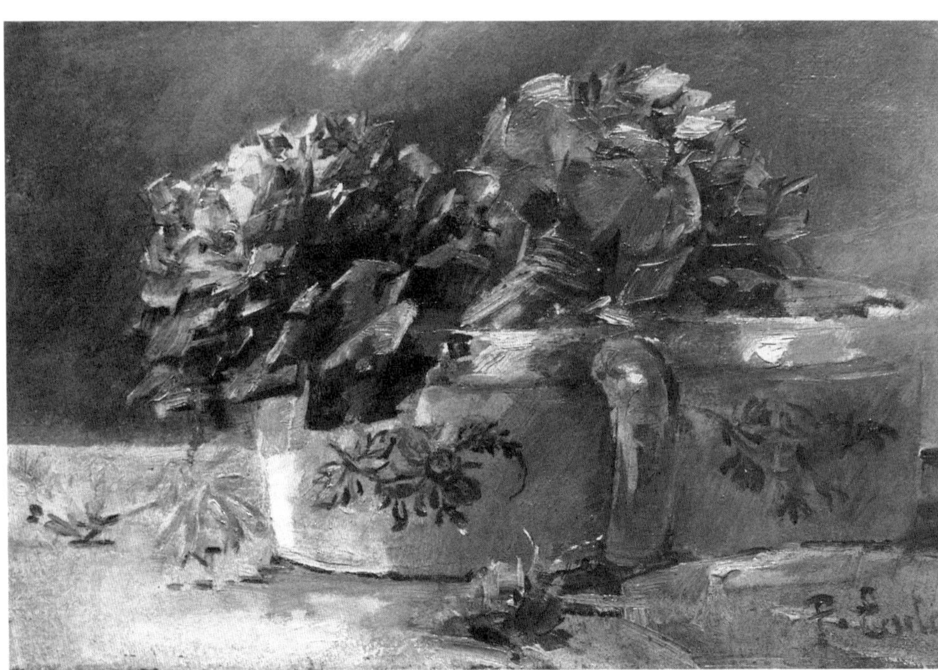

Pierre-Nicolas Euler

Oil on canvas, 8¾ × 12½ in. (22 × 32 cm.), signed
Private collection

F

F.A.
Painted *Rosier*, wc, *Rose*, wc, dated 1814, Paris BMAD (Maciet coll.)
LIT *Paris BMAD*

FABRE, Joseph ***b.1867***
Pupil of Castex-Dégrange, Lyon BA (CFD 1889–91)
LIT *Hardouin-Fugier Grafe*

FABREGUETTES, François-Jean ***b.1801***
b. Privas (Ardèche). Pupil of Girodet, Paris BA. Painted fruit, still-lifes and, occasionally, flowers. Exhib. Paris Salon 1833–1850 e.g. *Bouquet de dahlias*, 1850
LIT *Bellier*; *Bénézit*; *Thieme*

FAGEZ, ***see*** **FRANCHON**

FAGUET, Auguste
fl. 1864–1900. Designed plates for E. Bureau, *Monographie des bignoniacées*, Paris (Baillière) 1864; H.E. Baillon, *Dictionnaire de botanique*, Paris (Hachette) 1876–1892, and *Histoire des plantes*, 1867–1895. *Traité de botanique médicale phanérogamique*, Paris, 1883–1884
LIT *Nissen* I, 61, 298; *Paris MAD*

FAIVRE, Paul-Emile-Denis ***1821–1868***
b. Metz (Moselle). Pupil of Maréchal (Metz). Painted still-lifes and flowers. Exhib. Paris Salon 1855–1866 and *Fleurs et fruits d'automne*, *Roses trémières*, *Pavots et coquelicots*, Paris Exposition Universelle 1855; Lyon Salon *Le matin, fleurs*, 1858, *Bouquet de roses trémières et jasmin de Virginie*, 1861; *Pavots rouges et blancs*, Strasbourg Salon (300 francs), 1862; *Pivoines blanches et iris*, Lyon Salon 1863; *Pavots du caucase et tourneforts*, Strasbourg Salon 1864; M: Metz, Nancy
LIT *Bellier*; *Bénézit*; *Lyon Salon* 1858, 1861, 1863; *Paris Exposition Universelle* 1855; *Paris MAD*; *Strasbourg Salon* 1862, 1864; *Thieme*

FAIVRE, Tony ***1830–1905***
b. Besançon (Doubs). Pupil of Picot. Exhib. Paris Salon 1848–1898. Active in Italy, 1860, Russia 1862. Exhib. Paris Salon *La moisson de fleurs*, fan-leaf, 1861, *Fleurs*, tapestry cartoon, 1879
LIT *Orsay*; *Paris Salon* 1861, 1879; *Thieme*

FAJON, Rose-Jeanne, ***née*** **Boquet** ***b.1798***
b. Marseille. Pupil of Fajon and Hersent. Exhib. portraits and flowers in wc, Paris Salon 1833–1834. *Corbeille de fleurs*, Geneva sale, 1–2 June 1988, lot 23
LIT *Bellier*; *Bénézit*; *Paris Salon* 1833, 1834; *Thieme*

FAMCHON, Alphonse-Adolphe-Onésime ***b.1821***
b. Boulogne-sur-Mer (Pas-de-Calais). Pupil of Gobert. Exhib. Paris Salon 1864–1880 e.g. *Oiseaux et fleurs*, 1867, *Gibier et fleurs*, 1872
LIT *Bellier*; *Bénézit*; *Paris Salon* 1867, 1872; *Thieme*

FANO, Alice
Pupil of M. Carpentier. Exhib. Paris UFPS *Chrysanthèmes* et grenades, *Pavots et cerises*, *Lilas*, *Fleurs de Nice*, *Roses*, 1896, *Chrysanthèmes*, *Boules de neige*, 1898
LIT *Paris UFPS* 1896, 1898

FANTIN-LATOUR, Ignace Henri Jean-Théodore ***1836–1904***
b. Grenoble (Isère). Pupil of his father, an occasional flower painter, then of Lecoq de Boisbaudran *c.*1851, after the Fantin family settled in Paris. Fantin's early works were copies after old masters in the Louvre (where he met Whistler) and a few portraits. He may have taken to flower painting in 1856 to supplement his meagre earnings. In 1859 he paid his first visit to England, where, thanks to Ruth and Edwin Edwards who were to be life-long patrons and friends, he soon became a most sought-after flower painter. His flowers always sold well in England and found their way into many a private collection (e.g. Ionides). Fantin often stayed with the Edwardses at Sunbury and repeatedly exhibited flowers at the Royal Academy. In 1876 the painter married Victoria Dubourg, herself a flower painter, and from that time onwards painted flowers at his wife's Buré (Orne) country house. In France, Fantin's most admired works were his portraits and allegorical compositions, not his flower paintings. These came into their own after Fantin's death (cf. obituaries and reviews of the 1906 posthumous exhibition). Fantin-Latour is *the* 19th-century French flower painter *par excellence*

In the following list, Madame Fantin-Latour's catalogue numbers and dates have been kept. Through the generous help of Philippe and Sylvie Brame, the location of all flower paintings with Madame Fantin-Latour's catalogue numbers, which are today in museums, has been given. Descriptions have been omitted in some instances.

1856–1857
85, *Trois reines-marguerites blanches, petite branche de bruyère*
1860
147, 148, *Fleurs*; 149, *Bouquet de tournesols et autres fleurs dans une bouteille carrée en verre*; 180 (London)
1861
183, *Chrysanthèmes pompons dans un verre*; 184, *Lys, chrysanthèmes, véroniques*, roses . . . *dans un verre sombre*; 185, *Dahlias, reines-marguerites*,

roses, bleuets . . . dans un vase arrondi; 186, *Fleurs mêlées dans un pot vert*
1862
191, *Lys roses . . . dans un verre droit*; 192, *Branche de lys, rose, capucines . . . dans un verre bleu sombre coupé par le cadre*; 193, *Roses, phlox . . .* 195, *Narcisses et tulipes* (Paris, Orsay)
1863
218, *Lys pelargonium dans un vase de porcelaine blanche*; 220, *n.m. avec roses blanches dans un verre*; 221, *Fleurs dans un verre*
1864
239, *Roses blanches dans un verre droit* (London); 240, *Roses, narcisses, jacinthes, tulipes . . . dans une boule de verre*; 241, *Camélias, primevères, boules de neige dans une boule de verre*; 242, *Roses, lys, tulipes dans un boule de verre*; 243, *Roses, oeillets, véroniques . . . dans une boule de verre*; 244, (London); 245, (London); 248, (Saint Quentin)
1865
276 b. *n.m. avec bouquet de dahlias dans un vase blanc* (Paris, Orsay); 277. *n.m. avec bouquet de marguerites*; 278, *n.m. avec pot de primevère*; 279, *n.m. avec quelques jacinthes . . . mauves*; 280, *n.m. avec tulipes . . .*; 280b, *n.m. avec vase de fleurs diverses*
1866
285, *n.m. avec vase de camélias* (Washington); 286, *Lys du Japon . . .*; 288, *n.m. avec Lilas, giroflées* (New York); 289, *n.m. avec hortensias, anémones dans un vase rond en cristal* (Toledo); 290, *n.m. avec pot de primevère* (Otterlo); 291, *n.m. avec pot d'azalée*
1868
311, *n.m. avec dahlias dans un vase vert*
1869
325, *n.m. avec fleurs de printemps dans un vase cornet* (Grenoble); 326, *n.m. avec Camomille*; 327, *Pieds d'alouettes dans un vase, roses trémières, glaïeuls* (Edinburgh); 332, *Dahlias*; 333, *Coucous, jacinthes, giroflées dans un vase bleu foncé*
1870
428, *Roses . . . dans un vase sombre*; 436, *Phlox*, *442,Bouquet de dahlias*; 443, *n.m. avec Camélia dans un verre*; 446, *Narcisses, lilas blanc, tulipes jaunes, pivoines sur la table*; 453, *Fleurs blanches*; 454, *Étude d'hortensia*; 457, *Roses blanches noisettes* (Houston); 458, *n.m. avec julienne blanche* (San Francisco)
1871
528, *Aubépine rose*; 529, *Narcisses . . . dans un verre long*; 530, *Giroflées blanches dans un verre droit*; 532, *Jacinthes, tulipes, pensées*; (Hartford, Conn.); 533, *Pensées dans une bourriche*; 534, *Pieds d'alouette dans un verre*; 535, *n.m. avec delphinium, iris, giroflée blanche* (London); 536, *Roses . . . dans un verre à champagne*; 537, *Roses roses et blanches dans un vase en porcelaine* (San Diego); 539, *Chrysanthèmes*; 540, *Pivoines, blanches et bluets*; 541, *Camomilles dans un verre foncé, bouquet de dahlias*; 542, *Pensées et petites marguerites* (Otterlo); 543, *Roses blanches dans un verre droit*; 544, *Oeillets dans un verre long* (Oxford); 545, *Roses jaunes dans un verre long* (Oxford); 546, Bouquet de dahlias (Birmingham); 547, *Roses blanches dans un verre bas*; 548, *Phlox blanc*; 551, *Chrysanthèmes dans un vase de porcelaine blanche* (Huston); 552, *Chrysanthèmes dans un petit vase de verre vert foncé*; 553, *Chrysanthèmes blancs, jaunes, roses dans un petit verre long*; 554, *Roses blanches dans un vase de verre vert*; 556, *Dahlias, deux branches de lupin*; 557, *Pensées dans une bourriche*, 558; *n.m. avec bouquet de dahlias*; 559, *n.m. avec glaïeuls rouges*; 560, *Iris et jacinthes*
1872
600, 601, *Fleur de cerisier simple et double dans un verre*; 602, *Aubépines, lilas et feuilles* (Otterlo); 603, *Giroflées jaunes, jacinthes, lilas, roses, narcisses, jonquilles*; 604, *Giroflées, jacinthe, jonquilles, narcisses*; 605, *Pensées dans des petits pots*; 606, *Lilas dans une boule de verre*; 607, *Chrysanthèmes*; 608, *Pivoines dans un verre bleu foncé* (The Hague); 609, *Aubépines blanches et roses*; 610, *n.m. avec pivoines dans une boule de verre*; 612, *petite branche de pommier en fleurs* (Boulogne sur Mer); 613, *Giroflées blanches*; 614, *Oeillets blancs, roses . . . dans un verre*; 615, *Aubépines roses dans un verre à champagne*; 616, *Pivoines dans un vase bleu et blanc* (Los Angeles); 617, *Tulipes,*

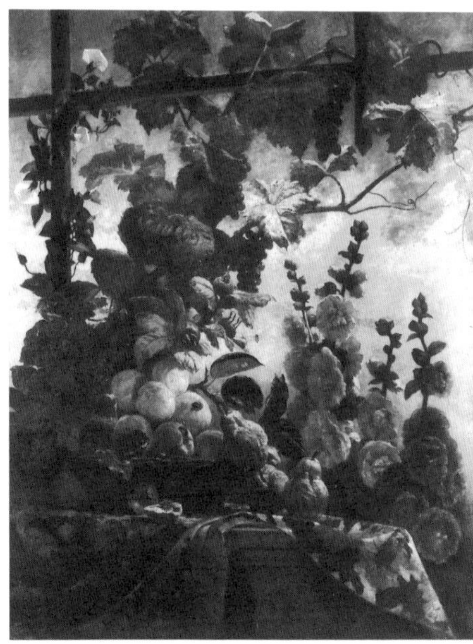

Paul-Emile-Denis Faivre

Oil on canvas, $61\frac{3}{4}$ × 50 in. (157 × 127 cm.), signed
Metz, Musée d'Art et d'Histoire

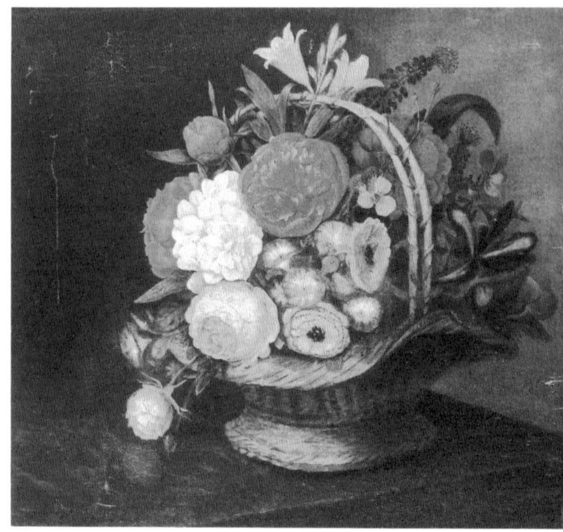

Rose-Jeanne Fajon

Oil on canvas, 18 × $21\frac{3}{4}$ in. (46 × 55 cm.), signed and dated 1842
Private collection

narcisses, jacinthes, jonquilles, giroflées; 618, *Oeillets dans un verre*; 619, *Narcisses, giroflées, jacinthes dans une flûte coupée au milieu* (Edinburgh); 620, *Narcisses*; 621, *Roses, jaunes de Perse, une rose*; 622, *Roses moussues roses*; 623, *n.m. avec chrysanthèmes blancs*; 624, *Roses blanches dans un verre à pied*; 625, *Roses dans un vase sombre*; 626, *Roses blanches*; 627, *Haut d'un rosier*; 628, *Dahlias sur une table*; 629, *Marguerites dans une boule de verre*; 630, *Marguerites et souci dans un verre*; 631, *Roses blanches dans un verre droit*; 632, *Trois roses blanches dans un verre à champagne*; 633, *Roses dans un verre sombre*; 634, *Roses blanches dans un verre droit* (Dublin); 635, *Chrysanthèmes jaunes dans un pot de terre*; 636, *n.m. avec roses blanches*; 637, *Gros bouquet sans vase* (Manchester); 639, *Roses blanches*; 640, *Roses dans un verre*; 641, *Dahlias et marguerites*; 642, *Roses de Malmaison dans un verre long* (Oxford); 644, *Roses dans un verre droit* (Bradford); 645; *Roses dans un verre à pied*; 646, *Bouquet de dahlias dans un vase de porcelaine blanc* (Boston); 647, *Roses de Malmaison dans un vase*

1873

671,. *n.m. avec touffe de rhododendrons* (Chicago); 672, *Narcisses, jacinthes, coucous, giroflées*; 673, *Dahlias; 674, Fleurs d'arbre fruitier*; 675, *Coucous*; 676, *Pensées*; 677, *Narcisses, jonquilles, jacinthes, giroflées et primevères* (Manchester); 678, *Lilas blanc*; 679, *n.m. avec roses blanches*; 680, *Roses dans un verre à pied*; 682, *Giroflée blanche*; 683, *Roses dans une flûte à champagne*; 685, *Roses dans un verre long*; 686, *Gros bouquet de dahlias, marguerites . . . sans vase* (Aberdeen); 687, *Bouquet de chrysanthèmes*; 688, *Petites dahlias dans un verre bleu sombre*, 689, *Dahlias dans une boule de verre*; 690, *Roses dans un verre* (Birmingham); 691, *Roses*; 692, *Fleurs de pommier*; 693, *n.m. avec roses blanches*; 694, *Bouquet de chrysanthèmes sans vase*; 695, *Roses de Nice*; 696, *Roses et mimosa dans un verre à pied*

1874

706, *n.m. avec azalées blancs* (Gothenburg); 707, *Azalées, bruyère et rose dans un cornet de porcelaine blanc*; 708, *Roses blanches dans un vase blanc*; 709, *Roses sans verre*; 710, *Touffe de rhododendrons* (Cologne); 711, *Pivoines, roses dans un pot*; 712, *Pivoines, boules de neige*; 714, *Roses* (Coventry); 715, *Pivoines dans un verre long*; 716; *Pivoines, oeillets blancs . . . esquisse*, 717, *Grand rosier blanc et laurier rose sans vase*; 718, *Bouquet de roses blanches dans un verre bleu foncé*; 719, *Dahlias dans un vase de porcelaine*; 720, *Oeillets sans vase*; 721, *Oeillets dans un verre à champagne*; 722, *Roses dans un verre haut*; 723, *Roses jaunes*; 731, *Fleurs et fruits*; 732, *"Gâchis" de roses*; 733, *Chrysanthèmes dans deux pots (Glasgow); 734, Chrysanthèmes dans un vase de porcelaine bleu*; 735, *n.m. avec pensées dans une bourriche et dans de petits pots* (New York); 736, *n.m. avec panier de roses thé*

1875

741, *Gros bouquet de chrysanthèmes*; 743, *Azalées blancs et violettes de Parme* (Buenos Aires); 744, *Narcisses blancs dans un verre opalin*; 745, *Pensées dans une bourriche*; 746, *Roses de Perse jaune dans un verre à pied*; 747, *Roses blanches et roses dans un verre*; 748, *Roses blanches dans un vase de verre*; 749, *Roses blanches dans un petit verre*; 750, *Branche de pommier en fleur*; 751, *Bouquet de roses choux dans un vase de porcelaine blanche*; 752, *Bouquet de roses blanches dans un haut verre à pied*; 753, *Petites roses blanches et jaunâtres dans un verre à pied*; 756, *Deux grands rosiers (in situ)* (Philadelphia); 757, *Grosses roses blanches*; 758, *Roses*, 759, *Dahlias sombres*; 760, *Dahlias clairs;* 761, *Marguerites dans un pot brun* (Saint Louis); 762, *Chrysanthèmes dans un pot brun*; 763, *Dahlias dans une corbeille*; 764, *Dahlias*; 766, *Gros bouquet de dahlias*; 767, *Roses de Malmaison dans un verre*; 768, *n.m. avec chrysanthèmes jaunes, rouges et violets*

1876

780, *Fleurs de cerisier, trois pensées*; 781, *Jacinthe, primevère, narcisses, tulipes sans vase*; 782, *Giroflées jaunes et cerisier double*; 783, *Roses jaunes et roses*; 784, *Pivoines* (Montreal); 785, *Roses*; 787, *n.m. avec des fleurs*; 788, *Pieds d'alouette*; 790, *Roses dans un panier*; 791, *Roses jaunes Falcon*; 792, *n.m. avec roses blanches*; 793, *Roses jaunes dans un verre haut*

1877

839, *Roses de Nice dans un verre*; 840, *Narcisses, jacinthe, tulipes, giroflées, coucous, impériales dans une jardinière désargentée* (Amsterdam); 841, *Giroflées* (San Francisco); 842, *Pivoines, boules de neige, myosotis*; 843, *Branche de lys* (London); 844, *n.m. avec balsamines*; 845, *Oeillets dans un verre long*: 846, *Trés petit bouquet de phlox . . .* (Oxford); 847, *Oeillets*; 848, *Roses jaunes et cramoisies* (Dordrecht); 849, *Roses blanches*; 850, *Bouquet avec souci*; 851, *n.m. avec dahlias, roses de Dijon*

1878

874, *Fleurs de printemps*; 875, *Roses sur une table*; 876, *Trois roses*; 877, *Roses de Nice*; 878, *Bouquet de roses*; 879, *Bouquet d'hiver*; 880, *Chrysanthèmes et giroflées*, 881, 883, *Bouquet de roses, pervenches . . .*; 884, *Petit bouquet de narcisses* (Glasgow); 885, *Dahlias*; 886, *Narcisses, tulipes, pensées*; 887, *Dahlias*; 888, *Spirée dans un vase*; 889, *Pivoines, roses, narcisses*; 890, *Pivoines*; 891, *Petit bouquet d'oeillets*; 892, *Pivoines et boules de neige* (Toronto); 893, 894, 895, *Fleurs des champs*; 896, *n.m. avec roses blanches*; 897, *Roses*, 900, *Fleurs des champs*; 902, *n.m. avec roses*; 903, *Pivoines et juliennes*; 904, *Petit bouquet*; 905, *Petit bouquet d'oeillets*; 906, *Roses*; 907, 908, *Oeillets* (Philadelphia); 909, *Roses*; 910, *Fleurs des champs*; 911, *Fleurs sans vase*

1879

933, *Petit bouquet*; 934, *Petit bouquet de printemps*; 935, *Fleurs des champs*; 936, *Fleurs de printemps dans un pot vert*; 937, *Hortensias, giroflées, deux pots de pensées*; 938, *Pensées*; 939, *Petit bouquet des champs*; 940, *Gros bouquet des champs*; 941, *Fleurs*; 942, *Pivoines, gros bouquet*; 943, *roses*; 945, *Fleurs des champs sans vase*; 946, *Glaïeuls*; 947, *Roses sans vase*; 948, *Roses dans un verre long*; 949, *Fleurs de printemps* (Bury); 950, *Roses Gloire de Dijon, Céline Forestier, dans un gros vase*; 951,

Bouquet de roses dans une flûte de champagne (Manchester); 952, *Petites roses*; 953, *Chrysanthèmes* (Glasgow); 955, *Dahlias dans un verre vert* (Buenos Aires); 956, *Roses*; 958, *Chrysanthèmes, lupins*; 959, *Dahlias, glaïeuls* (London), 960, *Pois de senteur, giroflées* (Tournai)

1880

990, *Coucous anémones*; 991, *Renoncules et narcisses*; 992, *Pensées dans des pots* (Oxford); 993, *Lilas et fleurs d'arbre fruitier dans une boule de verre*; 995, *Roses de janvier dans un pot gris*; 996, *Tulipes*; 997, *Branche de lilas* (San

Henri Fantin-Latour

Oil on canvas, $19\frac{3}{4} \times 24\frac{3}{8}$ in. (50.2 × 61.9 cm.)
signed and dated 'Fantin '87
Courtesy Christie's, London

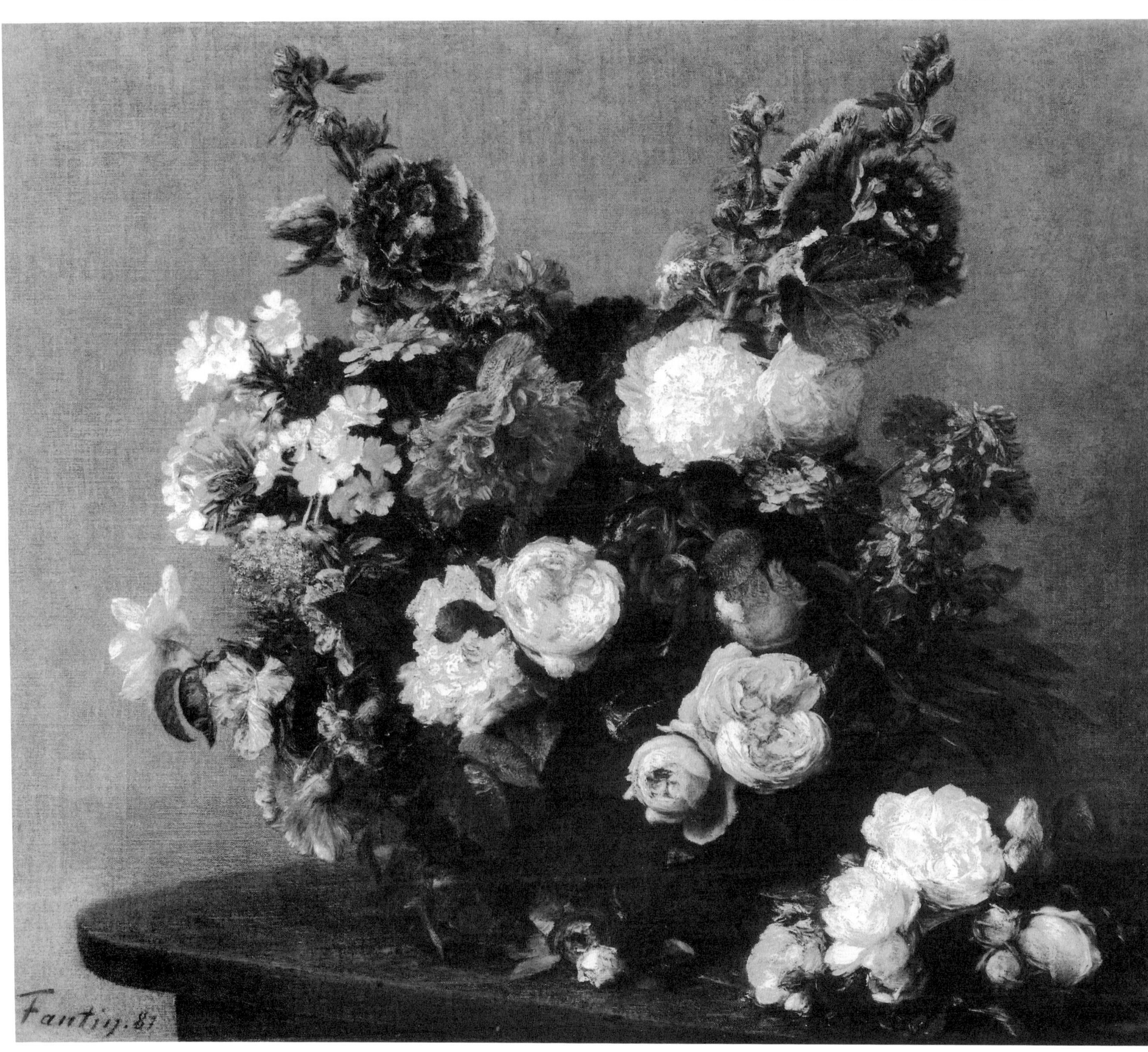

Francisco); 998, *Pluie d'or, aubépine*; 999, *Panier de roses*; 1,000, *Roses dans un petit verre*; 1,001, *Glaïeuls, pluie d'or, roses dans un panier*; 1,002, *Reines-marguerites, roses, violettes blanches*; 1,003, *Roses, Gloire de Dijon* (Otterlo); 1,004, *Capucine grimpant le long de bâtons* (London)

1881

1,002, *Grand bouquet de roses* (Tournai); 1,023, *Gros bouquet de phlox, roses...*; 1,024, *Azalées et pensées*; 1,025, *Jonquilles et capucines*, 1,026, *Narcisses, giroflées, primevères*; 1,027, *Primevères, deux ou trois violettes*; 1,028, *Gros bouquet de pivoines, roses et lilas*; 1,029, *Roses blanches et roses*; 1,030, 1,031, *Fleurs diverses, en pendant*; 1,032, *Glaïeuls et roses*; 1,033, *Pétunias* (Detroit); 1,034, *Roses dans une coupe*; 1,035, *Zinnias*; 1,036, *Roses et Vénus-dan-le-bois ou nigelles bleues* (San Franciso); 1037, *Roses*, 1,038, *Roses dans un pot de grès*; 1,039, *Capucines et fleurs*; 1,040, *Roses dans une boule verte* (Chicago); 1,041, *Roses dans un panier coupé*; 1,042, *Zinnias*; 1,043, *Roses*; 1,044, *Roses dans une boule verte*

1882

1,074, *Roses de Nice*; 1,077, *Fleurs de poirier*; 1,078, *Pivoines dans un vase vert*; 1,079, *Pensées* (Otterlo); 1,080, *Narcisses et fleurs diverses*; 1,082, *Bouquet de Proserpine, fleurs de genévrier*; 1,083, *Grand bouquet avec capucine tombant*; 1,084, *Roses trémières*; 1,085, *Pieds d'alouette*; 1,086, 1,087, 1,088, *Roses*; 1,089, *Roses Gloire de Dijon dans un verre, roses dans une corbeille*; 1,090, *Rose dans un verre droit*; 1,092, *Roses dans une coupe*; 1,093, *Trois roses*; 1,094, *Grand bouquet de chrysanthèmes*

1883

1,105, *Pensées...sans vase*; 1,106, *Roses*; 1,107, *Pensées*; 1,108, *Jacinthes, primevères, coucous...*; 1,109, *Jonquilles, narcisses*; 1,110, *Fleurs de pommier*; 1,111, *Lilas blanc*; 1,112, *Renoncules*; 1,113, *Roses*; 1,114, *Pensées sans vase*; 1,115, *Roses Maréchal Niel*; 1,116, *Pivoines, iris, narcisses doubles*, lys; 1,117, *Bouquet mêlé*; 1,118, *Lys sans vase*; 1,119, *Branche de roses dans une carafe-boule*; 1,120, *Oeillets blancs dans un verre allongé*; 1,122, *Grand bouquet de roses dans un vase rond, clématites bleues*; 1,123, *Cinq roses Malmaison dans une carafe*; 1,124, *Pavots dans un gros pichet brun*; 1,125, *Deux roses Céline Forestier, nigelles dans de petits verres*; 1,126, *Roses dans une coupe bleue*; 1,127, *Roses dans un pot de grès*; 1,128, *Bouquet de roses, en largeur*; 1,129, *Panier de roses*; 1,131, *Grand bouquet de fleurs diverses, roses, zinnias, dahlias*

1884

1,160, *Roses dans une coupe*; 1,161, *Gros bouquet de roses*; 1,162, *Petit bouquet dans une carafe boule*; 1,163, *Roses trémières sans vase*; 1,164, *Dahlias dans une bassine*; 1,165, *Gloire de Dijon dans une carafe boule*; 1,166, *Anémones blanches du Japon dans un vase de verre* (Aberdeen); 1,167, *Roses dans un vase et dans une bassine*; 1,168, *Chrysanthèmes dans un pot brun*; 1,169, *Cinq roses dans un verre droit*; 1,170, *Roses foncées dans une boule de verre* (Minneapolis)

1885

1,208, *Oeillets dans un vase de verre*; 1,209, *Roses Madame Pauvert dans un verre droit*; 1,210, *Roses dans un verre droit*; 1,211, *Roses dans une coupe* (Williamstown, Mass.); 1,212, *Pieds d'alouette dans un vase, coupe de roses*; 1,213, *Grand bouquet de roses dans un vase boule en verre*; 1,214, *Grand panier de roses*; 1,215 (Williamstown, Mass.); 1,216, *Roses*; 1,217, *Roses dans un pot de grès*; 1,218, *Bouquet de petites roses*; 1,219, Roses (Ottawa)

1886

1,256, *Pois de senteur, nigelles dans un petit verre*; 1,257, *Roses dans un verre droit*; 1,258, *Petit bouquet de roses*; 1,260, *Bouquet de dahlias*; 1,261, *Grand bouquet de roses*; 1,262, *Zinnias dans une coupe* (reprod. in *Lithographies*, Bénédite); 1,263, *Fleurs dans une bassine*; 1,264, *Fleurs dans un gros vase de verre à pieds cabochons* (London); 1,265, *Roses*; 1,266, *Roses jaunes*; 1,267, *Roses dans un gros verre* (Coventry); 1,268, *Quatre roses dans un verre à pied* (Oxford); 1,270, *n.m. avec rose rouge*

1887

1,296, *Chrysanthèmes d'été dans un verre à champagne*; 1,297, *Verveine*; 1,298, *Delphiniums*; 1,299, *Pensées dans un vase de grès*; 1,300, *Reine des prés*; 1,301, *Oeillets*; 1,302, *Capucines*; 1,303, *Zinnias dans un verre allongé* (Adelaide); 1,304, *Pied d'alouette dans une carafe boule*; 1,305, *Quatre roses dans un verre, roses dans une coupe*; 1,306, *Fleurs de Normandie dans un vase droit* (Amsterdam); 1,307, *Oeillets dans un verre droit*; 1,308, *Roses dans un gros verre*; 1,309, *Roses dan une vase bleu*; 1,310, *Roses*

1888

1,330, *Roses Maréchal Niel*; 1,331, *Pois de senteur dans un verre*; 1,332, *Lys dans un verre*; 1,333, *roses dan un panier*; 1,334, *Pieds d'alouette*; 1,335, *Phlox blanc dans un verre*; 1,336, *Capucines dans une carafe boule*; 1,337, *Pétunias doubles*; 1,338, *Géraniums*; 1,339, *Fleurs*; 1,341, *Roses dans un grand vase sur pied* (Philadelphia); 1,342, *Roses*; 1,343, *Roses dans un vase bleu vénitien* (Edinburgh); 1,344, *Roses blanches dans un verre vert à panse*

1889

1,371, *Roses Aimé Vibert*; 1,372, *Roses* (Lyon); 1,373, *Chrysanthèmes dans un verre à pied* (Kansas City); 1,374, *Bouquet de roses, roses trémières dans une bassine*; 1,375, *Roses trémières dans un vase*; 1,376, *roses dans une bassine*; 1,377, *Bouquet de roses* (Philadelphia)

1890

1,403, *Anémones et renoncules dans un verre*; 1,405, *Narcisses sans vase*; 1,406, *Pâquerettes et oreilles d'ours*; 1,407, *Roses sans vase*; 1,409, *Roses dans un vase bleu*; 1,410, *Rose dans un verre à pied*; 1,411, *Roses rouges*; 1,412, *Roses Aimé Vibert dans un vase boule*; 1,413, *Oeillets*; 1,414, *Dahlias dans une carafe*; 1,415, *Pavots dans un vase de cristal*; 1,416, *Roses trémières dans un vase*; 1,417, *Bouquet de dahlias, roses trémières, capucines roses*; 1,418, *Roses dans un broc de verre, capucines*; 1,420, *Petit bouquet de roses dans un vase rond*; 1,421, *Roses dans un panier plat* (London)

1891
1,442, *Pieds d'alouette dans un vase de cristal* (Philadelphia); 1,443, *Pieds d'alouette, roses trémières dans un vase de cristal*; 1,444, *Pavots blancs* (Adelaide); 1,445, *Oeillets d'Inde dans un verre vert à cabochons* (Melbourne); 1,446, *Zinnias dans une coupe*; 1,447, *Zinnias dans un panier*; 1,448, *Roses* (Waltham, Mass.) 1,449, *Bouquet dans un vase de verre*; 1,450, *Panier de roses* (Lisbon); 1,451, *Rose Coquette des Blanches dans une jardinière de verre*; 1,452, *Bouquet de pivoines dans un vase en verre opalin*; 1,453, *Roses Coquette des Blanches*; 1,454, *Roses jaunes Belles Lyonnaises*; 1,455, *Panier de roses*; 1,456, *Roses*
1892
1,473, *Bouquet de roses*; 1,474, *Reines marguerites dans un verre droit* (San Francisco), 1,476, *Oeillets d'Inde dans une boule de verre*; 1,477, *Zinnias dans une bassine*; 1,478, *Pieds d'alouette dans un vase* (Glasgow); 1,479, *Roses trémières dans un vase*; 1,480, *Fleurs variées*; 1,481, *Panier de fleurs*
1893
1,507, *Roses dans un vase de verre*; 1,508, *Zinnias dans un jardinière de cristal* (Boulogne sur Mer); 1,509, *Oeillets d'Inde dans ce même vase*; 1,510, *Panier de fleurs*; 1,512, *Dahlias*; 1,513, *Capucines dans un vase de verre*

1894
1,547, *Roses* (Oxford), 1,540, *Roses dans un vase à panse*; 1,549, *n.m. avec roses dans un vase de cristal*; 1,550, *Bouquet de fleurs dans une bassine*; 1,551, *Roses jaunes*; 1,552, *Roses dans un gros verre* (Durban); 1,554, *Pivoines*; 1,555, *Bouquet de roses*; 1,556, *Roses* (Rheims); 1,562, *Roses*; 1,563, *Roses dans une jardinière*
1895
1,590, *Roses Gloire de Dijon* (Edinburgh); 1,592, *Roses de la France* (Glasgow); 1,593, *Zinnias*; 1,594, *n.m. avec fleurs*; 1,595, *Mauves blanches et mauves dans un vase*; 1,596, *Roses trémières sans vase*; 1,597, *Bouquet de roses blanches, roses thé dans un verre*

1898
1,715, *Oeillets*
1899
1,765, *Roses dans un verre long*; 1,766, *Roses blanches*; 1,767, *Narcisses et giroflées*; 1,768, *Dahlias*; 1,769, *Anémones et renoncules*; 1,770, *Roses Gloire de Dijon*; 1,772, 1,773, *Roses*; 1,774, *Oeillets*; 1,775, *Roses* (Boulogne sur Mer); 1,776, *Roses Gloire de Dijon*; 1,777, *Oeillets sans vase* (Memphis); 1,778, *Oeillets dans un verre droit*; 1,779, *Capucines*; 1,780, *Pensées dans une coupe*; 1,781, *Quelques roses*; 1,782, *Chrysanthèmes sans vase*; 1,783, *Pieds d'alouette*; 1,784, *Fleurs sans vase*; 1,786, *Oeillets dans un verre*; 1,787, *Oeillets dans un verre droit* (Boulogne sur Mer); 1,788, *Petits oeillets*
1900
1,843, *Roses, verveines, dahlias dans un vase*; 1,844, *Bouquet*; 1,845, *Bouquet dans une bassine, glaïeuls, zinnias, dahlias*; 1,846, *Pensées*; 1,847, *Roses*; 1,848, *Fleurs*
1902
1,925, *Fleurs*; 1,926, *Oeillets*; 1,927, *Roses*; 1,928, *Fleurs*; 1,929, *Pensées* (Boulogne sur Mer); 1,930, *Oeillets blancs* (Philadelphia); 1,931, *Oeillets*; 1,932, *Fleurs* (Johannesburg); 1,933, *Zinnias, dahlias*; 1,934, *Petites roses*; 1,935, *Roses*; 1,936, *Roses*; 1,937, *Pivoines*; 1,938, *Chrysanthèmes*; 1,940, *Fleurs*; 1,941, *Phlox, chrysanthèmes, pieds d'alouette sans vase*; 1,942, *Roses*; 1,943, *Pieds d'alouette*; 1,944, *Oeillet* (The Hague); 1,945, *Bourriche de pensées*
1903
1,996, *Fleurs de printemps*; 1,997, *Pivoines*; 1,998, *Pensées*; 1,999, *Giroflées, iris*; 2,000, *Iris*; 2,001, *Botte d'oeillets*; 2,002, *Sept roses dans un verre*; 2,003, 2,004, 2,005, 2,006, *Roses*; 2,184 (Ghent); 2,217 (Paris)

LIT V. Fantin-Latour, *Catalogue de l'oeuvre complet de Fantin-Latour, 1849–1904*, Paris (Floury) 1911; *Orsay*; Paris Bibl. Nat. Est.; Paris, *Fantin-Latour*, Réunion des Musées Nationaux, Grand Palais, 1982; Brame and Lorenceau

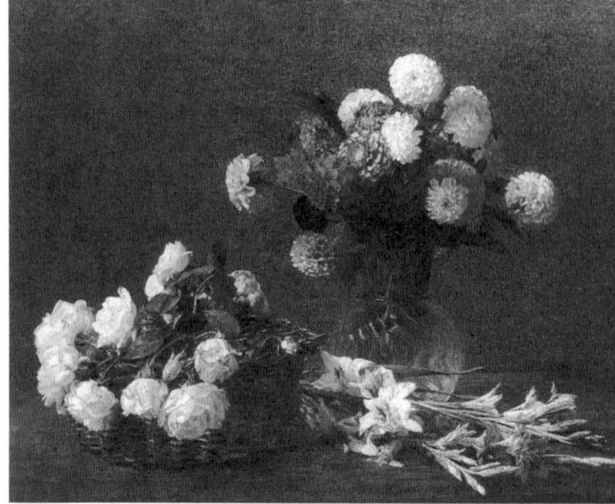

Henri Fantin-Latour

Oil on canvas
$23\frac{1}{4} \times 29$ in. (59 × 74 cm.)
Signed and dated '96
Courtesy Sotheby's, London

FANTIN-LATOUR, ***see*** **DUBOURG**

FANTY-LESCURE, Emma ***b.1835***
b. La Rochelle (Charente-Maritime). Pupil of Dumoulin, Pitolet and E. Claude. Exhib. Paris Salon from 1876 e.g. *Fleurs des champs*, *Anémones*, gouache, 1878, *Chrysanthèmes*, 1880, *Roses et boules de neige*, 1898
LIT *Bellier*; *Bénézit*; *Paris Salon* 1880, 1898; *Thieme*

FATIN, Jean-Antoine ***b.1824***
b. Lyon. Pupil of Thierriat, Lyon BA (CFD 1842). Painted landscapes and flowers
LIT *Bellier*; *Bénézit*; *Hardouin-Fugier Grafe*; *Thieme*

FAUCHÉ, Léon ***b.1868***
b. Briey (Meurthe-et-Moselle). Pupil of Nancy BA, Aimé Morot, Chartran, Friendly with Anquetin and Toulouse-Lautrec. Painted portraits, genre, landscapes and still-lifes. Exhib. *Fleurs*, Paris Indép. 1892
LIT *Bénézit*; *Paris Indép.* 1892; *Schurr* I, 127

FAUCHEUR, Léonie-Eugénie ***b.1873***
b. Paris. Pupil of Rivoire. Painted flowers
LIT *Bénézit*

FAUDI
Pupil of Berjon, Lyon BA (CFD 1813)
LIT *Hardouin-Fugier Grafe*

FAUGERON, Adolphe ***b.1866***
Exhib. *Fleurs et parfums*, Paris Salon 1896
LIT *Bénézit*; *Paris Salon* 1896 (ill.); *Thieme*

FAULCON, Louise-Adèle, ***née*** **Guichard** ***1817–1897***
b. Crémieu (Isère). Pupil of Lessore and Ravier. Friendly with Carrand and Fontanesi. Painted landscapes and flowers. Exhib. Paris Salon 1878–1894 Lyon Salon from 1878 e.g. *Fleurs*, 1979 and 1884, *Etude de fleurs*, 1880, *Soucis*, 1881, *Chardons et immortelles*, 1883. Her *Chardons et immortelles* is in the Musée de Grenoble
LIT *Bénézit*; A. Chagny *Un pays aimé des peintres, sites et monuments de la région de Crémieu*, 1929, p. 198; *Lyon Salon* 1879–1881, 1883, 1884; *Thieme*

FAURE, André ***b.1880***
Pupil of Castex-Dégrange, Lyon BA (CFD 1899)
LIT *Hardouin-Fugier Grafe*

FAURE, Charles-Louis
b. Tours (Indre-et-Loire). Pupil of Vernay. Exhib. *Fleurs et fruits*, Paris Salon 1880; Paris SNBA *Fleurs à la lampe*, 1893, *Fleurs au soleil*, 1894, *Pivoines et roses*, 1895
LIT *Paris Salon* 1880; *Paris SNBA* 1893 (ill.), 1894, 1895

FAURE, Eugène ***1822–1878***
b. Seyssinet (Isère). Pupil of David d'Angers and Rude. Painted portraits, landscapes and, occasionally, flowers e.g. *Fleurs*, Grenoble Salon 1850
LIT *Bellier*; *Bénézit*; *Grenoble Salon* 1850; *Thieme*

FAURE, Joannès ***1828–1913***
Pupil of Thierriat, Lyon BA (CFD 1845), op. textile designer
LIT *Hardouin-Fugier Grafe*

FAURE, Johanny ***1832–1906***
b. Saint-Etienne (Loire). Pupil of C. Soulary, Saint-Etienne BA. Thierriat, Lyon BA (CFD 1845), Gleyre and Beauverie. op. art teacher 1862–1897, Saint-Etienne BA where he taught flower design amongst other disciplines.
LIT *Bénézit*; *Hardouin-Fugier Bringuier*; *Thieme*

FAURE, Joseph-Antoine ***b.1813***
Pupil of Thierriat, Lyon BA (CFD 1834). Possibly the same as Joseph Faure who exhibited *Chrysanthèmes*, Lyon Salon 1885
LIT *Hardouin-Fugier Grafe*; *Lyon Salon* 1885

FAURE, Marie
b. Paris. Pupil of Barrias and Frémiet. Exhib. *Hortensias*, wc, Paris Salon 1890
LIT *Paris Salon* 1890

FAUTEL, Jean-Cécile
b. Le Havre (Seine-Maritime). Pupil of Leroux, Lhuillier and Rivoire. Exhib. *Pivoines, seringas et oeillets*, wc, Paris Salon 1890
LIT *Paris Salon* 1890

FAUVAGE, Blanche
Pupil of Thoret and Rivoire. Exhib. *Chrysanthèmes*, wc, Paris Salon 1895; *Roses trémières*, wc, *Paris UFPS* 1896; *Pivoines et iris*, wc, *Panier de giroflées*, wc, Paris Salon 1898; *Fleurs*, wc, *Paris UFPS* 1898
LIT *Paris Salon* 1895, 1898; *Paris UFPS* 1896, 1898

FAUVEL, Louise
b. Istanbul (Turkey). Pupil of Colin-Libour. Exhib. Paris Salon from 1876 e.g. *Fleurs et fruits*, 1879
LIT *Bellier*; *Bénézit*; Paris Arch. Nat. F21:438

FAUX-FROIDURE, Eugénie-Juliette
b. Noyen (Sarthe). Pupil of MacNab, O. de Champeaux, Galland, A. Maignan, Saint-Pierre and Quost. This most influential teacher exhibited *Chrysanthèmes*, *Iris*, wc, Paris Noir et Blanc Salon 1888; *Chrysanthèmes*, *Géraniums*, wc, Paris Salon 1890; Paris UFPS *Reines-marguerites*, *Bourriche de pensées*, *Roses jaunes*, *Roses et oeillets*, *jasmins*, 1896, *Pavots*, wc, 1898. M: Aubusson, Le Mans, Rouen
LIT *Bellier*; *Bénézit*; Paris Arch. Nat. F21:2132; *Paris Noir et Blanc Salon* 1888; *Paris Salon* 1890; *Paris UFPS* 1896, 1898; *Schurr* II, 64; *Thieme*

FAVERJON, Jean-Marie ***1823–1873***
Textile designer at Saint-Etienne then Lyon. Painted landscapes and religious subjects. Gave up flower painting to work with and imitate Hippolyte Flandrin
LIT *Hardouin-Fugier Bringuier*; *Schurr* I, 51

FAVIN, Jean-Marie
Pupil of Berjon, Lyon BA (CFD 1820)
LIT *Hardouin-Fugier Grafe*

FAVRE, Jean-Durand-Etienne ***b.1826***
Pupil of Thierriat, Lyon BA (CFD 1842) and, possibly, Saint-Jean. May be the painter who exhibited *Fleurs*, gouache, Lyon Salon 1842
LIT *Hardouin-Fugier Grafe*

FAVRE, *see* HÉNON

FAVRE, *see* MARITAIN

FAVROT, Louis-François-Joseph ***1812–1873***
Pupil of Lyon BA under Révoil, entered 1845 and 1846 FDC. Scarf manufacturer
LIT *Hardouin-Fugier Grafe*

FAY, Georges ***b.1871***
Pupil of Castex-Dégrange, Lyon BA (CFD 1889)
LIT *Hardouin-Fugier Grafe*

FAYETON, Joseph ***b.1826***
b. Lyon. Pupil of Lyon BA. Textile designer. Exhib. Lyon Salon 1868–1869
LIT *Bénézit*; *Hardouin-Fugier Grafe*; *Thieme*

FAYETON, Philippe ***1826–1888***
Pupil of Thierriat, Lyon BA (CFD 1844). op. Textile designer
LIT *Hardouin-Fugier Grafe*

FAYOLLE, Etienne ***b.1805***
Pupil of Lyon, BA and Thierriat, fl. Lyon *c.*1850. A Fayolle (no first name given) entered the 1849 FDC. His exhibit was in the 1849–1850 Lyon Société des Amis-des-Arts raffle
LIT *Bénézit*; *Hardouin-Fugier Grafe*; *Thieme*

FEHRENBACH, Marie
b. Paris. Exhib. *Chrysanthèmes*, on faience, Paris Salon 1880
LIT *Paris Salon* 1880

FELLOT, Louis
Pupil of Lyon BA. Exhib. *Tulipes*, wc, Lyon Salon 1869
LIT *Audin Vial*

FELON, Joseph ***1818–1896***
b. Bordeaux (Gironde). Self-taught. Painter, sculptor and lithographer. Exhib. Paris Salon 1840–1876. Designed stained-glass windows. Exhib. *Les abeilles et les fleurs*, Paris and Rouen Salons 1876
LIT *Bellier*; *Bénézit*; *Schurr* V, 102; *Thieme*

FENETRIER, Jean-Emile ***b.1879***
Pupil of Castex-Dégrange, Lyon BA (CFD 1899)
LIT *Hardouin-Fugier Grafe*

FERAUD, Mme
Exhib. *Fleurs*, wc, Paris Salon 1835. Possibly a relation of Vincent Féraud, painter and lithographer. In Paris, *c.*1834
LIT *Gabet*; *Paris Salon* 1835; *Thieme*

FEREY, Coralie
b. Rennes (Ille-et-Vilaine). Pupil of Libour. Painted portraits, animals, fruit and flowers e.g. *Fleurs et fruits d'hiver*, Paris Salon 1880
LIT *Paris Salon* 1880

FERNER
Designed plates for C. Gay *Historia ... de Chile*, 1845–1853; J. Deniker, *Atlas manuel de botanique*, Paris (Baillière) (1885–1889)
LIT *Nissen* I, 469, 695

FERNIER, *see* LEMORE

FERRAND, Ennemond ***b.1829***
Pupil of Reignier, Lyon BA (CFD 1854). Exhib. Paris Salon 1878, Lyon Salon 1881
LIT *Bénézit*; *Hardouin-Fugier Grafe*; *Thieme*

FERRÈRE, Cécile, *later* Mme Guérin ***b.1847***
b. Paris. Pupil of Lefebvre, Amaury-Duval and Chaplin. Painted genre, still-lifes and, occasionally, flowers. Exhib. Paris Salon from 1863
LIT *Bénézit*; *Thieme*

FERRIÉ, Blanche
Pupil of Chabal-Dussurgey. Musée de Draguignan, *Roses*
LIT *Bénézit*

FERRIER, Henry
b. Nevers (Nièvre). Pupil of Gleyre. Exhib. *Fleurs*, Paris Salon 1869
LIT *Bellier*; *Bénézit*

FERRON-FONTAN, François
Pupil of Berjon, Lyon BA (CFD 1818)
LIT *Hardouin-Fugier Grafe*

FEYDEAU, Diane
Exhib. *Anémones*, wc, Paris SNBA 1899. Musée de Dieppe, *Bouquet dans un vase corbeille*, wc, 1893 (1904 cat. 1792) (untraceable)
LIT *Bénézit*; *Paris SNBA* 1899

FICHEL-SAMSON, Jeanne
b. Lyon. Pupil of E. Fichel, her husband. Painted genre and flowers. Exhib. Paris Salon from 1869. e.g. *Bouquet de fleurs*, 1878, *La serre*, *La fleuriste*, 1879; *Fleurs* Paris UFPS 1898
LIT *Bellier*; *Bénézit*; *Paris UFPS* 1898; *Thieme*

FIGHIERA, Rosette
Pupil of Le Besgue. Exhib. Paris UFPS *Iris*, *Chrysanthèmes*, *Fleurs des champs*, *Iris et aubépines*, gouache, 1896, *Fleurs de Nice*, *Pavots*, *giroflées*, 1898. Avignon Musée Calvet. *Oeillets*, wc
LIT *Paris UFPS* 1896, 1898

FIGUIER, Mme Louis
Exhib. *Guirlande de fleurs*, wc, *Bouquet de dahlias*, wc, *Dahlias blancs et roses*, wc, Paris Salon 1861
LIT *Paris Salon* 1861

FILLET, Benoist
b. Cambrai (Nord). Pupil of Cuisal. Exhib. *Les trois couleurs*, *fleurs*, *Fleurs*, Paris Salon 1880
LIT *Paris Salon* 1880

FILLIARD, Ernest
b. Chambéry (Savoie). Pupil of B. Molin. Exhib. *Chrysanthèmes*, wc, Paris SNBA 1895; *Pivoines blanches*, wc, *Pavots rouges*, wc, Grenoble Salon 1899. M: Avignon, Chambéry
LIT *Grenoble Salon* 1899; *Paris SNBA* 1895 (ill.); *Pavière* III, pt. 2; *Thieme*

FIQUENET
op. Sèvres *c.*1862
LIT *Orsay*

FIRNHABER, Elise-Désirée
b. Lyon. Exhib. *Lilas blanc*, Paris Indép. 1896
LIT *Bénézit*; *Paris Indép.* 1896

FISCHER, Carlos
Pupil of Hochstuhl. Exhib. Strasbourg Salon *Primevères*, 1883, *Roses*, 1884
LIT *Strasbourg Salon* 1883, 1884

FIX-MASSEAU, Pierre-Félix ***1869–1937***
b. Lyon. Pupil of Paris BA. Painted genre and flowers
LIT *Bénézit*; *Schurr* III, 145; *Thieme*

FLAMENT, Ernest-Hippolyte
b. Paris. Pupil of Lucas and École des Gobelins. Exhib. Paris Salon from 1870 e.g. *roses*, 1880; *Fleurs*, 1890
LIT *Bellier*; *Bénézit*; *Paris Salon* 1880, 1890

FLAMENT, Mlle
Exhib. Paris Salon *Dahlias*, wc, *Géranium*, wc, 1835, *Vase de fleurs*, 1836
LIT *Annuaire statistique des artistes français*, Paris 1832–1836; *Bellier*

FLANDRIN, Jules-Léon ***1871–1947***
b. Corenc (Isère). Pupil of Paris BA, Gustave Moreau. Painted genre, portraits, landscapes, still-lifes and flowers e.g. *Fleurs et statuettes*, pastel, *Tulipes*, pastel, Grenoble Salon 1899; *Fleurs*, Paris SNBA 1899. Musée de Grenoble, *Roses d'automne*
LIT *Bénézit*; Grenoble-Corenc, *J. Flandrin*, 1972; *Grenoble Salon* 1899; *Paris SNBA* 1899; *Schurr* II, 133; *Thieme*

FLEURY, Edouard
b. Paris. Pupil of Couture. Painted still-lifes and flowers. Exhib. Paris Salon 1863–1868
LIT *Bénézit*

FLEURY, Emile
b. Nîmes (Gard). Exhib. *Reines-marguerites*, Paris Indép. 1891
LIT *Paris Indép.* 1891

FLEURY, Fanny, *née* Laurent
Pupil of Carolus-Duran and Henner. Exhib. Paris Salon 1869–1889. Painted figures and flowers e.g. *Bleuets*, Saint-Etienne Salon 1882; *Roses*, Dijon Salon 1892
LIT *Bénézit*; *Dijon Salon* 1892; *Saint-Etienne Salon* 1882; *Thieme*

FLEURY, Marie-Berthe ***b.1857***
Pupil of Rivoire. Exhib. *Pivoines et lilas*, wc, *Primevères et jacinthes*, wc, *Oeillets*, wc, Paris UFPS 1896; *Azalées*, Paris Salon 1898; *Roses*, *Anémones et giroflées*, Paris UFPS 1898
LIT *Bénézit*; *Paris Salon* 1898; *Paris UFPS* 1896, 1898

FLORENT, Alfred
b. Boulogne-sur-Mer (Pas-de-Calais). Exhib. flowers, Paris Salon from 1880
LIT *Bellier*; *Bénézit*

FLOTAL, Mme
Exhib. *Fleurs et fruits*, Dijon Salon 1880
LIT *Dijon Salon* 1880

FONTAINE, Jean-Joseph
Painted portraits and flowers on porcelain; Sèvres 1835–1836. Exhib. *Fleurs*, after E. Bruyère, 1836, Paris Salon 1836
LIT *Bellier*; *Bénézit*; *Paris Salon* 1836; *Thieme*

FONTAINE, Marie-Amélie
Exhib. *Roses*, pastel, Paris Salon 1866
LIT *Faré* 1962, p. 248; *Paris Salon* 1866

FONTAINE, Marie-Claire
b. Versailles (Yvelines), pupil of Edmé-Adolphe Fontaine, her father. Painted portraits and flowers. Exhib. Paris Salon *Roses*, pastel, 1875, *Fleurs*, pastel, 1876
LIT *Bellier*; *Bénézit*; *Paris Salon* 1875; *Thieme*

FONTAN, *see* FERRON

FONTANES, Louise de, *née* Méchin
b. Caen (Calvados). Pupil of École de la manufacture de Sèvres. op. Sèvres 1844–1879. Exhib. Paris Salon from 1841 e.g. *Fleurs*, on porcelain, 1841, 1861, 1864, 1868, and *Corbeille de fleurs* after Van Huysum, on porcelain, 1844, *Vase de fleurs sur une table de marbre*, after Bruyère, 1846. Designed a flower plate lithographed by Aubert
LIT *Bellier*; *Bénézit*; *Brunet Préaud*; Paris Bibl. Nat. Est. Jd 59; *Thieme*

FONTREAL, Albert de
b. Paris. Exhib. *Dahlias*, wc, Paris Salon 1885
LIT *Paris Salon* 1885

Blanche Ferrié (*right*)

Oil on canvas, signed
Draguignan, Musée Municipal (photo: J.L.A. Draguignan)

Ernest Filliard

Watercolour, 18½ × 23¼ in. (47 × 59 cm.), signed
Avignon, Musée Calvet

FORAIN, Jean-Louis *1852–1931*
b. Reims (Marne). Pupil of Gérôme, Paris BA. The famous cartoonist painted portraits, figures, genre and, occasionally, flowers
LIT *Bénézit*; Paris *J.-L. Forain*, Bibl. Nat. 1952; *J.-L. Forain*, Musée Marmottan, 1978; *J.-L. Forain*, Union Centrale des Arts Décoratifs, 1913; *Orsay*; *Thieme*

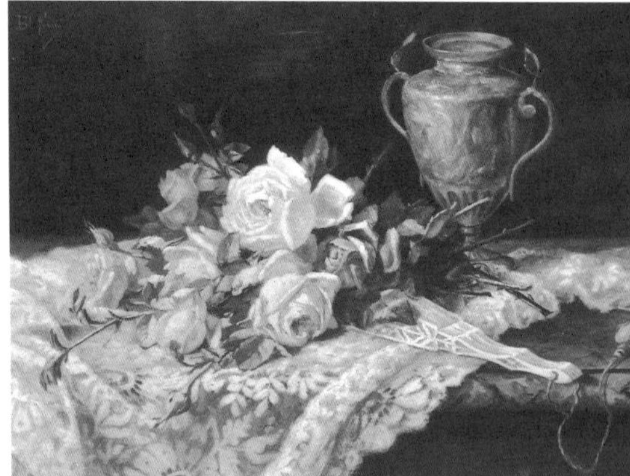

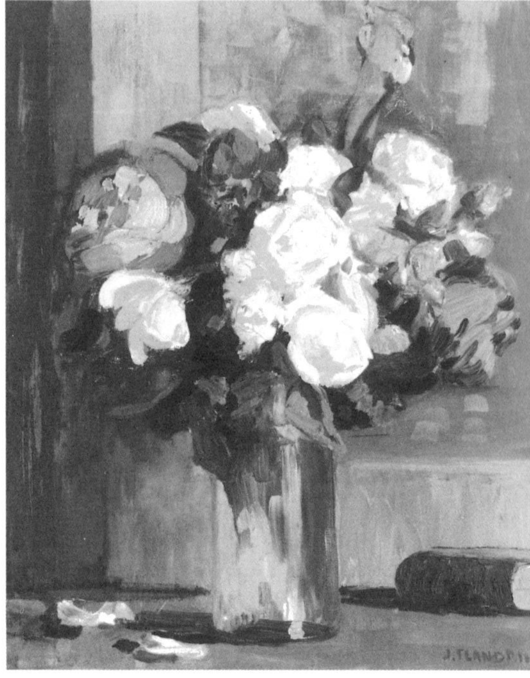

Jules-Léon Flandrin

Oil on canvas, 21¾ × 18 in. (55 × 46 cm.), signed
Grenoble, Musée de Peinture et de Sculpture

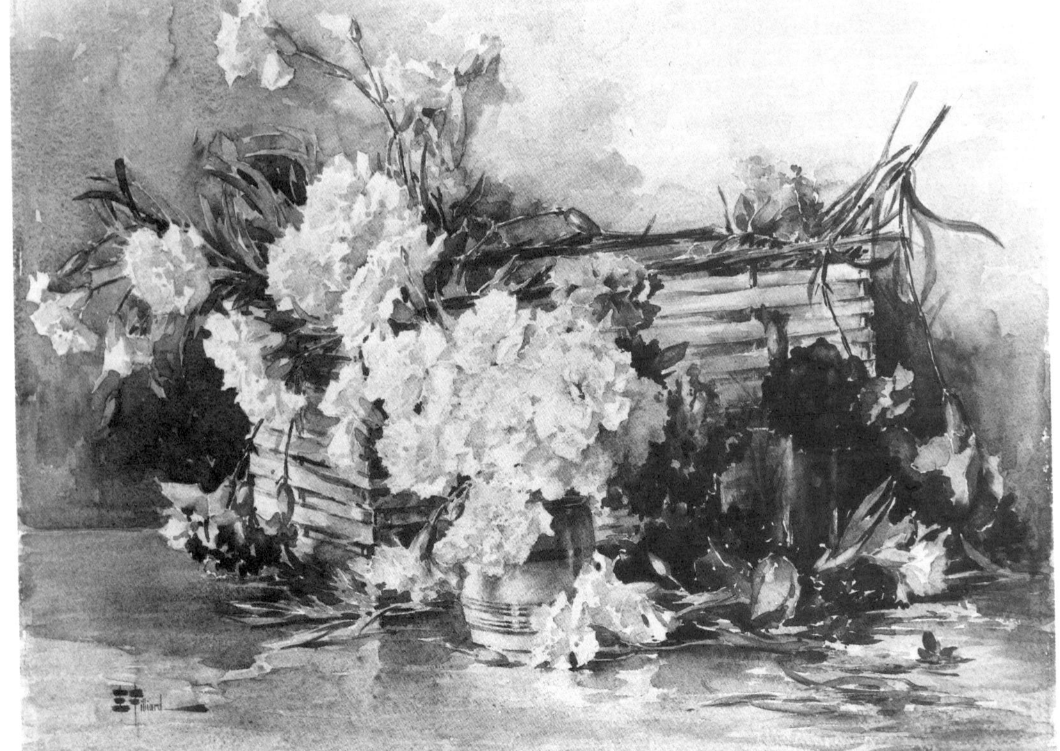

FORESTIER, Alice
b. Paris. Pupil of Jeannin. Painted landscapes and flowers. Exhib. *Dahlias* gouache, *Chrysanthèmes*, wc, Paris Salon 1890
LIT *Bellier*; *Paris Salon* 1890

FORET, Paul
b. Paris. Pupil of Goupil and Vollon. Painted birds, still-lifes and, occasionally, flowers e.g. *L'éventaire de la bouquetière*
LIT *Bellier*; *Bénézit*

FORMIGÉ, Marie-Emma
b. Bordeaux (Gironde). Pupil of Laurens, Carolus-Duran and Henner. Exhib. Paris Salon from 1876 e.g. *Pivoines*, wc, *Chrysanthèmes*, wc, 1880
LIT *Bénézit*; *Paris Salon* 1880

FOSSEY, André
b. Paris. Pupil of Fossey, Bouguereau and T. Robert-Fleury. Exhib. *Giroflées*, wc, Paris Salon 1890
LIT *Bénézit*; *Paris Salon* 1890

FOUACE, Guillaume-Romain ***1827–1895***
b. Réville (Manche). Pupil of Yvon. Painted still-lifes and, occasionally, flowers. Exhib. Paris Salon from 1870 and *Pensées*, Dijon Salon 1885. M: Bourges, Cherbourg, Mulhouse (lost in the war); Saint-Brieuc
LIT *Bellier*; *Bénézit*; *Dijon Salon* 1885; *Schurr* I, 31

FOUCAULT, *see* NUGENT

FOUCHARDIÈRE, Victoire de la,
To date, a pair of signed wc on vellum of the 1930s are known from this artist; another accomplished lady following Redouté's example. PM

FOUET, Louise-Berthe
b. Paris. Pupil of Mallou and Kuerniger. Painted flowers and genre. Exhib. Paris Salon from 1878 e.g. *Chrysanthèmes*, 1880
LIT *Bellier*; *Bénézit*; *Paris Salon* 1880

FOULON, Jeanne
b. La Rochelle (Charente-Maritime). Pupil of Lequien and Haquette. Exhib. *Roses* (150 francs) and *Giroflées* (200 francs) Strasbourg Salon 1891
LIT *Bénézit*; *Strasbourg Salon* 1891

FOUQUET, Félicie ***b.1845***
b. Paris. Pupil of Méry. Exhib. *Fleurs*, after Van Dael, on porcelain, Paris Salon 1868, 1870
LIT *Bellier*; *Bénézit*; *Thieme*

FOUR, *see* FRUCHARD

FOURAU or FOUREAU, Hughes ***1803–1873***
b. Paris. Pupil of Guérin and Gros. Painted genre and, occasionally, flowers
LIT *Bénézit*; *Schurr* V, 16; *Thieme*

FOURDRIN, Camille, *née* Lemaire
Exhib. Paris Salon 1831–1848 e.g. *Primevères, oreilles d'ours et impériales*, 1838, *Narcisses, tulipes, lilas*, wc, 1841, *Roses, tulipes, giroflées*, wc, 1843; *Camélias et roses*, wc, 1844
LIT *Bellier*; *Bénézit*; *Paris Salon* 1838, 1841, 1843

FOURNEL, *see* PELLETIER

FOURNEL, Jean-Baptiste
Pupil of Pizzetta and Laÿs. Exhib. Lyon Salon 1857–1892 e.g. *Les dernières fleurs*, *Fruits et fleurs*, 1858, *Groupe de fleurs*, wc, 1860, 1861
LIT *Bénézit*; *Hardouin-Fugier Grafe*; *Lyon Salon* 1858, 1860, 1861; *Thieme*

FOURNIER, *see* SCHNEIDER

FOURNIER, Anatole
op. Sèvres 1878–1904. Painted on glass
LIT *Bénézit*; *Thieme*

FOURNIER, Mme A.
Exhib. *Bouquet composé*, wc, Paris Salon 1835
LIT *Paris Salon* 1835

FOURREAU, Jules
op. 1870–1900. Designed plates for A. Jordan, *Icones ad Floram Europae* ... Paris 1866–1903
LIT *Nissen* I, 1008

FOYOT D'ALVAR, Marie-Madeleine
b. Paris. Pupil of Henry Cauchois. Exhib. *Chrysanthèmes*, Paris Salon 1895; *Chrysanthèmes*, *Cueillette de dahlias*, *Bouquet de dahlias*, Paris UFPS 1896
LIT *Bénézit*; *Paris Salon* 1895; *Paris UFPS* 1896

FRANCE, Wanda
Exhib. *Rhododendrons*, Dijon Salon 1890
LIT *Dijon Salon* 1890. CL

FRANCHON-FAGEL
b. Lille (Nord). Exhib. *Fleurs de printemps*, *Fleurs*, Lille Salon 1881
LIT *Lille Salon* 1881. G and LT

FRANC-LAMY, Pierre-Désiré Franc ***alias 1855–1919***
b. Clermont-Ferrand (Puy-de-Dôme). Pupil of Pils and Gérôme, Paris BA. Friendly with Renoir. Painted landscapes, genre and, occasionally, flowers e.g. *Bouquet devant une glace*, *Fleurs dans un verre*, *Roses dans un vase*, nos. 175, 176, 177 and the following ten lots of the Franc-Lamy sale, Paris Drouot 1919. M: Paris Musée d'Orsay, *Fleurs*
LIT *Bénézit*; *Orsay*; *Schurr* I, 107

FRAN LUCAIN
Pupil of Berjon, Lyon BA (CFD 1819)
LIT *Hardouin-Fugier Grafe*

FRANCO, Joseph-Napoléon *b.1811*
Painted on porcelain and alabaster. Exhib. *Fruits et fleurs*, Paris Salon 1850
LIT *Bénézit*; *Paris Salon* 1850

FRANÇON, Ernest
Exhib. Paris Indép. *Lilas, Chrysanthèmes, Fleurs et fruits d'automne*, 1898, *Fleurs et fruits, Poires et chrysanthèmes, Fleurs de printemps*, 1899
LIT *Paris Indép.* 1898, 1899

FRANQUEBALME, *see* COUSIN

FRAQUIER, Gabriel-Auguste-Claire-Arnaud de *1803–1873*
b. Besançon (Doubs). Pupil of Roqueplan. Painted genre and flowers. Exhib. Paris Salon 1833–1859 e.g. *Fleurs et fruits sur un bas-relief*, 1859. Musée de Besançon *Fleurs et fruits*, 1865 (gift of the artist 1866)
LIT *Bellier*; *Bénézit*; *Thieme*

FRÉCON, Henri *b.1870*
Pupil of Castex-Dégrange, Lyon BA (CFD 1888)
LIT *Hardouin-Fugier Grafe*

FRÉMONT, Gabrielle-Caroline-Céline *b.1850*
b. Lille (Nord). Pupil of Cossmann and Dessart. Exhib. *Fleur des blés*, on porcelain, Paris Salon 1880
LIT *Bellier*; *Bénézit*; *Paris Salon* 1880; *Thieme*

FRÈRE, Jérôme
Exhib. *Guimauves*, Saint-Etienne Salon 1882
LIT *Hardouin-Fugier Bringuier*; *Saint-Etienne Salon* 1882

FREULER, Gaspard *1837–1899*
b. Glarus (Switzerland). op. Lyon, then Paris. Textile designer. Painted flowers in oils and wc. Works in Glarus Museum
LIT *Audin Vial*; *Bénézit*; *Hardouin-Fugier Grafe*; *Thieme*

FREULER, Rodolphe *1830–1896*
b. Glarus (Switzerland). Lyon textile designer
LIT *Audin Vial*

FREUNDSTEIN DE WALDNER, Mme de
Exhib. *Fleurs*, on faience, Paris Salon 1880
LIT *Paris Salon* 1880

FRICK, Paul de *1864–1935*
b. Paris. Pupil of L.-O. Merson. Exhib. Dijon Salon *Lauriers en fleurs à la Giudecca*, 1892, *Pivoines*, 1894
LIT *Bénézit*; *Dijon Salon* 1882, 1884; *Schurr* V, 128. CL

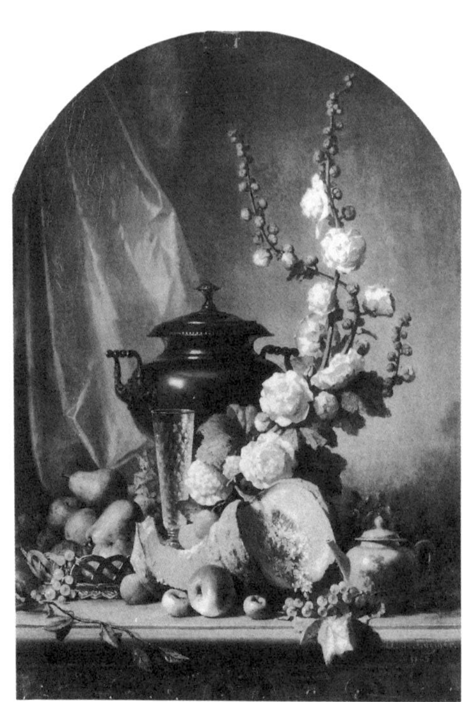

Gabriel-Auguste-Claire Arnaud de Fraquier

Oil on canvas, $49\frac{1}{2} \times 35\frac{3}{4}$ in. (126 × 91 cm.), signed and dated 1865
Besançon, Musée des Beaux-Arts et d'Archéologie

FRIES, Emmanuel *1778–1852*
b. Mulhouse (Haut-Rhin). Pupil of Regnault, Paris BA. Textile designer, Mulhouse 1797–1824. Exhib. Paris Salon e.g. *Fleurs*, 1837. Works in Musée de Mulhouse, *Vase de fleurs*, 1830 (artist's legacy 1898); *Fleurs et fruits*, 1832–1833
LIT *Histoire documentaire*; *MISE*; *Paris Salon* 1837; *Sitzmann*; *Thieme*. BJ

FROIDURE, *see* FAUX

FRUCHARD, Amélie, *née* Four
b. Tulle (Corréze). Pupil of Rivoire, Lefebvre, J.-P. Laurens and Benjamin Constant. Exhib. *Roses trémières*, Paris Salon 1895. Musée de Tulle, *Fleurs*, wc (disappeared in a flood in the 1960s)
LIT *Bénézit*; *Paris Salon* 1895

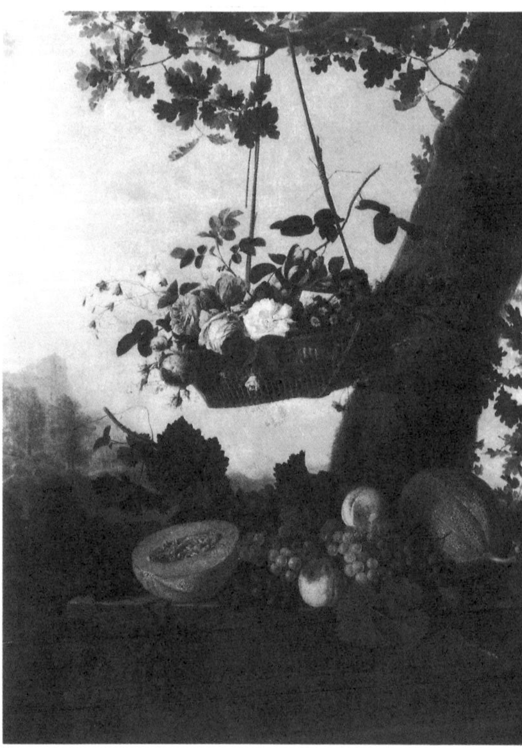

Emmanuel Fries

Oil on canvas, $51\frac{1}{4} \times 39\frac{1}{4}$ in. (130 × 100 cm.), signed and dated 1832–3
Mulhouse, Musée de l'Impression sur Etoffes

FUCHS, Joseph ***1814–1888***
b. Thann (Haut-Rhin). Worked in Mulhouse. Textile designer. Operated a design studio with G. Zippelius. Co-designed the Zuber Eldorado wallpaper LIT *Histoire documentaire*; B. Jacqué "Les papiers peints panoramiques Zuber ..." In *Bulletin du Musée ... de Mulhouse*", 1981. BJ

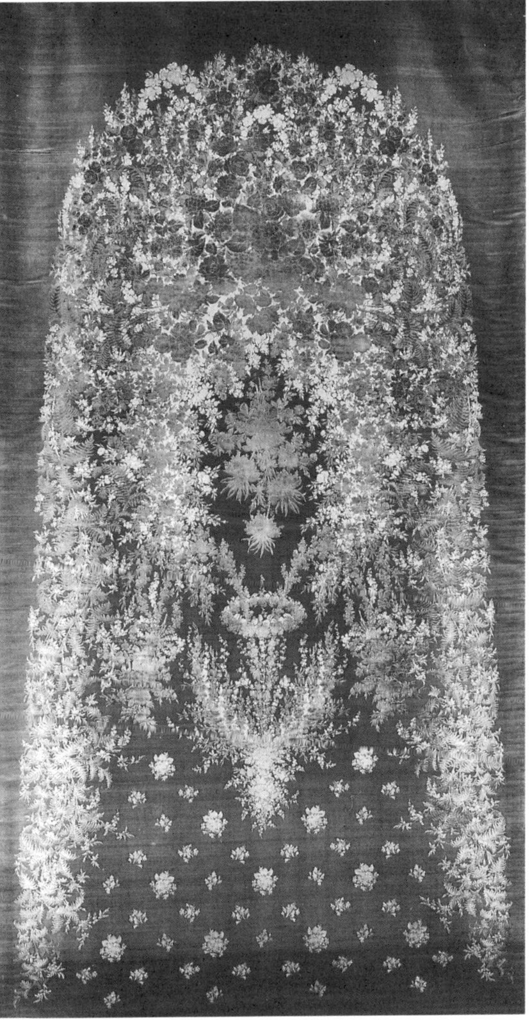

Joseph Fuchs

Design attributed to Joseph Fuchs and Georges Zipelius court robe of Gandin ciselé velvet with silk and gold thread, manufactured Eugène Schultz & Co., Lyon *c.* 1853, 141½ × 74¾ in. (360 × 190 cm.), Lyon, Musée Historique des Tissus, (photo: Studio Basset, Lyon)

FUCHS, Mlle N.
Exhib. Paris SNBA *Chrysanthèmes*, 1893; *Panneau de fleurs*, 1894, *Boules de neige et oeillets*, *Bouquets de roses rouges*, 1895, *Roses et violettes*, wc, 1896, *Oeillets*, wc, *Chardons*, wc, 1899 LIT *Paris SNBA* 1893, 1894, 1895, 1896, 1899

FULIGNY-DUMAS, *see* GROLLIER

FURCY DE LAVAULT, Albert-Tibulle ***1847–1915***
b. Saint-Genis (Charente-Maritime). Curator of Musée de la Rochelle 1882–1913. Exhib. *Fleurs de printemps*, Paris Salon 1880; Dijon Salon *Fleurs d'automne*, 1883, *Oeillets*, 1887; *Brouettée de chrysanthèmes*, Poitiers Salon 1887; *Un coin de jardin*, Paris Salon 1889; *Fleurs*, Dijon Salon 1890; *Fleurs d'été*, Paris Salon 1890; Dijon Salon *Chrysanthèmes*, 1892, *Fleurs d'automne*, 1894, *Fleurs et fruits d'automne*, 1897. M: Barbézieux, Cambrai, La Rochelle, Rochefort, Saintes LIT *Bénézit*; *Dijon Salon* 1883, 1887, 1890, 1892, 1894, 1897; *Paris Salon* 1880, 1889 (ill.); *Poitiers Salon* 1887; *Thieme*. BG and CL
See illustration on page 53

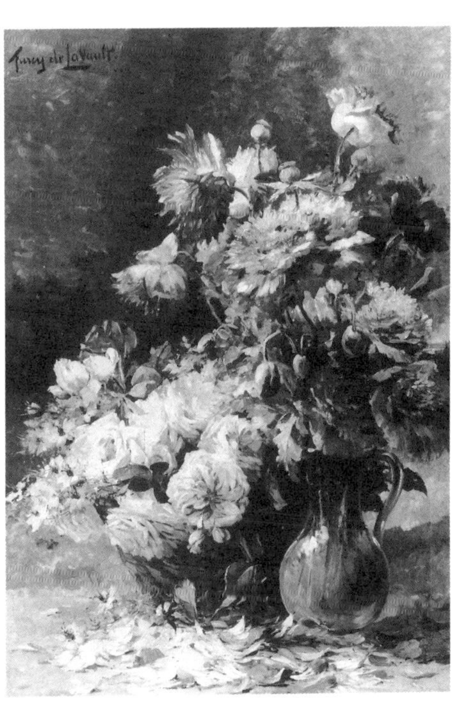

Albert-Tibulle Furcy de Lavault

Oil on canvas, 39 × 28 in. (99 × 71 cm.), signed
Courtesy Sotheby's, London

FURSTER, Joseph-Louis ***b.1880***
Pupil of Castex-Dégrange, Lyon BA (CFD 1898)
LIT *Hardouin-Fugier Grafe*

G

GAB, Mme J.
Pupil of E. Puyroche-Wagner. Exhib. *Groupe de roses*, Lyon Salon 1875
LIT *Lyon Salon* 1875

GABERT, Emile
Exhib. *Boules de neige*, *Roses*, Saint-Etienne Salon 1882
LIT *Hardouin-Fugier Bringuier*; *Saint-Etienne Salon* 1882

GABERT, Paul ***b.1802***
Pupil of Berjon, Lyon BA (CFD 1822)
LIT *Hardouin-Fugier Grafe*

GACHET, Paul
b. Lille (Nord). Exhib. *Lys rouge*, Paris Indép. 1892
LIT *Paris Indép.* 1892

GAGNIARD, E.
Exhib. *Fleurs*, wc, Paris Salon 1841, 1843
LIT *Paris Salon* 1841, 1843

GAILLARD, Louis
Pupil of Berjon, Lyon BA (CFD 1813). *Peonies*, 1888, Christie's, London, 30 May 1986, lot 37, may well be by the artist
LIT *Hardouin-Fugier Grafe*

GAILLARD, *see* BEAUREPAIRE

GAITET, Mlle
Exhib. *Pavots*, Dijon Salon 1897
LIT *Dijon Salon* 1897. CL

GALLAND, Joséphine
b. Lyon. Painted landscapes, still-lifes and flowers. Exhib. Lyon Salon from 1892
LIT *Bénézit*

GALLAND, Pierre-Victor ***1822–1892***
b. Geneva (Switzerland) of French parentage. Pupil of Drolling (Paris BA), Labrouste and Ciceri. op. decorator. Painted a ceiling at the Palais de l'Elysée, Paris. Designed a Gobelins tapestry cartoon. An influential teacher. *Poppies*, and *Amours et fleurs*, Paris BMAD
LIT *Bénézit*; M.N. de Garry, *V. Galland*, Paris BMAD 1980; *Orsay*; *Schurr* V, 191; *Thieme*

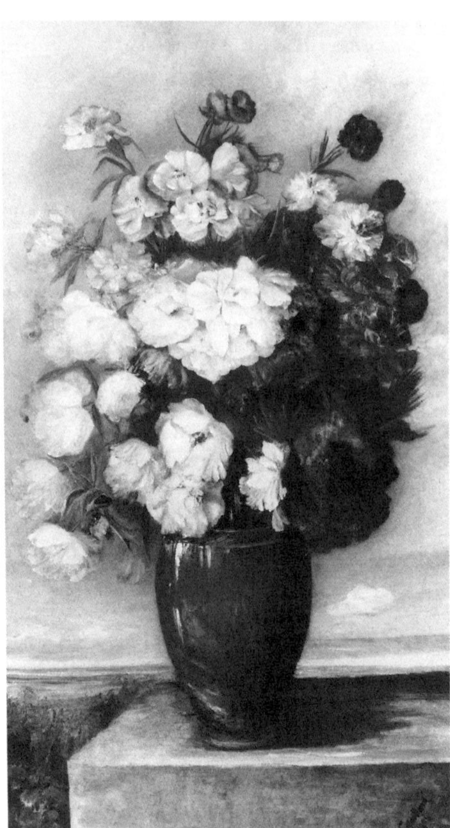

Louis Gaillard

Oil on canvas, 58 × 32½ in. (147.3 × 82.5 cm.), signed and dated 1888
Courtesy Christie's, London

GALLAY, N.
Exhib. *Anémones et roses*, pastel, Paris SNBA 1896
LIT *Paris SNBA* 1896

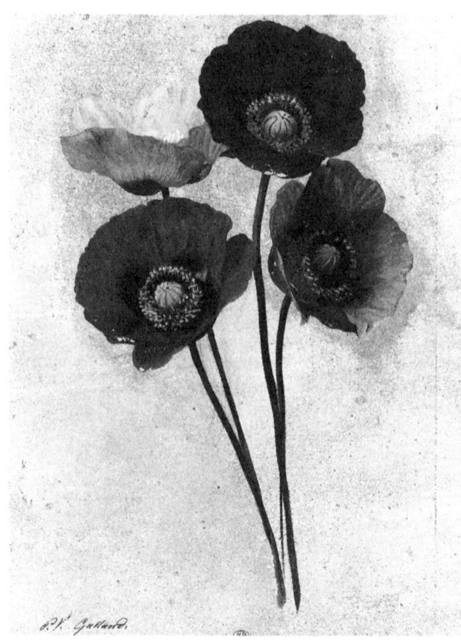

Pierre-Victor Galland

Oil on paper, 15¾ × 11½ in. (40 × 29 cm.), signed
Paris, Musée des Arts Décoratifs

GALLÉ, Emile ***1846–1904***
The many-sided master of Art Nouveau was a keen botanist and flower-lover. He produced a few flower-pieces, e.g. *Nature morte: Le dessert*, Geneva sale, 1–2 June 1988, lot 24
LIT *Bellier*; Gallé E. *Ecrits pour l'art*, Paris (Renouard) 1908; Paris BMAD; *Thieme*; Zurich, Museum Bellerive, *Gallé . . .* 1980

GALLET, Jean-Baptiste ***1820–1848***
b. Lyon. Pupil of Thierriat, Lyon BA (CFD 1838). Exhib. Lyon Salon 1842–1848, Paris Salon 1847–1848. Musée des Beaux-Arts, Lyon, *Reines-marguerites et dahlias* Musée de l'Ain, Bourg-en-Bresse
LIT *Hardouin-Fugier Grafe* (ill.); *Hardouin-Fugier Grafe* 1979: (ill.) *Hardouin-Fugier Grafe* 1982 (ill.)

GALTON, Mme L.
Exhib. *Oeillets*, wc, *Roses*, wc, Paris SNBA 1899
LIT *Paris SNBA* 1899

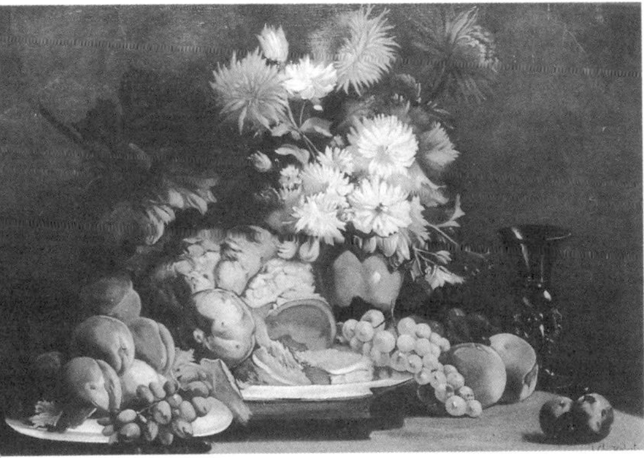

Emile Gallé

Oil on canvas, 23½ × 35½ in. (60 × 90 cm.), signed and dated 1894 and dedicated 'à Charles Hubert, son ami'
Private collection

Jean-Baptiste Gallet

Oil on canvas, 9½ × 7½ in. (24 × 19 cm.), signed
Bourg-en-Bresse, Musée de l'Ain

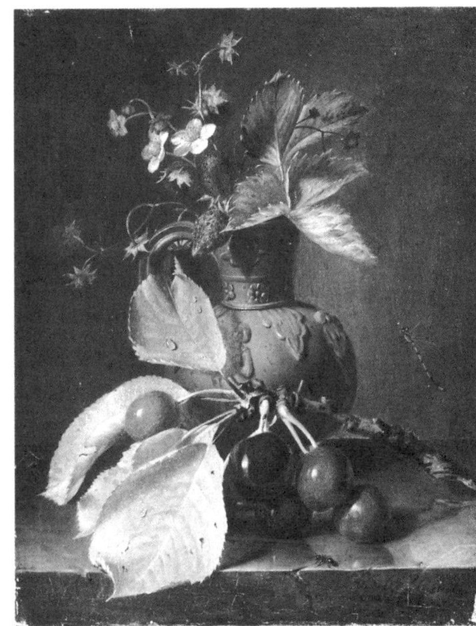

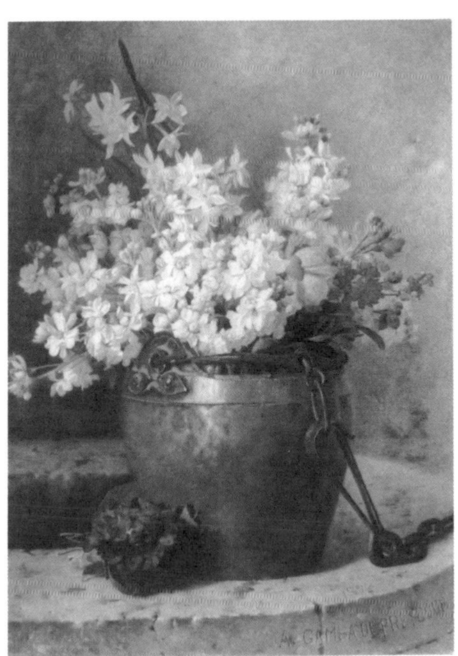

Alexandre-Jules Gamba de Preydour

Oil on canvas, 24½ × 18½ in. (62 × 47 cm.), signed and dated 1896
Private collection

GAMBA DE PREYDOUR, Alexandre-Jules ***b.1846***
b. Paris. Pupil of Gérôme. Painted portraits, landscapes, still-lifes and flowers. Exhib. *Fleurs d'eucalyptus et verre de Venise*, Paris Salon 1890, *Giroflées*, Dijon Salon 1894; *Fleurs*, Paris Salon 1895; *Roses dans un vase* and *Fleurs blanches*, Geneva sale, 1–2 June 1988, lots 25 and 26
LIT *Bellier*; *Bénézit*; *Dijon Salon* 1894; *Paris Salon* 1890, 1895; *Thieme*

GAMOT, Stanislas
Pupil of Berjon, Lyon BA (CFD 1820)
LIT *Hardouin-Fugier Grafe*

GARDE, Ferdinand
b. 1872. Pupil of Castex-Dégrange, Lyon BA (CFD 1890–1891)
LIT *Hardouin-Fugier Grafe*

GARDON, Félix-Justin
b. Choisy-le-Roy (Val-de-Marne). Pupil of Bellet and Lequien. Exhib. Paris Salon *Roses, premières fleurs*, wc, 1890, *Pivoines, Matinée de juin*, 1895, *A l'ombre, fleurs*, 1896. M: Limoges, *Chrysanthèmes*
LIT *Bénézit*; *Paris Salon* 1890, 1895 (ill.), 1896 (ill.)

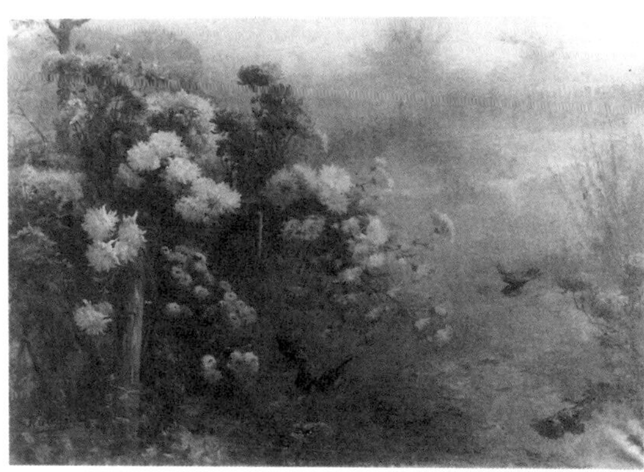

Félix-Justin Gardon

Oil on canvas, 39½ × 56 in. (100 × 142 cm.), signed
Limoges, Musée Municipal

GARDOT, Jules
b. Toulouse (Haute-Garonne). Pupil of Toulouse and Paris BA. Exhib. Paris Salon 1861–1880. Exhib. *Roses thé*, Lyon Salon 1880
LIT *Bénézit*; *Lyon Salon* 1880; *Thieme*

GARGALON
Pupil of Berjon, Lyon BA (CFD 1810)
LIT *Hardouin-Fugier Grafe*

GARIN, Charles
b. 1796. Pupil of Berjon, Lyon BA (CFD 1822)
LIT *Hardouin-Fugier Grafe*

GARNERAY, Ambroise-Louis
1783–1857
b. Rouen (Seine-Maritime). Son of François-Jean Garneray. op. Sèvres 1839–1848. Painted seascapes and, occasionally, flowers. Brother of Auguste-Louis Garneray
LIT *Bellier*; *Bénézit*; *Brunet-Préaud*; *Schurr* I, 36

GARNERAY, Auguste-Louis *1785–1824*
Pupil of his father François-Jean Garneray and J.B. Isabey. Flower painter to Queen Hortense and the Duchesse de Berry. Exhib. Paris Salon from 1808 e.g. *Guirlande de roses d'espèces variées*, 1817; *Roses trémières sur un tapis de velours*, 1819, *Fleurs*, 1822; Flowers figure in a watercolour portrait of Queen Hortense, and in an ensemble of watercolours representing views of the *Parc de Malmaison* in the Musée de Malmaison; M: Dunkerque
LIT *Bellier*; *Bénézit*; *Gabet*; *Faré* 1962, p. 242; *Schidlof*; *Thieme*

GARNERAY, François-Jean
1755–1837
b. Paris. Pupil of David. Painted portraits, figures, historical subjects and, occasionally, flowers. Exhib. Paris Salon 1791–1835 e.g. *Fleurs*, 1810
LIT *Bénézit*; *Faré* 1962, p. 141; *Paris Salon* 1810; *Schurr* III, 7; *Thieme*; *Witt*

GARNEREY, *see* CABANNE

GARNIER, *see* DELACROIX

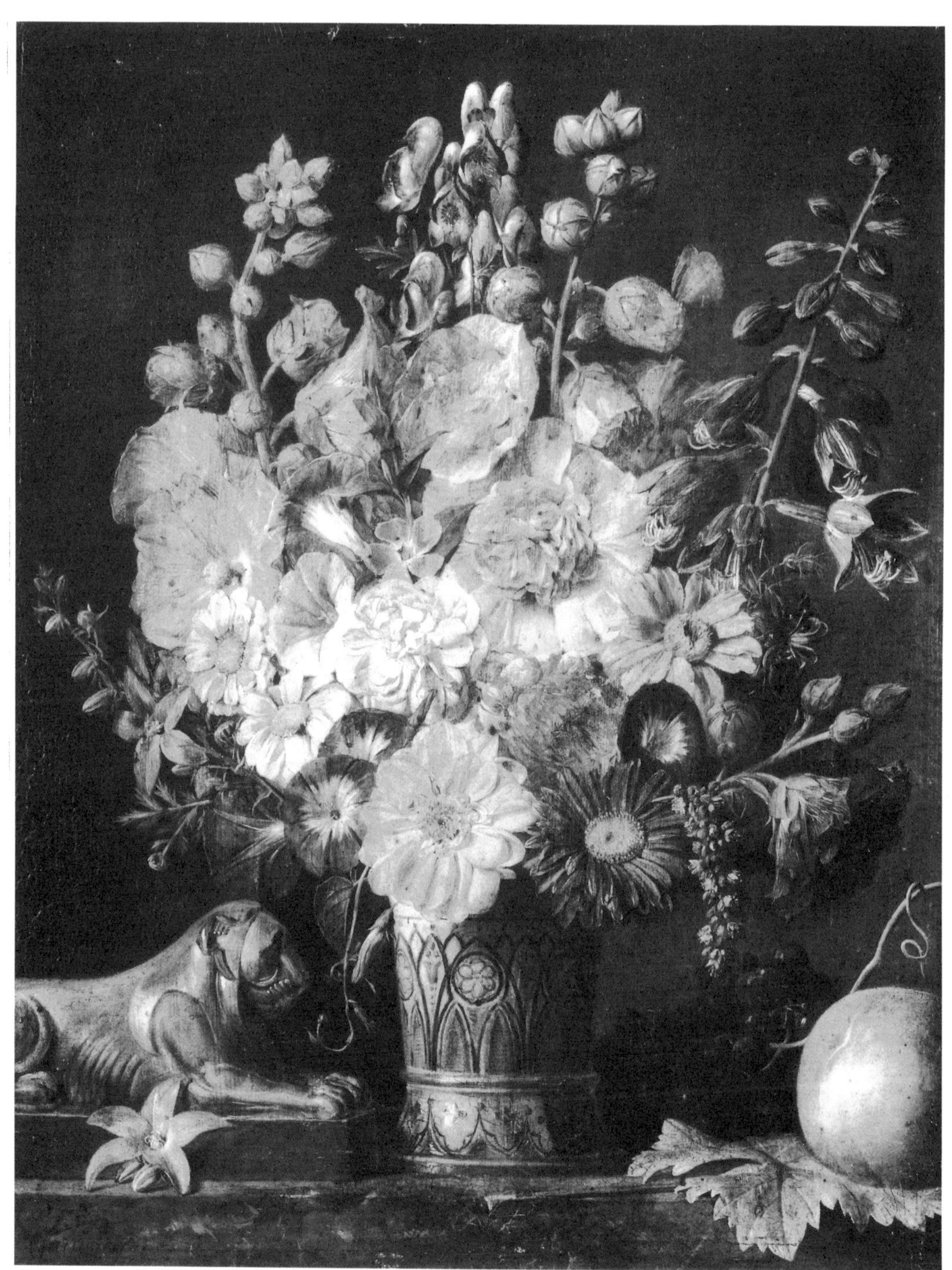

Auguste-Louis Garneray

Oil on canvas, signed
Dunkerque, Musée des Beaux-Arts (photo: Lauros-Giraudon)

GARNIER, M.L.
Jetée de fleurs, gouache 1882 (private coll.)

GARNIER, Michel ***1753–after 1819***
b. St. Cloud. Pupil of Pierre. Painter of elegant genre scenes (e.g. the pair in Musée Carnavalet, Paris). Salon debut in 1793. It has not been previously published that Garnier joined an expedition in 1800 to Australasia, commanded by Baudin. Together with the two other artists retained, Garnier was put ashore at Île de France (today Île de la Réunion) owing to ill health. He was obliged to remain there for five years painting portraits and giving drawing lessons but his principal task was painting studies of the rich variety of fruit found on the island. He finally returned to France in a frigate captured by the English and threw out all his belongings in order to fill his trunk with these precious oil paintings. There followed a long and frustrating attempt to sell the collection of 140 paintings depicting over 200 fruits to the Muséum. Finally in 1819 a committee, including Van Spaendonck, recommended their acquisition but was thwarted by the Minister with the familiar excuse of insufficient funds. Garnier died soon after and the collection was dispersed. By chance and the alertness of two people, the majority were acquired as anonymous items for the museum for derisory sums in two *tranches* in 1851 and 1876. Twenty-two years later Garnier's manuscript catalogue of 1815 was found, revealing the identity of the painter, as published by Hamy in 1898.
LIT *E.T. Hamy, Les peintures de Michel Garnier au Muséum d'Histoire Naturelle, Bulletin du Muséum* IV, 1898 (I am very grateful for the help of Jacqueline Mallet and her colleagues for providing me with a photocopy of this article). PM

GARNIER, Pierre ***1847–1937***
Pupil of Reignier, Lyon BA (CFD 1862). Entered 1869 Lyon Société des Amis-des-Arts FDC. Exhib. Paris Salon 1874–1879, Lyon Salon from 1878 to his death. Father of architect Tony Garnier. A successful painter whose favourite flowers were roses
LIT *Bénézit*; *Hardouin-Fugier Grafe*; *Hardouin-Fugier Grafe* 1982 (ill.)

GARNIER DE GRASSIN, Pierrette
b. Paris. Pupil of Petit. Exhib. *Géraniums*, Paris Salon 1880
LIT *Paris Salon* 1880

GARNOT, G.S.F
Exhib. Paris SNBA *Azalée blanche et vieux Chine*, 1897, *Les roses de Trianon*, 1899
LIT *Paris SNBA* 1897, 1899; *Thieme*

GARRAUD, Léon ***1877–1961***
b. Saint-Moreil (Creuse). Pupil of Lyon BA, Mangier, Bonnaud, Tollet. Painted portraits, nudes, landscapes and, occasionally, flowers
LIT *Bénézit*; Thiollier *Garraud*, Lyon 1981; *Thieme*

GASNIER, Charles-François ***1789–after 1835***
Son of P.G. Gasnier, the decorator, op. Mannheim (Germany). Painted flowers
LIT *Bénézit*; *Thieme*

GAUDELET, Charles
Exhib. *Fleurs* on glass, Paris Salon 1842. Exhib. Lille Salon 1866. May be a relation, a namesake of, or the same artist as the Gaudelet who exhibited *Lilas et Pivoines*, *Roses*, Dijon Salon 1890
LIT *Dijon Salon* 1890; *Paris Salon* 1842

GAUDIN, Augustine
b. Laval (Mayenne). Pupil of Carbillet, Parvillée and École de Laval. Exhib. *Fleurs* on faience, Paris Salon 1880
LIT *Paris Salon* 1880

GAUDISSARD or GAUDISSART, Emile ***b.1872***
b. Alger (Algeria). Sculptor and decorator. Painted genre, figures and flowers e.g. *L'âme des iris*, *L'âme des orchidées*, *L'âme des géraniums*
LIT *Bénézit*; *Orsay*; *Schurr* II, 23; *Thieme*

GAUGUIN, Paul ***1848–1903***
b. Paris. From Brittany to Tahiti, Gauguin painted flowers throughout his adventurous life. Their strong outlines, vibrant colours and sometimes puzzling arrangements have kept their mystery. His synthetic, intellectual approach to flower painting is a reaction against the more carefree, hedonistic or merely sensual Impressionist vision. *Nature-morte au livre ouvert*, 1872 (GW. 3); *Bouquet de fleurs dans un vase bleu*, 1874 (GW. 9); *Roses dans un verre*, 1875 (GW. 16); *Fleurs des champs dans un vase bleu*, 1876 (GW. 19); *Jacinthe et pommes sur un journal*, 1876 (GW. 19 bis); *Vase de fleurs sur une page de musique*, 1876 (GW. 20); *Pour faire un bouquet*, 1880 (GW. 49); *Vase de fleurs à la fenêtre*, 1881 (Rennes, GW. 63); *Jardinière et fleurs sur un tapis d'Orient*, 1881 (GW. 64); *Bouquet de fleurs*, 1882 (GW. 77); *Vase et cache-pot*, 1882 (Copenhagen, GW. 78); *Vase rond et tasse à thé*, 1882 (GW. 79); *Mandoline et cache-pot*, 1883 (GW. 91); *Les pivoines*, 1884 (GW. 131–2); *Corbeille de fleurs*, 1884 (Oslo, GW. 134); *Mandoline et fleurs*, 1885 (Orsay, GW. 173); *Les Dahlias*, 1885 (GW. 175); *Vase de fleurs*, 1885 (GW. 177); *Les vases et l'éventail*, 1885 (GW. 178); *Les glaïeuls*, 1885 (GW. 181); *Fleurs dans un panier*, 1885

(GW. 182); *Asters sur une commode*, 1886 (GW. 209); *Vase de fleurs et gourde*, 1886 (GW. 210); *Fleurs et feuillages, tambourins*, 1886 (GW. 212); *Fenêtre ouverte sur la mer*, 1888 (Orsay, GW. 292); *Van Gogh peignant des tournesols*, 1888 (GW. 296); *Nature-morte à l'estampe japonaise*, 1889
LIT *G. Wildenstein* (here GW), *Gauguin, Paris* 1964 *Paris Grand Palais, Réunion de Musées Nationaux*, 1989

GAUME, Marie-Madeleine
b. Versailles (Yvelines). Pupil of Collin and Foulongne. Exhib. *Fleurs et cuivres*, Paris Salon 1880
LIT *Bellier*; *Bénézit*; *Paris Salon* 1880

GAUPILLAT, Henri
b. Tonnerre (Yonne). Pupil of A. Dumarescq and H. Lamain. Exhib. *Orchidées* on faience, Paris Salon 1890
LIT *Bénézit*; *Paris Salon* 1890

GAUTHIER, Charles
b. Lyon. Pupil of Danguin and Bail. Exhib. *Fleurs et fruits*, Lyon Salon 1872, 1883
LIT *Lyon Salon* 1872, 1883

GAUTHIER, Marie
b. Lyon. Pupil of T. Tollet. Painted portraits, figures, genre and flowers. Exhib. Lyon Salon from 1889
LIT *Bénézit*; *Thieme*

GAUTHIER, Mathilde-Marie-Louise
b. Paris. Pupil of Leroux-Villeneuve. Exhib. *Premières fleurs d'été*, wc, Paris Salon 1895
LIT *Paris Salon* 1895

GAUTIER, Gabrielle
Exhib. Paris Indép. *Chrysanthèmes, Guirlandes de fleurs*, 1890, *Fleurs d'automne*, *Fleurs d'hiver*, 1894
LIT *Paris Indép.* 1890, 1894

GAUTIER, Georges
b. Le Havre (Seine-Maritime). Exhib. *Fleurs*, Paris Indép. 1894
LIT *Paris Indép.* 1894

GAUTIER, Marie, *later* Mme Antoni *b.1870*
b. Paris. Daughter of painter A.-D. Gautier (1825–1894). Exhib. Berlin, Dresden, Vienna, Paris e.g. *Glycine et soucis*, fan-leaf, wc, Paris SNBA 1894
LIT *Bénézit*; *Paris SNBA* 1894

GAUVIN, Mme J.M.
Exhib. *Un coin de serre*, Paris Salon 1895
LIT *Paris Salon* 1895 (ill.)

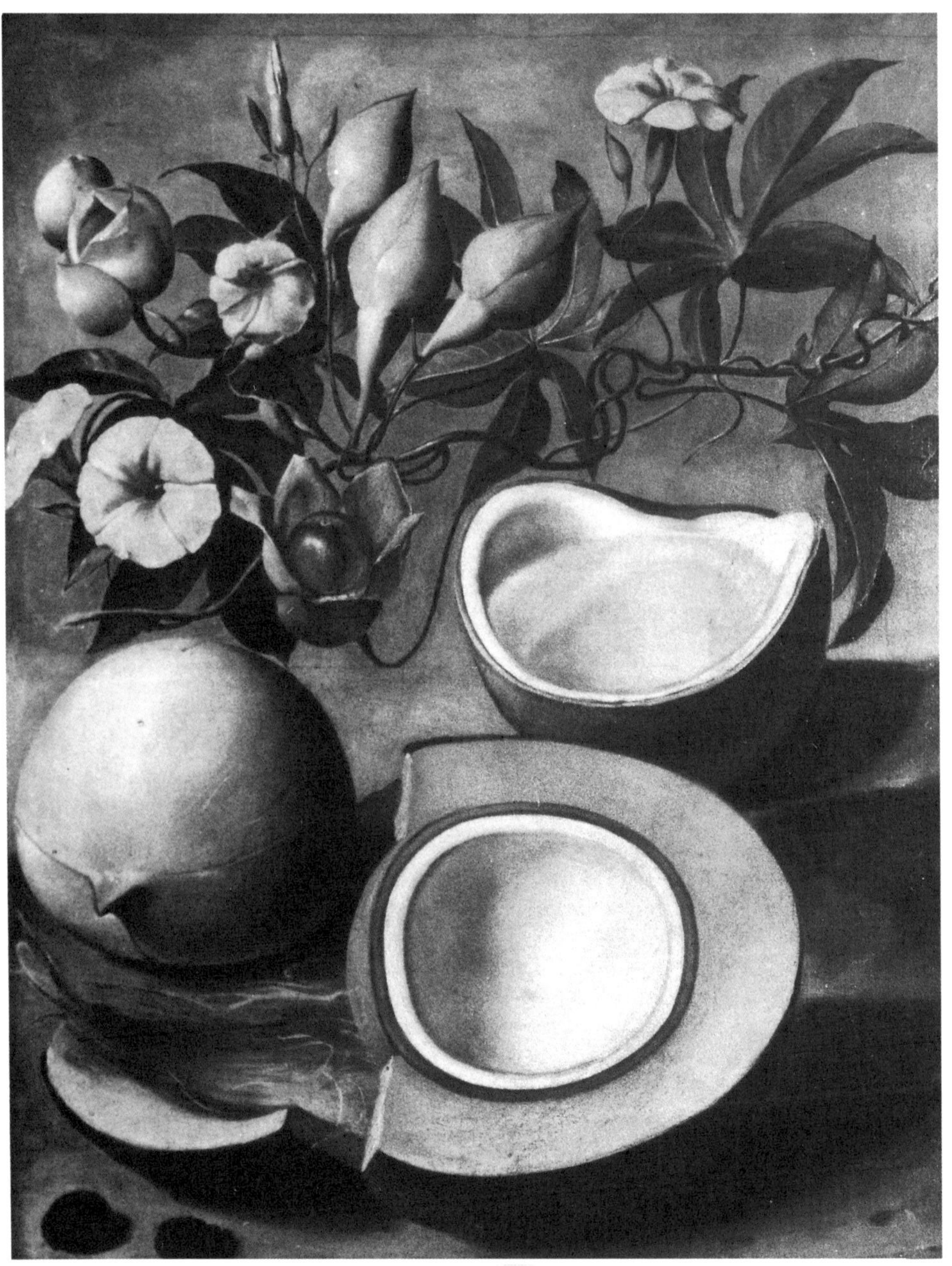

Michel Garnier

Oil on canvas
Paris, Muséum National d'Histoire Naturelle

GAUZI, François
b. Fronton (Haute-Garonne). Exhib. *Fleurs de printemps*, Paris Indép. 1893
LIT *Paris Indép.* 1893

GAVARRET, Eudoxie
b. Paris. Painted landscapes and flowers. Exhib. Paris Salon 1870–1879 e.g. *Chrysanthèmes*, wc, 1879
LIT *Bellier*; *Bénézit*

GAY, Jean-Claude ***b.1862***
Pupil of Castex-Dégrange, Lyon BA (CFD 1885)
LIT *Hardouin-Fugier Grafe*

GAYET, Etienne-Jules-Léonce ***b.1826***
Pupil of Thierriat, Lyon BA (CFD 1844). op. textile designer
LIT *Hardouin-Fugier Grafe* 1982 (ill.)

GAYET, Jules
Pupil of Berjon, Lyon BA (CFD 1820)
LIT *Hardouin-Fugier Grafe*

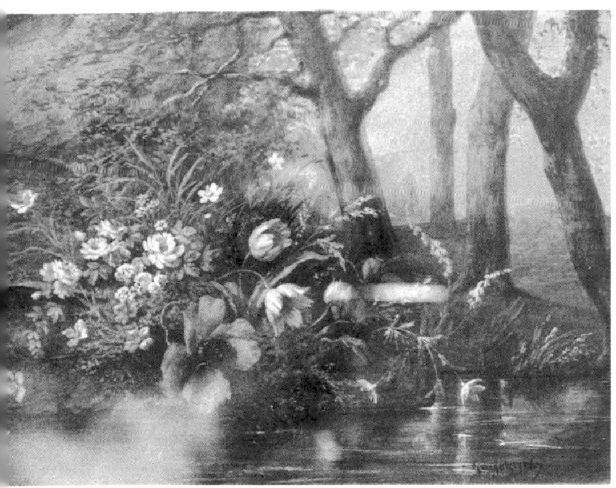

Etienne-Jules-Léonce Gayet

Gouache, 8¾ × 11 in. (22 × 28 cm.), signed and dated 1867
Private collection

GELFROY, Louise
Pupil of J. Amen. Exhib. *Bourriche d'oeillets*, Paris UFPS 1898
LIT *Paris UFPS* 1898

GELOT, Jean-Philippe ***b.1813***
b. Lyon. Pupil of Thierriat, Lyon BA (CFD 1832). Painted *Couronne de fleurs autour d'un médaillon*, Paris Salon 1849
LIT *Hardouin-Fugier Grafe*

GENEVOIS, Louis-Jean ***b.1879***
Pupil of Castex-Dégrange, Lyon BA (CFD 1899)
LIT *Hardouin-Fugier Grafe*

GENTELET
Pupil of Berjon, Lyon BA (CFD 1813)
LIT *Hardouin-Fugier Grafe*

GENY
Designed plates for A. Risso, *Flore de Nice*, 1844
LIT Paris Muséum MS 2047

GEOFFRAY, Blaise
Pupil of Thierriat, Lyon BA (CFD 1836). Exhib. Lyon Salon 1837
LIT *Hardouin-Fugier Grafe*

GEOFFROY, Noémi
b. Montluçon (Loire). Pupil of E. le Roux. Exhib. *Fleurs*, wc, *Chrysanthèmes*, fan-leaf, Paris Salon 1890
LIT *Paris Salon* 1890

GEORGE, Mlle L.B.
Exhib. *Roses et violettes*, *Roses Paul Nérin*, wc, Paris SNBA 1897
LIT *Paris SNBA* 1897

GEORGES-BONNARD, Mme
Pupil of S. Olivier and J. Médard, fl. Lyon. Exhib. *Roses et mimosas*, Lyon Salon 1884
LIT *Hardouin-Fugier Grafe*; *Lyon Salon* 1884

GEORGET, Elisa-Antoinette
b. Paris. Pupil of C. Georget and E. Claude. Exhib. 1880–1911: *Roses*, Paris Salon 1880; *Mimosas et violettes*, Dijon Salon 1892; *Chrysanthèmes et mimosas*, Paris Salon 1895; *Fleurs*, Dijon Salon 1897; *Chrysanthèmes*, Paris UFPS 1898
LIT *Bénézit*; *Dijon Salon* 1892, 1897; *Paris Salon* 1880, 1895; *Paris UFPS* 1898; *Thieme*

GEORGEVAL, Marie-Joséphine
Exhib. *Bouquet de fleurs*, on porcelain, Paris Salon 1845
LIT *Paris Salon* 1845

GÉRALDY, *see* REYNARD

GÉRARD, Gaston ***b.1859***
b. Saint-Mandé (Val-de-Marne). Pupil of J. Lefebvre, École des Arts et Métiers and Paris BA. op. decorator. Exhib. *Roses thé*, Paris Noir et Blanc Salon 1886
LIT *Bénézit*; *Orsay*; *Paris Noir et Blanc Salon* 1886; *Thieme*

GERBAULT, Jules
b. Reims (Marne). Painted flowers and fruit *c.*1875. Musée de Reims: *Pivoines* (disappeared *c.*1914–1918)
LIT *Bénézit*; *Thieme*

GERBAUT, Jenny ***1822–1894***
Sister of portrait painter Alfred Gerbaut. Miniature painter. Musée de Troyes: *Fleurs et fruits*
LIT *Bénézit*; *Thieme*

GERDERES, Jeanne, *later* Mme Freyssenge
b. Saint-Dizier (Haute-Marne). Pupil of Bourgouin and F. Rivoire. Exhib. *Camélias*, *Boules de neige*, Paris Noir et Blanc Salon 1886; *Chrysanthèmes*, wc, Paris Salon 1890; *Prunes et roses*, *Roses trémières*, wc, Paris SNBA 1898; *Fleurs des champs*, wc, *Eglantier*, pastel, Paris SNBA 1899
LIT *Bénézit*; *Paris Noir et Blanc Salon* 1886; *Paris Salon* 1890; *Paris SNBA* 1898, 1899

GERET, Jeanne-Alphonsine
b. Paris. Pupil of her father and Périn. Exhib. Paris Salon from 1877 e.g. *Pensées*, fan-leaf, gouache, 1878
LIT *Bellier*; *Bénézit*

GERMAIN, Louis
b. Niort (Deux-Sèvres). Painted religious subjects, still-lifes and flowers. Exhib. Paris Salon from *c.*1860 e.g. *Bouquet de fleurs*, 1882
LIT *Bénézit*; *Paris Salon* 1882

GERMAIN DE SAINT-PIERRE, Jacques-Ernest
b. Saint-Pierre-Moûtier (Nièvre). Designed plates for E. Cosson *Flore ... des environs de Paris*, Paris, 1845
LIT *Bénézit*; *Nissen* I, 415

GÉRÔME, Pauline, *later* Regnard
b. Paris. Pupil of Rottée and Thoret. Exhib. *Flowers*, gouache, Paris Salon 1875
LIT *Bénézit*; *Paris Salon* 1875

GERONO, Huberte or Hubertine *b.1797*
Pupil of Jaquotot, Robert and Redouté. Exhib. paintings on porcelain Paris Salon 1817, 1819, 1822, 1824
LIT *Bénézit*; *Hardouin-Fugier* 1981

GERVAIS
Spray of Flowers and Grasses, 1832, wc, Cambridge, Fitzwilliam Museum (Broughton coll.). JLC

GERVEX, Henri *1852–1929*
b. Paris. Pupil of Cabanel and Fromentin. Popular portrait, figure and genre painter occasionally produced some flowers (wc)
LIT *Bellier*; *Bénézit*; *Orsay*; *Thieme*

GHÉQUIER, Alexis de *1817–1869*
b. Dunkerque (Nord). Exhib. Paris Salon 1846–1868 e.g. *Fleurs et fruits*, *Bouquet de fleurs*, Paris Salon 1861
LIT *Paris Salon* 1861; *Thieme*

GIACOMELLI, Hector *1822–1904*
op. book illustrator. Painted birds and occasionally, flowers e.g. *Oiseaux et fleurs*, Paris Salon 1878, 1879
LIT *Bellier*; *Bénézit*; *Orsay*; *Schurr* IV, 91; *Thieme*

GIBAUT, Maxime
b. Bois-le-Roi (Seine-et-Marne). Exhib. Paris Indép. e.g. *Roses*, *Chrysanthèmes*, 1891, *Roses*, 1892, *Brassée de Chrysanthèmes*, 1894, *Roses*, 1896, *Phlox*, 1898, *Panier de chrysanthèmes*, 1899
LIT *Paris Indép.* 1891, 1892, 1894, 1896, 1898, 1899

GIBAULT, Eugène
b. Brest (Finistère). Exhib. Paris Salon from 1876 e.g. *Roses jaunes*, 1879
LIT *Bellier*; *Bénézit*

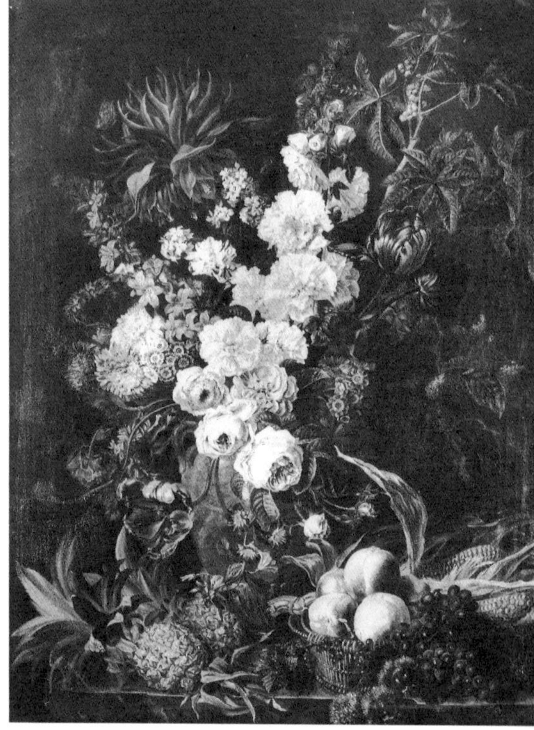

Jenny Gerbaut

Oil on canvas, 45¾ × 35¼ in. (116.5 × 89.5 cm.), signed
Troyes, Musée des Beaux-Arts

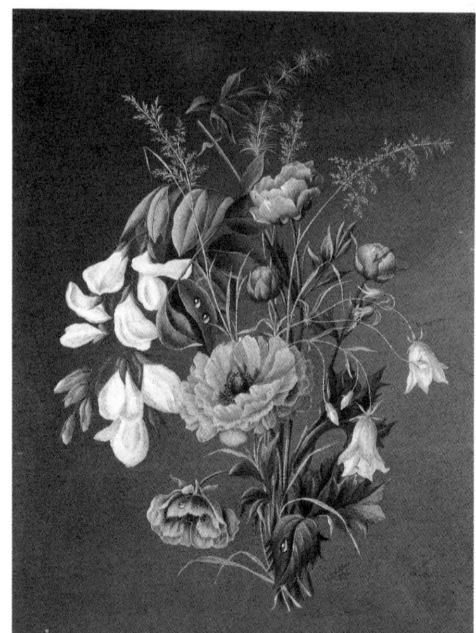

Gervais

Watercolour on paper, 10½ × 8 in. (26.6 × 20.4 cm.), signed and dated 1832
Cambridge, Fitzwilliam Museum (Broughton Collection)

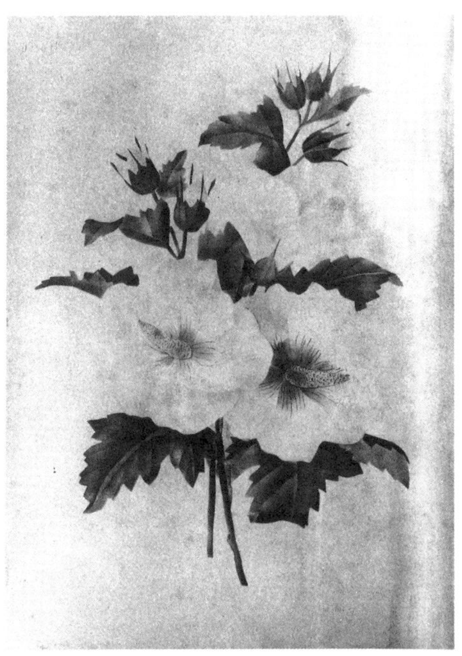

N. D. de Giradot

Watercolour on paper
Le Puy, Musée Crozatier

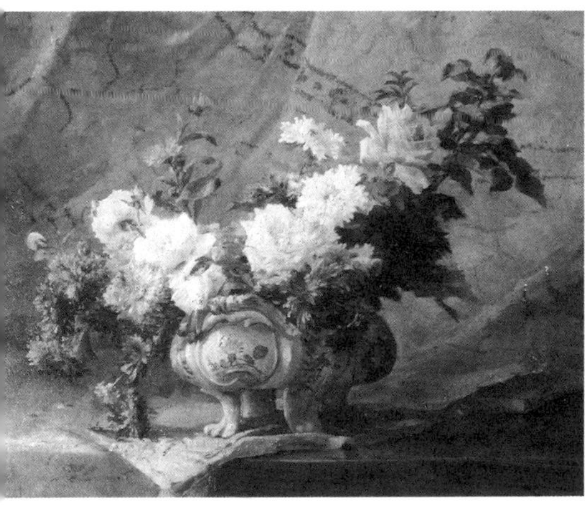

Marie-Charlotte Girard-Nauwelaers

Oil on canvas, 31½ × 39½ in. (80 × 100 cm.), signed
Private collection (photo: Musée des Beaux-Arts, Lyon)

GIBBAUD, Mme Alfred J.B.E
b. Paris. Exhib. *Fleurs et oiseaux*, on faience, Paris Salon 1890
LIT *Paris Salon* 1890

GIBERT, Louise
Exhib. *Pensées*, Dijon Salon 1890
LIT *Dijon Salon* 1890

GIESLER, Anna-Frédérique
b. Paris. Pupil of Seebuch. Exhib. *Pavots*, Paris Salon 1895; *Chrysanthèmes, Soleils et reines-marguerites*, Dijon Salon 1897; *Roses trémières et reines-marguerites*, Paris Salon 1898
LIT *Dijon Salon* 1897; *Paris Salon* 1895, 1898

GILBERT, Flore-Amélie, *née* Bienaimé *1808–1867*
b. Paris. Pupil of Ingres and Redouté. Exhib. *Bouquet de dahlias et géranium blanc*, wc, *Bouquet de tulipes, géranium rouge, rose et pensée*, wc, Paris Salon 1835
LIT *Bellier*; *Bénézit*; *Paris Salon* 1835; *Thieme*

GILBERT, Marthe
Pupil of Furcy de Lavault and Auguin. Exhib. *Marguerites et bluets*, Paris UFPS 1898
LIT *Paris UFPS* 1898

GILBERT, Victor-Gabriel *1847–after 1933*
b. Paris. Pupil of Levasseur, Busson and Adan. Painted genre, portraits and, occasionally, flowers. Exhib. *Roses*, *Fleurs coupées*, Paris Noir et Blanc Salon 1889
LIT *Bénézit*; *Paris Noir et Blanc Salon* 1889, *Schurr* I, 90; *Thieme*

GILLARD, Aline
Exhib. Dijon Salon: *Chrysanthèmes*, *Lilas*, 1887, *Lilas*, 1890, *Reines-marguerites*, 1892
LIT *Dijon Salon* 1887, 1890, 1892. CL

GILLES, Louis
Exhib. *Roses*, *Fleurs*, *Chrysanthèmes*, Paris Indép. 1888
LIT *Paris Indép.* 1888

GILON, Félix
b. Paris. Exhib. *Fleurs*, Paris Indép. 1894
LIT *Paris Indép.* 1894

GINISTY, Delphine-Julienne-Alice
Exhib. Paris Salon from 1876. Her *Chrysanthèmes* was bought by the government in 1892, 150 francs, for the Musée de Montélimar
LIT *Bénézit*; Paris Arch. Nat. F21:2135

GINTRAC-JOUASSET
b. Bordeaux (Gironde). Exhib. *Coquelicots*, pastel, Paris Indép. 1889
LIT *Paris Indép.* 1889

GIRADOT, N.D. de
M: Le Puy: *Fleurs de Mauves*, 1832
LIT *Bénézit*

GIRALDON, Adolphe-Paul *1855–1933*
b. Marseille. Pupil of Français, Lequien and L.O. Merson. Painted landscapes. Book illustrator and engraver. Designed flower plates
LIT *Bellier*; *Bénézit*; *Schurr* II, 70; *Thieme*

GIRARD, Claude *b.1796*
Pupil of Berjon, Lyon BA (CFD 1813)
LIT *Hardouin-Fugier Grafe*

GIRARD, Pierre-Florentin ***fl.c.1860***
Worked in Lyon. Painted still-lifes and, occasionally, flowers. Lyon, private coll.
LIT *Lyon Salon* 1858

GIRARD, Protais ***b.1870***
Pupil of Castex-Dégrange, Lyon BA (CFD 1887)
LIT *Hardouin-Fugier Grafe*

GIRARD-CONDAMIN, Jeanne
Pupil of Guichard, L. Guy and Reignier. Exhib. Lyon Salon from 1869, Paris Salon from 1874 e.g. *Chrysanthèmes*, Lyon Salon 1883, *Roses dans un arrosoir*, Lyon Salon 1898
LIT *Bénézit*; *Hardouin-Fugier Grafe*; *Lyon Salon* 1883, 1898

GIRARD-NAUWELAERS, Marie-Charlotte ***1865–1934***
Pupil of T. Tollet and A. Perrachon. Excelled at painting Malmaison roses. Exhib. Lyon Salon 1889–1934 and Dijon Salon e.g. *Coquelicots*, *Feuillages et fleurs d'automne*, 1890
LIT *Bénézit*; *Dijon Salon* 1890; *Hardouin-Fugier Grafe*; M. Moyne in *Fleurs de Lyon* (*Hardouin-Fugier Grafe* 1982 ill.)

GIRARDIN, Eugène **c.*1861–1898***
b. Plombières (Vosges). Pupil of Boulanger and Lefebvre. Exhib. Paris Salon 1880–1898 e.g. *Fleurs décoratives*, 1880
LIT *Bénézit*; *Paris Salon* 1880; *Schurr* V, 128; *Thieme*; *Witt*

GIRARDIN, Julien
b. Plombières (Vosges). Painted landscapes and genre. Exhib. Paris Salon 1855–1869 e.g. *Pivoines en arbre*, *Pavots vivaces*, *Bouillon blanc*, *Chardon*, 1861
LIT *Bellier*; *Paris Salon* 1861

GIRARDIN, Pauline, *née* Joannis ***b.1818***
b. Belleville-sur-Seine (Paris XX°). Pupil of L.A. Girardin and Redouté. Designed flower plates. Exhib. wc, Paris Salon 1838–1875. *Tulipes*, 1838, *Grand bouquet de camélias et fleurs diverses*, wc, *Branche de lauriers-rose*, wc, *Branche de lilas*, wc, *Une rose*, wc, *Bouquet de camélias*, wc; *Bouquet d'oeillets*, wc, Dijon Salon 1849; *Fleurs des champs*, *Volubilis*, *Oeillets*, *Roses cent feuilles*, *Camélia*, *Accacia*, Paris Salon 1850. M: Chambéry, Chartres, Dijon; Fitzwilliam Museum, Cambridge (Broughton coll.)
LIT *Bellier*; *Bénézit*; Dijon Salon 1849; *Faré* 1962, p. 246; *Hardouin-Fugier* 1981 (ill.); Paris Arch. Nat. F21:44, 4600, 4500; *Thieme*

GIRARDOT, Henri ***1878–1935***
b. Grenoble (Isère). Pupil of Girot and J. Flandrin. Painted landscapes and flowers. M: Grenoble: *Bouquet de roses*
LIT *Bénézit*; Grenoble Bibl. Mun. man. Sainson; Musée de Grenoble doc.; *Thieme*

GIRAUD, Alfred ***b.1868***
Pupil of Castex-Dégrange, Lyon BA (CFD 1889–1891)
LIT *Hardouin-Fugier Grafe*

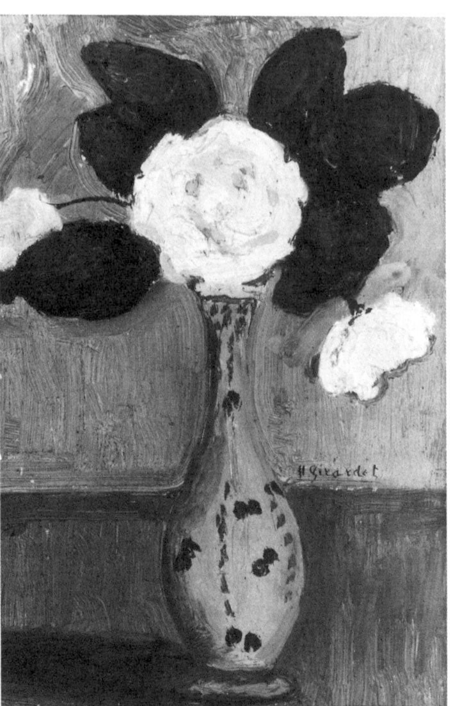

GIRAUD, Jules
b. Digne (Alpes-de-Haute-Provence). Exhib. Paris Salon 1879–1891 e.g. *Fleurs*, 1880, *Dans les ruines*, 1883
LIT *Paris Salon* 1880, 1883

GIRAUD, Jules-Lazare ***1804–1869***
Exhib. Paris Salon 1847–1861 e.g. *Fleurs dans un bonnet de femme accroché à une lanterne*, 1848, *Fleurs et fruits*, 1861
LIT *Bellier*; *Bénézit*; *Paris Salon* 1861; *Thieme*

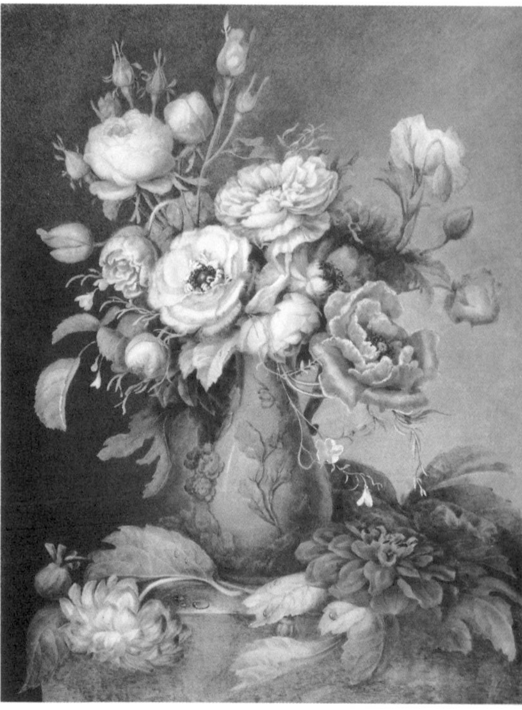

Pauline Girardin

Watercolour on vellum, 22½ × 17¼ in. (57 × 43.7 cm.), signed
Cambridge, Fitzwilliam Museum (Broughton Collection)

Henri Girardot

Oil on canvas, 23¼ × 22½ in. (59 × 57 cm), Grenoble, Musée de Peinture et de Sculpture

Héloïse-Augustine Girault née Lesourd-Delisle

Watercolour on paper, 10¾ × 9¼ in.
(27.5 × 23.5 cm.), signed
(photo: Musée d'Angers)

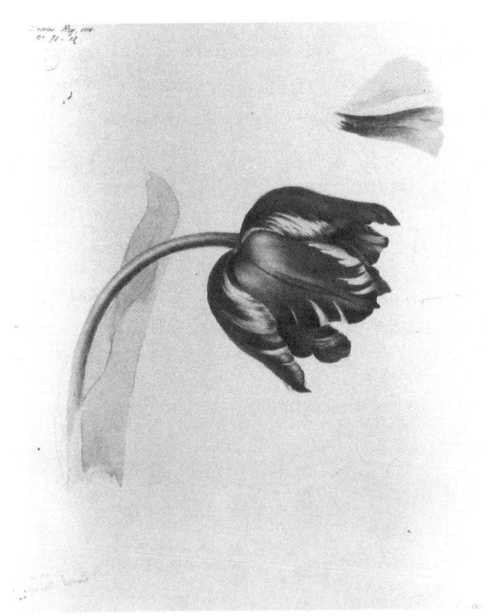

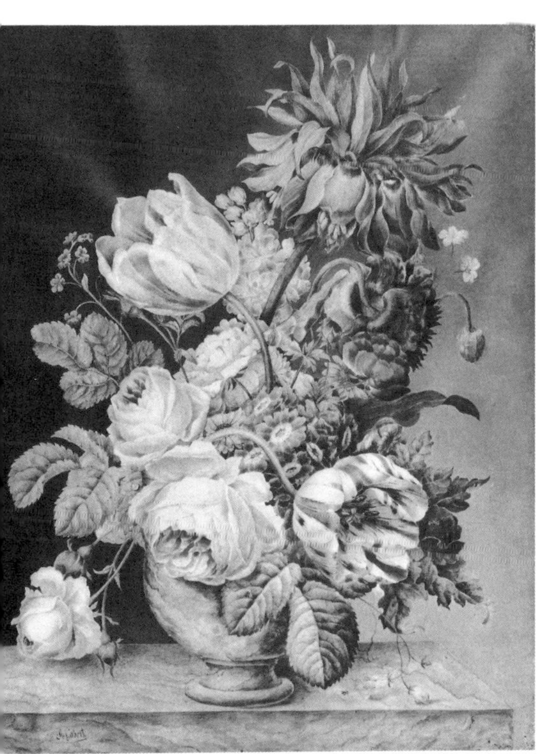

GIRAUD, Sébastien-Charles ***1819–1892***
b. Paris. Pupil of E. Giraud, his brother and Paris BA (1835). Painted landscapes, interiors, genre, still-lifes and, occasionally, flowers. Exhib. Paris Salon 1839–1876
LIT *Bellier*; *Bénézit*; Paris, Musée Jacquemart André, *S. Giraud* ... 1957; *Witt*

GIRAULT DE SAINT-FARGEAU, Amanda
b. Troyes (Aube). Pupil of L. de Mirbel. Painted portrait miniatures, and, occasionally, flowers (e.g. after Van Dael). Exhib. Paris Salon 1845–1870
LIT *Bellier*; *Bénézit*; *Thieme*

GIRAULT, Héloïse-Augustine, *née* Lesourd-Deslisle ***1810–1890***
b. Paris. Pupil of Redouté. Exhib. wc., Paris Salon 1835, 1836, 1838. M: Angers
LIT *Bénézit; Faré* 1962, p. 246; *Hardouin-Fugier* 1981 (ill.)

GIRAUT, Jean-Charles
Exhib. *Fleurs*, Paris Salon 1850
LIT *Paris Salon* 1850

GIRBAUD, Mme Alfred-Elaine
b. Paris. Exhib. Paris Salon from 1849 e.g. *Roses et jasmins blancs* (after Van Spaendonck, bought by the State); *Roses, Jasmins*, Paris Exposition Universelle 1855; *Groupe de roses*, *Rose et jacinthe dans un verre*, on porcelain, 1867, *Corbeille de fleurs*, miniature, 1885. op. Sèvres 1844–1870. Sister-in-law of Jeanne and Jenny Girbaud
LIT *Bellier*; *Bénézit*; Paris Arch. Nat. F.21:32; *Paris Exposition Universelle* 1855; *Paris Salon* 1861, 1867, 1885; *Thieme*

Auguste Gobert

Watercolour on paper, 18 × 14½ in.
(45.6 × 36.8 cm.), signed
Cambridge, Fitzwilliam Museum
(Broughton Collection)

GIRBAUD, Jeanne-Bathilde-Eliane
b. Paris. Exhib. *Groupe de fleurs*, pastel, Paris Salon 1880
LIT *Paris Salon* 1880

GIRBAUD, Jenny
Miniature painter. Exhib. Paris Salon 1845–80, often copies, e.g. *Branche de roses*, after Van Spaendonck, on porcelain, 1847
LIT *Bellier*; *Bénézit*; *Thieme*

GIRERD, Charles
Exhib. *Glaïeuls*, Paris Indép. 1888
LIT *Paris Indép.* 1888

GIROT, François-Joseph ***1873–1917***
b. Grenoble (Isère). Pupil of Grenoble BA and G. Moreau. Painted landscapes, portraits and, occasionally, flowers
LIT *Bénézit*

GIROT, Marie-Antoine ***1809–1895***
b. Paris. Painted still-lifes and, occasionally, flowers
LIT *Bénézit*; *Thieme*; *Witt*

GIROU, Marie
Exhib. *Argémones*, Roanne Salon 1890
LIT *Roanne Salon* 1890

GLORGET, P.E.
Exhib. Paris SNBA *Roses, capucines, iris*, *Roses et bluets*, wc, 1896, *Rose gloire de Dijon*, *Pavots*, *Roses mousse*, wc, 1897, *Hortensias*, *Pétunias*, wc, 1899
LIT *Paris SNBA* 1896, 1897, 1899

GOBERT, Auguste
Exhib. Paris Salon from 1841 e.g. *Renoncules*, wc, 1841, *Groupe de dahlias*, wc, *Roses cent feuilles et mousseuses*, wc, *Bouquet de fleurs*, wc, 1842
LIT *Bellier*; *Bénézit*

GOBILLARD, Paule *1867–1946*
b. Quimperlé (Finistère). Pupil of Berthe Morisot, her aunt. Painted landscapes, still-lifes and flowers. Exhib. Paris Indép. from 1894
LIT *Bénézit*; *Witt*

GOBLET, Jean-Pierre-Joachim
op. Sèvres 1847–1848. Exhib. *Vase de fleurs*, étude, Paris Salon 1842
LIT *Brunet Préaud*; *Paris Salon* 1842

GODARD, E.
Designed plates for Vilmorin, *Les fleurs*
LIT *P. de Vilmorin, Les fleurs*, Paris (Baillière) 1892

GODCHAUX *or* GODECHAUX *b.c.1860*
Painted landscapes and flowers c.1890 e.g. *Fleurs* Grenoble sale, 1983; *Chrysanthèmes* and *Dahlias*, Geneva sale, 1–2 June 1988, lots 28 and 29
LIT *Grenoble*, Blache, 25 Apr. 1983; *Schurr* III, 41

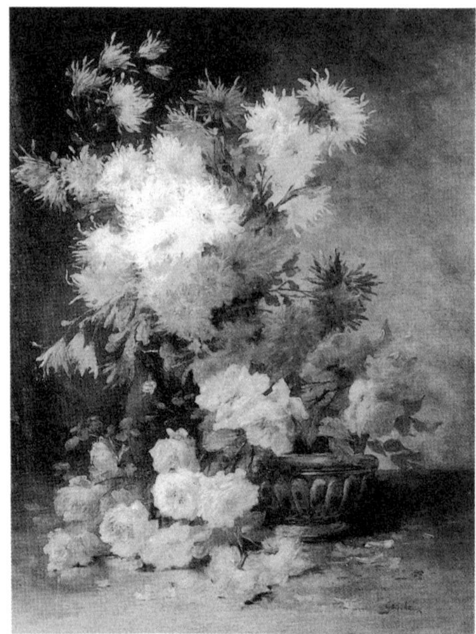

Godchaux or Godechaux

Oil on canvas, 51 × 36 in. (130 × 93 cm.), signed
Private collection

GODIEN, Adrien *1873–1949*
Pupil of Lyon BA and T. Tollet. Painted landscapes, genre, portraits and flowers. M: Lyon, *Fleurs dans un vase*
LIT *Bénézit*; *Hardouin-Fugier Grafe*; *Hardouin-Fugier Grafe* 1979 (ill.); *Thieme*

GODIN, Charles-Henri
b. Etampes (Essonne). Pupil of Vandremer and F. de Courcy. Exhib. Paris Salon 1878–1879 (Bénézit incorrectly cites a work by the artist in the Sheffield Art Gallery)
LIT *Bellier*; *Bénézit*

GOENEUTTE, Norbert *1854–1894*
b. Paris. Pupil of Pils. Painter and engraver. Painted figures, landscapes, genre and flowers e.g. *Bouquet de pavots*, *Fleurs*, *Jacinthes et jonquilles*
LIT *Bénézit*; G. de Knyff, *N. Goeneutte*, Paris (Mayer) 1978; *Orsay*; *Schurr* I, 92

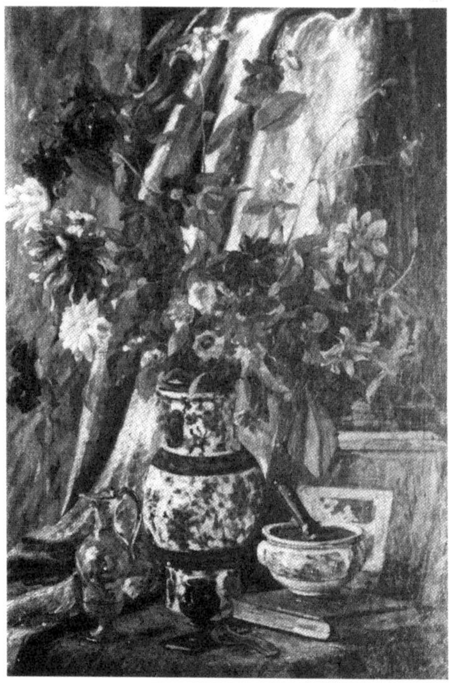

Adrien Godien

Oil on canvas, signed
Lyon, Musée des Beaux-Arts

GOGH, Vincent van *1853–1890*
b. Zundert, Netherlands. The recent sensational auctions of two major flower paintings by Van Gogh (Christie's, London, 30 Mar. 1987—£24m; Sotheby's, New York, 11 Oct. 1987—$55m) have, if conceivable, drawn yet further attention to a much reproduced and justly world-famous type of Van Gogh. They represent the continuation or culmination of a line to be traced back to *Cabbages and Clogs* (FI) of 1881, now in the Vincent Van Gogh Museum, Amsterdam. The latter also contains a uniquely large group of sixteen flower paintings. Unlike other great non-specialists included in the Dictionary, such as Renoir and Monet, the approach of the still-life painter is inseparable from our understanding of Van Gogh. Paintings such as the late *Sunflowers* and *Irises*, redolent of Japanese art or,

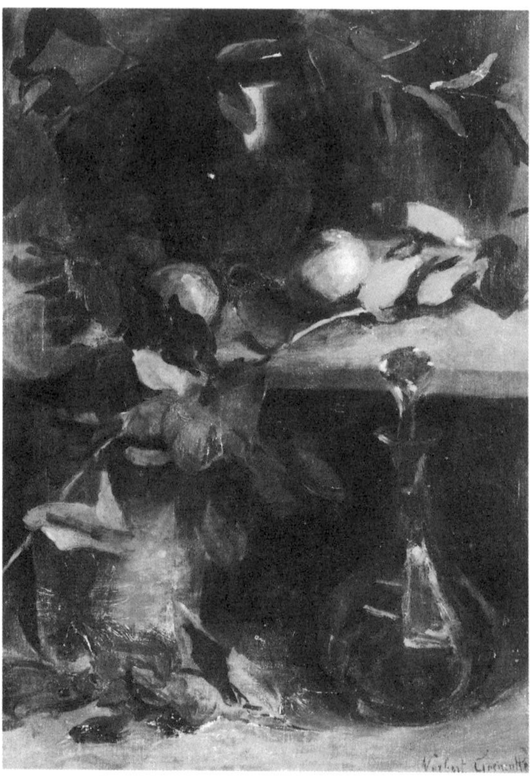

Norbert Goeneutte

Oil on canvas, 22 × 17 in. (56 × 42 cm.), signed
Courtesy Christie's, London

perhaps more accurately, of Van Gogh's vision of it, are clearly not isolated achievements. The list of numbers from the de la Faille catalogue below indicates that over eighty flower paintings are extant; and there are, in addition, many canvases of trees, corners of fields and gardens which include flowers. All are essential forerunners to the *Irises*. He studied and painted, with equal intensity, in the manner of a Dutch specialist of the 17th century, chairs, shoes, fruits, bottles, pots, pans, glasses, birds' nests, moths, fish, sacks, and books. None is more lovingly observed than the small basket of sprouting bulbs (F.334). The influence of Monticelli was transitory. Van Gogh's painting of flowers, whether cut or growing, developed strongly from the summer of 1886 in Paris to the end of his life in the Midi with ever-greater understanding and empathy with his subjects. Flowers helped him to bring undreamed of colour harmonies to his palette and he repaid them with incandescent immortality.
de la Faille: 76, 197, 198, 199, 201, 213, 214, 217, 218, 220, 234, 235, 236, 237, 241, 242, 243, 243a, 244, 245, 246, 247, 248, 248a, 248b, 249, 250, 251, 252, 258, 259, 278, 279, 280, 282, 286, 286a, 286b, 287, 322, 323, 324, 324a, 327, 362, 375, 376, 377, 392, 393, 452, 453, 454, 455, 456, 457, 458, 459, 579, 583, 588, 589, 591, 592, 593, 594, 595, 596, 597, 598, 599, 600, 601, 608, 610, 666, 666a, 671, 678, 680, 681, 682, 748, 749, 763, 764, 764a, 821. M: Amsterdam, Bern, Buffalo, Copenhagen, The Hague, Hartford, Laren, Leningrad, London, Mannheim, Merion, Munich, New York, Ottawa, Otterlo, Paris, Philadelphia, Rotterdam, Stockholm, Winnipeg, Wuppertal, Zürich
LIT *J.B. de la Faille, The Works of Vincent van Gogh, His Paintings and Drawings*, Amsterdam 1970, no. F.608, illus.; Jan Hulsker, *The Complete Van Gogh, Paintings, Drawings, Sketches*, New York, 1980, p. 390, no. 1691, illus.; Susan Alyson Stein, *Van Gogh, A Retrospective*, New York, 1986, pp. 157, 158, 181, 310, 313, illus. in colour p. 247, also on cover. PM

GOMIER, Marie-Eugénie
b. Paris. Pupil of Gosse. Painted portraits and, occasionally, flowers e.g. *Giroflée*, Paris Salon 1880
LIT *Bellier*; *Bénézit*; *Paris Salon* 1880

GONAZ, François or Francisque *b.1826*
b. Lyon. In Brazil 1846–1858. Exhib. Paris *Le Brésil ou la Nature des Tropiques*, 1866. Exhib. Paris Salon e.g. *Fleurs et fruits des régions tropicales*, 1864, *Fleurs et fruits d'Europe*, 1866, *Vase de fleurs*, 1883. M: Cincinnati, USA (untraceable); Paris Muséum d'Histoire Naturelle; Saint-Malo (destroyed in the war)
LIT *Bellier*; *Bénézit*; *Hardouin-Fugier Grafe*; *Paris Salon* 1883; *Thieme*

GONSSOLIN, Gabrielle
b. Lyon. Pupil of Puyroche-Wagner. Exhib. *Groupe de pivoines*, *Fleurs du mois d'avril*, gouache, fan-leaf, *Roses mousseuses*, gouache, fan-leaf, Lyon Salon 1882; *Fleurs*, Grenoble Salon 1899
LIT *Grenoble Salon* 1899; *Lyon Salon* 1882. MW

GONTIER, Clément
b. Lavaur. Pupil of J.P. Laurens. Third class medal 1904
LIT *Bénézit*. PM

GONTIER, Jean *d.1851*
Exhib. Paris Salon from 1835. Designed plates e.g. for C.H. Gaudichaud-Beaupré, *Voyage autour du monde ... 1836–1837*, Paris 1846–1866, H.F. Jaubert, E. Spach, *Choix de plantes ... de l'Asie occidentale*, Paris (Roret) 1842–1857. Exhib. Paris Salon 1835–1839 e.g. *Dahlias*, wc, 1835, *Fleurs d'après nature*, 1837. Works in Paris Muséum d'Histoire Naturelle (not botanical)
LIT *Bellier*; *Bénézit*; *Laissus*; *Nissen* I, 556, 690, 985, 1712–14, 2380; *Paris Salon* 1835, 1837; *Sitwell*

GONTIER, L.
Two flower-pieces dated 1879 formerly in the Musée de Saint-Omer
LIT *Bénézit*; *Orsay*

GONTIER, Pierre-Camille
Exhib. Paris Salon from 1863 e.g. *Panier de fleurs*, 1864, *Couronne de fleurs*, 1868; *Fleurs de printemps*, Paris Indép. 1884. *Roses* signed C. Gontier, Dorotheum, Vienna, 18–21 Sept. 1979. One work in Bowes Museum, Barnard Castle
LIT *Bellier*; *Bénézit*; *Orsay*; *Paris Indép.* 1884; *Witt*

GONZALÈS, Eva, *later* Mme Henri Guérard *1849–1883*
b. Paris. Pupil of C. Chaplin, G. Brinon and Manet. Painted figures, genre and flowers. Exhib. *La plante favorite*, Paris Salon 1872. *Le bouquet*, Galliera, Paris, 12 Mar. 1914, 25 Nov. 1967, *Roses dans un vase*, Sotheby's, London, 25 Nov. 1967, *Nature morte au bouquet*, *c*.1880, Sotheby's, London, 7 Dec. 1978 etc.
LIT *Bellier*; *Bénézit*; *Orsay*; *Paris Salon* 1872; C. Roger-Marx, *Eva Gonzalès ...* Saint-Germain-en-Laye (Neuilly) 1950; Saint-Tropez, Musée de l'Annonciade, *Fleurs de Fantin-Latour à Marquet*, 1982, no. 27; *Schurr* I, 90; *Witt*

GONZALÈS, Jeanne, after 1883 Mme Guérard *1856–1924*
b. Paris. Sister of Eva Gonzalès. Painted genre and flowers. Exhib. Paris Salon from 1879 e.g. *Géraniums*, 1880, *Fleurs et légumes*, 1882
LIT *Bellier*; *Bénézit*; *Orsay*; *Schurr* IV, 83

GORLIER, Jean-Baptiste *1829–1895*
op. textile designer. Exhib. Lyon Salon. His *Fleurs* was in the Lyon Société des Amis-des-Arts raffle 1873. Exhib. *Fleurs et fruits*, Saint-Etienne Salon 1882
LIT *Audin Vial*; *Hardouin-Fugier Grafe*; *Saint-Etienne Salon* 1882

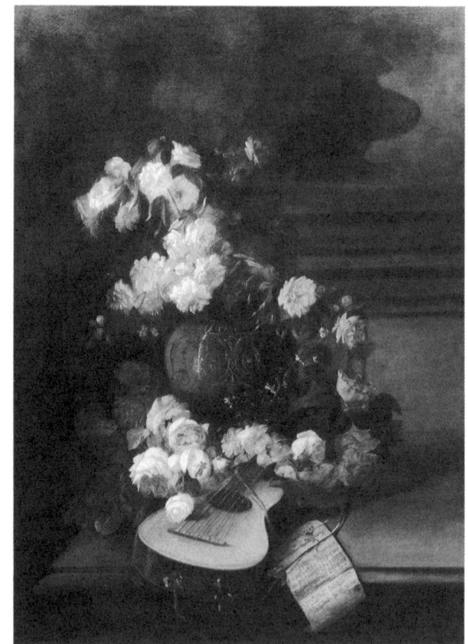

Clément Gontier (*right*)

Oil on canvas, $51\frac{1}{4} \times 38$ in. (130.2 × 96.5 cm.), signed
Courtesy Christie's, London

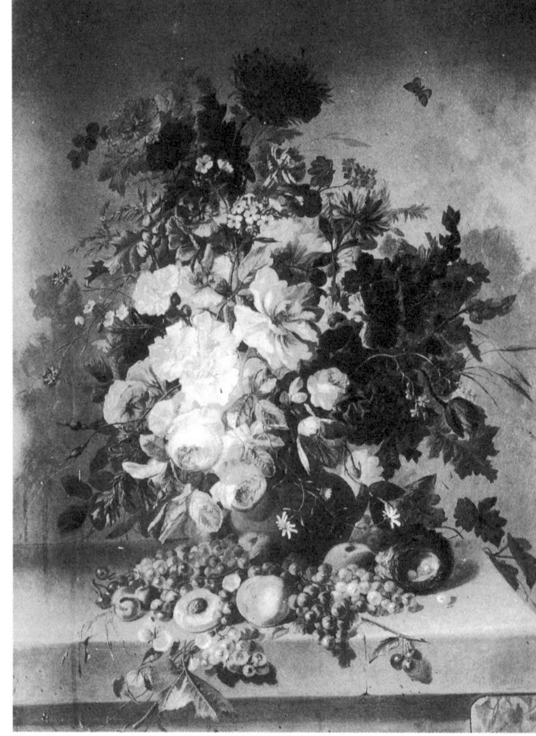

Pierre-Camille Gontier

Oil on canvas, $21\frac{3}{4} \times 15$ in. (55 × 38 cm.), signed
Private collection, France

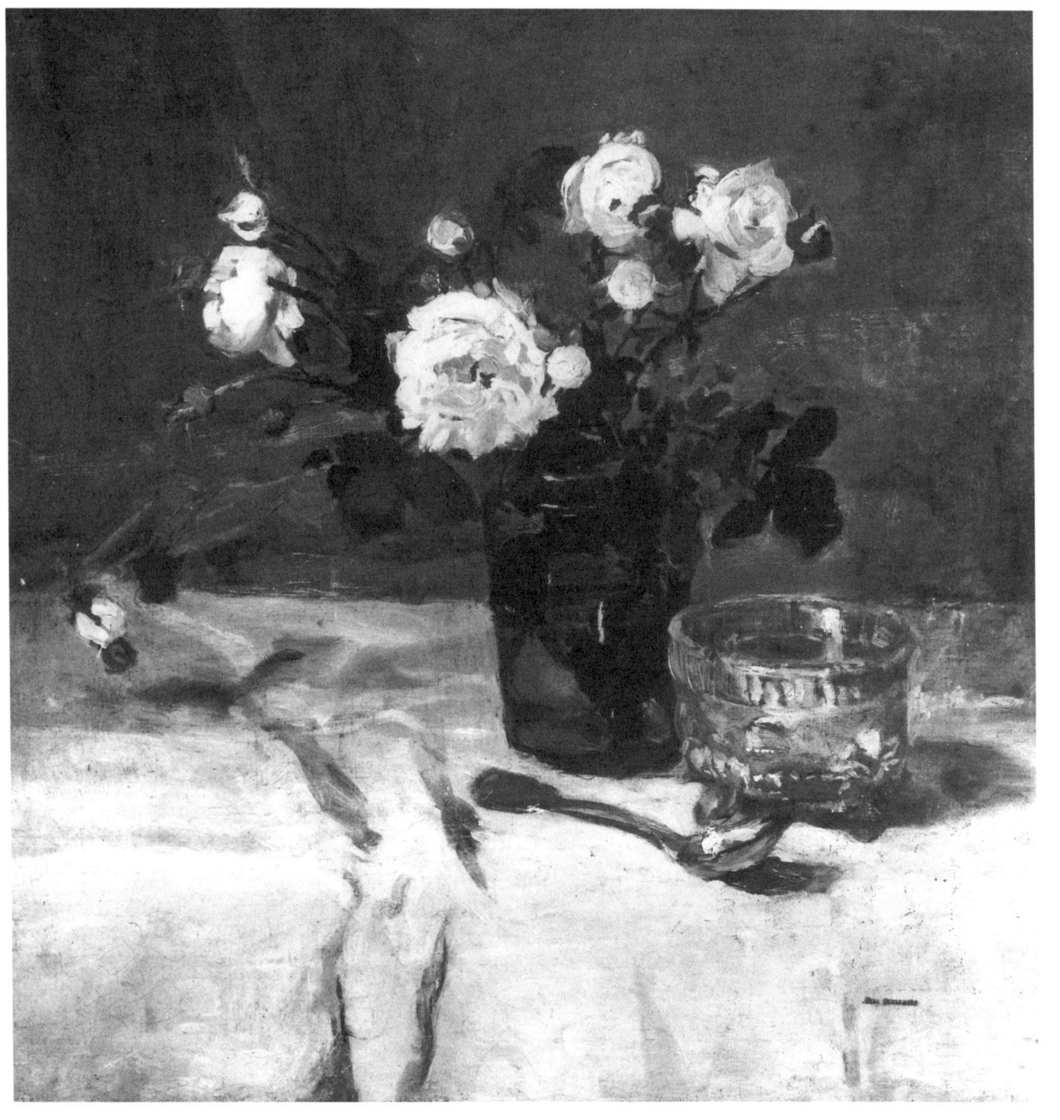

Eva Gonzalès

Oil on canvas, $16\frac{1}{2} \times 16\frac{1}{2}$ in. (42 × 42 cm.),
Josefowitz Collection

GORLIN, Eugène
b. Clermont (Oise). Exhib. *Yucca, Glaïeuls*, Paris Indép. 1893
LIT *Paris Indép.* 1893

GOROCHAND
Designed and lithographed botanical plates e.g. *Roscoea, Andromeda fastigiata*, Paris BMAD (Maciet coll.)
LIT *Paris BMAD*

GOTTSCHALK, Rose-Caroline
Pupil of L. Louppe. Exhib. *Fleurs de printemps*, wc, Paris UFPS 1898
LIT *Paris UFPS* 1898

GOUDEX, Joseph ***b.1874***
Pupil of Castex-Dégrange, Lyon BA (CFD 1892)
LIT *Hardouin-Fugier Grafe*

GOUILLET, Armand
b. Paris. Pupil of J. Gouillet, his father. Exhib. *Fleurs*, on faience, Paris Salon 1880
LIT *Paris Salon* 1880

GOUILLET, Jules ***b.1826***
b. Versailles (Yvelines). Pupil of Chazal and Wachsmuth. Painted flowers and fruit, mostly on faience, 1874–1882. Exhib. Paris Salon from 1847 e.g. *Fleurs*, 1850, 1861; *Roses*, 1859, Dorotheum, Vienna, 21 Mar. 1973
LIT *Bellier*; *Bénézit*; *Paris Salon* 1850, 1861; *Thieme*; *Witt*

GOUPIL, Marie-Mathilde
b. Paris. Pupil of Hardivillier and Matignon. Painted genre and flowers. Exhib. *Pensées*, on porcelain, Paris Salon 1880
LIT *Bellier*; *Bénézit*; *Paris Salon* 1880

GOUSSAINCOURT DE GAUVAIN, Louise de
b. Nancy (Meurthe-et-Moselle). Pupil of Lalanne and Beauverie. Exhib. *Fleurs*, Paris Salon 1880; Dijon Salon: *Lilas, Pavots*, 1885, *Fleurs de printemps*, 1887, *Roses*, 1890, *Rhododendrons et boules de neige*, 1894, *Rhododendrons, roses et marguerites*, 1894; *Rhododendrons*, Paris Indép. 1891
LIT *Bellier*; *Bénézit*; *Dijon Salon* 1885, 1887, 1890, 1894; *Paris Indép.* 1891; *Paris Salon* 1880; *Thieme*

GOYET, J.
Designed *Novembre* plate of *Naissance des fleurs* set. This may be Jean-Baptiste Goyet 1779–1854, who exhib. allegorical flowers e.g. *La Mélancolie*, Paris Salon 1841
LIT *Bellier*; *Paris Salon* 1841; *Thieme*

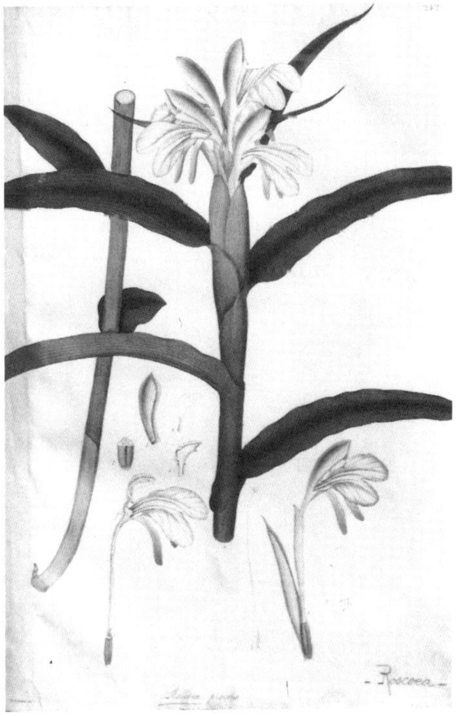

Gorochand

Watercolour on paper, 19 × 13½ in. (48 × 34 cm.), signed
Paris, BMAD (Maciet Collection)

GRABAL
Exhib. *Couronne de fleurs antour d'un portrait de SAR le duc d'Orléans*, Paris Salon 1846
LIT *Paris Salon* 1846

GRABOWSKA, Olga
Pupil of Jeanniot and Emeric-Bouvret. Exhib. watercolours: *Bouquet de fleurs des champs, Chrysanthèmes, Roses*, Lyon Salon 1882; *Chrysanthèmes*, Saint-Etienne Salon 1882; *Fleurs et oiseaux*, Dijon Salon 1892
LIT *Dijon Salon* 1892; *Lyon Salon* 1882; *Saint-Etienne Salon* 1882

GRADYN, Octavie
One signed and dated work from the 1830s, a watercolour on vellum, is known to date—typical of the Redouté-inspired works of this period. PM

GRAF, Emilie-Anna, *née* Reinhart ***1809–1884***
Pupil of Redouté. Drawing mistress
LIT *Hardouin-Fugier* 1981

GRAND
b. Lyon. Exhib. flowers Paris Salon 1804, 1806, 1812. Perhaps one of the Grand brothers, Lyon textile designers
LIT *Audin Vial*; *Bellier*; *Bénézit*; *Hardouin-Fugier Grafe*; *Hardouin-Fugier Grafe* 1982 (ill.); *Thieme*

GRAND, Clément-Jean-Pierre ***b.1820***
Pupil of Thierriat, Lyon BA (CFD 1843)
LIT *Hardouin-Fugier Grafe*

GRAND, Paul-Ange ***b.1818***
Pupil of Thierriat, Lyon BA (CFD 1838)
LIT *Hardouin-Fugier Grafe*

GRAND, Pierre-Etienne ***b.1811***
Pupil of Thierriat, Lyon BA (CFD 1831)
LIT *Hardouin-Fugier Grafe*

GRAND-PIÉGAY, Jean-Etienne ***b.1776 d. after 1858***
b. Lyon. Brother of J.F. Zacharie who ran the successful Maison Grand frères, silk weavers by appointment to Napoléon. Jean-Etienne Grand is possibly the silk manufacturer who was a member of the 1810 Lyon BA selection committee. May be the same artist as Grand who exhibited *Fleurs*, Lyon Salon 1827, *Groupe de fleurs et de fruits*, then *Fleurs*, Lyon Salon 1858 under Grand-Piégay was the name of his wife, herself a silk manufacturer's daughter—married 1813
LIT *Hardouin-Fugier Grafe* 1892 (ill.)

GRANDVAL, Georges de
b. Le Mans (Sarthe). Exhib. Paris Salon from 1879 e.g. *Roses et livres*, *Giroflées et pensées*, 1885; *Fleurs*, Paris Noir et Blanc Salon 1885, *Oeillets et prunes*, wc; *Fleurs des champs*, Paris SNBA 1893
LIT *Bellier*; *Bénézit*; *Paris Noir et Blanc Salon* 1885; *Paris Salon* 1885; *Paris SNBA* 1893

GRANDVILLE, Jean-Ignace-Isidore ***1803–1847***
b. Nancy (Meurthe-et-Moselle). Pupil of his father (1767–1854). Designed *Les Fleurs Animées*, Paris (de Gonet) 1847 and ed. Peter A. Wick, Paris (Vito) 1981. M: Nancy
LIT J. Adhémar, *Oeuvre graphique complet* ... Paris Hubschmid 1975; A. Avila, *Grandville* ... Paris (Limase) 1978; Topor, *Grandville* ... Paris (Garnier) 1979
See illustration on page 55

GRANGE, Pierre-Jean ***b.1818***
Pupil of Thierriat, Lyon BA (CFD 1838)
LIT *Hardouin-Fugier Grafe*

GRANGÉ, Claude ***b.1813***
Pupil of Thierriat, Lyon BA (CFD 1834)
LIT *Hardouin-Fugier Grafe*

GRANGER, Jean-Claude-Marie ***b.1824***
Pupil of Thierriat, Lyon BA (CFD 1842)
LIT *Hardouin-Fugier Grafe*

GRASSET, Jeanne
Exhib. *Fleurs*, wc, Paris Noir et Blanc Salon 1888
LIT *Paris Noir et Blanc Salon* 1888

GREBERT, Jules
Pupil of Rémond. Exhib. Paris Salon 1837–1870 e.g. *Fleurs*, 1850
LIT *Bellier*; *Bénézit*; *Paris Salon* 1850; *Thieme*

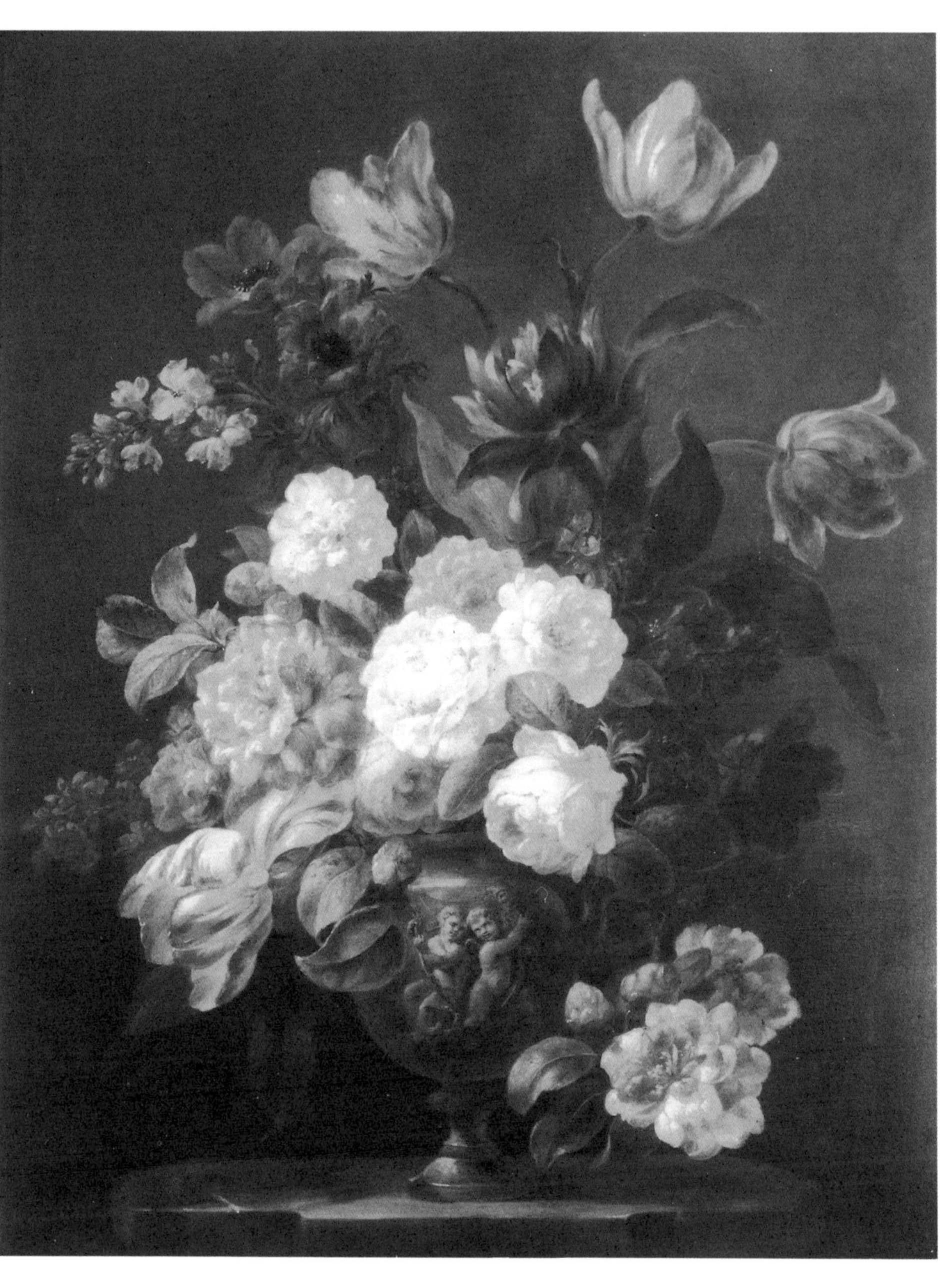

Jean-Etienne Grand-Piégay

Oil on panel, $27\frac{1}{2} \times 22\frac{3}{4}$ in. (70 × 58 cm.), signed and dated 1858
Private collection (photo: Musée des Beaux-Arts, Lyon)

GREDELUE, Clotilde
b. Paris. Pupil of Burat. Exhib. *Azalée*, fan-leaf, *Fleurs*, gouache, Paris Salon 1880
LIT *Paris Salon* 1880

GRENIER, Claude-Jules ***1817–1883***
b. Baume-les-Dames (Doubs). Pupil of Flajoulot, Paris BA. Delacroix and Picot. op. Barbizon in the Diaz. Français etc. circle. Painted landscapes and, occasionally, flowers. Exhib. Paris Salon 1847–1880
LIT *Bellier*; *Bénézit*; *Brune*; *Thieme*

GREUX, Gustave-Marie ***1838–1919***
b. Paris. Pupil of Gleyre and T. Robert-Fleury. Painter and engraver. Painted still-lifes and, occasionally, flowers. Exhib. Paris Salon from 1859 e.g. *Fleurs et fruits*, after Van Huysum, 1873
LIT *Bellier*; *Bénézit*; *Thieme*

GREVILLET, Mme M.
Exhib. *Roses*, Paris Indép. 1890
LIT *Paris Indép.* 1890

GRIMAUD, Joséphine, *later* Mme Eugène de Plas ***1826–1875***
b. Saint-Paul (La Réunion). Pupil of Arthur Grimaud, her father. Painted portraits, religious subjects and flowers
LIT *Bénézit*

GRIMOIN, Gustave ***b.1839***
b. Paris. Pupil of Paris BA. Painted flowers in oils and wc. Exhib. Paris Salon from 1869
LIT *Bénézit*

GRIVEL, Comtesse de
Exhib. *Corbeille de fleurs*, Lons-le-Saunier Salon 1876
LIT *Lons-le-Saunier Salon* 1876. JLM

GRIVOLAS, Antoine ***1843–1902***
b. Avignon (Vaucluse). Pupil of Pierre Grivolas, his brother. Painted landscapes and flowers. Exhib. Paris Salon from 1877. *Pivoines*, *Marguerites*, Lyon Salon 1879; *Pivoine*, Paris Salon 1880; *Bouquet*, Lyon Salon 1885; Paris Salon *Pivoines*, 1888, *Roses trémières à Trianon*, 1889, *Etalages de fleurs*, 1889, *Perron fleuri*, 1891, *Coin de jardin à Nérac*, 1893, *Roches fleuries* 1894, *Pivoines*, 1898; *Un bouquet*, Dijon Salon 1899. Musée Calvet, Avignon, *Roses d'hiver*, Hyères town hall, *Le jardin de mon propriétaire*
LIT *Bénézit*; *Bellier*; J. Bellendy, *J.A. Grivolas*, Académie du Vaucluse, Avignon n.d.; *Dijon Salon* 1899; E. Hild, "La peinture de fleurs en Provence" in *Fleurs de Fantin-Latour à Marquet*, Saint-Tropez, Musée de l'Annonciade 1982 (ill.); *Lyon Salon* 1879, 1885; *Orsay*; *Paris Arch. Nat. F21:2136; Paris Salon* 1880, 1888, 1889, 1891, 1893, 1894, 1898; *Schurr* I, 72; *Thieme*

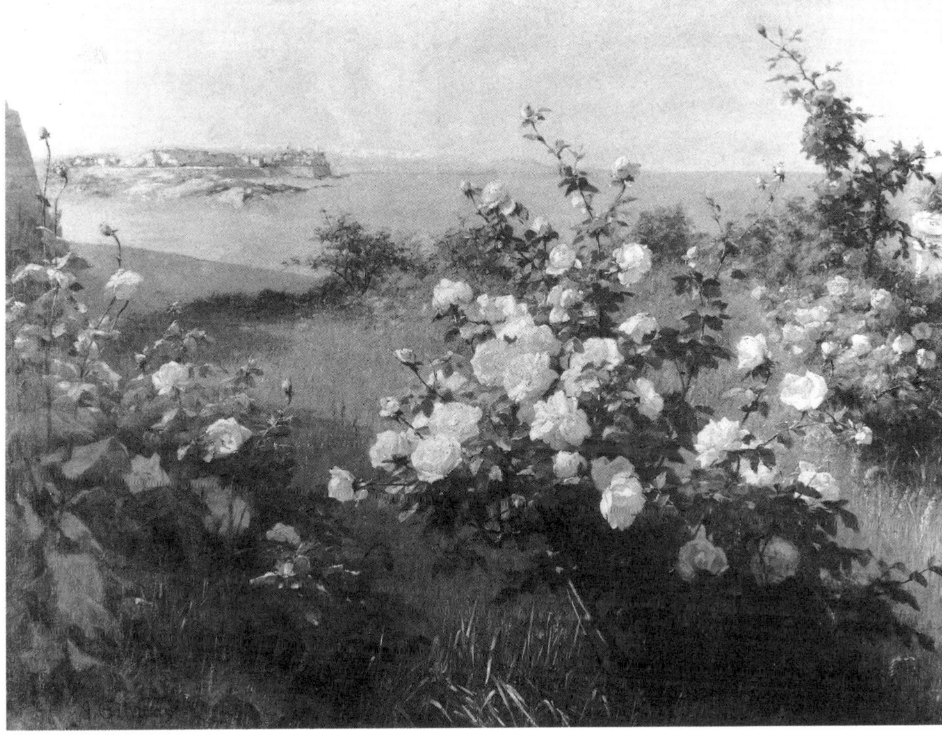

Antoine Grivolas
Oil on canvas, 44 × 50 in. (112 × 152 cm.), signed and dated
Avignon, Musée Calvet

Antoine Grivolas
Oil on canvas, 63 × 94½ in. (160 × 239 cm.), signed and dated 1885
Hyères, Musée Municipal, Courtesy Musée de L'Annonciade, Saint-Tropez

GRIVOLAS, Pierre ***1824–1905***
b. Avignon (Vaucluse). Pupil of C. Comte. Painted portraits, landscapes, genre and, occasionally, flowers. Exhib. Paris Salon from 1864. Designed plates for Seringe: *Description des mûriers* ... 1856. Musée Calvet, Avignon, *Cactus en fleurs*
LIT *Bénézit*; *Schurr* I, 70; *Witt*

GROBON, Anthelme-Eugène ***1820–1878***
b. Lyon. Pupil of F. Grobon, his brother, and Lyon BA (not in CFD). Exhib. Lyon Salon from 1838. Paris Salon 1852–1870
LIT *Hardouin-Fugier Grafe*; *Hardouin-Fugier Grafe* 1982

GROBON, François-Frédéric ***1815–1901***
b. Lyon. Pupil of Lyon BA and Orsel. With Eugène Grobon, his brother, co-designed and lithographed *Nouveau Cours gradué de fleurs et de fruits*, Paris (Delarue) for school purposes, and many flower plates. Operated a studio
LIT *Bénézit*; *Hardouin-Fugier Grafe* 1982 (ill.); *Thieme*

GROLLIER, Marquise de, *née* Fuligny-Dumas ***1742–1828***
Pupil of Van Spaendonck. Called by Canova "Le Raphaël des fleurs". Studio at Épinay, after the 1789 Revolution. *Palette et couronne de fleurs*, Exposition des femmes peintres, 1926
LIT *Bellier*; *Bénézit*; Sèvres, *Femmes peintres* ... 1926

GROMIER, Charles ***b.1814***
Pupil of Thierriat, Lyon BA (CFD 1836). Entered 1839 Lyon FDC
LIT *Hardouin-Fugier Grafe*

GROS, Adrienne
b. Fontaines-sur-Saône (Rhône). Pupil of Cartier and Brouillet. Exhib. *Roses*, Paris Salon 1890
LIT *Paris Salon* 1890

GROS, Jean-Marie ***b.1874***
Pupil of Castex-Dégrange, Lyon BA (CFD 1900)
LIT *Hardouin-Fugier Grafe*

GROS-RENAUD, Edouard
b. Cernay (Haut-Rhin). Pupil of Eck. Exhib. Paris Salon from 1874 e.g. *Pâquerettes*, *Primevères*, gouache, 1875, *Fleurs*, gouache, 1890
LIT *Bellier*; *Bénézit*; *Paris Salon* 1875, 1890

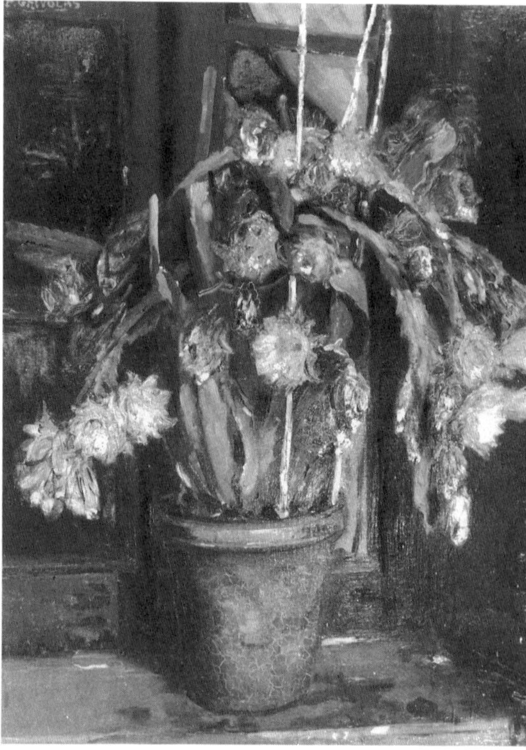

Pierre Grivolas

Oil on canvas, 32 × 25½ in. (81 × 65 cm.), signed
Avignon, Musée Calvet

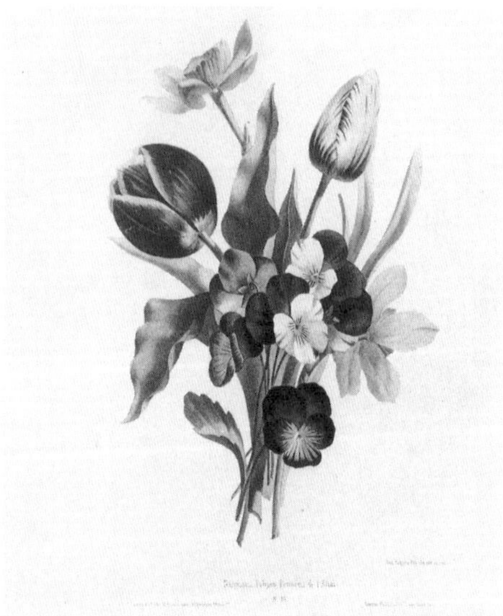

François-Frédéric Grobon (*left*)

Coloured lithograph, 13¼ × 10¼ in. (34 × 26 cm.), signed in the plate 'Grobon frères'
Private collection

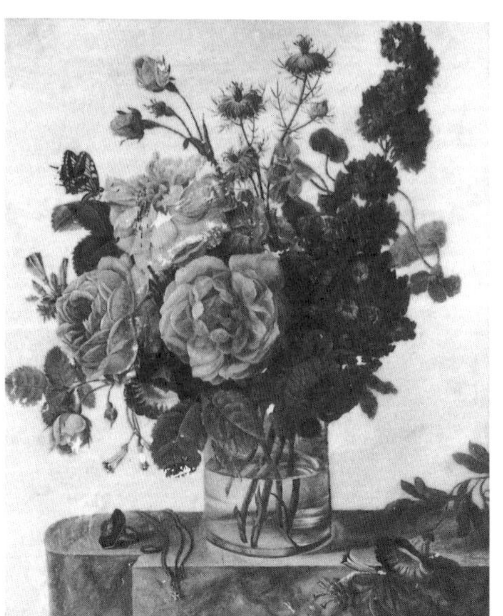

Marquise de Grollier

Oil on marble, signed
Private collection

GROSS, Emilie
Exhib. Strasbourg Salon e.g. *Fleurs*, 1883, *Pivoines*, 1884
LIT *Strasbourg Salon* 1883, 1884

GROSSE, *see* CHASSAGNE

GRÜN, Jules-Alexandre *1868–1934*
b. Paris. Pupil of Guillemet. Painted landscapes, genre, still-lifes, posters. M: Pontoise
LIT *Bénézit*; *Schurr* II, 21. PM

GRÜN, Maurice *b.1869*
b. Estonia (now USSR). Pupil of J. Lefebvre and B. Constant. Exhib. Paris Salon from 1890. Painted landscapes and, occasionally, flowers
LIT *Bénézit*; *Orsay*; Schurr III, 21

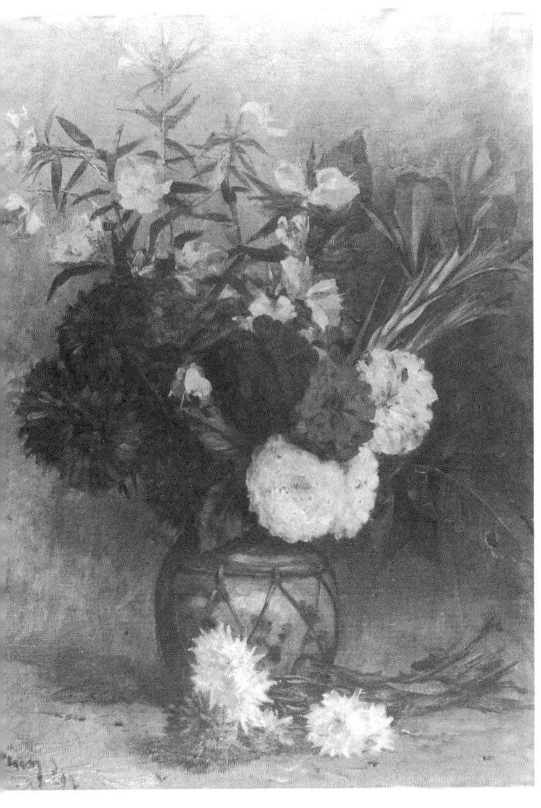

Jules-Alexandre Grün

Oil on canvas, 24 × 19¾ in. (60.9 × 50.1 cm.), signed
Pontoise, Musée Tavet-Delacour

GRUYER, Eugénie-Claire, *née* Brielman *b.1837*
b. Grenoble (Isère). Pupil of J.A. Brielman, her brother, and Serres. Painted landscapes, fruit and, occasionally, flowers in gouache. Exhib. Paris Salon from 1875
LIT *Bellier*; *Bénézit*; *Thieme*

GRUYER-HERBEMONT, Gabrielle *1875–1921*
b. Paris. Painted landscapes and flowers, mostly later works
LIT *Bénézit*

GUEDON, Alfred
Exhib. *Giroflées*, Paris Indép. 1893
LIT *Paris Indép.* 1893

GUEDON, Clément-Louis-Laurent *b.1817*
Pupil of Thierriat, Lyon BA (CFD 1836)
LIT *Hardouin-Fugier Grafe*

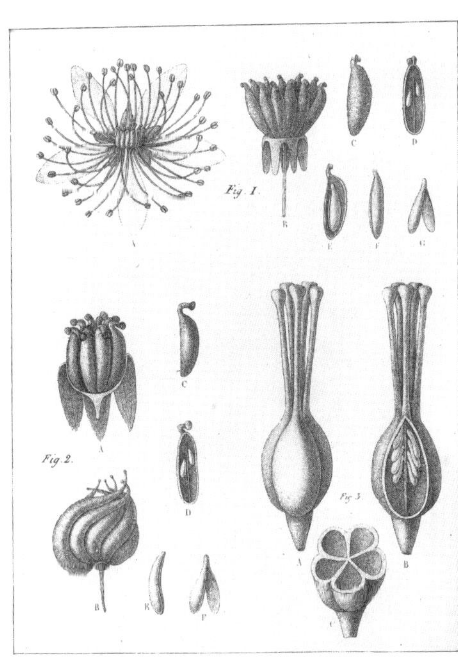

Eulalie Guérin

Engraving after, signed 'E., Guérin d'après'
Paris, Bibliothèque Centrale du Muséum National d'Histoire Naturelle

GUEMEAU
Pupil of Berjon, Lyon BA (CFD 1813)
LIT *Hardouin-Fugier Grafe*

GUENER, Eulalie de
Exhib. Paris Salon *Corbeille de roses*, wc, 1842, *Géranium*, wc, *Fleurs diverses dans un vase*, wc, 1843
LIT *Bellier*; *Bénézit*; *Paris Salon* 1842, 1843

GUENOT, Florimond *b.1825*
b. Metz (Moselle). Pupil of Tourneux. Painted still-lifes and, occasionally, flowers. Exhib. Paris Salon from 1866
LIT *Bellier*; *Bénézit*; *Thieme*

GUER, called GUERLIN, Jacques de
An *Étude de fleurs* dateable in the third quarter of the century was acquired by the Musée de Caens in 1912 and was destroyed during the war. PM

GUERARD, Henri-Charles *1846–1897*
b. Paris. This engraver married Eva Gonzalès. Exhib. *Fleurs et oiseaux*, five decorative panels, Paris SNBA 1893
LIT *Bénézit*; *Paris SNBA* 1893 (ill.); *Schurr* III, 78

GUÉRARD, *see* GONZALÈS, EVA

GUERIN, Eugénie, *née* Porché
b. Paris. Pupil of Trébuchet. Exhib. *Fleurs*, wc, Paris Salon 1880
LIT *Paris Salon* 1880

GUÉRIN, Eulalie
Painted portrait miniatures *c.*1825. Designed three flower plates lithographed by Noël aîné. The two wc on vellum dated 1824 and 1825 signed Guérin in the Paris Museum d'Histoire Naturelle may be by this artist
LIT *Bénézit*; *Laissus*; Paris Bibl. Nat. Est. snr; *Thieme*

GUÉRIN, Marie
b. Paris. Pupil of Marchard. Exhib. *Mimosa*, pastel, Paris Noir et Blanc Salon 1890
LIT *Paris Noir et Blanc Salon* 1890

GUÉRIN, Marie-Louise-Anna
Painted still-lifes and, occasionally, flowers. Exhib. Paris Salon from 1877
LIT *Bénézit*

GUÉRIN, Renée
Exhib. *Giroflées*, wc, *Pavots*, fan-leaf, Dijon Salon 1897
LIT *Dijon Salon* 1897

GUÉRIN, Thérèse *1861–1933*
b. Lyon. Pupil of Médard and A. Perrachon. Exhib. Lyon Salon from 1885. *Fleurs*, Dijon Salon 1887, 1890. op. teacher (Lyon École Municipale). Operated a successful studio. Exhib. Nîmes, Dijon, Grenoble, Paris 1889 Exposition Universelle
LIT *Bénézit*; *Dijon Salon* 1887, 1890; *Hardouin-Fugier Grafe*; *Hardouin-Fugier Grafe* 1982 (ill.)

GUÉRIN, *see* FERRÈRE

GUÉRINOT, Gustave
Exhib. *Fleurs*, Paris Indép. 1888
LIT *Paris Indép.* 1888

GUÉRITE
Designed flowers surrounding a portrait of Empress Eugénie for a wallpaper (Zuber), Paris BMAD (Maciet coll.). This may be by Victor Guéritte, b. Paris, pupil of Couder
LIT *Bulletin des Monuments historiques*, April 1979 (ill.)

GUERLIN, Jean-Gaspard
b. Paris. Pupil of Régerau. Exhib. *Primevères*, wc, Paris Salon 1880
LIT *Paris Salon* 1880

GUERNE, Jules-Germain-Maloteau de
b. Douai (Nord). Pupil of Petit. Exhib. *Pensées*, gouache, Paris Salon 1877
LIT *Bellier*; *Bénézit*

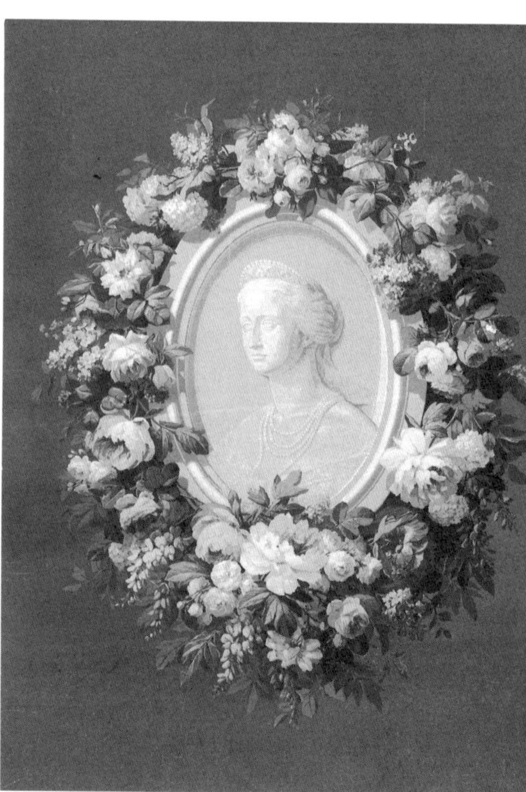

Guérite (*above*)

Gouache on paper, (designed the flowers surrounding the Empress Eugénie for a wallpaper) 79 × 49 in. (200 × 125 cm.), dated 1865
Paris, Musée des Arts Décoratifs

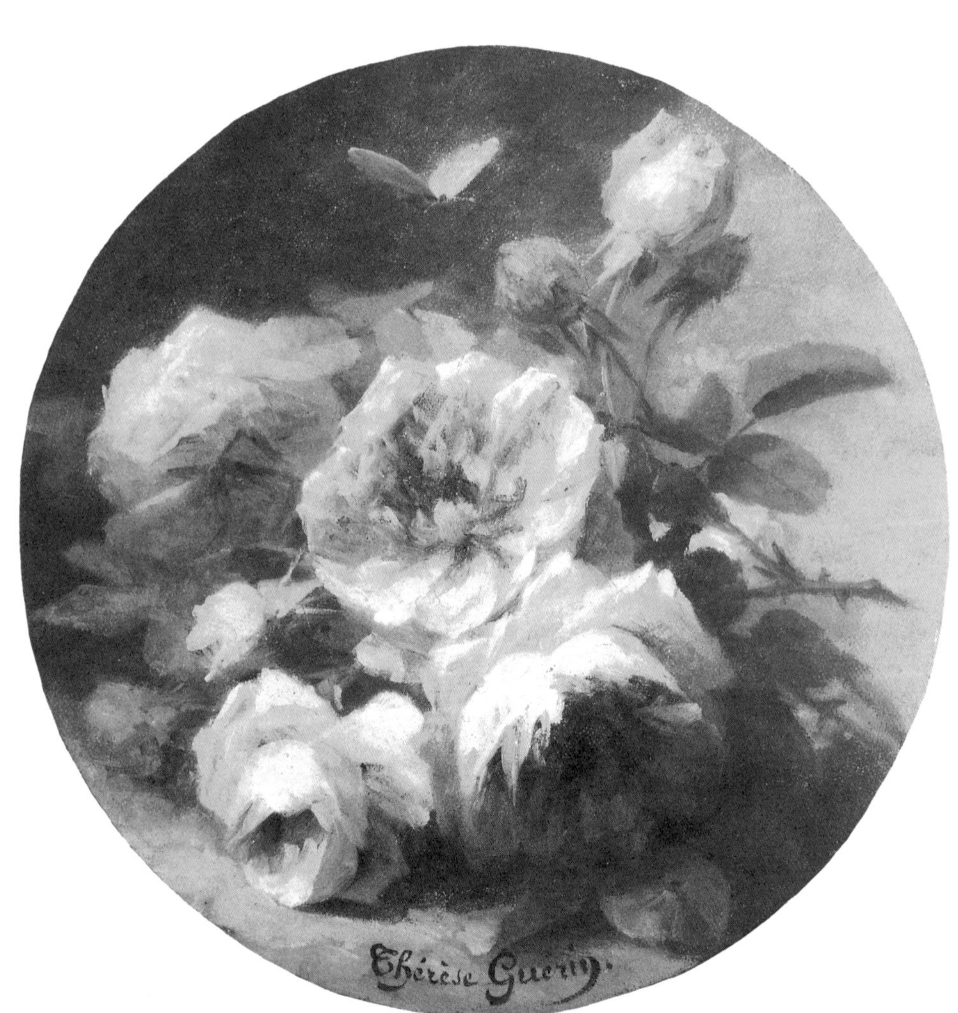

Thérèse Guérin

Oil on canvas, diameter 11 in. (28 cm.), signed
Private collection (photo: L'Image Fixe, Lyon)

GUÉROU, Pierre-Joseph
b. Paris. op. Sèvres 1847–1848. Exhib. Paris Salon 1849–1866 *Fleurs*, after Saint-Jean, on porcelain, 1864, *Pivoines*, wc, 1866. M: Paris Muséum d'Histoire Naturelle
LIT *Bellier*; *Bénézit*; *Brunet-Préaud*; *Faré* 1962, p. 247; *Thieme*

GUIBERT, Marguerite
b. Paris. Pupil of T. Robert-Fleury and F. Rivoire. Exhib. *Bleuets*, wc, Paris Salon 1895
LIT *Paris Salon* 1895

GUICHADOR
Pupil of Berjon, Lyon BA (CFD 1813)
LIT *Hardouin-Fugier Grafe*

GUICHARD, Charles-Paul *b.1827*
Pupil of Thierriat, Lyon BA (CFD 1845)
LIT *Hardouin-Fugier Grafe*

GUICHARD, Claude *b.1827*
Pupil of Thierriat, Lyon BA (CFD 1847)
LIT *Hardouin-Fugier Grafe*

GUICHARD, *see* DONNEUX

GUICHARD, *see* FAULCON

GUICHARDET, Paul
Pupil of Berjon, Lyon BA (CFD 1813)
LIT *Hardouin-Fugier Grafe*

GUIGNEBERT, Marie
b. Fronsac (Gironde). Pupil of École Sully and Lefebure. Drawing mistress (Saint-Denis Légion d'Honneur School). Exhib. *Glaïeuls*, wc, *Roses trémières*, wc, Paris Salon 1890
LIT *Bénézit*; *Paris Salon* 1890

GUIGNET, Mlle
Exhib. *Fleurs*, after Van Spaendonck, on porcelain, Paris Salon 1850
LIT *Paris Salon* 1850

GUILBERT, André
b. Paris. Pupil of E. Adam. Exhib. Paris Salon from 1879 e.g. *Anémones*, gouache, 1880
LIT *Bellier*; *Bénézit*; *Paris Salon* 1880

GUILLAUD, Dominique *b.1870*
Pupil of Castex-Dégrange, Lyon BA (CFD 1886)
LIT *Hardouin-Fugier Grafe*

GUILLAUMIN, Jean-Baptiste-Armand *1841–1927*
b. Moulins (Allier). Met Pissarro and Cézanne and worked with them. Though mostly a landscape painter, e.g. *Allée des Capucines*, 1880 (Copenhagen, Serret Fabiani 77), Guillaumin did paint a few flower-pieces e.g. *Nature-morte aux chrysanthèmes* (Genève, Petit-Palais, Serret Fabiani 127); *Nature-morte au vase de fleurs*, *c.*1900 (Serret Fabiani 543); *Vase de fleurs*, *c.*1900 (Serret Fabiani 544). M: Copenhagen, Ny Carlsberg Glyptotek; Genève; Paris, Petit Palais; Paris, Jeu de Paume
LIT G. Serret, D. Fabiani, *Armand Guillaumin*, Paris (Mayer) 1971; *Witt*. AC

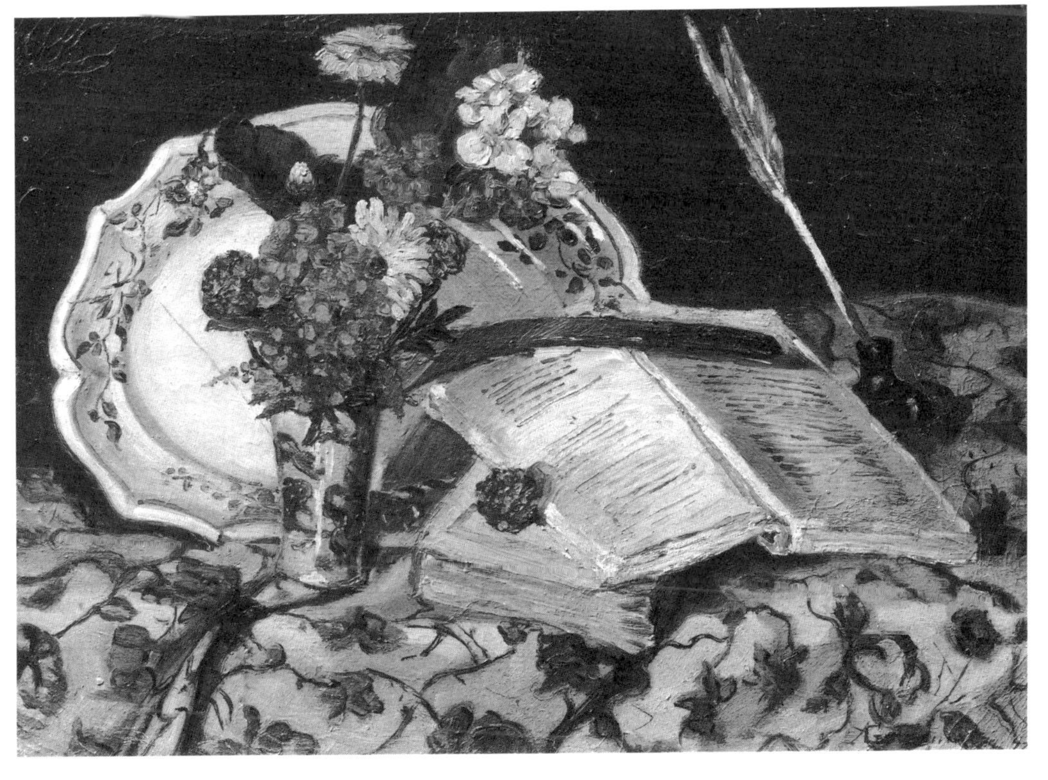

Jean-Baptiste-Armand Guillaumin

Oil on canvas, 12¾ × 18 in. (32.5 × 46 cm.), signed and dated 1872
Paris, Musée du Louvre

GUILLEMARD, Lucile
Pupil of L. Carrier-Belleuse. Exhib. *Jardinière de primevères*, wc, Paris UFPS 1898
LIT *Paris UFPS* 1898

GUILLEMOT, Joseph
Exhib. *Chrysanthèmes*, Dijon Salon 1887
LIT *Dijon Salon* 1887. CL

GUILLERMAIN, Léonie
One signed watercolour, with traces of bodycolour on vellum, is known. PM

GUILLERMIN, Bruno-Francisque *1878–c.1949*
op. Lyon. Pupil of Bardey and Guiget. Painted landscapes, portraits and flowers
LIT *Hardouin-Fugier Grafe*

GUILLET, Jean-Adolphe *b.1813*
Pupil of Thierriat, Lyon BA (CFD 1833)
LIT *Hardouin-Fugier Grafe*

GUILLIN, Jacques *b.1794*
Pupil of Berjon, Lyon BA (CFD 1812)
LIT *Hardouin-Fugier Grafe*

GUILLON, Adolphe-Irénée *1829–1896*
b. Paris. Pupil of J. Noël and Gleyre. Painted landscapes and, occasionally, flowers. Exhib. Paris Salon from 1863 e.g. *Tamaris et lauriers roses*, 1866; *Plantes, ronces*, Paris Noir et Blanc Salon 1888
LIT *Bellier*; *Bénézit*; *Paris Noir et Blanc Salon* 1888; *Schurr* II, 33

GUILLON, Nanine *fl.c.*1830
Possibly a pupil of Redouté. Lithographer. Illustrated Jaume de Saint-Hilaire, *Dahlias*, Paris (Didot) n.d.
LIT *Hardouin-Fugier* 1981; *Nissen* I, 986

GUILLON, Pierre-Joseph *b.1822*
Pupil of Thierriat, Lyon BA (CFD 1841). Entered 1843 FDC. Exhib. Lyon Salon 1844, 1845
LIT *Audin Vial*; *Hardouin-Fugier Grafe*

GUILLOT, Aimé *b.1826*
Pupil of Thierriat, Lyon BA (CFD 1844)
LIT *Hardouin-Fugier Grafe*

GUILLOT, Clément *b.1870*
Pupil of Castex-Dégrange, Lyon BA (CFD 1890)
LIT *Hardouin-Fugier Grafe*

GUILLOT D'OISY, Azémia-Vedastine
Painted portraits and flowers. Exhib. *Fleurs et oiseaux*, Paris Salon 1850
LIT *Bénézit*; *Paris Salon* 1850

GUINARD, Joseph *b.1872*
Pupil of Castex-Dégrange, Lyon BA (CFD 1895)
LIT *Hardouin-Fugier Grafe*

GUIRAND, Jean-Baptiste-Edouard *b.1812*
Pupil of Thierriat, Lyon BA (CFD 1833)
LIT *Hardouin-Fugier Grafe*

GUITEL, *see* PILON

GUY, Henri-Marius *b.1874*
Pupil of Castex-Dégrange, Lyon BA (CFD 1893)
LIT *Hardouin-Fugier Grafe*

Léonie Guillermain

Watercolour and bodycolour, $15\frac{3}{4} \times 12\frac{3}{8}$ in. (40 × 31 cm.), signed
Private collection

GUY, Victor *b.1804*
Pupil of Berjon, Lyon BA (CFD 1822)
LIT *Hardouin-Fugier Grafe*

GUYON, François-Casimir *b.1827*
Pupil of Thierriat, Lyon BA (CFD 1845)
LIT *Hardouin-Fugier Grafe*

GUYON, Pierre-Charles *b.1817*
Pupil of Thierriat, Lyon BA (CFD 1835)
LIT *Hardouin-Fugier Grafe*

GUYONNET, Anatole
Exhib. *Fleurs*, Poitiers Salon 1887
LIT *Poitiers Salon* 1887. BG

GUYOT, Jean-François
Pupil of Thierriat, Lyon BA (CFD 1827)
LIT *Hardouin-Fugier Grafe*

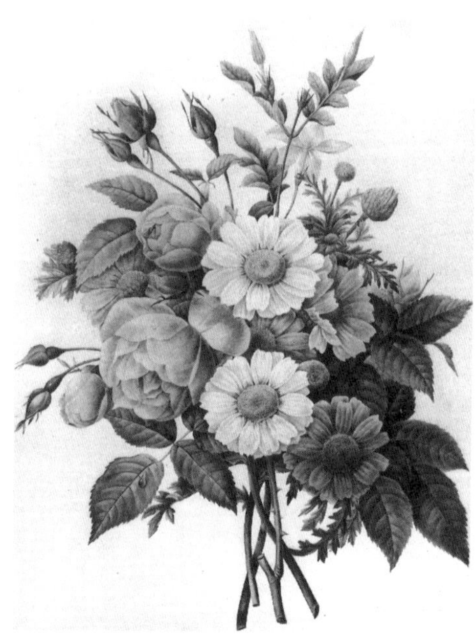

Nanine Guillon

Watercolour on vellum, $13\frac{1}{2} \times 9\frac{3}{4}$ in. (34 × 25 cm.), signed
Private collection

H

H.
Pupil of Puyroche-Wagner. Exhib. *Coquelicots et muguets*, gouache, Lyon Salon 1864
LIT *Lyon Salon* 1864

HABERT, Eugène ***d.1916***
b. Paris. Pupil of Gleyre and Bonnat. Exhib. Paris Salon from 1876. Exhib. Dijon Salon *Fleur mystique* 1890, *Fleurs de mai*, 1892
LIT *Bellier*; *Bénézit*; *Dijon Salon* 1892; *Thieme*. CL

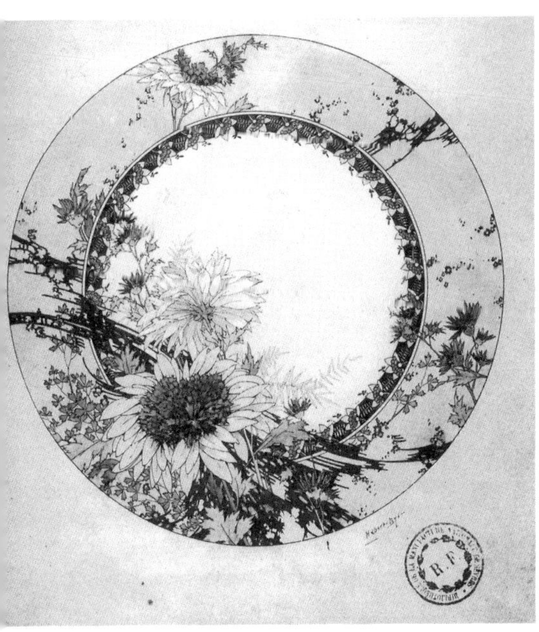

Jules-Auguste Habert-Dys

Gouache on paper, (project for a plate decoration) signed,
Sèvres, Manufacture Nationale de Sèvres

HABERT-DYS, Jules-Auguste ***b.1850***
b. Fresnes (Loir-et-Cher). Pupil of Ulysse Bernard at Blois, then of Gérome and Braquemond. Gifted decorative artist. Hon. mention 1884 for engraving; hon. mention 1891 for painting. Collaborated in the magazine *L'Art*. M: Sèvres. PM

HACHET, Marie, *née* Souplet
b. Saint-Quentin (Aisne). Painted still-lifes and flowers. Exhib. Paris Salon from 1875 e.g. *Fleurs d'hiver*, 1875, *Roses*, 1880, *Fleurs d'été*, 1881
LIT *Bellier*; *Bénézit*; *Mireur*; *Paris Salon* 1875, 1880 (ill.); *Thieme*

HADAMARD, Blanche
b. London. Pupil of L. Abbéma and Formstecker, Exhib. Paris Salon. *Pensées*, wc, 1890, *Iris*, wc, 1895
LIT *Paris Salon* 1890, 1895

HADENGUE, Louis-Michel
Pupil of Bonnat. Painted landscapes, still-lifes and flowers. Exhib. Paris Salon 1875–1893 e.g. *Fleurs des champs*, wc, 1890
LIT *Bénézit*; *Paris Salon* 1890; *Thieme*; *Witt*

HAILLECOURT, Caroline-Anne ***1817–1869***
b. Metz (Mozelle). Pupil of L. de Mirbel and Maréchal (Metz). Painted portrait miniatures and flowers. Exhib. Paris Salon 1840–1863 e.g. *Fleurs*, pastel, 1844; *Pivoines*, pastel, Lyon Salon 1865
LIT *Bellier*; *Bénézit*; *Lyon Salon* 1865; *Paris Salon* 1844; *Schidlof*; *Thieme*

HAIN, Marguerite ***b. 1876***
b. Rouen (Seine-Maritime). Painted landscapes and flowers. Exhib. *Bouquet de marguerites*, Dijon Salon 1890, *Bouquet de fleurs des champs*, Roanne Salon 1890 M: Rouen
LIT *Bénézit*; *Dijon Salon* 1890; *Roanne Salon* 1890; *Thieme*

HALLINBOURG, *see* HERVÉ

HALPHEN, Mme Cl.
b. Paris. Pupil of Rebeyrol. Exhib. *Bignonia et orchidée*, on faience, Paris Salon 1890
LIT *Paris Salon* 1890

HAMEL, Adolphe ***b.1820***
b. Fontainebleau (Seine-et-Marne). Pupil of G. Jadin. Painted landscapes, still-lifes and flowers. Exhib. Paris Salon 1848–1868 e.g. *Fleurs et fruits*, 1861
LIT *Bénézit*; *Paris Salon* 1861; *Thieme*

HAMON, Adrienne
b. Paris. Exhib. Paris Salon from 1878 e.g. *Pivoines et marguerites*, wc, *Bourriche de pensées*, wc, 1880
LIT *Bellier*; *Bénézit*; *Paris Salon* 1880

HAMON, Pierre-Paul ***1817–1860***
b. Livarot (Calvados). Pupil of L. Cogniet. Painted portraits, still-lifes and flowers
LIT *Bénézit*; *Thieme*

HANNEQUAND, Léonie
b. Briare (Loiret). Pupil of Toupillier and Rosa Bonheur. Exhib. *Bouquet de pensées*, wc, Paris Salon 1867
LIT *Paris Salon* 1867

HAQUENBACH, Frédéric ***b.1838***
Pupil of Reignier, Lyon BA (CFD 1854)
LIT *Hardouin-Fugier Grafe*

HAQUETTE, Georges-Jean-Marie ***1853–1906***
b. Paris. Pupil of A. Millet and Cabanel. Painted genre, figures, seascapes. Decorator. Four overdoors (flowers) for the Cherbourg theatre were commissioned from G. Haquette (2,200 francs) and exchanged for other subjects

1881–1882. Exhib. *Fleurs*, fan-leaf, wc, Paris Salon 1875
LIT *Bénézit*; Paris Arch. Nat. F21:2086; *Paris Salon* 1875; *Schurr* II, 37; *Thieme*

HAQUETTE, Jenny, *née* Bouffé
Pupil of École de Sèvres (1878). Exhib. Paris Salon from 1878. Musée de Bayeux: *Glaïeuls*, wc, Musée de Morlaix, *Fleurs*, wc (bought by the State in 1881, 400 francs)
LIT *Bénézit*; Paris Arch. Nat. F21:2186; *Thieme*

HARCHIES d', *see* BIRAT

HARDORFF, André
b. Saint-Etienne (Loire). Exhib. *Vase de fleurs*, Saint-Etienne Salon 1882
LIT *Hardouin Bringuier*; *Saint-Etienne Salon* 1882

HARDY, Berthe
b. Paris. Pupil of Colin-Libour. Exhib. Paris Salon *Roses trémières*, 1890, *Pavots*, wc, 1895
LIT *Paris Salon* 1890, 1895

HARDY, Blanche
b. Paris. Pupil of Colin-Libour. Exhib. *Roses, pommes et mirabelles*, wc, Paris Noir et Blanc Salon 1888
LIT *Paris Noir et Blanc Salon* 1888

HARTAUT *b.1817*
Pupil of Thierriat, Lyon BA (CFD 1835). Textile designer
LIT *Hardouin-Fugier Grafe*

HARVILLE, Berthe
b. Paris. Pupil of E. Girard and A. Cyb. Exhib. *Roses*, wc, Paris Salon 1880
LIT *Paris Salon* 1880

HATIN, Gabrielle
Pupil of Faux-Froidure. Exhib. *Roses*, Paris UFPS 1898
LIT *Paris UFPS* 1898

HAUREZ, Pierre *1826–1900*
b. Choisy-le-Roi (Val-de-Marne). Pupil of Chabal-Dussurgey. Active in Mulhouse. Textile designer specialising in flower designs
LIT *Histoire Documentaire*. BJ

HAUTEL, Virginie d', *b.1816*
b. Paris. Pupil of Lequien and Cogniet. Painted flowers and fruit. Exhib. Paris Salon from 1861 e.g. *Fleurs et fruits*, 1861; *Fleurs*, Lyon Salon 1869
LIT *Bellier*; *Bénézit*; *Lyon Salon* 1869; *Paris Salon* 1861, 1867; *Thieme*

HAUTIER, Virginie-Eugénie *1822–1909*
b. Rennes (Ille-et-Vilaine). Pupil of Robert-Fleury and E. Isabey. Painted portraits and flowers. Exhib. Paris Salon 1848–1863 e.g. *Fleurs au bord de l'eau*, 1850, *Camélias*, 1861. Musée d'Amiens: *Fleurs*, 1860 (acquired by the museum 1880)
LIT *Bellier*; *Bénézit*; *Paris Salon* 1850; *Thieme*

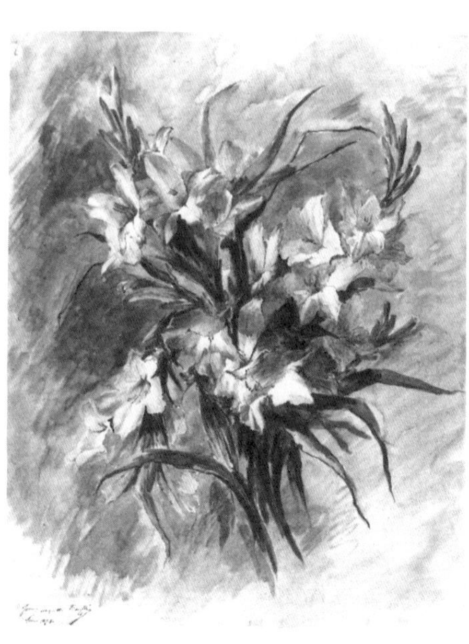

Jenny Haquette née Bouffé

Watercolour, $22\frac{1}{2}$ × 18 in. (57 × 46 cm.), signed and dated 1878
Bayeux, Musée Baron Gérard

HAZARD, Juliette
b. Rouen (Seine-Maritime). Painted flowers. Exhib. Paris Salon from 1893
LIT *Bénézit*; *Thieme*

HAZARD, Marthe
b. Paris. Pupil of Riottot. Exhib. Paris Salon from 1878 e.g. *Fleurs*, on faience, 1880
LIT *Bellier*; *Paris Salon* 1880

HEBERT, Antoine-Marc *b.1821*
Pupil of Thierriat, Lyon BA (CFD 1839). Textile designer
LIT *Audin Vial*; *Hardouin-Fugier Grafe*

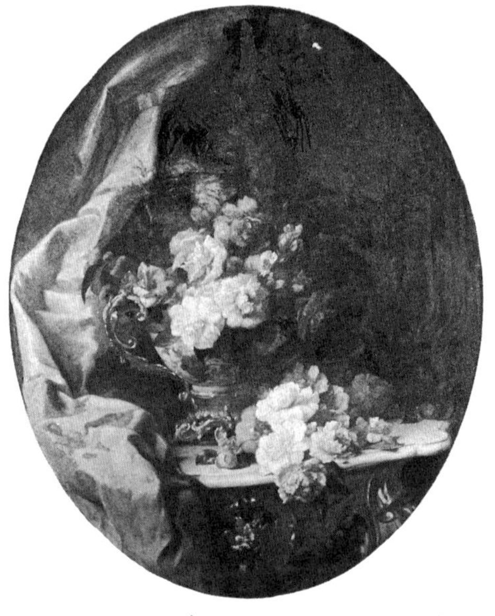

Virginie-Eugénie Hautier

Oil on canvas, oval, 78 × $43\frac{3}{4}$ in. (198 × 111 cm.), signed and dated 1860
Amiens, Musée de Picardie

HÉBERT-STEVENS, Jeanne
b. Paris. Pupil of A. and G. Hébert-Stevens. Exhib. *Les derniers chrysanthèmes*, Paris Salon 1895; *Chrysanthèmes aux couleurs d'automne*, *Branche de roses en plein air*, Paris Indép. 1899
LIT *Paris Indép.* 1899; *Paris Salon* 1895

HEIM, Victor ***b.1838***
Pupil of Reignier, Lyon BA (CFD 1862)
LIT *Hardouin-Fugier Grafe*

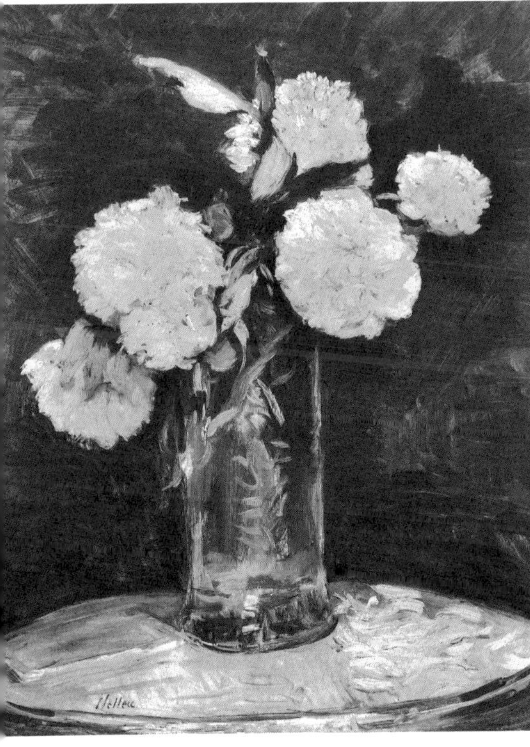

Paul-César Helleu

Oil on canvas, 32 × 25½ in. (81 × 65 cm.), signed
Courtesy Christian Delorme, Paris

T. Herzog

Watercolour over pencil outline on vellum, 12¾ × 10¼ in. (32 × 26 cm.), signed
Cambridge, Fitzwilliam Museum
(Broughton Collection)

HELLEU, Paul-César ***1859–1927***
b. Vannes (Morbihan). Pupil of Gérôme (Paris BA) and Deck. Painted portraits, landscapes and flowers. Famous for his dry-points. Proust's Elstir exhib. e.g. *Hortensias*, Paris SNBA 1892. *Les hortensias bleus*, pastel, Drouot, Paris, 15 Dec. 1969, *Pivoines sur un plateau d'argent*, Galliéra, Paris, 30 Nov. 1970, and Drouot, Paris, 26 May 1978. *Still-life with roses* Hirsch and Adler Gallery, New York, and Christian Delorme, Paris, 14 Mar. 1984
LIT *Apollo*, July 1975 (ill.); *Bellier*; *Bénézit*; London, Ferrers Gallery, *Helleu* 1970 (ill.); *Orsay*; Paris Galerie Charpentier, *Helleu ...* 1931; *Paris SNBA* 1892; *Thieme*; *Witt*

HENAULT, Antoine ***b.1810***
b. Lyon. Pupil of Thierriat, Lyon BA (CFD 1831) and Ingres. Painted portraits, genre, still-lifes and flowers. Exhib. Lyon Salon 1833, 1838, 1839 e.g. *Fleurs et fruits*, 1838. Exhib. Paris Salon 1842 to 1867 e.g. *Corbeille de fleurs*, 1865, *Fleurs*, 1867
LIT *Audin Vial*; *Bellier*; *Bénézit*; *Hardouin-Fugier Grafe*; *Lyon Salon* 1838; *Paris Salon* 1867; *Thieme*

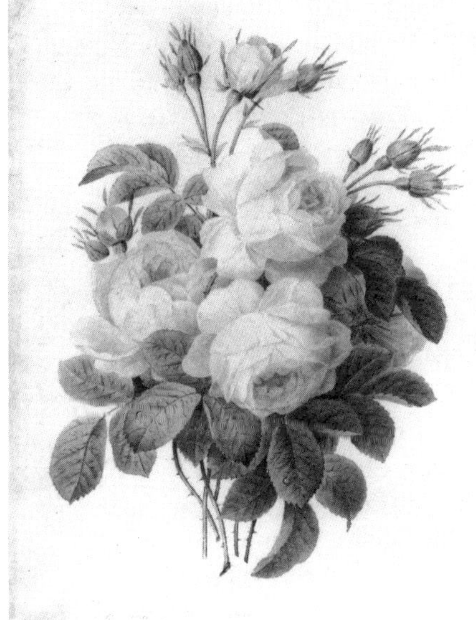

HENNEQUIN, Victor
Exhib. Paris Salon *Giroflées*, wc, *Fleurs*, after Van Spaendonck, on porcelain, 1841, *Groupe de fleurs*, wc, *Capucines*, wc, 1842
LIT *Bénézit*; *Paris Salon* 1841, 1842

HÉNON-FAVRE, Aurélie ***1814–1889***
b. Geneva (Switzerland). Botanical designer. Married botanist J.L. Hénon (1802–72), mayor of Lyon (1870–2). Painted flowers in wc and gouache
LIT E. Davies in *Fleurs de Lyon* (*Hardouin-Fugier Grafe* 1982, ill.); *Hardouin-Fugier Grafe*

HENRIET, Marie, *née* Larroque ***b.1837***
b. Limoges (Haute-Vienne). Pupil of Lesourd de Beauregard. Exhib. Paris Salon 1864–1868 e.g. watercolours: *Roses trémières*, *Glaïeuls*, *Géraniums*, 1864 (Larroque), *Bouquet de roses*, *Chrysanthèmes*, 1868 (Henriet)
LIT *Bellier*; *Bénézit*; *Faré* 1962, p. 245

HENRIOT, Pamphile ***b.1821***
Pupil of Thierriat, Lyon BA (CFD 1842)
LIT *Hardouin-Fugier Grafe*

HENRITT, Clémence
b. Paris. Pupil of E. Claude. Exhib. *Chrysanthèmes*, wc, Paris Noir et Blanc Salon 1888; *Giroflées*, Roanne Salon 1890
LIT *Paris Noir et Blanc Salon* 1888; *Roanne Salon* 1890

HENRY
Pupil of Thierriat, Lyon BA (CFD 1834)
LIT *Hardouin-Fugier Grafe*

HENRY, Aimé-Constant-Fidèle ***1801–75***
b. Douai (Nord). Designed plates for *Die Giftpflanzen Deutschlands*, Bonn (Henry & Cohen) 1836
LIT *Nissen* I, 853

HENRY, Geneviève
b. Paris. Pupil of Henry, her father. Exhib. *Chardons à Ballancourt*, pastel, Paris Salon 1895
LIT *Paris Salon* 1895

HENRY, Marie
b. Grenoble (Isère). Pupil of T. Robert-Fleury and J. Lefebvre. Exhib. Grenoble Salon, mostly flowers in wc, e.g. *Collection de pensées*, 1899
LIT *Grenoble Salon* 1899. MW

HENRY, Victor ***1855–1942***
Pupil of Allongé and Rivoire. Art teacher. Painted landscapes and flowers. Exhib. Dijon Salon *Fleurs*, wc, 1892, *Iris et boules de neige*, pastel, 1894
LIT *Bénézit*; *Dijon Salon* 1892, 1894. CL

HERBEMONT, *see* GRUYER

HERINCQ, Mme B.
Designed plates e.g. for E. Bonnet *Illustration des espéces ... de la Tunisie*, Paris, 1892, and for D. Bois, *Atlas des plantes de jardins et d'appartements*, Paris (Klincksieck) 1896
LIT *Nissen* I, 94, 187, 203, 377, 1504, 2150, 2380

HERPIN-MASSERAS, Marguerite ***d.1888***
b. Boston (USA). Pupil of Carteron, Valleray and Colin-Libour. Painted still-lifes and flowers. Exhib. Paris Salon from 1874 e.g. *Fleurs*, 1880
LIT *Bénézit*; *Paris Salon* 1880; *Thieme*

HERTL, Adelina ***1832–1872***
b. Sedan (Ardennes). Pupil of Coignet. Exhib. Paris Salon 1857–1870. *Pivoines de Chine et Azalées*, *Clématites*, *Géraniums*, *Roses*, pastels, Lyon Salon 1858; *Fleurs*, pastel, Strasbourg Salon 1858 (200 francs), *Fleurs*, pastel, Strasbourg Salon 1859 (200 francs)
LIT *Bellier*; *Bénézit*; *Lyon Salon* 1858; *Strasbourg Salon* 1858, 1859; *Thieme*

HERVÉ, Isabelle, *née* Hallinbourg
b. Paris. Pupil of Debillemont-Chardon, Gervais, Fouriès, Dagnan and Dessarts. Painted portraits and flowers. Exhib. *Chrysanthèmes*, wc, Paris UFPS 1898
LIT *Paris UFPS* 1898; *Thieme*

HERZOG, T.
Pupil of Redouté. Her 1843 exhibit was rejected by the Paris Salon selection committee. Fitzwilliam Museum, Cambridge (Broughton coll.)
LIT *Broughton* 1977; *Hardouin-Fugier* 1981 (ill.)

HÉSÈQUE, *see* ANDERS

HEUZÉ, *see* MAZELINE

HEUZÉ, Rosine-Victorine
b. Rouen (Seine-Maritime). Pupil of Voitelhier. Flower and porcelain painter. Exhib. Paris Salon 1861 and 1864 e.g. *Fleurs dans un vase*, after Bruyère, on porcelain, 1861, *Pivoines et iris*, 1864
LIT *Bellier*; *Bénézit*

HEWITT, Clémence
b. Paris. Pupil of Lanjalley. Exhib. Dijon Salon *Pêches et chrysanthèmes*, 1890, *Bourriche d'anémones*, 1892
LIT *Bénézit*; *Dijon Salon* 1890, 1892. CL

HEYNE, Louis ***b.1839***
Pupil of Reignier, Lyon BA (CFD 1862)
LIT *Hardouin-Fugier Grafe*

HIARD, Elisa
b. Brest (Finistère). Pupil of E. Benner and F. Louben. Exhib. Paris Noir et Blanc Salon, *Pensées*, *géraniums*, *chèvrefeuilles*, drawings, *Pivoines et capucines*, 1886, *Pivoines et capucines*, 1888; *Iris et mimosas*, on porcelain, Paris Salon 1898
LIT *Paris Noir et Blanc Salon* 1886, 1888; *Paris Salon* 1898

HIGELIN ***b.1838***
Pupil of Reignier, Lyon BA (CFD 1855)
LIT *Hardouin-Fugier Grafe*

HILDEBRAND, Claire
b. Colmar (Haut-Rhin). Pupil of D. de Cool and C. Chaplin. Painted miniatures on porcelain and enamel, landscapes, copies, genre and flowers. Exhib. Paris Salon from 1873. Exhib. *Roses*, Dijon Salon 1881
LIT *Bénézit*; *Dijon Salon* 1881; *Thieme*

HIRN, Jean-Georges ***1777–1839***
b. Mulhouse (Haut-Rhin). Textile designer. Painted flowers and fruit. Exhib. Paris Salon 1812–1838 e.g. *Fleurs sur les ruines d'un autel antique*, 1812, *Groupe de fleurs et de fruits sur des ruines*, *Bouquet de roses*, 1814, *Vase rempli de fleurs posé sur une pierre*, 1817, *Vase de fleurs sur un piedestal*, 1891, *Fleurs dans un vase*, *Fleurs sur une table de marbre*, 1827 *Fleurs dans un vase*, *Groupe de fleurs*, *sur le bord d'un ruisseau*, 1831, *Panier de fleurs et de fruits*, *Vase de fleurs*, 1833, *Vase de fleurs*, *Corbeille de fleurs*, 1836, M: Basle, Kunstmuseum; Colmar (fourteen works); Mulhouse; Paris (Louvre)
LIT *Bellier*; *Bénézit*; *Faré* 1962, p. 246; *Gabet*; *Histoire Documentaire*; *Paris Salon* 1812, 1814, 1817, 1819, 1827, 1833, 1836; *Sitzmann*; *Thieme*. *BJ*

HISTA, Louis
b. Aire-sur-Lys (Pas-de-Calais). Pupil of L. Rey and Galland. Decorator (Paris Hôtel-de-Ville). Exhib. *Six chassis*, *flore décorative*, Paris Noir et Blanc Salon 1888
LIT *Bénézit*; *Paris Noir et Blanc Salon* 1888; *Thieme*

HODIEUX, Jean-Baptiste
Pupil of Thierriat, Lyon BA (CFD 1832)
LIT *Hardouin-Fugier Grafe*

HODIEUX-BELOUS, Julie-Marie-Magdeleine ***c.1860–1897***
Pupil of A. Perrachon. Exhib. Lyon Salon 1882–1892. Paris *c*.1895 e.g. *Chrysanthèmes*, *Panier de roses*, Lyon Salon 1885; Dijon Salon *Panier de roses renversé*, 1887, *Roses*, *Fleurs de printemps*, 1890, *Vase de fleurs*, *Pivoines*, 1892; *Fleurs de printemps*, *Vase de fleurs*, Paris UFPS 1896. Lyon Musée des Beaux-Arts: *Vase de fleurs*
LIT *Bénézit*; *Dijon Salon* 1887, 1890, 1892; *Hardouin-Fugier Grafe*; *Hardouin-Fugier Grafe* 1982 (ill.); *Lyon Salon* 1885; *Paris UFPS* 1896

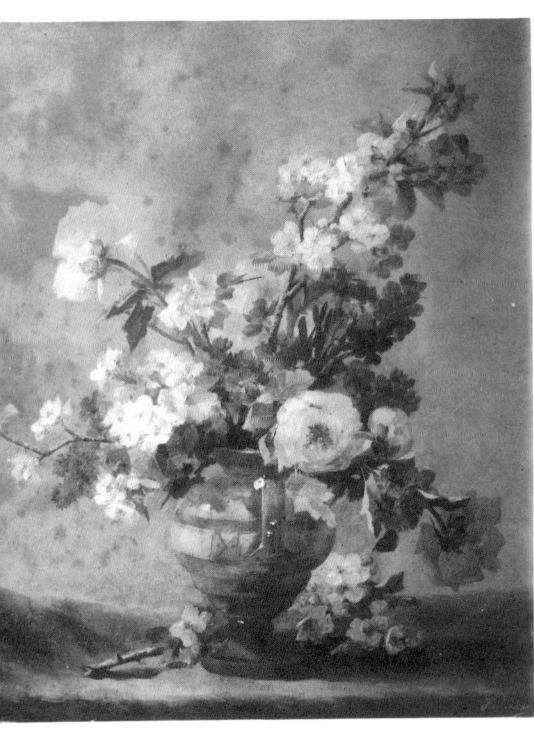

Julie-Marie-Magdeleine Hodieux-Belous

Oil on canvas, 39¼ × 32 in. (100 × 81 cm.), signed
Lyon, Musée des Beaux-Arts

HOMBRON, Henri
b. Lambezellec (Finistère). Pupil of L. Caradec. Painted still-lifes and landscapes. Exhib. Paris Salon from 1876. Exhib. *Fleurs d'automne et accessoires*, Dijon Salon 1897
LIT *Bénézit*; *Dijon Salon* 1897

HORR, Emile
Exhib. *Fleurs*, Lyon Salon 1863, 1864
LIT *Lyon Salon* 1863, 1864

Hubellin

Oil on canvas, 31½ × 25½ in. (80 × 65 cm.), signed
Private collection

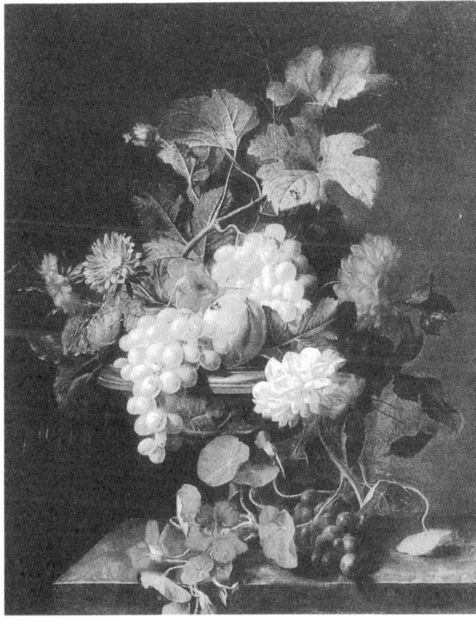

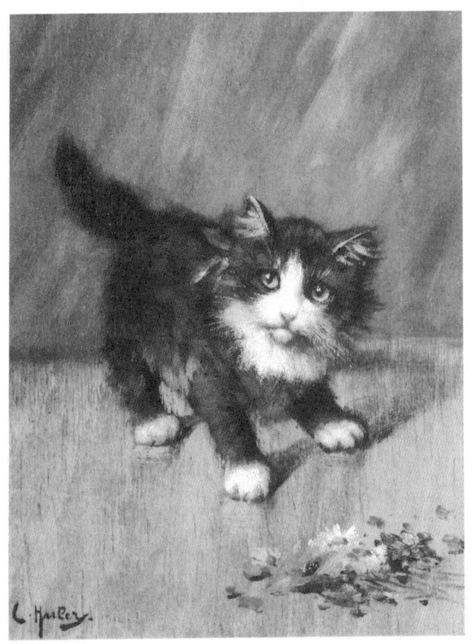

HORTENSE, Queen of Holland, ***see*** **BEAUHARNAIS**

HOSCHEDÉ-MONET, Blanche ***1865–1947***
Married Jean Monet, Claude Monet's eldest son. Painted landscapes and flowers, these mostly later works
LIT *Orsay*; *Schurr* II, 122

HOUSEL, ***see*** **TRÉBUCHET**

HOUSSAY, Joséphine ***b.1840***
b. Nantes (Loire-Atlantique). Pupil of Henner and Robert-Fleury. Exhib. Paris Salon from 1868. Exhib. *Fleurs et fruits*, Paris Noir et Blanc Salon 1886
LIT *Bénézit*; *Paris Noir et Blanc Salon* 1886

HOUSSIAUX, Ernest ***b.1873***
Pupil of Castex-Dégrange, Lyon BA (CFD 1892)
LIT *Hardouin-Fugier Grafe*

HUARD, ***see*** **CHARLES**

HUAS, Pierre-Adolphe ***1838–1900***
b. La Rochelle (Charente-Maritime). Painted portraits, genre and flowers. Exhib. Paris Salon from 1863. *Pivoines et iris*, Paris Indép. 1891; *Giroflées* (500 francs), Strasbourg Salon 1891
LIT *Bellier*; *Bénézit*; *Paris Indép.* 1891; *Strasbourg Salon* 1891; *Thieme*

HUBAUT, Marie-Joseph ***b.1829***
Pupil of Thierriat, Lyon BA (CFD 1850)
LIT *Hardouin-Fugier Grafe*

Léon Charles Huber

Oil on panel, 12 × 9½ in. (30.5 × 24.1 cm.), signed
Courtesy Christie's, London

HUBELLIN
A signed work by this artist was recently sold at auction: Geneva, 1–2 June 1988. PM

HUBER, Léon-Charles ***1858–1928***
b. Paris. Pupil of Paris BA (Dawant and J. Grün). The cat painter produced some still-lifes and flower-pieces
LIT *Bénézit*; *Orsay*; *Thieme*

HUBLIER, Charlotte, *née* Mast, *later* Mme N.H. Jacob ***b.1817***
b. Paris. Pupil of N.H. Jacob. Painted flowers and fruit in wc. Designed plates for H.F. Jaubert, D. Spach, *Choix de plantes ... de l'Asie occidentale*, Paris (Roret) 1842–1857. Exhib. Paris Salon 1837–1844 wc e.g. *Vase rempli de fleurs*, *Etude de fleurs*, 1838, *Vase de fleurs*, *Bouquet de tulipes*, 1843, *Fleurs et fruits*, 1844. Exhib. Dijon Salon *Fleurs*, wc, 1837
LIT *Bellier*; *Bénézit*; *Dijon Salon* 1837; *Nissen* I, 985; *Paris Salon* 1838, 1843, 1844; *Sitwell*; *Thieme*

HUET, Mlle M.
Exhib. *Lavande de mer*, wc, Paris SNBA 1894
LIT *Paris SNBA* 1894

HUET, Paul ***1803–1869***
b. Paris. Pupil of Gros and Guérin. Painted landscapes and, occasionally, flowers. Exhib. Paris Salon *Datura et volubilis*, 1866 (Versailles Trianon Palace, 30 Nov. 1962); *Basket of flowers*, Heim Gallery, London, winter 1969
LIT *Bénézit*; *Faré* 1962, p. 242; Heim Gallery, London, *Paintings by Huet*, 1969; P. Miquel, *P. Huet*, 1962, p. 165; C. Roger-Marx, *P. Huet* (Le Pavillon des Arts); *Thieme*; *Witt*

HUGONNET, *see* JOUANNE

HUGOT, Louis-Ernest
Exhib. Paris Salon from 1879. Exhib. *Hortensias*, Paris Indép. 1898
LIT *Bénézit Paris Indép.* 1898

HUILLIARD, Jeanne-Marie-Iréne-Esther
b. Sedan (Ardennes). Pupil of MacNab. Exhib. *Chrysanthèmes*, Paris Salon 1880
LIT *Bénézit*; *Paris Salon* 1880

HUMBERT-VIGNOT, Léonie ***1878–1960***
b. Lyon. Pupil of T. Tollet, Bonnardel, Toudouze, Baschet and Royer. Painted portraits, figures and, occasionally, flowers. Exhib. Lyon Salon from 1896
LIT *Bénézit*; *Hardouin-Fugier Grafe*; *Thieme*

HUOT, Magdelaine
Pupil of Beck. Exhib. *Violettes*, Paris UFPS 1898; *Boules de neige*, Paris SNBA 1899
LIT *Paris SNBA* 1899; *Paris UFPS* 1898

HURTEAU, Alexandre-Louis-Marie
Flower and porcelain painter. Exhib. Paris Salon *Raisins et vase de fleurs*, *Corbeille de fleurs*, on porcelain, 1845, *Fleurs dans un vase*, on porcelain, *Fleurs diverses*, five pencil drawings, 1848
LIT *Bellier*; *Bénézit*

HUSSARD, Louis-Charles ***d.1857***
Exhib. Paris Salon 1837–1852 e.g. *Fleurs et fruits*, 1839, *Roses trémières*, 1844
LIT *Bellier*; *Bénézit*; *Paris Salon* 1839; *Thieme*

HUTEAU, Auguste-François
b. Paris. Pupil of T. Robert-Fleury. Exhib. *Fleurs*, on faience, Paris Salon 1880
LIT *Paris Salon* 1880

HUTIN, Charles ***1847–1898***
Pupil of Le Gas. Exhib. Paris Salon 1874–1888. *Roses*, Dijon Salon 1892
LIT *Bénézit*; *Dijon Salon* 1892; *Thieme*. CL

HUZART, Félicie
Exhib. *Pavots*, wc, Paris Salon 1842
LIT *Paris Salon 1842*

HYVERNAT, Claude
b. 1872. Pupil of Castex-Dégrange, Lyon BA (CFD 1890)
LIT *Hardouin-Fugier Grafe*

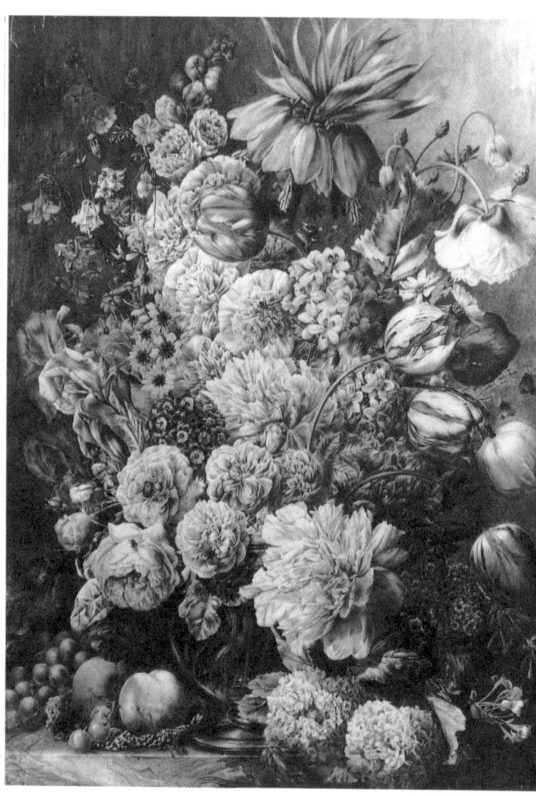

Charlotte Hublier

Gouache, 33½ × 26 in. (85 × 66 cm.), signed
Courtesy Sotheby's, Monaco

IJK

IMBERT, Bruno-Antoine *b.1865*
Pupil of Reignier, Lyon BA (CFD 1884)
LIT *Hardouin-Fugier Grafe*

IMBERT, Suzanne
Pupil of Alliod and Charbonnier. Exhib. *Fleurs*, Lyon Salon 1885; *Pivoines*, Dijon Salon 1885
LIT *Dijon Salon* 1885; *Lyon Salon* 1885. CL

ISBERT, Camille-Cornélie, *née* Paillard *1825–1911*
b. Paris. Pupil of H. Scheffer and Meuret. Painted portrait miniatures and flowers. Exhib. *Etude de fleurs*, Paris Salon 1867
LIT *Bénézit*; *Paris Salon* 1867

ISBERT, Valentine
b. Paris. Pupil of C. Isbert, her mother, and Grandhomme. Exhib. *Anémones et libellules*, fan-leaf, wc, Lyon Salon 1882; *Fleurs*, wc, Paris UFPS 1896
LIT *Lyon Salon* 1882; *Paris UFPS* 1896

ISNARD, des Joséphine
op. Sèvres 1835–1848. Exhib. *Groupe de fleurs composé*, on porcelain, Paris Salon 1836
LIT *Brunet Préaud*; *Paris Salon* 1836

JABOULAY, Etienne-Justin *b.1825*
Pupil of Thierriat, Lyon BA (CFD 1842). Exhib. Lyon Salon 1846
LIT *Hardouin-Fugier Grafe*

JABOULAY, Jacques
Exhib. *Groupe de fleurs*, wc, Lyon Salon 1861
LIT *Lyon Salon* 1861

JACOB
Pupil of A. Perrachon fl. Lyon, *c.*1890. Specialized in peonies
LIT *Hardouin-Fugier Grafe*

JACOB, Mlle A.M.
Exhib. *Envoi de Nice*, Paris Salon 1891
LIT *Paris Salon* 1891 (ill.)

JACOB, Eugénie
b. Riom (Puy-de-Dôme). Pupil of Jacobber. Painted flowers on porcelain. Exhib. Paris Salon 1859 and 1864
LIT *Bellier*; *Faré* 1962, p. 246

JACOB, Moïse
Exhib. *Giroflées*, Paris Indép. 1884
LIT *Paris Indép.* 1884

JACOBBER, Jakob Ber, *alias* Moïse *1786–1863*
b. Metz (Moselle) or Bavaria. Naturalized French. Pupil of G. Van Spaendonck. op. Sèvres 1814–1848. Painted flowers and fruit on porcelain, in oils or wc. An influential teacher, who exhibited at Cambria, Douai, Lille, and was the most popular porcelain painter of his day. Exhib. Paris Salon *Fleurs*, 1822, *Fleurs et fruits*, 1827, 1831, *Fruits et fleurs*, after Van Huysum, on porcelain, 1833, *Fleurs et fruits*, after Van Spaendonck, on porcelain, 1839, *Fleurs et fruits*, four watercolours, 1842, *Couronne de fleurs*, 1843, *Couronne de roses*, 1850; *Fleurs et fruits*, Paris Exposition Universelle, 1855. M: Paris (Louvre, Marmottan), Lyon
LIT *Bellier*; *Bénézit*; *Brunet Préaud*; *Faré* 1962, p. 246; *Gabet*; *Mitchell*; Paris Arch. Nat. F21:31, 250; *Paris Exposition Universelle*, 1855, *Paris Salon* 1822, 1827, 1831, 1833, 1839, 1842, 1843, 1850; *Thieme*; *Witt*

JACQUAND, Antoine *b.1797*
Pupil of Berjon, Lyon BA (CFD 1813)
LIT *Hardouin-Fugier Grafe*

JACQUELIN, Marguerite
b. Bordeaux (Gironde). Pupil of Augin, Lalanne, T. Robert-Fleury and Bonnat. Painted flowers. Exhib. Paris Salon 1879–1903 e.g. *Fleurs*, 1885
LIT *Bellier*; *Bénézit*; *Paris Salon* 1885; *Thieme*

JACQUEMART, Albert *1808–1875*
b. Paris. Pupil of Paris BA. Botanical illustrator, decorator, collector, writer, author of *La Flore des dames*, 1840; *Le nouveau langage des fleurs*, 1841. Exhib. Paris Salon from 1835
LIT *Bellier*; *Bénézit*; *Laissus*; *Thieme*

JACQUEMART, Jules-Ferdinand *1837–1880*
b. Paris. Pupil of A. Jacquemart, his father. Collector of Japanese art. Popular engraver and wc painter. Friendly with Burty. His *Compositions de fleurs* was published by Cadart in 1862: 22 *Roses trémières*, 23 *Géraniums*, 25 *Boules de neige*, 26 *Narcisses doubles*, 28 *Magnolias* (Jacquemart sale), *Boules de neige* (Bing sale)
LIT *Bellier*; *Bénézit*; *Bing sale*, Drouot, Paris, 17 May 1900; *Jacquemart sale*, Drouot, Paris, 1881; *Orsay*; *Schurr* I, 52; *Thieme*

JACQUES, Charles
Exhib. *Etude de Pivoines*, wc, Dijon Salon 1894
LIT *Dijon Salon* 1894

JACQUET, Edmond
b. Guichen (Ille-et-Vilaine). Pupil of M. Carpentier. Painted genre, landscapes and flowers. Exhib. *Chrysanthèmes*, Angers Salon 1886
LIT *Bénézit*

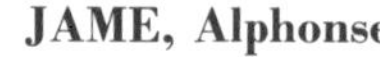

JACQUET, Gustave-Jean ***1846–1909***
b. Paris. Pupil of Bouguereau. Painted genre, portraits and, occasionally, flowers. Exhib. Paris Salon 1864–1909
LIT *Bellier*; *Bénézit*; *Thieme*

JACQUET, Henri-Léon ***b.1856***
b. Anzin (Nord). Active in Tourcoing and Paris. Painted genre and, occasionally, flowers. Exhib. *Sous les dahlias*, *La consultation des fleurs*, Dijon Salon 1897
LIT *Bénézit*; *Dijon Salon* 1897; *Thieme*. CL

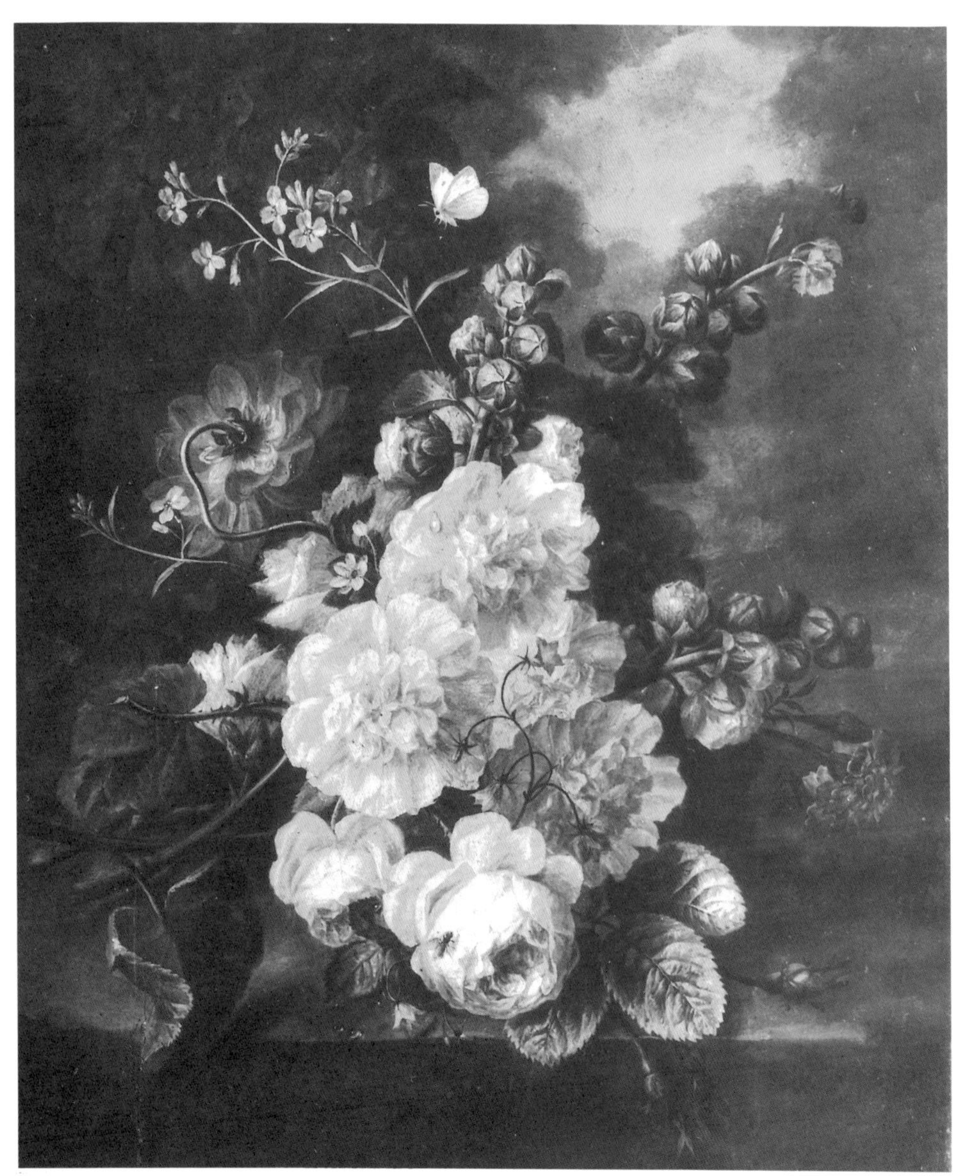

Moïse Jacobber

Oil on wood, 21¼ × 17¾ in. (54 × 45 cm.)
Lyon, Musée des Beaux-Arts

JACQUET, Henriette
b. Narbonne (Aude). Pupil of E. Jacquet. Exhib. Angers Salon 1886
LIT *Bénézit*

JADOT
Lawyer. Exhib. *Chrysanthèmes*, Dijon Salon 1894
LIT *Dijon Salon* 1894. CL

JAEGER, Paul ***b.1875***
Pupil of Castex-Dégrange, Lyon BA (CFD 1893)
LIT *Hardouin-Fugier Grafe*

JAMBON, *see* LAUBIÈS

JAME, Alphonse
b. Lyon. Pupil of Lyon BA. Painted miniatures, figures and flowers. Exhib. Paris Salon 1839–1880 e.g. *Fleurs et fruits*, 1880
LIT *Bellier*; *Hardouin-Fugier Grafe*; *Paris Salon* 1880; *Schidlof*; *Thieme*

JAMET, *see* ALLAIN

JANCE, Paul-Claude ***b.1840***
b. Lyon. Pupil of Lyon BA (1855–1861) and Gleyre. Painted portraits, genre, still-lifes and flowers. Exhib. Paris Salon from 1863. Exhib. Lyon Salon *Fleurs*, 1879, *Anémones du Japon*, 1881, *Vase de fleurs, chrysanthèmes*, 1882; Saint-Etienne Salon *Pivoines roses*, *Chrysanthèmes*, 1882; Dijon Salon *Roses*, *Chrysanthèmes*, 1880, *Chrysanthèmes*, 1881, 1883, *Pivoines roses*, 1883, *Dielytras et narcisses*, *Roses*, 1885, *Chrysanthèmes*,

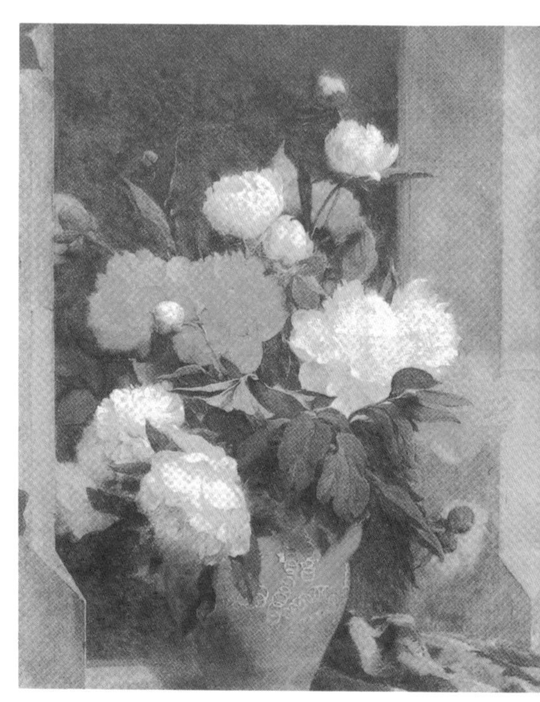

Paul-Claude Jance

Oil on canvas, 36 × 28¾ in. (92 × 73 cm.), signed and dated 1883
Private collection

Roses et abricots, *Roses*, 1887, *Panier de fleurs*, *Chrysanthèmes*, *Roses*, 1890, *Giroflées*, *Pivoines*, 1892, *Roses et cerises* 1897. *Vase de pivoines*, 1883, Geneva sale, 1–2 June 1988, lot 32
LIT *Bellier*; *Bénézit*; *Dijon Salon* 1880, 1881, 1883, 1885, 1887, 1890, 1892, 1897; *Hardouin-Fugier Grafe*; *Lyon Salon* 1879, 1881, 1882; *Saint-Etienne Salon* 1882; *Thieme*

JANE, Marie
b. La Boulaye (Saône-et-Loire). Pupil of Trébuchet. Exhib. Paris Salon from 1879 e.g. *Tulipes*, *Roses trémières*, gouache, 1880
LIT *Bellier*; *Paris Salon* 1880

JANET, Adèle ***d.1877***
Pupil of Redouté. Co-designer of Chavant's *Naissance des Fleurs* set, 1837. Some of her designs were lithographed by Chirat. Exhib. wc, Paris Salon 1833, 1836–1838, 1843
LIT *Bellier*; *Bénézit*; *Hardouin-Fugier* 1981

JANNOT, Marie
Exhib. wc, Dijon Salon *Fleurs*, 1892, 1897, *Chrysanthèmes*, 1894
LIT *Dijon Salon* 1892, 1894, 1897. CL

JAQUOTOT or JACQUOTOT, Marie-Victoire, *née* Leguay ***1772–1855***
b. Paris. Pupil of Leguay. op. Sèvres 1801–1842. Painted figures and, occasionally, flowers on porcelain. A most successful artist
LIT *Bellier*; *Bénézit*; *Brunet Préaud*; *Gabet*; P. Gualandi, *Maria Vittoria Jaquotot*, Venice (Antonelli) 1855; *Schidlof*; *Thieme*

JARRY, Louis François ***b.1821***
Pupil of Thierriat, Lyon BA (CFD 1839)
LIT *Hardouin-Fugier Grafe*

JAUBERT, Jacques-Léonard
Pupil of Thierriat, Lyon BA (CFD 1843)
LIT *Hardouin-Fugier Grafe*

JAUME-SAINT-HILAIRE, Jean-Henri ***1772–1845***
Illustrated his own *Plantes de la France décrites et peintes d'après Nature*, Paris 1808–1822, *La Flore et la Pomone françaises*, Paris 1828–1833
LIT *Nissen* I, 988, 989; *Sitwell*; *Thieme*

JAVELLE, Jean-Baptiste ***b.1835***
Pupil of Reignier, Lyon BA (CFD 1857)
LIT *Hardouin-Fugier Grafe*

JAVERZAT, Mlle
Exhib. *Vase de fleurs*, wc, Paris Salon 1839
LIT *Paris Salon* 1839

JEANDEL, *see* BIARD

JEANNIN, Georges ***1841–1925***
b. Paris. Pupil of Vincelet. This most prolific and popular flower painter decorated the Paris Hôtel de Ville's Salon de Passage with A. Cesbron. He was chairman of the Société des Peintres de Fleurs. Many of his flower-pieces were bought by the State. Exhib. Paris Salon e.g. *Roses et branche d'aubépine*, 1875, *Charretée de fleurs*, 1879, *Embarquement de fleurs*, 1880, *Camélias et tulipes*, 1890, *Dahlias*, gouache, 1890, *Camélias*, *Roses*, 1895; Lyon Salon e.g. *Pivoines*, 1884, *Roses*, *Dahlias*, 1885; Dijon Salon e.g. *Fleurs*, 1891, *Roses et dahlias*, 1897. *Pivoines*, Dorotheum, Vienna, 18–21 Mar. 1969, *Fleurs*, 1889, Dorotheum, Vienna, 16–19 Mar. 1971, *Roses et éventail*, Dorotheum, Vienna, 19 Sept. 1972, *Pensées*, Dorotheum, Vienna, 28 Nov. 1972, *Lilas*, 1912, Dorotheum, Vienna, 6 June 1972, *Roses*, Dorotheum, Vienna, 4 Dec. 1973, *Still-life with peonies and mayflower in a blue and gilded vase*, Bonham's, London, 3 Mar. 1977, *Still-life of summer flowers in a vase*, Sotheby's, London, 2 Nov. 1977, *Vase de fleurs*, Drouot, Paris, 15 Mar. 1976, *Jetée de roses*, Versailles, 19 Dec. 1981. Works in many museums and art galleries e.g. Beziers, Cambrai, Epinal, Mulhouse, Nancy, Paris (Petit Palais), Rochefort, Rouen, Valenciennes etc.
LIT *Bellier*; *Bénézit*; *Orsay*; Paris Arch. Nat. F21:228, 4317; Saint-Tropez, Musée de l'Annonciade, *Fleurs de Fantin-Latour à Marquet*, 1982, no. 30 (ill.); *Schurr* II, 62; *Thieme*; *Witt*

JEANNIOT, Pierre-Alexandre ***1826–1892***
Pupil of Diday and Calame. Professor at Dijon BA from 1851, then director. Painted landscapes and, occasionally, flowers e.g. *Chrysanthèmes*, Nancy Salon 1874
LIT *Bellier*; *Bénézit*; *Nancy Salon* 1874; *Schurr* I, 51; *Thieme*

JOANNIS, *see* GIRARDIN

JOANNIS, *see* MÉDARD

JOANNON, Jean-Joseph-Camille ***b.1826***
Pupil of Thierriat, Lyon BA (CFD 1844)
LIT *Hardouin-Fugier Grafe*

JOANNON-NAVIER, Etienne-Albert, *alias* Eugène ***b.1857***
b. Lyon. Pupil of Lyon BA, F.A. Clément and Cabanel. Painted genre and, occasionally, flowers. Exhib. Lyon Salon from 1878, Paris Salon 1884–1911. *Narcisses*, Lyon Salon 1879
LIT *Bénézit*; *Hardouin-Fugier Grafe*; *Thieme*; *Witt*

JOBBÉ-DUVAL, Félix-Armand-Marie ***1821–1889***
b. Carhaix (Finistère). Pupil of Paris BA, Delaroche and Gleyre. Painted genre, figures, landscapes and, occasionally, flowers e.g. *Bouquet de roses*, Paris Salon 1872. Musée de Reims: *Fleurs*, 1854
LIT *Bénézit*; *Paris Salon* 1872; *Thieme*; *Witt*

JOBBÉ-DUVAL, Jacques
b. Paris. Pupil of F. Jobbé-Duval, his father, and Gérôme. Painted figures and, occasionally, flowers e.g. *Bouquet de fleurs*, Paris Salon 1880
LIT *Bellier*; *Bénézit*; *Paris Salon* 1880

JOBEY DE LIGNY, Mme C.
This apparently needy flower-painter was granted state "encouragements" 1852–1856, 1860–1874
LIT Paris Arch. Nat. F21:279, 287

JOGUES, Jean-Louis-Laurent ***b.1818***
b. Bourg (Ain). Pupil of Grobon and Bonnefond. At BA at Marseille in 1836, and later pupil of Saint Jean. Exhib. Lyon Salon 1857–1873 landscapes in watercolour and crayon
LIT *Bénézit*. PM

JOIGNY, Dominique-Grenet de
Musée de Troyes: *Fleurs et fruits*
LIT *Bénézit*; *Thieme*

JOISEAU, Hélène
b. Paris. Pupil of Allongé. Exhib. *Fleurs*, wc, Paris Noir et Blanc Salon 1888
LIT *Paris Noir et Blanc Salon* 1888

JOLIBOIS, Berthe-Jeanne
Pupil of J. Duval. Exhib. *Chévrefeuille*, *Iris*, *Faux-ébénier*, *Petits soleils*, Paris UFPS 1896
LIT *Paris UFPS* 1896

JONAS, ***see*** **DESBORDES**

JONNART, M.J., ***née*** **Aynard**
Exhib. *Fleurs*, wc, Paris SNBA 1896
LIT *Paris SNBA* 1896

Félix-Armand-Marie Jobbé-Duval

Oil on canvas, signed
Reims, Musée des Beaux-Arts

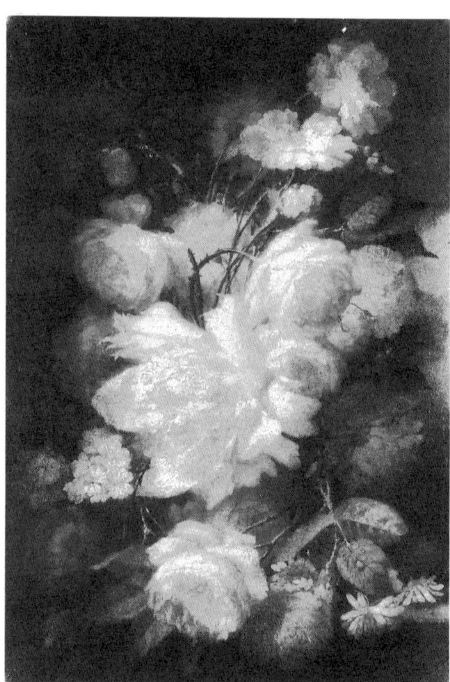

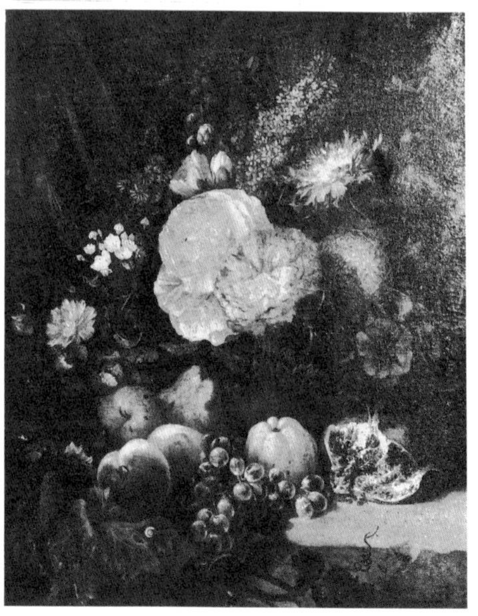

JORAS, Paul
b. Paris. Exhib. *Roses trémières*, wc, Paris Noir et Blanc Salon 1888
LIT *Paris Noir et Blanc Salon* 1888

JOSEPH, Lucy N.
b. Paris. Pupil of Henry and B. Constant. Exhib. *Bourriche de giroflées*, wc, Paris Salon 1898; *Giroflées*, Paris UFPS 1898
LIT *Bénézit*; *Paris Salon 1898; Paris UFPS* 1898

JOSEPH, Marguerite ***1856–1905***
b. Rixheim (Haut-Rhin). Pupil of Courtois. Exhib. *Géraniums*, Paris UFPS 1896
LIT *Bénézit*; *Paris UFPS* 1896; *Thieme*

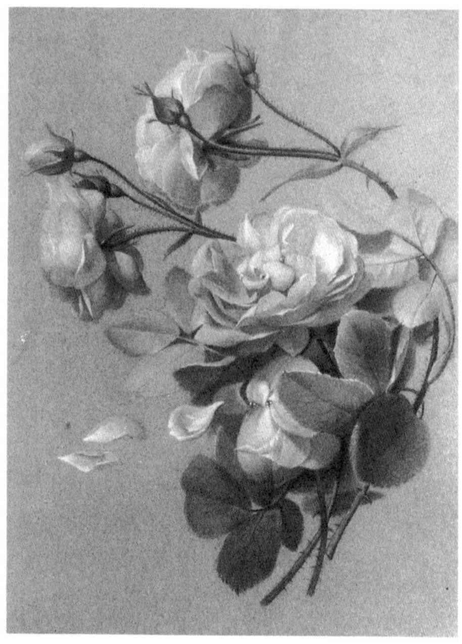

Jean-Louis-Laurent Jogues

Pencil heightened with white and pink gouache, 13¾ × 10½ in. (35 × 27 cm.), signed
Private collection

Dominique-Grenet de Joigny (*left*)

Oil on canvas, 31 × 25¼ in. (79 × 64 cm.), signed
Troyes, Musée des Beaux-Arts

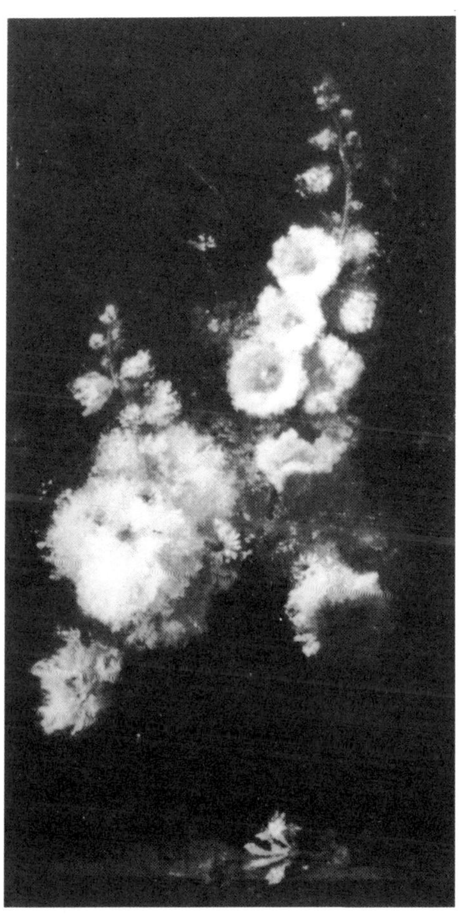

Auguste Jouve

Oil on canvas, $45\frac{3}{4}$ × 25 in. (116 × 64 cm.), signed
Amsterdam, Rijksmuseum

JOUANNE-HUGONNET, Marthe ***b.1871***
b. Paris. Pupil of Léandre and Saubes. Painted portraits, genre and flowers. Exhib. Paris Salon 1894–*c.*1914. Her *Vase de fleurs* was formerly in the Musée de Caen (destroyed)
LIT *Bénézit*; *Thieme*

JOUASSET, *see* GINTRAC

JOUFFROY D'ALBANS, Marthe
b. Paris. Pupil of Pallandre and Melicourt. Exhib. Paris Salon 1878 and 1879; *Reines-marguerites*, Lyon Salon 1878; *Fleurs*, Limoges Salon 1879; *Chrysanthèmes oranges et grenades*, Versailles Salon 1878; *Une corbeille de roses*, Dijon Salon 1883
LIT *Bellier*; *Bénézit*; *Dijon Salon* 1883; *Lyon Salon* 1878; *Versailles Salon* 1878

JOULIN, Lucien ***b.1842***
b. Paris. Pupil of Palizzi and Barrias. Painted genre, landscapes and flowers e.g. *Camélia*, Paris Salon 1867; *Pensées*, Lyon Salon 1872; *Chrysanthèmes* Lyon Salon 1876
LIT *Lyon Salon* 1872, 1876; *Paris Salon* 1867; *Thieme*

JOURDAIN, Roger-Joseph ***1845–1918***
b. Louviers (Eure). Pupil of Cabanel, Chabanne and Pils. Painted landscapes, genre and flowers. Exhib. Paris Société des Aquarellistes e.g. *Fleurs sauvages*, 1885, *Etude de fleurs*, 1886, *Chrysanthèmes*, *Pavots*, *Roses trémières*, *Iris*, 1894
LIT *Bénézit*; *Paris Aquar.* 1885, 1886, 1894; *Thieme*; *Witt*

JOURDAIN, *see* PERRARD

JOURDAN, Joseph-Antoine ***b.1814***
Pupil of Thierriat, Lyon BA (CFD 1834)
LIT *Hardouin-Fugier Grafe*

JOURNET, Elise-Marie-Thomate ***d.1866***
b. Paris. Painted still-lifes and flowers (cf. *L'Artiste*). Exhib. Paris Salon 1833–1845. Applied for a state allowance in 1855
LIT *L'Artiste*, Salon 1837, XIII, p. 97; *Bellier*; *Bénézit*; *Faré* 1962, p. 248; Paris Arch. Nat. F.21:38, 288; *Schurr* I, 30; *Thieme*

JOUVE, Auguste ***b.1846***
b. Lyon. Pupil of Lyon BA (Reignier and Guichard) 1861–1864 and Comte. Painted figures, landscapes, still-lifes and flowers. Exhib. Lyon Salon from 1866, Paris Salon from 1877 e.g. *Pivoines et lilas*, 1879; *Roses trémières*, *Pavots*, Paris Indép. 1893. Amsterdam (Rijksmuseum) *Still-life with flowers*
LIT *Bellier*; *Bénézit*; *Hardouin-Fugier Grafe*; *Paris Indép.* 1893; *Thieme*; *Witt*

JUBIN, Claude ***b.1818***
Pupil of Thierriat, Lyon BA (CFD 1835)
LIT *Hardouin-Fugier Grafe*

JUBREAUX, Joseph ***b.1834***
b. Reims (Marne). Pupil of Lequien. Exhib. Paris Salon from 1869 e.g. *Aubépine, boules de neige*, 1877; *Chrysanthèmes*, *Roses*, Lyon Salon 1879
LIT *Bellier*; *Lyon Salon* 1879; *Thieme*

JULIAN, Th.
Exhib. *Bouquet de roses*, Paris Salon 1850
LIT *Paris Salon* 1850

JULIEN de, *see* CHOISY

JULIENNE, Eugène
op. Sèvres until 1874. Painted flowers. Author of *L'ornemêniste des arts industriels*
LIT *Bénézit*; *Thieme*

JULLIARD
His *Chrysanthèmes* and *Lilas blancs et roses* used to be in the Musée de Brest
LIT *Bénézit*

JULLIEN
Designed flower plates lithographed by Monrocq, Paris BMAD (Maciet coll.). This may be Marie-Pauline Laurent, née Jullien (1785–1860), or Amédée Jullien b. Clamecy. *c.*1820–1887
LIT *Bellier*; Paris Bibl. Nat. Est. Jd 67; *Paris BMAD*; *Schurr* V, 50

JULLIEN, *see* LAURENT

JUMON, Agathe
b. Lyon. Pupil of D. de Cool. Painted portraits, genre and flowers. Exhib. 1873–1880 e.g. *Fleurs des champs*, Lyon Salon 1878; *Fleurs de février*, wc, Paris Salon 1880
LIT *Bellier*; *Bénézit*; *Hardouin-Fugier Grafe*; *Lyon Salon* 1878; *Paris Salon* 1880; *Schidlof*; *Thieme*

JUNCKER, Frederick *d.1906*
b. Paris. Pupil of Cogniet. Exhib. Paris Salon 1839–1882 e.g. *Fleurs et fruits*, pastel, 1861
LIT *Bénézit*; *Paris Salon* 1861; *Schurr* II, 31; *Thieme*

JUNDT, Gustave-Adolphe *1830–1884*
b. Strasbourg (Bas-Rhin). Pupil of Drolling, Picot, Biennoury, Paris BA. Painted landscapes, still-lifes and, occasionally, flowers. Exhib. Paris Salon 1857–1883. *Le bouquet dans les blés*, Lyon Salon 1867. His *Fleurs de Mai* (destroyed in war) was bought by the State, 16 June 1876 (2,000 francs) for the Musée de Saint-Malo
LIT *Bellier*; *Bénézit*; *Lyon Salon* 1867; Paris Arch. Nat. F21:228; *Schurr* II, 33; *Thieme*

JUNG, Charles-Frédéric *1865–1936*
b. Lyon. Pupil of Reignier and Castex-Dégrange, Lyon BA (CFD 1884–1885). Painted still-lifes and flowers often featuring thistles and copperware. Exhib. Lyon Salon from 1886, Paris Salon from 1905. M: Lyon, three works; Narbonne; Saint-Tropez
LIT *Hardouin-Fugier Grafe*; *Hardouin-Fugier Grafe* 1979 (ill.); *Hardouin-Fugier Grafe* 1982 (ill.)

JUNIQUE, Léon-Régis *1875–1945*
Pupil of Castex-Dégrange, Lyon BA (CFD 1892). Exhib. Lyon Salon from *c.*1900
LIT *Hardouin-Fugier Grafe*

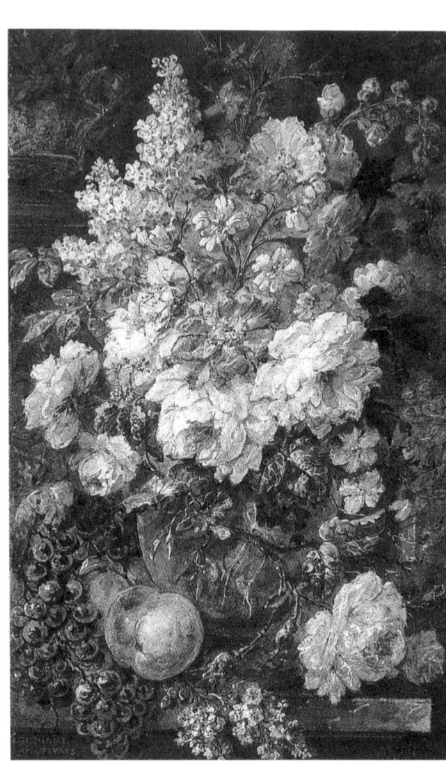

Eugène Julienne

Gouache, $8\frac{1}{4} \times 6$ in. (21.1. × 15.3 cm.), signed: 'E. Julienne/Ex à Sèvres'
Courtesy Sotheby's, London

JURREAUX, Joseph
b. Reims (Marne). Exhib. *Lilas et boules de neige*, Paris Salon 1880
LIT *Paris Salon* 1880

JUSSIEU, Adrien de *1797–1853*
Pupil of Laurent. Illustrated his own botanical works e.g. *De Euphorbiacearum*, Paris (Didot) 1824 and F. Gingins La Sarra, *Histoire Naturelle des lavandes*, Geneva 1826
LIT *Nissen* I, 712, 1014, 1017

JUSSIOME, Antoinette, *née* Clément
b. Nantes (Loire-Atlantique). Exhib. Paris Indép. e.g. *Violiers et giroflées*, 1886, *Marguerites*, *Roses*, *Pensées en bourriche* 1887
LIT *Paris Indép.* 1886, 1887

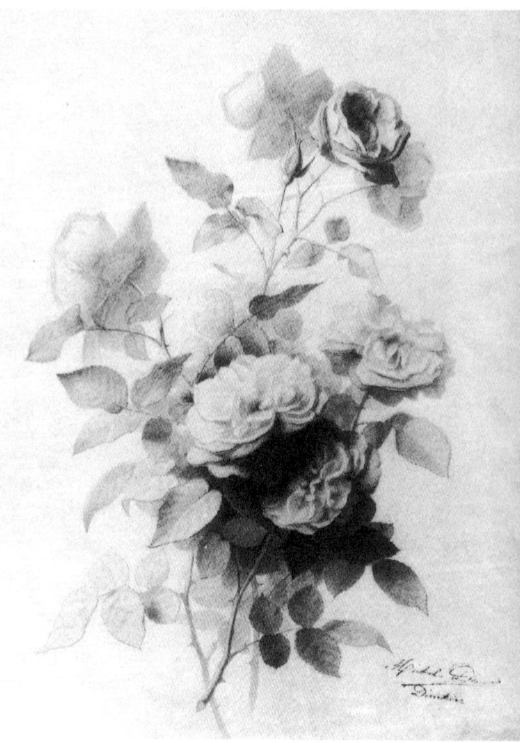

Charles-Frédéric Jung

Black crayon and chalk on paper, $21\frac{3}{4} \times 16\frac{1}{2}$ in. (55 × 42 cm.), signed and inscribed 'Michel Dumas Directeur'
Private collection

JUSTEAU, Emma-Cécile *b.1875*
b. Le Havre (Seine-Maritime). Painted flowers in wc. *Fleurs* formerly in the Musée de Mulhouse
LIT *Bénézit*

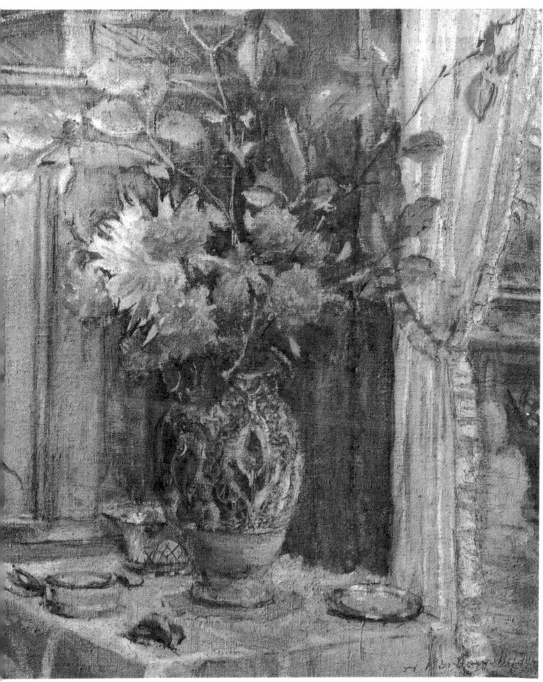

Adrien Karbowski

Oil on canvas, 21½ × 18 in. (54.5 × 46 cm.), signed and dated 1914
Paris, Musée d'Orsay

KAHN, Louise
Art teacher. Exhib. *Fleurs*, gouache, fan-leaf, Paris Indép. 1884
LIT *Paris Indép.* 1884

KAMMERER, Chrétien *1822–1903*
b. Illzach (Haut-Rhin). Textile designer. Three works once catalogued in the Musée de Mulhouse are now untraceable
LIT *Bénézit*; Musée de Mulhouse *cat.* 1922; *Thieme*. BJ

KARBOWSKI, Adrien *1855–1945*
b. Paris. Pupil of Lavastre, Lequien and Puvis de Chavannes. Theatre designer, decorator, occasionally painted flowers. Three *Fleurs*, wc, Paris SNBA 1893. M: Orsay
LIT *Bénézit*; *Paris SNBA* 1893; *Thieme*

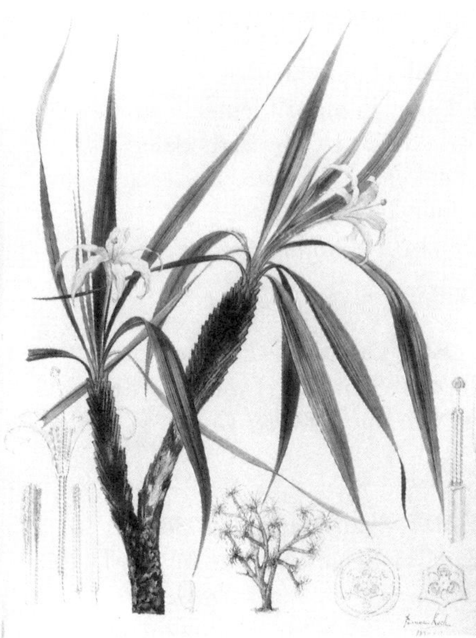

Jeanne de Kock

Watercolour on vellum, Vélins vol. 75, no. 87, signed and dated 1890
Paris, Bibliothèque Centrale du Muséum National d'Histoire Naturelle

KARCHER, Gustave *1831–1908*
b. Colmar (Haut-Rhin). Pupil of Fonville. Active in Lyon. Painted landscapes and, occasionally, flowers. Exhib. *Fleurs de printemps*, Lyon Salon 1882
LIT *Bénézit*; *Lyon Salon* 1882; *Schurr* III, 53; *Thieme*

KELLER, *see* DUSSIEUX

KERMABON, Adeline-Marie
b. Saint-Malo (Ille-et-Vilaine). Pupil of D. de Cool and Beauregard. Painted portraits and, occasionally, flowers. Exhib. *Roses*, fan-leaf, wc, Paris Salon 1882
LIT *Bellier*; *Bénézit*

KHANN, Eugéne *b.1834*
Pupil of Thierriat, Lyon BA (CFD 1849)
LIT *Hardouin-Fugier Grafe*

KIND, Auguste *b.1863*
b. Forbach (Moselle). Pupil of P. Thomas and P. Bourgogne. Exhib. Paris Salon *Chrysanthèmes*, 1895, *Fleurs*, 1898
LIT *Bénézit*; *Paris Salon* 1895, 1898

KNOERTZER, Gustave
Exhib. *Roses*, Strasbourg Salon 1883 (500 francs)
LIT *Strasbourg Salon* 1883

KOCH, *see* BARBAUD

KOCK, Jeanne de
b. Versailles (Yvelines). Pupil of Louis de Kock, her father. Exhib. Paris Salon *c.*1860 e.g. *Roses Trémières*, 1861; *Pavots*, *Roses Trémières*, Lyon Salon 1869. Museum d'Histoire Naturelle, Paris, one wc on vellum, 1890
LIT *Bellier*; Laissus; *Lyon Salon* 1869; *Thieme*

KOENIG, ***see*** **LECHENET**

KOHLER, Mathias or Mathieu ***b.1841***
b. Niederbronn (Bas-Rhin). Pupil of Reignier, Lyon BA (CFD 1856). Textile designer (Mulhouse). Exhib. Paris Salon 1877, 1878; *Retour du jardin*, *Roses*, Dijon Salon 1894
LIT *Bellier*; *Bénézit*; *Dijon Salon* 1894; *Hardouin-Fugier Grafe*; *Histoire Documentaire*. BJ

KREMER, Marie
Exhib. *Violettes* (100 francs), Strasbourg Salon 1891
LIT *Strasbourg Salon* 1891

KREYDER, Alexis ***1839–1912***
b. Andlau (Bas-Rhin). Pupil of Français, Zippelius and Fuchs. Exhib. Paris Salon from 1863. *Un rosier en automne*, 1867, *Bouquet de roses*, 1883, *Fleurs de printemps*, 1898. Exhib. Paris SNBA *Roses 1890*, *Bouquet de roses*, *Roses trémières*, *Boules de neige* 1891; *Roses*, Dijon Salon 1892. M: Auch. Colmar, Epinal, Paris (Louvre, Orsay), Strasbourg, Baltimore. Mulhouse, *Pivoines* 1866, *Un coin de Parc* 1885
LIT *Bellier*; *Bénézit*; *Dijon Salon* 1892; *Paris Salon* 1867, 1875, 1885, 1898; *Paris SNBA* 1890, 1891; Paris, Grand Palais, *Le Musée du Luxembourg en 1874*, G. Lacambre, 1874; *Sitzmann*; *Thieme*; *Witt*. BJ

KROPF, Simon-Paul ***b.1832***
Pupil of Reignier, Lyon BA (CFD 1858)
LIT *Hardouin-Fugier Grafe*

L

LABARRE, Anatole ***d.1906***
b. Paris. Pupil of S. Labarre. Painted still-lifes and flowers. Exhib. Paris Salon from 1874 e.g. *Camélia*, gouache, 1879
LIT *Bellier*; *Bénézit*; *Thieme*

LABBÉ, Charles-Emile ***d.1885***
b. Mussy-sur-Seine (Aube). Painted flowers, then landscapes. Director of Alger BA. Exhib. Paris Salon 1836–1876 e.g. *Dahlias*, wc, 1836, *Roses blanches*, 1839. Designed flower lithographs published by Michalot and Lemercier. Musée d'Alger: *Chrysanthèmes*
LIT *Bellier*; *Bénézit*; Paris Bibl. Nat. Est. Jd 67; *Paris BMAD*; *Paris Salon* 1836; *Thieme*

LABBÉ, Louis-Charles
b. Paris. Pupil of Clément. op. Sèvres 1847–1853. Exhib. Paris Salon *Bouquet de pivoines*, wc, 1848, *Bouquet de roses*, on porcelain, 1852
LIT *Bellier*; *Brunet Préaud*

LABIT, Christophe-Etienne ***b.1833***
Pupil of Thierriat, Lyon BA (CFD 1851)
LIT *Hardouin-Fugier Grafe*

LABIT, Jean-Marie ***b.1836***
Pupil of Reignier, Lyon BA (CFD 1856)
LIT *Hardouin-Fugier Grafe*

LABOUCHÈRE, A.M.
Painted *Pivoines roses* and *Bouquet* wc on vellum, one s.d. 1835. *Peonies* reproduced by A. Janet and lithographed by Chirat for the publisher Chavant
LIT *Hardouin-Fugier* 1981 (ill.)

LABOUREY, Jeanne
Exhib. Dijon Salon *Lilas*, 1885, *Anémones*, 1887
LIT *Dijon Salon* 1885, 1887. CL

LACAZETTE, Amélie
b. Cuba. Pupil of A. Tissier, E. Girard, Carolus-Duran and Henner. Exhib. Paris Salon 1877–1893. Exhib. *Fleurs et roman*, Lyon Salon 1881
LIT *Bénézit*; *Lyon Salon* 1881; *Thieme*

LACHAPELLE, Antoine-Elie ***1822–c.1890***
Pupil of Lyon BA. Exhib. Lyon Salon 1870–1889, Paris Salon 1877. Lyon Salon *Roses*, 1877, *Vase de fleurs*, 1878, *Giroflées*, 1884, 1885; *Vase de fleurs*, Dijon Salon 1887
LIT *Audin Vial*; *Bénézit*; *Dijon Salon* 1887; *Lyon Salon* 1877, 1878, 1884, 1885

LACHASSAIGNE, ***see*** **DEMIANNAY**

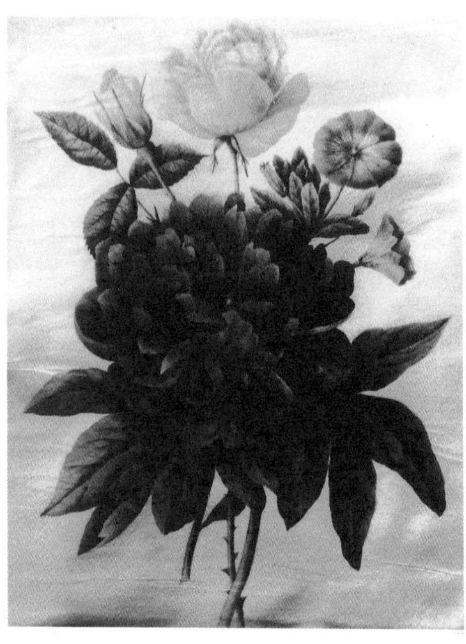

A.M. Labouchère

Watercolour on vellum, 9½ × 7 in. (24 × 18 cm.), signed and dated 1835
Private collection

LACHENY, Edward
b. Etampes (Essonne). Exhib. Paris Indép. *Lilas*, *Fleurs*, *Bruyéres*, *Géraniums*, 1891, *Fleurs*, *Giroflées*, Oeillets, *Iris*, *Vase de fleurs*, 1892
LIT *Paris Indép.* 1891, 1892

LACOSTE, *see* BRUNNER

LACOUR, Charles *1863–1940*
Painted landscapes and, occasionally, flowers. Exhib. Lyon Salon 1890–1938
LIT *Hardouin-Fugier Grafe*

LACOUR, Laurent-Louis *b.1858*
Pupil of Reignier, Lyon BA (CFD 1875)
LIT *Hardouin-Fugier Grafe*

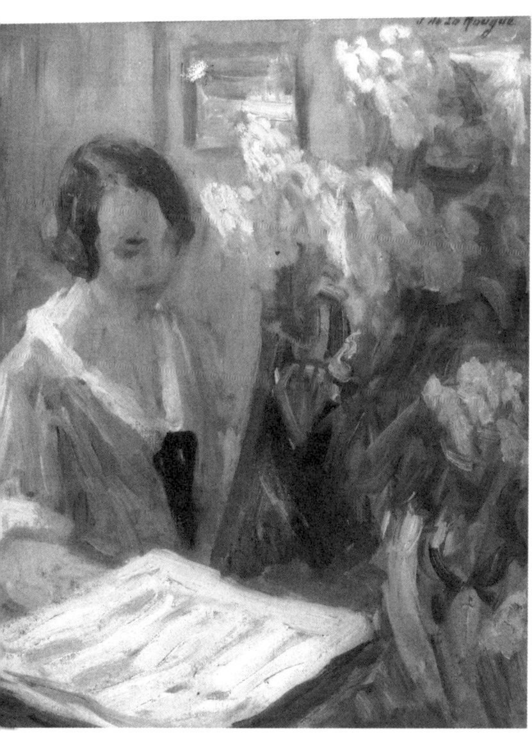

Jean de La Hougue

Oil on canvas, 15¾ × 19¾ in. (40 × 50 cm.), signed
Avranches, Musée d'Avranches

LACROIX, Claude-Marie *b.1835*
Pupil of Thierriat, Lyon BA (CFD 1852). Exhib. Lyon Salon 1868, 1873, 1877, 1878
LIT *Hardouin-Fugier Grafe*

LACROIX, Gabrielle *d.1894*
b. Chatellerault (Vienne). Pupil of D. de Cool and Chaplin. Exhib. *Phlox*, Paris Noir et Blanc Salon 1886; *Roses de Juin*, wc, Paris Salon 1890
LIT *Bénézit*; *Paris Noir et Blanc Salon* 1886; *Paris Salon* 1890

LACROIX, Mme
b. Vienne (Isère). Pupil of D. de Cool and Chaplin. Exhib. *Bouquet de roses*, Paris Noir et Blanc Salon 1888
LIT *Paris Noir et Blanc Salon* 1888

LACURIA, Thérèse, *née* Chatt *1816–1892*
b. Lyon. Pupil of Janmot. Exhib. Lyon Salon *Fleurs*, 1851, 1852
LIT *Lyon Salon* 1851, 1852

LADEVÈZE *d.1874*
Pupil of Thierriat, Lyon BA. Wallpaper designer
LIT *Hardouin-Fugier Grafe*

LA FARGUE, Ambroisine-Laure-Gabrielle de, *née* Boucher de Léoménil
b. Lyon. Pupil of J.B. Laurens and Viguier. Painted flowers in wc. Exhib. Paris Salon from 1878 e.g. *Roses trémières*, wc., 1880
LIT *Bellier*; *Bénézit*; *Hardouin-Fugier Grafe*; *Paris Salon* 1880

LAFERRERIE
In Toulouse *c.*1800. Designed plates for P. Picot de Lapeyrouse, *Flore des Pyrénées*, Paris 1795–1801, and for K. Sternberg. *Revisio Saxifragum ...* Ratisbon 1810
LIT *Nissen* I, 1141, 1896

LAFFITE, Gérard
Exhib. Strasbourg Salon *Azalées*, *Hortensia* (1,000 francs), 1891; Paris SNBA *Azalées*, *Lophophore*, 1893, *Roses trémières*, *fleurs*, fan-leaf, 1894, *Roses*, *Rose du Bengale*, *Chrysanthèmes*, *Roses de Nice*, wc, 1895, *Roses Capitaine Christie*, 1895, *Roses Maréchal Niel*, *Roses trémières*, *Roses du Bengale*, *Chrysanthèmes*, 1897, *Roses de Nice*, *Orchidées*, 1898
LIT *Paris SNBA* 1893, 1894, 1895, 1897, 1898; *Strasbourg Salon* 1891

LAFOND, Eugène-André *b.1837*
Pupil of Thierriat, Lyon BA (CFD 1851)
LIT *Hardouin-Fugier Grafe*

LAFOND, Victor
b. Paris. Pupil of E. Claude. Exhib. *Panneaux de fleurs*, Paris Noir et Blanc Salon 1886
LIT *Paris Noir et Blanc Salon* 1886

LAFONT, Jean-Joseph *b.1827*
Pupil of Thierriat, Lyon BA (CFD 1839)
LIT *Hardouin-Fugier Grafe*

LA FOREST, Pauline de
Pupil of Grönland. Exhib. Paris Salon from 1869 e.g. *Fleurs des champs*, *Aster*, 1872
LIT *Bénézit*; *Paris Salon* 1872

LAFORGE, Edouard
Exhib. Lyon Salon 1846, 1848
LIT *Audin Vial*

LAFORGUE, Emile-Paul
Exhib. *Capucines de Nice*, *Fleurs*, Paris Indép. 1884
LIT *Paris Indép.* 1884

LA FOSSE de, *see* DESPORTES

LALIGANT, Marie
Exhib. Dijon Salon *Marguerite et chicorée*, *Coquelicots et scabieuses*, 1890, *Fleurs*, four gouaches, 1892
LIT *Dijon Salon* 1890, 1892. CL

LALLEMAND, Mme Hippolyte, *née* Adèle Le Corbeiller *b.1807*
b. Paris. Pupil of Belloc. Painted portraits, fruit and flowers. Exhib. under her married name from 1840. Exhib. Paris Salon from 1835 watercolours e.g. *Fleurs* 1840, 1842, *Fleurs et fruits*, 1843, *Fleurs*, 1844, *Printemps*, *Automne*, *Fleurs et fruits*, 1850; Dijon Salon *Vase de fleurs diverses*, 1840. Some of her flower designs were published by Desjardins. *Corbeille de fleurs*, Sotheby's, London, 2 June 1985, lot 6. M: Château d'Azay-le-Ferron: *Vase de fleurs*, 1836
LIT *Bellier*; *Bénézit*; *Dijon Salon* 1840; *Faré* 1962, p. 248; Paris Bibl. Nat. Est. Jd 66; *Paris Salon* 1840, 1842, 1843, 1844, 1850; *Schurr* I, 30

LALUYÉ, Léopold-Charles-Antoine *1826–1899*
Paris BMAD (Maciet coll.): *Astrantia major*. Paris Muséum d'Histoire Naturelle: one watercolour on vellum, one watercolour on paper (not botanical).
LIT *Bénézit*; *Laissus*; *Paris BMAD*

LALYRE, Adolphe *b.1850*
b. Rouvres (Meuse). Pupil of Lyon BA and Paris BA. Painted religious and mythological subjects, nudes and portraits. Exhib. Paris Salon from 1876. Musée de Tours, *Fleurs de Touraine*
LIT *Bénézit*; Musée de Tours doc.; *Schurr* III, 115; *Thieme*

LAMBERT, Edmond-Eugène *b.1864*
Pupil of Reignier, Lyon BA (CFD 1880)
LIT *Hardouin-Fugier Grafe*

LAMBERT, *see* BOUILLET

LAMBERT-TRISTAN, Louise Baronne, *née* Chanton *c.1847–1899*
b. Neuilly-sur-Seine (Hauts-de-Seine). Pupil of P. Bourgogne, G. Jeannin and Bergeret. Exhib. Paris Salon from 1878 e.g. *Pivoines*, 1880; *Chrysanthèmes*, pastel, 1895; *Pivoines blanches*, Dijon Salon 1883; *Pivoines roses*, Lyon Salon 1884. *Chrysanthèmes*, *Dahlias*, *Oeillets*, *Fleurs de printemps*, *Roses trémières*, pastel, *Fleurs et fruits*, Paris UFPS 1896
LIT *Bellier*; *Bénézit*; *Dijon Salon* 1883; *Lyon Salon* 1884; *Paris Salon* 1880, 1895; *Paris UFPS* 1896; *Thieme*

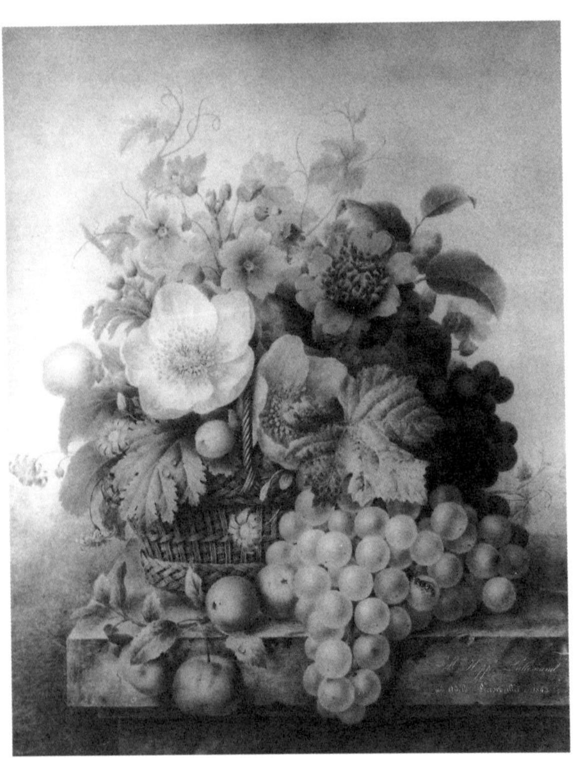

Mme Hippolyte Lallemand

Gouache and watercolour, 17¾ × 14½ in. (45 × 37 cm.), signed 'Mme Hippolyte Lallemand/née Adèle Le Corbeiller 1843'
Courtesy Sotheby's, London

Léopold-Charles-Antoine Laluyé

Engraving after a drawing, 8¼ × 5 in. (20.8 × 13 cm.), signed
Paris, BMAD (Maciet Collection)

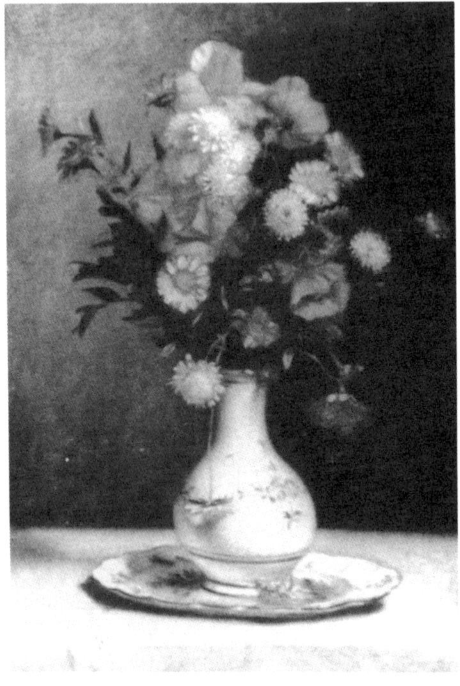

Charles-Zacharie Landelle

Oil on canvas, 30 × 24 in. (76 × 61 cm.), signed and dated 1888
Private collection

LAFRETE DE PONTBELLANGER, Marie
b. Paris. Pupil of Leroy. Exhib. *Fuchsia*, *Azalées*, Paris Salon 1880
LIT *Paris Salon* 1880

LAGARDE, Pierre ***1853–1910***
b. Paris. Pupil of Busson, F. Humbert, Dubufe and Mazerolle. Painted figures, landscapes, historical subjects, genre and, occasionally, flowers. Exhib. Paris Salon from 1878. Exhib. *Urne de fleurs*, Paris SNBA 1897
LIT *Bénézit*; *Paris SNBA* 1897; *Thieme*; *Witt*

LAGROST, Marguerite ***b.1865***
b. Mâcon (Saône-et-Loire). Pupil of Krug and Feyen-Perrin. Painted flowers. Exhib. Paris Salon. Dijon Salon *Narcisses et jacinthes*, 1887, *Fleurs de printemps*, 1892; Paris Noir et Blanc Salon, *Primevères*, 1886, *Cinéraires*, wc, 1888
LIT *Bénézit*; *Dijon Salon* 1887, 1892; *Paris Noir et Blanc Salon* 1886, 1888; *Thieme*

LAHAYE, Alexis-Marie ***1850–1914***
b. Nîmes (Gard). Pupil of Pils, Corot and Carolus-Duran. Director of Nîmes BA and curator of Nîmes Museum. Painted landscapes, figures and, occasionally, flowers. Exhib. Paris SNBA from 1894 e.g. *Iris*, *Hortensia*, *Glaïeul*, 1898
LIT *Bénézit*; *Paris SNBA* 1898; *Schurr* IV, 113; *Thieme*; *Witt*

LAHAYE, Gustave ***b.1873***
Pupil of Castex-Dégrange, Lyon BA (CFD 1893)
LIT *Hardouin-Fugier Grafe*

LAHOGUE, Léon
Painted still-lifes, fruit and flowers. Exhib. Paris Salon 1841–1850 e.g. *Fleurs*, 1847
LIT *Bellier*; *Bénézit*

LA HOUGUE, Jean de
His *Chrysanthèmes* (currently untraceable) was bought by the State for the Musée d'Avranches. *Pois de senteur*, *Parterre de fleurs* (both private coll.). M: Avranches, *Pianiste et lilas*
LIT Paris Arch. Nat. F21:4500

LAINÉ, *see* VOITELLIER

LAIR, Albert-Eugène
Painted flowers. Two works by Lair used to be in the Musée de Caen, *Oeillets*, acquired 1905 (lost)
LIT *Bénézit*

LAJALLET, Hélène de, *later* Mme Baude de Meurceley ***b.1858***
b. Saint-Jean-d'Angély (Charente-Maritime). Pupil of J. Lefebvre, G. Jeannin and Baschet, and B. Constant. Painted flowers. Exhib. Paris Salon from 1882 e.g. *Hotte de chrysanthèmes*, 1887, *Pavots*, 1888; Poitiers Salon, *Roses trémières* (600 francs), *Pavots* (400 francs), 1887; *Dijon Salon*, *Puits fleuri*, *Lilas* 1892. M: La Ferté-Macé, La Rochelle (bought by State 1896); Toulouse
LIT *Dijon Salon* 1892; *Orsay*; Paris Arch. Nat. F21:2137; *Paris Salon* 1887, 1888; *Poitiers Salon* 1887; *Thieme*

LALANNE, Maxime ***1827–1886***
b. Bordeaux (Gironde). Pupil of Gigoux. This popular etcher and draughtsman painted landscapes and, occasionally, flowers. Exhib. Paris Salon from 1852. *Plant de tabac dans un coin de jardin*, charcoal (Lalanne atelier sale, Drouot, Paris, March 1890)
LIT *Artistes contemporains du Pays de Guyenne*, Bordeaux (Gounouilhou) 1889; *Bellier*; *Bénézit*; *Orsay*; *Schurr* I, 70; *Witt*

LALAUZE, Adolphe ***1838–1905***
b. Rive-de-Gier (Louvre). Pupil of Gaucherel. The popular book illustrator exhibited flowers Paris Salon 1881
LIT *Bénézit*; A. Patouy, *A. Lalauze*, Saint-Quentin, Poette 1894. *Thieme*; *Witt*

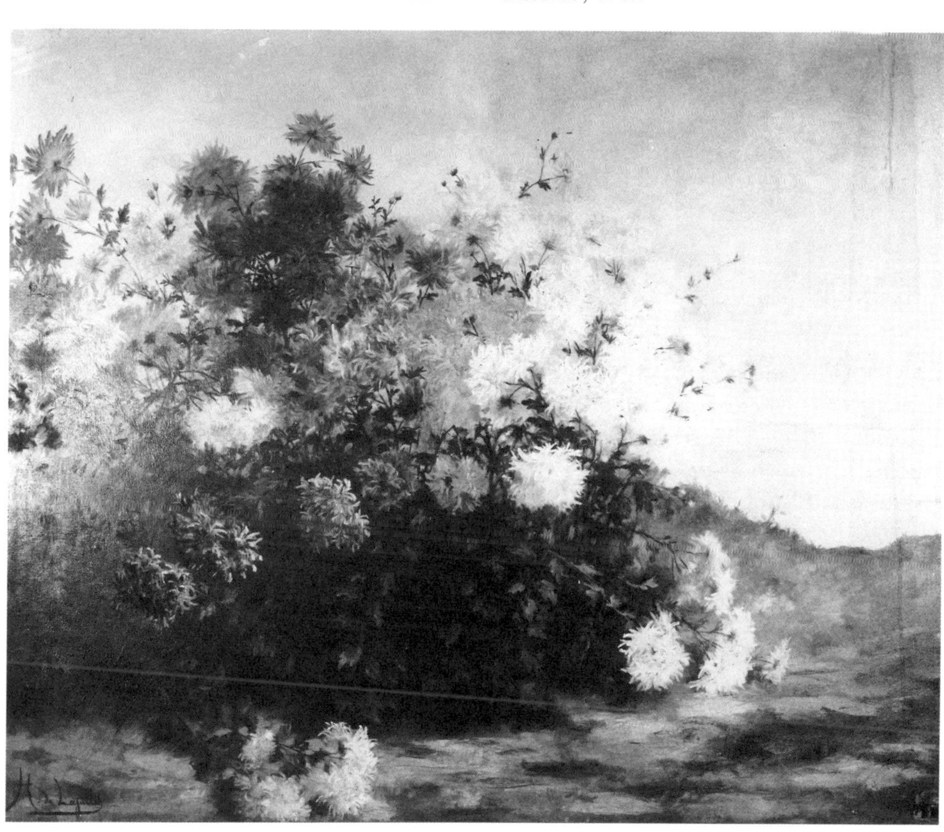

Hélène de Lajallet

Oil on canvas, 47½ × 55 in. (120 × 140 cm.), signed
La Rochelle, Musée d'Orbigny-Bernon

LAMBINET, Emile-Charles ***1815–1877***
b. Versailles (Yvelines). Pupil of Drolling and H. Vernet. Exhib. Paris Salon 1833–1878. The popular landscape painter occasionally exhib. flowers e.g. *Mai et ses fleurs*, Paris Salon 1863.
LIT *Bellier*; *Bénézit*; *Schurr* I, 48; *Thieme*; *Witt*

LAMEIRE, Charles-Joseph ***1832–1910***
b. Paris. Pupil of Dénuelle. Decorator. Produced tapestry and stained-glass window cartoons. His decorations sometimes feature flowers
LIT *Bénézit*; *Orsay*

LAMOTHE, Charles-Ferdinand
b. Paris. Pupil of Levasseur. Exhib. *Bourriche de pensées*, Paris Salon 1880
LIT *Paris Salon* 1880

LAMOUROUX, Rose
Designed flower plates lithographed by Engelmann
LIT Paris Bibl. Nat. Est. Jd 59, a,b

LAMY, Aline ***b.1862***
b. Paris. Pupil of F. Rivoire, Allongé and Laurent-Desrousseaux. Exhib. *Roses trémières*, Paris Salon 1895; *Iris, Bégonias, Boules de neige*, wc, Paris UFPS 1896
LIT *Bénézit; Paris Salon* 1895; *Paris UFPS* 1896; *Witt*

LAMY, ***see*** **FRANC**

LANDEAU, Rémy E. ***b.1859***
b. Sèvres (Hauts-de-Seine). Pupil of Pallandre. Painted genre, landscape and flowers. Chairman of the Société des Peintres de Fleurs. Exhib. 1899–1914
LIT *Bénézit*; *Thieme*

LANDELLE, Charles-Zacharie ***1812–1908***
b. Laval (Mayenne). Pupil of P. Delaroche and A. Scheffer. Painted genre, historical and religious subjects and, occasionally, flowers. Exhib. Paris Salon from 1841. *Roses dans une cruche en grès*, 1892, *Violettes et mimosas*, 1899, *Le papillon et la rose* (Landelle atelier sale 1908)
LIT *Bellier*; *Bénézit*; *Orsay*; *Schurr* II, 80; *Thieme*

LANDRÉ, Louise-Amélie ***b.1852***
b. Paris. Pupil of Chaplin and Barrias. Painted portraits, landscapes and flowers. Exhib. Paris Salon from 1876. Exhib. *Chrysanthèmes*, Saint-Etienne Salon 1882; *Fleurs de mai* (200 francs), Strasbourg Salon 1884; *Bourriche de pensées*, Dijon Salon 1885
LIT *Bénézit*; *Dijon Salon* 1885; *Saint-Etienne Salon* 1882; *Strasbourg Salon* 1884; *Schurr* V, 122

LANDRES, M. de
Exhib. *Gerbe de roses*, Paris SNBA 1898
LIT *Paris SNBA* 1898

LANEAU
Designed plates for E.P. Ventenat, *Description des plantes ... cultivées dans le jardin de M. Cels*, Paris 1800–1803. Worked with Redouté at Malmaison
LIT *Sitwell*

LANGLE, Pierre-Jean-Victor-Amable
op. Sèvres, 1837–1845. Painter and lithographer. Exhib. Paris Salon 1841, 1844, 1845 e.g. *Fleurs d'automne*, 1841
LIT *Brunet Préaud*; *Bellier*; *Paris Salon* 1841

LANGLOIS, Paul ***1858–1906***
b. Paris. Pupil of Cabanel, Bonnat and Humbert. Painted figures and landscapes. Exhib. *Fleurs*, Saint-Etienne Salon 1882
LIT *Bénézit*; *Saint-Etienne Salon* 1882

LANGRAND, E.
A signed flower painting, dated 1858, was at auction (Sotheby's, New York, 21 May 1987, lot 200). PM

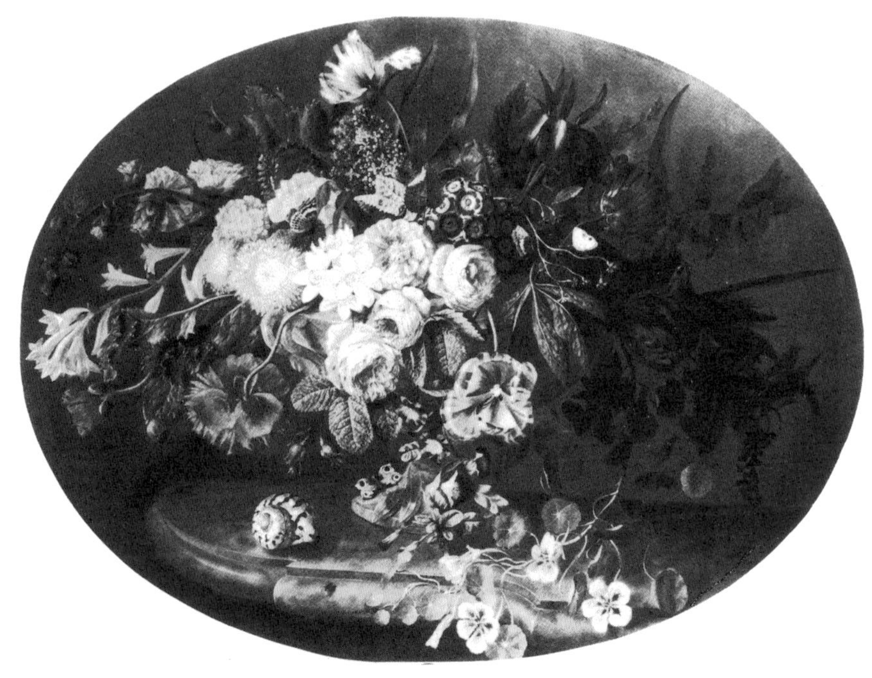

E. Langrand

Oil on canvas, oval, 34¼ × 45¼ in. (87 × 115 cm.), signed and dated '58
Courtesy Sotheby's, London

LANSSE, Blanche, *née* Salanson
b. Paris. Exhib. *Panier de géraniums*, wc, Paris Salon 1898
LIT *Paris Salon* 1898

LANSYER, Emmanuel-Maurice *1835–1893*
b. Ile Bouin (Vendée). Pupil of Viollet-le-Duc, Harpignies and Courbet. Painted landscapes and, occasionally, flowers. Exhib. Paris Salon from 1861 e.g. *Capucines*, *Cyclamens*, wc, 1874, *Flore champêtre*, tapestry cartoon for Gobelins, 1880, *Fuchsia, pétunia, érable*, 1881. Musée de Limoges, *Fleurs*, four watercolours
LIT *Bellier*; *Bénézit*; Lannyer, *Les maitres vendéens*, n.d., Paris (Bibl. Doucet D 9932); F. Loriot *E. Lansyer ...* Paris 1905; *Paris Salon* 1880; *Schurr* I, 51; *Witt*

LANTZ, Georges
Drawing master, Lyon. Exhib. Lyon Salon 1848
LIT *Audin Vial*

LA PEÑA de, *see* DIAZ

LAPORTE, or PORTE, or DE LA PORTE, Adèle
b. Paris. Pupil of Steuben. Painted portraits, cats, dogs and flowers. Exhib. Paris Salon 1842–1870 e.g. *Regrets, fleurs jetées*, 1849, *Mois de Marie, couronne de fleurs*, 1855, *Hommage à Van Spaendonck*, 1861
LIT *Bellier*; *Bénézit*; *Thieme*

LA POUZE, Louis
Exhib. *Pivoines*, Saint-Etienne Salon 1882
LIT *Saint-Etienne Salon* 1882

LAPRADE, Pierre *1875–1931*
b. Narbonne (Aude). Painted landscapes, figures and flowers. Most of these are later works. M: Grenoble, Paris, Musée d'Art Moderne
LIT *Bénézit*; Gebhard, L. Cann, *Laprade*, Paris (Crès) 1930; E. Jaloux, *P. Laprade*, Paris (NRF) 1925; Narbonne, Palais des Archevêques, *Centenaire de la naissance de Laprade*, 1975; *Pavière* III, pt. 1; Saint-Tropez, *Fleurs de Fantin-Latour à Marquet*, Musée de l'Annonciade, 1982 (ill.); *Witt*

LAQUESON
Designed flower plates lithographed by Demanne (1823, 1833), Paris BMAD (Maciet coll.)
LIT *Paris BMAD*

LARD, François-Maurice *1864–1908*
b. Paris. Pupil of Boulanger and Hébert. Painted genre and flowers. Exhib. Paris Salon from 1886. *Roses dans un verre*, *Violettes*, *Roses* (Lard atelier sale). A work formerly in the Musée de Mulhouse was lost in the war
LIT *Bénézit*; *Lard atelier sale*, Drouot, Paris, 24 Mar. 1909, no. 32, 34, 63; *Orsay*; *Thieme*; *Witt*

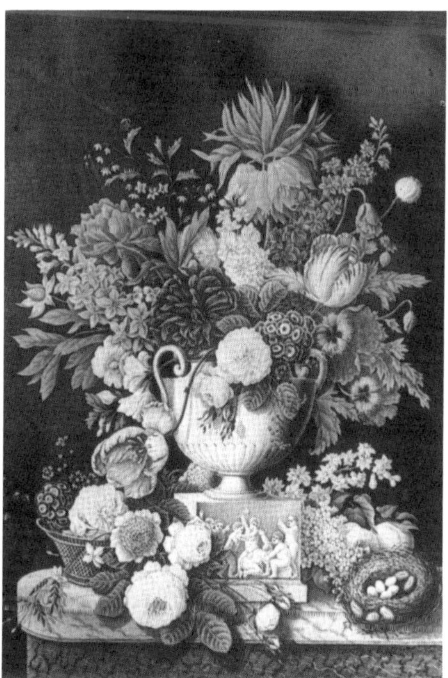

Georges Lantz

Gouache and watercolour, 11 × 8½ in. (28.1 × 21.4 cm.), signed
Courtesy Sotheby's, London

LARDET
Musée de Saint-Etienne, *Fleurs*, 1838
LIT Saint-Etienne Musée doc.

LARDILLON, Lucie or Lucy *d.1904*
b. Binges (Côte d'Or). Pupil of D. de Cool and Serres. Painted portraits, enamels and, occasionally, flowers. Exhib. Paris Salon from 1878. Exhib. *Panier de violettes*, wc, *Giroflées*, wc, Dijon Salon 1892
LIT *Bénézit*; *Dijon Salon* 1892

LARDIN, Camille-Antoine *b.1825*
Pupil of Thierriat, Lyon BA (CFD 1845)
LIT *Hardouin-Fugier Grafe*

LARHOVEN, *see* VAN LARHOVEN

LARROQUE, Madeleine
Exhib. *Cyclamens* (300 francs), *Nature morte de fleurs*, Poitiers Salon 1887
LIT *Poitiers Salon* 1887. BG

LARROQUE, Mathilde
b. Grenoble (Isère). Pupil of Lesourd de Beauregard. Exhib. Paris Salon 1864–1868 e.g. *Iris*, wc, 1866, *Bouquet de pensées*, 1868
LIT *Bellier*; Grenoble Bibl. Mun. Fichier R9909

LASSALE, Claude *b.1824*
Pupil of Thierriat, Lyon BA (CFD 1845)
LIT *Hardouin-Fugier Grafe*

LASSALLE, *see* CABAILLOT

LASSALLE, *see* DURAT

LASSARE, *see* BONVOISIN

LASSELAZ, Gustave
Exhib. Paris Indép. *Reines-marguerites*, 1888, *Fleurs sauvages*, 1896
LIT *Paris Indép.* 1888, 1896

LASSERRE, Laurent-Charles-Louis *b.1813*
Pupil of Thierriat, Lyon BA (CFD 1832)
LIT *Hardouin-Fugier Grafe*

LASSERRE, Prosper-Pierre *1832–1900*
b. Tirent-Pontejac (Gers). Active in Lisbon. Painted flowers. M: Lisbon, *Fleurs*
LIT *Bénézit*; *Thieme*

LA TOUCHE, Gaston *1854–1913*
b. Saint-Cloud (Hauts-de-Seine). Painted landscapes, interiors, figures and, occasionally, flowers. Exhib. *Pivoines, Phlox*, Paris SNBA 1890
LIT *Bénézit*; *Orsay*; Paris Arch. Nat. F21:37; *Paris SNBA* 1890; *Schurr* II, 102; M.A. Stevens, in *Post-Impressionism*, London, RA, 1979–1980; *Witt*

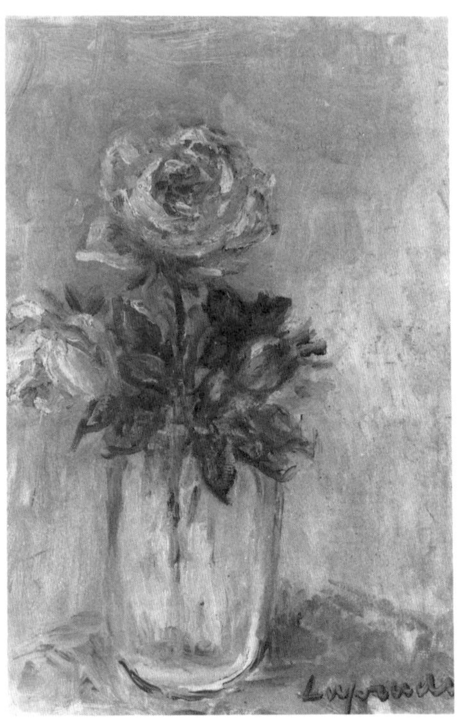

Pierre Laprade

Oil on canvas, 13¼ × 9in. (30.5 × 23 cm.), signed
Courtesy Christie's, London

LATOUR, Alexandre-Hilaire *b.1827*
Pupil of Lyon BA (1844), perhaps the Latour who entered the 1846 Lyon FDC or a namesake
LIT *Audin Vial*

LATOUR, Anna-Théodorine
b. Belleville (Paris XX°). Pupil of Dukette and École Normale de dessin. Exhib. *Chrysanthèmes*, Paris Salon 1880
LIT *Paris Salon* 1880

LATOUR, *see* CHABOURET

LATOUR, Fantin-Latour, *see* DUBOURG

LATTEUX, Eugène *1805–1850*
Painted landscapes and flowers, often in wc. Exhib. Paris Salon 1833–1840 e.g. *Roses de différentes espèces*, wc, 1833
LIT *Bellier*; *Bénézit*; *Paris Salon* 1833; *Schurr* I, 50; *Thieme*; *Witt*

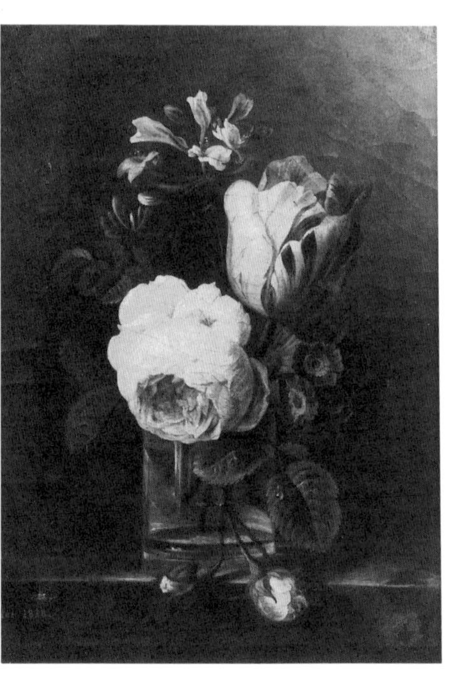

Lardet

Oil on canvas, signed and dated 1838
Saint-Etienne, Musée d'Art et d'Industrie

LAUBIÈS-JAMBON, Marie
Pupil of Pachot d'Arzve and Mareux-Baclet. op. Grenoble. Exhib. Grenoble Salon from 1899 e.g. *Primevères*, *Chrysanthèmes dans un vase*, *Chrysanthèmes à grandes fleurs*, 1899
LIT *Grenoble Salon* 1899. MW

LAUGÉ, Achille-Guillaume *1861–1944*
b. Arzens (Aude). Pupil of Toulouse BA, Cabanel and J.P. Laurens. Painted portraits, figures, landscapes and flowers (often later works). Exhib. Paris Indép. from 1894 e.g. *Fleurs*, 1894. Musée de Bourbon-Lancy, *Fleurs*
LIT *Bénézit*; Galerie Marcel Flavia, *Laugé*, Paris 1969; *Orsay*; *Paris Indép.* 1894; *Schurr* II, 58; *Thieme*

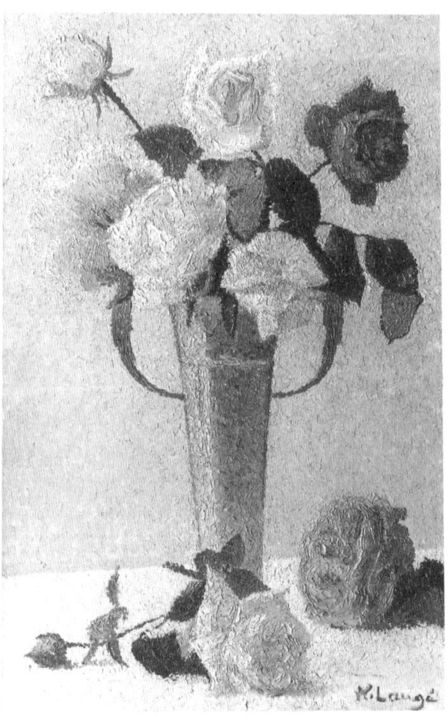

Achille-Guillaume Laugé

Oil on canvas, 21 × 14¼ in. (53 × 36 cm.), signed
Courtesy Sotheby's, London

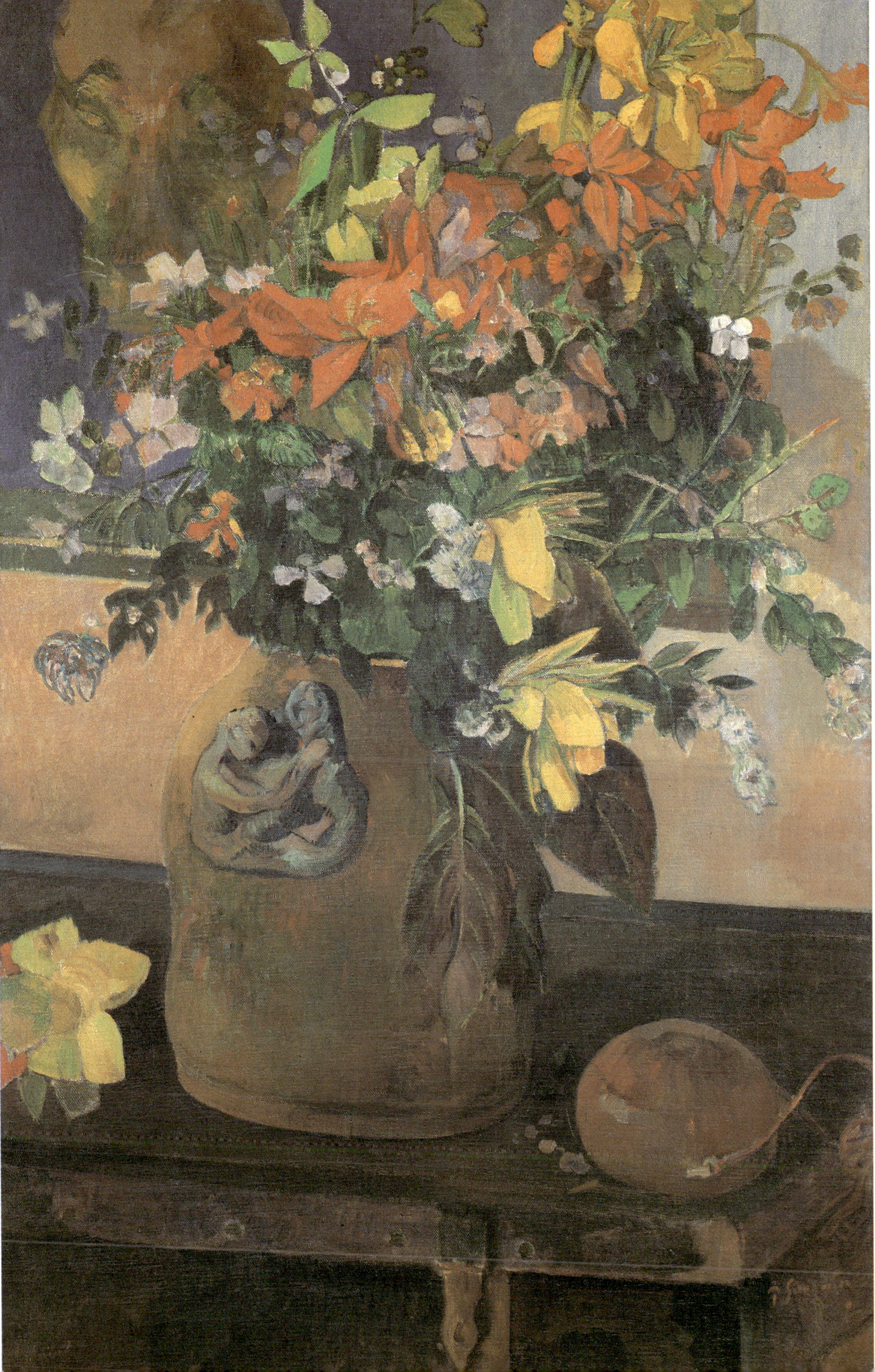

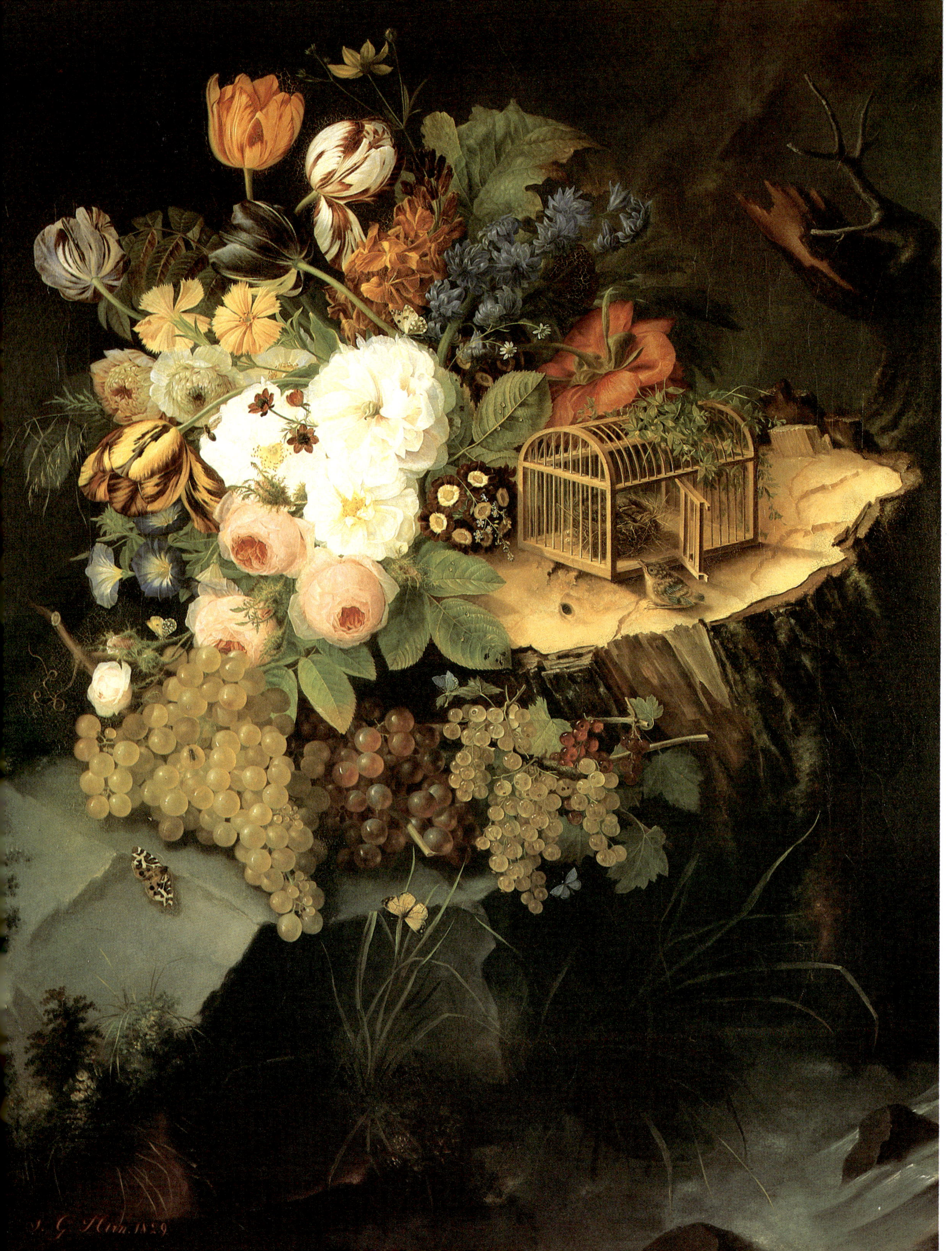
J. G. Hirn. 1829

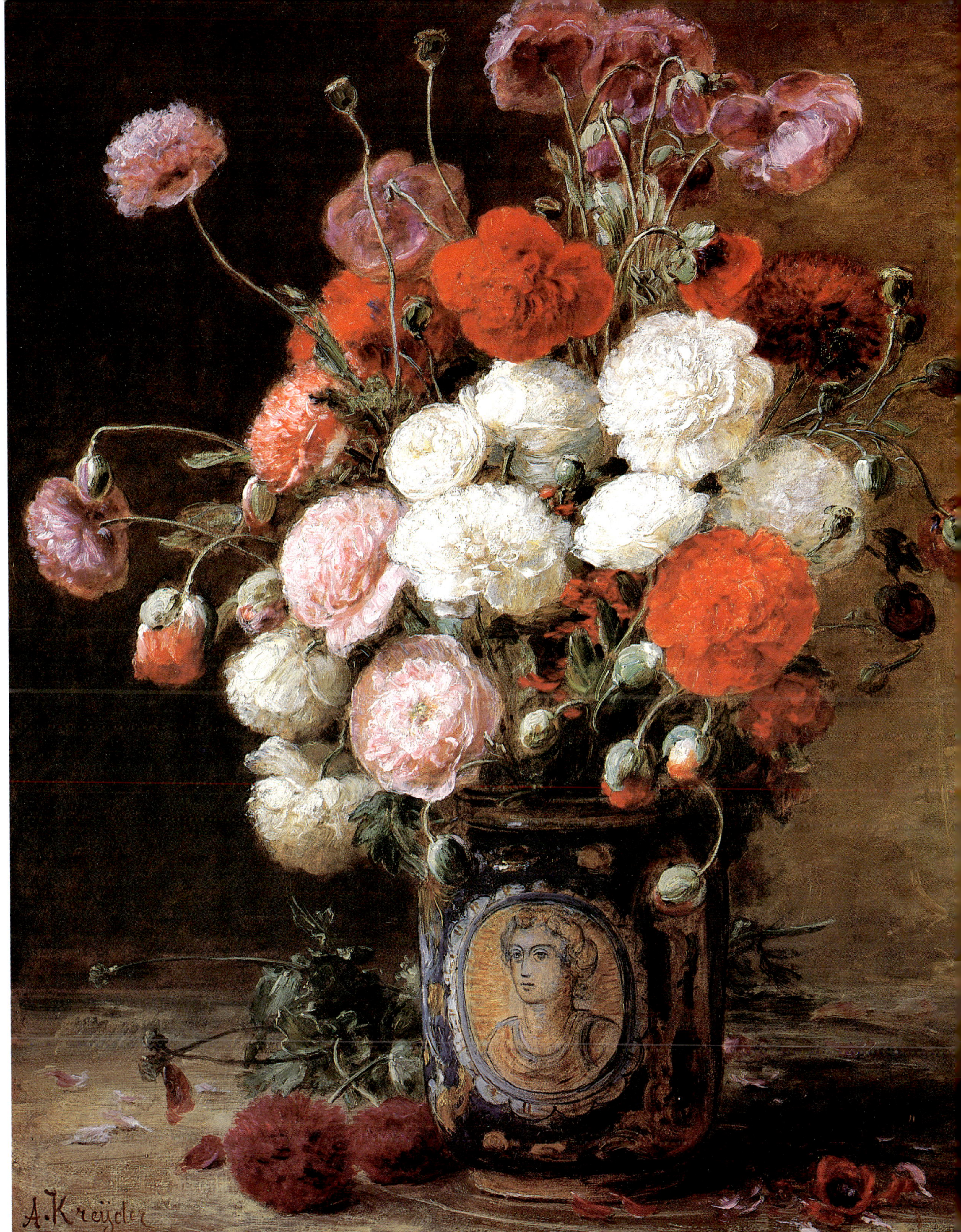
A. Kreÿder

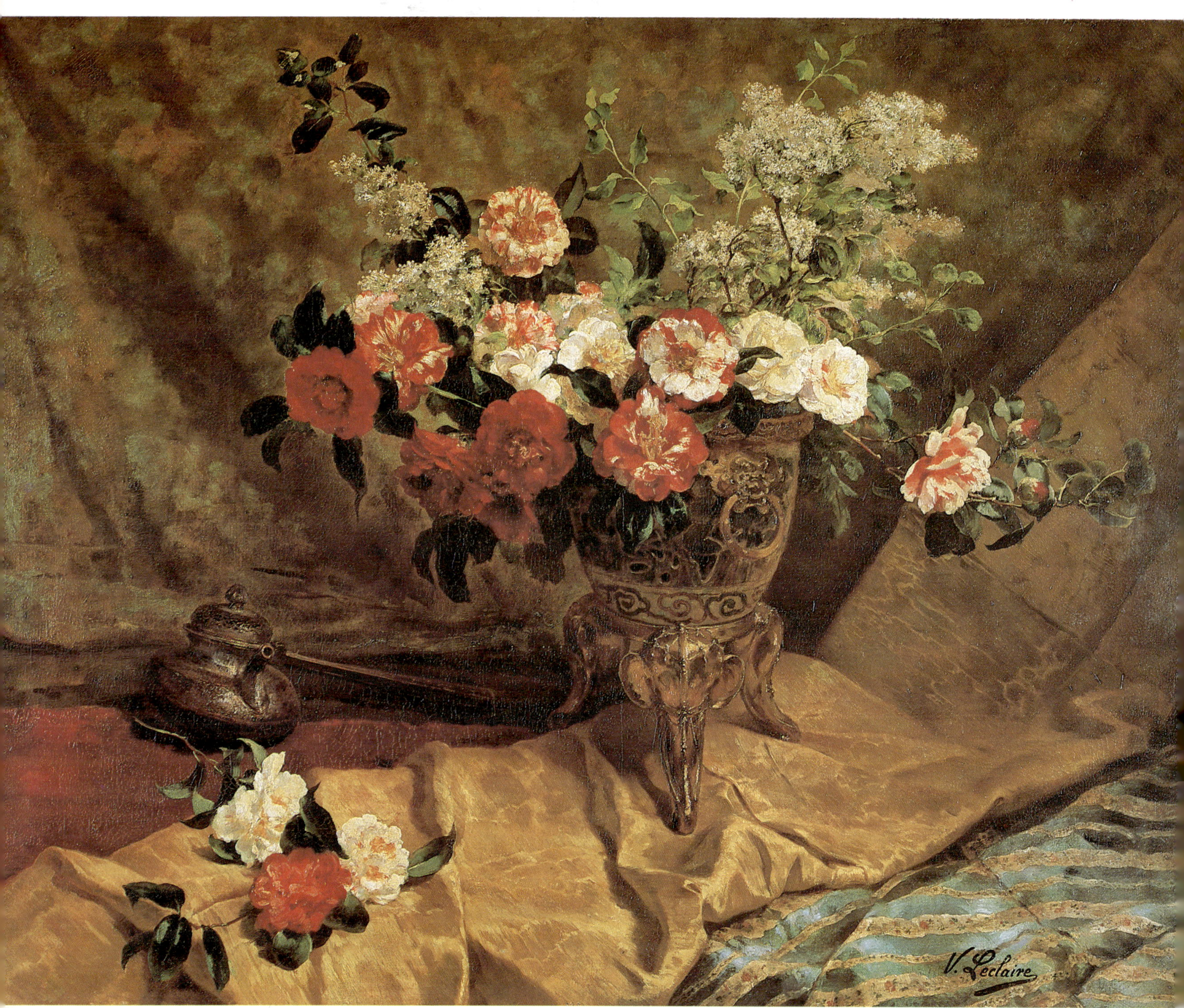
V. Leclaire

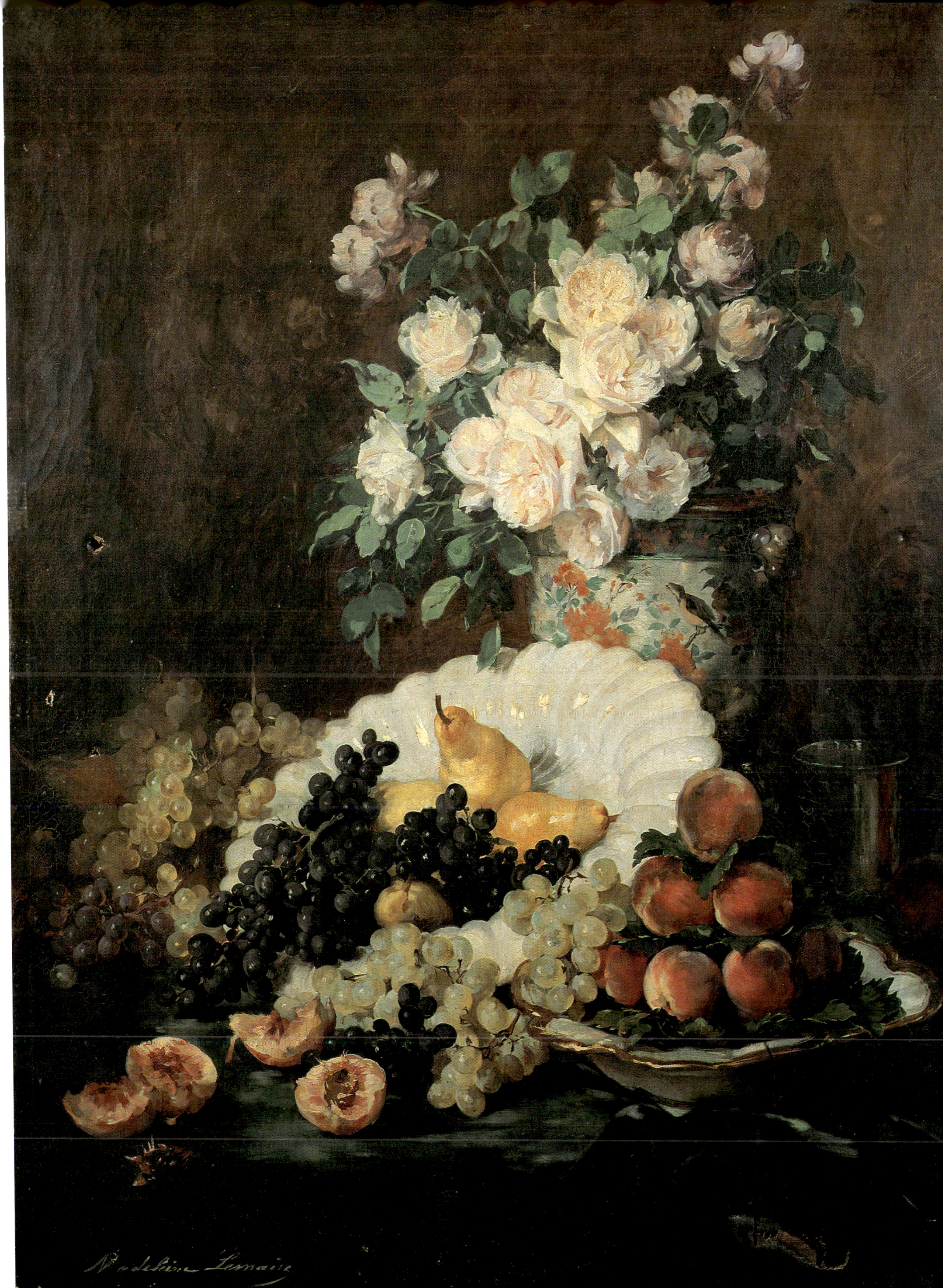

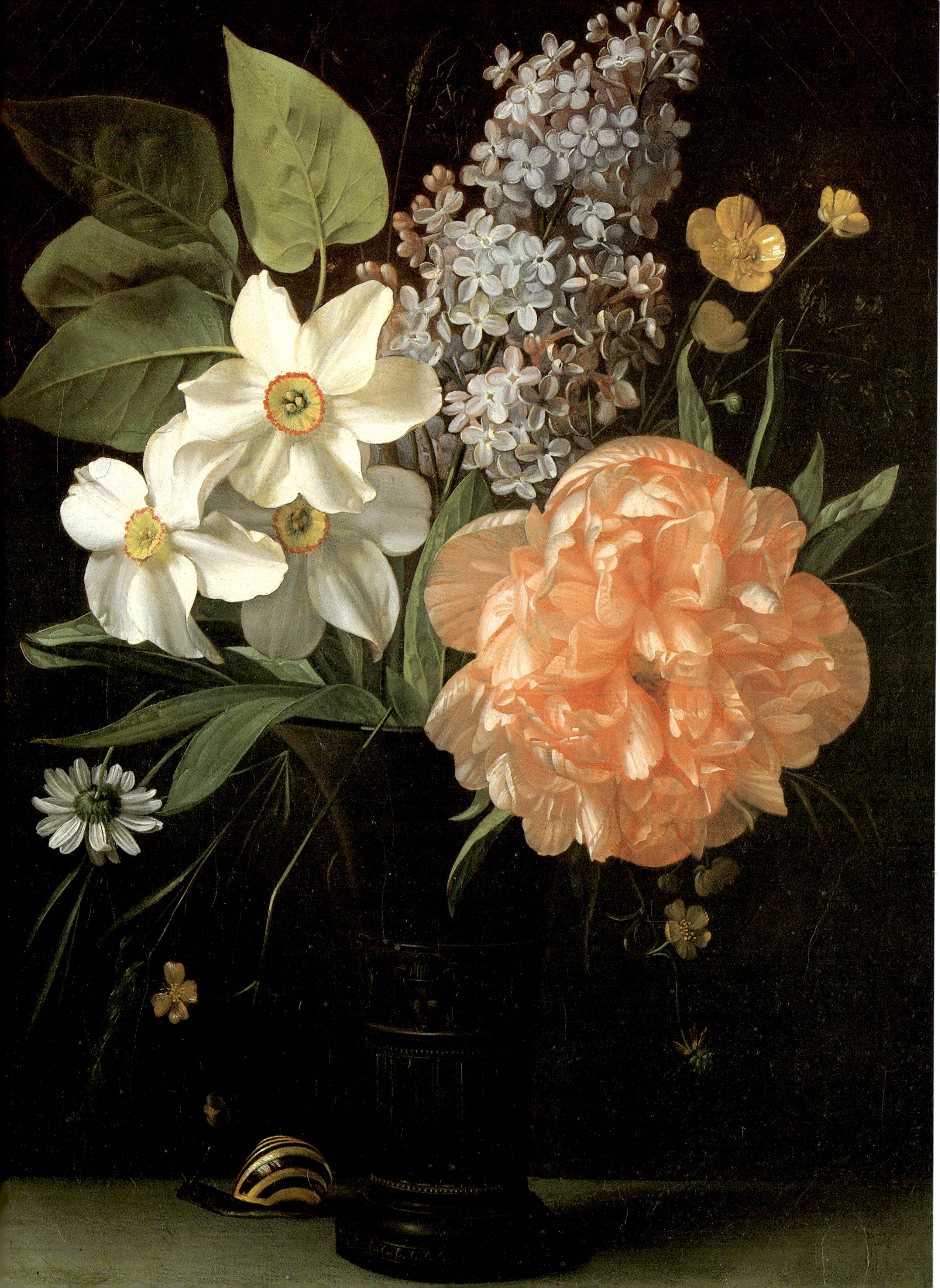

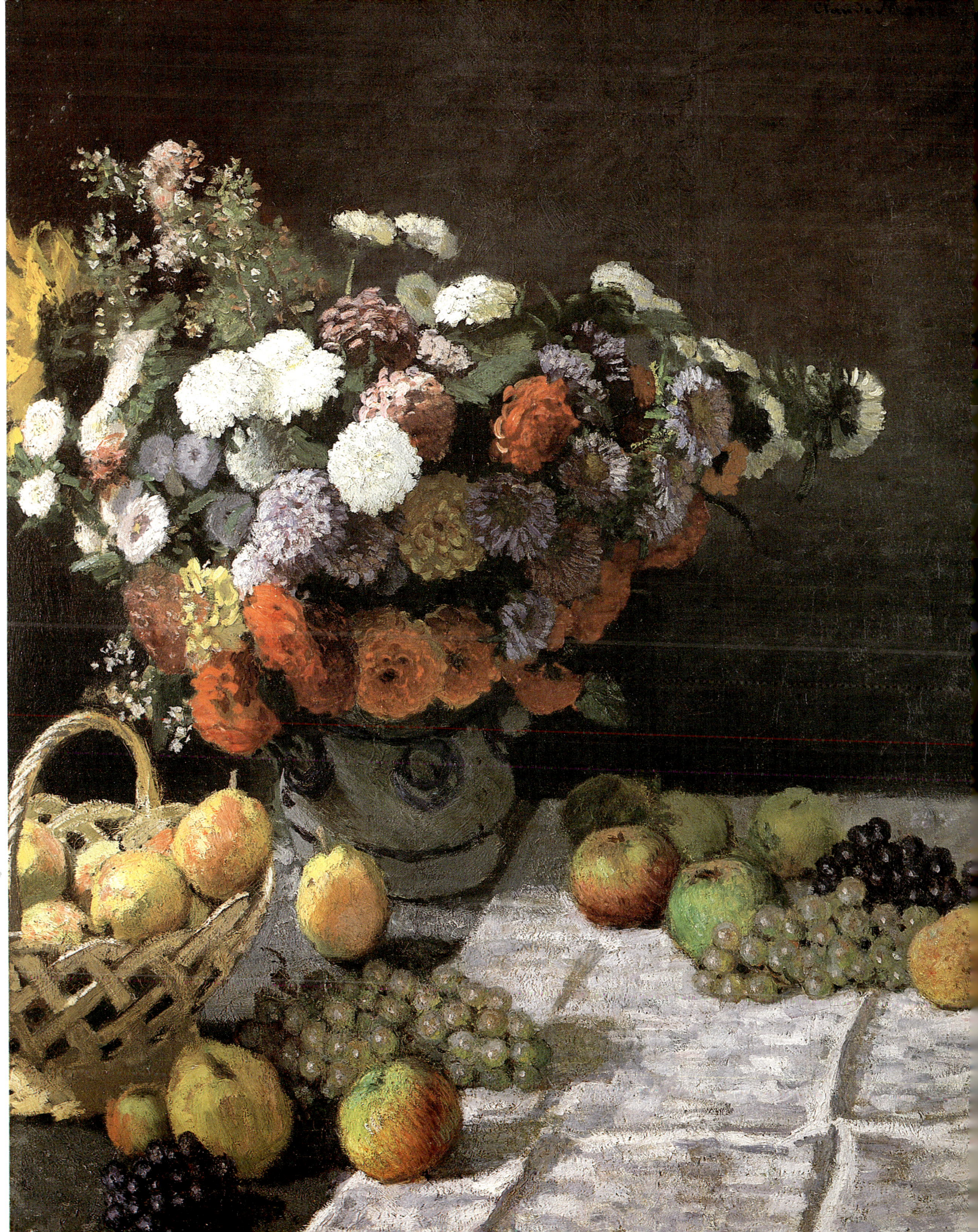

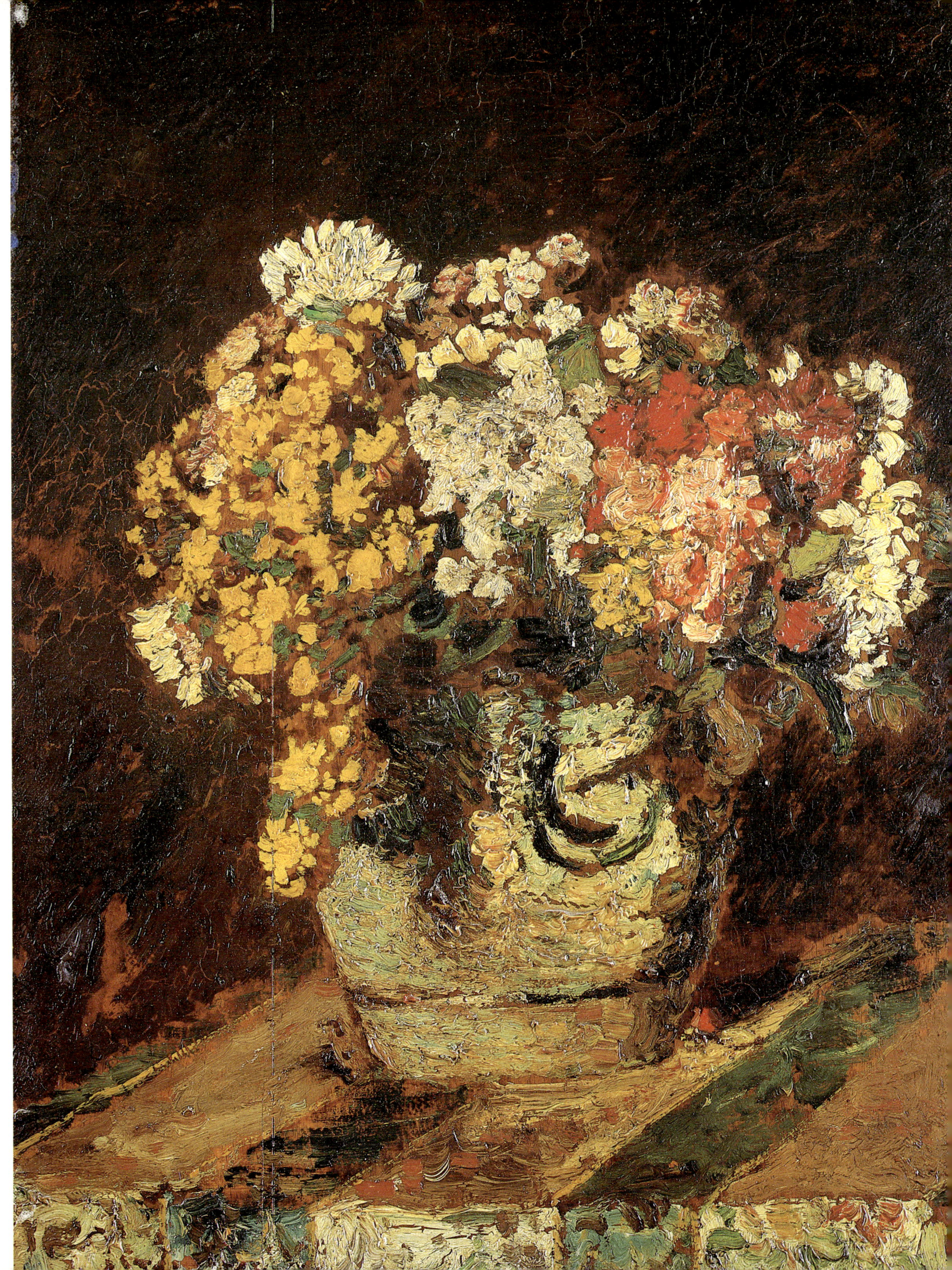

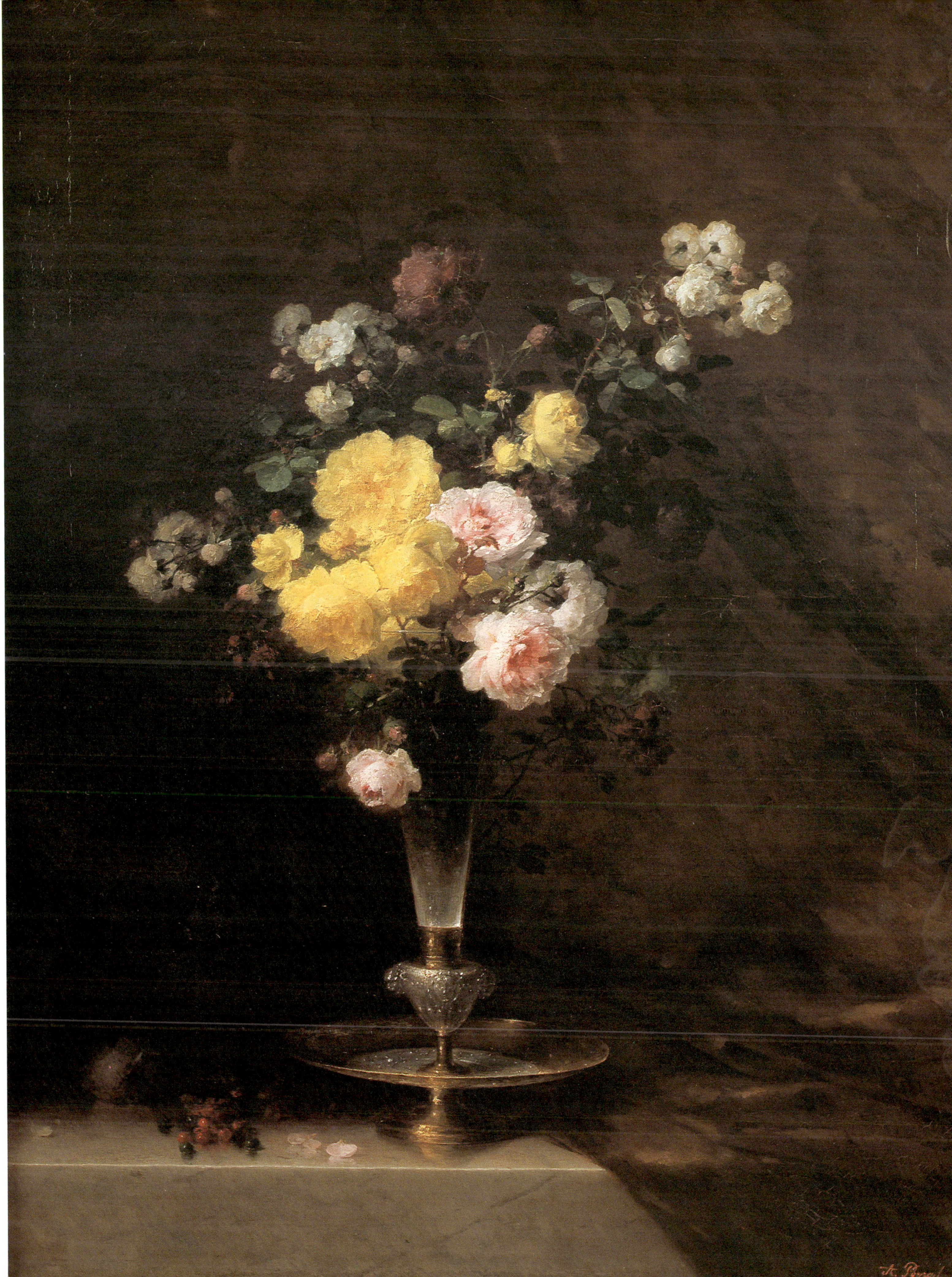

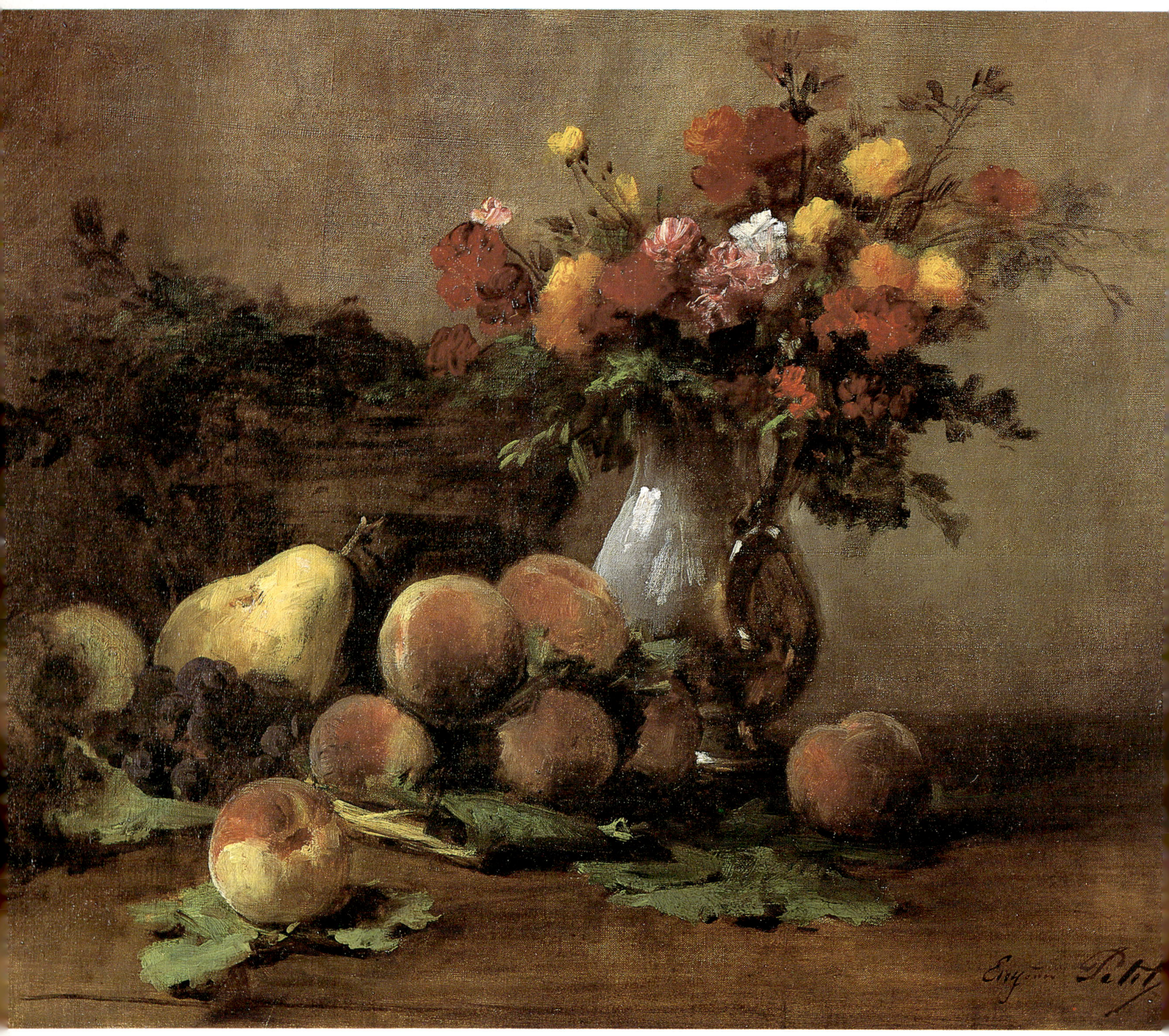

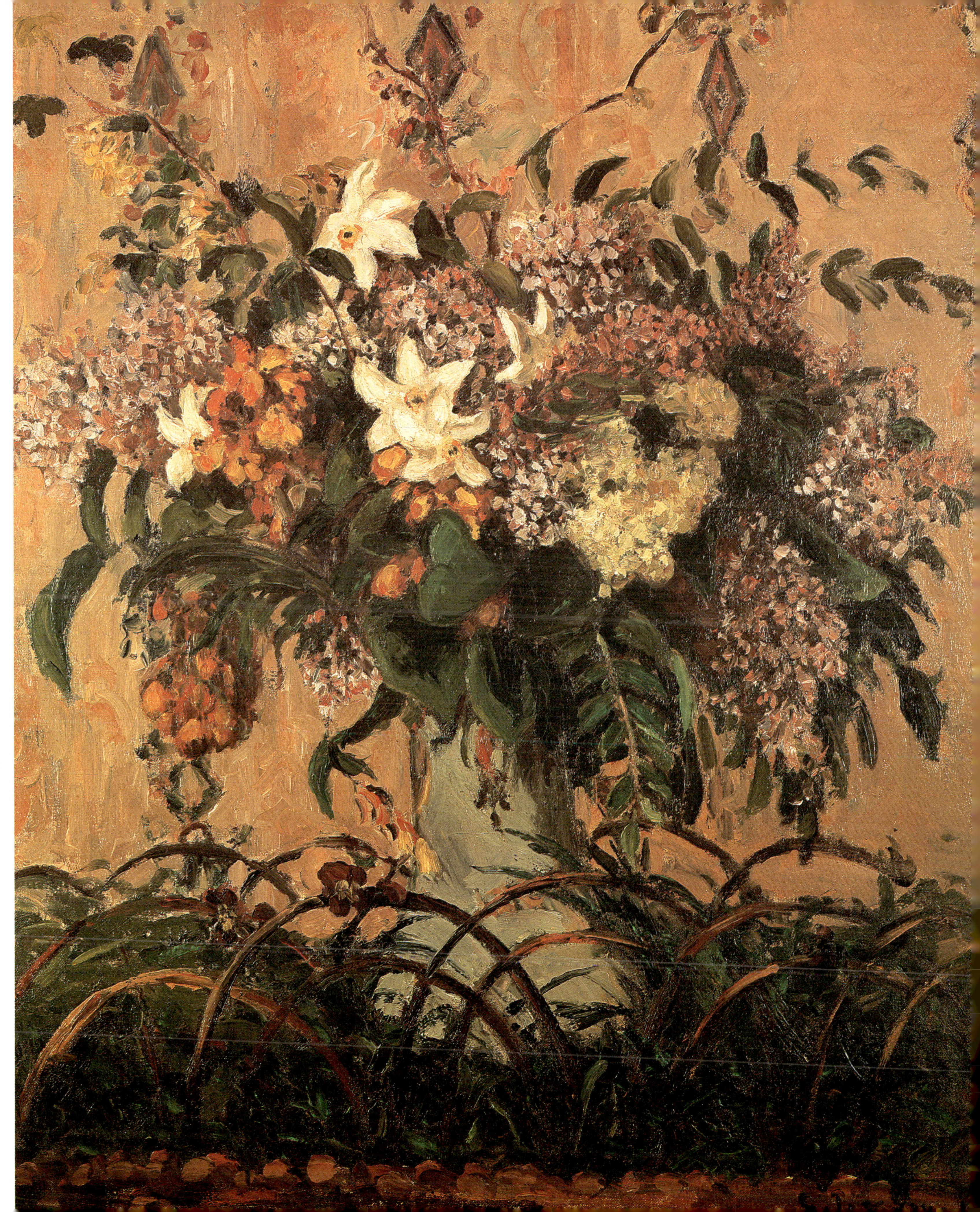

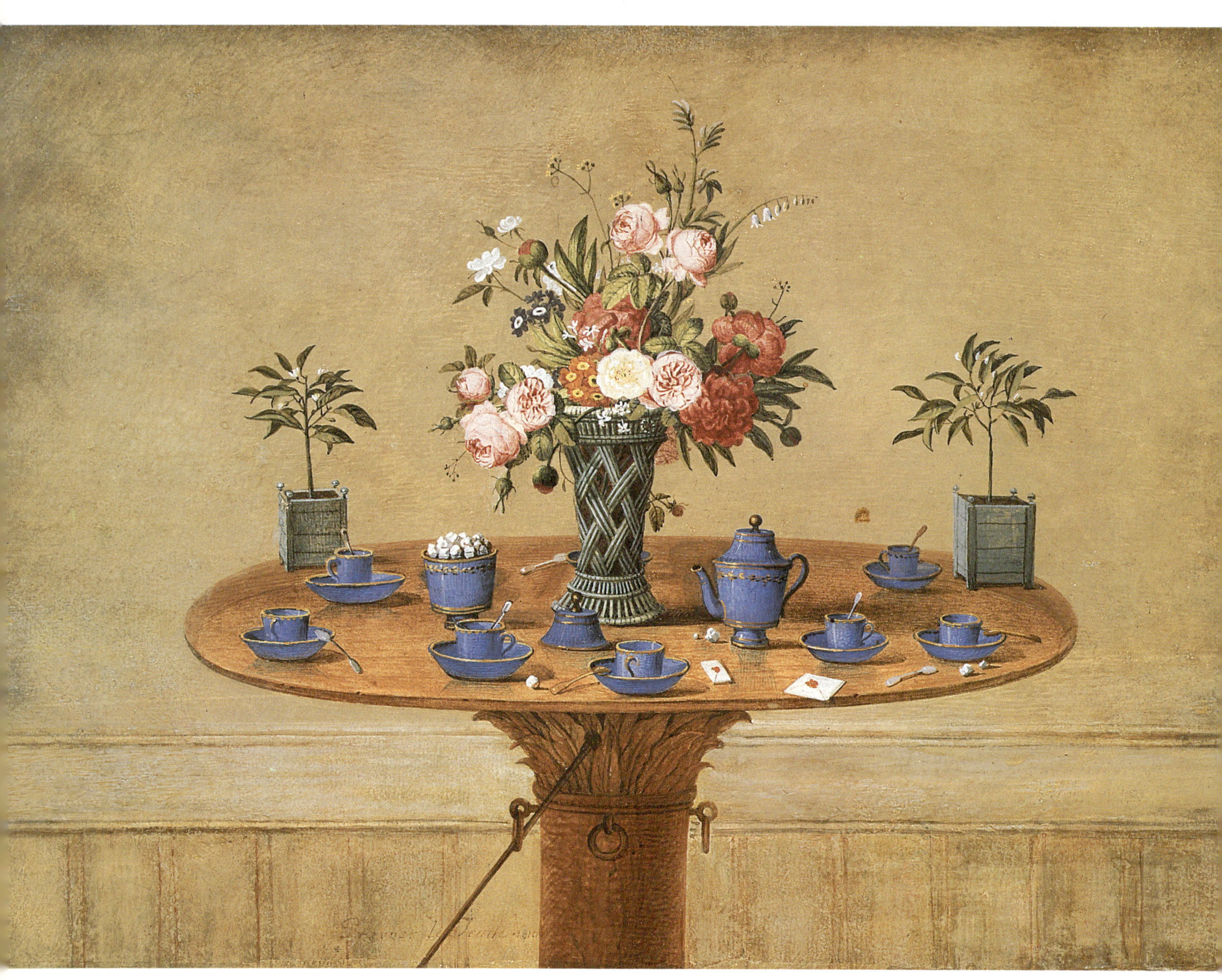

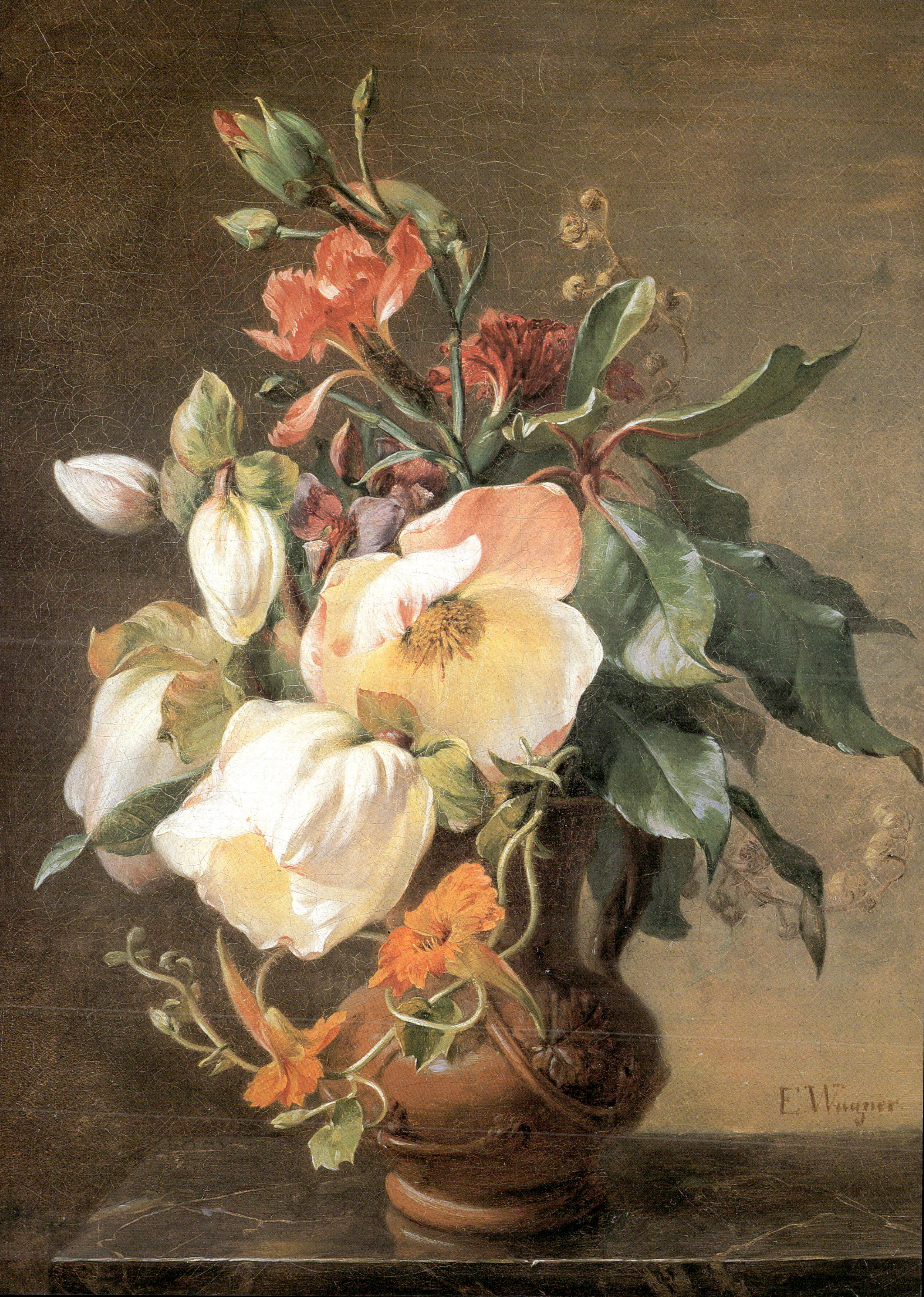
E. Wagner.

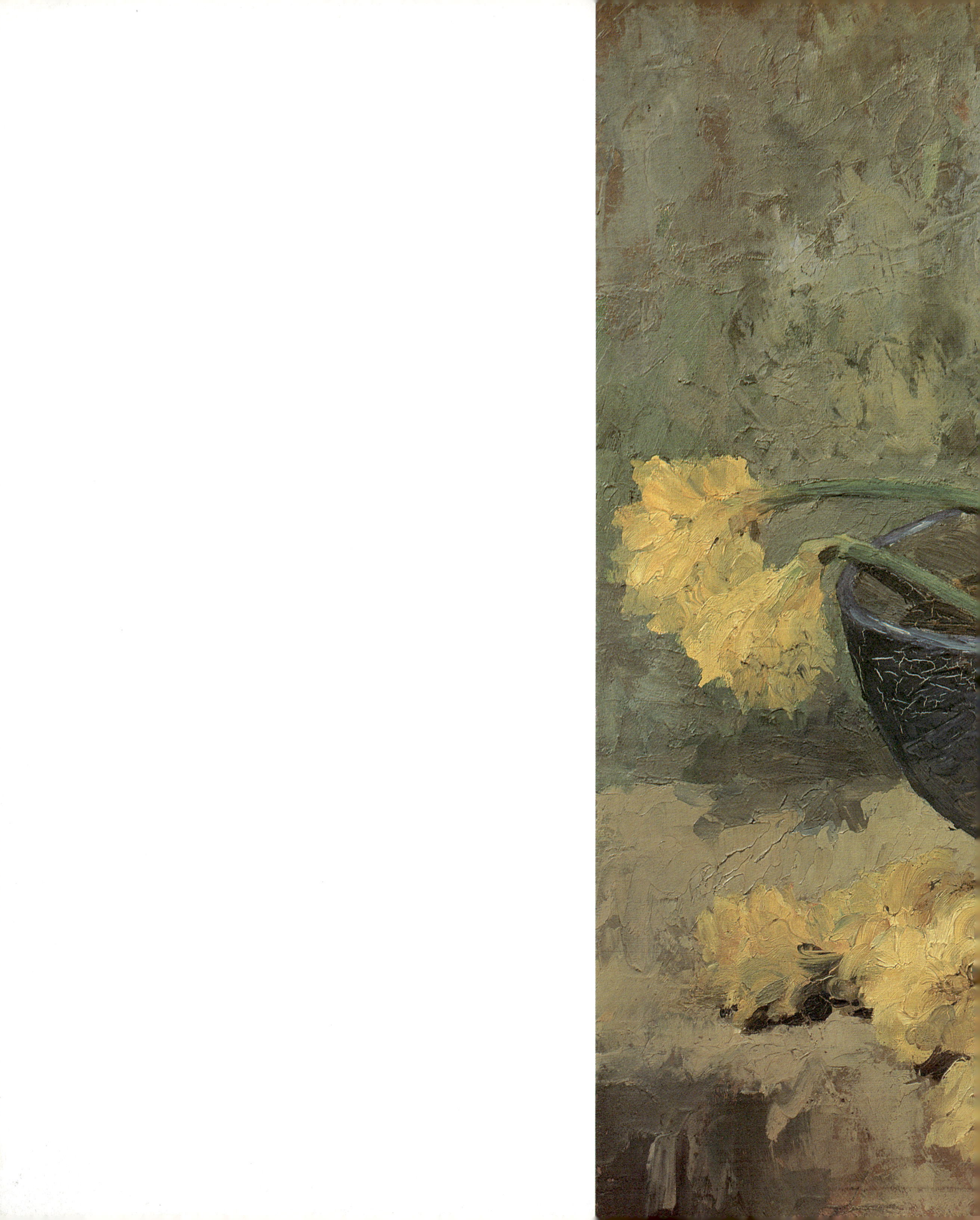

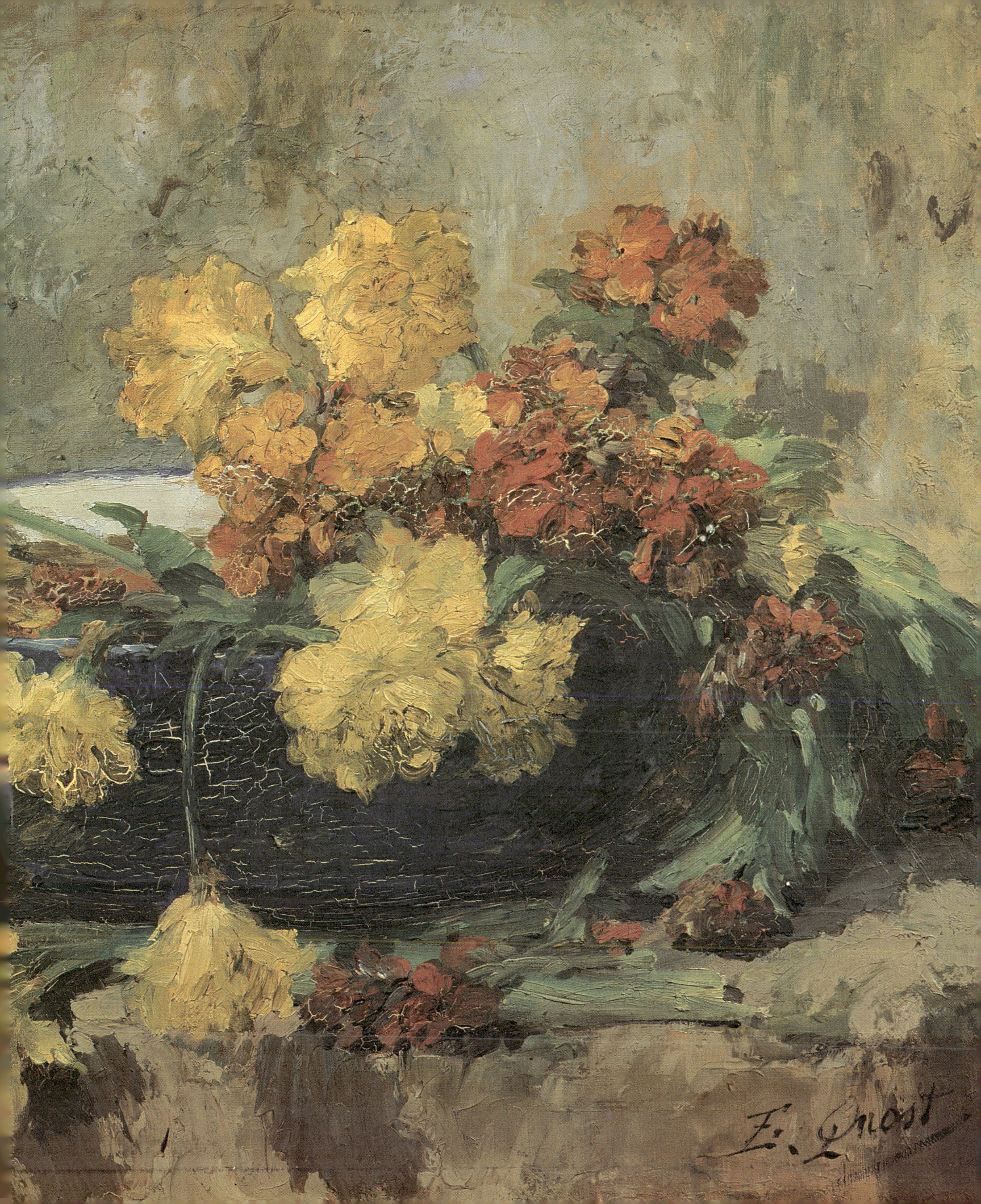

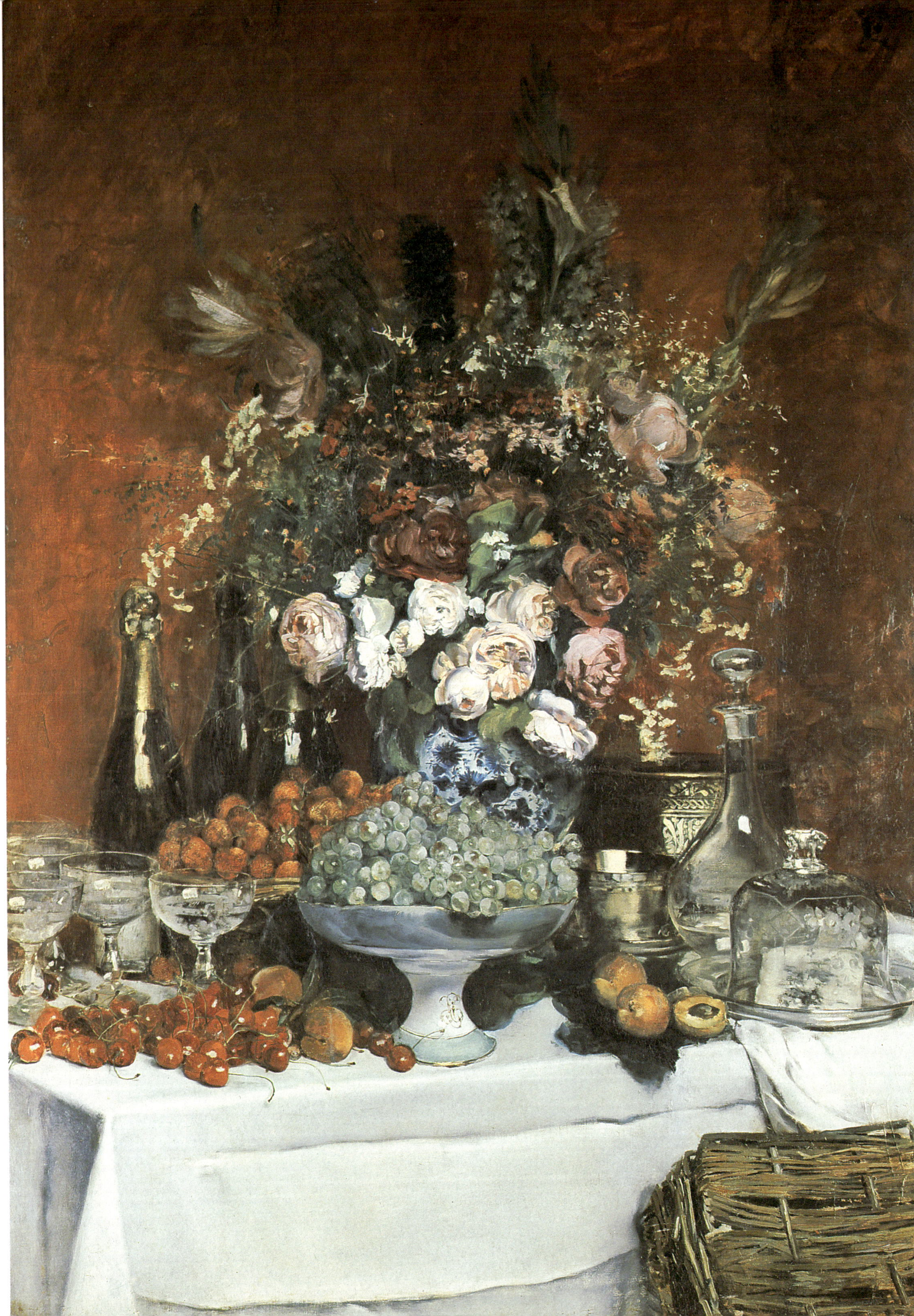

LAUGÉE, Désiré-François-Paul
1823–1896
b. Maromme (Seine-Maritime). Pupil of Picot. Painted religious subjects, genre and, occasionally, flowers. Exhib. Paris Salon 1845–1880. Exhib. *Bouquet*, Lyon Salon 1878, *Récolte de pavots*, Dijon Salon 1887
LIT *Bénézit*; *Dijon Salon* 1887; *Lyon Salon* 1878; *Schurr* IV, 102; *Thieme*; *Witt*

LAUGIER, *see* DEHARME

Fernand de Launay

Oil on canvas, 23 × 28½ in. (58.4 × 72.3 cm.), signed and stamped 'Vente de Launay 1905'
Courtesy Christie's, London

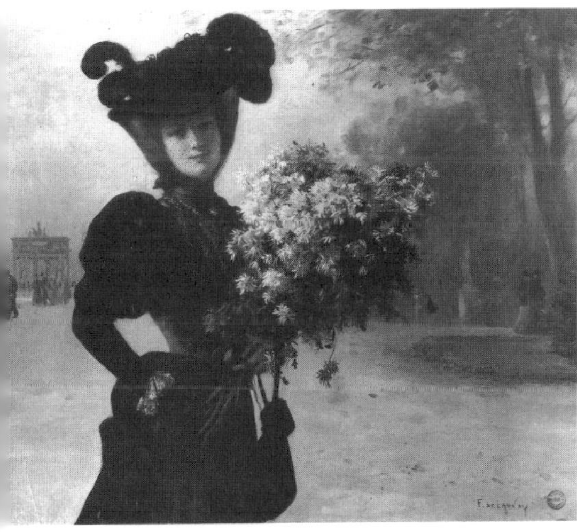

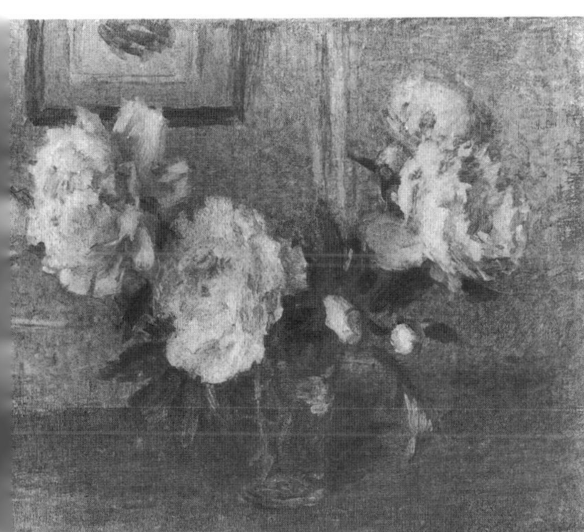

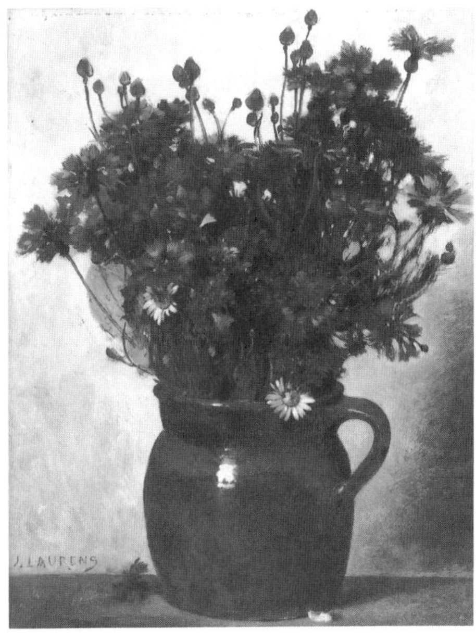

Jules-Joseph-Augustin Laurens

Oil on canvas, 13¾ × 10½ in. (35 × 27 cm.), signed
Montpellier, Musée Fabre

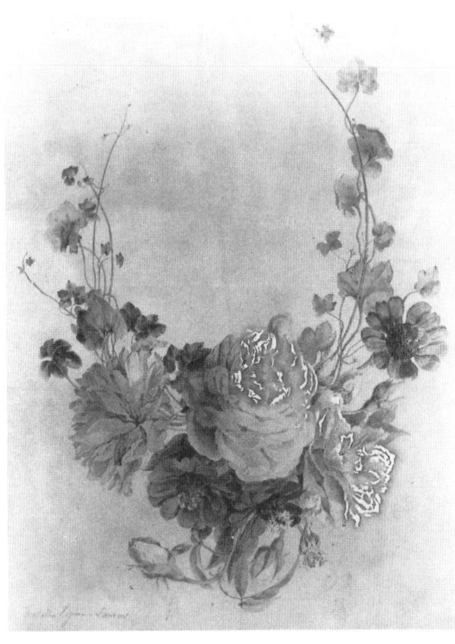

Rosalba Viguée Laurens

Watercolour, 15 × 11½ in. (38 × 29 cm.), signed
Avignon, Musée Calvet

Ernest-Joseph Laurent (*left*)

Oil on canvas, 18 × 20 in. (46 × 55.5 cm.), signed and dated 1907
Paris, Musée d'Orsay

LAUNAY, Fabien, Vieillard
1877–1904 alias
b. Paris. Engraver and illustrator. Exhib. *Fleurs*, Paris Indép. 1896
LIT *Bénézit*; *Paris Indép.* 1896; *Schurr* I, 97

LAUNAY, Fernand de
b. Lyon. Painter and engraver. Exhib. Paris S.A.F. Hon. mention 1896
LIT *Bénézit*. PM

LAUNAY, Regina-Marie de
b. Loué (Sarthe). Pupil of F. Rivoire, J. Lefebvre, T. Robert-Fleury. Exhib. Paris Salon *Iris et Pivoines*, *Roses*, wc, 1895, *Roses de Nice et pensées*, wc, 1898; Paris UFPS *Iris et marguerites jaunes*, *Roses et prunelles*, *Anémones*, *Oeillets*, *Pensées*, 1896
LIT *Paris Salon* 1895, 1898; *Paris UFPS* 1896

LAUREAU or LAUREAUX, Paul
1847–1901
b. Dijon (Côte-d'Or). Pupil of Dijon BA. Exhib. *Fleurs*, Dijon Salon 1881, 1887
LIT *Dijon Salon* 1881, 1887. CL

LAURENCEAU, Agénorie
b. Beaugency (Loiret). Pupil of E. Muraton. op. Tours. Painted landscapes, still-lifes and flowers. Exhib. Paris Salon 1864–1879 e.g. *Fleurs*, 1867
LIT *Bénézit*; *Paris Salon* 1867; *Thieme*

LAURENS, Jules-Joseph-Augustin
1825–1901
b. Carpentras (Vaucluse). Pupil of Matet, Montpellier BA, J.B. Laurens (his brother) and Delaroche. Painted landscapes and flowers. Exhib. Paris Salon 1853–1880, flowers from 1866. An influential teacher and popular painter. Lyon Salon *Dahlias de Provence*, 1879, *Fleurs*, 1881; Paris Salon *Chrysanthèmes*, *Etude de fleurs*, 1885, *Grands Chrysanthèmes*, 1895. M: Montpellier, *Giroflées et Chrysanthèmes*, *Coquelicots*

et marguerites, *Chrysanthèmes jaunes et blancs dans un vase de verre*, *Vase de roses*, *Dahlias variés*, *Chrysanthèmes*; M: Tulle, *Bouquet de fleurs*
LIT *Bellier*; *Bénézit*; *Lyon Salon* 1879, 1881; *Paris Salon* 1885, 1895; *Thieme*; *Witt*. MTC

LAURENS, Nicolas-Auguste *1829–1908*
b. Pontailler-sur-Saône (Côte-d'Or). Pupil of Couture. Painted landscapes, genre and flowers. Exhib. Paris Salon from 1859. Exhib. Dijon Salon *Fleurs*, 1881, *Couronne de bluets*, 1885, *Fleurs*, 1887, *Violettes et primevères*, 1897
LIT *Bénézit*; *Dijon Salon* 1881, 1885, 1887, 1897. CL

LAURENS, Rosalba Viguée
Pupil of J.B. Laurens (1801–1890), her father. Painted landscapes and flowers. Musée Calvet, Avignon, *Tiges de roses et d'anémones*, wc
LIT *Bénézit*; *Thieme*

LAURENS, *see* VIGUIER

LAURENT or LAURANT
op. Sèvres 1807–1816 and 1820
LIT *Brunet Préaud*

LAURENT
op. Sèvres 1829
LIT *Brunet Préaud*

LAURENT, Charles-Louis-Vivant *b.1813*
Pupil of Thierriat, Lyon BA (CFD 1832). Exhib. *Couronne de fleurs suspendue à un tombeau*, Lyon Salon 1833
LIT *Hardouin-Fugier Grafe*

LAURENT, Elie-Joseph *1841–1926*
b. Lyon. Pupil of Reignier, Lyon BA (CFD 1862). Jules Lefebvre and Bouguereau. Painted figures, religious subjects, portraits and, occasionally, flowers. Exhib. Paris Salon from 1870
LIT *Hardouin-Fugier Grafe*

LAURENT, Ernest-Joseph *1859–1929*
b. Paris. Pupil of Paris BA, L.O. Merson, Hébert, Lehmann and a friend of Seurat's. He painted portraits, figures, still-lifes and flowers, these mostly later works. Professor at Paris BA. Exhib. Paris 1882–1921
LIT *Bénézit*; *Orsay*; *Schurr* I, 115; *Thieme*; *Witt*

LAURENT, Eugène-Auguste *b.1872*
Pupil of Castex-Dégrange, Lyon BA (CFD 1886)
LIT *Hardouin-Fugier Grafe*

LAURENT, François-Nicolas *c.1785–1828*
d. Orléans (Loiret). Pupil of Gérard. "Peintre de fleurs et de fruits du Garde-Meuble de la Couronne". Exhib. Paris Salon 1801–1819 e.g. *Fleurs*, 1817, 1819.

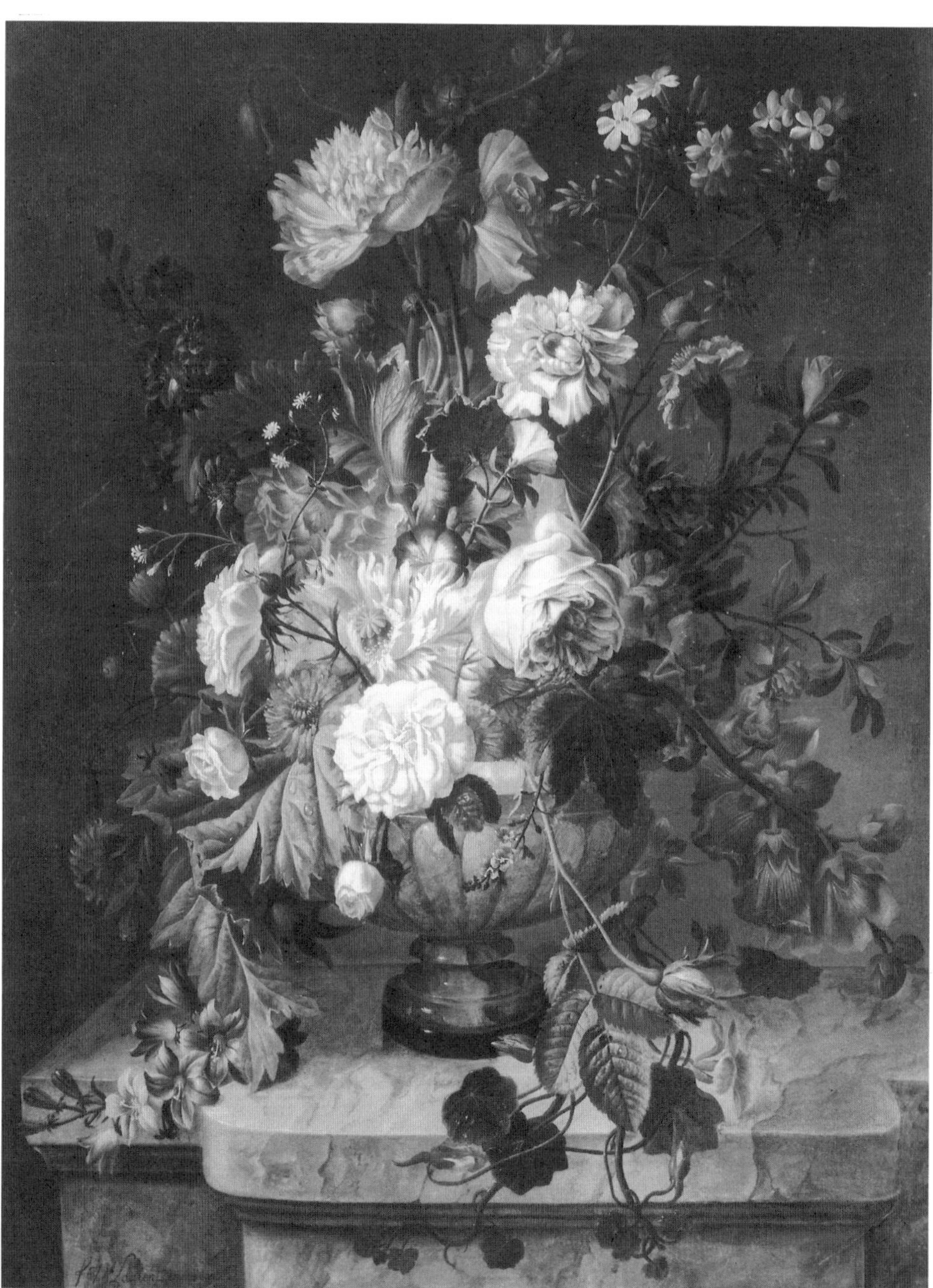

François-Nicolas Laurent

Oil on vellum mounted on canvas, $27\frac{1}{2} \times 21$ in. (70 × 53 cm.), signed
Cambridge, Fitzwilliam Museum
(Broughton Collection)

M: Cambridge, Fitzwilliam Museum
LIT *Bellier*; *Bénézit*; *Gabet*; *Mitchell* (ill.); *Paris Salon* 1817; *Thieme*; *Witt*

LAURENT, Henri-Adolphe-Louis
b. Valenciennes *c.*1840. Painted landscapes. Pupil of Palizzi and Ernest Hébert. Exhib. Paris Salon 1866–1885
LIT *Bénézit*. PM

LAURENT, Jean-Antoine ***1763–1832***
Flowers and Fruit, Cambridge, Fitzwilliam Museum (Broughton coll.) may be by this artist, who studied with Durand at Nancy and exhibited still-lifes, flowers, miniatures and portraits at the Paris Salon from 1791
LIT *Bellier*; *Thieme*. JLC

LAURENT, Julie
Exhib. *Un vase de fleurs de Baptiste*, Dijon Salon 1837
LIT *Dijon Salon* 1837. CL

LAURENT, Marie
Exhib. *Pivoine*, gouache, Saint-Etienne Salon 1882
LIT *Saint-Etienne Salon* 1882

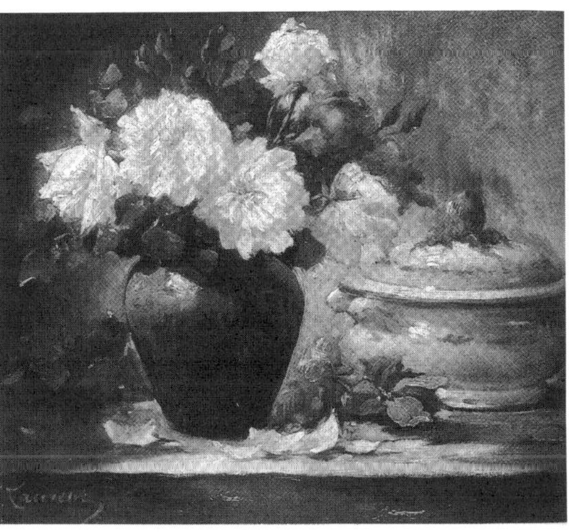

Henri-Adolphe-Louis Laurent

Oil on canvas, 14 × 17¾ in. (36 × 45 cm.), signed
Private collection

LAURENT, Marie-Louise
Pupil of Dumoulin. Exhib. *Pavots*, Lyon Salon 1883
LIT *Lyon Salon* 1883

LAURENT, T.
Exhib. Paris Salon *Tableau de fleurs*, on porcelain, 1831, 1833
LIT *Paris Salon* 1831, 1833

LAURENT, *see* FLEURY

LAURENT DE VALOIS, Michel-Charles ***b.1858***
Pupil of Reignier, Lyon BA (CFD 1875)
LIT *Hardouin-Fugier Grafe*

LAURON, Albin-Frédéric ***b.1841***
b. Wesserling (Haut-Rhin). Pupil of Reignier, Lyon BA (CFD 1861). Painted dogs, genre and flowers. Exhib. Paris Salon 1865–1873 e.g. *Fleurs*, 1867, *Fleurs et fruits sauvages*, 1868; Lyon Salon *Fleurs*, 1866, 1867. A work was formerly in the Musée de Mulhouse
LIT *Bellier*; *Bénézit*; *Hardouin-Fugier Grafe*; *Lyon Salon* 1866, 1867; *Paris Salon* 1867; *Thieme*

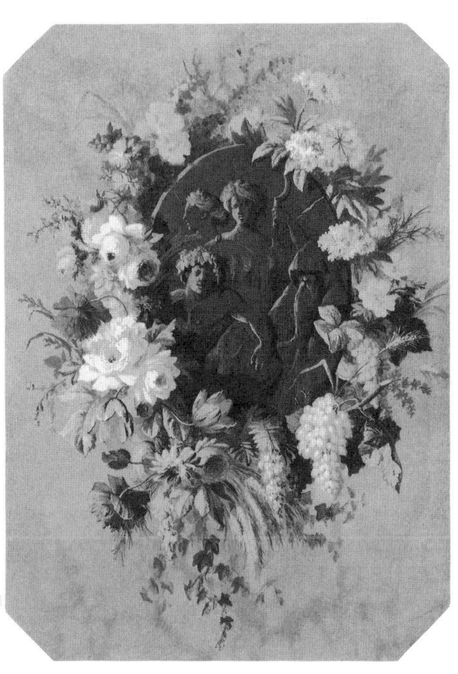

Jean-Antoine Laurent

Bodycolour on paper, 13⅝ × 10 in. (34.8 × 25.3 cm), signed 'J.L.'
Cambridge, Fitzwilliam Museum, (Broughton Collection)

LAURY, Pierre
b. Angers (Maine-et-Loire). Painted landscapes and flowers. Exhib. Angers Salon 1886
LIT *Bénézit*

LAUVERNAY-PETITJEAN, Jeanne ***b.1875***
b. Amiens (Somme). Pupil of Attendu and Delécluze. Exhib. *Roses*, Paris UFPS 1890
LIT *Bénézit*; *Paris UFPS* 1890

LAVAL, Charles ***1862–1894***
Pupil of Bonnat. Worked at Pont-Aven with Gauguin and his circle. Mostly a landscape and figure painter. *Fleurs* was exhibited at the Café Volpini show, Paris, 1889
LIT *Bénézit*; *Schurr*; Toronto-Amsterdam *Van Gogh and the birth of Cloisonism*, 1981; Zurich Kunsthaus: *Pont-Aven, Gauguin und sein Kreis*, 1966

LA VALETTE de, *see* EUZIÈRE

LAVAULT de, *see* FURCY

LAVERGNE, Marin ***1795–1881***
b. Lyon. Pupil of Berjon, Lyon BA (CFD 1813). This heraldic painter occasionally produced flowers
LIT *Bénézit*; *Hardouin-Fugier Grafe*

LAVERPILLIÈRE, *see* MONNET

LAVEUR, Jean-Benoit ***b.1839***
Pupil of Reignier, Lyon BA (CFD 1859)
LIT *Hardouin-Fugier Grafe*

LAVIER, A.
Exhib. *Fleurs*, Dijon Salon 1892
LIT *Dijon Salon* 1892. CL

LAVIGNE, Lucienne
b. Mennecy (Seine-et-Oise). Pupil of her father and Keller. Exhib. *Primevère de Chine*, on faience, Paris Salon 1880
LIT *Paris Salon 1880*

LAVIROTTE, Jane-Danièla
b. Paris. Pupil of Miciol and T. Tollet. Painted portraits, figures, fruit and flowers. Exhib. Lyon Salon from 1888, Paris Salon from 1890
LIT *Bénézit*

LAVIROTTE, Jules *b.1866*
Pupil of Castex-Dégrange, Lyon BA (CFD 1886)
LIT *Hardouin-Fugier Grafe*

LAŸS, Jean-Pierre *1825–1887*
b. Saint-Barthélémy-Lestra (Loire). Became Saint-Jean's valet at 15. Learnt wc painting from him. Started copying in oils some of his master's flower-pieces in 1848. Exhibited a large wc at the 1855 Paris Exposition Universelle. A popular flower painter. Exhib. Philadelphia, London, Genève, Bordeaux, Clermont-Ferrand, Le Havre, Montpellier, Lyon and Paris Salon (from 1852). Exhib. Paris Société des Amis-des-Arts *Giroflées, Fleurs et framboises*, 1874. Exhib. Dijon Salon *Rosier Cent feuilles*, 1880, *Offrande à Saint-François d'Assise, Fleurs*, 1881, *Corbeille de fleurs*, 1887. M: Bagnères de Bigorre, Lyon, Saint-Etienne
LIT *Bellier*; *Bénézit*; Hardouin-Fugier in *Les Laÿs vus par un Laÿs*, Lyon (A. Laÿs), 1981 (ill.); *Hardouin-Fugier Grafe*; *Hardouin-Fugier Grafe* 1982 (ill.) *Paris Amis-des-Arts* 1874; *Thieme*

Jean-Pierre Laÿs

Watercolour, 18 × 15½ in. (46 × 39 cm.), signed and dated 1848, stamped 'Vente Laÿs'
Private collection

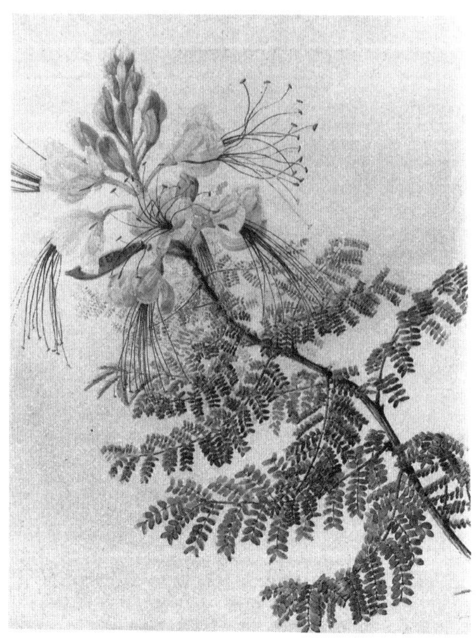

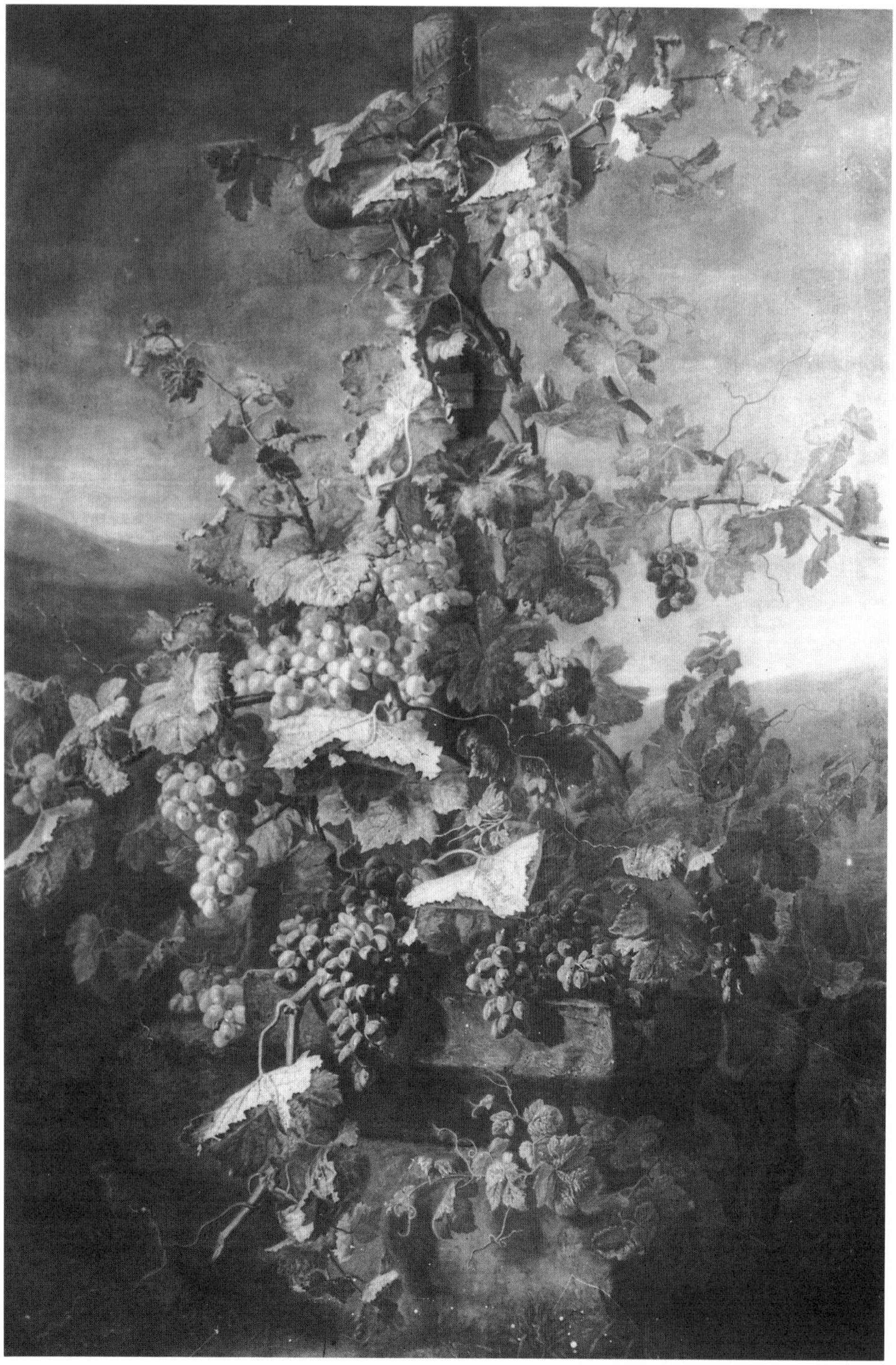

Jean-Pierre Laÿs (*left*)

Oil on canvas, 79 × 53½ in. (210 × 136 cm.), signed and dated 1862
Lyon, Musée des Beaux-Arts

L.B.
Pupi of Laÿs. Exhib. Lyon Salon 1868
LIT *Hardouin-Fugier Grafe*

LE BARBIER, *see* BRUYÈRE

LE BEL, Jean-Nicolas
Exhib. *Fleurs et fruits*, on porcelain, Paris Salon 1806
LIT *Paris Salon* 1806

LEBERT, Antoine-Henri *1794–1862*
b. Thann (Haut-Rhin). Textile designer. Produced landscapes and flowers. Exhib. Paris Salon 1822, 1836, 1848 e.g. *Vase de fleurs sur le tombeau d'un guerrier troubadour*, 1822
LIT *Bellier*; *Bénézit*; *Faré* 1962, p. 249; *Paris Salon* 1822; *Sitzmann*; *Thieme*. BJ

LE BESGUE, *see* DELBARRE

LEBORNE, Gabrielle
Pupil of J. Quesnet. Exhib. Paris UFPS *Chrysanthèmes*, *Glaïeuls*, 1896, *Pensée*, on faience, 1898
LIT *Paris UFPS* 1896, 1898

LEBOURG, Albert-Charles *1849–1928*
L. Montfort-sur-Risle (Eure). Pupil of Rouen BA and J.P. Laurens, painted landscapes and, occasionally, flowers, these being mostly later works.
LIT *Bénézit*; *Orsay*

LEBRUN, Marie
b. Toulon (Var). Exhib. Paris Salon from 1879 e.g. *Fleurs*, 1880
LIT *Paris Salon* 1880

LECHAT, Albert-Eugène *1863–1918*
b. Lille (Nord). Engraver. Painted landscapes, still-lifes and flowers e.g. *Fleurs des prés*, Paris SNBA 1890
LIT *Bénézit*; *Paris SNBA* 1890; *Schurr* V, 94; *Thieme*

LECHAT, Baptiste-Joseph *d.1890*
b. La Rochelle (Charente-Maritime). Exhib. Paris Indép. *Branche de lilas*, *Bourriche de géraniums*, *Reines-marguerites*, 1886, *Fruits et fleurs, d'automne*, 1887, *Roses*, 1888
LIT *Bénézit*; *Paris Indép*. 1886, 1887, 1888

LECHENE, Alice
Exhib. Paris Société des Amis-des-Arts *Branche de fleurs*, wc, 1855, *Fleurs*, wc, 1856
LIT *Paris Amis-des-Arts* 1855, 1856

LECHENE, Amicie, *née* Blagny
b. Dijon (Côte-d'Or). Pupil of S. Rude. Exhib. *Fleurs*, Paris Exposition Universelle 1855; *Panier fleuri*, Paris Salon 1857
LIT *Bellier*; *Bénézit*; *Paris Exposition Universelle* 1855

LECHENET, Camille-Alexandra, *née* Koenig
b. Paris. Pupil of her father. Exhib. *Fleurs*, fan-leaf, Paris Salon 1880
LIT *Paris Salon* 1880

LECLAIRE, Léon-Louis *b.1829*
b. Paris. Pupil of Cogniet. Painted historical subjects, genre and, occasionally, flowers. Exhib. Paris Salon from 1857. His *Fleurs d'automne* was bought by the State (800 francs) in 1879 for the Musée de Semur-en-Auxois
LIT *Bénézit*; Paris Arch. Nat. F21:232

LECLAIRE, Victor *1830–1885*
b. Paris. Pupil of L. Leclaire, his brother. Painted genre, still-lifes and flowers. Exhib. Paris Salon from 1861 e.g. *Fleurs des bois*, *Fleurs d'automne*, 1867, *Fleurs*, *Fleurs de pommier*, 1872, *Aubépine*, 1873, *Fleurs* 1875, *Fleurs d'hiver*, *Fleurs d'automne*, 1879, *Fleurs des Champs*, 1880; *Fleurs*, Limoges Salon 1879. His *Fleurs d'automne* was bought by the State (800 francs) in 1879 for the Musée d'Amiens. M: Paris (Orsay), Reims, Saint-Denis, Tourcoing
LIT *Bellier*; *Bénézit*; *L'Oeil*, August 1979 (ill.); *Orsay*; Paris Arch. F21:4500; Paris Petit Palais, *Peintres de fleurs en France*, 1979 (ill.); *Paris Salon* 1867, 1872, 1873, 1875, 1879, 1880; *Thieme*

LECOCQ, Maria
b. Paris. Pupil of P. Flandrin and Pichon. Exhib. *Mauvaises herbes*, Paris Noir et Blanc Salon 1886
LIT *Paris Noir et Blanc Salon* 1886

LECOMTE, Victor *1856–1920*
b. Paris. Pupil of Pignot and A. Gilbert. Painted genre, portraits, still-lifes and, occasionally, flowers. Exhib. Paris Salon from 1876 e.g. *Fleurs*, 1876
LIT *Bellier*; *Bénézit*; *Schurr* III, 118; *Thieme*; *Witt*

LECOMTE, *see* CHERPIN

LECONTE-ROUCH, Mme
Exhib. *Chrysanthèmes*, Dijon Salon 1894
LIT *Dijon Salon* 1894. CL

LECOQ, Caroline
Worked with Hector Giacomelli (1822–1904), the bird painter. Sister-in-law of Henri Lecoq, the botanist, botanical designer and wc painter
LIT *Orsay*

LECOQ DE BOISBAUDRAN, from 1831 Mme Cyane *1802–1897*
Pupil of Regnault, sister of H. Lecoq de Boisbaudran, an art teacher. Painted portraits, miniatures and flowers. Exhib. Paris Salon 1824–1838 watercolours e.g. *Bouquet*, 1833, *Vase de fleurs*, *Bouquet de roses*, *Camélias*, 1834.
LIT *Bellier*; *Bénézit*; *Faré* 1962, p. 218; F. Régamey Horace *Lecoq de Boisbaudran et ses élèves*, Paris (Champion) 1903; *Thieme*; *Witt*

LE CORBEILLER, *see* LALLEMAND

LECOURIEUX, *see* PINCHON

LECREUX, Gaston-Alfred *c.1846–1914*
b. Paris. Pupil of N. Bouchet, Bonnefoy and J. Noel. Painted landscapes, still-lifes and flowers. Exhib. Paris Salon from 1877 e.g. *Fleurs*, 1880, *Pivoines*, *Géranium*, 1885, *Pavots*, 1889, *Fleurs*, 1891, *Fleurs de printemps*, 1892. M: Paris, formerly in Musée de Luxembourg, *Fleurs dans un vase*
LIT *Bellier*; *Bénézit*; *Paris Salon* 1880, 1885 (ill.), 1889 (ill.), 1891 (ill.), 1892 (ill.); *Thieme*

LECUYER, Léon-Louis
b. Paris. Pupil of Dupuis senior and P. Baudry. op. decorator. Exhib. Paris Salon 1854–1868 e.g. *Fleurs, 1866, Vase et fleurs du Midi*, 1868
LIT *Bellier*; *Bénézit*

LEDOUX, Eugène *b.1841*
b. Paris. Exhib. Paris Salon *Fleurs et fruits*, 1869, *Bouquet de fleurs d'été*, 1870
LIT *Bellier*; *Bénézit*

LE FANU, B.
Exhib. *Roses*, wc, Paris SNBA 1896
LIT *Paris SNBA* 1896

LEFÉBURE, Eugénie
Pupil of Collin and École Nationale de dessin. Exhib. *Fleurs*, on faience, Paris Salon 1880
LIT *Paris Salon* 1880

LEFÉBURE, Marie
b. Paris. Pupil of Allix. Exhib. *Fleurs*, on porcelain, Paris Salon 1880
LIT *Paris Salon* 1880

LEFEBVRE, Ernest-Eugène *1850–1889*
b. Le Havre (Seine-Maritime). Pupil of G. Morin. Painted still-lifes and, occasionally, flowers. Exhib. Paris Salon from 1879
LIT *Bénézit*; *Thieme*

LEFEBVRE, Lucien
b. Varennes (Meuse). Pupil of Foré. Painted portraits and flowers. Exhib. Paris Salon 1872–1873 e.g. *Violettes*, 1873
LIT *Bellier*; *Bénézit*; *Witt*

LEFEBVRE-GLAIZE, Maguelonne
b. Montpellier (Hérault). Pupil of Humbert. Exhib. *Orchidées*, Paris UFPS 1898
LIT *Bénézit*; *Paris UFPS* 1898

LEFEVRE, A.
Active *c*.1870. Designed plates for H.E. Baillon, *Iconographie de la Flore française*, Paris (Doin) 1885–1894
LIT *Nissen* I, 64

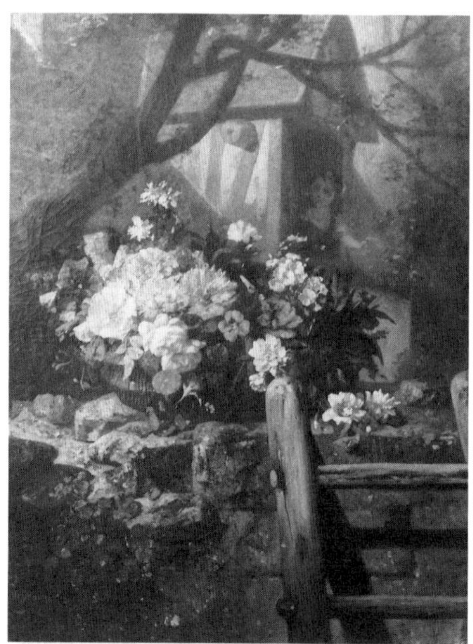

Isidore-Julien Legendre-Tilde

Oil on canvas, 45½ × 35½ in. (115 × 90 cm.), signed
Musée de Blois
(photo: Château de Blois, J. Marinier)

LEFEVRE, C.
Exhib. *Études de plantes*, Paris SNBA 1897
LIT *Paris SNBA* 1897

LEFEVRE, Hippolyte
b. Aubusson (Creuse). Pupil of Wauquier. Exhib. *Chrysanthèmes*, Paris Salon 1885
LIT *Paris Salon* 1885

LE FONT or LEFRONT, Léon
b. Fontainebleau (Seine-et-Marne). Pupil of his father and Lamain. Exhib. *Fleurs des champs*, *Ronces*, on faience, Paris Salon 1880
LIT *Bellier*; *Paris Salon* 1880

LEGAT, Léon *b.1829*
b. Paris. Pupil of Martinet. Painted genre, landscapes and, occasionally, flowers. Exhib. Paris Salon from 1848 e.g. *Fleurs et cristaux*, 1875
LIT *Bénézit*; *Paris Salon* 1875; *Schurr* IV, 63; *Witt*

LEGENDRE, Mlle F.
Active *c*.1840. Designed plates for E. Spach, *Histoire Naturelle des végétaux* . . . Paris, 1834–1848
LIT *Nissen* I, 1878; *Sitwell*

LEGENDRE, Louise-Inès
b. Étampes (Essonne). Pupil of Mlle Le Sueur and Mme Pichon. Exhib. Paris Salon from 1868 e.g. *Groupe de fleurs*, on porcelain, 1869, *Volubilis*, on porcelain, 1880
LIT *Bellier*; *Paris Salon* 1880

LEGENDRE-TILDE, Isidore-Julien *b.1811*
b. Blois (Loir-et-Cher). Pupil of Roqueplan, Delacroix and J. Blondel. Director of the Musée de Blois. Painted

animals, landscapes and flowers. Exhib. Paris Salon 1838–1872 e.g. *Pavots*, 1870, *Chrysanthèmes*, 1872. M: Blois, *Azalées* (currently untraceable); *Le mur mitoyen*, Blois Salon 1866; Orléans, *Fleurs*
LIT *Bellier*; *Thieme*

LEGER, H.P.
Exhib. *Fleurs et fruits*, Paris Salon 1885
LIT *Paris Salon* 1885 (ill.)

LÉGEROT, *see* ESCALLIER

LEGRAND, René *b.1847*
b. Paris. Pupil of Pils. Painted genre and flowers. Exhib. Paris Salon from 1891
LIT *Bénézit*; *Thieme*

LEGROS, Adèle
Exhib. Paris Salon 1843–1848 e.g. *Fleurs et fruits*, 1843, 1845, *Fleurs dans un oratoire*, 1846, *Roses trémières*, 1847
LIT *Bellier*; *Faré* 1962, p. 249; *Paris Salon* 1843, 1845

LEJOUTEUX, Jules-Gontran *d.1916*
b. Chateaudun (Eure-et-Loir). Pupil of Munie and Dardouze. Painted landscapes and flowers. Exhib. Paris Salon from 1877 e.g. *Primevères*, *Chrysanthèmes*, 1877
LIT *Bellier*; *Bénézit*; *Thieme*

LE LEDIER, Marie
b. Rouen (Seine-Maritime). Pupil of D. de Cool. Exhib. Paris Salon from 1877 e.g. *Chrysanthèmes*, *Camélias*, gouache, 1881
LIT *Bellier*

LELEUX, Armand-Hubert-Simon *1818–1885*
b. Paris. Pupil of Ingres. Painted genre. Exhib. Paris Salon. Lyon Salon *Les marguerites* (intérieur), 1854, 1862, *Fleurs des champs*, 1878; *Fleurs de printemps*, Paris Société des Amis-des-Arts 1874
LIT *Bénézit*; *Lyon Salon* 1854, 1862, 1878; *Paris Amis-des-Arts* 1874; *Schurr* I, 82; *Thieme*; *Witt*

LELIÈVRE, Jeanne
b. Lons-le-Saunier (Jura). Pupil of Saintpierre. Exhib. *Fleurs de mai*, Paris Salon 1898
LIT *Paris Salon* 1898

LELOIR, Louis-Alexandre *1843–1884*
b. Paris. Pupil of Auguste Leloir, his father, and A. Colin, his grandfather. Popular book illustrator and wc painter. Exhib. Paris Salon from 1863; *Paris Société des Aquarellistes*, *Les marguerites*, wc, 1879, *Le bouquet*, wc, 1880
LIT *Bénézit*; *Paris aquar.* 1879, 1880; *Thieme*; *Witt*

LELONG *fl.1800–1850*
A still-life painter. Six watercolours, all variations of *Still-Life with Vase of Flowers*, are in Cambridge, Fitzwilliam Museum (Broughton coll.)
LIT *Bénézit*; *Busse*; Mayer, *Annuaire des Prix*, 1970. JLC

LE LYRE, Caroline
b. Chatou (Yvelines). Pupil of F. Barrias. Exhib. *Oeillets*, *Roses trémières*, *Primevères*, wc, Paris Noir et Blanc Salon 1888
LIT *Paris Noir et Blanc Salon* 1888

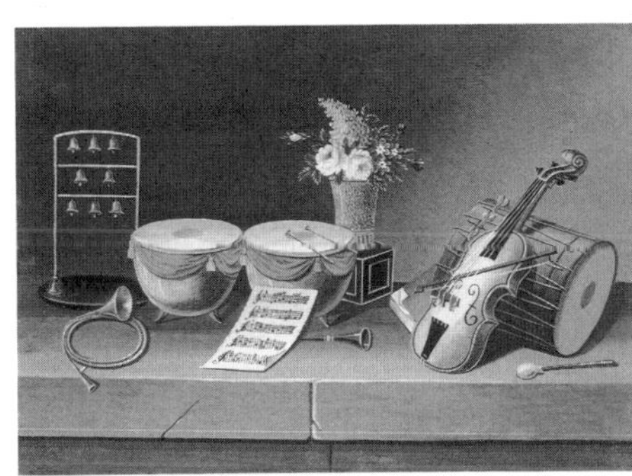

Lelong

Watercolour, $6\frac{1}{4} \times 8\frac{3}{8}$ in. (15.8 × 21.2 cm.), signed
Cambridge, Fitzwilliam Museum, (Broughton Collection)

LEMAIRE, Amélie
Exhib. *Corbeille de fleurs diverses*, wc, Paris Salon 1842
LIT *Paris Salon* 1842

LEMAIRE, Louis-Marie *1824–1910*
Pupil of J. Dupré and Boulard. Painted landscapes and flowers. Exhib. Lyon Salon *Pivoines et iris*, *Roses dans un verre*, 1876. *Pivoines sur une console dorée*, 1884. Exhib. Paris Salon from 1849 e.g. *Lilas*, *Fleurs dans un vase*, 1865, *Bouquet de pavots*, 1868, *Roses cent feuilles*, 1875, *Massif de pivoines*, 1884, *Roses et pivoines*, 1885, *Bouquet de fleurs*, 1889, *La saison des roses*, 1892, *Bouquet de roses*, 1898. M: Compiègne, *Roses coupées*, Rouen, *Lilas*, London (Victoria and Albert) *Vase de fleurs* (etching)
LIT *Bellier*; *Bénézit*; *Orsay*; *Lyon Salon* 1876, 1884; *Paris Salon* 1875, 1884 (ill.), 1885 (ill.), 1889 (ill.), 1892 (ill.), 1898; *Schurr* IV, 60; *Thieme*

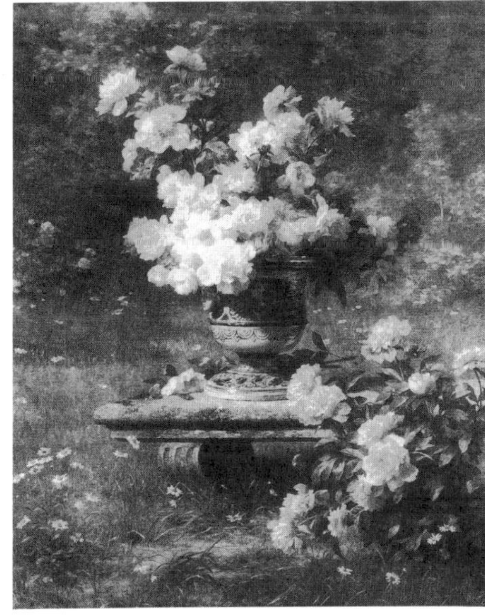

Louis-Marie Lemaire

Oil on canvas, 91 × 73 in. (231.2 × 185.5 cm.), signed
Courtesy Christie's, London

LEMAIRE, Madeleine-Jeanne, *née* Coll *1845–1928*
b. Sainte-Rossoline (Var). Pupil of Herbelin and Chaplin. Painted genre and flowers. Illustrated books e.g. M. Proust *Les plaisirs et les jours*, Paris; T. Villard, *Les fleurs à travers les âges* ... Paris 1900. Proust wrote of her "C'est elle qui a crée le plus de roses après Dieu" (*Les Plaisirs et les Jours*). This most successful and prolific flower painter exhib. Paris Salon from 1864, Paris Société des Aquarellistes from 1879, Paris SNBA from 1890. Paris Société des Aquarellistes, *Pensées*, *Fleurs des champs*, *Roses trémières*, 1879, *Roses et chèvrefeuilles*, *Oeillets*, Pavots, 1880, *Dans la serre*, *Chrysanthèmes et violettes*, *Roses*, 1881, *Autel de la Vierge*, 1883, *Capucines*, *Hotte de fleurs*, *Pavots*, *Fleurs des champs*, *Panier de fleurs*, *Chrysanthèmes et violettes*, 1887, *Oeillets*, *Violettes*, *Fleurs de haies* 1888, *Violettes*, 1892, *Chrysanthèmes*, *Violettes*, *Roses jaunes*, *Fleurs* 1894; *Paris SNBA Les Quatre Saisons*, *Fleurs*, 1894, *Violettes*, *Roses*, 1898, *Dahlias*, *Violettes*, *Fleurs de pommier*, 1899; Paris Noir et Blanc Salon *Panier de roses*, 1886; Dijon Salon *Fleurs*, wc, 1894; Roanne Salon, *Oeillets*, 1890. *Les Roses*, Orsoldi sale, Drouot, Paris, 25 May 1923, *Nature morte aux violettes*, wc, Sotheby's, London, 31 Oct. 1973 etc. M: Mulhouse, Reims, Toulouse
LIT *Bellier*; *Bénézit*; *Dijon Salon* 1894; *Nissen* 2063 n; *Orsay*; *Paris Noir et Blanc Salon* 1886; *Paris aquar.* 1879, 1880, 1881, 1883, 1885, 1887, 1888, 1892, 1894; *Paris SNBA* 1894, 1898, 1899; *Schurr* II, 63; *Thieme*; *Witt*

LEMAIRE, Marie-Thérèse *b.1861*
b. Paris. Painted flowers. Exhib. Paris Salon from 1908
LIT *Bénézit*

LEMAIRE, Suzanne
Daughter of Madeleine Lemaire. Exhib. Paris SNBA from 1890 e.g. *Azalées*, wc, 1890, *Glaïeuls*, 1892, *Pavots*, gouache, *Fleurs d'automne*, gouache, *Roses trémières*, gouache, *Lilas et boules de neige*, gouache, *Chrysanthèmes*, gouache, *Fleurs d'été*, gouache, *Bruyère*, fan-leaf, 1894
LIT *Paris SNBA* 1890, 1892, 1894; *Thieme*

LEMAIRE, *see* PIOT

LEMAITRE, Claire
Pupil of J. Béraud. Exhib. Paris Salon from 1888, Paris SNBA 1890–1912. Exhib. Paris Noir et Blanc Salon *Géraniums*, 1888. Exhib. Paris SNBA e.g. *Fleurs d'automne*, 1891, *Chardons jaunes et iris*, pastel, 1892, *Envoi de fleurs*, *Chrysanthèmes*, *Pavots*, *Anémones*, pastels, 1894, *Oeillets*, *Chrysanthèmes*, *Iris*, wc, 1896. Her *Fleurs d'automne* was bought by the State (1,200 francs) for the Musée de Toulouse, 1892. This often-reproduced painting, inspired by Armand Silvestre's poem was her most popular work (Paris BMAD, Maciet coll.)
LIT *Bellier*; *Bénézit*; Paris Arch. Nat. F21:2138; *Paris BMAD*; *Paris Noir et Blanc Salon* 1888; *Paris SNBA* 1891, 1892, 1894, 1896; *Thieme*

LEMAÎTRE, Louise
b. La Fère (Aisne). Pupil of Thoret. Exhib. Paris Salon from 1878 e.g. *Fleurs de pommiers doubles*, gouache, 1879; *Fleurs des champs*, *Coquelicots*, gouaches, 1880
LIT *Bellier*; *Bénézit*; *Paris Salon* 1880

LEMAÎTRE, *see* CLÉMENT

LEMARCHAND, Anne, *née* Bénard
b. Moulins (Allier). Pupil of Grönland, Yvon, D. de Cool, Le Gay. Painted still-lifes, fruit and flowers. Exhib. Paris Salon 1855–1877 e.g. *Roses trémières*, *Fleurs et fruits*, 1861; *Fleurs et fruits*, Lyon Salon 1864. *Raisins et fleurs*, Geneva sale, 1–2 June 1988, lot 47
LIT *Bellier*; *Bénézit*; *Lyon Salon* 1864; *Paris Salon* 1861

Marie-Thérèse Lemaire

Oil on canvas, 25¾ × 31½ in. (65.4 × 80 cm.), signed
Courtesy Sotheby's, London

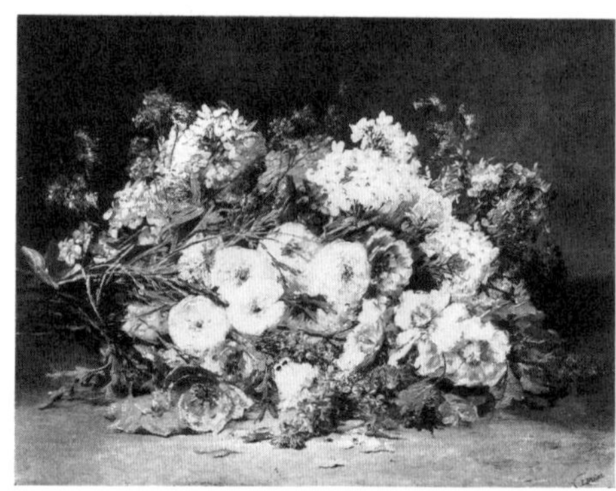

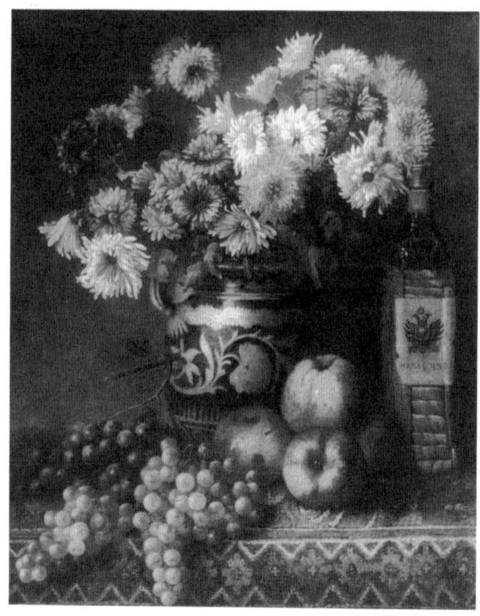

Anne Lemarchand née Bénard

Oil on canvas, 28½ × 21½ in. (72.5 × 59.5 cm.), signed
Private collection

LEMERCIER, Charles-Nicolas *1797–1859*
b. Paris. Pupil of his father, Regnault and Lethière. Painted landscapes, still-lifes and flowers, often in pastels. Exhib. Lille Salon, Cambrai Salon. Exhib. Paris Salon 1822–1852 e.g. *Groupe de fleurs et de fruits*, pastel, 1850. His *Fleurs et fruits* was bought by the State for the Musée de Limoges, 1852 Musée de Laon 1855, Musée de Saint-Denis (Maison de la Légion d'Honneur), Musée de Montargis (untraceable)
LIT *Bellier*; *Bénézit*; Paris Arch. Nat. F21:42A, 233, 438, 439; *Paris Salon* 1850; *Thieme*; *Witt*

LEMERCIER, L.
Designed plates for A.T. Brongniart, *Description de quelques plantes remarquables de la Nouvelle Calédonie*, Paris, 1808
LIT *Nissen*, 243n.

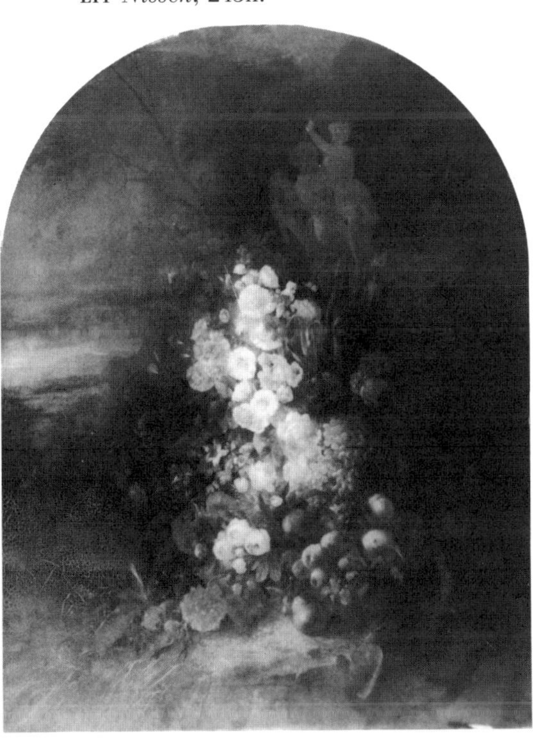

Charles-Nicolas Lemercier

Oil on canvas, 90 × 68½ in. (232 × 174 cm.), signed and dated 1852
Limoges, Musée Municipal

Elisabeth-Emilie Lemire, alias Elisa, née Navarre

Watercolour and bodycolour on vellum, 17 × 13¼ in. (43.4 × 33.9 cm.), signed and dated 1840
Cambridge, Fitzwilliam Museum
(Broughton Collection)

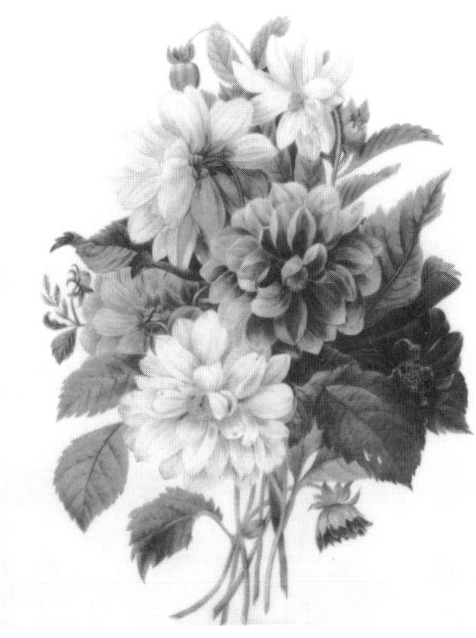

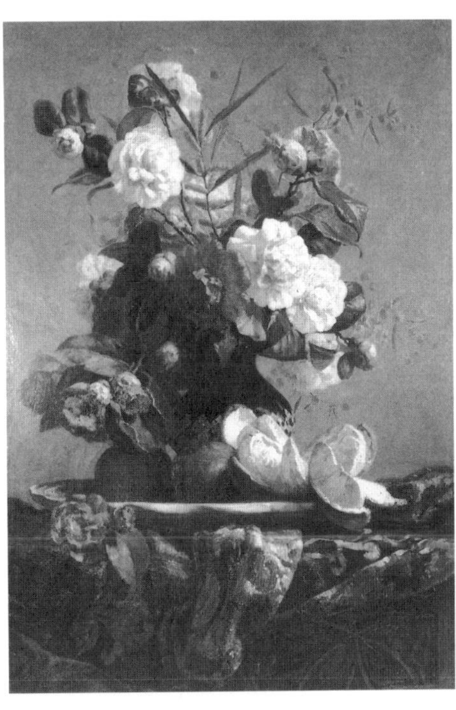

François Lepagnez

Oil on canvas, signed
Private collection (photo: Musée des Beaux-Arts, Lyon)

LEMIRE, Elisabeth-Emilie, *alias* Elisa, *née* Navarre *1807–1868*
b. Paris. Pupil of Redouté, Van Dael and Vidal. Operated a Ladies' Academy of Fine Arts. Exhib. wc, Paris Salon 1836, 1841, 1845, 1848, 1854. Her exhibit was rejected by the 1843 Paris Salon selection committee. M: Fitzwilliam Museum, Cambridge (Broughton coll.)
LIT *Broughton* 1977; *Broughton* 1978; *Bénézit*; *Hardouin-Fugier* 1981 (ill.)

LEMORE, Gabrielle, *née* Fernier
b. Paris. Pupil of Mme Leloir. Exhib. Paris Salon 1874–1878 e.g. *Pivoines et lilas*, wc, *Giroflées*, wc, 1874, *Dahlias*, 1877, *Marguerites et figures*, wc, 1878
LIT *Bellier*; *Bénézit*

LEMPEREUR, Antoine *b.1808*
Pupil of Thierriat, Lyon BA (CFD 1828). Textile designer
LIT *Hardouin-Fugier Grafe*

LÉONCE
Exhib. *Eperviers et fleurs*, Paris SNBA 1891
LIT *Paris SNBA* 1891

LEOTHAUD, Jeanne-Emilie-Marie *b.1871*
b. Livron (Drôme). Pupil of G. Debillemont. Exhib. *Chardon*, *Volubilis*, *Eglantines et mésanges*, Paris Indép. 1893
LIT *Bénézit*; *Paris Indép.* 1893

LEPAGE, François *1796–1871*
b. Lyon. Pupil of Revoil, Lyon BA. Textile designer at Saint-Etienne and drawing master at Lyon, then taught designing (mise-en-carte) at Lyon BA (1825–1827). Operated a studio. Among his pupils were Saint-Jean and Gallet. Exhib. Lyon Salon. Exhib. Paris Salon from 1824 *Offrande à la Sainte Vierge*, 1824, *La réunion des roses rouges et des roses blanches*, 1826, *La rose blanche et la rose rouge, ou Plus de Tories, plus de Whigs*, 1827

LIT *Hardouin-Fugier Grafe* 1982 (ill.); Paris, Petit Palais, *Peinture de fleurs en France*, 1979 (ill.)

LEPAGNEZ, François *1828–1870*
b. Lyon. Pupil of Lyon BA (engraving under V. Vibert 1842–1844 then 1850–1854). Lithographer. Painted genre, landscapes, still-lifes and flowers. Exhib. Lyon Salon from 1858 e.g. *Fleurs et fruits*, 1861, *Fleurs* 1869. Exhib. Paris Salon 1864, 1866. Musée des Beaux-Arts, Lyon, *Fleurs*, 1868
LIT E. Grafe, "Lepagnez" in *Bulletin des Musées et Monuments Lyonnais*, 1983 no. 3; *Hardouin-Fugier Grafe*; *Hardouin-Fugier Grafe* 1979 (ill.); *Hardouin-Fugier Grafe* 1982 (ill.); *Witt*

LEPAULLE, François-Gabriel-Guillaume *1804–1866*
b. Versailles (Yvelines). Pupil of Regnault, Vernet and Bertin. Painted portraits, historical and religious subjects, genre and flowers. Exhib. Paris Salon 1824–1879 e.g. *Vase de fleurs*, *Fleurs*, 1845, *Vase de fleurs*, 1849
LIT *Bellier*; *Bénézit*; *Paris Salon* 1845; *Thieme*

LEPELLE, Marie
Exhib. Paris Salon *Roses thé*, 1846, *Roses du Bengale*, 1848
LIT *Bellier*; *Bénézit*

LE PEU, Fanny-Marie
Pupil of Peseux. Exhib. *Orchidées*, wc, *Boules de neige*, wc, Paris UFPS 1898
LIT *Paris UFPS* 1898

LEPRINCE, Céline du Beaufort
Musée de Bagnères de Bigorre, *Bouquet de roses*, wc, and *Dahlias*, wc, both 1854; Musée de Toulouse, *Dahlias*, wc. This may be the artist who designed and lithographed a flower plate published by Lemercier (Paris Bibl. Nat. Est.)
LIT *Bénézit*; Paris Bibl. Nat. Est. Jd 59

Céline du Beaufort Leprince

Watercolour, signed and dated 1854
Dedicated to M. Achille Jubinal, Deputé
Bagnères-de-Bigorre, Musée Salies

LEQUEUX, Martial
Painted portraits, historical subjects, genre and, occasionally, flowers. Exhib. Paris Salon 1847–1849. Paris, Louvre Cabinet des Dessins, *Fleurs*, wc, in *Album Ingres*
LIT *Bénézit*; Paris, Louvre Cabinet des Dessins

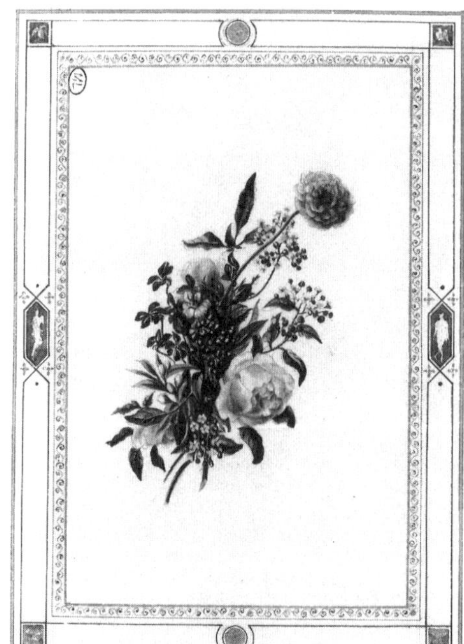

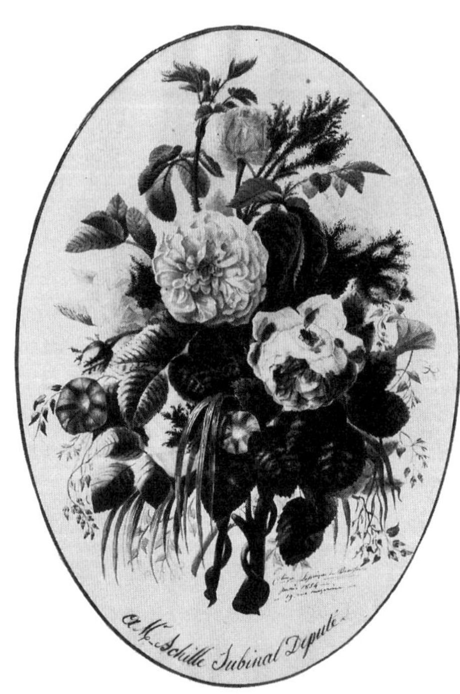

LERICHE
Suite de quatre compositions florales: Fleurs posées près d'un vase sur un entablement, 1821, 1823, Charpentier, Paris, 8–9 June 1959
LIT *Witt*

LE RICHE, Pierre *fl.c.1780–1813*
Decorator. *Vases et corbeilles de fleurs*, 1808, (Paris, private coll.), *Roses et lilas dans un vase bleu*, 1812, Mme Doucet sale, Drouot, Paris, 21–22 Nov. 1966, *Vases et gerbe de fleurs*, Paris, Pardo coll.
LIT *Bénézit*; *Faré* 1976, p. 274; *Mitchell*; *Witt*

LEROLLE, Henri *1848–1929*
b. Paris. Pupil of Lamothe, Paris BA 1864. Painted murals, decorations,

Martial Lequeux (*left*)

Watercolour on paper (from *Album Ingres*), signed
Paris, Musée du Louvre (Cabinet des Dessins)

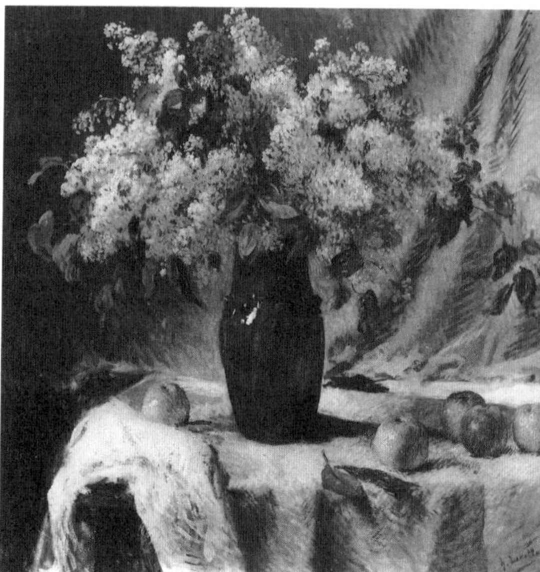

Henry Lerolle

Oil on canvas, $25\frac{1}{2} \times 25\frac{1}{2}$ in. (65 × 65 cm.), signed
Courtesy Noortman, London

religious subjects, occasionally flowers. Prominent collector, friend of Degas and Renoir. Exhib. Paris Salon 1868–1928
LIT *Bénézit*; *Schurr* V, 119. PM

LEROUDIER
His FDC exhibit was in the Lyon Société des Amis-des-Arts 1863 raffle
LIT *Compte-rendus annuels de la Société des Amis-des-Arts*, Lyon, (Perrin) 1863

LEROUDIER, Barthélémy *b.1870*
Pupil of Castex-Dégrange, Lyon BA (CFD 1890)
LIT *Hardouin-Fugier Grafe*

Jules Leroy

Oil on canvas, 31½ × 51 in. (80 cm × 130 cm.), signed and dated 1863
Varzy, Musée Municipal

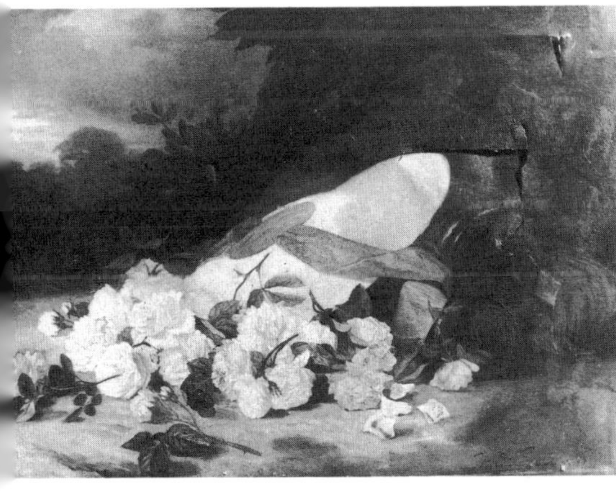

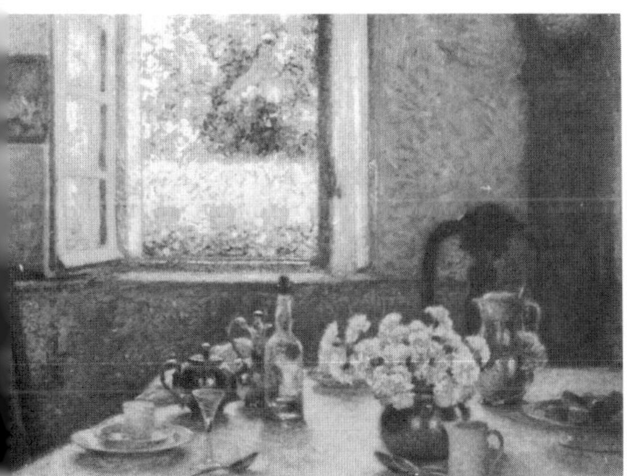

LE ROUX, Jeanne
b. Le Havre (Seine-Maritime). Pupil of Mazeline and Lhuillier. Exhib. *Chrysanthèmes*, wc, Paris Salon 1885
LIT *Paris Salon* 1885

LEROY, Augustine
fl.*c*.1834–1859. Pupil of Isabey and, possibly, Redouté. Contributed designs to Humboldt's *Mimoses* (vol. IV). Exhib. flowers in wc, Paris Salon 1834–1859
LIT *Bénézit*; *Hardouin-Fugier* 1981; *Thieme*

LEROY, Célestine or Céline-Emilie *b.1807*
Pupil of Redouté. Sold a flower in wc to the Duchesse de Berry. Exhib. Paris Salon 1831, 1833, 1834, 1835
LIT *Hardouin-Fugier* 1981

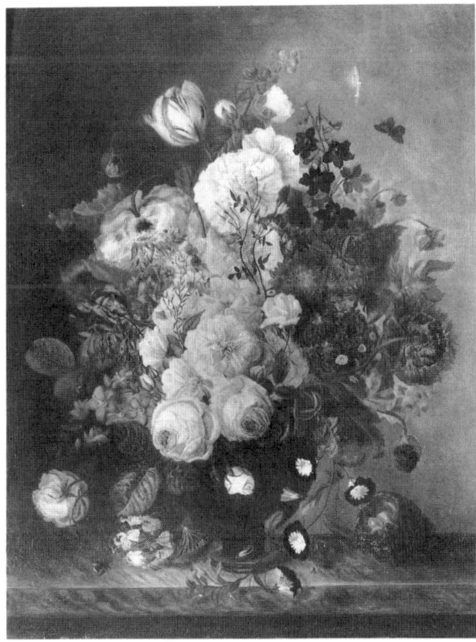

Louisa Lesca (*above*)

Oil on canvas, 36 × 28½ in. (92 × 72 cm.), signed and dated 1852
Besançon, Musée des Beaux-Arts

Henri-Eugène-Augustin Le Sidaner

Oil on canvas, 25½ × 32½ in. (65 × 82 cm.)
Gray, Musée Baron Martin

LEROY, Charles *d.1898*
b. Paris. Pupil of Defaux and Krug. Exhib. *Roses trémières*, Paris Salon 1895
LIT *Bénézit*; *Paris Salon* 1895

LEROY, Claire
b. Paris. Pupil of F. Rivoire. Exhib. Paris Salon from 1879 e.g. *Lilas*, *Chrysanthèmes*, gouache, 1879, *Lilas, roses, primevères*, gouache, *Azalées*, gouache, *Chrysanthèmes*, gouache 1880, *Giroflées*, 1885
LIT *Bellier*; *Bénézit*; *Paris Salon* 1885

LEROY, François *b.1797*
b. Nîmes (Gard). Pupil of Berjon, Lyon BA (CFD 1813). Exhib. Lyon Salon 1818
LIT *Hardouin-Fugier Grafe*

LEROY, Jules *1833–1865*
b. Le Mans (Sarthe). Pupil of Paris BA and P. Rousseau. Painted still-lifes, fruit, flowers. Exhib. Paris Salon 1859–1865 e.g. *Fleurs*, 1861. His *Fleurs et fruits* was bought by the State (800 francs) for Varzy, Nièvre, in 1864 (untraceable). M: Varzy, *Le Bouquet de roses et chapeaux*
LIT *Bellier*; *Bénézit*; Paris Arch. Nat. F21:157, 452; *Paris Salon* 1861; *Thieme*

LEROY, N., Vicomte de Barde, *alias* *1777–1828*
b. Montreuil-sur-Mer (Seine-Maritime). This natural history painter occasionally produced flower studies. Musée de Boulogne-sur-Mer
LIT *Bellier*; *Bénézit*

LESAGE, Céline
b. Lille (Nord). Pupil of Mazeline and F. Rivoire. Exhib. *Chrysanthèmes*, Paris Noir et Blanc Salon 1888; *Chrysanthèmes*, wc, Paris Salon 1890
LIT *Paris Noir et Blanc Salon* 1888; *Paris Salon* 1890

LESAGE, Gabrielle
Exhib. *Roses*, wc, Strasbourg Salon 1884; *Chrysanthèmes*, *Fleurs des champs*, Roanne Salon 1890; *Pivoines et aubépines*, wc, Dijon Salon 1892
LIT *Dijon Salon* 1892; *Roanne Salon* 1890; *Strasbourg Salon* 1884. CL

LESCA, Louisa, *née* Etevénot
Painted flowers, mostly copies e.g. *Fleurs*, after Van Dael, 1850, *Fleurs* after Van Spaendonck, 1861, *Notre Dame des Roses*, after Saint-Jean, 1863, *Fleurs dans les ruines*, after Saint-Jean, 1864, *Fleurs*, after Van Huysum, 1865, *Fleurs dans un vase d'agate*, after Van Dael, 1869. These were commissioned or bought from her by the State (800–1,000 francs each) for various public buildings e.g. Mâcon Préfecture. M: Angoulême, Auch, Auxonne, Besançon, Guéret
LIT *Bénézit*; Paris Arch. Nat. F21:42, 155, 157, 234, 436, 440, 445, 4500

LESCURE, *see* FANTY

LESÉBLE, E.
op. *c*.1850. Designed plates for H.F. Jaubert, E. Spach, *Choix de plantes ... de l'Asie occidentale*, Paris (Roret) 1841–1857
LIT *Nissen* I, 985; *Sitwell*

LE SIDANER, Henri-Eugène-Augustin *1862–1939*
b. Mauritius. Painted landscapes, interiors and flowers e.g. *Bouquet à la fenêtre*, *Pots de fleurs*, Drouot, Paris, 18 Jan. 1936. Musée de Gray, *Le dessert* (Carnations)
LIT *Bénézit*; E. Langlade, *Le Sidaner*, Arras, (INSAF) 1933; Saint-Tropez, Musée de l'Annonciade, *Fleurs de Fantin-Latour à Marquet*, 1982, no. 36 (ill.); *Witt*

LESOURD DE BEAUREGARD, Ange-Louis-Guillaume *1800–1885*
b. Paris. Pupil of C. and G. Van Spaendonck. Took over Redoutés' professorship of botanical drawing at the Paris Muséum d'Histoire Naturelle (1840). A most popular drawing master. Exhib. Paris Salon from 1822 e.g. *Fleurs et fruits*, 1842, *Fruits et fleurs*, 1861. Exhib. Strasbourg Salon *Bouquet* (250 francs), 1854, *Flowers and fruit*, New York, Newhouse Galleries, 1972. M: Paris Muséum d'Histoire Naturelle
LIT *Hardouin-Fugier* 1981 (ill.); *Strasbourg Salon* 1854; *Witt*

LESOURD-DESLISLE, *see* GIRAULT

LESPARDA, Louise de
Exhib. Paris Salon 1831–1841 wc., e.g. *Fleurs et fruits*, 1831, *Feuilles de vigne vierge*, *Géranium blanc*, *Oeillets*, 1841
LIT *Bellier*; *Bénézit*; *Paris Salon* 1831, 1841

LESPINASSE, Joseph *b.1866*
Pupil of Castex-Dégrange, Lyon BA (CFD 1887)
LIT *Hardouin-Fugier Grafe*

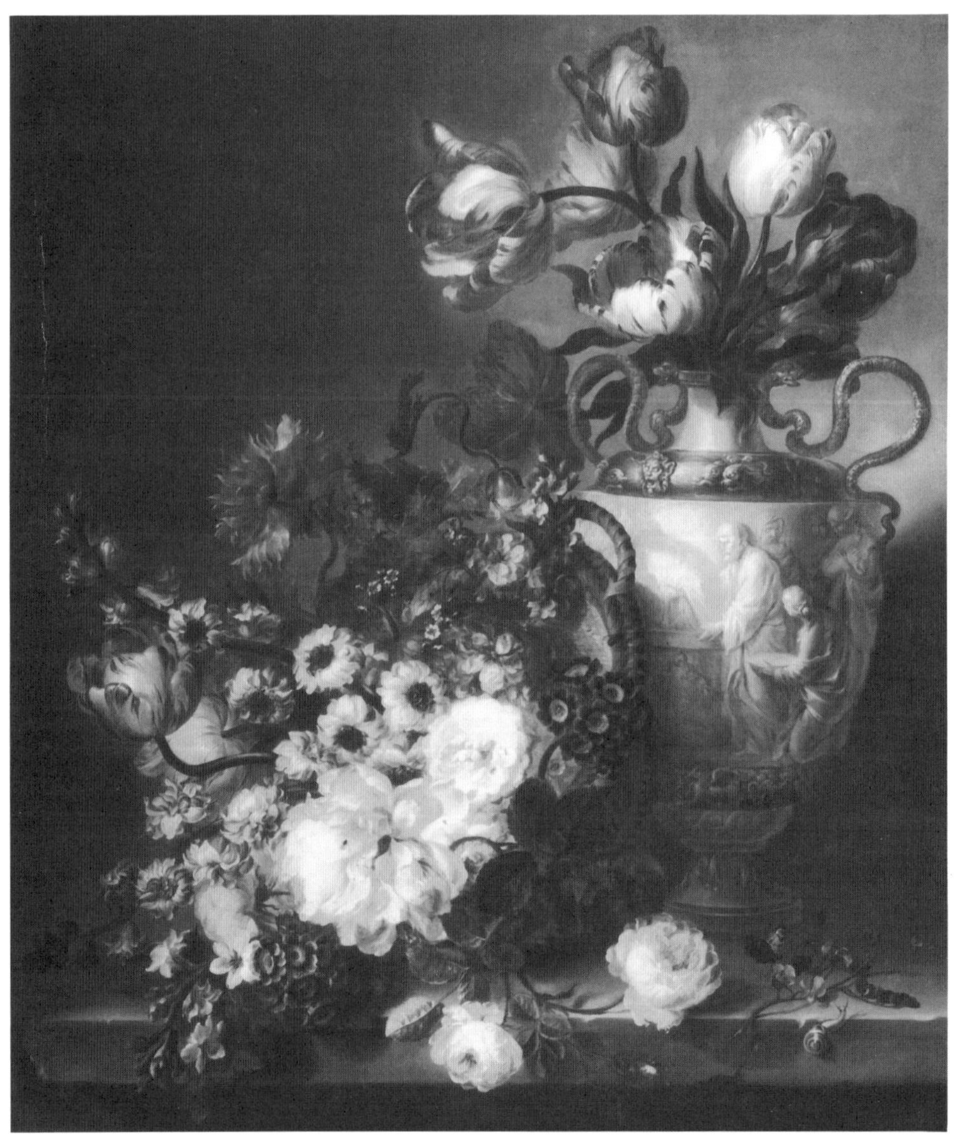

Ange-Louis-Guillaume Lesourd de Beauregard

Oil on canvas, $34\frac{1}{2} \times 28\frac{1}{2}$ in. (88 × 72 cm.)
Private collection

LESSIEUX, Louis-Ernest *1874–1925*
b. Rochefort-sur-mer (Charente-Maritime). Pupil of Lessieux and M. Lalanne. Exhib. *Rose et chardon*, wc, Paris Salon 1898
LIT *Bénézit*; *Paris Salon* 1898; *Schurr* III, 134; *Witt*

LESSORE, Jules *d.1892*
b. Paris. Painted landscapes and marines, occasionally flowers. Son and pupil of Emile Aubert and pupil of Barrias. Exhib. Paris Salon from 1864–1877
LIT *Bénézit*. PM

LESUEUR, Charles-Alexandre *1770–1846*
b. Le Havre (Seine-Maritime). Exhib. Paris Salon 1808 and 1821. Draughtsman. Illustrated *Missions en Australie* ... 1788–1802
LIT *Faré* 1962, p. 247; *Laissus*; A. Loir, *C. Lesueur* ... Paris 1921; *Witt*

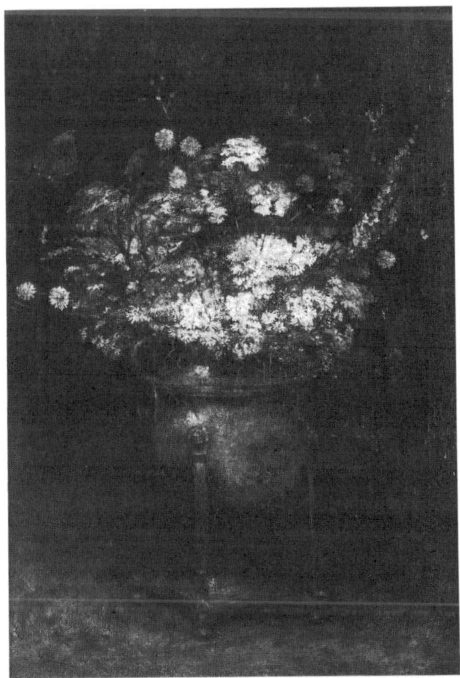

Jules Lessore

Oil on canvas, 36 × 24¼ in. (91.4 × 61.6 cm.), signed
Courtesy Christie's, London

LESUEUR, Claire
Exhib. Dijon Salon e.g. *Panier de fleurs*, *Lilas*, 1887, *Roses trémières*, 1892
LIT *Dijon Salon* 1887, 1892

LETELLIER, Mlle
Worked in Redouté's circle
LIT *Hardouin-Fugier* 1981

LETORSAY-TAINE, Virginie
b. Vouziers (Ardennes). Pupil of Duchesne and Sabatier. Painted portraits, fruit and, occasionally, flowers. Exhib. Paris Salon from 1876
LIT *Bellier*; *Bénézit*

LETOURNEUR, Angéline
Pupil of D. de Cool. Exhib. *Fleurs*, *Giroflées*, *Myosotis*, Paris UFPS 1898
LIT *Paris UFPS* 1898

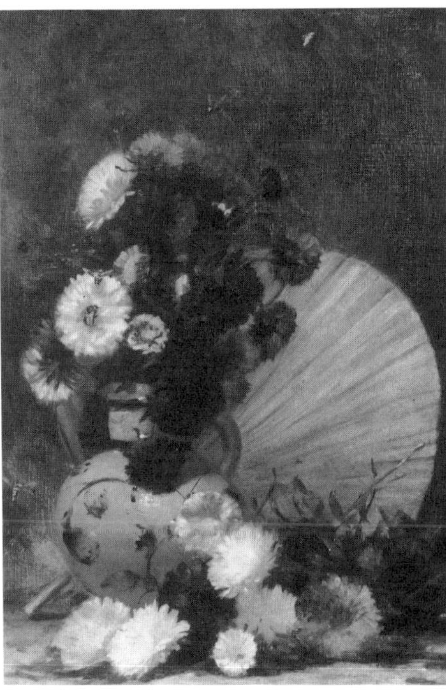

Betsy Libert

Oil on canvas, 21½ × 15 in. (55 × 38 cm.), signed and dated 'Paris '85'
Courtesy Christie's, London

LEVASSEUR, Léon
b. Paris. Pupil of C. Polisch. Exhib. flowers and still-lifes in gouache, Paris Salon from 1876 e.g. *Marguerites*, *Glaïeuls*, 1878
LIT *Bellier*; *Bénézit*

LEVASSEUR, Mme, *née* Fariau-Saint-Ange
Exhib. *Roses trémières en pleine terre et panier de fruits sur un banc*, wc, *Bouquet de roses thé*, wc, Paris Salon 1843
LIT *Paris Salon* 1843

LEVEQUE, Marie
Exhib. *Une brassée de fleurs*, wc, Dijon Salon 1892
LIT *Dijon Salon* 1892. CL

LEVERNE, H.
Exhib. *Fleurs des champs*, *Bouquet de roses*, Dijon Salon 1880
LIT *Dijon Salon* 1880. CL

LEVESQUE, *see* CHENOU

LEVEUX, Gaston *1846–1914*
b. Paris. Pupil of A. Bouchet and J. Noel. Painted landscapes and flowers. Exhib. Paris Salon 1877–1895. M: Paris, formerly in Musée du Luxembourg, *Fleurs et fruits dans un vase*
LIT *Thieme*

LEVIGNE, Théodore *1848–1912*
Pupil of Lyon BA (1860–1862). Laÿs, Gérôme and Cabanel. This prolific genre and landscape painter occasionally produced some flower-pieces. Exhib. Lyon Salon from 1863, Paris Salon from 1865
LIT *Hardouin-Fugier Grafe*

LE VILLAIN, Ernest-Auguste *d.1916*
b. Paris. Pupil of Guiaud. Painted landscapes, still-lifes and flowers. Exhib. Paris Salon 1870–1914 *Bouquet de fleurs*,

wc, 1880; *Bourriche de pensées*, Paris Indép. 1896
LIT *Bellier*; *Bénézit*; *Paris Indép.* 1896; *Paris Salon* 1880; *Witt*

LEVILLY
Lithographer and painter. Exhib. Paris Salon 1833–1836. Designed a flower plate published by Noel (Paris Bibl. Nat. Est.)
LIT *Bellier*; *Bénézit*; Paris Bibl. Nat. Est. Jd 59

LÉVY-DHURMER, Lucien *1865–1953*
b. Algiers. Pupil of Collin and Wallet. Exhib. AF then SNBA. Mostly a figure and portrait painter. Painted flowers on earthenware dishes and vases by Clément Massier e.g. Grand Palais 44, 48, 51. Most of his few flower paintings are later works, e.g. Grand Palais 79, *Chrysanthèmes*, *c.*1900 (Zagorowsky coll., Paris) and 91, *Glycines*, pastel, *c.*1922 (Paris, Petit Palais)
LIT *Bénézit*; Paris, *Autour de Lévy-Dhurmer*, Grand Palais, Réunion des Musées Nationaux, 1973; *Witt*

LEYRAS, François-Jean *b.1817*
Pupil of Thierriat, Lyon BA (CFD 1837)
LIT *Hardouin-Fugier Grafe*

LEZOUET-FEROUELLE, Gabrielle
Pupil of Jacomin and A. Cesbron. Exhib. *Fleurs*, Paris UFPS 1898
LIT *Paris UFPS* 1898

L'HAY, Michel-Eude de
b. Paris. Pupil of Defaux. Painted landscapes and flowers. Exhib. Paris Salon 1874–1898. Exhib. Lyon Salon *Roses* 1879, *Roses variées*, *Roses trémières*, 1880. Exhib. Saint-Etienne Salon *Roses*, 1882
LIT *Bénézit*; *Lyon Salon* 1879, 1880; *Saint-Etienne Salon* 1882; *Thieme*

LHERMITTE, Léon *1844–1925*
b. Mont-Saint-Pierre (Aisne). Pupil of Lecoq de Boisboudran. Painted figures, landscapes, genre and, occasionally, flowers. Exhib. Paris Salon from 1864 e.g. *Fleurs et fruits*, 1867
LIT *Bénézit*; Cleveland, *Realist Tradition*, 1980; *Paris Salon* 1867; *Schurr* I, 89; *Thieme*

LIANDRAT, Antoine
Pupil of Berjon, Lyon BA (CFD 1820)
LIT *Hardouin-Fugier Grafe*

LIBERT, Betsy
One canvas, signed and dated "Paris '85" has recently been sold at Christie's, London, 20 May 1988, lot 171. PM

LIBOUR, *see* COLIN

LIESSE, Jules
b. Versailles (Yvelines). Exhib. *Bouquet*, Paris Indép. 1893
LIT *Paris Indép.* 1893

LIÈVREMONT
Pupil of Thierriat, Lyon BA (CFD 1835). Exhib. Lyon Salon 1842
LIT *Hardouin-Fugier Grafe*

LIGNEVILLE, A. de
op. *c.*1850–1860. Designed plates for H.F. Jaubert, E. Spach *Choix de plantes ... de l'Asie occidentale*, Paris (Roret) 1842–1857
LIT *Nissen* I, 985; *Sitwell*

LIGNY, Elisabeth-Léonie de, *née* Mercier *b.1816*
Exhib. wc, Paris Salon 1844, 1845. M: Cambridge, Fitzwilliam (Broughton coll.)
LIT *Broughton* 1977; *Hardouin-Fugier Grafe* 1981 (ill.)

LIMONIER, Pierre-Victor *b.1839*
Pupil of Reignier, Lyon BA (CFD 1859)
LIT *Hardouin-Fugier Grafe*

LIMONNIER, Gaspard *b.1869*
Pupil of Castex-Dégrange, Lyon BA (CFD 1886)
LIT *Hardouin-Fugier Grafe*

LINDEN VAN, *see* ROZIER

LINT, Alphonse
b. Nancy (Meurthe-et-Moselle). Pupil of J. Lefebvre and T. Robert-Fleury. Exhib. *Roses*, Paris Salon 1895
LIT *Paris Salon* 1895

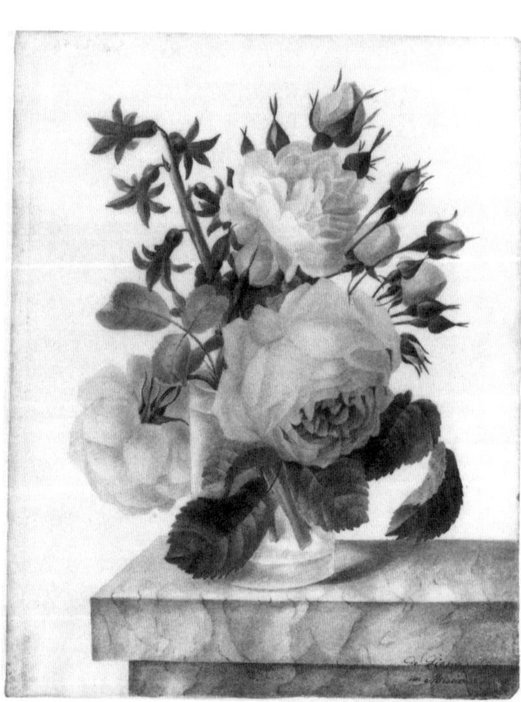

Elisabeth-Léonie de Ligny née Mercier

Pencil and watercolour on vellum, $11\frac{1}{4} \times 8\frac{3}{4}$ in. (28.4 × 22.5 cm.), signed
Cambridge, Fitzwilliam Museum
(Broughton Collection)

LIOT, A.
A single surviving work by the artist, *Bowl of Flowers*, oil on canvas, now in Cambridge, Fitzwilliam Museum (Broughton coll.) suggests a strong influence of C. van Spaendonck
LIT *Broughton* 1952. JLC

LIPPE, C.J.
Exhib. *Premières fleurs*, Dijon Salon 1894
LIT *Dijon Salon* 1894. CL

LIREAUX, *see* DELARUE

LISBETH
Exhib. Paris Indép. *Fleurs*, 1896, *Orchidées*, *Anémones*, *Chrysanthèmes et verre de Venise*, 1898. This may be Lisbeth Devolvé-Carrière, Eugène Carrière's daughter
LIT *Paris Indép.* 1896, 1898

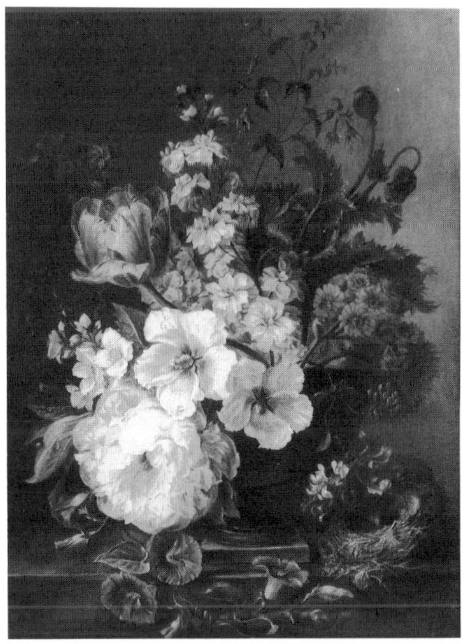

A Liot

Oil on canvas, 21 × 16 in. (53.9 × 40.6 cm.), signed
Cambridge, Fitzwilliam Museum
(Broughton Collection)

LIZAUBERT, André
b. Grenoble (Isère). Exhib. *Fleurs*, Grenoble Salon 1899
LIT *Grenoble Salon* 1899. MW

Louise Logerot

Watercolour and bodycolour on vellum, $11\frac{1}{2} \times 8\frac{1}{4}$ in (30 × 21.8 cm.), signed 'Louise Logerot/née Linet'
Cambridge, Fitzwilliam Museum
(Broughton Collection)

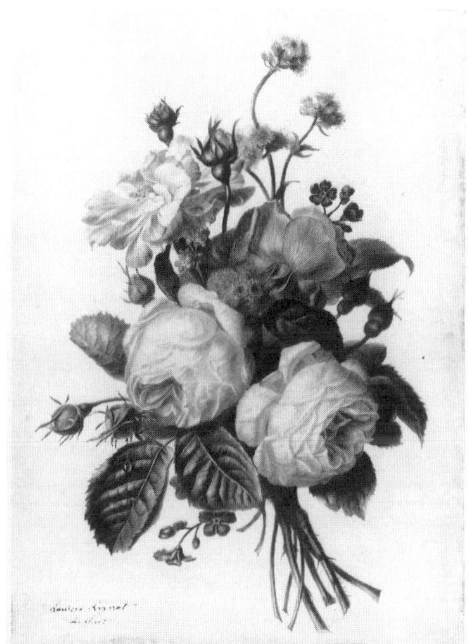

Gustave Loiseau

Oil on canvas, $25\frac{1}{4} \times 21$ in. (64 × 53 cm.), signed
Courtesy Christie's, London

LIZÉ, Charles
b. Elbeuf (Seine-Maritime). Pupil of Langlois, Flameng and G. Ferrier. Exhib. Paris Salon from 1876. Exhib. *Pensée*, *Violettes*, Saint-Etienne Salon 1882
LIT *Bénézit*; *Saint-Etienne Salon* 1882

LOBINHES, Olympe
b. Saint-Etienne (Loire). Exhib. *Fleurs des champs*, Saint-Etienne Salon 1882
LIT *Hardouin-Fugier Bringuier*; *Saint-Etienne Salon* 1882

LOGEROT, Louise, *née* Linet
Exhib. Paris Salon 1838–49, under Linet: *Fleurs dans un vase étrusque*, wc, 1838, *Roses*, 1839; under Logerot from 1842 e.g. *Fleurs* (four exhibits) 1843, eight *Études de fleurs*, wc, 1844. Possibly the artist who designed plates for J.L.A. Loiseleur Deslongchamps; *Flore générale de la France*, Paris (Baillière) 1828–1832
LIT *Bellier*; *Bénézit*; *Nissen* I, 1224; *Paris Salon* 1838, 1839, 1843, 1844; *Sitwell*

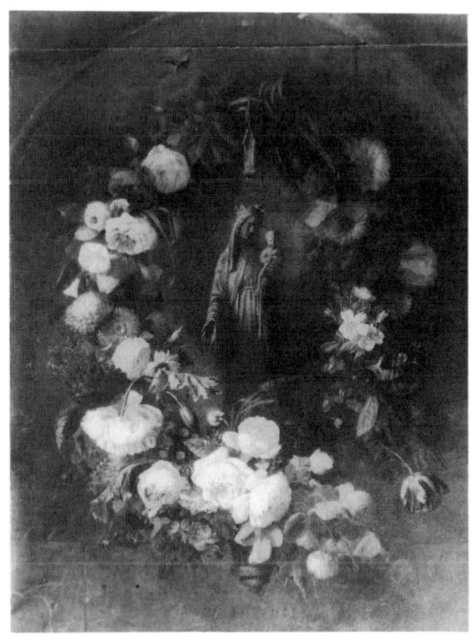

Henriette de Longchamp

Oil on canvas, $46 \times 35\frac{1}{2}$ in. (118 × 90 cm.), signed
Limoges, Musée Municipal

LOISEAU, Gustave ***1865–1935***
Worked at Pont-Aven with Gauguin. Mostly a landscape painter. His *Pivoines rouges*, 1899, seems to be his only early flower painting traced so far. Most of his flower-pieces are later works, *c.*1921
LIT *J.M. Kyriaz, Gustave Loiseau*, Paris-Lausanne (Bibliothèque des Arts) 1979; Paris, *Exposition Gustave Loiseau*, Durand-Ruel, 1957; *Pavière* III, pt. 2; *Witt*. AC

LOLETTE, *see* OZANNE

LONGAYRON
Pupil of Deschamps. Exhib. Lyon Salon 1874
LIT *Hardouin-Fugier Grafe*

LONGCHAMP, Henriette de ***b.1818***
b. Saint-Dizier (Haute-Marne). Exhib. Paris Salon 1841–1885 e.g. *Panier de fleurs*, wc, 1841, *Fleurs et fruits*, 1843, *Offrande à la Vierge*, 1846, *Guirlande de roses*, *Guirlande de marguerites*, Paris Exposition Universelle 1855, *Rose cent feuilles*, 1861, *Reines-marguerites*, 1867, *Roses remontantes*, *Roses cent feuilles*, 1875. Her *Fleurs* was bought by the State for the Musée de Limoges; her *Vierge aux roses* for the church of Courpalay (sent 19 Sept. 1885)
LIT *Bellier*; *Bénézit*; Paris Arch. Nat. F21:43, 439; *Paris Exposition Universelle* 1855; *Paris Salon* 1841, 1843, 1850, 1861, 1867, 1875; *Pavière* III, pt. 1; *Thieme*

LONGPRÉ, *see* MAUCHERAT

LOPES-SILVA, Lucien
Exhib. *Bouquet des champs*, Dijon Salon 1897
LIT *Dijon Salon* 1897. CL

LOUIS, Antoine
Pupil of Berjon, Lyon BA (CFD 1819)
LIT *Hardouin-Fugier Grafe*

LOUISE, Queen of the Belgians, *née* d'Orléans ***1812–1850***
Pupil of Redouté. M: Cambridge, Fitzwilliam (Broughton coll.): album of twenty-eight watercolours
LIT *Broughton* 1983/84; *Hardouin-Fugier* 1981 (ill.)

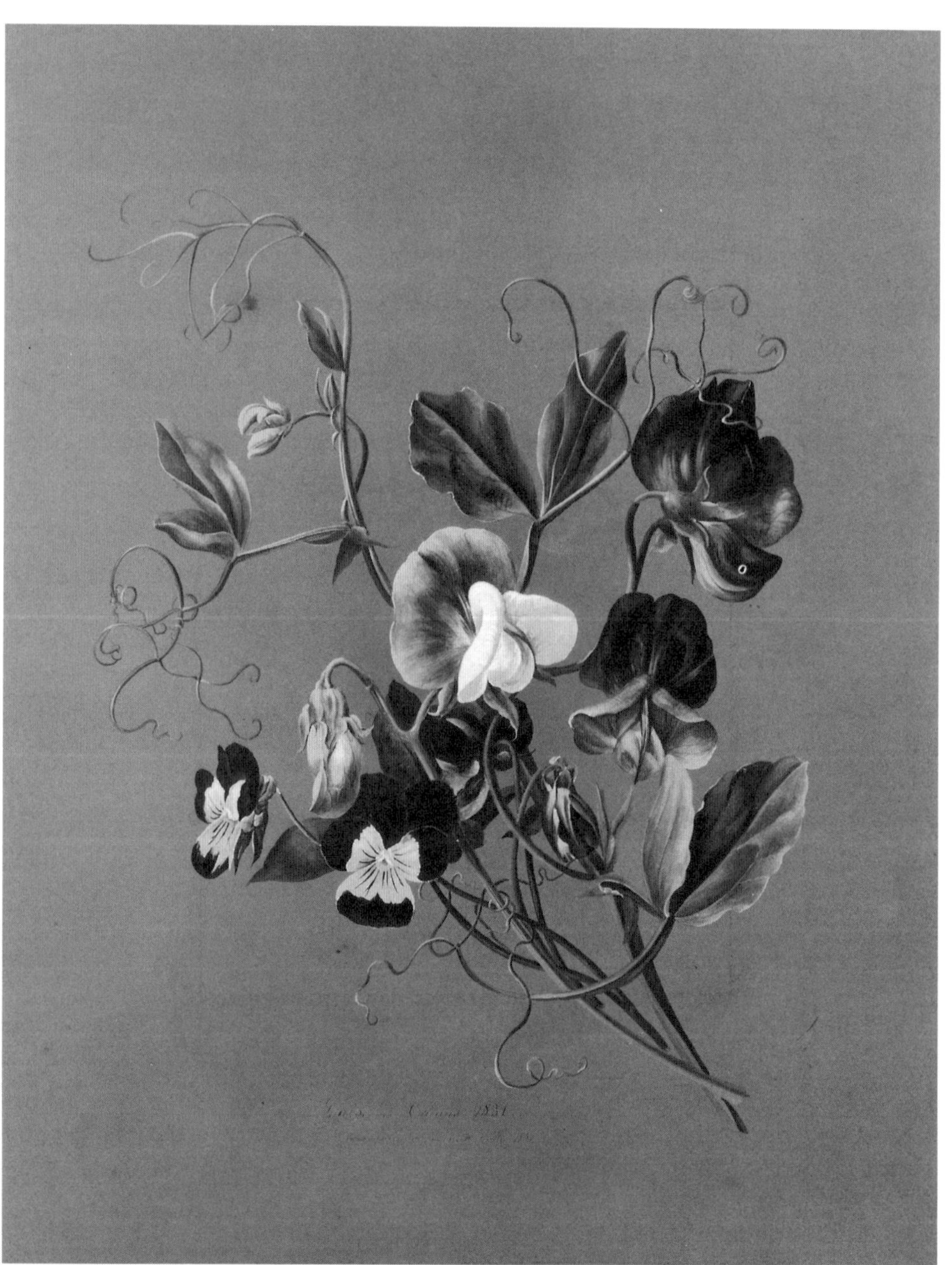

Louise, Queen of the Belgians, née d'Orléans

Watercolour and bodycolour on paper, 11¼ × 8¾ in. (28.3 × 22 cm.), signed, dated and inscribed 'Louise d'Orléans, 1831/commencé au mois Juillet 1830'
Cambridge, Fitzwilliam Museum
(Broughton Collection)

LOUPPE, Léonie, *alias* Léo Louppe ***b.1869***
b. Reims (Marne). Exhib. *Fleurs de printemps*, *Dahlias*, Paris Salon 1898
LIT *Bénézit*; *Paris Salon* 1898

Jacques-Auguste-Gaston Louvrier de Lajolais

Oil on canvas, 18 × 21¾ in. (46 × 55 cm.)
Gray, Musée Baron Martin

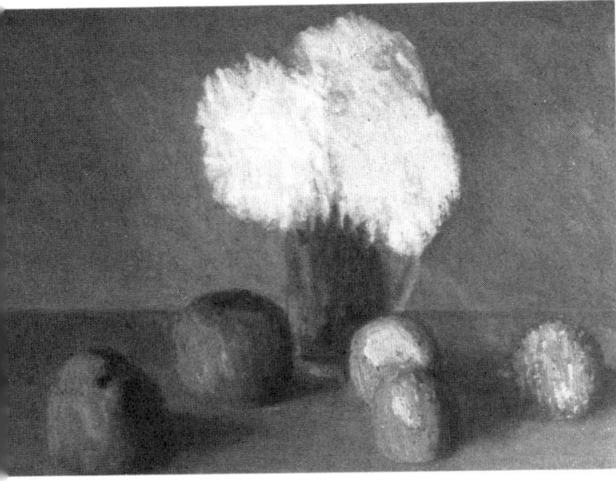

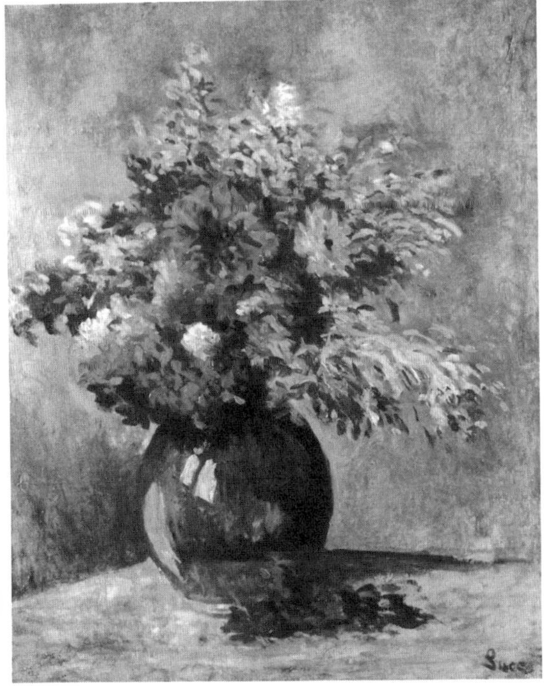

Maximilien Luce

Oil on canvas, 28¾ × 23½ in. (73 × 60 cm.), signed
Courtesy Maître Loudmer, Paris

LOUPPE, Lucie
Pupil of F. Rivoire. Exhib. Dijon Salon *Roses et boules de neige*, *Violettes*, wc, 1897; Paris UFPS *Roses et chrysanthèmes*, *Roses et violettes*, *Azalée*, 1896, *Pivoines et lilas*, *Roses*, *Violettes et oeillets*, wc, 1898
LIT *Bénézit*; *Dijon Salon* 1897; *Paris UFPS* 1896, 1898

LOUSTAU, Marie-Euphrosine, *née* Jacque
b. Paris. Painted flowers and fruit. Exhib. Paris Salon 1857–1866 e.g. *Lilas et boules de neige*, 1859, *Lilas et fleurs de poirier*, 1865, *Pavots*, 1866
LIT *Bellier*; *Bénézit*

LOUVEL, Marie-Louise
Pupil of Burat. Exhib. *Orchidées*, Paris UFPS 1898
LIT *Paris UFPS* 1898

LOUVET, Marie-Marguerite
Pupil of Thoret, Meyer and F. Rivoire. Exhib. *Bluets*, wc, *Chrysanthèmes*, wc, Paris UFPS 1898
LIT *Paris UFPS* 1898

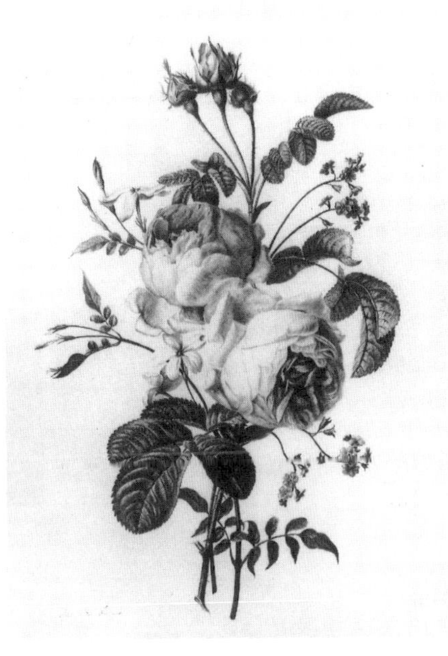

Sophie de Luisin

Watercolour, 16½ × 11¾ in. (42 × 30 cm.), signed
Courtesy Bonhams, London

LOUVRIER DE LAJOLAIS, Jacques-Auguste-Gaston
M: Baron Martin, Gray: *Chrysanthèmes et pommes*
LIT Gray Musée doc.

LOYER, Auguste-Stanislas *b.1797*
b. Rennes (Ille-et-Vilaine). Pupil of P. Guérin, Decorator. Painted religious subjects, portraits and, occasionally, flowers. Exhib. Paris Salon 1841–1870 e.g. *Fleurs d'automne*, 1867
LIT *Bénézit*; *Paris Salon* 1867; *Thieme*

LOYEUX, Charles-Antoine-Joseph
b. Paris 1823 d. 1898. Pupil of Delaroche. Portraitist and genre painter, occasionally painted flowers
LIT *Bénézit*

LOZIER, Gustave-Charles-Alexandre
b. Paris. Pupil of Henry. Exhib. Paris Salon *Bouquet de roses*, wc, 1867, *Gloxinias*, wc, *Daturas et phlox*, gouache, 1875; Dijon Salon *Fleurs*, 1881, *Fleurs et fruits*, 1883; Paris Indép. *Fleurs et fruits*, 1884
LIT *Dijon Salon* 1881, 1883; *Paris Indép.* 1884; *Paris Salon* 1867, 1875

LUCE, Maximilien *1858–1941*
b. Paris. Pupil of Carolus Duran and École de dessin des Gobelins. Worked with Camille Pissarro. Mostly a figure and landscape painter. His *Jardin au grand Montrouge*, 1877, and *Femme au bouquet*, 1890, feature flowers but his flower-pieces as such are later works (from *c.*1906) e.g. *Bouquet de fleurs*, *c.*1910, Sotheby's, New York, 14 Nov. 1985, lot 204
LIT *P. Cazeau, Maximilien Luce*, Lausanne-Paris (Bibliothèque des Arts) 1982; J. Sutter, *Luce, les travaux et les jours*, Paris-Lausanne (Bibliothèque des Arts) 1971; *Witt*. AC

LUCOTTE, Marie
Exhib. *Étude de roses*, Dijon Salon 1897
LIT *Dijon Salon* 1897. CL

LUIGNÉ, Sophie de
Designed plates for A.M.F. Palisot de Beauvais, *Flore … de Bénin*, Paris 1804 (1807)
LIT *Nissen* I, 1481

LUISIN, Sophie de
One signed watercolour has recently been sold at auction. Bonhams, London, 23 May 1988, lot 96. PM

LUIZET, François ***b.1803***
Pupil of Thierriat, Lyon BA (CFD 1826)
LIT *Hardouin-Fugier Grafe*

LUMINAIS, Evariste-Vital ***1822–1896***
b. Nantes (Loire-Atlantique). Pupil of Cogniet and Troyon. Painted figures, genre and historical subjects. Exhib. Paris Salon from 1843. Exhib. *Un bouquet*, Paris Salon 1867, Marseille Salon 1867
LIT *Bellier*; *Bénézit*; *Paris Salon* 1867; *Schurr* I, 48; *Thieme*; *Witt*

LUQUET DE SAINT-GERMAIN, Louise
Pupil of Leyssenne. Exhib. Paris UFPS *Fleurs des champs*, fan-leaf, 1896, *Roses rouges*, 1898
LIT *Paris UFPS 1896, 1898*

LUQUIN, Clément ***b.1836***
Pupil of Thierriat, Lyon BA (CFD 1856)
LIT *Hardouin-Fugier Grafe*

LUSY, Louis-Joseph ***b.1820***
Pupil of Thierriat, Lyon BA (CFD 1840)
LIT *Hardouin-Fugier Grafe*

LYONNET, Henry
b. Dorceny (Nièvre). Exhib. *Bouquets de fleurs*, Paris Indép. 1892
LIT *Paris Indép.* 1892

M

M., Mme
Exhib. *Fleurs*, wc, Paris Salon 1839
LIT *Paris Salon* 1839

MACHEREZ, Madeleine
Pupil of G. Roussin. Exhib. *Cyclamen*, pastel, Paris UFPS 1898
LIT *Paris UFPS* 1898

MAC NAB, Marie, ***née*** **d'Anglars** ***d.1911***
b. Bonny-sur-Loire (Loiret). Pupil of Rudder. Painted genre, portraits and flowers. Exhib. Strasbourg Salon *Pensée*, (375 francs) 1883, *Pivoines et boules de neige* (800 francs) 1884
LIT *Bénézit*; *Strasbourg Salon* 1883, 1884

MADINIER, Benoit ***b.1836***
Pupil of Thierriat, Lyon BA (CFD 1851)
LIT *Hardouin-Fugier Grafe*

MAGAUD, Adolphe-Jacques-Gabriel
b. Lyon. Pupil of Saint-Jean. Exhib. Paris Salon 1845–1861 e.g. *Bouquet de narcisses jaunes*, 1850, *Panier de fraises et fleurs des champs*, 1859. Exhib. Lyon Salon 1839–1868 e.g. *Groupe de fleurs*, 1846; Dijon Salon *Bouquet de fleurs*, 1849 Musée de Bagnères-de-Bigorre (currently untraceable)
LIT *Bellier*; *Dijon Salon* 1849; *Faré* 1962, p. 58; *Hardouin-Fugier Grafe*; *Paris Salon* 1850

MAGDE, Maria
Pupil of E. Claude. Exhib. *Lilas*, Paris UFPS 1898
LIT *Paris UFPS 1898*

MAGLIONE, André
b. Marseille. Pupil of Loubon. Painted landscapes and, occasionally, flowers. Musée de Marseille, *Fleurs* (acquired from the artist 1882)
LIT *Bénézit*

MAGNE, Delphine
b. Paris. Exhib. Paris Indép. *Chrysanthèmes*, 1890, *Mimosa*, fan-leaf, *Fleurs*, screen, 1893, *Fleurs*, 1894
LIT *Paris Indép.* 1890, 1893, 1894

MAGNE, Désiré-Alfred 1855–1936
b. Lusignan (Vienne). Pupil of Poitiers BA, Cabanel, J. Bertrand, Monginot, J. Lefebvre. Painted still-lifes and flowers, sometimes on porcelain. Exhib. Paris Salon from 1879. M: Arras, Compiègne (untraceable); Pontoise (not a flower painting)
LIT *Bellier*; *Bénézit*; B. Gaudichon, "La peinture au XIX° siècle …" in *Bulletin de la Société des Antiquaires de l'Ouest*" 1983; BG

MAGNIN, François-Gabriel b. 1835
Pupil of Reignier, Lyon BA (CFD 1854)
LIT *Hardouin-Fugier Grafe*

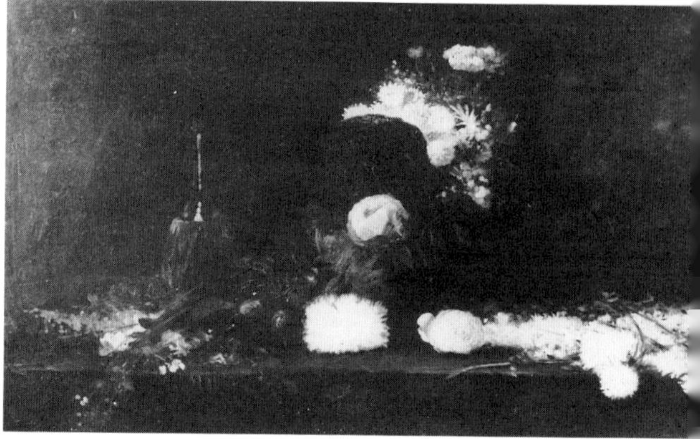

André Maglione

Oil on panel, 21½ × 36 in. (55 × 91.5 cm.)
Marseille, Musée des Beaux-Arts

MAIGNAN, Albert-Pierre-René *1845–1908*
b. Beaumont-sur-Sarthe (Sarthe). Pupil of J. Noël and E. Luminais. Painted landscapes, religious, allegorical and historical subjects. Exhib. Paris Salon from 1867. Musée de Picardie, Amiens, *Étude de pavots*, 1892, *Printemps de la Vie*, 1883, *Roses*, *Rosiers*
LIT *Béńzit*; *Schurr* II, 16; *Thieme*; Witt

MAIGNIEZ, Florence
Exhib. *Fleurs*, gouache, Lyon Salon 1879
LIT *Lyon Salon* 1879

MAILLET DU BOULLAY Thérèse
Pupil of E. Lefebure. Exhib. *Chrysanthèmes*, *Fleurs*, *Pavots*, Paris UFPS 1896
LIT *Paris UFPS* 1896

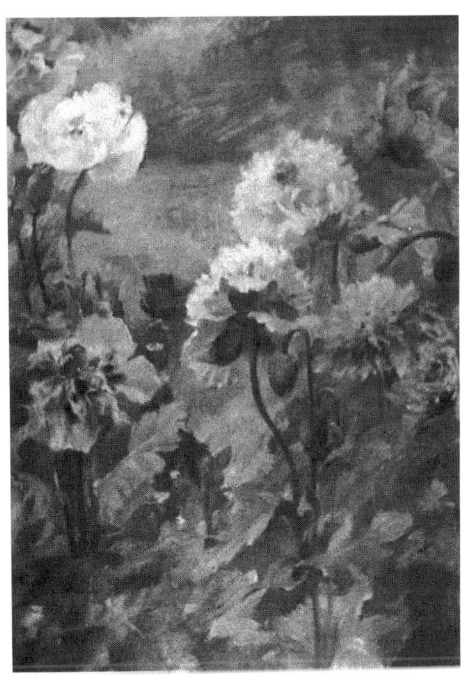

Albert-Pierre-René Maignan

Oil on canvas, 32 × 25¾ in. (81 × 65.5 cm.), signed and dated 1892
Amiens, Musée de Picardie

MAIN, Marie-Françoise-Alice
b. Paris. Pupil of Mme MacNab and F. Rivoire. Exhib. *Fleurs*, wc, *Anémomes*, wc, Paris Salon 1895
LIT *Paris Salon* 1895

MAISIAT, Etienne *1794–1848*
Pupil of Berjon, Lyon BA (CFD 1818). Professor of designing at Lyon BA. Joanny Maisiat's father
LIT *Hardouin-Fugier Grafe*; G. Vial, E. Grafe in *Hardouin-Fugier Grafe* 1981

MAISIAT, Joanny *1824–1910*
b. Lyon. Pupil of Thierriat, Lyon BA (CFD 1843) and Lehmann. Painted flowers, often in situ. Exhib. Paris and Lyon Salons *c.* 1852–1900. Lyon Salon e.g. *Fleurs de ronces*, *Fouillis*, *Marécage*, 1853, *Fruits et fleurs d'automne*, *Bords d'un taillis*, 1855, *Fleurs posées sur le sol*, 1867, *Rosiers dan un vieux parc*, 1885; Paris Salon e.g. *Un chemin en Touraine*, 1857, *La Marne à Vignely*, 1872. M: Valenciennes
LIT *Bénézit*; *Hardouin-Fugier Grafe*; *Hardouin-Fugier Grafe* 1982 (ill.). *Lyon Salon* 1853, 1855; *Thieme*

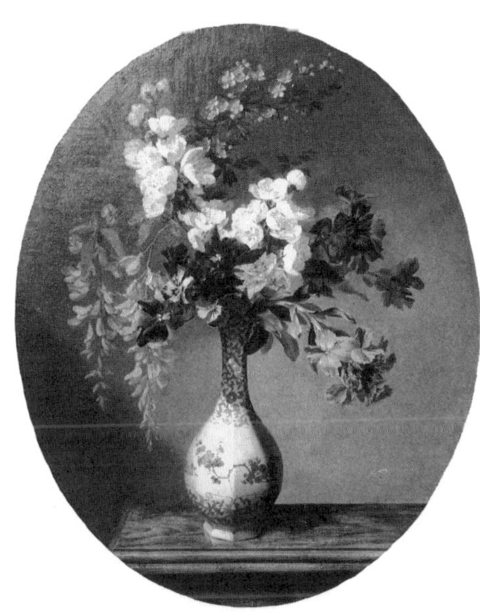

Joanny Maisiat

Oil on canvas, oval, 21¾ × 17¾ in. (55 × 45 cm.), signed Private collection

MALAINE, Joseph-Laurent *1745–1809*
b. Tournai (Belgium). Designed cartoons for Gobelins tapestries and wallpapers. Active in Alsace (Mulhouse, Thann, Rixheim). Exhib. Paris Salon from 1791 e.g. *Fleurs*, 1801–2, *Fleurs et fruits*, 1808. *Vase de fleurs*, Charpentier; Paris, 27 Apr. 1951. M: Cognac, Madrid, Mulhouse, Tournai
LIT *Bellier*; *Bénézit*; *Paris Salon* 1801, 1802; *Witt*

MALAINE, Louis-Joseph-Alphonse *1782–1856 or 1858*
b. Paris. Pupil of J.L. Malaine, his father. Textile designer (Mulhouse and Thann). Musée de Mulhouse (untraceable)
LIT *Histoire Documentaire*; *MISE cat. Sitzmann* BJ

MALANDRIN, Henriette
b. Paris. Pupil of Colin-Libour. Exhib. *Bouquet de coquelicots doubles*, wc, Paris Noir et Blanc Salon 1888; *Iris et pélargonium*, wc, Paris Salon 1890
LIT *Paris Noir et Blanc Salon* 1888; *Paris Salon* 1890

MALASSEZ, Jeanne
Exhib. Paris Indép. *Fleurs du Midi*, *Anémones*, 1892, *Chrysanthémes*, *Anthémis*, 1893
LIT *Paris-Indép.* 1892, 1893

MALASSIS Edmond
Exhib. *Fleurs*, Paris Indép. 1898
LIT *Paris Indép.* 1898

MALBERT, Ennemond ***b. 1859***
Pupil of Reignier, Lyon BA (CFD 1878)
LIT *Hardouin-Fugier Grafe*

MALBET, Aurélie-Léontine
b. Vienna (Austria) of French parentage. Pupil of her father, Vidal and Gleyre. Painted flowers and fruit. Exhib. Paris Salon 1868–1906 e.g. *Fleurs et fruits*, 1877, *Azalées et pensées*, 1878, *Fruits et fleurs*, *Fleurs*, 1880. One of her works belonged to Franz Josef, Emperor of Austria. Musée de Troyes, *Sur une table, fleurs et fruits*
LIT *Bellier*; *Bénézit*; *Paris Salon* 1880

MALBET, Olivia-Delphine
b. Paris. Pupil of Gleyre. Painted genre, still-lifes, fruit and flowers. Exhib. Paris Salon 1870–1888 e.g. *Fleurs et fruits*, 1878, 1881
LIT *Bellier*; *Bénézit*

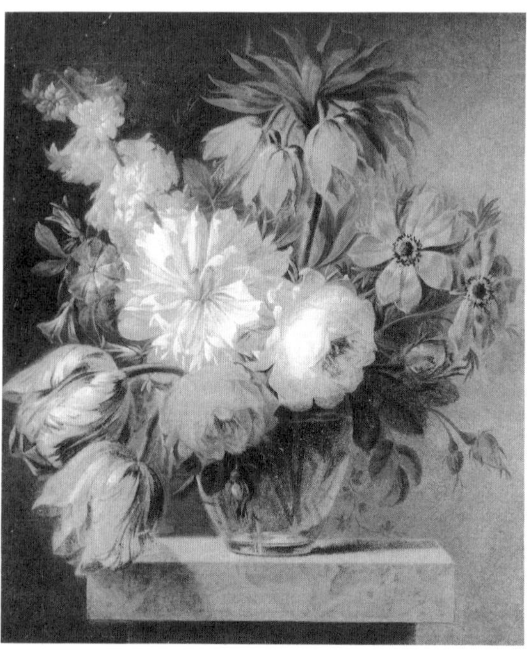

Joseph-Laurent Malaine

Oil painting on linen mounted on glass, 7 × 6 in. (17.8 × 15 cm.), signed
Collection of W. Graham Arader III, New York

MALIQUET, ***b. 1826***
Pupil of Thierriat, Lyon BA (CFD 1842)
LIT *Hardouin-Fugier Grafe*

MALLET, Joseph-Emile
b. Paris. Pupil of Nallet and B. Léonce. Exhib. *Fleurs*, on faience, Paris Salon 1880
LIT *Paris Salon* 1880

MALLEVAL, Antoine ***b. 1802***
Pupil of Berjon, Lyon BA (CFD 1822)
LIT *Hardouin-Fugier Grafe*

MALLEVAL, Félix ***b. 1864***
Pupil of Reignier, Lyon BA (CFD 1883)
LIT *Hardouin-Fugier Grafe*

MALPERTUY, Joseph-Augustin, ***alias*** **Auguste** ***1823–1897***
Textile designer (Lyon). Exhib. flowers and fruit Lyon 1851–1891. His *Primevères de Chine* was in the Lyon Société des Amis-des-Arts 1877 raffle, his *Fleurs* in the 1888 raffle
LIT *Hardouin-Fugier Grafe*; *Hardouin-Fugier Grafe* 1982 (ill.)

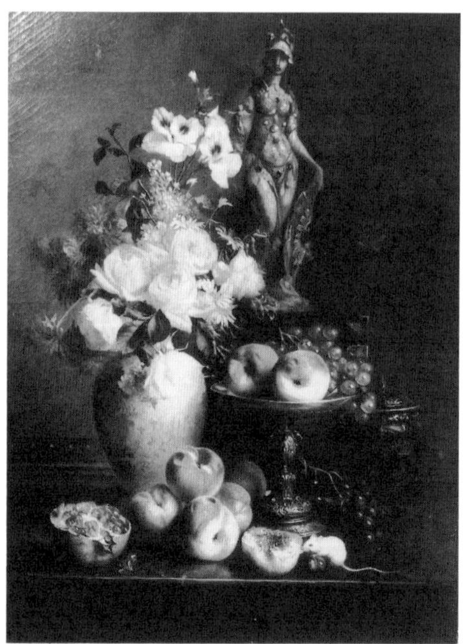

Aurélie-Léontine Malbet

Oil on canvas, 32 × 23¼ in. (81.5 × 59.8 cm.)
Troyes, Musée des Beaux-Arts

MANCEAU, Clémence
b. Rocroi (Ardennes). Pupil of MacNab and de Champeaux. Exhib. *Bouquet de roses*, wc, Paris Noir et Blanc Salon 1888; *Chrysanthèmes*, wc, Paris Salon 1890
LIT *Paris Noir et Blanc Salon* 1888; *Paris Salon* 1890

MANET, Edouard ***1832–1883***
b. Paris. Pupil of Thomas Couture. Women and flowers, sometimes represented together e.g. *Jeune femme dans les fleurs*, 1879 or *Madame Manet dans la serre*, 1879, were Manet's favourite subjects. Flowers growing in his Bellevue (c. 1880) or Rueil (c. 1882) gardens were a constant delight and source of inspiration to him. His favourite blooms are mostly garden flowers—peonies, roses or lilacs. *Chardons*, 1858 (RW. 16); *Vase de pivoines sur piédouche*, 1864, (Orsay,

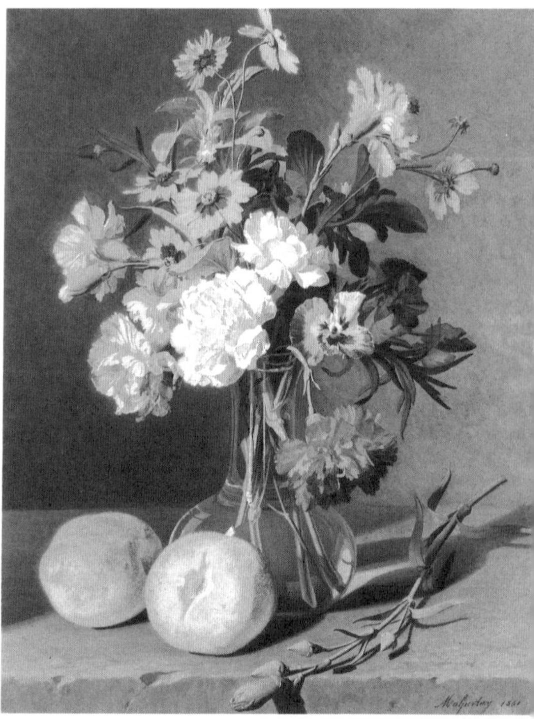

Joseph-Augustin Malpertuy

Oil on canvas, 19¾ × 15¾ in. (52 × 40 cm.), signed and dated 1861
Private collection

RW. 86); *Bouquet de pivoines*, 1864; (RW. 87); *Branches de pivoines et sécateur*, 1864 (Orsay, RW. 88); *Bouquet de pivoines*, 1864 (RW. 89); *Pivoines dans une bouteille*, 1864 (RW. 90); *Tiges de pivoines et sécateur*, 1864 (Orsay, RW. 91); *Bouquet de violettes*, 1872 (RW. 180); *Vase de fleurs*, c. 1877 (RW. 266); *Vase de jardin*, 1879 (RW. 288); *Plantes grimpantes sur un treillage*, 1881 (RW. 378); *Deux roses*, c. 1881 (RW. 380); *Lilas dans un verre à trois pieds*, 1881 (RW. 381); *Roses, tulipes, lilas blanc dans un vase de cristal*, 1881 (RW. 382); *Dahlias* (fan-leaf), 1881 (RW. 384); *Chrysanthèmes* (fan-leaf), 1881 (RW. 385, 386); *Vase de fleurs, roses et lilas*, 1882 (RW. 417) *Lilas et roses*, 1882 (RW. 416); *Lilas blanc dans un vase de cristal*, 1882 (RW. 418); *Roses dans un verre à champagne*, 1882 (Glasgow, RW. 419); *Roses, oeillets, pensées*, 1882 (Washington, RW. 420); *Bouquet de fleurs*, 1882 (Winterthur, RW. 421); *Fleurs dans un vase*, 1882 (RW. 422); *Oeillets et clématites dans un vase de cristal*, c. 1882 (Orsay, RW. 423); *Roses et pétales*, 1882 (RW. 424); *Roses mousseuses dans un vase*, 1882 (Williamstown, RW. 425); *Bouquet de pivoines*, 1882 (RW. 426); *Lilas blanc dans un vase de verre*, c. 1882 (Berlin RW. 427); *Lilas blanc dans un vase de verre*, 1883 (RW. 428); *Fleurs*, 1883 (RW. 430); *Roses dans un vase de verre*, 1883 (RW. 431). Many of his flowers in watercolours are dated 1880 (RW. 662–667). M: Berlin, National Galerie; Glasgow Art Gallery and Museum; Paris, Louvre and Orsay; Washington, National Gallery of Art; Williamstown, Mass., Sterling and Francine Clark Institute; Winterthur, Oskar Reinhard Sammlung
LIT D. Rouart, D. Wildenstein (here RW.) *Eugène Manet*, Paris-Lausanne (Bibliothèque des Arts) 1975; R. Gordon and Andrew Forge, *The Last Flower Paintings of Manet*, London, 1986; *Witt*. AC.

MANET, Julie, later Mme Ernest Rouart
Berthe Morisot's daughter exhib. *Dahlias*, Paris Indép. 1898
LIT *Paris Indép.* 1898

MANGIER, Marius 1867–c. 1952
Pupil of Lyon BA. Painted landscapes, portraits, figures and, occasionally, flowers
LIT *Hardouin-Fugier Grafe*

MANGONOT, Auguste
Exhib. *Fleurs*, wc, Dijon Salon 1897
LIT *Dijon Salon* 1897. CL

MANIQUET, Augustin, *alias* Maniquet-Barjon *1812–1879*
b. Lyon. Pupil of Lyon BA (1827–1830). Exhib. Lyon Salon. Exhib. Paris Salon 1852–1865 e.g. *Ronces et fleurs au bord d'un ruisseau*, 1852
LIT *Bellier*; *Bénézit*; *Hardouin-Fugier Grafe*; *Schurr* III, 68

MANIQUET, Jérôme-Auguste
Exhib. Lyon Salon e.g. *Fleurs*, 1860, 1864
LIT *Lyon Salon* 1860, 1864

MANTE, Jean-Charles *b. 1808*
Pupil of Thierriat, Lyon BA (CFD 1825)
LIT *Hardouin-Fugier Grafe*

MAQUERET, Mme
At Sèvres 1796–1798, 1817–1820
LIT *Brunet Préaud*

MARC-BONNEHÉE, Louise-Mathilde, *née* Marquet *d. 1900*
b. Bordeaux (Gironde). Pupil of A. Tissier. Painted portraits and flowers. Exhib. Paris Indép. *Chrysanthèmes et souvenirs de l'Exposition de 1889*, 1890, *Mûrier en fleurs*, 1891, *Bourriche de pensées*, 1898
LIT *Bénézit*; *Paris Indép.* 1890, 1891, 1898; *Thieme*

MARCELLE, Abel-Antoine
b. Saint-Quentin (Aisne). Exhib. *Fleurs des champs*, on faience, Paris Salon 1880
LIT *Paris Salon* 1880

MARCELLIN, Jeanne
Exhib. *Eglantine*, Saint-Etienne Salon 1882
LIT *Saint-Etienne Salon* 1882

MARCEUIL, Marie-Louise
Exhib. *Fleurs*, Paris Indép. 1884
LIT *Paris Indép.* 1884

MARCHAND, Eugène-Antoine
Exhib. *Roses trémières*, wc, Paris Salon 1844
LIT *Paris Salon* 1844

MARCHAND, J.
Designed and engraved flower plates. Exhib. watercolours Paris Salon 1834–1837 *Branche de groseillier*, *Groupe de giroflées*, 1834, *Fleurs*, 1836, *Bouquet composé*, *Fleurs d'arbustes*, 1837
LIT *Bellier*; *Bénézit*; *Paris Salon* 1834, 1836, 1837

MARCHAND, Jean-Albert *1828–1886*
b. Chartres (Eure-et-Loir). Pupil of P. Gilbert. Painted landscapes, birds and flowers. Exhib. Paris Salon 1877, 1878 and 1880. Musée de Louviers, *Anémones*, pastel (currently untraceable)
LIT *Bénézit*; *Thieme*

MARCHAUX, Aimé *b. c.1840*
Pupil of Hébert. Painted genre and flowers. Exhib. Paris Salon 1864–1868. Exhib. *Roses trémières*, Lyon Salon 1868
LIT *Bénézit*; *Lyon Salon* 1868, *Schurr* V, 114

MARCHEIX, Alice
Pupil of F. Rivoire. Exhib. watercolours *Fleurs*, *Violettes et chrysanthèmes*, *Pensées et giroflées*, *Primevères*, fan-leaf, Paris UFPS 1890; *Fleurs de printemps*, *Fleurs d'automne*, Paris Salon 1895
LIT *Paris Salon* 1895; *Paris UFPS* 1890

MARCKE, *see* VAN MARCKE.

MARCON, Joseph *b.1875*
Pupil of Castex-Dégrange, Lyon BA (CFD 1893)
LIT *Hardouin-Fugier Grafe*

MARCOTTE, Marie-Antoinette *b.1869*
b. Troyes (Aube). Pupil of Brussels BA and J. Lefebvre. Painted genre and flowers. Her *Serre d'Azalées* was bought by the State
LIT *Bénézit*; Paris Arch. Nat. F21: 4163; Witt

MARDUEL, Charles-Etienne *b.1839*
Pupil of Reignier, Lyon BA (CFD 1855)
LIT *Hardouin-Fugier Grafe*

MARÉCHAL, Gabriel
Exhib. *Fleurs*, wc, Dijon Salon 1894
LIT *Bénézit*; *Dijon Salon* 1894. CL

MARÉCHAL, Nicolas *1753–1802*
b. Paris. Pupil of G. Van Spaendonck. Described as "Peintre attaché au Muséum". Painted animals and flowers. Designed plates for R. Desfontaines, *Flora Atlantica*... Paris, 1798–1799; E. P. Ventenat, *Description des plantes... cultivées dans le Jardin de M. Cels*, Paris 1800–1803. M. Malmaison (album of drawings) Paris Muséum d'Histoire Naturelle (not botanical)
LIT *Bénézit*; P. Jovet, "Un aspect peu connu de l'oeuvre de P. J. Redouté" in *Bulletin du Jardin Botanique National Belge*, 37, pp. 53–60, 1967; *Laissus*; *Sitwell*; *Thieme*

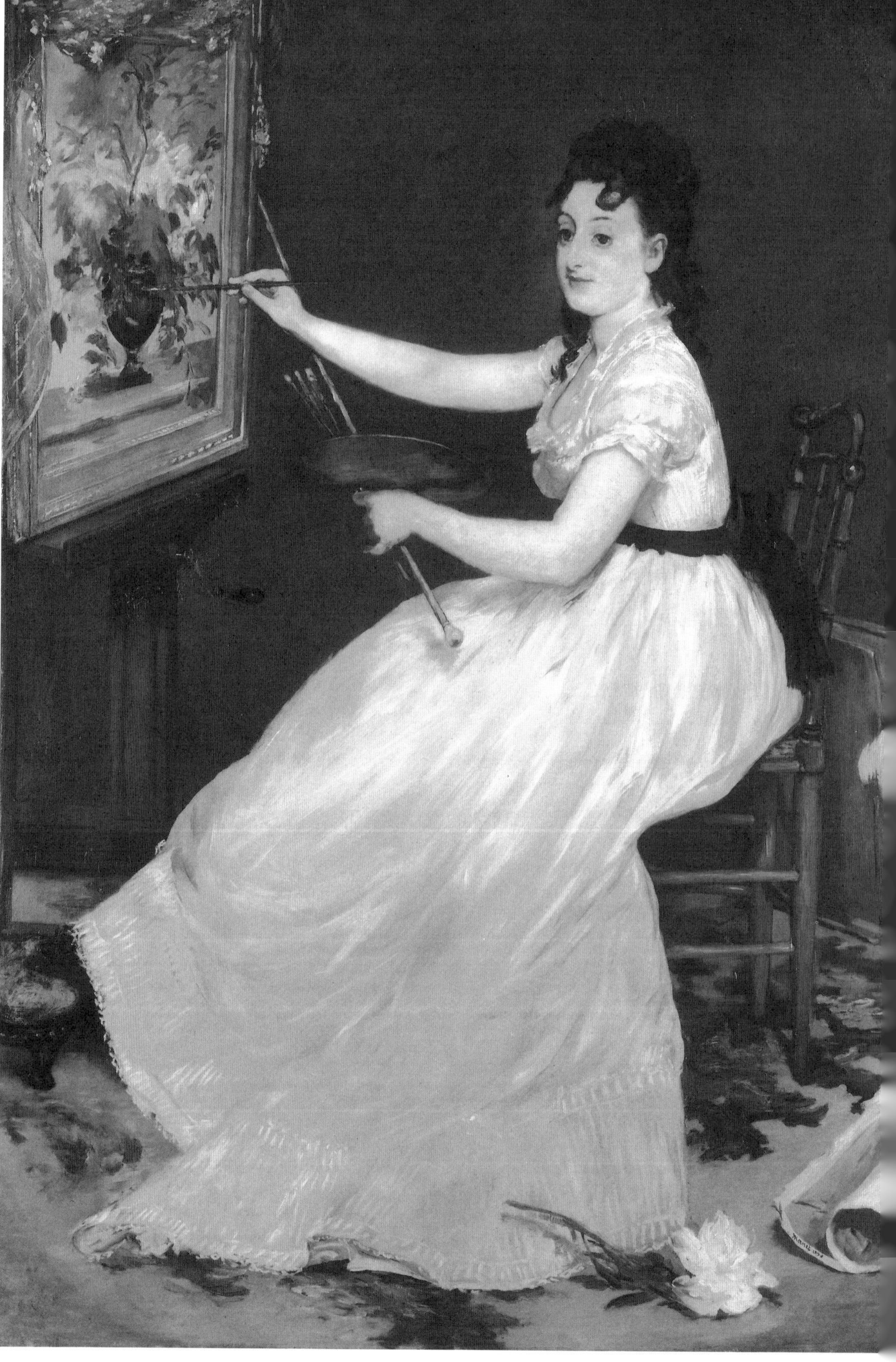

Edouard Manet

Portrait of Eva Gonzalès
Oil on canvas, 74½ × 52½ in. (188.5 × 133.3 cm.), signed and dated 1870
National Gallery, London

MARÉCHAL or MARESCHAL, Olympe
Painted flowers, often in wc. Exhib. Paris Salon 1839–1843 e.g. *Fleurs diverses*, 1839, *Fleurs et fruits dans un panier*, wc, 1840, *Fleurs et fruits*, wc, 1843. The same artist or a namesake was at Sèvres 1844–1848
LIT *Bellier*; *Bénézit*; *Brunet Préaud*; *Faré* 1962, p. 248; *Paris Salon* 1839, 1840, 1843

MAREL, Louis-Aimé *b.1807*
Pupil of Thierriat, Lyon BA (CFD 1827). Drawing master
LIT *Hardouin-Fugier Grafe*

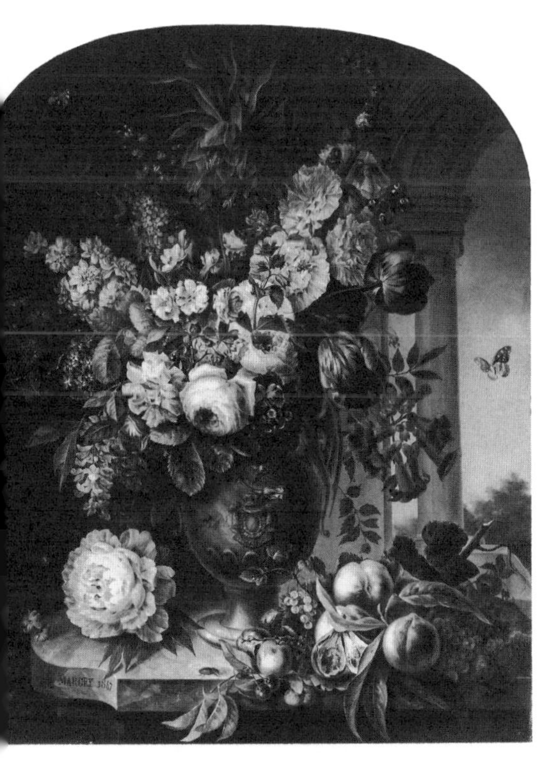

Antoine Margry

Oil on canvas, 39¼ × 32¼ in. (100 × 82 cm.), signed and dated 1847
Courtesy Christie's, London

MAREST, Julie
b. Paris. Pupil of Chaplin and Gervex. Painted genre, copies and, occasionally, flowers. Exhib. Paris Salon 1875–1920 e.g. *Roses*, pastel, 1890
LIT *Bellier*; *Bénézit*; *Paris Salon* 1890; *Thieme*

MAREY, Blanche
b. Paris. Exhib. *Fleurs*, Paris Indép. 1890
LIT *Paris Indép.* 1890

MARGRY, Antoine
Designed flower plates for *Principes de fleurs*.
Kaepelin (Paris Bibl. Nat. Est.).
Christie's London 29 Apr. 1988, Lot 94 *Roses and tulips*, 1847
LIT Paris Bibl. Nat. Est. Jd 59

MARGUERIT, Mlle G.
Exhib. *Plantes*, Paris Indép. 1900
LIT *Paris Indép.* 1900

MARIE, Louise-Sophie
b. Crécy-Couvé (Eure-et-Loir). Pupil of A. Bruxel-Rocque. Exhib. Paris Salon *Blé de Turquie*, after Van Spaendonck, 1868, *Fleurs*, on porcelain, 1869
LIT *Bellier*; *Bénézit*

MARIE-AMÉLIE, Queen of the French *1782–1866*
Pupil of Van Spaendonck, Van Dael and Redouté
LIT *Hardouin-Fugier* 1981

MARIE-LOUISE, Empress of the French *1791–1847*
Pupil of Prud'hon, Isabey and Redouté. Her *Rose et églantine* was formerly in the Sciolette collection
LIT *Bénézit*; *Hardouin-Fugier* 1981; *Paris MAD*; *Thieme*

MARIE, Raoul-Edmond
b. Paris. Pupil of Gérome. Painted genre, occasionally flowers. Exhib. Paris Salon 1873–1878
LIT *Bénézit*. PM

MARION, Joseph
Pupil of Thierriat, Lyon BA (CFD 1834)
LIT *Hardouin-Fugier Grafe*

MARIOTTE, Ernest
b. Paris. Pupil of Lesourd de Beauregard. Exhib. Paris Salon 1867–1870 e.g. *Fleurs*, on porcelain, 1867
LIT *Bénézit*; *Paris Salon* 1867

MARITAIN, Geneviève, *née* Favre
b. Paris. Pupil of A. Legrand. Painted still-lifes and flowers. Exhib. Paris Salon from 1878 e.g. *Panier de roses*, 1880
LIT *Bellier*; *Bénézit*

MARKAROFF-WARTAN *b.1863*
Pupil of Reignier, Lyon BA (CFD 1882)
LIT *Hardouin-Fugier Grafe*

MARLIER, Marie
b. Remiremont (Vosges). Pupil of Adler and Waidmann. Exhib. Paris Salon e.g. *Roses*, *Mauves et chrysanthèmes*, 1895, *Chèvrefeuilles*, 1898
LIT *Paris Salon* 1895, 1898

MARNAUD
Exhib. *Fleurs*, Dijon Salon 1881
LIT *Dijon Salon* 1881. CL

MARQUET, Auguste
Pupil of Berjon, Lyon BA (CFD 1822)
LIT *Hardouin-Fugier Grafe*

MARQUET, Pierre-Albert *1875–1947*
b. Bordeaux (Gironde). Pupil of Paris BA and Académie Ranson. Mostly a landscape painter. Among his early flowers *Pivoines dans un vase de verre*, panel, c. 1898, is a double-sided painting, on the verso *Paris, le point du jour*, c. 1904 (private coll.); *Les Tulipes*, 1900 (Lyon, 1962); *Oeillets et moulage égyptien*, c. 1900 (Paris, 1975)
LIT Lyon, *Albert Marquet*, Musée des Beaux-Arts, 1962; Baltimore, *Albert Marquet*, Museum of Art, 1958; Paris, *Marquet: Aspects insolites*, Jean-Claude and Jacques Bellier, 1962; Paris, *Marquet*, Galerie Schmit, 1967; Paris, *Albert Marquet*, Orangerie des Tuileries, Réunion des Musées Nationaux, 1975–1976. Tokyo, *Albert Marquet*, Wildenstein, 1982. AC.

MARQUET, *see* MARC-BONNEHÉE

MARQUIS, Alexandre-Louis *1777–1828*
Designed plates for J. L. A. Loiseleur, *Flora Gallia*, Paris (Baillerè) 1828
LIT *Nissen* I, 1224

MARROUX, Pierre *b.1816*
Pupil of Thierriat, Lyon BA (CFD 1837)
LIT *Hardouin-Fugier Grafe*

MARTIN, Charlotte
Exhib. *Giroflées*, Dijon Salon 1897
LIT *Dijon Salon* 1897

MARTIN, Edmée-Elizabeth-Pauline
b. Paris. Pupil of Thoret and Trébuchet. Exhib. *Roses*, wc, Paris Salon 1880
LIT *Paris Salon* 1880

MARTIN, Emilie-Elisabeth-Pauline
b. Paris. Pupil of Keller and Trébuchet. Painted flowers in wc and gouache. Exhib. Paris Salon from 1878 e.g. *Oeillets*, *Nid et fleurs d'amandier*, fan-leaf, 1878, *Lauriers-roses*, *Roses*, wc, 1879
LIT *Bellier*; *Bénézit*

Raoul-Edmond Marie

Oil on canvas, $25\frac{1}{2} \times 32$ in. (65 × 81 cm.), signed
Private collection

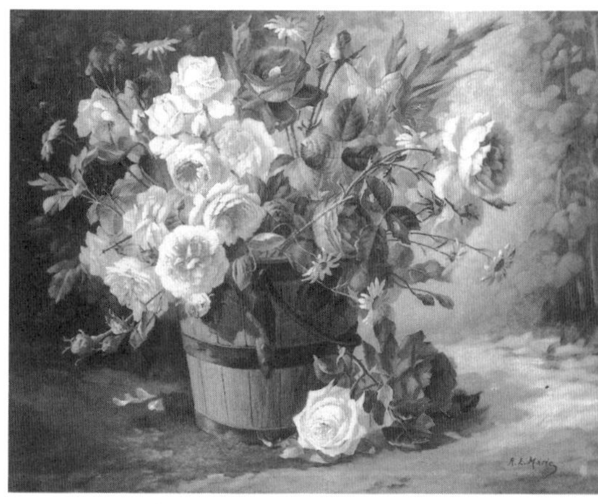

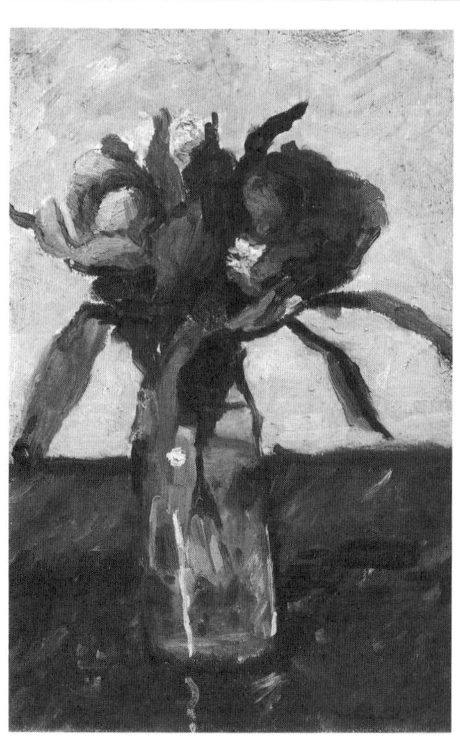

Pierre-Albert Marquet

Oil on panel, $13\frac{1}{4} \times 8\frac{1}{2}$ in. (33.5 × 21.7 cm.), signed
Private collection

MARTIN, F
Exhib. *Fleurs d'automne*, Lyon Salon 1879
LIT *Lyon Salon* 1879

MARTIN, Francisque *1870–1933*
Painted landscapes and, occasionally, flowers. In Lyon c. 1900–1930
LIT H. Béraud, *L'Ecole lyonnaise de peinture moderne*, Paris (Basset) 1912; *Hardouin-Fugier Grafe*

MARTIN, Francois *b.1826*
Pupil of Thierriat, Lyon BA (CFD 1842)
LIT *Hardouin-Fugier Grafe*

Jacques Martin

Oil on canvas, 31½ × 45¾ in. (80 × 116 cm.), signed
Private collection (photo: Musée des Beaux-Arts, Lyon)

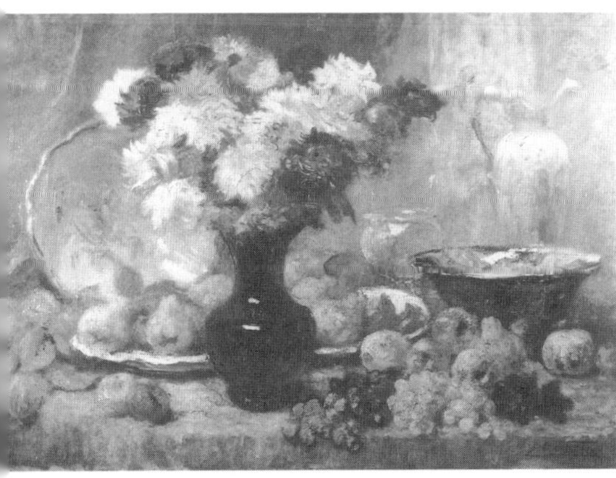

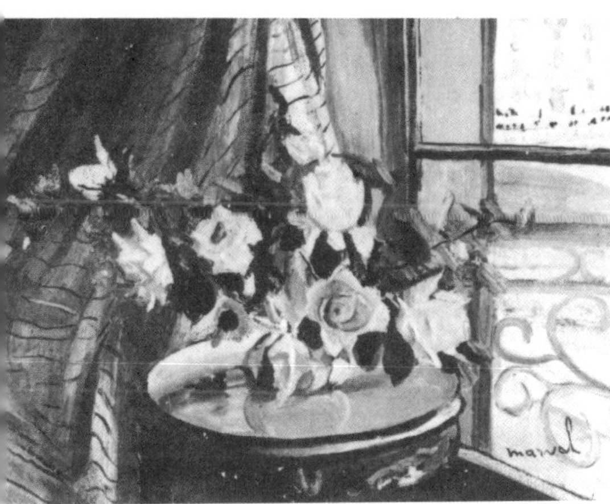

MARTIN, Mlle H.
Exhib. *Fleurs*, on porcelain, Paris Salon 1834
LIT *Paris Salon* 1834

MARTIN, Jacques *1844–1919*
b. Villeurbanne (Rhône). Chemical engineer. Self-taught. Exhib. Lyon Salon from 1881 and Paris Indép. e.g. *Fleurs*, 1896. Influenced by F. Vernay, admired by Puvis de Chavannes and Renoir. M: Digne, *Roses et cerises* Lyon: *Fleurs* Narbonne, *Fleurs de printemps*, formerly in Musée du Luxembourg, Paris, *Fleurs et fruits* now Louvre
LIT *Bénézit*; R. Caudal, in *Fleurs de Lyon*, p. 237 (*Hardouin-Fugier Grafe* 1982, ill); *Hardouin-Fugier Grafe* (ill.); *Hardouin-Fugier Grafe* 1979 (ill.); *Paris Indép.* 1896

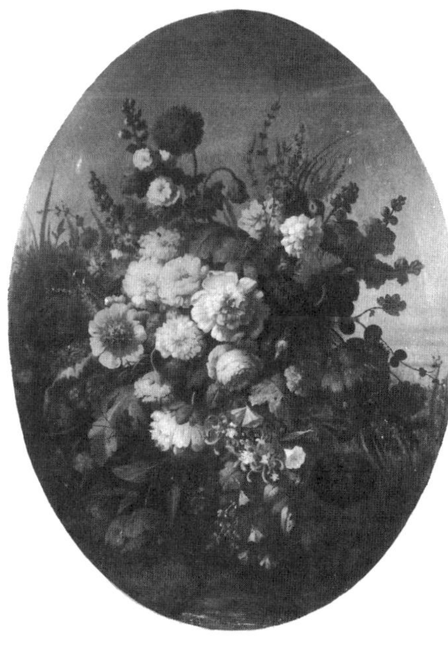

Louis Martinet

Oil on canvas, oval, 51¼ × 38¼ in. (130.2 × 97.1 cm.), signed and dated 1862
Chambéry, Musée d'Art et d'Histoire

Jacqueline-Marie-Joséphine Marval, alias Vallet

Oil on canvas, 28¾ × 39½ in. (73 × 100 cm.), signed
Private collection

MARTIN, Jean *b.1825*
Pupil of Thierriat, Lyon BA (CFD 1842)
LIT *Hardouin-Fugier Grafe*

MARTIN, Joseph
Fleurs, Paris Indép. 1884
LIT *Paris Indép.* 1884

MARTIN, Pierre *b. 1857*
Pupil of Reignier, Lyon BA (CFD 1874)
LIT *Hardouin-Fugier Grafe*

MARTIN, Pierre *b.1871*
Pupil of Castex-Dégrange, Lyon BA (CFD 1890)
LIT *Hardouin-Fugier Grafe*

MARTINAT *b.1830*
Pupil of Thierriat, Lyon BA (CFD 1848)
LIT *Hardouin-Fugier Grafe*

MARTINET, Louis *1810–1894*
b. Paris. Pupil of Gros. Painted portraits, landscapes and flowers. Exhib. Paris Salon 1833–1882. His works were bought by the state e.g. *Fleurs et fruits*, for the Musée de Blois. 1859 (gift of State 1859, Salon 1858 and 1869) *Fleurs* for Carcassonne 1857, *Fleurs et fruits*, for Chambéry, 1862. *Fleurs et fruits* for Lisieux, 1857, *Fleurs*, for Nancy, 1856, *Fleurs et fruits*, for Poitiers, 1856–1857, 1871.
LIT *Bellier*; *Bénézit*; Paris Arch. Nat. F21:437, 439, 444, 2199, 4500; *Thieme*

MARVAL, Jacqueline-Marie-Joséphine Vallet *alias* *1866–1932*
b. Quaix (Isère). Pupil of J. Flandrin. Painted figures, genre and flowers, these mostly 20th century works. Nicknamed "la fée aux fleurs". M: Paris (Orsay), *La coupe fleurie*
LIT *Bénézit*; Grenoble Bibl. Mun. man. Sainson; Grenoble, Musée des Beaux-Arts, *J. Marval*, 1932; *Orsay*; Paris Arch. Nat. F21: 4244, 4326 (20th century); Paris Salon d'Automne, *J. Marval*, 1932; *Schurr* III, 151; Witt

MARY, Mlle
Pupil of P. Jance. Exhib. *Chrysanthèmes*, Dijon Salon 1892
LIT *Dijon Salon* 1892. CL

MARZO, Antoine *1853–c.1946*
b. Domo (Italy). Painted flowers and fruit. op. Lyon. Exhib. Lyon Salon from 1884
LIT *Hardouin-Fugier Grafe*; *Lyon Salon d'Automne*, 1948 Marzo retrospective

MASSEAU, *see* Fix

MASSENOT, Charles-Antoine-Auguste *1821–1871*
b. Dijon (Côte-d'Or). Pupil of Drolling. Professor at Dijon BA. Painted landscapes, genre and, occasionally, flowers. *Bouquet de marguerites*, *Bouquet de pensées*, drawings, Dijon Salon 1849
LIT *Bénézit*; *Dijon Salon* 1849; *Thieme*

MASSERAS, *see* HERPIN

MASSON, Bénédict *1819–1893*
b. Sombernon (Côte-d'Or). Pupil of Delaroche and P. Chenavard. Painted historical, allegorical and religious subjects. Exhib. Paris Salon 1840–1881. His *Les Fleurs*, *composition allégorique*, was bought by the State (2,400 francs) in 1848 for the Musée de Tours (disappeared 1940). A small pair of oils at Sotheby's, New York, 30 Oct. 1985, signed and dated 1849, may be by this artist
LIT *Bénézit*; Paris Arch. Nat. F21: 45, 2201; *Thieme*; Witt

MASSON, François
Exhib. *Fleurs, peinture orientale*, Dijon Salon 1837
LIT *Dijon Salon* 1837. CL

MASSON, *see* BEAUCHARD

MASSYN, Anaïs
b. Paris. Pupil of Bellay. Exhib. *Couronnes Impériales*, Paris Noir et Blanc Salon 1888
LIT *Paris Noir et Blanc Salon* 1888

MAST, *see* HUBLIER

MATHEY, Paul *1844–1929*
b. Paris. Pupil of Léon Cogniet. Salon debut 1868. Portrait, landscape, marine and flower painter, also engraver. Exhib. Paris. Etalage de fleuriste 1927. Museum works: Luxembourg, Dieppe, Château-Thierry.
LIT *Bénézit*, *Schurr* II. 114

MATHIEU, Alexis
b. Paris. Pupil of Billod. Painted flowers and fruit. Exhib. Paris Salon 1865–1870 e.g. *Fleurs et fruits*, 1867, *Pelargoniums en pots et fruits*, 1868. M: Cambridge, Fitzwilliam (Broughton Coll.)
LIT *Bellier*; *Bénézit*; *Paris Salon* 1867

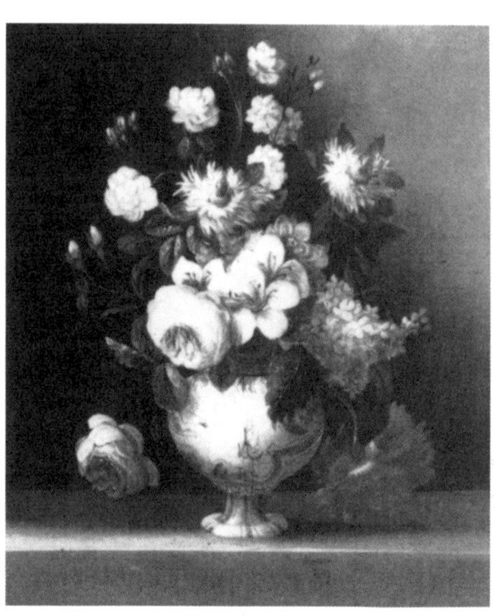

Bénédict Masson

Oil on canvas, 21½ × 18 in. (54.6 × 45.7 cm.) one of a pair
signed and dated 1849
Courtesy Sotheby's, London

MATHIEU, Frank
Exhib. *Lys et bleuets, souvenir*, Dijon Salon 1883
LIT *Dijon Salon* 1883. CL

MATHILDE-LAETITIA-WILHELMINE DEMIDOFF Princesse *née* Bonaparte *1820–1904*
Pupil of Eugène Giraud and C. Popelin. Painted figures, portraits and flowers. Exhib. Paris Salon 1859–1867
LIT F. Bac, *La Princesse Mathilde*, Paris (Hachette) 1928; *Bellier*; A. D. Gaigneron, "*Le salon de la Princesse Mathilde*" *in Connaissance des Arts*, *Dec. 1977*; *Thieme*; Witt

MATHILDE, Mme
Pupil of T. Robert-Fleury and Gerald-Laffite. Exhib. *Fleurs*, *Chrysanthèmes*, fan-leaf, wc, Paris Salon 1885
LIT *Paris Salon* 1885

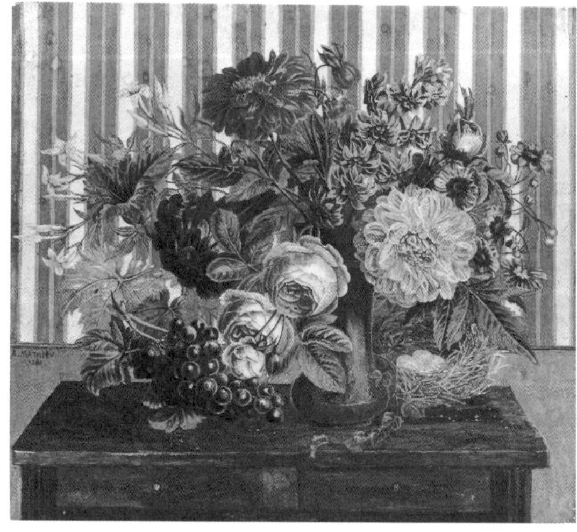

Alexis Mathieu

Watercolour on paper, 7½ × 8⅜ in. (19 × 21.2 cm.), signed and dated 1865
Cambridge, Fitzwilliam Museum
(Broughton Collection)

MATIFAS, Louis-Rémy 1847–1896
b. Amiens. Painted landscapes and still-lifes. Pupil of Cauchois and Vollon at Amiens BA. Exhib. Paris Salon. 1876–1891
LIT *Bénézit*. PM

MATISSE, Henri *1869–1954*
b. Cateau-Cambrésis (Nord). Pupil of Gabriel Ferrier, Bouguereau and Gustave Moreau in whose Paris BA studio he befriended Marquet, Puy and Rouault. Most of his flowers are later works dating, at least, from his Fauve period c.1904. *La desserte*, 1897 (Paris, Grand Palais 13) is a rare exception
LIT Paris, *Henri Matisse*, Grand Palais, Réunion des Musées Nationaux, 1970
See illustration on page 61

MATRAT, Charles *b.1797*
Pupil of Berjon, Lyon BA (CFD 1813)
LIT *Hardouin-Fugier Grafe*

MATTHEY-GUENET, Jean *b.1809*
Pupil of Thierriat, Lyon BA (CFD 1826)
LIT *Hardouin-Fugier Grafe*

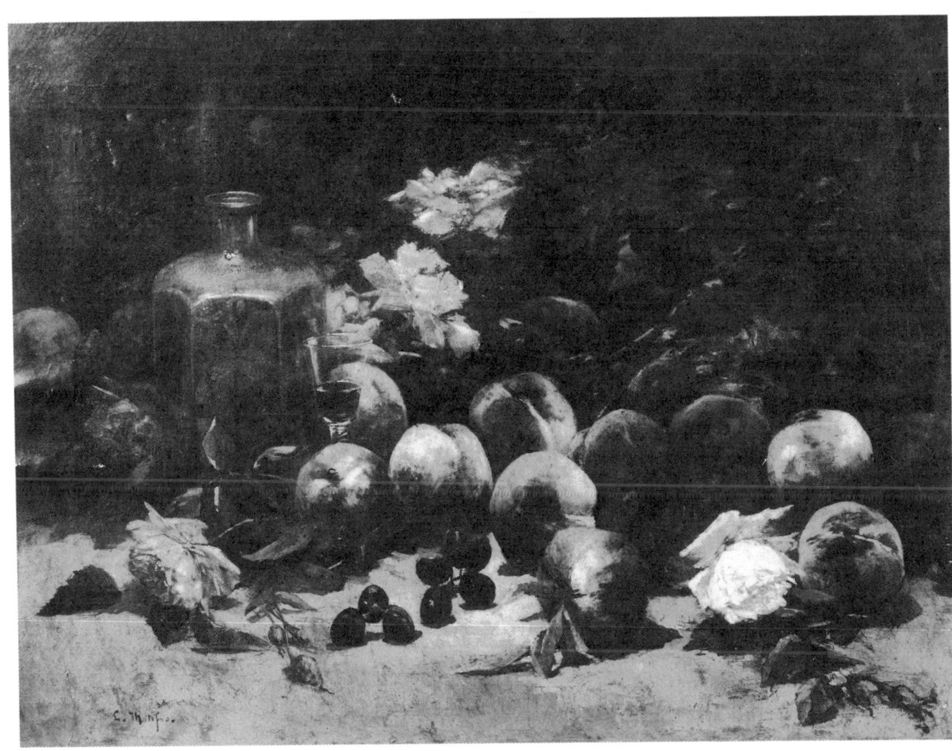

MAUBERT *op. 1840–1860*
Botanical draughtsman. Designed plates e.g. for H.F. Jaubert, E. Spach, *Choix de plantes... de l'Asie*, Paris (Roret) 1842–1857. Plates in Vilmorin coll. BMAD (Maciet coll.). Musée du Château, Azay-le-Férron, *Iris et orchidées*
LIT *Album Vilmorin*; *Nissen* I, 210, 985, 1169, 2118, 2231, 2240, 2380; Paris Bibl. Nat. Est. Jd 67; *Paris BMAD*

MAUCHERAT DE LONGPRÉ, Jean-Antoine-Marie-Victor *b.1815 or 1820*
b. Paris. Exhib. flowers Lyon Salon e.g. 1850, 1857, Paris Salon e.g. 1877, 1880. Designed sets of plates lithographed by Compte-Calix, some of which, *Fleurs poétiques*, *Les grandes et les petites myriades de fleurs et d'effets nouveaux*, are fancy flowers influenced by Pillement's *Fleurs idéales*
LIT *Audin Vial*; *Lyon Salon*, 1850, 1857; Paris MAD; Paris Salon 1877, 1880; G. Picard, "Les Lyonnais au Salon de 1877" in *La Revue du Lyonnais* 1877 II, p. 72

MAUCHERAT DE LONGPRÉ, Paul-Henri-Georges *1855–1911*
b. Lyon. Active in Paris, New York from 1890, Hollywood from 1901. Exhib. Paris Salon 1877, 1879, 1880. Exhib. *Marguerites*, *Roses*, *Pivoines*, gouaches, Paris Indép. 1884
LIT *Hardouin-Fugier Grafe*; *Hardouin-Fugier Grafe* 1982 (ill.); *Paris Indép.* 1884; *Thieme*; James J. White, Letter to E. Hardouin-Fugier, 1982; *Broughton* 1974

MAUCHERAT DE LONGPRÉ, Raoul-Henry *b. 1859*
Son of Jean-Antoine. Exhibited flowers at the Paris Salon: 1877, *Lilas*, gouache, and *Lilas et chrysanthèmes*: 1880, *Pivoines et lilas*. Three watercolours of flowers in Cambridge, Fitzwilliam Museum (Broughton coll.)
LIT *Bénézit*; *Broughton* 1974; *Hardouin-Fugier Grafe* 1982 (ill.). JLC

MAUCROY, Edmée
b. Nevers (Nièvre). Exhib. *Fleurs*, Paris Salon 1880
LIT *Paris Salon* 1880

MAUCUER, Claude-Etienne *b.1826*
Pupil of Thierriat, Lyon BA (CFD 1843)
LIT *Hardouin-Fugier Grafe*

MAUDUIT, Léonie, later (after 1839) Hersent
Painted portraits, genre and flowers, often in wc Exhib. Paris Salon 1838–1839
LIT *Bellier*; *Bénézit*; *Thieme*

Louis-Rémy Matifas

Oil on canvas, 21 × 28½ in. (53.5 × 72.5 cm.), signed
Courtesy Christie's, London

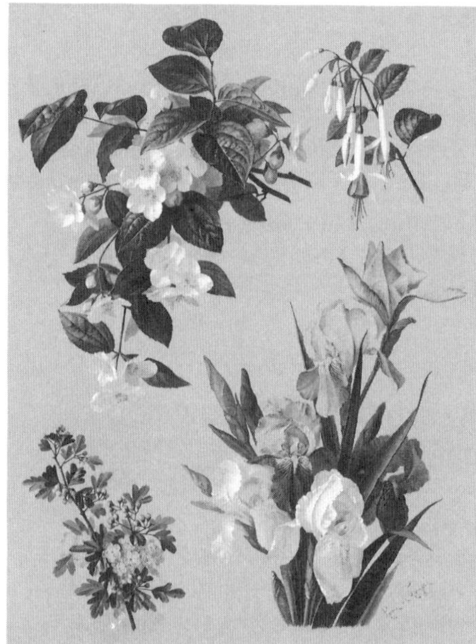

Paul-Henri-Georges Maucherat de Longpré

Oil on canvas, $20\frac{1}{2} \times 15\frac{3}{4}$ in. (51.7×39.8 cm.), signed
Cambridge, Fitzwilliam Museum
(Broughton Collection)

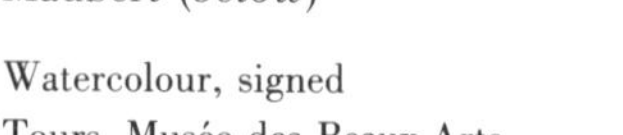

Maubert (*below*)

Watercolour, signed
Tours, Musée des Beaux-Arts
(on loan from Château d'Azay-le-Ferron)

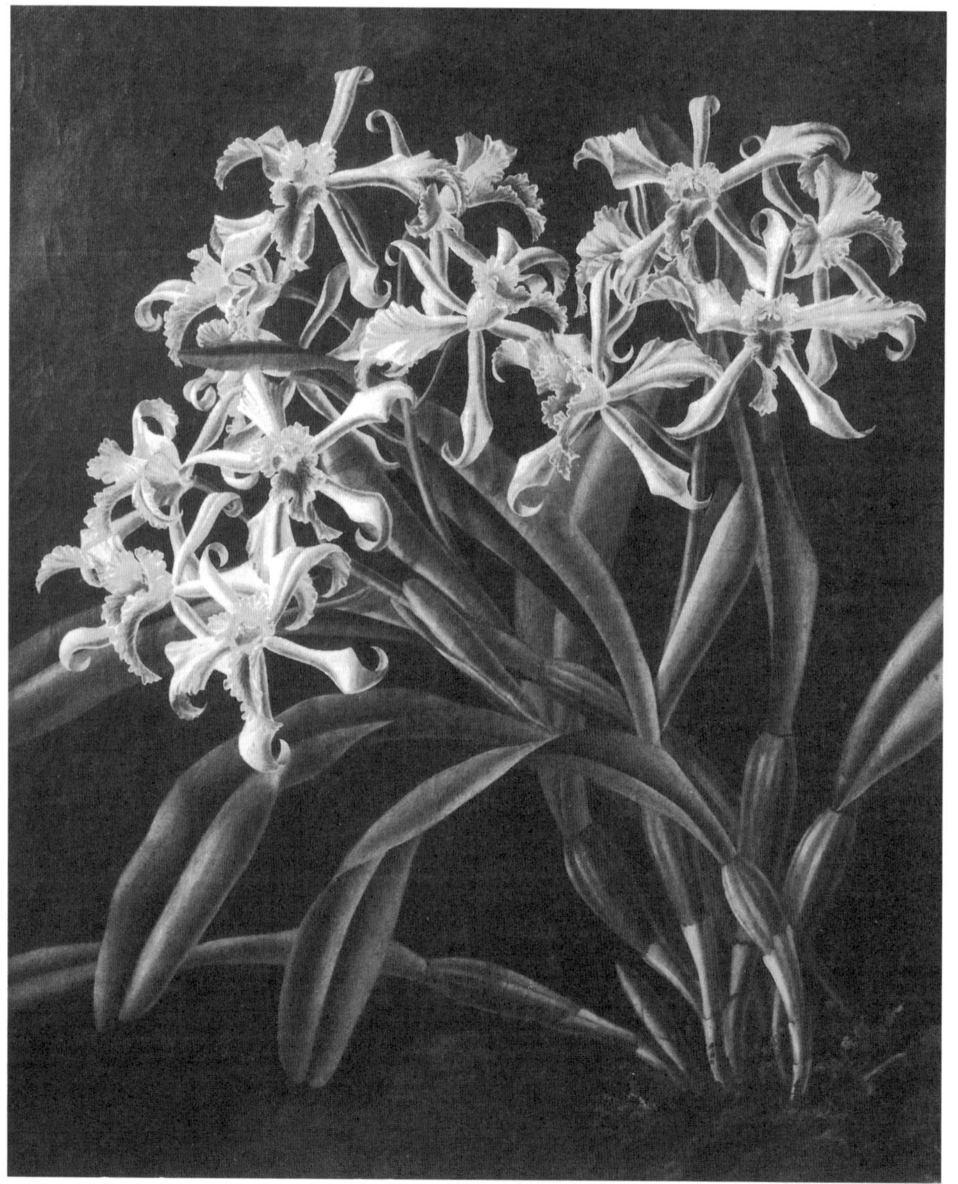

Raoul-Henry Maucherat de Longpré

Gouache on brown paper, $25\frac{1}{2} \times 19\frac{1}{2}$ in.
(64.8×49.5 cm.), signed
Courtesy Christie's, New York

Maxime-Emile-Louis-Maufra

Oil on canvas, $25\frac{1}{2} \times 21\frac{3}{4}$ in. (65.2 × 80.6 cm.), signed and dated 1909
Courtesy Sotheby's, London

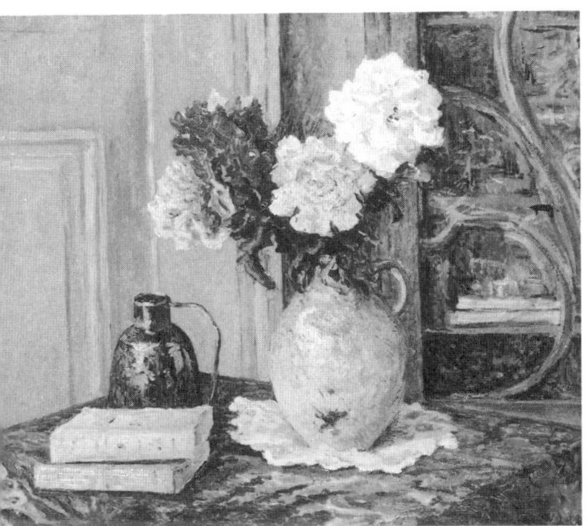

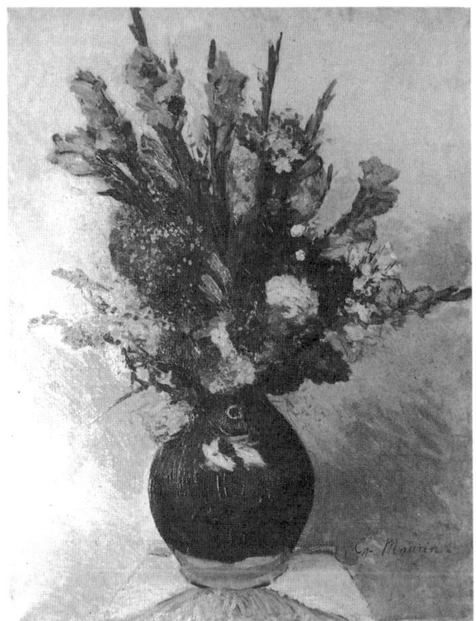

Charles Maurin

Oil on canvas, $38\frac{1}{4} \times 30\frac{3}{4}$ in. (97 × 78 cm.), signed
Private collection (photo: Musée Crozatier, Le-Puy-en-Vélay)

MAUFRA, Maxime-Emile-Louis
1861–1918
b. Nantes. A prolific landscape painter of the Post-Impressionist period who occasionally painted flowers. Friend of Gauguin and Sérusier; frequent contacts with the Nabis. A notable retrospective was held in Paris in 1950 by Rene Domerque.
LIT Arsène Alexandre, *Maxime Maufra*, Paris 1926. PM

MAULNOIR, Esther de, *née* Clavier
1796–1843
Pupil of Redouté, perhaps the same as or a namesake of the miniature painter (1796–1843). Exhib. *Bouquet de roses, acacias et belles de jour*, wc, Dijon Salon 1840. The Paris Salon selection committee rejected her 1843 exhibit
LIT *Dijon Salon* 1840; *Hardouin-Fugier* 1981; *Schidlof*; *Thieme*

MAURIN, Charles *1854–1914*
b. Le Puy (Haute-Loire). Painted genre, figures and, occasionally, flowers e.g. *Vases rustiques avec fleurs*, c.1890. Musée Crozatier, Le Puy

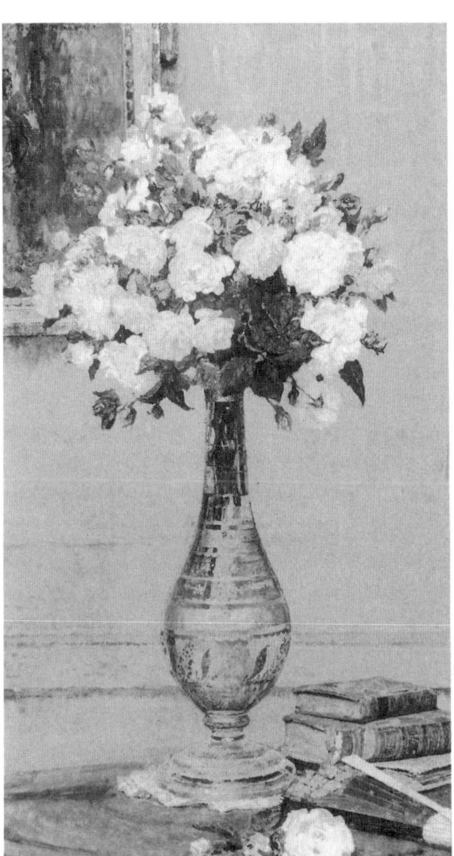

LIT *Bénézit*; R. Gounot, *C. Maurin*, Le Puy. Musée Crozatier, 1978; Witt

MAURIN, Pierre
Pupil of Berjon, Lyon BA (CFD 1820)
LIT *Hardouin-Fugier Grafe*

MAUVOISIN, Louis-François
Sannois (Val-d'Oise). Exhib. *Bourriche de giroflées*, *Bourriche de pensées*, Paris Indép. 1893
LIT *Paris Indép.* 1893

MAUZET, François-Antoine *b.1821*
Pupil of Thierriat, Lyon BA (CFD 1838)
LIT *Hardouin-Fugier Grafe*

MAVUYOT, Mlle
Exhib. *Fleurs*, Paris Indép. 1884
LIT *Paris Indép.* 1884

MAXENCE, Edgar *1871–1954*
b. Nantes (Loire-Atlantique). Pupil of G. Moreau and E. Delaunay. Painted portraits, figures, landscapes and, occasionally, flowers. Exhib. Paris Salon from 1898. Paris BMAD (Maciet coll.) *Fleurs*; Paris Musée d'Orsay, *Bouquet de fleurs des champs*
LIT *Bénézit*; *Paris BMAD*; *Schurr* I, 128; *Thieme*; Witt

MAYOUX, Jean-Etienne *b.1823*
Pupil of Thierriat, Lyon BA (CFD 1842)
LIT *Hardouin-Fugier Grafe*

MAYOUX, Jean-François-Marie
Pupil of Thierriat, Lyon BA (CFD 1842)
LIT *Hardouin-Fugier Grafe*

Edgar Maxence

Oil on board, $35\frac{1}{2} \times 19\frac{3}{4}$ in. (90 × 50 cm.), signed
Courtesy Sotheby's, London

MAYRE, Charles-Etienne-Nicolas
b. Choisy-le-Roy (Val-de-Marne). Pupil of Drolling and Cogniet. Painted genre, portraits, still-lifes and flowers. Exhib. Paris Salon from 1846. e.g. *Fleurs*, 1870, 1880
LIT *Bellier*; *Bénézit*; *Paris Salon* 1880; *Thieme*

MAYRÉNA de, *see* DAVID

MAZAROZ, Antoine-Désiré *1814–c.1876*
b. Lons-le-Saunier (Jura). Pupil of Dijon BA. Painted genre and flowers. Exhib. *Vase de fleurs dans un paysage*, Lons-le-Saunier Salon 1876
LIT *Bénézit*; *Brune*; *Lons-le-Saunier Salon* 1876. JLM

MAZAYER, Benoit *b.1832*
Pupil of Reignier, Lyon BA (CFD 1855)
LIT *Hardouin-Fugier Grafe*

MAZEAU, *see* CHOPARD

MAZELINE, Jehanne, *née* Heuzé
b. Rouen (Seine-Maritime). Pupil of C. Giraud, Giacomelli and Lemaire. Painted landscapes, portraits and flowers, mostly in wc. Exhib. Paris Salon 1878–1909 e.g. *Roses de Nice*, wc, 1879, *Rhododendron*, wc, 1880
LIT *Bellier*; *Bénézit*; *Orsay*; *Thieme*

MAZOT, Angeline
Exhib. wc Paris Salon *Bouquet de roses cent feuilles et roses mousseuses*, 1844, *Fleurs diverses dans un vase avec couronne de roses sur une table de marbre*, 1845
LIT *Bellier*; *Bénézit*; *Paris Salon* 1844, 1845

MÉCHIN, Louis
b. Paris. Exhib. *Roses*, gouache, Paris Noir et Blanc Salon 1888
LIT *Paris Noir et Blanc Salon* 1888

MÉCHIN, *see* FONTANES

MÉDARD, Jules *1855–c.1925*
b. Anzin (Nord). Pupil of Reignier, Lyon BA (CFD 1871). A popular painter and teacher. Exhib. Lyon Salon from *c.*1880. Lyon, Musée des Beaux-Arts, *Couronne de camélias*
LIT *Hardouin-Fugier Grafe*; *Hardouin-Fugier Grafe* 1979 (ill.); *Hardouin-Fugier Grafe* 1982 (ill.)

MÉDARD, Virginie, *née* Joannis
Pupil of Redouté, Van Dael and L. Cogniet. Exhib. Paris Salon 1835–1870, e.g. *Roses dans une carafe*, 1842, *Plante d'eau*, pastel, 1868. Exhib. Dijon Salon *Corbeille de fleurs*, 1840. M: Cambridge, Fitzwilliam Museum (Broughton coll.), Bordeaux (signed *élève de Van Dael*, 1875); Orléans
LIT *Bellier*; *Bénézit*; *Hardouin-Fugier* 1981 (ill.); *Thieme*

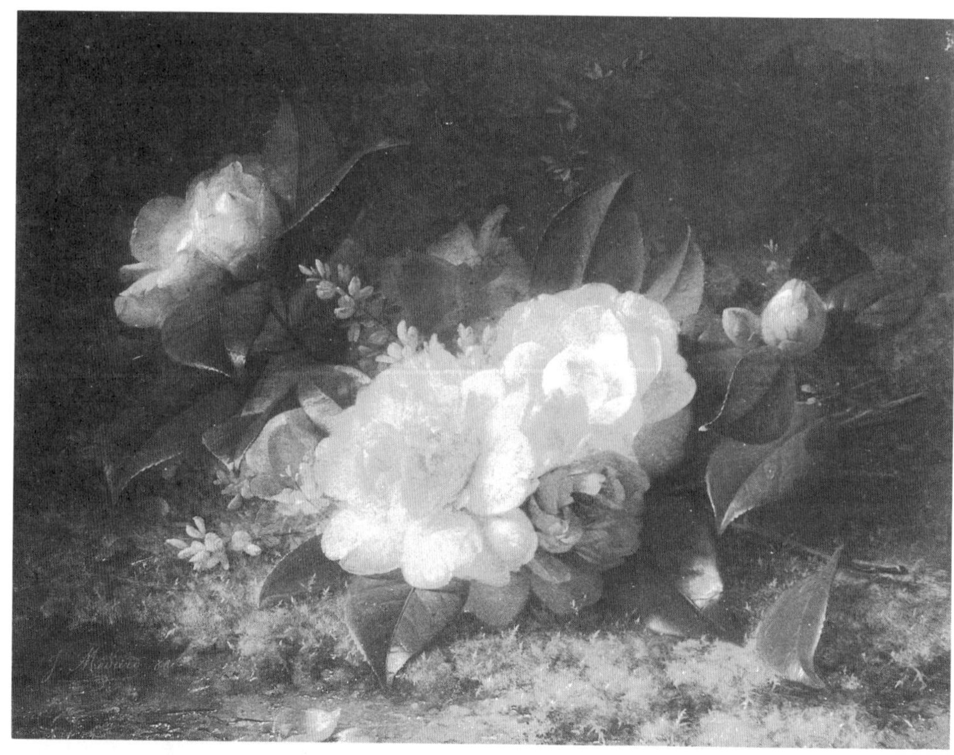

Jules Médard

Oil on panel, 13 × 16 in. (33 × 41 cm.), signed and dated 1888
Private collection, Courtesy Musée des Beaux-Arts, Lyon

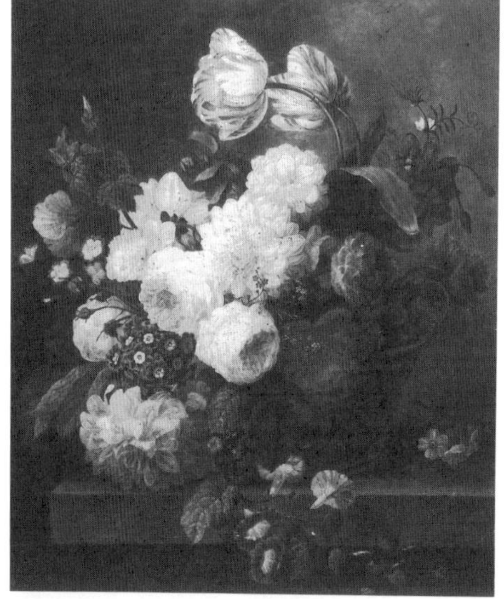

Virginie Médard

Watercolour, $24\frac{1}{2}$ × 21 in. (63 × 53 cm.), signed 'Virg. Médard, élève de Vandael. 1840'
Bordeaux, Musée des Beaux-Arts

MEGE, Lydia-Marie, *née* Hugot
Exhib. Paris Salon *Roses*, wc 1841, *Fleurs*, wc, 1842, *Bouquet composé*, on porcelain, 1843, *Fleurs*, wc, 1844
LIT *Bellier*; *Bénézit*; *Paris Salon* 1841–1844

MEISTER, Pierre *b.1814*
b. Colmar (Haut-Rhin). Pupil of H. Lebert. Exhib. Paris Salon 1861–1880 e.g. *Vase de fleurs*, 1861, *Fleur des champs*, 1867. Exhib. Strasbourg Salon *Croix entourée de guirlandes*, *Vierge entourée de guirlandes* (100 francs), 1856, *Bouquet de fleurs des champs* (800 francs) 1883. Musée de Colmar, *Roses dans un vase*
LIT *Bellier*; *Bénézit*; *Paris Salon* 1861, 1867; *Strasbourg Salon* 1856 *Thieme*

MELET, Hippolyte, *b.1870*
Pupil of Castex-Dégrange, Lyon BA (CFD 1891)
LIT *Hardouin-Fugier Grafe*

MELEY, *see* MILLIOUD

MELINAND, Antoine *b.1875*
Pupil of Castex-Dégrange, Lyon BA (CFD 1891)
LIT *Hardouin-Fugier Grafe*

MELLETON, Jean *1832–1899*
Textile designer, Lyon. Designed set of plates, *Compositions pittoresques à l'usage de l'industrie*. Exhib. gouaches Lyon Salon 1877, 1879
LIT *Hardouin-Fugier Grafe*

MENAGER, Fernand-Louis
b. Nantes (Loire-Atlantique). Pupil of Boisville. Exhib. *Capucines*, Paris Salon 1898
LIT *Paris Salon* 1898

MÉNARD, *see* BINET

MÉNÉTRIER
Designed a chromolithograph *Bouquet dans une coupe*, *c.*1885, Paris BMAD (Maciet coll.)
LIT *Paris BMAD*

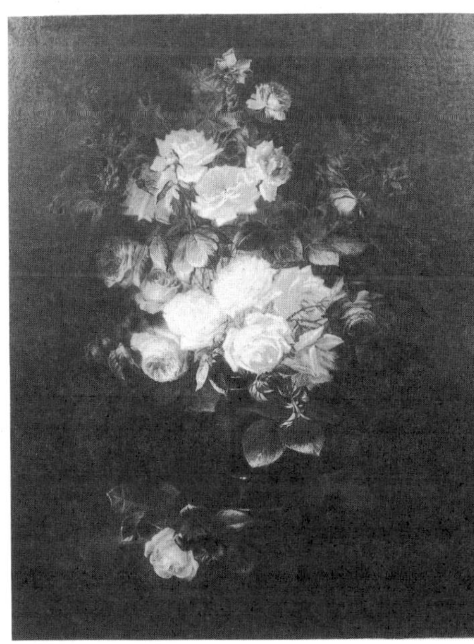

Pierre Meister

Oil on canvas, $39\frac{1}{2} \times 32$ in. (100 × 81 cm.), signed
Colmar, Musée d'Unterlinden

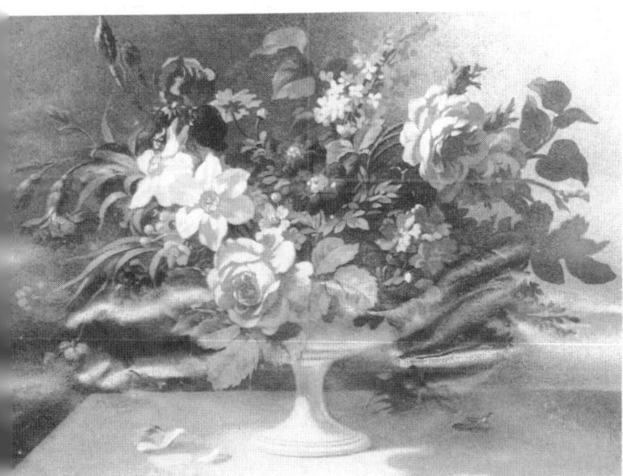

Ménétrier

Chromolithograph after a drawing, $8\frac{3}{4} \times 7\frac{1}{2}$ in. (22 × 19 cm.)
Paris, BMAD (Maciet Collection)

MÉRARD, Marguerite
Pupil of Barriot, T. Tollet and Filliard. Active in Lyon. Exhib. Lyon Salon from *c.*1894
LIT *Hardouin-Fugier Grafe*

MERAY, Hugues
Exhib. *Chrysanthèmes*, Dijon Salon 1894
LIT *Dijon Salon* 1894. CL

MERCIER, Louise
b. Paris. Pupil of C. J. Mercier, her father, and Jules Lefebvre. Exhib. 1879–1907 e.g. *Pivoines et cytises*, Paris UFPS 1896
LIT *Bénézit*; *Paris UFPS* 1896

MERCIER, Ruth
Cannes (Alpes-Maritimes) address (1894). Painted landscapes and flowers often in wc. Exhib. Paris Salon from 1880 and SNBA *Fleurs*, pastel, 1890, *Oeillets*, 1892, *Pensées*, wc, 1893, *Anémones blanches et violettes*, *Anémones rouges et blanches*, 1894, *Roses blanches, magenta et jaunes*, *Roses et pot noir*, wc, *Anémones sur fond vert*, *Oeillets magenta et rose*, wc, 1895, *Violettes*, *Roses*, fan-leaf, *Couronne de roses blanches*, 1897. Musée de Dax, *Roses* (currently untraceable). Presented her 1895 *Étude de roses* to the Musée du Luxembourg (Paris)
LIT *Bénézit*; *Orsay*; Paris Arch. Nat. F21: 2148; *Paris SNBA* 1890, 1892–1895, 1897

MERCIER, *see* LIGNY

MERIGOT, Maximilien-Ferdinand *1822–1884*
b. Paris. op. Sèvres 1845–1872. Musée de Sèvres
LIT *Bénézit*; *Brunet Préaud*; *Thieme*

MÉRINO
Exhib. *Fleurs et fruits*, Paris Société des Amis-des-Arts 1874
LIT *Paris Amis-des-Arts* 1874

MERKLIN, Jules
Exhib. *Pivoines* (100 francs) Strasbourg Salon 1891
LIT *Strasbourg Salon* 1891

MERLET ***b.1841***
Pupil of Reignier, Lyon BA (CFD 1858)
LIT *Hardouin-Fugier Grafe*

MERMET, Hippolyte ***b.1867***
Pupil of Castex-Dégrange, Lyon BA (CFD 1887)
LIT *Hardouin-Fugier Grafe*

MERWART, Paul ***1855–1902***
b. Marianowska (Russia). Naturalized French. Pupil of Vienna and Dusseldorf art schools and H. Lehmann. Exhib. *Fleurs* Paris Noir et Blanc Salon 1886
LIT *Paris Noir et Blanc Salon* 1886; *Thieme*

MÉRY, Alfred-Emile ***1824–1896***
b. Paris. Pupil of Beaucé. Painted landscapes, birds, insects and, occasionally, flowers. Exhib. Paris Salon from 1848 e.g. *Digitale*, gouache, 1867. His *Fleurs de l'air et fleurs de la terre* was bought by the government (1,200 francs) in 1893. M: Montauban
LIT *Bellier*; *Bénézit*; Paris Arch. Nat. F21: 41; D. Ternois, *Ingres et son temps*, Musée Ingres, Montauban, 1965 (ill.); Witt

MÉRY, Eugénie
b. Paris. Pupil of Mme Cavé and Pommayrac. Painted figures, animals and flowers (wc 1870 after the Van Dael in the Louvre)
LIT *Bénézit*

MESNIER, Marie
Pupil of B. Copreaux. Exhib. *Coquelicots*, *Soleils*, *Roses trémières*, *Paris UFPS* 1896
LIT Paris UFPS 1896

METRAT ***b.1812***
Pupil of Thierriat, Lyon BA (CFD 1832)
LIT *Hardouin-Fugier Grafe*

METZ, Emilie de
Exhib. *Bourriche d'anémones*, *Panier de chrysanthèmes*, Paris UFPS 1896
LIT *Paris UFPS* 1896

MEUNIÉ, Paul-Henri
b. Paris. Exhib. Paris Indép. *Fleurs*, 1892, *Chrysanthèmes*, wc 1896; Paris SNBA *Boules de neige*, wc, 1894, *Roses trémières*, wc, 1895, 1897
LIT *Paris Indép.* 1892, 1896; *Paris SNBA* 1894, 1895, 1897

MEUNIER
Active in Lyon. Entered 1842 FDC
LIT *Hardouin-Fugier Grafe*

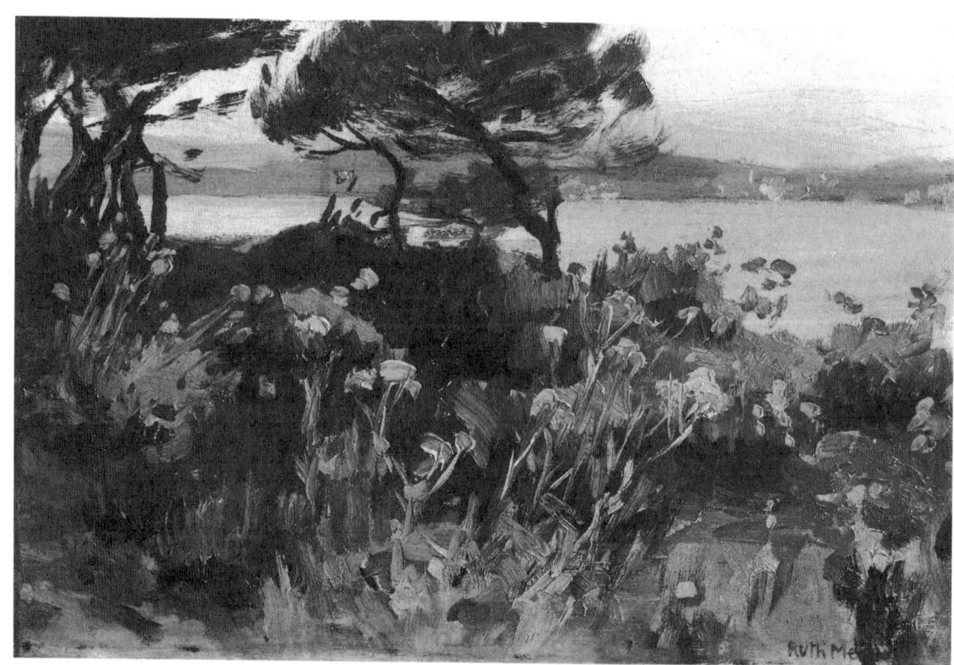

Ruth Mercier

Oil on canvas, $6\frac{7}{8} \times 10\frac{1}{2}$ in. (15.4 × 26.7 cm.), signed
Courtesy Christie's, London

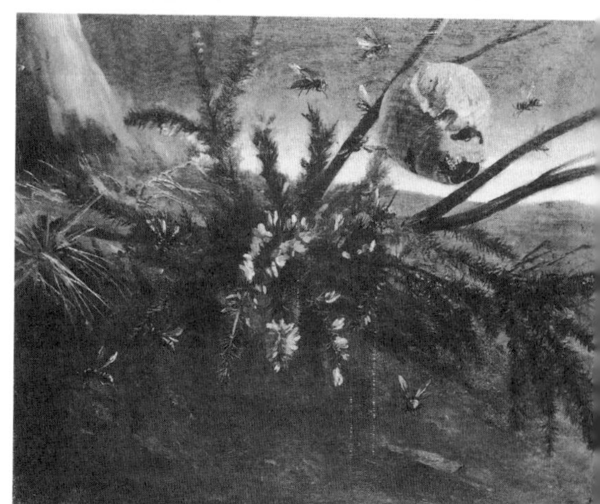

Alfred-Emile Méry

'Nid de Guêpes'
Oil on canvas, signed and dated '65
$13 \times 15\frac{3}{4}$ in. (33 × 40 cm.)
Montauban, Musée Ingres

MEUNIER, Caroline
Exhib. *Bourriche de marguerites*, Paris Indép. 1884
LIT *Paris Indép.* 1884

MEUNIER, Henriette-Caroline
Pupil of L. Desnos. Painted still-lifes and flowers. Exhib. Paris Salon 1866 and 1870 e.g. *Fleurs et fruits*, 1866
LIT *Bellier*; *Bénézit*

MEUNIER, J. A.
Exhib. *Roses trémières*, Paris SNBA 1890
LIT *Paris SNBA* 1890

MEYER, Auguste
b. Paris. Pupil of F. Dubois. Exhib. Paris Salon 1859–1868. e.g. *Fleurs*, 1861. *Roses*, signed A. Meyer, in the Musée des Beaux-Arts Bordeaux, may be by this artist
LIT *Bénézit*; *Paris Salon* 1861

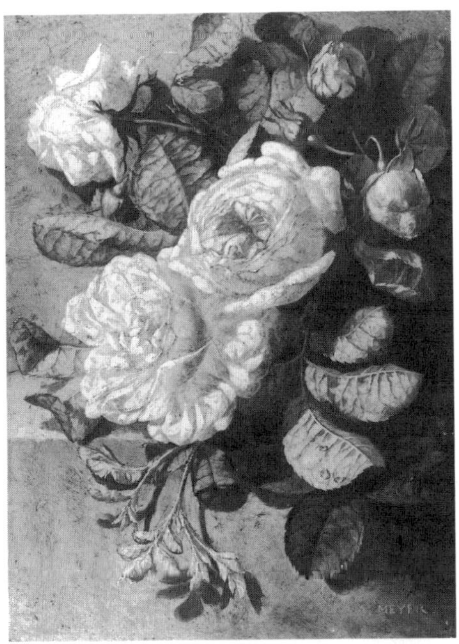

Auguste Meyer

Oil on canvas, 12½ × 9½ in. (32 × 24 cm.), signed
Bordeaux, Musée des Beaux-Arts

MEYER, Paul-Eugène ***b.1839***
Pupil of Reignier, Lyon BA (CFD 1859)
LIT *Hardouin-Fugier Grafe*

MEZ, Jeanne
Exhib. *Chrysanthèmes*, Paris Indép. 1884
LIT *Paris Indép.* 1884

MICARD, Etienne
Pupil of Berjon, Lyon BA (CFD 1811)
LIT *Hardouin-Fugier Grafe*

MICARD, Philippe
Pupil of Berjon, Lyon BA (CFD 1812)
LIT *Hardouin-Fugier Grafe*

MICHALLOT, Jean-Marie ***b.1819***
Pupil of Thierriat, Lyon BA (CFD 1839)
LIT *Hardouin-Fugier-Grafe*

MICHAUD, Antoine
b. Châlon-sur-Saône (Saône-et-Loire). Pupil of Thierriat, Lyon BA (CFD 1834). Exhib. *Groupe de fleurs*, wc, Lyon Salon 1867
LIT *Hardouin-Fugier Grafe*; *Lyon Salon* 1867

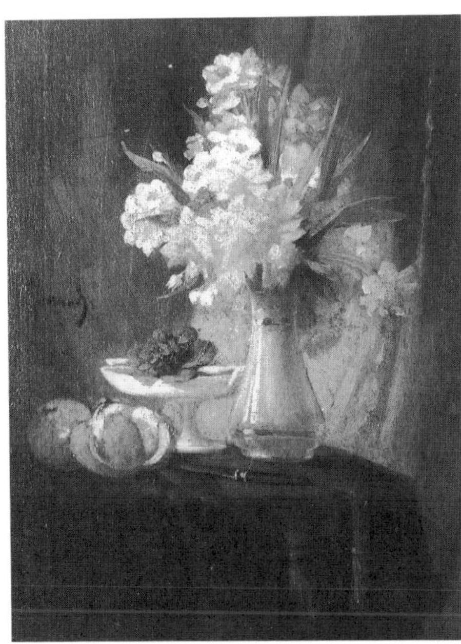

Joseph-François Michaud

Oil on panel, 12½ × 10 in. (32 × 25 cm.), signed
Private collection

MICHAUD, Hippolyte ***1813–1886***
b. Beaune (Côte-d'Or). Pupil of Devosge. Painted still-lifes, fruit and, occasionally, flowers
LIT *Schurr* I, 84; *Thieme*

MICHAUD, Joseph-François
Active in Lyon. Pupil of Reignier. Exhib. Lyon Salon 1867–1884 e.g. *Le jour des morts, fleurs*, 1884
LIT *Hardouin-Fugier Grafe*; *Lyon Salon* 1884

MICHAUD-MEUNIER
Pupil of Reignier. Exhib. Lyon Salon *Fleurs*, gouache, 1863, *Fleurs*, 1865
LIT *Lyon Salon* 1863, 1865

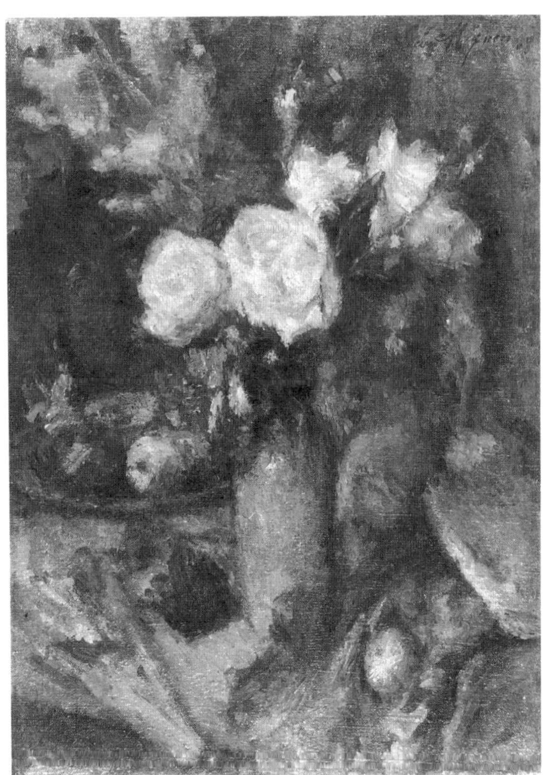

Lucien Mignon

Oil on canvas, 17¾ × 20¾ in. (45 × 53 cm.), signed and dated 1898
Angers, Musée des Beaux-Arts

MICHEA, Laure
Active Lyon. Pupil of S. Olivier and Castex-Dégrange. Exhib. Lyon Salon e.g. *Chrysanthèmes*, 1894
LIT *Hardouin-Fugier Grafe*

MICHEL
Exhib. Lyon Salon 1861, *Fleurs*
LIT *Hardouin-Fugier Grafe*; *Lyon Salon* 1861

MICHEL, Mlle Camille
Exhib. Dijon Salon *Primevères*, 1892, *Fleurs d'automne*, 1894
LIT *Dijon Salon* 1892, 1894. CL

MICOL, Antoine *b.1821*
Pupil of Thierriat, Lyon BA (CFD 1841)
LIT *Hardouin-Fugier Grafe*

MICOL, Jules *b.1822*
Pupil of Thierriat, Lyon BA (CFD 1841). Exhib. Lyon Salon 1867
LIT *Hardouin-Fugier Grafe*

MIEL, *see* VERNAY

MIGNON, Lucien *1865–1944*
b. Château-Gontier (Mayenne). Pupil of Gérôme, Paris BA. Painted figures, still-lifes and flowers, these being often 20th-century works. Exhib. Paris SNBA *Chrysanthèmes*, wc, 1894. Musée d'Angers. *Fleurs et fruits*, 1898 (gift of State 1909)
LIT *Bénézit*; Paris Arch. Nat. F21: 2099, 4500; *Paris SNBA* 1894; *Schurr* III, 143; *Thieme*; Witt

MIGNOT, A. Edouard
Active *c*.1870–1903. Designed plates for A. Jordan *Icones ad floram Europae* ...Paris 1866–1903
LIT *Nissen* I, 1008

MIGNOT, André *1839–1874*
Co-designed (with Ramboz) *Eléments généraux de botanique pratique*...Lyon 1869
LIT *Audin Vial*

MIKEL, Ferté *fl.1809–1818*
Painted flowers. One known work, *Spray of Flowers*, 1813, wc, in Cambridge, Fitzwilliam Museum (Broughton coll.)
LIT *Busse*. JLC

MILET, *see* DECAUX

MILLERON, Jean *b.1828*
Pupil of Thierriat, Lyon BA (CFD 1845)
LIT *Hardouin-Fugier Grafe*

MILLET, Jean-François *1814–1875*
b. Gruchy near Cherbourg (Manche). Pupil of Paul Delaroche. Mostly a landscape and figure painter. His Orsay *Bouquet de marguerites*, 1871–1874

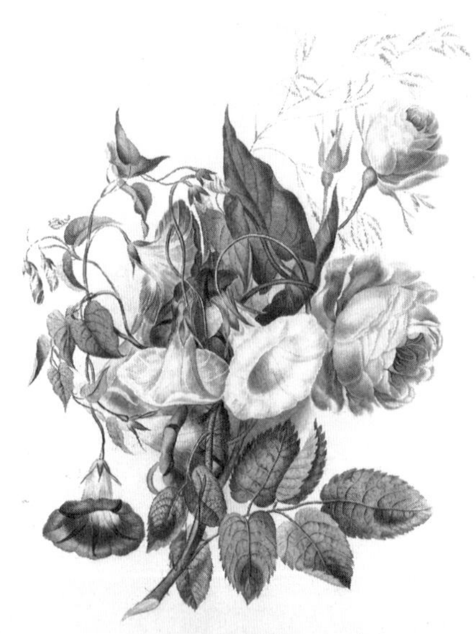

Ferté Mikel

Watercolour, $14\frac{5}{8} \times 11\frac{5}{8}$ in. (37.2 × 29.9 cm.), signed and dated 'Ferté Mikel Del, Sept. 1813'
Cambridge, Fitzwilliam Museum
(Broughton Collection)

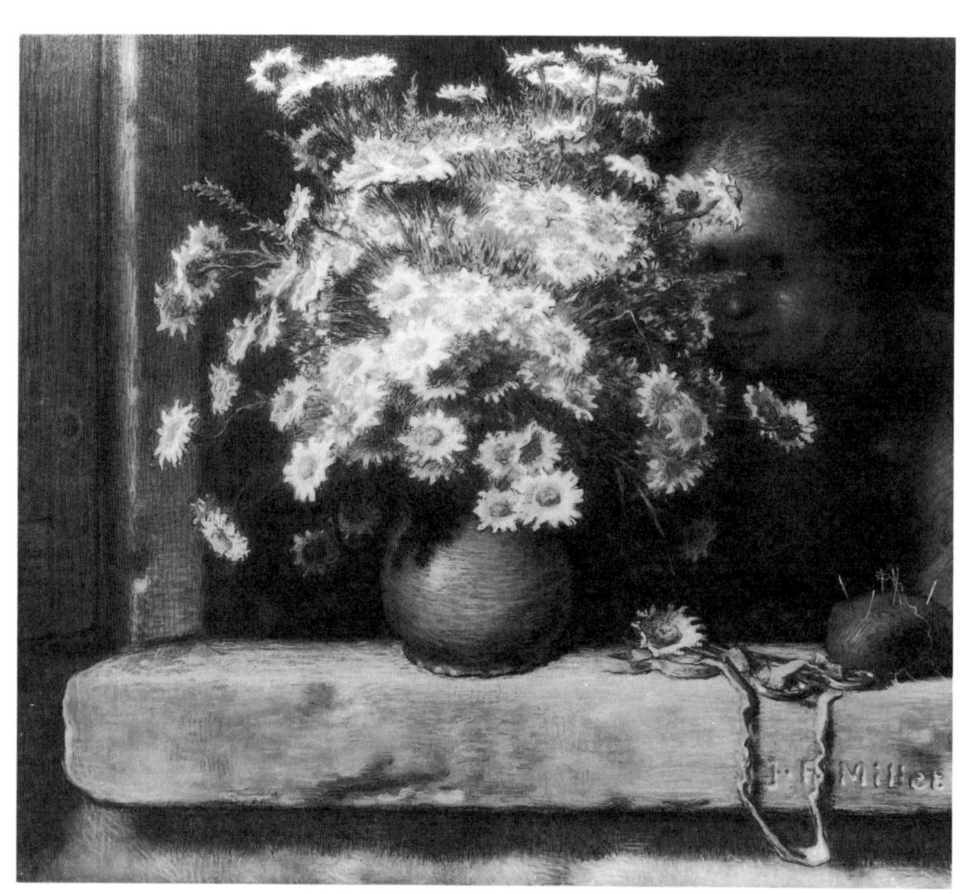

Jean-François Millet

Pastel on paper, $27 \times 32\frac{3}{4}$ in. (68 × 83 cm.), signed
Paris, Musée d'Orsay

(pastel) and his *Jonquilles* (pastel) *c.*1867 are two of his very few paintings of flowers. M: Paris, Louvre, Orsay
LIT Paris, *J. F. Millet*, Grand Palais, Réunion des Musées Nationaux, 1975–1976; L. Le Poittevin. *J. F. Millet ou l'ambiguîté de l'image*, Paris (Laget) 1973; *Witt* AC

MILLIOUD-MELEY, Gabrielle ***1875–1931***
Pupil of F. Vernay, Lyon BA, J. Martin and C. Bret-Charbonnier. Painted landscapes, still-lifes and flowers. Exhib. Lyon Salon e.g. *Fleurs de géranium*, gouache, 1895
LIT *Hardouin-Fugier Grafe*

MILLIOZ, Jules ***b.1834***
Pupil of Reignier, Lyon BA (CFD 1860)
LIT *Hardouin-Fugier Grafe*

MILLON, Jean ***b.1826***
Pupil of Thierriat, Lyon BA (CFD 1843)
LIT *Hardouin-Fugier Grafe*

MILLOT, Lucie
Pupil of F. Delacroix and Mme Delacroix-Garnier. Exhib. Paris UFPS *Chrysanthèmes*, *Envoi de roses*, pastel, 1896
LIT *Paris UFPS* 1896

MINET, Louis-Emile ***d.c.1920***
b. Rouen (Seine-Maritime). Pupil of Rudaux and H. Morin. Painted landscapes and, occasionally, flowers. Exhib. Paris Salon from 1876 e.g. *Fleurs des champs* 1878, 1881; Dijon Salon, *Primevères et pensées*, 1881. His *Fleurs* used to be in the Musée de Caen (acquired 1883; destroyed)
LIT *Bellier*; *Bénézit*; *Dijon Salon* 1881; *Thieme*; *Witt*

MINGARD, Jean-Louis-Clément
Pupil of Thierriat, Lyon BA (CFD 1843)
LIT *Hardouin-Fugier Grafe*

MINOT, Blanche
b. Charenton (Val-de-Marne). Pupil of L. Mercier. Exhib. *Chrysanthèmes*, *Iris d'eau*, Paris Salon 1885; *Ronces*, wc, Paris Noir et Blanc Salon 1888
LIT *Paris Noir et Blanc Salon* 1888; *Paris Salon* 1885

MIRBEL, B.
Designed plates for Palisot *Flore...de Bénin*, Paris 1804. This may be Brisseau de Mirbel, the botanist who married Lizinka Rue, the famous miniature painter (1796–1849) in 1824
LIT *Nissen* I, 1481

MIROL, Michel
Exhib. Paris Indép. *Fleurs*, 1890, *Fleurs des champs*, 1893
LIT *Paris Indép.* 1890, 1893

MISSET, Adèle
Pupil of Attendu and P. Bourgogne. Exhib. *Lilas*, Paris UFPS 1898
LIT *Paris UFPS* 1898

MITTEY, Joseph ***b.1853***
b. Vix (Côte-d'Or). Pupil of Jeannin, Lequien, Hugot and Turin. Painted figures and flowers; Ceramic artist (Petit-Lancy near Geneva) and art teacher (École des Arts Industriels, Geneva). Painted figures and flowers. Exhib. Paris Salon from 1877 e.g. *Giroflées*, 1877, *Fleurs*, wc, 1880, *Une terrasse à Glion*, 1885. Exhib. Dijon Salon *Le renouveau, fleurs*, 1890
LIT *Bellier*; *Bénézit*; *Brune*; *Dijon Salon* 1890; *Paris Salon* 1880, 1885 (ill.); *Thieme*

MITTON, Mathilde
Pupil of Perrachon. Exhib. Lyon Salon e.g. *Roses*, 1894
LIT *Hardouin-Fugier Grafe*

ML., Mlle
Pupil of Puyroche-Wagner and F. Rivoire.
Exhib. *Fleurs*, wc, Lyon Salon 1885
LIT *Lyon Salon* 1885

MODAMEY, Marguerite
Exhib. Dijon Salon *Lilas*, 1890, *Gloire de Dijon*, 1892, *Fleurs*, 1894
LIT *Dijon Salon* 1890, 1892, 1894

MODERAT d'OTEMAR, Marie-Adolphe-Edouard
b. Paris. Pupil of Giraud. Painted genre, portraits, still-lifes and, occasionally, flowers. Exhib. Paris Salon from 1880 e.g. *Chrysanthèmes du Japon*, 1885; *Plantes*, *Pavots*, Paris Indép. 1893
LIT *Bellier*; *Bénézit*; *Paris Indép.* 1893.; *Paris Salon* 1885; *Thieme*

MOINE, Guillaume-César ***b.1827***
Pupil of Thierriat, Lyon BA (CFD 1844)
LIT *Hardouin-Fugier Grafe*

MOINECOURT, ***b.1804***
Pupil of Berjon, Lyon BA (CFD 1822)
LIT *Hardouin-Fugier Grafe*

MOIRAND, Emilie
Pupil of Mme Emeric-Bouvret and Barré. Exhib. Paris Salon from 1864 e.g. *Fleurs*, after Van Spaendonck, on porcelain, 1864, 1865, *Fleurs dans un vase bleu*, on porcelain, 1868
LIT *Bellier*

MOISSON-DESROCHES, Elise
b. Rodez (Aveyron). Pupil of Couture and Emeric. Painted genre and flowers. Exhib. Paris Salon 1861–1869 e.g. *Fleurs*, 1861
LIT *Bellier*; *Bénézit*; *Paris Salon* 1861; *Thieme*

MOISSONNIER, Julie
Pupil of J. Médard Exhib. Lyon Salon *Roses*, 1880, *Fleurs*, 1881, 1882, 1883, *Roses et coquille*, *Portrait et chrysanthèmes*, 1884; Dijon Salon *Azalées et marguerites*, 1880, *Roses*, *Pivoines*, 1881, *Chrysanthèmes*, gouache, *Fleurs et fruits*, 1892; Grenoble Salon, *Fleurs*, gouache, 1880

LIT *Dijon Salon* 1880, 1881, 1892; *Grenoble Salon* 1880; *Hardouin-Fugier Grafe*; *Lyon Salon* 1880–1884

MOLAS, Marie-Désiré ***b.1832***
Pupil of Reignier, Lyon BA (CFD 1854)
LIT *Hardouin-Fugier Grafe*

MOLET, Joseph ***b.1817***
Pupil of Thierriat, Lyon BA (CFD 1836)
LIT *Hardouin-Fugier Grafe*

MOLET, Joseph ***1829–c.1851***
Pupil of Thierriat, Lyon BA (CFD 1848)
LIT *Hardouin-Fugier Grafe*

MOLLARD, Jean-Louis ***b.1841***
Pupil of Reignier, Lyon BA (CFD 1858)
LIT *Hardouin-Fugier Grafe*

MOLLIET, C.
Exhib. Paris SNBA *Fleurs des prés*, pastel, 1896, *Le Lis*, 1899
LIT *Paris SNBA* 1896, 1899

MOLTER, Jacques ***b.1812***
Pupil of Thierriat, Lyon BA (CFD 1836). Textile designer, Lyon
LIT *Hardouin-Fugier Grafe*

MONATON, Philippe-Antoine ***b.1826***
Pupil of Thierriat, Lyon BA (CFD 1844)
LIT *Hardouin-Fugier Grafe*

MONBLOND, Charles
b. Paris. Pupil of C. Polisch. Painted still-lifes and flowers. Exhib. Paris Salon 1866–1870
LIT *Bénézit*

MONCHICOURT-DREVET, Madeleine
Pupil of Mme de Chatillon. Exhib. *Rose rouge*, wc, Paris UFPS 1898
LIT *Paris UFPS* 1898

MONDAN, Pierre-Louis ***b.1856***
Pupil of Reignier, Lyon BA (CFD 1872)
LIT *Hardouin-Fugier Grafe*

MONDON, Jean ***b.1852***
Pupil of Reignier, Lyon BA (CFD 1871)
LIT *Hardouin-Fugier Grafe*

MONET, Claude ***1840–1926***
b. Paris. The father of Impressionism was a pupil of Boudin and Gleyre, in whose studio he befriended Renoir, Sisley and Bazille. Monet's life-long love for flowers evolved with his gardens at Argenteuil (from 1872), Vétheuil (from 1878) and Giverny (from 1883). These he painted to the end of his life with all their features: lilacs in cloudy weather or sunshine (DW. 203, 204), flowerbeds of every kind (DW. 412, 414), blossoming apple (DW. 201, 523, 524) or plum (DW. 519, 521) trees and, of course, countless iris borders and water-lilies at Giverny. Monet was attracted by field flowers, mostly poppies, as well (e.g. DW. 377, 1146, 1255–60) and often used his various gardens as backgrounds for his figures or outdoor scenes. For brevity's sake, the following list has been restricted to flower-pieces, thus excluding a sizeable part of Monet's paintings of gardens. His contribution to decorative flower painting is represented by the six Durand-Ruel drawing-room doors, a unique achievement of his middle period. Monet painted very few roses. His favourite blooms were chrysanthemums, marguerites, asters, peonies, sunflowers, dahlias, gladioli, lilies and azaleas. He seems to have painted few bouquets after 1887 when he devoted most of his time to painting his beloved water-lilies. *Fleurs*, 1864 (DW. 21); *Fleurs et fruits*, 1869 (DW. 139); *Fleurs dans un pot*, 1878 (DW. 471); *Bouquet de glaïeuls et de marguerites*, 1878 (DW. 472); *Chrysanthèmes*, 1878 (Louvre DW. 492); *Capucines dans un vase bleu*, 1879 (DW. 547); *Vase de capucines*, 1879 (DW. 548); *Dahlias*, 1880 (DW. 625); *Bouquet de mauves*, 1880 (London, Courtauld DW. 626); *Asters*, 1880 (DW. 627); *Bouquet de soleils*, 1880 (New-York, Metropolitan, DW. 628); *Fleurs de topinambours*, 1880 (Washington, DW. 629) *Chrysanthèmes*, 1880 (New York, Metropolitan, DW. 634)

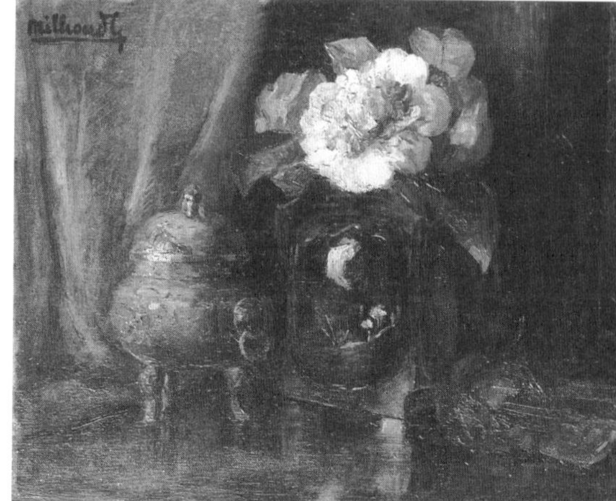

Gabrielle Millioud-Meley

Oil on canvas, 13 × 17 in. (33 × 43 cm.), signed
Private collection

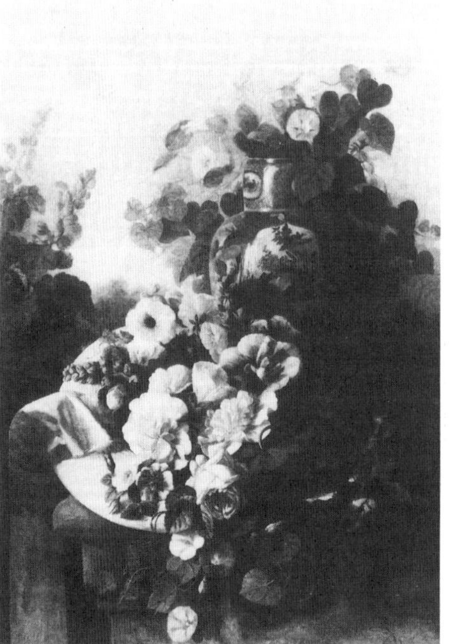

Louis-Emile Minet

Oil on canvas, 40 × 28¾ in. (101.5 × 73 cm.), signed
Courtesy Sotheby's, London

Chrysanthèmes rouges, 1880 (DW.635); *Glaïeuls*, 1881 (DW. 694, 695); *Vase de pivoines*, 1882 (DW.809); *Vase de fleurs*, 1882 (DW.810); *Roses dans un pichet bleu*, 1882 (DW.811); *Vase de chrysanthèmes*, 1882 (DW.812); *Mauves*, 1882–1883 (DW.813); *Vase de pavots*, 1883 (DW.848); *Pavots dans un vase de Chine*, 1883 (DW.849). Flowers and fruit painted on Durand-Ruel's drawing-room doors: Door A: *Pavots rouges et roses*, 1883 (DW.919); *Pavot blanc*, 1883 (DW.920); *Anémones*, 1885 (DW.921); *Jonquilles*, 1884, (DW.922); *Branche de citronnier*, 1884 (DW.923); *Oranges sur une branche*, 1884 (DW.924). Door B: *Chrysanthèmes dans un vase*, 1883 (DW.925); *Soleils*, 1883 (DW.926); *Chrysanthèmes*, 1883 (DW.927); *Jonquilles*, 1885 (DW.928); *Azalées blanches en pot*, 1885 (DW.929); *Anémones en pot*, 1885 (DW.930). Door C: *Vase de dahlias*, 1883 (DW.931); *Dahlias*, 1883 (DW.932); *Marguerites jaunes*, 1883 (DW.933); *Marguerites blanches*, 1883 (DW.934); *Pêches*, 1883–1885 (DW.935); *Pommes*, 1883–1885 (DW.936). Door D: *Dahlias*, 1883 (DW.937); *Claïeuls*, 1883 (DW.938); *Anémones*, 1885 (DW.939); *Marguerites jaunes*, 1883 (DW.940); *Trois pots de tulipes*, 1885 (DW.941); *Vase de tulipes*, 1885 (DW.942). Door E: *Azalées rouges en pot*, 1883 (DW.943), *Coléas*, 1883 (DW.944); *Branche d'azalées blanches et roses*, 1885 (DW.945, 946); *Vase de chrysanthèmes*, 1883 (DW.947); *Pot d'azalées blanches*, 1885 (DW.948). Door F: *Lys rouges*, 1883 (DW.949); *Lys du Japon*, 1883 (DW.950); *Pêches*, 1882 (DW.951, 952); *Roses de Noël*, 1883, (DW.953); *Panier de raisins, coings et poires*, 1883 (DW.954). *Tulipes dans un vase*, 1885 (DW.956); *Tulipes en pot*, 1885 (DW.957); *Pots de tulipes*, 1885 (DW.958); *Anémones*, *c*.1885 (DW.959); *Pivoines*, 1887 (Tokyo, DW. 1140); id DW. 1141, 1142, 1143); *Clématites blanches*, 1887 (Paris, Marmottan DW.1144); *Clématites*, 1887 (DW.1145); *Deux vases de chrysanthèmes*, 1888 (DW.1212). M: London, Courtauld Institute of Art; Malibu, J. Paul Getty Museum; New York, Metropolitan Museum of Art; Paris, Louvre, Orsay, Marmottan; Tokyo, National Museum of Western Art; Washington, National Gallery of Art etc.
LIT J. P. Hoschedé, *Claude Monet, ce mal connu*, Genève (Cailler) 1960; D. Wildenstein (here DW.) *Claude Monet, biographie et catalogue raisonné*, Paris-Lausanne (Bibliothèque des Arts) 1974–1979. AC

MONFREID, Georges-Daniel de 1856–1929
b. Paris. Gauguin's now well-known friend. Exhib. *Fleurs de cognassiers*, Paris Indép. 1893. M: Paris, Petit Palais, *Nature morte aux giroflées*, 1900
Lit. *Bénézit*; Galerie Charpentier, Paris *G.D. Monfreid...*1938; Galerie Jaubert, Paris, *G.D. Monfreid*, 1976; *Orsay*; *Paris Indép.* 1893; R. Puig *Gauguin...G.D. Monfreid...*Perpignan (la Tramontane) 1958; *Thieme*

MONGE, Edouard *b.1869*
Pupil of Castex-Dégrange, Lyon BA (CFD 1897)
LIT *Hardouin-Fugier Grafe*

MONGE, Joseph-Julien
b. Toulon (Var.) Exhib. *Derniers chrysanthèmes*, Paris Indép. 1893
LIT *Paris Indép.* 1893

MONGINOT, Charles *1825–1900*
b. Brienne (Aube). Pupil of Couture. Engraved and painted genre, animals and flowers. Exhib Paris Salon 1855–1881 e.g. *Un coin de palais, fleurs et fruits*, 1865, *Un camélia*, 1872; Lyon Salon *Singerie et fleurs*, 1872. M: Antwerp, Boston, Metz, Mulhouse (lost in the war); Nancy, Narbonne, Nice, Poitiers, Semur, Troyes
LIT *Bellier*; *Bénézit; Lyon Salon* 1872; *Paris Salon* 1872; *Schurr* I; 31; *Thieme*

MONGINOT, François-Antoine
Exhib. Paris Salon 1822–1850 e.g. *Fleurs*, on porcelain, 1822, *Mouchoir rempli de fleurs sur un coin de table*, 1831, *Fleurs et fruits sur une table*, *Bouquet de fleurs attaché par un ruban bleu*, wc, 1841, *Bouquet de fleurs*, on porcelain, 1848, *Fleurs*, 1850. Designed flower plates lithographed by Engelman, one dated February 1822 (Paris Bibl. Nat. Est. and BMAD Maciet coll). A namesake or the same artist known at Sèvres 1798–1799, 1801–1803
LIT *Bellier*; *Brunet Préaud*; *Bénézit*; *Faré* 1962, p. 249; Paris Bibl. Nat. Est. Jd 596; *Paris BMAD*; *Paris Salon* 1841, 1850

MONIER, Adrien *b.1868*
Pupil of Castex-Dégrange, Lyon BA (CFD 1885)
LIT *Hardouin-Fugier Grafe*

MONLUÇON, Alphonse c.*1882–1903*
Flower painter, decorator and engraver
LIT *Bénézit*; *Thieme*

MONNET-LAVERPILLIÈRE, Estelle
Lyon pupil of S. Saint-Jean. Exhib. Lyon Salon *c*.1860
LIT *Hardouin-Fugier Grafe*; *Hardouin-Fugier Grafe* 1982 (ill.)

MONPEUR, *see* VIGNAUD

MONTAGNEUX, Jean-François *b.1860*
Pupil of Reignier, Lyon BA (CFD 1881)
LIT *Hardouin-Fugier Grafe*

MONTAGNON, Jeanne-Marie-Léa
b. Gray (Haute-Saône). Pupil of E. Denis. Exhib. *Fleurs*, Paris Salon 1880
LIT *Paris Salon* 1880

MONTAGNON, Léon ***b.1879***
Pupil of Castex-Dégrange, Lyon BA (CFD 1892)
LIT *Hardouin-Fugier Grafe*

MONTAGNON, Pierre-Paul ***b.1864***
Pupil of Castex-Dégrange, Lyon BA (CFD 1885)
LIT *Hardouin-Fugier Grafe*

MONTAIGNAC-BILLOTEY, Marie-Elisabeth
b. Limoges (Haute-Vienne). Pupil of her father. Exhib. *Iris*, gouache, Paris Noir et Blanc Salon 1888; *Phlox et aster*, gouache, Paris UFPS 1898
LIT *Paris Noir et Blanc Salon* 1888; *Paris UFPS* 1898

MONTALIER, Jean-François ***b.1831***
Pupil of Thierriat, Lyon BA (CFD 1851)
LIT *Hardouin-Fugier Grafe*

MONTERBAN, Mathilde de
Exhib. *Pivoines* (180 francs), Poitiers Salon 1887
LIT *Poitiers Salon* 1887. BG

MONTESSUY, Jean-François ***1804–1876***
Painted genre, often scenes from Italian life. Exhib. Lyon Salon e.g. *Violettes*, wc, 1868
LIT *Hardouin-Fugier Grafe* 1981

MONTICELLI, Adolphe-Joseph-Thomas ***1824–1886***
b. Marseille. Pupil of Rey, Aubert and P. Delaroche. Painted figures, genre, portraits, still-lifes and flowers. Worked with Diaz. *Vase avec des fleurs*, exhib. Rotterdam, Boymans Museum 1959; *Giroflées c.*1875 exhib. Saint-Etienne *Natures mortes* 1955; *Vase de fleurs, La jardinière fleurie, Le vase renversé*, exhib. Rotterdam, Boymans Museum 1959; *Vase de fleurs*, Daber, coll., exhib. *Monticelli*, Hamburg Kunsthalle 1950; *Fleurs diverses*, exhib. Amsterdam, Van Wisselingh, 1962; *Fleurs dans une carafe*, exhib. London, A. Tooth, 1965; *Vase de marguerites*, exhib. New York, Hammer gallery 1968; *Fleurs dans un vase*, exhib. Tokyo, Sun Motoyama gallery 1971; *Vase de fleurs*, exhib. London, Fischer Fine Art 1973; *Vase de fleurs*, exhib. Paris, Galerie Schmidt, 1973. M. Lyon, Marseille, Paris (Louvre), USA Williamstown, Mass. Clark Institute etc.
LIT *Bénézit*; Galerie Cailleux, Genève, *Monticelli*, 1981–1982, A. Gouirand, *Monticelli*, Paris 1982 (Société d'Edition d'Art) 1900; G. Isnard *Monticelli*, Genève (Cailler) 1967; E. Martin *Monticelli*, Académie de Marseille 1922; Mitchell; A. Sheon, *Monticelli, his contemporaries and influence*, Pittsburgh 1978; S. Stammegna *Monticelli, catalogue des oeuvres*, Vence (Remparts) 1981

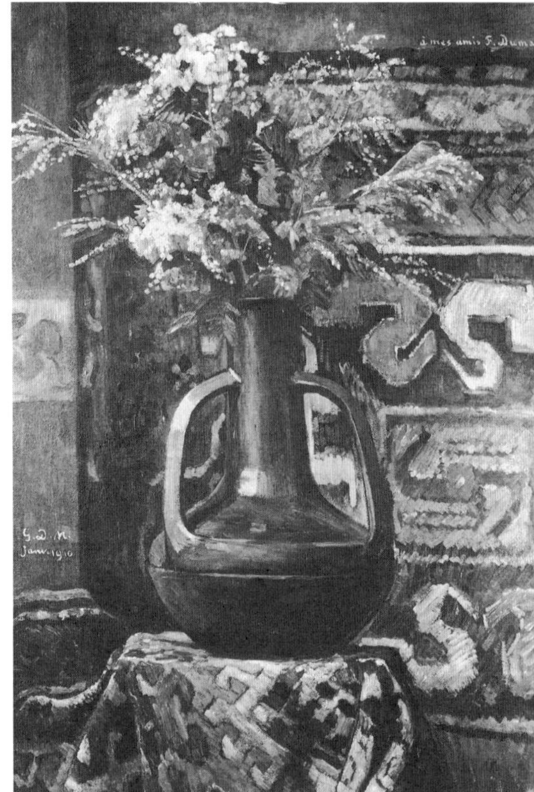

Georges Daniel de Montfreid (*right*)

Oil on paper mounted on canvas, 38 × 27¾ in. (97 × 70.5 cm.), signed and dated 'G.D.M. Janv. 1910', dedicated 'à mes amis F. Dumas'
Paris, Musée d'Orsay

Charles Monginot

Oil on panel, 12½ × 8¼ in. (32 × 21 cm.), signed
Private collection, The Netherlands
Courtesy John Mitchell & Son

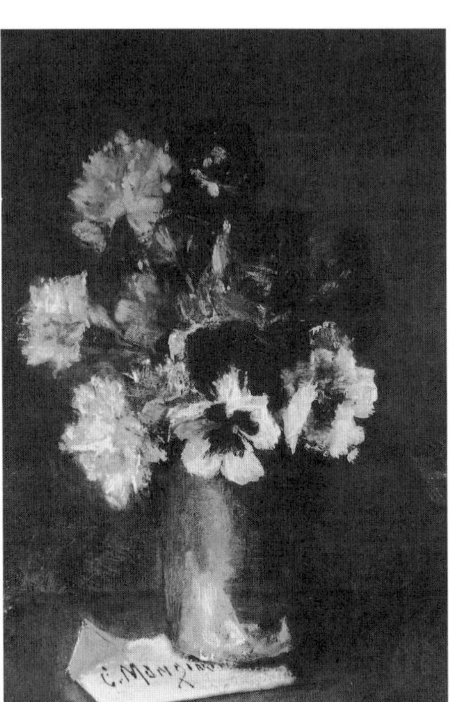

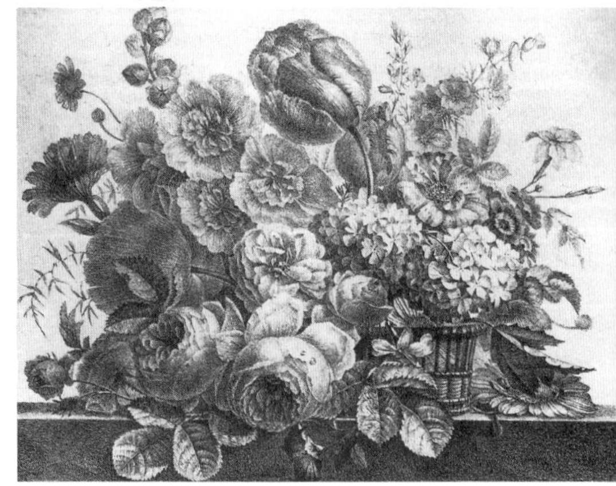

François-Antoine Monginot

Engraving after a drawing, signed
Paris, BMAD (Maciet Collection)

Camille Moreau née Nélaton

Footed dish: tin-enamelled earthenware with polychrome enamelled decoration 11¾ in. (30 cm.), in diameter, signed and dated 'Clle M'68'
Limoges, Musée National Adrien Dubouché

MONTIGNY, Léonie
b. Paris. Exhib. Paris Indép. *Brassée de roses*, 1886, *Roses*, *Fleurs*, 1888, *Pensées*, *Roses*, 1889, *Pensées*, 1890
LIT *Paris Indép.* 1886, 1888–1890

MONTPERLIER, Etienne *b.1796*
Pupil of Berjon, Lyon BA (CFD 1812)
LIT *Hardouin-Fugier Grafe*

MONVOISIN, Domenica, *née* Festa *d.1881*
b. Rome (Italy). Pupil of F. Festa, her father. Married painter R. Monvoisin (1794–1870). Painted portrait miniatures, portraits and flowers. Exhib. Paris Salon from 1831 e.g. *Fleurs*, wc, 1833. The same artist or a namesake known at Sèvres 1841–1842. Musée de Bordeaux (not a flower picture)
LIT *Bellier*; *Bénézit*; *Brunet Préaud*; *Paris Salon* 1833; *Thieme*

MOORE, Mathilde
b. Boulogne-sur-Mer (Pas-de-Calais). Pupil of Fantin-Latour senior and Burat. Exhib. *Fleur de pommier*, gouache, Paris Salon 1880; *Chrysanthèmes blancs*, Paris SNBA 1892
LIT *Bénézit*; *Paris Salon* 1880; *Paris SNBA* 1892

MORAND, Eugène-Edouard *b.1855*
b. Saint-Petersburg (Russia). Pupil of Galland. Art teacher. Director of Paris École des Arts Décoratifs. Exhib. Paris Salon *Fleurs*, wc, 1880; Paris Société des Aquarellistes, *Corbeille fleurie*, *Roses*, *Encore des roses*, 1889, *Roses et chrysanthèmes*, *Envoi de fleurs*, *Roses trémières dans une fontaine en vieux Rouen*, *Fleurs de mai*, *Roses de juin*, 1890
LIT *Bénézit*; *Paris Salon* 1880; *Paris aquar.* 1889, 1890; *Thieme*; Witt

MORAT, Jeanne
Pupil of Castex-Dégrange. Exhib. *Chrysanthèmes*, Lyon Salon 1894
LIT *Hardouin-Fugier Grafe*

MOREAU, Adolphe-Ferdinand *1827–1882*
b. Paris. Pupil of V. Tasson, A. Bonheur, C. Roqueplan and Cassagne. Painted genre, landscapes and, occasionally, flowers. Exhib. Paris Salon from 1849 e.g. *Pensées dans un pot de grès*, wc, 1873, *Fleurs*, wc, 1880.
LIT *Bellier*; *Bénézit*; *Paris Salon* 1880; *Thieme*

MOREAU, Adrien *1843–1906*
b. Troyes (Aube). Pupil of Pils. Painted genre, landscapes and, occasionally, flowers. Exhib. Paris Salon from 1868. Exhib. Paris Société des Aquarellistes *Buisson de roses*, *Iris d'eau*, 1891; *Roses trémières*, *Bouquet de fleurs*, Moreau atelier sale, Drouot, Paris, 19 Dec. 1909
LIT *Bénézit*; *Orsay*; *Paris aquar.* 1891; *Schurr* III, 73; *Thieme*

MOREAU, Camille, *née* Nélaton *1840–1897*
b. Paris. Pupil of J. Nélaton, her father and A. Bonheur. Painted genre and on porcelain. Exhib. *Hortensia*, *Mahonia*, Lyon Salon 1870
LIT *Bénézit*; K. B. Hiesinger, "C. Moreau" in *L'Art français sous le Second Empire*, Paris, Grand Palais 1979, p. 233 (ill.) *Lyon Salon* 1870; E. Moreau-Nélaton, *C. Moreau*, Paris 1899

André-Benoit Perrachon

Oil on canvas, 45¾ × 35 in. (116 × 89 cm.), signed
Lyon, Musée des Beaux-Arts

MOREAU, Gustave ***1826–1898***
b. Paris. Pupil of Picot. Flowers fraught with symbolism play an important part in Moreau's works e.g. *Fée au griffon*, 1876, *Galathée*, 1880; *Rêve oriental* (La Péri), 1881; *Filles et fleurs*, fan-leaf, 1882 (Paris, Musée Gustave Moreau). M: Paris Orsay and Gustave Moreau.
LIT P. Bittler *Catalogue des dessins de G. Moreau*, Paris, Réunion des Musées Nationaux, 1983; P. L. Mathieu, *G. Moreau*, Paris-Lausanne (Bibliothèque des Arts) 1976; *Orsay doc*; Paris, Musée Gustave Moreau doc.; *Witt*

MOREAU-FICATIER, Rosa
b. Troyes (Aube). Pupil of A. Moreau and Kreyder. Exhib. Paris Salon from 1875 e.g. *Branche de géraniums*, wc, fan-leaf, 1875, *Primevères et géraniums*, fan-leaf, 1875, *Primevères et géraniums*, fan-leaf, gouache, 1877, *Printemps en bourriche*, fan-leaf 1880
LIT *Bellier*; *Bénézit*; *Paris Salon* 1875

MOREAUX, Pierre ***b.1829***
Pupil of Thierriat, Lyon BA (CFD 1847)
LIT *Hardouin-Fugier Grafe*

MOREIGNE, Stéphanie
Pupil of Deubergue. Exhib. *Roses*, Paris UFPS 1898
LIT *Paris UFPS* 1898

MOREL, Charles-Alphonse ***b.1862***
Pupil of Reignier, Lyon BA (CFD 1878). Exhib. *Fleurs*, Lyon Salon 1885
LIT *Hardouin-Fugier Grafe*; *Lyon Salon* 1885

MOREL, Charlotte-Marie
b. Nantes (Loire-Atlantique). Pupil of Guay, J. Lefebvre and Doucet. Exhib. *Marguerites et violettes*, wc, *Bleuets*, wc, Paris Salon 1895
LIT *Paris Salon* 1895

MOREL, Hippolyte
Exhib. *Fleurs*, Paris Indép. 1884
LIT *Paris Indép.* 1884

MOREL, Julien ***b.1828***
Pupil of Thierriat, Lyon BA (CFD 1845)
LIT *Hardouin-Fugier Grafe*

MOREL, Marin
Pupil of Berjon, Lyon BA (CFD 1822)
LIT *Hardouin-Fugier Grafe*

MORELON, Charles ***b.1819***
Pupil of Thierriat, Lyon BA (CFD 1837)
LIT *Hardouin-Fugier Grafe*

MORFOUILLET, Pierre ***b.1793***
Pupil of Berjon, Lyon BA (CFD 1813)
LIT *Hardouin-Fugier Grafe*

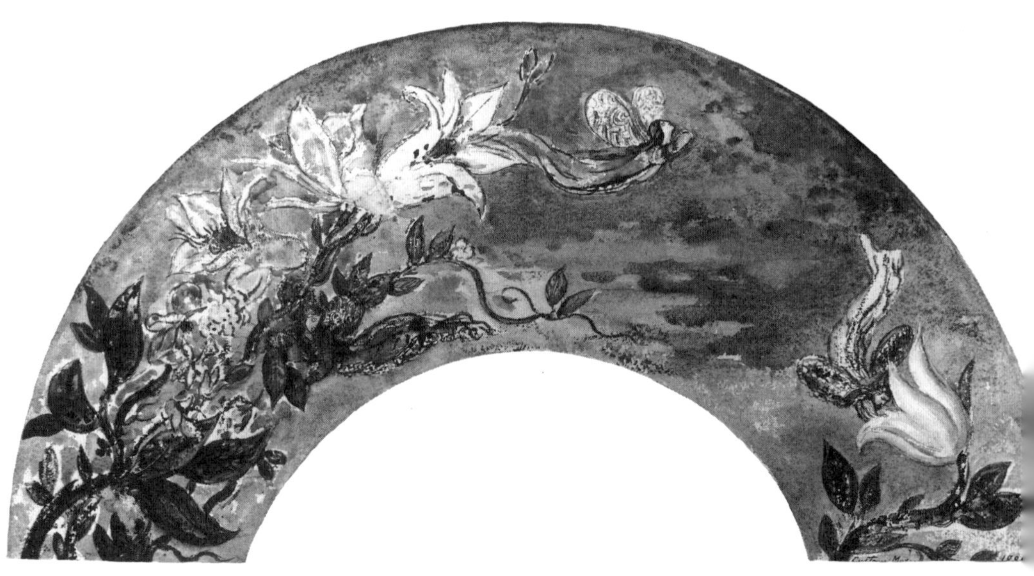

Gustave Moreau

Watercolour, signed and dated 1880
Paris, Musée Gustave Moreau

MORIN, Mathilde
Exhib. *Primevères* (250 francs), Strasbourg Salon 1891. Musée de Louviers *Chrysanthèmes et roses de Noël*
LIT *Strasbourg Salon* 1891

MORIOT, François-Adolphe ***b.1817***
op. Sèvres 1837–1844
LIT *Bénézit*; *Brunet Préaud*

MORISOT, Auguste-Ernest ***1859–1953***
b. Seurre (Côte-d'Or). Pupil of Reignier, Lyon BA (CFD 1880). Painted landscapes, figures, portraits and, occasionally, flowers
LIT *Hardouin-Fugier Grafe*; *Schurr* II, 90.

MORISOT, Berthe-Marie-Pauline, Madame Eugène Manet ***1841–1895***
b. Bourges (Cher.) Pupil of Chocarne and Guichard. Worked with Fantin-Latour, Corot and Manet. Painted mostly landscapes, portraits, figures and interiors. Painted in the garden planted by her husband or in the Bois de Boulogne. She "introduced flowers wherever she could either as a backdrop. . .or as the central theme in the gardens she loved to paint; their fragile nature presented a special challenge to an artist intent on seizing the essence of things fleeting" (Mongan). Among her flower paintings are *Roses trémières à Bougival*, 1884 (Limoges 5); *Anémones et sac de bonbons*, 1891 (Braun 52); *Vase de fleurs*, 1894 (Braun 59); *Coupe de fleurs* (Tokyo 21). M: Boston, Museum of Fine Art
LIT M. Bataille, G. Wildenstein, *B. Morisot*, Paris 1961; *Berthe Morisot*,

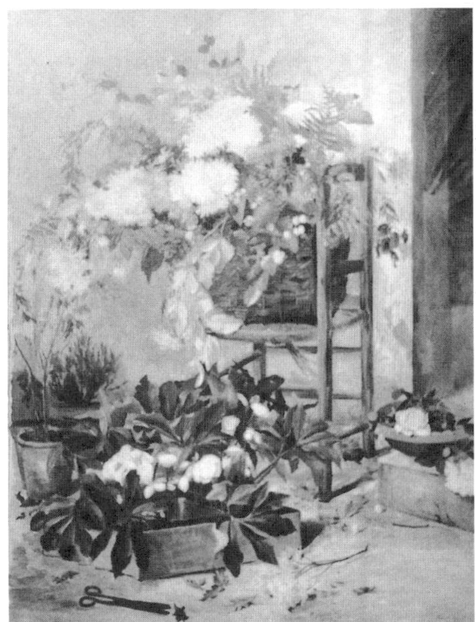

Mathilde Morin

Oil on canvas, $57\frac{1}{2} \times 44\frac{1}{2}$ in. (146 × 113 cm.), signed
Louviers, Musée des Beaux-Arts

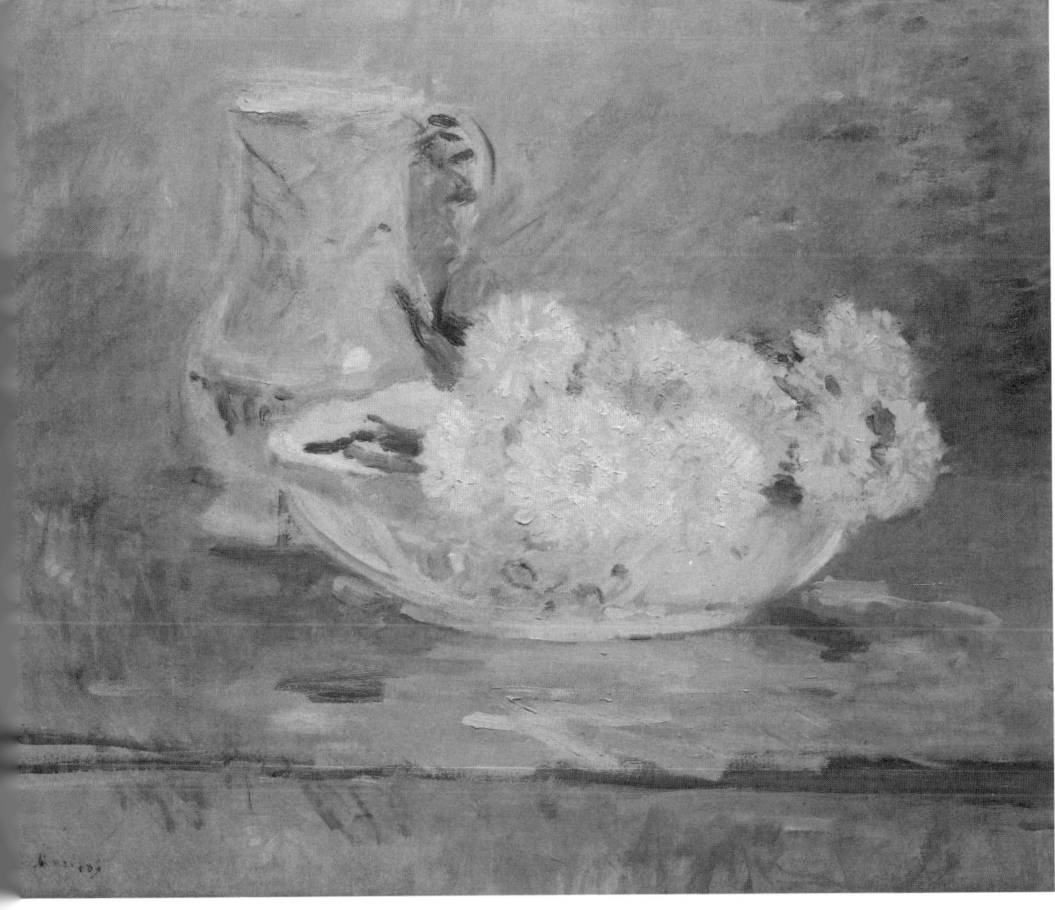

Berthe Morisot (*left*)

Oil on canvas, $18\frac{1}{8} \times 21\frac{5}{8}$ in. (46 × 55 cm.), signed
Boston, Museum of Fine Arts (Spaulding Bequest)

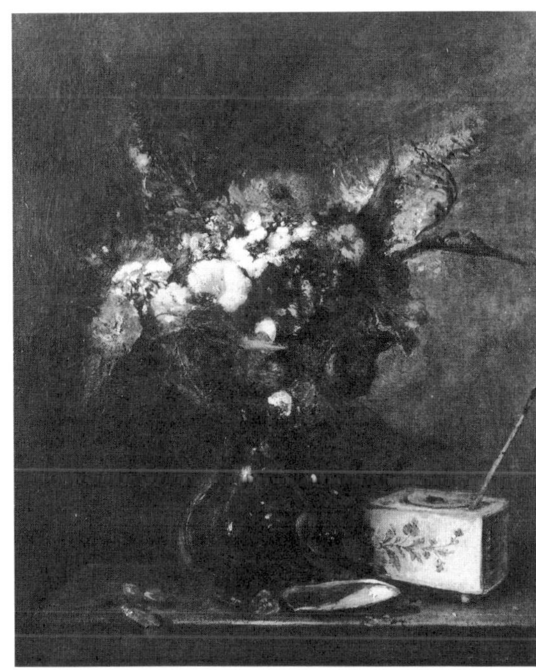

Alphonse-Alexis Morlot

Oil on canvas, signed
Paris, Galerie du Lethé

coll. des Maîtres, Braun n.d. *Renoir, B. Morisot, Limoges, Musée Municipal 1952*; *Bénézit*; E. Mongan, *B. Morisot*, New York, Slatkin, 1960; B. Morisot *Correspondance*, Paris (Editart) 1950; Tokyo, Japan Art Center n.d. *Witt*. AC

MORLOT, Alphonse-Alexis ***1838–1918***
b. Isômes (Haute-Marne). Pupil of Corot and Henner. Painted still-lifes, figures, landscapes. Paris Salon debut in 1864 with a still-life. Exhib. from 1883, with no fewer than sixty works at the 1908 Salon
LIT *Bénézit*; *Schurr* II, 35. PM

MORNARD, *see* THUILLIER de

MOROT, Ernest-Victor-Paul
b. Paris. Pupil of C. Jacque. Exhib. Paris Salon 1880–1920. Exhib. *Fleurs des champs*, Saint-Etienne Salon 1882
LIT *Bénézit*; *Hardouin-Fugier Bringuier*; *Saint-Etienne Salon* 1882

MORTAMAIS, Pierre-Marie ***b.1845***
Pupil of Reignier, Lyon BA (CFD 1869)
LIT *Hardouin-Fugier Grafe*

MORY, Pierre ***b.1804***
Pupil of Berjon, Lyon BA (CFD 1822)
LIT *Hardouin-Fugier Grafe*

MOSTERMAN, Louis
b. Paris. Exhib. Paris Indép. *Fleurs, Fruits et fleurs, Marguerites*, 1888, *Fleurs*, 1889, 1890, *Bouquet*, 1893
LIT *Paris Indép.* 1888–1890, 1893

MOTTE, Pierre-Jean ***b.1854***
Pupil of Reignier, Lyon BA (CFD 1878)
LIT *Hardouin-Fugier Grafe*

MOTTE-BEAUMANOIR, Mad. de la
Nothing is known of the artist other than a wc *Design for a Crest*, with a detailed floral surround in Cambridge, Fitzwilliam Museum (Broughton Coll.) JLC

MOUCHET, Jean-Antoine ***b.1811***
Pupil of Thierriat, Lyon BA (CFD 1826). Exhib. *Fleurs et fruits*, Lyon Salon 1831
LIT *Hardouin-Fugier Grafe*

MOUILLARD, Louis-Pierre ***b.1834***
Pupil of Reignier, Lyon BA (CFD 1854)
LIT *Hardouin-Fugier Grafe*

MOUILLET, Louis
Exhib. *Azalée dans un coin d'atelier*, Dijon Salon 1890
LIT *Dijon Salon* 1890. CL

MOUJET, Marie
Exhib. *Cueillette de roses*, on faience, Dijon Salon 1892
LIT *Dijon Salon* 1892. CL

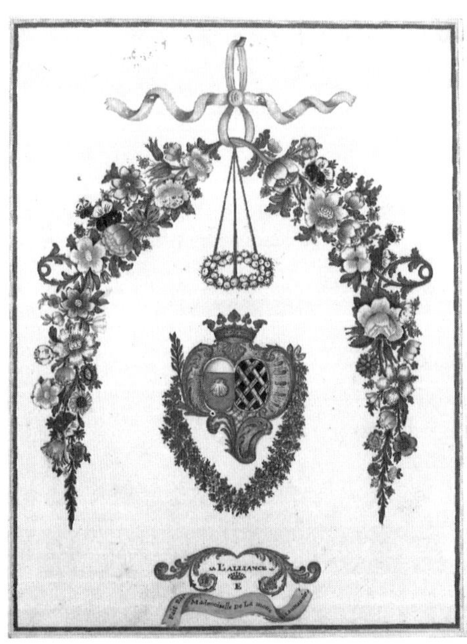

Mlle de la Motte-Beaumanoir

Watercolour, $9\frac{3}{4} \times 7\frac{1}{2}$ in. (24.7 × 19 cm.), signed and inscribed 'Fait par Mademoiselle de la Motte Beaumanoir'
Cambridge, Fitzwilliam Museum
(Broughton Collection)

MOULIN, Jules-Henri ***b.1862***
Pupil of Reignier, Lyon BA (CFD 1880)
LIT *Hardouin-Fugier Grafe*

MOUNIER
Pupil of Berjon, Lyon BA (CFD 1813)
LIT *Hardouin-Fugier Grafe*

MOURAD, Mohamed
Exhib. Paris Salon *Corbeille de dahlias*, *Vase de fleurs*, 1838, *Vase de fleurs*, 1839
LIT *Bellier*; *Paris Salon* 1838

MOUREAUX, Jean-François-Marie ***b.1825***
Pupil of Thierriat, Lyon BA (CFD 1842) Entered 1844 FDC
LIT *Hardouin-Fugier Grafe*.

MOURGUE, Eugénie-Julie
Pupil of Lemaire and E. Lambert. Exhib. *Narcisses et mimosas*, Paris UFPS 1898
LIT *Paris UFPS* 1898

MOUSSET, Pierre-Joseph ***d.1894***
b. Paris. Pupil of Villa. Painted genre and flowers. Exhib. Paris Salon from 1880 e.g. *Chrysanthèmes*, 1880; *Pivoines*, Lyon Salon 1883
LIT *Bellier*; *Bénézit*; *Lyon Salon* 1883; *Thieme*

MOUSSON, Michel
Pupil of Berjon, Lyon BA (CFD 1819)
LIT *Hardouin-Fugier Grafe*

MOUSSY, Jean-Michel ***b.1814***
Pupil of Thierriat, Lyon BA (CFD 1835). Entered 1838 FDC. Textile designer. Exhib. flowers (pastels) Lyon Salon 1858, 1869
LIT *Hardouin-Fugier Grafe*; *Lyon Salon* 1858

MOUSSY, Léonie
b. Paris. Pupil of Lefebure, Durban and Rousteau. Exhib. *Giroflées*, wc, Dijon Salon 1892; *Violettes de Parme*, Paris UFPS 1898; *Mimosas et roses*, Paris Salon 1898
LIT *Dijon Salon* 1892; *Paris Salon* 1898; *Paris UFPS* 1898

MOUTET-CHOLÉ, Célestine
b. Lunéville (Meurthe-et-Moselle). Pupil of Bléry, Carrand and Gaucherel. Exhib. Paris Salon 1874–1909; *Giroflées*, Lyon Salon 1879
LIT *Bénézit*; *Lyon Salon* 1879; *Thieme*

MOUTH, Ernest
Exhib. Lyon Salon 1868, 1869, 1872–1874
LIT *Hardouin-Fugier Grafe*

MOYSA
Designed flower plates for *Album Vilmorin*
LIT *Album Vilmorin*

MUENIER, Jules-Alexis ***b.1863 or 1869***
b. Vesoul (Haute-Saône) or Lyon. Painted landscapes, genre, figures, religious subjects. Exhib. Paris Salon from 1887. Exhib. *Roses trémières*, Paris SNBA 1890, 1892
LIT *Bénézit*; *Paris SNBA* 1890, 1892; *Schurr* II 92

MUGNIER, Henry
Exhib. Dijon Salon *Fleurs*, 1885, *Chrysanthèmes*, 1887, 1892
LIT *Dijon Salon* 1885, 1887, 1892. CL

MUIBLED, Hélène
Painted landscapes and flowers. Exhib. Paris Salon 1824–1835 e.g. *Fleurs posées sur un marbre*, on porcelain, 1835
LIT *Bellier*; *Paris Salon* 1835

MULINEN, Comtesse de, *née* Rougemont de Lowenberg ***fl. c.1825***
Possibly a pupil of Redouté
LIT *Hardouin-Fugier* 1981

MULLER, Camille-Victor-Louis ***1861–1880***
Painted flowers and fruit. Exhib. Paris Salon 1878, 1879
LIT *Bénézit*; *Thieme*

MULLER, Edouard, *alias* Rosenmuller ***1823–1876***
b. Glarus (Switzerland) or Mulhouse

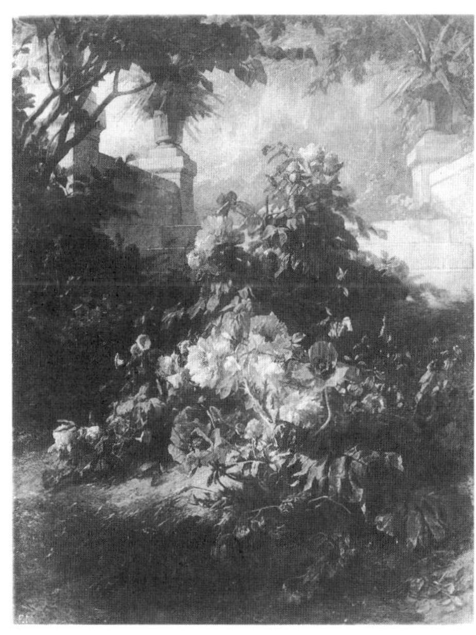

Edouard Muller, alias Rosenmuller

Oil on canvas, 91 × 68½ in. (230 × 174 cm.), signed and dated 1861
Lyon, Musée des Beaux-Arts

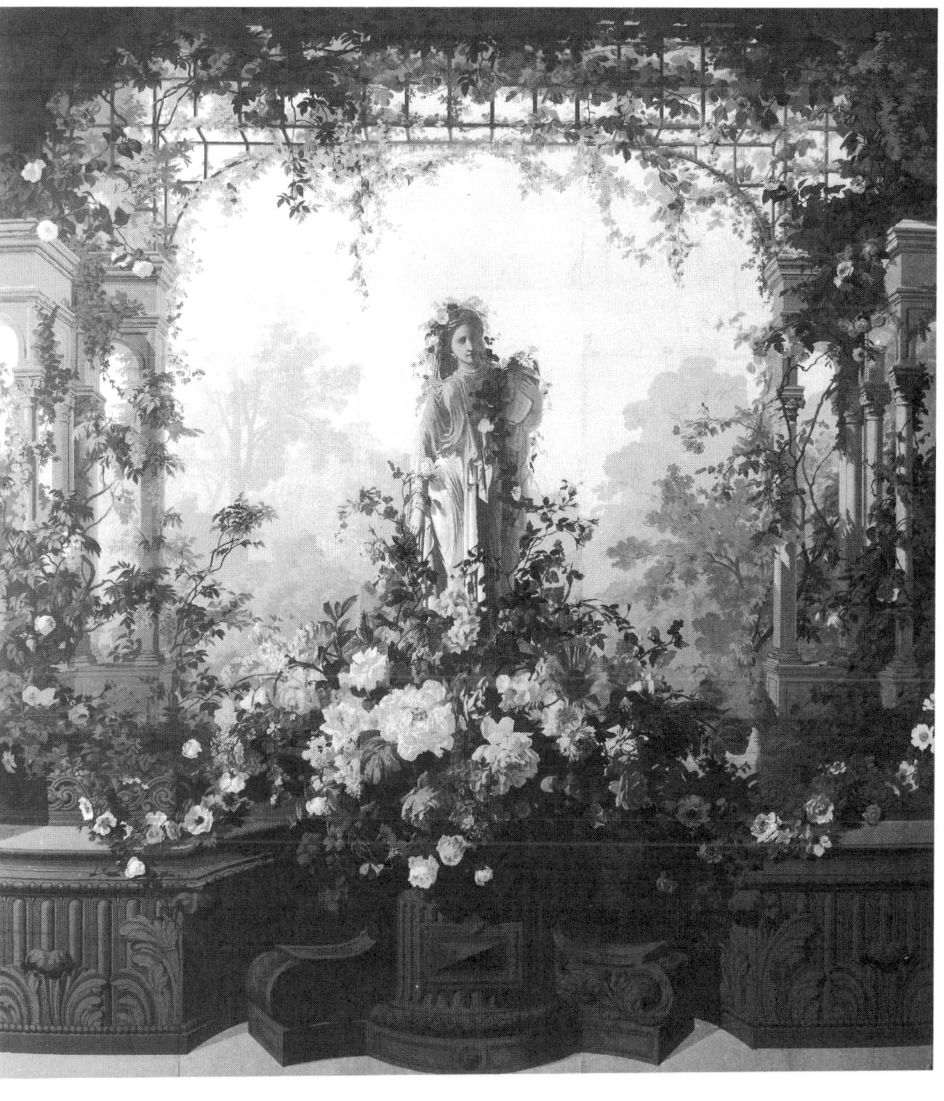

Edouard Muller, alias Rosenmuller (*right*)

Block printed wallpaper, 153 × 132½ in. (389 × 337 cm.), dated 1854
Paris, Musée des Arts Décoratifs

(Haut-Rhin). op. textile and wallpaper designer (Mulhouse). Designed *Le Jardin d'Armide*, 1854, for Jules Desfossé, wallpaper manufacturer. Designed twenty-four flower plates for *La flore pittoresque*, (Claesen), Paris and Berlin 1872. Exhib. Paris and Lyon Salons *Groupe de fleurs et de plantes*, 1861; *Still-life with flowers, Weinmuller, Munich, 28–29 Jan. 1970. M:* Lyon *Groupe de fleurs et de plantes, 1861, Paris* BMAD (*Maciet coll.*)
LIT *Bellier*; *Bénézit*; *Lyon Salon* 1861; O. Nouvel, in *L'Art français sous le Second Empire, Paris*, Grand Palais 1979; *Paris Salon* 1861; *Thieme*; *Witt*

MULON, Elisabeth, *née* Pêtre
Painted flowers and fruit. Exhib. Paris Salon 1844–1857 e.g. *Fleurs*, 1844, *Bouquet*, 1846, *Dahlias*, 1849, *Fleurs et fruits*, 1852
LIT *Bellier*; *Bénézit*; *Paris Salon* 1844

MURATON, Euphémie, *née* Duhanot *b.1840*
b. Beaugency (Loiret). Wife and pupil of A. Muraton (1824–1911). Painted genre, animals, still-lifes and flowers. Exhib. Paris Salon from 1863 e.g. *Camélia, Cinéraire*, 1863, *Bouquet d'automne*, 1867, 1872; Rouen Salon, *Chrysanthèmes*, 1872; Lyon Salon *Fleurs*, 1873; Dijon Salon *Bouquet de Chrysanthèmes*, 1892. Forty of her paintings were sold at Drouot, Paris 26 Mar. 1888 e.g. *Pivoines et boules de neige*, *Bouquet dans un vase du Japon*, *Anémones* etc. Musée de Rouen, *Fleurs*
LIT *Bellier*; *Bénézit*; *Dijon Salon* 1892, *Lyon Salon* 1873, *Orsay*; *Paris Salon* 1867, 1872; *Rouen Salon* 1872; *Schurr* IV, 81; *Thieme*

MUREAU de, *see* DECAUX

MYON, René *b.1840*
Pupil of Reignier, Lyon BA (CFD 1856)
LIT *Hardouin-Fugier Grafe*

N O

NADAILLAC or NADEILLAC, Comtesse de, *née* Delessert
b. Passy (Paris XVI°). Pupil of S. Petit. Painted portraits, copies of old masters and flowers. Exhib. Paris Salon from 1859 e.g. *Orchidées*, wc, 1863, *Roses d'automne*, wc, 1881. M: Bayonne
LIT *Bellier*; *Bénézit*

NAEYER de C.
Exhib. *Le bouquet*, *Fruits et fleurs*, Dijon Salon 1883
LIT *Dijon Salon* 1883. CL

NANCY, Anatole
b. Metz (Moselle). Pupil of S. Saint-Jean and Picot. Husband of Claire Nancy. Painted genre, historical subjects and flowers. Exhib. Paris Salon 1845–1870 e.g. *Fleurs d'hiver*, wc, 1845, *Fleurs et fruits au bas d'un escalier de jardin*, 1859, *Fleurs*, 1861
LIT *Bellier*; *Bénézit*; *Paris Salon* 1845, 1861; *Thieme*

NANCY, Auguste
Pupil of S. Saint-Jean. Exhib. Lyon Salon 1859–1861
LIT *Hardouin-Fugier Grafe*

NANCY, Claire, *née* Rey
b. Paris. Pupil of Scheffer and Robert-Fleury. Painted genre, portraits, copies and flowers. Exhib. Paris Salon 1859–1874 e.g. *Roses dans une coupe antique*, 1859, *Guirlande de fleurs entourant une Madone*, 1861, *Roses dans un vase étrusque*, 1864
LIT *Bellier*; *Bénézit*; *Paris Salon* 1861; *Thieme*

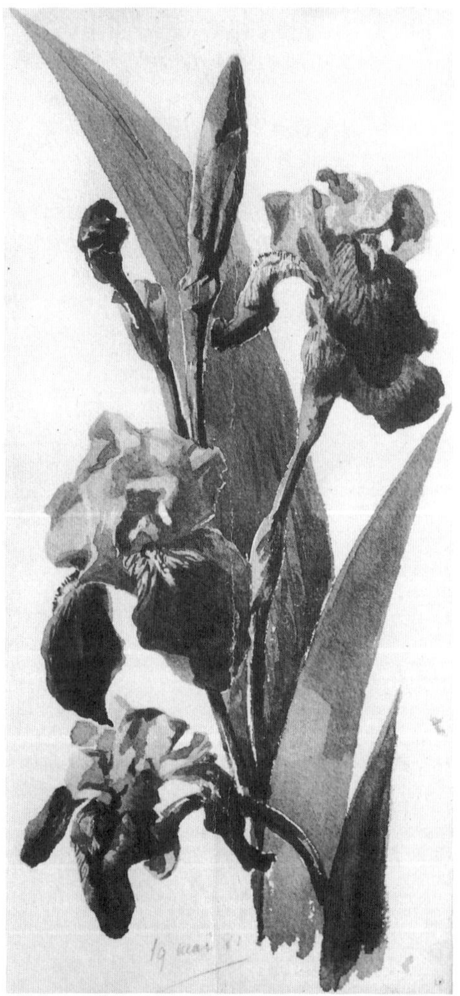

Comtesse de Nadaillac or Nadeillac

Watercolour, 14 × 6¼ in. (35.4 × 16.8 cm.), inscribed '19 mai 81'
Bayonne, Musée Bonnat

NARDEUX, Henri
Painted still-lifes and flowers. Exhib. Paris Salon 1833–1850 e.g. *Corbeille de fleurs*, 1836, *Fleurs dans un verre d'eau*, 1838
LIT *Bellier*; *Bénézit*; *Paris Salon* 1836, 1838

NAUWELAERS, *see* GIRARD

NAVARRE, Jean-Alexandre-Edmond *b.1848*
b. Paris. Architect. Exhib. Paris Salon *Bouquet de baptême*, wc, 1885
LIT *Paris Salon* 1885; *Thieme*

NAVARRE, *see* LEMIRE

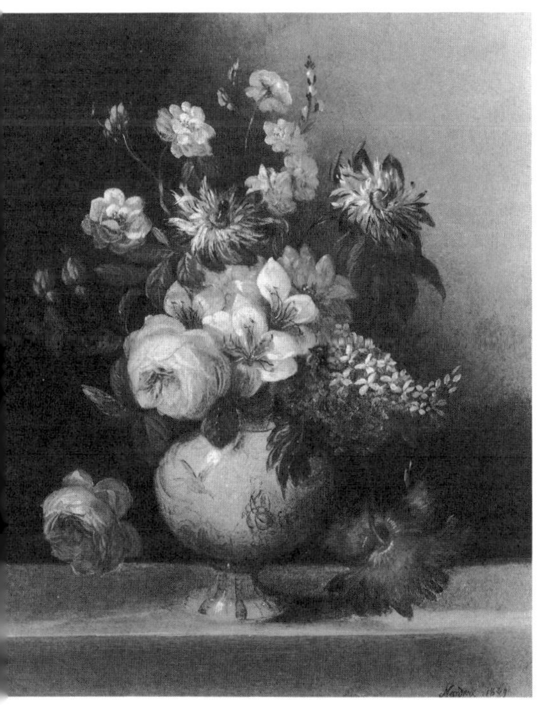

Henri Nardeux

Oil on canvas, 21 × 18 in. (53.5 × 46 cm.), signed and dated 1849

Frank S. Schwarz & Son, Philadelphia

NEPVEU, Aimable-Marie, *née* Chippel
op. Versailles. Exhib. Paris Salon 1833 and 1837 e.g. *Fleurs*, 1833. A relation of architect Frédéric-Eugène Nepveu 1777–1862
LIT *Bellier*; *Bénézit*; *Paris Salon* 1833; *Thieme*

NEUCHÈZE, Ferdinand de
Pupil of Gleyre and Couture. Exhib. *Fleurs*, Paris Salon 1880
LIT *Paris Salon* 1880

NEUVILLE, de, *see* BRUNEL

NICOLAS, Antoine
Pupil of Reignier, Lyon BA (CFD 1858). Exhib. Lyon Salon 1876
LIT *Hardouin-Fugier Grafe*

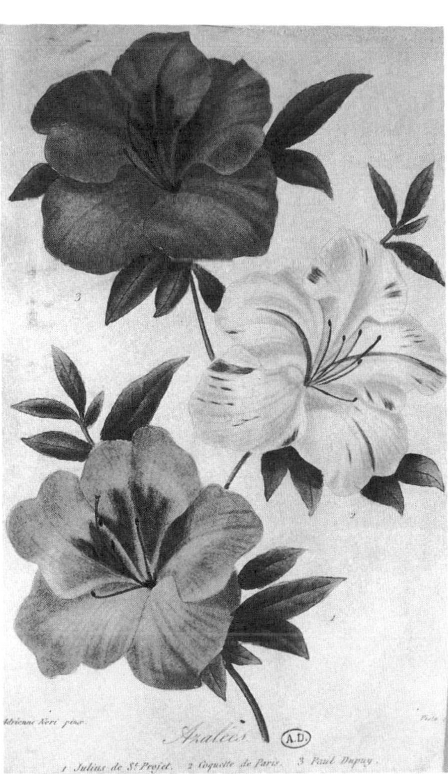

Adrienne Nori

Engraving after a drawing, $8\frac{3}{4} \times 5\frac{1}{2}$ in. (22 × 14 cm.) signed

Paris, BMAD (Maciet Collection)

NICOLAS, Marie
Pupil of Louis Guy. op. Lyon. Exhib. Lyon Salon e.g. *Vase de fleurs*, 1877, *Fleurs*, gouache, 1883; Dijon Salon e.g. *Fleurs d'automne*, 1887, *Fleurs d'hiver*, 1890; Saint-Etienne Salon e.g. *Fleurs*, 1891; Grenoble Salon e.g. *Fleurs*, 1899
LIT *Dijon Salon* 1887, 1890; *Grenoble Salon* 1899; *Hardouin-Fugier Grafe*; *Lyon Salon* 1877, 1883; *Saint-Etienne Salon* 1891

NICOUD, Théophile *b.1854*
Pupil of Reignier, Lyon BA (CFD 1870). Entered 1873 FDC. Exhib. Lyon Salon 1876
LIT *Hardouin-Fugier Grafe*

NOAILLES, Anna-Elisabeth, Comtesse Mathieu de, *née* Brancovan *1876–1933*
The famous poet painted flowers, often in pastels
LIT *Bénézit*

NOBILLET, Auguste-Michel
b. Vitré (Ille-et-Vilaine). Pupil of Vernier and P. Vayson. Painted genre, still-lifes and flowers Exhib. Paris Salon 1884–1914 e.g. *Coquelicots*, *Fleurs d'automne*, 1895; Dijon Salon *Fleurs (cinéraire)*, *Fleurs (roses dans l'eau)*, 1885, *Fleurs (pivoines)*, 1887
LIT *Bellier*; *Bénézit*; *Dijon Salon* 1885, 1887; *Paris Salon* 1895; *Thieme*

NOBLE-PIJEAUD, Claire-Julienne
b. Toulon (Var). Pupil of J. L. Noble (1834–1878), her husband and Courdouan. Exhib. Lyon Salon e.g. *Fleurs*, 1874, *Fleurs dans un verre*, 1875; Paris Salon from 1861 e.g. *Fleurs*, 1861, *Marguerites*, 1875
LIT *Bellier*; *Bénézit*; *Lyon Salon* 1874, 1875; *Paris Salon* 1861, 1875

NODE, Charles-Joseph ***1811–1886***
b. Montpellier (Hérault). Painted landscapes, genre, still-lifes and flowers. Designed plates for B. Delessert, *Icones selectae plantarum*, Paris, 1820–1846. Exhib. Paris Salon from 1845 e.g. *Fruits et fleurs*, 1845, 1846, *Guirlande de roses et de liserons*, wc, 1848; Exhib. Lyon Salon e.g. *Corbeille de fleurs et de fruits dans un paysage*, *Corbeille de fleurs et de fruits sur une table de marbre*, 1853, *Fruits et fleurs dans un paysage*, 1868. Musée de Montpellier, *Fruits et fleurs* (Paris Salon 1846)
LIT *Bellier*; *Bénézit*; *Lyon Salon* 1853, 1868; *Paris Salon* 1845; *Sitwell*; *Thieme*; *Witt*
See illustration on page 28

NODE, *see* Véran

NODE SAINT-ANGE, Charles
b. Montpellier (Hérault). Pupil of Charles-Joseph Node, his father. Painted landscapes, genre, still-lifes and flowers. Exhib. Paris Salon 1848, 1855, 1859 e.g. *Fleurs et fruits*, 1848
LIT *Bellier*; *Bénézit*; *Thieme*

NOEL, Hippolyte ***b. 1828***
b. Paris. Pupil of E. Fromentin. Painted landscapes and flowers. Exhib. Paris Salon 1850–1880 *Fleurs*, 1861, *Fleurs dans l'eau*, 1867, *Dernières fleurs*, 1874. Exhib. Lyon Salon e.g. *Fleurs, chrysanthèmes*, 1869. M: Chartres (lost in war); Draguignan.
LIT *Bellier*; *Bénézit*; *Lyon Salon* 1869; *Paris Salon* 1861, 1867; *Thieme*

NOEL, Joseph
Pupil of Delaroche. Exhib. *Fleurs*, Paris Salon 1873
LIT *Paris Salon* 1873

NOEL, Marie, *née* Postel
b. Cherbourg (Manche). Pupil of Mornand. Exhib. *Roses trémières*, Paris Salon 1898
LIT *Paris Salon* 1898

NOELLY, Marie
Pupil of Amen. Exhib. *Lilas blancs et roses*, Paris UFPS 1898
LIT *Paris UFPS* 1898

NONCLERCQ, Elie ***b.1847***
b. Valenciennes (Nord). Pupil of Cabanel. Painted historical subjects, landscapes and, occasionally, flowers. Exhib. *Bouquet de fleurs*, Saint-Etienne Salon 1882
LIT *Bénézit*; *Saint-Etienne Salon* 1882; *Thieme*

NORI, Adrienne
Designed botanical plates e.g. *Azalées*, *Berberis dulcis*, Paris BMAD (Maciet coll.) and for *Album Vilmorin*.
LIT *Album Vilmorin: Paris BMAD*

NOUVEAU, Louis ***b.1826***
Pupil of Thierriat, Lyon BA (CFD 1845)
LIT *Hardouin-Fugier Grafe*

NUGENT, Marie de ***b.1844***
b. Nantes (Loire-Atlantique). Pupil of Lepic and Rapin. Painted on enamel, portraits and flowers. Exhib. Paris Salon from 1874 e.g. *Iris*, 1890
LIT *Bellier*; *Bénézit*; *Paris Salon* 1890

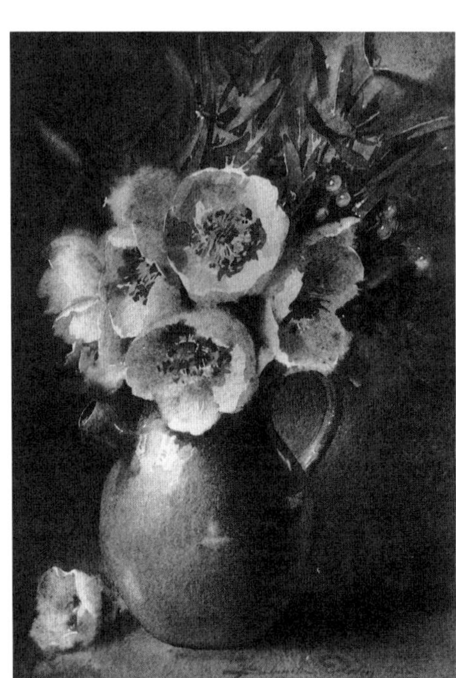

OBERLIN, Amélie-Pauline
Exhib. Paris Salon 1844–1846 e.g. *Fleurs et fruits*, on porcelain, 1844, *Fleurs*, after Jacobber, on porcelain, 1845
LIT *Bellier*; *Paris Salon* 1844, 1845

ODET, Antoine-Jean ***b.1807***
Pupil of Thierriat, Lyon BA (CFD 1827)
LIT *Hardouin-Fugier Grafe*

ODIN, Blanche ***b.1865***
b. Paris. Pupil of D. de Cool and M. Lemaire. Exhib. flowers, often in wc, Paris Salon from 1883. *Corbeille de fleurs*, wc, Drouot Paris, 8 Nov. 1974. Musée de Bagnères de Bigorre, *Roses variées*
LIT *Bénézit*; *Orsay*; Paris Arch. Nat. F21: 4500

OFFNER, Marguerite
b. Versailles (Yvelines). Pupil of C. Bertin and E. d'Apvril. op. Grenoble. Exhib. *Roses et cerises*, *Roses*, *Fleurs*, *Gerbe de giroflées*, Grenoble Salon 1899
LIT *Grenoble Salon* 1899. MW

OFFRAY, Victor ***b.1871***
Pupil of Castex-Dégrange, Lyon BA (CFD 1890)
LIT *Hardouin-Fugier Grafe*

OGER, Jean-Pierre ***b.1814***
Pupil of Thierriat Lyon BA (CFD 1833). Textile designer (Lyon)
LIT *Hardouin-Fugier Grafe*

OGIER, Jean-Baptiste-Léon
Pupil of Thierriat, Lyon BA (CFD 1844). Exhib. *Roses de Dijon*, Lyon Salon 1870
LIT *Hardouin-Fugier Grafe*

Blanche Odin

Watercolour, signed
Bagnères-de-Bigorre, Musée Salies

O.L. Mlle
Exhib. *Tableau de fleurs*, Lyon Salon 1846
LIT *Hardouin-Fugier Grafe*

OLIVE, Jacques
Painted landscapes and flowers. Op. Montpellier. Exhib. Paris Salon 1846 and 1847 e.g. *Corbeille de fleurs sur une banquette*, 1847
LIT *Bellier*; *Bénézit*

OLIVE, Jean-Baptiste-Joseph *1848–1936*
b. Marseille. Pupil of A. Vollon, J. Gustave and G. Julien. Painted landscapes, seascapes, still-lifes and, occasionally, flowers. Exhib. Paris Salon from 1874
LIT *Bénézit*; J. C. and G. Gamet and J. B. Olive. . .Paris (Frébert) 1977; *Schurr* I, 72; *Thieme*

OLIVIER, Mme Georges
Pupil of Champeaux, MacNab and J. Lefebvre. Exhib. *Panier de pommes et reines-marguerites*, Paris Salon 1890; *Anémones*, Dijon Salon 1892; *Fleurs, Lilas et boutons d'or*, Paris UFPS 1898
LIT *Dijon Salon* 1892; *Paris Salon* 1890; *Paris UFPS* 1898

OLIVIER, Henri
Pupil of Berjon, Lyon BA (CFD 1822)
LIT *Hardouin-Fugier Grafe*

OLIVIER, Sophie *1854–1908*
Pupil of A. Chaine and G. Chaine. Painted portraits and flowers. Exhib. *Chrysanthèmes*, Lyon Salon 1874, 1875
LIT *Hardouin-Fugier Grafe*; *Lyon Salon* 1874, 1875

OLLAT, Thomas-François
Pupil of Thierriat, Lyon BA (CFD 1848)
LIT *Hardouin-Fugier Grafe*

ORLÉANS Princesse Eugénie-Adelaide-Louise-d', *1777–1847*
Sister of Louis-Philippe. Most likely a pupil of Redouté, like her niece Louise d'Orléans to whom *Spray of Summer Flowers*, 1829 wc, Cambridge, Fitzwilliam Museum (Broughton coll.), has also been attributed. This picture is a copy of a drawing by Redouté also in the Broughton collection
LIT *Broughton*, 1978; *Broughton*, 1979; *Hardouin-Fugier*, 1981; *Broughton*, 1983. JLC

ORLÉANS, Princesse Marie-Amélie-Françoise-Hélène d' *1865–1909*
Daughter of the Duc de Chartres. Married Prince Waldemar of Denmark (1885). Painted flowers and still-lifes
LIT *Bénézit*; *Thieme*

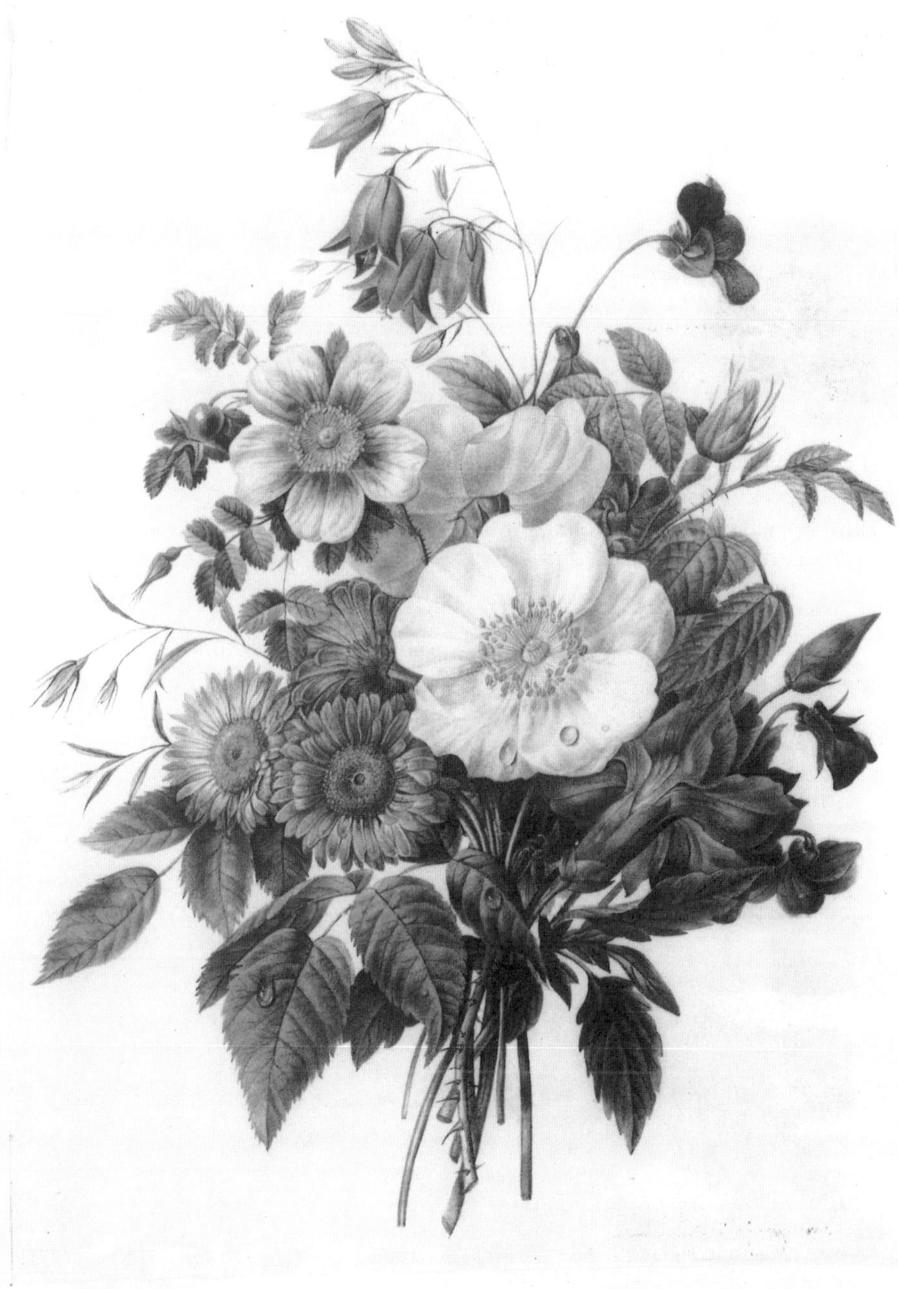

Princesse Eugénie Adelaide Louise d'Orléans

Watercolour on vellum, signed and dated 1820
Cambridge, Fitzwilliam Museum,
(Broughton Collection)

ORLÉANS, Princesse Marie-Christine-Caroline-Adelaïde-Francoise d' ***1813–1839***
Pupil of Redouté. Better known as a sculptress
LIT *Hardouin-Fugier* 1981

ORSEL, Jacques-Alphée-Antoine ***b. 1825***
Pupil of Thierriat, Lyon BA (CFD 1845)
LIT *Hardouin-Fugier Grafe*

ORSET, Isaac
Pupil of Berjon, Lyon BA (CFD 1813)
LIT *Hardouin-Fugier Grafe*

OSTROHOVE, Louise de
b. Paris. Pupil of Trébuchet. Exhib. *Roses trémières*, wc, Paris Salon 1885
LIT *Paris Salon* 1885

OTTMANN, Henri ***1877–1927***
b. Ancenis (Loire-Atlantique). Painted figures, genre, interiors, nudes and, occasionally, flowers. M: Grenoble
LIT *Bénézit*

OUDART, Paul-Louis ***1796–c.1860***
b. Paris. Pupil of G. van Spaendonck. Painted and lithographed animals, insects and, occasionally, flowers. Exhib. Paris Salon from 1819. op. Sèvres 1820–1821. Designed plates for many books e.g. C. Gay, *Historia...de Chile*, Paris 1845–1843 and sets of plates e.g. *Calendrier de Flore* (A. Bès et Dubreuil fils). Designed and lithographed a flower plate printed by Engelman (1826), Paris BMAD (Maciet coll.)
LIT *Bénézit*; *Brunet Préaud*; *Faré* 1962, p. 245; *Hardouin-Fugier* 1981; *Nissen* I, 242, 556, 695, 1471, 2240; Paris Arch. Nat. F21: 270, 287; Paris Bibl. Nat. Est. Jd 59; *Paris BMAD*

OURI, Alphonse-Antoine-Joseph ***1828–1891***
b. Versailles (Yvelines). Pupil of Bin, F. Gosse and E. Delacroix. Exhib. Paris Salon from 1849 *Pavots et plantes*, *Fleurs et fruits*, 1861, *Fleurs de mai*, 1867
LIT *Bénézit*; *Paris Salon* 1861, 1867; *Thieme*

OYEX, Eugène ***1816–1886***
Pupil of Thierriat, Lyon BA (CFD 1834). Wallpaper designer (Lyon). Designed a set of line lithographs. Co-designed other sets with Reybaud. M: Musée Historique des Tissus, Lyon
LIT *Hardouin-Fugier Grafe*; *Hardouin-Fugier Grafe* 1982 (ill.)

Henri Ottmann (*right*)

Oil on canvas, 28¾ × 36¼ in. (72 × 92 cm.), signed
Grenoble, Musée de Peinture et de Sculpture

Paul-Louis Oudart

Engraving after a drawing, 11 × 7½ in. (28 × 19cm.), signed
Paris, BMAD (Maciet Collection)

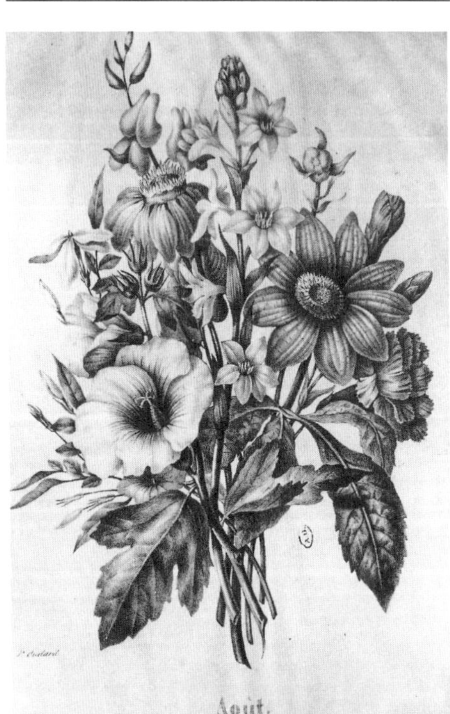

OYEX, Jean-Marie ***b.1811***
Pupil of Thierriat, Lyon BA (CFD 1829)
LIT *Hardouin-Fugier Grafe*

OYEX, Louis-Jules ***b.1861***
Pupil of Reignier, Lyon BA (CFD 1883)
LIT *Hardouin-Fugier Grafe*

OZANNE-LOLETTE, Alice
Pupil of Sain and Carpentier. Exhib. *Pavots*, Paris UFPS 1896
LIT *Paris UFPS* 1896

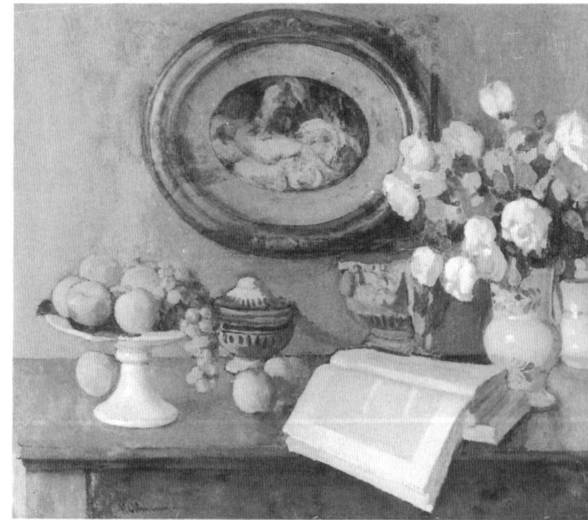

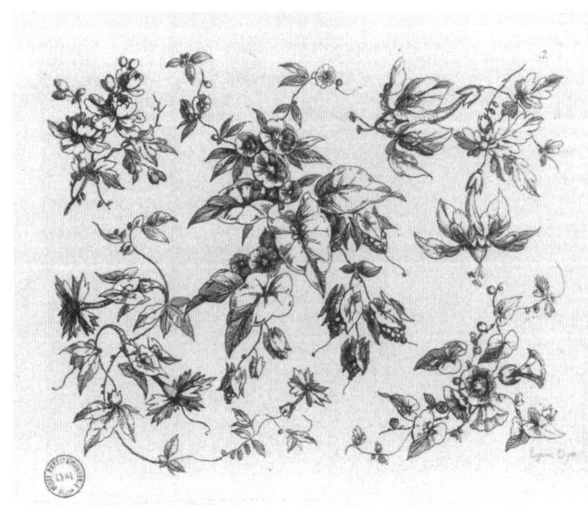

Eugène Oyex

Engraved page from *Album du Dessinateur*, Lyon, 1840 (With J . Reyband)
Lyon, Musée Historique des Tissus
(photo: M. Bessac)

P

P., Mlle
Exhib. *Roses de mai*, Lyon Salon 1866
LIT *Lyon Salon* 1866

PACAUD, Claude ***b.1807***
Pupil of Thierriat, Lyon BA (CFD 1827)
LIT *Hardouin-Fugier Grafe*

PAGERIE de la, *see* BEAUHARNAIS

PAHUD, Mme J.
Pupil of J. Médard. Exhib. *Azalée et Camélia*, *Primevère*, gouache, Lyon Salon 1884
LIT *Lyon Salon* 1884

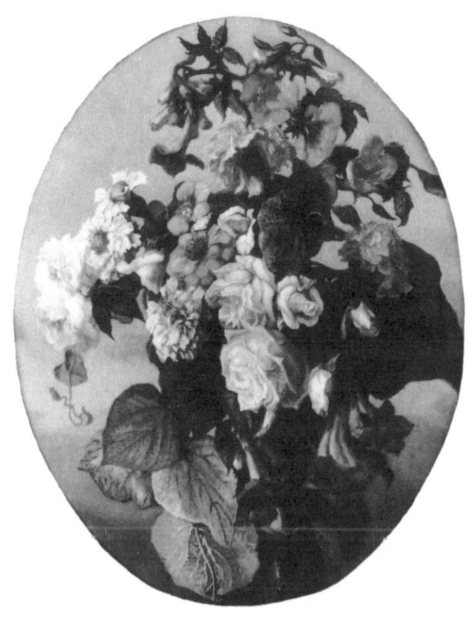

Mélanie Paigné

Pastel, oval, $28\frac{3}{4} \times 23\frac{3}{4}$ in. (73 × 60 cm.)
Metz, Musée d'Art et d'Histoire

PAIGNÉ, Mélanie ***1817–1872***
b. Metz (Moselle). Sister of Octavie Paigné-Sturel. Pupil of C. L. Maréchal (Metz). Painted portraits, landscapes and flowers. Exhib. Paris Salon 1845–1866 e.g. *Bouquet delphiniums, clématites, capucines*, pastel 1863, *Chrysanthèmes et capucines*, pastel, 1866; Lyon Salon *Groupe de cactus et clématites*, wc, 1858, *Pavots du Caucase*, pastel, *Roses trémières*, pastel, *Pavots et liserons*, pastel, 1860, *Glaïeuls et capucines*, pastel, 1865
LIT *Bellier*; *Bénézit*; *Lyon Salon* 1858, 1860, 1865; Paris Arch Nat. F21: 522; *Thieme*

PAIN, Gabriel ***b.1819***
Pupil of Thierriat, Lyon BA (CFD 1837)
Lit. *Hardouin-Fugier Grafe*

PAIVET, François ***b.1813***
Pupil of Thierriat, Lyon BA (CFD 1831)
LIT *Hardouin-Fugier Grafe*

PALLANDRE, Albert ***b.1870***
b. Versailles (Yvelines), son of H. L. Pallandre (b. 1831, active at Sèvres.) Painted landscapes and flowers
LIT *Bénézit*; *Thieme*

PALLÉ, Jeanne
b. Paris. Pupil of Deschamps, Laporte and Billotey. Exhib. *Fleurs*, fan-leaf, gouache, Paris Noir et Blanc Salon 1888
LIT *Paris Noir et Blanc Salon* 1888

PALLIÈRE, Marie-Louise
b. Orville (Côte-d'Or). Pupil of her father. Exhib. Paris Salon from 1880 e.g. *Fleurs*, 1880, *Aiguière et Chrysanthèmes*, 1881
LIT *Bellier*; *Bénézit*; *Paris Salon* 1880

PALLUIS, Philippe ***b.1864***
Pupil of Castex-Dégrange, Lyon BA (CFD 1880)
LIT *Hardouin-Fugier Grafe*

PALLUIS, Pierre-Marie ***b.1829***
Pupil of Thierriat, Lyon BA (CFD 1848)
LIT *Hardouin-Fugier Grafe*

PANCKOUCKE, Anne-Ernestine, *née* Désmoreaux ***1784–1860***
Pupil of Prud'hon, Van Spaendonck and Redouté. Co-designer of Chaumeton, *Flore médicale*, Panckoucke, *Flore usuelle*, Paris 1831. *Fleurs*, Duc de Berry sale, 1834. M: Cambridge, Fitzwilliam (Broughton coll., *Flowers on a ledge*, wc, 1814); Paris BMAD (Maciet coll.)
LIT *Bénézit*; *Hardouin-Fugier* 1981 (ill.); *Paris BMAD*; *Thieme*

PANNIER-PERNOLET, Zoé
b. Poullaouen (Finistère). Pupil of Luminais. Exhib. Paris Salon from 1869. Exhib. *Bouquet de roses*, wc, *Fruits et fleurs*, wc, Paris Aquar 1880
LIT *Bénézit*; *Paris Aquar*, 1880

PANSERON, *see* DOLL

PAPEGAY, Alexandre
Exhib. *Bouquet de lilas*, *roses*, *camélias*, *Vase de chrysanthèmes*, Paris Indép. 1890
LIT *Paris Indep*. 1890

PAPIN, Jean-Baptiste ***b.1837***
Pupil of Reignier, Lyon BA (CFD 1855)
LIT *Hardouin-Fugier Grafe*

PARAVEY, Marianne
Pupil of Cyane-Lecoq de Boisbaudran. Painted flowers
LIT *Faré* 1962, p. 248

PARENT, Elyma
b. Vesoul (Haute-Saône). Pupil of Mme Paigné (Metz). Exhib. *Corbeille de fleurs*, pastel, Metz Salon 1861. M: Gray, *Le bouquet tricolore*
LIT *Metz. Salon* 1861

PARGON, Victor-Wilfrid
Pupil of Cabanel and Vayson. Exhib. *Les premières fleurs*, Dijon Salon 1887
LIT *Bénézit*; *Dijon Salon* 1887. CL

PARIS, Cécile
Exhib. Dijon Salon *Branches de lilas*, 1880, *Violettes*, 1881, *Branches de lilas*, *Fleurs des champs*, 1883, *Chrysanthèmes*, 1887, *Fleurs de pommier*, 1892
LIT *Dijon Salon* 1880, 1881, 1883, 1887, 1892. CL

PARIS, Jeanne
b. Reims (Marne). Pupil of Burat. Exhib. Paris Salon from 1878 e.g. *Bouquet*, gouache, 1878, *Premières fleurs*, on faience, 1879
LIT *Bellier*

PARISSOT, Albert-Georges
b. Paris. Pupil of Bouchet and Bergeret. Painted flowers and fruit. Exhib. Paris Salon from 1879 e.g. *Envoi de fleurs*, 1880
LIT *Bellier*; *Bénézit*; *Paris Salon* 1880

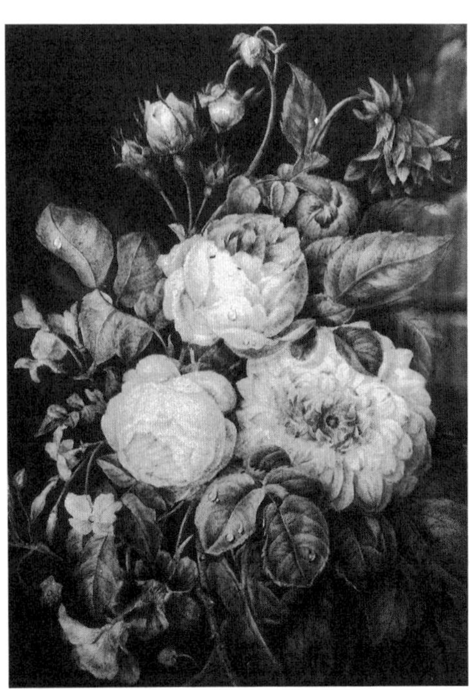

Anne-Ernestine Panckoucke

Watercolour, $15\frac{3}{4} \times 12\frac{1}{4}$ in. (40 × 21 cm.)
Private collection

PARISY, Eugène-Edmond *fl. 1876–1882*
b. Acy-en-Multien (Oise) Pupil of V. Leclaire. Painted still-lifes and, occasionally, flowers
LIT *Bellier*; *Bénézit*; *Thieme*

PARMENTIER, Edouard-Edmond-Ernest *1834–after 1877*
b. Paris. Pupil of E. Lecomte. Exhib. Paris Salon 1857–1878 e.g. *Fleurs et fruits*, 1873, *Fleurs et objets d'art*, 1874
LIT *Bellier*; *Bénézit*

PARMENTIER, Henri-Marie
b. Paris. Pupil of Langlacé. Painted still-lifes and, occasionally, flowers. Exhib. Paris Salon 1824–1850
LIT *Bénézit*; *Gabet*; *Thieme*

PARPALET
b. Longwy (Meurthe-et-Moselle). Exhib. *Fleurs*, Paris Indép. 1888
LIT *Paris Indép.* 1888

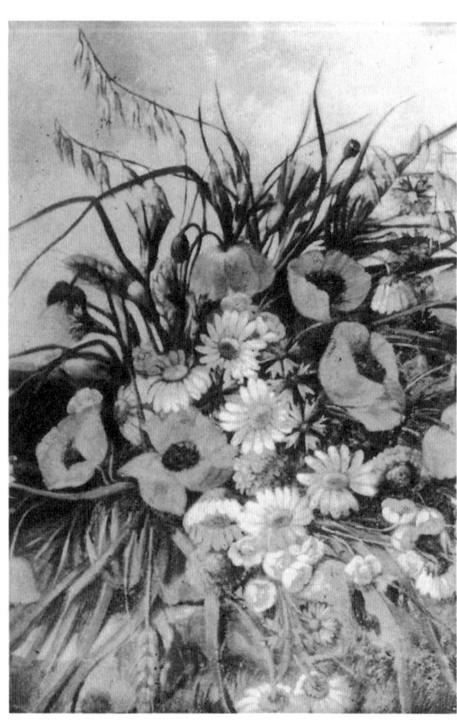

Elyma Parent

Oil on canvas, $21\frac{3}{4} \times 18$ in. (55 × 46 cm.)
Gray, Musée Baron Martin

PARRAYON, François *b.1824*
Pupil of Thierriat, Lyon BA (CFD 1840)
LIT *Hardouin-Fugier Grafe*

PARROT *b.1821*
Pupil of Thierriat, Lyon BA (CFD 1840)
LIT *Hardouin-Fugier Grafe*

PARVILLÉE, Achille
b. Istanbul (Turkey). Pupil of his father. Exhib. Paris Noir et Blanc Salon *Fleurs*, 1886, *Fleurs*, wc, 1888
LIT *Paris Noir et Blanc Salon* 1886, 1888

PARVILLÉE, Louis
b. Istanbul (Turkey), brother of A. Parvillée. Painted landscapes and flowers e.g. *Fleurs*, on faience, Paris Salon 1880, 1885
LIT *Paris Salon* 1880, 1885

PASCAL, Antoine *1803–1859*
b. Macon (Saône-et-Loire). Pupil of Redouté. Painted genre, landscapes, flowers and fruit. Designed flower plates published by Delaporte and Langlumé. Designed plates for Thory. *Monographie*

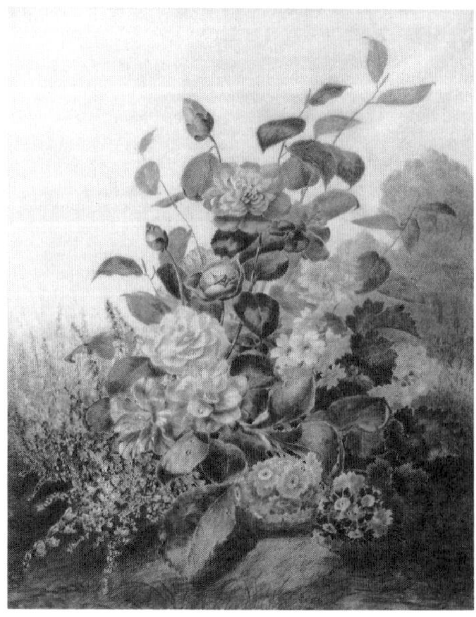

Antoine Pascal

Watercolour on vellum, $23\frac{3}{4} \times 18\frac{1}{2}$ in. (60.4 × 47 cm.)
Cambridge, Fitzwilliam Museum
(Broughton Collection)

du genre groseillier, *L'aquarelle ou les fleurs peintes d'après la méthode de Redouté*, Paris 1836; Chavant, *Cours des Fleurs du jardin des Plantes*. . .Exhib. Paris Salon 1843–1847, 1853 e.g. *Bouquet de fleurs*, 1843 (Private coll. Béziers) exhib. Béziers 1967. M: Autun, Nevers, Cambridge, Fitzwilliam Museum (Broughton coll), *Flowers in a landscape*, wc
LIT *Bellier*; *Bénézit*; *Faré* 1962, p. 246; *Hardouin-Fugier* 1981 (ill.); Nissen I 1493; Paris Arch. Nat. F21: 120, 199, 436, 4500; Paris Bibl. Nat. Est. Jd 59; *Thieme*; *Witt*

PASCAL, Antoine ***b.1821***
Pupil of Thierriat, Lyon BA (CFD 1839)
LIT *Hardouin-Fugier Grafe*

PASCAL, Antoine-Jean-Marie ***b.1865***
Pupil of Castex-Dégrange, Lyon BA (CFD 1885)
LIT *Hardouin-Fugier Grafe*

PASCAL, Marianne
Active in Paris. Exhib. Paris Salon 1835–1845 e.g. *Dahlias*, wc, 1835; *Tulipes*, on alabaster, *Roses trémières*, wc, 1839, nine flower medallions on alabaster, 1845.
LIT *Bellier*; *Bénézit*; *Hardouin-Fugier* 1981

PASQUET, Philippe-Victor ***b.1845***
Pupil of Reignier, Lyon BA (CFD 1861)
LIT *Hardouin-Fugier Grafe*

PASQUIER, Raymond-Etienne ***b.1818***
Pupil of Thierriat, Lyon BA (CFD 1835)
LIT *Hardouin-Fugier Grafe*

PASSEPONT, Jules-Joseph ***1811–1875***
b. Seignelay (Yonne). Pupil of A. B. Passepont, his father. Painted landscapes, birds, still-lifes and flowers. Exhib. Paris Salon from 1876 e.g. *Fuchsia*, wc, 1880
LIT *Bellier*; *Bénézit*; *Paris Salon* 1880; *Thieme*

PASSY, *see* AURE d'

PASTORET, Adélaïde de, *nee* Piscatory ***1765–1843***
Pupil of Redouté. An aristocratic amateur flower painter
LIT *Hardouin-Fugier* 1981

PATAUD, Henriette
b. Paris. Pupil of Barré. Exhib. *Fleurs*, on porcelain, Paris Salon 1867
LIT *Paris Salon* 1867

PATÉ, Suzanne
b. Saint-Omer (Pas-de-Calais). Pupil of Claire Leroy. Exhib. *Pétunias*, wc, *Fleurs des champs*, Paris Salon 1880
LIT *Paris Salon* 1880

PAULE, Louis ***b.1823***
Pupil of Thierriat, Lyon BA (CFD 1841)
LIT *Hardouin-Fugier Grafe*

PAUPORTE, Edouard-Xavier ***b.1868***
Pupil of Castex-Dégrange, Lyon BA (CFD 1886)
LIT *Hardouin-Fugier Grafe*

PAUPY, Pierre ***b.1820***
Pupil of Thierriat, Lyon BA (CFD 1837)
LIT *Hardouin-Fugier Grafe*

PAUQUET, Laure
Pupil of M. Charpentier. Exhib. *Roses*, *Oeillets*, wc, Paris UFPS 1896
LIT *UFPS* 1896

PAYET, Gabriel
Pupil of Thierriat, Lyon BA (CFD 1839)
LIT *Hardouin-Fugier Grafe*

PEADELEU, Mme
Exhib. *Fleurs*, Dijon Salon 1894
LIT *Dijon Salon* 1894. CL

PEALAT, Louis ***b.1818***
Pupil of Thierriat, Lyon BA (CFD 1835)
LIT *Hardouin-Fugier Grafe*

PEGGI, Marie
Exhib. *Azalées*, *Roses*, Dijon Salon 1887
LIT *Dijon Salon* 1887

PEILLON, Charles ***b.1828***
Pupil of Thierriat, Lyon BA (CFD 1845)
LIT *Hardouin-Fugier Grafe*

PELIN, Gaspard ***b.1822***
Pupil of Thierriat, Lyon BA (CFD 1839)
LIT *Hardouin-Fugier Grafe*

PELLEGRIN, René ***b.1792***
Pupil of Berjon, Lyon BA (CFD 1812)
LIT *Hardouin-Fugier Grafe*

PELLET, Joseph ***1817–1885***
b. Béziers (Hérault). Painted animals, landscapes and flowers. M: Béziers, *Bouquet de pétunias blancs*, *Fleurs*; Montpellier, *Fleurs*
LIT *Bénézit*; *Thieme*

PELLETIER, Antoine-Jules
b. Amsterdam (Netherlands). Pupil of Rudder and Couture. Painted portraits, genre, flowers and fruit. Exhib. Paris Salon from 1848 e.g. *Fleurs oubliées*, 1859, *Gibier, fleurs et fruits*, 1868, *Roses*, 1880; *Fleurs oubliées*, Lyon Salon 1861. M: Cambridge, Fitzwilliam (Broughton coll.), *Study of plants*, wc, and *Bouquet of flowers*, wc 1867
LIT *Bellier*; *Bénézit*; *Lyon Salon* 1861; *Thieme*

PELLETIER, Mme Laurent, *née* Eugénie Fournel
Pupil of Maréchal (Metz). Married Laurent Pelletier (1811–1892), landscape painter and lithographer, of Metz. Painted portraits, flowers and fruit.

Exhib. Paris Salon 1833–1877 e.g. *Fruits et fleurs*, 1863
LIT *Bellier*; *Bénézit*; *Thieme*

PELOSSE
op. Lyon. Exhib. *Groupe de fleurs sur une roche*, *Vase de fleurs*, Lyon Salon 1858
LIT *Lyon Salon* 1858

PELTE
Designed a flower plate lithographed by Garron
LIT Paris Bibl. Nat. Est. Jd 59

PENSA, Hélène, *née* Humblot
Exhib. *Violettes et marguerites jaunes*, wc, Dijon Salon 1892
LIT *Dijon Salon* 1892

PERIAUX, op. c.*1850*
Designed plates for C. Gaudichaud Beaupré *Voyage autour du monde*, Paris 1844
LIT *Nissen* I, 690

PERONET, Claudius, *b.1823*
Pupil of Thierriat, Lyon BA (CFD 1839)
LIT *Hardouin-Fugier Grafe*

PERRACHON, André-Benoit *1828–1909*
b. Lyon. Pupil of Lyon BA and Lepage. In Paris after 1847; Lyon after 1853. A most popular art teacher and rose painter. Exhib. Lyon Salon e.g. *L'Eucharistie* (after Saint-Jean) *c*.1845, *Guirlande de fleurs*, 1847, *La parure*, 1852, *Nid dans les bruyères*, 1853, *Trophée de la danse*, 1854, *Nid dans les roses*, 1855, *Richesse et simplicité*, 1856, *Fleurs*, 1857, *Intérieur de cuisine*, 1857, *Vase de fleurs*, *Groupe de giroflées*, 1858, *Groupe de giroflées*, 1859, *Roses trémières*, *Primevères*, *Fleurs d'hiver*, *Roses mousseuses*, *Groupe de mauves*, *Vase de bruyères et camélias*, *Bruyère, primevère, vase bleu, bijoux*, 1860, *Hommage à Saint-Jean*, *Vase de lilas, glaïeuls, mauves*, *Groupe de fleurs d'hiver*, *Roses dans un vase d'or*, 1861, *Fleurs, fruits*, 1862, *Roses, tournesols, glaïeuls, queues de renard dans un vase vert*, 1865, *Vase de fleurs*, *Fleurs dans un verre*, 1867, *Buisson de roses*, 1868 (Paris), *Hommage au Christ*, 1870 (Paris), *Nid de fauvette*, 1872, *Roses sur la mousse*, *Amours d'un papillon*, 1872, *Rosier*, *Rose sur la mousse*, 1873, *Rose et sureaux*, 1874 (Paris), *Roses*, 1875 (Paris), *Roses et glaïeuls* (Paris), *Roses et amarante*, 1876, *Roses*, *Roses en deuil*, 1877, *Bouquet*, *Buisson de roses*, 1879, *Roses dans un verre de Bohème*, *Roses sur la mousse*, *Les deux couronnes l'une après l'autre*, 1880, *Roses*, 1881, *La veille d'une fête*, 1882, *Roses dans un vase de cristal*, 1884, *Roses Général Jacqueminot*, *Hommage aux Poètes du Siècle*, 1888, *Marchande de fleurs*, 1890, *Pivoines et roses trémières*, 1892, *Sous les roses*, *Vase de roses*, 1893, *Le jour des Noces*, 1894, *A l'ombre, panier de roses*, *Amarantes et soucis*, 1895, *Roses de Malmaison*, 1897, *Chez la marchande de fleurs*, *Pivoines et iris, avant, pendant, après*, 1898, *L'amour dans les roses (avant)*, *Fauvette dans le rosier*, *Pivoines et iris*, *Arrivage de fleurs*, 1898, *Fête-Dieu*, 1900, *Les préparatifs d'une fête*, 1903. *Roses blanches*, 1909. Exhib. Paris Salon e.g. *Nid dans un rosier*, 1852, *Roses trémières dans un vase de cristal*, 1861, *Vase de fleurs*, 1863, *Vase de fleurs*, 1867, *Roses*, *Fleurs*, 1872, *Roses*, 1873, *Roses*, 1874, *Roses sur un drap d'argent*, *Rose sur un drap d'or*, 1876, *Roses*, 1880, Exhib. Saint-Etienne Salon *Roses d'automne*, *Nid de guêpes dans un buisson d'églantier*, 1860; Dijon Salon *La coquille, roses*, 1881, (*Fleurs*, 1858); M: Lyon, Musée des Beaux-Arts; Saint-Etienne; Tournus
LIT *Hardouin-Fugier Grafe* (ill.): *Hardouin-Fugier Grafe* 1979 (ill.); *Hardouin-Fugier Grafe* 1982 (ill.)

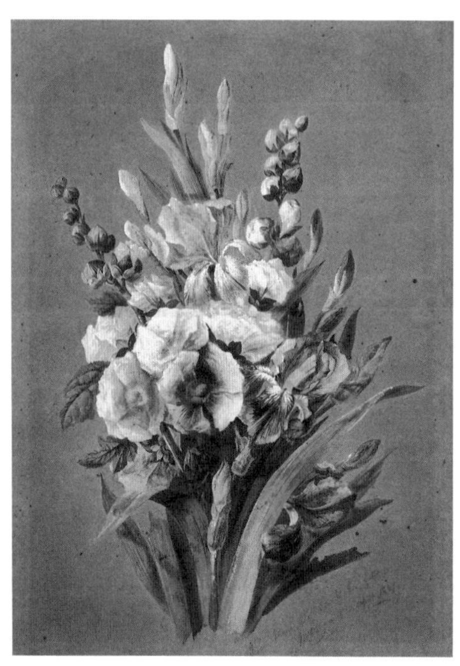

Antoine-Jules Pelletier

Bodycolour on paper, $24\frac{1}{2} \times 17\frac{3}{8}$ in. (62 × 44.2 cm.), signed, dated 1867 and inscribed. Cambridge, Fitzwilliam Museum (Broughton Collection)

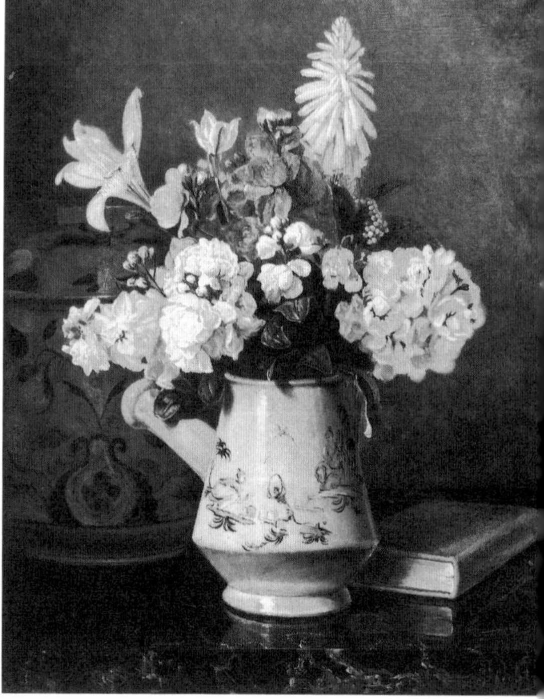

Joseph Pellet

Oil on canvas, $15\frac{3}{4} \times 12\frac{1}{2}$ in. (40 × 32 cm.), signed Montpellier, Musée Fabre

PERRARD, Constance-Adélaïde, later Jourdain ***1838–1871***
b. Poligny (Jura). Pupil of V. A. Maire. Painted still-lifes and, occasionally, flowers
LIT *Bénézit*; *Brune*; *Thieme*

PERRAUD, Louis
b. Lyon. Pupil of Bonnat and Boulanger. Exhib. *Pivoines herbacées*, *Lyon Salon* 1885
LIT *Lyon Salon* 1885

PERRAULT, Henri ***1867–1932***
b. Versailles (Yvelines). Pupil of Léon Perrault (1832–1908), his father, and A. Richemont. Painted figures, genre and, occasionally, flowers. Exhib. *Fleurs*, Poitiers Salon 1887
LIT *Poitiers Salon* 1887; *Witt*; BG

PERRE, Jean ***b.1809***
Pupil of Thierriat, Lyon BA (CFD 1833)
LIT *Hardouin-Fugier Grafe*

PERRÉE, Berthe
Exhib. *Roses*, Dijon Salon 1892
LIT *Dijon Salon* 1892. CL

PERRET, Aimé ***1847–1927***
b. Lyon. Pupil of Guichard, Vollon and Lyon BA. Painted genre, landscape, portraits, occasionally flowers. Debut at Paris Salon 1869. One of the founders of the SNBA
LIT *Bénézit*; Schurr III, 113. PM

PERRET, Antoine-Louis
Pupil of Lyon BA and Mettling. His *Fruits et fleurs* was in the 1873 Lyon Société des Amis-des-Arts raffle. Exhib. *Chrysanthèmes*, Paris Salon 1880; *Fleurs d'automne*, Paris Indép. 1884
LIT *Compte-rendu annuel de la Société des Amis-des-Arts de Lyon*, Lyon 1873; *Paris Indép.* 1884; *Paris Salon* 1880

PERRET, Charles
Pupil of Thierriat, Lyon BA (CFD 1843). Exhib. *Fleurs*, Saint-Etienne Salon 1882
LIT *Hardouin-Fugier Grafe*; *Saint-Etienne Salon* 1882

PERRIER, Henri ***b.1880***
Pupil of Castex-Dégrange, Lyon BA (CFD 1899)
LIT *Hardouin-Fugier Grafe*

PERRIN ***b.1809***
Pupil of Thierriat, Lyon BA (CFD 1826)
LIT *Hardouin-Fugier Grafe*

PERRIN, Gabriel
b. Lyon. Pupil of Lyon BA. First prize in the 1859 Lyon Société-Amis-des-Arts FDC. Exhib. Lyon Salon e.g. *Fleurs* 1870, *Lilas de serre et Camélia*, 1877, *Fruits et fleurs*, 1880 (Lyon Société des Amis-des-Arts raffle). Exhib. Paris Salon 1869–1896 e.g. *Fleurs et fruits*, 1870, *Roses*, 1895
LIT *Bellier*; *Bénézit*; *Lyon Salon* 1870; *Paris Salon* 1895; *Thieme*

PERRIN, Léonie
b. Paris. Pupil of Voruz and F. Barrias. Exhib. *Coquelicots*, wc, Paris Noir et Blanc Salon 1888
LIT *Paris Noir et Blanc Salon* 1888

PERRIOUD, Joseph-Victor ***b.1816***
Pupil of Thierriat, Lyon BA (CFD 1835)
LIT *Hardouin-Fugier Grafe*

PERROUDON, Lucien
b. Ferté-Gaucher (Seine-et-Marne). Exhib. *Roses mousseuses*, Paris Indép. 1887
LIT *Bénézit*; *Paris Indép.* 1887

PERSIN, Marie
b. Paris. Pupil of Cogniet and Nicolas. Painted genre, fruit and, occasionally, flowers. Exhib. Paris Salon from 1870
LIT *Bénézit*

PERSIN, Thérèse
Worked in Redouté's circle
LIT *Hardouin-Fugier* 1981

PERTUE, Marie
b. Paris. Pupil of Delattre, Saintpierre and Delacroix. Exhib. *Pavots rouges*, wc, Paris Salon 1898
LIT *Bénézit*; *Paris Salon* 1898

PETINIAUD-DUBOS, Charles
b. Limoges (Haute-Vienne). Painted genre and flowers. Exhib. Paris Salon from 1894. Exhib. *Fleurs d'automne*, Paris Indép. 1899
LIT *Bénézit*; *Paris Indép.* 1899

PETIT, Didier ***b. 1793***
b. USA. Pupil of Berjon, Lyon BA (CFD 1813). Textile manufacturer. S. Saint-Jean's first employer. Eager collector, garden lover and influential member of *Oeuvre de la Propagation de la Foi* (Lyon). His flowers are early works
LIT Hardouin-Fugier. *Simon Saint-Jean* (Lewis Leigh-on-Sea) 1981, p. 15

PETIT, Etienne ***b.1814***
Pupil of Thierriat, Lyon BA (CFD 1833)
LIT *Hardouin-Fugier Grafe*

PETIT, Eugène ***1839–1886***
b. Paris. Pupil of E. Muller and Diéterle. Exhib. Paris Salon from 1863 e.g. *Fleurs de printemps*, 1869, *Le bouquet du jardinier*, 1875, *Fleurs*, tapestry cartoon for Palais du Luxembourg, 1878, *Fleurs*, tapestry cartoon (Beauvais) 1879, *Pivoines*, 1880, *Fleurs*, *Pivoines*, 1885; Lyon Salon e.g. *Vase de chrysanthèmes*, 1875, *Pêches et giroflées*, 1880. *Cornflowers, daisies and poppies in a glass vase*, Parke-Bernet, New York, 3 Oct. 1975. *Fleurs*, Lasson Gallery, London, Nov. 1976. M: Carcassonne, *Fleurs et argenterie*, Compiègne, *Fleurs*; Courtrai, *Fleurs*; Rouen, *Roses*; Saint-Etienne, *Fleurs*

LIT *Bellier*; *Bénézit*; *Lyon Salon* 1875, 1880; *Orsay*; *Paris Salon* 1875, 1878–1880, 1885; *Thieme*; *Witt*

PETIT, François ***b.1827***
Pupil of Thierriat, Lyon BA (CFD 1844)
LIT *Hardouin-Fugier Grafe*

PETIT, Ida
b. Boulogne-sur-mer (Pas-de-Calais). Pupil of Solange Petit. Exhib. *Tulipes*, gouache, Paris Salon 1880
LIT *Paris Salon* 1880

PETIT, Jacob, ***alias*** **Jacob-Petit** ***1806–1868***
Pupil of Gros. At Sèvres from 1822. Owner of the Fontainebleau porcelain factory. Flower and porcelain painter
LIT *Bénézit*; *Thieme*

PETIT, P. J.
op. Sèvres 1808–1811
LIT *Brunet Préaud*

PETIT, Solange, ***née*** **Poirson**
b. Autun (Saône-et-Loire). Pupil of Dumoulin. Painted flowers in gouache and wc. Exhib. Paris Salon from 1878 e.g. *Fleurs des champs*, gouache, 1878, *Buisson de roses*, gouache, 1879, *Coquelicots*, wc, 1881
LIT *Bellier*; *Bénézit*

PETITEAU, Madeleine
Pupil of E. Claude. Exhib. *Chrysanthèmes*, Paris UFPS 1896
LIT *Paris UFPS* 1896

PETITFRÈRE, René
Exhib. *Fleurs des champs*, Dijon Salon 1894
LIT *Dijon Salon* 1894

PETITJEAN, Jeanne ***b.1828***
b. Paris. Pupil of Thénot and Watelet. Painted landscapes, fruit and flowers. Exhib. Paris Salon from 1863
LIT *Bellier*; *Bénézit*

PETITJEAN, ***see*** **LAUVERNAY**

PETRÉ, Hippolyte-Antoine ***b.1835***
Pupil of Thierriat, Lyon BA (CFD 1853). Exhib. *Pensées*, gouache, Lyon Salon 1858
LIT *Hardouin-Fugier Grafe*; *Lyon Salon* 1858

PÊTRE, ***see*** **MULON**

PETUA, Léon-Jean ***1846–1921***
b. Besançon (Doubs). Pupil of Gérôme. Exhib. Paris Salon 1875. Painted figures, landscapes and, occasionally, flowers. Exhib. *Pour faire un bouquet*, Dijon Salon 1887
LIT *Bénézit*; *Dijon Salon* 1887

PEYRON, Joseph ***c.1841–1910***
b. Saint-Etienne (Loire). op. decorator (Saint-Etienne Bourse and Hôtel-de-Ville,

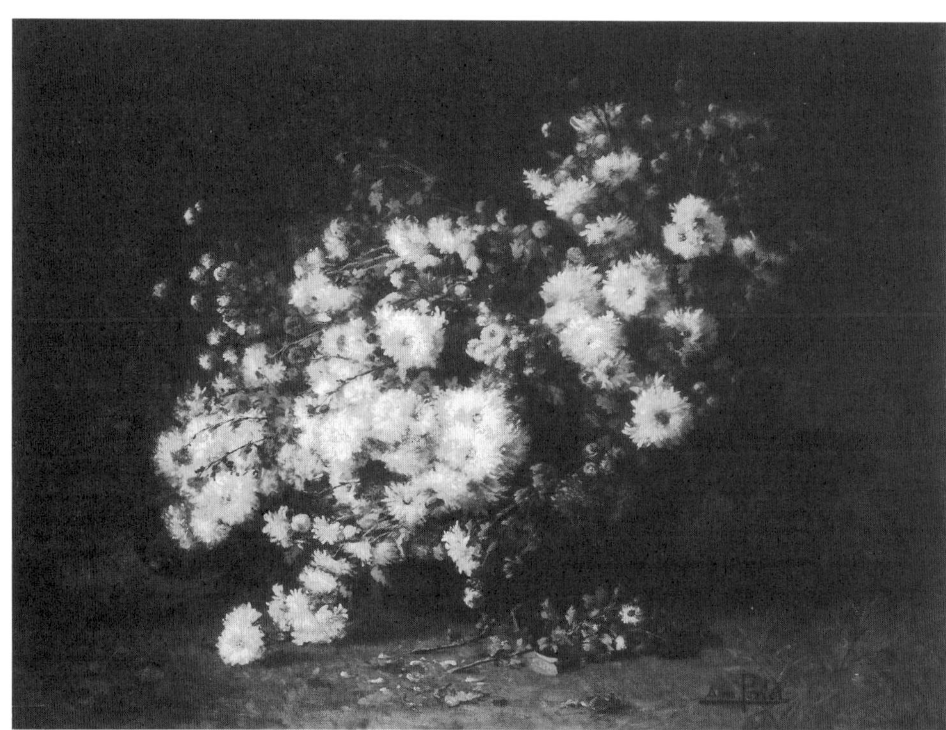

Aimé Perret

Oil on canvas, 38½ × 54 in., (96.5 × 130.2 cm.), signed
Courtesy Sotheby's, New York

Gabriel Perrin

Watercolour, 14½ × 21¼ in. (37 × 54 cm.), signed
(photo: Marie-Jane Garoche, Paris)

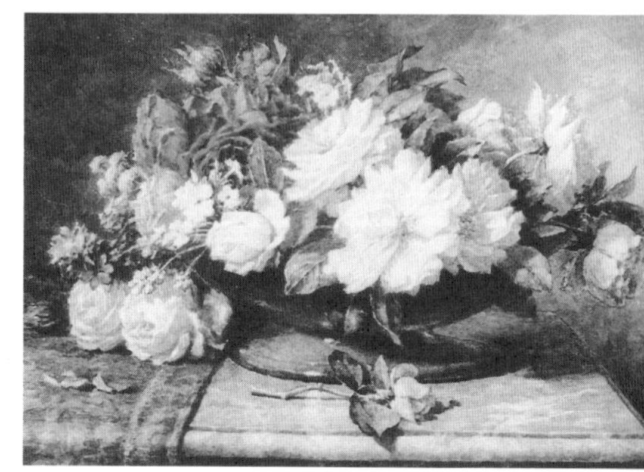

various cafés). Painted landscapes, still-lifes and flowers. Exhib. *Fleurs et fruits*, gouache, *Roses trémières*, Saint-Etienne Salon 1882; *Fleurs*, Lyon Salon 1888. Musée de Saint-Etienne, *Roses trémières*, *Fleurs*
LIT *Hardouin-Fugier Bringuier*; G. Joubert *Dossiers*, *Saint-Etienne* BA

PEYSSONEAU, Claire
Exhib. *Les roses*, Dijon Salon 1897
LIT *Dijon Salon* 1897. CL

PFLUCHER, M.
Exhib. *Roses d'automne*, Paris Salon 1885
LIT *Paris Salon* 1885 (ill.)

PHALIPON, Adolphe
Painted portraits, genre, fruit and flowers. Exhib. Paris Salon 1846–1848 e.g. *Fruits et fleurs*, 1846
LIT *Bellier*; *Bénézit*

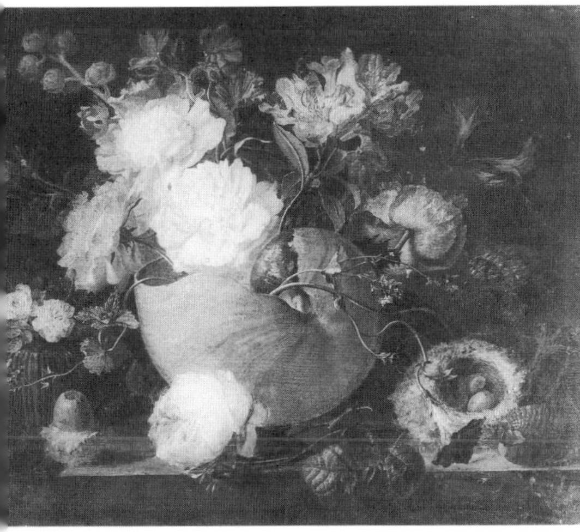

Jean-François Philippine

Oil on canvas, 15 × 18¾ in. (38 × 48 cm.)
Sèvres Manufacture Nationale de Sèvres

PHALIPON, Louise, *née* Vincent
Painted portraits, fruit and, occasionally, flowers, often on porcelain. Exhib. Paris Salon 1837–1850
LIT *Bellier*; *Bénézit*

PHILIBERT, Marie
Exhib. Paris Indép. *Chrysanthèmes du Japon*, 1893, *Chrysanthèmes du Japon*, *Roses*, 1894, *Roses*, 1898
LIT *Paris Indép.* 1893, 1894, 1898

PHILIPARD, Charles
b. Auxerre (Yonne). Pupil of Van Spaendonck and Lesourd de Beauregard. Painted flowers and fruit. Exhib. Paris Salon 1863–1868 e.g. *Fleurs, fraises et cerises*, 1864, *Fleurs et fruits*, 1865
LIT *Bellier*; *Bénézit*; *Faré* 1962, p. 245; *Thieme*

PHILIPPINE, Jean-François *1771–1840*
Pupil of Jacobber, op. Sèvres. Exhib. Paris Salon *Fleurs*, on porcelain, 1819, *Bouquets* (2), porcelain, 1840. Many namesakes worked at Sèvres. M: Sèvres (Manufacture Nationale) *Fleurs dans une coquille et nid*
LIT *Bellier*; *Bénézit*; *Faré* 1962, p. 246; *Gabet*; *Mitchell*; *Paris Salon* 1840; *Thieme*

PHILIPPON, Augustine, *née* Simonet
Pupil of Levasseur, Donzel and Glaize. Exhib. *Etude de pivoines*, pastel, Paris UFPS 1896
LIT *Bénézit*; *Paris UFPS* 1896

PHILT, Marie
b. Paris. Exhib. *Roses*, Paris Indép. 1891
LIT *Paris Indép.* 1891

PICARD, Augustine
Pupil of Cogniet, Painted portraits, still-lifes and, occasionally, flowers. Exhib. Paris Salon 1841–1865
LIT *Bénézit*; *Faré* 1962, p. 248; *Thieme*

PICARD, Edmond-Marie-André *1861–1899*
b. Besançon (Doubs). Pupil of Rapin and J. P. Laurens. Painted genre and, occasionally, flowers. Exhib. Paris Indép. *Grosses roses, bouquet pour cuisinière*, 1886, *Laurier rose*, 1887
LIT *Bénézit*; *Paris Indép.* 1886, 1887; Edmond Picard, Sale Drouot, Paris, Dec. 1900; *Schurr* III, 59; Witt

PICARD, Julie-Ange, *née* Wasset *1802–1842*
Pupil of Redouté. Designed plates for *Cours des Fleurs du Jardin des Plantes*, Paris (Chavant); *Choix de 15 bouquets de fleurs*, Paris (Chavant). Exhib. wc Paris Salon 1831, 1833, 1836, 1838, 1840
LIT *Bénézit*; *Hardouin-Fugier* 1981

PICARD, Martin
op. Paris. Painted animals, still-lifes and, occasionally, flowers. Exhib. Paris Salon 1837, 1839, 1844
LIT *Bénézit*

PICARD, *see* CHAVANT

PICARD-FOUBERT, Elie-Ernest
b. Paris. Pupil of Cogniet and Bonnat. Painted portraits, landscapes and flowers. Exhib. Paris Salon from 1880. Exhib. Paris Indép. *Fleurs*, *Giroflées*, 1888, *Pivoines*, 1890
LIT *Bénézit*; *Paris Indép.* 1888, 1890

PICHAT, Ennemond *b.1816*
Pupil of Thierriat, Lyon BA (CFD 1835)
LIT *Hardouin-Fugier Grafe*

PICHON, Marguerite
Pupil of Lefebure and T. Robert-Fleury, Exhib. *Chrysanthèmes*, *Tulipes*, *Cueillette*, wc, Paris UFPS 1896
LIT *Paris UFPS* 1896

PICOU, Eugène *b.1831*
b. Nantes (Loire-Atlantique). Pupil of Debret. Painted landscapes and flowers. Exhib. Paris Salon from 1879. Exhib. Dijon Salon *Fleurs et fruits*, 1883, *Chrysanthèmes*, wc, 1892, *Panier de roses*, wc, 1894. Exhib. Strasbourg Salon *Chrysanthèmes*, wc (150 francs) 1891. Musée de Nantes, *Pavots*
LIT *Bénézit*; *Dijon Salon* 1883, 1892, 1894; *Strasbourg Salon* 1891

PIERDON, François *1821–1904*
b. Saint-Gerand-le-Puy (Allier). Pupil of Hanoteau. Etcher. Painted landscapes and, occasionally, flowers. Exhib. Paris Salon from 1853. Exhib. *Bouquet d'automne*, Lyon Salon 1869
LIT *Bénézit*; *Lyon Salon* 1869; *Schurr* IV, 47

PIERON, Georges
b. Paris. Painted still-lifes, game and flowers. Exhib. Paris Salon 1869, 1870, e.g. *Fleurs*, 1869
LIT *Bellier*; *Bénézit*

PIERRAT, Nicolas-Constant 1829–1910
b. Münster (Haut-Rhin). Pupil of Vollon and Guillemet. Painter and lithographer. Painted landscapes, still-lifes and flowers. Exhib. Paris Salon from 1867 e.g. *Chrysanthèmes*, *Glycines*, 1875, *Roses Malmaison*, 1878, *Fleurs*, 1890
LIT *Bellier*; *Bénézit*; *Paris Salon* 1875, 1890; *Thieme*

PIERRE, Caroline, *née* Bailly
b. Annecy (Haute-Savoie). Pupil of Cabanel and Cellières. Exhib. Paris Salon *Lilas et pensées*, on porcelain, 1879, *Roses*, on porcelain, 1880
LIT *Bellier*; *Paris Salon* 1880

PIERRESON, Marthe
Exhib. *Fleurs*, Paris UFPS 1896
LIT *Paris UFPS* 1896

PIERRET, Gabrielle
b. Compiègne (Oise). Exhib. *Pivoines*, *Roses*, Paris Indép. 1894. Compiègne, Musée Vivenel, *Lilas et Pivoines*
LIT *Bénézit*; *Paris Indép.* 1894

PIERRON, Blanche
Exhib. *Panier de lilas*, wc, Dijon Salon 1892
LIT *Dijon Salon* 1892

PIERROT or PIERRET
Entered 1859 Lyon Société des Amis-des-Arts FDC
LIT *Compte-rendu annuel de la Société des Amis-des-Arts de Lyon*, (Perrin) 1859

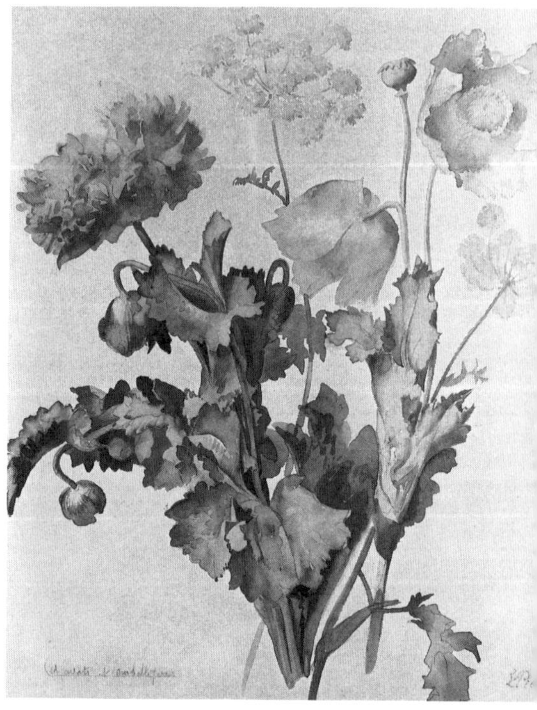

Eugène Picou

Watercolour, 16½ × 13¾ in., (42 × 35 cm), signed (photo: Musée des Beaux-Arts, Nantes)

PIERSON, Blanche-Adeline
b. La Réunion. Pupil of Dubasty and Clairin. Painted genre and still-lifes. Many of her works feature flowers e.g. *Accessoires de la danse sacrée au Japon*, 1880, *Noël*, Paris Salon 1882
LIT *Bénézit*; *Witt*

PIETTE, Ludovic ***1826–1877***
b. Niort (Deux-Sevres). Pupil of Couture and Pils. Friend of Pissarro and Manet. Painted landscapes, figures and flowers. Exhib. Lyon Salon *Fleurs*, 1858; Paris Salon from 1875 e.g. *Fleurs*, 1861. M: Pontoise (not flowers)
LIT *Bellier*; *Bénézit*; *Lyon Salon* 1858; *Paris Salon* 1861; *Schurr* I, 105; *Thieme*

PIGNANT, Marie-Marguerite
Exhib. Dijon Salon *Quelques fleurs du clos, pivoines*, 1881, *Quelques fleurs de printemps*, 1887, *Bouquet de pivoines*, 1890, *Une botte de pavots*, *Fleurs*, 1894
LIT *Dijon Salon* 1881, 1887, 1890, 1894

PIJEAUD, *see* NOBLE

PILET, Laure
b. Paris. Pupil of École de la rue Dupuytren and Thoret. Exhib. *Branche d'églantier*, fan-leaf, wc and gouache, Paris Salon 1875
LIT *Paris Salon* 1875

PILLEMENT, Jean-Baptiste ***1728–1808***
b. Lyon. Pupil of Sarrabat at Lyon. A neglected but excellent individual landscape painter and pioneer of the Chinoiserie taste, travelled throughout Europe. Belongs to the 18th century, but such is his influence on the designs of silk fabrics and materials that he must be included as a forerunner of a sustained tradition at Lyon. Two hundred of his drawings were engraved under the title *Fleurs naturelles, Fleurs idéales et de fantaisie dans le gout chinois propres aux manufactures de soie et d'indienne*
LIT *Hardouin-Fugier Grafe*. PM

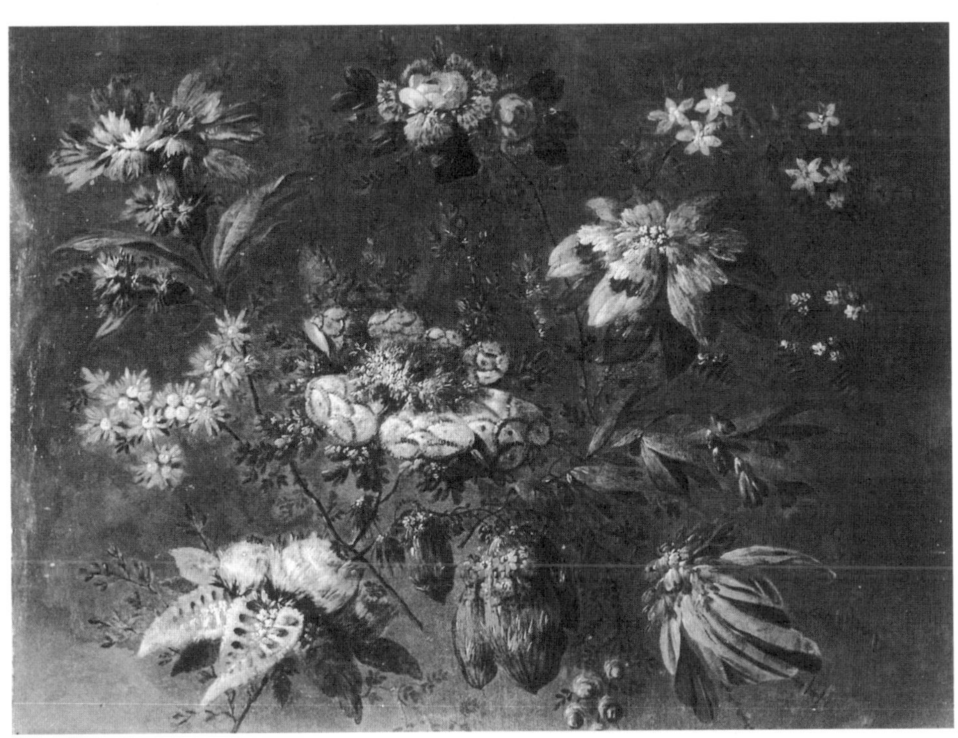

Jean-Baptiste Pillement

Oil on canvas, 18 × $21\frac{3}{4}$ in. (46 × 55 cm.), signed and dated 'l'an 7R'
Lyon, Musée des Arts Décoratifs

PILLET, Celina
Exhib. Paris Indép. *Fleurs*, 1893, *Fleurs*, pastel, 1894
LIT *Paris Indép*. 1893, 1894

PILLET, *see* DUBOIS

PILON, Agathe
Pupil of Couton. Exhib. Paris Salon 1838–1847 e.g. *Fleurs*, 1838, *Fleurs et raisins dans un panier*, 1841, *Reines-marguerites*, 1846; *Fleurs*, Lyon Salon 1839
LIT *Bellier*; *Bénézit*; *Lyon Salon* 1839; *Paris Salon* 1838, 1841, 1846

PILON-GUITEL, Flore
Pupil of Cavaillé-Coll, Odin and Cox. Exhib. wc, *Pavots*, screen, *Iris et roses trémières*, *Chrysanthèmes*, Paris UFPS 1898
LIT *Bénézit*; *Paris UFPS* 1898

PINCHON-LECOURIEUX, Madeleine ***b.1868***
b. Mesnil-Esnard (Seine-Maritime) or Philippeville (Algeria). Pupil of Allongé. Exhib. Paris UFPS *Passe-roses*, *Chrysanthèmes*, 1896, *Cognassier du Japon*, wc, 1898. Musée de Rouen; *Livres et fleurs*
LIT *Bénézit*; *Paris Indép*. 1896, 1898

PINEL, François ***b.1827***
Pupil of Thierriat, Lyon BA (CFD 1843)
LIT *Hardouin-Fugier Grafe*

PINEL, Georges
Painted still-lifes and flowers. Apart from the illustrated example of 1878, a still-life is recorded at the Musée de Pontoise, as having been exhibited there in 1897. Has been confused with Gustave Pinel
LIT *Bénézit*. PM

PINET, Claude-Nicolas ***b.1818***
Pupil of Thierriat, Lyon BA (CFD 1838)
LIT *Hardouin-Fugier Grafe*

PINET, Marie
Exhib. *Roses*, Grenoble Salon 1899
LIT *Grenoble Salon* 1899. MW

PINGOT, Henri-Auguste
b. Mantes (Seine-et-Oise). Pupil of Lazerges and Lafosse. Exhib. Paris Salon 1848–1876
LIT *Bénézit*. PM

PIOGÉ-BRIELMAN, Julie-Eugénie
b. Paris. Pupil of Brielman. Exhib. *Roses*, *Glycines*, gouaches, Paris Noir et Blanc Salon 1888
LIT *Paris Noir et Blanc Salon* 1888

PIOT, Adolphe-Etienne
b. Dijon (Côte-d'Or). Pupil of L. Cogniet. Painted portraits, figures and flowers. Exhib. Paris Salon from 1883 e.g. *Bouquet*, 1890
LIT *Bellier*; *Bénézit*; *Paris Salon* 1890

PIOT, Catherin-Ernest
b. Paris. Pupil of Bergeret. Exhib. *Lilas*, Paris Indép. 1884; *Chrysanthèmes*, Paris Salon 1890
LIT *Paris Salon* 1890; *Paris Indép.* 1884

PIOT, Mme Charles, *née* Jeanne-Adèle Lemaire
b. Paris. Pupil of Jacobber, Redouté and O. Arson. Painted flowers and fruit. Exhib. watercolours at Paris Salon 1843–1865 e.g. *Bouquet de roses*, 1844, *Roses trémières*, *Groupe de fleurs*, 1845; *Pivoines de Sibérie*, *pieds d'alouette*, wc., *Roses cent-feuilles*, wc., *Roses*, Paris Ex position Universelle 1855
LIT *Bellier*; *Bénézit*; *Faré* 1962, p. 246; *Paris Exposition Universelle* 1855; *Paris Salon* 1844, 1845

PIOT, René ***1869–1934***
b. Paris. Pupil of G. Moreau and Andrieu. Designed theatre sets, costumes and tapestry cartoons (Gobelins). M: Belfort, *Dahlias*; Grenoble, *Fleurs*, wc (legacy of Agutte-Sembat, 1923)
LIT *Bénézit*; Paris Arch. Nat. F21: 4500; *Schurr* 1, 128; *Thieme*, Witt

PIPARD, Charles ***b.1832***
b. Versailles (Yvelines). Pupil of Gigoux. Lithographer. Painted portraits and still-lifes. Exhib. Paris Salon 1859–1902. e.g. *Fruits et fleurs dans un paysage*, 1867
LIT *Bénézit*; *Béraldi*; *Paris Salon* 1867; *Thieme*

Georges Pinel

Oil on canvas, 32 × 25½ in. (81 × 65 cm.), signed and dated 1878
Private collection

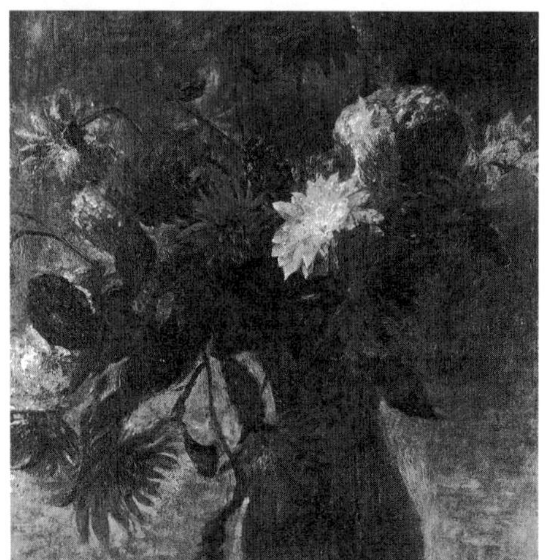

PIQUET, Pierre ***1828–1878***
b. Lyon. Pupil of Bonnefond. Painted genre and, occasionally, flowers. Exhib. *Roses*, Lyon Salon 1863
LIT *Bénézit*; *Lyon Salon* 1863; *Thieme*

PIQUET de, *see* BRIENNE

PIRON
Designed plates for J. J. La Billardière, *Novae Hollandiae Plantarum Specimen*, Paris 1804–1806, with Poiteau, Redouté, Sauvage and Turpin
LIT *Sitwell*

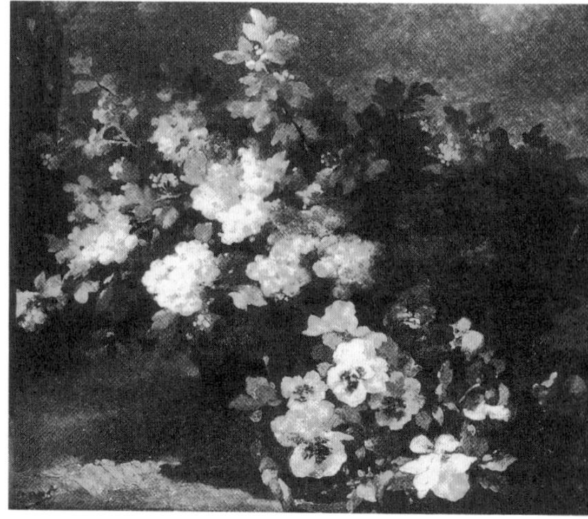

Henri-August Pingot

Oil on canvas, 19¼ × 25½ in. (49 × 65 cm.), signed
Private collection

René Piot (*left*)

Oil on canvas, 19¾ × 19¾ in. (50 × 50 cm.), dated 1904
Belfort, Musée d'Art et d'Histoire

PISCATORY, *see* PASTORET

PISSARRO, Camille *1830–1903*
b. Saint-Thomas (Danish West Indies). Mostly self-taught. Mainly a landscape and figure painter but a flower-lover who occasionally painted flowers when rainy weather kept him from working out of doors. His wife, who worked for a florist, was particularly proud of her pink peonies (Rewald). *Chrysanthèmes dans un vase*, 1870; *Bouquet de pivoines*, 1873 (Oxford); *Roses dans un vase*, 1877; *Bouquet de fleurs*, 1878 (Minneapolis); *Bouquet de fleurs*, 1878 (Sotheby's 1961); *Bouquet de fleurs, iris, coquelicots*, 1898; *Bouquet de fleurs*, 1898 (San Francisco); *Bouquet*, 1900; *Bouquet of flowers* (Atlanta 1984); *Nature-morte et fleurs dans un vase*. M: Minneapolis Institute of Art; Oxford, Ashmolean; San Francisco, Fine Arts Museum
LIT *Bénézit*; Orsay; L. R. Pissarro and L. Venturi, *Camille Pissarro, son art, son oeuvre*, Paris (Rosenberg) 1939; J. Rewald, *Pissarro* Paris (Braun) 1948

PITET, *see* CHAMPIN

PITOLET, Fanny-Jeanne
b. Paris. Pupil of Dumoulin and Barré. Exhib. flowers in gouache, Paris Salon from 1877
LIT *Bénézit*

PITRA, Claude-Antoine *b.1807*
Pupil of Thierriat, Lyon BA (CFD 1827)
LIT *Hardouin-Fugier Grafe*

PITRE, Hubert
Exhib. *Boutons de roses*, Saint-Etienne Salon 1882
LIT *Saint-Etienne Salon* 1882

PITRE, Jean-Gaspard *b.1830*
Pupil of Thierriat, Lyon BA (CFD 1848)
LIT *Hardouin-Fugier Grafe*

PITTOUD, Joséphine-Louisa de
b. Paris. Painted genre, landscapes and flowers. Exhib. Paris Salon from 1866 e.g. *Bouquet de fleurs des champs*, 1866
LIT *Hardouin-Fugier-Grafe*

PIVOT, Alexandre *b.1868*
Pupil of Reignier, Lyon BA (CFD 1884)
LIT *Hardouin-Fugier Grafe*

PIZZETY or PIZZETAY, Jacques-Claude, Claudius, from 1881 Pizzeta *alias* *1832–1894*
b. Belley (Ain). Pupil of Thierriat, Lyon BA (CFD 1850). Exhib. Lyon Salon from 1858 to 1864, from 1881 to 1887 and from 1892 to 1894. Painted still-lifes and flowers. op. art teacher
LIT *Hardouin-Fugier Grafe*; *Hardouin-Fugier Grafe* 1982 (ill.)

PLACE-FONTAINE, Mme
Painted still-lifes and flowers. Musée de Louviers (not a flower picture)
LIT *Bénézit*; Musée de Louviers doc.

PLANSON, Joseph-Alphonse *b.1799*
b. Orléans (Loiret). Painted landscapes, animals, fruit and flowers. Exhib. Paris Salon 1836–1859 e.g. *Fleurs et fruits*, 1836, *Fleurs dans un vase étrusque*, *Corbeille de fleurs*, 1837, *Fleurs dans un vase de bronze*, 1841, *Fleurs dans une corbeille sur une table de marbre*, 1844
LIT *Bellier*; *Bénézit*; *Faré*, 1962, p. 249; *Paris Salon* 1836, 1837, 1841, 1844; *Thieme*

PLANTET
Exhib. *Fleurs et fruits*, copy. Dijon Salon 1849
LIT *Dijon Salon* 1849. CL

PLAS Mme de, *see* GRIMAUD

PLÉE, François
Son of Auguste Plée (1787–1825). Designed plates for A. Plée *Herborisations...aux environs de Paris*, Paris 1811, and *Types...de plantes croissant spontanément en France*, Paris 1844–1860, and for many other books
LIT *Nissen* I, 207, 459, 461, 954, 1016, 1534, 1535, 1630, 1635, 1715

PLUCHART, Flore
Exhib. *Couronne de fleurs des champs*, wc, Paris Salon 1844
LIT *Paris Salon* 1844

POCHAT, Antoine-Eugène *b.1822*
Pupil of Thierriat, Lyon BA (CFD 1840)
LIT *Hardouin-Fugier Grafe*

PODEVIN, Séraphin *1822–1878*
op. Cambrai. Pupil of B. Martho (1747–1832). Portrait and flower painter
LIT *Bénézit*; *Thieme*

POILEUX, Edwige
Exhib. *Violettes et jacinthes roses*, wc, Dijon Salon 1892
LIT *Dijon Salon* 1892

POILEY, *alias* Jean de Chaville
Exhib. Fleurs, *Paris Indép*. 1898
LIT *Paris Indép*. 1898

POILPOT, Théophile
b. Saint-Brieuce (Côtes-du-Nord). Pupil of Cogniet. Exhib. Paris Salon e.g. *Tulipes de races*, 1841
LIT *Bellier*; Paris Arch. Nat. F21: 301; *Paris Salon* 1841; *Schurr* IV, 92

POINT, Armand *1861–1932*
b. Alger (Algeria). Pupil of A. Herst. The now popular symbolist painted a few works featuring flowers e.g. *Mimosas*, Paris SNBA 1893
LIT *Bénézit*; J. Daurelle, *A. Point*, Paris (La Plume) 1901; *Schurr* I, 121; *Thieme*

POINTEL DU PORTAIL
Active 1820–1845. Designed and lithographed *Fleurs de la Chine*, n.d. (*c*1835) Paris BMAD (Maciet coll.) and a set of twelve flower plates with lithographer Prévost, Paris 1835
LIT *Brune*; *Nissen* I, 1598 n; *Paris BMAD*; *Thieme*

POIRET, A. fils
op. *c*.1820–1830. Designed plates e.g. for *Histoire . . . des plantes d'Europe* 1825–1829
LIT *Nissen*, I, 461, 1552, 2244

POIRIER, Paul-Théodore ***d.1895***
b. Paris. Pupil of J. Lequien. Painted flowers on faience and in oils. Exhib. Paris Salon from 1878 e.g. *Roses*, on faience, 1880, *Fleurs de mai*, 1882, *Fleurs (fin d'automne)*, 1885; *Chrysanthèmes* (150 francs), Strasbourg Salon 1891
LIT *Bellier*; *Bénézit*; *Paris Salon* 1880, 1885; *Strasbourg Salon* 1891; *Thieme*

POIRSON, *see* PETIT

POITEAU, Antoine ***1766–1854***
b. Ambleny (Aisne). Pupil of Redouté. Gardener at the Paris Jardin des Plantes. Trained as a botanist. Sailed to Santo Domingo, Cayenne etc. Co-designer of Ventenat's and Mordant de Launay's botanical books and, with Turpin, of *Flora Parisiensis*, Paris (Schoell), 1808–1813, etc. M: Cambridge; Paris, Muséum d'Histoire Naturelle
LIT Broughton 1983/84; *Hardouin-Fugier* 1981 (ill.)

POLAILLON, Jean-Baptiste
Pupil of Berjon, Lyon BA (CFD 1820)
LIT *Hardouin-Fugier Grafe*

POLY, Jean-Baptiste ***b.1827***
Pupil of Thierriat, Lyon BA (CFD 1844)
LIT *Hardouin-Fugier Grafe*

POMARET, Gabrielle de
b. Mende (Lozère). Pupil of J. Salles, F. Barrias and J. Laurens. Painted portraits, folk scenes and flowers. Exhib. Paris Salon from 1878 e.g. *Roses trémières*, wc, 1890; Paris Noir et Blanc Salon, *Fleurs*, 1886, 1888
LIT *Bellier*; *Paris Noir et Blanc Salon* 1886, 1888; *Paris Salon* 1890

POMEY, *see* DUCLOUX

POMPASKY, Jean-Baptiste ***1818–1895***
Pupil of Thierriat, Lyon BA (CFD 1837). Exhib. Lyon Salon 1838–1878
LIT *Hardouin-Fugier Grafe*

PONCET, Jean-Baptiste ***1827–1901***
Pupil of Thierriat, Lyon BA (CFD 1845). Mostly genre and history painter
LIT *Bénézit*; *Hardouin-Fugier Grafe*; *Thieme*

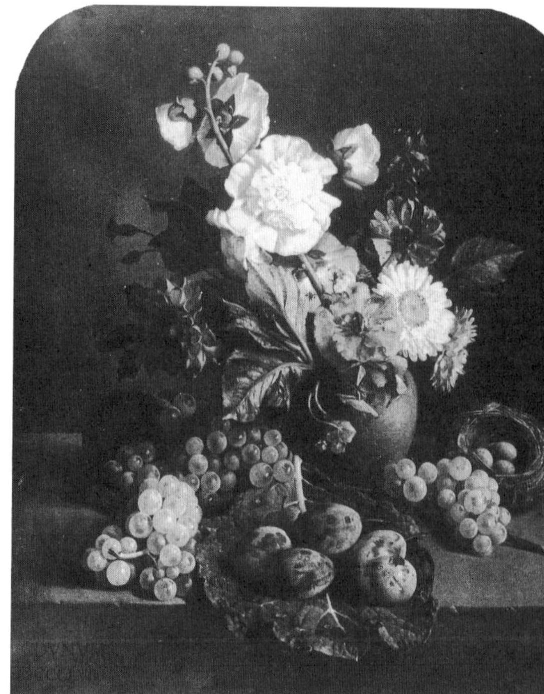

Jacques-Claude Pizzety or Pizzetay

Oil on panel, 34¾ × 29½ in. (88 × 75 cm.), signed and dated 1858
Lyon, Musée des Beaux-Arts

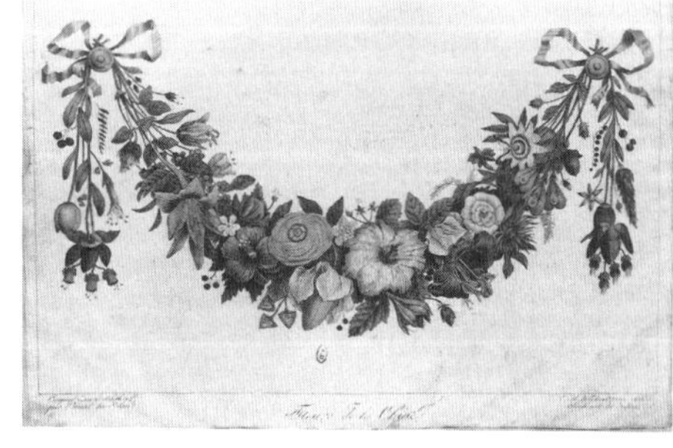

Pointel du Portail

Engraving after a drawing, 10 × 13¾ in. (25 × 35 cm.)
Paris, BMAD (Maciet Collection)

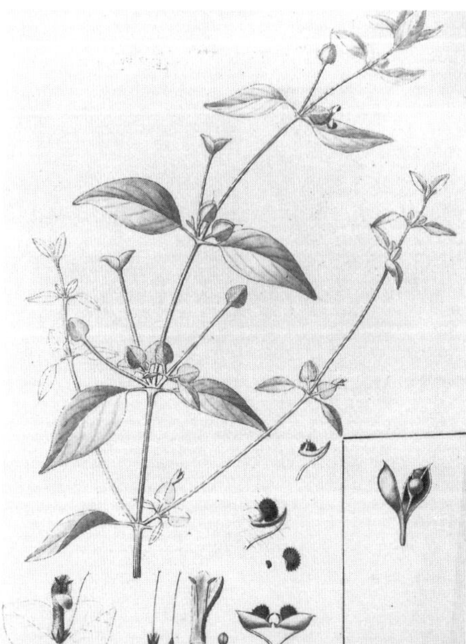

Antoine Poiteau (*left*)

Watercolour on vellum, Vélins, ms. 337, signed
Paris, Bibliothèque Centrale du Muséum National d'Histoire Naturelle

PONCET, Joseph ***b.1821***
Pupil of Thierriat, Lyon BA (CFD 1839)
LIT *Hardouin-Fugier Grafe*

PONCET, Léopold
Pupil of Castex-Dégrange, Lyon BA (CFD 1893)
LIT *Hardouin-Fugier Grafe*

PONIATOWSKA, Aurore
fl. *c.*1817. Pupil of Redouté
LIT *Hardouin-Fugier* 1981

PONS, Jean-Claude ***b.1823***
Pupil of Thierriat, Lyon BA (CFD 1841)
LIT *Hardouin-Fugier Grafe*

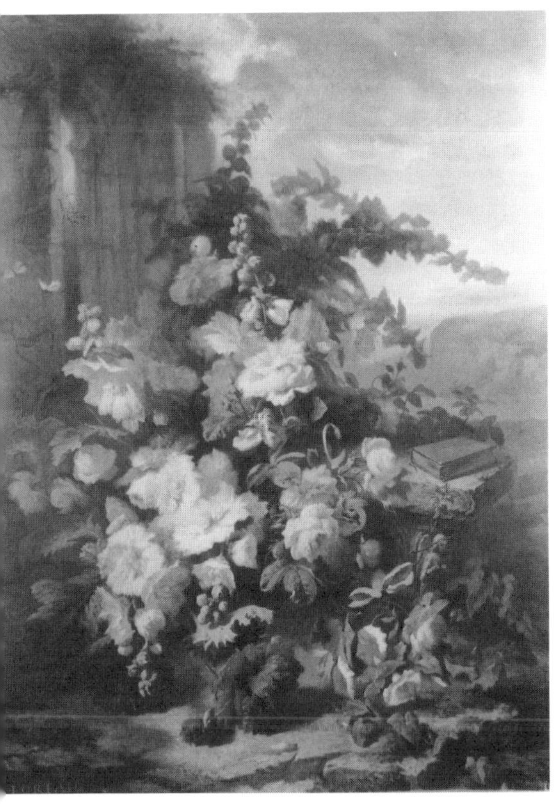

Amédée-Louis Portail

Oil on canvas, 63 × 46½ in. (160 × 118 cm.), signed
Dijon, Musée des Beaux Arts

PONS, Michel ***b.1872***
Pupil of Castex-Détgrange, Lyon BA (CFD 1889)
LIT *Hardouin-Fugier Grafe*

PONSAN, ***see*** **DEBAT**

PONSARD, Andrée
Pupil of Thoret and F. Rivoire. Exhib. *Bourriche d'oeillets*, wc, Paris UFPS 1898
LIT *Paris UFPS* 1898

PONSON, Etienne-Aimé ***b.1850***
b. Marseille. Pupil of L. R. Ponson, his brother. Painted genre, still-lifes and, occasionally, flowers. Exhib. Paris Salon from 1876
LIT *Bellier*; *Bénézit*; *Orsay*; *Schurr* I, 73; *Thieme*

PORCHÉ, ***see*** **GUÉRIN**

PORCHER, Charles-Albert ***1834–1895***
b. Orléans (Loiret). Painted landscape and flowers. Exhib. Paris Salon from 1865
LIT *Bellier*; *Bénézit*; *Orsay*; *Thieme*

PORTAIL, Amédée-Louis
Pupil of Van Spaendonck and Lesourd de Beauregard. Exhib. Paris Salon 1865–1874 e.g. *Vase de fleurs*, 1865, *Fleurs*, fan-leaf, wc, 1966. His copy of a still-life by S. Saint-Jean was bought (800 francs) by the State for the Musée de Dijon (1865)
LIT *Bellier*; *Bénézit*; *Faré* 1962, p. 243; Paris Arch. Nat. F21: 173, 445

PORTE, Adèle de la
Exhib. Paris Salon 1845–1850 e.g. *Roses*, 1845
LIT *Faré* 1962, p. 248; *Paris Salon* 1845

PORTIER
Pupil of Suvée. Painted birds, insects, shells and, occasionally, flowers. Exhib. Paris Salon 1806, 1814, 1819. A signed watercolour sold at Sotheby's, Monaco, 22 Feb. 1986 may be by the artist
LIT *Bellier*; *Bénézit*; *Paris Salon* 1814

POSTEL, ***see*** **NOEL**

POTEAU, Clara
Exhib. *Roses*, Paris Salon 1850
LIT *Paris Salon* 1850

POTEMONT, Adolphe-Théodore-Jules-Martial ***1828–1883***
b. Paris. Pupil of Cogniet and Brissot de Warville. Painter and engraver. Painted landscapes and, occasionally, flowers. Exhib. Paris Salon from 1848 e.g. *Bouquet de pensées*, 1880
LIT *Bellier*; *Bénézit*; *Paris Salon* 1880; *Schurr* II, 46

POTHIER, Claude-Charles ***b.1809***
Pupil of Thierriat, Lyon BA (CFD 1829)
LIT *Hardouin-Fugier Grafe*

POTTIER, Constance
b. Paris. Pupil of A. Bonheur. Painted flowers. Exhib. Paris Salon from 1864
LIT *Bénézit*

POTY, Laurent ***b.1828***
Pupil of Thierriat, Lyon BA (CFD 1846)
LIT *Hardouin-Fugier Grafe*

POURCHET, Edouard ***1839–1888***
Pupil of Thierriat, Lyon BA (CFD 1854). Exhib. Lyon Salon from 1865 e.g. *Vase de roses*, 1866, *Fleurs*, 1875, *Diane de Poitiers entourée de roses*, 1880
LIT *Hardouin-Fugier Grafe*; *Lyon Salon* 1866, 1875

POURCHET, Philippe ***1873–1941***
Pupil of Castex-Dégrange, Lyon BA (CFD 1892) Active in Lyon. Painted mostly landscapes
LIT *Hardouin-Fugier Grafe*

POUSSIN
Fleur d'amandier, after Pithou, 1825 (Sèvres)
LIT Sèvres Arch

POY, Jean-Marie, ***alias*** **Joannès** ***b.1843***
Pupil of Reignier, Lyon BA (CFD 1859). Two of his exhibits were in the Lyon Société des Amis-des-Arts raffles: *Fleurs* 1863, *Roses de Dijon dans un verre*, 1866
LIT *Compte-rendu annuel de la Société des Amis-des-Arts*, 1863, 1866; *Hardouin-Fugier Grafe*

POYET, Antoine ***b.1834***
Pupil of Reignier, Lyon BA (CFD 1858)
LIT *Hardouin-Fugier Grafe*

PRADEL, Michel ***b.1831***
Pupil of Thierriat, Lyon BA (CFD 1849). Mostly a landscape painter
LIT *Hardouin-Fugier Grafe*

PRADIN, Michel-Hubert ***b.1838***
Pupil of Reignier, Lyon BA (CFD 1858)
LIT *Hardouin-Fugier Grafe*

PRANDIÈRE de, ***see*** **CHOMEL**

PRELLE, Aimé ***1873–1959***
Pupil of Castex-Dégrange, Lyon BA (CFD 1889). Textile designer and manufacturer (Lyon)
LIT *Hardouin-Fugier Grafe*

PRELLE, Alexandre ***1875–1945***
Pupil of Castex-Dégrange, Lyon BA (CFD 1893). Textile designer and manufacturer (Lyon)
LIT *Hardouin-Fugier Grafe*

PRELLE, Eugène ***d.1907***
Pupil of Reignier. Exhib. Lyon Salon 1867, 1869, 1870, 1872, 1874
LIT *Hardouin-Fugier Grafe*

PRETRE, Jean-Gabriel
op. *c*1820. Designed plates e.g. for Palisot de Beauvois *Flore...de Bénin*, Paris 1804–1807 and *Flore des Antilles*, Paris 1808–1827. M: Paris Muséum d'Histoire Naturelle
LIT *Nissen* I, 354, 1480, 1481, 2017, 2233, 2236, 2239, 2375; *Thieme*; Witt

PREVEL, Charlotte, ***née*** **Cozier**
Pupil of Bourgogne. Exhib. *Narcisses, giroflées, violettes, Oeillets*, fan-leaf, gouache, Paris UFPS 1890
LIT *Paris UFPS* 1890

PREVOST, A.
b. Paris. Exhib. *Fleurs*, Paris Salon 1861. This may be Alexandre-Céleste Gabriel Prévost, pupil of Lassalle and Jeanron. Exhib. Paris Salon from 1861
LIT *Bénézit*; *Paris Salon* 1861; *Thieme*; Witt

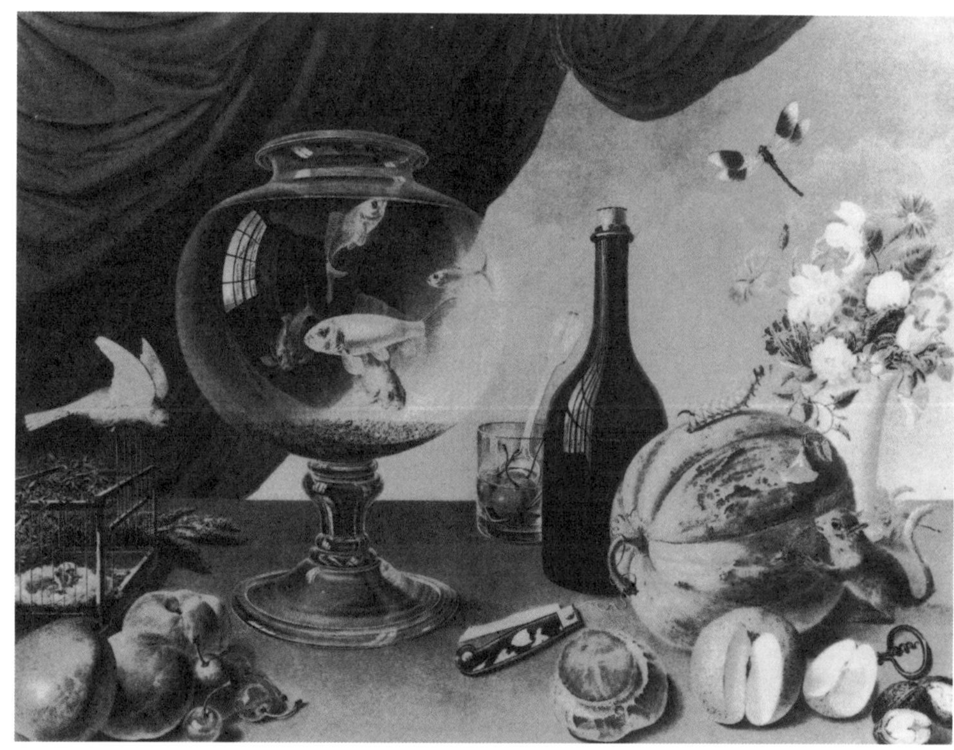

Portier

Watercolour, 23¼ × 29½ in. (59 × 75 cm.), signed and dated 1824
Courtesy Sotheby's, London

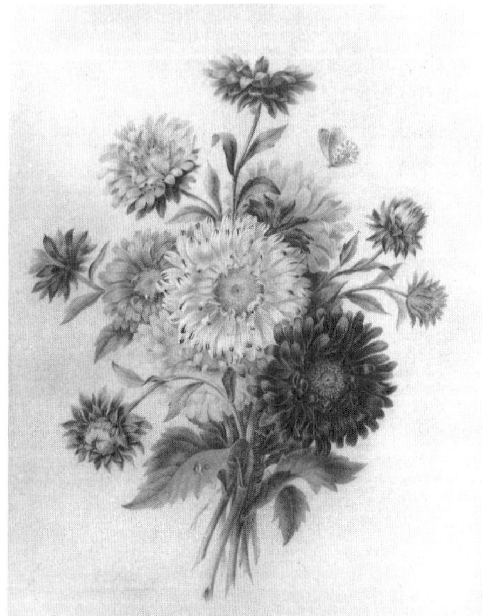

Clara Poteau

Watercolour on vellum, 16 × 12¾ in. (26.5 × 21.5 cm.), signed, dated 1830 and inscribed 'd'après Lesourd de Beauregard'
Private collection

PREVOST, A.
May be the same artist as A. Prévost who designed flower plates after Redouté for teaching purposes, *Méthode Tirpenne V, Cours de fleurs sous la direction de M. Redouté par M. Prévost*, Paris 1840
LIT *Nissen*, Künstler Register; Paris Bibl. Muséum 25066–7; *Sitwell*

PREVOST, AL.
Designed and lithographed *Réunion de douze planches de fleurs*, Paris 1835 (co-designer Pointel du Portail)
LIT *Nissen* I, 1598 n.

PREVOST, Eugène-Joseph ***b.1812***
Pupil of Redouté. Exhib. Paris Salon 1837, 1839 e.g. *Vase de fleurs*, wc, 1837. M: Cambridge, Fitzwilliam (Broughton coll.), *Roses, ipomoea and grapevine*, wc
LIT Broughton 1977; *Bénézit*; *Hardouin-Fugier* 1981; *Paris Salon* 1837.

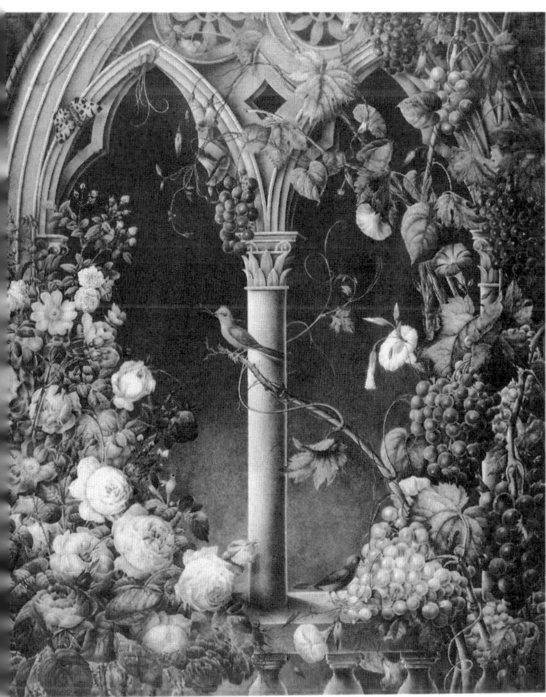

Eugène-Joseph Prévost

Watercolour and bodycolour on paper, 31½ × 29½ in. (88 × 75 cm.)
Cambridge, Fitzwilliam Museum
(Broughton Collection)

PREVOST, Jean-Baptiste
b. Paris. Exhib. Paris Salon 1848–1866 e.g. *Fleurs*, 1848, *Roses dans les ruines*, 1863
LIT *Bellier*; *Bénézit*

PRÉVOST, Jean-Louis, *called* le jeune ***1760–1810***
b. Nointel (Seine-et-Oise). Pupil of Bachelier. Among his later works are *Tableau de fleurs*, *Fleurs et fruits*, gouache, Paris Salon 1798–1799; *Fleurs dans une corbeille*, 1810 (Musée de Besançon private donation 1843); *Vases of flowers*, s. 1802, gouache, Christie's, London, 23 Apr. 1926: *Deux vases de fleurs*, 1797–1798. Charpentier, Paris, 1 June, 1949; Spink, London, 1982 (two works). Schwarz, Philadelphia, *Flowers*, 1988. This most successful flower painter designed sets of flower plates for teaching purposes e.g. *Collection de fleurs et de fruits*, Paris (Vilquin), 1805. M: Angers, Besançon, Cambridge, Fitzwilliam; Langres, Stockholm
LIT *Bellier*; *Bénézit*; Broughton 1983–1984; *Faré* 1962, p. 247; *Faré* 1976 p. 188, 190, 294, 297; *Mitchell* (ill.); *Nissen* I, 1568; Paris Bibl. Nat. Est. Jd 34, 61; *Paris BMAD*; *Sitwell*; *Thieme*; *Witt*

PREVOST, Jeanne-Henriette
b. Paris. Pupil of Rivoire and Monacé. Exhib. *Oeillets*, wc, *Cerises et bluets*, wc, Paris Salon 1898.
LIT *Paris Salon* 1898.

PREVOST, Mme
Exhib. *Plantes*, on vellum, Paris Salon 1801–1802
LIT *Paris Salon* 1801–1802

PRÉVOST-ROQUEPLAN, Camille
Pupil of Stevens. Painted genre and flowers. Exhib. Paris Salon from 1878 e.g. *Roses trémières*, 1878. Musée de Sens: *Fleurs* (donated by Mme. Prevost-Roqueplan 1889)
LIT *Bellier*; *Bénézit*; *Thieme*

PREVOST-THIBAULT
Exhib. Paris Salon 1834–1836 e.g. *Bouquet de pivoines*, wc, 1835, *Fleurs dans un vase chinois*, wc, 1836
LIT *Bellier*; *Bénézit*; *Faré* 1962, p. 249; *Paris Salon* 1835

PREVOT-VALERI, Auguste *1857–1930*
b. Villeneuve-sur-Yonne (Yonne). Pupil of J. Lefebvre and Guillemot. Painted landscapes, animals and flowers. Exhib. *Pensées*, Dijon Salon 1890
LIT *Dijon Salon* 1890; *Witt*. CL

PRIEUR, Jules-Félix
Exhib. Paris Indép. *Chrysanthèmes*, 1892, 1893, 1899, *Pivoines*, 1896, *Chrysanthèmes*, *Pavots*, 1898
LIT *Paris Indép*. 1892, 1893, 1896, 1898, 1899

PRIGNOL, Benoit *b.1842*
Pupil of Reignier, Lyon BA (CFD 1859)
LIT *Hardouin-Fugier Grafe*

PUVIS, Isabelle
fl. *c.*1860. Exhib. Lyon Salon e.g. *Géranium*, *Narcisses blancs*, *roses rouges et jasmins*, 1860, *Azalée et tulipes d'Ecully*, *Raisins*, *pêches et violettes*, *Clochettes blanches*, *liserons*, *roses et violettes* 1861, *Corbeille d'azalées et autres fleurs*, *Groupe de roses*, *tulipes et lilas*, 1862. M. Cambridge, Fitzwilliam Museum (Broughton Coll.): *Bouquet de fleurs*, wc
LIT *Lyon Salon* 1860–1862

PUX, Marie
Active in Lyon. Pupil of J. Médard. Exhib. Lyon Salon e.g. *Fleurs*, gouache, 1883, 1884, *Fleurs dans un verre*, gouache, 1885
LIT *Lyon Salon* 1883–1885

Camille Prévost-Roqueplan

Oil on canvas, signed
(photo: Musée de Sens)

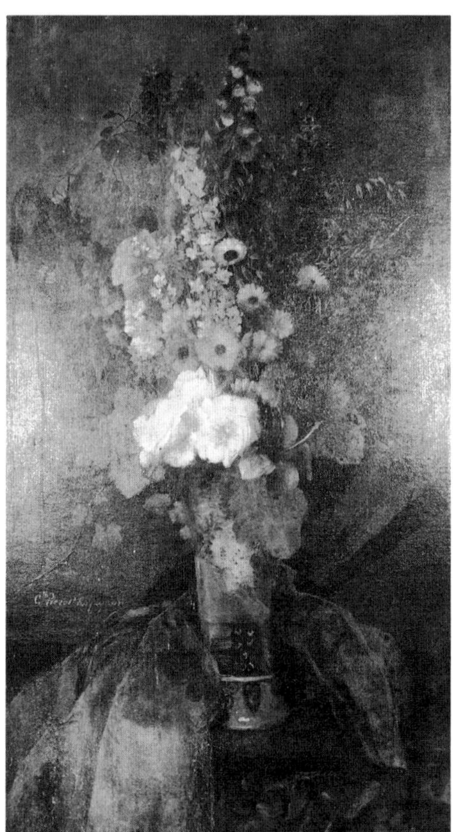

PUYROCHE-WAGNER, Elise
1828–1895
b. Dresden (Germany), of French parentage (Bellier). Pupil of E. Humblot, Grönland and S. Saint-Jean (Lyon). Exhib. Lyon Salon e.g. *La force vaincue* (*pavots*) 1864; Exhib. Dijon Salon e.g. *Roses thé dans un vase oriental*, 1887, *Capucines dans un vase*, 1890, *Roses blanches sur le balcon d'un chalet*, *Lilas dans un vase*, 1892, *Coquelicots de Chine*, 1894. M: Dresden, Leipzig, Saint-Etienne
Hardouin-Fugier Grafe; *Hardouin-Fugier Grafe* 1982 (ill.), *Lyon Salon* 1864; *Thieme*

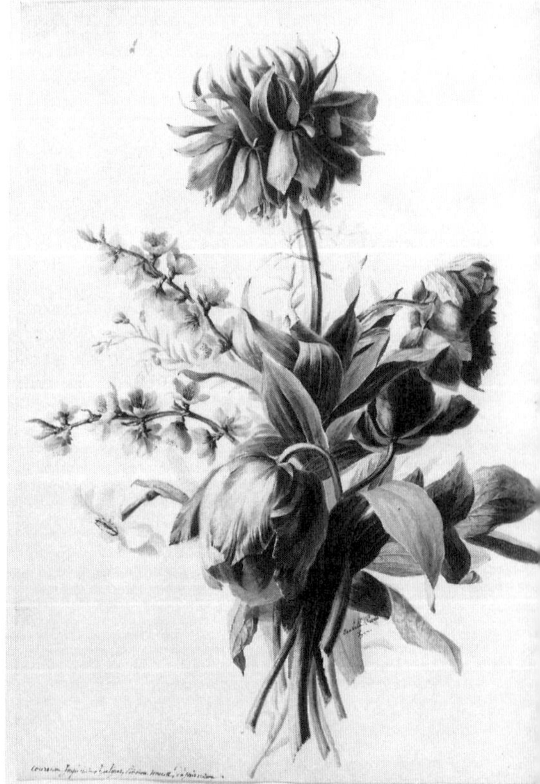

Isabelle Puvis

Bodycolour on paper, $20\frac{1}{2} \times 14\frac{1}{2}$ in. (51.7 × 37 cm.), signed and inscribed 'Isabelle Puvis, Lyon, Couronne Imperiale Tulipes, Pivoine noi . . d'après nature'
Cambridge, Fitzwilliam Museum
(Broughton Collection)

Q R

QUARRE, Marie
This flower painter was granted "encouragements" in 1848
LIT Paris Arch. Nat. F21: 287

QUELLAIN, Louis-Eugène
Pupil of Vauchelet. Painted still-lifes and flowers. Exhib. Paris Salon from 1869. Exhib. *Pivoines*, Paris Indép. 1887
LIT *Bénézit; Paris Indép.* 1887

QUENTIN, Léon-Adolphe
Exhib. *Pivoines dans un vase*, Paris SNBA 1893
LIT *Paris SNBA* 1893 (ill.)

QUERIAU or QUERIOT
Pupil of Berjon, Lyon BA (CFD 1811)
LIT *Hardouin-Fugier Grafe*

QUESTROY, Elisabeth
b. Paris. Pupil of Bergeret. Exhib. Paris Salon from 1880 e.g. *Fleurs*, 1880, *Fleurs des champs*, 1882
LIT *Bellier*; *Bénézit*; *Paris Salon* 1880

QUINIER, Adèle
b. Paris. Pupil of Grosclaude, Lesourd de Beauregard, Grönland and H. de Longchamp. Exhib. Paris Salon 1852, 1859, 1863 and 1868 e.g. *Vase de fleurs*, 1852
LIT *Bellier*; *Bénézit*; *Faré* 1962, p. 245

QUOST, Ernest *1844–1931*
b. Avallon (Yonne). Pupil of H. Aumont. Painted flowers, fruit and still-lifes. Exhib. Paris Salon from 1866 e.g. *Fleurs d'hiver*, 1872, *Fleurs*, 1880, *Roses*, wc, 1895, *Fleurs de printemps*, 1898; *Bouquet de fleurs*, Pau Salon 1877; *Trois tableaux de fleurs*, Limoges Salon 1879. Produced tapestry cartoons for Beauvais and Gobelins. A most popular flower painter and art teacher. Many of his works were purchased by the State to decorate public buildings e.g. Prefecture, Seine-et-Oise. M: Avallon, Bernay, Castres, Gray, Limoges. Paris (Orsay) Nancy
LIT *Bellier*; *Bénézit*; Paris Arch. Nat. F21: 2146, 4260; Paris, Musée Marmottan, *Monet et ses amis*, 1971; *Schurr* II, 114; *Thieme*; *Witt*

RABY, Daniel-Henri *b.1879*
Pupil of Castex-Dégrange, Lyon BA (CFD 1899)
LIT *Hardouin-Fugier Grafe*

RACHOU, *see* YMART

RACINE, Jean-Baptiste
Designed plates for C. Mirbel *Histoire naturelle des végétaux*, Paris (Deterville) 1803
LIT *Bénézit*; *Nissen* I, 1392 n.

RACINE, Joseph-Eugène
b. Guadeloupe. Pupil of E. Lejeune. Exhib. from 1866 e.g. *Roses et cerises*, Paris Salon 1880; *Reines marguerites*, *Roses et cerises*, Paris Indép. 1893; *Roses*, Paris Indép. 1894
LIT *Bellier*; *Bénézit*; *Paris Indép.* 1893, 1894; *Paris Salon* 1880; *Thieme*

RAFFAËLLI, Jean-François *1850–1924*
b. Paris. Pupil of Gérôme. Painted figures, portraits, landscapes and flowers. Exhib. Paris Salon from 1870, Exhib. Paris SNBA e.g. *Fleurs*, 1892, 1893, *Fleurs jaunes et blanches*, 1896, *Fleurs roses, jaunes et blanches*, *Dahlias*, 1898, *Fleurs*, Parke-Bernet, New York, 5 Feb. 1947; *Vase de fleurs*, Parke-Bernet, New York, 26 Apr. 1951; *Fleurs*, Parke-Bernet, New-York, 11 Oct. 1961; *Grand vase de fleurs*, Sotheby's London, *31 Mar. 1965; Grand vase de fleurs variées*, Sotheby's London, 26 Apr. 1967; *Dahlias panachés*, Parke-Bernet, New York 12 Apr. 1967; *Fleurs dans un pichet*, Sotheby's, London, 5 July 1973; *Table laden with fruit, glasses and flowers in a vase*, Sotheby's, London, 25 Nov. 1987
LIT *Bellier*; *Bénézit*; J. K. Huysmans, *Certains*, Paris, (Tresse) 1889; G. Lecomte, *Raffaëlli*, Paris, (Rieder), 1927; *Mitchell*; *Paris SNBA* 1892, 1893, 1896, 1898; Pavière III, pt. 2; *Thieme*; *Witt*

RAGONOT, Henri
Exhib. *Fleurs*, Paris Indép. 1884
LIT *Paris Indép.* 1884

RAGOT, Jules-Félix
b. Paris. Pupil of Murat and Picot. Painted still-lifes and flowers. Exhib. Paris Salon from 1867 e.g. *Roses et anémones*, 1888. *Nature-morte aux roses*, Geneva sale 1–2 June 1988, lot 57
LIT *Bellier*; *Bénézit*; *Paris Salon* 1888 (ill.); *Thieme*

RAGUET, Jean-Baptiste
b. Dijon (Côte-d'Or). Pupil of Chocarne and Dijon BA. Painted still-lifes and, occasionally, flowers. Exhib. Paris Salon 1861–1866
LIT *Bellier*; *Bénézit*

RAIMOND, Barthélémy *b.1820*
Pupil of Thierriat, Lyon BA (CFD 1839)
LIT *Hardouin-Fugier Grafe*

RAMAIN, Ambroise *b.1831*
Pupil of Reignier, Lyon BA (CFD 1856)
LIT *Hardouin-Fugier Grafe*

RAMBAUD, Joseph-Henri
Pupil of Thierriat, Lyon BA (CFD 1826)
LIT *Hardouin-Fugier Grafe*

RAMÉE, Marquis de la
Exhib. *Fleurs*, wc, Paris Indép. 1900
LIT *Paris Indép.* 1900

RANSON
Flowers, fruit, gardening tools and musical instruments, wc, Cambridge, Fitzwilliam Museum (Broughton coll.). JLC

RANVIER, Joseph-Victor ***1832–1896***
b. Lyon. Pupil of Janmot and Richard. Painted figures prolific painter on faience. Worked for Th. Deck, exhib. faiences Paris Exposition Universelle 1867. May have produced flowers in pencil or wc
LIT *Audin Vial*; *Bénézit*; *Schurr* III, 104; *Thieme*

RAPALLEY
Designed *Roses* Paris BMAD (Maciet coll.)
LIT *Paris BMAD*

RASSAT, Félix
fl. *c*1840. Pupil of Redouté. Designed plates for Vérat. *Plantes des environs de Paris*. . .Paris, Muséum d'Histoire Naturelle
LIT *Hardouin-Fugier* 1981

RASTOUX, Jules-Gaspard
b. Nîmes (Gard). Pupil of Boucoiran. Painted portraits and flowers. Exhib. Paris Salon from 1878. Musée de Bagnols-sur-Cèze, *Vase de fleurs, jacinthes et fleurs variées*
LIT *Bellier*; *Bénézit*

RATHELOT, Jules
Painted portraits, animals, fruit and occasionally, flowers. Exhib. Paris Salon 1847–1850
LIT *Bellier*; *Bénézit*

RATON, Amédée ***b. 1838***
Painted flowers in gouache. Pupil of Reignier, Lyon BA (CFD 1854)
LIT *Hardouin-Fugier Grafe*

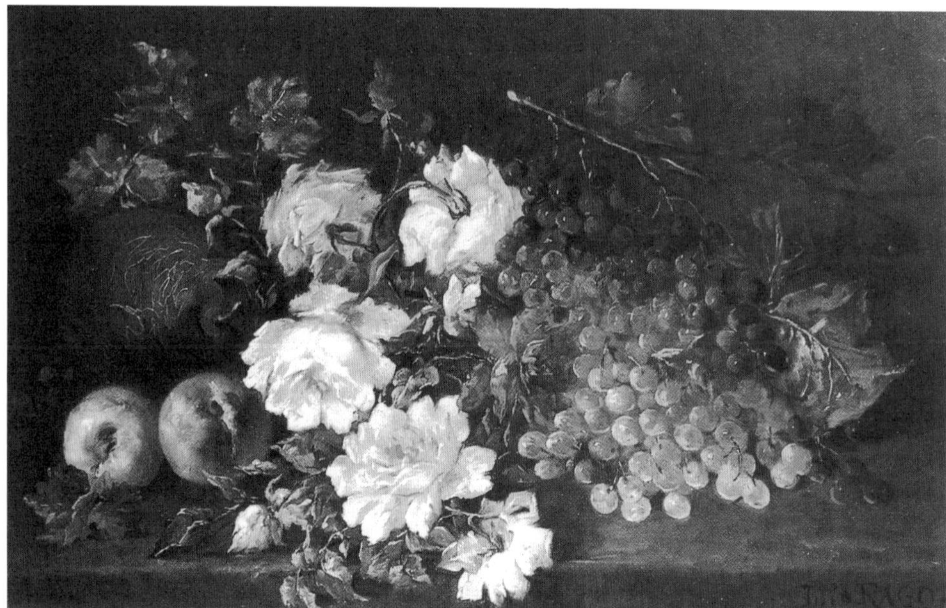

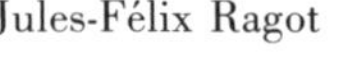

Jules-Félix Ragot

Oil on canvas, $19\frac{3}{4} \times 31$ in. (50 × 80 cm.), signed
Private collection

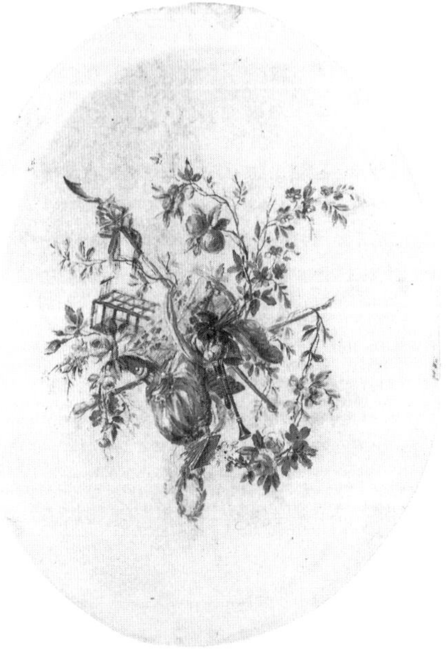

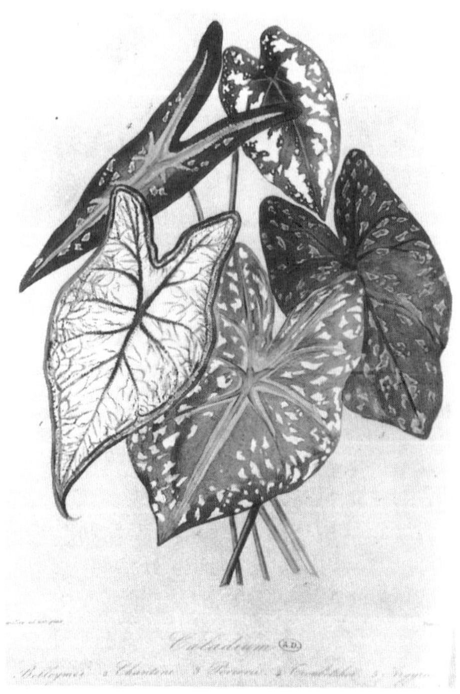

Rapalley

Engraving after
$10\frac{3}{4} \times 7\frac{1}{4}$ in. (27.5 × 18.5 cm.), signed
Paris, BMAD (Maciet Collection)

RAULT
Painted flowers on porcelain e.g. *Service au muguet*, 1896, *Service aux chrysanthèmes*, *Écritoire aux pensées*, 1897 etc.
LIT *Orsay*

RAVE, Joanny *1827–1882*
b. Lyon. Pupil of Bonnefond and Drolling. Exhib. *Fleurs d'aubépine*, Lyon Salon 1856
LIT *Bénézit*; *Lyon Salon* 1856; *Thieme*

RAVENEL, Jules *1824–1910*
b. Caen. Painter of highly finished still-lifes in the Dutch 17th-century tradition, of which two examples are at the Musée d'Alençon. Of his occasional work where flowers are included the example at Musée de Caen was destroyed in World War II
LIT *Schurr* II, 62. PM

RAVERAT, Robert-Michel-Antoine-Pascal
Pupil of Thierriat, Lyon BA (CFD 1829)
LIT *Hardouin-Fugier Grafe*

RAVIER, Jeanne *b.1865*
b. Void (Meuse). Pupil of J. Lefebvre, B. Constant and Boulanger. Exhib. Paris Salon from 1888. Exhib. *Corbeille de pivoines*, Dijon Salon 1892
LIT *Bénézit*; *Dijon Salon* 1892

RAY, Noémie
Exhib. Paris Salon 1847–1850 e.g. *Bouquet*, *Corbeille de fleurs*, 1848, *Bouquet de fleurs*, on porcelain, 1850
LIT *Bellier*; *Bénézit*; *Paris Salon* 1850

REBEYROL, Mlle C.
b. Paris. Pupil of Ledoyen and Lesourd de Beauregard. Exhib. flowers on porcelain Paris Salon from 1876
LIT *Bellier*; *Bénézit*; *Paris Salon* 1880

REBOUR, Charles *1831–1897*
b. Grand (Vosges). Pupil of Paris BA. Textile designer. Established in Saint-Etienne 1852. Exhib. Paris Exposition Universelle 1878; Antwerp 1885
LIT *Audin Vial*; *Hardouin-Fugier Bringuier*; *Le Mémorial de la Loire* 1 May 1897

REBOURS, Alexandrine-Esther
Pupil of Redouté. Exhib. *Bouquet de giroflées*, wc, Paris Salon 1844. The Paris Salon selection committee rejected her 1843 exhib.
LIT *Paris Salon* 1844; Louvre arch.

REBUT, Michel-Antoine-Paul *b.1809*
Pupil of Thierriat, Lyon BA (CFD 1828)
LIT *Hardouin-Fugier Grafe*

REDELSPERGER, Charles-Louis-Emile-Jacques
b. Paris. Pupil of J. H. Belloc, whose daughter Jeanne he married, and Madeleine Lemaire. Painted landscapes, flowers and fruit. Exhib. Paris Salon from 1876 e.g. *Roses, violettes, primevères*, 1878, *Cinéraires*, 1882
LIT *Bellier*; *Bénézit*, *Thieme*

REDON, Georges *1869–1943*
b. Paris. Flower painter and lithographer
LIT *Bénézit*; *Thieme*

REDON, Odilon *1840–1916*
b. Bordeaux (Gironde). Pupil of Gerôme. Botanist Clavaud introduced Redon to the world of plants and flowers. Most of his flowers, whether in oils or pastel, were painted after 1900. Vibrant and mysteriously silent, they are the work of a deeply inquisitive, restless soul. Unlike most painters, Redon's approach combines the decorative, naturalistic and symbolistic features of flowers into unique, timeless, dream-like creations. Among Redon's early flowers are *Rose dans un vase*, 1866–1867 (Algiers); *Volubilis et marguerites dans un vase gris*, *c*.1867 (Paris 1956, 121); *Oeillets blancs et rouges dans une tasse de Chine*, 1884 (Paris 1956, 128); *La prière, visage, fleurs*, *c*.1893 (Bordeaux); *Fleurs dans une coupe bleue*, 1900 (Paris 1956, 139); *Grand bouquet de fleurs des champs*, 1900 (Paris, 1956, 140); *Petit bouquet aux quatre anémones*, *c*.1900–1903 (Paris 1956). M: Algiers, Musée des Beaux-Arts; Bordeaux, Musée des Beaux-Arts; Paris, Petit Palais etc.
LIT Paris, *O. Redon*, Orangerie des Tuileries, Réunion des Musées Nationaux, 1956 K. Berger, "The Reconversion of Odilon Redon", *Art Quarterly*, 1958 (ill.); Paris, *Donation Ari et Suzanne Redon*, Musée du Louvre, Réunion des Musées Nationaux, 1984; J. Selz, *O. Redon*, Paris (Flammarion) 1971; Witt; AC

REDOUTÉ, Pierre-Joseph *1759–1840*
b. Saint-Hubert (Ardennes). This most celebrated and productive artist and teacher began, at the age of 13, a career as an itinerant decorator and painter in the family tradition, travelling in Luxembourg, Flanders and Holland. It was in the latter country that he encountered the work of the great Dutch masters e.g. Van Huysum, Rachel Ruysch, an experience which he later recalled as decisive for his career. 1782: followed his elder brother to Paris learning engraving and colour printing with Demarteau and came under the instruction of the great Gérard van Spaendonck. His practice of studying in the Jardin du Roi brought him to the attention of a wealthy and gifted amateur botanist, Charles Louis l'Heritier de Brutelle, first in what was to be a long and illustrious list of patrons. Working on illustrations for l'Heritier's *Sertum Anglicum* took Redouté to London, 1787, where he met Sir Joseph Banks and furthered his knowledge of the process in which Van Spaendonck had probably first instructed him, stipple engraving. The foundations of his success derived from a mastery of watercolour over pencil on

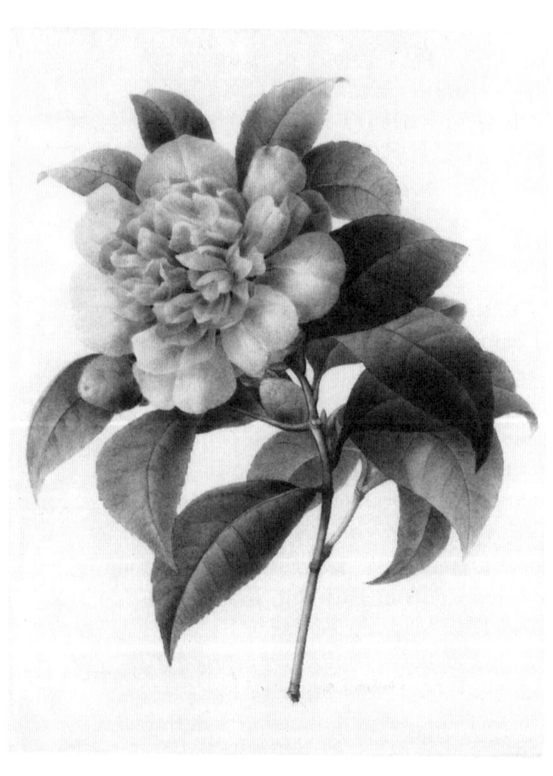

Pierre-Joseph Redouté

Watercolour on vellum, $9\frac{3}{4} \times 7$ in. (23.7 × 17.7 cm.)
signed
Private collection

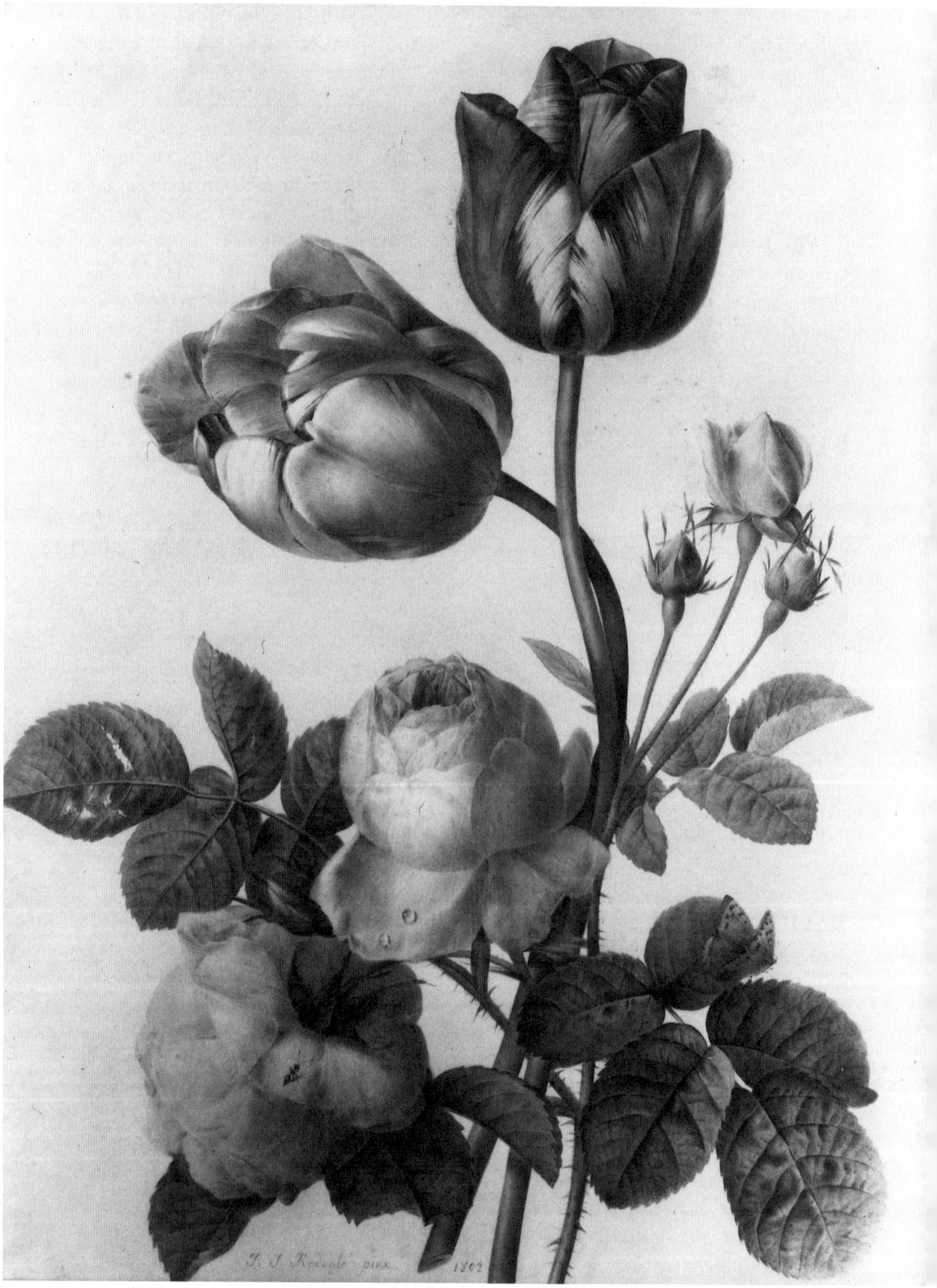

Pierre-Joseph Redouté

Watercolour on vellum, $14\frac{1}{2} \times 10\frac{1}{2}$ in.
(37 × 26.5 cm.), signed and dated 1802
Private Collection

prepared vellum and superb taste in arranging his specimens, allied to the means of accurately reproducing his work. These skills allowed him to take charge of major projects from inception to publication. It is relevant to add that his admirable personal qualities found him ready acceptance in court and aristocratic circles, both as artist and teacher, throughout a career begun with Marie-Antoinette's *Ancien Régime* to end with the daughters of Louis Philippe.

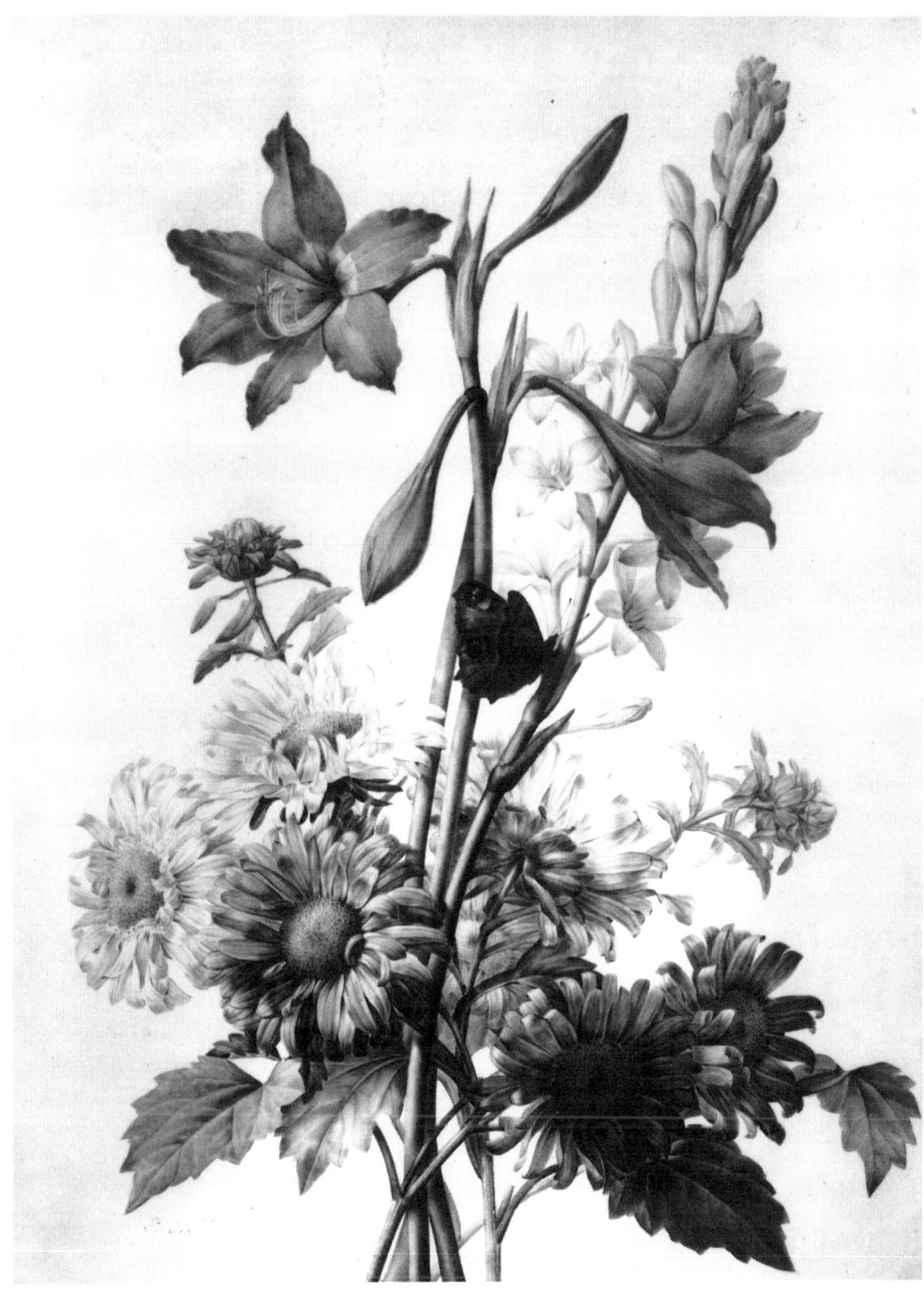

Pierre-Joseph Redouté

Watercolour on vellum, 19 × 14 in. (48.6 × 35.7 cm.) signed and dated 'XI'

Private collection

After succeeding Van Spaendonck, he contributed over six hundred vellums to the Vélins du Roi, and thousands more, mainly for the illustration of printed botanical and flower books. Often the quality of commentary, engraving and printing of these works equalled that of Redouté's contribution. The most famous are *Les roses* and *Les liliacées*. The original 486 watercolours for the latter passed to Eugène Beauharnais after Josephine's death and recently sold at auction for $5 million and are now dispersed in numerous private collections. Although equalled technically by Spaendonck and Bauer, in terms of sustained consistency of quality over a vast output, Redouté has no parallel in the history of flower painting. Self-evidently his influence in 19th-century France and far beyond is incalculable and prints from his work continue to be reproduced throughout the world today. His exceptionally long and productive career obliges a summary here: 1785; contributed 54 plates *Stirpes Novae*; 1786: married Marie-Marthe Gobert; 1787; called to London; 1788: l'Héritier's *Sertum Anglicum* published (plants observed at Kew); 1789: appointed Dessinateur du cabinet de Marie Antoinette; 1792: appointed Dessinateur de l'Académie des Sciences; 1798–1799: Desfontaine's *Flora Atlantica* published; 1799: Empress Joséphine buys Malmaison (650 acres) to be expanded nearly threefold by the time of her death in 1814; 1799: de Candolle's *Histoire des plantes grasses* published; 1800: l'Héritier assassinated; Joséphine commissions six vellums (shown at Salon), Redouté appointed her "Peintre de fleurs", Ventenat's *Jardin de Monsieur Cels* published; 1801–1817: Duhamel's *Traité des arbres*, 1802–1816: *Les liliacées* published (486 plates); 1803: Redouté buys country property at Fleury (Meudon); 1803–1804: Ventenat's *Jardin de la Malmaison*, dedicated to Napoléon published; 1805: J. J. Rousseau's *La Botanique*; 1810–1813: Michaux's *Histoire des arbres forestières de l'Amerique septentrionale* published; 1813: Bonpland's *Plantes rares cultivées à Malmaison et à Navarre* published; 1817–1821: *Les roses* published, text by Thory (168 plates); 1822: deprived of proper post at Muséum on death of Van Spaendonck; embarks on sixteen years of public lessons there; 1824: Redouté's *Album de Redouté* published, dedicated to the Duchesse de Berry; 1827: Redouté purchased extra land at Fleury, leading to financial difficulties in the following decade; sustained by constant friendship of Baron Gérard; 1827–1833: Redouté's *Choix des plus belles fleurs* published, dedicated to Louise and Marie d'Orléans; 1840: Refused government grant. His funeral attended by large following. Salon exhibits (Redouté made his Salon debut in 1796 and not 1793 as given by Léger through confusion with exhibits of elder brother Antoine-Fernand—a slight error in an otherwise invaluable monograph): 1796: *Un vase de cristal rempli de différentes fleurs posé sur un socle d'albâtre*—1804; six *tableaux de fleurs*, watercolours (property of the Empress Joséphine); 1810: *tableau de fleurs à l'aquarelle, il resprésente un vase d'albâtre posé sur un stylobate dans un jardin*, watercolour; 1814; flower-piece, watercolour; 1822: *tableau de fleurs, le fond represente un paysage*; 1833: *Bouquet de roses*, watercolour; *Bouquet de pivoines*, watercolour; *Bouquet de roses trémières*, watercolour; *Vase d'oreilles d'ours*, watercolour; 1834: *Offrande à Bacchus*, large watercolour (Maison du roi); 1835: *Fruits et fleurs*, watercolour; *Fleurs*, watercolour; 1836: *Oreilles d'ours et camelias*, watercolour; 1837: *Roses trémières, raisins et le lory cramoisi*, watercolour; *Pivoines et tulipes*, watercolour; *Altheas et roses trémières*, watercolour; *Renoncules*; *Bouquet composé de plusieurs fleurs*; 1838: *Pivoines*, watercolour; *Grappes de raisin*, watercolour; *Fruits*, watercolour; *Roses groupées dans un vase et camelias*, (sketch); 1840: *Reines-marguerites, Roses sur fond brun, Fleurs et fruits*, watercolours (Maison du roi); posthumously, 1841: *Fleurs diverses*; *Pivoines sur fond brun*, watercolour. M: Brussels, Cambridge, New York (Morgan Library), Paris, Muséum National d'Histoire naturelle, Malmaison. Pittsburgh, Hunt Botanical Institute, Leiden, Leige, Séures, Namur, Mendon, Berlin

LIT C. Léger, *Redouté et son temps*, Paris, 1945. Y. Laissus, Redouté, *Les vélins du Muséum National d'Histoire Naturelle*, 1980. Paris: *Le Raphael de Fleurs*, 1982 (André Lawalrée). PM

† See illustration on page 20 and colour illustration on page 23

REGNIER, Antony-Ludovic *1851–1930*

b. Paris. Pupil of Pils. Friend of Th. Deck. Designed plates for Album Vilmorin. Exhib. Paris Salon from 1877 e.g. *Fleurs d'hiver*, 1880, *Fleurs des champs*, on faience, 1890; Paris Indép. *Fleurs des champs*, *Cinéraires*, *Pavots*, *Pensée*, 1892, *Bouquet de narcisses*, *Roses trémières*, *Pavots*, 1893, *Fleurs des champs*, 1894

LIT *Bellier*; *Bénézit*; *Paris Indép.* 1892, 1893, 1894; *Paris Salon* 1880 (ill.), 1890

REHM, Marie

Pupil of Henner, R. Collin, Carolus-Duran and Courtois. Exhib. *Anémones*, wc, Paris UFPS 1898

LIT *Bénézit*; *Paris UFPS* 1898

REIBEL, Marguerite

Exhib. *Fleurs*, pastel, Dijon Salon 1897.

LIT *Dijon Salon* 1897. CL

REICHENECKER, Joseph-Henri *b.1836*

Pupil of Reignier, Lyon BA (CFD 1854)

LIT *Hardouin-Fugier Grafe*

REIGNIER, Félix *b.1838*

Pupil of Reignier, Lyon BA (CFD 1855)

LIT *Hardouin-Fugier Grafe*

REIGNIER, Gaspard-Elie *b.1828*

Pupil of Thierriat, Lyon BA (CFD 1843) Nephew of J. M. Reignier

LIT *Hardouin-Fugier Grafe*

REIGNIER, Jean-Marie *1815–1886*

b. Lyon. Pupil of Thierriat, Lyon BA (CFD 1833–1885) and possibly Saint-Jean and Berjon. Textile designer. Operated a private studio from 1845. Professor of flower design at Lyon BA 1853–1884. Exhib. Lyon Salon from 1838 and Exhib. Paris Salon from 1842 e.g. *Hommage à SM la Reine des Belges, deux pensées*, 1852, *Hommage à Jean Gerson*, 1855, *Hommage à la Reine Hortense*, 1857, *Hommage à la Sainte Vierge*, 1867. Works in Musée de Beaux-Arts, Lyon, Musée des Arts Décoratifs, Lyon, Musée du Mans

LIT *Hardouin-Fugier Grafe* (ill.); *Hardouin-Fugier Grafe* 1979 (ill.); *Hardouin-Fugier Grafe* 1982 (ill.); Witt

REIGNIER, Louis *b.1838*

Pupil of Reignier, Lyon BA (CFD 1855)

LIT *Hardouin-Fugier Grafe*

REILLY, N. P.

Exhib. Paris SNBA e.g. *Fleurs de marronnier d'Inde*, *Fleurs de saule*, wc, 1895, *Fleurs de juillet*, wc, *Lis du Japon*, wc, 1896, *Chrysanthèmes jaunes*, wc, *Anémones*, wc, 1899

LIT *Paris SNBA* 1895, 1896, 1899

REINHART, *see* GRAF

REMBAUD, Joseph-Henri *b.1807*

Pupil of Thierriat, Lyon BA (CFD 1828)

LIT *Hardouin-Fugier Grafe*

REMILLIEUX, Pierre-Etienne *1811–1856*

b. Vienne (Isère). Pupil of Thierriat, Lyon BA (CFD 1831). Operated a private studio; seems to have painted about thirty flower and fruit pieces. Exhib.

Lyon Salon from 1833, Paris Salon from 1841 to 1855 e.g. *Hommage rendu à la mémoire de SAR Marie de France*, 1844. M: Lyon, Musée des Beaux-Arts, *Fleurs et fruits*, Montpellier, *Vase de fleurs*
LIT *Hardouin-Fugier Grafe* (ill.); *Hardouin-Fugier Grafe*, 1979 (ill.). *Fleurs de Lyon* (*Hardouin-Fugier Grafe* 1982, ill.)

RÉMY, J.
op. *c.*1850. Designed plates for C. Gay *Historia...de Chile*, Paris 1845–1853
LIT *Nissen* I, 695

RENARD, Mme Camille
Pupil of Rozier. Exhib. Paris Salon from 1877 e.g. *Fleurs des champs*, 1880
LIT *Bellier*; *Bénézit*; *Paris Salon* 1880

RENARD, Léonie
Exhib. Dijon Salon *Lilas*, *Chrysanthèmes*, 1890, *Premières fleurs*, 1894
LIT *Dijon Salon* 1890, 1894. CL

RENAUD, Gabrielle
Pupil of Laligant. Exhib. *Épine-vinette et pensées*, Dijon Salon 1894
LIT *Dijón Salon* 1894. CL

RENAUD, Louis *b.1874*
Pupil of Castex-Dégrange, Lyon BA (CFD 1892)
LIT *Hardouin-Fugier Grafe*; *Witt*

RENAUD, Pierre-Gustave *b.1836*
Pupil of Thierriat, Lyon BA (CFD 1850)
LIT *Hardouin-Fugier Grafe*

RENAUD, *see* ESMÉNARD

RENAUDIN, Alfred *b.1866*
b. La Neuveville-les-Raon (Vosges). Pupil of Nancy BA and Petitjean. Exhib. *Pavots*, *Chrysanthèmes*, Dijon Salon 1892; *Fleurs*, wc, Paris Salon 1895
LIT *Bénézit*; *Dijon Salon* 1892; *Paris Salon* 1895; *Thieme*. CL

RENAUDIN, Rosalie
Pupil of Girodet. Portrait, flower, fruit and miniature painter. Exhib. Paris Salon 1819–1824
LIT *Bellier*; *Bénézit*; *Gabet*; *Thieme*

RENOIR, Pierre-Auguste *1841–1919*
b. Limoges (Vienne). Apprenticed as a porcelain painter at the age of 13, then painted fan-leaves and curtains. Pupil of Gleyre, in whose studio he befriended Bazille, Monet and Sisley, all to become Impressionists. Like Manet, he sometimes painted women and flowers e.g. *La femme aux lilas*, 1877 or *La cueillette des fleurs*, *c.*1878–1880 (Chicago Art Institute). His early *Arums et plantes de serre* (1864, Winterthur, Oskar Reinhardt Sammlung) are still in the Courbet tradition. His favourite blooms are roses, peonies and, to a lesser extent, chrysanthemums and anemones. In 1879 Renoir met Paul Bérard who had a country house and rose garden at Wargemont near Dieppe, where many of his most shimmering flower-pieces were painted. At the turn of the century, his flowers are more and more suffused in a pink, reddish, golden haze. In the last years of his life, when, crippled with arthritis Renoir painted with a brush tied to his hand, his sketchy flowers, sometimes mere blotches of colour, are pathetic reminders of his past achievements. *Arums et plantes de serre*, 1864 (Winterthur Z. 8); *Bouquet printanier*, 1866 (Cambridge, Z.12); *Roses*, *c.*1868 (id. Z.31); *Fleurs dans un vase*, 1869 (Boston, Z.37); *Nature-morte au melon et au vase de fleurs*, 1872 (Lisbon, Z.76); *Pivoines dans un vase*, 1872 (Mannheim, Z.88); *Bouquet de fleurs*, *c.*1872 (Z.89); *Roses*, 1875 (Z.183); *Glaïeuls* (Z.194); *Bouquet devant la glace*, 1876 (Z.263); *Pivoines*, *c.*1876–1878 (Z.264); *Bouquet dans un vase*, (Indianapolis, Z.305); *Bouquet de lilas* *c.*1878 (Z.320); *Roses et chèvrefeuilles*, 1878 (Z.321); *Roses dans un vase de cristal*, 1879 (Z.373); *Le bouquet*, 1879 (Williamstown, Z.372); *Fleurs*, 1879 (Z.374); *Le bouquet dans une loge*, 1880 (Paris, Orangerie Z.384); *Géraniums dans une bassine de cuivre*, 1880 (Z.426); *Pivoines*, 1880 (Williamstown, Z.427); *Roses et dahlias*, *c.*1880 (Z.428); *Vase de roses*, *c.*1880 (Z.429); *Arums et plantes de serre*, 1881 (Hamburg, Z.8A); *Vase de chrysanthèmes* (Z.481); *Chrysanthèmes*, 1880–1882 (Z.482); id. *c.*1882 (Chicago, Z.483); *Fleurs*, *c.*1883 (Z.564); *Vase de fleurs*, (Z.565); *Chrysanthèmes*, 1884 (Rouen, Z.574); *Fleurs et figues de Barbarie*, 1884 (Z.575); *Fleurs*, 1884 (New-York, Guggenheim Z.576); *Vase de fleurs*, 1885 (Z.577); *Les roses de Wargemont*, 1885 (Limoges, 1952); *Anémones*, 1885 (Merion, Z.578); *Fleurs et fruits*, 1889 (Z.611); *Vase, corbeille de fleurs et de fruits*, 1889–1890 (Philadelphia, Z.612); *Roses mousseuses*, *c.*1890 (Paris, Orsay, Z.613); *Grande corbeille de fleurs d'été*, 1890 (Z.619); *Vase de fleurs*, 1895 (Z.649); *Anémones*, *c.*1898 (Z.658); *Chrysanthèmes*, *c.*1895 (Z.662); *Roses blanches*, 1901 (Z.680). M: Boston, Museum of Fine Arts; Cambridge, Mass, Fogg Art Museum; Chicago, Art Institute; Hamburg, Kunsthalle; Indianapolis, Museum of Art; Lisbon, Calouste Gulbenkian Foundation; Mannheim, Kunstalle; Merion, Barnes Foundation; New York, Salomon R. Guggenheim Foundation; Paris, Orangerie des Tuileries, Musée d'Orsay; Philadelphia, Museum of Art; Rouen, Musée des Beaux-Arts; Williamstown, Sterling and Francine Clark Institute; Winterthur, Oskar Reinhardt Sammlung
LIT *F. Daulte* 1971, Limoges, *Renoir-Berthe Morisot*, Musée Municipal, 1952; London, *Renoir*, Hayward Gallery, 1985, then Boston, Museum of Fine Arts and Paris, Grand Palais; Pavière III, pt. 2; E. Zezzi (here Z.) *Tout l'œuvre peint de Renoir*, Paris, (Flammarion) 1985; *Witt*; AC

RENOUARD, Edmond
Pupil of S. Saint-Jean. Exhib. *Roses*, wc, Lyon Salon 1844
LIT *Hardouin-Fugier Grafe*

RETY, Marguerite
Exhib. *Lilas*, Dijon Salon 1881
LIT *Dijon Salon* 1881. CL

REVERCHON, Claude-André *b.1808*
Pupil of Thierriat, Lyon BA (CFD 1824)
LIT *Hardouin-Fugier Grafe*

REVERCHON, François-Prosper *b.1844*
Pupil of Reignier, Lyon BA (CFD 1861)
LIT *Hardouin-Fugier Grafe*

REVOL, Claude-Louis-Marie, *alias* Claudius
Pupil of Thierriat, Lyon BA (CFD 1842). Exhib. Lyon Salon 1848–1870
LIT *Hardouin-Fugier Grafe*

REVOL, Marc-Régis
Pupil of Reignier, Lyon BA (CFD 1856)
LIT *Hardouin-Fugier Grafe*

REY, B.
op. *c.*1840. Designed plates for Seringe, *Eléments de botanique*, Paris (Hachette) 1841, Lyon (Giberton. Brun)
LIT *Nissen* I, 1834

REY, Gabrielle
b. Seine-Port (Seine-et-Marne). Pupil of Thoret. Exhib. *Fleurs*, wc, fan-leaf, Paris Salon 1880
LIT *Paris Salon* 1880

REY, Louis *1816–1888*
b. Orléans (Loiret). Pupil of Dussance. Decorator. Painted flowers and plants "*médicinales*" for the museum of the Physicians Hall, London (perhaps the room called the "museum" in the 19th-century documents relating to the former premises of the Royal College of Physicians)
LIT *Bellier*; *Bénézit*

REY, Rita-Pauline
b. Cramoisy (Oise). Pupil of E. H. Delacroix and E. Sain. Exhib. Paris Indép. *Pavots*, *Pivoines*, 1890, *Iris et muguet*, 1893, *Lilas*, *Roses*, 1894, *Bouquet de roses*, 1898, *Pavots et digitales*; *Roses*, Paris UFPS 1898
LIT *Bénézit*; *Paris Indép.* 1890, 1893, 1894, 1898; *Paris UFPS* 1898

REY, *see* NANCY

REYBAUD, Joseph-Marie-Jules *1807–c.1868*
Pupil of Thierriat, Lyon BA (CFD 1827). op. textile designer. Engraved sets of plates (E. Oyex co-designer) e.g. *Groupes de fleurs dessinées*, 1840
LIT *Hardouin-Fugier Grafe*

REYBER, Benoit *b.1797*
Pupil of Berjon, Lyon BA (CFD 1813)
LIT *Hardouin-Fugier Grafe*

REYNARD, Flora, *née* Géraldy
Pupil of Redouté. Exhib. flowers in wc. Paris Salon 1836–1842
LIT *Hardouin-Fugier* 1981

REYS, Jenny-Augustine, *née* Allais *b.1798*
b. Paris. Pupil of Mme Allais, her mother, and Van Spaendonck. Exhib. flowers in wc 1824 and 1831
LIT *Bellier*; *Bénézit*; *Paris Salon* 1831; *Thieme*

REYSSIÉ
Exhib. *Vase de fleurs*, Lyon Salon 1862
LIT *Lyon Salon* 1862

RHENTER, André *b.1808*
Pupil of Thierriat, Lyon BA (CFD 1827)
LIT *Hardouin-Fugier Grafe*

RIBARZ, Rudolf *1848–1904*
Exhib. a screen featuring hollyhocks, Paris SNBA 1890
LIT *Paris SNBA* 1890; *Schurr* II, 57

RIBELOT, Eugénie
b. Paris. Pupil of Dubreuil, Faux-Froidure and Pelz. Exhib. Paris Salon e.g. *Fleurs*, wc, 1895, *Bleuets*, wc, 1898
LIT *Paris Salon* 1895, 1898

RIBET, Charles
Pupil of Berjon, Lyon BA (CFD 1822)
LIT *Hardouin-Fugier Grafe*

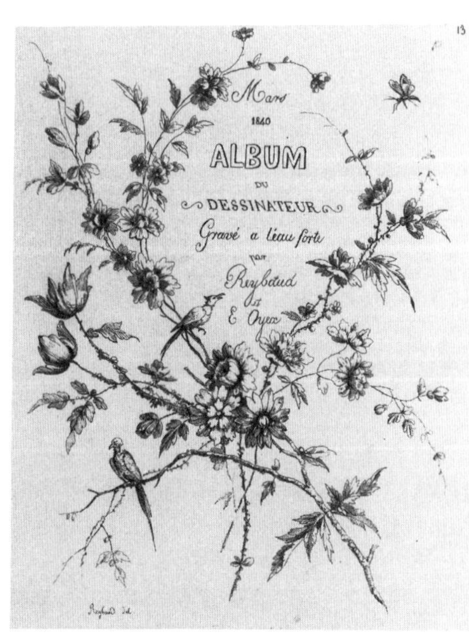

Joseph-Marie-Jules Reybaud

Etching: 'March 1840', $8\frac{3}{4} \times 6\frac{3}{4}$ in. (22 × 17 cm.), signed
Private collection

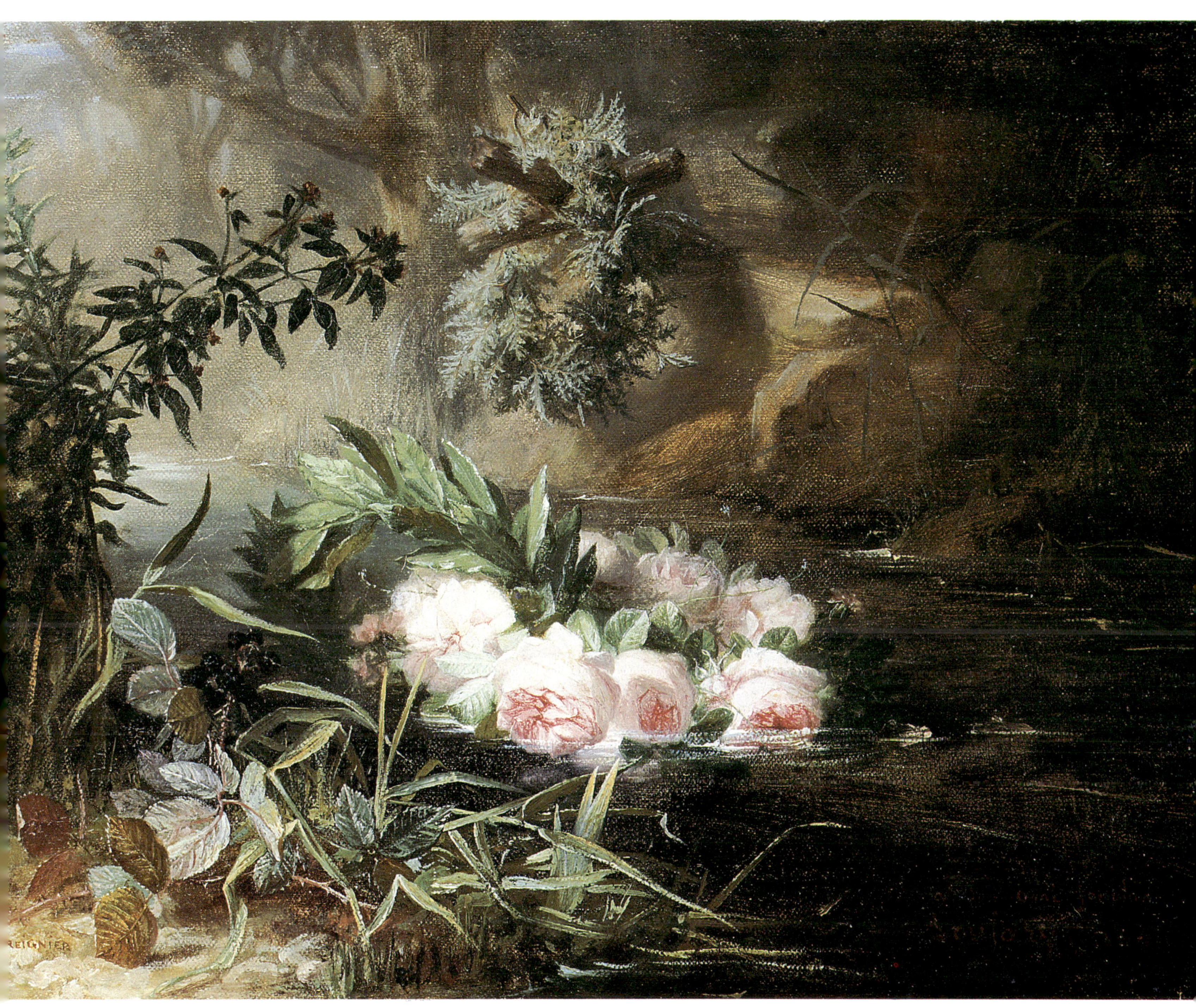
REIGNIER

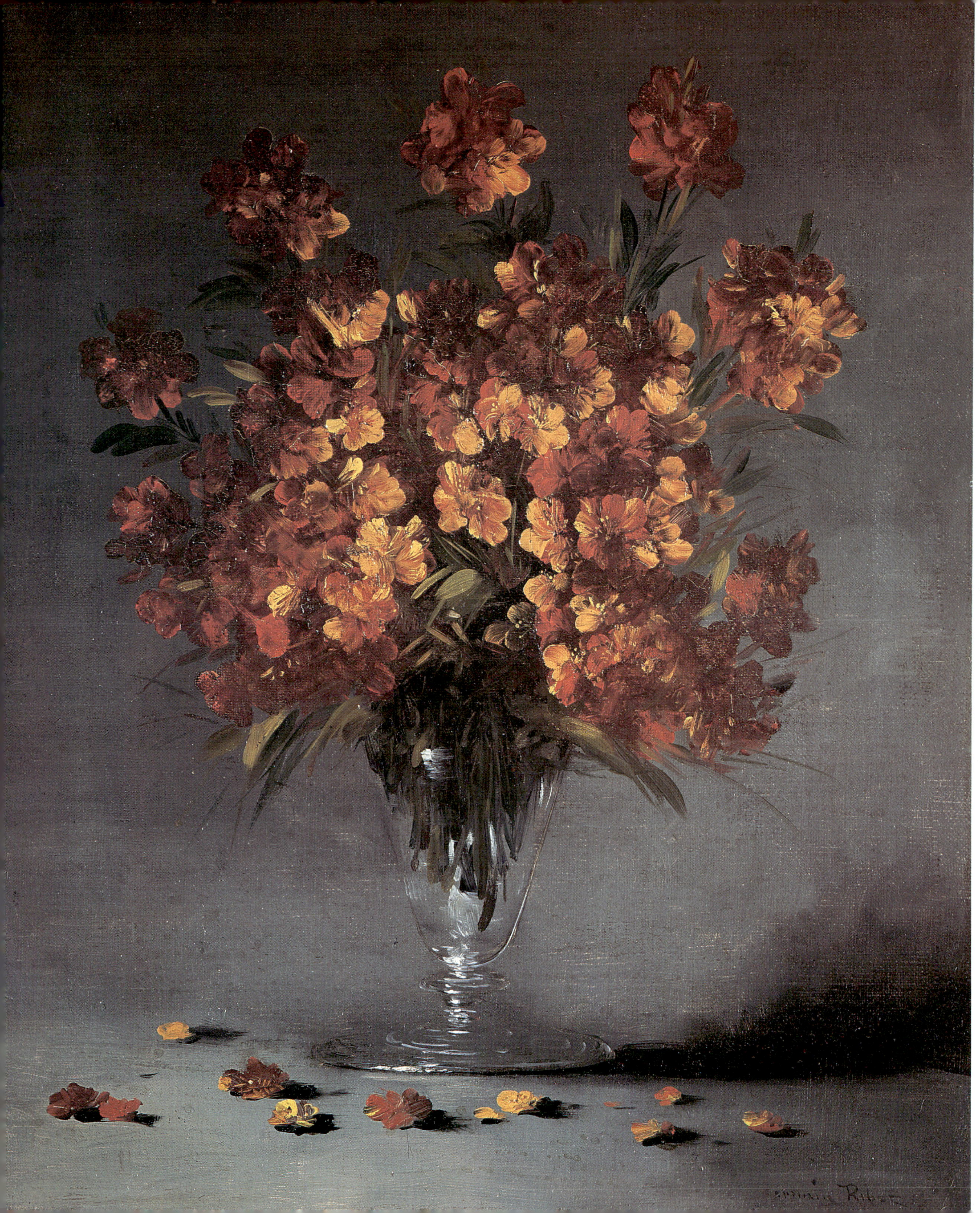

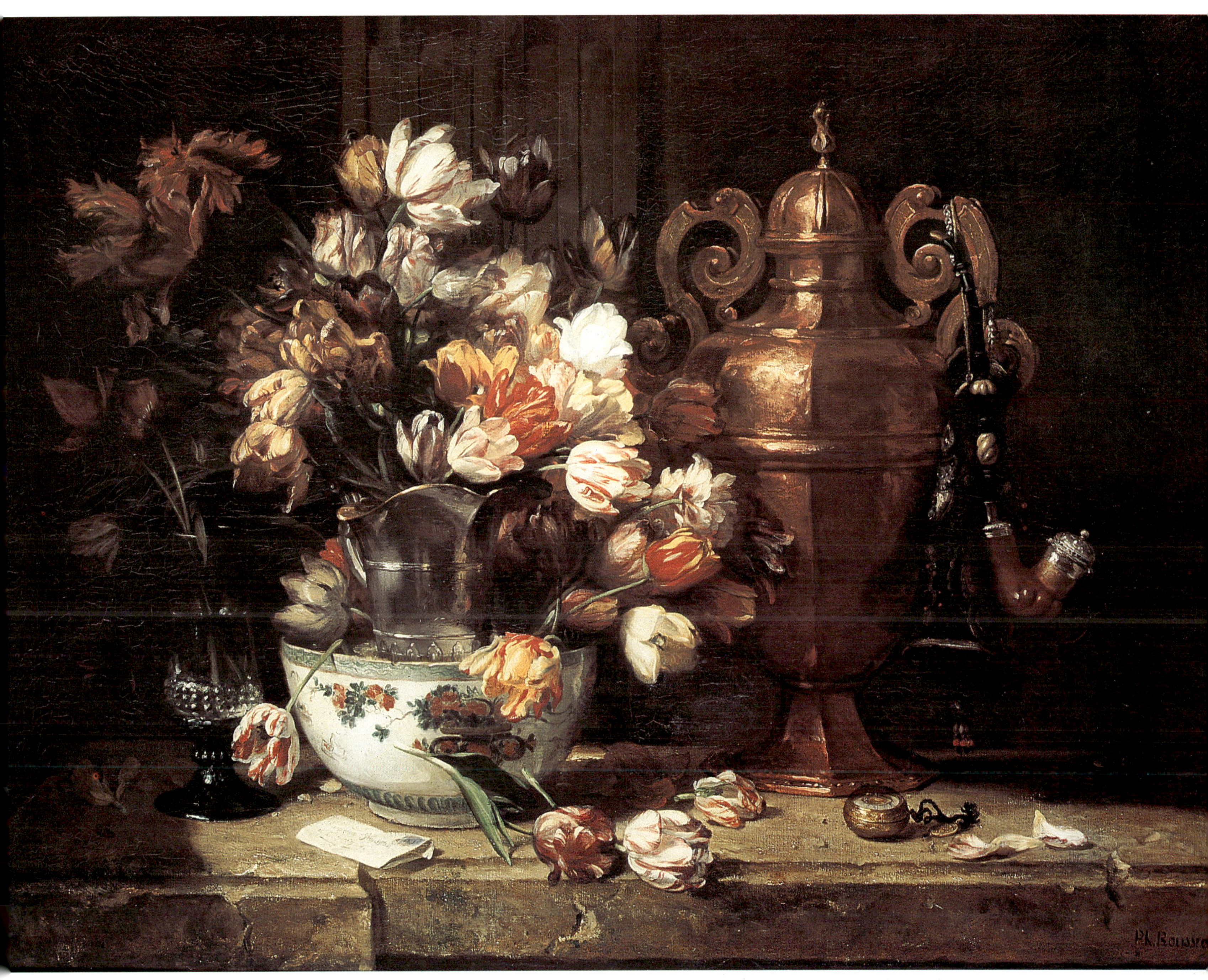

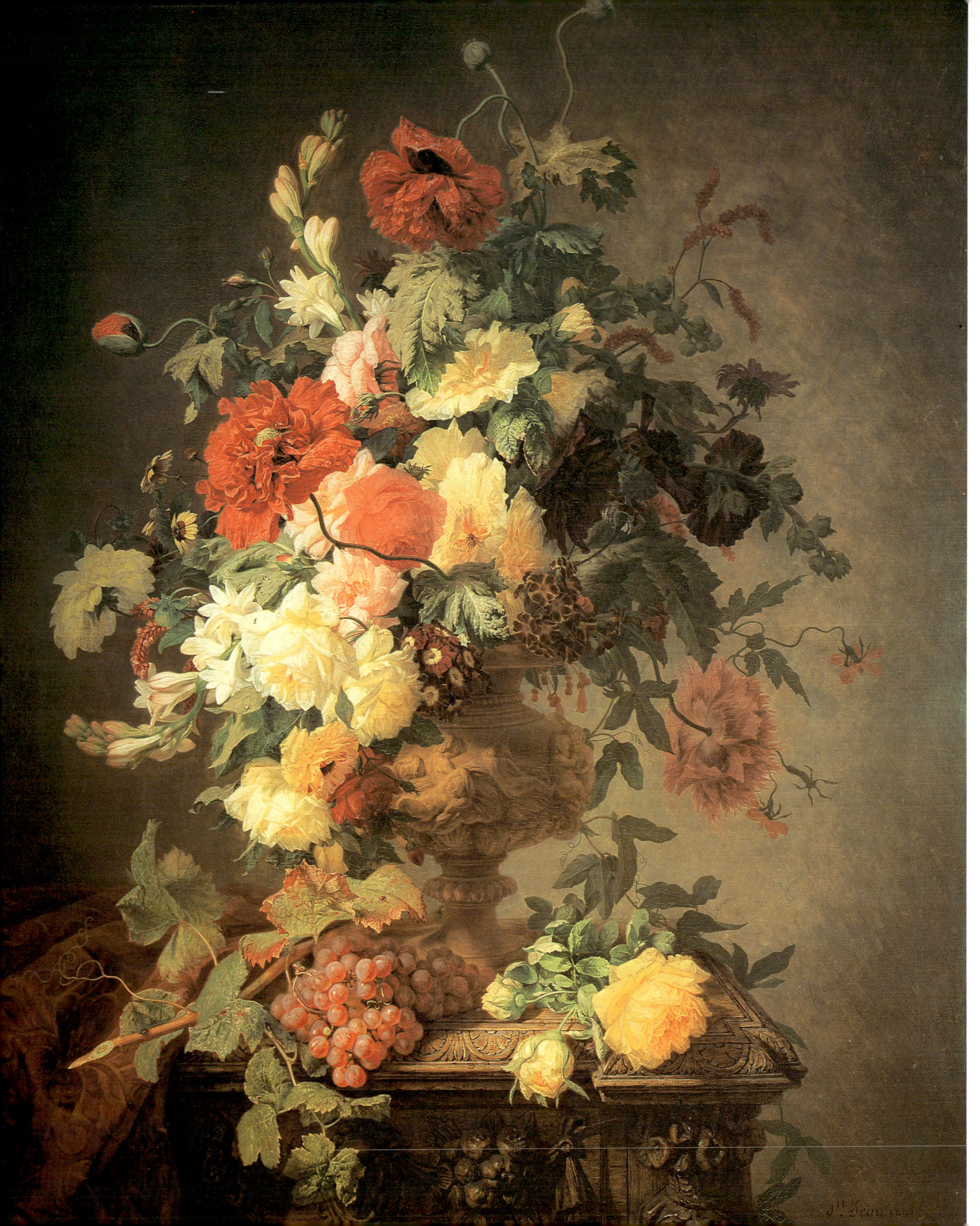

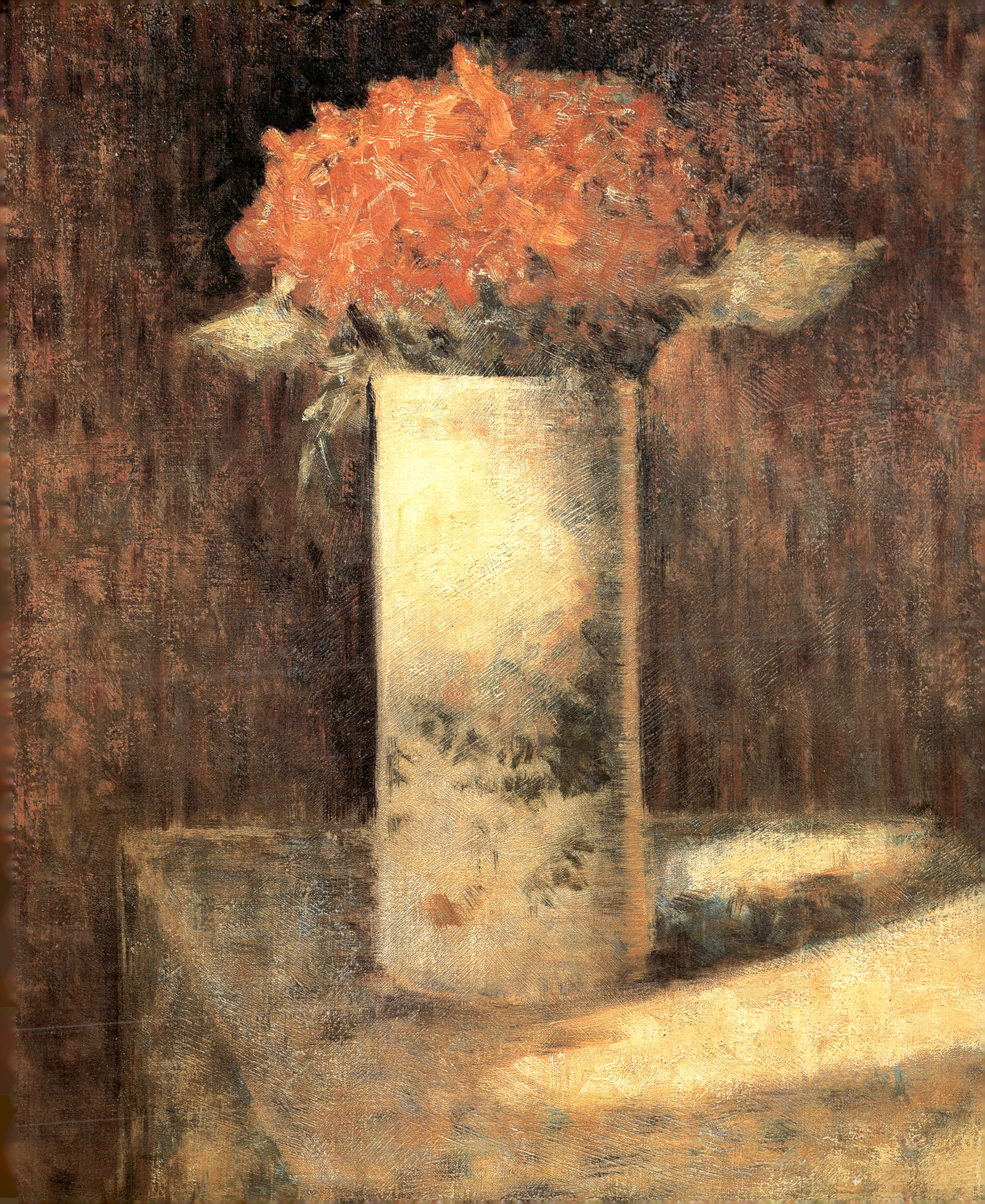

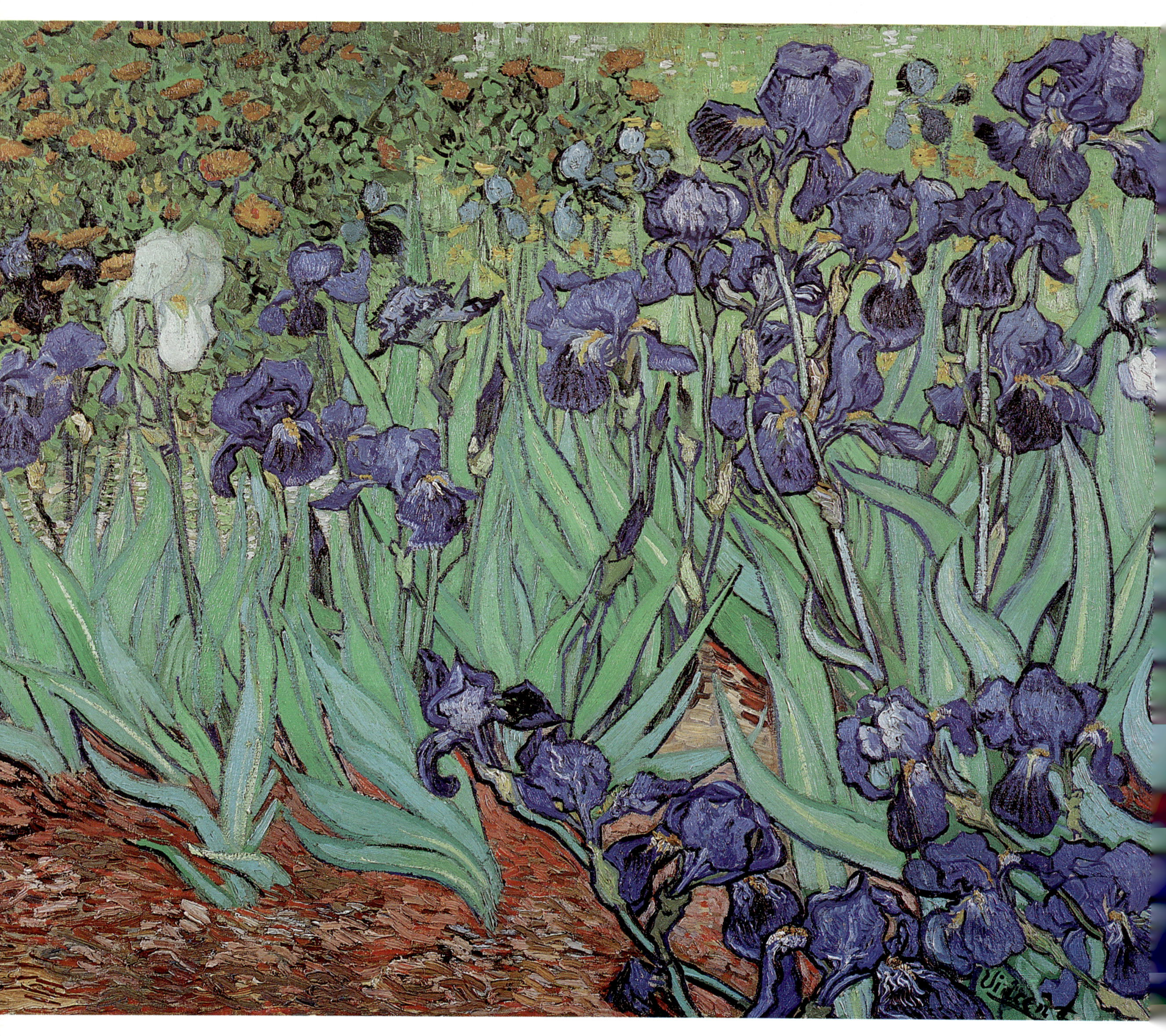
Vincent

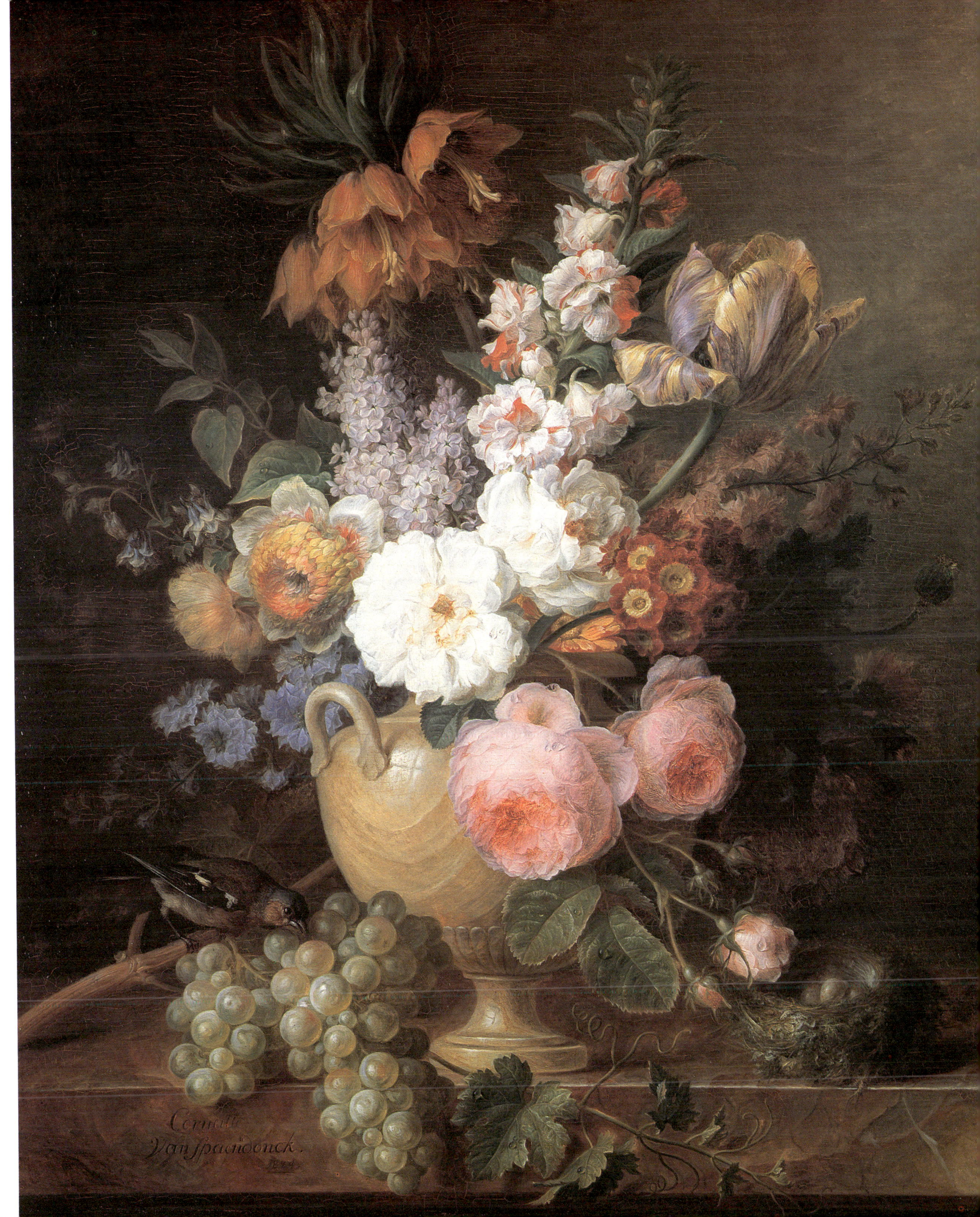
Vanspaendonck.

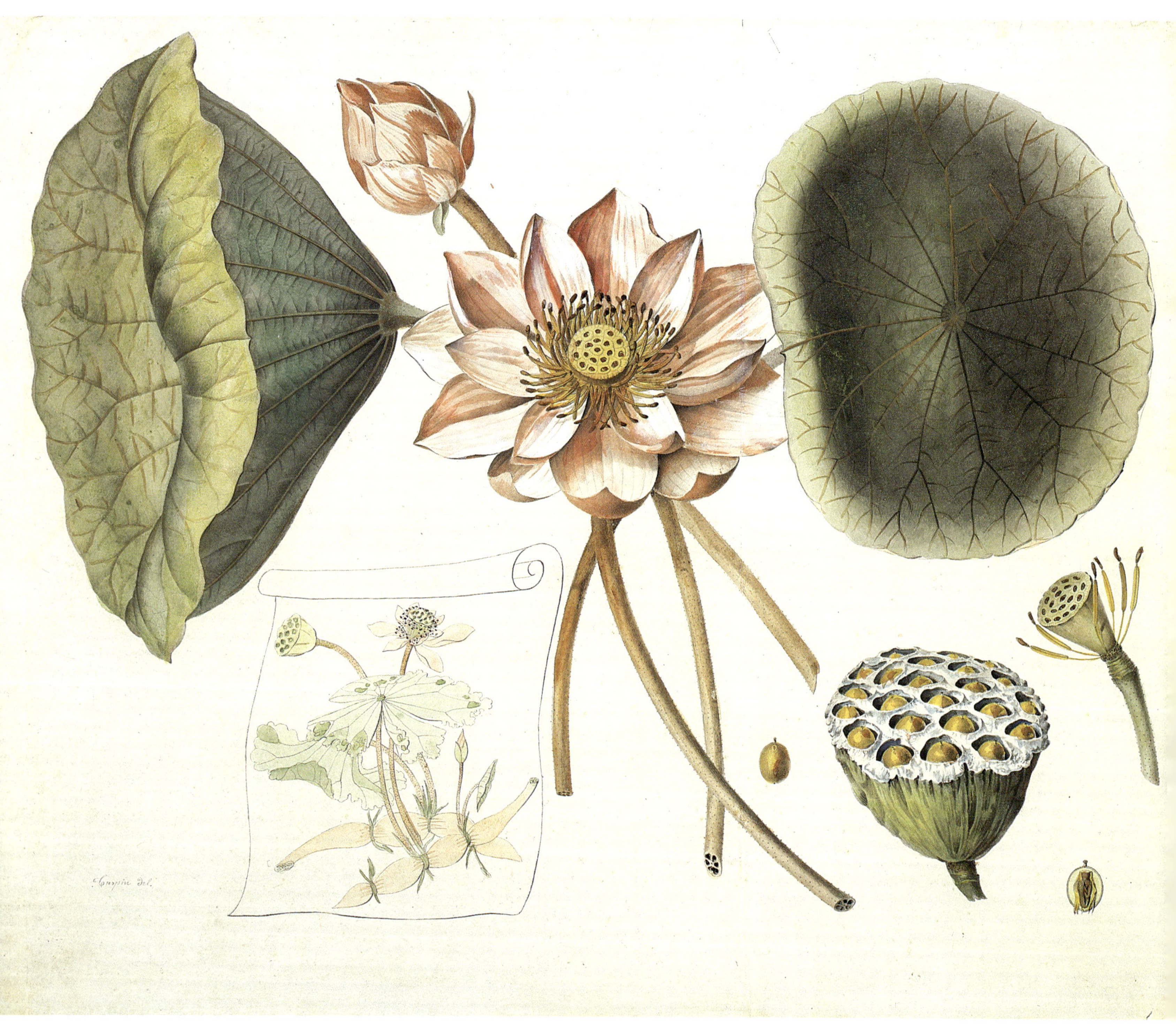
Turpin del.

RIBOT, Germain-Théodore c.*1845–1893*
b. Paris. Pupil of T. Ribot, his father and A. Vollon. Painted genre, still-lifes and flowers. Exhib. Paris Salon from 1870 e.g. *Fleurs*, 1875. *Flowers*, Galerie Abels, Cologne, cat. 1961; *Chrysanthemums in a vase*, Christie's, London, 30 Apr. 1979. *Pansies in a basket*, Marshall Spink, London, Nov. 1980–Jan. 1981
LIT *Bellier*; *Bénézit*; London, *Three centuries of flower and still-life painting*, Marshall Spink, 1980 (ill.); *Paris Salon* 1875; Pavière III, pt. 1; *Thieme*; G. Weisberg, *Chardin and the Still-Life Tradition*, Cleveland, 1979 (ill.); *Witt*

RIBOT, Louise-Aimée
b. Fontenay-aux-Roses (Hauts-de-Seine). Pupil of Ribot, her father. Painted genre, still-lifes and flowers. Exhib. Paris Salon from 1877
LIT *Bellier*; *Bénézit*; *Schurr* V, 84; *Thieme*

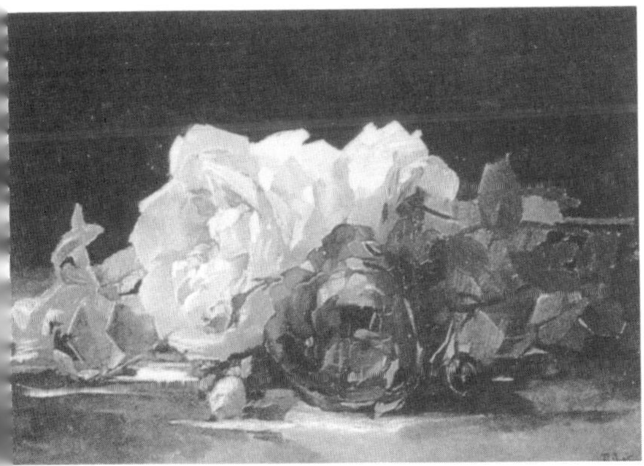

Louise-Aimée Ribot

Oil on canvas, 10 × 15¾ in. (25.5 × 40 cm.), signed *c.*1825
Private collection

Germain-Théodore Ribot

Oil on canvas, signed
Philadelphia Museum of Art, John C. Johnson Collection

RIBOT, Théodule-Augustin *1823–1891*
b. Saint-Nicolas-d'Attez (Eure). Pupil of Glaize. Painted history, genre, portraits and still-lifes. e.g. *Still-life with flowers*, exhib. Allentown, 1959–1960 lent by Silberman Galleries; *A bed of chrysanthemums*, Philadelphia (Johnson coll).
LIT *Bénézit*; G. Lacambre, "Ribot" in *L'Art en France sous le Second Empire*, Paris, Grand Palais 1979, p. 405; Paris, *Ribot*, École des Beaux-Arts 1892; G. Weisberg, *Chardin and the Still-Life Tradition*, Cleveland, 1979 (ill.); G. Weisberg, *The Realist Tradition*, Cleveland 1981

RICHAN, Eugène-Hilaire *b.1814*
Pupil of Thierriat, Lyon BA (CFD 1835)
LIT *Hardouin-Fugier Grafe*

RICHARD
Pupil of S. Saint-Jean. Exhib. *Fleurs*, white chalks, Lyon Salon 1843
LIT *Lyon Salon* 1843

RICHARD, Achille *1794–1852*
b. Paris. Illustrated his own books e.g. *Monographie des orchidées*, Paris 1841
LIT *Nissen* I, 1630, 1631, 1632

RICHARD, Emile
op. Sèvres 1859–1900. Painted flowers
LIT *Bénézit*; Sèvres Arch.; *Thieme*

RICHARD, Eugène *b.1808*
b. Paris. op. Sèvres 1833–1872. Exhib. Paris Salon 1833–1847 e.g. *Bouquet de fleurs dans un vase*, on porcelain, 1842
LIT *Bellier*; *Bénézit*; *Brunet Préaud*; *Paris Salon* 1842; *Thieme*

RICHARD, François
Sèvres Archives, flower designs dated 1858–1859
LIT Sèvres arch.

RICHARD, Irénée *1821–1906*
b. Vienne (Isère). Painted portraits, figures, religious subjects and, occasionally, flowers. Exhib. *Fleurs d'aubépine*, Lyon Salon 1858
LIT *Lyon Salon* 1858; Hardouin-Fugier in *Les peintres de l'Ame* (*Hardouin-Fugier Grafe* 1981), p. 53

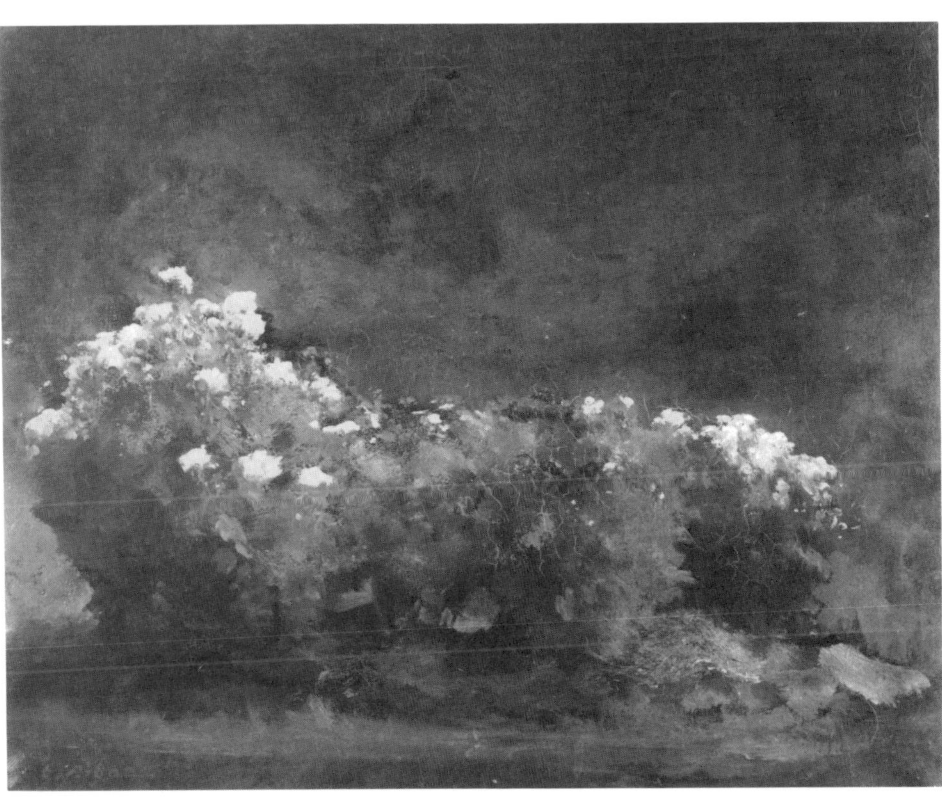

RICHARD, Jules-Gédéon
b. Paris. Painted landscapes and flowers. Exhib. Paris Indép. from 1891
LIT *Bénézit*

RICHARD, Louise-Aurélie or Amélie
Pupil of Burat, T. Robert-Fleury and D. de Cool. Painted copies, flowers and fruit
LIT *Orsay*; *Paris Salon* 1875

RICHARD, Nicolas-Joseph *b.1805*
op. Sèvres 1830–1872
LIT *Bénézit*; *Thieme*

RICHARD, P.
Recorded as flower painter late 19th to early 20th centuries.
LIT *Bénézit*. PM

RICHARD-CHAPONET, Marie-Eugénie *b.1867*
b. Paris. Pupil of Quost and Académie de la Plante. Figure, miniature and flower painter
LIT *Bénézit*

RICHARD-LAGERIE, Marie-Justine
Pupil of Thoret. Exhib. *Bleuets*, *Envoi de Cannes*, Paris Noir et Blanc Salon 1886
LIT *Paris Noir et Blanc Salon* 1886

RICHÉ, Adèle *1791–1887*
A gardener's daughter. Pupil of Van Spaendonck, Van Dael and, possibly, Redouté. Co-designer of *Annales du Muséum d'Histoire Naturelle* and Michaux *Histoire des arbres forestiers*. Exhib. wc, Paris Salon 1819, 1824, 1831, 1833, 1836. M: Paris Muséum d'Histoire Naturelle, forty watercolours (1834–1850), Musée de Tours, Cambridge, Fitzwilliam, (Broughton coll.)
LIT *Bellier*; *Bénézit*; *Hardouin-Fugier* 1981 (ill.); *Laissus*; *Thieme*; *Witt*
See illustration on page 24

RICHE, Jean-Pierre-Gabriel *b.1823*
Pupil of Thierriat, Lyon BA (CFD 1841)
LIT *Hardouin-Fugier Grafe*

RICHEBÉ, Horace *1871–1964*
b. Alger (Algeria). Pupil of Gérôme. Painted figures, landscapes, fruit and, occasionally, flowers
LIT *Bénézit*; *Orsay*; *Schurr* I, 74

RICHET, Léon *1847–1907*
b. Solesmes (Sarthe). Painted landscapes, occasionally flowers. Pupil of Diaz, Lefebure and Boulanger. Paris Salon debut 1869. Inspired by the Barbizon School.
LIT *Bénézit* PM

RICHEY, Clémence
b. Bourg (Ain.). Pupil of Barrias and Hautier. Painted portraits, genre and flowers. Exhib. Paris Salon from 1875. Exhib. *Chrysanthèmes*, Dijon Salon 1887
LIT *Bénézit*; *Dijon Salon* 1887. CL

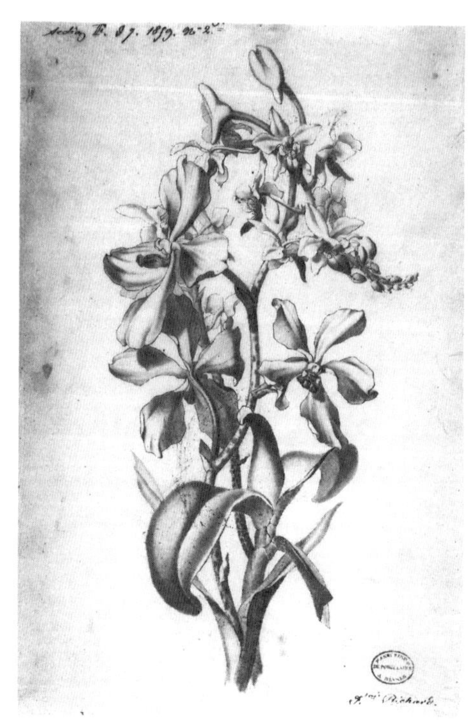

François Richard

Ink and watercolour design for porcelain signed
Sèvres, Manufacture Nationale de Sèvres

RICHNER, *b.1852*
Pupil of Reignier, Lyon BA (CFD 1867)
LIT *Hardouin-Fugier Grafe*

RICORDY de, *see* RENAUD

RICOTTIER, Henri-Martin *b.1835*
Pupil of Thierriat, Lyon BA (CFD 1851). Exhib. Lyon Salon 1858
LIT *Hardouin-Fugier Grafe*

P. Richard

Oil on canvas, $21\frac{1}{4} \times 25$ in. (54 × 65 cm.), signed
Private collection

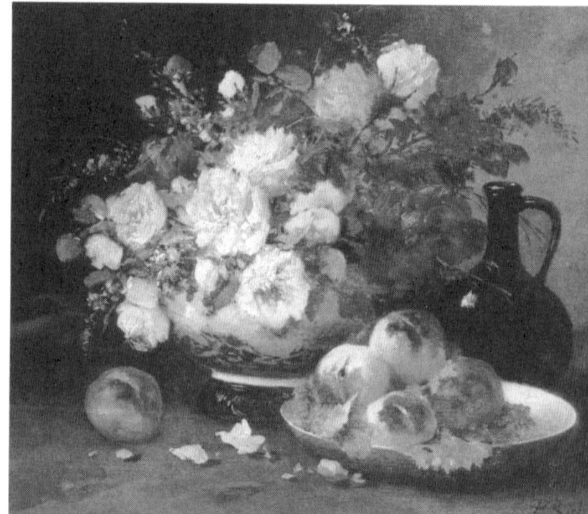

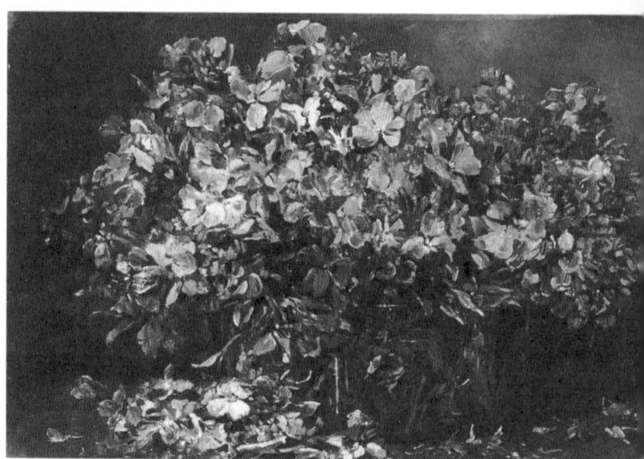

Léon Richet

Oil on panel, 11 × 16 in. (28 × 41 cm.), signed
Courtesy Christie's, London

RIDEAU du SAL, ***see*** **Vincent**

RIDEAU-PAULET, Marie-Thélika ***b.1853***
b. Bordeaux (Gironde). Pupil of Legras and D. de Cool. Exhib. Paris Salon from 1879; *Roses trémières*, wc, Paris Noir et Blanc Salon 1888
LIT *Bénézit*; *Paris Noir et Blanc Salon* 1888; *Thieme*

RIDEL, Louis-Marie-Joseph ***b.1866***
b. Vannes (Morbihan). Pupil of E. Delaunay and G. Moreau. The State acquired Ridel's *Au bord de l'eau* in 1897 (2,000 francs) for the Musée de Nantes, and his *Dernières fleurs* in 1900 (2,500 francs) for the Musée de Lille

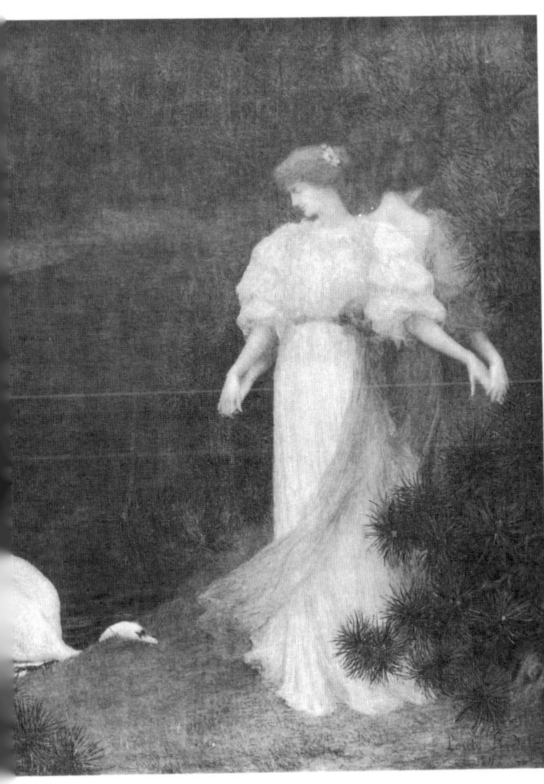

Louis-Marie-Joseph Ridel

Oil on canvas, 98¾ × 74¾ in. (251 × 190 cm.), signed and dated 1897
Nantes, Musée des Beaux-Arts (photo: Patrick Jean)

LIT Paris Arch. Nat. F21: 2147; *Schurr* II, 108 *Thieme*

RIEDER, Marcel ***b.1852***
b. Thann (Haut-Rhin). Pupil of Cabanel. Painted genre and flowers e.g. *Envoi de Nice* (Musée de Mulhouse—currently untraceable)
LIT *Bénézit*; *Orsay*; *Thieme*

RIEGER, Jenny
b. Paris. Pupil of F. Rivoire. Exhib. *Mimosas et anémones*, Paris Indép. 1890; *Chrysanthèmes*, wc, Paris Salon 1895
LIT *Paris Indép.* 1890; *Paris Salon* 1895

RIEHL, Philippe-Thiébaut
b. Paris. Pupil of Laveille. Exhib. Paris Salon from 1879 e.g. *Fleurs et fruits d'automne*, 1880
LIT *Bellier*; *Bénézit*; *Paris Salon* 1880

RIESENER, Louis-Antoine-Léon ***1808–1878***
Pupil of H. F. Riesener, his father, and Gros. Painted still-lifes and, occasionally, flowers
LIT *Bénézit*; *Faré* 1962, p. 242; Paris, *Gros, ses amis, ses élèves*, Petit Palais 1936; *Schurr* I, 15; *Witt*

RIGAL
Exhib. *Fleurs*, Paris Indép. 1884
LIT *Paris Indép.* 1884

RINGARD, Louis-Clément ***b.1824***
Pupil of Thierriat, Lyon BA (CFD 1843) Entered 1845 Lyon Société des Amis-des-Arts FDC
LIT *Hardouin-Fugier Grafe*

RIOCREUX, Alfred ***1820–1912***
Pupil of D. D. Riocreux, his father and Redouté. Illustrated many botanical works. Exhib. Paris Salon 1837, 1838, 1855 M: two watercolours at Cambridge, Fitzwilliam (Broughton coll.), one of these exhibited Marseilles, 1984; Sèvres, Paris Muséum d'Histoire Naturelle, wc on vellum, 1843–1855.
LIT *Hardouin-Fugier* 1981; *Laissus*; Marseille, Musée d'Art et d'Archéologie, *Les Orchidées*, 1984

RIOCREUX, Denis-Désiré ***1791–1872***
op. Sèvres from 1807. Curator of Sèvres Museum from 1840. Painted flowers
LIT *Bénézit*; *Hardouin-Fugier* 1981; *Thieme*

RIOT, Mlle
Exhib. Paris Salon 1830, 1831 e.g. *Camélia, jacinthe, narcisse, oreille d'ours, cinéraire, cynoglosse*, 1831
LIT *Bellier*; *Faré* 1962, p. 248; *Paris Salon* 1831

RIOTTOT, Adolphe ***b. c.1850***
Pupil of Fontaine. Flower and porcelain painter. Exhib. Paris Salon from 1870 e.g. *Pivoines*, on porcelain, 1874; *Fleurs*, on porcelain, Paris Indép. 1884; gouache, Paris Noir et Blanc Salon 1886
LIT *Bellier*; *Bénézit*; *Paris Indép.* 1884; *Paris Noir et Blanc Salon* 1886; *Schurr* IV, 82

RIPAULT, Alexandre ***1839–1911***
b. Tours (Indre-et-Loire). Exhib. *Chrysanthèmes*, Paris Salon 1880. Musée de Tours, *Fleurs*, wc
LIT *Paris Salon* 1880

RIPPOZ, Auguste-Félix ***d.1890***
b. Paris. Pupil of Bin. Painted flowers and fruit. Exhib. Paris Salon from 1874 e.g. *Bourriche d'anémones*, 1876
LIT *Bellier*; *Bénézit*

RIS-PAQUOT, Mme
Exhib. *Fleurs de printemps*; Amiens Salon 1868
LIT *Amiens Salon* 1868

RITLENG, Georges *b.1875*
b. Strasbourg (Bas-Rhin). Pupil of Académie Julian and G. Thurner. Painted flowers. M: Haguenau, Strasbourg
LIT *Bénézit*; *Schurr* II, 41; *Thieme*
See illustration on page 54

RITTIG, J.
Exhib. Paris SNBA *Pivoines*, wc, *Roses trémières*, wc, 1896, *Roses trémières*, 1897
LIT *Paris SNBA* 1896, 1897

RIVEMALE, Paul
Exhib. *Fleurs*, Dijon Salon 1892
LIT *Dijon Salon* 1892. CL

RIVES, Cécile-Marthe-Elise *b.1880*
b. Carcassonne (Aude). Pupil of A. Rives. Painted landscapes, still-lifes and flowers
LIT *Bénézit*; *Thieme*

RIVIÈRE, Charles *1848–1920*
b. Orléans (Loiret). Pupil of Bergeret. Painted still-lifes, animals and, occasionally, flowers
LIT *Bénézit*; *Thieme*

RIVIÈRE, Désiré *b.1826*
Pupil of Thierriat, Lyon BA (CFD 1843)
LIT *Hardouin-Fugier Grafe*

RIVIÈRE, Mlle
Pupil of F. Grobon. Exhib. Lyon Salon 1845
LIT *Hardouin-Fugier Grafe*

RIVOIRE, François 1842–1919
b. Lyon. Pupil of Thierriat and Reignier. op. textile designer. Exhib. Lyon Salon from 1862 e.g. *Vase de fleurs*, 1862, Paris Salon from 1867. Exhib. Dijon Salon e.g. *Chrysanthèmes*, wc, *Fleurs dans un verre*, wc, 1892, *Bleuets et giroflées*, wc, 1897. A watercolourist of international fame and influential teacher. *Giroflées, violettes primevères*, wc, is at the Musée d'Amiens. *Bouquet de Fleurs*, pastel, *c.*1890 (Musée des Beaux-Arts, Arras)
LIT *Bénézit*; *Dijon Salon* 1892, 1897; *Hardouin-Fugier Grafe*; *Hardouin-Fugier Grafe* 1982 (ill.); *Lyon Salon* 1862; Saint Tropez, *Fleurs de Fantin-Latour à Marquet*, Musée de l'Annonciade, 1982 (ill.); *Thieme*
See illustration on page 40

RIZET, Méline
b. La Roche-sur-Yon (Vendée). Pupil of Pallandre and Bourgogne. Exhib. Paris Salon *Lilas et roses*, on faience, 1880, *Fleurs de printemps*, 1885
LIT *Paris Salon* 1880, 1885

ROBERT, Mme
op. Sèvres 1819–1827
LIT *Brunet Préaud*

ROBERT, Eugène
b. Paris. Pupil of Lequien and Simon. Exhib. Paris Salon from 1866 e.g. *Fleurs dans un verre*, 1873, *Primevère*, wc, 1890
LIT *Bellier*; *Paris Salon* 1890

ROBERT, Mlle G.
Exhib. *Oiseaux et fleurs*, Lyon Salon 1881
LIT *Lyon Salon* 1881

ROBERT, Gabriel
op. Sèvres 1846–1852. Painted animals, still-lifes and, occasionally, flowers. Exhib. Paris Salon 1838–1841
LIT *Bellier*; *Bénézit*; *Brunet Préaud*

ROBERT, Héléna-Joséphine
b. Gravelines (Nord). Pupil of Lebour. Painted still-lifes and, occasionally, flowers. Exhib. Paris Salon 1857–1859
LIT *Bellier*; *Bénézit*

ROBERT, Mme Louis
op. Sèvres 1835–1840. Exhib. Paris Salon 1835, 1836, 1837 e.g. *Bouquet*, 1835
LIT *Bellier*; *Bénézit*; *Brunet Préaud*; *Thieme*

ROBERT, N.
Designed plates for H. F. Jaubert, E. Spach *Choix de plantes. . .de l'Asie occidentale*, Paris (Roret) 1842–1857
LIT *Nissen* I, 985; *Sitwell*

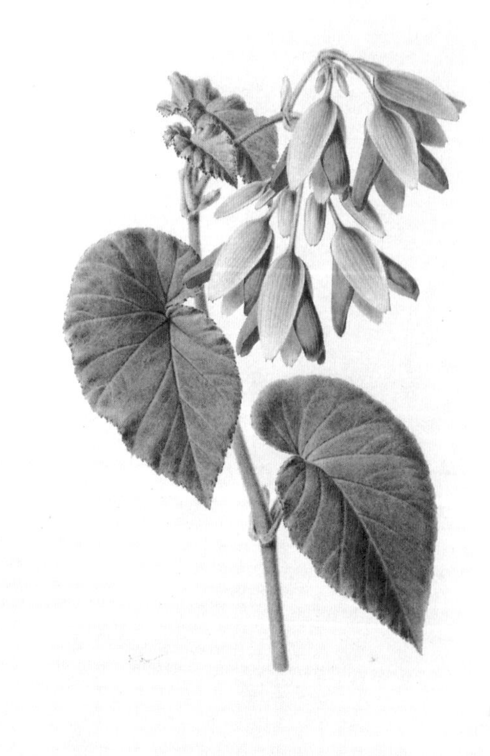

Alfred Riocreux

Watercolour, $11\frac{1}{8}$ × 8 in. (28.3 × 20.5 cm.), signed
Cambridge, Fitzwilliam Museum
(Broughton Collection)

ROBILLOT, Marthe-Blanche ***b.1856***
b. Troyes (Aube). Pupil of E. Vaudé. Musée de Troyes, *Fleurs de mai*, *Roses et lilas*
LIT *Bénézit*; *Thieme*; Troyes Musée doc.

ROBIN, Elise, *née* Renolt
Exhib. *Attributs de chasse, fleurs et fruits*, *Cruche renversée et couronne de fleurs des champs*, Paris Salon 1842
LIT *Paris Salon* 1842

ROBIN, Marie
Pupil of Lyon École Municipale du Quai Saint-Antoine. Exhib. *Bouquet de roses*, Lyon Salon 1881
LIT *Lyon Salon* 1881

ROBLOT-DELANDE, Louise-Marie
b. Paris. Pupil of F. Rivoire. Exhib. *Bouquet de fleurs*, wc, Paris Salon 1895
LIT *Paris Salon* 1895

ROCHAT
Pupil of Lyon BA and J. Guichard. Exhib. *Vase de fleurs*, Lyon Salon 1880
LIT *Lyon Salon* 1880

ROCHE, Jenny
Her *Giroflées et pensées* was sold at the 1879 Lyon Salon
LIT *Compte-rendu annuel de la Société des Amis-des-Arts de Lyon*, Lyon (Perrin) 1879

ROCHE, P.
Exhib. Paris SNBA *Muguet*, wc, 1892, *Orchidée*, wc, 1896
LIT *Paris SNBA*, 1892, 1896

ROCHE, Pierre ***b.1823***
Pupil of Thierriat, Lyon BA (CFD 1842)
LIT *Hardouin-Fugier Grafe*

ROCHE de la, Claire
Exhib. *Bouquet de roses*, Dijon Salon 1850
LIT *Dijon Salon* 1850. CL

ROCHE, *see* VILLEBESSEYX

ROCHETTE, Pierre, *alias* Pétrus ***b.1818***
Pupil of Thierriat, Lyon BA (CFD 1836). Entered 1845 Lyon Sociéte des Amis-des Arts FDC
LIT *Hardouin-Fugier Grafe*

ROCHON, François
Pupil of Berjon, Lyon BA (CFD 1812)
LIT *Hardouin-Fugier Grafe*

RODET, Anne-Charlotte-Claudine
b. Moret (Seine-et-Marne). Pupil of A. Riché and H. Scheffer. Painted landscapes and flowers. Exhib. Paris Salon 1839–1859. e.g. *Roses*, wc, 1848, *Vases de fleurs sur table de marbre*, 1859
LIT *Bellier*; *Bénézit*

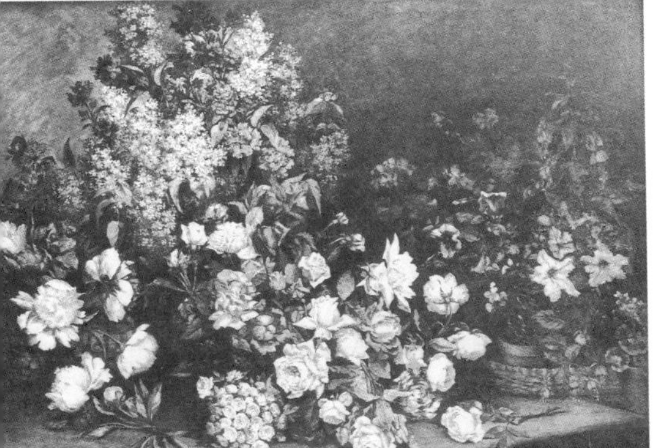

Marthe-Blanche Robillot

Oil on canvas, 35¾ × 51¼ in. (90.5 × 130.5 cm.), signed
Troyes, Musée des Beaux-Arts

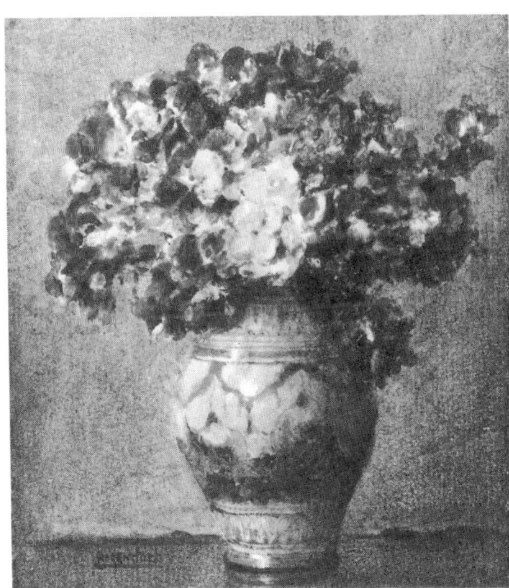

Isidore Rosenstock

Watercolour, 5 × 4 in. (12.5 × 10 cm.), signed
Private collection

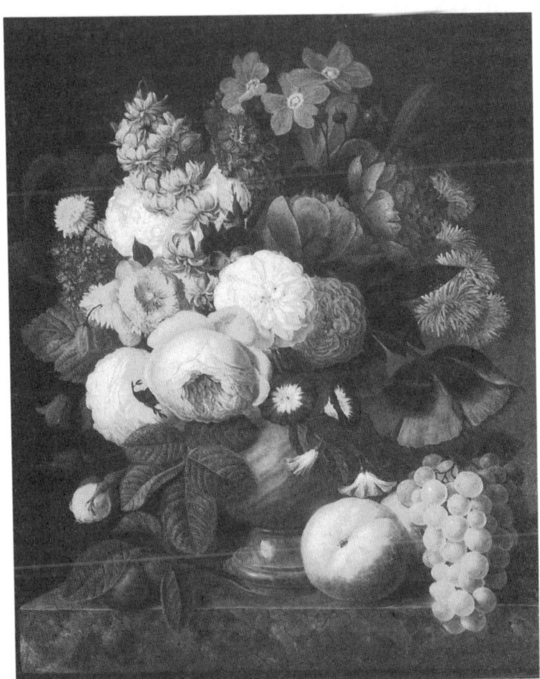

Ferdinand Rossignol

Oil on canvas, 23¼ × 19 in. (59 × 48.5 cm), signed and dated 1848 (destroyed by fire)
(photo: John Mitchell & Son, London)

ROEHN, Jean-Alphonse *1799–1864*
b. Paris. Pupil of A. E. G. Roehn, his father, Regnault and Gros, Paris BA. Painted religious subjects, genre and, occasionally, flowers e.g. *Fleurs*, Lyon Salon 1842; *Couronne de fleurs*, Paris Salon 1842
LIT *Bellier*; *Bénézit*; *Lyon Salon* 1842; *Paris Salon* 1842; *Schurr* I, 78; *Thieme*; *Witt*

ROGER, Marie-Blanche *b.1873*
b. Villeneuve-Saint-Georges (Val-de-Marne). Pupil of F. Rivoire. Painted landscapes and flowers. Exhib. Paris Salon from 1897 e.g. *Iris*, screen, 1898
LIT *Bénézit*; *Paris Salon* 1898; *Thieme*

ROGIER-ROBERT, Marie-Alice
b. Paris. Pupil of Barrias and G. Béthune. Exhib. *Bourriche de pensées*, wc, *Chrysanthèmes*, wc, Dijon Salon 1897
LIT *Bénézit*; *Dijon Salon* 1897. CL

ROGNIAT, Louis *1852–1934*
Pupil of A. Louvier and H. Daume. Architect. Exhib. wc, Lyon Salon from *c.*1892 and *Pivoines*, Paris Salon 1895
LIT *Bellier*; *Hardouin-Fugier Grafe*; *Paris Salon* 1895

ROLL, Alfred-Philippe *1847–1919*
b. Paris. Pupil of Gérôme, Bonnat and Harpignies, painted genre, figures, landscapes and, occasionally, flowers e.g. *Fleurs*, Strasbourg Salon 1884 (2,000 francs)
LIT *Bénézit*; Paris *Equivoques*, MAD 1973; L. Roger-Milès *A. Roll*, Paris (Lahure) 1904; *Strasbourg Salon* 1884; *Thieme*

ROLLIN, Gilbert-Joseph *b.1875*
Pupil of Castex-Dégrange, Lyon BA (CFD 1895)
LIT *Hardouin-Fugier Grafe*

ROMAIN, Nicolas *b.1808*
Pupil of Thierriat, Lyon BA (CFD 1827). op. textile designer
LIT *Hardouin-Fugier Grafe*

ROMANET, Ernest-Victor *b.1876*
b. Paris. Painted flowers
LIT *Bénézit*; *Thieme*

ROMANNE, Valentine
b. Boursonne (Oise). Pupil of Vautier. Exhib. Paris Salon from 1877 e.g. *Fleurs*, 1880
LIT *Bellier*; *Paris Salon* 1880

ROQUEPLAN, *see* PRÉVOST

ROSENMULLER, *see* MULLER

ROSENSTOCK, Isidore *b.1880–1956*
b. Strasbourg. Painted landscapes and flowers, principally in watercolour; Versailles gardens a frequent subject. Exhib. Paris Salon and Société Internationale des Aquarellistes
LIT *Bénézit*. PM

ROSLIN, Emma-Adèle, *née* Blanche *d.1883*
b. Auxerre (Yonne). Pupil of Cogniet and Clinchamp. Exhib. Paris Salon from 1864. Her *Premières fleurs* was sold at the 1870 Lyon Salon
LIT *Compte-rendu annuel de la Société des Amis-des-Arts*, Lyon (Perrin) 1870; *Thieme*

ROSSET, Nicolas-Jules *b.1818*
Pupil of Thierriat, Lyon BA (CFD 1837)
LIT *Hardouin-Fugier Grafe*

ROSSI
Pupil of Chometon, op. Lyon. Designed lithograph *Althea et épi de blé*, 1882
LIT *Hardouin-Fugier Grafe*; Paris Bibl. Nat. Est. Jd 59

ROSSIGNOL, Ferdinand
Exhib. *Flowers* Paris Salon 1848 (private coll.)
LIT *Bénézit*

ROSTAIN
Pupil of Thierriat, Lyon BA (CFD 1824)
LIT *Hardouin-Fugier Grafe*

ROSTAIN, Claude or Mathieu *1829–1887*
Pupil of Thierriat, Lyon BA. Silk manufacturer
LIT *Hardouin-Fugier Grafe*

ROSTAN, Mlle A.
Painted landscapes and flowers. Exhib. *Fleur d'aristoloche du jardin du roi*, wc, Paris Salon 1835
LIT *Bénézit*; *Paris Salon* 1835

ROSZCZEWSKI, Henri-Dominique
b. Chezal-Benoit (Cher). Pupil of Maillard. Exhib. Paris Salon from 1868. Exhib. *Fleurs et bijoux*, Lyon Salon 1870
LIT *Bénézit*; *Lyon Salon* 1870

ROUAIX-DUNEAU, Jeanne
Exhib. Dijon Salon *Brioches et violettes*, 1894, *Chrysanthèmes et raisins*, 1897
LIT *Dijon Salon* 1894, 1897

ROUART, Ernest *1874–1942*
b. Paris. Married Julie Manet, Berthe Morisot's daughter. Pupil of Degas. Painted figures, landscapes and, occasionally, flowers. Musée de Bagnols-sur-Cèze, *Fleurs*
LIT *Bénézit*; *Thieme*

ROUBY, Alfred-Jean ***b.1849***
b. Paris. Pupil of Beyle. Painted still-lifes and flowers. Exhib. Paris Salon e.g. *Fleurs*, 1880, *Giroflées*, 1895. His 1890 exhibit was bought by the State (800 francs) for the French Embassy at Saint-Petersburg. *Giroflées*, Drouot, Paris, 24 Mar 1909. Musée de Sète, *Chrysanthèmes*
LIT *Bénézit*; Paris Arch. Nat. F21: 2110; *Paris Salon* 1880, 1895; *Witt*

ROUCH, Caroline
Exhib. *Bouquet de roses*, *Botte de chrysanthèmes*, Dijon Salon 1890
LIT *Dijon Salon* 1890. CL

ROUGEMONT DE LOWENBERG, ***see*** **MULINEN**

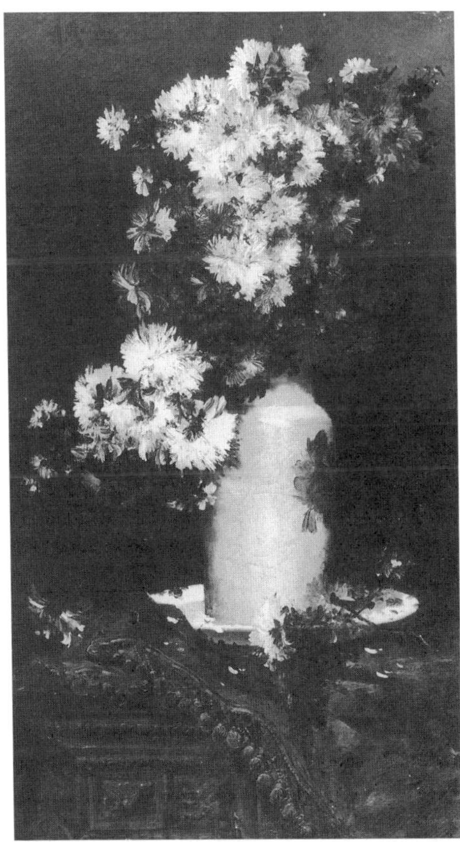

Alfred-Jean Rouby

Oil on canvas, 38¼ × 20½ in. (97.5 × 51.7 cm.), signed
Sète, Musée Paul Valéry

ROUGET, Marie
b. Paris. Pupil of École Professionnelle and A. Bonnefoy. Exhib. *Fleurs*, ink, Paris Noir et Blanc Salon 1886
LIT *Paris Noir et Blanc Salon* 1886

ROUGNY, Jean-François ***b.1814***
Pupil of Thierriat, Lyon BA (CFD 1832)
LIT *Hardouin-Fugier Grafe*

ROUGY
Pupil of Thierriat, Lyon BA (CFD 1833)
LIT *Hardouin-Fugier Grafe*

ROULLIER, Blanche
b. San Francisco (USA). Pupil of Delonce. Exhib. *Mimosa*, pastel, Paris Salon 1890; *Bleuet*, Roanne Salon 1890
LIT *Paris Salon* 1890; *Roanne Salon* 1890

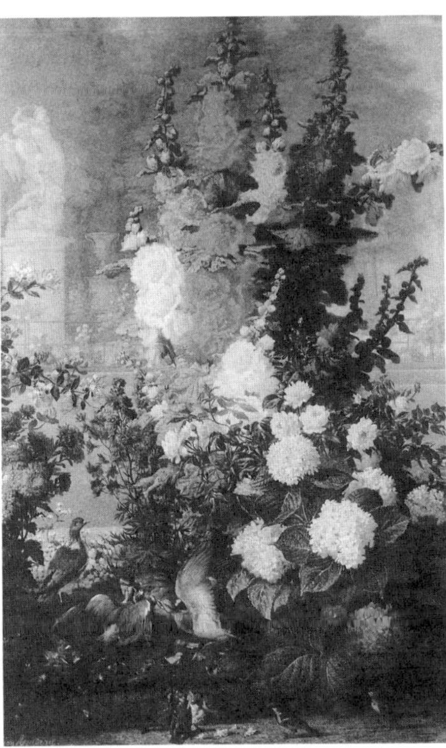

Léon Rousseau

Oil on canvas, 92 × 60 in. (234 × 152 cm.), signed
Courtesy Maître Francis Briest

ROULLIET, Nicolas-Amaranthe ***b.1810***
b. Lyon. Pupil of Lyon BA. Painted landscapes and flowers. Designed plates for many lithographed sets e.g. *Naissance des fleurs*, Paris 1837, *Redouté des Dames* etc.
LIT *Bellier*; *Bénézit*; *Hardouin-Fugier* 1981; *Thieme*

ROUSSEAU, Henri-Julien-Félix called Le Douanier ***1844–1910***
b. Laval (Mayenne). Self-taught. Among his earlier listed flower paintings are *Corbeille de fleurs*, 1883–1884 (Bourret, 55); *Fleurs de Poète*, *c.*1890 (Bourret, 68); *Bonne fête*, 1892 (Vallier, 53); *Bouquet de fleurs*, 1892 (Vallier, 55); *Autoportrait au bouquet de fleurs*, 1899 (Bourret, 120); *Fleurs dans un vase*, c. 1899 (Bourret, 116). Other flowers are either undated or later works, e.g. London, Tate Gallery, *Flowers*, *c.*1909
LIT *Bénézit*; J. Bourret, *Henri Rousseau*, Neuchâtel (Ides et Calandes) 1961; D. Vallier, *Tout l'œuvre peint d'Henri Rousseau*, Paris (Flammarion) 1970. AC

ROUSSEAU, Léon ***b. c.1825***
b. Pontoise (Val-d'Oise). Pupil of Ciceri and Pingret. Exhib. Paris Salon 1849–1881 e.g. *Fruits et fleurs*, *Fleurs*, 1850, *Pivoines*, 1867, *Splendeur et modestie, fleurs*, 1869. *Massif de fleurs aux oiseaux*, Drouot, Paris, 30 Nov. 1981. M: Angers, Bagneres-de-Bigorre (currently untraceable), Pontoise, Le Puy (not a flower picture)
LIT *Bellier*; *Bénézit*; *Paris Salon* 1850, 1867; *Schurr* IV, 80; *Thieme*

ROUSSEAU, Léonie
b. Paris. Pupil of Léon Rousseau, her father. Painted landscapes, still-lifes and flowers. Exhib. Paris Salon 1865–1869
LIT *Bellier*; *Bénézit*

ROUSSEAU, Pauline
Exhib. *Fleurs dans une carafe*, Paris Salon 1842
LIT *Paris Salon* 1842

ROUSSEAU, Philippe ***1816–1887***
b. Paris. Pupil of Gros and Bertin. One of the most popular artists of his day. Painted animals, still-lifes and, occasionally, flowers e.g. *Fleurs* Stasbourg Salon 1859, *Le banc aux fleurs et à la cornemuse*, Roussel coll. sale, G. Petit, Paris, March 1912. *Still-life with roses and hollyhocks*, Deutman coll., Brandt Amsterdam, 14–25 Feb. 1949. *Nature morte aux fleurs*, Rosset, Geneva 28 June 1973. *Fleurs*, Sotheby's, London, 17 June 1986, Lot 64. M: Rotterdam, Boymans Van Beuningen Museum
LIT C. Baudelaire, *Le Salon de 1845*, *Le Salon de 1846*, Gallimard 1973, I, p. 395; *Bellier*; *Bénézit*; H. D. Davenport, "Rousseau" in *L'Art en France sous le Second Empire* Paris, Grand Palais 1979, p. 406; *Faré* 1962, p. 242; *Mitchell* (ill.); Paris Arch. Nat. F21: 522, *Pavière III*, pt. 1; *Strasbourg Salon* 1859; *Thieme*; G. Weisberg, *Chardin and the Still-Life Tradition*, Cleveland, 1979 (ill.); *Witt*

ROUSSEL, Ker-Xavier ***1867–1944***
b. Lorry-lès-Metz (Moselle). Pupil of D. N. Maillart, T. Robert-Fleury and Bouguereau. Painted figures, landscapes, and, occasionally, flowers. Six of his flower pieces exhibited 27 Mar.–14 Apr.

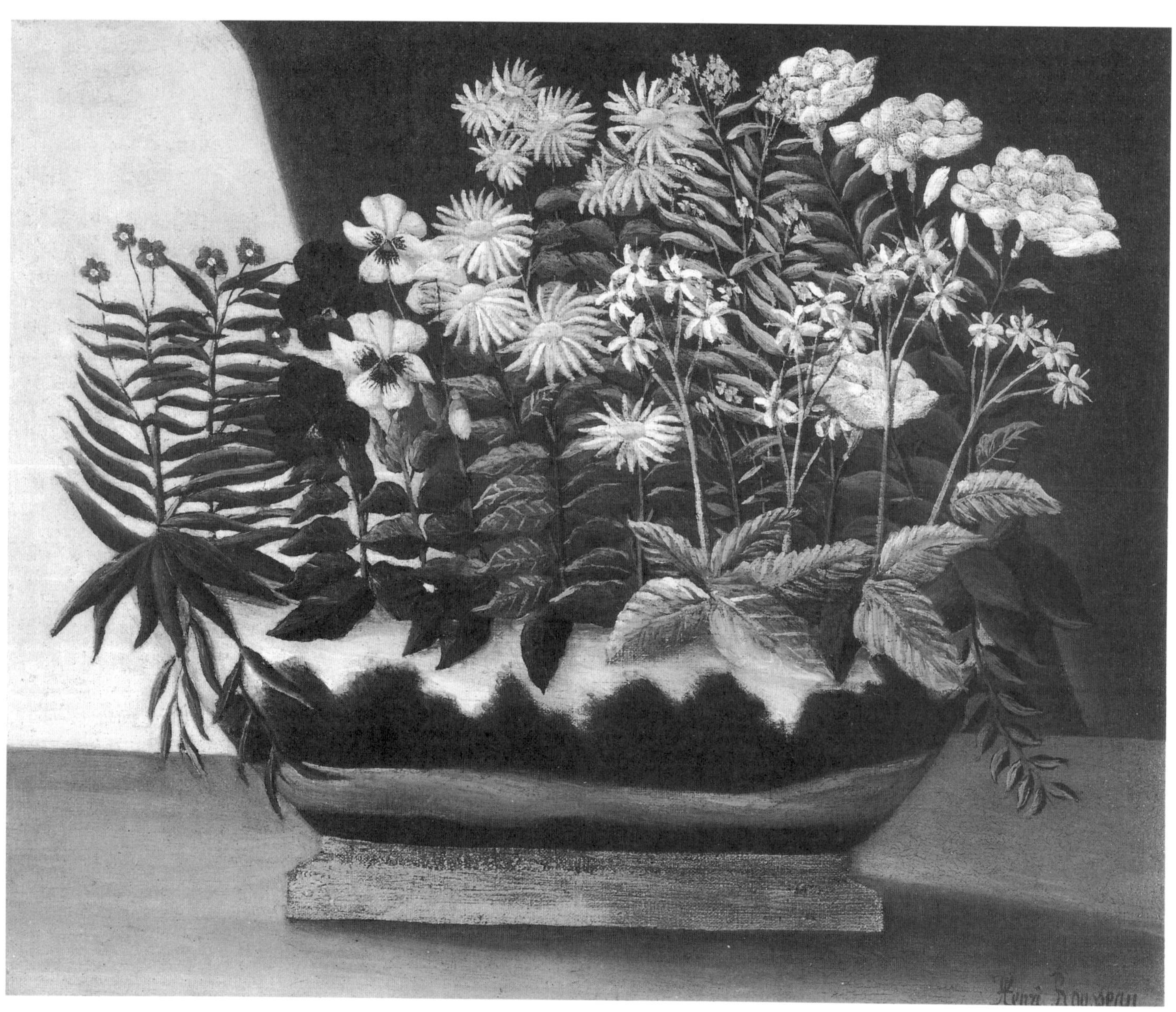

Henri Rousseau

Oil on canvas, 15 × 18 in. (38 × 46 cm.), signed
Upperville, Virginia, Collection of Mr and Mrs Paul Mellon

1911 at Galerie Bernheim-Jeune, Paris. *Fleurs des Arbres*, Christie's, London, 13 Dec. 1985, lot 127
LIT K.-X. Roussel, Galerie Bernheim-Jeune, Paris 1906. Brussels, *K.-X. Roussel*, Musée Royal des Beaux Arts, 1975; Paris, Orangerie des Tuileries, *K.X. Roussel*, 1968; M. A. Stevens in *Post-Impressionism*, London RA 1979–1880; G. Weisberg, *The Realist Tradition*, Cleveland 1981; *Witt*

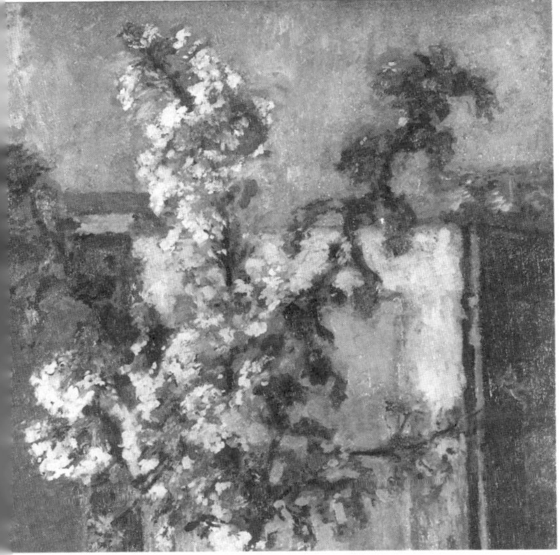

Ker-Xavier Roussel

Oil on board, 23¼ × 25½ in. (59 × 65.5 cm.), signed
Courtesy Christie's, London

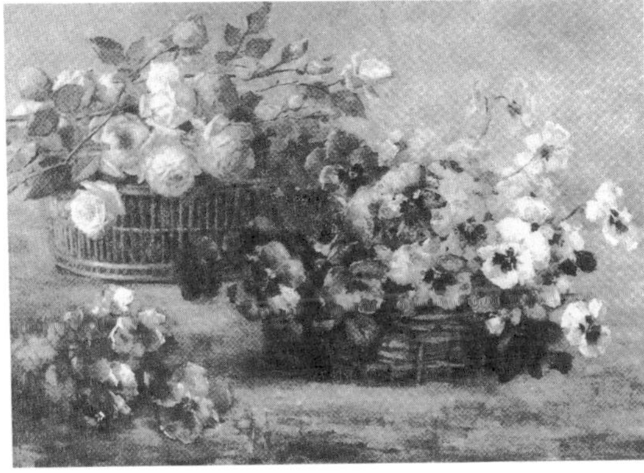

ROUSSELIN-CORBEAU DE SAINT-ALBIN, *see* SAINT-ALBIN

ROUSSET, Charles *b.1824*
Pupil of Thierriat, Lyon BA (CFD 1844)
LIT *Hardouin-Fugier Grafe*

ROUX, François *b.1822*
Pupil of Thierriat, Lyon BA (CFD 1841)
LIT *Hardouin-Fugier Grafe*

ROUX, Hippolyte *b.1852*
b. Sainte-Euphémie (Drôme). Painted landscapes and flowers.
LIT *Bénézit*

ROUX, Marie
b. Ivry (Val-de-Marne). Pupil of Barré

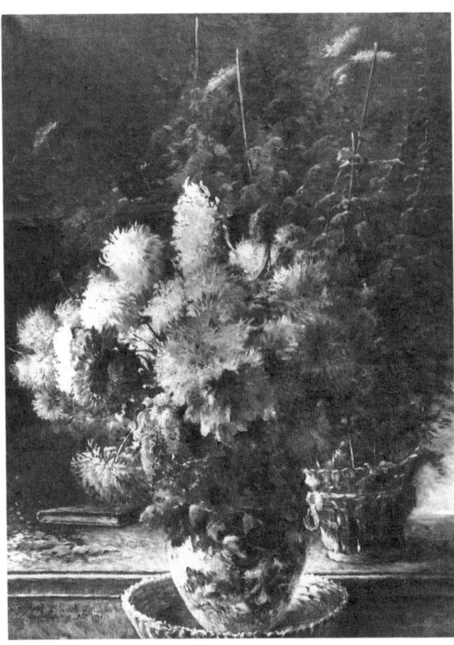

Dieudonné-Auguste Royer

Oil on canvas, 36¼ × 27½ in. (92 × 70 cm.), signed, dated 1898, and inscribed 'D. Royer a son ami Ernest Baltet 9bre 1898 souvenir affectueux'
Troyes, Musée des Beaux-Arts

Dominique-Hubert Rozier

Oil on canvas, 21¼ × 28¾ in. (54 × 73 cm.), signed
Private collection

and Lesourd de Beauregard. Exhib. *Fleurs et éventail*, wc, Paris Salon 1872
LIT *Bénézit*; *Paris Salon* 1872

ROUX, Pierre-Louis *b.1819*
Pupil of Thierriat, Lyon BA (CFD 1836). Textile designer
LIT *Hardouin-Fugier Grafe*

ROY
Exhib. *Fleurs* Lyon Salon 1875
LIT *Lyon Salon* 1875

ROY, Marguerite
Pupil of Bourgogne. Exhib. *Bourriche de pensées*, Paris UFPS 1898
LIT *Paris UFPS* 1898

ROYBON, Antoine
b. Paris. Exhib. *Fleurs*, Paris Indép. 1890
LIT *Paris Indép.* 1890

ROYER, Charles
b. Langres (Haute-Marne). Pupil of Lugardon. Worked at Langres. Exhib.

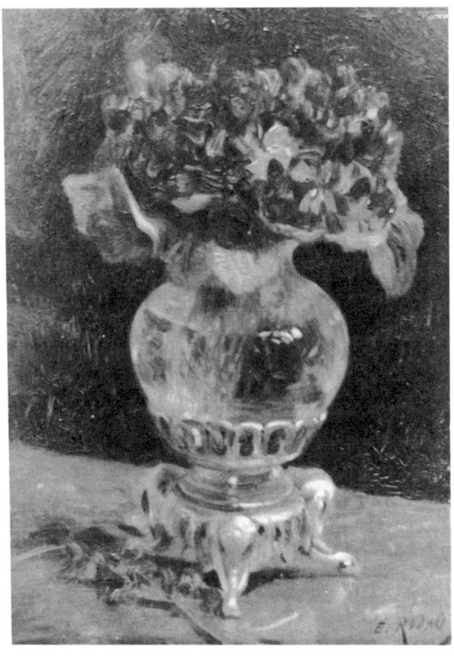

Edmond-Adolphe Rudaux

Oil on panel, 10½ × 4¼ in. (26.5 × 10.8 cm.), signed
Gray, Musée Baron Martin

Paris Salon from 1880 and Dijon Salon *Lilas*, 1883, *Chrysanthèmes*, 1885, *Pivoines*, 1890. Musée de Langres, *Chrysanthèmes*
LIT *Bellier*; *Bénézit*; *Dijon Salon* 1883, 1885, 1890

ROYER, Dieudonné-Auguste *1835–1920*
b. Troyes (Aube). Pupil of Lancelot and Français. Drawing master. Musée de Troyes *Gerbe de chrysanthèmes*, 1898, *Bouquet de chrysanthemes*
LIT *Bénézit*; Musée de Troyes doc.; *Thieme*

ROYER, Marcel
Exhib. *Bleuets*, *Chrysanthèmes*, Paris Indép. 1894
LIT *Paris Indép.* 1894

ROYET, Journoud *alias* *b.1851*
Pupil of Reignier, Lyon BA (CFD 1871)
LIT *Hardouin-Fugier Grafe*

ROZE, Emile-Louis
Exhib. *Anémones et mimosas*, *Coquelicots et marguerites*, Paris Indép. 1896
LIT *Paris Indép.* 1896

ROZET, Pierre *b.1880*
Pupil of Castex-Dégrange, Lyon BA (CFD 1899)
LIT *Hardouin-Fugier Grafe*

ROZIER, Dominique-Hubert *1840–1901*
b. Paris. Pupil of Vollon. Painted still-lifes, game and flowers. Exhib. Paris Salon from 1872 e.g. *Aiguière et fleurs*, 1873, *Bouquet de roses, glace et objets divers*, 1875, *Panier fleuri*, 1885, *Fleurs*, 1895, *Roses et pensées* (private coll.). M: Castellane, Privas
LIT *Bellier*; *Bénézit*; *Orsay*; Paris Arch. Nat. F21: 4711 4510; *Paris Salon* 1873, 1875, 1885 (ill.) 1895; *Schurr* IV, 81; *Thieme*; *Witt*

ROZIER VAN LINDEN, Geneviève
b. Paris. Exhib. *Pavots*, Paris Indép. 1890
LIT *Paris Indép.* 1890

RUBELLIN or RUBELIN, Jean-Claude *alias* Joannes *b.1827*
Pupil of Thierriat, Lyon BA (CFD 1846). Exhib. Lyon Salon 1849–1900 e.g. *Vase de fleurs*, 1861; *Fruits et fleurs dans un surtout de table*, Dijon Salon 1897
LIT *Dijon Salon* 1897; *Hardouin-Fugier Grafe*; *Lyon Salon* 1861

RUDAUX, Edmond-Adolphe *1865–1925*
b. Verdun (Meuse). Pupil of Laveille and Boulanger. Exhib. *Anémones*, wc, Paris Salon 1898 M: Gray, *Violettes*
LIT *Paris Salon* 1898; *Schurr* IV, 93; *Thieme*

RUPIED, Ernestine *fl. c.1863*
Pupil of Maréchal (of Metz). Musée de Dieppe
LIT *Bénézit*

RUPRICH-ROBERT, Victor-Marie-Charles *1820–1887*
b. Paris. Pupil of Constant Dufeux. Designed plates for *Flore ornementale* 1866–1876. Paris BMAD (Maciet coll.) *Rosa Indica*
LIT *Bellier*; *Nissen* I, 1705; *Paris BMAD*; C. Samoyault-Verlet, "Ruprich-Robert" in *L'Art en France sous le Second Empire*, p. 139; *Thieme*

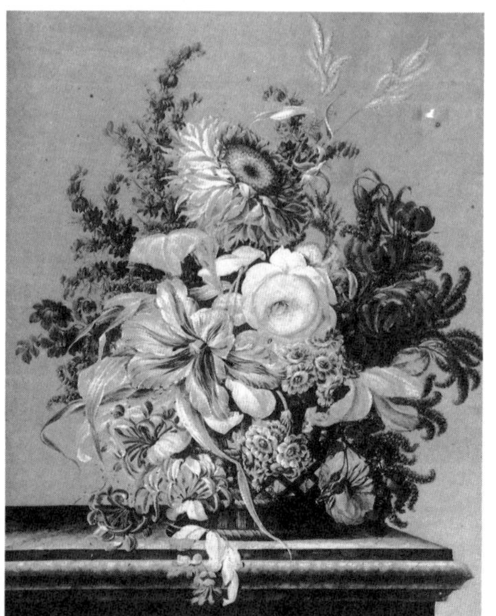

RUSTERHOLZ, Henri *b.1821*
Pupil of Thierriat, Lyon BA (CFD 1839)
LIT *Hardouin-Fugier Grafe*; *Witt*

RUTOWSKY, Louis de
A pair of signed gouaches of 1803 were recently sold at auction: Sotheby's, London, 24 June 1987, lot 519. PM

RUYER, Mlle J.
Exhib. *Oeillets*, Paris Salon 1895
LIT *Paris Salon* 1895 (ill.)

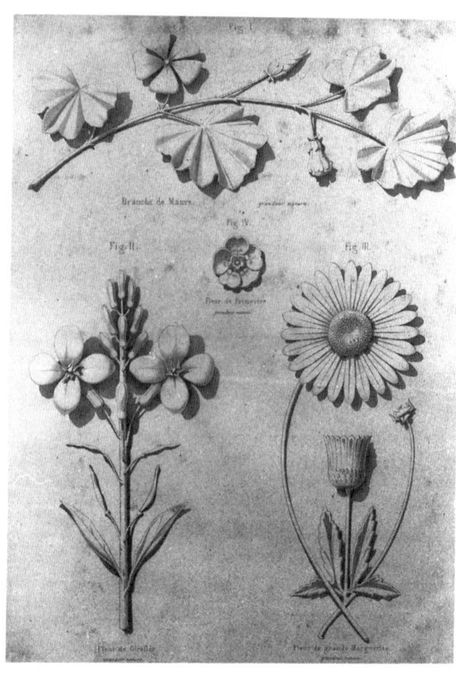

Victor-Marie-Charles Ruprich-Robert

12 × 7¼ in. (30 × 18.5 cm.), signed
Paris, BMAD (Maciet Collection)

Louis de Rutowsky

Gouache, 20¼ × 16 in. (52.5 × 41 cm.), signed and dated 'Sept 20 1803'
Courtesy Sotheby's, London

S

SABOURET, *see* DESCAMPS

SACÉ de, *see* BOIS

SACHY, Henri-Emile de
b. Paris. Pupil of Colin, Cabanel and Dubufe. Painted landscapes and flowers. Exhib. *Bouquet des champs*, Lyon Salon 1879
LIT *Bénézit*; *Lyon Salon* 1879

SAGLIER, Jeanne
Pupil of Hervé. Exhib. *Fleurs* Paris UFPS 1898
LIT *Paris UFPS* 1898

SAGNIMORTE, Louis-Claude *1843*
b. Lyon. Pupil of Reignier, Lyon BA (CFD 1859)
LIT *Hardouin-Fugier Grafe*

SAIGNEMORTE, Claude *b.1816*
Pupil of Thierriat, Lyon BA (CFD 1833)
LIT *Hardouin-Fugier Grafe*

SAILLET, Charles de
Designed flower plates lithographed by Genty
LIT Paris Bibl. Nat. Est. Jd 59

SAINT-ALBIN ROUSSELIN-CORBEAU, Céline Hortensius de, *née* Duhameau *1817–1874*
b. Mayenne (Mayenne). Pupil of Jacobber. Exhib. flowers on porcelain Paris Salon 1843–1874 e.g. *Corbeille de fleurs et de fruits*, 1843, *Fleurs et fruits*, after Jacobber 1845, *Orchidées*, *Fleurs et coquillages*, 1869. M: Alençon, Bagnères de Bigorre
LIT *Bellier*; *Bénézit*; *Paris Salon* 1845; *Thieme*

SAINT-AMOUR, Constance de
Pupil of Institut Fénelon. Exhib. *Fleurs des champs*, Lille Salon 1881
LIT *Lille Salon* 1881; G and PT

SAINT-ANGE CHASSELAT, *see* CHASSELAT

SAINT-CÈNE, Antoine *b.1837*
Pupil of Reignier, Lyon BA (CFD 1856)
LIT *Hardouin-Fugier Grafe*

SAINTE MARIE de, *see* ENFANTO

SAINT-ETIENNE, Mme
Painted landscapes, interiors and flowers. Exhib. Paris Salon 1835, 1836 *Anémones* wc, *Jacinthes*, *Primevères*, 1836
LIT *Bellier*; *Bénézit*

SAINT-GENOIST, de
Exhib. *Les violettes*, Dijon Salon 1885
LIT *Dijon Salon* 1885. CL

SAINT-HILAIRE, Mme C.
Exhib. *Fleurs*, Lyon Salon 1877
LIT *Hardouin-Fugier Grafe*

SAINTIN, Henri or Louis-Henri *1846–1899*
b. Paris. Pupil of Pils, Segé and Saint-Marcel. Painted landscape, town views, occasionally flowers. Paris Salon debut 1867.
LIT *Bénézit*; *Schurr* I, 85. PM

SAINTIN, Jules-Emile *1829–1894*
b. Lemée (Aisne). Pupil of Drolling, Picot and Leboucher. Paris BA 1845. Painted figures and genre. Exhib. Paris Salon from 1848 e.g. *Fleurs de Nice*, 1880 and Lyon Salon 1884
LIT *Bellier*; *Bénézit*; *Lyon Salon* 1884; *Paris Salon* 1880; *Schurr* V, 108

SAINT-JEAN, Paul 1842–1875
b. Lyon. Pupil of Simon Saint-Jean, his father. Exhib. Paris and Lyon Salon 1866–1875. Painted genre and, occasionally, flowers. M: Utrecht *Fleurs*, (disposed of at sale, 1944)
LIT *Bellier*; *Bénézit*; *Hardouin-Fugier Grafe*; *Hardouin-Fugier* 1980 *Thieme*

SAINT-JEAN, Simon *1808–1860*
b. Lyon. Pupil of Thierriat, Lyon BA (CFD 1826) and F. Lepage. Exhib. Lyon Salon 1827, 1828, 1831, 1833 and 1836–1859. Paris Salon 1834–1859. Baudelaire's pet-hate was the most successful of all Lyonnais flower painters. M: London, Wallace coll.; Paris, Louvre; Musée des Beaux-Arts, Lyon; Rouen
LIT *Hardouin-Fugier* 1980; Hardouin-Fugier "Baudelaire et S. Saint-Jean" in *Bulletin Baudelairien*, Vanderbilt University, Upperville Tenn. 1978, pp. 3–11

SAINT-MAXIN, Marthe
Pupil of A. Jourdeuil and G. Debillemont-Chardon. Exhib. *Chardons de Berck*, wc, Paris UFPS 1898
LIT *Paris UFPS* 1898

SAINT-QUENTIN, Désiré de
b. Valenciennes (Nord.) Pupil of Abel de Pujol. Exhib. Paris Salon 1847–1848. M: Tourcoing
LIT *Bénézit*

SAINT-SAENS *d.1890*
b. Paris. The famous composer's mother was a flower and fruit painter. Musée de Dieppe: wc of birds, flowers and fruit
LIT *Bénézit*

SAINT-SUPERI, Francisque ***b.1871***
b. Lyon. Pupil of Castex-Dégrange, Lyon BA (CFD 1888)
LIT *Hardouin-Fugier Grafe*

SAINT-VINCENT de, *see* BORY

SALANSON, *see* LANSSE

SALARD, Céline
b. Paris. Pupil of Voruz. Exhib. *Roses*, wc, Paris Salon 1890; *Pavots*, wc (200 francs), *Pensées et giroflées*, Strasbourg Salon 1891; *Fleurs et fruits d'automne*, *Roses*, Paris Salon 1895; *Roses*, *Boules de neige*, *Chèvrefeuille*, *roses*, *Marguerites*, Paris UFPS 1898; *Dahlias blancs et Fuchsias*, wc, Paris Salon 1898. Her *Lilas and faux-ébénier*, wc, was bought by the State (300 francs) in 1900
LIT Paris Arch. Nat. F21: 2149; *Paris Salon* 1890, 1895, 1898; *Paris UFPS* 1898; *Strasbourg Salon* 1891

SALAVIN ***b.1821***
b. Lyon. Pupil of Thierriat, Lyon BA (CFD 1841)
LIT *Hardouin-Fugier Grafe*

SALEMFELS, Olga de
b. Paris. Pupil of Faux-Froidure and Saint-Pierre. Exhib. *Pavots*, wc, Paris Salon 1898
LIT *Paris Salon* 1898

SALMON, Charles
b. Cepoy (Nord). Pupil of E. Bruyère. Exhib. Paris Salon 1842 and 1852 e.g. *Vase de fleurs dans une niche*, 1842. A Salmon (first name unknown) op. Sèvres 1809
LIT *Bellier*; *Bénézit*; *Brunet Préaud*; *Paris Salon* 1842

SALOMÉ, Jeanne
Musée de Louviers *Violettes*
LIT Musée de Louviers doc.

SALOMON, Anne-Elodie
b. Marseille. Pupil of Cesbron, Cogniet and Troyon. Painted still-lifes and, occasionally, flowers. Exhib. Paris Salon 1859, 1861
LIT *Bellier*; *Bénézit*; *Faré* 1962, p. 242; Paris Arch. Nat. F21: 302, 2201; *Thieme*

SAMSON, *see* FICHEL

SANDIER, Albert
Exhib. *Chrysanthèmes*, Dijon Salon 1887
LIT *Dijon Salon* 1887. CL

SANDIER, Alexandre
Exhib. *Orchidées*. Textile design. Paris SNBA 1897
LIT *Paris SNBA* 1897

SANDT, Alice de
b. Neuilly-sur-Seine (Hauts-de-Seine). Exhib. *Géraniums*, Paris Noir et Blanc Salon 1880; *Roses de Noël*, gouache, Lyon Salon 1884
LIT *Lyon Salon* 1884; *Paris Noir et Blanc Salon* 1880

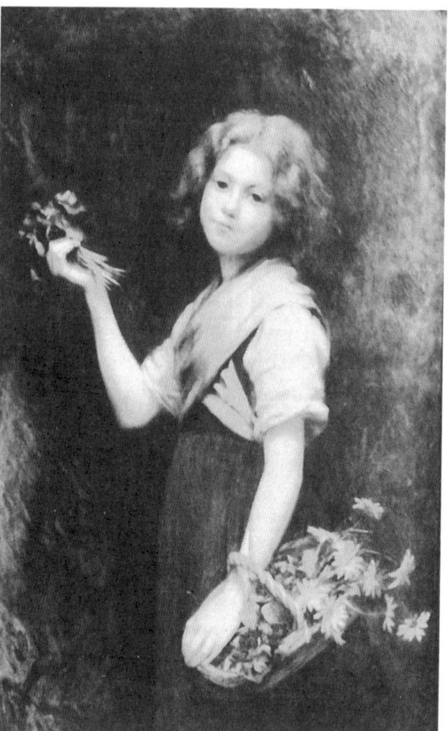

SANTÉ, Etienne
Pupil of Berjon, Lyon BA (CFD 1820)
LIT *Hardouin-Fugier Grafe*

Céline Hortensius de Saint-Albin Rousselin-Corbeau

Oil on canvas, 11 × 13 in. (28 × 33 in.), signed
Bagnères-de-Bigorre, Musée Salies

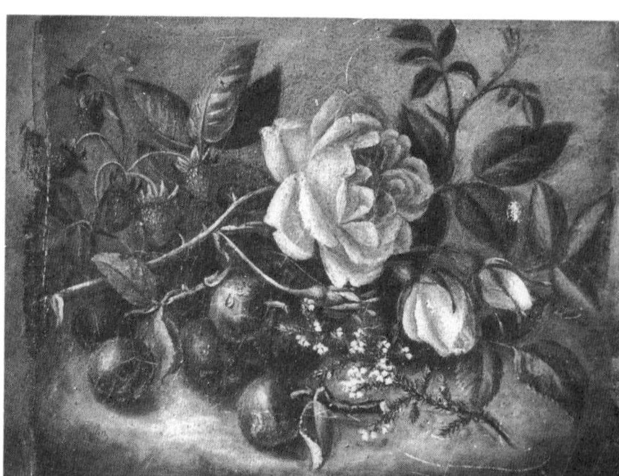

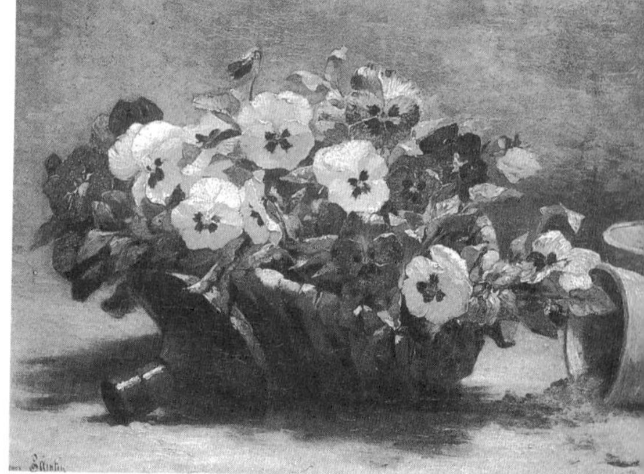

Henri Saintin

Oil on canvas, 18 × 24 in. (46 × 61 cm.), signed and dated 1884
Private collection

Jeanne Salomé

Oil on canvas, 43¼ × 28¼ in. (110 × 72 cm.), signed
Louviers, Musée des Beaux-Arts

SANTOIRE, ***see*** **VARENNE**

SARGANT-FLORENCE, Mary
Pupil of L. O. Merson. Exhib. *Fleurs décoratives*, Paris Noir et Blanc Salon 1888
LIT *Paris Noir et Blanc Salon* 1888

SARRAZIN
Exhib. *Fleurs*, *Chrysanthèmes*, Dijon Salon 1894
LIT *Dijon Salon* 1894. CL

SAUGET, Louis-Marie
b. Besançon (Doubs). Exhib. *Chrysanthèmes*, Grenoble Salon 1899
LIT *Grenoble Salon* 1899. MW

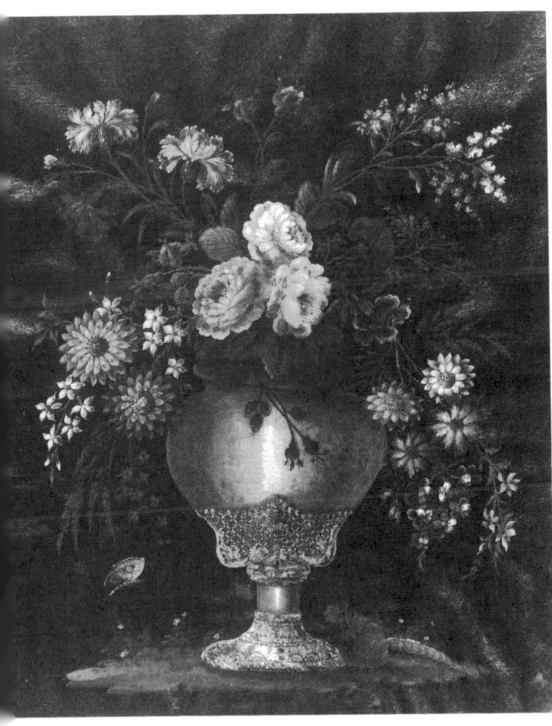

Mme N.E. Saunier de Gadancourt

Oil on paper, 11 × 9 in. (28 × 23 cm.), Monogrammed and inscribed '1810 à l'âge de 78 ans'
Pontoise, Musée Tavet-Delacour

SAUNIER DE GADANCOURT, Mme N.E.
One work is known at Pontoise dated 1810 and inscribed 'à l' âge de 78 ans'
PM

Charles Gabriel Sauvage

Engraving after a drawing, $16\frac{1}{2}$ × 11 in. (42 × 28 cm.), signed verso 'Berthollet: Bon à être gravé.. Vu en commission le 4 juillet 1808'
Courtesy John Mitchell & Son, London

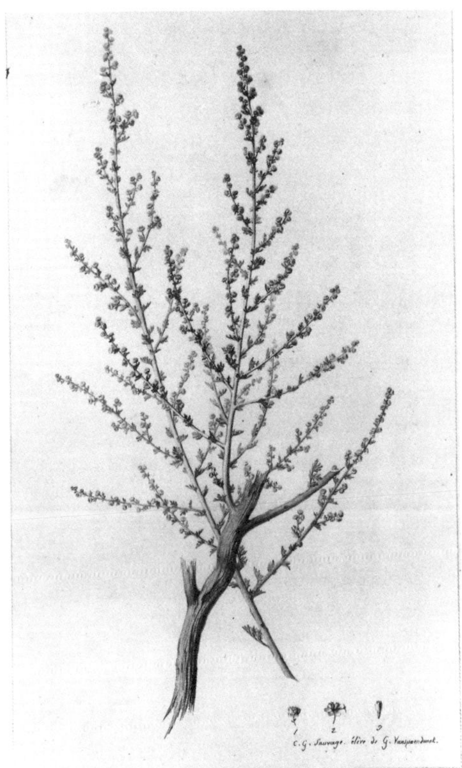

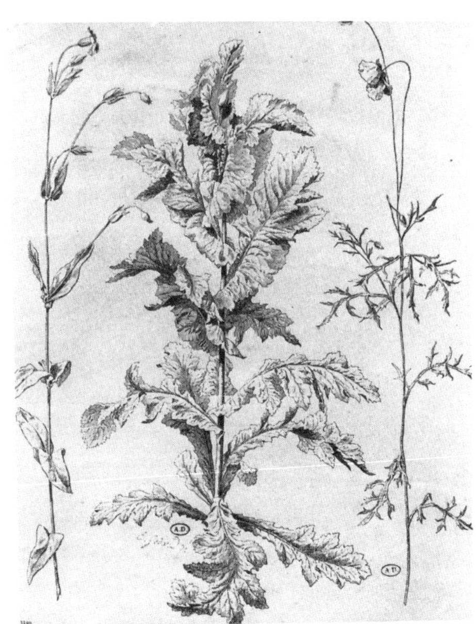

SAUVAGE, Charles Gabriel ***d.1817***
Pupil of Piat-Joseph Sauvage. Active 1800–1817. Designed plates for E. P. Ventenat, *Description des plantes nouvelles et peu connues cultivées dans le jardin de M. Cels*, Paris 1800–1803; J. J. La Billardière, *Novae hollandiae plantarum specimen*, Paris (Huzard) 1804–1806
LIT *Laissus*; *Nissen* I, 451, 1116, 2048; *Sitwell*

SAUVAGE, Henri ***1853–1912***
b. Blois (Loir-et-Cher). Pupil of Bonnat and Humbert. Painted portraits, still-lifes and flowers. *Fleurs*, Blois 1877
LIT *Bellier*; *Bénézit*; *Blois H. Sauvage*, cat. 1977; *Orsay*; *Schurr* IV, 117

SAUVAGEOT, Claude ***1823–1885***
b. Santenay (Côte-d'Or). Pupil of Gaucherel. Exhib. Paris Salon from 1855. Designed and engraved *Fleurs et plantes d'après nature, Paris* BMAD (Maciet coll.)
LIT *Bellier*; *Bénézit*; *Paris BMAD*; *Thieme*

SAUZÉ, Léopold ***b.1872***
Pupil of Castex-Dégrange, Lyon BA (CFD 1891)
LIT *Hardouin-Fugier Grafe*

SAVOYE, Jean-Joseph
Pupil of Reignier, Lyon BA (CFD 1883) Designed plates of *Flore appliquée à l'ornement gravé*
LIT *Hardouin-Fugier Grafe*

SAVOYE, Sophie
Designed a flower plate, 1839, published by Brunet
LIT Paris Bibl. Nat. Est. Jd 59

Claude Sauvageot

Engraving after a drawing, 12 × $10\frac{1}{4}$ in. (31 × 26 cm.), signed
Paris, BMAD (Maciet Collection)

SAVY, Marie
Pupil of Laÿs. Exhib. Lyon Salon 1867, 1868, 1870, 1881 e.g. *Vase de fleurs*, 1867, *Fleurs des champs*, 1881
LIT *Hardouin-Fugier Grafe*; *Lyon Salon* 1867, 1881

SCALBERT, Jules ***b.1851***
b. Douai (Nord). Pupil of Petit and Lehmann. Painted genre, still-lifes and, occasionally, flowers. Exhib. Paris Salon from 1876
LIT *Bellier*; *Bénézit*; *Schurr* V, 121; *Thieme*

SCHALL, Pierre ***b.1804***
Pupil of Berjon, Lyon BA (CFD 1823)
LIT *Hardouin-Fugier Grafe*

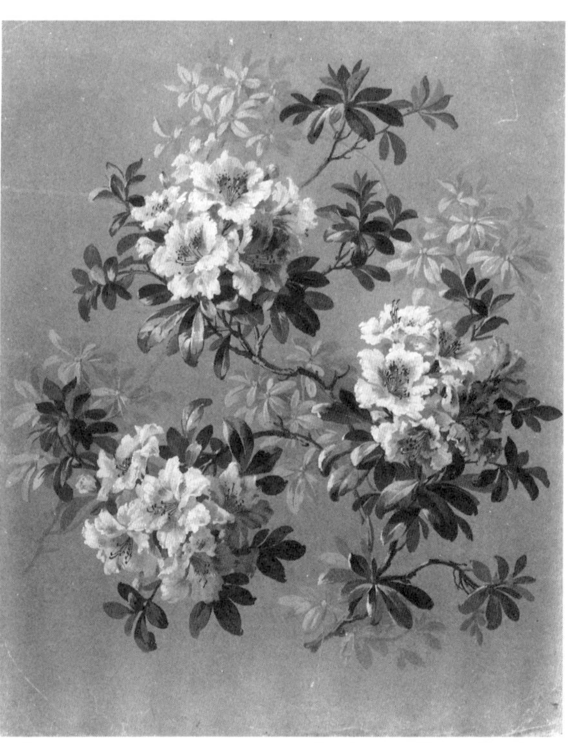

Jacques Schaub

Gouache on paper — cartoon for printed fabric, 30½ × 25½ in. (77.8 × 67.3 cm.),
Mulhouse, Musée de l'Impression sur Etoffes

SCHAUB, Fernand ***b.1860***
b. Mulhouse (Haut-Rhin). Textile designer Mulhouse and Paris, in partnership with J. Schaub, his father, and took over direction of the Atelier Schaub 1887–1910
LIT *Histoire Documentaire*; B. Jacqué, *Chefs d'œuvre du MISE*, Tokyo (Gakken) 1978. BJ

SCHAUB, Jacques ***1827–1889***
b. Ilzach (Haut-Rhin). Pupil of J. U. Tournier. Textile designer, Mulhouse where he directed an atelier of fabric designers 1873–1887. Produced designs and drawings for fabrics (Musée Mulhouse) e.g. *Rhododendrons*
LIT *Histoire Documentaire*; B. Jacqué, *Chefs d'œuvre du MISE*, Tokyo (Gakken) 1978. BJ

SCHEURER, Henriette
Exhib. *Fleurs*, Grenoble Salon 1899
LIT *Grenoble Salon* 1899. MW

SCHILT, François-Philippe-Abel ***1818–1855***
Son of porcelain painter Louis-Pierre Schilt. Pupil of Roqueplan. M: Sèvres arch. *Robinier faux acacia*, *Pois*, *Acacia rose*, *Baguenaudier moyen*, *Fève des marais*, ink and wc, 1829. Namesake op. Sèvres 1845–1880
LIT Sèvres Arch. B VIII 1829; *Thieme*

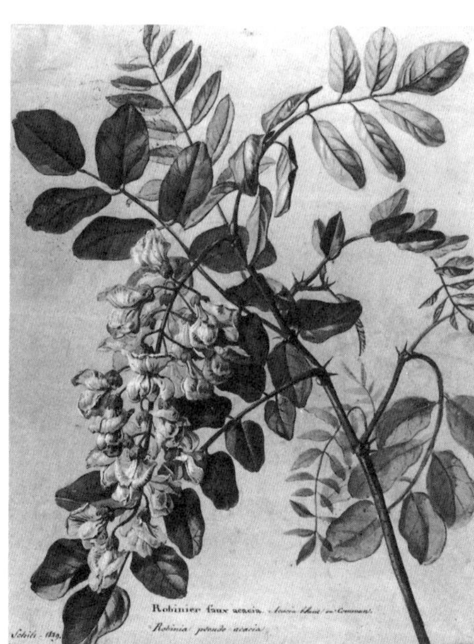

François-Philippe-Abel Schilt

Ink and watercolour design, signed and dated 1829,
Sèvres, Archives Manufacture Nationale de Sèvres

SCHILT, Louis-Pierre ***1790–1859***
b. Paris. Pupil of Constant then Lefebvre. Entered Sèvres porcelain factory 1822. op. Sèvres. Painted flowers and fruit on porcelain. Jacobber's only rival, lithographed sets of flower plates e.g. *Les mois fleurs et fruits*. Exhib. *Fleurs sur un rocher*, Paris Salon 1839. Cambridge, Fitzwilliam Museum (Broughton coll.), two water-colours, *Bouquet de fleurs*, both dated 1833
LIT *Bénézit*; Broughton 1976; *Brunet Préaud*; Conches de in *L'Artiste*, 1832, p. 787; *Paris Salon* 1839; *Thieme*

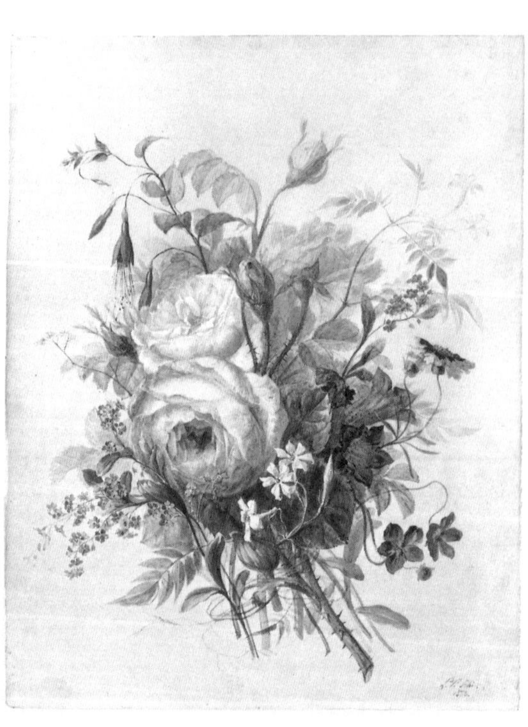

Louis-Pierre Schilt

Watercolour on paper, 15⅞ × 12½ in. (40.5 × 31.6 cm.), signed and dated 1833
Cambridge, Fitzwilliam Museum
(Broughton Collection)

SCHIRMANN, Mlle Auguste
Exhib. *Pervenches et giroflées*, wc, *Giroflées*, wc, *Dijon Salon* 1897
LIT *Dijon Salon* 1897. CL

SCHLESINGER, Jeanne
Exhib. Lyon Salon 1875
LIT *Hardouin-Fugier Grafe*; *Lyon Salon* 1875

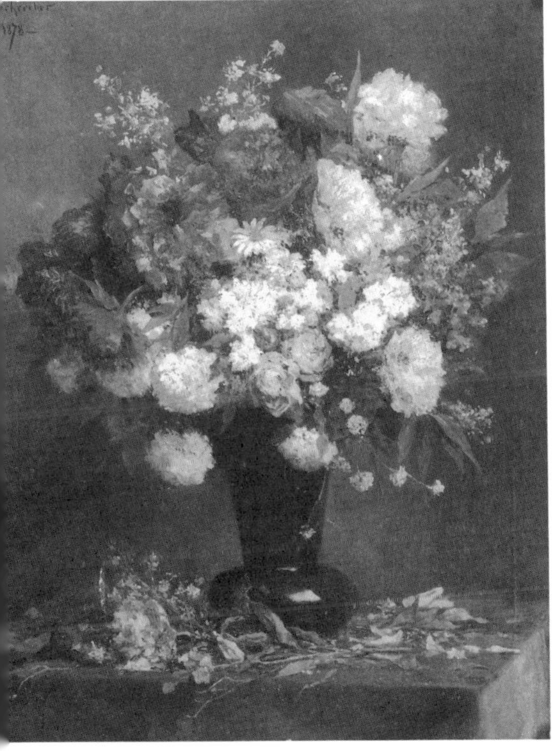

Charles-Baptiste Schreiber

Oil on canvas, 28 × 22¾ in. (71 × 58 cm.), signed and dated 1878
Courtesy Sotheby's, London

SCHLUMBERG, Cécile-Elisabeth, *née* Meyer
b. Mulhouse (Haut-Rhin). Pupil of Pallandre and Meyer. Exhib. Paris Salon from 1880 e.g. *Roses des haies*, *Iris blanc*, on faience, 1880
LIT *Bellier*; *Paris Salon* 1880

SCHLUMBERGER, Camille-Gabriel *b.1864*
b. Strasbourg (Bas-Rhin). Exhib. *Etude de fleurs*, Paris SNBA 1895
LIT *Bénézit*; *Paris SNBA* 1895

SCHLUMBERGER, Georges *1807–1862*
b. Mulhouse (Haut-Rhin) Painted flowers
LIT *Bénézit*; *Thieme*

SCHMIDT, Jeanne
b. Lille (Nord). Exhib. *Oeillets*, *Roses*, Lille Salon 1881
LIT *Lille Salon* 1881. G and LT

SCHMIDT, Mlle M
Exhib. *Oeillets*, *Violettes*, wc, Paris SNBA 1893
LIT *Paris SNBA* 1893

SCHMITT, Georgette
b. Paris. Pupil of Roux and Porée. Exhib. Paris Salon *Fleurs*, fan-leaf, 1880, *Marguerites*, on porcelain, 1882
LIT *Bellier*; *Bénézit*; *Paris Salon* 1880

SCHMUTZ, Gustave-Emmanuel *b.1823*
b. Colmar (Haut-Rhin). Pupil of Lyon BA and F. Grobon. Exhib. Lyon Salon 1845
LIT *Audin Vial*

SCHNEIDER, Félicie, *née* Fournier *1831–1888*
b. Saint-Cloud (Hauts-de-Seine). Pupil of N. Fournier, her father, and L. Cogniet. Exhib. Paris Salon from 1849. Painted and engraved genre, portraits, and, occasionally, flowers e.g. *Dernières fleurs d'automne*, 1852, *Fleurs*, wc, 1877. *Fleurs*, wc, Drouot sale, Paris, in aid of Bonvin, 1885
LIT *Bellier*; *Bénézit*; *Orsay*; *Thieme*

SCHOUTETTEN, Louis *1833–1907*
b. Lille (Nord). Painted landscapes and flowers. Exhib. Paris Salon from 1864. *Fleurs*, Dijon Salon 1885
LIT *Bénézit*; *Dijon Salon* 1885; *Thieme*. CL

SCHREIBER, Charles-Baptiste *d.1903*
b. Paris. Pupil of Bonnat and Brandon. Painted portraits and genre, occasionally flowers. Paris Salon debut 1868. Honourable mention 1901
LIT *Bénézit*. PM

SCHRYVER, Louis-Marie de ***1862–1942***
b. Paris. Pupil of G. Ferrier. Painted genre, still-lifes and flowers. Exhib. Paris Salon. *Roses*, Dijon Salon 1880; *Roses*, Saint-Etienne Salon, 1882; *Au marché de la Madeleine*, Paris Salon 1889; *Fleurs d'amour*, Dijon Salon 1890. *A flower seller, avenue de l'Opéra Paris*, 1891, Sotheby's London, 14 Nov. 1973; *The flower vendor*, Parke-Bernet, New York, 12 Jan. 1974; *The flower market*, Monaco Fine Arts, 1977; *A flower vendor, rue Royale*, Paris, 1898, Newman's, London, 1977; *Pansies and violets*, 1880, *Marigolds and chrysanthemums* 1881, Sotheby's, London, 1 Oct. 1980; *Roses in a Bowl*, 1881, Christie's, London, 26 June 1987, lot 82. M: Cambrai, Pontoise, Tourcoing
LIT *Bellier*; *Bénézit*; *Dijon Salon* 1880, 1890; *Orsay*; *Saint-Etienne Salon* 1882; *Thieme*; *Witt*

Louis-Marie de Schryver

Oil on canvas, 19¼ × 25½ in. (49 × 65 cm.), signed and dated 1881
Courtesy Christie's, London

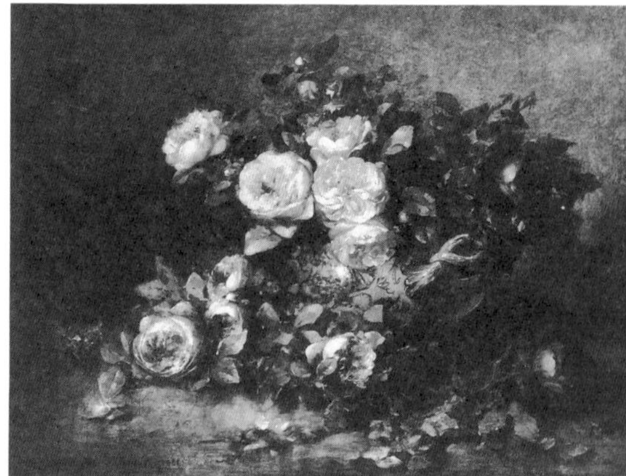

SCHUFFENECKER, Claude-Emile ***1851–1934***
b. Fresne-Saint-Mamès (Haute-Saône). Pupil of Grellet, Baudry and Carolus-Duran. Friendly with Pissarro, Seurat and Gauguin. Drawing master. Painted landscapes and, occasionally, flowers e.g. *Pivoines*, 1886, Paris Indép. 1926
LIT *Bénézit*; *Paris Indép*. 1926; *Schurr* I, 120; M. A. Stevens in *Post-Impressionism*, London RA, 1979–1980

SCHULLER, Joseph-Paul
b. Husseren (Haut-Rhin). Pupil of E. Benner and Damoye. Exhib. Paris Salon from 1880. *Bouquet*, wc, *Roses*, wc, 1880, *Fleurs d'automne*, wc, 1885; *Marguerites et glaïeuls*, *Premiers lilas*, Paris Noir et Blanc Salon 1886; *Pivoines, étude*, Paris SNBA 1892. M: Caen, *Chrysanthèmes* (acquired 1886; destroyed in World War II); Morlaix, *Soleils, fin d'été*
LIT *Bellier*; *Bénézit*; *Paris Noir et Blanc Salon* 1886; *Paris Salon* 1880, 1885; *Paris SNBA* 1892

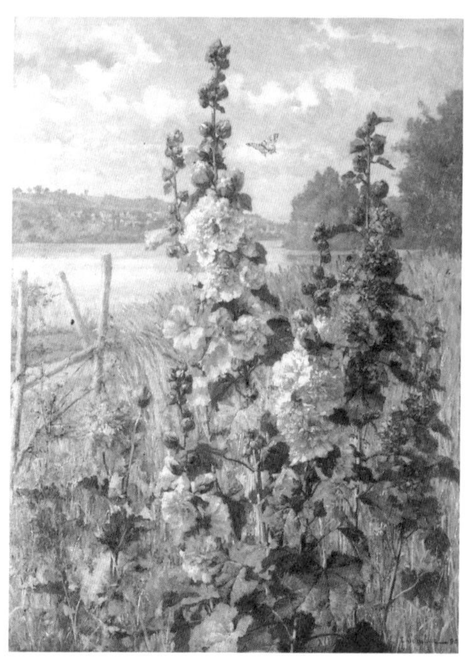

Joseph-Paul Schuller

Oil on canvas, 55 × 39 in. (140 × 101 cm.) signed and dated '90
Courtesy Sotheby's, London

SCHWARTZ, Berthe
b. Paris. Pupil of Bergeret and M. Lemaire. Exhib. *Bourriche de pensées*, wc, Paris Salon 1880
LIT *Paris Salon* 1880

SCHWOB, ME.
Exhib. Paris SNBA *Oeillets*, 1894, *Giroflées*, 1896
LIT *Paris SNBA* 1894, 1896

SCIOT, Lucie
Exhib. *Iris*, fan-leaf, gouache, Paris Noir et Blanc Salon 1888
LIT *Paris Noir et Blanc Salon* 1888

SCOHY, Jean ***1824–1896***
b. Lyon. Pupil of Thierriat, Lyon BA (CFD 1842). Entered 1842 FDC. Painted figures, portraits and, occasionally, flowers
LIT *Bellier*; *Bénézit*; V. Féroldi in *Les Peintres de l'Ame* (*Hardouin-Fugier Grafe* 1981); *Hardouin-Fugier Grafe*; *Thieme*

SEE, Mathilde ***d.1935***
b. Paris. Pupil of Gérald-Laffitte, T. Robert-Fleury and L. Breslau. Painted flowers. Exhib. *Roses*, Paris Noir et Blanc Salon 1886; *Pivoines*, wc, Paris Salon 1890; Paris SNBA *Lilas*, wc, *Hortensias bleus*, fan-leaf, 1892, *Pavots*, fan-leaf, *Cinéraires*, wc, 1894. Works in the former Musée du Luxembourg (Paris)
LIT *L'Art et les Artistes*, April 1913; *Bénézit*; *Orsay*; *Paris Noir et Blanc* 1886; *Paris Salon* 1890; *Paris SNBA* 1892, 1894; *Thieme*

SEGUIN, Edouard
b. Paris. Pupil of L. Mouchet. Painted flowers and fruit. Exhib. Paris Salon from 1877 e.g. *Fleurs*, 1879
LIT *Bellier*; *Bénézit*

SEGUIN, Gérard, *alias* Gérard-Seguin ***1805–1875***
b. Paris. Pupil of Langlois. Painted religious subjects. Illustrated A. Karr, *Le Royaume des roses*
LIT *Bénézit*; *Thieme*

SEGUIN-BERTAULT, Paul ***1869–1964***
Pupil of G. Moreau and Cabanel. Designed tapestry cartoons (Gobelins) and plates for *Album Vilmorin*. Painted landscapes, figures and, occasionally, flowers e.g. *Bouquet de fleurs, gaillardes et pieds d'alouette* (atelier sale 1980)
LIT Album Vilmorin; *Bénézit*; *Orsay*; *Seguin-Bertault sale, Drouot, Paris, 1980*; *Schurr* III 145; *Thieme*, *Witt*

SEGUY, Claude-François-Edouard ***b.1809***
b. Lyon. Pupil of Thierriat, Lyon BA (CFD 1825). Exhib. *Groupe de fleurs*, gouache, Lyon Salon 1841
LIT *Hardouin-Fugier Grafe*; *Lyon Salon* 1841

SEIGNEMARTIN, Jean ***1848–1875***
b. Lyon. Pupil of Guichard (Lyon BA). Worked with F. Vernay. Exhib. Lyon Salon 1864–1875. M: Lyon *Camélias*, *Lilas et gant*, *Fleurs*; Paris (Louvre), *Fleurs*
LIT *Bénézit*; *Hardouin-Fugier Grafe* (ill.); *Hardouin-Fugier Grafe* 1979 (ill.) *Hardouin-Fugier Grafe* 1982 (ill.); *Thieme*; *Witt*

SEIGNOL, Claudius ***1858–1926***
Painted landscapes and, occasionally, flowers. Exhib. Lyon Salon from *c.*1890
LIT *Hardouin-Fugier Grafe*

SEITTE, Charles ***b.1872***
b. Montluçon (Loire). Painted flowers in wc. Exhib. Lyon Salon from *c.*1900
LIT *Hardouin-Fugier Grafe*

SELMERSHEIM-DESGRANGE, Jeanne ***1879–1958***
Painted flowers, often in pointillist style. M. St Tropez
LIT: *Saint Tropez, Musée de l'Annonciade*, 1982

SEMBAT, *see* AGUTTE

SÉNARD, Charles ***1878–1934***
Pupil of Castex-Dégrange, Lyon BA (CFD 1896). Painted figures, still-lifes and flowers. Exhib. Lyon from *c.*1900
LIT *Hardouin-Fugier Grafe*

SENGEL, Andrée
b. Paris. Pupil of Bouguereau and Ferrier. Exhib. *Pivoines*, wc, Paris Salon 1895
LIT *Paris Salon* 1895

SÉON, Alexandre ***1855–1917***
b. Chazelles-sur-Lyon (Loire). Pupil of Lyon BA, Lehmann and Puvis de Chavannes: Exhib. Paris Salon from 1872. This symbolist artist occasionally painted flowers e.g. *Genêts fleuris*, Saint-Etienne Salon 1882; *Les Fleurs*, Paris SNBA 1890; *Fleurs*, Saint-Etienne Salon 1891
LIT *Bénézit*; *Orsay*; *Paris SNBA* 1890; *Saint-Etienne Salon* 1882, 1891; *Thieme*; *Witt*

SÉRAPHINE LOUIS, *alias* Séraphine de Senlis ***1864–1942***
b. Assy (Oise). Though most flower paintings by this naïve artist belong to our century, she may have produced some earlier ones
LIT *Bénézit*; J. P. Foucher *Séraphine de Senlis*, Paris (Le Temps) 1968; *Witt*

SERENDAT de Belzim, Louis ***1854–1933***
b. Port-Louis (Martinique). Pupil of Cabanel and Carolus-Duran. Exhib. *Roses*, Paris Indép. 1896
LIT *Paris Indép.* 1896; *Thieme*

SERINGE, Nicolas-Charles ***1776–1858***
Director of the Lyon botanical gardens (1830). Botanical draughtsman
LIT *Hardouin-Fugier Grafe*

SERPOLLET, Joseph ***b.1871***
b. Lyon. Pupil of Castex-Dégrange, Lyon BA (CFD 1891)
LIT *Hardouin-Fugier Grafe*

SERRES, Henri-Charles de ***1823–1883***
b. Paris. Pupil of Rudder. Painted portraits, landscapes and flowers. Exhib. Paris Salon from 1846, flowers from 1865 e.g. *Corbeille de fleurs d'automne*, *Vase de dahlias*, 1872, *Fleurs de printemps*, *Fleurs d'automne*, 1873, *Reines-marguerites*, 1875, *Fleurs d'hiver*, 1880. M: Bagnols-sur-Cèze, *Fleurs et fruits*, 1874, Coutance, *Corbeille de fleurs*, 1872, Rennes, *Bourriche de pensées*, 1875
LIT *Bellier*; *Bénézit*; *Michelez*, cl. 80, II, 22; *Orsay*; Paris Arch. Nat. F21: 253, 456, 461, 4500; *Thieme*

SERRIERE, Joseph
Pupil of Berjon, Lyon BA (CFD 1820)
LIT *Hardouin-Fugier Grafe*

SÉRUSIER, Louis-Paul-Henri ***1863–1927***
b. Paris. Pupil of Académie Julian. Mostly a landscape, figure and portrait painter. His few flower paintings are often later works except *Nature-morte, pommes et violettes*, 1891 (Paris 1955, 147; Guicheteau, 44), *Fleurs*, 1891 (Guicheteau, 43), *Nature-morte au livre*, 1893 (Guicheteau, 83), and *Femme au bouquet*, 1893, Paris, Petit Palais (Guicheteau, 79). M: Paris, Petit Palais
LIT Paris, *Bonnard, Vuillard et les Nabis*, Musée National d'Art Moderne, 1955; M. Guicheteau, *Paul Sérusier*, Paris, 1976; *Witt*. AC, JLC

SERVAIS, Joseph
Exhib. Paris Salon *Bouquet de fleurs sur bois verni*, gouache, 1831, *Bouquet de fleurs*, gouache, 1833, *Fleurs*, on alabaster, 1839
LIT *Bellier*; *Bénézit*; *Paris Salon* 1831, 1833, 1839

SERVAN, Florentin ***1811–1879***
b. Lyon. Pupil of Thierriat, Lyon BA (CFD 1831). Painted landscapes
LIT *Hardouin-Fugier Grafe* 1981, pp. 131–132

SERVANT, Guillaume ***b.1802***
Pupil of Berjon, Lyon BA (CFD 1822)
LIT *Hardouin-Fugier Grafe*

SETTE, Jules
Painted portraits, still-lifes, fruit and, occasionally, flowers. Exhib. Paris Salon 1836–1846. Lithographed a flower plate after Vitasse (Paris Bibl. Nat. Est.)
LIT *Bellier*; *Bénézit*; *Faré* 1962, p. 247; Paris Bibl. Nat. Est. Jd 67; *Thieme*

Paul Seguin-Bertault

Oil on canvas, $28\frac{3}{4} \times 23\frac{3}{4}$ in. (73 × 60 cm.), signed
Private collection

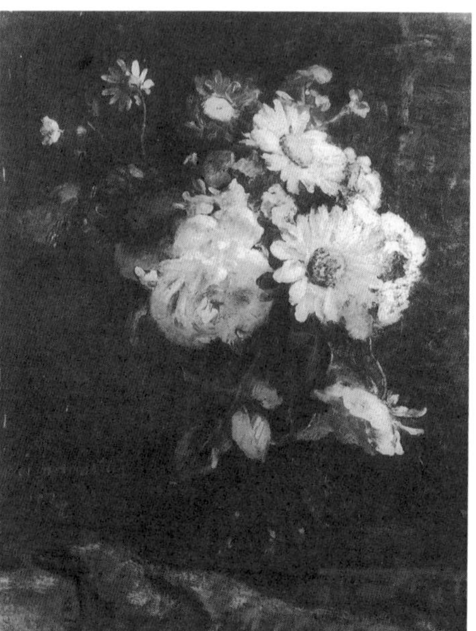

SEURAT, Georges-Pierre ***1859–1891***
b. Paris. Pupil of Henri Lehmann at Paris Beaux-Arts. Founder member of Paris Indépendants. Painted figures, landscapes and portraits. *Fleurs dans un vase*, c.1880 (Cambridge); *L'arrosoir, jardin au Raincy*, c.1883. M: Cambridge, Mass, Fogg Art Museum
LIT *Bénézit*; J. O'Brian, *Degas to Matisse, Maurice Wertheim Collection*, New York, 1988; H. Dorra, J. Rewald, *Seurat*, Paris, (Éditions d'études et documents) 1959; F. Minervino, *Tout l'œuvre peint de Seurat*, Paris (Flammarion) 1973. *Witt*; AC

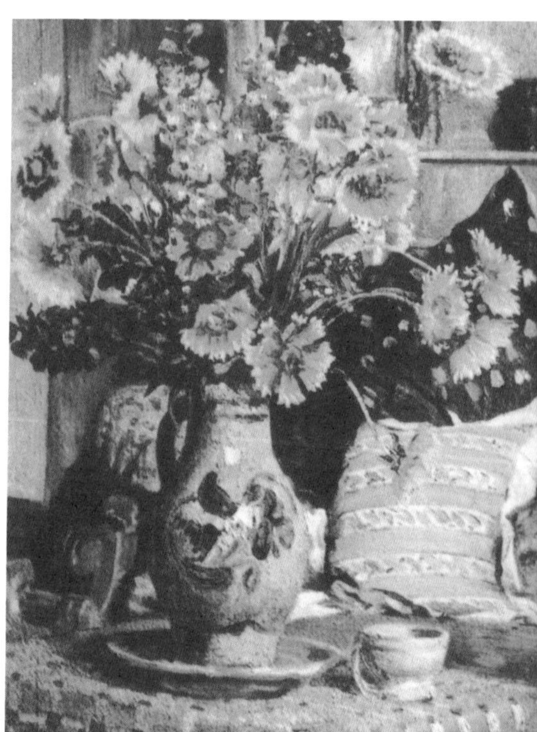

Jean Seignemartin

Oil on canvas, 18 × 15 in. (46 × 38 in.), signed and dated 1874
Paris, Musée du Louvre

SEVERAC, Gilbert-Alexandre de 1834–1897
b. Saint-Sulpice-sur-Leyre (Haute-Garonne). Pupil of L. Cogniet. Portrait and history painter. Exhib. Paris Salon from 1859. Musée de Béziers, *Roses dans un vase*, and *Bouquet de fleurs*, 1886 (gift from the artist to the museum in that year)
LIT *Bellier*; *Bénézit*; *Schurr* I, 71, V, 21; *Witt*

SEYS, Camille
Exhib. *Etude de fleurs*, Lyon Salon 1868.
LIT *Lyon Salon* 1868

SEYSSAUD, René *1867–1952*
b. Marseille. Pupil of Marseille BA and Grivolas (Avignon). Painted landscapes, figures, still-lifes and flowers. Other than *Tournesois sur la mer*, 1898 (private coll.) these are mostly 20th-century works.
LIT Albi, *Seyssaud*, 1959; Aix-en-Provence, *Rétrospective Seyssaud*, Hôtel des Ventes, 1957; *Bénézit*; *Orsay*; Oxford, *Seyssaud*, cat. by Roger-Marx, *c.*1957; Paris, *Seyssaud*, Galerie Bernheim-Jeune, 1911; Saint-Tropez, *Fleurs de Fantin-Latour à Marquet*. Musée de l'Annonciade, 1982 (ill.); Y. Silvestre, *Seyssaud*, Saint-Chamas, 1959; *Thieme*; *Witt*

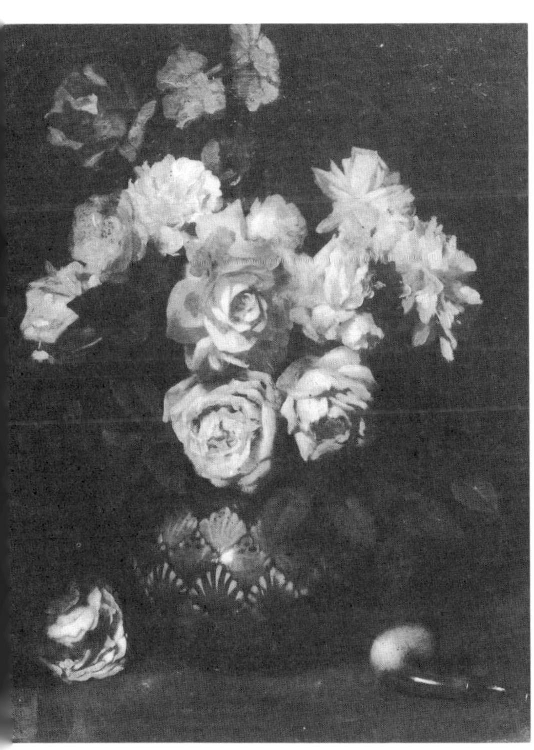

Gilbert-Alexandre de Séverac

Oil on canvas, 181 × 153½ in. (461 × 381 cm.), signed and dated 1886
Béziers, Musée des Beaux-Arts

René Seyssaud

Oil on canvas, 36¼ × 28¾ in. (92 × 73 cm.), signed and dated 1878
Private collection (courtesy Musée de L'Annonciade, Saint-Tropez)

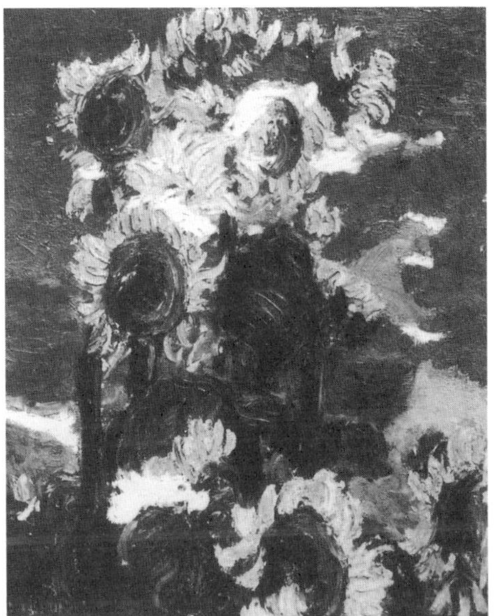

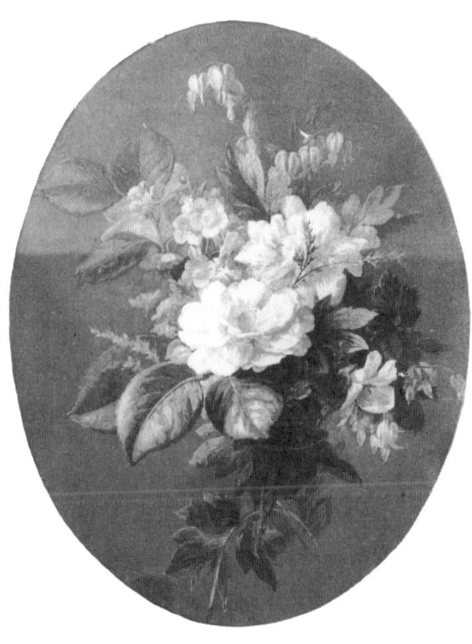

Claude-Louis Sibuet

Gouache, oval, 18½ × 14½ in. (47 × 37 cm.), signed
Private collection

SIBUET, Claude-Louis *1831–1879*
b. Lyon. Pupil of Lyon BA and Reignier. Exhib. Lyon Salon 1854–1879
LIT *Bénézit*; *Hardouin-Fugier Grafe* (ill.); *Thieme*

SICARD, Louis-Apollinaire *1807–1881*
b. Lyon. Pupil of Thierriat, Lyon BA (CFD 1824) and, possibly, Berjon. Exhib. Lyon Salon from 1837, Paris Salon from 1857. M: Dijon, *Fleurs* (private legacy
LIT *Bénézit*; *Hardouin-Fugier Grafe* (ill.); *Hardouin-Fugier Grafe* 1982 (ill.); *Thieme*

SICART, Eugène *b.1860*
Pupil of Castex-Dégrange, Lyon BA (CFD 1887)
LIT *Hardouin-Fugier Grafe*

SIEFFERT, Clémentine, after 1870 Bost-Sieffert
Exhib. *Primevères*, fan-leaf, wc, Lyon Salon 1870
LIT *Lyon Salon* 1870

SIGNAC, Paul *1863–1935*
b. Paris. Pupil of Seurat. Founder-member of Paris Indépendants, where he exhibited. Mostly a landscape painter. Among his early flowers are *Nature-morte, livre et violettes*, *c.*1883 (Louvre, 1963) and *Les coquelicots*, *c.*1894
LIT F. Cachin, *Signac*, Paris (Bibliothèque des Arts) 1971; Paris, *Signac*, Musée du Louvre, Réunion des Musées Nationaux, 1963–1964. *Witt*. AC

SIGNARD, Claude
b. Gray (Haute-Saône). Exhib. *Bouquet de roses*, *Fleurs*, Paris Indép. 1892. Musée Baron Martin, Gray, *Chrysanthèmes*
LIT *Paris Indép.* 1892

SILVENT, Antoine-Alexandre *b.1810*
b. Lyon. Pupil of Thierriat Lyon BA (CFD 1828) and F. Lepage. Painted landscapes and flowers
LIT *Hardouin-Fugier Grafe*

SILVENT, Mme Marie-Louise
Pupil of Reignier. Exhib. *Roses thé*, *Chrysanthèmes*, Lyon Salon 1885; *Roses thé*, Dijon Salon 1885
LIT *Dijon Salon* 1885; *Lyon Salon* 1885. CL

SILVENT, Victor-Albin *b.1837*
Pupil of Reignier, Lyon BA (CFD 1854)
LIT *Hardouin-Fugier Grafe*

SILVESTRE, Pierre
Exhib. *Fleurs*, Dijon Salon 1881. This may be Edmond-Pierre-Henri-Adolphe Silvestre du Perron 1823–1889
LIT *Brune*; *Dijon Salon* 1881; *Thieme*

SIMEON or SIMON, Claudette
Pupil of Bonirote. fl. Lyon *c.*1850–1875. Painted genre and flowers e.g. *Fleurs*, Lyon Salon 1854
LIT *Hardouin-Fugier Grafe*; *Hardouin-Fugier Grafe* 1981 (ill.); *Lyon Salon* 1854

SIMON, Adèle
b. Paris. Pupil of Colin-Libour. Exhib. *Azalées*, *Livre et oeillets*, wc, Paris Salon 1885; Paris Noir et Blanc Salon *Pivoines* 1886, *Pensées*, 1888
LIT *Paris Noir et Blanc Salon* 1886, 1888; *Paris Salon* 1885

SIMON, Ernest-Constant *d.1895*
b. Paris. Painted landscapes, Orientalist, died Cairo. Paris Salon debut 1880
LIT *Bénézit*. PM

SIMONET, Paul-Léon
b. Versailles (Yvelines). Pupil of Bin and Lavastre. Painted still-lifes and flowers. Exhib. Paris Salon from 1876 e.g. *Eventails et Camélias*, 1878
LIT *Bellier*; *Bénézit*

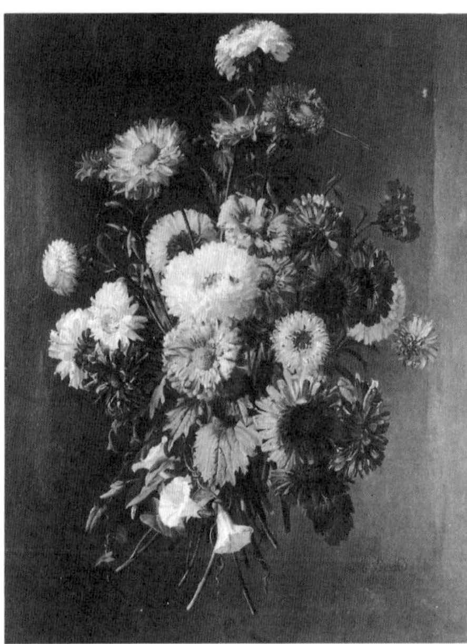

Louis-Apollinaire Sicard

Oil on canvas, 32¾ × 21¾ in. (83 × 55 cm.), signed
Dijon, Musée des Beaux-Arts

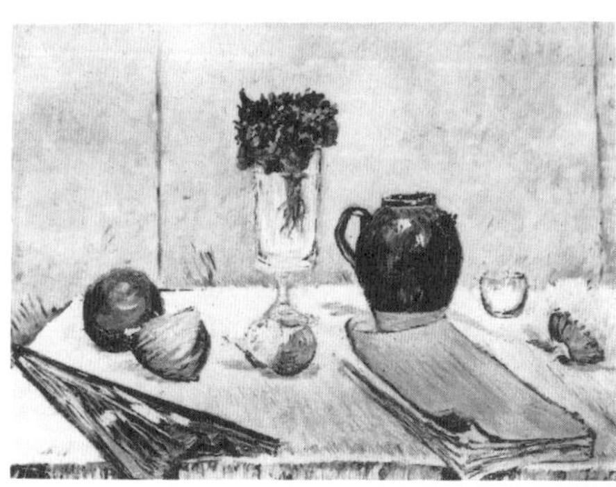

Paul Signac

Oil on canvas, 21¼ × 28¾ in. (54 × 73 cm.), signed and dated 1883
Private collection

SIMONIN, Henri-Alexis
b. Paris. Pupil of L. Cogniet. Painted genre, portraits and flowers. Exhib. Paris Salon from 1877 e.g. *Violon, fleurs et statuette*, 1880
LIT *Bellier*; *Bénézit*, *Paris Salon* 1880; *Witt*

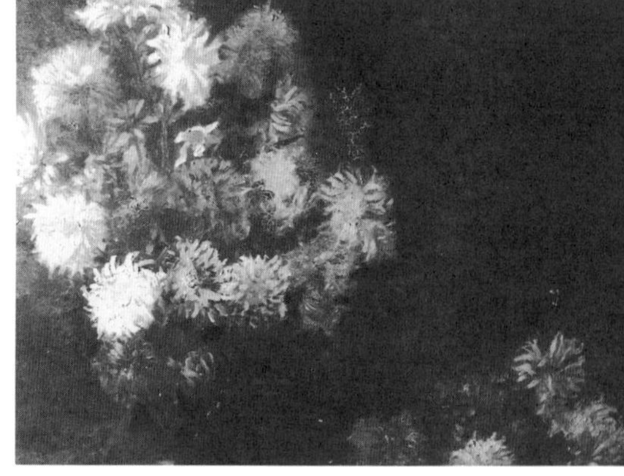

Claude Signard

Oil on canvas, 35½ × 46 in. (90 × 117 cm.)
Gray, Musée Baron Martin

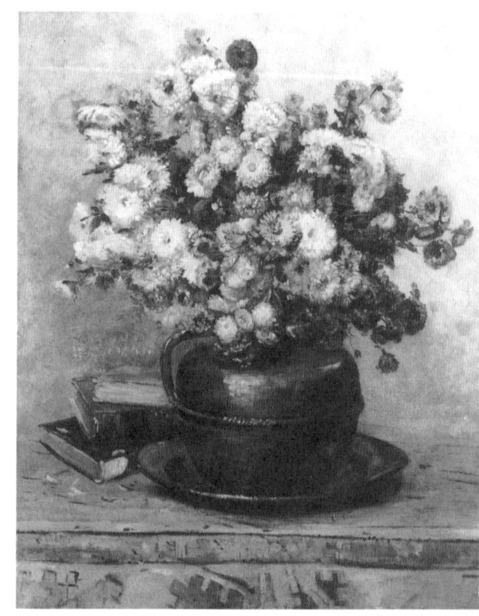

Ernest-Constant Simon

Oil on canvas, 29 × 23¾ in. (73.5 × 60.5 cm.), signed and dated 1886
Courtesy Sotheby's, London

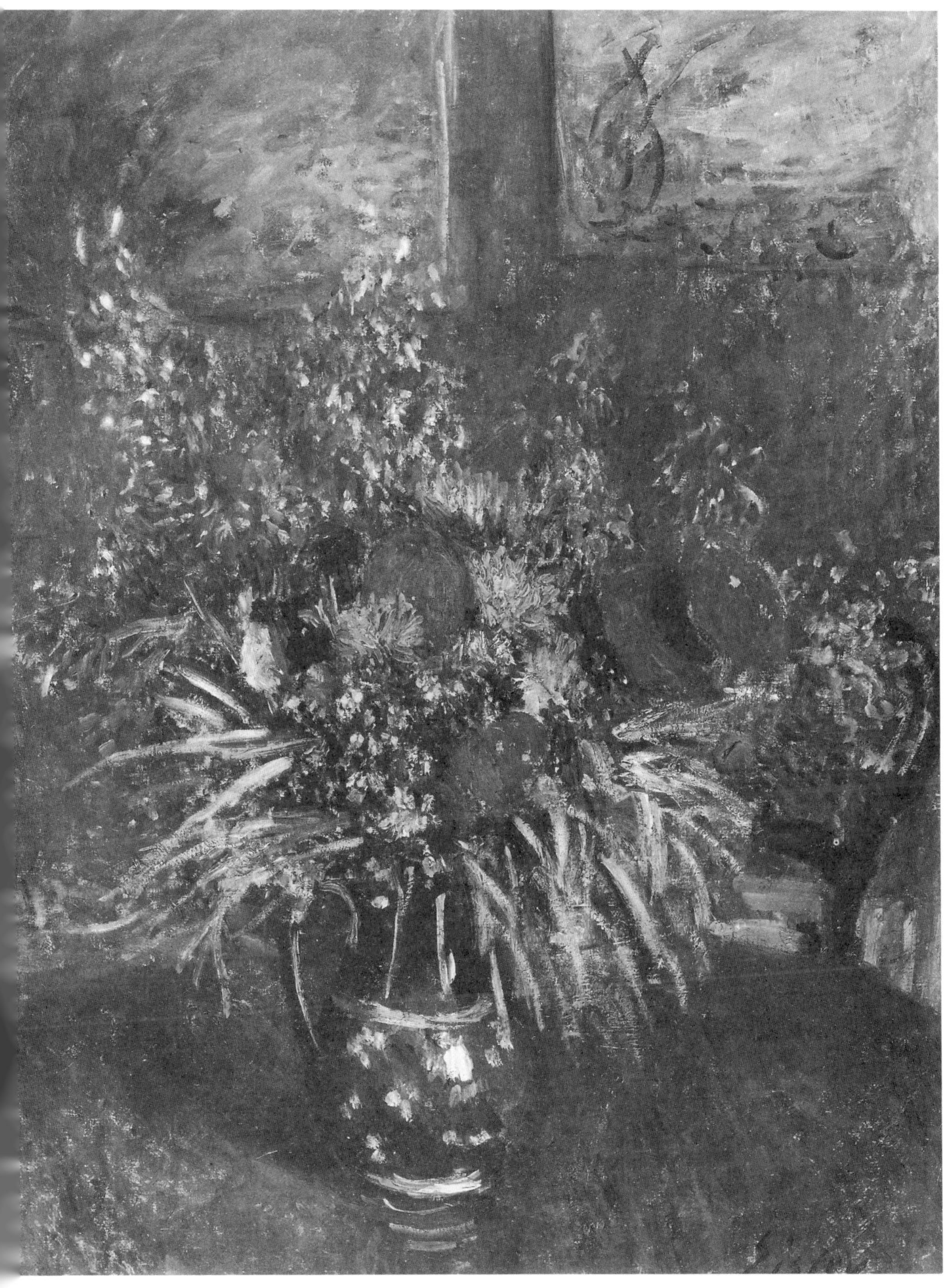

Alfred Sisley

Oil on canvas, $25\frac{3}{4} \times 19\frac{7}{8}$ in. (65.5 × 50.5 cm.), signed
Private collection, Courtesy Christie's, London

SINSSON, Louis ***b.1815***
At Sèvres 1830–1847. Exhib. *Fleurs*, after Van Spaendonck, on porcelain, Paris Salon 1836
LIT *Paris Salon* 1836; *Brunet Préaud*

SINSSON or SISSON, Pierre
op. Sèvres 1818–1848
LIT *Brunet Préaud*

SIRAND, Marie
Pupil of Médard. Exhib. *Couronne de fleurs*, Lyon Salon 1885
LIT *Lyon Salon* 1885

SISLEY, Alfred ***1839–1899***
b. Paris. Pupil of Gleyre in whose studio he befriended Renoir, Monet and Bazille, all of them early Impressionists. Mostly a landscape painter. *Bouquet de fleurs*, 1875, is a rare flower painting. Exhibited: Basle, Kunsthalle, *Impressionisten*, 1949, No. 92 (ill.); Wildenstein, New York, *Magic of Flowers*, 1954, no. 74; Philadelphia, Museum of Art, *World of Flowers*, 1963; Washington, National Gallery of Art, *French Paintings from the Collections of Mr and Mrs Paul Mellon*, 1966, no. 74 (ill.); sale Christie's, London, 27 Nov. 1964, Lot 41 (ill.), Christie's, New York, 15 Nov. 1983, Lot 13 (ill.)
LIT *Bénézit*; R. Cogniat, *Sisley*, Paris (Flammarion) 1978; F. Daulte, *Les Impressionnistes, Sisley*, Wildenstein (Delta) 1974; F. Daulte, "Découverte de Sisley" in *Connaissance des Arts*, no. 60, Feb. 1957; *Thieme*; *Witt*

SIVEL, Emilie
One signed gouache is known in a private collection, dated 1872. The artist has proudly inscribed above her signature 'Médaille d'or 1870', but where she achieved this award remains to be discovered. PM

SOLEIL, Alexandre-François
Exhib. Paris Salon from 1877 e.g. *Giroflées*, gouache, *Premières fleurs*, gouache, 1878, *Pivoines*, gouache, 1879
LIT *Bellier*; *Bénézit*

SON, Joannès *1859–1942*
b. Lyon. Pupil of E. Yon. Painted landscapes and flowers. Exhib. Paris Indép. *Fleurs au soleil dans mon jardin*, 1891, *Fleurs*, 1892, 1893, *Roses*, 1894; *Fleurs*, Dijon Salon 1894
LIT *Bénézit*; *Dijon Salon* 1894; *Paris Indép.* 1891–1894; *Thieme*

SONNERAT, Pierre *1748–1814*
b. Lyon. Botanical designer
LIT *Bénézit*; *Laissus*; *Thieme*

SONNIER, Léon-Julien-Ernest
b. Paris. Pupil of J. P. Laurens and Montenard. Painted landscapes and, occasionally, flowers. Exhib. *Reines des prés*, pastel, Paris SNBA 1893. M: Louviers, Musée Municipal, *Femme du 1er Empire à sa toilette*, pastel
LIT *Bénézit*; *Paris SNBA* 1893

SOTTAS, Marguerite
Pupil of Dagnaux, Chaumet, Tournay and Keller. Exhib. *Roses*, wc, Paris UFPS 1898
LIT *Paris UFPS* 1898

SOULANGE-TEISSIER, Mme
Painted flowers in wc. Exhib. Paris Salon *Vase de fleurs*, 1843, *Camélias*, 1848
LIT *Bellier*; *Bénézit*; *Paris Salon* 1843

SOULARY, Claude *1792–1870*
b. Lyon (Rhône) Pupil of Berjon, Lyon BA (CFD 1812) and Révoil. Painted genre, portraits and, occasionally, flowers
LIT *Audin Vial*; *Bénézit*; *Hardouin-Fugier Bringuier*; *Hardouin-Fugier Grafe*; *Thieme*

SOUPLET, *see* HACHET

SPACH, Mme Edouard
Designed plates e.g. for E. Spach *Histoire Naturelle des végétaux.*. Paris, 1834–1848; E. Spach, H. F.Jaubert, *Choix de plantes...de l'Asie occidentale* Paris (Roret) 1842–1857
LIT*Nissen* I, 985, 1878, 2116, 2118; *Sitwell*

SPAENDONCK, Corneille (Cornelius) van *1756–1840*
b. Tilburg, Netherlands. Younger brother, pupil and collaborator of Gérard; followed him to Paris in 1773, aged 17, after an apprenticeship with Herryns at Antwerp. 1789: member of the Académie. 1785–1800: director at Sèvres and continued as a designer there until 1808. Little is known of his life. Unlike Gérard, Corneille continued to exhibit, and most of his output was in oils and gouache rather than watercolour. The brothers were personally close and continued to collaborate, but, from his Salon debut in 1789, the stature and individuality of Corneille is evident, with a softer touch and more romantic or fanciful composition. 1840: (February) studio sale following his death. Exhib. Paris Salon 1789: *Une corbeille renversée et remplie de differentes fleurs* (*morceau de reception de l'auteur*), *Un vase rempli de differentes fleurs*, *Autres petits tableaux de fleurs, sous le même numero*; 1791: *Un tableau de fleurs*, *Un tableau de fleurs*, *Tableau de fleurs*; 1793: *Des roses dans un gobelet*, *Un vase d'albâtre rempli de differentes fleurs posé sur un socle où se trouvent quelques fruits dans un plat de cristal et en bas un autre vase rempli de differentes fleurs*, *Quelques pêches et une grappe de raisin de Maroc*,

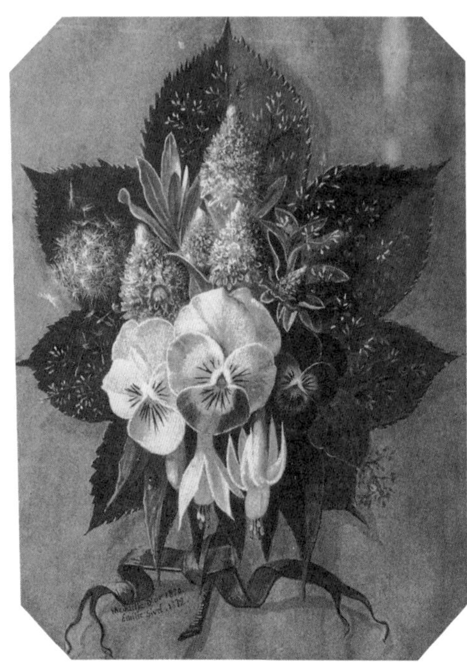

Emilie Sivel

Gouache on vellum, $7\frac{1}{2} \times 5\frac{1}{2}$ in. (19 × 14 cm.), signed and dated 1872 and inscribed 'Medaille d'or 1870'
Private collection

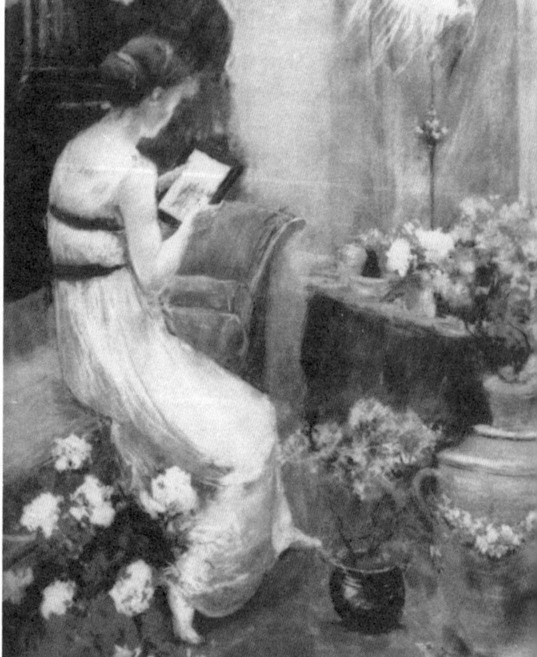

Léon-Julien-Ernest Sonnier

Pastel, signed
Louviers, Musée Municipal

peint sur marbre blanc; 1795: *Un vase d'albâtre rempli de differentes fleurs posé sur une table de marbre où sont quelques fruits et une branche de lilas*, *Differents fruits jetés sur une table de marbre sur laquelle on voit un vase d'albâtre rempli de differents pavots*, *Petit tableau peint sur marbre blanc representant quelques pêches et une grappe de raisin*; 1796: *Des fleurs dans un vase d'albâtre et accessoires*, *des roses dans un vase de cristal*, *Un oiseau, un nid, corbeille de fleurs et de fruits sur une table de marbre*; 1798: *Des pêches jetées sur une table de marbre avec un ananas et une grappe de raisin de Maroc*, *Roses dans un gobelet*, *Differentes fleurs dans un vase d'albâtre*; 1800: *Un tableau representant un panier de fleurs sur une table de marbre, sur laquelle on voit differentes espèces de raisins, ananas, pêches, etc.*, *Tableau representant des lilas et des roses jetés sur une table de marbre où l'on voit un vase de la lave du Vesuve*; 1801: *Des fleurs sur une table de marbre prêtes à être mises dans un vase d'albâtre oriental qu'on voit dans le fond*, *Plusieurs gouaches et différentes espèces de raisins, posées sur une table d'albâtre*; 1802: *Des fleurs dans un vase de cristal posé sur une table d'albâtre sur laquelle on voit des grenades et une grappe de raisin*, *Des raisins sur une table de granit*, *Deux tableaux pendants representant des fleurs dans une corbeille*; 1804; *Corbeille de differentes fleurs, ananas et raisins, blé de Turquie et pêches*; 1806; *Un tableau de fleurs*, *Un vase de marbre rempli de différentes espèces de roses et posé sur une table de marbre*, *Tableau de fruits, des pêches, du raisin et du blé de Turquie sur une table de marbre*; 1808: *Un vase d'albâtre rempli de fleurs*, *Des grenades et des raisins jetés sur une table d'albâtre. Des fleurs dans un vase de cristal avec un nid d'oiseaux*, *Des fleurs dans une corbeille*; 1810: *Des fleurs sur une table où l'on voit un nid d'oiseaux*, *Des fleurs dans une corbeille placée sur une table de granit*, *Lilas et roses sur une table*, *Pêches, ananas et raisins peints sur un marbre*; 1812: *Un vase d'albâtre rempli de différentes fleurs, posé sur un stylobate où se trouvent des pêches et raisins, un bouvreuil et son nid*, *Un panier rempli de différentes fleurs posé sur une table de marbre*, *Des pêches et raisins sur une table d'albâtre*; 1814: *Corbeille de fleurs posée sur un chapiteau corinthien*, *Panier de fleurs posé sur une table de marbre*, *Branches de lilas et de roses sur une table d'albâtre*; 1817: *Vase d'albâtre oriental rempli de differentes fleurs, posé sur un banc de marbre où l'on voit une branche de lilas*, *Un bouquet de roses, de seringat et de lilas sur une table de marbre*, *Rose althea et pieds d'alouette dans une corbeille*, *Une grappe de raisin attaché à son cep*; 1819: *Fleurs et fruits*, *Fleurs avec un nid, raisins et bouvreuil*, *Deux petits tableaux de fleurs faisant pendants*, *Fleurs faisant pendants*; 1822: *Une corbeille de differentes fleurs*, *Une corbeille de fleurs*, *Roses à cent feuilles, fruits, grenades et raisins*; 1824: *Tableau de fleurs*, *Fleurs et fruits*, *Tableau de fleurs*, *Deux petits tableaux de fleurs*; 1827: *Fleurs jetées sur une table de marbre sur laquelle est posé un vase d'albâtre contenant des fleurs*, *Tableaux de fleurs, même numero*; 1833: *Fleurs, roses, hyacinthes, oreilles d'ours, etc., jetées sur une table d'albâtre*, *Raisins, pêches*, etc., *posées sur une table de marbre*, *Fleurs dans une corbeille posée sur une table de marbre.* M: Antwerp (Smidt van Gelder Museum), Cambridge (Fitzwilliam), Carcassonne, Hague (Dienst Verspreide Rijkscollecties), Luxembourg (J. P. Pescatore Museum), Lyon, Paris (Louvre), Rijssel, Sèvres

LIT *Bellier*; Faré 1976; M: van Boven, S. Segal, *Gerard & Cornelis van Spaendonck* (Twee Brabantse bloemenschilders in Parijs) 1980. PM

SPAENDONCK, Gérard van ***1746–1822***
b. Tilburg, Netherlands. The key figure in flower and fruit painting in France in the period of transition from the late 18th to the 19th centuries. The status of his extraordinarily versatile work, in all mediums and in every format from miniatures on ivory to large-scale oils on canvas, is equalled by his stature as a teacher. Pupil of Herryns at Antwerp from 1764 until 1769, when he left for Paris, there to spend the remainder of his career. 1774: appointed miniaturist to the King. 1777: Salon debut. 1780: succeeded Madeleine Basseporte as "Professeur de peinture de fleurs" at the Jardin des Plantes. 1781: member of l'Académie. 1781–1785: contributed over fifty vellums to the Vélins du Roi, and in the course of doing so changed from the traditional gouache to pure watercolour; the task and the medium were assumed by his pupil Redouté. Also, at this period, continually active in designing for Sèvres, a role to be taken up by his brother and pupil, Corneille. 1783: sent five paintings and two vélins (part of the contribution to the Vélins du Roi) to the Salon to particular critical acclaim. 1785: Comte d'Angivillier commissioned, "pour le service du Roy", the painting now at Fontainebleau. 1788: appointed *conseiller* to l'Académie. 1789: despite political upheavals his work, together with that of other academicians, remained on display at the Louvre. 1791: Salon exhibits included a painting on marble—a support also employed by Corneille and Van Dael. 1793: in the reorganization of the Muséum d'Histoire Naturelle the post of "Professeur d'Iconographie naturelle" was created for him. 1795: one of the founders of the Institut. 1799–1801: publication of his *Fleurs dessinées d'après Nature*, twenty-four plates considered by Blunt to be "probably the finest engravings of flowers ever made". 1804: Legion of Honour. 1805: Napoleon honoured him with the title of "Count". 1822: Baron Cuvier gave his funeral oration. 1826: engravings after his work published under the title *Souvenirs de van Spaendonck* by his pupils as a posthumous tribute. 1830: Antoine

Chazal painted his *Hommage à Spaendonck* (Musée de Tourcoing). The rarity of Gérard van Spaendonck's work, which today is mostly in established collections, and the universal celebrity of his pupil, Redouté, have in the past hindered a proper appreciation of this great and extremely influential master. However, the exhibition of 1980 (see Boven and Segal) and the recent sales at auction of two major paintings (1987, 1988) have helped to redress the balance. Exhib. Paris Salon 1777: *Fleurs dans un vase d'agathe*, *Étude de raisins d'Alexandrie et de muscats*, *Un bouquet de fleurs peint sur papier—aquarelle*, *Vase de marbre jaune antique rempli de fleurs*; 1779: *Différentes fleurs dans un vase de marbre blanc, mêlées avec des fruits comme ananas, pêches, raisins, etc.*, *Des fleurs dans un vase de marbre jaune*, *Un bouquet de fleurs peint sur papier blanc—gouache*, *Bouquet de fleurs—dessiné sur papier bleu*; 1781: *Un tableau représentant un vase sculpté en bas-relief, rempli de fleurs et de fruits se détachant sur un fond d'architecture*, *Quatre dessins peints à la gouache et à l'aquarelle de fleurs et de fruits*, *Un tableau représentant un vase de marbre rempli de fleurs, et dans le bas, un groupe de fleurs et de fruits (morceau de réception de l'auteur)*; 1783 *Un vase d'albâtre oriental rempli de différentes fleurs posé sur un socle où sont représentés des enfants en bas-relief*, *Deux tableaux ovales, l'un vase de lapis lazulis, et l'autre, un vase de porphyre, tous deux remplis de différentes fleurs*, *Étude de pêches posées sur une pierre*, *Autre tableau de pêches posées dans une assiette*, *Deux plantes etrangères peintes sur vélin faisant suite de la collection*

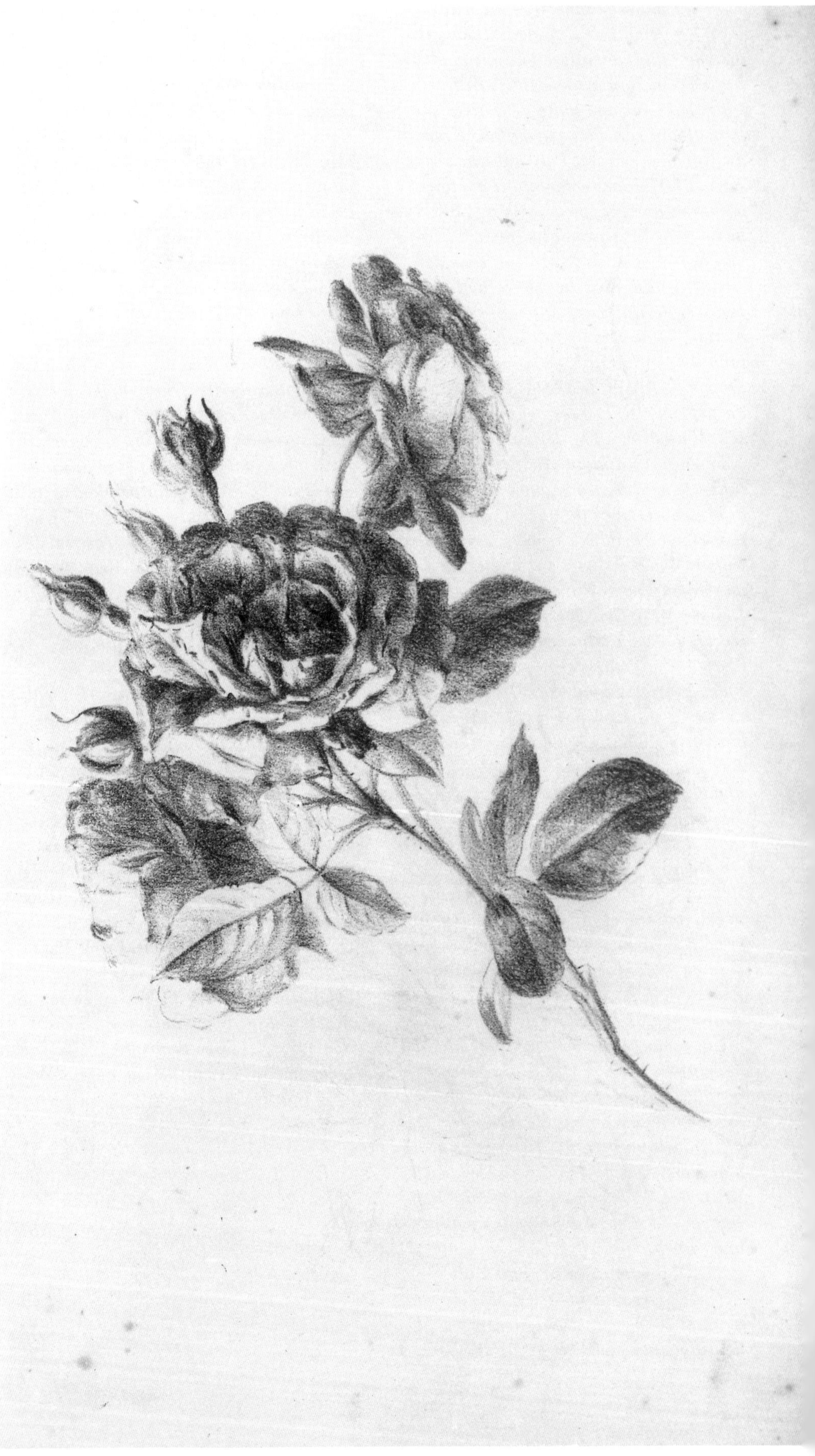

Gérard van Spaendonck

Black chalk — from an album of flower studies, $12\frac{1}{2} \times 9\frac{1}{2}$ in. (31.5 × 24 cm.),
Private collection, Courtesy John Mitchell & Son, London

des plantes pour le roi; 1785: *Tableau représéntant un piédestal d'albâtre enrichi de bas-relief sur lequel est posée une corbeille de fleurs et à côté un vase de bronze (appartient au roi), Vase de porphyre garni de fleurs, Un bouquet de fleurs—dessin à l'aquarelle*; 1787: *Un tableau représentant un piédestal de marbre, enrichi de bas-reliefs et sur lequel est posée une corbeille remplie de différentes fleurs, à côté se trouve un vase rempli de roses (appartient au roi), Tableau représentant une corbeille remplie de diverses fleurs posée sur une encoignure de marbre sculpté, à côté se voit un piédestal de marbre blanc sur lequel est un vase (appartient à Mgr. le comte d'Artois)*; 1789: *Vase rempli de différentes fleurs et posé sur une table de marbre où se trouvent deux ananas et une corbeille garnie de différents fruits, Petit tableau de pêches posées sur un appui de marbre*; 1791: *Grappe de raisin, peinte sur marbre blanc, Cadre contenant quelques petits tableaux de fleurs en miniature*; 1793: *Plusieurs pêches et une grappe de raisin de Maroc peints sur marbre blanc*; 1795: *Un dessin fait à l'aquarelle représentant plusieurs pêches et du raisin de Maroc*; 1796: *Une corbeille et un vase remplis de différentes fleurs, Un bouquet de roses, tulipes et pavots peints sur marbre blanc, Des pêches et des raisins au pastel, Une étude de rose sur marbre blanc*; *Salon de la Correspondance*, 1779: *Une corbeille de fleurs de la plus grande fraicheur et d'une imitation belle comme nature.* M: Paris, Louvre; Fontainebleau; Montpellier; Quincy
LIT *Bellier*; W. Blunt, *The Art of Botanical Illustration*, 1950 Faré 1976; M. van Boven, S. Segal, *Gérard & Cornelis van Spaendonck* Twee Brabantse bloemenschilders in Parijs 1980 PM

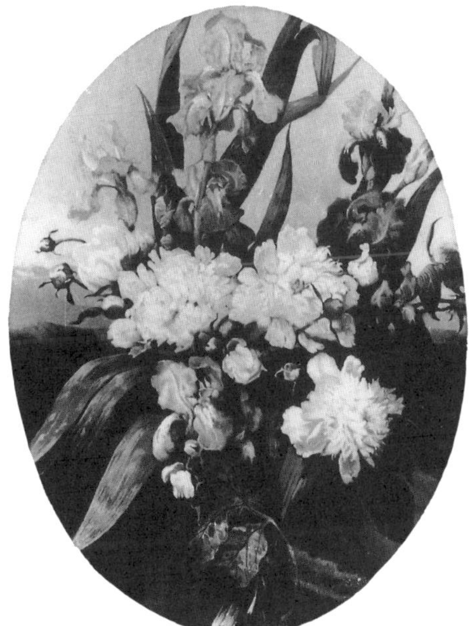

Octavie-Marie Sturel

Pastel, oval, 31½ × 24¾ in. (80 × 63 cm.), Metz, Musée d'Art et d'Histoire

SPITZ, C.
Exhib. *Azalées*, Strasbourg Salon 1883
LIT *Strasbourg Salon* 1883

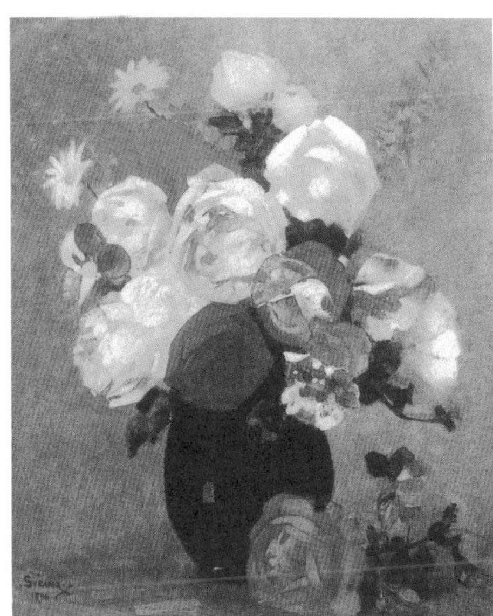

Gustave Surand

Oil on canvas, 18 × 15 in. (46 × 38 cm.), signed and dated 1894
Private collection

STEINHEIL, Adolphe-Charles-Edouard *1850–1908*
b. Paris. Pupil of L. C. A. Steinheil, his father. Painted historical subjects, still-lifes, game and flowers. Exhib. Paris Salon from 1870 e.g. *Chrysanthèmes*, 1872, *Fleurs*, 1880
LIT *Bellier*; *Bénézit*; *Paris Salon* 1872, 1880; *Thieme*; *Witt*

STEINHEIL, Louis-Charles-Auguste *1814–1885*
b. Strasbourg (Bas-Rhin). Pupil of Paris BA, Decaisne and David d'Angers. Painted portraits, genre, historical subjects and, occasionally, flowers. Designed plates for *Leçons élémentaires de botanique* (vol. II). Exhib. Paris Salon from 1836 e.g. *Giroflées*, 1849, 1863; *Fleurs*, 1850
LIT *Bellier*; *Bénézit*; *Schurr* IV, 99; *Thieme*

STENGELIN, Alphonse *1852–1938*
b. Lyon. Pupil of Guichard, Chenu and N. Cabane. Painted landscapes and flowers. These are mostly late works
LIT *Bénézit*; E. Christen, Oberkampf de Dabrun. *A. Stengelin*, Geneva 1932; Ecully (Rhônc) *A. Stengelin*, 1979; *Hardouin-Fugier Grafe*; *Thieme*; *Witt*

STEVENS, *see* HÉBERT-STEVENS

STOLK, Alida *d.1897*
b. The Hague (Netherlands). Pupil of S. Saint-Jean and Puyroche-Wagner. Exhib. Paris and Lyon 1861–1885 e.g. Lyon Salon, *Vase de camélias et cinéraires, Roses entourées d'une guirlande de verveines, Mauves et pavots du Caucase*, 1862, *La guirlande de Julie, Fleurs des bois*, 1863, *Fleurs dans une bourriche*, 1868, *Primevères*, 1879; Paris Salon, *Pivoines*, wc, 1885; *Chrysanthèmes*, wc, *Pivoines*, *wc*, *Pavots*, wc. Paris Noir et Blanc Salon 1888
LIT *Hardouin-Fugier Grafe*; *Lyon Salon* 1862, 1863, 1868, 1879; *Paris Noir et Blanc Salon* 1888; *Paris Salon* 1885

STUGOCKI, Jules-Georges ***b.1880***
b. Paris. Pupil of Castex-Dégrange Lyon BA (CFD 1898)
LIT Lyon Beaux-Arts arch.

STUMM, Mme
Pupil of L. O. Merson and J. Dupré. Exhib. *Violettes de Parme*, wc, *Paris Salon* 1895
LIT *Paris Salon* 1895

STUREL, Octavie-Marie, ***née*** **Paigné** ***1819–1854***
b. Metz (Moselle). Pupil of M. Paigné, her sister and Maréchal (Metz). Exhib. Paris Salon from 1844 e.g. *Fleurs*, pastel, 1844, *Bouquet de roses trémières*, pastel, *Pavots Tournefort et ordinaires*, pastel, Paris Exposition Universelle 1855. M: Metz, Troyes
LIT *Bellier*; *Bénézit*; *Faré* 1962, p. 248; *Paris Exposition Universelle* 1855; *Paris Salon* 1844, 1850; *Thieme*

SUAU, Edmond-Eugène ***1871–1929***
b. Mulhouse (Haut-Rhin). Pupil of B. Constant, J. Leblanc, J. Lefebvre, and T. Robert-Fleury. Painted genre and flowers. Exhib. Paris Salon from 1897
LIT *Bénézit*; *Orsay*; *Schurr* V, 143; *Thieme*

SURAND, Gustave ***b.1860***
b. Paris. Pupil of J. P. Laurens. Painted genre and figures. Exhib. Paris Salon from 1881. Exhib. *Roses* Dijon Salon 1897. *Roses mousseuses*, 1894, Geneva sale 1–2 June 1988, lot 64
LIT *Bénézit*; *Dijon Salon* 1897; *Thieme*; *Witt*

SYLVESTRE, Marie-Elise
Exhib. Dijon Salon *Primevères et cinéraires*, 1890, *Fleurs et fruits*, *Chrysanthèmes*, 1897
LIT *Dijon Salon* 1890, 1897. CL

T U

TACONNET, Jeanne
Pupil of Devosges, Bourgogne and F. Rivoire. Exhib. Dijon Salon *Primevères*, 1880, *Pavots*, 1885, *Premières fleurs*, *Roses*, 1894, *Chrysanthèmes*, *Roses*, 1897; Paris UFPS *Raisins et chrysanthèmes*, *Roses et violettes*, *Mandarines et violettes*, 1896, *Pivoines*, *Roses trémières*, 1898
LIT *Dijon Salon* 1880, 1885, 1894, 1897; *Paris UFPS* 1896, 1898. CL

TANNERON, Marcelin ***1818–1869***
b. Toulon (Var). Painted still-lifes and, occasionally, flowers
LIT *Bénézit*; *Thieme*

TANTE, Claude-Aimé ***b.1818***
b. Lyon. Pupil of Thierriat, Lyon BA (CFD 1837). Exhib. Lyon Salon 1839–1849
LIT *Hardouin-Fugier Grafe*

TAPISSIER, Jean-Joseph ***b.1825***
b. Lyon. Pupil of Thierriat, Lyon BA (CFD 1842)
LIT *Hardouin-Fugier Grafe*

TAPISSIER, Jean-Louis ***b.1841***
Pupil of Reignier, Lyon BA (CFD 1861)
LIT *Hardouin-Fugier Grafe*

TARDIEU, Jean-Claude ***b.1837***
Pupil of Reignier, Lyon BA (CFD 1854)
LIT *Hardouin-Fugier Grafe*

TARGE, Mme Mathieu
Exhib. Lyon Salon 1867, 1870, 1874, 1878
LIT *Hardouin-Fugier Grafe*

TARIN
Designed a flower plate lithographed by Thierry
LIT Paris Bibl. Nat. Est. Jd 59

TASCHER DE LA PAGERIE, ***see*** **BEAUHARNAIS**

TAUPIER, Edmond
One known work *Fleurs et fruits*, 1810, Drouot, Paris, 10 Dec. 1948
LIT *Bénézit*

TAUPIN, Maurice-Hippolyte-Edouard
b. Paris. Pupil of Van Spaendonck and Budelot. Picture restorer. Painted landscapes and flowers
LIT *Bénézit*; *Thieme*

TEILLARD-BUSSY, Pierre
Pupil of M. Bruyas. Exhib. *Primevères*, Lyon Salon 1870
LIT *Hardouin-Fugier Grafe*

TEISSIER, Emile ***b.1874***
b. Lyon. Pupil of Castex-Dégrange, Lyon BA (CFD 1892)
LIT *Hardouin-Fugier Grafe*

TEISSIER, ***see*** **SOULANGE**

TERNOIS
Pupil of Berjon, Lyon BA (CFD 1810)
LIT *Hardouin-Fugier Grafe*

TETART, André
Exhib. *Roses*, Paris Indép. 1896
LIT *Paris Indép.* 1896

THENOT, Vincent-Léopold ***1835–1890***
b. Bordeaux (Gironde). Painted landscapes and flowers. Exhib. Paris Salon from 1880. M: Bordeaux: *Pivoines* (currently untraceable); Paris Muséum d'Histoire Naturelle (not original works)
LIT *Hardouin-Fugier Grafe*

THÉRON, Jean-Germain ***b.1817***
b. Lyon. Pupil of Thierriat. Lyon BA (CFD 1835)
LIT Lyon Beaux-Arts arch.

THEURIET
Pupil of Thierriat. Textile designer
LIT *Hardouin-Fugier Grafe*

THEVENET, Louis ***1837–1898***
b. Varennes (Saône-et-Loire). Pupil of Lyon BA. Exhib. *Roses et Cerises*, Lyon Salon 1884
LIT *Hardouin-Fugier Grafe*; *Lyon Salon* 1884

THEVENOT or THEUVENOT, Alexandre-Jean-Baptiste
b. Port-sur-Saône (Haute-Saône). Pupil of Gleyre and Gérôme. op. drawing master. Painted birds and flowers. Exhib. Paris Salon 1862–1876 and *Fruits et fleurs*, Lons-le-Saunier Salon, 1876
LIT *Bellier*; *Bénézit*; *Lons-le-Saunier Salon* 1876; *Thieme*. JLM

THIBAUDIER, Jean-François ***b.1809***
Pupil of Thierriat, Lyon BA (CFD 1830)
LIT *Hardouin-Fugier Grafe*

THIEBAUD, Mlle
Exhib. *Trois cadres de fleurs*, Dijon Salon 1837
LIT *Dijon Salon* 1837. CL

THIEBAULT, Louis
Exhib. *Fleurs*, *Boules de neige*, Strasbourg Salon 1884
LIT *Strasbourg Salon* 1884

THIEBLIN, Reine-Joséphine
b. Mery-sur-Seine (Aube). Pupil of Royer. Painted fruit and flowers. Exhib. Paris Salon from 1878
LIT *Bellier*; *Bénézit*

THIEGHEM, *see* VAN THIEGHEM

THIERCELIN-BARBIER, Mathilde
b. Paris. Pupil of Marest. Exhib. *Roses trémières*, Paris Salon 1895
LIT *Paris Salon* 1895 (ill.)

THIERRIAT, Augustin ***1789–1870***
b. Lyon. Pupil of Grognard, Lyon BA and possibly, Berjon. Professor of CFD at Lyon BA (1823–1853). Designed *Fleurs, fruits. . .d'après nature* 1824–1827. Exhib. Lyon Salon *Fleurs*, 1821, *Bouquet de fleurs*, 1882; *Groupe* or *Gerbe de fleurs*, *Fleurs*, wc Paris Salon 1822; Lyon Salon *Grand bouquet*, *Petit bouquet*, 1823; *Fleurs dans un vase de Sarreguemines*, wc, 1824; *Vase de fleurs*, 1826; *Fleurs*, wc, Paris Salon 1827; Lyon Salon *Corbeille de fleurs*, wc, 1827; *Fleurs, fruits, ornements*, lithographs, 1828, *Fleurs*, wc, 1828; *Fleurs*, wc, *Bouquet de tulipes, jacinthes, giroflées*, wc, 1833; *Bouquet*, 1836; *Gerbe de roses trémières*; 1838; *Bouquet de fleurs*, wc, Paris Salon 1840; Lyon Salon *Bouquet de fleurs*, wc, 1840; *Bouquet de pensées et roses mousseuses roses liées avec un ruban rose*, 1842; *Fleurs sans épine*, *Vase de fleurs*, 1848, *Prunes et chardon*, wc, *Guirlande*, wc, *Fleurs et nature morte*, wc, 1848, (*Vase de capucines*?), *Fleurs, fruits*, 1850; *Le mois d'avril*, 1850; *Avril, Mai*, wc, Marseille Salon 1851; *Groupe de fleurs dans un vase du Japon*, Paris Salon 1854; Lyon Salon *Fables de Rousset*, 1854; *Pensées*, 1856; *Vase de fleurs*, 1859; *Vase de fleurs*, 1860, *Groupe de jonquilles, premières fleurs*, 1861. An influential teacher who, strangely enough, produced more landscape drawings than flower-pieces. Musée des Beaux-Arts de Lyon, *Fleurs dans un vase du Japon*, 1854
LIT *Hardouin-Fugier Grafe*; *Hardouin-Fugier Grafe* 1982 (ill.); *Witt*

THIERRY, Clémentine
Exhib. flowers in wc, Paris Salon 1844, 1846, 1850
LIT *Bellier*; *Bénézit*; *Paris Salon* 1844, 1850

THIERRY, Louis-Jules
b. Paris. Pupil Exhib. *Fleurs*, gouache, Paris Salon 1895
LIT *Paris Salon* 1895

THIMOTÉE
Designed *Bouquets dessinés d'après nature*, published by Desmaisons, Dauty
LIT Paris Bibl. Nat. Est. Jd 59

THIVILLON, Alphonse ***b.1804***
Pupil of Berjon, Lyon BA (CFD 1822)
LIT *Hardouin-Fugier Grafe*

THOLER, Raymond ***b.1859***
b. Paris. Pupil of Bergeret and Gérôme. Painted still-lifes and flowers. Exhib. Paris Salon from 1877. M: Niort (currently untraceable); Leipzig
LIT *Bellier*; *Bénézit*; *Thieme*

THOLIN, Henri
Pupil of Castex-Dégrange, Lyon BA (CFD 1899)
LIT Lyon Beaux-Arts arch.

THOLLOT, Benoit ***b.1817***
b. Lyon. Pupil of Picot, Paris BA. Painted figures and, occasionally, flowers, e.g. *Fleurs de mars*, Lyon Salon 1875
LIT *Bénézit*; *Hardouin-Fugier Grafe*; *Lyon Salon* 1875; *Thieme*

THOLOZAN, Auguste
Pupil of Berjon, Lyon BA (CFD 1820)
LIT *Hardouin-Fugier Grafe*

THOMAS, André-Félix
b. Paris. Pupil of Starke. Painted still-lifes and flowers. Exhib. Paris Salon from 1865 e.g. *Fruits et fleurs dans un jardin*, 1867
LIT *Bellier*; *Bénézit*; *Paris Salon* 1867

THOMAS, Charles-Armand-Etienne *1857–1892*
b. Paris. Pupil of V. Leclaire. Painted genre, landscapes, still-lifes and flowers. Exhib. Paris Salon from 1878 e.g. *Un gai matin*, 1882, *Entrée de cour à Seisy*, 1888. M: Le Havre, *Veille de fête* (last painting), Nantes, *Le cellier du Père Jacquemin*
LIT *Bénézit*; *Paris Salon* 1882 (ill.), 1888 (ill.); *Thieme*

THOMASSIN, Edouard *b.1817*
b. Paris. Pupil of Thierriat, Lyon BA (CFD 1832).
LIT *Hardouin-Fugier Grafe*

THOUARS, *see* DUPETIT

THOUAULT, Blanche
Pupil of Attendu and Poinsot. Exhib. Paris UFPS e.g. *Pivoines*, 1890, *Anémones*, pastel, 1898; Paris SNBA e.g. *Fleurs*, wc, 1894
LIT *Paris SNBA* 1894; *Paris UFPS* 1890, 1898

THOUBILLON, Stéphanie
Pupil of Lyon École Municipale du quai Saint-Antoine and Médard. Exhib. *Fleurs et légumes*, Lyon Salon 1882
LIT *Lyon Salon* 1882

THUILLIER DE MORNARD, Louise
b. Amiens (Somme). Pupil of her father and Chaplin. Exhib. *Panerée de roses*, wc, Paris Salon 1890
LIT *Bénézit*; *Paris Salon* 1890.

THURNER, Gabriel-Edouard *1840–1907*
b. Mulhouse (Haut-Rhin). Pupil of Chabal-Dussurgey. Professor of flower design at École des Gobelins. Exhib. Paris Salon from 1865 e.g. *Fleurs de mai*, 1872, *Pivoines*, 1873, *Bouquet de la cuisinière*, 1888, *Azaléa*, 1889, *Rosée du matin à Saint-Germain*, 1893; Dijon Salon e.g. *Vase de roses*, 1894; *Fleurs de printemps* 1897; Lyon Salon e.g. *Chrysanthèmes roses*, 1881, Mulhouse Salon e.g. *Fleurs*, 1876. M: Amiens, Clamecy, Epinal, Mulhouse, Rouen, Strasbourg, Tourcoing

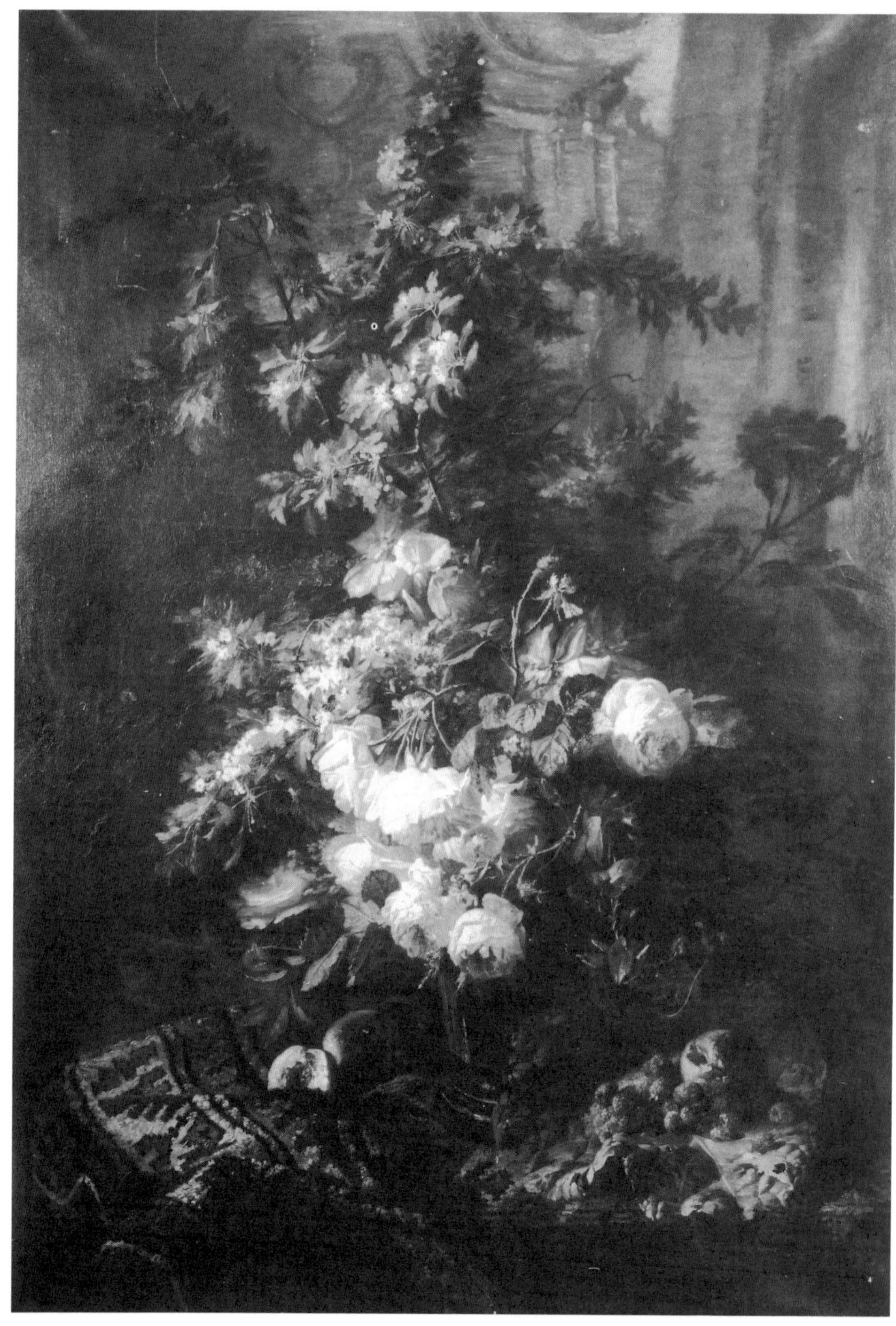

Gabriel-Edouard Thurner

Oil on canvas, 55 × 39½ in. (140 × 100 cm.), signed
Mulhouse, Musée de l'Impression sur Etoffes

LIT *Bellier*; *Bénézit*; *MISE*; *Dijon Salon* 1894, 1897; *Lyon Salon* 1881; Paris Arch. Nat. F21: 2114; *Paris Salon* 1872, 1873, 1880, 1889, 1893; *Thieme*. BJ

TICARD, Anna
b. Paris. Pupil of Carbillet, Bellay and Parvillée. Exhib. Paris Salon from 1881 e.g. *Chrysanthèmes*, 1895
LIT *Bellier*; *Paris Salon* 1895

TIGÉ, Léonie
Exhib. *Fleurs des champs*, Lyon Salon 1857
LIT *Lyon Salon* 1857

TIGER, Adolphe
Painted portraits and flowers. Exhib. *Fleurs*, on porcelain, Paris Salon 1850
LIT *Bénézit*; *Paris Salon* 1850

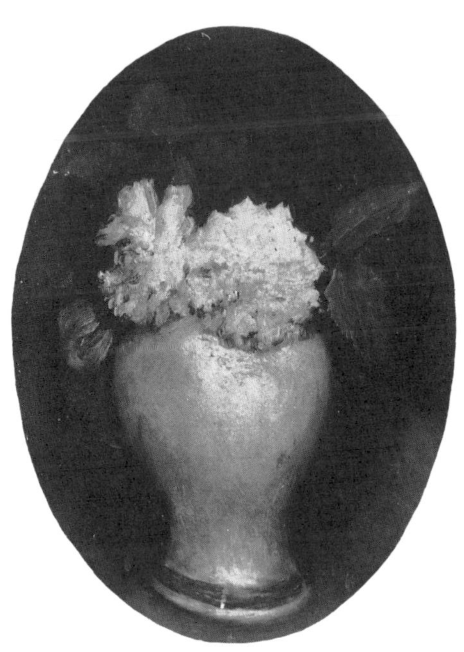

Stanislas-Pierre-Nolasque Torrents y de Amat

Oil on panel, oval, 20 × 12 in. (51 × 30 cm.), Marseille, Musée des Beaux-Arts

TINEIRE, Martial
Pupil of Thierriat, Lyon BA (CFD 1826)
LIT *Hardouin-Fugier Grafe*

TINEL, Jean
Exhib. *Chrysanthèmes*, Dijon Salon 1885
LIT *Dijon Salon* 1885. CL

TIPHAGNE, Adrienne-Edmond
Exhib. *Corbeille de fleurs*, after Van Spaendonck, on porcelain, Paris Salon 1844. Designed *Bouquets de fleurs dessinés d'après nature et composés*
LIT Paris Bibl. Nat. Est. Jd 66; *Paris Salon* 1844

TISSOT, Ferdinand-Joseph *b.1804*
Pupil of Lyon BA 1818–1827. Exhib. Lyon Salon 1836
LIT *Audin Vial*

TIXIER, Marie-Antoinette
Exhib. *Pivoines et lilas*, Dijon Salon 1890; *Pivoine*, Roanne Salon 1890
LIT *Dijon Salon* 1890; *Roanne Salon* 1890

Victor Tortez

Oil on canvas, signed and dated 1868
Chambéry, Musée d'Art et d'Histoire

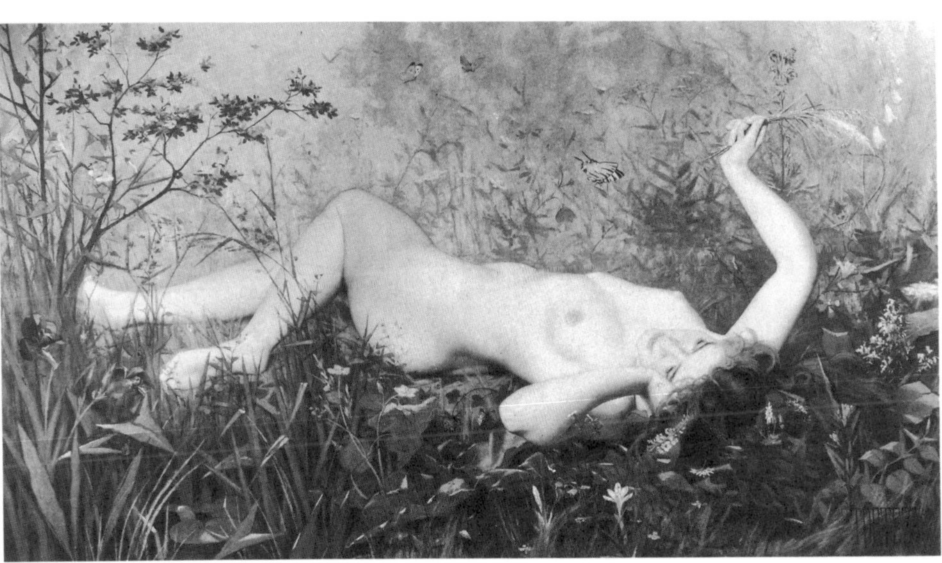

TOCHÉ, Charles *1851–1916*
b. Nantes (Loire-Atlantique). Self-taught. Exhib. *Fleurs*, fan-leaf, Paris, Aquar. 1891
LIT *Paris Aquar.* 1891; *Thieme*

TOILLIEZ, Edmond
Exhib. *Récolte de fleurs*, Lyon Salon 1867
LIT *Lyon Salon* 1867

TOINON, Renée-Marguerite
b. Angers (Maine-et-Loire). Exhib. *Fleurs*, fan-leaf, Paris Salon 1880
LIT *Paris Salon* 1880

TORRENTS Y DE AMAT, Stanislas-Pierre-Nolasque *1839–1916*
b. Marseille. Pupil of Couture, fl. Marseille *c.*1870–1910. Painted genre, figures and flowers. Musée de Marseille, *Roses*
LIT *Bénézit*; J. R. Soubiran, "Torrents" in *Renaissance du Musée des Beaux Arts de Cannes*, Musées de Cannes, 1983, p. 196; *Thieme*

TORTEZ, Victor *d.1890*
b. Paris. Pupil of Gérôme, Gleyre and Henner. Painted genre and flowers. Exhib. Paris Salon from 1868. His *Papillons et fleurs*, 1868, was bought by

the State in 1869 for the Musée de Chambery (1,200 francs)
LIT *Bellier*; *Bénézit*; Paris Arch. Nat. F21: 185, 444

TOSCAN, *see* ROSTAN

TOUDOUZE, Edouard *1848–1907*
b. Paris. Pupil of Pils and Leloir. Painted figures, mythological subjects, tapestry cartoons and, occasionally, flowers e.g. *Fleurs d'automne*, Paris Salon 1890
LIT *Bellier*; *Bénézit*; *Paris Salon* 1890; *Thieme*; *Witt*

TOUDOUZE, Isabelle
b. Paris. Pupil of A. Toudouze, née Colin, her mother (1822–1899). Exhib. Paris Salon 1868–1875, e.g. *Fleurs*, wc, 1872, 1873, *Roses trémières*, *Bouquet*, wc, 1875
LIT *Bellier*; *Bénézit*; *Paris Salon* 1872, 1873, 1875; *Thieme*

TOUDOUZE, Marie-Anne
b. Lyon. Pupil of Edouard Toudouze, her husband. Painted flowers
LIT *Bénézit*

TOUDOUZE, *see* DESGRANGE

TOULET, Th.
Draughtsman and lithographer. Designed plates for P. Champy, *Flore Algérienne*, Paris (Delahaye) 1844
LIT *Nissen* I, 346

TOULMOUCHE, Auguste *1829–1890*
b. Nantes (Loire-Atlantique). Pupil of Gleyre. Many works by this popular genre painter feature flowers e.g. *Dans la serre*, Musée de Nantes, *Girl and roses*, Saint-Louis, USA (untraceable). He produced some flower paintings
LIT *Bellier*; *Bénézit*; *Schurr* IV, 105; *Thieme*; *Witt*

TOULMOUCHE, Marie
b. Nantes (Loire-Atlantique). Wife of Auguste Toulmouche. Exhib. Paris SNBA e.g. *Fleurs de ronces*, 1890, *Jacinthe*, 1892. Musée de Soissons, *Violettes et raisins*
LIT *Bénézit*; *Paris SNBA* 1890, 1892; *Thieme*

TOURNES, Etienne *1857–1931*
b. Seix (Ariège). Pupil of Cabanel. Some of his genre paintings feature flowers e.g. *Le bouquet*, Paris SNBA 1894
LIT *Bénézit*; *Paris SNBA* 1894; *Thieme*; *Witt*

TOURNIER, Georges
b. Paris. Exhib. Paris Salon from 1879 e.g. *Lilas et roses*, 1880; *Choix de fleurs de mars*, Saint-Etienne Salon 1882
LIT *Bellier*; *Bénézit*; *Saint-Etienne Salon* 1882

TOURNIER, Jean-Ulrich *1802–1865*
b. Illzach (Haut-Rhin). Pupil of Van Dael. Textile designer (Mulhouse), Designs manufactured by Schwartz-Huguenin in Mulhouse. Exhib. Paris Salon 1822–1833. e.g. *Fleurs*, 1822, *Guirlande*, 1827; *Fleurs*, Lyon Salon 1834. Designed *Bouquet de roses*, lithographed by Turgis, Paris BMAD (Maciet coll.). M:Lyon, Mulhouse
LIT *Bellier*; *Bénézit*; *Faré* 1962, p. 245; B. Jacqué, *Chefs d'oeuvre du MISE*, Tokyo (Gakken) 1978; *Lyon Salon* 1834; *Mitchell*; *Paris BMAD*; *Paris Salon* 1822; *Thieme*; *Witt*. BJ
See illustration on page 37

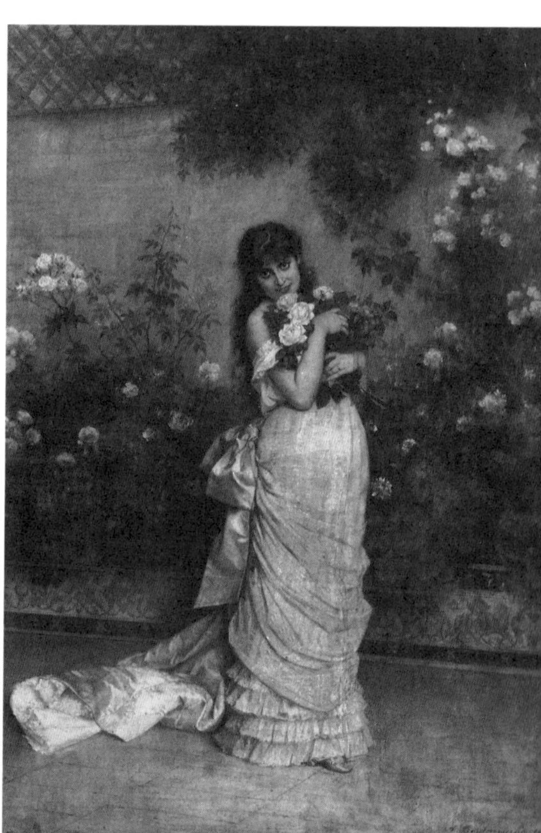

Auguste Toulmouche

Oil on canvas, signed and dated 1883
Nantes, Musée des Beaux-Arts

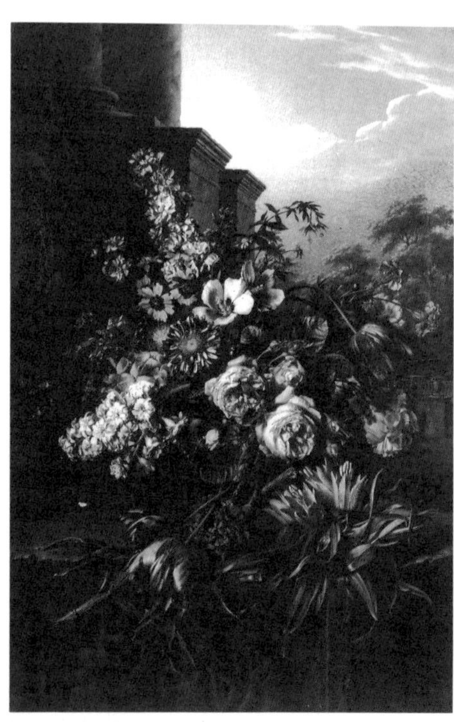

Jean-Ulrich Tournier

Oil on canvas, 42 × 28½ in. (107 × 72 cm.)
Mulhouse, Musée de l'Impression sur Etoffes

TOURNY, Joseph-Gabriel ***1817–1880***
b. Paris. Pupil of Martinet. Painted portraits, figures and copies. Engraver and wc painter. Exhib. Paris Salon from 1857. His *Coquelicots et cerises* was in the Lyon Société des Amis-des-Arts 1869 raffle
LIT *Bénézit*; *Schurr* V, 20; *Thieme*

TOUSSAINT, Lucie
Exhib. *Eventail de fleurs*, Paris Indép. 1884.
LIT *Paris Indép.* 1884

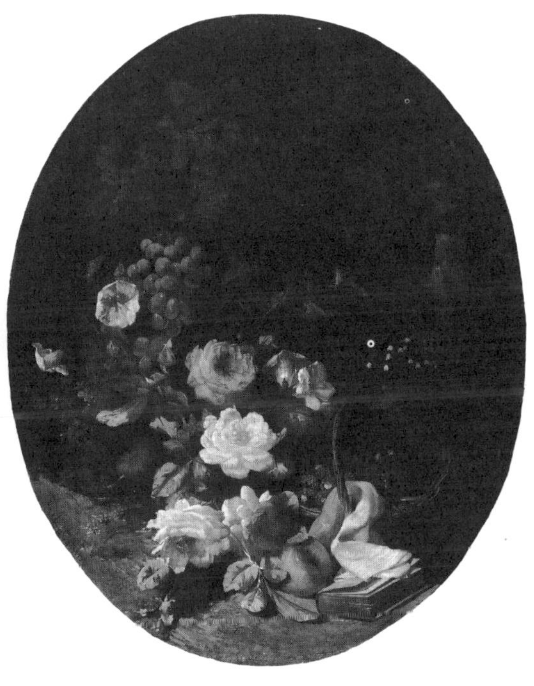

Etienne-Léon Trébutien

Oil on canvas, oval, 39 × 31½ in. (99 × 80 cm.), signed
Courtesy Christie's, London

TOUSSAINT, Pierre
b. Laroque d'Antheron (Bouches-du-Rhône). Studied at Marseille BA with Jeanron and Joanny Rave. Painted figures, genre, portraits and flowers. Exhib. Paris Salon 1865–1872 e.g. *Livres et fleurs*, 1867. Musée de Marseille, *Roses* (acquired 1874) and *Pivoines*, wc (from the artist 1881)
LIT *Bellier*; *Bénézit*; *Paris Salon* 1867; *Thieme*

TRABACH, Fernande
Pupil of Le Besgue-Delbarre. Exhib. *Roses*, *Chrysanthèmes*, gouaches, Paris UFPS 1898
LIT *Paris UFPS* 1898

TRAENKLE, Jacques ***b.1832***
Pupil of Reignier Lyon BA (CFD 1861)
LIT *Hardouin-Fugier Grafe*

TRANCHAND, Jeanne
Exhib. *Giroflées*, Dijon Salon 1887.
LIT *Dijon Salon* 1887. CL

TRANCHARD, Joseph ***b.1850***
b. Lyon. Pupil of Reignier, Lyon BA (CFD 1867). Exhib. Paris Salon 1876–1878, 1880 e.g. *Bourriche de pensées*, 1880
LIT *Bellier*; *Bénézit*; *Hardouin-Fugier Grafe*, *Paris Salon* 1880

TRAVIÈS, Edouard ***b.1809***
b. Doulléns (Somme). The popular bird and insect painter also produced *Macédoines variées de fleurs*
LIT *Bénézit*; *Laissus*; *Thieme*

TRÉBUCHET, Louise-Marie, *née* Housel
b. Paris. Pupil of Thoret and Dessart. Painted flowers and genre. An influential teacher. Exhib. Paris Salon from 1875 e.g. *Roses trémières*, wc, 1880; *Fleurs*, Paris Noir et Blanc Salon 1886
LIT *Bellier*; *Paris Noir et Blanc Salon* 1886; *Paris Salon* 1880

TRÉBUTIEN, Etienne-Léon ***1823–1871***
b. Bayeux (Calvados). Exhib. Paris Salon from 1857 e.g. *Fleurs*, 1861, His *Fleurs et fruits* was bought by the State for the Musée de Bayeux; *Fleurs*, for the Musée de Montargis (1866, 1,000 francs); *A un ami, fleurs*, for the Musée de la Réunion (1868, 1,000 francs); *Fleurs et fruits*, for the Musée de Saint-Etienne. *Basket of Raspberries*, Christie's, London, 10 Dec. 1984, lot 43
LIT *Bellier*; *Bénézit*; Paris Arch. Nat. F21: 185, 446, 448; *Paris Salon* 1861; *Thieme*

TRÉMOLIÈRES, Raoul
Exhib. *Iris et cerises*, Dijon Salon 1892
LIT *Dijon Salon* 1892

TRINQUIER, Antonin or Antoine-Guillaume ***b.1833***
b. Le Vigan (Gard). Pupil of Matet. Professor at Montpellier BA. Painted genre, still-lifes and, occasionally, flowers. Exhib. Paris Salon from 1864. *Fleurs*; 1874, Sotheby's Monaco, 23 Feb. 1986
LIT *Bénézit*; *Thieme*

TRINQUIER, Fernand ***b.1863***
b. Montpellier (Hérault). Pupil of Bideau. Sète, Musée Paul Valéry, *Oeillets* (donated by the artist, 1891)
LIT *Bénézit*; *Thieme*

TRIPONEL, Marie
b. Mulhouse (Haut-Rhin). Pupil of Pallandre, Meyer and Bourgogne. Exhib. *Jonquilles*, *Amaryllis*, *Pois de senteur*, wc, Saint-Etienne Salon 1882; *Acacias*, on faience (160 francs); *Ronces*, fan-leaf (80 francs), Strasbourg Salon 1883; *Chrysanthèmes*, gouache, Paris Salon 1885; *Fleurs*, *Pavots*, fan-leaf, Paris Noir et Blanc Salon 1886
LIT *Lyon Salon* 1883; *Paris Noir et Blanc Salon* 1886; *Paris Salon* 1885. *Saint-Etienne Salon* 1882; *Strasbourg Salon* 1883

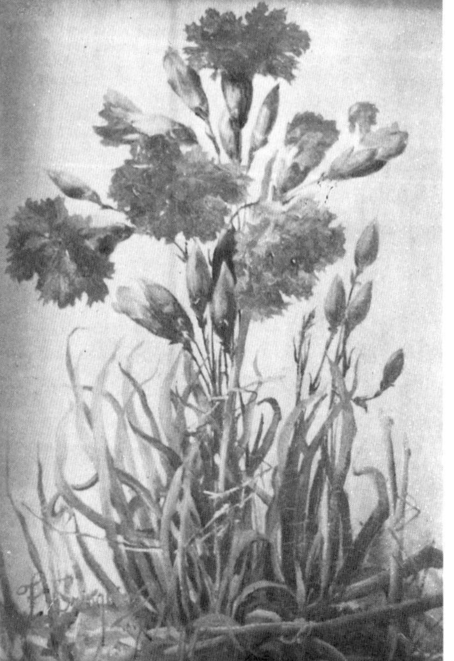

LAMBERT-TRISTAN, ***see*** **CHANTON**

TRITSCH, François ***1814–1865***
b. Sansheim (Haut-Rhin). Textile designer Paris and Mulhouse, specializing in flower design
LIT *Histoire Documentaire*. BJ

TROUILLET, Joseph
Pupil of Berjon, Lyon BA (CFD 1820)
LIT *Hardouin-Fugier Grafe*

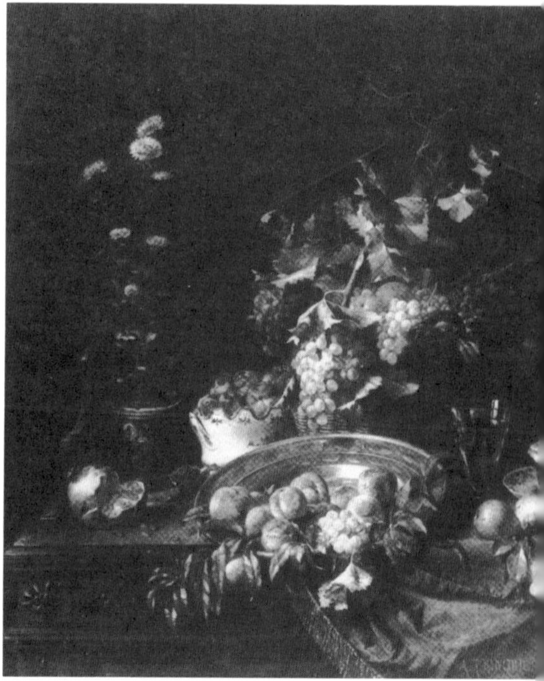

Antonin or Antoine-Guillaume Trinquier

Oil on canvas, signed and datged 1874
Courtesy Sotheby's, London

Fernand Trinquier

Oil on canvas, signed and dated 1887
Sète, Musée Paul Veléry

TROUILLEUX, Joseph-Jean-Jacques *1819–1899*
b. Saint-Héand (Loire). Pupil of Lyon BA (1839–1843) and Lalanne. Textile designer, Saint-Etienne. Landscape, figure and flower painter. Etchings issued by Cadart, Paris, e.g. *Fleurs et papillons*, *Roses*, etc. Exhib. *Marguerite des prés et lézards*, Saint-Etienne Salon 1857; *Le mois de Marie*, Lyon Salon 1860
LIT *Bellier*; *Bénézit*; *Hardouin-Fugier Bringuier*; *Hardouin-Fugier Grafe*; *Lyon Salon* 1860; *Saint-Etienne Salon* 1857; *Thieme*

TROUPEAU, Ferdinand
b. Bordeaux (Gironde). Pupil of Utin, Pignot and Lambotte. Exhib. Paris Salon from 1878 e.g. *Camélias*, *Pensées*, gouache, 1885; *Pavots*, 1890; *Roses*, *Lys*, Roanne Salon 1890; *Iris* (*matin*), Dijon Salon 1892, *Pavots*, *Chrysanthèmes*, gouache, Dijon Salon 1894 and Paris Salon 1895
LIT *Bellier*; *Bénézit*; *Dijon Salon* 1892, 1894; *Paris Salon* 1885, 1890, 1895; *Roanne Salon* 1890. CL

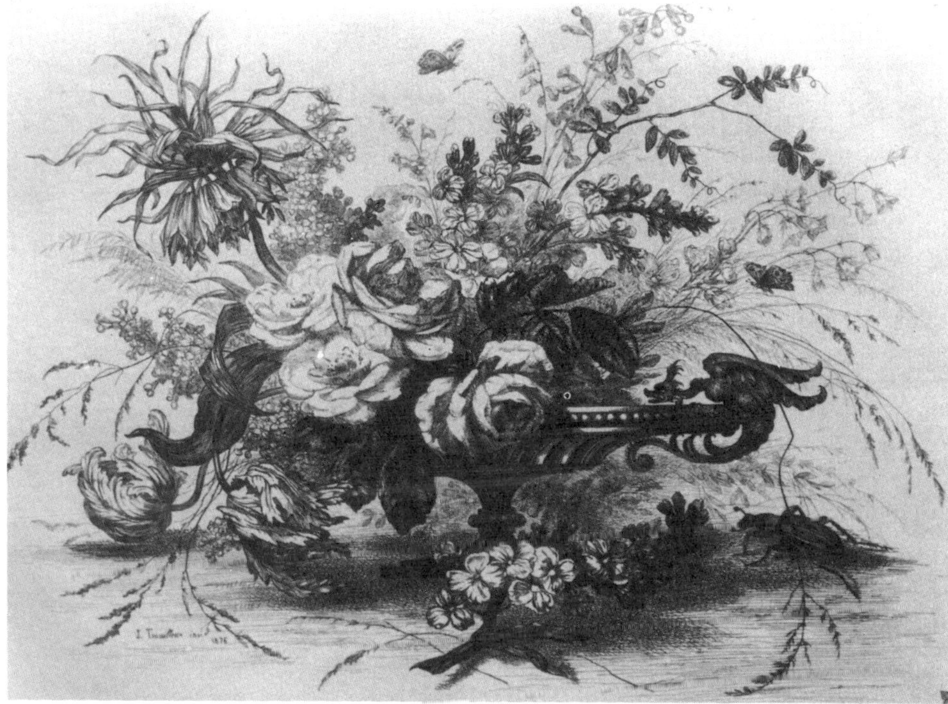

Joseph-Jean-Jacques Trouilleux

Etching, $8\frac{3}{4} \times 5\frac{3}{4}$ in. (22 × 14.5 cm.)
Private collection

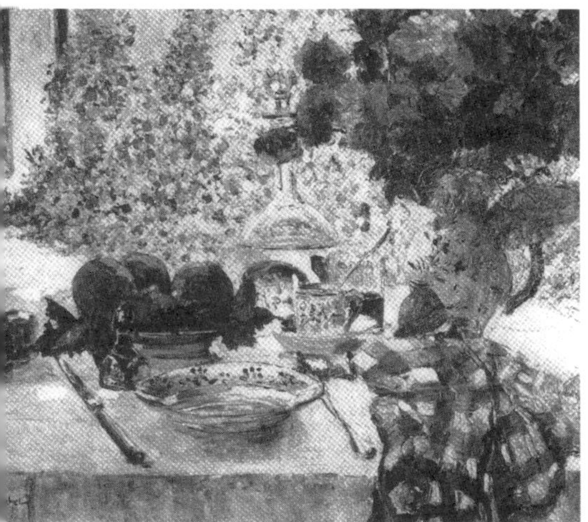

Abel Truchet

Oil on canvas, $25\frac{1}{2} \times 32$ in. (65 × 81 cm.), signed
Private collection

TROUVÉ, Nicolas-Eugène *1808–1888*
b. Paris. Pupil of Bertin and Picot. Painted copies, genre, fruit and flowers. Exhib. Paris Salon 1836–1877 e.g. *Fleurs et fruits*, 1875
LIT *Bénézit*; *Paris Salon* 1875; *Schurr* I, 50; *Thieme*

TRUCHET, Abel *1857–1918*
b. Versailles (Yvelines). Pupil of Académie Julian. Painted landscapes, figures and, occasionally, flowers. Lithographer and engraver. Exhib. *Les coquelicots*, Dijon Salon 1894. *Le déjeuner au jardin* (private coll.)
LIT *Bénézit*; *Dijon Salon* 1894; *Schurr* I, 92; *Thieme*. CL

TRUCHOT, Pierre-Victor
Exhib. *Bouquet de chrysanthèmes*, Dijon Salon 1894
LIT *Dijon Salon* 1894. CL

TRUCHY, Prudence-Marie
Exhib. Paris Salon 1843–1849 e.g. *Panier de fleurs*, wc, 1843, *Vase de fleurs*, after Van Dael, wc, 1846
LIT *Bellier*; *Bénézit*; *Faré* 1962, p. 248; *Paris Salon* 1843; *Thieme*

TSCHARNER de, *see* EGLÉ

TUFFET, François *1809–1854*
b. Mâcon (Saône-et-Loire). Pupil of Thierriat, Lyon BA (CFD 1824). Designed *Flore du dessinateur* (Thomassin, engraver)
LIT *Audin Vial*; *Hardouin-Fugier Grafe*

TULPIN, Mme
Her *Roses blanches* was formerly in the Musée de Tours
LIT *Bénézit*

TURIQUE de, *see* BERR

TURLIN, Henri-Jean
b. Paris. Exhib. Paris Salon from 1870 e.g. *Primevères*, *Chrysanthèmes*, 1875
LIT *Bellier*; *Bénézit*; *Paris Salon* 1875; *Thieme*

TURPIN, Pierre-Jean-François *1775–1840*
b. Vire (Calvados). Self-taught. This well-known botanical artist painted over six thousand watercolours and illustrated numerous botanical works e.g. *Essai d'iconographie... des Végétaux*, Paris (Panckoucke) 1820; Illustrated his own *Flore Visuelle*, Paris, 1834 etc., and collaborated with Pierre-Antoine Poiteau 1834 and after. *Nelumbo nucifera* (Lotus or Lily of the Nile), wc, exhib. *Discovery of Nature*, Eyre & Hobhouse, London, 1983. op. Sèvres 1825. London, Royal Horticultural Society, twenty-five watercolours on vellum. M: Cambridge, Fitzwilliam.
LIT *Bénézit*; *Brunet-Préaud*; Broughton 1983–1984; Alice M. Coats. *The Treasury of Flowers*, London (Phaidon) 1975; *Faré* 1962 p. 247; *Hardouin-Fugier* 1981; *Nissen* I, 2014, 2015, 2016; *Thieme*; *Witt*

TUSSAC, Mlle de
This needy flower painter was granted a state allowance (180 francs) in 1852
LIT Paris Arch. Nat. F21: 288

ULYSSE BERNARD, *see* BONHEUR

UMBRICHT, Honoré-Louis *b.1860*
b. Obernai (Bas-Rhin). Pupil of Bonnat. Painted genre, landscapes, portraits, still-lifes and flowers. Exhib. Paris Salon from 1881
LIT *Bénézit*; *Orsay*; *Schurr* III, 20; *Thieme*

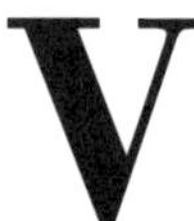

V

VAILLANT, A. J. B. *c.1817–1852*
Designed a botanical plate n.d. for *Voyage au pôle sud*, Paris Muséum d'Histoire Naturelle
LIT Paris Muséum d'Histoire Naturelle, MS 584; *Thieme*

VAILLANT, *see* BAUDRY

VALADON, Maria-Clémentine *alias* Suzanne *1865–1938*
b. Bessines (Haute-Vienne). Earliest listed flower painting *Camélias rouges et blancs*, 1903
LIT P. Petridès, *L'oeuvre complet de Suzanne Valadon*, Paris, (Compagnie française des Arts Graphiques) 1971. *Witt*. AC

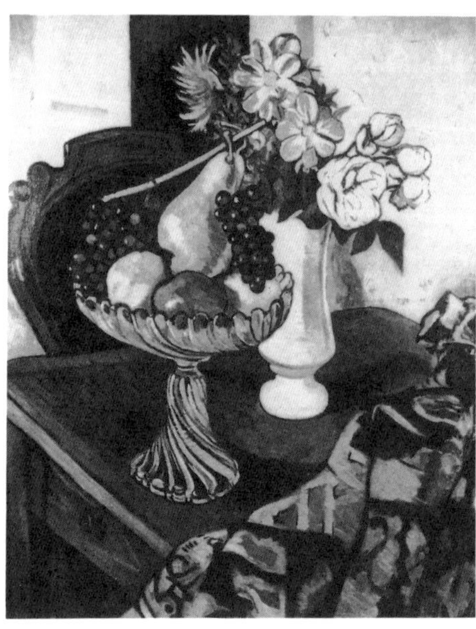

Suzanne Valadon

Oil on canvas, 24 × 19¾ in. (61 × 50 cm.), signed and dated 1918
Courtesy Sotheby's, London

VALANTIN, Paul-Louis *b.1838*
b. Lyon. Pupil of Reignier, Lyon BA (CFD 1858). Exhib. Paris and Lyon from 1861 e.g. *Vase d'oeillets*, Paris Salon 1861; *Groupe de fleurs*, Lyon Salon 1862. His *Vase de roses* was bought by the Lyon Société des Amis-des-Arts in 1864
LIT *Bellier*; *Bénézit*; *Hardouin-Fugier Grafe*; *Lyon Salon* 1862; *Paris Salon* 1861

VALENTIN, Louis
b. 1833. Pupil of Thierriat, Lyon BA (CFD 1850)
LIT *Hardouin-Fugier Grafe*

VALLAYER-COSTER, Anne-Dorothée *1744–1818*
Among the late flower-pieces by this famous painter are *Fleurs*, drawing, Paris Salon 1801–1802, *Roses et raisins*, 1803–1804, cf. Roland-Michel 1884;

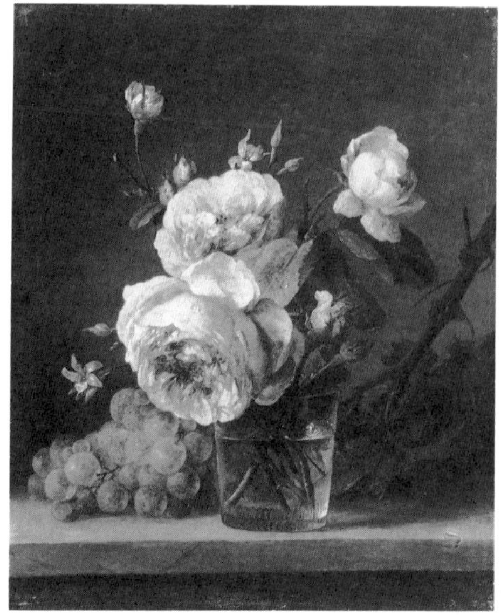

Anne-Dorothée Vallayer-Coster

Oil on canvas, 12½ × 10½ in. (32 × 26.5 cm.), signed and dated 'an 12'
Courtesy Sotheby's, Monaco

Bouquet de fleurs, 1812, ink and wash cf. Roland-Michel 396, *Fleurs dans un vase de porcelaine de Chine*, Paris Salon 1817, *Table chargée d'un grand vase*, Paris Salon 1817, cf. Roland-Michel 228 (Paris, Mobilier National). Earlier works, *Roses dans un verre et Raisin* (Salon "An XII, N. 480.") Sotheby's, Monaco, 29 Mar. 1986, lot 365. M: Cambridge, Fitzwilliam; Laval, Nancy, Narbonne, Reims, Versailles etc.
LIT *Bénézit*; *Bellier*; Broughton 1983–1984; *Faré* 1962; *Faré* 1976; *Mitchell*; M. Roland-Michel, *Anne-Vallayer Coster*, Paris 1970; *Thieme*; *Witt*

VALLÉE, Pauline
Exhib. *Pivoines roses et aubépines*, Dijon Salon 1890
LIT *Dijon Salon* 1890. CL

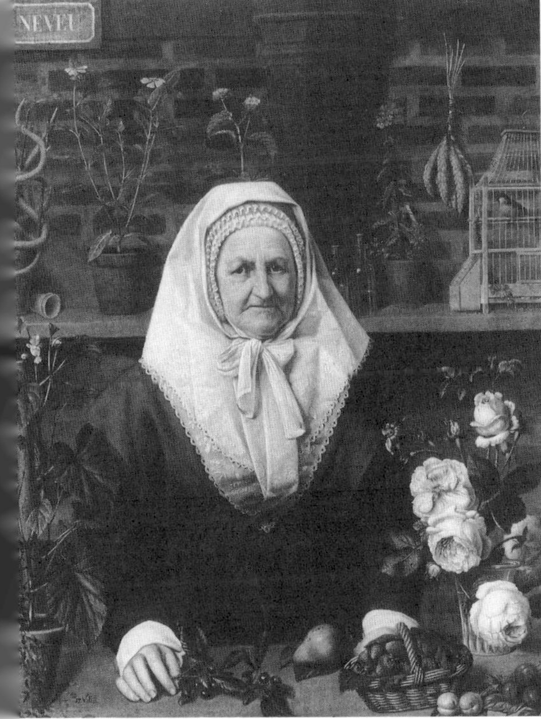

Jean-Pierre Vallet

Oil on canvas, 39½ × 24 in. (100 × 61 cm.), signed
Tours, Musée des Beaux-Arts

VALLERAY, *see* CARTERON

VALLET, Jean-Pierre *1809–1886*
Pupil of Ingres. His *Madame Neveu, marchande de fleurs et de fruits* is in the Musée de Tours
LIT *Thieme*; Tours Musée doc.

VALLET, *see* MARVAL

VALLY, Jules *b.1820*
b. Bourg-en-Bresse (Ain). Pupil of Thierriat, Lyon BA (CFD 1838)
LIT *Hardouin-Fugier Grafe*

VALMON, Léonie
b. Paris. Pupil of T. Chauvel. This still-life painter and engraver produced some flower-pieces e.g. *Roses dans un vase* Drouot, Paris, 19 Jan. 1942. Exhibited Paris Salon from 1882
LIT *Bellier*; *Bénézit*; *Béraldi*; *Thieme*

VALNAUD, Léonie
b. Paris. Pupil of Trébuchet. This flower painter exhibited in the Paris Salon from 1879
LIT *Bénézit*

VALON, Mme B. de
One signed canvas in the Musée Ernest Rupin, Brive, dated 1885. PM

VALOTTE, Octavie
Exhib. Dijon Salon *Fleurs des champs*, *Bourriche de pensées*, 1881, *Le bouquet de la cuisine*, 1883, *Toutes mes pensées à mon ami*, 1885, *Chrysanthèmes*, 1887
LIT *Dijon Salon* 1881, 1883, 1885, 1887. CL

VALOUIS, Balthazar
Pupil of Berjon, Lyon BA (CFD 1811)
LIT *Hardouin-Fugier Grafe*

VALTAT, Louis *1869–1952*
b. Dieppe (Seine-Maritime). Pupil of Paris BA (under Gustave Moreau). Exhib. Paris Indép. from 1894. Painted figures, portraits, landscapes, still-lifes and flowers, most of the latter being either undated or later works except *Les pensées*, 1899
LIT *Bénézit*; Genève, *Louis Valtat*, Petit Palais, 1969 J. Valtat, *Louis Valtat, Catalogue de l'Oeuvre Peint*, Neuchâtel, 1977; *Thieme*; *Witt*

VALTON, Edmond Eugène *1836–1910*
Pupil of F. Fossey and T. Couture. Exhib. Paris Indép. *Fleurs* 1892; *Panier de fleurs*, 1894
LIT *Paris Indép.* 1892, 1894; *Thieme*

VAN ASSCHE, Marie
b. Paris. Exhib. *Fleurs* wc Paris Noir et Blanc Salon 1888; *Pivoines et glycines*, Strasbourg Salon 1891
LIT *Paris Noir et Blanc Salon* 1888; *Strasbourg Salon* 1891

VAN COPPENOLLE, Jacques *d.1915*
b. Montigny-sur-Loing (Seine-et-Marne). Painted landscapes, animals and flowers. *Jonquilles et giroflées*, Versailles sale, 8 Mar. 1981. Four works recently in Geneva sale 1–2 June 1988
LIT *Bénézit*; *Orsay*; *Schurr* II, 124; *Thieme*

VAN DER SYP, Armand
Pupil of Lefebvre. Exhib. flowers Lyon Salon 1881
LIT *Lyon Salon* 1881

VAN DOREN, Benoit-Marc *b.1802*
Pupil of Lyon BA (1820–1822). Exhib. *Vase de fleurs*, Lyon Salon 1845, *Fleurs*, Lyon Salon 1847, Paris Salon 1846
LIT *Audin Vial*; *Bénézit*; *Hardouin-Fugier Grafe*

VAN DOREN, Charles-François-Clément *1830–1893*
b. Lyon. Son of Benoit-Marc (above) and pupil of Thierriat, Lyon BA (CFD 1850). Exhib. Lyon Salon 1851–1892
LIT *Audin Vial*; *Hardouin-Fugier Grafe*; *Thieme*

VAN DOREN, François-Fréderic *b.1806*
b. Lyon. Pupil of Thierriat, Lyon BA (CFD 1831). Textile designer, Saint-Etienne
LIT *Audin Vial*; *Hardouin-Fugier Grafe*

VAN DOREN, Joannès *b.1877*
Pupil of Castex-Dégrange Lyon BA (CFD 1897)
LIT *Hardouin-Fugier Grafe*

VAN LARHOVEN
Exhib. *Roses*, *Vases de roses*, Dijon Salon 1890
LIT *Dijon Salon* 1890. CL

VAN MARCKE, Julie-Palmyre, *née* Robert *1801–1875*
Wife of J. B. alias Jules van Marcke (1798–1849). Active at Sèvres. Daughter of J. F. Robert, op. Sèvres. Painted flowers. e.g. *Vase de fleurs*, 1843 (private coll.)
LIT *Bénézit*

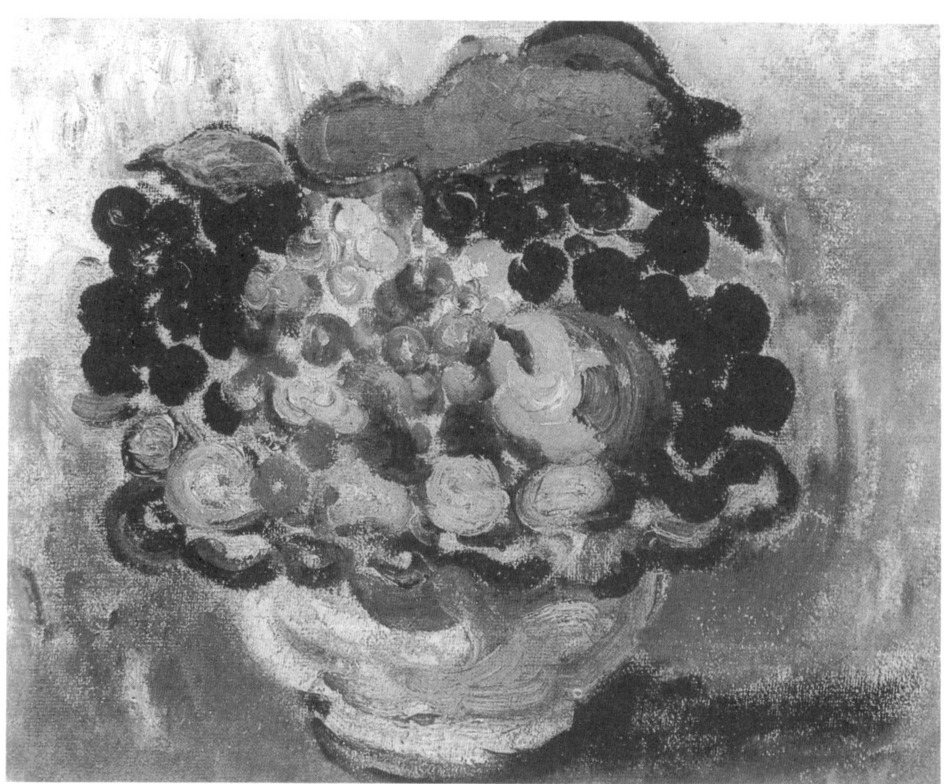

Louis Valtat

Oil on canvas, 14⅞ × 18⅛ in. (38 × 46 cm.), signed with initials *c.*1898
Courtesy Sotheby's, London

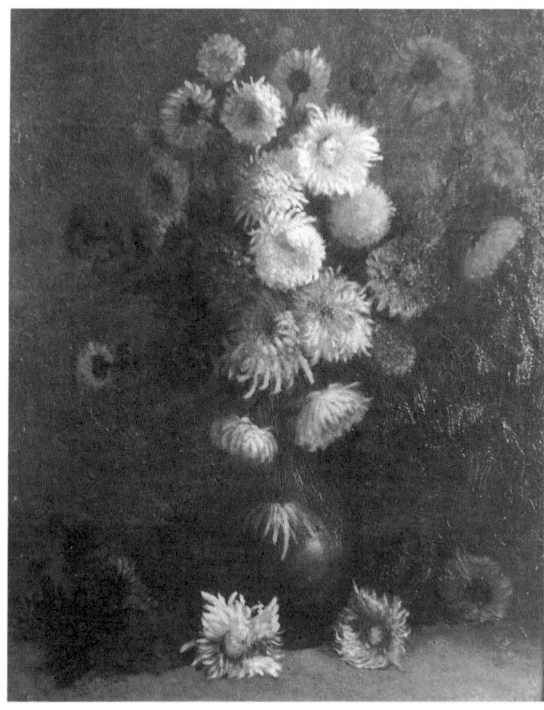

Mme B. de Valon

Oil on canvas, 28 × 23¼ in. (71 × 59 cm.), signed
Brive, Musée Ernest Rupin

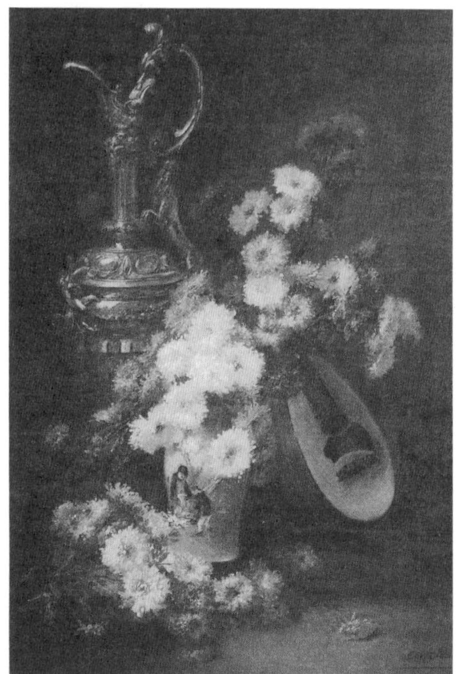

Jacques van Coppenolle

Oil on canvas, 45¾ × 32 in. (116 × 81 cm.), signed
Private collection

VAN PARYS, Marie-Fernande
b. Lille (Nord). Pupil of Dasq, E. Boutry, P. de Winter. Exhib. *Amaryllis*, wc, Paris Salon 1898
LIT *Paris Salon* 1898

VAN TIEGHEM, Philippe ***1839–1914***
Illustrated his own *Recherches sur la structure du pistil*, Paris (Imprimerie Nationale) 1871
LIT *Nissen* I, 1965

VAQUEZ, Emile-Modeste-Nicolas ***1841–1900***
b. Paris. Exhib. Paris Salon from 1873 e.g. *Iris, Campanules, capucines*, gouache, 1876, *Camélias, jonquilles*, 1878, *Camélias*, 1879, *Roses, lys et anémones*, 1880, *Dahlias et glaïeuls*, 1881, *Chrysanthèmes*, 1882
LIT *Bellier*; *Bénézit*; *Thieme*

VARENNE, Dorothée Santoire de ***b. c.1804***
Her father was the painter Charles Santoire de Varenne. According to Gabet's Yearbook, she was born *c.*1804 and studied under Redouté, probably at the Paris Muséum d'Histoire Naturelle. Exhib. miniatures Paris Salon 1824–1826 and at Lebrun's in 1827. Gave tuition in her Paris studio
LIT *Hardouin-Fugier* 1981

VASSEL, Antoine-Henri
b. 1826. Pupil of Thierriat. Lyon BA (CFD 1843)
LIT *Hardouin-Fugier Grafe*

VASSELON, Alice
b. Paris. Pupil of M. Vasselon. Exhib. Paris and Lyon *c.*1870–1881. Paris Salon *Fleurs dans un vase*, 1870, *Fleurs d'automne*, 1876, *Couronne à la Vierge*, 1877, *Couronne de fleurs*, 1880; Lyon Salon *Fleurs d'automne*, 1881
LIT *Bellier*; *Lyon Salon* 1881; *Thieme*

VASSELON, Marius
b. Saint-Etienne (Loire). Pupil of Chabal-Dussurgey and Bonnat. Exhib. Paris and Lyon 1863–1880 e.g. *Coupe de fleurs*, Paris Salon 1863; *Matinée de printemps*, 1864; *Fleurs*, Lyon Salon 1865. His *Coupe de fleurs* was won by Paul Saint-Jean at the 1864 Lyon Société des Amis-des-Arts raffle
LIT *Bellier*; *Bénézit*; *Hardouin-Fugier Bringuier*; *Hardouin-Fugier Grafe*; *Thieme*

VASSELON, *see* DURY

VAUCHELET, Antoine ***1763–1819***
Painted flowers on velvet e.g. *Corbeille de fleurs et de fruits*, Paris Salon 1817
LIT *Bellier*; *Thieme*

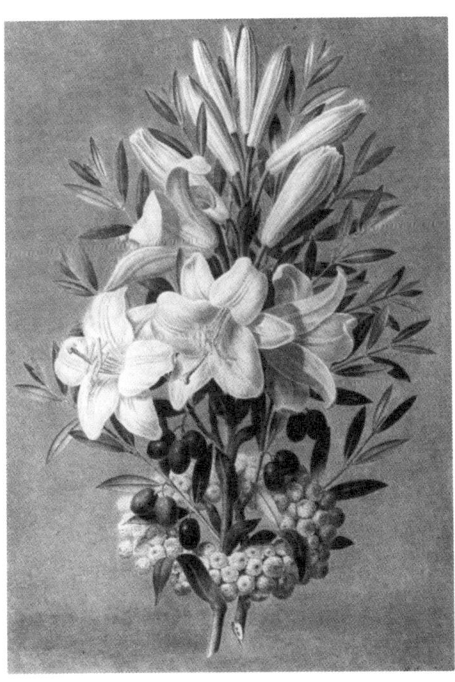

Véran or Node-Véran

Watercolour and gouache, 19 × 13½ in. (48.5 × 34cm.), signed and inscribed 'Node-Veran, peintre de fleurs du jardin du Roi à Montpellier'
Courtesy Maître Paul Renaud, Paris

VAUCHELET, Théophile-Auguste ***1802–1873***
b. Passy (Paris XVI°). Pupil of Abel de Pujol, Hersent and Antoine Vollon. This decorator painted flowers in the Paris Mairie du VII° arrondissement
LIT *Bellier*; *Thieme*

VAUTHIER, Antoine-Charles ***1790–1850***
Designed plates e.g. for R. Gaudichaud-Beaupré, *Voyage autour du monde*, Paris, 1844 and A. Richard *Tentamen Florae...Abyssinicae*, Paris (Bertrand) 1847, and D. Gay *Historia...de Chile*, Paris 1845–1853
LIT *Nissen* I, 555, 766, 690, 695, 1633, 1712–4, 2235; *Thieme*

VAUTIER, Louise
b. Caen (Calvados). Pupil of de Jonghe. Exhib. *Premières roses*, Paris Salon 1875
LIT *Paris Salon* 1875

VAYSON, Paul ***1842–1911***
b. Gordes (Tarn). Pupil of Gleyre and J. Laurens. Painted landscapes, animals (mostly sheep) and flowers. Exhib. Paris Salon 1865–1882 e.g. *Fleurs* 1867, *Pensées*, 1873. Paul Vayson was director of the École des Beaux-Arts d'Avignon. Musée de Villeneuve-les-Avignon, *Bourriche de pensées*
LIT *Bellier*; *Orsay*; *Paris Salon* 1867, 1873; *Schurr* II, 85; *Thieme*

VELAY, Amédée
Pupil of Jeannot, Lalanne and V. Lecler. Exhib. *Fleurs et fruits*, Lyon Salon 1879
LIT *Lyon Salon* 1879

VENO, Lor
Pupil of Loubet and Barriot. Exhib. flowers Lyon Salon from *c.*1895
LIT *Hardouin-Fugier Grafe*

VENOT, *see* AUTEROCHE d'

VÉRAN or NODE-VÉRAN
Designed plates for Benjamin Delessert *Icones selectae plantarum*, Paris 1820
LIT *Nissen* I, 461; *Sitwell*; *Thieme*

VERD, Pierre-Marie *b.1827*
Pupil of Thierriat, Lyon BA (CFD 1844)
LIT *Hardouin-Fugier*

VERDIER, Denis *b.1820*
b. Lyon. Pupil of Thierriat, Lyon BA (CFD 1838)
LIT *Hardouin-Fugier Grafe*

VERNAY, Armand *1868–1930*
Exhib. *Fleurs*, Dijon Salon 1894
LIT *Dijon Salon* 1894. CL

VERNAY, François Miel *alias 1821–1896*
Pupil of Thierriat, Lyon BA (CFD 1840). Textile designer. Exhib. Lyon Salon from 1855, Paris Salon 1868, 1876, 1880. Vernay's boldly painted flowers were admired by Renoir. M: Bagnols-sur-Cèze, *Bouquet de Roses*, 1870; Lyon; Paris, Louvre etc.
LIT *Hardouin-Fugier Grafe* (ill.); *Hardouin-Fugier Grafe* 1979 (ill.); *Hardouin-Fugier Grafe* 1982 (ill.). Saint Tropez, *Fleurs de Fantin-Latour à Marquet*, Musée de l'Annonciade, 1982

VERNET, Jean-Antoine *b.1824*
b. Lyon. Pupil of Thierriat, Lyon BA (CFD 1841)
LIT *Hardouin-Fugier Grafe*

VERNON, Emile
b. Blois (Loir-et-Cher). Pupil of Bouge and Truphème. Exhib. *Oeillets de Nice*, wc, Paris Salon 1898
LIT *Paris Salon 1898*

VERON, Alexandre-Paul-Joseph, *alias* Veron-Bellecourt *b.1773*
b. Paris. Pupil of David and Van Spaendonck. Exhib. Paris Salon 1801–1838, e.g. *Fleurs*, wc, 1817, *Roses et oeillets*, 1831, *Offrande à Marie*, 1837, *Corbeille de fleurs au bord d'un ruisseau* after Delille's lines "Offert par l'amitié, hasardé par l'amour" 1838
LIT *Bellier*; *Bénézit*; *Faré* 1962, p. 241; *Paris Salon* 1817, 1831, 1837, 1838; *Thieme*

VERRIÈRE
Designed plates for the 1900 *Album Vilmorin*
LIT *Album Vilmorin*

VESVRES, Henriette de
One large and excellent pair of watercolours on vellum is known by this artist, dated 1837 and 1840. PM

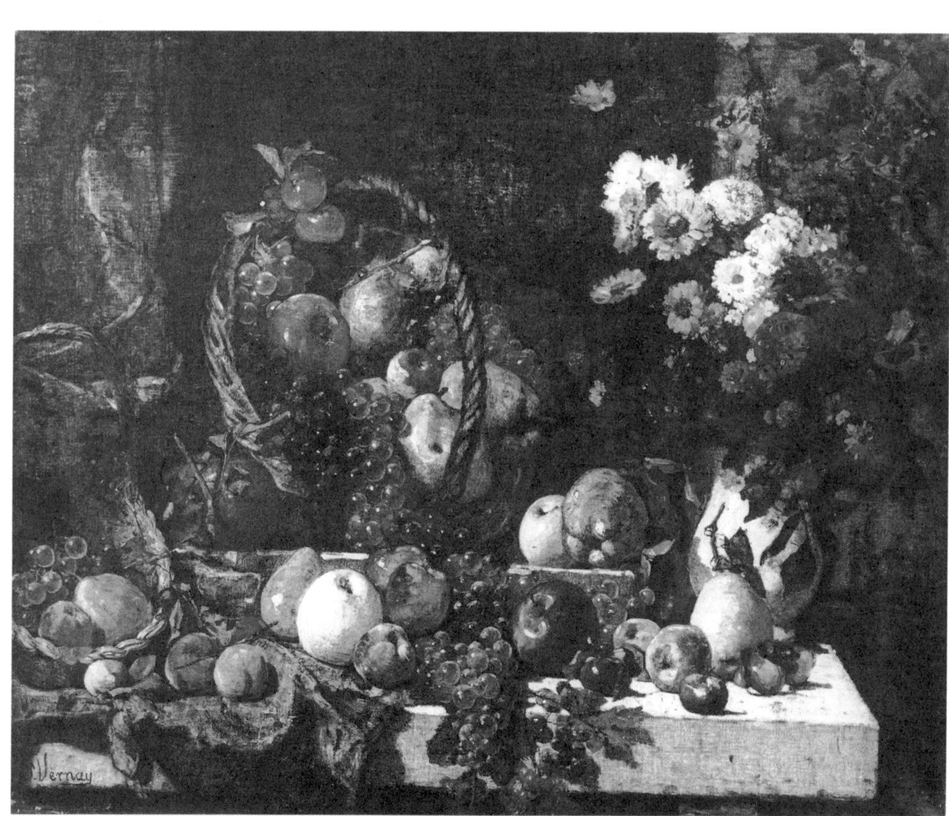

François Miel, alias Vernay

Oil on canvas, 29 × 36¼ in. (74 × 92 cm.), signed
Paris, Musée du Louvre

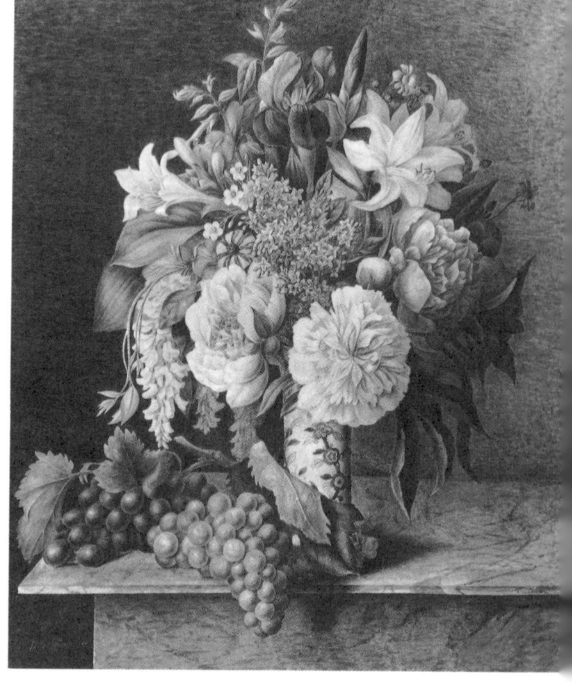

Henriette de Vesvres

Watercolour on vellum, 24½ × 20 in. (62 × 51 cm.), signed and dated 1837
Private collection, Courtesy Jeremy Ltd., London

VETARD, François
Pupil of Thierriat, Lyon BA (CFD 1824)
LIT *Hardouin-Fugier Grafe*

VETAULT, *see* CORNÉE

VETU, Adolphe
Pupil of Thierriat, Lyon BA (CFD 1830)
LIT *Hardouin-Fugier Grafe*

VETU, Alphonse-Louis-Guillaume *b.1811*
b. Lyon. Pupil of Thierriat, Lyon BA (CFD 1828)
LIT *Hardouin-Fugier Grafe*

Benoit-Josephus Veyrat

Oil on canvas, 14½ × 13¼ in. (37 × 34 cm.), signed
Private collection (photo: Musée des Beaux-Arts, Lyon)

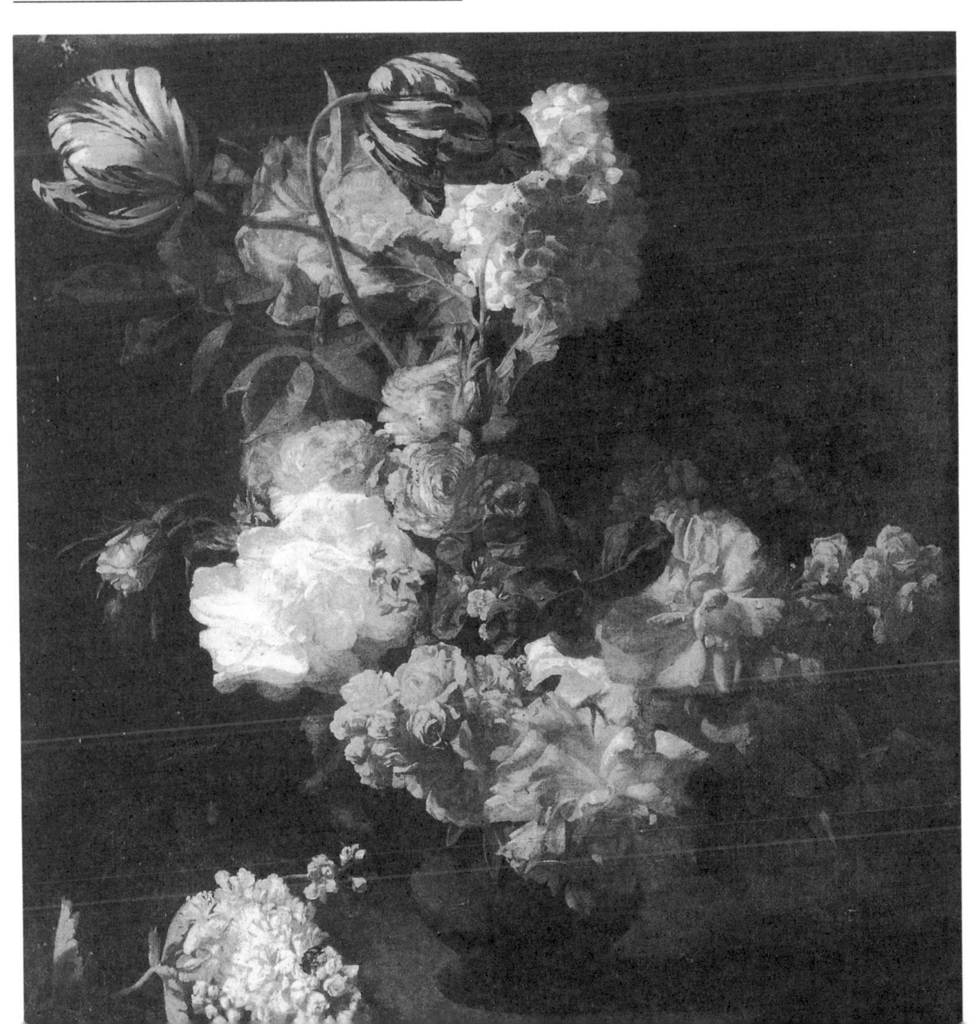

VEYRAT, Benoit-Josephus *d.1887 or 1888*
Pupil of Simon Saint-Jean. fl. Lyon
LIT C. Servan in *Hardouin-Fugier Grafe* 1982 (ill.)

VEYRON
Exhib. *Offrande à la Vierge*, Lyon Salon 1827
LIT *Hardouin-Fugier Grafe*

VEZU, *see* VOISIN

VIAL, André *b.1865*
Pupil of Castex-Dégrange, Lyon BA (CFD 1882)
LIT *Hardouin-Fugier Grafe*

VIAL, Louis *b.1867*
Pupil of Castex-Dégrange, Lyon BA (CFD 1885)
LIT *Hardouin-Fugier Grafe*

VIANNE
Designed plates for Gay, *Historia...de Chile*, Paris 1845–1853. One plate by Vianne lithographed by Lemercier is in Paris BMAD (Maciet coll.)
LIT *Nissen* I, 695; *Paris BMAD*

VIARD, Claude-Victor *b.1820*
Pupil of Thierriat, Lyon BA (CFD 1840)
LIT *Hardouin-Fugier Grafe*

VIARD, Georges
Exhib. *Fleurs dans un vase*, Lyon Salon 1867. A Viard, Georges, exhib. Paris Salon 1831–1848; A Viard exhibited Paris Salon 1863–1869: these exhibitors may be related or may even be the same artist
LIT *Lyon Salon* 1867; *Thieme*

VIARGUES, Marie
b. Paris. Exhib. *Tulipes*, *Bouquet de lilas*, Paris Indép. 1890
LIT *Paris Indép.* 1890

VIBERT, Jean-Georges *1840–1902*
Pupil of Barriat and Picot. Exhib. Paris Aquar. *Fleurs d'automne*, 1884, *Fleurs des champs*, 1891
LIT *Paris Aquar.* 1884, 1891; *Schurr* II, 16; *Thieme*

VIDAL, Jacques-Joseph *b.1795*
b. Marseille. Pupil of Guérin and Paris BA (1814). Painted landscapes, portraits and, occasionally, flowers e.g. *Fruits et fleurs*, Paris Salon 1819
LIT *Bellier*

VIDAL, Louis *c.1754–after 1805*
b. Marseille. In England 1790–1792. Exhib. London RA. Painted still-lifes and flowers. Works in Cambridge, Fitzwilliam Museum (Broughton coll.), and Musée de Lille, *Fleurs, fruits, gibier*, 1805
LIT *Bénézit*; *Faré* 1962, p. 328; *Mitchell*; *Thieme*; *Witt*

VIDAL-BOISSON, Élise
Exhib. Dijon Salon *Bouquet de fleurs*, 1890, *Bouquet d'iris*, wc 1894
LIT *Dijon Salon* 1890, 1894

VIDECOQ, Lucie-Marie
b. Paris. Pupil of Courtois. Painted still-lifes, landscapes and, occasionally, flowers. Exhib. Paris Salon 1878 and 1880
LIT *Bellier*; *Bénézit*

VIEN, Joseph-Marie ***1716–1809***
Pupil of Vincent. *Fleurs dans un verre*, 1806 (private coll., USA). M: J. B. Speed Art Museum, Louisville, Kentucky
LIT *Faré* 1976, p. 213; *Thieme*

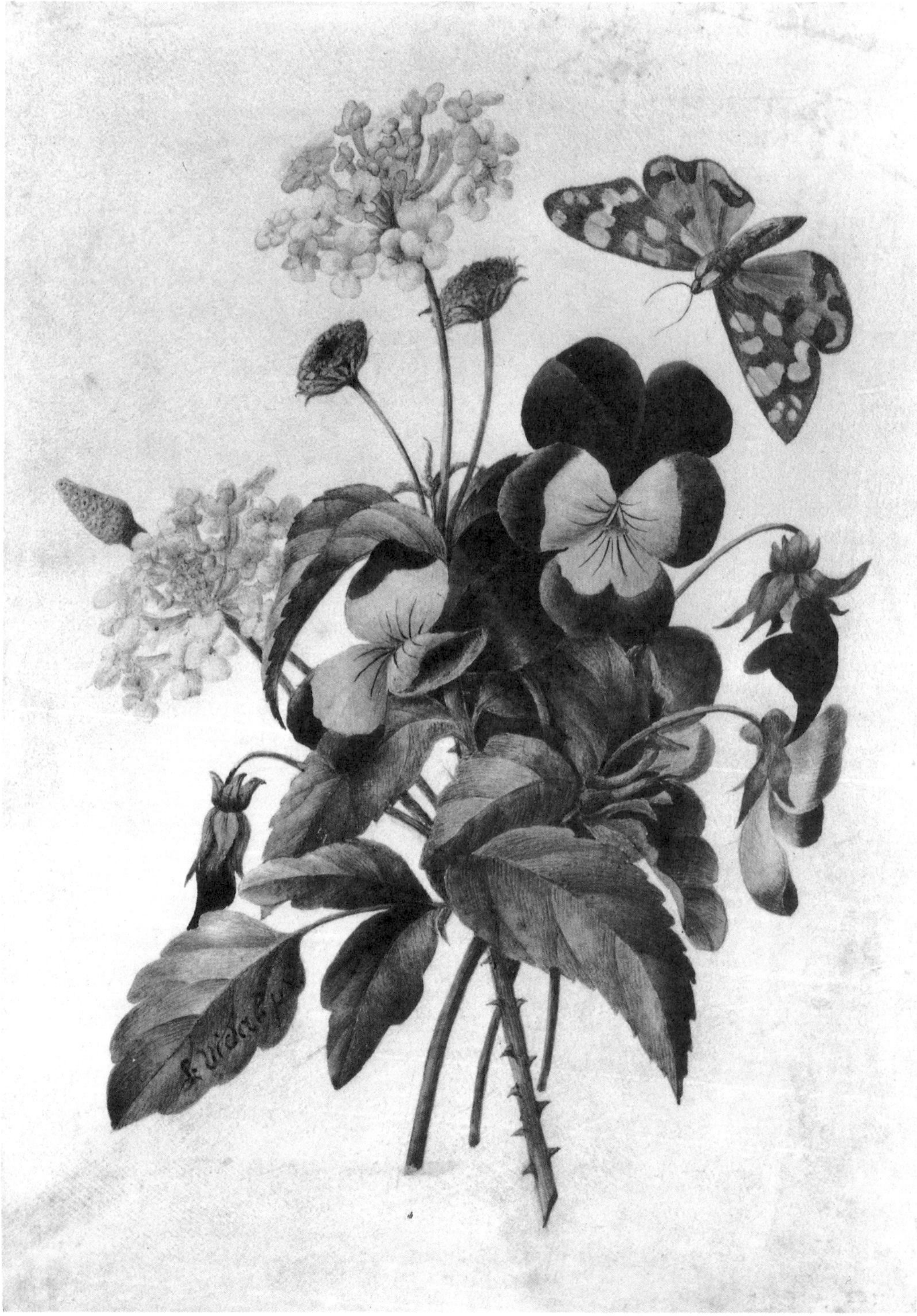

Louis Vidal

Watercolour on vellum, 7 × 5¼ in. (17.5 × 13 cm.), signed
Private collection

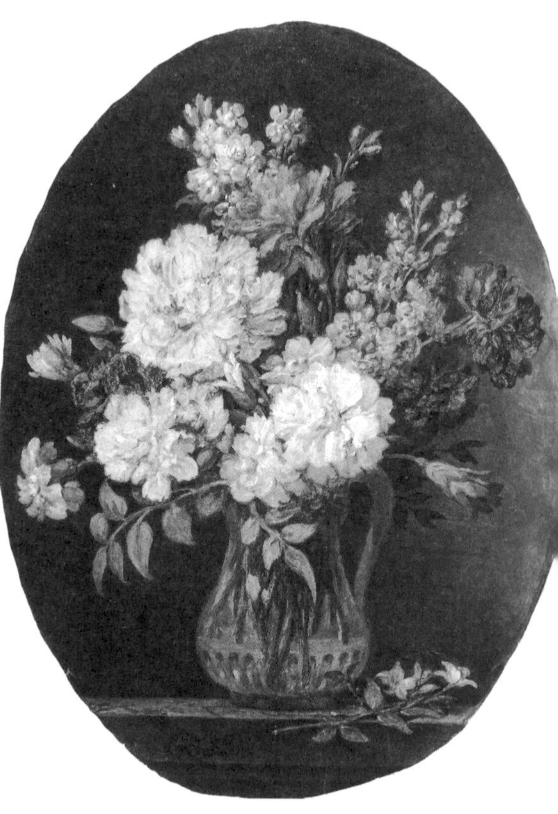

Joseph-Marie Vien

Oil on panel, oval, 16¼ × 12½ in. (41.5 × 31.5 cm.), signed and dated 1806; inscribed 'à la 91 Année'
Louisville, Kentucky, J.B. Speed Art Museum

Jenny Villebesseyx

Oil on canvas, 45½ × 31½ in. (115.5 × 80 cm.), signed
Courtesy Sotheby's, London

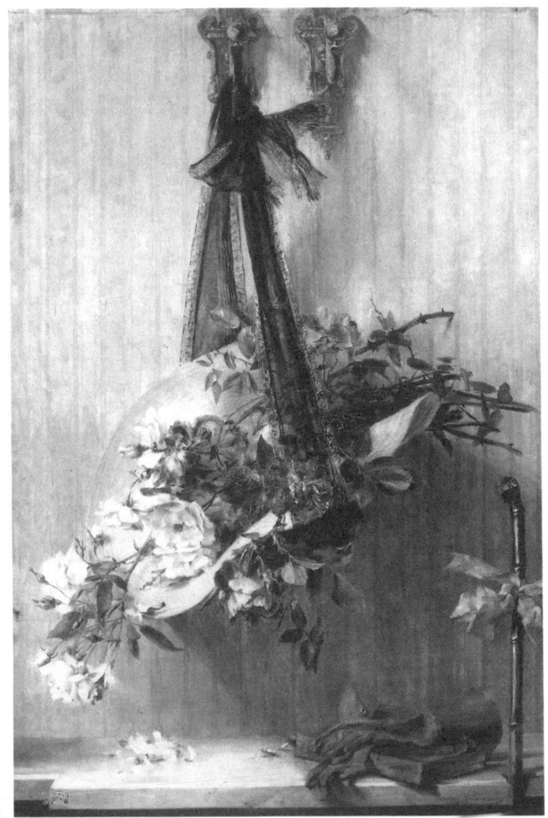

VIGESSY
Pupil of S. Saint-Jean. Exhib. Lyon Salon 1843–1845
LIT *Hardouin-Fugier Grafe*

VIGNAUD, Marie-Antoinette, *née* Monpeur *1825–1869*
b. Paris. Painted flowers and fruit
LIT *Bellier*; *Bénézit*

VIGNERON, Mira *1817–1884*
Exhib. *Touffe de marguerites*, pastel, Lyon Salon 1857
LIT *Lyon Salon* 1857; *Schurr* III, 68; *Thieme*

VIGNEUX, A.
Designed plates for his own *Flore pittoresque des environs de Paris*, 1812. Exhib. Paris Salon 1799–1814
LIT *Nissen* I. 2063: *Thieme*

VIGNOT, *see* HUMBERT

Elise Bonamy de Villermeuil

Watercolour, 17¼ × 10¾ in. (44 × 27.5 cm.), signed and dated 1861
Troyes, Musée des Beaux-Arts

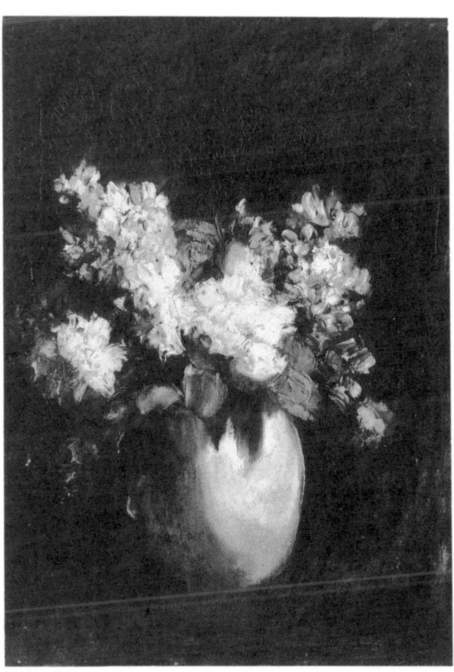

Victor Vincelet

Oil on canvas, 21½ × 15½ in. (54.5 × 34.3 cm.)
Glasgow, Glasgow Art Gallery and Museum

VIGUIER, Mme *née* Laurens
Exhib. *Couronne de liserons*, wc, Lyon Salon 1862
LIT *Lyon Salon* 1862

VILLAIN, Eugène *b.1821*
b. Paris. Pupil of Cogniet and Charlet. Painted still-lifes and, occasionally, flowers. Exhib. Paris Salon 1844–1882
LIT Paris Arch. Nat. F21: 2199; *Schurr* III, 100; *Thieme*

VILLAIN, G.
Exhib. Paris SNBA e.g. *Chrysanthèmes*, *Hortensias blancs*, 1898, *Géraniums*, *Roses blanches*, wc, 1899
LIT *Paris SNBA* 1898, 1899

VILLARD, Damien *b.1835*
Pupil of Reignier, Lyon BA (CFD 1854)
LIT *Hardouin-Fugier Grafe*

VILLARD, François *b.1806*
Pupil of Berjon, Lyon BA (CFD 1820)
LIT *Hardouin-Fugier Grafe*

VILLARD, Gabriel *b.1835*
Pupil of Thierriat, Lyon BA (CFD 1853) and Chatigny. Painted genre, figures, portraits and, occasionally, flowers, e.g. *Fleurs*, Lyon Salon 1878
LIT *Lyon Salon* 1878

VILLARD, Jean
Pupil of Lyon BA. Exhib. Lyon Salon 1879
LIT *Audin-Vial*

VILLEBESSEYX, Jenny, *née* Roche *b.1854*
b. Lyon. Pupil of P. Rousseau, A. Millet, Gallois and Colin. Exhib. *Iris et pivoines*, Strasbourg Salon 1884 (650 francs); *Au temps des roses*, *Dernière fleurs*, Paris Salon 1890; *Au temps des roses* (1,500 francs) *Tulipes* (300 francs), Strasbourg Salon 1891; Paris Salon *Fontaine de*

cuivre et lilas, 1892 *Fin de saison*, 1893, *Roses et pensées*, 1894, *Coquelicots doubles*, 1898; *Retour du Parc*, exhib. Avignon 1903, Versailles 1909, sale Sotheby's, London, 6 Oct. 1982, lot 140. M: Compiègne, *Coquelicots*, Château-Thierry, *Dernières fleurs*
LIT *Bénézit*; *Hardouin-Fugier Grafe*; *Paris Salon* 1890, 1892, (ill.), 1893 (ill.), 1894 (ill.); *Strasbourg Salon* 1884, 1891; *Thieme*; *Witt*

VILLENEUVE, Laure-Jeanne de
b. Paris. Exhib. *Fleurs*, wc, Paris Salon 1895
LIT *Paris Salon* 1895

VILLENEUVE, Marie-Thérèse-Félicie
Exhib. *Chrysanthèmes* (100 francs) Poitiers Salon 1887
LIT *Poitiers Salon* 1887. BG

VILLERMEUIL, Elisa BONAMY de
Musée de Troyes, *Fleur*, 1861, wc (gift from the artist 1862)
LIT *Bénézit*

VILLOTEAU
Exhib. *Roses trémières*, Paris Salon 1880
LIT *Bellier*

VILMORIN, Charles-Philippe-Henry de *1843–1899*
VILMORIN, Maurice de *1849–1918*
VILMORIN, Pierre-Louis-François Levêque de *1816–1860*
The well-known seed merchants and nurserymen published beautifully illustrated albums and catalogues. Madame Louis de Vilmorin drew flowers and plants, e.g. *Les fleurs de pleine terre*, Paris (Vilmorin et Andrieux) 1863
LIT *Nissen* I, 2065

VINÇARD, Charles
Exhib. *Fleurs*, wc, Paris Indép. 1884.
LIT *Paris Indép.* 1884

VINCELET, Victor *1840–1871*
b. Thiers (Puy-de-Dôme). Pupil of Lhullier. Exhib. Paris Salon *Bourriche de giroflées*, 1869, *Pieds de jacinthes*, 1870; Lyon Salon *Fleurs et coupe*, 1870. *Fleurs dans un vase*, *Beurdeley sale*, Paris, 6 May 1920. M: Clermont-Ferrand, Saint-Etienne, Troyes (*Fleurs dans une jardinière*), Glasgow.
LIT *Bellier*; *Bénézit*; *Lyon Salon* 1870; *Orsay*; *Thieme*; G. Viatte, *Collection George et Adèle Besson*, 1964–5; *Witt*

VINCENDON, Berthe
Exhib. *Chrysanthèmes*, Dijon Salon 1890; *Bourriche de chrysanthèmes*, Strasbourg Salon 1891; *Roses trémières* (200 francs), Dijon Salon 1894
LIT *Dijon Salon* 1890, 1894; *Strasbourg Salon* 1891

VINCENS, Daniel *1820–1888*
b. Aubenas (Ardèche). Draughtsman and lithographer of landscapes. A collection of twenty-eight drawings at Musée du Puy
LIT Museum communication. PM

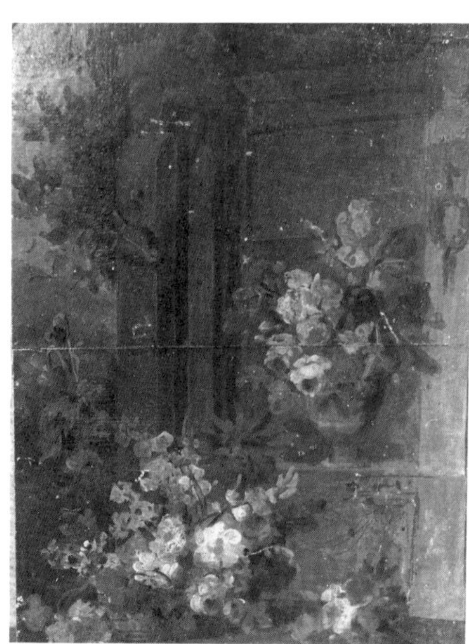

Daniel Vincens

Oil on paper laid down on panel, $10\frac{1}{4} \times 8$ in. (26 × 20 cm.), Mongrammed 'V.D.' on verso
Le Puy-en-Velay, Musée Crozatier

VINCENT, Alexandre-Gabriel *b.1821*
b. Lyon. Pupil of Thierriat, Lyon BA (CFD 1837). op. Lyon, textile designer
LIT *Hardouin-Fugier Grafe*

VINCENT, Eugène
b. Lyon. Exhib. *Bouquet de roses* Saint-Etienne Salon 1882
LIT *Hardouin-Fugier Bringuier*; *Saint-Etienne Salon* 1882

VINCENT, Henriette-Antoinette, *née* Rideau du Sal *1786–1830*
b. Brest (Finistère). Pupil of Van Spaendonck and Redouté. Exhib. flowers

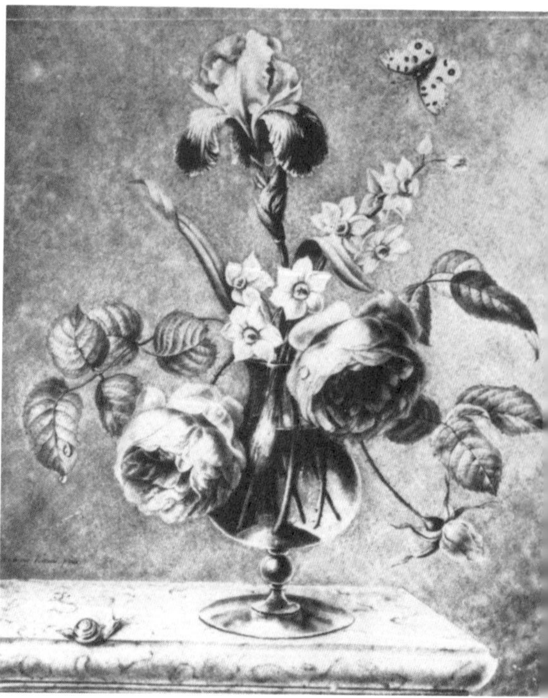

Henriette-Antoinette Vincent

Watercolour and gouache, $13\frac{1}{4} \times 11\frac{1}{4}$ in. (34 × 28.5 cm.), signed
Private collection

in wc, Paris Salon 1814, 1819, 1822, 1824. Co-designed many lithographed sets of flower plates. M: Paris (Marmottan, Muséum d'Histoire Naturelle)
LIT *Bénézit*; *Hardouin-Fugier* 1981; *Laissus*; *Thieme*; *Witt*

VINCENT, Jean ***b.1836***
b. Lyon. Pupil of Reignier, Lyon BA (CFD 1854)
LIT *Hardouin-Fugier Grafe*

VINCENT, Jean-Hughes ***b.1842***
b. Saint-Etienne (Loire). Pupil of Reignier, Lyon BA (CFD 1863)
LIT *Hardouin-Fugier Grafe*

VINCENT, Joannès ***b.1865***
Pupil of Castex-Dégrange, Lyon BA (CFD 1886)
LIT *Hardouin-Fugier Grafe*

VINCENT, Lucie
Exhib. *Fleurs*, Dijon Salon 1881
LIT *Dijon Salon* 1881. CL

VINCENT, *see* PHALIPON

VIOLA, Ferdinand ***1853–1911***
b. Marseille. Pupil of Paris BA. Exhib. Paris Salon 1865–1882. Friend of Monticelli. Painted genre, still-lifes and flowers. Father of R. Viola. Musée de Digne, *Reines-marguerites*
LIT *Bellier*; *Bénézit*; *Orsay*; *Schurr* IV, 76; *Thieme*

VIOLA, Raoul
b. Marseille. Pupil of G. Boulanger and J. Lefebvre. This opera singer painted still-lifes and flowers. Exhib. Paris Salon from 1880 e.g. *Bourriche de pensées*, 1881, *Bourriche de fleurs*, 1882
LIT *Bellier*; *Bénézit*

VIOLAINE-BRINQUANT
b. Soissons (Aisne). Pupil of J. Lefebvre. Exhib. *Gerbe de pavots et de coquelicots*, pastel, Paris Salon 1895
LIT *Paris Salon* 1895

VIOLET, Paul
b. Paris. Pupil of Richomme. Exhib. *Iris*, gouache, Paris Salon 1880
LIT *Paris Salon* 1880

VIOLET, Pierre-Auguste ***b.1856***
b. Lyon. Pupil of Reignier, Lyon BA (CFD 1875)
LIT *Hardouin-Fugier Grafe*

VIRET, Frédéric
Exhib. *Fleurs*, Paris Salon 1850
LIT *Bellier*; *Bénézit*

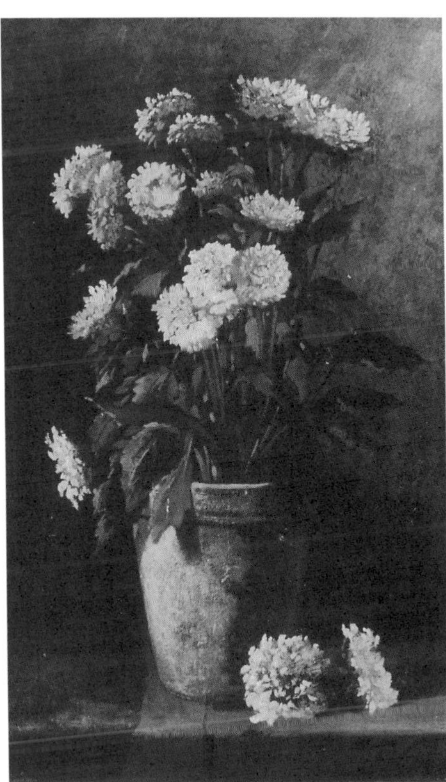

Ferdinand Viola

Oil on canvas, 26 × 15¾ in. (66 × 40 cm.), signed
Digne, Musée Municipal

VISCONTI, Alphonse
b. Milan (Italy). Naturalized French. Exhib. Paris Salon. Painted still-lifes and flowers; decorator
LIT *Bénézit*; *Orsay*; *Thieme*

VISIEN, Charles-Antoine
b. Troyes (Aube). Pupil of L. Cogniet and O. Mathieu. Painted still-lifes and, occasionally, flowers. Exhib. Paris Salon 1867–1868
LIT *Bellier*; *Bénézit*

VITASSE, Jean-Louis-Nicolas
Exhib. Paris Salon 1792–1814, 1831–5. Designed flower plates lithographed by Derebergue, Paris (Letouzé) n.d.
LIT *Bellier*; Paris Bibl. Nat. Est. Jd 59b

VITEAU, *see* CASTAGNARY

VIVIER, *see* BARDOUX

VLAMINCK, Maurice de ***1876–1958***
b. Paris. Listed flowers are later works (from *c.*1910) but the artist may have painted earlier ones
LIT *Bénézit*; A. Mantaigne, *Maurice Vlaminck*, Paris (Crès) 1929. AC

VOECKER
Exhib. *Guirlande de fleurs*, Strasbourg Salon 1853, *Pyritz Pommen*, Paris 1865
LIT *Strasbourg Salon* 1853; *Thieme*

VOGEL, Adolphe
Exhib. *Roses*, Strasbourg Salon 1853 (80 francs)
LIT *Strasbourg Salon* 1853

VOHANE, Mlle de
Exhib. *Chrysanthèmes*, *Pivoines*, Dijon Salon 1883
LIT *Dijon Salon* 1883. CL

VOILLEMOT, André Charles ***1823–1893***
b. Paris. Pupil of Drolling. Decorative painter. Salon debut 1845, 2nd class medal 1870. Carried out the decoration of the Imperial Pavilion at the Exposition of 1867 and the theatre at Fontainebleau and a commission in Santiago, Chile. Frequent use of flowers in his figure pictures and decors, e.g. in the canvas at Pontoise
LIT *Bénézit*. PM

VOISIN-VEZU, Louise
Pupil of O. Piquet. fl. Lyon. Exhib. *Roses de Noël*, Lyon Salon 1875
LIT *Hardouin-Fugier Grafe*; *Lyon Salon 1875*

VOITELLIER, Marie-Théophile, ***née*** **Lainé**
b. Paris. Pupil of Fontaine. At Sèvres 1845–1849. Exhib. Paris Salon from 1845 e.g. *Bouquet de fleurs*, on porcelain, 1845. *Bouquet de fleurs d'après nature*, 1846
LIT *Bellier*; *Bénézit*; *Brunet Préaud*; *Paris Salon* 1845; *Thieme*

VOLAND, Auguste ***b.1875***
Pupil of Castex-Dégrange, Lyon BA (CFD 1893)
LIT *Hardouin-Fugier Grafe*

VOLATIER, Charles ***b.1875***
Pupil of Castex-Dégrange, Lyon BA (CFD 1893)
LIT *Hardouin-Fugier Grafe*

VOLATIER, Marie-Gaspard ***b.1837***
b. Pont-de-Vaux (Ain). Pupil of Thierriat, Lyon BA (CFD 1854)
LIT *Hardouin-Fugier Grafe*

VOLL, Mathias
b. Munster (Haut-Rhin). Pupil of Thierriat, Lyon BA (CFD 1826)
LIT *Hardouin-Fugier Grafe*

VOLLE, François-Catherin-Marie ***b.1831***
Pupil of Lyon BA (1852). Exhib. Paris Exposition Universelle, 1855 and Lyon Salon 1853–1858. His *Pivoines* was in the 1856 and his *Camélia*, wc, in the 1857 Lyon Société des Amis-des-Arts raffle
LIT *Bénézit*; *Hardouin-Fugier Grafe*

VOLLON, Alexis. ***1865–1945***
b. Paris. Pupil of his father Antoine Vollon. Frequent exhibitor at Paris A.F. from 1885. 2nd class Medal 1889. Silver medal 1900 at l'Exposition Universelle. His work is similar in style to that of his father's
LIT *Bénézit: Schurr I*, 60

VOLLON, Antoine ***1833–1900***
b. Lyon. Pupil of Lyon BA. The famous landscape and still-life painter produced many flower pieces e.g. *Fleurs et fruits*, Lyon Salon 1865, *Vase de chrysanthèmes*, Lyon Salon 1867; *Flowers in a vase*, coll. Marquis of Salisbury, Hatfield, cat. 1891, no. 223; *Still-life with bunch of violets on a yellow book, Lyall sale, American Art Association, New York, 10 Feb. 1903, no. 25*; *Fruit and flowers (formerly in P. Palmer coll.) Chicago*, exhib. H. Young galleries, New York 1922; *Flowers and fruit, ex coll. Dhainaut, American Art Association sale, Paris, 4 Jan 1923, lot 43*; *Flowers and fruit, Roland, Browse & Delbanco, London, 1948*; *Potted flowers, Worcester Art Museum, Worcs, UK, News Bulletin, Dec. 1967*; *Corbeille de fleurs, Christie's, London, 4 July 1969, lot 75*; *Vase of chrysanthemums, H. Shickman gallery Feb. 1970*; *Still-life with flowers* in *The neglected XIXth Century*, II, Oct. 1971, H. Shickman Gallery; *Bouquet*, 1857, Musée d'Arras, Paris BMAD, *Equivoques*, 1973, (ill.); *Pivoines blanches et roses*, ex. coll. Lord Astor of Hever, Sotheby's, London, 5 July 1973, lot 10; *Roses et cerises*, Christie's, London, 5 Apr. 1974, lot 16; *Marguerites dans un verre*, Christie's, London, 9 Apr. 1976, lot 129; *Still-life of mixed flowers in a vase*, Sotheby's, London, 30 Nov. 1977, lot 224; *Flowers in a vase*, M. Newman, London, in *Connoisseur* Apr. 1977, p. 304; *Fleurs dans un vase*, London, Marshall Spink 1980–1981, no. 29. M: Arras; Amsterdam (Rijksmuseum); Edinburgh, Lille, Toledo etc.
LIT *Bellier*; Cleveland Museum, *The realist tradition*, 1980; *Hardouin-Fugier Grafe*; *Orsay*; *Thieme*; G. Weisberg, "A still-life by Vollon, painter of two traditions" in *Bulletin of the Detroit Institute of Arts*, 1978, pp. 223–228; G. Weisberg, *Chardin and the Still-Life Tradition*, Cleveland, 1979 (ill.); *Witt*
† See colour illustration on page 392

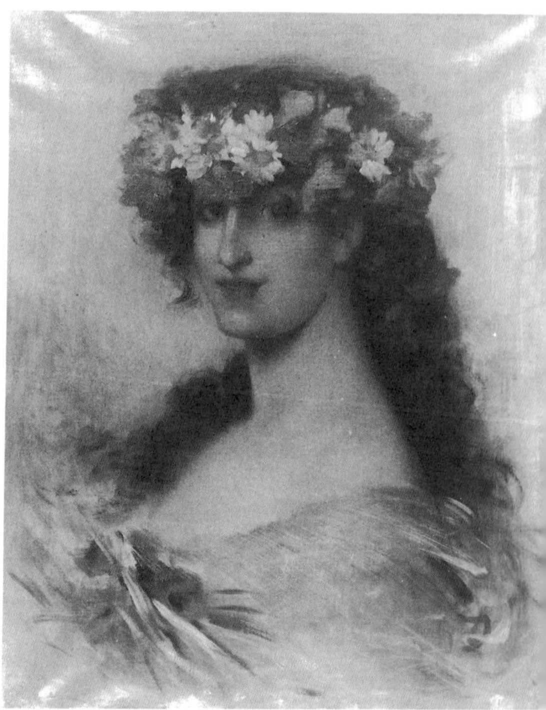

André-Charles Voillemot

Oil on canvas, $21\frac{3}{4}$ × 18 in. (55.7 × 45.8 cm.), signed
Pontoise, Musée Tavet-Delacour

VOLLON, Pierre ***b.1816***
b. Lyon. Pupil of Thierriat, Lyon BA (CFD 1835)
LIT *Hardouin-Fugier Grafe*

VOLTER, Elise
b. Bordeaux (Gironde). Pupil of M. Dumas. Exhib. *Envoi de Nice*, *Roses et oeillets*, Paris Salon 1898
LIT *Paris Salon* 1898

VOMANE, Mlle Rose-Marie de
b. Montpellier (Hérault). Pupil of Baudry. This shadowy, needy flower painter applied for a state allowance. Her *Fleurs et fruits* was bought from her (1,000 francs, 13 Apr. 1881). Exhib. *Bourriche de pensées*, Strasbourg Salon 1884 (250 francs). Exhib. Paris Salon 1866–1881
LIT Paris Arch. Nat. F21: 2118; *Strasbourg Salon* 1884; *Thieme*

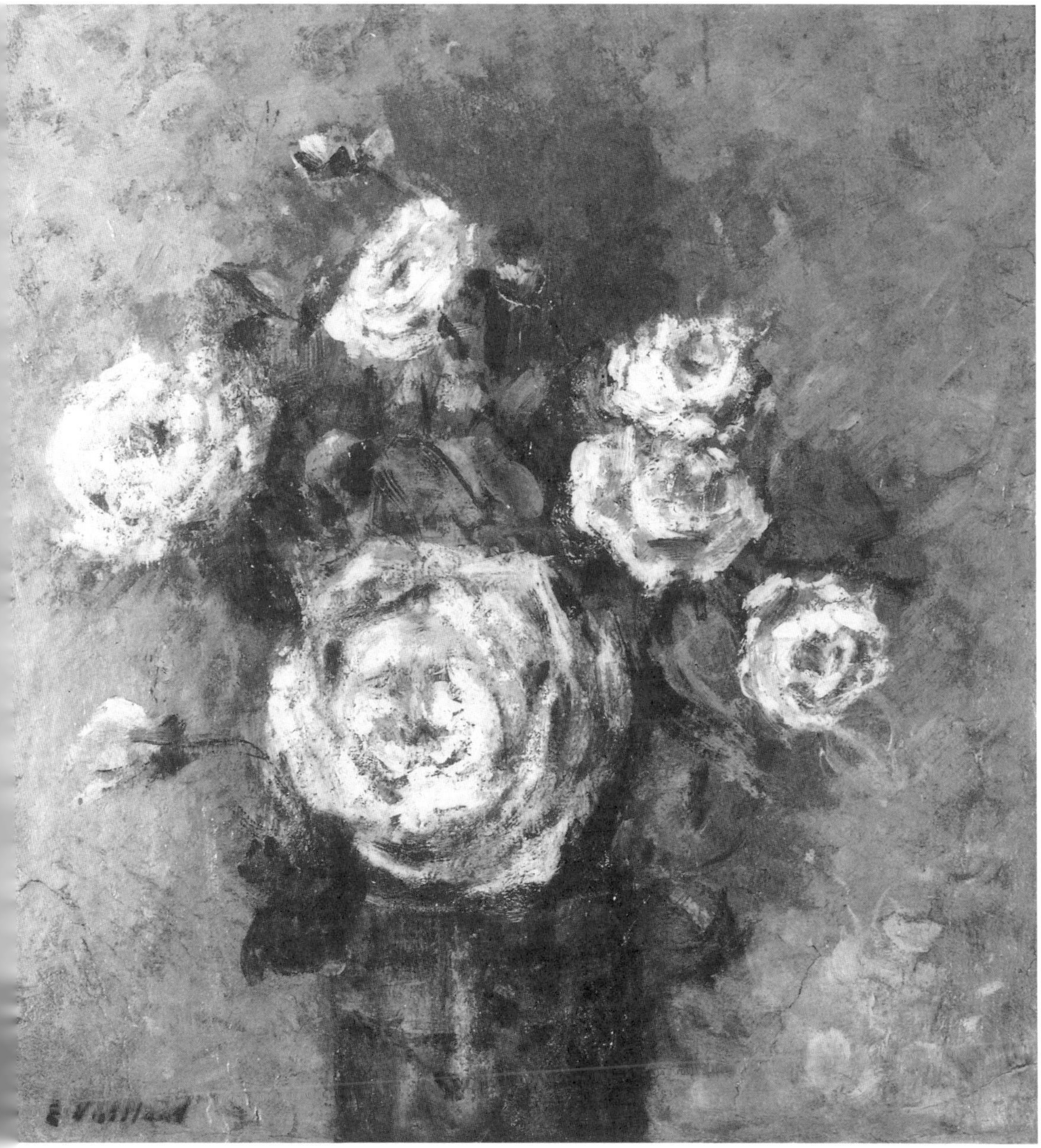

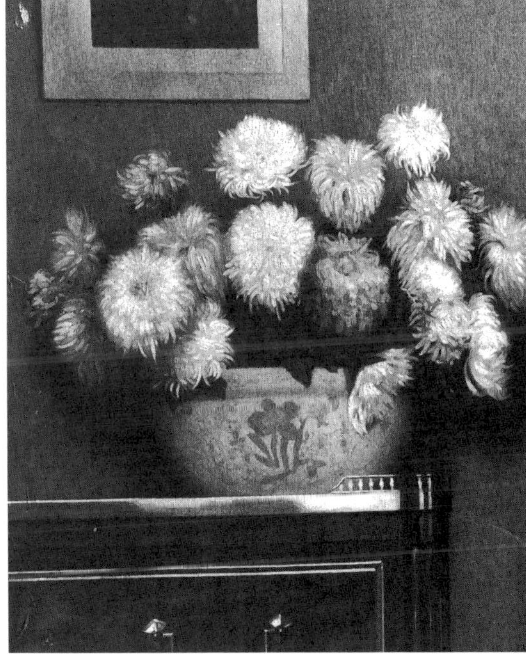

Henri Vouillemont

Oil on canvas, $28\frac{3}{4} \times 23\frac{1}{2}$ in. (73×60 cm.), signed and dated 1904
Troyes, Musée des Beaux-Arts

Edouard Vuillard

Oil on board laid down on panel $11 \times 10\frac{3}{4}$ in. (28×27.5 cm.), signed *c.*1899
Courtesy Sotheby's, London

VOSS, Charles
Exhib. Lyon Salon *Couronne de fleurs*, 1863; *Fleurs*, 1868
LIT *Lyon Salon* 1863, 1868; *Thieme*

VOUILLEMONT, Henri *1878–1911*
b. Troyes (Aube). Musée de Troyes, *Chrysanthèmes*, 1904
LIT Troyes Musée doc.

VUBOST, Jean-Baptiste
Pupil of Thierriat, Lyon BA (CFD 1834)
LIT *Hardouin-Fugier Grafe*

VUILLARD, Edouard *1868–1940*
b. Cuiseaux (Saône-et-Loire). Pupil of Paris BA (Maillard and Gérôme) and Académie Julian. Though flowers are prominent features in many of Vuillard's early interiors or garden scenes e.g. *Dans les fleurs*, *c.*1894, *Conversation*, *c.*1894 or *La musique*, 1896 (Paris, Musée National d'Art Moderne), he did paint quite a few flower-pieces, most of them later works. Belonging to his early period are *Fleurs*, 1890, pastel (sold New York 1951); *Fleurs*, *c.*1899 (Sotheby's, London, 7 Dec. 1983, lot 120); *Marguerites*, *c.*1900 (Chastel, p. 56); *Bouquet de myosotis et de pâquerettes*, *c.*1900 (repr. Rythmes et couleurs). M: Cambridge, Fitzwilliam, *Pot de grès et fleurs*, *c.*1909; Minneapolis Institute of Art, *Les Boules de neige*, 1903; Paris, Musée National d'Art Moderne, Louvre, *Fleurs*, 1904
LIT *Bénézit*; A. Chastel, *Vuillard*, Paris (Floury) 1946; London, Wildenstein, *Vuillard*, 1948; Paris, *Vuillard*, *KX. Roussel*, Orangerie des Tuileries, Réunion des Musées Nationaux, 1968; *Rythmes et couleurs*, Lausanne, (Librex), 1968; *Witt*. AC

W Y Z

WABLE, Mathilde
Exhib. *Fleurs et fruits*, Paris UFPS 1896
LIT *Paris UFPS* 1896

WAGNER, *see* PUYROCHE

WAGREZ, Jacques-Clément
b. Paris. Pupil of his father, Farochon, Lenepveu, Pils and Lehmann. Exhib. genre, mythological figures and, occasionally, flowers
LIT *Bellier*; *Witt*

WAHL, Léa, Rachel
b. Paris. Pupil of Lefebvre and B. Constant. Exhib. *Fleurs d'été*, Paris Salon 1890
LIT *Paris Salon* 1890

WALDNER de, *see* FREUNDSTEIN

WALTZ, Jacques 1873–1951
Pupil of Castex-Dégrange, Lyon BA (CFD 1894). This is Hansi, the popular Alsatian illustrator
LIT *Hardouin-Fugier Grafe*

WANNER, Isabelle
Exhib. wc, Dijon Salon *Anémones et mimosas*, *Oeillets*, fan-leaf, *Bégonias*, fan-leaf, 1894; *Roses*, 1897
LIT *Dijon Salon* 1894, 1897

WASSET, *see* PICARD

WATELET, Eugénie-Sophie
b. Soissons (Aisne). Painted flowers and landscapes. Exhib. Paris Salon *Iris au bord de l'eau*, 1869, *Pavots*, 1870
LIT *Bellier*; *Bénézit*; *Thieme*

WATTERNAU, Françoise
Exhib. *Bouquet de roses*, wc, Paris Indép. 1884
LIT *Paris Indép.* 1884

WAUQUIER, Alix
b. Paris. Exhib. *Fleurs*, Paris Salon 1867
LIT *Paris Salon* 1867

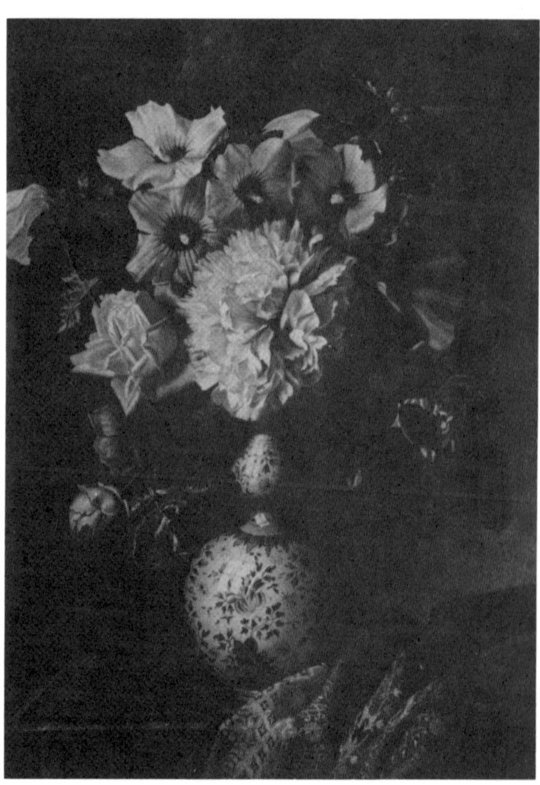

Eugénie-Sophie Watelet

Oil on canvas, $25\frac{1}{2} \times 18\frac{1}{2}$ in. (65 × 47 cm.)
signed and dated 1879
Private collection

Julie Weber née Arnaud *(right)*

Watercolour on paper, 14 × 10¼ in. (35.5 × 27.5 cm), signed
Courtesy Sotheby's, London

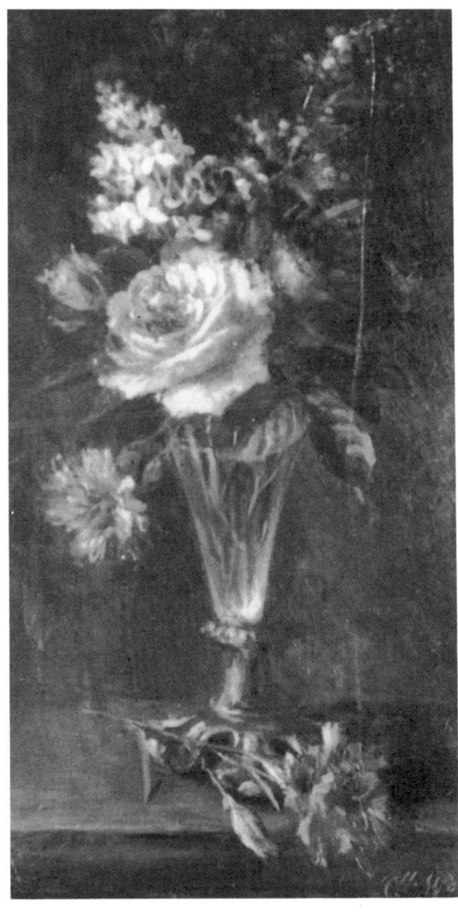

Camille-Aimé-François Wolf

Oil on panel, 15 × 8 in. (38 × 20 cm.), signed
Private collection

WEBER, Julie, *née* Arnaud
Pupil of Redouté. Painted flowers. Exhib. wc, Paris Salon 1838–1844 and *Pivoines*, Paris Amis-des-Arts, 1855
LIT *Bénézit*; *Hardouin-Fugier* 1981; *Paris Amis-des-Arts* 1855; *Thieme*

WILLERMOZ, Vincent-Claude-Auguste *b.1862*
Pupil of Reignier, Lyon BA (CFD 1878)
LIT *Hardouin-Fugier Grafe*

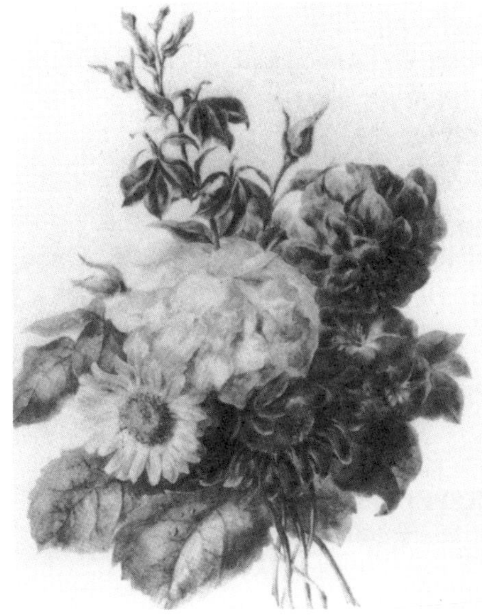

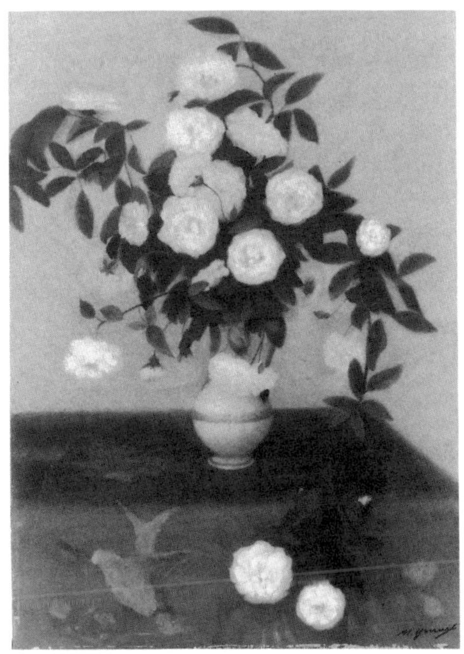

Marguerite Ymart (Ymart-Rachou)

Oil on canvas, signed
Cognac, Musée Municipal

WILLMANN, Rudolf-Bernhardt *1868–1919*
b. Strasbourg (Bas-Rhin). Pupil of Gysis (Munich Academy of Art). Painted still-lifes
LIT *Bénézit*; *Thieme*

WILLY, F.
Designed plates for H. F. Jaubert and E. Spach *Choix de plantes...de l'Asie Occidentale*, Paris (Roret) 1842–1857
LIT *Laissus*; *Nissen* I, 985; *Sitwell*; *Thieme*

WINCKEL, Georges
Exhib. *Fruits et fleurs*, Strasbourg Salon 1884
LIT *Strasbourg Salon* 1884

WOLF, Camille-Aimé-François *b.1837*
Pupil of Thierriat, Lyon BA (CFD 1854). Painted fruit and flowers. Exhib. Lyon Salon from *c.*1870. His *Bouquet de violettes* was in the 1869 Lyon Société des Amis-des-Arts raffle
LIT *Hardouin-Fugier Grafe*

WOLOWSKA
Exhib. *Bouquet de fleurs*, Paris Salon 1837
LIT *Paris Salon* 1837

WOS, Carl
Painted still-lifes and flowers. Exhib. Lyon Salon 1851, 1852, 1865
LIT *Hardouin-Fugier Grafe*

YMART, later YMART-RACHOU, Marguerite
b. Castres (Tarn). Exhib. Paris Indép. *Chrysanthèmes*, *Lilas*, *Roses*, *Pavots*, *Coquelicots*, 1893, *Capucines*, *Bleuets*, 1894, *Cyclamens*, 1896. Musée de Cognac, *Roses blanches*
LIT Paris Arch. Nat. F21: 4500; *Paris Indép.* 1893, 1894, 1896

YON, Edmond ***1836–1897***
The well-known landscape and genre painter exhib. *Chrysanthèmes*, wc, Paris Salon 1887
LIT *Paris Salon* 1887; *Schurr* I, 52

ZACHARIE, Charles ***b.1795***
Pupil of Berjon, Lyon BA (CFD 1810)
LIT *Hardouin-Fugier Grafe*

ZACCHEO, Jean
b. Roanne (Loire). Landscape painter. Exhib. *Fleurs*, Saint-Etienne Salon 1891
LIT *Saint-Etienne Salon* 1891

ZIEM, Félix-François-Georges-Philibert ***1821–1911***
b. Beaune (Côte-d'Or). Pupil of Dijon BA. The well-known landscape painter produced comparatively few still-lifes and flower paintings. With a few exceptions e.g. *Rose*, ink, 1842, most of these bold paintings are undated and may be later works featuring peonies and often unidentifiable semi-abstract flowers e.g. *Fleurs dans un vase*, *Fleurs jetées* (Saint-Tropez, 1982); *Fleurs* (Dijon M.4); *Fleurs* (Paris, Petit Palais M. 110); *Fouillis de fleurs*, (M. 113, M. 1753, M. 1779); *Fleurs de soleil*, (M. 163); *Fleurs* (M. 182, 250, 279); *Jetée de fleurs* (M. 280); *Jonchée de fleurs* (M. 458); *Bouquet*, (M. 580); *Fleurs*, *c*.1868 (M. 589); *Roses*, (M. 620); *Fleurs de pommier* (Beaune M. 817); *Fleurs et fruits* (Douai, M. 1166); *Fleurs disposées en arbuste* (M. 1181); *Fleurs et fruits*, (M. 1206); *Pivoines* (Paris, Petit Palais M. 1583); *Fleurs* (Châlon-sur-Saône M. 1610). M: Beaune, Châlon-sur-Saône, Dijon, Douai, Paris, (Petit Palais)
LIT *Bénézit*; E. Hild, in *Fleurs de Fantin-Latour à Marquet*, Saint-Tropez, Musée de l'Annonciade, 1982; P. Miquel (here M.), *F. Ziem*, Maurs-la-Jolie, 1978; *Thieme*

ZILLHARDT, Jenny
Exhib. *Chrysanthèmes*, Dijon Salon 1892
LIT *Dijon Salon* 1892

ZIPCY, *see* DUPONT

ZIPPELIUS, Georges ***1808–1890***
b. Mulhouse (Haut-Rhin) Pupil of Paris BA. op. decorator. Worked with Joseph Fuchs
LIT *Sitzmann*

ZO, Achille or Jean-Baptiste Achille ***1826–1901***
b. Bayonne. (Pyrénées-Atlantiques) Pupil of Couture. Painted genre, portraits, occasionally still life. Salon debut 1852. Gold medal 1865. Settled at Bordeaux, appointed director of BA there and the École des Arts Decoratifs
LIT *Bénézit*. PM

ZUBER, Anna-Elise ***1872–1932***
b. Rixheim (Haut-Rhin). Pupil of her father, Henri Zuber (1844–1909), the landscape painter. Painted landscapes and flowers. Exhib. *Oeillets*, *Mufliers*, wc, Paris Salon 1898. M: Dieppe, Mulhouse (currently untraceable), Pontoise, Rouen, Saumur
LIT *Bénézit*; *Paris Salon* 1898

Antoine Vollon

Oil on canvas, 24½ × 20 in. (61.5 × 50.5 cm.), signed
Lille, Musée des Beaux-Arts (donation Brasseur)

Felix-François-Georges-Philibert Ziem

Oil on canvas, signed
Paris, Petit Palais

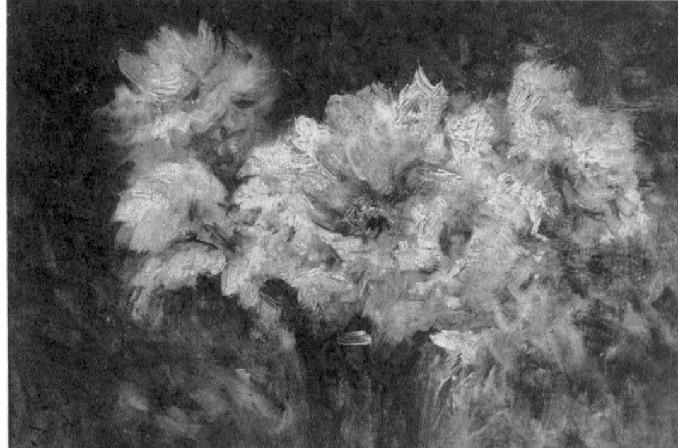

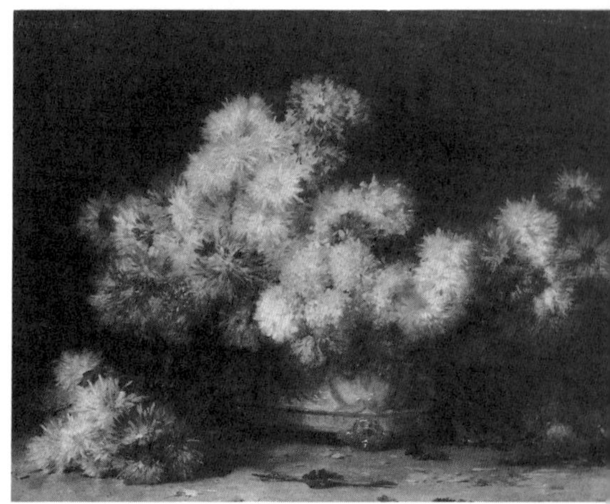

Achille Zo

Oil on canvas, 25½ × 31 in. (64.8 × 80.7 cm.), signed
Courtesy Christie's, London

Glossary

Aiguière: ewer
Amandier: almond tree
Aristoloche: birthwort
Arrosoir: watering can
Aubépine: hawthorn

Baguenaudier: bladder-senna
Blé de Turquie: maize
Bleuet or bluet: cornflower
Botte: bunch
Bouillon blanc: Aaron's rod
Boule de neige: guelder rose
Bourriche: hamper
Bouton: bud
Brassée: armful
Brouette: wheelbarrow
Bruyère: heather

Capucine: nasturtium
Campanule: campanula, blue bell, bell flower
Cerisier: cherry tree
Chardon: thistle
Charretée: cartful
Chèvrefeuille: honeysuckle
Cigüe: hemlock
Clochette: small bell flower
Coquelicot: corn-poppy
Corbeille: basket
Coucou: cowslip
Couronne: wreath
Couronne Impériale: crown imperial
Cruche: pitcher
Cueillette: a gathering or picking

Eglantine: wild rose
Eventaire: street stall or hawker's tray

Faux-ébénier: laburnum

Genet: gorse
Gerbe: large bunch, sheaf
Giroflée: wallflower
Glaïeul: gladiolus
Glycine: wistaria

Haie: hedge
Hotte: pannier, basket

Impériale: crown imperial

Jacinthe: hyacinth
Jardinière: flower-stand

Laurier: laurel
Laurier thym: laurustine, a virburnum
Lilas: lilac
Lis or lys: lily
Liseron: convolvulus, bind weed

Marguerite: ox-eye daisy
Marronnier d'Inde: horse-chestnut tree
Mauve: mallow
Mignardise: garden pink
Muflier: snapdragon, antirrhinum
Muguet: lily-of-the-valley
Myosotis: forget-me-not

Nénuphar: water-lily

Oeillet: carnation
Oeillet d'Inde: African marigold
Oreille d'ours: bear's ear, auricula

Panaché: variegated
Panerée: basketful
Panier: basket
Pâquerette: daisy
Parterre: flower bed
Pavot: Poppy
Pavot Tournefort: oriental poppy
Pêcher: peach tree
Pensée: pansy
Pervenche: periwinkle
Pied d'alouette: larkspur
Pissenlit: dandelion
Pivoine: peony
Poirier: pear tree
Pois de senteur: sweet pea
Pomme d'api: Lady-apple (small, sweet apple)

Pommier: apple tree
Primevère: primula, primrose
Prunier: plum tree

Reine des prés: meadow-sweet
Reine-marguerite: China-aster
Ronce: bramble
Rose de Noël: Christmas rose
Rose trémière: hollyhock

Sauge: sage
Serre: greenhouse
Soleil: sunflower
Souci: marigold
Sureau: elder tree
Surtout: épergne, table centre-piece

Touffe: bunch, cluster, clump
Tournesol: sunflower
Trèfle: clover

Verre: glass
Verveine: verbena
Vigne vierge: Virginia creeper
Violier: stock
Volubilis: convolvulus

For spelling and hyphenation, the glossary has followed T.W. Sanders, *Sanders' Encyclopaedia of Gardening*, London (Collinsridge) 1953, which is generally accepted as the standard work

Abbreviations

A.F.
Salon des Artistes Français

Album Vilmorin
Collection of flower designs in watercolour. Bibliothèque de l'Institut de Recherche Vilmorin, 49250 La Ménitré, France

Arch.
Archives

Arch. Nat.
Archives Nationales

Audin Vial
Audin M. Vial E. *Dictionnaire des artistes et ouvriers d'art de la France, Lyonnais.* Paris (Bibliothèque d'Art et d'Archéologie) 1918

b.
born

BA
École des Beaux-Arts

Bellier
Bellier de la Chavignerie, Auvray L. *Dictionnaire des artistes de l'École française*, Paris (Renouard) 1882, and *Supplément*

Bénézit
Dictionnaire des peintres, Paris (Grund) 1976

Béraldi
Béraldi H. *Les Graveurs du XIX° siècle*, Paris, 1885–1892

Bibl. Mun.
Bibliothèque Municipale

Broughton 1952
Grant, M.H., *Flower Paintings through Four Centuries*, A Descriptive Catalogue of the collection formed by.... Henry Rogers Broughton, Leigh-on-Sea, (Lewis) 1952

Broughton 1973
1st Selection of Flower Drawings from the Broughton Collection, Fitzwilliam Museum, Cambridge, Dec.–Jan. 1973–1974

Broughton 1974
Botanical Drawings from the Broughton Collection, Fitzwilliam Museum, Cambridge, June-Sep. 1974

Broughton 1976
Gardener's Pride, a 3rd Selection of Drawings, Fitzwilliam Museum, Cambridge, July–Sep. 1976

Broughton 1977
Roses, Roses ... a 4th Selection of Drawings, Fitzwilliam Museum, Cambridge, July–Sep. 1977

Broughton 1978
Pick of the Bunch, a 5th Selection of Drawings, Fitzwilliam Museum, Cambridge, July–Sep. 1978

Broughton 1979
Men versus Women, a 6th Selection of Drawings, Fitzwilliam Museum, Cambridge, July–Oct. 1979

Broughton 1983/84
D. Scrase, *Flowers of Three Centuries, One Hundred Drawings and Watercolours from the Broughton Collection*, Washington DC, 1983–1984

Brune
Brune P. *Dictionnaire des artistes et ouvriers d'art de la France, Franche-Comté*, Paris (Bibliothèque d'Art et d'Archéologie) 1912

Brunet Préaud
Brunet, M. Préaud T. *Sèvres des origines à nos jours*, Fribourg, (Office du Livre), 1978

Busse
Busse, J. *Internationales Handbuch aller Maler und Bildhauer des 19. Jahrhunderts*, Wiesbaden 1977

c.
circa

cat.
catalogue

cat. Mise
Catalogue du Musée de l'Impression sur Étoffes de Mulhouse, Bulletin de la Société industrielle de Mulhouse No. 761, 4/1975

CFD
class of flower design, École des Beaux-Arts de Lyon (Classe de Fleur)

coll.
collection

d.
died or dated

doc.
documentation

Faré 1962
Faré, M. *La Nature-morte en France*, Genève (Cailler) 1962

Faré 1976
Faré, M. *La Vie silencieuse en France*, Fribourg (Office du Livre) 1976

FDC
Flower design contest (Concours de la Fleur, Lyon)

Gabet
Gabet, C. *Dictionnaire des artistes de l'École française au XIX° siècle*, Paris 1831

Hardouin-Fugier 1980
Hardouin-Fugier, E. *Simon Saint-Jean*, Leigh-on-Sea (Lewis) 1980

Hardouin-Fugier, 1981
Hardouin-Fugier, E. *The Pupils of Redouté*, Leigh-on-Sea (Lewis) 1981

Hardouin-Fugier Bringuier
Hardouin-Fugier, E., Bringuier, H., 'La peinture à Saint-Etienne' in *L'Encyclopédie du Forez*, Roanne (Horvath) 1984

Hardouin-Fugier Grafe
Hardouin-Fugier, E., Grafe, E. *The Lyon School of Flower Painting*, Leigh-on-Sea (Lewis) 1978

Hardouin-Fugier Grafe 1979
Peintures de Fleurs de l'École lyonnaise,

Lyon, Musée des Beaux-Arts, 1979

Hardouin-Fugier Grafe 1981
Les Peintres de l'Ame, Lyon, Musée des Beaux-Arts, 1981

Hardouin-Fugier Grafe 1982
Fleurs de Lyon, Lyon, Musée des Beaux-Arts, 1982

Hist. doc.
Histoire Documentaire de l'Industrie de Mulhouse et de ses environs au XIX° siècle, Mulhouse 1902

(ill.)
illustration or illustrated

Laissus
Laissus, Y. *Les Vélins du Muséum*, Université de Paris, Palais de la Découverte, 1967

Louvre
Musée du Louvre, Paris

Louvre Arch.
Archives du Louvre

Louvre doc.
Service de documentation des Peintures du Musée du Louvre

MAD
Paris, Musée des Arts Décoratifs

Mireur
Mireur, H. *Dictionnaire des ventes d'art en France et à l'étranger*, Paris 1910

Mitchell
Mitchell, P. *European Flower Painters*, London (Black) 1973

MS.
manuscript

Nissen
Nissen, C. *Die Botanische Buchillustration, ihre Geschichte und Bibliographie*, 2te Auflage, Stuttgart, (Hiersemann) 1966. Nissen I: Bibliography (1st part of vol. II); Nissen II: Bibliography (2nd part of vol. II); Nissen n: bibliography (supplement to vol. II)

n.d.
no date

n.m.
nature-morte (still-life)

op.
operavit, active

Orsay
Service de Documentation des Peintures, Musée du XIX° siècle, Paris

Paris Amis-des-Arts
Société des Amis-des-Arts de Paris, scarce handbooks

Paris Aquar.
Société des Aquarellistes français, Paris (Jouaust) from 1879

Paris Arch. Nat.
Paris Archives Nationales

Paris Bibl. Nat. Est.
Paris, Bibliothèque Nationale, Cabinet des Estampes

Paris Indép.
Société des Artistes Indépendants, Paris, from 1884

Paris BMAD (Maciet coll.)
Paris, Bibliothèque du Musée des Arts Décoratifs

Paris Noir et Blanc Salon
Exposition internationale de Blanc et Noir, Paris (Bernard) from 1885

Paris Muséum
Paris, Bibliothèque Centrale du Muséum National d'Histoire Naturelle

Paris Salon
Explication des ouvrages de peinture, sculpture, architecture, Paris, 1673–1881; from 1881: Société des Artistes Français

Paris Salon (ill.)
Le Salon illustré, Paris, (Baschet)

Paris SNBA
Société Nationale des Beaux-Arts, from 1890

Pavière
Pavière, S. *A Dictionary of Flower, Fruit and Still-Life Painters*, Leigh-on-Sea (Lewis) 1962

s.
signed

Sèvres Arch.
Archives de la Manufacture Nationale de Porcelaine de Sèvres

Schidlof
Schidlof, L. *La Miniature en Europe*, Graz 1964

Schurr
Schurr, G. *Les Petits Maîtres de la peinture*, Paris (L'Amateur) 1975 etc.

Sitwell
Sitwell, S., Blunt, W. *Great Flower Book*, London (Collins) 1956

Sitzmann
Sitzmann, E.S. *Dictionnaire biographique des hommes célèbres de l'Alsace*, Rixheim 1909–1910

Thieme
Thieme, Becker. *Allgemeines Lexikon der bildenden Künstler*, Leipzig (Seeman) 1907–1940

UFPS
Union des Femmes peintres et sculpteurs, Paris, founded 1881

Witt
London, Witt Library, Courtauld Institute

Select Bibliography

Adhèmar, J., Lethéve, J. *Inventaire du fonds français après 1800*, Paris, Bibliothèque Nationale, 1954

Aix-en-Provence, (Bouches-du-Rhone) *Rétrospective Seyssaud*, Hôtel des Ventes, 1957

Ajalbert, J., *Anquetin*, Paris (Rey) 1930

Albi, (Tarn) *Seyssaud*, Musée 1959

Amis de V. Charreton, *V. Charreton*, Paris (Imprimerie Mazarine) 1964–1966

Amiens Salon (Somme)

Amsterdam-Toronto, *Van Gogh and the birth of Cloisonism*, 1981

Annuaire statistique des artistes français, Paris, 1832–1836

***Apollo*,** 'Helleu', July 1975

***Apollo*,** 'Bonvin', Sep. 1965

Artistes contemporains du pays de Guyenne, Bordeaux, Gounouilhou, 1889

Auxerre, (Yonne) *E. Bernard*, Musée des Beaux-Arts, 1968

Baudelaire, C., *Le Salon de 1845*, Paris (Labitte) 1845

Bazalgette, L., *A. Dubois-Pillet*, Villejuif (Bazalgette) 1976

Bellendy, J., *J.A. Grivolas*, Académie du Vaucluse, Avignon, n.d.

Béraud, H., *L'École moderne de peinture lyonnaise*, Paris (Basset) 1912

Berger, K., 'The Reconversion of Odilon Redon' *Art Quarterly*, 1958 (ill.)

Berhaut, M., *Caillebotte, sa vie, son oeuvre*, Paris (Bibliothèque des Arts) 1978

Bernard, E., 'Anquetin' in *La Gazette des Beaux-Arts*, 1934

Bernheim-Jeune Galerie, *M. Bracquemond*, Paris 1962

Bertauts-Couture, T., *Couture*, Paris (le Garrec) 1932

Bittler, P., *Catalogue des dessins de Gustave Moreau*, Paris (Réunion des Musées Nationaux) 1983

Blois, (Loir-et-cher) *H. Sauvage*, Musée 1977

Blunt, W., The Art of Botanical Illustration, 1950

Bordeaux, (Gironde) *Anquetin*, Centre Régional de Documentation pédagogique, 1965

Bouillon, J. P., *Félix et Marie Bracquemond*, Mortagne 1972

Bouillon, J. P., Weisberg, G., 'Bracquemond et le baron Vitta' in *The Bulletin of the Cleveland Museum of Art*, Nov. 1979

Bourg-en-Bresse Salon (Ain)

Bourret, J., *Henri Rousseau*, Neuchâtel (Ides et Calendes) 1961

Boven, M. van, and Segal, S., *Gérard and Cornelis van Spaendonck*, Paris 1980

Bremen, *E. Bernard*, Kunsthalle 1967

Brame, Philippe and **Lorenceau,** Bernard, *Catalogue raisonée of the complete works of Henri Fantin-Latour*, (in preparation)

Brussels, *X.K. Roussel*, Musée des Beaux-Arts, 1975

***Bulletin des Monuments historiques*,** 'Guèrite', Apr. 1971

***Burlington Magazine*,** 'Couture', Sep. 1954

Cachin, F., *Signac*, Paris (Bibliothèque des Arts) 1971

Cailleux Galerie, *Monticelli*, Genève 1981–1982

Caudal, R., 'Martin J.' in *Hardouin-Fugier Grafe*, 1982

Cazeau, P., *M. Luce*, Paris (Bibliothèque des Arts) 1982

Chagny, A., *Un Pays aimé des peintres ... la région de Crémieu*, Lyon (Masson) 1929

Charpentier Galerie, *Helleu*, Paris 1931

Charpentier Galerie, *G. D. Monfried*, Paris 1938

Charrin, A., 'Deyrieux' in *Hardouin-Fugier Grafe*, 1982

Chastel, A., *Vuillard*, Paris (Floury) 1946

Cleveland Museum, *The Realist Tradition*, 1980

Coats, A., *A Book of Flowers*, London 1973–1974

Coats, A., *The Great Book of Flowers*, London (Phaidon) 1975

Cogniat, R., *Sisley*, Paris (Flammarion) 1978

Commerre, G. and D., *L. Commerre*, Paris (La Presse artistique) 1980

Compin, I., *H.E. Cross*, Paris (Quatre-Chemins) 1964

Compte-rendu annuel de la Société des Amis-des-Arts de Lyon, Lyon, (Perrin), e.g. 1852, 1863, 1870, 1879

Connoisseur, 'Bonvin', Sep. 1978

Corenc (Isère), *J. Flandrin*, Mairie, 1972

Courbevoie, (Hauts-de-Seine) *J. B. Carpeaux*, Musée des Beaux-Arts, 1975–1976

Dagnan-Bouveret, *Catalogue des oeuvres*, Paris (Meunier) 1901

Daulte, F., *Frédéric Bazille et son temps*, Genève (Cailler) 1952

Dorra, H. and **Rewald J.,** *Seurat*, Paris (Éditions d'études et documents) 1959

Daurelle, J., *A. Point* (La Plume) 1901

Davies, E., 'Favre-Hénon' in *Hardouin-Fugier Grafe* 1982

Desgoffe, A., *B. A. Desgoffe*, Paris (Mersch) 1888

Desvernay, F., *Le Vieux Lyon à l'exposition de 1914*, Lyon (Rey) 1914

Dieppe, (Seine-Maritime) *J. E. Blanche*, Musée des Beaux-Arts, 1954

Dijon Salon (Côte-d'Or)

Dubourg, J., Galerie. *A. Cals*, Paris 1979

Dubray, J. P., *E. Carrière*, Paris (Seheur) 1931

Durand-Ruel Galerie, *Gustave Loiseau*, Paris 1957

Dussieux, L., *Les Artistes Français à l'étranger*, Paris (Didron) 1852

Dutilleux, P., *Nos artistes peintres*, Lille 1911

Ecully (Rhône), *A. Stengelin*, Mairie 1979

Estignard, A., *H. Baron*, Besançon (Louys) 1896

Fernier, R., *La Vie et l'oeuvre de Gustave Courbet*, Paris-Lausanne (Bibliothèque des Arts) 1977

Ferrers Gallery, *Helleu*, London 1970

Flavia, Galerie, M., *Laugé*, Paris 1969

Flescher, *Z. Astruc*, New York, London (Garland) 1978

Forge, A., and Gordon, R., *The Last Flower Paintings of Manet*, London 1986

Forneris, J., 'T. Coquelin', in *Renaissance du Musée des Beaux-Arts de Cannes*, 1983, p. 142

Foucher, J.P., *Séraphine de Senlis*, Paris (Le Temps) 1968

Gallé, E., *Écrits sur l'art*, Paris (Renouard) 1908

Gamet, J. C. and G., *J. B. Olive*, Paris (Frebert) 1977

Garry, M. N. de, *V. Galland*, Paris, Musée des Arts Décoratifs, 1980

Gaudichon, B., 'La Peinture au XIX° siècle' in *Bulletin de la Société des Antiquaires de l'ouest*, 1983

Geffroy, G., *L'Oeuvre de Carrière*, Paris, 1901; *Marie Bracquemond*, Paris, 1919

Genaille, J., 'Baudry de Balzac' in *Archives de l'Art français*, Paris, (de Nobele), 1978, p. 301–305

Genève, *L. Valtat*, Petit Palais, 1969

Georgel, P., Bortolatto, L. R. *Tout l'oeuvre peint de Delacroix*, Paris (Flammarion) 1975

Germain, A., *Les Artistes lyonnais*, Lyon, (Lardanchet), 1911

Gouirand, A., *Monticelli*, Paris, Société d'édition d'art, 1900

Gounot, R., *C. Maurin*, Le Puy, Musée Crozatier, 1978

Grandville, J. I., *Les fleurs animées*, Paris (de Gonet) 1847

Grenoble (Isère), J. Marval, Musée des Beaux-Arts, 1932

Grenoble Salon

Gualandi, P., *Maria Vittoria Jaquotot*, Venezia (Antonelli) 1855

Guicheteau, M., *Paul Sérusier*, Paris 1976

Guillot, G., 'Les Solitaires de Lyon', *Apollo*, Oct. 1964, pp. 301–305

Hardouin-Fugier, E., 'Baudelaire et S. Saint-Jean' in *Bulletin Baudelairien*, Vanderbilt University, Nashville, 1978, pp. 3–11; 'I. Richard' in *Hardouin-Fugier Grafe*, 1981, p. 53. *S. Saint Jean*, Leigh-on-Sea, (Lewis), 1981.

Hardouin-Fugier, E., Grafe, E., *Répertoire des peintres lyonnais du XIX° siècle en Bugey*, Lacoux, 1980

Hardouin-Fugier, E., Grafe, E., *Portraitistes Lyonnais*, Lyon, Musée des Beaux-Arts, 1986

Harisse, H., *L. L. Boilly*, Paris, (Société de propagation des Livres d'Art), 1898

Heim Gallery, *Paintings by Huet*, London 1969

Hiesinger, K. B., 'C. Moreau' in *l'Art français sous le Second Empire*, Paris, Grand Palais, 1979, 'Escallier' *id*

Hild, E., 'La peinture en Provence 1870–1920'; 'Ziem' in *Fleurs de Fantin-Latour à Marquet*, Musée de l'Annonciade, Saint-Tropez 1982

Hofstätter, H. H., *Geschichte des Europäischen Jugendstilmalerei*, *Köln* (Dumont) 1972

Hoschedé, J.P., *CL. Monet, ce mal connu*, Genève (Cailler) 1960

House, J., 'Angrand' in *Post-Impressionism*, London, RA 1979–1980

Huysmans, J.K., *Certains*, Paris (Tresse) 1889

Isle-Adam (L') (Seine-et-Oise), *Les Amis de l'Isle-Adam*, Musée Louis Senlecq, 1979

Isnard, G., *Monticelli*, Genève (Cailler) 1967

Jacqué, B., *Chefs d'oeuvre du MISE*, Tokyo (Gakken) 1978 'Les papiers peints panoramiques de Zuber au XIX° siècle' in *Bulletin du Musée historique de Mulhouse*, 1981

Jaubert Galerie, *G. D. Monfreid*, Paris 1976

Jouin, H., 'Piquet de Brienne' in *Nouvelles Archives de l'Art français*, Paris (Charavay) 1890

Jovet, P., 'Un Aspect peu connu de l'oeuvre de P. J. Redouté' in *Bulletin du Jardin botanique national Belge*, 37, 1967, pp. 53–60

Knyff, G. de., *N. Goeneutte*, Paris (Mayer) 1978

Kyriazi, J. M., *Gustave Loiseau*, Paris-Lausanne (La Bibliothèque des Arts) 1979

Lacambre, G., 'Brune' in *Société de l'Histoire de l'Art Français*, Paris, de Nobele 1969; 'Desgoffe', Kreyder in *Le Musée du Luxembourg en 1874*, Paris, Grand Palais 1974; 'Ribot' in *L'Art en France sous le Second Empire*, Paris, Grand Palais 1979

Laissus, Y., *Redouté, Les Vélins du Muséum National d'Histoire Naturelle*, 1980

Lambeau, L., *L'Hôtel de Ville de Paris*, Paris (Laurens) 1908

Landon, 'Bruyère' in *Salon de 1819*, Paris (Landon) p. 107

Langlade, E., *Le Sidaner*, Arras, (INSAF) 1933

Lannyer, *Les Maîtres vendéens*, n.d. (Paris, Bibl. Doucet D 9932)

Laÿs, A., *Les Laÿs vus par un Laÿs*, Lyon (A. Laÿs) 1981

Lecocq, G., *L. Abbéma*, Paris (Librairie des Bibliophiles) 1879

Lecomte, G., *Raffaëlli*, Paris (Rieder) 1927

Lepoittevin, L., *J.F. Millet ou l'ambiguïté de l'image*, Paris (Laget) 1973

Léger, C., *Redouté et son temps*, Paris (Galerie Charpentier) 1945

Lespinasse, F., *Angrand*, Rouen (Le Cerf) 1982

Leymarie, J., *Corot*, Genève, 1966 (reprint 1979)

Limoges (Haute-Vienne), *Renoir, Berthe Morisot*, Musée Municipal, 1952

Limoges Salon

Lille (Nord), *E. Bernard*, Musée des Beaux-Arts, 1967

Lille Salon

Loir, A.C., *Lesueur*, Paris 1921

London, *Renoir*, Hayward Gallery, 1985

Lons-le-Saunier Salon (Jura)

Loriot, F., *E. Lansyer*, Paris 1905

Lossky, B., 'Le Peintre fleuriste Jean-Francois van Dael et ses oeuvres au Château de Fontainebleau', *Bulletin de la Société d'Histoire de l'art français*, 1967, pp. 122–136

Lyon, *Albert Marquet*, Musée des Beaux-Arts, 1962

Lyon, *Dufrénoy*, Lyon, Musée des Beaux-Arts, 1983–1984

Magnin, J., *La Peinture au Musée de Dijon*, Besançon (Demontrand) 1933

Mantaigne, A., *Maurice Vlaminck*, Paris (Crès) 1929

Marseille (Bouches-du-Rhône), *L'Orient en question*, Musée Cantini, 1982

Marseille, *Monticelli*, Musée des Beaux-Arts, 1986

Marshall Spink Gallery, *Three Centuries of Flower and Still-Life Painting*, London 1980

Martin, E., *Monticelli*, Académie de Marseille, 1922

Marumo, C., *Barbizon*, Paris (L'Amateur) 1975

Mas, N., 'Durand' in *Hardouin-Fugier Grafe*, 1982

Masson, F., *C. Chaplin*, Paris (Boussod-Valadon) 1888

Mathew, B., *P.J. Redouté, Lilies and Related Flowers*, London 1982

Mathieu, P. L., *G. Moreau*, Paris-Lausanne (La Bibliothèque des Arts) 1976

Mazeyrie, A., *Cécile et Marie Desliens*, Tulle 1953

Mermillon, M., *A. André*, Paris (Cres) 1927

Metz Salon (Moselle)

Michelez, *Album photographique des Salons parisiens*, 1873 etc.

Minervino, F., *Tout l'oeuvre peint de Seurat*, Paris (Flammarion) 1973

Minervino, F., *Tout l'oeuvre peint de Degas*, Paris (Flammarion) 1974

Miquel, P., *P. Huet*, 1962
F. Ziem, Maurs-la-Jolie 1978

Mongan, E., *B. Morisot*, New York (Slatkine) 1960

Moreau-Nélaton, E., *F. Bonvin*, Paris (Laurens) 1927

Morisot, B., *Correspondance*, Paris (Editart) 1950

Moulins Salon (Allier)

Nancy Salon (Meurthe-et-Moselle)

Nantes Salon (Loire-Maritime)

Nice (Alpes-Maritimes), *H.E. Cross*, Musée des Ponchettes, 1972–1973

Nice, *J.B. Carpeaux*, Musée des Ponchettes, 1980

Nouvel, O., 'E. Muller' in *L'Art français sous le Second Empire*, Paris, Grand Palais, 1979

Paris, Bibliothèque Nationale, *J. L. Forain*, 1952

Paris, Drouot, Jacquemart sale, 1881

idem Bing sale, 17 May 1900

idem E.C. Dameron sale, 8 Apr. 1908

Paris, École des Beaux-Arts, *Ribot*, 1892

Paris, Grand Palais, *L'Art en France sous le Second Empire*, 1979

Paris, Grand Palais, *Degas*, 1988

Paris, Grand Palais, *H. Matisse*, 1970; *Autour de Lévy-Dhurmer*, 1973; *J. Millet*, 1975–1976; *Courbet*, 1978; *Cézanne, les dernières années*, 1978; *Manet*, 1981; *Fantin-Latour*, 1982

Paris, Jacquemard-André, *S. Giraud*, 1957

Paris, Louvre—Signac, 1963–1964; *Donation Ari et Suzanne Redon*, 1984

Paris, Marmottan, *Monet et ses amis*, 1971; *J. L. Forain*, 1978

Paris, Musée des Arts Décoratifs, *J. L. Forain*, 1913; *Equivoques*, 1973

Paris, Musée des Arts Décoratifs, *P. V. Galland, la Flore et l'Ornement*, 1980

Paris, Musée National d'Art Moderne. *Bonnard, Vuillard et les Nabis*, 1955

Paris, Orangerie des Tuileries, *Redon*, 1956; *Vuillard, X. K. Roussel*, 1968; *A. Marquet*, 1975–1976

Paris, Petit Palais, *Gros, ses amis ...*, 1936; *Peintres de fleurs en France*, 1979

Paris, Pierre-Joseph Redouté, 'Le Raphaël des Fleurs', 1982

Paris, Salon d'Automne, *J. Marval*, 1932

Parrocel, E., *Annales de la peinture provençale*, Paris-Marseille (Albessard Beraud) 1862

Pathoy, A., *A. Lalauze*, Saint-Quentin (Poette) 1894

Pau (Pyrénées-Atlantiques), *L. Bonnat*, Musée des Beaux-Arts, 1978

Pau Salon

Petridès, P., *L'Oeuvre complet de Suzanne Valadon*, Paris (Compagnie française des Arts graphiques) 1971

Poitiers Salon (Vienne)

Pontoise (Seine-et-Oise). *T. Couture*, Musée des Beaux-Arts, 1972

Preston, H., 'Facets of French Art', *Apollo*, January, 1985, pp. 40–47

Prévost, Roman d'Amat, *Dictionnaire de biographies françaises*, Paris (Letouzay) 1959

Proust, M., *Les plaisirs et les jours*, Paris (Calmann-Lévy) 1896

Puig, R., *Gauguin, G. D. Monfreid*, Perpignan (La Tramontane) 1958

Régamey, F., *Horace Lecoq de Boisbaudran et ses élèves*, Paris (Champion) 1903

Reims Salon (Marne)

Roanne Salon (Loire)

Robaut, A., *L'oeuvre de Corot*, Paris (Laget) 1955

Roger-Marx, C., *Eva Gonzalès*, Saint-Germain-en-Laye (Editions Neuilly) 1950; Seyssaud, Musée Galliera, 1956

Roger-Miles, *A. Roll*, Paris (Lahure) 1904

Roland-Michel, M., *Anne Vallayer-Coster*, Paris 1970

Rouart, D., Wildenstein, D., *E. Manet*, Paris-Lausanne (La Bibliothèque des Arts) 1975

Rouen Salon (Seine-Maritime)

Saint-Etienne Salon (Loire)

Saint-Fargeau, (Yonne) *E. Bernard*, 1980

Saint-Germain-en-Laye (Seine-et-Oise), *Symbolistes et nabis, M. Denis et son temps*, Musée du Prieuré, n.d.

Saint-Tropez (Var), *Fleurs de Fantin-Latour à Marquet*, Musée de l'Annonciade, 1982

Samoyault-Verlet, 'Ruprich-Robert' in *L'Art en France sous le Second Empire*, p. 139

Schmit, R., *Eugène Boudin 1824–1898*, 3 vols., Paris 1973

Selz, J., *O. Redon*, Paris (Flammarion) 1971

Senlis (Oise), *T. Couture*, Musée des Beaux-Arts, 1980

Serret, G., Fabiani, D., *Armand Guillaumin*, Paris (Mayer) 1971

Silvestre, V., *Seyssaud*, Saint-Chamas, 1959

Stammegna, S., *Monticelli*, catalogue des oeuvres, Vence (Remparts) 1981

Stevens, M. A., 'Anquetin', Dagnan-Bouveret', 'La Touche', Schuffenecker etc., in *Post-Impressionism*, London, RA 1979–1980

Strasbourg Salon (Bas-Rhin)

Sutter, J., *Luce, les travaux et les jours*, Paris-Lausanne (La Bibliothèque des Arts) 1971

Taylor, Baron, *Annuaire de l'Association des artistes-peintres*, Paris 1845–1852

Vaillat, L., *Oeuvres de F. Bracquemond exposées à la SNBA*, Paris 1907

Vallier, D., *Tout l'oeuvre peint d'H. Rousseau*, Paris (Flammarion) 1970

Valmy-Baysse, *Joseph Bail*, Paris (Juven) 1910

Valtat, J., *Louis Valtat*, Neuchâtel 1977

Varnedoc, K., *Gustave Caillebotte*, London and New Haven 1987

Viatte, G., *Collection George et Adèle Besson*, 1964–1965

Vilmorin, P. de, *Les Fleurs*, Paris (Baillière) 1892

Weisberg, G., *The Early Years of P. Burty*, Ph.D. Dissertation, John Hopkins University 1967; F. Bonvin, Paris (Geoffroy-Dechaume) 1979; *Chardin and the still life tradition in France*, Cleveland 1979

Welsh-Orcharov, B., *The Early Work of Charles Angrand*, The Hague 1971

Wildenstein, G., *Gauguin*, Paris, l'Art Français, 1964; *C. Monet, biographie et catalogue raisonné*, Paris-Lausanne (La Bibliothèque des Arts) 1974–1979

Zezzi, F., *Tout l'oeuvre peint de Renoir*, Paris (Flammarion) 1985

Zurich, *Pont-Aven, Gauguin und sein Kreis*, Kunsthaus, 1966; *Gallé*, Museum Bellerive, 1980